PHILOSOPHY OF MIND

PHILOSOPHY OF
MIND

Classical and Contemporary Readings

David J. Chalmers

New York   Oxford
OXFORD UNIVERSITY PRESS
2002

Oxford University Press

Oxford   New York
Auckland   Bangkok   Buenos Aires   Cape Town   Chennai
Dar es Salaam   Delhi   Hong Kong   Istanbul   Karachi   Kolkata
Kuala Lumpur   Madrid   Melbourne   Mexico City   Mumbai   Nairobi
São Paulo   Shanghai   Singapore   Taipei   Tokyo   Toronto

and an associated company in Berlin

Published by Oxford University Press, Inc.
198 Madison Avenue, New York, New York, 10016
http://www.oup-usa.org

Oxford is a registered trademark of Oxford University Press

Library of Congress Cataloging-in-Publication Data
Chalmers, David John, 1966–
    Philosophy of mind : classical and contemporary readings / David J. Chalmers.
        p. cm.
    Includes bibliographical references.
    ISBN 0-19-514580-1 (hardback : alk. paper)—ISBN 0-19-514581-X (pbk. : alk. paper)
        1. Philosophy of mind.   I. Title.

  BD418.3 .C435 2002
  128′.2—dc21   2002072403

Printing number: 9 8 7 6 5 4 3

Printed in the United States of America
on acid-free papers

CONTENTS

3 Content 473

4 Miscellaneous 653

PREFACE

What is the mind? What is the relationship between mind and body? Is the mind the same as the brain? How can the mind affect the physical world? What is consciousness? Could a purely physical system be conscious? Can we explain subjective experience in objective terms? How does the mind represent the world? What is the nature of belief and desire? What is the relationship between consciousness and representation? Is the mind in the head or in the environment? What can we know about other minds, in humans, animals, and machines? What is the self?

These are some of the central questions in the philosophy of mind. This book is a collection of articles addressing them. If the book has a thematic focus, it is on the many aspects of the mind–body problem: What is the relationship between mind, brain, and body and between the mental and the physical? This is unquestionably the central problem in the philosophy of mind, and it ramifies into any number of different questions, concerning different aspects of this relationship and concerning different aspects of the mind. The articles in this book address these questions from many different angles.

This collection has three main parts, representing what are arguably the three main streams in the philosophy of mind. The first concerns foundational questions about the metaphysics of mind: What is the nature of the mind, and what is the relationship between the mental and the physical? The second concerns questions about consciousness: What is the place of consciousness in the natural world, is consciousness a physical process, and how can consciousness be understood? The third concerns questions about mental content: How can the mind represent the world, what is the nature of thought, and are the contents of our thoughts determined by the brain or by the environment? In addition, there is a brief fourth part addressing the problems of other minds, personal identity, free will, and artificial intelligence.

The collection includes both classical articles that make up much of the standard history of the field and contemporary articles that represent recent directions in the area. Much of the classical background to recent debates, from Descartes' dualism to various twentieth-century forms of materialism, can be found in the first part of the book. The second and third parts concentrate largely on material from the last few decades, with a good representation of material at the edge of current research. The book contains a combination of highly accessible articles and more sophisticated articles, so it should be suitable for use in undergraduate courses at all levels as well as in graduate courses. I hope that the book will also be interesting to general readers interested in these issues.

The philosophy of mind has become an enormous and diverse area of research in recent years, and it is impossible to cover the entire field in a book like this. In general, I have aimed for depth of coverage in the central areas of the field, but difficult omissions have had to be made. In particular, one cannot do justice to the thriving and sprawling area of the philosophy of cognitive science as a mere section in a book like this. Instead, this topic will be covered in a forthcoming companion volume, *Philosophy of Cognitive Science*.

I have written introductions to each of the parts, giving relevant background for the material in those parts as well as pointers for further reading. I have also put together a website for this book containing links to relevant online material, including extensive bibliographies and online articles and reference works. This website will be continually updated to cover recent developments in the field. Readers are encouraged to consult it at **http://www.u.arizona.edu/~chalmers/pom.html.**

I would like to thank Robert Miller of Oxford University Press for inviting me to put this book together and for all his help on the editorial front. Brad Thompson was a great help in chasing down permissions and in preparing the manuscript. Thanks are due also to Fiona Cowie, George Graham, Jaegwon Kim, and two other reviewers for their helpful comments on the contents and organization of the book. Finally, I owe a debt to the editors of previous anthologies in the area—especially Ned Block (*Readings in the Philosophy of Psychology*), David Rosenthal (*The Nature of Mind*), and William Lycan (*Mind and Cognition*)—for their example.

1 Foundations

The articles in this part address foundational questions about the nature of the mind and about the relationship between the mental and the physical. Many of these questions concern the nature of mental states: states such as seeing red, feeling pain, experiencing anger, and desiring happiness. What is the nature of a mental state? And how are mental states related to physical states, such as states of the brain, of one's body and behavior, and of the physical world more generally?

Traditionally, views on these issues can be divided into two main classes. *Dualist* views hold that the mind is quite distinct from the body and the brain (although they may be associated in some fashion), and/or that mental states are fundamentally distinct from physical states. *Materialist* views hold that the mind is itself a broadly physical entity, and/or that mental states are derivative on physical states. There also exist *idealist* views, according to which physical states are derivative on mental states, but these will not be as central here. The papers in this part discuss many varieties of dualist and materialist views, as well as other foundational questions about relation between the mental and the physical.

A. Dualism

Dualist views come in two main varieties. *Interactionism* holds that the mental and physical are fundamentally distinct but interact in both directions: Physical states affect mental states, and mental states affect physical states. *Epiphenomenalism* holds that the mental and physical are fundamentally distinct and that physical states affect mental states, but denies that mental states affect physical states.

In the history of philosophy, the most important dualist view is the interactionism of René Descartes. Descartes' most important work is his *Meditations on First Philosophy*. This is a series of six meditations, the second and sixth of which are reproduced here as chapter 1. In the first meditation, Descartes attempts to cast doubt on all of his beliefs and finds that he cannot be certain that the external world exists. In the second meditation, Descartes finds that there is one thing he can be certain of: his own mind, and thus his own existence ("I think, therefore I am"). He concludes that he is fundamentally "a thing that thinks." In the third through fifth meditations, Descartes infers the existence of God and uses this to justify his belief in the external world (since God would not deceive him). In the sixth meditation, Descartes reflects on the differences between the mental and the physical and concludes that they are fundamentally distinct. He uses a number of arguments here: One can be certain about the mental but not about the physical; the mind is indivisible while any physical entity is divisible; and most famously, one can imagine oneself existing without a body, so one must be distinct from one's body and likewise from any physical entity.

The *Meditations* argue for the distinctness of mind and body but do not say much about their relationship. This question is addressed in more depth in Descartes' *Passions of the Soul* (chapter 2), which discusses the interaction between mind and body. Humans have a rational soul, which receives perceptions as "passions" from the brain and performs actions through acts of will that affect the brain. Signals are passed between the brain and the soul via the pineal gland (a small gland centrally located in the brain). On this picture, mind and body involve separate substances but interact in both directions.

Descartes' ideas about the mind have been highly influential, but today they are widely rejected. Many objections have been raised to the idea that a nonphysical mind controls the movement of a physical body. It is not clear just how a nonphysical substance and a physical substance can interact: The idea that the pineal gland mediates this interaction has long since been rejected on physiological grounds, and it is unclear whether any better causal nexus could exist. Further, it is often held that this interaction cannot be reconciled with physics, which postulates a closed network of physical interactions, with no room for a nonphysical mind to play any role.

In reaction to objections of this sort, some have embraced epiphenomenalism, retaining the distinctness of mind and body but denying any causal role for mind in the physical world. Such a view is put forward by Thomas Huxley (chapter 3). Huxley addresses Descartes' view that nonhuman animals are mere automata, whose behavior is controlled entirely by their brain and which lack minds altogether. Huxley suggests that contemporary evidence favors the first aspect of this view, but does not favor the second: That is, animals' behavior is controlled entirely by their brain, but they have minds nevertheless. On this view, the mind is a sort of by-product of the brain that has no effect on it. At the end of his article, Huxley suggests that the same goes for humans.

Epiphenomenalism has the advantage of being easier to reconcile with science than interactionist dualism, but it has the disadvantage of running strongly counter to common sense. Intuitively, it is hard to accept that our thoughts and feelings have no effect on our behavior. Another problem is raised by Raymond Smullyan in his short fable "An Unfortunate Dualist" (chapter 4): If mind has no effect on behavior, then it has no effect on what we say about the mind, so it seems that one could remove the mind and we would go on talking about it just the same. Smullyan raises the issue as a problem for dualism in general, but it is particularly pressing for an epiphenomenalist.

FURTHER READING

Objections to interactionism and epiphenomenalism are discussed in more detail by Kim (chapter 22) and Chalmers (chapter 27). Chalmers gives a limited defense of both interactionism and epiphenomenalism, while Jackson (chapter 28) defends an epiphenomenalist view. Elsewhere, interactionist views are defended by Foster (1991), Hodgson (1991), Popper and Eccles (1977), and Swinburne (1986), while an epiphenomenalist view is defended by Robinson (1988) and to a limited extent by Chalmers (1996). A relevant collection is Smythies and Beloff (1989).

Chalmers, D. J. 1996. *The Conscious Mind: In Search of a Fundamental Theory.* Oxford University Press.

Foster, J. 1991. *The Immaterial Self: A Defense of the Cartesian Dualist Conception of Mind.* Routledge.

Hodgson, D. 1991. *The Mind Matters: Consciousness and Choice in a Quantum World.* Oxford University Press.

Popper, K., and Eccles, J. 1977. *The Self and Its Brain: An Argument for Interactionism.* Springer.

Robinson, W. S. 1988. *Brains and People: An Essay on Mentality and Its Causal Conditions.* Temple University Press.

Smythies, J. R., and Beloff, J. (eds.). 1989. *The Case for Dualism.* University of Virginia Press.

Swinburne, R. 1986. *The Evolution of the Soul.* Oxford University Press.

B. Behaviorism

In the second half of the twentieth century, dualism was widely rejected, and many different forms of materialism were explored. This was both a reaction to the problems of dualism and a product of the success of physical explanations in many different domains.

Gilbert Ryle's 1949 book *The Concept of Mind* is recognizably the antecedent of much recent work in the philosophy of mind. This book argues against dualist views and puts forward a positive view of its own. Included here is the first chapter of the book, "Descartes' Myth" (chapter 5). As the title suggests, this chapter is largely directed against the dualism of Descartes. He accuses Descartes and others of subscribing to the "dogma of the ghost in the machine" and suggests that these views rest on a "category mistake" in posing questions about the relationship between mind and body. The mind is not to be seen as something distinct from the body and steering it from the inside, but as an aspect of the body's own activities.

Ryle's positive views (developed in other chapters of his book) are subtle and hard to summarize, but one strand in these views seems to involve a sort of *behaviorism:* roughly, the view that the mind is an aspect of behavior. On this view, to be in a given mental state (such as pain) is to be in a certain behavioral state (such as wincing), or at least to have a disposition to behave in certain ways (such as the disposition to express pain if queried). Thus mind is seen as a public aspect of human activity, rather than as a private inner aspect.

This sort of behaviorism is more explicit in Rudolf Carnap's "Psychology in Physical Language" (chapter 6). Carnap was a logical positivist, holding roughly that all meaningful claims can be translated into claims about observable, verifiable phenomena. In the case of the mind, this comes to the claim that meaningful claims about the mind can be translated into claims about behavior. This is a form of *logical* behaviorism, holding ultimately that what we *mean* when we make claims about the mind involves underlying claims about behavior. (This differs from scientific behaviorism, which holds roughly that the scientific study of the mind is the study of behavior.) Given that behavior itself seems to be a physical phenomenon, behaviorism can be seen as a form of materialism.

Like dualism, behaviorism has been subject to a number of objections. It seems more intuitive to say that mind is an inner cause of behavior, rather than an aspect of behavior itself. More concretely, one can argue that any given mental state is distinct from any given behavioral state or behavioral disposition. This sort of argument is mounted by Hilary Putnam in "Brains and Behavior" (chapter 7). Putnam argues that specially trained beings ("super-spartans") might feel pain while having no associated behavioral dispositions at all. Likewise, it can be argued that a perfect actor might have any given behavioral disposition without the associated mental state. If so, mental states cannot be behavioral dispositions.

FURTHER READING

Apart from being the classic statement of a broadly behaviorist view, Ryle (1949) contains nuanced discussions of many aspects of the mind and mentality. The views of Hempel (1949), Wittgenstein (1953), and Quine (1960) also have some affinity with behaviorism. Dennett (chapter 52), who was a student of Ryle's, puts forward a view that can be seen as a sophisticated contemporary descendant of behaviorism. Important objections to behaviorism are given by Geach (1957) and Block (1981). Scientific behaviorism is advocated by Watson (1930) and Skinner (1971).

Block, N. 1981. Psychologism and behaviorism. *Philosophical Review* 90:5–43.

Dennett, D. C. 1987. *The Intentional Stance.* MIT Press.

Geach, P. 1957. *Mental Acts.* Routledge and Kegan Paul.

Hempel, C. 1949. The logical analysis of psychology. In H. Feigl and W. Sellars, eds., *Readings in Philosophical Analysis,* pp. 373–84. Appleton-Century-Crofts.

Quine, W. V. 1960. *Word and Object.* MIT Press.

Ryle, G. 1949. *The Concept of Mind.* Hutchinson and Co.

Skinner, B. F. 1971. *Beyond Freedom and Dignity.* Alfred A. Knopf.

Watson, J. 1930. *Behaviorism.* Norton.

Wittgenstein, L. 1953. *Philosophical Investigations.* Blackwell.

C. The Identity Theory

The mind–brain identity theory holds that mental states are brain states. Most theorists accept that mental states are at least associated or correlated with brain states: For example, feeling pain might be correlated with a certain sort of brain activity. The identity theory goes further to hold that mental states are *identical* to the associated brain states: These states are one and the same. This identification, unlike the behaviorist thesis, is not intended to be grounded in an analysis of our concepts. Rather, it is supposed to be an empirical claim, analogous to the claim that lightning is identical to electrical discharge or that water is identical to H_2O. In this way, the identity theory can be seen as driven by scientific developments, especially in neuroscience.

The identity theory in its modern form was put forward by U. T. Place, J. J. C. Smart, and Herbert Feigl in the late 1950s. The original statement of the view was given by Place (chapter 8) and was refined and elaborated by his colleague Smart (chapter 9). Both Place and Smart recognize the strong intuitive resistance to the claim that mental states are brain states, especially in the case of conscious experiences. They try to defuse this resistance by careful diagnoses of its source: Place locates this in a "phenomenological fallacy," while Smart addresses a number of objections to the thesis, putting forward the idea that mental concepts can be analyzed in a "topic-neutral way," so that nothing in these concepts alone dictates whether or not mental states are physical. This suggests that while it may not seem antecedently that mental states are physical, we can discover their physical nature through empirical science.

Feigl's form of the identity theory has a somewhat different flavor from Place's and Smart's. Feigl gives more weight to intuitions about the special nature of conscious experience than do Place and Smart, but he argues that these can be reconciled with an identity view once we correctly understand the nature of physical understanding. Physical theory characterizes its entities structurally and leaves open their intrinsic nature. This raises the possibility that mental states are tied to the intrinsic aspect of physical states. This possibility is explored in the selection from Feigl here (chapter 10), which is a short excerpt from his article "The 'Mental' and the 'Physical.' "

An objection to the identity theory, developed by Putnam (chapter 11), is that states such as pain cannot be identical to any particular brain states, since a creature such as a Martian might have pain without having the brain state in question. As Putnam put it, it is plausible that mental states are *multiply realizable.* If this is right, one cannot identify a mental state *type,* such as being in pain, with a physical state type, such as a specific sort of brain state. This still leaves open the possibility that one can identify mental state *tokens,* such as a specific pain of a subject, with physical state tokens, such as a specific biological state of that subject. Many philosophers think that the type identity theory is refuted by this objection but that the token identity theory is left open.

FURTHER READING

Feigl's long and interesting 1958 article is reprinted with an afterword as Feigl (1967). The identity theory provoked a great deal of critical discussion in the 1960s, some of which is collected in Borst (1970); another collection is Presley (1967). Influential objections to the identity theory are developed by Putnam (chapter 11) and Kripke (chapter 32). Hill (chapter 33; see also Hill 1991) advocates a version of the type identity theory.

Borst, C. V. (ed.). 1970. *The Mind/Brain Identity Theory.* Macmillan.

Feigl, H. 1967. *The 'Mental' and the 'Physical.'* University of Minnesota Press.

Hill, C. S. 1991. *Sensations: A Defense of Type Materialism.* Cambridge University Press.

Presley, C. P. (ed.). 1967. *The Identity Theory of Mind.* University of Queensland Press.

D. Functionalism

Functionalism is a descendant of both behaviorism and the identity theory. Broadly speaking, it holds that mental states correspond to *functional* states: states of playing a certain role within the cognitive system. Some forms of functionalism identify mental states with functional states, while other forms identify mental states with the physical states that play the functional role in question. Functionalism was developed in the 1960s by Hilary Putnam, David Armstrong, and David Lewis, in somewhat different forms.

In Putnam's "The Nature of Mental States" (chapter 11), he argues against behaviorism and the identity theory and proposes instead a hypothesis that has come to be known as *machine functionalism,* according to which mental states are functional states of a computational machine. This makes mental states more abstract than any particular biological state, and so allows the possibility of multiple realization. It also allows a loose tie between mental states and behavior, without an absolute tie. This analogy between minds and machines has been very influential in contemporary philosophy of mind and cognitive science and has been developed in many different directions.

Armstrong (chapter 12) puts forward a different form of functionalism, cast not in terms of machines, but in terms of the general idea that mental states are defined in terms of their causal role. Specifically, he holds that the concept of a mental state is the concept of a state that is apt to be the cause of certain effects or apt to be the effect of certain causes. Where Putnam viewed his thesis as a sort of empirical hypothesis (like the identity theory), Armstrong puts forward his thesis as a sort of conceptual analysis (like logical behaviorism). It is a view about what we mean when we talk about the mind. Because of this, the view is often known as *analytic functionalism.* Unlike Putnam, Armstrong sees his view as supporting the identity theory rather than competing with it. If it turns out that in humans, a specific brain state plays the causal role associated with pain, then that brain state is itself a pain.

This sort of functionalism is developed in much more detail by Lewis (chapter 13). One might ask: *Which* causal roles are relevant to defining mental states? Lewis suggests that these roles are given by our everyday *theory* of the mind, as reflected in common-sense claims about mental states, their connections to one another, and their role in guiding behavior. If these claims are gathered together, they can be seen as providing a sort of definition of what it is to be the mental state in question: So pain is whatever state plays the role that common sense associates with pain, and so on. For this purpose, Lewis adapts Frank Ramsey's idea that the claims of a theory can be represented in a single long sentence (the "Ramsey sentence"), and then used to identify the entities that satisfy the theory. Like Armstrong's view, Lewis' functionalism is a form of analytic functionalism, put forward as an analysis of what mental concepts mean.

A common objection to functionalism holds that it cannot deal with the "qualitative" aspects of conscious experience, such as the experience of seeing red or feeling pain. Ned Block (chapter 14) develops the "absent qualia" objection, according to which a system could have the same functional states as a conscious system, while having no qualitative states at all. He argues for this thesis using a thought-experiment involving a vast number of people causally organized to realize the given organization. Martine Nida-Rümelin (chapter 15) develops a version of the "inverted qualia" objection, according to which two systems could have the same relevant functional states as a conscious system while having *different* qualitative states. If these objections are correct, then qualitative states are not identical to functional states, so functionalism is false.

FURTHER READING

There is an enormous and scattered literature on functionalism; some relevant papers are collected in Biro and Shahan (1982). Putnam's version of functionalism is developed in a series of papers collected in Putnam (1975) and is repudiated in Putnam (1987). Armstrong's functionalism is developed at length in Armstrong (1968). The idea that mental states are defined in terms of a theory is also present in Sellars (chapter 50) and is developed further by Churchland (chapter 53). Searle (chapter 63) gives an argument against machine functionalism that is closely related to the absent qualia argument. Dennett (chapter 26) tries to deflate the idea of absent and inverted qualia, while Shoemaker (1975) and White (1986) give important defenses of functionalism against absent qualia objections. See also a number of related papers on this topic (e.g., those by Nagel, Chalmers, Kripke, and Hill) in Part 2 of this book. Shoemaker (1982) and Palmer (1999) discuss inverted qualia from a philosophical and empirical standpoint, respectively.

Armstrong, D. M. 1968. *A Materialist Theory of the Mind.* Routledge and Kegan Paul.

Biro, J. I., and Shahan, R. W. (eds.). 1982. *Mind, Brain and Function.* Oklahoma University Press.

Palmer, S. 1999. Color, consciousness, and the isomorphism constraint. *Behavioral and Brain Sciences* 22:1–21.

Putnam, H. 1975. *Mind, Language, and Reality.* Cambridge University Press.

Putnam, H. 1987. *Representation and Reality.* MIT Press.

Shoemaker, S. 1975. Functionalism and qualia. *Philosophical Studies* 27:291–315. Reprinted in *Identity, Cause, and Mind* (Cambridge University Press, 1984).

Shoemaker, S. 1982. The inverted spectrum. *Journal of Philosophy* 79:357–81. Reprinted in *Identity, Cause, and Mind* (Cambridge University Press, 1984).

White, S. 1986. Curse of the qualia. *Synthese* 68:333–68. Reprinted in N. Block, O. Flanagan, and G. Güzeldere (eds.), *The Nature of Consciousness* (MIT Press, 1997).

E. Other Psychophysical Relations

A number of other views about the relationship between the mental and the physical have been put forward. One important view is the *emergentism* of C. D. Broad (chapter 16) and others, holding that the mental is an emergent property of an underlying physical substrate. A property is *emergent* in Broad's sense when it is a property of an underlying physical substance but cannot be deduced in principle from the low-level physical properties of that substance. Broad illustrates emergence in the domains of chemistry and biology, contrasting emergentism with *mechanism,* on which high-level properties are deducible from low-level properties, and with *substantial vitalism,* on which separate substances are involved. Broad argues both for emergent qualities (high-level qualities that cannot be deduced from underlying qualities) and for emergent behavior (high-level behavior that cannot be deduced from the principles governing low-level behavior). This view of chemistry and biology is now widely rejected, although many theorists embrace a sort of *weak emergence* where high-level properties are surprising consequences of low-level properties, while still (unlike Broad's *strong emergence*) being deducible from them in principle. In the case of the mind (to which Broad applies the framework in a later chapter), strong emergence is more popular. In this domain, Broad's view has something in common with the interactionism of Descartes, but with just one underlying substance and two sorts of properties.

Another important view is the *anomalous monism* of Donald Davidson (chapter 17). This view can be seen as an attempt to preserve materialism without any strong reduction of the mental to the physical. On Davidson's view, any given mental event is identical to a physical event (a form of token identity theory), but there are no strict laws that connect mental events to physical events, and there are no strict laws governing mental events themselves. Davidson argues for this view by considering the distinct character of mental and physical concepts along with the causal connections between mental events and physical events.

There has been much discussion of whether the mental can be *reduced* to the physical, where this is understood as requiring more than the mere truth of materialism. Jerry Fodor (chapter 18) argues that in general, one cannot expect that the theories of a high-level "special science" should be reducible to the theories of a low-level science such as physics. Because of the many ways in which a high-level kind can be realized at a low level, the general principles in a high-level science cannot be captured by a low-level science except in a very complex and arbitrary way. This applies especially to the science of psychology, suggesting that one cannot expect that psychology can be reducible to physics, or even to neuroscience. Instead, it will always have a degree of autonomy.

In a more recent paper (chapter 19), Jaegwon Kim replies to Fodor's argument, suggesting that multiple realizability does not pose an obstacle to reduction. We may still be able to reduce the psychological principles that apply to *humans* (or some other particular species) to lower-level principles and to reduce species-specific psychological kinds to lower-level kinds. One should not expect anything more, since there may not be any general principles that apply to all possible minds. Where one has multiple realizability, one has multiple psychological principles. So the important principles and kinds always lie at a species-specific level.

It has also been suggested that the mental–physical relationship can be analyzed using the notion of *supervenience*. A class of high-level properties supervenes on a class of low-level properties when any two possible systems (or possible worlds) that have the same low-level properties have the same high-level properties. This captures the intuitive materialist idea that a system's physical properties might determine its mental properties, without making further commitments about the relationship. The idea is discussed critically by Terence Horgan (chapter 20). Horgan sketches the history and the various versions of supervenience and argues that while supervenience is a useful tool, it needs to be augmented to yield a full materialist theory of the mental–physical relations. In particular, we need an *explanation* of why the mental properties supervene on physical properties. Supervenience augmented by this sort of explanation yields what Horgan calls *superdupervenience.*

Finally, Frank Jackson (chapter 21) argues for an important role for *conceptual analysis* in understanding the mental–physical relation. Jackson argues that the truth of materialism requires a sort of supervenience of the mental on the physical and he argues that this in turn requires that mental concepts can be analyzed in such a way so that there is a sort of a priori entailment from physical truths to mental truths. This sort of analyzability can be seen as one way of answering Horgan's request for an explanation of supervenience. At the same time, the requirement of conceptual analyzability, if accepted, imposes a significant burden on the materialist.

FURTHER READING

Broad's emergentist view is developed in more depth in Broad (1925). The general program of British emergentists such as Broad is carefully described and analyzed by McLaughlin (1992). Beckermann, Flohr, and Kim (1992) is an excellent collection of papers on both emergence and reduction. Davidson's anomalous monism is criticized briefly by Kim (chapter 19) and is analyzed in more depth by papers in McLaughlin and Lepore (1985) and Heil and Mele (1993). Fodor (1997) responds to Kim's arguments (as do other papers in the same volume). Bickle (1997) argues at length for a reductionist view. Wilson (1999) responds to Horgan's arguments. Important papers on supervenience are collected in Kim (1993) and in the 1984 supplement to the *Southern Journal of Philosophy*. Jackson (1998) gives a more extensive treatment of the issues addressed in his paper here. Block and Stalnaker (chapter 37) argue against Jackson's requirement of conceptual analyzability.

Beckermann, A., Flohr, H., and Kim, J. (eds.). 1992. *Emergence or Reduction? Prospects for Nonreductive Physicalism.* De Gruyter.

Bickle, J. 1997. *Psychoneural Reductionism: The New Wave.* MIT Press.

Broad, C. D. 1925. *The Mind and Its Place in Nature.* Routledge and Kegan Paul.

Fodor, J. 1997. Special sciences: Still autonomous after all these years. *Philosophical Perspectives* 11:149–63.

Heil, J., and Mele, A. 1993. *Mental Causation.* Oxford University Press.

Jackson, F. 1998. *From Metaphysics to Ethics: A Defence of Conceptual Analysis.* Oxford University Press.

Kim, J. 1993. *Supervenience and Mind.* Cambridge University Press.

McLaughlin, B. P. 1992. The rise and fall of British emergentism. In Beckermann, Flohr, and Kim 1992.

McLaughlin, B. P., and Lepore, E. 1985. *Action and Events.* Blackwell.

Wilson, J. 1999. How superduper does a physicalist supervenience need to be? *Philosophical Quarterly* 49:33–52.

F. Mental Causation

One of the central problems in the metaphysics of mind is the problem of mental causation: How can the mind affect the physical world? This problem was central in Descartes' discussion of the mind–body problems, and it proved to be a serious difficulty for any form of dualism. More recently, it has been argued that mental causation also poses a problem for many forms of materialism.

Jaegwon Kim's article in this section (chapter 22) summarizes a number of different problems of mental causation. The first is a problem specifically for Davidson's anomalous monism: If there are no strict laws connecting mental states to physical states, how can mental states be causally relevant? The second is a problem specifically for externalist views about the mind (see Part 3, Section C): If mental states depend on factors outside the head, how can they affect behavior? The third is a problem raised for any view: Given that one can give a full causal explanation of behavior in physical terms, how can mental states be causally relevant? This third problem can be called the "exclusion problem," since it suggests that mental states are excluded from causal explanation. (Note that this problem might apply to any high-level states, not just to mental states.) Kim focuses on the exclusion problem, analyzing it in terms of supervenience, but not reaching firm conclusions.

Stephen Yablo (chapter 23) discusses the exclusion problem in more detail and offers an original solution to the problem. Yablo suggests that mental properties stand to physical properties as determinables stand to determinates—that is, in the way that a property such as *being colored* stands to a property such as *being red*. He argues that the fact that one can give a full causal account in terms of determinables does not make determinables irrelevant: For example, explaining an object's effects in terms of its redness does not make its being colored irrelevant. In this way, we might see how mental properties can be causally efficacious even in a physical world.

FURTHER READING

Many aspects of the problem of mental causation are discussed by the papers in Heil and Mele (1993). Kim's ideas are developed further in Kim (1998). In this volume, problems about mental causation in the case of consciousness are addressed by Chalmers (chapter 27) and Jackson (chapter 28).

Heil, J., and Mele, A. 1993. *Mental Causation.* Oxford University Press.

Kim, J. 1998. *Mind in a Physical World.* MIT Press.

A. Dualism

1 Meditations on First Philosophy
René Descartes

Second Meditation

The Nature of the Human Mind, and How It Is Better Known Than the Body

So serious are the doubts into which I have been thrown as a result of yesterday's meditation that I can neither put them out of my mind nor see any way of resolving them. It feels as if I have fallen unexpectedly into a deep whirlpool which tumbles me around so that I can neither stand on the bottom nor swim up to the top. Nevertheless I will make an effort and once more attempt the same path which I started on yesterday. Anything which admits of the slightest doubt I will set aside just as if I had found it to be wholly false; and I will proceed in this way until I recognize something certain, or, if nothing else, until I at least recognize for certain that there is no certainty. Archimedes used to demand just one firm and immovable point in order to shift the entire earth; so I too can hope for great things if I manage to find just one thing, however slight, that is certain and unshakeable.

I will suppose then, that everything I see is spurious. I will believe that my memory tells me lies, and that none of the things that it reports ever happened. I have no senses. Body, shape, extension, movement and place are chimeras. So what remains true? Perhaps just the one fact that nothing is certain.

Yet apart from everything I have just listed, how do I know that there is not something else which does not allow even the slightest occasion for doubt? Is there not a God, or whatever I may call him, who puts into me[1] the thoughts I am now having? But why do I think this, since I myself may perhaps be the author of these thoughts? In that case am not I, at least, something? But I have just said that I have no senses and no body. This is the sticking point: what follows from this? Am I not so bound up with a body and with senses that I cannot exist without them? But I have convinced myself that there is absolutely nothing in the world, no sky, no earth, no minds, no bodies. Does it now follow that I too do not exist? No: if I convinced myself of something[2] then I certainly existed. But there is a deceiver of supreme power and cunning who is deliberately and constantly deceiving me. In that case I too undoubtedly exist, if he is deceiving me; and let him deceive me as much as he can, he will never bring it about that I am nothing so long as I think that I am something. So after considering everything very thoroughly, I must finally conclude that this proposition, *I am, I exist,* is necessarily true whenever it is put forward by me or conceived in my mind.

But I do not yet have a sufficient understanding of what this 'I' is, that now necessarily exists. So I must be on my guard against carelessly taking something else to be this 'I', and so making a mistake in the very item of knowledge that I maintain is the most certain and evident of all. I will therefore go back and meditate on what I originally believed myself to be, before I embarked on this present train of thought. I will then subtract anything capable of being weakened, even minimally, by the arguments now introduced, so that what is left at the end may be exactly and only what is certain and unshakeable.

What then did I formerly think I was? A man. But what is a man? Shall I say 'a rational animal'? No; for then I should have to inquire what an animal is, what rationality is, and in this way one question would lead me down the slope to other harder ones, and I do not now have the time to waste on subtleties of this kind. Instead I propose to concentrate on what came into my thoughts spontaneously and quite naturally whenever I used to consider what I was. Well, the first thought to come to mind was that I had a face, hands, arms and the whole mechanical structure of limbs which can be seen in a corpse, and which I called the body. The next thought was that I was nourished, that I moved about, and that I engaged in sense-perception and thinking; and these actions I attributed to the soul. But as to the nature of this soul, either I did not think about this or else I imagined it to be something tenuous, like a wind or fire or ether, which permeated my more solid parts. As to the body, however, I had no doubts about it, but thought I knew its nature distinctly. If I had tried to describe the mental conception I had of it, I would have expressed it as follows: by a body I understand whatever has a determinable shape and a definable location and can occupy a space in such a way as to exclude any other body; it can be perceived by touch, sight, hearing, taste or smell, and can be moved in various ways, not by itself but by whatever else comes into contact with it. For, according to my judgement, the power of self-movement, like the power of sensation or of thought, was quite foreign to the nature of a body; indeed, it was a source of wonder to me that certain bodies were found to contain faculties of this kind.

But what shall I now say that I am, when I am supposing that there is some supremely powerful and, if it is permissible to say so, malicious deceiver, who is deliberately trying to trick me in every way he can? Can I now assert that I possess even the most insignificant of all the attributes which I have just said belong to the nature of a body? I scrutinize them, think about them, go over them again, but nothing suggests itself; it is tiresome and pointless to go through the list once more. But what about the attributes I assigned to the soul? Nutrition or movement? Since now I do not have a body, these are mere fabrications. Sense-perception? This surely does not occur without a body, and besides, when asleep I have appeared to perceive through the senses many things which I afterwards realized I did not perceive through the senses at all. Thinking? At last I have discovered it—thought; this alone is inseparable from me. I am, I exist—that is certain. But for how long? For as long as I am thinking. For it could be that were I totally to cease from thinking, I should totally cease to exist. At present I am not admitting anything except what is necessarily true. I am, then, in the strict sense only a thing that thinks;[3] that is, I am

a mind, or intelligence, or intellect, or reason—words whose meaning I have been ignorant of until now. But for all that I am a thing which is real and which truly exists. But what kind of a thing? As I have just said—a thinking thing.

What else am I? I will use my imagination.[4] I am not that structure of limbs which is called a human body. I am not even some thin vapour which permeates the limbs—a wind, fire, air, breath, or whatever I depict in my imagination; for these are things which I have supposed to be nothing. Let this supposition stand;[5] for all that I am still something. And yet may it not perhaps be the case that these very things which I am supposing to be nothing, because they are unknown to me, are in reality identical with the 'I' of which I am aware? I do not know, and for the moment I shall not argue the point, since I can make judgements only about things which are known to me. I know that I exist; the question is, what is this 'I' that I know? If the 'I' is understood strictly as we have been taking it, then it is quite certain that knowledge of it does not depend on things of whose existence I am as yet unaware; so it cannot depend on any of the things which I invent in my imagination. And this very word 'invent' shows me my mistake. It would indeed be a case of fictitious invention if I used my imagination to establish that I was something or other; for imagining is simply contemplating the shape or image of a corporeal thing. Yet now I know for certain both that I exist and at the same time that all such images and, in general, everything relating to the nature of body, could be mere dreams <and chimeras>. Once this point has been grasped, to say 'I will use my imagination to get to know more distinctly what I am' would seem to be as silly as saying 'I am now awake, and see some truth; but since my vision is not yet clear enough, I will deliberately fall asleep so that my dreams may provide a truer and clearer representation.' I thus realize that none of the things that the imagination enables me to grasp is at all relevant to this knowledge of myself which I possess, and that the mind must therefore be most carefully diverted from such things[6] if it is to perceive its own nature as distinctly as possible.

But what then am I? A thing that thinks. What is that? A thing that doubts, understands, affirms, denies, is willing, is unwilling, and also imagines and has sensory perceptions.

This is a considerable list, if everything on it belongs to me. But does it? Is it not one and the same 'I' who is now doubting almost everything, who nonetheless understands some things, who affirms that this one thing is true, denies everything else, desires to know more, is unwilling to be deceived, imagines many things even involuntarily, and is aware of many things which apparently come from the senses? Are not all these things just as true as the fact that I exist, even if I am asleep all the time, and even if he who created me is doing all he can to deceive me? Which of all these activities is distinct from my thinking? Which of them can be said to be separate from myself? The fact that it is I who am doubting and understanding and willing is so evident that I see no way of making it any clearer. But it is also the case that the 'I' who imagines is the same 'I'. For even if, as I have supposed, none of the objects of imagination are real, the power of imagination is something which really exists and is part of my thinking. Lastly, it is also the same 'I' who has sensory perceptions, or is aware of bodily things as it were through the senses. For example, I am now seeing light, hearing a noise, feeling heat. But I am asleep, so all this is false. Yet I certainly *seem* to see, to hear, and to be warmed. This cannot be false; what is called 'having a sensory perception' is strictly just this, and in this restricted sense of the term it is simply thinking.

From all this I am beginning to have a rather better understanding of what I am. But it still appears—and I cannot stop thinking this—that the corporeal things of which images are formed in my thought, and which the senses investigate, are known with much more distinctness than this puzzling 'I' which cannot be pictured in the imagination. And yet it is surely surprising that I should have a more distinct grasp of things which I realize are doubtful, unknown and foreign to me, than I have of that which is true and known—my own self. But I see what it is: my mind enjoys wandering off and will not yet submit to being restrained within the bounds of truth. Very well then; just this once let us give it a completely free rein, so that after a while, when it is time to tighten the reins, it may more readily submit to being curbed.

Let us consider the things which people commonly think they understand most distinctly of all; that is, the bodies which we touch and see. I do not mean bodies in general—for general perceptions are apt to be somewhat more confused—but one particular body. Let us take, for example, this piece of wax. It has just been taken from the honeycomb; it has not yet quite lost the taste of the honey; it retains some of the scent of the flowers from which it was gathered; its colour, shape and size are plain to see; it is hard, cold and can be handled without difficulty; if you rap it with your knuckle it makes a sound. In short, it has everything which appears necessary to enable a body to be known as distinctly as possible. But even as I speak, I put the wax by the fire, and look: the residual taste is eliminated, the smell goes away, the colour changes, the shape is lost, the size increases; it becomes liquid and hot; you can hardly touch it, and if you strike it, it no longer makes a sound. But does the same wax remain? It must be admitted that it does; no one denies it, no one thinks otherwise. So what was it in the wax that I understood with such distinctness? Evidently none of the features which I arrived at by means of the senses; for whatever came under taste, smell, sight, touch or hearing has now altered—yet the wax remains.

Perhaps the answer lies in the thought which now comes to my mind; namely, the wax was not after all the sweetness of the honey, or the fragrance of the flowers, or the whiteness, or the shape, or the sound, but was rather a body which presented itself to me in these various forms a little while ago, but which now exhibits different ones. But what exactly is it that I am now imagining? Let us concentrate, take away everything which does not belong to the wax, and see what is left: merely something extended, flexible and changeable. But what is meant here by 'flexible' and 'changeable'? Is it what I picture in my imagination: that this piece of wax is capable of changing from a round shape to a square shape, or from a square shape to a triangular shape? Not at all; for I can grasp that the wax is capable of countless changes of this kind, yet I am unable to run through this immeasurable number of changes in my imagination, from which it follows that it is not the faculty of imagination that gives me my grasp of the wax as flexible and changeable. And what is meant by 'extended'? Is the extension of the wax also unknown? For it increases if the wax melts, increases again if it boils, and is greater still if the heat is increased. I would not be making a correct judgement about the nature of wax unless I believed it capable of being extended in many more different ways than I will ever encompass in my imagination. I must therefore admit that the nature of this piece of wax is in no way revealed by my imagination, but is perceived by the mind alone. (I am speaking of this particular piece of wax; the point is even clearer with regard to wax in general.) But what is this wax which is perceived by the mind alone?[7] It is of course the same wax which I see, which I touch, which I picture in my imagination, in short the same wax which I thought it to be from the start. And yet, and here is the point, the perception I have of it[8] is a case not of vision or touch or imagination—nor has it ever been, despite previous appearances—but of purely mental scrutiny; and this can be imperfect and confused, as it was before, or clear and distinct as it is now, depending on how carefully I concentrate on what the wax consists in.

But as I reach this conclusion I am amazed at how <weak and> prone to error my mind is. For although I am thinking about these matters within myself, silently and without speaking, nonetheless the actual words bring me up short, and I am almost tricked by ordinary ways of talking. We say that we see the wax itself, if it is there before us, not that we judge it to be there from its colour or shape; and this might lead me to conclude without more ado that knowledge of the wax comes from what the eye sees, and not from the scrutiny of the mind alone. But then if I look out of the window and see men crossing the square, as I just happen to have done, I normally say that I see the men themselves, just as I say that I see the wax. Yet do I see any more than hats and coats which could conceal automatons? I *judge* that they are men. And so something which I thought I was seeing with my eyes is in fact grasped solely by the faculty of judgement which is in my mind.

However, one who wants to achieve knowledge above the ordinary level should feel ashamed at having taken ordinary ways of talking as a basis for doubt. So let us proceed, and consider on which occasion my perception of the nature of the wax was more perfect and evident. Was it when I first looked at it, and believed I knew it by my external senses, or at least by what they call the 'common' sense[9]—that is, the power of imagination? Or is my knowledge more perfect now, after a more careful investigation of the nature of the wax and of the means by which it is known? Any doubt on this issue would clearly be foolish; for what distinctness was there in my earlier perception? Was there anything in it which an animal could not possess? But when I distinguish the wax from its outward forms—take the clothes off, as it were, and consider it naked—then although my judgement may still contain errors, at least my perception now requires a human mind.

But what am I to say about this mind, or about myself? (So far, remember, I am not admitting that there is anything else in me except a mind.) What, I ask, is this 'I' which seems to perceive the wax so distinctly? Surely my awareness of my own self is not merely much truer and more certain than my awareness of the wax, but also much more distinct and evident. For if I judge that the wax exists from the fact that I see it, clearly this same fact entails much more evidently that I myself also exist. It is possible that what I see is not really the wax; it is possible that I do not even have eyes with which to see anything. But when I see, or think I see (I am not here distinguishing the two), it is simply not possible that I who am now thinking am not something. By the same token, if I judge that the wax exists from the fact that I touch it, the same result follows, namely that I exist. If I judge that it exists from the fact that I imagine it, or for any other reason, exactly the same thing follows. And the result that I have grasped in the case of the wax may be applied to everything else located outside me. Moreover, if my perception of the wax seemed more distinct[10] after it was established not just by sight or touch but by many other considerations, it must be admitted that I now know myself even more distinctly. This is because every consideration whatsoever which contributes to my perception of the wax, or of any other body, cannot but establish even more effectively the nature of my own mind. But besides this, there is so much else in the mind itself which can serve to make my knowledge of it more distinct, that it scarcely seems worth going through the contributions made by considering bodily things.

I see that without any effort I have now finally got back to where I wanted. I now know that even bodies are not strictly perceived by the senses or the faculty of imagination but by the intellect alone, and that this perception derives not from their being touched or seen but from their being understood; and in view of this I know plainly that I can achieve an easier and more evident perception of my own mind than of anything else. But since the habit of holding on to old opinions cannot be set aside so quickly, I should like to stop here and meditate for some time on this new knowledge I have gained, so as to fix it more deeply in my memory.

Sixth Meditation

The Existence of Material Things, and the Real Distinction between Mind and Body[11]

It remains for me to examine whether material things exist. And at least I now know they are capable of existing, in so far as they are the subject-matter of pure mathematics, since I perceive them clearly and distinctly. For there is no doubt that God is capable of creating everything that I am capable of perceiving in this manner; and I have never judged that something could not be made by him except on the grounds that there would be a contradiction in my perceiving it distinctly. The conclusion that material things exist is also suggested by the faculty of imagination, which I am aware of using when I turn my mind to material things. For when I give more attentive consideration to what imagination is, it seems to be nothing else but an application of the cognitive faculty to a body which is intimately present to it, and which therefore exists.

To make this clear, I will first examine the difference between imagination and pure understanding. When I imagine a triangle, for example, I do not merely understand that it is a figure bounded by three lines, but at the same time I also see the three lines with my mind's eye as if they were present before me; and this is what I call imagining. But if I want to think of a chiliagon, although I understand that it is a figure consisting of a thousand sides just as well as I understand the triangle to be a three-sided figure, I do not in the same way imagine the thousand sides or see them as if they were present before me. It is true that since I am in the habit of imagining something whenever I think of a corporeal thing, I may construct in my mind a confused representation of some figure; but it is clear that this is not a chiliagon. For it differs in no way from the representation I should form if I were thinking of a myriagon, or any figure with very many sides. Moreover, such a representation is useless for recognizing the properties which distinguish a chiliagon from other polygons. But suppose I am dealing with a pentagon: I can of course understand the figure of a pentagon, just as I can the figure of a chiliagon, without the help of the imagination; but I can also imagine a pentagon, by applying my mind's eye to its five sides and the area contained within them. And in doing this I notice quite clearly that imagination requires a peculiar effort of mind which is not required for understanding; this additional effort of mind clearly shows the difference between imagination and pure understanding.

Besides this, I consider that this power of imagining which is in me, differing as it does from the power of understanding, is not a necessary constituent of my own essence, that is, of the essence of my mind. For if I lacked it, I should undoubtedly remain the same individual as I now am; from which it seems to follow that it depends on something distinct from myself. And I can easily understand that, if there does exist some body to which the mind is so joined that it can apply itself to contemplate it, as it were, whenever it pleases, then it may possibly be this very body that enables me to imagine corporeal things. So the difference between this mode of thinking and pure understanding may simply be this: when the mind understands, it in some way turns towards itself and inspects one of the ideas which are within it; but when it imagines, it turns towards the body and looks at something in the body which conforms to an idea understood by the mind or perceived by the senses. I can, as I say, easily understand that this is how imagination comes about, if the body exists; and since there is no other equally suitable way of explaining imagination that comes to mind, I can make a probable conjecture that the body exists. But this is only a probability; and despite a careful and comprehensive investigation, I do not yet see how the distinct idea of corporeal nature which I find in my imagination can provide any basis for a necessary inference that some body exists.

But besides that corporeal nature which is the subject-matter of pure mathematics, there is much else that I habitually imagine, such as colours, sounds, tastes, pain and so on—though not so distinctly. Now I perceive these things much better by means of the senses, which is how, with the assistance of memory, they appear to have reached the imagination. So in order to deal with them more fully, I must pay equal attention to the senses, and see whether the things which are perceived by means of that mode of thinking which I call 'sensory perception' provide me with any sure argument for the existence of corporeal things.

To begin with, I will go back over all the things which I previously took to be perceived by the senses, and reckoned to be true; and I will go over my reasons for thinking this. Next, I will set out my reasons for subsequently calling these things into doubt. And finally I will consider what I should now believe about them.

First of all then, I perceived by my senses that I had a head, hands, feet and other limbs making up the body which I regarded as part of myself, or perhaps even as my whole self. I also perceived by my senses that this body was situated among many other bodies which could affect it in various favourable or unfavourable ways; and I gauged the favourable effects by a sensation of pleasure, and the unfavourable ones by a sensation of pain. In addition to pain and pleasure, I also had sensations within me of hunger, thirst, and other such appetites, and also of physical propensities towards cheerfulness, sadness, anger and similar emotions. And outside me, besides the extension, shapes and movements of bodies, I also had sensations of their hardness and heat, and of the other tactile qualities. In addition, I had sensations of light, colours, smells, tastes and sounds, the variety of which enabled me to distinguish the sky, the earth, the seas, and all other bodies, one from another. Considering the ideas of all these qualities which presented themselves to my thought, although the ideas were, strictly speaking, the only immediate objects of my sensory awareness, it was not unreasonable for me to think that the items which I was perceiving through the senses were things quite distinct from my thought, namely bodies which produced the ideas. For my experience was that these ideas came to me quite without my consent, so that I could not have sensory awareness of any object, even if I wanted to, unless it was present to my sense organs; and I could not avoid having sensory awareness of it when it was present. And since the ideas perceived by the senses were much more lively and vivid and even, in their own way, more distinct than any of those which I deliberately formed through meditating or which I found impressed on my memory, it seemed impossible that they should have come from within me; so the only alternative was that they came from other things. Since the sole source of my knowledge of these things was the ideas themselves, the supposition that the things resembled the ideas was bound to occur to me. In addition, I remembered that the use of my senses had come first, while the use of my reason came only later; and I saw that the ideas which I formed myself were less vivid than those which I perceived with the senses and were, for the most part, made up of elements of sensory ideas. In this way I easily convinced myself that I had nothing at all in the intellect which I had not previously had in sensation. As for the body which by some special right I called 'mine', my belief that this body, more than any other, belonged to me had some justification. For I could never be separated from it, as I could from other bodies; and I felt all my appetites and emotions in, and on account of, this body; and finally, I was aware of pain and pleasurable ticklings in parts of this body, but not in other bodies external to it. But

why should that curious sensation of pain give rise to a particular distress of mind; or why should a certain kind of delight follow on a tickling sensation? Again, why should that curious tugging in the stomach which I call hunger tell me that I should eat, or a dryness of the throat tell me to drink, and so on? I was not able to give any explanation of all this, except that nature taught me so. For there is absolutely no connection (at least that I can understand) between the tugging sensation and the decision to take food, or between the sensation of something causing pain and the mental apprehension of distress that arises from that sensation. These and other judgements that I made concerning sensory objects, I was apparently taught to make by nature; for I had already made up my mind that this was how things were, before working out any arguments to prove it.

Later on, however, I had many experiences which gradually undermined all the faith I had had in the senses. Sometimes towers which had looked round from a distance appeared square from close up; and enormous statues standing on their pediments did not seem large when observed from the ground. In these and countless other such cases, I found that the judgements of the external senses were mistaken. And this applied not just to the external senses but to the internal senses as well. For what can be more internal than pain? And yet I had heard that those who had had a leg or an arm amputated sometimes still seemed to feel pain intermittently in the missing part of the body. So even in my own case it was apparently not quite certain that a particular limb was hurting, even if I felt pain in it. To these reasons for doubting, I recently added two very general ones.[12] The first was that every sensory experience I have ever thought I was having while awake I can also think of myself as sometimes having while asleep; and since I do not believe that what I seem to perceive in sleep comes from things located outside me, I did not see why I should be any more inclined to believe this of what I think I perceive while awake. The second reason for doubt was that since I did not know the author of my being (or at least was pretending not to), I saw nothing to rule out the possibility that my natural constitution made me prone to error even in matters which seemed to me most true. As for the reasons for my previous confident belief in the truth of the things perceived by the senses, I had no trouble in refuting them. For since I apparently had natural impulses towards many things which reason told me to avoid, I reckoned that a great deal of confidence should not be placed in what I was taught by nature. And despite the fact that the perceptions of the senses were not dependent on my will, I did not think that I should on that account infer that they proceeded from things distinct from myself, since I might perhaps have a faculty not yet known to me which produced them.[13]

But now, when I am beginning to achieve a better knowledge of myself and the author of my being, although I do not think I should heedlessly accept everything I seem to have acquired from the senses, neither do I think that everything should be called into doubt.

First, I know that everything which I clearly and distinctly understand is capable of being created by God so as to correspond exactly with my understanding of it. Hence the fact that I can clearly and distinctly understand one thing apart from another is enough to make me certain that the two things are distinct, since they are capable of being separated, at least by God. The question of what kind of power is required to bring about such a separation does not affect the judgement that the two things are distinct. Thus, simply by knowing that I exist and seeing at the same time that absolutely nothing else belongs to my nature or essence except that I am a thinking thing, I can infer correctly that my essence consists solely in the fact that I am a thinking thing. It is true that I may have (or, to anticipate, that I certainly have) a body that is very closely joined to me. But nevertheless, on the one hand I have a clear and distinct idea of myself, in so far as I am simply a thinking, non-extended thing; and on the other hand I have a distinct idea of body,[14] in so far as this is simply an extended, non-thinking thing. And accordingly, it is certain that I[15] am really distinct from my body, and can exist without it.

Besides this, I find in myself faculties for certain special modes of thinking,[16] namely imagination and sensory perception. Now I can clearly and distinctly understand myself as a whole without these faculties; but I cannot, conversely, understand these faculties without me, that is, without an intellectual substance to inhere in. This is because there is an intellectual act included in their essential definition; and hence I perceive that the distinction between them and myself corresponds to the distinction between the modes of a thing and the thing itself.[17] Of course I also recognize that there are other faculties (like those of changing position, of taking on various shapes, and so on) which, like sensory perception and imagination, cannot be under-

stood apart from some substance for them to inhere in, and hence cannot exist without it. But it is clear that these other faculties, if they exist, must be in a corporeal or extended substance and not an intellectual one; for the clear and distinct conception of them includes extension, but does not include any intellectual act whatsoever. Now there is in me a passive faculty of sensory perception, that is, a faculty for receiving and recognizing the ideas of sensible objects; but I could not make use of it unless there was also an active faculty, either in me or in something else, which produced or brought about these ideas. But this faculty cannot be in me, since clearly it presupposes no intellectual act on my part,[18] and the ideas in question are produced without my cooperation and often even against my will. So the only alternative is that it is in another substance distinct from me—a substance which contains either formally or eminently all the reality which exists objectively[19] in the ideas produced by this faculty (as I have just noted). This substance is either a body, that is, a corporeal nature, in which case it will contain formally <and in fact> everything which is to be found objectively <or representatively> in the ideas; or else it is God, or some creature more noble than a body, in which case it will contain eminently whatever is to be found in the ideas. But since God is not a deceiver, it is quite clear that he does not transmit the ideas to me either directly from himself, or indirectly, via some creature which contains the objective reality of the ideas not formally but only eminently. For God has given me no faculty at all for recognizing any such source for these ideas; on the contrary, he has given me a great propensity to believe that they are produced by corporeal things. So I do not see how God could be understood to be anything but a deceiver if the ideas were transmitted from a source other than corporeal things. It follows that corporeal things exist. They may not all exist in a way that exactly corresponds with my sensory grasp of them, for in many cases the grasp of the senses is very obscure and confused. But at least they possess all the properties which I clearly and distinctly understand, that is, all those which, viewed in general terms, are comprised within the subject-matter of pure mathematics.

What of the other aspects of corporeal things which are either particular (for example that the sun is of such and such a size or shape), or less clearly understood, such as light or sound or pain, and so on? Despite the high degree of doubt and uncertainty involved here, the very fact that

God is not a deceiver, and the consequent impossibility of there being any falsity in my opinions which cannot be corrected by some other faculty supplied by God, offers me a sure hope that I can attain the truth even in these matters. Indeed, there is no doubt that everything that I am taught by nature contains some truth. For if nature is considered in its general aspect, then I understand by the term nothing other than God himself, or the ordered system of created things established by God. And by my own nature in particular I understand nothing other than the totality of things bestowed on me by God.

There is nothing that my own nature teaches me more vividly than that I have a body, and that when I feel pain there is something wrong with the body, and that when I am hungry or thirsty the body needs food and drink, and so on. So I should not doubt that there is some truth in this.

Nature also teaches me, by these sensations of pain, hunger, thirst and so on, that I am not merely present in my body as a sailor is present in a ship,[19] but that I am very closely joined and, as it were, intermingled with it, so that I and the body form a unit. If this were not so, I, who am nothing but a thinking thing, would not feel pain when the body was hurt, but would perceive the damage purely by the intellect, just as a sailor perceives by sight if anything in his ship is broken. Similarly, when the body needed food or drink, I should have an explicit understanding of the fact, instead of having confused sensations of hunger and thirst. For these sensations of hunger, thirst, pain and so on are nothing but confused modes of thinking which arise from the union and, as it were, intermingling of the mind with the body.

I am also taught by nature that various other bodies exist in the vicinity of my body, and that some of these are to be sought out and others avoided. And from the fact that I perceive by my senses a great variety of colours, sounds, smells and tastes, as well as differences in heat, hardness and the like, I am correct in inferring that the bodies which are the source of these various sensory perceptions possess differences corresponding to them, though perhaps not resembling them. Also, the fact that some of the perceptions are agreeable to me while others are disagreeable makes it quite certain that my body, or rather my whole self, in so far as I am a combination of body and mind, can be affected by the various beneficial or harmful bodies which surround it.

There are, however, many other things which I may appear to have been taught by nature, but which in reality I acquired not from nature but from a habit of making ill-considered judgements; and it is therefore quite possible that these are false. Cases in point are the belief that any space in which nothing is occurring to stimulate my senses must be empty; or that the heat in a body is something exactly resembling the idea of heat which is in me; or that when a body is white or green, the selfsame whiteness or greenness which I perceive through my senses is present in the body; or that in a body which is bitter or sweet there is the selfsame taste which I experience, and so on; or, finally, that stars and towers and other distant bodies have the same size and shape which they present to my senses, and other examples of this kind. But to make sure that my perceptions in this matter are sufficiently distinct, I must more accurately define exactly what I mean when I say that I am taught something by nature. In this context I am taking nature to be something more limited than the totality of things bestowed on me by God. For this includes many things that belong to the mind alone—for example my perception that what is done cannot be undone, and all other things that are known by the natural light;[20] but at this stage I am not speaking of these matters. It also includes much that relates to the body alone, like the tendency to move in a downward direction, and so on; but I am not speaking of these matters either. My sole concern here is with what God has bestowed on me as a combination of mind and body. My nature, then, in this limited sense, does indeed teach me to avoid what induces a feeling of pain and to seek out what induces feelings of pleasure, and so on. But it does not appear to teach us to draw any conclusions from these sensory perceptions about things located outside us without waiting until the intellect has examined[21] the matter. For knowledge of the truth about such things seems to belong to the mind alone, not to the combination of mind and body. Hence, although a star has no greater effect on my eye than the flame of a small light, that does not mean that there is any real or positive inclination in me to believe that the star is no bigger than the light; I have simply made this judgement from childhood onwards without any rational basis. Similarly, although I feel heat when I go near a fire and feel pain when I go too near, there is no convincing argument for supposing that there is something in the fire which resembles the heat, any more than for supposing that there is something which resembles the pain. There is simply reason to suppose that there is something in the fire, whatever it may eventually turn out to be, which produces in us the feelings of heat or pain. And likewise, even though there is nothing in any given space that stimulates the senses, it does not follow that there is no body there. In these cases and many others I see that I have been in the habit of misusing the order of nature. For the proper purpose of the sensory perceptions given me by nature is simply to inform the mind of what is beneficial or harmful for the composite of which the mind is a part; and to this extent they are sufficiently clear and distinct. But I misuse them by treating them as reliable touchstones for immediate judgements about the essential nature of the bodies located outside us; yet this is an area where they provide only very obscure information.

I have already looked in sufficient detail at how, notwithstanding the goodness of God, it may happen that my judgements are false. But a further problem now comes to mind regarding those very things which nature presents to me as objects which I should seek out or avoid, and also regarding the internal sensations, where I seem to have detected errors[22]—e.g. when someone is tricked by the pleasant taste of some food into eating the poison concealed inside it. Yet in this case, what the man's nature urges him to go for is simply what is responsible for the pleasant taste, and not the poison, which his nature knows nothing about. The only inference that can be drawn from this is that his nature is not omniscient. And this is not surprising, since man is a limited thing, and so it is only fitting that his perfection should be limited.

And yet it is not unusual for us to go wrong even in cases where nature does urge us towards something. Those who are ill, for example, may desire food or drink that will shortly afterwards turn out to be bad for them. Perhaps it may be said that they go wrong because their nature is disordered, but this does not remove the difficulty. A sick man is no less one of God's creatures than a healthy one, and it seems no less a contradiction to suppose that he has received from God a nature which deceives him. Yet a clock constructed with wheels and weights observes all the laws of its nature just as closely when it is badly made and tells the wrong time as when it completely fulfils the wishes of the clockmaker. In the same way, I might consider the body of a man as a kind of machine equipped with and made up of bones, nerves, muscles, veins, blood and skin in such a way that, even if there were no mind in it, it would

still perform all the same movements as it now does in those cases where movement is not under the control of the will or, consequently, of the mind.[23] I can easily see that if such a body suffers from dropsy, for example, and is affected by the dryness of the throat which normally produces in the mind the sensation of thirst, the resulting condition of the nerves and other parts will dispose the body to take a drink, with the result that the disease will be aggravated. Yet this is just as natural as the body's being stimulated by a similar dryness of the throat to take a drink when there is no such illness and the drink is beneficial. Admittedly, when I consider the purpose of the clock, I may say that it is departing from its nature when it does not tell the right time; and similarly when I consider the mechanism of the human body, I may think that, in relation to the movements which normally occur in it, it too is deviating from its nature if the throat is dry at a time when drinking is not beneficial to its continued health. But I am well aware that 'nature' as I have just used it has a very different significance from 'nature' in the other sense. As I have just used it, 'nature' is simply a label which depends on my thought; it is quite extraneous to the things to which it is applied, and depends simply on my comparison between the idea of a sick man and a badly-made clock, and the idea of a healthy man and a well-made clock. But by 'nature' in the other sense I understand something which is really to be found in the things themselves; in this sense, therefore, the term contains something of the truth.

When we say, then, with respect to the body suffering from dropsy, that it has a disordered nature because it has a dry throat and yet does not need drink, the term 'nature' is here used merely as an extraneous label. However, with respect to the composite, that is, the mind united with this body, what is involved is not a mere label, but a true error of nature, namely that it is thirsty at a time when drink is going to cause it harm. It thus remains to inquire how it is that the goodness of God does not prevent nature, in this sense, from deceiving us.

The first observation I make at this point is that there is a great difference between the mind and the body, inasmuch as the body is by its very nature always divisible, while the mind is utterly indivisible. For when I consider the mind, or myself in so far as I am merely a thinking thing, I am unable to distinguish any parts within myself; I understand myself to be something quite single and complete. Although the whole mind seems to be united to the whole body, I recognize that if a foot or arm or any other part of the body is cut off, nothing has thereby been taken away from the mind. As for the faculties of willing, of understanding, of sensory perception and so on, these cannot be termed parts of the mind, since it is one and the same mind that wills, and understands and has sensory perceptions. By contrast, there is no corporeal or extended thing that I can think of which in my thought I cannot easily divide into parts; and this very fact makes me understand that it is divisible. This one argument would be enough to show me that the mind is completely different from the body, even if I did not already know as much from other considerations.

My next observation is that the mind is not immediately affected by all parts of the body, but only by the brain, or perhaps just by one small part of the brain, namely the part which is said to contain the 'common' sense.[24] Every time this part of the brain is in a given state, it presents the same signals to the mind, even though the other parts of the body may be in a different condition at the time. This is established by countless observations, which there is no need to review here.

I observe, in addition, that the nature of the body is such that whenever any part of it is moved by another part which is some distance away, it can always be moved in the same fashion by any of the parts which lie in between, even if the more distant part does nothing. For example, in a cord ABCD, if one end D is pulled so that the other end A moves, the exact same movement could have been brought about if one of the intermediate points B or C had been pulled, and D had not moved at all. In similar fashion, when I feel a pain in my foot, physiology tells me that this happens by means of nerves distributed throughout the foot, and that these nerves are like cords which go from the foot right up to the brain. When the nerves are pulled in the foot, they in turn pull on inner parts of the brain to which they are attached, and produce a certain motion in them; and nature had laid it down that this motion should produce in the mind a sensation of pain, as occurring in the foot. But since these nerves, in passing from the foot to the brain, must pass through the calf, the thigh, the lumbar region, the back and the neck, it can happen that, even if it is not the part in the foot but one of the intermediate parts which is being pulled, the same motion will occur in the brain as

occurs when the foot is hurt, and so it will necessarily come about that the mind feels the same sensation of pain. And we must suppose the same thing happens with regard to any other sensation.

My final observation is that any given movement occurring in the part of the brain that immediately affects the mind produces just one corresponding sensation; and hence the best system that could be devised is that it should produce the one sensation which, of all possible sensations, is most especially and most frequently conducive to the preservation of the healthy man. And experience shows that the sensations which nature has given us are all of this kind; and so there is absolutely nothing to be found in them that does not bear witness to the power and goodness of God. For example, when the nerves in the foot are set in motion in a violent and unusual manner, this motion, by way of the spinal cord, reaches the inner parts of the brain, and there gives the mind its signal for having a certain sensation, namely the sensation of a pain as occurring in the foot. This stimulates the mind to do its best to get rid of the cause of the pain, which it takes to be harmful to the foot. It is true that God could have made the nature of man such that this particular motion in the brain indicated something else to the mind; it might, for example, have made the mind aware of the actual motion occurring in the brain, or in the foot, or in any of the intermediate regions; or it might have indicated something else entirely. But there is nothing else which would have been so conducive to the continued well-being of the body. In the same way, when we need drink, there arises a certain dryness in the throat; this sets in motion the nerves of the throat, which in turn move the inner parts of the brain. This motion produces in the mind a sensation of thirst, because the most useful thing for us to know about the whole business is that we need drink in order to stay healthy. And so it is in the other cases.

It is quite clear from all this that, notwithstanding the immense goodness of God, the nature of man as a combination of mind and body is such that it is bound to mislead him from time to time. For there may be some occurrence, not in the foot but in one of the other areas through which the nerves travel in their route from the foot to the brain, or even in the brain itself; and if this cause produces the same motion which is generally produced by injury to the foot, then pain will be felt as if it were in the foot. This deception of the senses is natural, because a given motion in the brain must always produce the same sensation in the mind; and the origin of the motion in question is much more often going to be something which is hurting the foot, rather than something existing elsewhere. So it is reasonable that this motion should always indicate to the mind a pain in the foot rather than in any other part of the body. Again, dryness of the throat may sometimes arise not, as it normally does, from the fact that a drink is necessary to the health of the body, but from some quite opposite cause, as happens in the case of the man with dropsy. Yet it is much better that it should mislead on this occasion than that it should always mislead when the body is in good health. And the same goes for the other cases.

This consideration is the greatest help to me, not only for noticing all the errors to which my nature is liable, but also for enabling me to correct or avoid them without difficulty. For I know that in matters regarding the well-being of the body, all my senses report the truth much more frequently than not. Also, I can almost always make use of more than one sense to investigate the same thing; and in addition, I can use both my memory, which connects present experiences with preceding ones, and my intellect, which has by now examined all the causes of error. Accordingly, I should not have any further fears about the falsity of what my senses tell me every day; on the contrary, the exaggerated doubts of the last few days should be dismissed as laughable. This applies especially to the principal reason for doubt, namely my inability to distinguish between being asleep and being awake. For I now notice that there is a vast difference between the two, in that dreams are never linked by memory with all the other actions of life as waking experiences are. If, while I am awake, anyone were suddenly to appear to me and then disappear immediately, as happens in sleep, so that I could not see where he had come from or where he had gone to, it would not be unreasonable for me to judge that he was a ghost, or a vision created in my brain,[25] rather than a real man. But when I distinctly see where things come from and where and when they come to me, and when I can connect my perceptions of them with the whole of the rest of my life without a break, then I am quite certain that when I encounter these things I am not asleep but awake. And I ought not to have even the slightest doubt of their reality if, after calling upon all the senses as well as my memory and my intellect in order to check them, I receive no conflicting reports from any of these sources. For from the fact that God is not a deceiver it follows that in cases like these I am completely free from error. But since the pressure of things to be done does not always allow us to stop and make such a meticulous check, it must be admitted that in this human life we are often liable to make mistakes about particular things, and we must acknowledge the weakness of our nature.

NOTES

1. '. . . puts into my mind' (French version).
2. '. . . or thought anything at all' (French version).
3. The word 'only' is most naturally taken as going with 'a thing that thinks', and this interpretation is followed in the French version. When discussing this passage with Gassendi, however, Descartes suggests that he meant the 'only' to govern 'in the strict sense'; cf. AT IXA 215; CSM II 276.
4. '. . . to see if I am not something more' (added in French version).
5. Lat. *maneat* ('let it stand'), first edition. The second edition has the indicative *manet*: 'The proposition still stands, *viz.* that I am nonetheless something.' The French version reads: 'without changing this supposition, I find that I am still certain that I am something'.
6. '. . . from this manner of conceiving things' (French version).
7. '. . . which can be conceived only by the understanding or the mind' (French version).
8. '. . . or rather the act whereby it is perceived' (added in French version).
9. See note 24 below.
10. The French version has 'more clear and distinct' and, at the end of this sentence, 'more evidently, distinctly and clearly.'
11. '. . . between the soul and body of a man' (French version).
12. Cf. Med. 1.
13. Cf. Med. III.
14. The Latin term *corpus* as used here by Descartes is ambiguous as between 'body' (i.e., corporeal matter in general) and 'the body' (i.e., this particular body of mine). The French version preserves the ambiguity.
15. '. . . that is, my soul, by which I am what I am' (added in French version).
16. '. . . certain modes of thinking which are quite special and distinct from me' (French version).
17. '. . . between the shapes, movements and other modes or accidents of a body and the body which supports them' (French version).
18. '. . . cannot be in me in so far as I am merely a thinking thing, since it does not presuppose any thought on my part' (French version).
19. '. . . as a pilot in his ship' (French version).

20. '. . . without any help from the body' (added in French version).
21. '. . . carefully and maturely examined' (French version).
22. '. . . and thus seem to have been directly deceived by my nature' (added in French version).
23. '. . . but occurs merely as a result of the disposition of the organs' (French version).
24. The supposed faculty which integrates the data from the five specialized senses (the notion goes back ultimately to Aristotle). 'The seat of the common sense must be very mobile, to receive all the impressions coming from the senses, but must be moveable only by the spirits which transmit these impressions. Only the *conarion* [pineal gland] fits these conditions' (letter to Mersenne, 21 April 1641).
25. '. . . like those that are formed in the brain when I sleep' (added in French version).

2 | The Passions of the Soul
René Descartes

17. The Functions of the Soul

Having thus considered all the functions belonging solely to the body, it is easy to recognize that there is nothing in us which we must attribute to our soul except our thoughts. These are of two principal kinds, some being actions of the soul and others its passions. Those I call its actions are all our volitions, for we experience them as proceeding directly from our soul and as seeming to depend on it alone. On the other hand, the various perceptions or modes of knowledge present in us may be called its passions, in a general sense, for it is often not our soul which makes them such as they are, and the soul always receives them from the things that are represented by them.

18. The Will

Our volitions, in turn, are of two sorts. One consists of the actions of the soul which terminate in the soul itself, as when we will to love God or, generally speaking, to apply our mind to some object which is not material. The other consists of actions which terminate in our body, as when our merely willing to walk has the consequence that our legs move and we walk.

19. Perception

Our perceptions are likewise of two sorts: some have the soul as their cause, others the body. Those having the soul as their cause are the perceptions of our volitions and of all the imaginings or other thoughts which depend on them. For it is certain that we cannot will anything without thereby perceiving that we are willing it. And although willing something is an action with respect to our soul, the perception of such willing may be said to be a passion in the soul. But because this perception is really one and the same thing as the volition, and names are always determined by whatever is most noble, we do not normally call it a 'passion', but solely an 'action'.

30. The Soul Is United to All the Parts of the Body Conjointly

But in order to understand all these things more perfectly, we need to recognize that the soul is really joined to the whole body, and that we cannot properly say that it exists in any one part of the body to the exclusion of the others. For the body is a unity which is in a sense indivisible because of the arrangement of its organs, these being so

Excerpted from J. Cottingham, R. Stoothoff, and D. Murdoch, eds./trans., *The Philosophical Writings of Descartes*, Volume 1 (Cambridge University Press, 1996), with the permission of Cambridge University Press. Copyright © 1996 Cambridge University Press.

related to one another that the removal of any one of them renders the whole body defective. And the soul is of such a nature that it has no relation to extension, or to the dimensions or other properties of the matter of which the body is composed: it is related solely to the whole assemblage of the body's organs. This is obvious from our inability to conceive of a half or a third of a soul, or of the extension which a soul occupies. Nor does the soul become any smaller if we cut off some part of the body, but it becomes completely separate from the body when we break up the assemblage of the body's organs.

31. There Is a Little Gland[1] in the Brain Where the Soul Exercises Its Functions More Particularly Than in the Other Parts of the Body

We need to recognize also that although the soul is joined to the whole body, nevertheless there is a certain part of the body where it exercises its functions more particularly than in all the others. It is commonly held that this part is the brain, or perhaps the heart—the brain because the sense organs are related to it, and the heart because we feel the passions as if they were in it. But on carefully examining the matter I think I have clearly established that the part of the body in which the soul directly exercises its functions is not the heart at all, or the whole of the brain. It is rather the innermost part of the brain, which is a certain very small gland situated in the middle of the brain's substance and suspended above the passage through which the spirits in the brain's anterior cavities communicate with those in its posterior cavities. The slightest movements on the part of this gland may alter very greatly the course of these spirits, and conversely any change, however slight, taking place in the course of the spirits may do much to change the movements of the gland.

32. How We Know That This Gland Is the Principal Seat of the Soul

Apart from this gland, there cannot be any other place in the whole body where the soul directly exercises its functions. I am convinced of this by the observation that all the other parts of our brain are double, as also are all the organs of our external senses—eyes, hands, ears and so on. But in so far as we have only one simple thought about a given object at any one time, there must necessarily be some place where the two images coming through the two eyes, or the two impressions coming from a single object through the double organs of any other sense, can come together in a single image or impression before reaching the soul, so that they do not present to it two objects instead of one. We can easily understand that these images or other impressions are unified in this gland by means of the spirits which fill the cavities of the brain. But they cannot exist united in this way in any other place in the body except as a result of their being united in this gland.

33. The Seat of the Passions Is Not in the Heart

As for the opinion of those who think that the soul receives its passions in the heart, this is not worth serious consideration, since it is based solely on the fact that the passions make us feel some change in the heart. It is easy to see that the only reason why this change is felt as occurring in the heart is that there is a small nerve which descends to it from the brain—just as pain is felt as in the foot by means of the nerves in the foot, and the stars are perceived as in the sky by means of their light and the optic nerves. Thus it is no more necessary that our soul should exercise its functions directly in the heart in order to feel its passions there, than that it should be in the sky in order to see the stars there.

34. How the Soul and the Body Act on Each Other

Let us therefore take it that the soul has its principal seat in the small gland located in the middle of the brain. From there it radiates through the rest of the body by means of the animal spirits, the nerves, and even the blood, which can take on the impressions of the spirits and carry them through the arteries to all the limbs. Let us recall what we said previously about the mechanism of our body. The nerve-fibres are so distributed in all the parts of the body that when the objects of the senses produce various different movements in these parts, the fibres are occasioned to open the pores of the brain in various different ways. This, in turn, causes the animal spirits contained in these cavities to enter the muscles in various different ways. In this manner the spirits can move the limbs in all the different ways they are capable of being moved. And all the other causes that can move the spirits in different ways are sufficient to direct them into different muscles. To this we may now add that the small gland which is the principal seat of the soul is suspended within the cavities containing these spirits, so that it can be moved by them in as many different ways as there are perceptible differences in the objects. But it can also be moved in various different ways by the soul, whose nature is such that it receives as many different impressions—that is, it has as many different perceptions as there occur different movements in this gland. And conversely, the mechanism of our body is so constructed that simply by this gland's being moved in any way by the soul or by any other cause, it drives the surrounding spirits towards the pores of the brain, which direct them through the nerves to the muscles; and in this way the gland makes the spirits move the limbs.

35. Example of the Way in which the Impressions of Objects Are United in the Gland in the Middle of the Brain

Thus, for example, if we see some animal approaching us, the light reflected from its body forms two images, one in each of our eyes; and these images form two others, by means of the optic nerves, on the internal surface of the brain facing its cavities. Then, by means of the spirits that fill these cavities, the images radiate towards the little gland which the spirits surround: the movement forming each point of one of the images tends towards the same point on the gland as the movement forming the corresponding point of the other image, which represents the same part of the animal. In this way, the two images in the brain form only one image on the gland, which acts directly upon the soul and makes it see the shape of the animal.

36. Example of the Way in which the Passions Are Aroused in the Soul

If, in addition, this shape is very strange and terrifying—that is, if it has a close relation to things which have previously been harmful to the body—this arouses the passion of anxiety in the soul, and then that of courage or perhaps fear and terror, depending upon the particular temperament of the body or the strength of the soul, and upon whether we have protected ourselves previously by defence or by flight against the harmful things to which the present impression is related. Thus in certain persons these factors dispose their brain in such a way that some of the spirits reflected from the image formed on the gland proceed from there to the nerves which serve to turn the back and move the legs in order to flee. The rest of the spirits go to nerves which expand or constrict the orifices of the heart, or else to nerves which agitate other parts of the body from which blood is sent to the heart, so that the blood is rarefied in a different manner from usual and spirits are sent to the brain which are adapted for maintaining and strengthening the passion of fear—that is, for holding open or re-opening the pores of the brain which direct the spirits into these same nerves. For merely by entering into these pores they produce in the gland a particular movement which is ordained by nature to make the soul feel this passion. And since these pores are related mainly to the little nerves which serve to contract or expand the orifices of the heart, this makes the soul feel the passion chiefly as if it were in the heart.

NOTE

1. The pineal gland.

3 | On the Hypothesis That Animals Are Automata, and Its History

Thomas H. Huxley

... Thus far, the propositions respecting the physiology of the nervous system which are stated by Descartes have simply been more clearly defined, more fully illustrated, and, for the most part, demonstrated, by modern physiological research. But there remains a doctrine to which Descartes attached great weight, so that full acceptance of it became a sort of note of a thoroughgoing Cartesian, but which, nevertheless, is so opposed to ordinary prepossessions that it attained more general notoriety, and gave rise to more discussion, than almost any other Cartesian hypothesis. It is the doctrine that brute animals are mere machines or automata, devoid not only of reason, but of any kind of consciousness, which is stated briefly in the "Discours de la Méthode," and more fully in the "Réponses aux Quatrièmes Objections," and in the correspondence with Henry More.[1]

The process of reasoning by which Descartes arrived at this startling conclusion is well shown in the following passage of the "Réponses":—

> But as regards the souls of beasts, although this is not the place for considering them, and though, without a general exposition of physics, I can say no more on this subject than I have already said in the fifth part of my Treatise on Method; yet, I will further state, here, that it appears to me to be a very remarkable circumstance that no movement can take place, either in the bodies of beasts, or even in our own, if these bodies have not in themselves all the organs and instruments by means of which the very same movements would be accomplished in a machine. So that, even in us, the spirit, or the soul, does not directly move the limbs, but only determines the course of that very subtle liquid which is called the animal spirits, which, running continually from the heart by the brain into the muscles, is the cause of all the movements of our limbs, and often may cause many different motions, one as easily as the other.
>
> And it does not even always exert this determination; for among the movements which take place in us, there are many which do not depend on the mind at all, such as the beating of the heart, the digestion of food, the nutrition, the respiration of those who sleep; and even in those who are awake, walking, singing, and other similar actions, when they are performed without the mind thinking about them. And, when one who falls from a height throws his hands forward to save his head, it is in virtue of no ratiocination that he performs this action; it does not depend upon his mind, but takes place merely because his senses being affected by the present danger, some change arises in his brain which determines the animal spirits to pass thence into the nerves, in such a manner as is required to produce this motion, in the same way as in a machine, and without the mind being able to hinder it. Now since we observe this in ourselves, why should we be so much astonished if the light reflected from the body of a wolf into the eye of a sheep has the same force to excite in it the motion of flight?
>
> After having observed this, if we wish to learn by reasoning, whether certain movements of beasts are comparable to those which are effected in us by the operation of the mind, or, on the contrary, to those which depend only on the animal spirits and the disposition of the organs, it is necessary to consider the difference between the two, which I have explained in the fifth part of the Discourse on Method (for I do not think that any others are discoverable), and then it will easily be seen, that all the actions of beasts are similar only to those which we perform without the help of our minds. For which reason we shall be forced to conclude, that we know of the existence in them of no other principle of motion than the disposition of their organs and the continual affluence of animal spirits produced by the heat of the heart, which attenuates and subtilises the blood; and, at the same time, we shall acknowledge that we have had no reason for assuming any other principle, except that, not having distinguished these two principles of motion, and seeing that the one, which depends only on the animal spirits and the organs, exists in beasts as well as in us, we have hastily concluded that the other, which depends on mind and on thought, was also possessed by them.

Excerpted from *Fortnightly Review* 16:555–80, 1874.

Descartes' line of argument is perfectly clear. He starts from reflex action in man, from the unquestionable fact that, in ourselves, co-ordinate, purposive, actions may take place, without the intervention of consciousness or volition, or even contrary to the latter. As actions of a certain degree of complexity are brought about by mere mechanism, why may not actions of still greater complexity be the result of a more refined mechanism? What proof is there that brutes are other than a superior race of marionettes, which eat without pleasure, cry without pain, desire nothing, know nothing, and only simulate intelligence as a bee simulates a mathematician?[2]

The Port Royalists adopted the hypothesis that brutes are machines, and are said to have carried its practical applications so far as to treat domestic animals with neglect, if not with actual cruelty. As late as the middle of the eighteenth century, the problem was discussed very fully and ably by Bouillier, in his "Essai philosophique sur l'Ame des Bêtes," while Condillac deals with it in his "Traite des Animaux"; but since then it has received little attention. Nevertheless, modern research has brought to light a great multitude of facts, which not only show that Descartes' view is defensible, but render it far more defensible than it was in his day.

It must be premised, that it is wholly impossible absolutely to prove the presence or absence of consciousness in anything but one's own brain, though, by analogy, we are justified in assuming its existence in other men. Now if, by some accident, a man's spinal cord is divided, his limbs are paralysed, so far as his volition is concerned, below the point of injury; and he is incapable of experiencing all those states of consciousness which, in his uninjured state, would be excited by irritation of those nerves which come off below the injury. If the spinal cord is divided in the middle of the back, for example, the skin of the feet may be cut, or pinched, or burned, or wetted with vitriol, without any sensation of touch, or of pain, arising in consciousness. So far as the man is concerned, therefore, the part of the central nervous system which lies beyond the injury is cut off from consciousness. It must indeed be admitted, that, if any one think fit to maintain that the spinal cord below the injury is conscious, but that it is cut off from any means of making its consciousness known to the other consciousness in the brain, there is no means of driving him from his position by logic. But assuredly there is no way of

proving it, and in the matter of consciousness, if in anything, we may hold by the rule, "De non apparentibus et de non existentibus eadem est ratio." However near the brain the spinal cord is injured, consciousness remains intact, except that the irritation of parts below the injury is no longer represented by sensation. On the other hand, pressure upon the anterior division of the brain, or extensive injuries to it, abolish consciousness. Hence, it is a highly probable conclusion, that consciousness in man depends upon the integrity of the anterior division of the brain, while the middle and hinder divisions of the brain,[3] and the rest of the nervous centres, have nothing to do with it. And it is further highly probable, that what is true for man is true for other vertebrated animals.

We may assume, then, that in a living vertebrated animal, any segment of the cerebro-spinal axis (or spinal cord and brain) separated from that anterior division of the brain which is the organ of consciousness, is as completely incapable of giving rise to consciousness as we know it to be incapable of carrying out volitions. Nevertheless, this separated segment of the spinal cord is not passive and inert. On the contrary, it is the seat of extremely remarkable powers. In our imaginary case of injury, the man would, as we have seen, be devoid of sensation in his legs, and would have not the least power of moving them. But, if the soles of his feet were tickled, the legs would be drawn up just as vigorously as they would have been before the injury. We know exactly what happens when the soles of the feet are tickled; a molecular change takes place in the sensory nerves of the skin, and is propagated along them and through the posterior roots of the spinal nerves, which are constituted by them, to the grey matter of the spinal cord. Through that grey matter the molecular motion is reflected into the anterior roots of the same nerves, constituted by the filaments which supply the muscles of the legs, and, travelling along these motor filaments, reaches the muscles, which at once contract, and cause the limbs to be drawn up.

In order to move the legs in this way, a definite co-ordination of muscular contractions is necessary; the muscles must contract in a certain order and with duly proportioned force; and moreover, as the feet are drawn away from the source of irritation, it may be said that the action has a final cause, or is purposive.

Thus it follows, that the grey matter of the segment of the man's spinal cord, though it is devoid of consciousness, nevertheless responds to a simple stimulus by giving rise to a complex set of muscular contractions, co-ordinated towards a definite end, and serving an obvious purpose.

If the spinal cord of a frog is cut across, so as to provide us with a segment separated from the brain, we shall have a subject parallel to the injured man, on which experiments can be made without remorse; as we have a right to conclude that a frog's spinal cord is not likely to be conscious, when a man's is not.

Now the frog behaves just as the man did. The legs are utterly paralysed, so far as voluntary movement is concerned; but they are vigorously drawn up to the body when any irritant is applied to the foot. But let us study our frog a little farther. Touch the skin of the side of the body with a little acetic acid, which gives rise to all the signs of great pain in an uninjured frog. In this case, there can be no pain, because the application is made to a part of the skin supplied with nerves which come off from the cord below the point of section; nevertheless, the frog lifts up the limb of the same side, and applies the foot to rub off the acetic acid; and, what is still more remarkable, if the limb be held so that the frog cannot use it, it will, by and by, move the limb of the other side, turn it across the body, and use it for the same rubbing process. It is impossible that the frog, if it were in its entirety and could reason, should perform actions more purposive than these: and yet we have most complete assurance that, in this case, the frog is not acting from purpose, has no consciousness, and is a mere insensible machine.

But now suppose that, instead of making a section of the cord in the middle of the body, it had been made in such a manner as to separate the hindermost division of the brain from the rest of the organ, and suppose the foremost two-thirds of the brain entirely taken away. The frog is then absolutely devoid of any spontaneity; it sits upright in the attitude which a frog habitually assumes; and it will not stir unless it is touched; but it differs from the frog which I have just described in this, that, if it be thrown into the water, it begins to swim, and swims just as well as the perfect frog does. But swimming requires the combination and successive co-ordination of a great number of muscular actions. And we are forced to conclude, that the impression made upon the sensory nerves of the skin of the frog by the contact with the water into which it is thrown, causes the transmission

to the central nervous apparatus of an impulse which sets going a certain machinery by which all the muscles of swimming are brought into play in due co-ordination. If the frog be stimulated by some irritating body, it jumps or walks as well as the complete frog can do. The simple sensory impression, acting through the machinery of the cord, gives rise to these complex combined movements.

It is possible to go a step farther. Suppose that only the anterior division of the brain—so much of it as lies in front of the "optic lobes"—is removed. If that operation is performed quickly and skilfully, the frog may be kept in a state of full bodily vigour for months, or it may be for years; but it will sit unmoved. It sees nothing: it hears nothing. It will starve sooner than feed itself, although food put into its mouth is swallowed. On irritation, it jumps or walks; if thrown into the water it swims. If it be put on the hand, it sits there, crouched, perfectly quiet, and would sit there for ever. If the hand be inclined very gently and slowly, so that the frog would naturally tend to slip off, the creature's fore paws are shifted on to the edge of the hand, until he can just prevent himself from falling. If the turning of the hand be slowly continued, he mounts up with great care and deliberation, putting first one leg forward and then another, until he balances himself with perfect precision upon the edge; and if the turning of the hand is continued, he goes through the needful set of muscular operations, until he comes to be seated in security, upon the back of the hand. The doing of all this requires a delicacy of coordination, and a precision of adjustment of the muscular apparatus of the body, which are only comparable to those of a rope-dancer. To the ordinary influences of light, the frog, deprived of its cerebral hemispheres, appears to be blind. Nevertheless, if the animal be put upon a table, with a book at some little distance between it and the light, and the skin of the hinder part of its body is then irritated, it will jump forward, avoiding the book by passing to the right or left of it. Therefore, although the frog appears to have no sensation of light, visible objects act through its brain upon the motor mechanism of its body.[4]

It is obvious, that had Descartes been acquainted with these remarkable results of modern research, they would have furnished him with far more powerful arguments than he possessed in favour of his view of the automatism of brutes. The habits of a frog, leading its natural life, involve such simple adaptations to surrounding conditions, that the machinery which is competent to do so much without the intervention of consciousness, might well do all. And this argument is vastly strengthened by what has been learned in recent times of the marvellously complex operations which are performed mechanically, and to all appearance without consciousness, by men, when, in consequence of injury or disease, they are reduced to a condition more or less comparable to that of a frog, in which the anterior part of the brain has been removed. A case has recently been published by an eminent French physician, Dr. Mesnet, which illustrates this condition so remarkably, that I make no apology for dwelling upon it at considerable length.[5]

A sergeant of the French army, F—, twenty-seven years of age, was wounded during the battle of Bazeilles, by a ball which fractured his left parietal bone. He ran his bayonet through the Prussian soldier who wounded him, but almost immediately his right arm became paralysed; after walking about two hundred yards, his right leg became similarly affected, and he lost his senses. When he recovered them, three weeks afterwards, in hospital at Mayence, the right half of the body was completely paralysed, and remained in this condition for a year. At present, the only trace of the paralysis which remains is a slight weakness of the right half of the body. Three or four months after the wound was inflicted, periodical disturbances of the functions of the brain made their appearance, and have continued ever since. The disturbances last from fifteen to thirty hours; the intervals at which they occur being from fifteen to thirty days.

For four years, therefore, the life of this man has been divided into alternating phases—short abnormal states intervening between long normal states.

In the periods of normal life, the ex-sergeant's health is perfect; he is intelligent and kindly, and performs, satisfactorily, the duties of a hospital attendant. The commencement of the abnormal state is ushered in by uneasiness and a sense of weight about the forehead, which the patient compares to the constriction of a circle of iron; and, after its termination, he complains, for some hours, of dulness and heaviness of the head. But the transition from the normal to the abnormal state takes place in a few minutes, without convulsions or cries, and without anything to indicate the change to a bystander. His movements remain free and his expression calm, except for a contraction of the brow, an in-

cessant movement of the eyeballs, and a chewing motion of the jaws. The eyes are wide open, and their pupils dilated. If the man happens to be in a place to which he is accustomed, he walks about as usual; but, if he is in a new place, or if obstacles are intentionally placed in his way, he stumbles gently against them, stops, and then, feeling over the objects with his hands, passes on one side of them. He offers no resistance to any change of direction which may be impressed upon him, or to the forcible acceleration or retardation of his movements. He eats, drinks, smokes, walks about, dresses and undresses himself, rises and goes to bed at the accustomed hours. Nevertheless, pins may be run into his body, or strong electric shocks sent through it, without causing the least indication of pain; no odorous substance, pleasant or unpleasant, makes the least impression; he eats and drinks with avidity whatever is offered, and takes asafœtida, or vinegar, or quinine, as readily as water; no noise affects him; and light influences him only under certain conditions. Dr. Mesnet remarks, that the sense of touch alone seems to persist, and indeed to be more acute and delicate than in the normal state: and it is by means of the nerves of touch, almost exclusively, that his organism is brought into relation with the external world. Here a difficulty arises. It is clear from the facts detailed, that the nervous apparatus by which, in the normal state, sensations of touch are excited, is that by which external influences determine the movements of the body, in the abnormal state. But does the state of consciousness, which we term a tactile sensation, accompany the operation of this nervous apparatus in the abnormal state? or is consciousness utterly absent, the man being reduced to an insensible mechanism? . . .

As I have pointed out, it is impossible to prove that F— is absolutely unconscious in his abnormal state, but it is no less impossible to prove the contrary; and the case of the frog goes a long way to justify the assumption that, in the abnormal state, the man is a mere insensible machine.

If such facts as these had come under the knowledge of Descartes, would they not have formed an apt commentary upon that remarkable passage in the "Traité de l'Homme," which I have quoted elsewhere, but which is worth repetition?—

All the functions which I have attributed to this machine (the body), as the digestion of food, the pulsation of the heart and of the arteries; the nutrition and the growth of the limbs; respiration, wakefulness, and sleep; the reception of light, sounds, odours, flavours, heat, and such like qualities, in the organs of the external senses; the impression of the ideas of these in the organ of common sensation and in the imagination; the retention or the impression of these ideas on the memory; the internal movements of the appetites and the passions; and lastly the external movements of all the limbs, which follow so aptly, as well the action of the objects which are presented to the senses, as the impressions which meet in the memory, that they imitate as nearly as possible those of a real man; I desire, I say, that you should consider that these functions in the machine naturally proceed from the mere arrangement of its organs, neither more nor less than do the movements of a clock, or other automaton, from that of its weights and its wheels; so that, so far as these are concerned, it is not necessary to conceive any other vegetative or sensitive soul, nor any other principle of motion or of life, than the blood and the spirits agitated by the fire which burns continually in the heart, and which is no wise essentially different from all the fires which exist in inanimate bodies.

And would Descartes not have been justified in asking why we need deny that animals are machines, when men, in a state of unconsciousness, perform, mechanically, actions as complicated and as seemingly rational as those of any animals?

But though I do not think that Descartes' hypothesis can be positively refuted, I am not disposed to accept it. The doctrine of continuity is too well established for it to be permissible to me to suppose that any complex natural phenomenon comes into existence suddenly, and without being preceded by simpler modifications; and very strong arguments would be needed to prove that such complex phenomena as those of consciousness, first make their appearance in man. We know, that, in the individual man, consciousness grows from a dim glimmer to its full light, whether we consider the infant advancing in years, or the adult emerging from slumber and swoon. We know, further, that the lower animals possess, though less developed, that part of the brain which we have every reason to believe to be the organ of consciousness in man; and as, in other cases, function and organ are proportional, so we have a right to conclude it is with the brain; and that the brutes, though they may not possess our intensity of consciousness, and though, from the absence of language, they can have no trains of thoughts, but only trains of feelings, yet have a consciousness which, more or less distinctly, foreshadows our own.

I confess that, in view of the struggle for existence which goes on in the animal world, and of the frightful quantity of pain with which it must be accompanied, I should be glad if the probabilities were in favour of Descartes' hypothesis; but, on the other hand, considering the terrible practical consequences to domestic animals which might ensue from any error on our part, it is as well to err on the right side, if we err at all, and deal with them as weaker brethren, who are bound, like the rest of us, to pay their toll for living, and suffer what is needful for the general good. As Hartley finely says, "We seem to be in the place of God to them"; and we may justly follow the precedents He sets in nature in our dealings with them.

But though we may see reason to disagree with Descartes' hypothesis that brutes are unconscious machines, it does not follow that he was wrong in regarding them as automata. They may be more or less conscious, sensitive, automata; and the view that they are such conscious machines is that which is implicitly, or explicitly, adopted by most persons. When we speak of the actions of the lower animals being guided by instinct and not by reason, what we really mean is that, though they feel as we do, yet their actions are the results of their physical organisation. We believe, in short, that they are machines, one part of which (the nervous system) not only sets the rest in motion, and co-ordinates its movements in relation with changes in surrounding bodies, but is provided with special apparatus, the function of which is the calling into existence of those states of consciousness which are termed sensations, emotions, and ideas. I believe that this generally accepted view is the best expression of the facts at present known.

It is experimentally demonstrable—any one who cares to run a pin into himself may perform a sufficient demonstration of the fact—that a mode of motion of the nervous system is the immediate antecedent of a state of consciousness. All but the adherents of "Occasionalism," or of the doctrine of "Pre-established Harmony" (if any such now exist), must admit that we have as much reason for regarding the mode of motion of the nervous system as the cause of the state of consciousness, as we have for regarding any event as the cause of another. How the one phenomenon causes the other we know, as much or as little, as in any other case of causation; but we have as much right to believe that the sensation is an effect of the molecular change, as we have to believe that motion is an effect of impact; and there is as much propriety in saying that the brain evolves sensation, as there is in saying that an iron rod, when hammered, evolves heat.

As I have endeavoured to show, we are justified in supposing that something analogous to what happens in ourselves takes place in the brutes, and that the affections of their sensory nerves give rise to molecular changes in the brain, which again give rise to, or evolve, the corresponding states of consciousness. Nor can there be any reasonable doubt that the emotions of brutes, and such ideas as they possess, are similarly dependent upon molecular brain changes. Each sensory impression leaves behind a record in the structure of the brain—an "ideagenous" molecule, so to speak, which is competent, under certain conditions, to reproduce, in a fainter condition, the state of consciousness which corresponds with that sensory impression; and it is these "ideagenous molecules" which are the physical basis of memory.

It may be assumed, then, that molecular changes in the brain are the causes of all the states of consciousness of brutes. Is there any evidence that these states of consciousness may, conversely, cause those molecular changes which give rise to muscular motion? I see no such evidence. The frog walks, hops, swims, and goes through his gymnastic performances quite as well without consciousness, and consequently without volition, as with it; and, if a frog, in his natural state, possesses anything corresponding with what we call volition, there is no reason to think that it is anything but a concomitant of the molecular changes in the brain which form part of the series involved in the production of motion.

The consciousness of brutes would appear to be related to the mechanism of their body simply as a collateral product of its working, and to be as completely without any power of modifying that working as the steam-whistle which accompanies the work of a locomotive engine is without influence upon its machinery. Their volition, if they have any, is an emotion indicative of physical changes, not a cause of such changes.

This conception of the relations of states of consciousness with molecular changes in the brain—of *psychoses* with *neuroses*—does not prevent us from ascribing free will to brutes. For an agent is free when there is nothing to prevent him from doing that which he desires to do. If a greyhound chases a hare, he is a free agent, because his action is in entire accordance with his strong desire to catch the hare; while so long as he is held back by the leash he is not free, being prevented by external force from following his inclination. And the ascription of freedom to the greyhound under the former circumstances is by no means inconsistent with the other aspect of the facts of the case—that he is a machine impelled to the chase, and caused, at the same time, to have the desire to catch the game by the impression which the rays of light proceeding from the hare make upon his eyes, and through them upon his brain.

Much ingenious argument has at various times been bestowed upon the question: How is it possible to imagine that volition, which is a state of consciousness, and, as such, has not the slightest community of nature with matter in motion, can act upon the moving matter of which the body is composed, as it is assumed to do in voluntary acts? But if, as is here suggested, the voluntary acts of brutes—or, in other words, the acts which they desire to perform—are as purely mechanical as the rest of their actions, and are simply accompanied by the state of consciousness called volition, the inquiry, so far as they are concerned, becomes superfluous. Their volitions do not enter into the chain of causation of their actions at all.

The hypothesis that brutes are conscious automata is perfectly consistent with any view that may be held respecting the often discussed and curious question whether they have souls or not; and, if they have souls, whether those souls are immortal or not. It is obviously harmonious with the most literal adherence to the text of Scripture concerning "the beast that perisheth"; but it is not inconsistent with the amiable conviction ascribed by Pope to his "untutored savage," that when he passes to the happy hunting-grounds in the sky, "his faithful dog shall bear him company." If the brutes have consciousness and no souls, then it is clear that, in them, consciousness is a direct function of material changes; while, if they possess immaterial subjects of consciousness, or souls, then, as consciousness is brought into existence only as the consequence of molecular motion of the brain, it follows that it is an indirect product of material changes. The soul stands related to the body as the bell of a clock to the works, and consciousness answers to the sound which the bell gives out when it is struck.

Thus far I have strictly confined myself to the problem with which I proposed to deal at starting—the automatism of brutes. The question is, I believe, a perfectly open one, and I feel happy in running no risk of either Papal or Presbyterian condemnation for the views which I have ventured to put forward. And there are so very few interesting questions which one is, at present, allowed to think out scientifically—to go as far as reason leads, and stop where evidence comes to an end—without speedily being deafened by the tattoo of "the drum ecclesiastic"— that I have luxuriated in my rare freedom, and would now willingly bring this disquisition to an end if I could hope that other people would go no farther. Unfortunately, past experience debars me from entertaining any such hope, even if

> *. . . that drum's discordant sound*
> *Parading round and round and round,*

were not, at present, as audible to me as it was to the mild poet who ventured to express his hatred of drums in general, in that well-known couplet.

It will be said, that I mean that the conclusions deduced from the study of the brutes are applicable to man, and that the logical consequences of such application are fatalism, materialism, and atheism—whereupon the drums will beat the *pas de charge.*

One does not do battle with drummers; but I venture to offer a few remarks for the calm consideration of thoughtful persons, untrammelled by foregone conclusions, unpledged to shore-up tottering dogmas, and anxious only to know the true bearings of the case.

It is quite true that, to the best of my judgment, the argumentation which applies to brutes holds equally good of men; and, therefore, that all states of consciousness in us, as in them, are immediately caused by molecular changes of the brain-substance. It seems to me that in men, as in brutes, there is no proof that any state of consciousness is the cause of change in the motion of the matter of the organism. If these positions are well based, it follows that our mental conditions are simply the symbols in consciousness of the changes which takes place automatically in the organism; and that, to take an extreme illustration, the feeling we call volition is not the cause of a voluntary act, but the symbol of that state of the brain which is the immediate cause of that act. We are conscious automata, endowed with free will in the only intelligible sense of that much-abused term—inasmuch as in many respects we are able to do as we like— but nonetheless parts of the great series of causes and effects which, in unbroken continuity, composes that which is, and has been, and shall be—the sum of existence. . . .

NOTES

1. *Réponse de M. Descartes a M. Morus.* 1649. *Œuevres,* tome x. p. 204. "Mais le plus grand de tous les préjugés que nous ayons retenus de notre enfance, est celui de croire que les bêtes pensent," etc.

2. Malebranche states the view taken by orthodox Cartesians in 1689 very forcibly: "Ainsi dans les chiens, les chats, et les autres animaux, il n'y a ny intelligence, ny âme spirituelle comme on l'entend ordinairement. Ils mangent sans plaisir; ils crient sans douleur; ils croissent sans le sçavoir; ils ne desirent rien; ils ne connoissent rien; et s'ils agissent avec adresse et d'une maniere qui marque l'intelligence, c'est que Dieu les faisant pour les conserver, il a conformé leurs corps de telle manière, qu'ils évitent organiquement, sans le sçavoir, tout ce qui peut les de truire et qu'ils semblent craindre." *Feuillet de Conches. Méditations Métaphysiques et Correspon-*

dance de. N. Malebranche. Neuvième Méditation. 1841.

3. Not to be confounded with the anterior middle and hinder parts of the hemispheres of the cerebrum.

4. See the remarkable essay of Göltz, *Beitrage zur Lehre von den Functionen der Nervencentren des Frosches,* published in 1809. I have repeated Göltz's experiments, and obtained the same results.

5. "De l'Automatisme de la Mémoire et du Souvenir, dans le Somnambulisme pathologique." Par le Dr. E. Mesnet, Médecin de l'Hôpital Saint-Antoine. *L'Union Médicale,* Juillet 21 et 23, 1874. My attention was first called to a summary of this remarkable case, which appeared in the *Journal des Débats* for the 7th of August, 1874, by my friend General Strachey, F.R.S.

4 An Unfortunate Dualist

Raymond M. Smullyan

Once upon a time there was a dualist. He believed that mind and matter are separate substances. Just how they interacted he did not pretend to know—this was one of the "mysteries" of life. But he was sure they were quite separate substances.

This dualist, unfortunately, led an unbearably painful life—not because of his philosophical beliefs, but for quite different reasons. And he had excellent empirical evidence that no respite was in sight for the rest of his life. He longed for nothing more than to die. But he was deterred from suicide by such reasons as: (1) he did not want to hurt other people by his death; (2) he was afraid suicide might be morally wrong; (3) he was afraid there *might* be an afterlife, and he did not want to risk the possibility of eternal punishment. So our poor dualist was quite desperate.

Then came the discovery of *the* miracle drug! Its effect on the taker was to annihilate the soul or mind entirely but to leave the body functioning *exactly* as before. Absolutely no observable change came over the taker; the body continued to act just as if it still had a soul. Not the closest friend or observer could possibly know that the taker had taken the drug, unless the taker informed him.

Do you believe that such a drug is impossible in principle? Assuming you believe it possible, would you take it? Would you regard it as immoral? Is it tantamount to suicide? Is there anything in Scriptures forbidding the use of such a drug? Surely, the *body* of the taker can still fulfill all its responsibilities on earth. Another question: Suppose your spouse took such a drug, and you knew it. You would know that she (or he) no longer had a soul but acted just as if she did have one. Would you love your mate any less?

To return to the story, our dualist was, of course, delighted! Now he could annihilate himself (his *soul,* that is) in a way not subject to any of the foregoing objections. And so, for the first time in years, he went to bed with a light heart, saying: "Tomorrow morning I will go down to the drugstore and get the drug. My days of suffering are over at last!" With these thoughts, he fell peacefully asleep.

Now at this point a curious thing happened. A friend of the dualist who knew about this drug, and who knew of the sufferings of the dualist, decided to put him out of his misery. So in the middle of the night, while the dualist was fast asleep, the friend quietly stole into the house and injected the drug into his veins. The next morning the body of the dualist awoke—without any soul indeed—and the first thing it did was to go to the drugstore to get the drug. He took it home and, before taking it, said, "Now I shall be released." So he took it and then waited the time interval in which it was supposed to work. At the end of the interval he angrily exclaimed: "Damn it, this stuff hasn't helped at all! I still obviously have a soul and am suffering as much as ever!"

Doesn't all this suggest that perhaps there might be something just a *little* wrong with dualism?

From *This Book Needs No Title* (Prentice-Hall, 1980), pp. 53–55. Reprinted by permission of the author.

5 | Descartes' Myth
Gilbert Ryle

1. The Official Doctrine

There is a doctrine about the nature and place of minds which is so prevalent among theorists and even among laymen that it deserves to be described as the official theory. Most philosophers, psychologists and religious teachers subscribe, with minor reservations, to its main articles and, although they admit certain theoretical difficulties in it, they tend to assume that these can be overcome without serious modifications being made to the architecture of the theory. It will be argued here that the central principles of the doctrine are unsound and conflict with the whole body of what we know about minds when we are not speculating about them.

The official doctrine, which hails chiefly from Descartes, is something like this. With the doubtful exceptions of idiots and infants in arms every human being has both a body and a mind. Some would prefer to say that every human being is both a body and a mind. His body and his mind are ordinarily harnessed together, but after the death of the body his mind may continue to exist and function.

Human bodies are in space and are subject to the mechanical laws which govern all other bodies in space. Bodily processes and states can be inspected by external observers. So a man's bodily life is as much a public affair as are the lives of animals and reptiles and even as the careers of trees, crystals and planets.

But minds are not in space, nor are their operations subject to mechanical laws. The workings of one mind are not witnessable by other observers; its career is private. Only I can take direct cognisance of the states and processes of my own mind. A person therefore lives through two collateral histories, one consisting of what happens in and to his body, the other consisting of what happens in and to his mind. The first is public, the second private. The events in the first history are events in the physical world, those in the second are events in the mental world.

It has been disputed whether a person does or can directly monitor all or only some of the episodes of his own private history; but, according to the official doctrine, of at least some of these episodes he has direct and unchallengeable cognisance. In consciousness, self-consciousness and introspection he is directly and authentically apprised of the present states and operations of his mind. He may have great or small uncertainties about concurrent and adjacent episodes in the physical world, but he can have none about at least part of what is momentarily occupying his mind.

It is customary to express this bifurcation of his two lives and of his two worlds by saying that the things and events which belong to the physical world, including his own body, are external, while the workings of his own mind are internal. This antithesis of outer and inner is of course meant to be construed as a metaphor, since minds, not being in space, could not be described as being spatially inside anything else, or as having things going on spatially inside themselves. But relapses from this good intention are common and theorists are found speculating how stimuli, the physical sources of which are yards or miles outside a person's skin, can generate mental responses inside his skull, or how decisions framed inside his cranium can set going movements of his extremities.

Even when 'inner' and 'outer' are construed as metaphors, the problem how a person's mind and body influence one another is notoriously charged with theoretical difficulties. What the

From Gilbert Ryle, *The Concept of Mind* (Hutchinson, 1949), pp. 11–24. Reprinted with permission of the publisher and the Principal, Fellows, and Scholars of Hertford College in the University of Oxford.

mind wills, the legs, arms and the tongue execute; what affects the ear and the eye has something to do with what the mind perceives; grimaces and smiles betray the mind's moods and bodily castigations lead, it is hoped, to moral improvement. But the actual transactions between the episodes of the private history and those of the public history remain mysterious, since by definition they can belong to neither series. They could not be reported among the happenings described in a person's autobiography of his inner life, but nor could they be reported among those described in some one else's biography of that person's overt career. They can be inspected neither by introspection nor by laboratory experiment. They are theoretical shuttlecocks which are forever being bandied from the physiologist back to the psychologist and from the psychologist back to the physiologist.

Underlying this partly metaphorical representation of the bifurcation of a person's two lives there is a seemingly more profound and philosophical assumption. It is assumed that there are two different kinds of existence or status. What exists or happens may have the status of physical existence, or it may have the status of mental existence. Somewhat as the faces of coins are either heads or tails, or somewhat as living creatures are either male or female, so, it is supposed, some existing is physical existing, other existing is mental existing. It is a necessary feature of what has physical existence that it is in space and time; it is a necessary feature of what has mental existence that it is in time but not in space. What has physical existence is composed of matter, or else is a function of matter; what has mental existence consists of consciousness, or else is a function of consciousness.

There is thus a polar opposition between mind and matter, an opposition which is often brought out as follows. Material objects are situated in a common field, known as 'space,' and what happens to one body in one part of space is mechanically connected with what happens to other bodies in other parts of space. But mental happenings occur in insulated fields, known as 'minds,' and there is, apart maybe from telepathy, no direct causal connection between what happens in one mind and what happens in another. Only through the medium of the public physical world can the mind of one person make a difference to the mind of another. The mind is its own place and in his inner life each of us lives the life of a ghostly Robinson Crusoe. People can see, hear and jolt one another's bodies, but they are irremediably blind and deaf to the workings of one another's minds and inoperative upon them.

What sort of knowledge can be secured of the workings of a mind? On the one side, according to the official theory, a person has direct knowledge of the best imaginable kind of the workings of his own mind. Mental states and processes are (or are normally) conscious states and processes, and the consciousness which irradiates them can engender no illusions and leaves the door open for no doubts. A person's present thinkings, feelings and willings, his perceivings, rememberings and imaginings are intrinsically 'phos-phorescent'; their existence and their nature are inevitably betrayed to their owner. The inner life is a stream of consciousness of such a sort that it would be absurd to suggest that the mind whose life is that stream might be unaware of what is passing down it.

True, the evidence adduced recently by Freud seems to show that there exist channels tributary to this stream, which run hidden from their owner. People are actuated by impulses the existence of which they vigorously disavow; some of their thoughts differ from the thoughts which they acknowledge; and some of the actions which they think they will to perform they do not really will. They are thoroughly gulled by some of their own hypocrisies and they successfully ignore facts about their mental lives which on the official theory ought to be patent to them. Holders of the official theory tend, however, to maintain that anyhow in normal circumstances a person must be directly and authentically seized of the present state and workings of his own mind.

Besides being currently supplied with these alleged immediate data of consciousness, a person is also generally supposed to be able to exercise from time to time a special kind of perception, namely inner perception, or introspection. He can take a (non-optical) 'look' at what is passing in his mind. Not only can he view and scrutinize a flower through his sense of sight and listen to and discriminate the notes of a bell through his sense of hearing; he can also reflectively or introspectively watch, without any bodily organ of sense, the current episodes of his inner life. This self-observation is also commonly supposed to be immune from illusion, confusion or doubt. A mind's reports of its own affairs have a certainty superior to the best that is possessed by its reports of matters in the physical world. Sense-perceptions can, but consciousness and introspection cannot, be mistaken or confused.

On the other side, one person has no direct access of any sort to the events of the inner life of another. He cannot do better than make problematic inferences from the observed behaviour of the other person's body to the states of mind which, by analogy from his own conduct, he supposes to be signalised by that behaviour. Direct access to the workings of a mind is the privilege of that mind itself; in default of such privileged access, the workings of one mind are inevitably occult to everyone else. For the supposed arguments from bodily movements similar to their own to mental workings similar to their own would lack any possibility of observational corroboration. Not unnaturally, therefore, an adherent of the official theory finds it difficult to resist this consequence of his premises, that he has no good reason to believe that there do exist minds other than his own. Even if he prefers to believe that to other human bodies there are harnessed minds not unlike his own, he cannot claim to be able to discover their individual characteristics, or the particular things that they undergo and do. Absolute solitude is on this showing the ineluctable destiny of the soul. Only our bodies can meet.

As a necessary corollary of this general scheme there is implicitly prescribed a special way of construing our ordinary concepts of mental powers and operations. The verbs, nouns and adjectives, with which in ordinary life we describe the wits, characters and higher-grade performances of the people with whom we have to do, are required to be construed as signifying special episodes in their secret histories, or else as signifying tendencies for such episodes to occur. When someone is described as knowing, believing or guessing something, as hoping, dreading, intending or shirking something, as designing this or being amused at that, these verbs are supposed to denote the occurrence of specific modifications in his (to us) occult stream of consciousness. Only his own privileged access to this stream in direct awareness and introspection could provide authentic testimony that these mental-conduct verbs were correctly or incorrectly applied. The onlooker, be he teacher, critic, biographer or friend, can never assure himself that his comments have any vestige of truth. Yet it was just because we do in fact all know how to make such comments, make them with general correctness and correct them when they turn out to be confused

or mistaken, that philosophers found it necessary to construct their theories of the nature and place of minds. Finding mental-conduct concepts being regularly and effectively used, they properly sought to fix their logical geography. But the logical geography officially recommended would entail that there could be no regular or effective use of these mental-conduct concepts in our descriptions of, and prescriptions for, other people's minds.

2. The Absurdity of the Official Doctrine

Such in outline is the official theory. I shall often speak of it, with deliberate abusiveness, as 'the dogma of the Ghost in the Machine.' I hope to prove that it is entirely false, and false not in detail but in principle. It is not merely an assemblage of particular mistakes. It is one big mistake and a mistake of a special kind. It is, namely, a category-mistake. It represents the facts of mental life as if they belonged to one logical type or category (or range of types or categories), when they actually belong to another. The dogma is therefore a philosopher's myth. In attempting to explode the myth I shall probably be taken to be denying well-known facts about the mental life of human beings, and my plea that I aim at doing nothing more than rectify the logic of mental-conduct concepts will probably be disallowed as mere subterfuge.

I must first indicate what is meant by the phrase 'Category-mistake.' This I do in a series of illustrations.

A foreigner visiting Oxford or Cambridge for the first time is shown a number of colleges, libraries, playing fields, museums, scientific departments and administrative offices. He then asks 'But where is the University? I have seen where the members of the Colleges live, where the Registrar works, where the scientists experiment and the rest. But I have not yet seen the University in which reside and work the members of your University.' It has then to be explained to him that the University is not another collateral institution, some ulterior counterpart to the colleges, laboratories and offices which he has seen. The University is just the way in which all that he has already seen is organized. When they are seen and when their coordination is understood, the University has been seen. His mistake lay in his innocent assumption that it was correct to speak of Christ

Church, the Bodleian Library, the Ashmolean Museum *and* the University, to speak, that is, as if 'the University' stood for an extra member of the class of which these other units are members. He was mistakenly allocating the University to the same category as that to which the other institutions belong.

The same mistake would be made by a child witnessing the march-past of a division, who, having had pointed out to him such and such battalions, batteries, squadrons, etc., asked when the division was going to appear. He would be supposing that a division was a counterpart to the units already seen, partly similar to them and partly unlike them. He would be shown his mistake by being told that in watching the battalions, batteries and squadrons marching past he had been watching the division marching past. The march-past was not a parade of battalions, batteries, squadrons *and* a division; it was a parade of the battalions, batteries and squadrons *of* a division.

One more illustration. A foreigner watching his first game of cricket learns what are the functions of the bowlers, the batsmen, the fielders, the umpires and the scorers. He then says 'But there is no one left on the field to contribute the famous element of team-spirit. I see who does the bowling, the batting and the wicket-keeping; but I do not see whose role it is to exercise *esprit de corps.*' Once more, it would have to be explained that he was looking for the wrong type of thing. Team-spirit is not another cricketing-operation supplementary to all of the other special tasks. It is, roughly, the keenness with which each of the special tasks is performed, and performing a task keenly is not performing two tasks. Certainly exhibiting team-spirit is not the same thing as bowling or catching, but nor is it a third thing such that we can say that the bowler first bowls *and* then exhibits team-spirit or that a fielder is at a given moment *either* catching *or* displaying *esprit de corps.*

These illustrations of category-mistakes have a common feature which must be noticed. The mistakes were made by people who did not know how to wield the concepts *University, division* and *team-spirit.* Their puzzles arose from inability to use certain items in the English vocabulary.

The theoretically interesting category-mistakes are those made by people who are perfectly competent to apply concepts, at least in the situations with which they are familiar, but are still liable in their abstract thinking to allocate those concepts to logical types to which they do not belong. An instance of a mistake of this sort would be the following story. A student of politics has learned the main differences between the British, the French and the American Constitutions, and has learned also the differences and connections between the Cabinet, Parliament, the various Ministries, the Judicature and the Church of England. But he still becomes embarrassed when asked questions about the connections between the Church of England, the Home Office and the British Constitution. For while the Church and the Home Office are institutions, the British Constitution is not another institution in the same sense of that noun. So inter-institutional relations which can be asserted or denied to hold between the Church and the Home Office cannot be asserted or denied to hold between either of them and the British Constitution. 'The British Constitution' is not a term of the same logical type as 'the Home Office' and 'the Church of England.' In a partially similar way, John Doe may be a relative, a friend, an enemy or a stranger to Richard Roe; but he cannot be any of these things to the Average Taxpayer. He knows how to talk sense in certain sorts of discussions about the Average Taxpayer, but he is baffled to say why he could not come across him in the street as he can come across Richard Roe.

It is pertinent to our main subject to notice that, so long as the student of politics continues to think of the British Constitution as a counterpart to the other institutions, he will tend to describe it as a mysteriously occult institution; and so long as John Doe continues to think of the Average Taxpayer as a fellow-citizen, he will tend to think of him as an elusive insubstantial man, a ghost who is everywhere yet nowhere.

My destructive purpose is to show that a family of radical category-mistakes is the source of the double-life theory. The representation of a person as a ghost mysteriously ensconced in a machine derives from this argument. Because, as is true, a person's thinking, feeling and purposive doing cannot be described solely in the idioms of physics, chemistry and physiology, therefore they must be described in counterpart idioms. As the human body is a complex organised unit, so the human mind must be another complex organised unit, though one made of a different sort of stuff and with a different sort of structure. Or, again, as the human body, like any other parcel of matter, is a field of causes and ef-

fects, so the mind must be another field of causes and effects, though not (Heaven be praised)
mechanical causes and effects.

3. The Origin of the Category-Mistake

One of the chief intellectual origins of what I
have yet to prove to be the Cartesian category-
mistake seems to be this. When Galileo showed
that his methods of scientific discovery were
competent to provide a mechanical theory which
should cover every occupant of space, Descartes
found in himself two conflicting motives. As a
man of scientific genius he could not but endorse
the claims of mechanics, yet as a religious and
moral man he could not accept, as Hobbes accepted, the discouraging rider to those claims,
namely that human nature differs only in degree
of complexity from clockwork. The mental
could not be just a variety of the mechanical.

He and subsequent philosophers naturally but
erroneously availed themselves of the following
escape-route. Since mental-conduct words are
not to be construed as signifying the occurrence
of mechanical processes, they must be construed as signifying the occurrence of non-
mechanical processes; since mechanical laws
explain movements in space as the effects of
other movements in space, other laws must explain some of the non-spatial workings of minds
as the effects of other non-spatial workings of
minds. The difference between the human be-
haviours which we describe as intelligent and
those which we describe as unintelligent must
be a difference in their causation; so, while
some movements of human tongues and limbs
are the effects of mechanical causes, others
must be the effects of non-mechanical causes,
i.e. some issue from movements of particles of
matter, others from workings of the mind.

The differences between the physical and the
mental were thus represented as differences inside the common framework of the categories of
'thing,' 'stuff,' 'attribute,' 'state,' 'process,'
'change,' 'cause' and 'effect'. Minds are things,
but different sorts of things from bodies; mental
processes are causes and effects, but different
sorts of causes and effects from bodily movements. And so on. Somewhat as the foreigner
expected the University to be an extra edifice,
rather like a college but also considerably different, so the repudiators of mechanism represented minds as extra centres of causal processes, rather like machines but also considerably
different from them. Their theory was a para-
mechanical hypothesis.

That this assumption was at the heart of the
doctrine is shown by the fact that there was from
the beginning felt to be a major theoretical difficulty in explaining how minds can influence and
be influenced by bodies. How can a mental
process, such as willing, cause spatial movements like the movements of the tongue? How
can a physical change in the optic nerve have
among its effects a mind's perception of a flash
of light? This notorious crux by itself shows the
logical mould into which Descartes pressed his
theory of the mind. It was the self-same mould
into which he and Galileo set their mechanics.
Still unwittingly adhering to the grammar of
mechanics, he tried to avert disaster by describing minds in what was merely an obverse vocabulary. The workings of minds had to be described by the mere negatives of the specific
descriptions given to bodies; they are not in
space, they are not motions, they are not modifications of matter, they are not accessible to public observation. Minds are not bits of clockwork, they are just bits of not-clockwork.

As thus represented, minds are not merely
ghosts harnessed to machines, they are themselves just spectral machines. Though the
human body is an engine, it is not quite an ordinary engine, since some of its workings are governed by another engine inside it—this interior
governor-engine being one of a very special
sort. It is invisible, inaudible and it has no size
or weight. It cannot be taken to bits and the laws
it obeys are not those known to ordinary engineers. Nothing is known of how it governs the
bodily engine.

A second major crux points the same moral.
Since, according to the doctrine, minds belong to
the same category as bodies and since bodies are
rigidly governed by mechanical laws, it seemed
to many theorists to follow that minds must be
similarly governed by rigid non-mechanical
laws. The physical world is a deterministic system, so the mental world must be a deterministic
system. Bodies cannot help the modifications
that they undergo, so minds cannot help pursuing the careers fixed for them. *Responsibility,
choice, merit* and *demerit* are therefore inapplicable concepts—unless the compromise solution is adopted of saying that the laws governing
mental processes, unlike those governing physical processes, have the congenial attribute of
being only rather rigid. The problem of the Free-

dom of the Will was the problem how to reconcile the hypothesis that minds are to be described in terms drawn from the categories of mechanics with the knowledge that higher-grade human conduct is not of a piece with the behaviour of machines.

It is an historical curiosity that it was not noticed that the entire argument was broken-backed. Theorists correctly assumed that any sane man could already recognise the differences between, say, rational and non-rational utterances or between purposive and automatic behaviour. Else there would have been nothing requiring to be salved from mechanism. Yet the explanation given presupposed that one person could in principle never recognise the difference between the rational and the irrational utterances issuing from other human bodies, since he could never get access to the postulated immaterial causes of some of their utterances. Save for the doubtful exception of himself, he could never tell the difference between a man and a Robot. It would have to be conceded, for example, that, for all that we can tell, the inner lives of persons who are classed as idiots or lunatics are as rational as those of anyone else. Perhaps only their overt behaviour is disappointing; that is to say, perhaps 'idiots' are not really idiotic, or 'lunatics' lunatic. Perhaps, too, some of those who are classed as sane are really idiots. According to the theory, external observers could never know how the overt behaviour of others is correlated with their mental powers and processes and so they could never know or even plausibly conjecture whether their applications of mental-conduct concepts to these other people were correct or incorrect. It would then be hazardous or impossible for a man to claim sanity or logical consistency even for himself, since he would be debarred from comparing his own performances with those of others. In short, our characterisations of persons and their performances as intelligent, prudent and virtuous or as stupid, hypocritical and cowardly could never have been made, so the problem of providing a special causal hypothesis to serve as the basis of such diagnoses would never have arisen. The question, 'How do persons differ from machines?' arose just because everyone already knew how to apply mental-conduct concepts before the new causal hypothesis was introduced. This causal hypothesis could not therefore be the source of the criteria used in those applications. Nor, of course, has the causal hypothesis in any degree improved our handling of

those criteria. We still distinguish good from bad arithmetic, politic from impolitic conduct and fertile from infertile imaginations in the ways in which Descartes himself distinguished them before and after he speculated how the applicability of these criteria was compatible with the principle of mechanical causation.

He had mistaken the logic of his problem. Instead of asking by what criteria intelligent behaviour is actually distinguished from non-intelligent behaviour, he asked 'Given that the principle of mechanical causation does not tell us the difference, what other causal principle will tell it to us?' He realised that the problem was not one of mechanics and assumed that it must therefore be one of some counterpart to mechanics. Not unnaturally psychology is often cast for just this role.

When two terms belong to the same category, it is proper to construct conjunctive propositions embodying them. Thus a purchaser may say that he bought a left-hand glove and a right-hand glove, but not that he bought a left-hand glove, a right-hand glove and a pair of gloves. 'She came home in a flood of tears and a sedan-chair' is a well-known joke based on the absurdity of conjoining terms of different types. It would have been equally ridiculous to construct the disjunction 'She came home either in a flood of tears or else in a sedan-chair.' Now the dogma of the Ghost in the Machine does just this. It maintains that there exist both bodies and minds; that there occur physical processes and mental processes; that there are mechanical causes of corporeal movements and mental causes of corporeal movements. I shall argue that these and other analogous conjunctions are absurd; but, it must be noticed, the argument will not show that either of the illegitimately conjoined propositions is absurd in itself. I am not, for example, denying that there occur mental processes. Doing long division is a mental process and so is making a joke. But I am saying that the phrase 'there occur mental processes' does not mean the same sort of thing as 'there occur physical processes,' and, therefore, that it makes no sense to conjoin or disjoin the two.

If my argument is successful, there will follow some interesting consequences. First, the hallowed contrast between Mind and Matter will be dissipated, but dissipated not by either of the equally hallowed absorptions of Mind by Matter or of Matter by Mind, but in quite a different way. For the seeming contrast of the two will be shown to be as illegitimate as would be the contrast of 'she came home in a flood of tears' and 'she came home in a sedan-chair.' The belief that there is a polar opposition between Mind and Matter is the belief that they are terms of the same logical type.

It will also follow that both Idealism and Materialism are answers to an improper question. The 'reduction' of the material world to mental states and processes, as well as the 'reduction' of mental states and processes to physical states and processes, presuppose the legitimacy of the disjunction 'Either there exist minds or there exist bodies (but not both).' It would be like saying, 'Either she bought a left-hand and a right-hand glove or she bought a pair of gloves (but not both).'

It is perfectly proper to say, in one logical tone of voice, that there exist minds and to say, in another logical tone of voice, that there exist bodies. But these expressions do not indicate two different species of existence, for 'existence' is not a generic word like 'coloured' or 'sexed.' They indicate two different senses of 'exist,' somewhat as 'rising' has different senses in 'the tide is rising,' 'hopes are rising,' and 'the average age of death is rising.' A man would be thought to be making a poor joke who said that three things are now rising, namely the tide, hopes and the average age of death. It would be just as good or bad a joke to say that there exist prime numbers and Wednesdays and public opinions and navies; or that there exist both minds and bodies. In the succeeding chapters I try to prove that the official theory does rest on a batch of category-mistakes by showing that logically absurd corollaries follow from it. The exhibition of these absurdities will have the constructive effect of bringing out part of the correct logic of mental-conduct concepts.

4. Historical Note

It would not be true to say that the official theory derives solely from Descartes' theories, or even from a more widespread anxiety about the implications of seventeenth century mechanism. Scholastic and Reformation theology had schooled the intellects of the scientists as well as of the laymen, philosophers and clerics of that age. Stoic-Augustinian theories of the will were embedded in the Calvinist doctrines of sin and grace; Platonic and Aristotelian theories of the intellect shaped the orthodox doctrines of the immortality of the soul. Descartes was reformulating already prevalent theological doctrines of the soul in the new syntax of Galileo. The theologian's privacy of conscience became the philosopher's privacy of consciousness, and what had been the bogy of Predestination reappeared as the bogy of Determinism.

It would also not be true to say that the two-worlds myth did no theoretical good. Myths often do a lot of theoretical good, while they are still new. One benefit bestowed by the para-mechanical myth was that it partly superannuated the then prevalent para-political myth. Minds and their Faculties had previously been described by analogies with political superiors and political subordinates. The idioms used were those of ruling, obeying, collaborating and rebelling. They survived and still survive in many ethical and some epistemological discussions. As, in physics, the new myth of occult Forces was a scientific improvement on the old myth of Final Causes, so, in anthropological and psychological theory, the new myth of hidden operations, impulses and agencies was an improvement on the old myth of dictations, deferences and disobedience.

6 Psychology in Physical Language

Rudolf Carnap

1. Introduction. Physical Language and Protocol Language

In what follows, we intend to explain and to establish the thesis that *every sentence of psychology may be formulated in physical language.* To express this in the material mode of speech: *all sentences of psychology describe physical occurrences, namely, the physical behavior of humans and other animals.* This is a sub-thesis of the general thesis of *physicalism* to the effect that *physical language is a universal language,* that is, a language into which every sentence may be translated. The general thesis has been discussed in an earlier article,[1] whose position shall here serve as our point of departure. Let us first briefly review some of the conclusions of the earlier study.

In meta-linguistic discussion we distinguish the customary *material mode of speech* (e.g., "The sentences of this language speak of this and that object.") from the more correct *formal mode of speech* (e.g., "The sentences of this language contain this and that word and are constructed in this and that manner."). In using the material mode of speech we run the risk of introducing confusions and pseudo-problems. If, because of its being more easily understood, we occasionally do use it in what follows, we do so only as a paraphrase of the formal mode of speech.

Of first importance for epistemological analyses are the *protocol language,* in which the primitive protocol sentences (in the material mode of speech: the sentences about the immediately given) of a particular person are formulated, and the *system language,* in which the sentences of the system of science are formulated. A person S *tests* (verifies) a system-sentence by deducing from it sentences of his own protocol language, and comparing these sentences with those of his actual protocol. The possibility of such a deduction of protocol sentences constitutes the *content* of a sentence. If a sentence permits no such deductions, it has no content, and is meaningless.

If the same sentences may be deduced from two sentences, the latter two sentences have the same content. They say the same thing, and may be translated into one another.

To every sentence of the system language there corresponds some sentence of the physical language such that the two sentences are inter-translatable. It is the purpose of this article to show that this is the case for the sentences of psychology. Moreover, every sentence of the protocol language of some specific person is inter-translatable with some sentence of physical language, namely, with a sentence about the physical state of the person in question. The various protocol languages thus become sub-languages of the physical language. The *physical language is universal and inter-subjective.* This is the thesis of physicalism.

If the physical language, on the grounds of its universality, were adopted as the system language of science, all science would become physics. Metaphysics would be discarded as meaningless. The various domains of science would become parts of unified science. In the material mode of speech: there would, basically, be only one kind of object—physical occurrences, in whose realm law would be all-encompassing.

Physicalism ought not to be understood as requiring psychology to concern itself only with physically describable situations. The thesis, rather, is that psychology may deal with whatever it pleases, it may formulate its sentences as it pleases—these sentences will, in every case, be translatable into physical language.

We say of a sentence P that it is *translatable* (more precisely, that it is reciprocally translatable) into a sentence Q if there are rules, independent of space and time, in accordance with which Q may be deduced from P and P from Q; to use the material mode of speech, P and Q describe the same state of affairs; epistemologically speaking, every protocol sentence which confirms P also confirms Q and *vice versa.* The definition of an expression "a" by means of ex-

Originally published in *Erkenntnis*, 3:107–42, 1932/33. Reprinted with permission of Kluwer Academic Publishers.

pressions "b," "c" ..., represents a translation-rule with the help of which any sentence in which "a" occurs may be translated into a sentence in which "a" does not occur, but "b," "c," ... do, and *vice versa*. The translatability of all the sentences of language L_1 into a (completely or partially) different language L_2 is assured if, for every expression of L_1, a definition is presented which directly or indirectly (i.e., with the help of other definitions) derives that expression from expressions of L_2. Our thesis thus states that a definition may be constructed for every psychological concept (i.e., expression) which directly or indirectly derives that concept from physical concepts. We are not demanding that psychology formulate each of its sentences in physical terminology. For its own purposes psychology may, as heretofore, utilize its own terminology. All that we are demanding is the production of the definitions through which psychological language is linked with physical language. We maintain that these definitions can be produced, since, implicitly, they already underlie psychological practice.

If our thesis is correct, the generalized sentences of psychology, the *laws* of psychology, are also translatable into the physical language. They are thus physical laws. Whether or not these physical laws are deducible from those holding in inorganic physics, remains, however, an open question. This question of the deducibility of the laws is completely independent of the question of the definability of concepts. We have already considered this matter in our discussion of biology.[2] As soon as one realizes that the sentences of psychology belong to the physical language, and also overcomes the emotional obstacles to the acceptance of this provable thesis, one will, indeed, incline to the conjecture, which cannot as yet be proved, that the laws of psychology are special cases of physical laws holding in inorganic physics as well. But we are not concerned with this conjecture here.

Let us permit ourselves a brief remark—apart from our principal point—concerning the emotional resistance to the thesis of physicalism. Such resistance is always exerted against any thesis when an Idol is being dethroned by it, when we are asked to discard an idea with which dignity and grandeur are associated. As a result of Copernicus' work, man lost the distinction of a central position in the universe; as a result of Darwin's, he was deprived of the dignity of a special supra-animal existence; as a result of Marx's, the factors by means of which histo-

ry can be causally explained were degraded from the realm of ideas to that of material events; as a result of Nietzsche's, the origins of morals were stripped of their halo; as a result of Freud's, the factors by means of which the ideas and actions of men can be causally explained were located in the darkest depths, in man's nether regions. The extent to which the sober, objective examination of these theories was obstructed by emotional opposition is well known. Now it is proposed that psychology, which has hitherto been robed in majesty as the theory of spiritual events, be degraded to the status of a part of physics. Doubtless, many will consider this an offensive presumption. Perhaps we may therefore express the request that the reader make a special effort in this case to retain the objectivity and openness of mind always requisite to the testing of a scientific thesis.

2. The Forms of Psychological Sentences

The distinction between singular and general sentences is as important in psychology as in other sciences. A *singular psychological sentence,* e.g., "Mr. A was angry at noon yesterday" (an analogue of the physical sentence, "Yesterday at noon the temperature of the air in Vienna was 28 degrees centigrade"), is concerned with a particular person at a particular time. *General psychological sentences* have various forms, of which the following two are perhaps the most important. A sentence may describe a specific quality of a specific kind of event, e.g., "An experience of surprise always (or: always for Mr. A, or: always for people of such and such a society) has such and such a structure." A physical analogy would be: "Chalk (or: chalk of such and such a sort) always is white." The second important form is that of universal-conditional statements concerning sequences of events, that is, of causal laws. For instance, "When, under such and such circumstances, images of such and such a sort occur to a person (or: to Mr. A, or: to anyone of such and such a society), an emotion of such and such a sort always (or: frequently, or: sometimes) is aroused." A physical analogy would be: "When a solid body is heated, it usually expands."

Research is primarily directed to the discovery of general sentences. These cannot, however, be established except by means of the so-called method of induction from the available

PSYCHOLOGY IN PHYSICAL LANGUAGE

singular sentences, i.e., by means of the construction of hypotheses.

Phenomenology claims to be able to establish universal synthetic sentences which have not been obtained through induction. These sentences about psychological qualities are, allegedly, known either a priori or on the basis of some single illustrative case. In our view, knowledge cannot be gained by such means. We need not, however, enter upon a discussion of this issue here, since even on the view of phenomenology itself, these sentences do not belong to the domain of psychology.

In physics it sometimes seems to be the case that a general law is established on the basis of some single event. For instance, if a physicist can determine a certain physical constant, say, the heat-conductivity of a sample of some pure metal, in a single experiment, he will be convinced that, on other occasions, not only the sample examined but any similar sample of the same substance will, very probably, be characterizable by the same constant. But here too induction is applied. As a result of many previous observations the physicist is in possession of a universal sentence of a higher order which enables him in this case to follow an abbreviated method. This higher-order sentence reads roughly: "All (or: the following) physical constants of metals vary only slightly in time and from sample to sample."

The situation is analogous for certain conclusions drawn in psychology. If a psychologist has, as a result of some single experiment, determined that the simultaneous sounding of two specific notes is experienced as a dissonance by some specific person A, he infers (under favorable circumstances) the truth of the general sentence which states that the same experiment with A will, at other times, have the same result. Indeed, he will even venture—and rightly—to extend this result, with some probability, to pairs of tones with the same acoustic interval if the pitch is not too different from that of the first experiment. Here too the inference from a singular sentence to a general one is only apparent. Actually, a sentence inductively obtained from many observations is brought into service here, a sentence which, roughly, reads: "The reaction of any specific person as to the consonance or dissonance of a chord varies only very slightly with time, and only slightly on a not too large transposition of the chord." It thus remains the case that every general sentence is inductively established on the basis of a number of singular ones.

Finally, we must consider sentences about psycho-physical interrelations, such as for instance, the connection between physical stimulus and perception. These are likewise arrived at through induction, in this case through induction in part from physical and in part from psychological singular sentences. The most important sentences of gestalt psychology belong also to this kind.

General sentences have the character of hypotheses in relation to concrete sentences, that is, the testing of a general sentence consists in testing the concrete sentences which are deducible from it. A general sentence has content insofar and only insofar as the concrete sentences deducible from it have content. Logical analysis must therefore primarily be directed towards the examination of the latter sort of sentences.

If A utters a singular psychological sentence such as "Yesterday morning B was happy," the epistemological situation differs according as A and B are or are not the same person. Consequently, we distinguish between sentences about *other minds* and sentences about *one's own mind*. As we shall presently see, this distinction cannot be made among the sentences of inter-subjective science. For the epistemological analysis of subjective, singular sentences it is, however, indispensable.

3. Sentences about Other Minds

The epistemological character of a singular sentence about other minds will now be clarified by means of an analogy with a sentence about a physical property, defined as a disposition to behave (or respond) in a specific manner under specific circumstances (or stimuli). To take an example: a substance is called "plastic" if, under the influence of deforming stresses of a specific sort and a specific magnitude, it undergoes a permanent change of shape, but remains intact.

We shall try to carry out this analogy by juxtaposing two examples. We shall be concerned with the epistemological situation of the example taken from psychology; the parallel example about the physical property is intended only to facilitate our understanding of the psychological sentence, and not to serve as a specimen of an argument from analogy. (For the sake of convenience, where the text would have been the same in both columns, it is written only once.)

A Sentence about a property of a physical substance.	A Sentence about a condition of some other mind.
Example: I assert the sentence P_1: "This wooden support is very firm."	Example: I assert the sentence P_1: "Mr. A is now excited."

tem sentence P_1. I would then say something like, "I made a mistake. The test has shown

that the support was not firm, even though it had such and such a form and color."	that A was not excited, even though his face had such and such an expression."

There are two different ways in which sentence P_1 may be derived. We shall designate them as the "rational" and the "intuitive" methods. The *rational* method consists of inferring P_1 from some protocol sentence p_1 (or from several like it), more specifically, from a perception-sentence

In practical matters the *intuitive* method is applied more frequently than this rational one, which presupposes theoretical knowledge and requires reflection. In accordance with the intuitive method, P_1 is obtained without the mediation of any other sentence from the identically sounding protocol sentence p_2.

about the shape and color of the wooden support.	about the behavior of A, e.g., about his facial expressions, his gestures, etc., or about physical effects of A's behavior, e.g., about characteristics of his handwriting.

"The support is firm."	"A is excited."

Consequently, one speaks in this case of *immediate perceptions*

of properties of substances, e.g., of the firmness of supports.	of other minds, e.g., of the excitement of A.

In order to justify the conclusion, a major premise O is still required, namely the general sentence which asserts that

when I perceive a wooden support to be of this color and form, it (usually) turns out to be firm. (A sentence about the perceptual signs of firmness.)	when I perceive a person to have this facial expression and handwriting he (usually) turns out to be excited. (A sentence about the expressional or graphological signs of excitement.)

But in this case too the protocol sentence p_2 and the system sentence P_1 have different contents. The difference is generally not noted because, on the ordinary formulation, both sentences sound alike. Here too we can best clarify the difference by considering the possibility of error. It may happen that, though p_2 occurs in my protocol, I am obliged, on the basis of further protocols, to retract the established system sentence P_1. I would then say "I made a mistake. Further tests have shown

The content of P_1 does not coincide with that of p_1, but goes beyond it. This is evident from the fact that to infer P_1 from p_1 O is required. The cited relationship between P_1 and p_1 may also be seen in the fact that under certain circumstances, the inference from p_1 to P_1 may go astray. It may happen that, though p_1 occurs in a protocol, I am obliged, on the grounds of further protocols, to retract the established sys-

that the support was not firm, although I had the intuitive impression that it was."	that A was not excited, although I had the intuitive impression that he was."

[The difference between p_2 and P_1 is the same as that between the identically sounding sentences p and P_1: "A red marble is lying on this table," of an earlier example.[3] The argument of that article shows that the inference of P_1 from p_2, if it is to be rigorous, also requires a major premise of general form, and that it is not in the least simple. Insofar as ordinary usage, for convenience's sake, assigns to both sentences the same sequence of words, the inference is, in practice, simplified to the point of triviality.]

Our problem now is: *what does sentence P_1 mean?* Such a question can only be answered by the presentation of a sentence (or of several sentences) which has (or which conjointly have) the same content as P_1. The viewpoint which will here be defended is that P_1 has the same content as a sentence P_2 which asserts the existence of a physical structure characterized by the disposition to react in a specific manner to specific physical stimuli. In our example, P_2 asserts the existence of that physical structure (micro-structure)

of the wooden support that is characterized by the fact that, under a slight load, the support undergoes no noticeable distortion, and, under heavier loads, is bent in such and such a manner, but does not break.	of Mr. A's body (especially of his central nervous system) that is characterized by a high pulse and rate of breathing, which, on the application of certain stimuli, may even be made higher, by vehement and factually unsatisfactory answers to questions, by the occurrence of agitated movements on the application of certain stimuli, etc.

On my view, there is here again a thoroughgoing analogy between the examples from physics and from psychology. If, however, we were to question the experts concerning the examples from their respective fields, the majority of them nowadays would give us thoroughly non-analogous answers. The identity of the content of P_2

and of the content of the physical sentence P_1 would be agreed to	and of the content of the psychological sentence P_1 would be de-

as a matter of course by all physicists.	nied by almost all psychologists (the exceptions being the radical behaviorists).

The contrary view which is most frequently advocated by psychologists is that, "A sentence of the form of P_1 asserts the existence of a state of affairs not identical with the corresponding physical structure, but rather, only accompanied by it, or expressed by it. In our example:

P_1 states that the support not only has the physical structure described by P_2, but that, besides, there exists in it a certain force, namely its *firmness.*	P_1 states that Mr. A not only has a body whose physical structure (at the time in question) is described by P_2, but that—since he is a *psychophysical being*—he has, besides, a consciousness, a certain power or entity, in which that excitement is to be found.

This firmness is not identical with the physical structure, but stands in some parallel relation to it in such a manner that the firmness exists when and only when a physical structure of the characterized sort exists.	This excitement cannot, consequently, be identical with the cited structure of the body, but stands in some parallel relation (or in some relation of interaction) to it in such a manner that the excitement exists when and only when (or at least, frequently when) a physical, bodily structure of the characterized sort exists.

Because of this parallelism one may consider the described reaction to certain stimuli—which is causally dependent	Because of this parallelism one may consider the described reaction to certain stimuli to be an *expression* of excitement.

upon that structure—
to be an *expression* of
firmness.

Firmness is thus an
occult property, an
obscure power which
stands behind physi-
cal structure, appears
in it, but itself remains
unknowable."

Excitement, or the
consciousness of
which it is an attrib-
ute, is thus an occult
property, an obscure
power which stands
behind physical struc-
ture, appears in it, but
itself remains un-
knowable."

This view falls into the error of a hypostatiza-
tion as a result of which a remarkable duplication occurs: besides or behind a state of affairs
whose existence is empirically determinable,
another, *parallel* entity is assumed, whose existence is not determinable. (Note that we are here
concerned with a sentence about other minds.)
But—one may now object—is there not really
at least one possibility of testing this claim,
namely, by means of the protocol sentence p_2
about the intuitive impression of

the firmness of the   the excitement of A?
support?

The objector will point out that this sentence,
after all, occurs in the protocol along with the
perception sentence p_1. May not then a system
sentence whose content goes beyond that of P_2
be founded on p_2? This may be answered as follows. A sentence says no more than what is
testable about it. If, now, the testing of P_1 consisted in the deduction of the protocol sentence
p_2, these two sentences would have the same
content. But we have already seen that this is impossible.

There is no other possibility of testing P_1 except by means of protocol sentences like p_1 or
like p_2. If, now, the content of P_1 goes beyond that
of P_2, the component not shared by the two sentences is not testable, and is therefore meaningless. If one rejects the interpretation of P_1 in
terms of P_2, P_1 becomes a metaphysical pseudo-
sentence.

The various sciences today have reached very
different stages in the process of their deconta-
mination from metaphysics. Chiefly because of
the efforts of Mach, Poincaré, and Einstein,
physics is, by and large, practically free of
metaphysics. In psychology, on the other hand,
the work of arriving at a science which is to be
free of metaphysics has hardly begun. The difference between the two sciences is most clearly seen in the different attitudes taken by experts
in the two fields towards the position which we
rejected as metaphysical and meaningless. In
the case of the example from physics, most
physicists would reject the position as anthropo-
morphic, or mythological, or metaphysical.
They thereby reveal their anti-metaphysical orientation, which corresponds to our own. On the
other hand, in the case of the example from psychology (though, perhaps, not when it is so
crudely formulated), most psychologists would
today consider the view we have been criticizing to be self-evident on intuitive grounds. In
this one can see the metaphysical orientation of
psychologists, to which ours is opposed.

NOTES

1. Carnap, "Die Physikalische Sprache als Universal-
sprache der Wissenschaft," *Erkenntnis* II, 1931, pp.
432–65. [The English translation of this article by
Max Black was published as a monograph under the
title *The Unity of Science* (London: Kegan Paul,
1934).]
2. Ibid., p. 449 ff. (*The Unity of Science,* p. 68 ff.).
3. See Ibid., p. 460 (*The Unity of Science*, p. 92).

7 | Brains and Behaviour[1]

Hilary Putnam

Once upon a time there was a tough-minded philosopher who said, 'What is all this talk about "minds," "ideas," and "sensations"? Really—and I mean *really* in the real world—there is nothing to these so-called "mental" events and entities but certain processes in our all-too-material heads.'

And once upon a time there was a philosopher who retorted, 'What a masterpiece of confusion! Even if, say, *pain* were perfectly correlated with any particular event in my brain (which I doubt) that event would obviously have certain properties—say, a certain numerical intensity measured in volts—which it would be *senseless* to ascribe to the feeling of pain. Thus, it is *two* things that are correlated, not *one*—and to call *two* things *one* thing is worse than being mistaken; it is utter contradiction.'

For a long time dualism and materialism appeared to exhaust the alternatives. Compromises were attempted ('double aspect' theories), but they never won many converts and practically no one found them intelligible. Then, in the mid-1930s, a seeming third possibility was discovered. This third possibility has been called *logical behaviourism.* To state the nature of this third possibility briefly, it is necessary to recall the treatment of the natural numbers (i.e., zero, one, two, three . . .) in modern logic. Numbers are identified with *sets,* in various ways, depending on which authority one follows. For instance, Whitehead and Russell identified zero with the set of all empty sets, one with the set of all one-membered sets, two with the set of all two-membered sets, three with the set of all three-membered sets, and so on. (This has the appearance of circularity, but they were able to dispel this appearance by defining 'one-membered set,' 'two-membered set,' 'three-membered set,' &c., without using 'one,' 'two,' 'three,' &c.) In short, numbers are treated as *logical constructions out of sets.* The number theorist is doing set theory without knowing it, according to this interpretation.

What was novel about this was the idea of getting rid of certain philosophically unwanted or embarrassing entities (numbers) without failing to do justice to the appropriate body of discourse (number theory) by treating the entities in question as logical constructions. Russell was quick to hold up this 'success' as a model to all future philosophers. And certain of those future philosophers—the Vienna positivists, in their 'physicalist' phase (about 1930)—took Russell's advice so seriously as to produce the doctrine that we are calling *logical behaviourism*—the doctrine that, just as numbers are (allegedly) logical constructions out of *sets,* so *mental events* are logical constructions out of actual and possible *behaviour events.*

In the set theoretic case, the 'reduction' of number theory to the appropriate part of set theory was carried out in detail and with indisputable technical success. One may dispute the philosophical significance of the reduction, but one knows exactly what one is talking about when one disputes it. In the mind–body case, the reduction was never carried out in even *one* possible way, so that it is not possible to be clear on just *how* mental entities or events are to be (identified with) logical constructions out of behaviour events. But, broadly speaking, it is clear what the view implies: it implies that all talk about mental events is translatable into talk about actual or potential overt behaviour.

It is easy to see in what way this view differs from both dualism and classical materialism. The logical behaviourist agrees with the dualist that what goes on in our brains has no connection whatsoever with what we *mean* when we say that someone is in pain. He can even take over the dualist's entire stock of arguments against the materialist position. Yet, at the same time, he can be as 'tough-minded' as the materialist in denying that ordinary talk of 'pains,' 'thoughts,' and 'feelings' involves reference to 'Mind' as a Cartesian substance.

Thus it is not surprising that logical behaviourism attracted enormous attention—both pro and con—during the next thirty years. Without doubt, this alternative proved to be a fruitful one to inject into the debate. Here, however, my intention is not to talk about the fruitfulness of the investigations to which logical behaviourism

From R. Butler, ed. *Analytical Philosophy: Second Series*, pp. 1–19. Blackwell, 1968. Reprinted with permission of the publisher.

has led, but to see if there was any upshot to those investigations. Can we, after thirty years, say anything about the rightness or wrongness of logical behaviourism? Or must we say that a third alternative has been added to the old two; that we cannot decide between three any more easily than we could decide between two; and that our discussion is thus half as difficult again as it was before?

One conclusion emerged very quickly from the discussion pro and con logical behaviourism: that the extreme thesis of logical behaviourism, as we just stated it (that all talk about 'mental events' is translatable into talk about overt behaviour) is false. But, in a sense, this is not very interesting. An extreme thesis may be false, although there is 'something to' the way of thinking that it represents. And the more interesting question is this: what, if anything, can be 'saved' of the way of thinking that logical behaviourism represents?

In the last thirty years, the original extreme thesis of logical behaviourism has gradually been weakened to something like this:

1. That there exist entailments between mind-statements and behaviour-statements; entailments that are not, perhaps, analytic in the way in which 'All bachelors are unmarried' is analytic, but that nevertheless follow (in some sense) from the meanings of mind words. I shall call these *analytic entailments.*

2. That these entailments may not provide an actual *translation* of 'mind talk' into 'behaviour talk' (this 'talk' talk was introduced by Gilbert Ryle in his *Concept of Mind*), but that this is true for such superficial reasons as the greater ambiguity of mind talk, as compared with the relatively greater specificity of overt behaviour talk.

I believe that, although no philosopher would today subscribe to the older version of logical behaviourism, a great many philosophers[2] would accept these two points, while admitting the unsatisfactory imprecision of the present statement of both of them. If these philosophers are right, then there is much work to be done (e.g., the notion of 'analyticity' has to be made clear), but the direction of work is laid out for us for some time to come.

I wish that I could share this happy point of view—if only for the comforting conclusion that first-rate philosophical research, continued for some time, will eventually lead to a solution to the mind–body problem which is independent of troublesome empirical facts about brains, central causation of behaviour, evidence for and against nonphysical causation of at least some behaviour, and the soundness or unsoundness of psychical research and parapsychology. But the fact is that I come to bury logical behaviourism, not to praise it. I feel that the time has come for us to admit that logical behaviourism is a mistake, and that even the weakened forms of the logical behaviourist doctrine are incorrect. I cannot hope to establish this in so short a paper as this one[3]; but I hope to expose for your inspection at least the main lines of my thinking.

Logical Behaviourism

The logical behaviourist usually begins by pointing out what is perfectly true, that such words as 'pain' ('pain' will henceforth be our stock example of a mind word) are not taught by reference to standard examples in the way in which such words as 'red' are. One can point to a standard red thing, but one cannot point to a standard pain (that is, except by pointing to some piece of *behaviour*) and say: 'Compare the feeling you are having with this one (say, Jones's feeling at time t_1). If the two feelings have the identical *quality,* then your feeling is legitimately called a feeling of *pain.*' The difficulty, of course, is that I cannot have Jones's feeling at time t_1—unless I *am* Jones, and the time *is* t_1.

From this simple observation, certain things follow. For example, the account according to which the *intension* of the word 'pain' is a certain *quality* which 'I know from my own case' must be wrong. But this is not to refute dualism, since the dualist need not maintain that I know the intension of the English word 'pain' from my own case, but only that I experience the referent of the word.

What then is the intension of 'pain'? I am inclined to say that 'pain' is a cluster-concept. That is, the application of the word 'pain' is controlled by a whole cluster of criteria, *all of which can be regarded as synthetic.*[4] As a consequence, there is no satisfactory way of answering the question 'What does "pain" mean?'

except by giving an exact synonym (e.g., 'Schmerz'); but there are a million and one different ways of saying what pain is. One can, for example, say that pain is that feeling which is normally evinced by saying 'ouch,' or by wincing, or in a variety of other ways (or often not evinced at all).

All this is compatible with logical behaviourism. The logical behaviourist would reply: 'Exactly. "Pain" is a cluster-concept—that is to say, it stands for *a cluster of phenomena.*' But that is not what I mean. Let us look at another kind of cluster-concept (cluster-concepts, of course, are not a homogeneous class): names of diseases.

We observe that, when a virus origin was discovered for polio, doctors said that certain cases in which all the symptoms of polio had been present, but in which the virus had been absent, had turned out not to be cases of polio at all. Similarly, if a virus should be discovered which normally (almost invariably) is the cause of what we presently call 'multiple sclerosis,' the hypothesis that this virus is *the* cause of multiple sclerosis would not be falsified if, in some few exceptional circumstances, it was possible to have all the symptoms of multiple sclerosis for some other combination of reasons, or if this virus caused symptoms not presently recognized as symptoms of multiple sclerosis in some cases. These facts would certainly lead the lexicographer to *reject* the view that 'multiple sclerosis' means 'the simultaneous presence of such and such symptoms.' Rather he would say that 'multiple sclerosis' means 'that disease which is normally responsible for some or all of the following symptoms. . . .'

Of course, he does not have to say this. Some philosophers would prefer to say that 'polio' *used to mean* 'the simultaneous presence of such-and-such symptoms.' And they would say that the *decision* to accept the presence or absence of a virus as a criterion for the presence or absence of polio represented a *change of meaning.* But this runs strongly counter to our common sense. For example, doctors used to say 'I believe polio is caused by a virus.' On the 'change of meaning' account, those doctors were *wrong, not right.* Polio, *as the word was then used,* was not always caused by a virus; it is only what *we* call polio that is always caused by a virus. And if a doctor ever said (many did) 'I believe this may not be a case of polio,' knowing that all of the text-book symptoms were present,

that doctor must have been contradicting himself (even if we, to-day, would say that he was right) or, perhaps, 'making a disguised linguistic proposal.' Also, this account runs counter to good linguistic methodology. The definition we proposed a paragraph back—'multiple sclerosis' means 'the disease that is normally *responsible* for the following symptoms. . . .'—has an exact analogue in the case of polio. This kind of definition leaves open the question whether there is a single cause or several. It is consonant with such a definition to speak of 'discovering a single origin for polio (or two or three or four),' to speak of 'discovering X did not have polio' (although he exhibited all the symptoms of polio), and to speak of 'discovering X did have polio' (although he exhibited *none* of the 'textbook symptoms'). And, finally, such a definition does not require us to say that any 'change of meaning' took place. Thus, this is surely the definition that a good lexicographer would adopt. But this entails *rejecting* the 'change of meaning' account as a philosopher's invention.[5]

Accepting that this is the correct account of the names of diseases, what follows? There *may* be analytic entailments connecting diseases and symptoms (although I shall argue against this). For example, it looks plausible to say that:

> 'Normally people who have multiple sclerosis have some or all of the following symptoms . . .'

is a necessary ('analytic') truth. But it does not follow that 'disease talk' is translatable into 'symptom talk.' Rather the contrary follows (as is already indicated by the presence of the word 'normally'): statements about multiple sclerosis are not translatable into statements about the symptoms of multiple sclerosis, not because disease talk is 'systematically ambiguous' and symptom talk is 'specific,' but because *causes* are not logical constructions out of their *effects.*

In analogy with the foregoing, both the dualist and the materialist would want to argue that, although the meaning of 'pain' may be *explained* by reference to overt behaviour, what we mean by 'pain' is not the presence of a cluster of responses, but rather the presence of an event or condition that normally causes those responses. (Of course the pain is not the whole cause of the pain behaviour, but only a suitably invariant part of that cause;[6] but, similarly, the virus-caused tissue damage is not the whole cause of the individual symptoms of polio in some individual case, but a suitably invariant part of the cause.) And they would want to argue further, that even if it *were* a necessary truth that

> 'Normally, when one says "ouch" one has a pain'

or a necessary truth that

> 'Normally, when one has a pain one says "ouch"'

this would be an interesting observation about what 'pain' means, but it would shed no metaphysical light on what pain *is* (or *isn't*). And it certainly would not follow that 'pain talk' is translatable into 'response talk', or that the failure of translatability is only a matter of the 'systematic ambiguity' of pain talk as opposed to the 'specificity' of response talk: quite the contrary. Just as before, *causes* (pains) are *not* logical constructions out of their *effects* (behaviour).

The traditional dualist would, however, want to go farther, and deny the *necessity* of the two propositions just listed. Moreover, the traditional dualist is right: there is nothing self-contradictory, as we shall see below, in talking of hypothetical worlds in which there are pains but *no* pain behaviour.

The analogy with names of diseases is still preserved at this point. Suppose I identify multiple sclerosis as the disease that normally produces certain symptoms. If it later turns out that a certain virus is the cause of multiple sclerosis, using this newly discovered criterion I may then go on to find out that multiple sclerosis has quite different symptoms when, say, the average temperature is lower. I can then perfectly well talk of a hypothetical world (with lower temperature levels) in which multiple sclerosis does *not* normally produce the usual symptoms. It is true that if the *words* 'multiple sclerosis' are used in any world in such a way that the above lexical definition is a good one, *then* many victims of the disease must have had some or all of the following symptoms . . . And in the same way it is true that *if* the explanation suggested of the word 'pain' is a good one (i.e., 'pain is the feeling that is normally being evinced when someone says "ouch," or winces, or screams, &c.'), *then* persons in pain must have at some time winced or screamed or said 'ouch'—but this does *not* imply that 'if someone ever had a pain, then someone must at some time have winced or screamed or said "ouch."' To conclude this would be to confuse preconditions for *talking* about pain as *we* talk about pain with preconditions for the existence of pain.

The analogy we have been developing is not an identity: linguistically speaking, mind words and names of diseases are different in a great many respects. In particular, *first person uses* are very different: a man may have a severe case of polio and not know it, even if he knows the word 'polio,' but one cannot have a severe pain and not know it. At first blush, this may look like a point in favour of logical behaviourism. The logical behaviourist may say: it is because the premisses 'John says he has a pain,' 'John knows English,' and 'John is speaking in all sincerity,'[7] *entail* 'John has a pain,' that pain reports have this sort of special status. But even if this is right, it does not follow that logical behaviourism is correct unless *sincerity* is a 'logical construction out of overt behaviour'! A far more reasonable account is this: one can have a 'pink elephant hallucination,' but one cannot have a 'pain hallucination,' or an 'absence of pain hallucination,' simply because any situation that a person cannot discriminate from a situation in which he himself has a pain *counts* as a situation in which he has a pain, whereas a situation that a person cannot distinguish from one in which a pink elephant is present does not necessarily *count* as the presence of a pink elephant.

To sum up: I believe that pains are not clusters of responses, but that they are (normally, in our experience to date) the causes of certain clusters of responses. Moreover, although this is an empirical fact, it underlies the possibility of talking about pains in the particular way in which we do. However, it does not rule out in any way the possibility of worlds in which (owing to a difference in the environmental and hereditary conditions) pains are not responsible for the usual responses, or even are not responsible for any responses at all.

Let us now engage in a little science fiction. Let us try to describe some worlds in which pains are related to responses (and also to causes) in quite a different way than they are in our world.

If we confine our attention to non-verbal responses by full grown persons, for a start, then matters are easy. Imagine a community of 'super-spartans' or 'super-stoics'—a community in which the adults have the ability to successfully suppress *all* involuntary pain behaviour. They may, on occasion, admit that they feel pain, but always in pleasant well-modulated voices—even if they are undergoing the agonies of the damned. They do *not* wince, scream, flinch, sob, grit their teeth, clench their fists, exhibit beads of sweat, or otherwise act like people in pain or people suppressing the unconditioned responses associated with pain. However, they do feel pain, and they dislike it (just as we do). They even admit that it takes a great effort of will to behave as they do. It is only that they have what they regard as important ideological reasons for behaving as they do, and they have, through years of training, learned to live up to their own exacting standards.

It may be contended that children and not fully mature members of this community will exhibit, to varying degrees, normal unconditioned pain behaviour, and that this is all that is necessary for the ascription of pain. On this view, the sine qua non for the significant ascription of pain to a species is that its immature members should exhibit unconditioned pain responses.

One might well stop to ask whether this statement has even a clear meaning. Supposing that there are Martians: do we have any criterion for something being an 'unconditioned pain response' for a Martian? Other things being equal, one *avoids* things with which one has had painful experiences: this would suggest that *avoidance* behaviour might be looked for as a universal unconditioned pain response. However, even if this were true, it would hardly be specific enough, since avoidance can also be an unconditioned response to many things that we do not associate with pain—to things that disgust us, or frighten us, or even merely bore us.

Let us put these difficulties aside, and see if we can devise an imaginary world in which there are not, even by lenient standards, any unconditioned pain responses. Specifically, let us take our 'super-spartans', and let us suppose that after millions of years they begin to have children who are born fully acculturated. They are born speaking the adult language, knowing the multiplication table, having opinions on political issues, and inter alia sharing the dominant spartan beliefs about the importance of not evincing pain (except by way of a verbal report,

and even that in a tone of voice that suggests indifference). Then there would not *be* any 'unconditioned pain responses' in this community (although there might be unconditioned *desires* to make certain responses—desires which were, however, always suppressed by an effort of will). Yet there is a clear absurdity to the position that one cannot ascribe to these people a capacity for feeling pain.

To make this absurdity evident, let us imagine that we succeed in converting an adult 'super-spartan' to *our* ideology. Let us suppose that he begins to evince pain in the normal way. Yet he reports that the pains he is feeling are not more *intense* than are the ones he experienced prior to conversion—indeed, he may say that giving expression to them makes them *less* intense. In this case, the logical behaviourist would have to say that, through the medium of this one member, we had demonstrated the existence of unconditioned pain responses in the whole species, and hence that ascription of pain to the species is 'logically proper.' But this is to say that had this one man never lived, and had it been possible to demonstrate only indirectly (via the use of *theories*) that these beings feel pain, then pain ascriptions *would* have been improper.

We have so far been constructing worlds in which the relation of pain to its non-verbal *effects* is altered. What about the relation of pain to *causes*? This is even more easy for the imagination to modify. Can one not imagine a species who feel pain only when a magnetic field is present (although the magnetic field causes no detectable damage to their bodies or nervous systems)? If we now let the members of such a species become converts *to* 'super-spartanism,' we can depict to ourselves a world in which pains, in our sense, are clearly present, but in which they have neither the normal causes nor the normal effects (apart from verbal reports).

What about verbal reports? Some behaviourists have taken these as the characteristic form of pain behaviour. Of course, there is a difficulty here: If 'I am in pain' means 'I am disposed to utter this kind of verbal report' (to put matters crudely), then how do we tell that any particular report is 'this kind of verbal report'? The usual answer is in terms of the unconditioned pain responses and their assumed supplantation by the verbal reports in question. However, we have seen that there are no *logical* reasons for the existence of unconditioned pain responses in all species capable of feeling pain (there *may* be logical reasons for the existence of avoidance desires, but avoidance *desires* are not themselves behaviour any more than pains are).

Once again, let us be charitable to the extent of waving the first difficulty that comes to mind, and let us undertake the task of trying to imagine a world in which there are not even pain *reports*. I will call this world the 'X-world.' In the X-world we have to deal with 'super-super-spartans.' These have been super-spartans for so long, that they have begun to suppress even *talk* of pain. Of course, each individual X-worlder may have his private way of thinking about pain. He may even have the *word* 'pain' (as before, I assume that these beings are born fully acculturated). He may *think* to himself: 'This pain is intolerable. If it goes on one minute longer I shall scream. Oh No! I mustn't do that! That would disgrace my whole family . . .' But X-worlders do not even admit to *having* pains. They pretend not to know either the word or the phenomenon to which it refers. In short, if pains are 'logical constructs out of behaviour', then our X-worlders behave so as not to have pains!—Only, of course, they do have pains, and they know perfectly well that they have pains.

If this last fantasy is not, in some disguised way, self-contradictory, then logical behaviourism is simply a mistake. Not only is the second thesis of logical behaviourism—the existence of a near-translation of pain talk into behaviour talk—false, but so is even the first thesis—the existence of 'analytic entailments.' Pains *are* responsible for certain kinds of behaviour—but only in the context of our beliefs, desires, ideological attitudes, and so forth. From the statement 'X has a pain' by itself *no* behavioural statement follows—not even a behavioural statement with a 'normally' or a 'probably' in it.

In our concluding section we shall consider the logical behaviourist's stock of counter-moves to this sort of argument. If the logical behaviourist's positive views are inadequate owing to an oversimplified view of the nature of cluster words—amounting, in some instances, to an open denial that it is *possible* to have a word governed by a cluster of indicators, *all* of which are synthetic—his negative views are inadequate owing to an oversimplified view of empirical reasoning. It is unfortunately characteristic of modern philosophy that its problems should overlap three different areas—to speak roughly, the areas of linguistics, logic, and 'theory of theories' (scientific methodology)—and that many of its practitioners should try to get by with an inadequate knowledge of at least two out of the three.

Some Behaviourist Arguments

We have been talking of 'X-worlders' and 'super-spartans.' No one denies that, in *some* sense of the term, such fantasies are 'intelligible.' But 'intelligibility' can be a superficial thing. A fantasy may be 'intelligible,' at least at the level of 'surface grammar,' although we may come to see, on thinking about it for a while, that some absurdity is involved. Consider, for example, the supposition that last night, just on the stroke of midnight, all distances were instantaneously doubled. Of course, we did not notice the change, for *we* ourselves also doubled in size! This story may seem intelligible to us at first blush, at least as an amusing possibility. On reflection, however, we come to see that a logical contradiction is involved. For 'length' means nothing more nor less than a relation to a standard, and it is a contradiction to maintain that the length of everything doubled, while the relations to the standards remained unchanged.

What I have just said (speaking as a logical behaviourist might speak) is false, but not totally so. It is false (or at least the last part is false), because 'length' does *not* mean 'relation to a standard.' If it did (assuming a 'standard' has to be a macroscopic material object, or anyway a material object), it would make no sense to speak of distances in a world in which there were only gravitational and electromagnetic fields, but no material objects. Also, it would make no sense to speak of the *standard* (whatever it might be) as having changed its length. Consequences so counter-intuitive have led many physicists (and even a few philosophers of physics) to view 'length' not as something operationally defined, but as a theoretical magnitude (like electrical charge), which can be measured in a virtual infinity of ways, but which is not explicitly and exactly definable in terms of any of the ways of measuring it. Some of these physicists—the 'unified field' theorists—would even say that, far from it being the case that 'length' (and hence 'space') depends on the existence of suitably related material bodies, material bodies are best viewed as local variations in the curvature of space—that is to say, local variations in the intensity of a certain magnitude (the tensor g_{ik}), one aspect of which we experience as 'length.'

Again, it is far from true that the hypothesis 'last night, on the stroke of midnight, everything doubled in length' has no testable consequences. For example, if last night everything did double in length, and the velocity of light did not also double, then this morning we would have experienced an apparent halving of the speed of light. Moreover, if g (the gravitational constant) did not double, then we would have experienced and apparent halving in the intensity of the gravitational field. And if h (Planck's constant) did not change, then. . . . In short, our world would have been bewilderingly different. And if we could survive at all, under so drastically altered conditions, no doubt some clever physicist would figure out what had happened.

I have gone into such detail just to make the point that in philosophy things are rarely so simple as they seem. The 'doubling universe' is a favourite classroom example of a 'pseudohypothesis'—yet it is the worst possible example if a 'clear case' is desired. In the first place, what is desired is a hypothesis with no testable consequences—yet *this* hypothesis, as it is always stated, *does* have testable consequences (perhaps some more complex hypothesis does not; but then we have to see this more complex hypothesis stated before we can be expected to discuss it). In the second place, the usual argument for the absurdity of this hypothesis rests on a simplistic theory of the meaning of 'length'—and a full discussion of *that* situation is hardly possible without bringing in considerations from unified field theory and quantum mechanics (the latter comes in in connection with the notion of a 'material standard'). But, the example aside, one can hardly challenge the point that a superficially coherent story may contain a hidden absurdity.

Or can one? Of course, a superficially coherent story may contain a hidden logical contradiction, but the whole point of the logical behaviourist's sneering reference to 'surface grammar' is that *linguistic coherence, meaningfulness of the individual terms,* and *logical consistency,* do not by themselves guarantee freedom from another kind of absurdity—there are 'depth absurdities' which can only be detected by more powerful techniques. It is fair to say that to-day, after thirty years of this sort of talk,

we lack both a single *convincing* example of such a depth absurdity, and a technique of detection (or alleged technique of detection) which does not reduce to 'untestable, *therefore* nonsense'.

To come to the case at hand: the logical behaviourist is likely to say that our hypothesis about 'X-worlders' is untestable in principle (if there *were* 'X-worlders,' by hypothesis we couldn't distinguish them from people who really didn't know what pain is); and *therefore* meaningless (apart from a certain 'surface significance' which is of no real interest). If the logical behaviourist has learned a little from 'ordinary language philosophy,' he is likely to shy away from saying 'untestable, therefore *meaningless,*' but he is still likely to say or at least think: 'untestable, therefore in *some* sense absurd.' I shall try to meet this 'argument' *not* by challenging the premiss, be it overt or covert, that 'untestable synthetic statement' is some kind of contradiction in terms (although I believe that premiss to be mistaken), but simply by showing that, on any but the most naive view of testability, our hypothesis *is* testable.

Of course, I could not do this if it were true that 'by hypothesis, we couldn't distinguish X-worlders from people who *really* didn't know what pain is.' But that isn't true—at any rate, it isn't true 'by hypothesis.' What is true by hypothesis is that we couldn't distinguish X-worlders from people who really didn't know what pain is *on the basis of overt behaviour alone.* But that still leaves many other ways in which we might determine what is going on 'inside' the X-worlders—in both the figurative and literal sense of 'inside.' For example, we might examine their *brains.*

It is a fact that when pain impulses are 'received' in the brain, suitable electrical detecting instruments record a characteristic 'spike' pattern. Let us express this briefly (and too simply) by saying that 'brain spikes' are one-to-one correlated with experiences of pain. If our X-worlders belong to the human species, then we can verify that they do feel pains, notwithstanding their claim that they don't have any idea what pain is, by applying our electrical instruments and detecting the tell-tale 'brain spikes.'

This reply to the logical behaviourist is far too simple to be convincing. 'It is true,' the logical behaviourist will object, 'that experiences of pain are one-to-one correlated with "brain spikes" in the case of normal human beings. But you don't know that the X-worlders are normal human beings, in this sense—in fact, you have every reason to suppose that they are *not* normal human beings.' This reply shows that no *mere* correlation, however carefully verified in the case of normal human beings, can be used to verify ascriptions of pain to X-worlders. Fortunately, we do not have to suppose that our knowledge will always be restricted to mere correlations, like the pain–'brain spike' correlation. At a more advanced level, considerations of simplicity and coherence can begin to play a rôle in a way in which they cannot when only crude observational regularities are available.

Let us suppose that we begin to detect waves of a new kind, emanating from human brains—call them 'V-waves.' Let us suppose we develop a way of 'decoding' V-waves so as to reveal people's unspoken thoughts. And, finally, let us suppose that our 'decoding' technique also works in the case of the V-waves emanating from the brains of X-worlders. How does this correlation differ from the pain—'brain spike' correlation?

Simply in this way: it is reasonable to say that 'spikes'—momentary peaks in the electrical intensity in certain parts of the brain—could have almost any cause. But waves which go over into coherent English (or any other language); under a relatively simple decoding scheme, could not have just any cause. The 'null hypothesis'—that this is just the operation of 'chance'—can be dismissed at once. And if, in the case of human beings, we verify that the decoded waves correspond to what we are in fact thinking, then the hypothesis that this same correlation holds in the case of X-worlders will be assigned an immensely high probability, simply because no other likely explanation readily suggests itself. But 'no other likely explanation readily suggests itself' isn't verification, the logical behaviourist may say. On the contrary. How, for example, have we verified that cadmium lines in the spectrographic analysis of sunlight indicate the presence of cadmium in the sun? Mimicking the logical behaviourist, we might say: 'We have verified that under normal circumstances, cadmium lines only occur when heated cadmium is present. But we don't know that circumstances on the sun are normal in this sense.' If we took this seriously, we would have to *heat cadmium on the sun* before we could say that the regularity

upon which we base our spectrographic analysis of sunlight had been verified. In fact, we have verified the regularity under 'normal' circumstances, and we can *show* (deductively) that *if* many other laws, that have also been verified under 'normal' circumstances and *only* under 'normal' circumstances (i.e., never on the surface of the sun), hold on the sun, *then* this regularity holds also under 'abnormal' circumstances. And if someone says, 'But perhaps *none* of the usual laws of physics hold on the sun,' we reply that this is like supposing that a random process always produces coherent English. The fact is that the 'signals' (sunlight, radio waves, &c.) which we receive from the sun cohere with a vast body of theory. Perhaps there is some other explanation than that the sun obeys the usual laws of physics; but *no other likely explanation suggests itself.* This sort of reasoning *is* scientific verification; and if it is not reducible to simple Baconian induction—well, then, philosophers must learn to widen their notions of verification to embrace it.

The logical behaviourist might try to account for the decodability of the X-worlders' 'V-waves' into coherent English (or the appropriate natural language) without invoking the absurd 'null hypothesis.' He might suggest, for example, that the 'X-worlders' are having fun at our expense—they are able, say, to produce misleading V-waves at will. If the X-worlders have brains quite unlike ours, this may even have some plausibility. But once again, in an advanced state of knowledge, considerations of coherence and simplicty may quite conceivably 'verify' that this is false. For example, the X-worlders may have brains quite like ours, rather than unlike ours. And we may have built up enough theory to say how the brain of a human being should 'look' if that human being were pretending not to be in pain when he was, in fact, in pain. Now consider what the 'misleading V-waves' story requires: it requires that the X-worlders produce V-waves in quite a different way than we do, without specifying what that different way is. Moreover, it requires that this be the case, although the reverse hypothesis—that X-worlders' brains function *exactly* as human brains do—in fact, that they *are* human brains—fits all the data. Clearly, this story is in serious methodological difficulties, and any other 'counter-explanation' that the logical behaviourist tries to invoke will be in similar difficulties. In short, the logical behaviourist's argument reduces to this: 'You cannot verify "psycho-physical" correlations in the case of X-worlders (or at least, you can't verify ones having to do, directly or indirectly, with *pain*), because, by hypothesis, X-worlders won't tell you (or indicate behaviourally) when they are in pain. "Indirect verification"—verification using theories which have been "tested" only in the case of human beings—is not verification at all, because X-worlders *may* obey different laws than human beings. And it is not incumbent upon *me* (the logical behaviourist says) to suggest what those laws might be: it is incumbent upon *you* to rule out *all* other explanations.' And this is a silly argument. The scientist does not have to rule out all the ridiculous theories that someone *might* suggest; he only has to show that he has ruled out any reasonable alternative theories that one might put forward on the basis of present knowledge.

Granting, then, that we might discover a technique for 'reading' the unspoken thoughts of X-worlders: we would then be in the same position with respect to the X-worlders as we were with respect to the original 'super-spartans.' The super-spartans were quite willing to tell us (and each other) about their pains; and we could see that their pain talk was linguistically coherent and situationally appropriate (e.g., a super-spartan will tell you that he feels intense pain when you touch him with a red hot poker). On this basis, we were quite willing to grant that the super-spartans did, indeed, feel pain—all the more readily, since the deviancy in their behaviour had a perfectly convincing ideological explanation. (Note again the rôle played here by considerations of coherence and simplicity). But the X-worlders also 'tell' us (and, perhaps, each other), exactly the same things, albeit *un*willingly (by the medium of the involuntarily produced 'V-waves'). Thus we have to say—at least, we have to say as long as the 'V-wave' theory has not broken down—that the X-worlders are what they, in fact, are—just 'super-super-spartans.'

Let us now consider a quite different argument that a logical behaviourist might use. 'You are assuming,' he might say, 'the following principle:

If someone's brain is in the same state as that of a human being in pain (not just at the moment of the pain, but before and after for a sufficient interval), then he is in pain.'

'Moreover, this principle is one which it would never be reasonable to give up (on your conception of "methodology"). Thus, you have turned it into a tautology. But observe what turning this principle into a tautology involves: it involves changing the meaning of "pain." What "pain" means for *you* is: the presence of pain, in the colloquial sense of the term, *or* the presence of a brain state identical with the brain state of someone who feels pain. Of course, in that sense we can verify that your "X-worlders" experience "pain"—but that is not the sense of "pain" at issue.'

The reply to this argument is that the premiss is simply false. It is just not true that, on my conception of verification, it would *never* be reasonable to give up the principle stated. To show this, I have to beg your pardons for engaging in a little more science fiction. Let us suppose that scientists discover yet another kind of waves—call them 'W-waves'. Let us suppose that W-waves do not emanate from human brains, but that they are detected emanating from the brains of X-worlders. And let us suppose that, once again, there exists a simple scheme for decoding W-waves into coherent English (or whatever language X-worlders speak), and that the 'decoded' waves 'read' like this: 'Ho, ho! Are we fooling those Earthians! They think that the V-waves they detect represent our thoughts! If they only knew that instead of pretending not to have pains when we really have pains, we are really pretending to pretend not to have pains when we really do have pains when we really don't have pains!' Under these circumstances, we would 'doubt' (to put it mildly) that the same psycho-physical correlations held for normal humans and for X-worlders. Further investigations might lead us to quite a number of different hypotheses. For example, we might decide that X-worlders don't think with their brains at all—that the 'organ' of thought is not just the brain, in the case of X-worlders, but some larger structure—perhaps even a structure which is not 'physical' in the sense of consisting of elementary particles. The point is that what is necessarily true is not the principle stated two paragraphs back, but rather the principle:

If someone (some organism) is in the same state as a human being in pain in all relevant respects, then he (that organism) is in pain.

—And *this* principle *is* a tautology by anybody's lights! The only a priori methodological restriction I am imposing here is this one:

> If some organism is in the same state as a human being in pain in all respects *known* to be relevant, and there is no reason to suppose that there exist *un*known relevant respects, then don't postulate any.

—But this principle is not a 'tautology'; in fact, it is not a *statement* at all, but a methodological directive. And deciding to conform to this directive is not (as hardly needs to be said) changing the meaning of the word 'pain', or of *any* word.

There are two things that the logical behaviourist can do: he can claim that ascribing pains to X-worlders, or even super-spartans, involves a 'change of meaning,'[8] or he can claim that ascribing pains to super-spartans, or at least to X-worlders, is 'untestable.' The first thing is a piece of unreasonable linguistics; the second, a piece of unreasonable scientific method. The two are, not surprisingly, mutually supporting: the unreasonable scientific method makes the unreasonable linguistics appear more reasonable. Similarly, the normal ways of thinking and talking are mutually supporting: reasonable linguistic field techniques are, needless to say, in agreement with reasonable conceptions of scientific method. Madmen sometimes have consistent delusional systems; so madness and sanity can both have a 'circular' aspect. I may not have succeeded, in this paper, in breaking the 'delusional system' of a committed logical behaviourist; but I hope to have convinced the uncommitted that that system need not be taken seriously. If we have to choose between 'circles,' the circle of reason is to be preferred to any of the many circles of unreason.

NOTES

1. This paper was read as a part of the programme of The American Association for the Advancement of Science, Section L (History and Philosophy of Science), December 27th, 1961.
2. E.g., these two points are fairly explicitly stated in Strawson's *Individuals.* Strawson has told me that he no longer subscribes to point (1), however.
3. An attempted fourth alternative—i.e., an alternative to dualism, materialism, *and* behaviourism—is sketched in 'The Mental Life of Some Machines,' which appeared in the Proceedings of the Wayne Symposium on the Philosophy of Mind. This fourth alternative is materialistic in the wide sense of being compatible with the view that organisms, including human beings, are physical systems consisting of elementary particles and obeying the laws of physics, but does not require that such 'states' as *pain* and *preference* be defined in a way which makes reference to either overt behaviour or physical-chemical constitution. The idea, briefly, is that predicates which apply to a system by virtue of its *functional organization* have just this characteristic: a given functional organization (e.g., a given inductive logic, a given rational preference function) may realize itself in almost any kind of overt behaviour, depending upon the circumstances, and is capable of being 'built into' structures of many different logically possible physical (or even metaphysical) constitutions. Thus the statement that a creature prefers A to B does not tell us whether the creature has a carbon chemistry, or a silicon chemistry, or is even a disembodied mind, nor does it tell us how the creature would behave under any circumstances specifiable without reference to the creature's other preferences and beliefs, but it does not thereby become something 'mysterious.'
4. I mean not only that *each* criterion can be regarded as synthetic, but also that the cluster is *collectively* synthetic, in the sense that we are free in certain cases to say (for reason of inductive simplicity and theoretical economy) that the term applies although the whole cluster is missing. This is completely compatible with saying that the cluster serves to fix the meaning of the word. The point is that when we specify something by a cluster of indicators we assume that people will *use their brains.* That criteria may be over-ridden when good sense demands is the sort of thing we may regard as a 'convention associated with discourse' (Grice) rather than as something to be stipulated in connection with the individual words.
5. Cf. 'Dreaming and "Depth Grammar,"' *Analytical Philosophy,* First Series.
6. Of course, 'the cause' is a highly ambiguous phrase. Even if it is correct in certain contexts to say that certain events in the brain are 'the cause' of my pain behaviour, it does *not* follow (as has sometimes been suggested) that my pain must be 'identical' with these neural events.
7. This is suggested in Wittgenstein's *Philosophical Investigations.*
8. This popular philosophical move is discussed in 'Dreaming and "Depth Grammar,"' *Analytical Philosophy,* First Series

8 | Is Consciousness a Brain Process?
U. T. Place

The thesis that consciousness is a process in the brain is put forward as a reasonable scientific hypothesis, not to be dismissed on logical grounds alone. The conditions under which two sets of observations are treated as observations of the same process, rather than as observations of two independent correlated processes, are discussed. It is suggested that we can identify consciousness with a given pattern of brain activity, if we can explain the subject's introspective observations by reference to the brain processes with which they are correlated. It is argued that the problem of providing a physiological explanation of introspective observations is made to seem more difficult than it really is by the "phenomenological fallacy," the mistaken idea that descriptions of the appearances of things are descriptions of the actual state of affairs in a mysterious internal environment.

I. Introduction

The view that there exists a separate class of events, mental events, which cannot be described in terms of the concepts employed by the physical sciences no longer commands the universal and unquestioning acceptance among philosophers and psychologists which it once did. Modern physicalism, however, unlike the materialism of the seventeenth and eighteenth centuries, is behavioristic. Consciousness on this view is either a special type of behavior, "sampling" or "running-back-and-forth" behavior as Tolman has it,[1] or a disposition to behave in a certain way, an itch, for example, being a temporary propensity to scratch. In the case of cognitive concepts like "knowing," "believing," "understanding," "remembering," and volitional concepts like "wanting" and "intending,"

there can be little doubt, I think, that an analysis in terms of dispositions to behave is fundamentally sound.[2] On the other hand, there would seem to be an intractable residue of concepts clustering around the notions of consciousness, experience, sensation, and mental imagery, where some sort of inner process story is unavoidable.[3] It is possible, of course, that a satisfactory behavioristic account of this conceptual residuum will ultimately be found. For our present purposes, however, I shall assume that this cannot be done and that statements about pains and twinges, about how things look, sound, and feel, about things dreamed of or pictured in the mind's eye, are statements referring to events and processes which are in some sense private or internal to the individual of whom they are predicated. The question I wish to raise is whether in making this assumption we are inevitably committed to a dualist position in which sensations and mental images form a separate category of processes over and above the physical and physiological processes with which they are known to be correlated. I shall argue that an acceptance of inner processes does not entail dualism and that the thesis that consciousness is a process in the brain cannot be dismissed on logical grounds.

II. The "Is" of Definition and the "Is" of Composition

I want to stress from the outset that in defending the thesis that consciousness is a process in the brain, I am not trying to argue that when we describe our dreams, fantasies, and sensations we are talking about processes in our brains. That is, I am not claiming that statements about sensations and mental images are reducible to or

From *British Journal of Psychology* 47:44–50, 1956. Reprinted with permission from the *British Journal of Psychology*.

analyzable into statements about brain processes, in the way in which "cognition statements" are analyzable into statements about behavior. To say that statements about consciousness are statements about brain processes is manifestly false. This is shown (a) by the fact that you can describe your sensations and mental imagery without knowing anything about your brain processes or even that such things exist, (b) by the fact that statements about one's consciousness and statements about one's brain processes are verified in entirely different ways, and (c) by the fact that there is nothing self-contradictory about the statement "X has a pain but there is nothing going on in his brain." What I do want to assert, however, is that the statement "Consciousness is a process in the brain," although not necessarily true, is not necessarily false. "Consciousness is a process in the brain" in my view is neither self-contradictory nor self-evident; it is a reasonable scientific hypothesis, in the way that the statement "Lightning is a motion of electric charges" is a reasonable scientific hypothesis.

The all but universally accepted view that an assertion of identity between consciousness and brain processes can be ruled out on logical grounds alone derives, I suspect, from a failure to distinguish between what we may call the "is" of definition and the "is" of composition. The distinction I have in mind here is the difference between the function of the word "is" in statements like "A square is an equilateral rectangle," "Red is a color," "To understand an instruction is to be able to act appropriately under the appropriate circumstances," and its function in statements like "His table is an old packing case," "Her hat is a bundle of straw tied together with string," "A cloud is a mass of water droplets or other particles in suspension." These two types of "is" statements have one thing in common. In both cases it makes sense to add the qualification "and nothing else." In this they differ from those statements in which the "is" is an "is" of predication; the statements "Toby is eighty years old and nothing else," "Her hat is red and nothing else," or "Giraffes are tall and nothing else," for example, are nonsense. This logical feature may be described by saying that in both cases both the grammatical subject and the grammatical predicate are expressions which provide an adequate characterization of the state of affairs to which they both refer.

In another respect, however, the two groups of statements are strikingly different. State-

ments like "A square is an equilateral rectangle" are necessary statements which are true by definition. Statements like "His table is an old packing-case," on the other hand, are contingent statements which have to be verified by observation. In the case of statements like "A square is an equilateral rectangle" or "Red is a color," there is a relationship between the meaning of the expression forming the grammatical predicate and the meaning of the expression forming the grammatical subject, such that whenever the subject expression is applicable the predicate must also be applicable. If you can describe something as red then you must also be able to describe it as colored. In the case of statements like "His table is an old packing-case," on the other hand, there is no such relationship between the meanings of the expressions "his table" and "old packing-case"; it merely so happens that in this case both expressions are applicable to and at the same time provide an adequate characterization of the same object. Those who contend that the statement "Consciousness is a brain process" is logically untenable, base their claim, I suspect, on the mistaken assumption that if the meanings of two statements or expressions are quite unconnected, they cannot both provide an adequate characterization of the same object or state of affairs: if something is a state of consciousness, it cannot be a brain process, since there is nothing self-contradictory in supposing that someone feels a pain when there is nothing happening inside his skull. By the same token we might be led to conclude that a table cannot be an old packing-case, since there is nothing self-contradictory in supposing that someone has a table, but is not in possession of an old packing-case.

III. The Logical Independence of Expressions and the Ontological Independence of Entities

There is, of course, an important difference between the table/packing-case and the consciousness/brain process case in that the statement "His table is an old packing-case" is a particular proposition which refers only to one particular case, whereas the statement "Consciousness is a process in the brain" is a general or universal proposition applying to all states of consciousness whatever. It is fairly clear, I think, that if we lived in a world in which all tables without exception were packing-cases, the concepts of "table" and "packing-case" in our language would not have their present logically independent status. In such a world a table would be a species of packing-case in much the same way that red is a species of color. It seems to be a rule of language that whenever a given variety of object or state of affairs has two characteristics or sets of characteristics, one of which is unique to the variety of object or state of affairs in question, the expression used to refer to the characteristic or set of characteristics which defines the variety of object or state of affairs in question will always entail the expression used to refer to the other characteristic or set of characteristics. If this rule admitted of no exception it would follow that any expression which is logically independent of another expression which uniquely characterizes a given variety of object or state of affairs must refer to a characteristic or set of characteristics which is not normally or necessarily associated with the object or state of affairs in question. It is because this rule applies almost universally, I suggest, that we are normally justified in arguing from the logical independence of two expressions to the ontological independence of the states of affairs to which they refer. This would explain both the undoubted force of the argument that consciousness and brain processes must be independent entities because the expressions used to refer to them are logically independent and, in general, the curious phenomenon whereby questions about the furniture of the universe are often fought and not infrequently decided merely on a point of logic.

The argument from the logical independence of two expressions to the ontological independence of the entities to which they refer breaks down in the case of brain processes and consciousness, I believe, because this is one of a relatively small number of cases where the rule stated above does not apply. These exceptions are to be found, I suggest, in those cases where the operations which have to be performed in order to verify the presence of the two sets of characteristics inhering in the object or state of affairs in question can seldom if ever be performed simultaneously. A good example here is the case of the cloud and the mass of droplets or other particles in suspension. A cloud is a large semi-transparent mass with a fleecy texture suspended in the atmosphere whose shape is subject to continual and kaleidoscopic change. When observed at close quarters, however, it is found to consist of a mass of tiny particles, usually water droplets, in continuous motion. On the basis of this second observation we conclude that a cloud is a mass of tiny particles and nothing else. But there is no logical connection in our language between a cloud and a mass of tiny particles; there is nothing self-contradictory in talking about a cloud which is not composed of tiny particles in suspension. There is no contradiction involved in supposing that clouds consist of a dense mass of fibrous tissue; indeed, such a consistency seems to be implied by many of the functions performed by clouds in fairy stories and mythology. It is clear from this that the terms "cloud" and "mass of tiny particles in suspension" mean quite different things. Yet we do not conclude from this that there must be two things, the mass of particles in suspension and the cloud. The reason for this, I suggest, is that although the characteristics of being a cloud and being a mass of tiny particles in suspension are invariably associated, we never make the observations necessary to verify the statement "That is a cloud" and those necessary to verify the statement "This is a mass of tiny particles in suspension" at one and the same time. We can observe the micro-structure of a cloud only when we are enveloped by it, a condition which effectively prevents us from observing those characteristics which from a distance lead us to describe it as a cloud. Indeed, so disparate are these two experiences that we use different words to describe them. That which is a cloud when we observe it from a distance becomes a fog or mist when we are enveloped by it.

IV. When Are Two Sets of Observations Observations of the Same Event?

The example of the cloud and the mass of tiny particles in suspension was chosen because it is one of the few cases of a general proposition involving what I have called the "is" of composition which does not involve us in scientific technicalities. It is useful because it brings out the connection between the ordinary everyday cases of the "is" of composition like the table/packing-case example and the more technical cases like "Lightning is a motion of electric charges" where the analogy with the consciousness/brain process case is most marked. The limitation of the cloud/tiny particles in suspension case is that it does not bring out sufficiently clearly the crucial problems of how the identity of the states of affairs referred to by the two expressions is established. In the cloud case the fact that something is a cloud and the fact that something is a mass of tiny particles in suspension are both verified by the normal processes of visual observation. It is arguable, moreover, that the identity of the entities referred to by the two expressions is established by the continuity between the two sets of observations as the observer moves towards or away from the cloud. In the case of brain processes and consciousness there is no such continuity between the two sets of observations involved. A closer introspective scrutiny will never reveal the passage of nerve impulses over a thousand synapses in the way that a closer scrutiny of a cloud will reveal a mass of tiny particles in suspension. The operations required to verify statements about consciousness and statements about brain processes are fundamentally different.

To find a parallel for this feature we must examine other cases where an identity is asserted between something whose occurrence is verified by the ordinary processes of observation and something whose occurrence is established by special procedures. For this purpose I have chosen the case where we say that lightning is a motion of electric charges. As in the case of consciousness, however closely we scrutinize the lightning we shall never be able to observe the electric charges, and just as the operations for determining the nature of one's state of consciousness are radically different from those involved in determining the nature of one's brain processes, so the operations for determining the occurrence of lightning are radically different from those involved in determining the occurrence of a motion of electric charges. What is it, therefore, that leads us to say that the two sets of observations are observations of the same event? It cannot be merely the fact that the two sets of observations are systematically correlated such that whenever there is lightning there is always a motion of electric charges. There are innumerable cases of such correlations where we have no temptation to say that the two sets of observations are observations of the same event. There is a systematic correlation, for example, between the movement of the tides and the stages of the moon, but this does not lead us to say that records of tidal levels are records of the moon's stages or vice versa. We speak rather of a causal connection between two independent events or processes.

The answer here seems to be that we treat the two sets of observations as observations of the same event in those cases where the technical scientific observations set in the context of the appropriate body of scientific theory provide an immediate explanation of the observations made by the man in the street. Thus we conclude that lightning is nothing more than a motion of electric charges, because we know that a motion of electric charges through the atmosphere, such as occurs when lightning is reported, gives rise to the type of visual stimulation which would lead an observer to report a flash of lightning. In the moon/tide case, on the other hand, there is no such direct causal connection between the stages of the moon and the observations made by the man who measures the height of the tide. The causal connection is between the moon and the tides, not between the moon and the measurement of the tides.

V. The Physiological Explanation of Introspection and the Phenomenological Fallacy

If this account is correct, it should follow that in order to establish the identity of consciousness and certain processes in the brain, it would be necessary to show that the introspective observations reported by the subject can be accounted for in terms of processes which are known to have occurred in his brain. In the light of this suggestion it is extremely interesting to find that when a physiologist, as distinct from a philosopher, finds it difficult to see how consciousness could be a process in the brain, what worries him is not any supposed self-contradiction involved in such an assumption, but the apparent impossibility of accounting for the reports given by the subject of his conscious processes in terms of the known properties of the central nervous system. Sir Charles Sherrington has posed the problem as follows:

> The chain of events stretching from the sun's radiation entering the eye to, on the one hand, the contraction of the pupillary muscles, and on the other, to the electrical disturbances in the brain-cortex are all straightforward steps in a sequence of physical "causation," such as, thanks to science, are intelligible. But in the second serial chain there follows on, or attends, the stage of brain-cortex reaction an event or set of events quite inexplicable to us, which both as to themselves and as to the causal tie between them and what preceded them science does not help us; a set of events seemingly incommensurable with

any of the events leading up to it. The self "sees" the sun; it senses a two-dimensional disc of brightness, located in the "sky," this last a field of lesser brightness, and overhead shaped as a rather flattened dome, coping the self and a hundred other visual things as well. Of hint that this is within the head there is none. Vision is saturated with this strange property called "projection," the unargued inference that what it sees is at a "distance" from the seeing "self." Enough has been said to stress that in the sequence of events a step is reached where a physical situation in the brain leads to a psychical, which however contains no hint of the brain or any other bodily part . . . The supposition has to be, it would seem, two continuous series of events, one physico-chemical, the other psychical, and at times interaction between them.[4]

Just as the physiologist is not likely to be impressed by the philosopher's contention that there is some self-contradiction involved in supposing consciousness to be a brain process, so the philosopher is unlikely to be impressed by the considerations which lead Sherrington to conclude that there arc two sets of events, one physico-chemical, the other psychical. Sherrington's argument, for all its emotional appeal, depends on a fairly simple logical mistake, which is unfortunately all too frequently made by psychologists and physiologists and not infrequently in the past by the philosophers themselves. This logical mistake, which I shall refer to as the "phenomenological fallacy," is the mistake of supposing that when the subject describes his experience, when he describes how things look, sound, smell, taste, or feel to him, he is describing the literal properties of objects and events on a peculiar sort of internal cinema or television screen, usually referred to in the modern psychological literature as the "phenomenal field." If we assume, for example, that when a subject reports a green after-image he is asserting the occurrence inside himself of an object which is literally green, it is clear that we have on our hands an entity for which there is no place in the world of physics. In the case of the green after-image there is no green object in the subject's environment corresponding to the description that he gives. Nor is there anything green in his brain; certainly there is nothing which could have emerged when he reported the appearance of the green after-image. Brain processes are not the sort of things to which color concepts can be properly applied. The phenomenological fallacy on which this argument is based depends on the mistaken assumption that because our ability to describe

things in our environment depends on our consciousness of them, our descriptions of things are primarily descriptions of our conscious experience and only secondarily, indirectly, and inferentially descriptions of the objccts and events in our environments. It is assumed that because we recognize things in our environment by their look, sound, smell, taste, and feel, we begin by describing their phenomenal properties, i.e. the properties of the looks, sounds, smells, tastes, and feels which they produce in us, and infer their real properties from their phenomenal properties. In fact, the reverse is the case. We begin by learning to recognize the real properties of things in our environment. We learn to recognize them, of course, by their look, sound, smell, taste, and feel; but this does not mean that we have to learn to describe the look, sound, smell, taste, and feel of things before we can describe the things themselves. Indeed, it is only after we have learned to describe the things in our environment that we learn to describe our consciousness of them. We describe our conscious experience not in terms of the mythological "phenomenal properties" which are supposed to inhere in the mythological "objects" in the mythological "phenomenal field," but by reference to the actual physical properties of the concrete physical objects, events, and processes which normally, though not perhaps in the present instance, give rise to the sort of conscious experience which we are trying to describe. In other words when we describe the after-image as green, we are not saying that there is something, the after-image, which is green; we are saying that we are having the sort of experience which we normally have when, and which we have learned to describe as, looking at a green patch of light.

Once we rid ourselves of the phenomenological fallacy we realize that the problem of explaining introspective observations in terms of brain processes is far from insuperable. We realize that there is nothing that the introspecting subject says about his conscious experiences which is inconsistent with anything the physiologist might want to say about the brain processes which cause him to describe the environment and his consciousness of that environment in the way he does. When the subject describes his experience by saying that a light which is in fact stationary appears to move, all the physiologist or physiological psychologist has to do in order to explain the subject's introspective observations is to show that the brain process which is causing the subject to describe his experience in this way is the sort of process which normally occurs when he is observing an actual moving object and which therefore normally causes him to report the movement of an object in his environment. Once the mechanism whereby the individual describes what is going on in his environment has been worked out, all that is required to explain the individual's capacity to make introspective observations is an explanation of his ability to discriminate between those cases where his normal habits of verbal descriptions are appropriate to the stimulus situation and those cases where they are not, and an explanation of how and why, in those cases where the appropriateness of his normal descriptive habits is in doubt, he learns to issue his ordinary descriptive protocols preceded by a qualificatory phrase like "it appears," "seems," "looks," "feels," etc.[5]

NOTES

1. E. C. Tolman, *Purposive Behaviour in Animals and Men* (Berkeley 1932).
2. L. Wittgenstein, *Philosophical Investigations* (Oxford 1953); G. Ryle, *The Concept of Mind* (1949).
3. Place, "The Concept of Heed," *British Journal of Psychology* XLV (1954), 243–55.
4. Sir Charles Sherrington, *The Integrative Action of the Nervous System* (Cambridge 1947), pp. xx–xxi.
5. I am greatly indebted to my fellow-participants in a series of informal discussions on this topic which took place in the Department of Philosophy, University of Adelaide, in particular to Mr. C. B. Martin for his persistent and searching criticism of my earlier attempts to defend the thesis that consciousness is a brain process, to Professor D. A. T. Gasking, of the University of Melbourne, for clarifying many of the logical issues involved, and to Professor J. J. C. Smart for moral support and encouragement in what often seemed a lost cause.

9 | Sensations and Brain Processes
J. J. C. Smart

Suppose that I report that I have at this moment a roundish, blurry-edged after-image which is yellowish towards its edge and is orange towards its centre. What is it that I am reporting?[1] One answer to this question might be that I am not reporting anything, that when I say that it looks to me as though there is a roundish yellowy orange patch of light on the wall I am expressing some sort of *temptation,* the temptation to say that there *is* a roundish yellowy orange patch on the wall (though I may know that there is not such a patch on the wall). This is perhaps Wittgenstein's view in the *Philosophical Investigations* (see paragraphs 367, 370). Similarly, when I "report" a pain, I am not really reporting anything (or, if you like, I am reporting in a queer sense of "reporting"), but am doing a sophisticated sort of wince. (See paragraph 244: "The verbal expression of pain replaces crying and does not describe it." Nor does it describe anything else?)[2] I prefer most of the time to discuss an after-image rather than a pain, because the word "pain" brings in something which is irrelevant to my purpose: the notion of "distress." I think that "he is in pain" entails "he is in distress," that is, that he is in a certain agitation-condition.[3] Similarly, to say "I am in pain" may be to do more than "replace pain behavior": it may be partly to report something, though this something is quite nonmysterious, being an agitation-condition, and so susceptible of behavioristic analysis. The suggestion I wish if possible to avoid is a different one, namely that "I am in pain" is a genuine report, and that what it reports is an irreducibly psychical something. And similarly the suggestion I wish to resist is also that to say "I have a yellowish orange after-image" is to report something irreducibly psychical.

Why do I wish to resist this suggestion? Mainly because of Occam's razor. It seems to me that science is increasingly giving us a viewpoint whereby organisms are able to be seen as physico-chemical mechanisms:[4] it seems that even the behavior of man himself will one day be explicable in mechanistic terms. There does seem to be, so far as science is concerned, nothing in the world but increasingly complex arrangements of physical constituents. All except for one place: in consciousness. That is, for a full description of what is going on in a man you would have to mention not only the physical processes in his tissue, glands, nervous system, and so forth, but also his states of consciousness: his visual, auditory, and tactual sensations, his aches and pains. That these should be *correlated* with brain processes does not help, for to say that they are *correlated* is to say that they are something "over and above." You cannot correlate something with itself. You correlate footprints with burglars, but not Bill Sikes the burglar with Bill Sikes the burglar. So sensations, states of consciousness, do seem to be the one sort of thing left outside the physicalist picture, and for various reasons I just cannot believe that this can be so. That everything should be explicable in terms of physics (together of course with descriptions of the ways in which the parts are put together—roughly, biology is to physics as radio-engineering is to electro-magnetism) except the occurrence of sensations seems to me to be frankly unbelievable. Such sensations would be "nomological danglers," to use Feigl's expression.[5] It is not often realized how odd would be the laws whereby these nomological danglers would dangle. It is sometimes asked, "Why can't there be psychophysical laws which are of a novel sort, just as the laws of electricity and magnetism were novelties from the standpoint of Newtonian mechanics?" Certainly we are pretty sure in the future to come across new ultimate laws of a novel type, but I expect them to relate simple constituents: for example, whatever ultimate particles are then in vogue. I cannot believe that ultimate laws of nature could relate simple constituents to configurations consisting of perhaps billions of neurons (and goodness knows how many billion billions of ultimate particles) all put together for all the world as though their main purpose in life was to be a negative feedback mechanism of a complicated sort. Such ultimate laws would be like nothing so far known in science. They have a queer "smell" to them. I am just unable to believe in the nomological danglers themselves, or in the laws whereby they would dangle. If any philosophical arguments seemed to compel us to believe in such things, I would suspect a catch in the argument. In any case it is the object of this paper to show that there are no philosophical arguments which compel us to be dualists.

The above is largely a confession of faith, but it explains why I find Wittgenstein's position (as I construe it) so congenial. For on this view there are, in a sense, no sensations. A man is a vast arrangement of physical particles, but there are not, over and above this, sensations or states of consciousness. There are just behavioral facts about this vast mechanism, such as that it expresses a temptation (behavior disposition) to say "there is a yellowish-red patch on the wall" or that it goes through a sophisticated sort of wince, that is, says "I am in pain." Admittedly Wittgenstein says that though the sensation "is not a something," it is nevertheless "not a nothing either" (paragraph 304), but this need only mean that the word "ache" has a use. An ache is a thing, but only in the innocuous sense in which the plain man, in the first paragraph of Frege's *Foundations of Arithmetic,* answers the question "what is the number one?" by "a thing." It should be noted that when I assert that to say "I have a yellowish-orange after-image" is to express a temptation to assert the physical-object statement "there is a yellowish-orange patch on the wall," I mean that saying "I have a yellowish-orange after-image" is (partly) the exercise of the disposition[6] which is the temptation. It is not to *report* that I have the temptation, any more than is "I love you" normally a report that I love someone. Saying "I love you" is just part of the behavior which is the exercise of the disposition of loving someone.

Though, for the reasons given above, I am very receptive to the above "expressive" account of sensation statements, I do not feel that it will quite do the trick. Maybe this is because I have not thought it out sufficiently, but it does seem to me as though, when a person says "I have an after-image," he *is* making a genuine report, and that when he says "I have a pain," he *is* doing more than "replace pain-behavior," and that "this more" is not just to say that he is in distress. I am not so sure, however, that to admit this is to admit that there are nonphysical correlates of brain processes. Why should not sensations just be brain processes of a certain sort? There are, of course, well-known (as well as lesser-known) philosophical objections to the view that reports of sensations are reports of brain-processes, but I shall try to argue that these arguments are by no means as cogent as is commonly thought to be the case.

Let me first try to state more accurately the thesis that sensations are brain processes. It is not the thesis that, for example, "after-image" or "ache" means the same as "brain process of sort X" (where "X" is replaced by a description of a certain sort of brain process). It is that, in so far as "after-image" or "ache" is a report of a process, it is a report of a process that *happens to be* a brain process. It follows that the thesis does not claim that sensation statements can be *translated* into statements about brain processes.[7] Nor does it claim that the logic of a sensation statement is the same as that of a brain-process statement. All it claims is that in so far as a sensation statement is a report of something, that something is in fact a brain process. Sensations are nothing over and above brain processes. Nations are nothing "over and above" citizens, but this does not prevent the logic of nation statements being very different from the logic of citizen statements, nor does it insure the translatability of nation statements into citizen statements. (I do not, however, wish to assert that the relation of sensation statements to brain-process statements is very like that of nation statements to citizen statements. Nations do not just *happen to be* nothing over and above citizens, for example. I bring in the "nations" example merely to make a negative point: that the fact that the logic of A-statements is different from that of B-statements does not insure that A's are anything over and above B's.)

Remarks on Identity

When I say that a sensation is a brain process or that lightning is an electric discharge, I am using "is" in the sense of strict identity. (Just as in the—in this case necessary—proposition "7 is identical with the smallest prime number greater than 5.") When I say that a sensation is a brain process or that lightning is an electric discharge I do not mean just that the sensation is somehow spatially or temporally continuous with the brain process or that the lightning is just spatially or temporally continuous with the discharge. When on the other hand I say that the

successful general is the same person as the small boy who stole the apples I mean only that the successful general I see before me is a time slice[8] of the same four-dimensional object of which the small boy stealing apples is an earlier time slice. However, the four-dimensional object which has the general-I-see-before-me for its late time slice is identical in the strict sense with the four-dimensional object which has the small-boy-stealing-apples for an early time slice. I distinguish these two senses of "is identical with" because I wish to make it clear that the brain-process doctrine asserts identity in the *strict* sense.

I shall now discuss various possible objections to the view that the processes reported in sensation statements are in fact processes in the brain. Most of us have met some of these objections in our first year as philosophy students. All the more reason to take a good look at them. Others of the objections will be more recondite and subtle.

Objection 1

Any illiterate peasant can talk perfectly well about his after-images, or how things look or feel to him, or about his aches and pains, and yet he may know nothing whatever about neurophysiology. A man may, like Aristotle, believe that the brain is an organ for cooling the body without any impairment of his ability to make true statements about his sensations. Hence the things we are talking about when we describe our sensations cannot be processes in the brain.

Reply

You might as well say that a nation of slugabeds, who never saw the morning star or knew of its existence, or who had never thought of the expression "the Morning Star," but who used the expression "the Evening Star" perfectly well, could not use this expression to refer to the same entity as we refer to (and describe as) "the Morning Star."[9]

You may object that the Morning Star is in a sense not the very same thing as the Evening Star, but only something spatiotemporally continuous with it. That is, you may say that the Morning Star is not the Evening Star in the strict sense of "identity" that I distinguished earlier. I can perhaps forestall this objection by considering the slug-abeds to be New Zealanders and the early risers to be Englishmen. Then the thing the New Zealanders describe as "the Morning Star" could be the very same thing (in the strict sense) as the Englishmen describe as "the Evening Star." And yet they could be ignorant of this fact.

There is, however, a more plausible example. Consider lightning.[10] Modern physical science tells us that lightning is a certain kind of electrical discharge due to ionization of clouds of water-vapor in the atmosphere. This, it is now believed, is what the true nature of lightning is. Note that there are not two things: a flash of lightning and an electrical discharge. There is one thing, a flash of lightning, which is described scientifically as an electrical discharge to the earth from a cloud of ionized water-molecules. The case is not at all like that of explaining a footprint by reference to a burglar. We say that what lightning really is, what its true nature as revealed by science is, is an electric discharge. (It is not the true nature of a footprint to be a burglar.)

To forestall irrelevant objections, I should like to make it clear that by "lightning" I mean the publicly observable physical object, lightning, not a visual sense-datum of lightning. I say that the publicly observable physical object lightning is in fact the electric discharge, not just a correlate of it. The sense-datum, or at least the having of the sense-datum, the "look" of lightning, may well in my view be a correlate of the electric discharge. For in my view it is a brain state *caused* by the lightning. But we should no more confuse sensations of lightning with lightning than we confuse sensations of a table with the table.

In short, the reply to Objection 1 is that there can be contingent statements of the form "A is identical with B," and a person may well know that something is an A without knowing that it is a B. An illiterate peasant might well be able to talk about his sensations without knowing about his brain processes, just as he can talk about lightning though he knows nothing of electricity.

Objection 2

It is only a contingent fact (if it is a fact) that when we have a certain kind of sensation there is a certain kind of process in our brain. Indeed it is possible, though perhaps in the highest degree unlikely, that our present physiological theories will be as out of date as the ancient theory connecting mental processes with goings on in the heart. It follows that when we report a sensation we are not reporting a brain-process.

Reply

The objection certainly proves that when we say "I have an after-image" we cannot *mean* something of the form "I have such and such a brain-process." But this does not show that what we report (having an after-image) is not *in fact* a brain process. "I see lightning" does not *mean* "I see an electric discharge." Indeed, it is logically possible (though highly unlikely) that the electrical discharge account of lightning might one day be given up. Again, "I see the Evening Star" does not *mean* the same as "I see the Morning Star," and yet "the Evening Star and the Morning Star are one and the same thing" is a contingent proposition. Possibly Objection 2 derives some of its apparent strength from a "Fido"—Fido theory of meaning. If the meaning of an expression were what the expression named, then of course it *would* follow from the fact that "sensation" and "brain-process" have different meanings that they cannot name one and the same thing.

Objection 3[11]

Even if Objections 1 and 2 do not prove that sensations are something over and above brain-processes, they do prove that the qualities of sensations are something over and above the qualities of brain-processes. That is, it may be possible to get out of asserting the existence of irreducibly psychic processes, but not out of asserting the existence of irreducibly psychic *properties*. For suppose we identify the Morning Star with the Evening Star. Then there must be some properties which logically imply that of being the Morning Star, and quite distinct properties which entail that of being the Evening Star. Again, there must be some properties (for example, that of being a yellow flash) which are logically distinct from those in the physicalist story.

Indeed, it might be thought that the objection succeeds at one jump. For consider the property of "being a yellow flash." It might seem that this property lies inevitably outside the physicalist framework within which I am trying to work (either by "yellow" being an objective emergent property of physical objects, or else by being a power to produce yellow sense-data, where "yellow," in this second instantiation of the word, refers to a purely phenomenal or introspectible quality). I must therefore digress for a moment and indicate how I deal with secondary qualities. I shall concentrate on color.

First of all, let me introduce the concept of a normal percipient. One person is more a normal percipient than another if he can make color discriminations that the other cannot. For example, if A can pick a lettuce leaf out of a heap of cabbage leaves, whereas B cannot though he can pick a lettuce leaf out of a heap of beetroot leaves, then A is more normal than B. (I am assuming that A and B are not given time to distinguish the leaves by their slight difference in shape, and so forth.) From the concept of "more normal than" it is easy to see how we can introduce the concept of "normal." Of course, Eskimos may make the finest discriminations at the blue end of the spectrum, Hottentots at the red end. In this case the concept of a normal percipient is a slightly idealized one, rather like that of "the mean sun" in astronomical chronology. There is no need to go into such subtleties now. I say that "This is red" means something roughly like "A normal percipient would not easily pick this out of a clump of geranium petals though he would pick it out of a clump of lettuce leaves." Of course it does not exactly mean this: a person might know the meaning of "red" without knowing anything about geraniums, or even about normal percipients. But the point is that a person can be *trained* to say "This is red" of objects which would not easily be picked out of geranium petals by a normal percipient, and so on. (Note that even a color-blind person can reasonably assert that something is red, though of course he needs to use another human being, not just himself, as his "color meter.") This account of secondary qualities explains their unimportance in physics. For obviously the discriminations and lack of discriminations made by a very complex neurophysiological mechanism are hardly likely to correspond to simple and nonarbitrary distinctions in nature.

I therefore elucidate colors as powers, in Locke's sense, to evoke certain sorts of discriminatory responses in human beings. They are also, of course, powers to cause sensations in human beings (an account still nearer Locke's). But these sensations, I am arguing, are identifiable with brain processes.

Now how do I get over the objection that a sensation can be identified with a brain process only if it has some phenomenal property, not possessed by brain processes, whereby one-half of the identification may be, so to speak, pinned down?

My suggestion is as follows. When a person says, "I see a yellowish-orange after-image," he is saying something like this: "*There is something going on which is like what is going on when* I have my eyes open, am awake, and there is an orange illuminated in good light in front of me, that is, when I really see an orange." (And there is no reason why a person should not say the same thing when he is having a veridical sense-datum, so long as we construe "like" in the last sentence in such a sense that something can be like itself.) Notice that the italicized words, namely "there is something going on which is like what is going on when," are all quasi-logical or topic-neutral words. This explains why the ancient Greek peasant's reports about his sensations can be neutral between dualistic metaphysics or my materialistic metaphysics. It explains how sensations can be brain-processes and yet how those who report them need know nothing about brain-processes. For he reports them only very abstractly as "something going on which is like what is going on when . . ." Similarly, a person may say "someone is in the room," thus reporting truly that the doctor is in the room, even though he has never heard of doctors. (There are not two people in the room: "someone" *and* the doctor.) This account of sensation statements also explains the singular elusiveness of "raw feels"—why no one seems to be able to pin any properties on them.[12] Raw feels, in my view, are colorless for the very same reason that *something* is colorless. This does not mean that sensations do not have properties, for if they are brain-processes they certainly have properties. It only means that in speaking of them as being like or unlike one another we need not know or mention these properties.

This, then, is how I would reply to Objection 3. The strength of my reply depends on the possibility of our being able to report that one thing is like another without being able to state the respect in which it is like. I am not sure whether this is so or not, and that is why I regard Objection 3 as the strongest with which I have to deal.

Objection 4

The after-image is not in physical space. The brain-process is. So the after-image is not a brain-process.

Reply

This is an *ignoratio elenchi*. I am not arguing that the after-image is a brain-process, but that the experience of having an after-image is a brain-process. It is the *experience* which is reported in the introspective report. Similarly, if it is objected that the after-image is yellowy-orange but that a surgeon looking into your brain would see nothing yellowy-orange, my reply is that it is the experience of seeing yellowy-orange that is being described, and this experience is not a yellowy-orange something. So to say that a brain-process cannot be yellowy-orange is not to say that a brain-process cannot in fact be the experience of having a yellowy-orange after-image. There is, in a sense, no such thing as an after-image or a sense-datum, though there is such a thing as the experience of having an image, and this experience is described indirectly in material object language, not in phenomenal language, for there is no such thing.[13] We describe the experience by saying, in effect, that it is like the experience we have when, for example, we really see a yellow-orange patch on the wall. Trees and wallpaper can be green, but not the experience of seeing or imagining a tree or wallpaper. (Or if they are described as green or yellow this can only be in a derived sense.)

Objection 5

It would make sense to say of a molecular movement in the brain that it is swift or slow, straight or circular, but it makes no sense to say this of the experience of seeing something yellow.

Reply

So far we have not given sense to talk of experiences as swift or slow, straight or circular. But I am not claiming that "experience" and "brain-process" mean the same or even that they have the same logic. "Somebody" and "the doctor" do not have the same logic, but this does not lead us to suppose that talking about somebody telephoning is talking about someone over and above, say, the doctor. The ordinary man when he reports an experience is reporting that something is going on, but he leaves it open as to what sort of thing is going on, whether in a material solid medium, or perhaps in some sort of gaseous medium, or even perhaps in some sort of non-spatial medium (if this makes sense). All that I am saying is that "experience" and "brain-process" may in fact refer to the same thing, and if so we may easily adopt a convention (which is not a change in our present rules for the use of experience words but an addition to them) whereby it would make sense to talk of an experience in terms appropriate to physical processes.

Objection 6

Sensations are private, brain processes are *public*. If I sincerely say, "I see a yellowish-orange after-image" and I am not making a verbal mistake, then I cannot be wrong. But I can be wrong about a brain-process. The scientist looking into my brain might be having an illusion. Moreover, it makes sense to say that two or more people are observing the same brain-process but not that two or more people are reporting the same inner experience.

Reply

This shows that the language of introspective reports has a different logic from the language of material processes. It is obvious that until the brain-process theory is much improved and widely accepted there will be no *criteria* for saying "Smith has an experience of such-and-such a sort" *except* Smith's introspective reports. So we have adopted a rule of language that (normally) what Smith says goes.

Objection 7

I can imagine myself turned to stone and yet having images, aches, pains, and so on.

Reply

I can imagine that the electrical theory of lightning is false, that lightning is some sort of purely optical phenomenon. I can imagine that lightning is not an electrical discharge. I can imagine that the Evening Star is not the Morning Star. But it is. All the objection shows is that "experience" and "brain-process" do not have the same meaning. It does not show that an experience is not in fact a brain process.

This objection is perhaps much the same as one which can be summed up by the slogan:

"What can be composed of nothing cannot be composed of anything."[14] The argument goes as follows: on the brain-process thesis the identity between the brain-process and the experience is a contingent one. So it is logically possible that there should be no brain-process, and no process of any other sort, either (no heart process, no kidney process, no liver process). There would be the experience but no "corresponding" physiological process with which we might be able to identify it empirically.

I suspect that the objector is thinking of the experience as a ghostly entity. So it is composed of something, not of nothing, after all. On his view it is composed of ghost stuff, and on mine it is composed of brain stuff. Perhaps the counter-reply will be[15] that the experience is simple and uncompounded, and so it is not composed of anything after all. This seems to be a quibble, for, if it were taken seriously, the remark "What can be composed of nothing cannot be composed of anything" could be recast as an a priori argument against Democritus and atomism and for Descartes and infinite divisibility. And it seems odd that a question of this sort could be settled a priori. We must therefore construe the word "composed" in a very weak sense, which would allow us to say that even an indivisible atom is composed of something (namely, itself). The dualist cannot really say that an experience can be composed of nothing. For he holds that experiences are something over and above material processes, that is, that they are a sort of ghost stuff. (Or perhaps ripples in an underlying ghost stuff.) I say that the dualist's hypothesis is a perfectly intelligible one. But I say that experiences are not to be identified with ghost stuff but with brain stuff. This is another hypothesis, and in my view a very plausible one. The present argument cannot knock it down a priori.

Objection 8

The "beetle in the box" objection (see Wittgenstein, *Philosophical Investigations,* paragraph 293). How could descriptions of experiences, if these are genuine reports, get a foothold in language? For any rule of language must have public criteria for its correct application.

Reply

The change from describing how things are to describing how we feel is just a change from un-inhibitedly saying "this is so" to saying "this looks so." That is, when the naive person might be tempted to say, "There is a patch of light on the wall which moves whenever I move my eyes" or "A pin is being stuck into me," we have learned how to resist this temptation and say "It *looks as though* there is a patch of light on the wallpaper" or "It *feels as though* someone were sticking a pin into me." The introspective account tells us about the individual's state of consciousness in the same way as does "I see a patch of light" or "I feel a pin being stuck into me": it differs from the corresponding perception statement in so far as (a) in the perception statement the individual "goes beyond the evidence of his senses" in describing his environment and (b) in the introspective report he withholds descriptive epithets he is inclined to ascribe to the environment, perhaps because he suspects that they may not be appropriate to the actual state of affairs. Psychologically speaking, the change from talking about the environment to talking about one's state of consciousness is simply a matter of inhibiting descriptive reactions not justified by appearances alone, and of disinhibiting descriptive reactions which are normally inhibited because the individual has learned that they are unlikely to provide a reliable guide to the state of the environment in the prevailing circumstances.[16] To say that something looks green to me is to say that my experience is like the experience I get when I see something that really is green. In my reply to Objection 3, I pointed out the extreme openness or generality of statements which report experiences. This explains why there is no language of private qualities. (Just as "someone," unlike "the doctor," is a colorless word.)[17]

If it is asked what is the difference between those brain processes which, in my view, are experiences and those brain processes which are not, I can only reply that this is at present unknown. But it does not seem to me altogether fanciful to conjecture that the difference may in part be that between perception and reception (in Dr. D. M. MacKay's terminology) and that the type of brain process which is an experience might be identifiable with MacKay's active "matching response."[18]

I have now considered a number of objections to the brain-process thesis. I wish now to conclude by some remarks on the logical status of the thesis itself. U. T. Place seems to hold that it is a straight-out scientific hypothesis.[19] If so, he is partly right and partly wrong. If the issue is between (say) a brain-process thesis and a heart thesis, or a liver thesis, or a kidney thesis, then the issue is a purely empirical one, and the verdict is overwhelmingly in favor of the brain. The right sorts of things don't go on in the heart, liver, or kidney, nor do these organs possess the right sort of complexity of structure. On the other hand, if the issue is between a brain-or-heart-or-liver-or-kidney thesis (that is, some form of materialism) on the one hand and epiphenomenalism on the other hand, then the issue is not an empirical one. For there is no conceivable experiment which could decide between materialism and epiphenomenalism. This latter issue is not like the average straight-out empirical issue in science, but like the issue between the nineteenth-century English naturalist Philip Gosse[20] and the orthodox geologists and paleontologists of his day. According to Gosse, the earth was created about 4000 B.C. exactly as described in Genesis, with twisted rock strata, "evidence" of erosion, and so forth, and all sorts of fossils, all in their appropriate strata, just as if the usual evolutionist story had been true. Clearly this theory is in a sense irrefutable: no evidence can possibly tell against it. Let us ignore the theological setting in which Philip Gosse's hypothesis had been placed, thus ruling out objections of a theological kind, such as "what a queer God who would go to such elaborate lengths to deceive us." Let us suppose that it is held that the universe just *began* in 4004 B.C. with the initial conditions just every-

where as they were in 4004 B.C., and in particular that our own planet began with sediment in the rivers, eroded cliffs, fossils in the rocks, and so on. No scientist would ever entertain this as a serious hypothesis, consistent though it is with all possible evidence. The hypothesis offends against the principles of parsimony and simplicity. There would be far too many brute and inexplicable facts. Why are pterodactyl bones just as they are? No explanation in terms of the evolution of pterodactyls from earlier forms of life would any longer be possible. We would have millions of facts about the world as it was in 4004 B.C. that just have to be *accepted.*

The issue between the brain-process theory and epiphenomenalism seems to be of the above sort. (Assuming that a behavioristic reduction of introspective reports is not possible.) If it be agreed that there are no cogent philosophical arguments which force us into accepting dualism, and if the brain process theory and dualism are equally consistent with the facts, then the principles of parsimony and simplicity seem to me to decide overwhelmingly in favor of the brain-process theory. As I pointed out earlier, dualism involves a large number of irreducible psychophysical laws (whereby the "nomological danglers" dangle) of a queer sort, that just have to be taken on trust, and are just as difficult to swallow as the irreducible facts about the paleontology of the earth with which we are faced on Philip Gosse's theory.

NOTES

1. This paper takes its departure from arguments to be found in U. T. Place's "Is Consciousness a Brain Process?" (*British Journal of Psychology,* XLVII, 1956, 44–50). I have had the benefit of discussing Place's thesis in a good many universities in the United States and Australia, and I hope that the present paper answers objections to his thesis which Place has not considered, and presents his thesis in a more nearly unobjectionable form. This paper is meant also to supplement "The 'Mental' and the 'Physical,' " by H. Feigl (in *Minnesota Studies in the Philosophy of Science,* II, 370–497), which argues for much the same thesis as Place's.

2. Some philosophers of my acquaintance, who have the advantage over me in having known Wittgenstein, would say that this interpretation of him is too behavioristic. However, it seems to me a very natural interpretation of his printed words, and whether or not it is Wittgenstein's real view it is certainly an interesting and important one. I wish to consider it here as a possible rival both to the "brain-process" thesis and to straight-out old-fashioned dualism.

3. See Ryle, *Concept of Mind* (New York, 1949), p. 93.

4. On this point see Paul Oppenheim and Hilary Putnam, "Unity of Science as a Working Hypothesis," in *Minnesota Studies in the Philosophy of Science,* II, 3–36; also my note "Plausible Reasoning in Philosophy," *Mind,* LXVI (1957), 75–78.

5. Feigl, op. cit., p. 428.

6. Wittgenstein did not like the word "disposition." I am using it to put in a nutshell (and perhaps inaccurately) the view which I am attributing to Wittgenstein. I should like to repeat that I do not wish to claim that my interpretation of Wittgenstein is correct. Some of those who knew him do not interpret him in this way. It is merely a view which I find myself extracting from his printed words and which I think is important and worth discussing for its own sake.

7. See Place, op. cit., p. 45, near top, and Feigl, op. cit., p. 390, near top.

8. See J. H. Woodger, *Theory Construction* (Chicago, 1939), p. 38 (International Encyclopedia of Unified Science, Vol. 2, No. 5). I here permit myself to speak loosely. For warnings against possible ways of going wrong with this sort of talk, see my note "Spatialising Time," *Mind,* LXIV (1955), 239–41.

9. Cf. Feigl, op. cit., p. 439.
10. See Place, op. cit., p. 47; also Feigl, op. cit. p. 438.
11. I think this objection was first put to me by Professor Max Black. I think it is the most subtle of any of those I have considered, and the one which I am least confident of having satisfactorily met.
12. See B. A. Farrell, "Experience," *Mind,* LIX (1950), especially 174.
13. Dr. J. R. Smythies claims that a sense-datum language could be taught independently of the material object language ("A Note on the Fallacy of the 'Phenomenological Fallacy,' " *British Journal of Psychology,* XLVIII, 1957, 141–144.) I am not so sure of this: there must be some public criteria for a person having got a rule wrong before we can teach him the rule. I suppose someone might *accidentally* learn color words by Dr. Smythies' procedure. I am not, of course, denying that we can learn a sense-datum language in the sense that we can learn to report our experience. Nor would Place deny it.

14. I owe this objection to Mr. C. B. Martin. I gather that he no longer wishes to maintain this objection, at any rate in its present form.
15. Martin did not make this reply, but one of his students did.
16. I owe this point to Place, in correspondence.
17. The "beetle in the box" objection is, *if it is sound,* an objection to *any* view, and in particular the Cartesian one, that introspective reports are genuine reports. So it is no objection to a weaker thesis that I would be concerned to uphold, namely, that if introspective reports of "experiences" are genuinely reports, then the things they are reports of are in fact brain processes.
18. See his article "Towards an Information-Flow Model of Human Behaviour," *British Journal of Psychology,* XLVII (1956), 30–43.
19. Op. cit.
20. See the entertaining account of Gosse's book *Omphalos* by Martin Gardner in *Fads and Fallacies in the Name of Science* (2nd ed., New York, 1957).

10 | The "Mental" and the "Physical"
Herbert Feigl

E. Arguments Concerning the Identification of Sentience with Neural Events

I shall now present, as explicitly as I can, the reasons for an empirical identification of raw feels with neural processes. I shall also discuss several apparently trenchant arguments that have been advanced against this identity theory of the mental and the physical. It will be advisable first to state my thesis quite succinctly, and to elaborate the arguments for and against it afterwards.

Taking into consideration everything we have said so far about the scientific and the philosophical aspects of the mind–body problem, the following view suggests itself: The raw feels of direct experience as we "have" them, are empirically identifiable with the referents of certain specifiable concepts of molar behavior theory, and these in turn (this was argued in the preceding subsection *D*) are empirically identifiable with the referents of some neurophysiological concepts. As we have pointed out, the word "mental" in present day psychology covers, however, not only the events and processes of direct experience (i.e., the raw feels), but also the unconscious events and processes, as well as the "intentional acts" of perception, introspective awareness, expectation, thought, belief, doubt, desire, volition, resolution, etc. I have argued above that since intentionality as such is to be analyzed on the one hand in terms of pure semantics (and thus falls under the category of the logical, rather than the psychological), it would be a category mistake of the most glaring sort to attempt a neurophysiological identification of this aspect of "mind." But since, on the other hand, intentional acts as occurrents in direct experience are introspectively or phenomenologically describable in something quite like raw-feel terms, a neural identification of this aspect of mind is prima facie not excluded on purely logical grounds. Unconscious processes, such as those described in psychoanalytic theory, are

Excerpted from H. Feigl, M. Scriven, and G. Maxwell, eds., *Concepts, Theories, and the Mind–Body Problem* (University of Minnesota Press, 1958). Copyright © 1958 University of Minnesota Press.

methodologically on a par with the concepts of molar behavior theories (as, e.g., instinct, habit strength, expectancy, drive, etc.) and hence offer in principle no greater difficulties for neurophysiological identification than the concepts of molar behavior theory which refer to conscious events or processes (e.g., directly experienced sensations, thoughts, feelings, emotions, etc.). As we have repeatedly pointed out, the crux of the mind–body problem consists in the interpretation of the relation between raw feels and the neural processes. The questions to be discussed are therefore these:

1. What does the identity thesis assert about the relation of raw feels to neural events?
2. What is the difference, if there is a difference, between psychophysiological parallelism (or epiphenomenalism) and the identity thesis?
3. Can the identity thesis be defended against empirical arguments which support an interactionistic dualism?
4. Can the identity thesis be defended against philosophical arguments which support dualism on the grounds of the alleged fundamental differences between the properties of direct experience and the features of physical (neurophysiological) processes?

Since I have already paved the way for at least partial replies to question 3, and to some extent also to 4, I shall now primarily concentrate on questions 1 and 2, and discuss the other issues more briefly whenever they will be relevant.

The identity thesis which I wish to clarify and to defend asserts that the states of direct experience which conscious human beings "live through," and those which we confidently ascribe to some of the higher animals, are identical with certain (presumably configurational) aspects of the neural processes in those organisms. To put the same idea in the terminology explained previously, we may say, what is had-in-experience, and (in the case of human beings) knowable by acquaintance, is identical with the object of knowledge by description provided first by molar behavior theory and this is in turn identical with what the science of neurophysiology describes (or, rather, will describe when sufficient progress has been achieved) as processes in the central nervous system, perhaps especially in the cerebral cortex. In its basic core this is the "double knowledge" theory held by many modern monistic critical realists.[1]

This view does not have the disadvantages of the Spinozistic doctrine of the unknown or unknowable third of which the mental and the physical are aspects. The "mental" states or events (in the sense of raw feels) are the referents (denotata) of both the phenomenal terms of the language of introspection, as well as of certain terms of the neurophysiological language. For this reason I have in previous publications called my view a "double-language theory." But, as I have explained above, this way of phrasing it is possibly misleading in that it suggests a purely analytic (logical) translatability between the statements in the two languages. It may therefore be wiser to speak instead of twofold access or double knowledge. The identification, I have emphasized, is to be empirically justified, and hence there can be no logical equivalence between the concepts (or statements) in the two languages.

On superficial reflection one may be tempted to regard the identification of phenomenal data with neurophysiological events as a case of the theoretically ascertainable identities of the natural sciences. "Theoretical identity" (explicated in section V D) means the sameness of the referent (universal or particular) of two or more intersubjective descriptions. For example, it is the atomic micro-structure of a crystal which is indicated ("described") by the optical refraction index, the dielectric constant, the magnetic permeability coefficient, and in greater detail evidenced by X-ray diffraction patterns. Similarly, the various behavioral indications for habit strength refer to a certain, as yet not fully specified, neurophysiological structure in a brain, which may ultimately be certified by more direct histological evidence. Logical Behaviorism admits only intersubjectively confirmable statements and hence defines mentalistic (phenomenal) terms explicitly on the basis of molar behavioral theoretical concepts. Thus, to ascribe to a person the experience of, e.g., an after-image amounts, within the intersubjective frame of reference, to the ascription of a hypothetical construct (theoretical concept), anchored in observable stimulus and response variables. This theoretical concept may then later be identified, i.e., come to be regarded as empirically co-referential with the more detailed and deductively more powerful neurophysiological concept.

The empirical character of the identification rests upon the extensional equivalences, or extensional implications, which hold between statements about the behavioral and the neurophysiological evidence. In our example this means that all persons to whom we ascribe an after-image, as evidenced by certain stimulus and response conditions, also have cerebral processes of a certain kind, and vice versa. In view of the uncertainties and inaccuracies of our experimental techniques we can at present, of course, assert only a statistical correlation between the two domains of evidence. That is to say, the equivalences or implications are, practically speaking, only probabilistic. But in any case, the correlations as well as the theoretical identification of the referents indicated by various items of evidence are formulated in intersubjectively confirmable statements.

The identification of raw feels with neural states, however, crosses what in metaphysical phraseology is sometimes called an "ontological barrier." It connects the "subjective" with the "intersubjective." It identifies the referents of subjective terms with the referents of certain objective terms. But in my view of the matter there is here no longer an unbridgeable gulf, and hence no occasion for metaphysical shudders. Taking into account the conclusions of the preceding analyses of "privacy," "acquaintance," "physical," and of "identification," private states known by direct acquaintance and referred to by phenomenal (subjective) terms can be described in a public (at least physical$_1$) language and may thus be empirically identifiable with the referents of certain neurophysiological terms. Privacy is capable of public (intersubjective) description, and the objects of intersubjective science can be evidenced by data of private experience.

The application of phenomenal terms in statements of knowledge by acquaintance is direct, and therefore the verification of such statements (about the present moment of subjective experience) is likewise immediate. Phenomenal terms applied to other persons or organisms are used indirectly, and the confirmation of statements containing phenomenal terms (thus used) is mediated by rules of inference, utilizing various strands in the nomological net as rules of inference. Judging by the structure of one's own experience, there seems to be no reason to assume the existence of absolutely private mental states; i.e., there are presumably no "captive minds" in our world. This is of course a basic ontological feature of nature as we have come to conceive it. It is an empirical feature of a very fundamental kind, similar in its "basic frame" character to the 3 + 1 dimensionality of space-time, or to the causal order of the universe. Such frame principles do not differ in kind, although

they differ in degree of generality, from the postulates of scientific theories. Their adoption is essentially regulated by the rules of the hypothetico-deductive method.

Logical empiricism as it has come to be formulated in recent years (Carnap, 1950, 1956; Feigl, 1963) recognizes the difference between direct observation (knowledge-by-acquaintance) statements and inferential statements as a contextual difference between direct and indirect confirmation. It does not matter precisely where, in our epistemological reconstruction, we draw the line between the observable and the inferred entities. But wherever we do draw it, the scope of the directly experienceable or of the directly observable depends on the identity of the experiencing and/or observing subject.[2] What is directly verifiable for one subject is only indirectly confirmable for another. And these very statements (expressed in the preceding two sentences) may be formalized in a pragmatic, intersubjective metalanguage.

Having formulated and in outline explicated the identity thesis, we now have to attend to several important points of philosophical interpretation. I reject the (Spinozistic) double aspect theory because it involves the assumption of an unknown, if not unknowable, neutral ("third") substance or reality-in-itself of which the mental (sentience) and the physical (appearance, properties, structure, etc.) are complementary aspects. If the neutral third is conceived as unknown, then it can be excluded by the principle of parsimony which is an essential ingredient of the normal hypothetico-deductive method of theory construction. If it is defined as in principle unknowable, then it must be repudiated as factually meaningless on even the most liberally interpreted empiricist criterion of significance. But our view does not in the least suggest the need for a neutral third of any sort. This will now be shown more explicitly.

If a brain physiologist were equipped with the knowledge and devices that may be available a thousand years hence, and could investigate my brain processes and describe them in full detail, then he could formulate his findings in neurophysiological language, and might even be able to produce a complete microphysical account in terms of atomic and subatomic concepts. In our logical analysis of the meanings of the word "physical" we have argued that the physical sciences consist of knowledge-claims-by-description. That is to say that the objects (targets, referents) of such knowledge claims are "triangulated" on the basis of various areas of observational (sensory) evidence. What these objects are acquaintancewise is left completely open as long as we remain within the frame of physical concept formation and theory construction. But, since in point of empirical fact, I am directly acquainted with the qualia of my own immediate experience, I happen to know (by acquaintance) what the neurophysiologist refers to when he talks about certain configurational aspects of my cerebral processes.

There is a danger at this point to lapse into the fallacies of the well-known doctrine of structuralism, according to which physical knowledge concerns only the form or structure of the events of the universe, whereas acquaintance concerns the contents or qualia of existence.[3] This doctrine is to be repudiated on two counts. First, by failing to distinguish acquaintance (the mere having of data, or the capacity for imaging some of them) from knowledge by acquaintance (propositions, e.g., about similarities or dissimilarities, rank-orders, etc., of the qualia of the given), the doctrine fails to recognize that even introspective or phenomenological knowledge claims are structural in the very same sense in which all knowledge is structural, i.e., that it consists in the formulation of relations of one sort or another. Second, the realistic interpretation of physical knowledge which we have defended implies that whatever we "triangulate" from various bases of sensory observation is to be considered as "qualitative" in a generalized sense of this term. In the vast majority of cases the qualitative content of the referents of physical descriptions is not "given," i.e., it is not part of a phenomenal field. But it is a given content in the case of certain specifiable neurophysiological processes.

If one wishes to trace the historical origins of this view, one might find it, if not in Aristotle, then certainly in Kant who came very close to saying that the experienced content is the Ding-an-sich which corresponds to the brain process as known in the spatio-temporal-causal concepts of natural science.[4] To put it more picturesquely, in the physical account of the universe as provided in the four-dimensional Minkowski diagram, there are sporadically some very small regions (representing the brains of living and awake organisms) which are "illuminated by the inner light" of direct experience or sentience. This view differs from panpsychism which assumes that the "internal illumination" pervades all of physical reality. But the panpsychists' hypothesis is inconsistent with the very principles of analogy which they claim to use as guides for their reasoning. If one really follows the analogies, then it stands to reason that the enormous differences in behavior (and neural processes) that exist between, e.g., human beings and insects, indicate equally great differences in their corresponding direct experience or sentience. Fancying the qualities of sentience of the lower animals is best left to poetic writers like Fechner, Bergson, or Maeterlinck. As regards the mental life of robots, or of Scriven's (1953) "androids," I cannot believe that they could display all (or even most) of the characteristics of human behavior unless they were made of the proteins that constitute the nervous systems—and in that case they would present no puzzle.

NOTES

1. Especially Alois Riehl, Moritz Schlick, Richard Gätschenberger, H. Reichenbach, Günther Jacoby, Bertrand Russell, Roy W. Sellars, Durant Drake, and C. A. Strong. To be sure, there are very significant differences among these thinkers. Russell has never quite freed himself from the neutral monism (phenomenalism) of his earlier neorealistic phase. R. W. Sellars and, following him on a higher level of logical sophistication, his son, Wilfrid, have combined their realistic, double-knowledge view with a doctrine of evolutionary emergence. Opposing the emergence view, Strong and Drake, originally influenced by F. Paulsen, adopted a panpsychistic metaphysics. My own view is a development in more modern terms of the epistemological outlook common to Riehl, Schlick, Russell, and to some extent of that of the erratic but brilliant Gätschenberger. The French philosopher Raymond Ruyer (1930, 1934) especially before he turned to a speculative and questionable neovitalism (1952) held a similar view. Among psychologists W. Köhler (1929, 1938), E. G. Boring (1933), and D. K. Adams (1954), again differing in many important respects, hold similar monistic positions. Personally, I consider sections 22–35 in Schlick (1925) as the first genuinely perspicacious, lucid and convincing formulation of the realistic-monistic point of view here defended. It is to be hoped that an English translation of this classic in modern epistemology will eventually become available.

2. As I understand Dewey and other pragmatists, as well as contextualists like S. C. Pepper (1950, 1960), this point has been explicitly recognized by them. Cf. also the discussions by analytic philosophers, such as Hampshire (1952), Watling (1954), and Ayer (1956). An exact logical account of the linguistic re-

flection of direct versus indirect verifiability has been given in the analysis of egocentric particulars (token-reflexive, indexical terms) by B. Russell (1940), Reichenbach (1947), Burks (1949), W. Sellars (1948, 1954), and Bar-Hillel (1954).

3. This doctrine has been espoused in various forms by Poincaré (1929), Eddington (1928), C. I. Lewis (1929), Schlick (1938), et al.

4. Cf. I. Kant, *Critique of Pure Reason,* section on "The Paralogisms of Pure Reason."

REFERENCES

Adams, D. K. "Learning and explanation," *Learning Theory, Personality Theory, and Clinical Research: The Kentucky Symposium,* pp. 66–80. New York: Wiley; London: Chapman & Hall, Ltd., 1954.

Ayer, A. J. *The Problem of Knowledge.* New York: St. Martin's Press, 1956.

Bar-Hillel, Y. "Indexical Expressions," *Mind,* 63:359–379 (1954).

Boring, E. G. *The Physical Dimensions of Consciousness.* New York, London: The Century Co., 1933.

Burks, A. W. "Icon, Index and Symbol," *Philosophical and Phenomenological Research,* 9:673–89 (1949).

Carnap, R. "Empiricism, Semantics, and Ontology," *Revue Internationale de Philosophie,* 4:20–40 (1950). Reprinted in P. P. Wiener (ed.), *Readings in the Philosophy of Science,* pp. 509–21. New York: Scribner, 1953. Also reprinted in L. Linsky (ed.), *Semantics and the Philosophy of Language,* pp. 208–30. Urbana (Ill.): Univ. of Illinois Press, 1952.

Carnap, R. "The Methodological Character of Theoretical Concepts," in *Minnesota Studies in the Philosophy of Science,* Vol. I, pp. 38–76. Minneapolis: Univ. of Minnesota Press, 1956.

Eddington, A. S. *The Nature of the Physical World.* New York: Macmillan, 1928.

Feigl, H. "Physicalism, Unity of Science and the Foundations of Psychology," in P. A. Schilpp (ed.), *The Philosophy of Rudolf Carnap,* LaSalle (Ill.): Open Court Pub. Co., 1963.

Hampshire, S. "The Analogy of Feeling," *Mind,* 61:1–12 (1952).

Köhler, W, "Ein altes Scheinproblem," *Die Naturwissenschaften,* 17:395–401 (1929).

Köhler, W. *The Place of Values in a World of Facts.* New York: Liveright, 1938.

Lewis, C. I. *Mind and the World Order.* New York: Scribner, 1929.

Pepper, S. C. "The Issue Over the Facts," in *Meaning and Interpretation.* Berkeley: Univ. of California Press, 1950.

Pepper, S. C. "A Neural Identity Theory," in S. Hook (ed.), *Dimensions of Mind,* pp. 37–56. New York: New York Univ. Press, 1960.

Poincaré, H. *The Foundations of Science.* New York: The Science Press, 1929.

Reichenbach, H. *Elements of Symbolic Logic.* New York: Macmillan, 1947.

Russell, B. *An Inquiry into Meaning and Truth.* New York: Norton & Co., 1940.

Ruyer, R. *Esquisse d'une Philosophie de la Structure,* Paris: F. Alcan, 1930.

Ruyer, R. "Les Sensations Sont-elles dans Notre Tête?" *Journal de Psychologie,* 31:555–80 (1934).

Ruyer, R. *Néo-Finalisme.* Paris: Presses Univ. de France, 1952.

Schlick, M. *Allgemeine Erkenntnislehre.* Berlin: Springer, 1925.

Schlick, M. *Gesammelte Aufsaetze.* Vienna: Gerold & Co., 1938.

Scriven, M. "The Mechanical Concept of Mind," *Mind,* 62:230–40 (1953).

Sellars, W. "Realism and the New Way of Words," *Philosophical and Phenomenological Research,* 8:601–34 (1948). Reprinted in H. Feigl and W. Sellars (eds.), *Readings in Philosophical Analysis,* pp. 424–56. New York: Appleton-Century-Crofts, 1949.

————. "Some Reflections on Language Games," *Philosophy of Science,* 21:204–228 (1954).

Watling, J. "Ayer on Other Minds," *Theoria,* 20:175–80 (1954).

11 | The Nature of Mental States

Hilary Putnam

The typical concerns of the Philosopher of Mind might be represented by three questions: (1) How do we know that other people have pains? (2) Are pains brain states? (3) What is the analysis of the concept *pain?* I do not wish to discuss questions (1) and (3) in this paper. I shall say something about question (2).[1]

I. Identity Questions

"Is pain a brain state?" (Or, "Is the property of having a pain at time *t* a brain state?")[2] It is impossible to discuss this question sensibly without saying something about the peculiar rules which have grown up in the course of the development of "analytical philosophy"—rules which, far from leading to an end to all conceptual confusions, themselves represent considerable conceptual confusion. These rules—which are, of course, implicit rather than explicit in the practice of most analytical philosophers—are (1) that a statement of the form "being *A* is being *B*" (e.g., "being in pain is being in a certain brain state") can be *correct* only if it follows, in some sense, from the meaning of the terms *A* and *B;* and (2) that a statement of the form "being *A* is being *B*" can be philosophically *informative* only if it is in some sense reductive (e.g. "being in pain is having a certain unpleasant sensation" is not philosophically informative; "being in pain is having a certain behavior disposition" is, if true, philosophically informative). These rules are excellent rules if we still believe that the program of reductive analysis (in the style of the 1930s) can be carried out; if we don't, then they turn analytical philosophy into a mug's game, at least so far as "is" questions are concerned.

In this paper I shall use the term 'property' as a blanket term for such things as being in pain, being in a particular brain state, having a particular behavior disposition, and also for magnitudes such as temperature, etc.—i.e., for things which can naturally be represented by one-or-more-place predicates or functors. I shall use the term 'concept' for things which can be identified with synonymy-classes of expressions. Thus the concept *temperature* can be identified (I maintain) with the synonymy-class of the word 'temperature.'[3] (This is like saying that the number 2 can be identified with the class of all pairs. This is quite a different statement from the peculiar statement that 2 *is* the class of all pairs. I do not maintain that concepts *are* synonymy-classes, whatever that might mean, but that they can be identified with synonymy-classes, for the purpose of formalization of the relevant discourse.)

The question "What is the concept *temperature?*" is a very "funny" one. One might take it to mean "What is temperature? Please take my question as a conceptual one." In that case an answer might be (pretend for a moment 'heat' and 'temperature' are synonyms) "temperature is heat," or even "the concept of temperature is the same concept as the concept of heat." Or one might take it to mean "What are *concepts,* really? For example, what is 'the concept of temperature'?" In that case heaven knows what an "answer" would be. (Perhaps it would be the statement that concepts *can be identified with* synonymy-classes.)

Of course, the question "What is the property temperature?" is also "funny." And one way of interpreting it is to take it as a question about the concept of temperature. But this is not the way a physicist would take it.

The effect of saying that the property P_1 can be identical with the property P_2 only if the terms P_1, P_2 are in some suitable sense "synonyms" is, to all intents and purposes, to collapse the two notions of "property" and "concept" into a sin-

Originally published as "Psychological Predicates," in (W. H. Capitan & D. D. Merrill, eds.) *Art, Mind, and Religion* (1973), pp. 37–48. Reprinted with permission of University of Pittsburgh Press.

gle notion. The view that concepts (intensions) *are* the same as properties has been explicitly advocated by Carnap (e.g., in *Meaning and Necessity*). This seems an unfortunate view, since "temperature is mean molecular kinetic energy" appears to be a perfectly good example of a true statement of identity of properties, whereas "the concept of temperature is the same concept as the concept of mean molecular kinetic energy" is simply false.

Many philosophers believe that the statement "pain is a brain state" violates some rules or norms of English. But the arguments offered are hardly convincing. For example, if the fact that I can know that I am in pain without knowing that I am in brain state S shows that pain cannot be brain state S, then, by exactly the same argument, the fact that I can know that the stove is hot without knowing that the mean molecular kinetic energy is high (or even that molecules exist) shows that it is *false* that temperature is mean molecular kinetic energy, physics to the contrary. In fact, all that immediately follows from the fact that I can know that I am in pain without knowing that I am in brain state S is that the concept of pain is not the same concept as the concept of being in brain state S. But either pain, or the state of being in pain, or some pain, or some pain state, might still be brain state S. After all, the concept of temperature is not the same concept as the concept of mean molecular kinetic energy. But temperature is mean molecular kinetic energy.

Some philosophers maintain that both 'pain is a brain state' and 'pain states are brain states' are unintelligible. The answer is to explain to these philosophers, as well as we can, given the vagueness of all scientific methodology, what sorts of considerations lead one to make an empirical reduction (i.e. to say such things as "water is H_2O," "light is electromagnetic radiation," "temperature is mean molecular kinetic energy"). If, without giving reasons, he still maintains in the face of such examples that one cannot imagine parallel circumstances for the use of 'pains are brain states' (or, perhaps, 'pain states are brain states') one has grounds to regard him as perverse.

Some philosophers maintain that "P_1 is P_2" is something that can be true, when the 'is' involved is the 'is' of empirical reduction, only when the properties P_1 and P_2 are (a) associated with a spatio-temporal region; and (b) the region is one and the same in both cases. Thus "temperature is mean molecular kinetic energy" is an admissible empirical reduction, since the temperature and the molecular energy are associated with the same space-time region, but "having a pain in my arm is being in a brain state" is not, since the spatial regions involved are different.

This argument does not appear very strong. Surely no one is going to be deterred from saying that mirror images are light reflected from an object and then from the surface of a mirror by the fact that an image can be "located" three feet *behind* the mirror! (Moreover, one can always find *some* common property of the reductions one is willing to allow—e.g., temperature is mean molecular kinetic energy—which is not a property of some one identification one wishes to disallow. This is not very impressive unless one has an argument to show that the very purposes of such identification depend upon the common property in question.)

Again, other philosophers have contended that all the predictions that can be derived from the conjunction of neurophysiological laws with such statements as "pain states are such-and-such brain states" can equally well be derived from the conjunction of the same neurophysiological laws with "being in pain is correlated with such-and-such brain states," and hence (sic!) there can be no methodological grounds for saying that pains (or pain states) *are* brain states, as opposed to saying that they are *correlated* (invariantly) with brain states. This argument, too, would show that light is only correlated with electromagnetic radiation. The mistake is in ignoring the fact that, although the theories in question may indeed lead to the same predictions, they open and exclude different *questions*. "Light is invariantly correlated with electromagnetic radiation" would leave open the questions "What is the light then, if it isn't the same as the electromagnetic radiation?" and "What makes the light accompany the electromagnetic radiation?"—questions which are excluded by saying that the light *is* the electromagnetic radiation. Similarly, the purpose of saying that pains are brain states is precisely to exclude from empirical meaningfulness the questions "What is the pain, then, if it isn't the same as the brain state?" and "What makes the pain accompany the brain state?" If there are grounds to suggest that these questions represent, so to speak, the wrong way to look at the matter, then those grounds are grounds for a theoretical identification of pains with brain states.

If all arguments to the contrary are unconvincing, shall we then conclude that it is meaningful (and perhaps true) to say either that pains are brain states or that pain states are brain states?

1. It is perfectly meaningful (violates no "rule of English," involves no "extension of usage") to say "pains arc brain states."
2. It is not meaningful (involves a "changing of meaning" or "an extension of usage," etc.) to say "pains are brain states."

My own position is not expressed by either (1) or (2). It seems to me that the notions "change of meaning" and "extension of usage" are simply so ill-defined that one cannot in fact say *either* (1) or (2). I see no reason to believe that either the linguist, or the man-on-the-street, or the philosopher possesses today a notion of "change of meaning" applicable to such cases as the one we have been discussing. The *job* for which the notion of change of meaning was developed in the history of the language was just a *much* cruder job than this one.

But, if we don't assert either (1) or (2)—in other words, if we regard the "change of meaning" issue as a pseudo-issue in this case—then how are we to discuss the question with which we started? "Is pain a brain state?"

The answer is to allow statements of the form "pain is *A*," where 'pain' and '*A*' are in no sense synonyms, and to see whether any such statement can be found which might be acceptable on empirical and methodological grounds. This is what we shall now proceed to do.

II. Is Pain a Brain State?

We shall discuss "Is pain a brain state?," then. And we have agreed to waive the "change of meaning" issue.

Since I am discussing not what the concept of pain comes to, but what pain is, in a sense of 'is' which requires empirical theory-construction (or, at least, empirical speculation), I shall not apologize for advancing an empirical hypothesis. Indeed, my strategy will be to argue that pain is *not* a brain state, not on a priori grounds, but on the grounds that another hypothesis is more plausible. The detailed development and verification of my hypothesis would be just as Utopian a task as the detailed development and verification of the brain-state hypothesis. But the putting-forward, not of detailed and scientifically "finished" hypotheses, but of schemata for hypotheses, has long been a function of philosophy. I shall, in short, argue that pain is not a brain state, in the sense of a physical-chemical state of the brain (or even the whole nervous system), but another *kind* of state entirely. I propose the hypothesis that pain, or the state of being in pain, is a functional state of a whole organism.

To explain this it is necessary to introduce some technical notions. In previous papers I have explained the notion of a Turing Machine and discussed the use of this notion as a model for an organism. The notion of a Probabilistic Automaton is defined similarly to a Turing Machine, except that the transitions between "states" are allowed to be with various probabilities rather than being "deterministic." (Of course, a Turing Machine is simply a special kind of Probabilistic Automaton, one with transition probabilities 0, 1.) I shall assume the notion of a Probabilistic Automaton has been generalized to allow for "sensory inputs" and "motor outputs"—that is, the Machine Table specifies, for every possible combination of a "statc" and a complete set of "sensory inputs," an "instruction" which determines the probability of the next "state," and also the probabilities of the "motor outputs." (This replaces the idea of the Machine as printing on a tape.) I shall also assume that the physical realization of the sense organs responsible for the various inputs, and of the motor organs, is specified, but that the "states" and the "inputs" themselves are, as usual, specified only "implicitly"—i.e., by the set of transition probabilities given by the Machine Table.

Since an empirically given system can simultaneously be a "physical realization" of many different Probabilistic Automata, I introduce the notion of a *Description* of a system. A Description of S where S is a system, is any true statement to the effect that S possesses distinct states $S_1, S_2 \ldots, S_n$ which are related to one another and to the motor outputs and sensory inputs by the transition probabilities given in such-and-such a Machine Table. The Machine Table mentioned in the Description will then be called the Functional Organization of S relative to that Description, and the S_i such that S is in state S_i at a given time will be called the Total State of S (at that time) relative to that Description. It should be noted that knowing the Total State of a system relative to a Description involves knowing a good deal about how the system is likely to "behave," given various combinations of sensory inputs, but does *not* involve knowing the physical realization of the S_i as, e.g., physical-chemical states of the brain. The S_i, to repeat, are specified only *implicitly* by the Description—i.e., specified *only* by the set of transition probabilities given in thc Machine Table.

The hypothesis that "being in pain is a functional state of the organism" may now be spelled out more exactly as follows:

1. All organisms capable of feeling pain are Probabilistic Automata.
2. Every organism capable of feeling pain possesses at least one Description of a certain kind (i.e., being capable of feeling pain *is* possessing an appropriate kind of Functional Organization.)
3. No organism capable of feeling pain possesses a decomposition into parts which separately possess Descriptions of the kind referred to in (2).
4. For every Description of the kind referred to in (2), there exists a subset of the sensory inputs such that an organism with that Description is in pain when and only when some of its sensory inputs are in that subset.

This hypothesis is admittedly vague, though surely no vaguer than the brain-state hypothesis in its present form. For example, one would like to know more about the kind of Functional Organization that an organism must have to be capable of feeling pain, and more about the marks that distinguish the subset of the sensory inputs referred to in (4). With respect to the first question, one can probably say that the Functional Organization must include something that resembles a "preference function," or at least a preference partial ordering, and something that resembles an "inductive logic" (i.e., the Machine must be able to "learn from experience"). (The meaning of these conditions, for Automata models, is discussed in my paper "The Mental Life of Some Machines.") In addition, it seems natural to require that the Machine possess "pain sensors," i.e., sensory organs which normally signal damage to the Machine's body, or dangerous temperatures, pressures, etc., which transmit a special subset of the inputs, the subset referred to in (4). Finally, and with respect to the second question, we would want to require at least that the inputs in the distinguished subset have a high disvalue on the Machine's preference function or ordering (further conditions are discussed in "The Mental Life of Some Machines"). The purpose of condition (3) is to rule out such "organisms" (if they can count as such) as swarms of bees as single pain-feelers. The condition (1) is, obviously, redundant, and is only introduced for expository reasons. (It is, in fact, empty, since everything is a Probabilistic Automaton under *some* Description.)

I contend, in passing, that this hypothesis, in spite of its admitted vagueness, is far *less* vague than the "physical-chemical state" hypothesis is today, and far more susceptible to investigation of both a mathematical and an empirical kind. Indeed, to investigate this hypothesis is just to attempt to produce "mechanical" models of organisms—and isn't this, in a sense, just what psychology is about? The difficult step, of course, will be to pass from models of *specific* organisms to a *normal form* for the psychological description of organisms—for this is what is required to make (2) and (4) precise. But this too seems to be an inevitable part of the program of psychology.

I shall now compare the hypothesis just advanced with (a) the hypothesis that pain is a brain state, and (b) the hypothesis that pain is a behavior disposition.

III. Functional State versus Brain State

It may, perhaps, be asked if I am not somewhat unfair in taking the brain-state theorist to be talking about *physical-chemical* states of the brain. But (a) these are the only sorts of states ever mentioned by brain-state theorists. (b) The brain-state theorist usually mentions (with a certain pride, slightly reminiscent of the Village Atheist) the incompatibility of his hypothesis with all forms of dualism and mentalism. This is natural if physical-chemical states of the brain are what is at issue. However, functional states of whole systems are something quite different. In particular, the functional-state hypothesis is *not* incompatible with dualism! Although it goes without saying that the hypothesis is "mechanistic" in its inspiration, it is a slightly remarkable fact that a system consisting of a body and a "soul," if such things there be, can perfectly well be a Probabilistic Automaton. (c) One argument advanced by Smart is that the brain-state theory assumes only "physical" properties, and Smart finds "non-physical" properties unintelligible. The Total States and the "inputs" defined above are, of course, neither mental nor physical per se, and I cannot imagine a functionalist advancing this argument. (d) If the brain-state theorist does mean (or at least allow) states other than physical-chemical states, then his hypothesis is completely empty, at least until he specifies *what* sort of "states" he *does* mean.

Taking the brain-state hypothesis in this way, then, what reasons are there to prefer the functional-state hypothesis over the brain-state hypothesis? Consider what the brain-state theorist has to do to make good his claims. He has to specify a physical-chemical state such that *any* organism (not just a mammal) is in pain if and only if (a) it possesses a brain of a suitable physical-chemical structure; and (b) its brain is in that physical-chemical state. This means that the physical-chemical state in question must be a possible state of a mammalian brain, a reptilian brain, a mollusc's brain (octopuses are mollusca, and certainly feel pain), etc. At the same time, it must *not* be a possible (physically possible) state of the brain of any physically possible creature that cannot feel pain. Even if such a state can be found, it must be nomologically certain that it will also be a state of the brain of any extra-terrestrial life that may be found that will be capable of feeling pain before we can even entertain the supposition that it may *be* pain.

It is not altogether impossible that such a state will be found. Even though octopus and mammal are examples of parallel (rather than sequential) evolution, for example, virtually identical structures (physically speaking) have evolved in the eye of the octopus and in the eye of the mammal, notwithstanding the fact that this organ has evolved from different kinds of cells in the two cases. Thus it is at least possible that parallel evolution, all over the universe, might *always* lead to *one and the same* physical "correlate" of pain. But this is certainly an ambitious hypothesis.

Finally, the hypothesis becomes still more ambitious when we realize that the brain-state theorist is not just saying that *pain* is a brain state; he is, of course, concerned to maintain that *every* psychological state is a brain state. Thus if we can find even one psychological predicate which can clearly be applied to both a mammal and an octopus (say "hungry"), but whose physical-chemical "correlate" is different in the two cases, the brain-state theory has collapsed. It seems to me overwhelmingly probable that we can do this. Granted, in such a case the brain-state theorist can save himself by ad hoc assumptions (e.g., defining the disjunction of two states to be a single "physical-chemical state"), but this does not have to be taken seriously.

Turning now to the considerations *for* the functional-state theory, let us begin with the fact that we identify organisms as in pain, or hungry, or angry, or in heat, etc., on the basis of their *behavior*. But it is a truism that similarities in the behavior of two systems are at least a reason to suspect similarities in the functional organization of the two systems, and a much *weaker* reason to suspect similarities in the actual physical details. Moreover, we expect the various psychological states—at least the basic ones, such as hunger, thirst, aggression, etc.—to have more or less similar "transition probabilities" (within wide and ill-defined limits, to be sure) with each other and with behavior in the case of different species, because this is an artifact of the way in which we identify these states. Thus, we would not count an animal as *thirsty* if its "unsatiated" behavior did not seem to be directed toward drinking and was not followed by "satiation for liquid." Thus any animal that we count as capable of these various states will at least *seem* to have a certain rough kind of functional organization. And, as already remarked, if the program of finding psychological laws that are not species-specific—i.e., of finding a normal form for psychological theories of different species—ever succeeds, then it will bring in its wake a delineation of the kind of functional organization that is necessary and sufficient for a given psychological state, as well as a precise definition of the notion "psychological state." In contrast, the brain-state theorist has to hope for the eventual development of neurophysiological laws that are species-independent, which seems much less reasonable than the hope that psychological laws (of a sufficiently general kind) may be species-independent, or, still weaker, that a species-independent *form* can be found in which psychological laws can be written.

IV. Functional State versus Behavior Disposition

The theory that being in pain is neither a brain state nor a functional state but a behavior disposition has one apparent advantage: it appears to agree with the way in which we verify that organisms are in pain. We do not in practice know anything about the brain state of an animal when we say that it is in pain; and we possess little if any knowledge of its functional organization, except in a crude intuitive way. In fact, however, this "advantage" is no advantage at all: for, although statements about how we verify that *x* is *A* may have a good deal to do with what the concept of being *A* comes to, they have precious little to do with what the property *A* is. To argue on the ground just mentioned that pain is neither a brain state nor a functional state is like arguing that heat is not mean molecular kinetic energy from the fact that ordinary people do not (they think) ascertain the mean molecular kinetic energy of something when they verify that it is hot or cold. It is not necessary that they should; what is necessary is that the marks that they take as indications of heat should in fact be explained by the mean molecular kinetic energy. And, similarly, it is necessary to our hypothesis that the marks that are taken as behavioral indications of pain should be explained by the fact that the organism is in a functional state of the appropriate kind, but not that speakers should *know* that this is so.

The difficulties with "behavior disposition" accounts are so well known that I shall do little more than recall them here. The difficulty—it appears to be more than "difficulty," in fact—of specifying the required behavior disposition except as "the disposition of *X* to behave as if *X* were in *pain*," is the chief one, of course. In contrast, we *can* specify the functional state with which we propose to identify pain, at least roughly, without using the notion of pain. Namely, the functional state we have in mind is the state of receiving sensory inputs which play a certain role in the Functional Organization of the organism. This role is characterized, at least partially, by the fact that the sense organs responsible for the inputs in question are organs whose function is to detect damage to the body, or dangerous extremes of temperature, pressure, etc., and by the fact that the "inputs" themselves, whatever their physical realization, represent a condition that the organism assigns a high disvalue to. As I stressed in "The Mental Life of Some Machines," this does *not* mean that the Machine will always *avoid* being in the condition in question ("pain"); it only means that the condition will be avoided unless not avoiding it is necessary to the attainment of some more highly valued goal. Since the behavior of the Machine (in this case, an organism) will depend not merely on the sensory inputs, but also on the Total State (i.e., on other values, beliefs, etc.), it seems hopeless to make any general statement about how an organism in such a condition *must* behave; but this does not mean that we must abandon hope of characterizing the condition. Indeed, we have just characterized it.[4]

Not only does the behavior-disposition theory seem hopelessly vague; if the "behavior" referred to is peripheral behavior, and the relevant stimuli are peripheral stimuli (e.g., we do not say anything about what the organism will do if its brain is operated upon), then the theory seems clearly false. For example, two animals with all motor nerves cut will have the same actual and potential "behavior" (viz., none to speak of); but if one has cut pain fibers and the other has uncut pain fibers, then one will feel pain and the other won't. Again, if one person has cut pain fibers, and another suppresses all pain responses deliberately due to some strong compulsion, then the actual and potential peripheral behavior may be the same, but one will feel pain and the other won't. (Some philosophers maintain that this last case is conceptually impossible, but the only evidence for this appears to be that *they* can't, or don't want to, conceive of it.)[5] If, instead of pain, we take some sensation the "bodily expression" of which is easier to suppress—say, a slight coolness in one's left little finger—the case becomes even clearer.

Finally, even if there *were* some behavior disposition invariantly correlated with pain (species-independently!), and specifiable without using the term 'pain,' it would still be more plausible to identify being in pain with some state whose presence *explains* this behavior disposition—the brain state or functional state—than with the behavior disposition itself. Such considerations of plausibility may be somewhat subjective; but if other things *were* equal (of course, they aren't) why shouldn't we allow considerations of plausibility to play the deciding role?

V. Methodological Considerations

So far we have considered only what might be called the "empirical" reasons for saying that being in pain is a functional state, rather than a brain state or a behavior disposition; viz., that it seems more likely that the functional state we described is invariantly "correlated" with pain, species-independently, than that there is either a physical-chemical state of the brain (must an organism have a *brain* to feel pain? perhaps some ganglia will do) or a behavior disposition so correlated. If this is correct, then it follows that the identification we proposed is at least a candidate for consideration. What of methodological considerations?

The methodological considerations are roughly similar in all cases of reduction, so no surprises need be expected here. First, identification of psychological states with functional states means that the laws of psychology can be derived from statements of the form "such-and-such organisms have such-and-such Descriptions" together with the identification statements ("being in pain is such-and-such a functional state," etc.). Secondly, the presence of the functional state (i.e., of inputs which play the role we have described in the Functional Organization of the organism) is not merely "correlated with" but actually explains the pain behavior on the part of the organism. Thirdly, the identification serves to exclude questions which (if a naturalistic view is correct) represent an altogether wrong way of looking at the matter, e.g., "What *is* pain if it isn't either the brain state or the functional state?" and "What causes the pain to be always accompanied by this sort of functional state?" In short, the identification is to be tentatively accepted as a theory which leads to both fruitful predictions and to fruitful *questions,* and which serves to discourage fruitless and empirically senseless questions, where by 'empirically senseless' I mean "senseless" not merely from the standpoint of verification, but from the standpoint of what there in fact *is.*

NOTES

1. I have discussed these and related topics in the following papers: "Minds and machines," in *Dimensions of Mind,* ed. Sidney Hook, New York, 1960, pp. 148–79; "Brains and behavior," in *Analytical Philosophy,* second series, ed. Ronald Butler, Oxford, 1965, pp. 1–20; and "The Mental Life of Some Machines," in *Intentionality, Minds, and Perception,* ed. Hector-Neri Castañeda, Detroit, 1967, pp. 177–200.
2. In this paper I wish to avoid the vexed question of the relation between *pains* and *pain states.* I only remark in passing that one common argument *against* identification of these two—viz., that a pain can be in one's arm but a state (of the organism) cannot be in one's arm—is easily seen to be fallacious.
3. There are some well-known remarks by Alonzo Church on this topic. Those remarks do not bear (as might at first be supposed) on the identification of concepts with synonymy-classes as such, but rather support the view that (in formal semantics) it is necessary to retain Frege's distinction between the normal and the "oblique" use of expressions. That is, even if we say that the concept of temperature *is* the synonymy-class of the word 'temperature,' we must not thereby be led into the error of supposing that 'the concept of temperature' is synonymous with 'the synonymy-class of the word "temperature"'—for then 'the concept of temperature' and 'der Begriff der Temperatur' would not be synonymous, which they are. Rather, we must say that 'the concept of temperature' *refers* to the synonymy-class of the word 'temperature' (on this particular reconstruction); but that class is *identified* not as "the synonymy class to which such-and-such a word belongs," but in another way (e.g., as the synonymy-class whose members have such-and-such a characteristic use).
4. In the "Mental life of some machines" a further, and somewhat independent, characteristic of the pain inputs is discussed in terms of Automata models—namely the spontaneity of the inclination to withdraw the injured part, etc. This raises the question, which is discussed in that paper, of giving a functional analysis of the notion of a spontaneous inclination. Of course, still further characteristics come readily to mind—for example, that feelings of pain are (or seem to be) *located* in the parts of the body.
5. Cf. the discussion of "super-spartans" in "Brains and behavior."

12 | The Causal Theory of the Mind
D. M. Armstrong

Is Philosophy Just Conceptual Analysis?

What can philosophy contribute to solving the problem of the relation to mind to body? Twenty years ago, many English-speaking philosophers would have answered: "Nothing beyond an analysis of the various mental *concepts*." If we seek knowledge of things, they thought, it is to science that we must turn. Philosophy can only cast light upon our concepts of those things.

This retreat from things to concepts was not undertaken lightly. Ever since the seventeenth century, the great intellectual fact of our culture has been the incredible expansion of knowledge both in the natural and in the rational sciences (mathematics, logic). Everyday life presents us with certain simple verities. But, it seems, through science and only through science can we build upon these verities, and with astonishing results.

The success of science created a crisis in philosophy. What was there for philosophy to do? Hume had already perceived the problem in some degree, and so surely did Kant, but it was not until the twentieth century, with the Vienna Circle and with Wittgenstein, that the difficulty began to weigh heavily. Wittgenstein took the view that philosophy could do no more than strive to undo the intellectual knots it itself had tied, so achieving intellectual release, and even a certain illumination, but no knowledge. A little later, and more optimistically, Ryle saw a positive, if reduced, role for philosophy in mapping the "logical geography" of our concepts: how they stood to each other and how they were to be analyzed.

On the whole, Ryle's view proved more popular than Wittgenstein's. After all, it retained a special, if much reduced, realm for philosophy where she might still be queen. There was better hope of continued employment for members of the profession!

Since that time, however, philosophers in the "analytic" tradition have swung back from Wittgensteinian and even Rylean pessimism to a more traditional conception of the proper role and tasks of philosophy. Many analytic philosophers now would accept the view that the central task of philosophy is to give an account, or at least play a part in giving an account, of the most general nature of things and of man. (I would include myself among that many.)

Why has this swing back occurred? Has the old urge of the philosopher to determine the nature of things by a priori reasoning proved too strong? To use Freudian terms, are we simply witnessing a return of what philosophers had repressed? I think not. One consideration that has had great influence was the realization that those who thought that they were abandoning ontological and other substantive questions for a mere investigation of concepts were in fact smuggling in views on the substantive questions. They did not acknowledge that they held these views, but the views were there; and far worse from their standpoint, the views imposed a form upon their answers to the conceptual questions.

For instance, in *The Concept of Mind* (1949), Gilbert Ryle, although he denied that he was a Behaviorist, seemed to be upholding an account of man and his mind that was extremely close to Behaviorism. Furthermore, it seemed in many cases that it was this view of the mind–body problem that led him to his particular analyses of particular mental concepts, rather than the other way around. Faced with examples like this, it began to appear that, since philosophers could not help holding views on substantive matters, and the views could not help affecting their analyses of concepts, the views had better be held and discussed explicitly instead of appearing in a distorted, because unacknowledged, form.

The swing back by analytic philosophers to first-order questions was also due to the growth of a more sophisticated understanding of the nature of scientific investigation. For a philosophical tradition that is oriented towards science, as, on the whole, Western philosophy is, the consideration of the *methods* of science must be

From *The Nature of Mind*, pp. 16–31. University of Queensland Press, 1981. Reprinted with permission of the publisher.

an important topic. It was gradually realized that in the past scientific investigation had regularly been conceived in far too positivistic, sensationalistic and observationalistic a spirit. (The influence of Karl Popper has been of the greatest importance in this realization.) As the central role of speculation, theory and reasoning in scientific investigation began to be appreciated by more and more philosophers, the border-line between science and philosophy began to seem at least more fluid, and the hope arose again that philosophy might have something to contribute to first-order questions.

The philosopher has certain special skills. These include the stating and assessing of the worth of arguments, including the bringing to light and making explicit suppressed premises of arguments, the detection of ambiguities and inconsistencies, and, perhaps especially, the analysis of concepts. But, I contend, these special skills do not entail that the *objective* of philosophy is to do these things. They are rather the special *means* by which philosophy attempts to achieve further objectives. Ryle was wrong in taking the analysis of concepts to be the end of philosophy. Rather, the analysis of concepts is a means by which the philosopher makes his contribution to great general questions, not about concepts, but about things.

In the particular case of the mind–body problem, the propositions the philosopher arrives at need not be of a special nature. They perhaps might have been arrived at by the psychologist, the neuro-physiologist, the biochemist or others, and, indeed, may be suggested to the philosopher by the results achieved or programs proposed by those disciplines. But the way that the argument is marshalled by a philosopher will be a special way. Whether this special way has or has not any particular value in the search for truth is a matter to be decided in particular cases. There is no a priori reason for thinking that the special methods of philosophy will be able to make a contribution to the mind–body problem. But neither is there an a priori reason for assuming that the philosopher's contribution will be valueless.

The Concept of a Mental State

The philosophy of philosophy is perhaps a somewhat joyless and unrewarding subject for reflection. Let us now turn to the mind–body problem itself, hoping that what is to be said

about this particular topic will confirm the general remarks about philosophy that have just been made.

If we consider the mind–body problem today, then it seems that we ought to take account of the following consideration. The present state of scientific knowledge makes it probable that we can give a purely physico-chemical account of man's body. It seems increasingly likely that the body and the brain of man are constituted and work according to exactly the same principles as those physical principles that govern other, non-organic, matter. The differences between a stone and a human body appear to lie solely in the extremely complex material set-up that is to be found in the living body and which is absent in the stone. Furthermore, there is rather strong evidence that it is the state of our brain that completely determines the state of our consciousness and our mental state generally.

All this is not beyond the realm of controversy, and it is easy to imagine evidence that would upset the picture. In particular, I think that it is just possible that evidence from psychical research might be forthcoming that a physico-chemical view of man's brain could not accommodate. But suppose that the physico-chemical view of the working of the brain is correct, as I take it to be. It will be very natural to conclude that mental states are not simply *determined* by corresponding states of the brain, but that they are actually *identical* with these brain-states, brain-states that involve nothing but physical properties.

The argument just outlined is quite a simple one, and it hardly demands philosophical skill to develop it or to appreciate its force! But although many contemporary thinkers would accept its conclusion, there are others, including many philosophers, who would not. To a great many thinkers it has seemed obvious a priori that mental states could not be physical states of the brain. Nobody would identify a number with a piece of rock: it is sufficiently obvious that the two entities fall under different categories. In the same way, it has been thought, a perception or a feeling of sorrow must be a different category of thing from an electro-chemical discharge in the central nervous system.

Here, it seems to me, is a question to which philosophers can expect to make a useful contribution. It is a question about mental concepts. Is our concept of a mental state such that it is an intelligible hypothesis that mental states are physical states of the brain? If the philosopher can show that it is an *intelligible* proposition (that is, a non-self-contradictory proposition) that mental states are physical states of the brain, then the scientific argument just given above can be taken at its face value as a strong reason for accepting the truth of the proposition.

My view is that the identification of mental states with physical states of the brain is a perfectly intelligible one, and that this becomes clear once we achieve a correct view of the analysis of the mental concepts. I admit that my analysis of the mental concepts was itself adopted because it permitted this identification, but such a procedure is commonplace in the construction of theories, and perfectly legitimate. In any case, whatever the motive for proposing the analysis, it is there to speak for itself, to be measured against competitors, and to be assessed as plausible or implausible independently of the identification it makes possible.

The problem of the identification may be put in a Kantian way: "How is it possible that mental states should be physical states of the brain?" The solution will take the form of proposing an *independently plausible* analysis of the concept of a mental state that will permit this identification. In this way, the philosopher makes the way smooth for a first-order doctrine, which, true or false, is a doctrine of the first importance: a purely physicalist view of man.

The analysis proposed may be called the Causal analysis of the mental concepts. According to this view, the concept of a mental state essentially involves, and is exhausted by, the concept of a state that is *apt to be the cause of certain effects or apt to be the effect of certain causes.*

An example of a causal concept is the concept of poison. The concept of poison is the concept of something that when introduced into an organism causes that organism to sicken and/or die.[1] This is but a rough analysis of the concept the structure of which is in fact somewhat more complex and subtle than this. If *A* pours molten lead down *B*'s throat, then he may cause *B* to die as a result, but he can hardly be said to have poisoned him. For a thing to be called a poison, it is necessary that it act in a certain *sort* of way: roughly, in a biological as opposed to a purely physical way. Again, a poison can be introduced into the system of an organism and that organism fail to die or even to sicken. This might occur if an antidote were administered promptly. Yet again, the poison may be present in insufficient quantities to do any damage. Other qualifications could be made.

But the essential point about the concept of poison is that it is the concept of *that, whatever it is, which produces certain effects.* This leaves open the possibility of the *scientific identification* of poisons, of discovering that a certain sort of substance, such as cyanide, is a poison, and discovering further what it is about the substance that makes it poisonous.

Poisons are accounted poisons in virtue of their active powers, but many sorts of thing are accounted the sorts of thing they are by virtue of their *passive* powers. Thus brittle objects are accounted brittle because of the disposition they have to break and shatter when sharply struck. This leaves open the possibility of discovering empirically what sorts of thing are brittle and what it is about them that makes them brittle.

Now *if* the concepts of the various sorts of mental state are concepts of that which is, in various sorts of ways, apt for causing certain effects and apt for being the effect of certain causes, then it would be a quite unpuzzling thing if mental states should turn out to be physical states of the brain.

The concept of a mental state is the concept of something that is, characteristically, the cause of certain effects and the effect of certain causes. What sort of effects and what sort of causes? The effects caused by the mental state will be certain patterns of behavior of the person in that state. For instance, the desire for food is a state of a person or animal that characteristically brings about food-seeking and food-consuming behavior by that person or animal. The causes of mental states will be objects and events in the person's environment. For instance, a sensation of green is the characteristic effect in a person of the action upon his eyes of a nearby green surface.

The general pattern of analysis is at its most obvious and plausible in the case of *purposes.* If a man's purpose is to go to the kitchen to get something to eat, it is completely natural to conceive of this purpose as a cause within him that brings about, or tends to bring about, that particular line of conduct. It is, furthermore, notorious that we are unable to characterize purposes *except* in terms of that which they tend to bring about. How can we distinguish the purpose to go to the kitchen to get something to eat from another purpose to go to the bedroom to lie down? Only by the different outcomes that the two purposes tend to bring about. This fact was an encouragement to Behaviorism. It is still more plausibly explained by saying that the concept of purpose is a causal concept. The further hypothesis that the two purposes are, in their own nature, different physical patterns in, or physical states of, the central nervous system is then a natural (although, of course, not logically inevitable) supplement to the causal analysis.

Simple models have great value in trying to grasp complex conceptions, but they are ladders that may need to be kicked away after we have mounted up by their means. It is vital to realize that the mental concepts have a far more complex logical structure than simple causal notions such as the concept of poison. The fact should occasion no surprise. In the case of poisons, the effect of which they are the cause is a gross and obvious phenomenon and the level of causal explanation involved in simply calling a substance "a poison" is crude and simple. But in the case of mental states, their effects are all those complexities of behavior that mark off men and higher animals from the rest of the objects in the world. Furthermore, differences in such behavior are elaborately correlated with differences in the mental causes operating. So it is only to be expected that the causal patterns invoked by the mental concepts should be extremely complex and sophisticated.

In the case of the notion of a purpose, for instance, it is plausible to assert that it is the notion of a cause within which drives, or tends to drive, the man or animal through a series of actions to a certain end-state. But this is not the whole story. A purpose is only a purpose if it works to bring about behavioral effects *in a certain sort of way.* We may sum up this sort of way by saying that purposes are *information-sensitive* causes. By this is meant that purposes direct behavior by utilizing *perceptions* and *beliefs,* perceptions and beliefs about the agent's current situation and the way it develops, and beliefs about the way the world works. For instance, it is part of what it is to be a purpose to achieve X that this cause will cease to operate, will be "switched off," if the agent perceives or otherwise comes to believe that X has been achieved.

At this point, we observe that an account is being given of that special species of cause that is a purpose in terms of *further* mental items: perceptions and beliefs. This means that if we are to give a purely causal analysis even of the concept of a purpose we also will have to give a purely causal analysis of perceptions and beliefs. We may think of man's behavior as brought about by the joint operation of two sets of causes: first, his purposes and, second, his perceptions of and/or beliefs about the world. But since perceptions and beliefs are quite different sorts of thing from purposes, a Causal analysis must assign quite different causal *roles* to these different things in the bringing about of behavior.

I believe that this can be done by giving an account of perceptions and beliefs as *mappings* of the world. They are structures within us that model the world beyond the structure. This model is created in us by the world. Purposes may then be thought of as driving causes that utilize such mappings.

This is a mere thumb-nail, which requires much further development as well as qualification. One point that becomes clear when that development is given is that just as the concept of purpose cannot be elucidated without appealing to the concepts of perception and belief, so the latter cannot be elucidated without appealing to the concept of purpose. (This comes out, for instance, when we raise Hume's problem: what marks off beliefs from the mere entertaining of the same proposition? It seems that we can only mark off beliefs as those mappings in the light of which we are prepared to *act,* that is, which are potential servants of our purposes.) The logical dependence of purpose on perception and belief, and of perception and belief upon purpose, is not circularity in definition. What it shows is that the corresponding concepts *must be introduced together or not at all.* In itself, there is nothing very surprising in this. Correlative or mutually implied concepts are common enough: for instance, the concepts of husband and wife or the concepts of soldier and army. No husbands without wives or wives without husbands. No soldiers without an army, no army without soldiers. But if the concepts of purpose, perception and belief are (i) correlative concepts and (ii) different species of purely causal concepts, then it is clear that they are far more complex in structure than a simple causal concept like poison. What falls under the mental concepts will be a complex and interlocking set of causal factors, which together are responsible for the "minded" behavior of men and the higher animals.

The working out of the Causal theory of the mental concepts thus turns out to be an extremely complex business. Indeed when it is merely baldly stated, the Causal theory is, to use the phrase of Imre Lakatos, a *research program* in conceptual analysis rather than a developed theory. I have tried to show that it is a hopeful program by attempting, at least in outline, a Causal analysis of all the main concepts in *A Materialist Theory of Mind* (1968); and I have supplemented the rather thin account given there of the concepts of belief, knowledge and inferring in *Belief, Truth and Knowledge* (1973).

Two examples of mental concepts where an especially complex and sophisticated type of Causal analysis is required are the notions of introspective awareness (one sense of the word "consciousness") and the having of mental imagery. Introspective awareness is analyzable as a mental state that is a "perception" of mental states. It is a mapping of the causal factors themselves. The having of mental imagery is a sort of mental state that cannot be elucidated in *directly* causal terms, but only by resemblance to the corresponding perceptions, which *are* explicated in terms of their causal role.

Two advantages of the Causal theory may now be mentioned. First, it has often been remarked by philosophers and others that the realm of mind is a shadowy one, and that the nature of mental states is singularly elusive and hard to grasp. This has given aid and comfort to Dualist or Cartesian theories of mind, according to which minds are quite different sorts of thing from material objects. But if the Causal analysis is correct, the facts admit of another explanation. What Dualist philosophers have grasped in a confused way is that our direct acquaintance with mind, which occurs in introspective awareness, is an acquaintance with something that we are aware of only as something that is causally linked, directly or indirectly, with behavior. In the case of our purposes and desires, for instance, we are often (though not invariably) introspectively aware of them. What we are aware of is the presence of factors within us that drive in a certain direction. We are not aware of the intrinsic nature of the factors. This emptiness or gap in our awareness is then interpreted by Dualists as immateriality. In fact, however, if the Causal analysis is correct, there is no warrant for this interpretation and, if the Physicalist identification of the nature of the causes is correct, the interpretation is actually false.

Second, the Causal analysis yields a still more spectacular verification. It shows promise of explaining a philosophically notorious feature of all or almost all mental states: their *intentionality*. This was the feature of mental states to which Brentano in particular drew attention, the fact that they may point towards certain objects or states of affairs, but that these objects and states of affairs need not exist. When a man strives, his striving has an objective, but that objective may never be achieved. When he

believes, there is something he believes, but what he believes may not be the case. This capacity of mental states to "point" to what does not exist can seem very special. Brentano held that intentionality set the mind completely apart from matter.

Suppose, however, that we consider a concept like the concept of poison. Does it not provide us with a miniature and unsophisticated model for the intentionality of mental states? Poisons are substances apt to make organisms sicken and die when the poison is administered. So it may be said that this is what poisons "point" to. Nevertheless, poisons may fail of their effect. A poison does not fail to be a poison because an antidote neutralizes the customary effect of the poison.

May not the intentionality of mental states, therefore, be in principle a no more mysterious affair, although indefinitely more complex, than the death that lurks in the poison? As an intermediate case between poisons and mental states, consider the mechanisms involved in a homing rocket. Given a certain setting of its mechanism, the rocket may "point" towards a certain target in a way that is a simulacrum of the way in which purposes point towards their objectives. The mechanism will only bring the rocket to the target in "standard" circumstances: many factors can be conceived that would "defeat" the mechanism. For the mechanism to operate successfully, some device will be required by which the developing situation is "mapped" in the mechanism (i.e. what course the rocket is currently on, etc.). This mapping is an elementary analogue of perception, and so the course that is "mapped" in the mechanism may be thought of as a simulacrum of the perceptual intentional object. Through one circumstance or another (e.g. malfunction of the gyroscope) this mapping may be "incorrect."

It is no objection to this analogy that homing rockets are built by men with purposes, who deliberately stamp a crude model of their own purposes into the rocket. Homing rockets might have been natural products, and non-minded objects that operate in a similar but far more complex way are found in nature. The living cell is a case in point.

So the Causal analyses of the mental concepts show promise of explaining both the transparency and the intentionality of mental states. One problem quite frequently raised in connection with these analyses, however, is in what sense they can be called "analyses." The welter of complications in which the so-called analyses are involved make it sufficiently obvious that they do not consist of *synonymous translations* of statements in which mental terms figure. But, it has been objected, if synonymous translations of mental statements are unavailable, what precisely can be meant by speaking of "analyses of concepts"?

I am far from clear what should be said in reply to this objection. Clearly, however, it does depend upon taking all conceptual analyses as claims about the synonymy of sentences, and that seems to be too simple a view. Going back to the case of poison: it is surely not an empirical fact, to be learnt by experience, that poisons kill. It is at the center of our notion of what poisons are that they have the power to bring about this effect. If they did not do that, they would not be properly called "poisons." But although this seems obvious enough, it is extremely difficult to give exact translations of sentences containing the word "poison" into other sentences that do not contain the word or any synonym. Even in this simple case, it is not at all clear that the task can actually be accomplished.

For this reason, I think that sentence translation (with synonymy) is too strict a demand to make upon a purported conceptual analysis. What more relaxed demand can we make and still have a conceptual analysis? I do not know. One thing that we clearly need further light upon here is the concept of a concept, and how concepts are tied to language. I incline to the view that the connection between concepts and language is much less close than many philosophers have assumed. Concepts are linked primarily with belief and thought, and belief and thought, I think, have a great degree of logical independence of language, however close the empirical connection may be in many cases. If this is so, then an analysis of concepts, although of course conducted *in* words, may not be an investigation *into* words. (A compromise proposal: analysis of concepts might be an investigation into some sort of "deep structure"—to use the currently hallowed phrase—which underlies the use of certain words and sentences.) I wish I were able to take the topic further.

The Problem of the Secondary Qualities

No discussion of the Causal theory of the mental concepts is complete that does not say some-

thing about the *secondary qualities*. If we consider such mental states as purposes and intentions, their "transparency" is a rather conspicuous feature. It is notorious that introspection cannot differentiate such states except in terms of their different objects. It is not so immediately obvious, however, that *perception* has this transparent character. Perception involves the experience of color and of visual extension; touch the experience of the whole obscure range of tactual properties, including tactual extension; hearing, taste and smell the experience of sounds, tastes and smells. These phenomenal qualities, it may be argued, endow different perceptions with different qualities. The lack of transparency is even more obvious in the case of bodily sensations. Pains, itches, tickles and tingles are mental states, even if mental states of no very high-grade sort, and they each seem to involve their own peculiar qualities. Again, associated with different emotions it is quite plausible to claim to discern special emotion qualities. If perception, bodily sensation and emotions involve qualities, then this seems to falsify a purely Causal analysis of these mental states. They are not mere "that whiches" known only by their causal role.

However, it is not at all clear how strong is the line of argument sketched in the previous paragraph. We distinguish between the intention and what is intended, and in just the same way we must distinguish between the perception and what is perceived. The intention is a mental state and so is the perception, but what is intended is not in general something mental and nor is what is perceived. What is intended may not come to pass, it is a merely intentional object, and the same may be said of what is perceived. Now in the case of the phenomenal qualities, it seems plausible to say that they are qualities not of the perception but rather of what is perceived. "Visual extension" is the shape, size, etc. that some object of visual perception is perceived to have (an object that need not exist). Color seems to be a quality of that object. And similarly for the other phenomenal qualities. Even in the case of the bodily sensations, the qualities associated with the sensations do not *appear* to be qualities of mental states but instead to be qualities of portions of our bodies: more or less fleeting qualities that qualify the place where the sensation is located. Only in the case of the emotions does it seem natural to place the quality on the mental rather than the object side: but then it is not so clear whether there really *are* peculiar qualities associated with the emotions. The different patterns of bodily sensations associated with the different emotions may be sufficient to do phenomenological justice to the emotions.

For these reasons, it is not certain whether the phenomenal qualities pose any threat to the Causal analysis of the mental concepts. But what a subset of these qualities quite certainly does pose a threat to, is the doctrine that the Causal analysis of the mental concepts is a step towards: Materialism or Physicalism.

The qualities of colour, sound, heat and cold, taste and smell together with the qualities that appear to be involved in bodily sensations and those that may be involved in the case of the emotions, are an embarrassment to the modern Materialist. He seeks to give an account of the world and of man purely in terms of *physical* properties, that is to say in terms of the properties that the physicist appeals to in his explanations of phenomena. The Materialist is not committed to the *current* set of properties to which the physicist appeals, but he is committed to whatever set of properties the physicist in the end will appeal to. It is clear that such properties as color, sound, taste and smell—the so-called "secondary qualities"—will never be properties to which the physicist will appeal.

It is, however, a plausible thesis that associated with different secondary qualities are properties that are respectable from a physicist's point of view. Physical surfaces *appear* to have color. They not merely appear to, but undoubtedly do, emit light-waves, and the different mixtures of lengths of wave emitted are linked with differences in color. In the same way, different sorts of sound are linked with different sorts of sound-wave and differences in heat with differences in the mean kinetic energy of the molecules composing the hot things. The Materialist's problem therefore would be very simply solved if the secondary qualities could be identified with these physically respectable properties. (The qualities associated with bodily sensations would be identified with different sorts of stimulation of bodily receptors. If there are unique qualities associated with the emotions, they would presumably be identified with some of the physical states of the brain linked with particular emotions.)

But now the Materialist philosopher faces a problem. Previously he asked: "How is it possible that mental states could be physical states of the brain?" This question was answered by the Causal theory of the mental concepts. Now he must ask: "How is it possible that secondary qualities could be purely physical properties of the objects they are qualities of?" A Causal analysis does not seem to be of any avail. To try to give an analysis of, say, the quality of being red in Causal terms would lead us to produce such analyses as "those properties of a physical surface, whatever they are, that characteristically produce *red sensations* in us." But this analysis simply shifts the problem unhelpfully from property of surface to property of sensation. Either the red sensations involve nothing but physically respectable properties or they involve something more. If they involve something more, Materialism fails. But if they are simply physical states of the brain, having nothing but physical properties, then the Materialist faces the problem: "How is it possible that red sensations should be physical states of the brain?" This question is no easier to answer than the original question about the redness of physical surfaces. (To give a Causal analysis of red sensations as the characteristic effects of the action of red surfaces is, of course, to move round in a circle.)

The great problem presented by the secondary qualities, such as redness, is that they are *unanalyzable*. They have certain relations of resemblance and so on to each other, so they cannot be said to be completely simple. But they are simple in the sense that they resist any analysis. You cannot give any complete account of the concept of redness without involving the notion of redness itself. This has seemed to be, and still seems to many philosophers to be, an absolute bar to identifying redness with, say, certain patterns of emission of light-waves.

But I am not so sure. I think it can be maintained that although the secondary qualities *appear* to be simple, they are not in fact simple. Perhaps their simplicity is *epistemological* only, not ontological, a matter of our awareness of them rather than the way they are. The best model I can give for the situation is the sort of phenomena made familiar to us by the Gestalt psychologists. It is possible to grasp that certain things or situations have a certain special property, but be unable to analyze that property. For instance, it may be possible to perceive that certain people are all alike in some way without being able to make it clear to oneself what the likeness is. We are aware that all these people have a certain likeness to each other, but are unable to define or specify that likeness. Later psychological research may achieve a specification of the likeness, a specification that may come as a complete surprise to us. Perhaps, therefore, the secondary qualities are in fact complex, and perhaps they are complex characteristics of a sort demanded by Materialism, but we are unable to grasp their complexity in perception.

There are two divergences between the model just suggested and the case of the secondary qualities. First, in the case of grasping the indefinable likeness of people, we are under no temptation to think that the likeness is a likeness in some simple quality. The likeness is indefinable, but we are vaguely aware that it is complex. Second, once research has determined the concrete nature of the likeness, our attention can be drawn to, and we can observe individually, the features that determine the likeness.

But although the model suggested and the case of the secondary qualities undoubtedly exhibit these differences, I do not think that they show that the secondary qualities cannot be identified with respectable physical characteristics of objects. Why should not a complex property appear to be simple? There would seem to be no contradiction in adding such a condition to the model. It has the consequence that percep-

tion of the secondary qualities involves an element of illusion, but the consequence involves no contradiction. It is true also that in the case of the secondary qualities the illusion cannot be overcome within perception: it is impossible to see a colored surface as a surface emitting certain light-waves. (Though one sometimes seems to *hear* a sound as a vibration of the air.) But while this means that the identification of color and light-waves is a purely *theoretical* one, it still seems to be a possible one. And if the identification is a possible one, we have general scientific reasons to think it a *plausible* one.

The doctrine of mental states and of the secondary qualities briefly presented in this paper seems to me to show promise of meeting many of the traditional philosophical objections to a Materialist or Physicalist account of the world. As I have emphasized, the philosopher is not professionally competent to argue the positive case for Materialism. There he must rely upon the evidence presented by the scientist, particularly the physicist. But at least he may neutralize the objections to Materialism advanced by his fellow philosophers.

NOTE

1. "Any substance which, when introduced into or absorbed by a living organism, destroys life or injures health." (*Shorter Oxford Dictionary,* 3rd edn., rev., 1978.)

13 | Psychophysical and Theoretical Identifications

David Lewis

Psychophysical identity theorists often say that the identifications they anticipate between mental and neural states are essentially like various uncontroversial theoretical identifications: the identification of water with H_2O, of light with electromagnetic radiation, and so on. Such theoretical identifications are usually described as pieces of voluntary theorizing, as follows. Theoretical advances make it possible to simplify total science by positing bridge laws identifying some of the entities discussed in one theory with entities discussed in another theory. In the name of parsimony, we posit those bridge laws forthwith. Identifications are made, not found.

In 'An Argument for the Identity Theory,'[1] I claimed that this was a bad picture of psychophysical identification, since a suitable physiological theory could *imply* psychophysical identities—not merely make it reasonable to posit them for the sake of parsimony. The implication was as follows:

Mental state M = the occupant of causal role R (by definition of M).
Neural state N = the occupant of causal role R (by the physiological theory).
∴ Mental state M = neural state N (by transitivity of =).

If the meanings of the names of mental states were really such as to provide the first premise, and if the advance of physiology were such as to provide the second premise, then the conclusion would follow. Physiology and the meanings of words would leave us no choice but to make the psychophysical identification.

In this sequel, I shall uphold the view that psychophysical identifications thus described would be like theoretical identifications, though they would not fit the usual account thereof. For the usual account, I claim, is wrong; theoretical identifications *in general* are implied by the theories that make them possible—not posited independently. This follows from a general hypothesis about the meanings of theoretical terms: that they are definable functionally, by reference to causal roles.[2] Applied to common-

sense psychology—folk science rather than professional science, but a theory nonetheless—we get the hypothesis of my previous paper[3] that a mental state M (say, an experience) is definable as the occupant of a certain causal role R—that is, as the state, of whatever sort, that is causally connected in specified ways to sensory stimuli, motor responses, and other mental states.

First, I consider an example of theoretical identification chosen to be remote from past philosophizing; then I give my general account of the meanings of theoretical terms and the nature of theoretical identifications; finally I return to the case of psychophysical identity.

I

We are assembled in the drawing room of the country house; the detective reconstructs the crime. That is, he proposes a *theory* designed to be the best explanation of phenomena we have observed: the death of Mr. Body, the blood on the wallpaper, the silence of the dog in the night, the clock seventeen minutes fast, and so on. He launches into his story:

> X, Y and Z conspired to murder Mr. Body. Seventeen years ago, in the gold fields of Uganda, X was Body's partner . . . Last week, Y and Z conferred in a bar in Reading . . . Tuesday night at 11:17, Y went to the attic and set a time bomb . . . Seventeen minutes later, X met Z in the billiard room and gave him the lead pipe . . . Just when the bomb went off in the attic, X fired three shots into the study through the French windows . . .

And so it goes: a long story. Let us pretend that it is a single long conjunctive sentence.

The story contains the three names 'X', 'Y' and 'Z'. The detective uses these new terms without explanation, as though we knew what they meant. But we do not. We never used them before, at least not in the senses they bear in the present context. All we know about their meanings is what we gradually gather from the story itself. Call these *theoretical terms* (*T-terms* for

From *Australasian Journal of Philosophy* 50:249–58, 1972. Reprinted with permission of the author's estate and the publisher.

short) because they are introduced by a theory. Call the rest of the terms in the story *O-terms.* These are all the *other* terms except the T-terms; they are all the *old, original* terms we understood before the theory was proposed. We could call them our 'pre-theoretical' terms. But 'O' does *not* stand for 'observational.' Not all the O-terms are observational terms, whatever those may be. They are just any old terms. If part of the story was mathematical—if it included a calculation of the trajectory that took the second bullet to the chandelier without breaking the vase—then some of the O-terms will be mathematical. If the story says that something happened because of something else, then the O-terms will include the intensional connective 'because,' or the operator 'it is a law that,' or something of the sort.

Nor do the theoretical terms name some sort of peculiar theoretical, unobservable, semi-fictitious entities. The story makes plain that they name *people.* Not theoretical people, different somehow from ordinary, observational people—just people!

On my account, the detective plunged right into his story, using 'X', 'Y' and 'Z' as if they were names with understood denotation. It would have made little difference if he had started, instead, with initial existential quantifiers: 'There exist X, Y and Z such that . . .' and then told the story. In that case, the terms 'X', 'Y' and 'Z' would have been bound variables rather than T-terms. But the story would have had the same explanatory power. The second version of the story, with the T-terms turned into variables bound by existential quantifiers, is the Ramsey sentence of the first. Bear in mind, as evidence for what is to come, how little difference the initial quantifiers seem to make to the detective's assertion.

Suppose that after we have heard the detective's story, we learn that it is true of a certain three people: Plum, Peacock and Mustard. If we put the name 'Plum' in place of 'X', 'Peacock' in place of 'Y', and 'Mustard' in place of 'Z' throughout, we get a true story about the doings of those three people. We will say that Plum, Peacock and Mustard together *realize* (or are a *realization* of) the detective's theory.

We may also find out that the story is not true of any other triple.[4] Put in any three names that do not name Plum, Peacock and Mustard (in that order) and the story we get is false. We will say that Plum, Peacock and Mustard *uniquely realize* (are the *unique realization* of) the theory.

We might learn both of these facts. (The detective might have known them all along, but held them back to spring his trap; or he, like us, might learn them only after his story had been told.) And if we did, we would surely conclude that X, Y and Z in the story were Plum, Peacock and Mustard. I maintain that we would be compelled so to conclude, given the senses borne by the terms 'X', 'Y' and 'Z' in virtue of the way the detective introduced them in his theorizing, and given our information about Plum, Peacock and Mustard.

In telling his story, the detective set forth three roles and said that they were occupied by X, Y and Z. He must have specified the meanings of the three T-terms 'X', 'Y' and 'Z' thereby; for they had meanings afterwards, they had none before, and nothing else was done to give them meanings. They were introduced by an implicit functional definition, being reserved to name the occupants of the three roles. When we find out who are the occupants of the three roles, we find out who are X, Y and Z. Here is our theoretical identification.

In saying that the roles were occupied by X, Y and Z, the detective implied that they were occupied. That is, his theory implied its Ramsey sentence. That seems right; if we learnt that no triple realized the story, or even came close, we would have to conclude that the story was false. We would also have to deny that the names 'X', 'Y' and 'Z' named anything; for they were introduced as names for the occupants of roles that turned out to be unoccupied.

I also claim that the detective implied that the roles were uniquely occupied, when he reserved names for their occupants and proceeded as if those names had been given definite referents. Suppose we learnt that two different triples realized the theory: Plum, Peacock, Mustard; and Green, White, Scarlet. (Or the two different triples might overlap; Plum, Peacock, Mustard; and Green, Peacock, Scarlet.) I think we would be most inclined to say that the story was false, and that the names 'X', 'Y' and 'Z' did not name anything. They were introduced as names for the occupants of certain roles; but there is no such thing as *the* occupant of a doubly occupied role, so there is nothing suitable for them to name.

If, as I claim, the T-terms are definable as naming the first, second, and third components of the unique triple that realizes the story, then the T-terms can be treated like definite descriptions. If the story is uniquely realized, they

name what they ought to name; if the story is
unrealized or multiply realized, they are like improper descriptions. If too many triples realize
the story, 'X' is like 'the moon of Mars'; if too
few triples—none—realize the story, 'X' is like
'the moon of Venus.' Improper descriptions are
not meaningless. Hilary Putnam has objected
that on this sort of account of theoretical terms,
the theoretical terms of a falsified theory come
out meaningless.[5] But they do not, if theoretical
terms of unrealized theories are like improper
descriptions. 'The moon of Mars' and 'The
moon of Venus' do not (in any normal way)
name anything here in our actual world; but they
are not meaningless, because we know very
well what they name in certain alternative possible worlds. Similarly, we know what 'X' names
in any world where the detective's theory is
true, whether or not our actual world is such a
world.

A complication: what if the theorizing detective has made one little mistake? He should
have said that Y went to the attic at 11:37, not
11:17. The story as told is unrealized, true of no
one. But another story is realized, indeed
uniquely realized: the story we get by deleting
or correcting the little mistake. We can say that
the story as told is *nearly realized,* has a unique
near-realization. (The notion of a near-realization is hard to analyze, but easy to understand.)
In this case the T-terms ought to name the components of the near-realization. More generally:
they should name the components of the nearest
realization of the theory, provided there is a
unique nearest realization and it is near enough.
Only if the story comes nowhere near to being
realized, or if there are two equally near nearest
realizations, should we resort to treating the
T-terms like improper descriptions. But let us
set aside this complication for the sake of simplicity, though we know well that scientific theories are often nearly realized but rarely realized, and that theoretical reduction is usually
blended with revision of the reduced theory.

This completes our example. It may seem
atypical; the T-terms are names, not predicates
or functors. But that is of no importance. It is a
popular exercise to recast a language so that its
nonlogical vocabulary consists entirely of predicates; but it is just as easy to recast a language
so that its nonlogical vocabulary consists entirely of names (provided that the logical vocabulary includes a copula). These names, of course,
may purport to name individuals, sets, attributes, species, states, functions, relations, magni-

tudes, phenomena or what have you; but they
are still names. Assume this done, so that we
may replace all T-terms by variables of the same
sort.

II

We now proceed to a general account of the
functional definability of T-terms and the nature
of theoretical identification. Suppose we have a
new theory, T, introducing the new terms $t_1 \ldots
t_n$. These are our T-terms. (Let them be names.)
Every other term in our vocabulary, therefore, is
an O-term. The theory T is presented in a sentence called the *postulate* of T. Assume this is a
single sentence, perhaps a long conjunction. It
says of the entities—states, magnitudes,
species, or whatever—named by the T-terms
that they occupy certain *causal roles;* that they
stand in specified causal (and other) relations to
entities named by O-terms, and to one another.
We write the postulate thus:[6]

$$T[\mathbf{t}].$$

Replacing the T-terms uniformly by free variables $x_1 \ldots x_n$, we get a formula in which only
O-terms appear:

$$T[\mathbf{x}].$$

Any n-tuple of entities which satisfies this formula is a realization of the theory T. Prefixing
existential quantifiers, we get the *Ramsey sentence* of T, which says that T has at least one realization:

$$\exists \mathbf{x}\, T[\mathbf{x}].$$

We can also write a *modified Ramsey sentence*
which says that T has a unique realization:[7]

$$\exists_1 \mathbf{x}\, T[\mathbf{x}].$$

The Ramsey sentence has exactly the same O-
content as the postulate of T; any sentence free
of T-terms follows logically from one if and
only if it follows from the other.[8] The modified
Ramsey sentence has slightly more O-content. I
claim that this surplus O-content does belong to
the theory T—there are more theorems of T than
follow logically from the postulate alone. For in
presenting the postulate as if the T-terms has
been well-defined thereby, the theorist has im-
plictly asserted that T is uniquely realized.

We can write the *Carnap sentence* of T: the
conditional of the Ramsey sentence and the postulate, which says that if T is realized, then the

T-terms name the components of some realization of T:

$$\exists \mathbf{x}\, T[\mathbf{x}] \supset T[\mathbf{t}].$$

Carnap has suggested this sentence as a meaning postulate for T;[9] but if we want T-terms of unrealized or multiply realized theories to have the status of improper descriptions, our meaning postulates should instead be a *modified Carnap sentence*, this conditional with our modified Ramsey sentence as antecedent:

$$\exists_1 \mathbf{x}\, T[\mathbf{x}] \supset T[\mathbf{t}],$$

together with another conditional to cover the remaining cases:[10]

$$\sim \exists_1 \mathbf{x}\, T[\mathbf{x}] \supset \mathbf{t} = *.$$

This pair of meaning postulates is logically equivalent[11] to a sentence which explicitly defines the T-terms by means of O-terms:

$$\mathbf{t} = \iota \mathbf{x}\, T[\mathbf{x}].$$

This is what I have called functional definition. The T-terms have been defined as the occupants of the causal roles specified by the theory T; as *the* entities, whatever those may be, that bear certain causal relations to one another and to the referents of the O-terms.

If I am right, T-terms are eliminable—we can always replace them by their definientia. Of course, this is not to say that theories are fictions, or that theories are uninterpreted formal abacuses, or that theoretical entities are unreal. Quite the opposite! Because we understand the O-terms, and we can define the T-terms from them, theories are fully meaningful; we have reason to think a good theory true; and if a theory is true, then whatever exists according to the theory really *does* exist.

I said that there are more theorems of T than follow logically from the postulate alone. More precisely: the theorems of T are just those sentences which follow from the postulate together with the corresponding functional definition of the T-terms. For that definition, I claim, is given implicitly when the postulate is presented as bestowing meanings on the T-terms introduced in it.

It may happen, after the introduction of the T-terms, that we come to believe of a certain n-tuple of entities, specified otherwise than as the entities that realize T, that they do realize T. That is, we may come to accept a sentence

$$T[\mathbf{r}]$$

where $r_1 \ldots r_n$ are either O-terms or theoretical terms of some other theory, introduced into our language independently of $t_1 \ldots t_n$. This sentence, which we may call a *weak reduction premise* for T, is free of T-terms. Our acceptance of it might have nothing to do with our previous acceptance of T. We might accept it as part of some new theory; or we might believe it as part of our miscellaneous, unsystematized general knowledge. Yet having accepted it, for whatever reason, we are logically compelled to make theoretical identifications. The reduction premise, together with the functional definition of the T-terms and the postulate of T, logically implies the identity:

$$\mathbf{t} = \mathbf{r}.$$

In other words, the postulate and the weak reduction premise definitionally imply the identities $t_i = r_i$.

Or we might somehow come to believe of a certain n-tuple of entities that they *uniquely* realize T; that is, to accept a sentence

$$\forall \mathbf{x}(T[\mathbf{x}] \equiv \mathbf{x} = \mathbf{r})$$

where $r_1 \ldots r_n$ are as above. We may call this a *strong reduction premise* for T, since it definitionally implies the theoretical identifications by itself, without the aid of the postulate of T. The strong reduction premise logically implies the identity

$$\mathbf{r} = \iota \mathbf{x}\, T[\mathbf{x}]$$

which, together with the functional definition of the T-terms, implies the identities $t_i = r_i$ by transitivity of identity.

These theoretical identifications are not voluntary posits, made in the name of parsimony; they are deductive inferences. According to their definitions, the T-terms name the occupants of the causal roles specified by the theory T. According to the weak reduction premise and T, or the strong reduction premise by itself, the occupants of those causal roles turn out to be the referents of $r_1 \ldots r_n$. Therefore, those are the entities named by the T-terms. That is how we inferred that X, Y and Z were Plum, Peacock and Mustard; and that, I suggest, is how we make theoretical identifications in general.

III

And that is how, someday, we will infer that[12] the mental states M_1, M_2, . . . are the neural states N_1, N_2, ...

Think of common-sense psychology as a term-introducing scientific theory, though one invented long before there was any such institution as professional science. Collect all the platitudes you can think of regarding the causal relations of mental states, sensory stimuli, and motor responses. Perhaps we can think of them as having the form:

> When someone is in so-and-so combination of mental states and receives sensory stimuli of so-and-so kind, he tends with so-and-so probability to be caused thereby to go into so-and-so mental states and produce so-and-so motor responses.

Add also all the platitudes to the effect that one mental state falls under another—'toothache is a kind of pain,' and the like. Perhaps there are platitudes of other forms as well. Include only platitudes which are common knowledge among us—everyone knows them, everyone knows that everyone else knows them, and so on. For the meanings of our words are common knowledge, and I am going to claim that names of mental states derive their meaning from these platitudes.

Form the conjunction of these platitudes; or better, form a cluster of them—a disjunction of all conjunctions of *most* of them. (That way it will not matter if a few are wrong.) This is the postulate of our term-introducing theory. The names of mental states are the T-terms.[13] The O-terms used to introduce them must be sufficient for speaking of stimuli and responses, and for speaking of causal relations among these and states of unspecified nature.

From the postulate, form the definition of the T-terms; it defines the mental states by reference to their causal relations to stimuli, responses, and each other. When we learn what sort of states occupy those causal roles definitive of the mental states, we will learn what states the mental states are—exactly as we found out who X was when we found out that Plum was the man who occupied a certain role, and exactly as we found out what light was when we found that electromagnetic radiation was the phenomenon that occupied a certain role.

Imagine our ancestors first speaking only of external things, stimuli, and responses—and perhaps producing what we, but not they, may call *Äusserungen* of mental states—until some genius invented the theory of mental states, with its newly introduced T-terms, to explain the regularities among stimuli and responses. But that did not happen. Our common-sense psychology

was never a newly invented term-introducing scientific theory—not even of prehistoric folk-science. The story that mental terms were introduced as theoretical terms is a myth.

It is, in fact, Sellars' myth of our Rylean ancestors.[14] And though it is a myth, it may be a good myth or a bad one. It is a good myth if our names of mental states do in fact mean just what they would mean if the myth were true.[15] I adopt the working hypothesis that it is a good myth. This hypothesis can be tested, in principle, in whatever way any hypothesis about the conventional meanings of our words can be tested. I have not tested it; but I offer one item of evidence. Many philosophers have found Rylean behaviorism at least plausible; more have found watered down, 'criteriological' behaviorism plausible. There is a strong odor of analyticity about the platitudes of common-sense psychology. The myth explains the odor of analyticity and the plausibility of behaviorism. If the names of mental states are like theoretical terms, they name nothing unless the theory (the cluster of platitudes) is more or less true. Hence it is analytic that *either* pain, etc., do not exist *or* most of our platitudes about them are true. If this *seems* analytic to you, you should accept the myth, and be prepared for psychophysical identifications.

The hypothesis that names of mental states are like functionally defined theoretical terms solves a familiar problem about mental explanations. How can my behavior be explained by an explanans consisting of nothing but particular-fact premises about my present state of mind? Where are the covering laws? The solution is that the requisite covering laws are implied by the particular-fact premises. Ascriptions to me of various particular beliefs and desires, say, cannot be true if there are no such states as belief and desire; cannot be true, that is, unless the causal roles definitive of belief and desire are occupied. But these roles can only be occupied by states causally related in the proper lawful way to behavior.

Formally, suppose we have a mental explanation of behavior as follows.

$$\frac{C_1[t], C_2[t], \ldots}{E}$$

Here E describes the behavior to be explained; $C_1[t], C_2[t], \ldots$ are particular-fact premises describing the agent's state of mind at the time. Various of the mental terms $t_1 \ldots t_n$ appear in these premises, in such a way that the premises would be false if the terms named nothing. Now let $L_1[\mathbf{t}]$, $L_2[\mathbf{t}]$, . . . be the platitudinous purported causal laws whereby—according to the myth—the mental terms were introduced. Ignoring clustering for simplicity, we may take the term-introducing postulate to be the conjunction of these. Then our explanation may be rewritten:

$$\frac{\exists_1\mathbf{x}\left(\begin{array}{l} L_1[\mathbf{x}] \,\&\, L_2[\mathbf{x}] \,\&\, \ldots \,\& \\ C_1[\mathbf{x}] \,\&\, C_2[\mathbf{x}] \,\&\, \ldots \end{array}\right)}{E}$$

The new explanans is a definitional consequence of the original one. In the expanded version, however, laws appear explicitly alongside the particular-fact premises. We have, so to speak, an existential generalization of an ordinary covering-law explanation.[16]

The causal definability of mental terms has been thought to contradict the necessary infallibility of introspection.[17] Pain is one state; belief that one is in pain is another. (Confusingly, either of the two may be called 'awareness of pain.') Why cannot I believe that I am in pain without being in pain—that is, without being in whatever state it is that occupies so-and-so causal role? Doubtless I am so built that this normally does not happen; but what makes it impossible?

I do not know whether introspection is (in some or all cases) infallible. But if it is, that is no difficulty for me. Here it is important that, on my version of causal definability, the mental terms stand or fall together. If common-sense psychology fails, all of them are alike denotationless.

Suppose that among the platitudes are some to the effect that introspection is reliable: 'belief that one is in pain never occurs unless pain occurs' or the like. Suppose further that these platitudes enter the term-introducing postulate as conjuncts, not as cluster members; and suppose that they are so important that an n-tuple that fails to satisfy them perfectly is not even a near-realization of common-sense psychology. (I neither endorse nor repudiate these suppositions.) Then the necessary infallibility of introspection is assured. Two states cannot be pain and belief that one is in pain, respectively (in the case of a given individual or species) if the second *ever* occurs without the first. The state that *usually* occupies the role of belief that one is in pain may, of course, occur without the state that *usually* occupies the role of pain; but in that case (under the suppositions above) the former no longer is the state of belief that one is in pain, and the latter no longer is pain. Indeed, the victim no longer is in any mental state whatever, since his states no longer realize (or nearly realize) common-sense psychology. Therefore it is impossible to believe that one is in pain and not be in pain.

NOTES

Previous versions of this paper were presented at a conference on Philosophical Problems of Psychology held at Honolulu in March, 1968; at the annual meeting of the Australasian Association of Philosophy held at Brisbane in August, 1971; and at various university colloquia. This paper is expected to appear also in a volume edited by Chung-ying Cheng.

1. *Journal of Philosophy,* 63 (1966): 17–25.

2. See my 'How to Define Theoretical Terms,' *Journal of Philosophy,* 67 (1970): 427–446.

3. Since advocated also by D. M. Armstrong, in *A Materialist Theory of the Mind* (New York: Humanities Press, 1968). He expresses it thus: 'The concept of a mental state is primarily the concept of a state of the person apt for bringing about a certain sort of behaviour [and secondarily also, in some cases] apt for being brought about by a certain sort of stimulus,' p. 82.

4. The story itself might imply this. If, for instance, the story said 'X saw Y give Z the candlestick while the three of them were alone in the billiard room at 9:17,' then the story could not possibly be true of more than one triple.

5. 'What Theories Are Not,' in Nagel, Suppes and Tars-

ki eds., *Logic, Methodology and Philosophy of Science* (Stanford University Press, 1962): 247.

6. Notation: boldface names and variables denote n-tuples; the corresponding subscripted names and variables denote components of n-tuples. For instance, $\mathbf{t}$ is $<t_1 \ldots t_n>$. This notation is easily dispensable, and hence carries no ontic commitment to n-tuples.

7. That is, $\exists\mathbf{y}\forall\mathbf{x}(\mathrm{T}[\mathbf{x}] \equiv \mathbf{y} = \mathbf{x})$. Note that $\exists_1 x_1 \ldots \exists_1 x_n \mathrm{T}[\mathbf{x}]$ does not imply $\exists_1\mathbf{x}\, \mathrm{T}[\mathbf{x}]$, and does not say that T is uniquely realized.

8. On the assumptions—reasonable for the postulate of a scientific theory—that the T-terms occur purely referentially in the postulate, and in such a way that the postulate is false if any of them are denotationless. We shall make these assumptions henceforth.

9. Most recently in *Philosophical Foundations of Physics* (New York: Basic Books, 1966): 265–274. Carnap, of course, has in mind the case in which the O-terms belong to an observation language.

10. $\mathbf{t} = *$ means that each t_i is denotationless. Let $*$ be some chosen necessarily denotationless name; then $*$ is $<* \ldots *>$ and $\mathbf{t} = *$ is equivalent to the conjunction of all the identities $t_i = *$.

11. Given a theory of descriptions which makes an iden-

tity true whenever both its terms have the status of improper descriptions, false whenever one term has that status and the other does not. This might best be the theory of descriptions in Dana Scott, 'Existence and Description in Formal Logic,' in R. Schoenman, ed., *Bertrand Russell: Philosopher of the Century* (London: Allen & Unwin, 1967).

12. In general, or in the case of a given species, or in the case of a given person. It might turn out that the causal roles definitive of mental states are occupied by different neural (or other) states in different organisms. See my discussion of Hilary Putnam 'Psychological Predicates' in *Journal of Philosophy,* 66 (1969): 23–25.

13. It may be objected that the number of mental states is infinite, or at least enormous; for instance, there are as many states of belief as there are propositions to be believed. But it would be better to say that there is one state of belief, and it is a relational state, relating people to propositions. (Similarly, centigrade temperature is a relational state, relating objects to numbers.) The platitudes involving belief would, of course, contain universally quantified proposition-variables. Likewise for other mental states with intentional objects.

14. Wilfrid Sellars, 'Empiricism and the Philosophy of Mind,' in Feigl and Scriven, eds., *Minnesota Studies in the Philosophy of Science,* I (University of Minnesota Press, 1956): 309–20.

15. Two myths which cannot both be true together can nevertheless both be good together. Part of my myth says that names of color-sensations were T-terms, introduced using names of colors as O-terms. If this is a good myth, we should be able to define 'sensation of red' roughly as 'that state apt for being brought about by the presence of something red (before one's open eyes, in good light, etc.).' A second myth says that names of colors were T-terms introduced using names of color-sensations as O-terms. If this second myth is good, we should be able to define 'red' roughly as 'that property of things apt for bringing about the sensation of red.' The two myths could not both be true, for which came first: names of color-sensations or of colors? But they could both be good. We could have a circle in which colors are correctly defined in terms of sensations and sensations are correctly defined in terms of colors. We could not discover the meanings *both* of names of colors and of names of color-sensations just by looking at the circle of correct definitions, but so what?

16. See 'How to Define Theoretical Terms': 440–441.

17. By Armstrong, in *A Materialist Theory of the Mind,* pp. 100–13. He finds independent grounds for denying the infallibility of introspection.

14 | Troubles with Functionalism
Ned Block

. . . One characterization of functionalism that is probably vague enough to be accepted by most functionalists is: each type of mental state is a state consisting of a disposition to act in certain ways *and to have certain mental states,* given certain sensory inputs and certain mental states. So put, functionalism can be seen as a new incarnation of behaviorism. Behaviorism identifies mental states with dispositions to act in certain ways in certain input situations. But as critics have pointed out (Chisholm, 1957; Putnam, 1963), desire for goal G cannot be identified with, say, the disposition to do A in input circumstances in which A leads to G, since, after all, the agent might not *know* A leads to G and thus might not be disposed to do A. Functionalism replaces behaviorism's "sensory inputs" with "sensory inputs and mental states"; and functionalism replaces behaviorism's "disposition to act" with "disposition to act and have certain mental states." Functionalists want to individuate mental states causally, and since mental states have mental causes and effects as well as sensory causes and behavioral effects, functionalists individuate mental states partly in terms of causal relations to other mental states. One consequence of this difference between functionalism and behaviorism is that there are organisms that according to behaviorism, have mental states but, according to functionalism, do not have mental states.

So, necessary conditions for mentality that are postulated by functionalism are in one respect stronger than those postulated by behav-

Excerpted from C. W. Savage, ed., *Perception and Cognition* (University of Minnesota Press, 1978), pp. 261–325, with permission of the publisher. Copyright © 1978 University of Minnesota Press.

iorism. According to behaviorism, it is necessary and sufficient for desiring that G that a system be characterized by a certain set (perhaps
infinite) of input-output relations; that is, according to behaviorism, a system desires that G
just in case a certain set of conditionals of the
form 'It will emit O given I' are true of it. According to functionalism, however, a system
might have these input-output relations, yet not
desire that G; for according to functionalism,
whether a system desires that G depends on
whether it has internal states which have certain
causal relations to other internal states (and to
inputs and outputs). Since behaviorism makes
no such "internal state" requirement, there are
possible systems of which behaviorism affirms
and functionalism denies that they have mental
states.[1] One way of stating this is that, according
to functionalism, behaviorism is guilty of *liberalism*—ascribing mental properties to things
that do not in fact have them. . . .

By 'physicalism,' I mean the doctrine that
pain, for example, is identical to a physical (or
physiological) state.[2] As many philosophers
have argued (notably Fodor, 1965, and Putnam,
1966; see also Block & Fodor, 1972), if functionalism is true, physicalism is false. The point
is at its clearest with regard to Turing-machine
versions of functionalism. Any given abstract
Turing machine can be realized by a wide variety of physical devices; indeed, it is plausible
that, given any putative correspondence between a Turing-machine state and a configurational physical (or physiological) state, there
will be a possible realization of the Turing machine that will provide a counterexample to that
correspondence. (See Kalke, 1969; Gendron,
1971; Mucciolo, 1974, for unconvincing arguments to the contrary; see also Kim, 1972.)
Therefore, if pain is a functional state, it cannot,
for example, be a brain state, because creatures
without brains can realize the same Turing machine as creatures with brains. . . .

One way of expressing this point is that, according to functionalism, physicalism is a *chau-
vinist* theory: it withholds mental properties
from systems that in fact have them. In saying
mental states are brain states, for example,
physicalists unfairly exclude those poor brain-
less creatures who nonetheless have minds. . . .

This chapter has three parts. The first [ex-
cerpted here—ed.] argues that functionalism is
guilty of liberalism, the second that one way of
modifying functionalism to avoid liberalism is
to tie it more closely to empirical psychology,

and the third that no version of functionalism
can avoid both liberalism and chauvinism.

1.1. More about What Functionalism Is

. . . One can also categorize functionalists in
terms of whether they regard functional identities as part of a priori psychology or empirical
psychology. (Since this distinction crosscuts the
machine/nonmachine distinction, I shall be able
to illustrate nonmachine versions of functionalism in what follows.) The a priori functionalists
(e.g., Smart, Armstrong, Lewis, Shoemaker) are
the heirs of the logical behaviorists. They tend
to regard functional analyses as analyses of the
meanings of mental terms, whereas the empirical functionalists (e.g., Fodor, Putnam, Harman) regard functional analyses as substantive
scientific hypotheses. In what follows, I shall
refer to the former view as 'Functionalism' and
the latter as 'Psychofunctionalism.' (I shall use
'functionalism' with a lowercase 'f' as neutral
between Functionalism and Psychofunctionalism. When distinguishing between Functionalism and Psychofunctionalism, I shall always
use capitals.)

Functionalism and Psychofunctionalism and
the difference between them can be made clearer in terms of the notion of the Ramsey sentence
of a psychological theory. Mental-state terms
that appear in a psychological theory can be defined in various ways by means of the Ramsey
sentence of the theory. All functional-state identity theories (and functional-property identity
theories) can be understood as defining a set of
functional states (or functional properties) by
means of the Ramsey sentence of a psychological theory—with one functional state corresponding to each mental state (or one functional property corresponding to each mental
property). The functional state corresponding to
pain will be called the 'Ramsey functional correlate' of pain, with respect to the psychological
theory. In terms of the notion of a Ramsey functional correlate with respect to a theory, the distinction between Functionalism and Psychofunctionalism can be defined as follows:
Functionalism identifies mental state S with S's
Ramsey functional correlate with respect to a
common-sense psychological theory; Psychofunctionalism identifies S with S's Ramsey
functional correlate with respect to a *scientific*
psychological theory. . . .

1.2. Homunculi-Headed Robots

In this section I shall describe a class of devices that embarrass all versions of functionalism in that they indicate functionalism is guilty of liberalism—classifying systems that lack mentality as having mentality.

Consider the simple version of machine functionalism already described. It says that each system having mental states is described by at least one Turing-machine table of a certain kind, and each mental state of the system is identical to one of the machine-table states specified by the machine table. I shall consider inputs and outputs to be specified by descriptions of neural impulses in sense organs and motor-output neurons. This assumption should not be regarded as restricting what will be said to Psychofunctionalism rather than Functionalism. As already mentioned, every version of functionalism assumes *some* specification of inputs and outputs. A Functionalist specification would do as well for the purposes of what follows.

Imagine a body externally like a human body, say yours, but internally quite different. The neurons from sensory organs are connected to a bank of lights in a hollow cavity in the head. A set of buttons connects to the motor-output neurons. Inside the cavity resides a group of little men. Each has a very simple task: to implement a "square" of a reasonably adequate machine table that describes you. On one wall is a bulletin board on which is posted a state card, i.e., a card that bears a symbol designating one of the states specified in the machine table. Here is what the little men do: Suppose the posted card has a 'G' on it. This alerts the little men who implement G squares—'G-men' they call themselves. Suppose the light representing input I_{17} goes on. One of the G-men has the following as his sole task: when the card reads 'G' and the I_{17} light goes on, he presses output button O_{191} and changes the state card to 'M'. This G-man is called upon to exercise his task only rarely. In spite of the low level of intelligence required of each little man, the system as a whole manages to simulate you because the functional organization they have been trained to realize is yours. A Turing machine can be represented as a finite set of quadruples (or quintuples, if the output is divided into two parts)—current state, current input; next state, next output. Each little man has the task corresponding to a single quadru-

ple. Through the efforts of the little men, the system realizes the same (reasonably adequate) machine table as you do and is thus functionally equivalent to you.

I shall describe a version of the homunculi-headed simulation, which is more clearly nomologically possible. How many homunculi are required? Perhaps a billion are enough; after all, there are only about a billion neurons in the brain.

Suppose we convert the government of China to functionalism, and we convince its officials that it would enormously enhance their international prestige to realize a human mind for an hour. We provide each of the billion people in China (I chose China because it has a billion inhabitants) with a specially designed two-way radio that connects them in the appropriate way to other persons and to the artificial body mentioned in the previous example. We replace the little men with a radio transmitter and receiver connected to the input and output neurons. Instead of a bulletin board, we arrange to have letters displayed on a series of satellites placed so that they can be seen from anywhere in China. Surely such a system is not physically impossible. It could be functionally equivalent to you for a short time, say an hour.

"But," you may object, "how could something be functionally equivalent to me for *an hour?* Doesn't my functional organization determine, say, how I would react to doing nothing for a week but reading *Reader's Digest?*" Remember that a machine table specifies a set of conditionals of the form: if the machine is in S_i and receives input I_j, it emits output O_k and goes into S_l. Any system that has a set of inputs, outputs, and states related in the way described realizes that machine table, even if it exists for only an instant. For the hour the Chinese system is "on," it *does* have a set of inputs, outputs, and states of which such conditionals are true. Whatever the initial state, the system will respond in whatever way the machine table directs. This is how *any* computer realizes the machine table it realizes.

Of course, there are signals the system would respond to that you would not respond to, e.g., massive radio interference or a flood of the Yangtze River. Such events might cause a malfunction, scotching the simulation, just as a bomb in a computer can make it fail to realize the machine table it was built to realize. But just as the computer *without* the bomb *can* realize the machine table, the system consisting of the people and artificial body can realize the machine table so long as there are no catastrophic interferences, e.g., floods, etc.

"But," someone may object, "there is a difference between a bomb in a computer and a bomb in the Chinese system, for in the case of the latter (unlike the former), inputs as specified in the machine table can be the cause of the malfunction. Unusual neural activity in the sense organs of residents of Chungking Province caused by a bomb or by a flood of the Yangtze can cause the system to go haywire."

Reply: the person who says what system he or she is talking about gets to say what counts as inputs and outputs. I count as inputs and outputs only neural activity in the artificial body connected by radio to the people of China. Neural signals in the people of Chungking count no more as inputs to this system than input tape jammed by a saboteur between the relay contacts in the innards of a computer count as an input to the computer.

Of course, the object consisting of the people of China + the artificial body has *other* Turing machine descriptions under which neural signals in the inhabitants of Chungking *would* count as inputs. Such a new system (i.e., the object under such a new Turing-machine description) would not be functionally equivalent to you. Likewise, any commercial computer can be redescribed in a way that allows tape jammed into its innards to count as inputs. In describing an object as a Turing machine, one draws a line between the inside and the outside. (If we count only neural impulses as inputs and outputs, we draw that line inside the body if *we* count only peripheral stimulations as inputs and only bodily movements as outputs, we draw that line at the skin.) In describing the Chinese system as a Turing machine, I have drawn the line in such a way that it satisfies a certain type of functional description—one that you *also* satisfy, and one that, according to functionalism, justifies attributions of mentality. Functionalism does not claim that every mental system has a machine table of a sort that justifies attributions of mentality with respect to *every* specification of inputs and outputs, but rather, only with respect to *some* specification.

Objection: The Chinese system would work too slowly. The kind of events and processes with which we normally have contact would pass by far too quickly for the system to detect them. Thus, we would be unable to converse with it, play bridge with it, etc.[3]

Reply: It is hard to see why the system's time scale should matter. What reason is there to believe that *your* mental operations could not be very much slowed down, yet remain mental operations? Is it really contradictory or nonsensical to suppose we could meet a race of intelligent beings with whom we could communicate only by devices such as time-lapse photography? When we observe these creatures, they seem almost inanimate. But when we view the time-lapse movies, we see them conversing with one another. Indeed, we find they are saying that the only way they can make any sense of us is by viewing movies greatly slowed down. To take time scale as all important seems crudely behavioristic. Further, even if the time-scale objection is right, I can elude it by retreating to the point that a homunculus-head that works in normal time is *metaphysically* possible, even if not nomologically possible. Metaphysical possibility is all my argument requires (see Section 1.3).[4]

What makes the homunculi-headed system (count the two systems as variants of a single system) just described a prima facie counter example to (machine) functionalism is that there is prima facie doubt whether it has any mental states at all—especially whether it has what philosophers have variously called "qualitative states," "raw feels," or "immediate phenomenological qualities." (You ask: What is it that philosophers have called qualitative states? I answer, only half in jest. As Louis Armstrong said when asked what jazz is, "If you got to ask, you ain't never gonna get to know.") In Nagel's terms (1974), there is a prima facie doubt whether there is anything which it is like to be the homunculi-headed system.

The force of the prima facie counterexample can be made clearer as follows: Machine functionalism says that each mental state is identical to a machine-table state. For example, a particular qualitative state, Q, is identical to a machine-table state, S_q. But if there is nothing it is like to be the homunculi-headed system, it cannot be in Q even when it is in S_q. Thus, if there is prima facie doubt about the homunculi-headed system's mentality, there is prima facie doubt that $Q = S_q$, i.e., doubt that the kind of functionalism under consideration is true.[5] Call this argument the Absent Qualia Argument.

NOTES

1. The converse is also true.
2. State type, not state token. Throughout the chapter, I shall mean by 'physicalism' the doctrine that says each distinct type of mental state is identical to a distinct type of physical state, for example, pain (the universal) is a physical state. Token physicalism, on the other hand, is the (weaker) doctrine that each particular datable pain is a state of some physical type or other. Functionalism shows that type physicalism is false, but it does not show that token physicalism is false.

   By 'physicalism,' I mean *first order* physicalism, the doctrine that, e.g., the property of being in pain is a first-order (in the Russell-Whitehead sense) physical property. (A first-order property is one whose definition does not require quantification over properties; a second-order property is one whose definition requires quantification over first-order properties.) The claim that being in pain is a second-order physical property is actually a (physicalist) form of functionalism. See Putnam, 1970.

   'Physical property' could be defined for the purposes of this chapter as a property expressed by a predicate of some true physical theory or, more broadly, by a predicate of some true theory of physiology, biology, chemistry, or physics. Of course, such a definition is unsatisfactory without characterizations of these branches of science. See Hempel, 1970, for further discussion of this problem.
3. This point has been raised with me by persons too numerous to mention.
4. One potential difficulty for Functionalism is provided by the possibility that one person may have two radically different Functional descriptions of the sort that justify attribution of mentality. In such a case, Functionalists might have to ascribe two radically different systems of belief, desire, etc., to the same person, or suppose that there is no fact of the matter about what the person's propositional attitudes are. Undoubtedly, Functionalists differ greatly on what they make of this possibility, and the differences reflect positions on such issues as indeterminacy of translation.
5. Shoemaker, 1975, argues (in reply to Block & Fodor, 1972) that absent qualia are logically impossible, that is, that it is logically impossible that two systems be in the same functional state yet one's state have and the other's state lack qualitative content. If Shoemaker is right, it is wrong to doubt whether the homunculi-headed system has qualia. I attempt to show Shoemaker's argument to be fallacious in Block, 1980.

REFERENCES

Block, N. Are absent qualia impossible? *Philosophical Review,* 1980, 89, 257–74.

Block, N. & Fodor, J. What psychological states are not. *Philosophical Review,* 1972, 81, 159–81.

Chisholm, Roderick. *Perceiving.* Ithaca: Cornell University Press, 1957.

Fodor, J. Explanations in psychology. In M. Black (Ed.), *Philosophy in America,* London: Routledge & Kegan Paul, 1965.

Gendron, B. On the relation of neurological and psychological theories: A critique of the hardware thesis. In R. C. Buck and R. S. Cohen (Eds.), *Boston studies in the philosophy of Science VIII.* Dordrecht: Reidel, 1971.

Hempel, C. Reduction: Ontological and linguistic facets. In S. Morgenbesser, P. Suppes & M. White (Eds.), *Essays in honor of Ernest Nagel.* New York: St. Martin's Press, 1970.

Kalke, W. What is wrong with Fodor and Putnam's functionalism? *Nous,* 1969, 3, 83–93.

Kim, J. Phenomenal properties, psychophysical laws, and the identity theory. *The Monist,* 1972, 56(2), 177–92.

Mucciolo, L. F. The identity thesis and neuropsychology. *Nous,* 1974, 8, 327–42.

Nagel, T. What is it like to be a bat? *Philosophical Review,* 1974, 83, 435–50.

Putnam, H. Brains and behavior. 1963. Reprinted as are all Putnam's articles referred to here (except "On properties") in *Mind, language and reality; philosophical papers,* Vol. 2). London: Cambridge University Press, 1975.

———. The mental life of some machines. 1966.

———. On properties. In *Mathematics, matter and method; philosophical papers,* Vol. 1. London: Cambridge University Press, 1970.

Shoemaker, S. Functionalism and qualia. *Philosophical studies,* 1975, 27, 271–315.

Pseudonormal Vision
An Actual Case of Qualia Inversion?

15

Martine Nida-Rümelin

1. Introduction

Is it possible that a person who behaves just like you and me in normal life situations and applies colour words to objects just as we do and makes the same colour discriminations and colour similarity judgements that we make, see green where we see red and red where we see green? Many philosophers assert that the description of such a case is somehow incoherent. Often the motivation for this assertion is "that they suspect that admitting that claim [the possibility of such a case] will put one on a slippery slope which will eventually land one in skepticism about other minds."[1]

Among philosophers, however, it does not seem to be common knowledge that there is scientific evidence for the existence of such cases. Theories about the physiological basis of colour vision deficiencies together with theories about the genetics of colour vision deficiencies lead to the prediction that some people are 'pseudonormal' (according to an estimation of Piantanida (1974) this occurs in around 14 of 10,000 males).[2] Pseudonormal people "would be expected to have normal colour vision except that the sensations of red and green would be reversed—something that would be difficult, if not impossible, to prove."[3]

Any philosophical theory of mind or more specifically about colour, colour appearances or colour concepts should meet the following plausible prima facie constraint: *No hypotheses accepted or seriously considered in colour vision science should be regarded according to a philosophical theory to be either incoherent or unstatable or false.* Therefore—regardless of whether the hypothesis of the existence of pseudonormal people is correct—the mere fact that the hypothesis is seriously considered in colour vision science, is philosophically relevant. Central claims of colour vision science when combined with specific empirical assumptions lead to the prediction that there are red-green-inverted people. Therefore any philo-

sophical theory which excludes such a case does not meet the above formulated constraint. The failure to meet this prima facie constraint does not in itself justify the rejection of a philosophical proposal, but it does represent a serious objection. This kind of criticism will be advanced against some widely held philosophical proposals in the present paper. But let me begin with a short sketch of the relevant parts of colour vision science.

2. Pseudonormal Vision. The Scientific Background

There are three types of photoreceptors on the retina that play a central role in human colour vision (B-, G- and R-cones). They are morphologically distinguishable, they play different roles in colour information processing and they normally contain three chemically different photopigments. For each cone type there is a characteristic function (the so-called sensitivity curve) which describes how the level of stimulation caused by monochromatic light in a cone of the given type depends on the wavelengths of the light at a given intensity level. It is assumed that the sensitivity curves are determined by the absorption spectra of the pigments contained in the receptors. The expected level of stimulation of a cone caused by non-monochromatic light (which is the normal case) can be calculated on the basis of the sensitivity curve characteristic for its type. When light reaches a given area on the retina, then some neural mechanism will calculate the average stimulation of the cones in the area of any of the three types. The average stimulation of the three cone types is then compared and information about the results is carried to the brain by two neural channels, the r-g-channel (responsible for red- and green-sensations) and the y-b-channel (responsible for blue- and yellow-sensations). If (b, g, r) represents the average stimulation of the B-, G- and R-cones in the area at issue then how the chan-

From *Philosophical Studies* 82:145–57, 1996. Reprinted with permission of the author and of Kluwer Academic Publishers.

nel states depend on the average stimulation (b, g, r) of the three cone types can be represented (according to a simple model of so-called opponent process theory presented in Boynton (1979)) by the following two functions.

(1) $C1((b, g, r)) = r - g$
(2) $C2((b, g, r)) = g + r - b$

It is assumed that the amount of greenness, yellowness, blueness and redness experienced by an observer in a concrete case can be predicted on the basis of the values of C1 and C2. In case $C1((b, g, r)) = O$, the corresponding object will appear neither greenish nor reddish to the person. At the zero-point of the second function, there will be no blue or yellow component in the perceived colour. For positive values of C1, the person does not sense any greenness and the amount of redness increases with the distance from zero. With negative values of C1, the person does not sense any redness, and the amount of greenness increases with the distance from zero. Analogously yellow-sensations are correlated with values of C2 greater than zero and blueness-sensations with values of C2 smaller than zero.

According to the prevailing theory about red-green blind vision these people differ from normal people in the following respect: their G-cones and R-cones contain the same photopigment. Therefore the average stimulation of their R- and G-cones will be equal for any light stimulus. The value of C1 consequently will always be zero and it follows from the theory that nothing will appear reddish or greenish to the subject. One group of red-green-blind people (so-called protanopes) have the photopigment normally contained in the G-cones not only in their G-cones, but also in their R-cones. For the other group of red-green blind people the reverse is true: their G-cones and their R-cones both contain the photopigment normally contained in R-cones. According to a widely accepted model of the inheritance of colour vision defects, both genes, the one that causes production of the G-cone photopigment in R-cones and the one that causes production of the R-cone photopigment in G-cones, may be active simultaneously in one single individual. In these cases the photopigments of the two cone types at issue are simply exchanged. The result should be a person which does not have any obvious colour vision defect. These people are called pseudonormal since they appear to be normal but really are not.

To any light stimulus their R-cones react like normally filled G-cones and their G-cones react like normally filled R-cones. The reversed filling of cones with photopigments only affects the causal interconnections between external stimuli and cone type activation. It does not, however, affect the causal interconnections between cone type activation and the states of the two chromatic channels. This second causal dependency is therefore assumed not to be altered in pseudonormal people. It follows that any light stimulus which causes the r-g-channel of a normal person to have the value y, will cause the r-g-channel of a pseudonormal person to have the value −y. If y corresponds to a reddish component in the perceived colour, then −y corresponds to a greenish component in the perceived colour (and vice versa). It therefore follows from received scientific theory about human colour vision, that pseudonormal people, if they exist, are red-green-inverted in the following sense: things that appear reddish to normal people to a certain degree, appear greenish to pseudonormal people to roughly the same degree (and vice versa) while the perception of yellowish or bluish components remains unaffected.[4]

3. Philosophical Consequences

3.1. A Problem for Wittgensteinians

Let us call an N-case a case where a person P is red-green-inverted and yet there is no behavioural difference between P and normally sighted people detectable in normal life situations that would give any reason to suspect that P's colour perceptions differ from those of normal people. Some of those philosophers who are influenced by Wittgensteinian ideas think that the possibility of an N-case can be excluded without empirical research on the basis of philosophical considerations alone. They would subscribe to the following view: Ripe tomatoes look red to a given person iff it is appropriate according to the rules of the relevant language game to assert that they look red to the person at issue. These rules do not require physiological examination of someone's visual system. Pseudonormal people are expected by colour vision science to behave roughly like normal people do in colour discrimination and colour judgement and therefore the conditions meant by Wittgensteinians for an appropriate ascription of normal colour perception are certainly fulfilled. So it seems that the Wittgensteinian must deny that pseudonormal people are red-green inverted and finds himself in conflict with what colour vision science asserts.

The Wittgensteinian however might defend his view claiming that the rules governing the use of colour appearance concepts in normal language are different from those governing scientific usage of these terms. He might then adopt one of the two following slightly different strategies: a) he might say that philosophy is concerned with everyday language and therefore need not care about how colour vision science describes the phenomenology of pseudonormal vision or b) he might admit that given the results of colour vision science sketched above we have reason to change the rules of the game and adopt the view that pseudonormal people are red-green inverted. In order to argue against both defence strategies it is necessary to show that colour vision science when using colour appearance terms does not introduce new concepts but rather uses these terms in their normal way. This indeed seems quite obvious, but to argue for this claim is a more complicated task which cannot be completed in the present paper.[5]

3.2. Pseudonormal Vision and Functionalism

It has been objected to functionalism that there could be what I will call an F-case. An F-case is a case where there is no relevant functional difference between a person P and normally sighted people although P is red-green-inverted.[6] Before we can begin discussing whether pseudonormals represent an F-case we need to distinguish different senses of "functional difference" and thereby different versions of functionalism.

Conceptual functionalism claims that the meaning of mental terms may be analysed in functionalist terminology. According to conceptual functionalism to see something as red means to be in a state which plays a specific causal role. This causal role, according to conceptual functionalism, can be specified by reference to a) typical causes of the state and b) typical causal influence of the state at issue upon other mental states. The proponent of conceptual functionalism therefore must deny the possibility of what I will call an F1-case: An F1-case would be realized if for a red-green-inverted person P something like the following two conditions hold: a) P does not differ from normals with respect to colour naming and colour discrimination behaviour and b) if there is a specific difference in the role red- and green-sensations play in connection with emotions, other modes of perception, space perception and the like, then these roles in the case of person P are reversed too. For N-cases it was required that the difference between P and normally sighted people could not be detected in normal life. It is required in addition for F1-cases that P will behave like a normal person even in sophisticated psychological and psychophysiological experiments. To the proponent of conceptual functionalism, we may ascribe the view that F1-cases are incoherent. To reject conceptual functionalism it is not necessary to show that pseudonormal people represent F1-cases. It suffices to argue that according to received colour vision science the question whether they do represent F1-cases or whether they do not needs to be settled by empirical research. This is enough since no hypotheses seriously considered in scientific theory should be regarded incoherent by any philosophical proposal. It has already been shown that pseudonormals, if they exist, are red-green inverted according to scientific theory. Whether they do represent an F1-case therefore only depends on the answer to the following question: Are there differences between red-sensations and green-sensations with respect to their causal influence upon other mental states which are innate and will not be overridden by learning processes? If the answer is 'yes', then pseudonormal people cannot represent F1-cases and could be detected by sophisticated psychological experiments. If the answer is 'no', then pseudonormal people could not be detected without direct investigation of their retina and they would represent F1-cases. Obviously the question needs to be settled by empirical research, and conceptual functionalism thus violates the above formulated prima facie constraint.[7]

Psychofunctionalism does not claim to give an analysis of the meaning of mental terms. Rather it proposes to accept the *empirical* hypothesis that mental terms will turn out to refer to functionally definable internal states. Colour vision science asserts that red sensations occur when the relevant r-g channel is in a specific type of state which is represented by positive values of C1. Let us call this type of state 'positive r-g channel state', analogously I will talk of negative

r-g channel states. The question of whether psychofunctionalism violates the above formulated
prima facie constraint then depends on whether
the difference between positive and negative r-g
channel states is a functional difference in the
sense of psychofunctionalism. At first sight it
seems that it is not: positive and negative r-g
channel states can be distinguished by reference
to their causes. Positive states are caused by a
predominance of R-cone activity, while negative
states are caused by a predominance of G-cone
activity. But this is a functionally describable
difference only if the two types of cones can be
functionally defined. The most obvious way to
define receptor types in the present context is by
reference to the way they react to light stimuli.
This strategy however is not available here. R-
cones can be filled with the photopigment normally contained in G-cones and thereby be
caused to behave like G-cones. But, as the hypothesis of pseudonormal vision shows, colour
vision science explicitly denies that a G-cone
filled with the wrong pigment thereby ceases to
be a G-cone. Of course there is a difference in
causal role between G-cones and R-cones: They
have different influences upon the channel
states. But this is what we started with. So the difference between positive and negative r-g channel states cannot be functionally specified by reference to the way these states are caused. Still,
the psychofunctionalist may hope that the two
channel states will turn out to play different functional roles on higher levels of information processing.

I have characterized psychofunctionalism
by the empirical hypothesis that terms for mental states will turn out to refer to functionally definable states. A somehow stronger claim is
however in the spirit of psychofunctionalism.
Those who subscribe to some kind of psychofunctionalism certainly would have expected
any theory of colour information processing to
be a functional theory from the outset. This
would mean that the central notions of colour
vision science at any of its historical stages
should be explicable in functionalist terminology. This stronger claim, however, is quite obviously wrong.[8]

3.3. Fixing the Reference of Physiological Concepts

The *real* story about the development of colour
vision science seems to be this: It is a central assumption of colour vision science which has

been accepted from the very beginning of this
empirical discipline and has turned out fruitful
that for any of the four phenomenally basic hues
there must be some specific physiological
process responsible for the occurrence of that
colour sensation. (The assumption is hold true
for the whole range of sighted people independently of their specific kind of—normal or abnormal—colour vision). One first step in the development of modern colour vision science was
to *postulate* the existence of one type of physiological process responsible for every basic hue
sensation and to assume that any of these four
processes allows for degrees which are correlated with the corresponding amount of f-ness
(where f is a basic hue) in the phenomenally
given colour. *Thus the reference of physiological
concepts was fixed in colour vision science by
definite descriptions formulated using phenomenal concepts* (e.g. "the process p such that the
'degree of p' is correlated with the amount of
redness"). It was assumed as a working hypothesis that these phenomenal descriptions are successful in picking out specific physiological
types.

If this description is correct, then phenomenal
concepts used in their everyday meaning did
play and still do play an essential role in the development of scientific terminology. If this is
true, then the psychofunctionalist who wishes to
uphold what I called his stronger claim, needs to
show that our phenomenal concepts really are
functional concepts. He thus has to support, in
addition, some kind of conceptual functionalism. Conceptual functionalist, however, has already been shown to be inadequate.[9]

4. Two Objections

Here is a possible objection that needs to be discussed: Someone might propose to redefine R-
cones, G-cones and B-cones in terms of their
corresponding spectral sensitivity curves. This
indeed would cause the argument to break
down. We then could not say of pseudonormal
people that their cones contain the 'wrong' pigment, since, by containing erythrolabe and
thereby a specific spectral sensitivity curve, a
receptor *by definition* becomes an R-cone. This
definition of cone-types, combined with a definition of the relevant states of the r-g-channel
according to its causal relations to the cone-
types, leads to the conclusion that in normal
subjects and in pseudonormal subjects the same

external conditions cause the same r-g-states. It would follow that red things appear red to pseudonormal people just as they do to normal ones. The philosopher proposing this redefinition might make his view still more difficult to attack by adding: My position does not need the assumption that the proposed definition is more adequate than a morphological individuation of cone types. It probably is a matter of practical convenience which definition should be preferred. Since it depends on what definition we choose whether opponent process theory predicts normal vision or inverted vision for pseudonormal subjects, the question whether an object appears red or green to a pseudonormal person turns out to be decidable by convention. It is then not a factual question about what really is the case. This result—the opponent might go on—is almost as good or even better than genuine impossibility of qualia inversion.

This counterargument can be met in two ways: First, redefining receptor types in the way proposed would by definition exclude specific cases of *acquired* red-green-inversion which seems quite unacceptable.[10] Second, the proposal violates the widely accepted principle of supervenience for mental properties upon the relevant physiological properties: Let us for the moment accept that the relevant states of the r-g-channel can be functionally defined in the way proposed, and let us call states represented by positive C1-values, positive states of the r-g-channel and the same for negative values. Since the neural hardware is not affected by exchanging photopigments, we must assume that the physiological state produced by a specific pattern of stimulation of concrete photoreceptors in a given person is the same regardless of whether the photopigments are reversed. The proposal, therefore, entails that the same physiological state that realizes a positive r-g-state, given normal distribution of photopigments, realizes a negative r-g-state, given pseudonormal distribution of photopigments. So the proposed definition, combined with opponent process theory, entails the prediction that the *very same* physiological state will lead to a red-sensation in the one case and to a green-sensation in the other. Since the only difference between the two cases lies in the way the physiological state is *caused* (by different patterns of light stimuli) and since the brain does not have any access to this information, this would seem rather mysterious.

David Lewis defended functionalism against the so-called Inverted Qualia Argument claiming that "object o looks red to person x" is ambiguous, needs to be relativized to a population P and means something like the following: "object o produces in x a state, which in people of population P plays the role of red-perceptions" where 'the role of red-perceptions' is assumed to be explicable in functional terms.[11] On this account the assumption that green things look red to pseudonormal people (in the sense in which it is true) would *mean:* when looking at grass the brain of pseudonormal people is in a physiological state which occupies the role of seeing something red in normally sighted people.[12] Lewis' proposal, however, yields an inadequate interpretation of the following central assumption in colour vision science: there is a specific physiological state which is responsible for red sensations in general (whoever is in that state has an experience of red and vice versa). This assumption is supposed to be true for all human beings in a non-trivial sense. This basic assumption, therefore, should not follow from the following 'weaker' claim: There is a physiological state (or process) which occupies a specific functional role F in normal subjects. On Lewis' account, however, it does.[13] This argument does not in itself show that the proposal violates the above formulated constraint for philosophical theories, but it does prove the violation of another plausible necessary condition for an adequate philosophical theory: *If a hypothesis H which is accepted or seriously considered in some well-established scientific theory contains a concept C and if the philosophical theory proposes a definition of C, then replacing C by the proposed definiens should not change the empirical content of H.*

5. Final Remark

The two constraints used in this paper only provide prima facie reasons for rejecting a given philosophical proposal. They may be overridden by philosophical considerations in some cases even if the scientific theory is empirically well-established. However, in such a case, the philosopher who wishes to reject scientific terminology, should be able to argue convincingly that the theory can be replaced by an alternative one, which does conform to the philosopher's intuitions and is yet in some relevant sense empirically equivalent to the original one.[14]

NOTES

1. Sydney Shoemaker, "The Inverted Spectrum," *The Journal of Philosophy* 79 (1982): 357–82, p. 364.
2. See T.P. Piantanida, "A replacement model of X-linked recessive colour vision defects." *Annals of Human Genetics* 37 (1974): 393–404 and Robert M. Boynton "Human Color Vision," New York et al. 1979, Holt Rinehart and Winston, p. 351–58.
3. Boynton in "Human Color Vision" op. cit., p. 356.
4. In an earlier paper and in my dissertation I discussed the case of photopigment exchange between R- and G-cones as an empirically possible but only imaginary case for which colour vision science would have to predict red-green inverted vision (see my "Irreduzibel mentale Prädikate in physiologischen Theorien der Farbwahrnehmung," *Berichte des Internationalen Wittgensteinsymposiums* 1988, Wien 1989 S. 59–62 and my "Farben und phänomenales Wissen," Conceptus Studienband 9, Wien 1993: Academia Verlag (St. Augustin)). Three years later I discovered that the imaginary case had actually appeared as a serious hypothesis in scientific literature. As far as I know pseudonormal vision has not yet been discussed in philosophical literature which might be due to the fact that the hypothesis can only be found in chapters or articles about the inheritance of colour vision deficiencies which philosophers might tend to skip.
5. If pseudonormal people exist, then normal subjects are systematically wrong about the colour experiences of these people as long as they believe them to be normal. Both strategies discussed above would commit the Wittgensteinian to the view that prior to the development of modern colour vision science there was no such error.
6. See, e.g., Ned Block and Jerry Fodor, "What Mental States Are Not," *Philosophical Review* 81 (1972): 158–82, pp. 172–74.
7. It violates the constraint in the following way: A hypothesis which according to colour vision science needs to be settled by empirical research (the hypothesis that there are F1-cases) is incoherent according to conceptual functionalism. The case shows that conceptual functionalism violates a further plausible prima facie constraint: No claim should be conceptually true according to a philosophical theory if it has to be settled by empirical research according to colour vision science. (Conceptual functionalism violates this further constraint with respect to the hypothesis that there are no F1-cases.)

  The argument against conceptual functionalism may also be put this way: According to received scientific theory (according to central claims of colour vision science plus the hypothesis of pseudonormal vision) there are F1-cases iff there are no innate differences in our reactions to red and green. Our colour concepts do not suffice to tell us that there are such innate differences. Therefore, contrary to conceptual functionalism, the existence of F1-cases cannot be excluded by conceptual considerations either. (I am grateful for a comment by Ned Block, which brought me to see this alternative way of making this point.)
8. It has been pointed out to me independently by Janet Levin and by Ned Block that the functionalist might reply claiming that normals and pseudonormals looking at a red thing simply have different *physiological realizations* of the same sensory quality. Of course, this is what some functionalists would like to say about the case. My point is that this description of pseudonormal vision (we would have to say, e.g., that red things look red to them) is in conflict with the way the case is described in color vision science. This reply, therefore, does not meet the above formulated prima facie constraint for philosophical theories: According to this account certain hypotheses accepted in colour vision science turn out false.
9. It is just a historical observation which is not in need of any philosophical argument that phenomenal concepts ("sensations of blue," "sensations of yellow" etc.) were used to pick out physiological types in the way roughly described in the text. For my argument I do not need the stronger claim that these concepts as used in these contexts cannot be interpreted in a behaviourist or functionalist manner (although I am certain they cannot). My point is, rather, that given the above historical observation, the stronger claim of the psychofunctionalist fails unless it is combined with some kind of conceptual functionalism.
10. Assume that someone's R-cones and G-cones start to produce the wrong photopigments at some point in his adult life. Colour vision science predicts such a person will experience and report a radical change in his colour perception. Who accepts the proposed redefinition of cone types and subscribes to opponent process theory, however, would have to insist that no such change has taken place: Those individual receptors that were R-cones before the inversion of photopigment distribution in the retina of the person at issue, *turned into G-cones* according to the proposed redefinition. Thus, green objects cause a predominance of G-cone-activity before the inversion *and* after the inversion. Therefore, the channel state produced by green things is a negative r-g-channel state before *and* after the change. So, according to the proposed redefinition, acquired photopigment inversion could not result in any change in the colour perceived by the subject.
11. See David Lewis "Mad Pain and Martian Pain," in *Philosophy of Psychology,* Vol. I, ed. Ned Block (Cambridge: Harvard University Press, 1980): 216–22, p. 200.
12. Assuming that pseudonormal and normal people are functionally equivalent in the relevant sense, on Lewis' account the following further assumptions hold: green things look green to pseudonormal people relative to the group of pseudonormal people, green things look red to normal people relative to the group of pseudonormal people, green things look green to normal people relative to their own group. Lewis's proposal, of course, should not be confused with the view that pseudonormal people and normal people simply refer to different subjective qualities when they use colour appearance concepts.
13. The argument can be formulated more precisely:

    (A) $\exists s \, \forall x \, (<s,x> \, \epsilon\alpha \leftrightarrow R(x))$
    (B) $\exists s \, \forall x \, (<s,x> \, \epsilon\alpha \leftrightarrow <\text{the } s'FR(s',P^*),x> \, \epsilon\alpha)$
    (C) there is exactly one s such that $FR(s,P^*)$
    $<s,x> \, \epsilon\alpha$: the brain of the person x is in the physiological state s

R(x)   : x has a sensation of red
FR(s,P)   : the state s occupies the functional role of
                  seeing something as red in population P
P*   : population of normally sighted people
The s ϕ[s] : the state s which satisfies ϕ. Quantifiers
                  followed by s or s' quantify over physio-
                  logical states, quantifiers followed by x
                  quantify over people.

(A) is the basic assumption at issue. (B) is the account of Lewis for this assumption (R(x) is replaced
by the proposed definiens). (B), however, logically
follows from (C) and therefore cannot be equivalent
to (A) as meant in colour vision science.

14. I have benefitted from discussions on this topic with
    Max Drömmer, Andreas Kemmerling, Martin Rech-
    enauer and Wolfgang Spohn. I am very grateful to
    Ned Block for detailed criticisms of an earlier version
    of the paper. The work was supported by the grant
    Nr. Sp. 279/4-1 from the *Deutsche Forschungs-
    gemeinschaft*. Special thanks is due to Edith Vangh-
    elof who helped with linguistic corrections.

16 | Mechanism and Its Alternatives
C. D. Broad

The Ideal of Pure Mechanism

. . . Let us first ask ourselves what would be the ideal of a mechanical view of the material realm. I think, in the first place, that it would suppose that there is only one fundamental kind of stuff out of which every material object is made. Next, it would suppose that this stuff has only one intrinsic quality, over and above its purely spatio-temporal and causal characteristics. The property ascribed to it might, e.g., be inertial mass or electric charge. Thirdly, it would suppose that there is only one fundamental kind of change, viz., change in the relative positions of the particles of this stuff. Lastly, it would suppose that there is one fundamental law according to which one particle of this stuff affects the changes of another particle. It would suppose that this law connects particles by pairs, and that the action of any two aggregates of particles as wholes on each other is compounded in a simple and uniform way from the actions which the constituent particles taken by pairs would have on each other. Thus the essence of Pure Mechanism is (a) a single kind of stuff, all of whose parts are exactly alike except for differences of position and motion; (b) a single fundamental kind of change, viz, change of position. Imposed on this there may of course be changes of a higher order, e.g., changes of velocity, of acceleration, and so on; (c) a single elementary causal law, according to which particles influence each other by pairs; and (d) a single and simple principle of composition, according to which the behaviour of any aggregate of particles, or the influence of any one aggregate on any other, follows in a uniform way from the mutual influences of the constituent particles taken by pairs.

A set of gravitating particles, on the classical theory of gravitation, is an almost perfect example of the ideal of Pure Mechanism. The single elementary law is the inverse-square law for any pair of particles. The single and simple principle of composition is the rule that the influence of any set of particles on a single particle is the vector-sum of the influences that each would exert taken by itself. An electronic theory of matter departs to some extent from this ideal. In the first place, it has to assume at present that there are two ultimately different kinds of particle, viz., protons and electrons. Secondly, the laws of electro-magnetics cannot, so far as we know, be reduced to central forces. Thirdly, gravitational phenomena do not at present fall within the scheme; and so it is necessary to ascribe masses as well as charges to the ultimate particles, and to introduce other elementary forces beside those of electro-magnetics.

On a purely mechanical theory all the apparently different kinds of matter would be made of the same stuff. They would differ only in the number, arrangement and movements of their constituent particles. And their apparently different kinds of behaviour would not be ultimately different. For they would all be deducible by a single simple principle of composition from the mutual influences of the particles taken by pairs; and these mutual influences would all obey a single law which is quite independent of the configurations and surroundings in which the particles happen to find themselves. The ideal which we have been describing and illustrating may be called "Pure Mechanism."

When a biologist calls himself a "Mechanist" it may fairly be doubted whether he means to assert anything so rigid as this. Probably all that he wishes to assert is that a living body is composed only of constituents which do or might occur in non-living bodies, and that its characteristic behaviour is wholly deducible from its structure and components and from the chemi-

Excerpted from C. D. Broad, *The Mind and Its Place in Nature* (Routledge & Kegan Paul, 1925), pp. 43–72, with permission of the publisher.

cal, physical and dynamical laws which these materials would obey if they were isolated or were in non-living combinations. Whether the apparently different kinds of chemical substance are really just so many different configurations of a single kind of particles, and whether the chemical and physical laws are just the compounded results of the action of a number of similar particles obeying a single elementary law and a single principle of composition, he is not compelled as a biologist to decide. I shall later on discuss this milder form of "Mechanism," which is all that is presupposed in the controversies between mechanistic and vitalistic biologists. In the meanwhile I want to consider how far the ideal of Pure Mechanism could possibly be an adequate account of the world as we know it.

Limitations of Pure Mechanism

No one of course pretends that a satisfactory account even of purely physical processes in terms of Pure Mechanism *has* ever been given; but the question for us is: How far, and in what sense, *could* such a theory be adequate to all the known facts? On the face of it external objects have plenty of other characteristics beside mass or electric charge, e.g., colour, temperature, etc. And, on the face of it, many changes take place in the external world beside changes of position, velocity, etc. Now of course many different views have been held about the nature and status of such characteristics as colour; but the one thing which no adequate theory of the external world can do is to ignore them altogether. I will state here very roughly the alternative types of theory, and show that none of them is compatible with Pure Mechanism as a complete account of the facts. . . .

I will now sum up the argument. The plain fact is that the external world, as perceived by us, seems not to have the homogeneity demanded by Pure Mechanism. If it *really* has the various irreducibly different sensible qualities which it *seems* to have, Pure Mechanism cannot be true of the whole of the external world and cannot be the whole truth about any part of it. The best that we can do for Pure Mechanism on this theory is to divide up the external world first on a macroscopic and then on a microscopic scale; to suppose that the macroscopic qualities which pervade any region are causally determined by the microscopic events and objects which exist within it; and to hope that the latter,

in their interactions with *each other* at any rate, fulfil the conditions of Pure Mechanism. . . .

If, on the other hand, we deny that physical objects have the various sensible qualities which they seem to us to have, we are still left with the fact that some things *seem* to be red, others to be blue, others to be hot, and so on. And a complete account of the world must include such events as "seeming red to me," "seeming blue to you," etc. We can admit that the ultimate physical objects may all be exactly alike, may all have only one non-spatio-temporal and non-causal property, and may interact with each other in such a way which Pure Mechanism requires. But we must admit that they are also cause-factors in determining the *appearance,* if not the *occurrence,* of the various sensible qualities at such and such places and times. And, in these transactions, the laws which they obey *cannot* be mechanical.

We may put the whole matter in a nutshell by saying that the appearance of a plurality of irreducible sensible qualities forces us, no matter what theory we adopt about their status, to distinguish two different kinds of law. One may be called "intra-physical" and the other "transphysical." The intra-physical laws may be, though there seems no positive reason to suppose that they are, of the kind required by Pure Mechanism. If so, there is just one ultimate elementary intra-physical law and one ultimate principle of composition for intra-physical transactions. But the trans-physical laws cannot satisfy the demands of Pure Mechanism; and, so far as I can see, there must be at least as many irreducible trans-physical laws as there are irreducible determinable sense-qualities. The nature of the trans-physical laws will of course depend on the view that we take about the status of sensible qualities. It will be somewhat different for each of the three alternative types of theory which I have mentioned, and it will differ according to which form of the third theory we adopt. But it is not necessary for our present purpose to go into further detail on this point.

The Three Possible Ways of Accounting for Characteristic Differences of Behaviour

So far we have confined our attention to pure qualities, such as red, hot, etc. By calling these "pure qualities" I mean that, when we say "This is red," "This is hot," and so on, it is no part of the meaning of our predicate that "this" stands in such and such a relation to something else. It is *logically* possible that this should be red even though "this" were the only thing in the world; though it is probably not *physically* possible. I have argued so far that the fact that external objects seem to have a number of irreducibly different pure qualities makes it certain that Pure Mechanism cannot be an adequate account of the external world. I want now to consider differences of *behaviour* among external objects. These are not differences of pure quality. When I say "This combines with that," "This eats and digests," and so on, I am making statements which would have no meaning if "this" were the only thing in the world. Now there are apparently extremely different kinds of behaviour to be found among external objects. A bit of gold and a bit of silver behave quite differently when put into nitric acid. A cat and an oyster behave quite differently when put near a mouse. Again, all bodies which would be said to be "alive," behave differently in many ways from all bodies which would be said not to be "alive." And, among nonliving bodies, what we call their "chemical behaviour" is very different from what we call their "merely physical behaviour." The question that we have now to discuss is this: "Are the differences between merely physical, chemical, and vital behaviour ultimate and irreducible or not? And are the differences in chemical behaviour between Oxygen and Hydrogen, or the differences in vital behaviour between trees and oysters and cats, ultimate and irreducible or not?" I do not expect to be able to give a conclusive answer to this question, as I do claim to have done to the question about differences of pure quality. But I hope at least to state the possible alternatives clearly, so that people with an adequate knowledge of the relevant empirical facts may know exactly what we want them to discuss, and may not beat the air in the regrettable way in which they too often have done.

We must first notice a difference between vital behaviour, on the one hand, and chemical behaviour, on the other. On the macroscopic scale, i.e., within the limits of what we can perceive with our unaided senses or by the help of optical instruments, *all* matter seems to behave chemically from time to time, though there may be long stretches throughout which a given bit of matter has no chance to exhibit any marked chemical behaviour. But only a comparatively few bits of matter *ever* exhibit vital behaviour. These are always very complex chemically; they are always composed of the same comparatively small selection of chemical elements; and they generally have a characteristic external form and internal structure. All of them after a longer or shorter time cease to show vital behaviour, and soon after this they visibly lose their characteristic external form and internal structure. We do not know how to make a living body out of non-living materials; and we do not know how to make a once living body, which has ceased to behave vitally, live again. But we know that plants, so long as they are alive, do take up inorganic materials from their surroundings and build them up into their own substance; that all living bodies maintain themselves for a time through constant chemical change of material; and that they all have the power of restoring themselves when not too severely injured, and of producing new living bodies like themselves.

Let us now consider what general types of view are possible about the fact that certain things behave in characteristically different ways.

[Special Component Theories]

[These theories] hold that the characteristic behaviour of a certain object or class of objects is in part dependent on the presence of a peculiar component which does not occur in anything that does not behave in this way. . . .

The doctrine which I will call "Substantial Vitalism" is logically a theory of this type about vital behaviour. It assumes that a necessary factor in explaining the characteristic behaviour of living bodies is the presence in them of a peculiar component, often called an "Entelechy," which does not occur in inorganic matter or in bodies which were formerly alive but have now died. I will try to bring out the analogies and differences between this type of theory as applied to vital behaviour and as applied to the behaviour of chemical compounds. (i) It is not supposed that the presence of an entelechy is sufficient to explain vital behaviour; as in chemistry, the structure of the complex is admitted to be also an essential factor. (ii) It is admitted that entelechies cannot be isolated, and that perhaps they cannot exist apart from the complex which is a living organism. But there is plenty of analogy to this in chemistry. In the first place, elements have been recognised, and the characteristic behaviour of certain compounds has been ascribed to their presence, long before they were isolated. Secondly, there are certain groups, like CH_3 and C_6H_5 in organic chemistry, which cannot exist in isolation, but which nevertheless play an essential part in determining the characteristic behaviour of certain compounds. (iii) The entelechy is supposed to exert some kind of directive influence over matter which enters the organism from outside. There is a faint analogy to this in certain parts of organic chemistry. The presence of certain groups in certain positions in a Benzene nucleus makes it very easy to put certain other groups and very hard to put others into certain positions in the nucleus. There are well-known empirical rules on this point.

Why then do most of us feel pretty confident of the truth of the chemical explanation and very doubtful of the formally analogous explanation of vital behaviour in terms of entelechies? I think that our main reasons are the following, and that they are fairly sound ones. (i) It is true that some elements were recognised and used for chemical explanations long before they were isolated. But a great many other elements had been isolated, and it was known that the process presented various degrees of difficulty. No entelechy, or anything like one, has ever been isolated; hence an entelechy is a purely hypothetical entity in a sense in which an as yet unisolated but suspected chemical element is not. If it be said that an isolated entelechy is from the nature of the case something which could not be perceived, and that this objection is therefore unreasonable, I can only answer (as I should to the similar assertion that the physical phenomena of mediumship can happen only in darkness and in the presence of sympathetic spectators) that it may be true but is certainly very unfortunate. (ii) It is true that some groups which cannot exist in isolation play a most important part in chemical explanations. But they are groups of known composition, not mysterious simple entities; and their inability to exist by themselves is not an isolated fact but is part of the more general, though imperfectly understood, fact of valency. Moreover, we can at least pass these groups from one compound to another, and can note how the chemical properties change as one compound loses such a group and another gains it. There is no known analogy to this with entelechies. You cannot pass an entelechy from a living man into a corpse and note that the former ceases and the latter begins to behave vitally. (iii) Entelechies are supposed to differ in kind from material particles; and it is doubtful whether they are literally in Space at all. It is thus hard to understand what exactly is meant by saying that a living body is a compound of an entelechy and a material structure; and impossible to say anything in detail about the structure of the total complex thus formed.

These objections seem to me to make the doctrine of Substantial Vitalism unsatisfactory, though not impossible. I think that those who have accepted it have done so largely under a misapprehension. They have thought that there was no alternative between Biological Mechanism (which I shall define a little later) and Substantial Vitalism. They found the former unsatisfactory, and so they felt obliged to accept the latter. We shall see in a moment, however, that there is another alternative type of theory, which I will call "Emergent Vitalism," borrowing the adjective from Professors Alexander and Lloyd Morgan. Of course positive arguments have been put forward in favour of entelechies, notably by Driesch. I do not propose to consider them in detail. I will merely say that Driesch's arguments do not seem to me to be in the least conclusive, even against Biological Mechanism, because they seem to forget that the smallest fragment which we can make of an organised body by cutting it up may contain an enormous number of similar microscopic structures, each of enormous complexity. And, even if it be held that Driesch has conclusively disproved Biological Mechanism, I cannot see that his arguments have the least tendency to prove Substantial Vitalism rather than the Emergent form of Vitalism which does not assume entelechies.

Emergent Theories

Put in abstract terms the emergent theory asserts that there are certain wholes, composed (say) of constituents A, B, and C in a relation R to each other; that all wholes composed of constituents of the same kind as A, B, and C in relations of the same kind as R have certain characteristic properties; that A, B, and C are capable of occurring in other kinds of complex where the relation is not of the same kind as R; and that the characteristic properties of the whole R(A, B, C) cannot, even in theory, be deduced from the most complete knowledge of the properties of A, B, and C in isolation or in other wholes which are not of the form R(A, B, C). The mechanistic theory rejects the last clause of this assertion.

Let us now consider the question in detail. If we want to explain the behaviour of any whole in terms of its structure and components we *always* need two independent kinds of information. (*a*) We need to know how the parts would behave separately. And (*b*) we need to know the law or laws according to which the behaviour of the separate parts is compounded when they are acting together in any proportion and arrangement. Now it is extremely important to notice that these two bits of information are quite independent of each other in every case. . . .

We will now pass to the case of chemical composition. Oxygen has certain properties and Hydrogen has certain other properties. They combine to form water, and the proportions in which they do this are fixed. Nothing that we know about Oxygen by itself or in its combinations with anything but Hydrogen would give us the least reason to suppose that it would combine with Hydrogen at all. Nothing that we know about Hydrogen by itself or in its combinations with anything but Oxygen would give us the least reason to expect that it would combine with Oxygen at all. And most of the chemical and physical properties of water have no known connexion, either quantitative or qualitative, with those of Oxygen and Hydrogen. Here we have a clear instance of a case where, so far as we can tell, the properties of a whole composed of two constituents could not have been predicted from a knowledge of the properties of these constituents taken separately, or from this combined with a knowledge of the properties of other wholes which contain these constituents.

Let us sum up the conclusions which may be reached from these examples before going further. It is clear that in no case could the behaviour of a whole composed of certain constituents be predicted *merely* from a knowledge of the properties of these constituents, taken separately, and of their proportions and arrangements in the particular complex under consideration. Whenever this *seems* to be possible it is because we are using a suppressed premise which is so familiar that it has escaped our notice. The suppressed premise is the fact that we have examined other complexes in the past and have noted their behaviour; that we have found a general law connecting the behaviour of these wholes with that which their constituents would show in isolation; and that we are assuming that this law of composition will hold also of the particular complex whole at present under consideration. For purely dynamical transactions this assumption is pretty well justified, because we have found a simple law of composition and have verified it very fully for wholes of very different composition, complexity, and internal structure. It is therefore not particularly rash to expect to predict the dynamical behaviour of any material complex under the action of any set of forces, however much it may differ in the details of its structure and parts from those complexes for which the assumed law of composition has actually been verified.

The example of chemical compounds shows us that we have no right to expect that the same simple law of composition will hold for chemical as for dynamical transactions. And it shows us something further. It shows us that, if we want to know the chemical (and many of the physical) properties of a chemical compound, such as silver-chloride, it is absolutely necessary to study samples of *that particular compound.* It would of course (on any view) be useless merely to study silver in isolation and chlorine in isolation; for that would tell us nothing about the law of their conjoint action. This would be equally true even if a mechanistic explanation of the chemical behaviour of compounds were possible. The essential point is that it would also be useless to study chemical compounds in general and to compare their properties with those of their elements in the hope of discovering a *general* law of composition by which the properties of any chemical compound could be foretold when the properties of its separate elements were known. So far as we know, there is no general law of this kind. It is useless even to study the properties of other compounds of silver and of other compounds of chlorine in the hope of discovering one general law by which the properties of silver-compounds could be predicted from those of elementary silver and another general law by which the properties of chlorine-compounds could be predicted from those of elementary chlorine. No doubt the properties of silver-chloride are completely *determined* by those of silver and of chlorine; in the sense that whenever you have a whole composed of these two elements in certain proportions and relations you have something with the characteristic properties of silver-chloride, and that nothing has these properties except a whole composed in this way. But the law connecting the properties of silver-chloride with those of silver and of chlorine and with the structure of the compound is, so far as we know, a *unique* and *ultimate* law. By this I mean (*a*) that it is not a special case which arises through substituting certain determinate values for determinable variables in a general law which connects the properties of *any* chemical compound with those of its separate elements and with its structure. And (b) that it is not a special case which arises by combining two more general laws, one of which connects the properties of *any* silver-compound with those of elementary silver, whilst the other connects the properties of *any* chlorine-compound with those of elementary chlorine. So far as we know there are no such laws. It is (c) a law which could have been discovered only by studying samples of silver-chloride itself, and which can be extended inductively *only* to other samples of the same substance.

We may contrast this state of affairs with that which exists where a mechanistic explanation is possible. In order to predict the behaviour of a clock a man need never have seen a clock in his life. Provided he is told how it is constructed, and that he has learnt from the study of *other* material systems the general rules about motion and about the mechanical properties of springs and of rigid bodies, he can foretell exactly how a system constructed like a clock must behave.

The situation with which we are faced in chemistry, which seems to offer the most plausible example of emergent behaviour, may be described in two alternative ways. These may be theoretically different, but in practice they are equivalent. (i) The first way of putting the case is the following. What we call the "properties" of the chemical elements are very largely propositions about the compounds which they form with other elements under suitable conditions E.g., one of the "properties" of silver is that it combines under certain conditions with chlorine to give a compound with the properties of silver-chloride. Likewise one of the "properties" of chlorine is that under certain conditions it combines with silver to give a compound with the properties of silver-chloride. These "properties" cannot be deduced from any selection of the other properties of silver or of chlorine. Thus we may say that we do not know all the properties of chlorine and of silver until they have been put in presence of each other; and that no amount of knowledge about the properties which they manifest in other circumstances will tell us what property, if any, they will manifest in these circumstances. Put in this way the position is that we do not know all the properties of any element, and that there is always the possi-

bility of their manifesting unpredictable properties when put into new situations. This happens whenever a chemical compound is prepared or discovered for the first time. (ii) The other way to put the matter is to confine the name "property" to those characteristics which the elements manifest when they do not act chemically on each other, i.e., the physical characteristics of the isolated elements. In this case we may indeed say, if we like, that we know all the properties of each element; but we shall have to admit that we do not know the laws according to which elements, which have these properties in isolation, together produce compounds having such and such other characteristic properties. The essential point is that the behaviour of an as yet unexamined compound cannot be predicted from a knowledge of the properties of its elements in isolation or from a knowledge of the properties of their other compounds; and it matters little whether we ascribe this to the existence of innumerable "latent" properties in each element, each of which is manifested only in the presence of a certain other element; or to the lack of any general principle of composition, such as the parallelogram law in dynamics, by which the behaviour of any chemical compound could be deduced from its structure and from the behaviour of each of its elements in isolation from the rest.

Let us now apply the conceptions, which I have been explaining and illustrating from chemistry, to the case of vital behaviour. We know that the bits of matter which behave vitally are composed of various chemical compounds arranged in certain characteristic ways. We have prepared and experimented with many of these compounds apart from living bodies, and we see no obvious reason why some day they might not all be synthesised and studied in the chemical laboratory. A living body might be regarded as a compound of the second order, i.e., a compound composed of compounds; just as silver-chloride is a compound of the first order, i.e., one composed of chemical elements. Now it is obviously possible that, just as the characteristic behaviour of a first-order compound could not be predicted from any amount of knowledge of the properties of its elements in isolation or of the properties of other first-order compounds, so the properties of a second-order compound could not be predicted from any amount of knowledge about the properties of its first-order constituents taken separately or in other surroundings. Just as the only way to find out the properties of silver-chloride is to study samples of silver-chloride, and no amount of study of silver and of chlorine taken separately or in other combinations will help us; so the only way to find out the characteristic behaviour of living bodies may be to study living bodies as such. And no amount of knowledge about how the constituents of a living body behave in isolation or in other and non-living wholes might suffice to enable us to predict the characteristic behaviour of a living organism. This possibility is perfectly compatible with the view that the characteristic behaviour of a living body is completely determined by the nature and arrangement of the chemical compounds which compose it, in the sense that any whole which is composed of such compounds in such an arrangement will show vital-behaviour and that nothing else will do so. We should merely have to recognise, as we had to do in considering a first-order compound like silver-chloride, that we are dealing with an *unique* and *irreducible* law; and not with a special case which arises by the substitution of particular values for variables in a more general law, nor with a combination of several more general laws.

We could state this possibility about living organisms in two alternative but practically equivalent ways, just as we stated the similar possibility about chemical compounds. (i) The first way would be this. Most of the properties which we ascribe to chemical compounds are statements about what they do in presence of various chemical reagents under certain conditions of temperature, pressure, etc. These various properties are not deducible from each other; and, until we have tried a compound with every other compound and under every possible condition of temperature, pressure, etc., we cannot possibly know that we have exhausted all its properties. It is therefore perfectly possible that, in the very special situation in which a chemical compound is placed in a living body, it may exhibit properties which remain "latent" under all other conditions. (ii) The other, and practically equivalent, way of putting the case is the following. If we confine the name "property" to the behaviour which a chemical compound shows in isolation, we may perhaps say that we know all the "properties" of the chemical constituents of a living body. But we shall not be able to predict the behaviour of the body unless we also know the laws according to which the behaviour which each of these constituents *would have* shown in isolation is compounded when they

are acting together in certain proportions and arrangements. We can discover such laws only by studying complexes containing these constituents in various proportions and arrangements. And we have no right to suppose that the laws which we have discovered by studying non-living complexes can be carried over without modification to the very different case of living complexes. It may be that the only way to discover the laws according to which the behaviour of the separate constituents combines to produce the behaviour of the whole in a living body is to study living bodies as such. For practical purposes it makes little difference whether we say that the chemical compounds which compose a living body have "latent properties" which are manifested only when they are parts of a whole of this peculiar structure; or whether we say that the properties of the constituents of a living body are the same whether they are in it or out of it, but that the law according to which these separate effects are compounded with each other is different in a living whole from what it is in any nonliving whole.

This view about living bodies and vital behaviour is what I call "Emergent Vitalism"; and it is important to notice that it is quite different from what I call "Substantial Vitalism." So far as I can understand them I should say that Driesch is a Substantial Vitalist, and that Dr J. S. Haldane is an Emergent Vitalist. But I may quite well be wrong in classifying these two distinguished men in this way.

Mechanistic Theories

The mechanistic type of theory is much more familiar than the emergent type, and it will therefore be needless to consider it in great detail. I will just consider the mechanistic alternative about chemical and vital behaviour, so as to make the emergent theory still clearer by contrast. Suppose it were certain, as it is very probable, that all the different chemical atoms are composed of positive and negative electrified particles in different numbers and arrangements; and that these differences of number and arrangement are the only ultimate difference between them. Suppose that all these particles obey the same elementary laws, and that their separate actions are compounded with each other according to a single law which is the same no matter how complicated may be the whole of which they are constituents. Then it would be theoretically possible to deduce the characteristic behaviour of any element from an adequate knowledge of the number and arrangement of the particles in its atom, without needing to observe a sample of the substance. We could, *in theory,* deduce what other elements it would combine with and in what proportions; which of these compounds would be stable to heat, etc.; and how the various compounds would react in presence of each other under given conditions of temperature, pressure, etc. And all this should be *theoretically* possible without needing to observe samples of these compounds.

I want now to explain exactly what I mean by the qualification "theoretically." (1) In the first place the mathematical difficulties might be overwhelming in practice, even if we knew the structure and the laws. This is a trivial qualification for our present purpose, which is to bring out the *logical* distinction between mechanism and emergence. Let us replace Sir Ernest Rutherford by a mathematical archangel, and pass on. (2) Secondly, we cannot directly perceive the microscopic structure of atoms, but can only infer it from the macroscopic behaviour of matter in bulk. Thus, in practice, even if the mechanistic hypothesis were true and the mathematical difficulties were overcome, we should have to start by observing enough of the macroscopic behaviour of samples of each element to infer the probable structure of its atom. But, once this was done, it should be possible to deduce its behaviour in macroscopic conditions under which it has never yet been observed. That is, if we could infer its microscopic structure from a selection of its observed macroscopic properties, we could henceforth *deduce* all its other macroscopic properties from its microscopic structure without further appeal to observation. The difference from the emergent theory is thus profound, even when we allow for our mathematical and perceptual limitations. If the emergent theory of chemical compounds be true, a mathematical archangel, gifted with the further power of perceiving the microscopic structure of atoms as easily as we can perceive hay-stacks, could no more predict the behaviour of silver or of chlorine or the properties of silver-chloride without having observed samples of those substances than we can at present. And he could no more deduce the rest of the properties of a chemical element or compound from a selection of its properties than we can.

Would there be any theoretical limit to the deduction of the properties of chemical elements and compounds if a mechanistic theory of chemistry were true? Yes. Take any ordinary statement, such as we find in chemistry books; e.g., "Nitrogen and Hydrogen combine when an electric discharge is passed through a mixture of the two. The resulting compound contains three atoms of Hydrogen to one of Nitrogen; it is a gas readily soluble in water, and possessed of a pungent and characteristic smell." If the mechanistic theory be true the archangel could deduce from his knowledge of the microscopic structure of atoms all these facts but the last. He would know exactly what the microscopic structure of ammonia must be; but he would be totally unable to predict that a substance with this structure must smell as ammonia does when it gets into the human nose. The utmost that he could predict on this subject would be that certain changes would take place in the mucous membrane, the olfactory nerves and so on. But he could not possibly know that these changes would be accompanied by the appearance of a smell in general or of the peculiar smell of ammonia in particular, unless someone told him so or he had smelled it for himself. If the existence of the so-called "secondary qualities," or the fact of their appearance, depends on the microscopic movements and arrangements of material particles which do not have these qualities themselves, then the laws of this dependence are certainly of the emergent type.

The mechanistic theory about vital behaviour should now need little explanation. A man can hold it without being a mechanist about chemistry. The minimum that a Biological Mechanist need believe is that, in theory, everything that is characteristic of the behaviour of a living body could be deduced from an adequate knowledge of its structure, the chemical compounds which make it up, and the properties which these show in isolation or in non-living wholes.

Logical Status of Emergence and Mechanism

I have now stated the two alternatives which alone seem worthy of serious consideration. It is not my business as a philosopher to consider detailed empirical arguments for or against mechanism or emergence in chemistry or in biology. But it is my business to consider the logical status of the two types of theory, and it is relevant to our present purpose to discuss how far the possibility of science is bound up with the acceptance of the mechanistic alternative.

(1) I do not see any a prior impossibility in a mechanistic biology or chemistry, so long as it confines itself to that kind of behaviour which can be completely described in terms of changes of position, size, shape, arrangement of parts, etc. I have already argued that this type of theory cannot be the whole truth about all aspects of the material world. For one aspect of it is that bits of matter have or seem to have various colours, temperatures, smells, tastes, etc. If the occurrence or the appearance of these "secondary qualities" depends on microscopic particles and events, the laws connecting the latter with the former are certainly of the emergent type. And no complete account of the external world can ignore these laws.

(2) On the other hand, I cannot see the least trace of self-evidence in theories of the mechanistic type, or in the theory of Pure Mechanism which is the ideal towards which they strive. I know no reason whatever why new and theoretically unpredictable modes of behaviour should not appear at certain levels of complexity, or why they must be explicable in terms of elementary properties and laws of composition which have manifested themselves in less complex wholes. . . .

Let us now sum up the theoretical differences which the alternatives of Mechanism and Emergence would make to our view of the external world and of the relations between the various sciences. The advantage of Mechanism would be that it introduces a unity and tidiness into the world which appeals very strongly to our aesthetic interests. On that view, when pushed to its extreme limits, there is one and only one kind of material. Each particle of this obeys one elementary law of behaviour, and continues to do so no matter how complex may be the collection of particles of which it is a constituent. There is one uniform law of composition, connecting the behaviour of groups of these particles as wholes with the behaviour which each would show in isolation and with the structure of the group. All the apparently different kinds of stuff are just differently arranged groups of different numbers of the one kind of elementary particle; and all the apparently peculiar laws of behaviour are simply special cases which could be deduced in theory from the structure of the whole under consideration, the one elementary law of behaviour for isolated particles, and the one universal law of composition. On such a view the external world has the greatest amount of unity which is conceivable. There is really only one science, and the various "special sciences" are just particular cases of it. This is a magnificent ideal; it is certainly much more nearly true than anyone could possibly have suspected at first sight; and investigations pursued under its guidance have certainly enabled us to discover many connexions within the external world which would otherwise have escaped our notice. But it has no trace of self-evidence; it cannot be the *whole* truth about the external world, since it cannot deal with the existence or the appearance of "secondary qualities" until it is supplemented by laws of the emergent type which assert that under such and such conditions such and such groups of elementary particles moving in certain ways have, or seem to human beings to have, such and such secondary qualities; and it is certain that considerable scientific progress can be made without assuming it to be true. As a practical postulate it has its good and its bad side. On the one hand, it makes us try our hardest to explain the characteristic behaviour of the more complex in terms of the laws which we have already recognized in the less complex. If our efforts succeed, this is sheer gain. And, even if they fail, we shall probably have learned a great deal about the minute details of the facts under investigation which we might not have troubled to look for otherwise. On the other hand, it tends to over-simplification. If in fact there are new types of law at certain levels, it is very desirable that we should honestly recognise the fact. And, if we take the mechanistic ideal too seriously, we shall be in danger of ignoring or perverting awkward facts of this kind. This sort of over-simplification has certainly happened in the past in biology and physiology under the guidance of the mechanistic ideal; and it of course reaches its wildest absurdities in the attempts which have been made from time to time to treat mental phenomena mechanistically.

On the emergent theory we have to reconcile ourselves to much less unity in the external world and a much less intimate connexion between the various sciences. At best the external world and the various sciences that deal with it will form a kind of hierarchy. We might, if we liked, keep the view that there is only one fundamental kind of stuff. But we should have to recognise aggregates of various orders. And there would be two fundamentally different types of law, which might be called "intra-ordinal" and "trans-ordinal" respectively. A transordinal law would be one which connects the properties of aggregates of adjacent orders. A and B would be adjacent, and in ascending order, if every aggregate of order B is composed of aggregates of order A, and if it has certain properties which no aggregate of order A possesses and which cannot be deduced from the A-properties and the structure of the B-complex by any law of composition which has manifested itself at lower levels. An intra-ordinal law would be one which connects the properties of aggregates of the same order. A trans-ordinal law would be a statement of the irreducible fact that an aggregate composed of aggregates of the next lower order in such and such proportions and arrangements has such and such characteristic and non-deducible properties. . . .

There is nothing, so far as I can see, mysterious or unscientific about a trans-ordinal law or about the notion of ultimate characteristics of a given order. A trans-ordinal law is as good a law as any other; and, once it has been discovered, it can be used like any other to suggest experiments, to make predictions, and to give us practical control over external objects. The only peculiarity of it is that we must wait till we meet with an actual instance of an object of the higher order before we can discover such a law; and that we cannot possibly deduce it beforehand from any combination of laws which we have discovered by observing aggregates of a lower order. There is an obvious analogy between the trans-ordinal laws which I am now discussing and the trans-physical laws which I mentioned in considering Pure Mechanism and said must be recognised in any complete account of the external world. The difference is this. Trans-physical laws, in the sense in which we are using the term, are *necessarily* of the emergent type. For they connect the configurations and internal motions of groups of microscopic particles, on the one hand, with the fact that the volume which contains the group is, or appears to be, pervaded by such and such a secondary quality. Since there are many irreducibly different *kinds* of secondary quality, e.g. colour, smell, temperature, etc., there must be many irreducible laws of this sort. Again, suppose we confine our attention to one *kind* of secondary quality, say colour. The concepts of the various colours—red, blue, green, etc.—are not contained in the general concept of Colour in the sense in which we might quite fairly say that the concepts of all possible motions are contained in the general concepts of Space and of Motion. We have no difficulty in conceiving and adequately describing determinate possible motions which we have never witnessed and which we never shall witness. We have merely to assign a determinate direction and a determinate velocity. But we could not possibly have formed the concept of such a colour as blue or such a shade as sky-blue unless we had perceived instances of it, no matter how much we had reflected on the concept of Colour in general or on the instances of other colours and shades which we *had* seen. It follows that, even when we know that a certain kind of secondary quality (e.g., colour) pervades or seems to pervade a region when and only when such and such a kind of microscopic event (e.g., vibrations) is going on within the region, we still could not possibly predict that such and such a determinate event of the kind (e.g., a circular movement of a certain period) would be connected with such and such a determinate shade of colour (e.g., sky-blue). The trans-physical laws are then necessarily of the emergent type. . . .

17 | Mental Events
Donald Davidson

Mental events such as perceivings, remember-ings, decisions, and actions resist capture in the nomological net of physical theory.[1] How can this fact be reconciled with the causal role of mental events in the physical world? Reconcil-ing freedom with causal determinism is a spe-cial case of the problem if we suppose that causal determinism entails capture in, and free-dom requires escape from, the nomological net. But the broader issue can remain alive even for someone who believes a correct analysis of free action reveals no conflict with determinism. *Au-tonomy* (freedom, self-rule) may or may not clash with determinism; *anomaly* (failure to fall under a law) is, it would seem, another matter.

I start from the assumption that both the causal dependence, and the anomalousness, of mental events are undeniable facts. My aim is therefore to explain, in the face of apparent dif-ficulties, how this can be. I am in sympathy with Kant when he says,

> it is as impossible for the subtlest philosophy as for the commonest reasoning to argue freedom away. Philosophy must therefore assume that no true contradiction will be found between free-dom and natural necessity in the same human actions, for it cannot give up the idea of nature any more than that of freedom. Hence even if we should never be able to conceive how freedom is possible, at least this apparent contradiction must be convincingly eradicated. For if the thought of freedom contradicts itself or nature . . . it would have to be surrendered in competi-tion with natural necessity.[2]

Generalize human actions to mental events, substitute anomaly for freedom, and this is a de-scription of my problem. And of course the con-nection is closer, since Kant believed freedom entails anomaly.

Now let me try to formulate a little more care-fully the "apparent contradiction" about mental events that I want to discuss and finally dissi-pate. It may be seen as stemming from three principles.

The first principle asserts that at least some mental events interact causally with physical events. (We could call this the Principle of Causal Interaction.) Thus for example if some-one sank the *Bismarck,* then various mental events such as perceivings, notings, calcula-tions, judgments, decisions, intentional actions and changes of belief played a causal role in the sinking of the *Bismarck.* In particular, I would urge that the fact that someone sank the *Bis-marck* entails that he moved his body in a way that was caused by mental events of certain sorts, and that this bodily movement in turn caused the *Bismarck* to sink.[3] Perception illustrates how causality may run from the physical to the men-tal: if a man perceives that a ship is approaching, then a ship approaching must have caused him to come to believe that a ship is approaching. (Nothing depends on accepting these as exam-ples of causal interaction.)

Though perception and action provide the most obvious cases where mental and physical events interact causally, I think reasons could be given for the view that all mental events ulti-mately, perhaps through causal relations with other mental events, have causal intercourse with physical events. But if there are mental events that have no physical events as causes or effects, the argument will not touch them.

The second principle is that where there is causality, there must be a law: events related as cause and effect fall under strict deterministic laws. (We may term this the Principle of the Nomological Character of Causality.) This prin-ciple, like the first, will be treated here as an as-sumption, though I shall say something by way of interpretation.[4]

The third principle is that there are no strict deterministic laws on the basis of which mental events can be predicted and explained (the Anomalism of the Mental).

The paradox I wish to discuss arises for someone who is inclined to accept these three assumptions or principles, and who thinks they are inconsistent with one another. The inconsis-tency is not, of course, formal unless more premises are added. Nevertheless it is natural to reason that the first two principles, that of causal

From L. Foster & J. Swanson, eds., *Experience and Theory*, pp. 79–101. Humanities Press, 1970. Reprinted with permission of the author.

interaction, and that of the nomological character of causality, together imply that at least some mental events can be predicted and explained on the basis of laws, while the principle of the anomalism of the mental denies this. Many philosophers have accepted, with or without argument, the view that the three principles do lead to a contradiction. It seems to me, however, that all three principles are true, so that what must be done is to explain away the appearance of contradiction; essentially the Kantian line.

The rest of this paper falls into three parts. The first part describes a version of the identity theory of the mental and the physical that shows how the three principles may be reconciled. The second part argues that there cannot be strict psychophysical laws; this is not quite the principle of the anomalism of the mental, but on reasonable assumptions entails it. The last part tries to show that from the fact that there can be no strict psychophysical laws, and our other two principles, we can infer the truth of a version of the identity theory, that is, a theory that identifies at least some mental events with physical events. It is clear that this "proof" of the identity theory will be at best conditional, since two of its premises are unsupported, and the argument for the third may be found less than conclusive. But even someone unpersuaded of the truth of the premises may be interested to learn how they may be reconciled and that they serve to establish a version of the identity theory of the mental. Finally, if the argument is a good one, it should lay to rest the view, common to many friends and some foes of identity theories, that support for such theories can come only from the discovery of psychophysical laws.

I

The three principles will be shown consistent with one another by describing a view of the mental and the physical that contains no inner contradiction and that entails the three principles. According to this view, mental events are identical with physical events. Events are taken to be unrepeatable, dated individuals such as the particular eruption of a volcano, the (first) birth or death of a person, the playing of the 1968 World Series, or the historic utterance of the words, "You may fire when ready, Gridley." We can easily frame identity statements about individual events; examples (true or false) might be:

The death of Scott = the death of the author of *Waverley;*

The assassination of the Archduke Ferdinand = the event that started the First World War;

The eruption of Vesuvius in A.D. 79 = the cause of the destruction of Pompeii.

The theory under discussion is silent about processes, states, and attributes if these differ from individual events.

What does it mean to say that an event is mental or physical? One natural answer is that an event is physical if it is describable in a purely physical vocabulary, mental if describable in mental terms. But if this is taken to suggest that an event is physical, say, if some physical predicate is true of it, then there is the following difficulty. Assume that the predicate 'x took place at Noosa Heads' belongs to the physical vocabulary; then so also must the predicate 'x did not take place at Noosa Heads' belong to the physical vocabulary. But the predicate 'x did or did not take place at Noosa Heads' is true of every event, whether mental or physical.[5] We might rule out predicates that are tautologically true of every event, but this will not help since every event is truly describable either by 'x took place at Noosa Heads' or by 'x did not take place at Noosa Heads.' A different approach is needed.[6]

We may call those verbs mental that express propositional attitudes like believing, intending, desiring, hoping, knowing, perceiving, noticing, remembering, and so on. Such verbs are characterized by the fact that they sometimes feature in sentences with subjects that refer to persons, and are completed by embedded sentences in which the usual rules of substitution appear to break down. This criterion is not precise, since I do not want to include these verbs when they occur in contexts that are fully extensional ('He knows Paris,' 'He perceives the moon' may be cases), nor exclude them whenever they are not followed by embedded sentences. An alternative characterization of the desired class of mental verbs might be that they are psychological verbs as used when they create apparently nonextensional contexts.

Let us call a description of the form 'the event that is M' or an open sentence of the form 'event x is M' a *mental description* or a *mental open sentence* if and only if the expression that replaces 'M' contains at least one mental verb essentially. (Essentially, so as to rule out cases where the description or open sentence is logically equivalent to one not containing mental vocabulary.) Now we may say that an event is mental if and only if it has a mental description, or (the description operator not being primitive) if there is a mental open sentence true of that event alone. Physical events are those picked out by descriptions or open sentences that contain only the physical vocabulary essentially. It is less important to characterize a physical vocabulary because relative to the mental it is, so to speak, recessive in determining whether a description is mental or physical. (There will be some comments presently on the nature of a physical vocabulary, but these comments will fall far short of providing a criterion.)

On the proposed test of the mental, the distinguishing feature of the mental is not that it is private, subjective, or immaterial, but that it exhibits what Brentano called intentionality. Thus intentional actions are clearly included in the realm of the mental along with thoughts, hopes, and regrets (or the events tied to these). What may seem doubtful is whether the criterion will include events that have often been considered paradigmatic of the mental. Is it obvious, for example, that feeling a pain or seeing an afterimage will count as mental? Sentences that report such events seem free from taint of nonextensionality, and the same should be true of reports of raw feels, sense data, and other uninterpreted sensations, if there are any.

However, the criterion actually covers not only the havings of pains and afterimages, but much more besides. Take some event one would intuitively accept as physical, let's say the collision of two stars in distant space. There must be a purely physical predicate 'Px' true of this collision, and of others, but true of only this one at the time it occurred. This particular time, though, may be pinpointed as the same time that Jones notices that a pencil starts to roll across his desk. The distant stellar collision is thus *the* event x such that Px and x is simultaneous with Jones' noticing that a pencil starts to roll across his desk. The collision has now been picked out by a mental description and must be counted as a mental event.

This strategy will probably work to show every event to be mental; we have obviously failed to capture the intuitive concept of the mental. It would be instructive to try to mend this trouble, but it is not necessary for present purposes. We can afford Spinozistic extravagance with the mental since accidental inclusions can only strengthen the hypothesis that all mental events are identical with physical events.

What would matter would be failure to include bona fide mental events, but of this there seems to be no danger.

I want to describe, and presently to argue for, a version of the identity theory that denies that there can be strict laws connecting the mental and the physical. The very possibility of such a theory is easily obscured by the way in which identity theories are commonly defended and attacked. Charles Taylor, for example, agrees with protagonists of identity theories that the sole "ground" for accepting such theories is the supposition that correlations or laws can be established linking events described as mental with events described as physical. He says, "It is easy to see why this is so: unless a given mental event is invariably accompanied by a given, say, brain process, there is no ground for even mooting a general identity between the two."[7] Taylor goes on (correctly, I think) to allow that there may be identity without correlating laws, but my present interest is in noticing the invitation to confusion in the statement just quoted. What can "a given mental event" mean here? Not a particular, dated, event, for it would not make sense to speak of an individual event being "invariably accompanied" by another. Taylor is evidently thinking of events of a given *kind*. But if the only identities are of kinds of events, the identity theory presupposes correlating laws.

One finds the same tendency to build laws into the statement of the identity theory in these typical remarks:

> When I say that a sensation is a brain process or that lightning is an electrical discharge, I am using 'is' in the sense of strict identity . . . there are not two things: a flash of lightning and an electrical discharge. There is one thing, a flash of lightning, which is described scientifically as an electrical discharge to the earth from a cloud of ionized water molecules.[8]

The last sentence of this quotation is perhaps to be understood as saying that for every lightning flash there exists an electrical discharge to the earth from a cloud of ionized water molecules with which it is identical. Here we have an honest ontology of individual events and can make literal sense of identity. We can also see how there could be identities without correlating laws. It is possible, however, to have an ontology of events with the conditions of individuation specified in such a way that any identity implies a correlating law. Kim, for example, suggests that Fa and Gb "describe or refer to the same event" if and only if $a = b$ and the property of being F = the property of being G. The identity of the properties in turn entails that (x) $(Fx \leftrightarrow Gx)$.[9] No wonder Kim says:

> If pain is identical with brain state B, there must be a concomitance between occurrences of pain and occurrences of brain state B.... Thus, a necessary condition of the pain–brain state B identity is that the two expressions 'being in pain' and 'being in brain state B' have the same extension.... There is no conceivable observation that would confirm or refute the identity but not the associated correlation.[10]

It may make the situation clearer to give a fourfold classification of theories of the relation between mental and physical events that emphasizes the independence of claims about laws and claims of identity. On the one hand there are those who assert, and those who deny, the existence of psychophysical laws; on the other hand there are those who say mental events are identical with physical and those who deny this. Theories are thus divided into four sorts: *Nomological monism,* which affirms that there are correlating laws and that the events correlated are one (materialists belong in this category); *nomological dualism,* which comprises various forms of parallelism, interactionism, and epiphenomenalism; *anomalous dualism,* which combines ontological dualism with the general failure of laws correlating the mental and the physical (Cartesianism). And finally there is *anomalous monism,* which classifies the position I wish to occupy.[11]

Anomalous monism resembles materialism in its claim that all events are physical, but rejects the thesis, usually considered essential to materialism, that mental phenomena can be given purely physical explanations. Anomalous monism shows an ontological bias only in that it allows the possibility that not all events are mental, while insisting that all events are physical. Such a bland monism, unbuttressed by correlating laws or conceptual economies, does not seem to merit the term "reductionism"; in any case it is not apt to inspire the nothing-but reflex ("Conceiving the *Art of the Fugue* was nothing but a complex neural event," and so forth.)

Although the position I describe denies there are psychophysical laws, it is consistent with the view that mental characteristics are in some sense dependent, or supervenient, on physical characteristics. Such supervenience might be taken to mean that there cannot be two events alike in all physical respects but differing in some mental respect, or that an object cannot alter in some mental respect without altering in some physical respect. Dependence or supervenience of this kind does not entail reducibility through law or definition: if it did, we could reduce moral properties to descriptive, and this there is good reason to *believe* cannot be done; and we might be able to reduce truth in a formal system to syntactical properties, and this we *know* cannot in general be done.

This last example is in useful analogy with the sort of lawless monism under consideration. Think of the physical vocabulary as the entire vocabulary of some language L with resources adequate to express a certain amount of mathematics, and its own syntax. L′ is L augmented with the truth predicate 'true-in-L,' which is "mental." In L (and hence L′) it is possible to pick out, with a definite description or open sentence, each sentence in the extension of the truth predicate, but if L is consistent there exists no predicate of syntax (of the "physical" vocabulary), no matter how complex, that applies to all and only the true sentences of L. There can be no "psychophysical law" in the form of a biconditional, '(x) (x is true-in-L if and only if x is ϕ)' where 'ϕ' is replaced by a "physical" predicate (a predicate of L). Similarly, we can pick out each mental event using the physical vocabulary alone, but no purely physical predicate, no matter how complex, has, as a matter of law, the same extension as a mental predicate.

It should now be evident how anomalous monism reconciles the three original principles. Causality and identity are relations between individual events no matter how described. But laws are linguistic; and so events can instantiate laws, and hence be explained or predicted in the light of laws, only as those events are described in one or another way. The principle of causal interaction deals with events in extension and is therefore blind to the mental–physical dichotomy. The principle of the anomalism of the mental concerns events described as mental, for events are mental only as described. The principle of the nomological character of causality must be read carefully: it says that when events are related as cause and effect, they have descriptions that instantiate a law. It does not say that every true singular statement of causality instantiates a law.[12]

II

The analogy just bruited, between the place of the mental amid the physical, and the place of the semantical in a world of syntax, should not be strained. Tarski proved that a consistent language cannot (under some natural assumptions) contain an open sentence 'Fx' true of all and only the true sentences of that language. If our analogy were pressed, then we would expect a proof that there can be no physical open sentence 'Px' true of all and only the events having some mental property. In fact, however, nothing I can say about the irreducibility of the mental deserves to be called a proof; and the kind of irreducibility is different. For if anomalous monism is correct, not only can every mental event be uniquely singled out using only physical concepts, but since the number of events that falls under each mental predicate may, for all we know, be finite, there may well exist a physical open sentence coextensive with each mental predicate, though to construct it might involve the tedium of a lengthy and uninstructive alternation. Indeed, even if finitude is not assumed, there seems no compelling reason to deny that there could be coextensive predicates, one mental and one physical.

The thesis is rather that the mental is nomologically irreducible: there may be *true* general statements relating the mental and the physical, statements that have the logical form of a law; but they are not *lawlike* (in a strong sense to be described). If by absurdly remote chance we were to stumble on a nonstochastic true psychophysical generalization, we would have no reason to believe it more than roughly true.

Do we, by declaring that there are no (strict) psychophysical laws, poach on the empirical preserves of science—a form of hubris against which philosophers are often warned? Of course, to judge a statement lawlike or illegal is not to decide its truth outright; relative to the acceptance of a general statement on the basis of instances, ruling it lawlike must be a priori. But such relative apriorism does not in itself justify philosophy, for in general the grounds for deciding to trust a statement on the basis of its instances will in turn be governed by theoretical and empirical concerns not to be distinguished from those of science. If the case of supposed laws linking the mental and the physical is different, it can only be because to allow the possibility of such laws would amount to changing the subject. By changing the subject I mean here: deciding not to accept the criterion of the mental in terms of the vocabulary of the propositional attitudes. This short answer cannot prevent further ramifications of the problem, however, for there is no clear line between changing the subject and changing what one says on an old subject, which is to admit, in the present context at least, that there is no clear line between philosophy and science. Where there are no fixed boundaries only the timid never risk trespass.

It will sharpen our appreciation of the anomological character of mental—physical generalizations to consider a related matter, the failure of definitional behaviorism. Why are we willing (as I assume we are) to abandon the attempt to give explicit definitions of mental concepts in terms of behavioral ones? Not, surely, just because all actual tries are conspicuously inadequate. Rather it is because we are persuaded, as we are in the case of so many other forms of definitional reductionism (naturalism in ethics, instrumentalism and operationalism in the sciences, the causal theory of meaning, phenomenalism, and so on—the catalogue of philosophy's defeats), that there is system in the failures. Suppose we try to say, not using any mental concepts, what it is for a man to believe there is life on Mars. One line we could take is this: when a certain sound is produced in the man's presence ("Is there life on Mars?") he produces another ("Yes"). But of course this shows he believes there is life on Mars only if he understands English, his production of the sound was intentional, and was a response to the sounds as meaning something in English; and so on. For each discovered deficiency, we add a new proviso. Yet no matter how we patch and fit the nonmental conditions, we always find the need for an additional condition (provided he *notices, understands,* etc.) that is mental in character.[13]

A striking feature of attempts at definitional reduction is how little seems to hinge on the question of synonymy between definiens and definiendum. Of course, by imagining counterexamples we do discredit claims of synonymy. But the pattern of failure prompts a stronger conclusion: if we were to find an open sentence couched in behavioral terms and exactly coextensive with some mental predicate, nothing could reasonably persuade us that we had found it. We know too much about thought and behavior to trust exact and universal statements linking them. Beliefs and desires issue in behavior only as modified and mediated by further beliefs and desires, attitudes and attendings, without limit. Clearly this holism of the mental realm is a clue both to the autonomy and to the anomalous character of the mental.

These remarks apropos definitional behaviorism provide at best hints of why we should not expect nomological connections between the mental and the physical. The central case invites further consideration.

Lawlike statements are general statements that support counterfactual and subjunctive claims, and are supported by their instances. There is (in my view) no nonquestion-begging criterion of the lawlike, which is not to say there are no reasons in particular cases for a judgment. Lawlikeness is a matter of degree, which is not to deny that there may be cases beyond debate. And within limits set by the conditions of communication, there is room for much variation between individuals in the pattern of statements to which various degrees of nomologicality are assigned. In all these respects, nomologicality is much like analyticity, as one might expect since both are linked to meaning.

'All emeralds are green' is lawlike in that its instances confirm it, but 'all emeralds are grue' is not, for 'grue' means 'observed before time *t* and green, otherwise blue,' and if our observations were all made before *t* and uniformly revealed green emeralds, this would not be a reason to expect other emeralds to be blue. Nelson Goodman has suggested that this shows that some predicates, 'grue' for example, are unsuited to laws (and thus a criterion of suitable predicates could lead to a criterion of the lawlike). But it seems to me the anomalous character of 'All emeralds are grue' shows only that the predicates 'is an emerald' and 'is grue' are not suited to one another: grueness is not an inductive property of emeralds. Grueness *is* however an inductive property of entities of other sorts, for instance of emerires. (Something is an emerire if it is examined before *t* and is an emerald, and otherwise is a sapphire.) Not only is 'All emerires are grue' entailed by the conjunction of the lawlike statements 'All emeralds are green' and 'All sapphires are blue,' but there is no reason, as far as I can see, to reject the deliverance of intuition, that it is itself lawlike.[14] Nomological statements bring together predicates that we know a priori are made for each other—know, that is, independently of knowing whether the evidence supports a connection between them. 'Blue,' 'red,' and 'green' are made for emeralds, sapphires, and roses; 'grue,' 'bleen,' and 'gred' are made for sapphalds, emerires, and emeroses.

The direction in which the discussion seems headed is this: mental and physical predicates are not made for one another. In point of lawlikeness, psychophysical statements are more like 'All emeralds are grue' than like 'All emeralds are green.'

Before this claim is plausible, it must be seriously modified. The fact that emeralds examined before *t* are grue not only is no reason to believe all emeralds are grue; it is not even a reason (if we know the time) to believe *any* unobserved emeralds are grue. But if an event of a certain mental sort has usually been accompanied by an event of a certain physical sort, this often is a good reason to expect other cases to follow suit roughly in proportion. The generalizations that embody such practical wisdom are assumed to be only roughly true, or they are explicitly stated in probabilistic terms, or they are insulated from counterexample by generous escape clauses. Their importance lies mainly in the support they lend singular causal claims and related explanations of particular events. The support derives from the fact that such a generalization, however crude and vague, may provide good reason to believe that underlying the particular case there is a regularity that could be formulated sharply and without caveat.

In our daily traffic with events and actions that must be foreseen or understood, we perforce make use of the sketchy summary generalization, for we do not know a more accurate law, or if we do, we lack a description of the particular events in which we are interested that would show the relevance of the law. But there is an important distinction to be made within the category of the rude rule of thumb. On the one hand, there are generalizations whose positive instances give us reason to believe the generalization itself could be improved by adding further provisos and conditions stated in the same general vocabulary as the original generalization. Such a generalization points to the form and vocabulary of the finished law: we may say that it is a *homonomic* generalization. On the other hand there are generalizations which when instantiated may give us reason to believe there is a precise law at work, but one that can be stated only by shifting to a different vocabulary. We may call such generalizations *heteronomic*.

I suppose most of our practical lore (and science) is heteronomic. This is because a law can hope to be precise, explicit, and as exceptionless as possible only if it draws its concepts from a comprehensive closed theory. This ideal theory may or may not be deterministic, but it is if any true theory is. Within the physical sciences we do find homonomic generalizations, generalizations such that if the evidence supports them, we then have reason to believe they may be sharpened indefinitely by drawing upon further physical concepts: there is a theoretical asymptote of perfect coherence with all the evidence, perfect predictability (under the terms of the system), total explanation (again under the terms of the system). Or perhaps the ultimate theory is probabilistic, and the asymptote is less than perfection; but in that case there will be no better to be had.

Confidence that a statement is homonomic, correctible within its own conceptual domain, demands that it draw its concepts from a theory with strong constitutive elements. Here is the simplest possible illustration; if the lesson carries, it will be obvious that the simplification could be mended.

The measurement of length, weight, temperature, or time depends (among many other things, of course) on the existence in each case of a two-place relation that is transitive and asymmetric: warmer than, later than, heavier than, and so forth. Let us take the relation *longer than* as our example. The law or postulate of transitivity is this:

(L) $L(x,y)$ and $L(y,z) \rightarrow L(x,z)$

Unless this law (or some sophisticated variant) holds, we cannot easily make sense of the concept of length. There will be no way of assigning numbers to register even so much as ranking in length, let alone the more powerful demands of measurement on a ratio scale. And this remark goes not only for any three items directly involved in an intransitivity: it is easy to show (given a few more assumptions essential to measurement of length) that there is no consistent assignment of a ranking to any item unless (L) holds in full generality.

Clearly (L) alone cannot exhaust the import of 'longer than'—otherwise it would not differ from 'warmer than' or 'later than.' We must suppose there is some empirical content, however difficult to formulate in the available vocabulary, that distinguishes 'longer than' from the other two-place transitive predicates of measurement and on the basis of which we may assert that one thing is longer than another. Imagine this empirical content to be partly given by the predicate '$O(x,y)$'. So we have this "meaning postulate":

(M) $O(x,y) \rightarrow L(x,y)$

that partly interprets (L). But now (L) and (M) together yield an empirical theory of great strength, for together they entail that there do

not exist three objects a, b, and c such that $O(a,b)$, $O(b,c)$, and $O(c,a)$. Yet what is to prevent this happening if '$O(x,y)$' is a predicate we can ever, with confidence, apply? Suppose we *think* we observe an intransitive triad; what do we say? We could count (L) false, but then we would have no application for the concept of length. We could say (M) gives a wrong test for length; but then it is unclear what we thought was the *content* of the idea of one thing being longer than another. Or we could say that the objects under observation are not, as the theory requires, *rigid* objects. It is a mistake to think we are forced to accept some one of these answers. Concepts such as that of length are sustained in equilibrium by a number of conceptual pressures, and theories of fundamental measurement are distorted if we force the decision, among such principles as (L) and (M): analytic or synthetic. It is better to say the whole set of axioms, laws, or postulates for the measurement of length is partly constitutive of the idea of a system of macroscopic, rigid, physical objects. I suggest that the existence of lawlike statements in physical science depends upon the existence of constitutive (or synthetic a priori) laws like those of the measurement of length within the same conceptual domain.

Just as we cannot intelligibly assign a length to any object unless a comprehensive theory holds of objects of that sort, we cannot intelligibly attribute any propositional attitude to an agent except within the framework of a viable theory of his beliefs, desires, intentions, and decisions.

There is no assigning beliefs to a person one by one on the basis of his verbal behavior, his choices, or other local signs no matter how plain and evident, for we make sense of particular beliefs only as they cohere with other beliefs, with preferences, with intentions, hopes, fears, expectations, and the rest. It is not merely, as with the measurement of length, that each case tests a theory and depends upon it, but that the content of a propositional attitude derives from its place in the pattern.

Crediting people with a large degree of consistency cannot be counted mere charity: it is unavoidable if we are to be in a position to accuse them meaningfully of error and some degree of irrationality. Global confusion, like universal mistake, is unthinkable, not because imagination boggles, but because too much confusion leaves nothing to be confused about and massive error erodes the background of true belief against which alone failure can be construed. To appreciate the limits to the kind and amount of blunder and bad thinking we can intelligibly pin on others is to see once more the inseparability of the question what concepts a person commands and the question what he does with those concepts in the way of belief, desire, and intention. To the extent that we fail to discover a coherent and plausible pattern in the attitudes and actions of others we simply forego the chance of treating them as persons.

The problem is not bypassed but given center stage by appeal to explicit speech behavior. For we could not begin to decode a man's sayings if we could not make out his attitudes towards his sentences, such as holding, wishing, or wanting them to be true. Beginning from these attitudes, we must work out a theory of what he means, thus simultaneously giving content to his attitudes and to his words. In our need to make him make sense, we will try for a theory that finds him consistent, a believer of truths, and a lover of the good (all by our own lights, it goes without saying). Life being what it is, there will be no simple theory that fully meets these demands. Many theories will effect a more or less acceptable compromise, and between these theories there may be no objective grounds for choice.

The heteronomic character of general statements linking the mental and the physical traces back to this central role of translation in the description of all propositional attitudes, and to the indeterminacy of translation.[15] There are no strict psychophysical laws because of the disparate commitments of the mental and physical schemes. It is a feature of physical reality that physical change can be explained by laws that connect it with other changes and conditions physically described. It is a feature of the mental that the attribution of mental phenomena must be responsible to the background of reasons, beliefs, and intentions of the individual. There cannot be tight connections between the realms if each is to retain allegiance to its proper source of evidence. The nomological irreducibility of the mental does not derive merely from the seamless nature of the world of thought, preference and intention, for such interdependence is common to physical theory, and is compatible with there being a single right way of interpreting a man's attitudes without relativization to a scheme of translation. Nor is the irreducibility due simply to the possibility of many equally eligible schemes, for this is compatible with an arbitrary choice of one scheme

relative to which assignments of mental traits are made. The point is rather that when we use the concepts of belief, desire and the rest, we must stand prepared, as the evidence accumulates, to adjust our theory in the light of considerations of overall cogency: the constitutive ideal of rationality partly controls each phase in the evolution of what must be an evolving theory. An arbitrary choice of translation scheme would preclude such opportunistic tempering of theory; put differently, a right arbitrary choice of a translation manual would be of a manual acceptable in the light of all possible evidence, and this is a choice we cannot make. We must conclude, I think, that nomological slack between the mental and the physical is essential as long as we conceive of man as a rational animal.

III

The gist of the foregoing discussion, as well as its conclusion, will be familiar. That there is a categorial difference between the mental and the physical is a commonplace. It may seem odd that I say nothing of the supposed privacy of the mental, or the special authority an agent has with respect to his own propositional attitudes, but this appearance of novelty would fade if we were to investigate in more detail the grounds for accepting a scheme of translation. The step from the categorial difference between the mental and the physical to the impossibility of strict laws relating them is less common, but certainly not new. If there is a surprise, then, it will be to find the lawlessness of the mental serving to help establish the identity of the mental with that paradigm of the lawlike, the physical.

The reasoning is this. We are assuming, under the Principle of the Causal Dependence of the Mental, that some mental events at least are causes or effects of physical events; the argument applies only to these. A second Principle (of the Nomological Character of Causality) says that each true singular causal statement is backed by a strict law connecting events of kinds to which the events mentioned as cause and effect belong. Where there are rough, but homonomic, laws, there are laws drawing on concepts from the same conceptual domain and upon which there is no improving in point of precision and comprehensiveness. We urged in the last section that such laws occur in the physical sciences. Physical theory promises to provide a comprehensive closed system guaranteed to yield a standardized, unique description of every physical event couched in a vocabulary amenable to law.

It is not plausible that mental concepts alone can provide such a framework, simply because the mental does not, by our first principle, constitute a closed system. Too much happens to affect the mental that is not itself a systematic part of the mental. But if we combine this observation with the conclusion that no psychophysical statement is, or can be built into, a strict law, we have the Principle of the Anomalism of the Mental: there are no strict laws at all on the basis of which we can predict and explain mental phenomena.

The demonstration of identity follows easily. Suppose *m,* a mental event, caused *p,* a physical event; then under some description *m* and *p* instantiate a strict law. This law can only be physical, according to the previous paragraph. But if *m* falls under a physical law, it has a physical description; which is to say it is a physical event. An analogous argument works when a physical event causes a mental event. So every mental event that is causally related to a physical event is a physical event. In order to establish anomalous monism in full generality it would be sufficient to show that every mental event is cause or effect of some physical event; I shall not attempt this.

If one event causes another, there is a strict law which those events instantiate when properly described. But it is possible (and typical) to know of the singular causal relation without knowing the law or the relevant descriptions. Knowledge requires reasons, but these are available in the form of rough heteronomic generalizations, which are lawlike in that instances make it reasonable to expect other instances to follow suit without being lawlike in the sense of being indefinitely refinable. Applying these facts to knowledge of identities, we see that it is possible to know that a mental event is identical with some physical event without knowing which one (in the sense of being able to give it a unique physical description that brings it under a relevant law). Even if someone knew the entire physical history of the world, and every mental event were identical with a physical, it would not follow that he could predict or explain a single mental event (so described, of course).

Two features of mental events in their relation to the physical—causal dependence and nomological independence—combine, then, to dissolve what has often seemed a paradox, the efficacy of thought and purpose in the material world, and their freedom from law. When we portray events as perceivings, rememberings, decisions and actions, we necessarily locate them amid physical happenings through the relation of cause and effect; but that same mode of portrayal insulates mental events, as long as we do not change the idiom, from the strict laws that can in principle be called upon to explain and predict physical phenomena.

Mental events as a class cannot be explained by physical science; particular mental events can when we know particular identities. But the explanations of mental events in which we are typically interested relate them to other mental events and conditions. We explain a man's free actions, for example, by appeal to his desires, habits, knowledge and perceptions. Such accounts of intentional behavior operate in a conceptual framework removed from the direct reach of physical law by describing both cause and effect, reason and action, as aspects of a portrait of a human agent. The anomalism of the mental is thus a necessary condition for viewing action as autonomous. I conclude with a second passage from Kant:

> It is an indispensable problem of speculative philosophy to show that its illusion respecting the contradiction rests on this, that we think of man in a different sense and relation when we call him free, and when we regard him as subject to the laws of nature. . . . It must therefore show that not only can both of these very well co-exist, but that both must be thought *as necessarily united* in the same subject. . . . [16]

NOTES

1. I was helped and influenced by Daniel Bennett, Sue Larson, and Richard Rorty, who are not responsible for the result. My research was supported by the National Science Foundation and the Center for Advanced Study in the Behavioral Sciences.

2. *Fundamental Principles of the Metaphysics of*

Morals, trans. T. K. Abbott (London, 1909), pp. 75–76.

3. These claims are defended in my "Actions, Reasons and Causes," *The Journal of Philosophy,* LX (1963), pp. 685–700 and in "Agency," a paper forthcoming in the proceedings of the November, 1968, colloqui-

um on Agent, Action, and Reason at the University of Western Ontario, London, Canada [in *Agent, Action, and Reason,* edited by Robert Binkley, Richard Bronaugh, and Ausonio Marras (Oxford: Basil Blackwell, 1971), pp. 3–25].

4. In "Causal Relations," *The Journal of Philosophy,* LXIV (1967), pp. 691–703, I elaborate on the view of causality assumed here. The stipulation that the laws be deterministic is stronger than required by the reasoning, and will be relaxed.

5. The point depends on assuming that mental events may intelligibly be said to have a location; but it is an assumption that must be true if an identity theory is, and here I am not trying to prove the theory but to formulate it.

6. I am indebted to Lee Bowie for emphasizing this difficulty.

7. Charles Taylor, "Mind-Body Identity, a Side Issue?" *The Philosophical Review,* LXXVI (1967), p. 202.

8. J. J. C. Smart, "Sensations and Brain Processes," *The Philosophical Review,* LXVIII (1959), pp. 141–56. The quoted passages are on pp. 163–65 of the reprinted version in *The Philosophy of Mind,* ed. V. C. Chappell (Englewood Cliffs, N.J., 1962). For another example, see David K. Lewis, "An Argument for the Identity Theory," *The Journal of Philosophy,* LXIII (1966), pp. 17–25. Here the assumption is made explicit when Lewis takes events as universals (p. 17, footnotes 1 and 2). I do not suggest that Smart and Lewis are confused, only that their way of stating the identity theory tends to obscure the distinction between particular events and kinds of events on which the formulation of my theory depends.

9. Jaegwon Kim, "On the Psycho-Physical Identity Theory," *American Philosophical Quarterly,* III (1966), p. 231.

10. Ibid., pp. 227–28. Richard Brandt and Jaegwon Kim propose roughly the same criterion in "The Logic of the Identity Theory," *The Journal of Philosophy* LIV (1967), pp. 515–37. They remark that on their conception of event identity, the identity theory "makes a stronger claim than merely that there is a pervasive phenomenal-physical correlation" (p. 518). I do not discuss the stronger claim.

11. Anomalous monism is more or less explicitly recognized as a possible position by Herbert Feigl, "The 'Mental' and the 'Physical,' " in *Concepts, Theories and the Mind–Body Problem,* vol. II, *Minnesota Studies in the Philosophy of Science* (Minneapolis, 1958); Sydney Shoemaker, "Ziff's Other Minds," *The Journal of Philosophy,* LXII (1965), p. 589; David Randall Luce, "Mind-Body Identity and Psycho-Physical Correlation," *Philosophical Studies,* XVII (1966), pp. 1–7; Charles Taylor, op. cit., p. 207. Something like my position is tentatively accepted by Thomas Nagel, "Physicalism," *The Philosophical Review,* LXXIV (1965), pp. 339–56, and briefly endorsed by P. F. Strawson in *Freedom and the Will,* ed. D. F. Pears (London, 1963), pp. 63–67.

12. The point that substitutivity of identity fails in the context of explanation is made in connection with the present subject by Norman Malcolm, "Scientific Materialism and the Identity Theory," *Dialogue,* III (1964–65), pp. 123–24. See also my "Actions, Reasons and Causes," *The Journal of Philosophy,* LX (1963), pp. 696–99 and "The Individuation of Events" in *Essays in Honor of Carl G. Hempel,* ed. N. Rescher, et al. (Dordrecht, 1969).

13. The theme is developed in Roderick Chisholm, *Perceiving* (Ithaca, New York, 1957), chap. 11.

14. This view is accepted by Richard C. Jeffrey, "Goodman's Query," *The Journal of Philosophy,* LXII (1966), p. 286 ff., John R. Wallace, "Goodman, Logic, Induction," same journal and issue, p. 318, and John M. Vickers, "Characteristics of Projectible Predicates," *The Journal of Philosophy,* LXIV (1967), p. 285. On pp. 328–29 and 286–87 of these journal issues respectively Goodman disputes the lawlikeness of statements like "All emerires are grue." I cannot see, however, that he meets the point of my "Emeroses by Other Names," *The Journal of Philosophy,* LXIII (1966), pp. 778–80.

15. The influence of W. V. Quine's doctrine of the indeterminacy of translation, as in chap. 2 of *Word and Object* (Cambridge, Mass., 1960), is, I hope, obvious. In § 45 Quine develops the connection between translation and the propositional attitudes, and remarks that "Brentano's thesis of the irreducibility of intentional idioms is of a piece with the thesis of indeterminacy of translation" (p. 221).

16. Op. cit., p. 76.

18 | Special Sciences (or: The Disunity of Science as a Working Hypothesis)

Jerry A. Fodor

A typical thesis of positivistic philosophy of science is that all true theories in the special sciences should reduce to physical theories in the long run. This is intended to be an empirical thesis, and part of the evidence which supports it is provided by such scientific successes as the molecular theory of heat and the physical explanation of the chemical bond. But the philosophical popularity of the reductivist program cannot be explained by reference to these achievements alone. The development of science has witnessed the proliferation of specialized disciplines at least as often as it has witnessed their reduction to physics, so the widespread enthusiasm for reduction can hardly be a mere induction over its past successes.

I think that many philosophers who accept reductivism do so primarily because they wish to endorse the generality of physics vis-à-vis the special sciences: roughly, the view that all events which fall under the laws of any science are physical events and hence fall under the laws of physics.[1] For such philosophers, saying that physics is basic science and saying that theories in the special sciences must rede to physical theories have seemed to be two ways of saying the same thing, so that the latter doctrine has come to be a standard construal of the former.

In what follows, I shall argue that this is a considerable confusion. What has traditionally been called 'the unity of science' is a much stronger, and much less plausible, thesis than the generality of physics. If this is true it is important. Though reductionism is an empirical doctrine, it is intended to play a regulative role in scientific practice. Reducibility to physics is taken to be a *constraint* upon the acceptability of theories in the special sciences, with the curious consequence that the more the special sciences succeed, the more they ought to disappear. Methodological problems about psychology, in particular, arise in just this way: the assumption that the subject-matter of psychology is part of the subject-matter of physics is taken to imply that psychological theories must reduce to physical theories, and it is this latter principle that

makes the trouble. I want to avoid the trouble by challenging the inference.

I

Reductivism is the view that all the special sciences reduce to physics. The sense of 'reduce to' is, however, proprietary. It can be characterized as follows.[2]

Let

(1) $S_1x \rightarrow S_2x$

be a law of the special science S. ((1) is intended to be read as something like 'all S_1 situations bring about S_2 situations.' I assume that a science is individuated largely by reference to its typical predicates, hence that if S is a special science 'S_1' and 'S_2' are not predicates of basic physics. I also assume that the 'all' which quantifies laws of the special sciences needs to be taken with a grain of salt; such laws are typically *not* exceptionless. This is a point to which I shall return at length.) A necessary and sufficient condition of the reduction of (1) to a law of physics is that the formulae (2) and (3) be laws, and a necessary and sufficient condition of the reduction of S to physics is that all its laws be so reducible.[3]

(2a) $S_1x \leftrightarrows P_1x$
(2b) $S_2x \leftrightarrows P_2x$
(3) $P_1x \rightarrow P_2x.$

'P_1' and 'P_2' are supposed to be predicates of physics, and (3) is supposed to be a physical law. Formulae like (2) are often called 'bridge' laws. Their characteristic feature is that they contain predicates of both the reduced and the reducing science. Bridge laws like (2) are thus contrasted with 'proper' laws like (1) and (3). The upshot of the remarks so far is that the reduction of a science requires that any formula which appears as the antecedent or consequent of one of its proper laws must appear as the reduced formula in some bridge law or other.[4]

Several points about the connective '$\rightarrow$' are

From *Synthese* 28:97–115, 1974. Reprinted with permission of the author and of Kluwer Academic Publishers.

in order. First, whatever other properties that connective may have, it is universally agreed that it must be transitive. This is important because it is usually assumed that the reduction of some of the special sciences proceeds via bridge laws which connect their predicates with those of intermediate reducing theories. Thus, psychology is presumed to reduce to physics via, say, neurology, biochemistry, and other local stops. The present point is that this makes no difference to the logic of the situation so long as the transitivity of '$\rightarrow$' is assumed. Bridge laws which connect the predicates of S to those of S^* will satisfy the constraints upon the reduction of S to physics so long as there are other bridge laws which, directly or indirectly, connect the predicates of S^* to physical predicates.

There are, however, quite serious open questions about the interpretations of '$\rightarrow$' in bridge laws. What turns on these questions is the respect in which reductivism is taken to be a physicalist thesis.

To begin with, if we read '$\rightarrow$' as 'brings about' or 'causes' in proper laws, we will have to have some other connective for bridge laws, since bringing about and causing are presumably *asymmetric*, while bridge laws express symmetric relations. Moreover, if '$\rightarrow$' in bridge laws is interpreted as any relation other than identity, the truth of reductivism will only guaranty the truth of a weak version of physicalism, and this would fail to express the underlying ontological bias of the reductivist program.

If bridge laws are not identity statements, then formulae like (2) claim at most that, by law, x's satisfaction of a P predicate and x's satisfaction of an S predicate are causally correlated. It follows from this that it is nomologically necessary that S and P predicates apply to the same things (i.e., that S predicates apply to a subset of the things that P predicates apply to). But, of course, this is compatible with a non-physicalist ontology since it is compatible with the possibility that x's satisfying S should not itself *be* a physical event. On this interpretation, the truth of reductivism does *not* guarantee the generality of physics vis-à-vis the special sciences since there are some events (satisfactions of S predicates) which fall in the domains of a special science (S) but not in the domain of physics. (One could imagine, for example, a doctrine according to which physical and psychological predicates are both held to apply to organisms, but where it is denied that the event which consists of an organism's satisfying a psychological predicate is, in any sense, a physical event. The up-shot would be a kind of psychophysical dualism of a non-Cartesian variety; a dualism of events and/or properties rather than substances.)

Given these sorts of considerations, many philosophers have held that bridge laws like (2) ought to be taken to express contingent event identities, so that one would read (2a) in some such fashion as 'every event which consists of x's satisfying S_1 is identical to some event which consists of x's satisfying P_1 and vice versa.' On this reading, the truth of reductivism would entail that every event that falls under any scientific law is a physical event, thereby simultaneously expressing the ontological bias of reductivism and guaranteeing the generality of physics vis-à-vis the special sciences.

If the bridge laws express event identities, and if every event that falls under the proper laws of a special science falls under a bridge law, we get the truth of a doctrine that I shall call 'token physicalism.' Token physicalism is simply the claim that all the events that the sciences talk about are physical events. There are three things to notice about token physicalism.

First, it is weaker than what is usually called 'materialism.' Materialism claims *both* that token physicalism is true *and* that every event falls under the laws of some science or other. One could therefore be a token physicalist without being a materialist, though I don't see why anyone would bother.

Second, token physicalism is weaker than what might be called 'type physicalism,' the doctrine, roughly, that every *property* mentioned in the laws of any science is a physical property. Token physicalism does not entail type physicalism because the contingent identity of a pair of events presumably does not guarantee the identity of the properties whose instantiation constitutes the events; not even where the event identity is nomologically necessary. On the other hand, if every event is the instantiation of a property, then type physicalism does ential token physicalism: two events will be identical when they consist of the instantiation of the same property by the same individual at the same time.

Third, token physicalism is weaker than reductivism. Since this point is, in a certain sense, the burden of the argument to follow, I shan't labour it here. But, as a first approximation, reductivism is the conjunction of token physicalism with the assumption that there are natural kind predicate in an ideally completed physics which correspond to each natural kind predicates in any ideally completed special science. It will be one of my morals that the truth of reductivism cannot be inferred from the assumption that token physicalism is true. Reductivism is a sufficient, but not a necessary, condition for token physicalism.

In what follows, I shall assume a reading of reductivism which entails token physicalism. Bridge laws thus state nomologically necessary contingent event identities, and a reduction of psychology to neurology would entail that any event which consists of the instantiation of a psychological property is identical with some event which consists of the instantiation of some neurological property.

Where we have got to is this: reductivism entails the generality of physics in at least the sense that any event which falls within the universe of discourse of a special science will also fall within the universe of discourse of physics. Moreover, any prediction which follows from the laws of a special science and a statement of initial conditions will also follow from a theory which consists of physics and the bridge laws, together with the statement of initial conditions. Finally, since 'reduces to' is supposed to be an asymmetric relation, it will also turn out that physics is *the* basic science; that is, if reductivism is true, physics is the only science that is general in the sense just specified. I now want to argue that reductivism is too strong a constraint upon the unity of science, but that the relevantly weaker doctrine will preserve the desired consequences of reductivism: token physicalism, the generality of physics, and its basic position among the sciences.

II

Every science implies a taxonomy of the events in its universe of discourse. In particular, every science employs a descriptive vocabulary of theoretical and observation predicates such that events fall under the laws of the science by virtue of satisfying those predicates. Patently, not every true description of an event is a description in such a vocabulary. For example, there are a large number of events which consist of things having been transported to a distance of less than three miles from the Eiffel Tower. I take it, however, that there is no science which contains 'is transported to a distance of less than three miles from the Eiffel Tower' as part of its descriptive vocabulary. Equivalently, I take it that there is no natural law which applies to events in virtue of their being instantiations of the property *is transported to a distance of less than three miles from the Eiffel Tower* (though I suppose it is conceivable that there is some law that applies to events in virtue of their being instantiations of some distinct but co-extensive property). By way of abbreviating these facts, I shall say that the property *is transported . . .* does not determine a *natural kind,* and that predicates which express that property are not natural kind predicates.

If I knew what a law is, and if I believed that scientific theories consist just of bodies of laws, then I could say that P is a natural kind predicate relative to S iff S contains proper laws of the form $P_x \rightarrow \alpha_x$ or $\alpha_x \rightarrow P_x$; roughly, the natural kind predicates of a science are the ones whose terms are the bound variables in its proper laws. I am inclined to say this even in my present state of ignorance, accepting the consequence that it makes the murky notion of a natural kind viciously dependent on the equally murky notions *law* and *theory.* There is no firm footing here. If we disagree about what is a natural kind, we will probably also disagree about what is a law, and for the same reasons. I don't know how to break out of this circle, but I think that there are interesting things to say about which circle we are in.

For example, we can now characterize the respect in which reductivism is too strong a construal of the doctrine of the unity of science. If reductivism is true, then *every* natural kind is, or is co-extensive with, a physical natural kind. (Every natural kind *is* a physical natural kind if bridge laws express property identities, and every natural kind is co-extensive with a physical natural kind if bridge laws express event identities.) This follows immediately from the reductivist premise that every predicate which appears as the antecedent or consequent of a law of the special sciences must appear as one of the reduced predicates in some bridge, together with the assumption that the natural kind predicates are the ones whose terms are the bound variables in proper laws. If, in short, some physical law is related to each law of a special science in the way that (3) is related to (1), then every natural kind predicate of a special science is related to a natural kind predicate of physics in the way that (2) relates 'S_1' and 'S_2' to 'P_1' and 'P_2'.

I now want to suggest some reasons for believing that this consequence of reductivism is intolerable. These are not supposed to be knock-down reasons; they couldn't be, given that the question whether reductivism is too strong is finally an *empirical* question. (The world could turn out to be such that every natural kind corresponds to a physical natural kind, just as it could turn out to be such that the property *is transported to a distance of less than three miles from the Eiffel Tower* determines a natural kind in, say, hydrodynamics. It's just that, as things stand, it seems very unlikely that the world *will* turn out to be either of these ways.)

The reason it is unlikely that every natural kind corresponds to a physical natural kind is just that (a) interesting generalizations (e.g., counter-factual supporting generalizations) can often be made about events whose physical descriptions have nothing in common, (b) it is often the case that *whether* the physical descriptions of the events subsumed by these generalizations have anything in common is, in an obvious sense, entirely irrelevant to the truth of the gencralizations, or to their interestingness, or to their degree of confirmation or, indeed, to any of their epistemologically important properties, and (c) the special sciences are very much in the business of making generalizations of this kind.

I take it that these remarks are obvious to the point of self-certification; they leap to the eye as soon as one makcs thc (apparently radical) move of taking the special sciences at all seriously. Suppose, for example, that Gresham's 'law' really is true. (If one doesn't like Gresham's law, then any true generalization of any conceivable future economics will probably do as well.) Gresham's law says something about what will happen in monetary exchanges under certain conditions. I am willing to believe that physics is general *in the sense that it implies that any event which consists of a monetary exchange* (hence any event which falls under Gresham's law) *has a true description in the vocabulary of physics and in virtue of which it falls under the laws of physics*. But banal considerations suggest that a description which covers all such events must be wildly disjunctive. Some monetary exchanges involve strings of wampum. Some involve dollar bills. And some involve signing one's name to a check. What are the chances that a disjunction of physical predicates which covers all these events (i.e., a disjunctive predicate which can form the right hand side of a bridge law of the form '*x* is a monetary exchange $\leftrightarrows \ldots$') expresses a physical natural

kind? In particular, what are the chances that such a predicate forms the antecedent or consequent of some proper law of physics? The point is that monetary exchanges have interesting things in common; Gresham's law, if true, says what one of these interesting things is. But what is interesting about monetary exchanges is surely not their commonalities under *physical* description. A natural kind like a monetary exchange *could* turn out to be co-extensive with a physical natural kind; but if it did, that would be an accident on a cosmic scale.

In fact, the situation for reductivism is still worse than the discussion thus far suggests. For, reductivism claims not only that all natural kinds are co-extensive with physical natural kinds, but that the co-extensions are nomologically necessary: bridge laws are *laws*. So, if Gresham's law is true, it follows that there is a (bridge) law of nature such that '*x* is a monetary exchange $\rightleftarrows$ *x* is *P*', where *P* is a term for a physical natural kind. But, surely, there is no such law. If there were, then *P* would have to cover not only all the systems of monetary exchange that there *are*, but also all the systems of monetary exchange that there *could be*; a law must succeed with the counterfactuals. What physical predicate is a candidate for '*P*' in '*x* is a nomologically possible monetary exchange iff P_x'?

To summarize: an immortal econophysicist might, when the whole show is over, find a predicate in physics that was, in brute fact, co-extensive with 'is a monetary exchange'. If physics is general—if the ontological biases of reductivism are true—then there must *be* such a predicate. But (a) to paraphrase a remark Donald Davidson made in a slightly different context, nothing but brute enumeration could convince us of this brute co-extensivity, and (b) there would seem to be no chance at all that the physical predicate employed in stating the co-extensivity is a natural kind term, and (c) there is still less chance that the co-extension would be lawful (i.e., that it would hold not only for the nomologically possible world that turned out to be real, but for any nomologically possible world at all).

I take it that the preceding discussion strongly suggests that economics is not reducible to physics in the proprietary sense of reduction involved in claims for the unity of science. There is, I suspect, nothing special about economics in this respect; the reasons why economics is unlikely to reduce to physics are paralleled by those which suggest that psychology is unlikely to reduce to neurology.

If psychology is reducible to neurology, then for every psychological natural kind predicate there is a co-extensive neurological natural kind predicate, and the generalization which states this co-extension is a law. Clearly, many psychologists believe something of the sort. There are departments of 'psycho-biology' or 'psychology and brain science' in universities throughout the world whose very existence is an institutionalized gamble that such lawful co-extensions can be found. Yet, as has been frequently remarked in recent discussions of materialism, there are good grounds for hedging these bets. There are no firm data for any but the grossest correspondence between types of psychological states and types of neurological states, and it is entirely possible that the nervous system of higher organisms characteristically achieves a given psychological end by a wide variety of neurological means. If so, then the attempt to pair neurological structures with psychological functions is foredoomed. Physiological psychologists of the stature of Karl Lashley have held precisely this view.

The present point is that the reductivist program in psychology is, in any event, *not* to be defended on ontological grounds. Even if (token) psychological events are (token) neurological events, it does not follow that the natural kind predicates of psychology are co-extensive with the natural kind predicates of any other discipline (including physics). That is, the assumption that every psychological event is a physical event does not guaranty that physics (or, *a fortiori,* any other discipline more general than psychology) can provide an appropriate vocabulary for psychological theories. I emphasize this point because I am convinced that the make-or-break commitment of many physiological psychologists to the reductivist program stems precisely from having confused that program with (token) physicalism.

What I have been doubting is that there are neurological natural kinds co-extensive with psychological natural kinds. What seems increasingly clear is that, even if there is such a co-extension, it cannot be lawlike. For, it seems increasingly likely that there are nomologically possible systems other than organisms (namely, automata) which satisfy natural kind predicates in psychology, and which satisfy no neurological predicates at all. Now, as Putnam has emphasized, if there are any such systems, then there are probably vast numbers, since equivalent automata can be made out of practically anything. If this observation is correct, then there can be no serious hope that the class of automata whose psychology is effectively identical to that of some organism can be described by *physical* natural kind predicates (though, of course, if token physicalisms is true, that class can be picked out by some physical predicate or other). The upshot is that the classical formulation of the unity of science is at the mercy of progress in the field of computer simulation. This is, of course, simply to say that that formulation was too strong. The unity of science was intended to be an empirical hypothesis, defeasible by possible scientific findings. But no one had it in mind that it should be defeated by Newell, Shaw and Simon.

I have thus far argued that psychological reductivism (the doctrine that every psychological natural kind is, or is co-extensive with, a neurological natural kind) is not equivalent to, and cannot be inferred from, token physicalism (the doctrine that every psychological event is a neurological event). It may, however, be argued that one might as well take the doctrines to be equivalent since the only possible *evidence* one could have for token physicalism would also be evidence for reductivism: namely, the discovery of type-to-type psychophysical correlations.

A moment's consideration shows, however, that this argument is not well taken. If type-to-type psychophysical correlations would be evidence for token physicalism, so would correlations of other specifiable kinds.

We have type-to-type correlations where, for every *n*-tuple of events that are of the same psychological kind, there is a correlated *n*-tuple of events that are of the same neurological kind. Imagine a world in which such correlations are *not* forthcoming. What is found, instead, is that for every *n*-tuple of type identical psychological events, there is a spatiotemporally correlated *n*-tuple of type *distinct* neurological events. That is, every psychological event is paired with some neurological event or other, but psychological events of the same kind may be paired with neurological events of different kinds. My present point is that such pairings would provide as much support for token physicalism as type-to-type pairings do *so long as we are able to show that the type distinct neurological events paired with a given kind of psychological event are identical in respect of whatever properties are relevant to type-identification in psy-*

chology. Suppose, for purposes of explication, that psychological events are type identified by reference to their behavioral consequences.[5] Then what is required of all the neurological events paired with a class of type homogeneous psychological events is only that they be identical in respect of their behavioral consequences. To put it briefly, type identical events do not, of course, have *all* their properties in common, and type distinct events must nevertheless be identical in *some* of their properties. The empirical confirmation of token physicalism does not depend on showing that the neurological counterparts of type identical psychological events are themselves type identical. What needs to be shown is only that they are identical in respect of those properties which determine which kind of *psychological* event a given event is.

Could we have evidence that an otherwise heterogeneous set of neurological events have these kinds of properties in common? Of course we could. The neurological theory might itself explain why an *n*-tuple of neurologically type distinct events are identical in their behavioral consequences, or, indeed, in respect of any of indefinitely many other such relational properties. And, if the neurological theory failed to do so, some science more basic than neurology might succeed.

My point in all this is, once again, not that correlations between type homogeneous psychological states and type heterogeneous neurological states would prove that token physicalism is true. It is only that such correlations might give us as much reason to be token physicalists as type-to-type correlations would. If this is correct, then the epistemological arguments from token physicalism to reductivism must be wrong.

It seems to me (to put the point quite generally) that the classical construal of the unity of science has really misconstrued the *goal* of scientific reduction. The point of reduction is *not* primarily to find some natural kind predicate of physics co-extensive with each natural kind predicate of a reduced science. It is, rather, to explicate the physical mechanisms whereby events conform to the laws of the special sciences. I have been arguing that there is no logical or epistemological reason why success in the second of these projects should require success in the first, and that the two are likely to come apart *in fact* wherever the physical mechanisms whereby events conform to a law of the special sciences are heterogeneous.

III

I take it that the discussion thus far shows that reductivism is probably too strong a construal of the unity of science; on the one hand, it is incompatible with probable results in the special sciences, and, on the other, it is more than we need to assume if what we primarily want is just to be good token physicalists. In what follows, I shall try to sketch a liberalization of reductivism which seems to me to be just strong enough in these respects. I shall then give a couple of independent reasons for supposing that the revised doctrine may be the right one.

The problem all along has been that there is an open empirical possibility that what corresponds to the natural kind predicates of a reduced science may be a heterogeneous and unsystematic disjunction of predicates in the reducing science, and we do not want the unity of science to be prejudiced by this possibility. Suppose, then, that we allow that bridge statements may be of the form

$$(4) \quad S_x \rightleftarrows P_1 x \vee P_2 x \vee \ldots \vee P_n x,$$

where '$P_1 \vee P_2 \vee \ldots \vee P_n$' is *not* a natural kind predicate in the reducing science. I take it that this is tantamount to allowing that at least some 'bridge laws' may, in fact, not turn out to be laws, since I take it that a necessary condition on a universal generalization being lawlike is that the predicates which constitute its antecedent and consequent should pick out natural kinds. I am thus supposing that it is enough, for purposes of the unity of science, that every law of the special sciences should be reducible to physics by bridge statements which express true empirical generalizations. Bearing in mind that bridge statements are to be construed as a species of identity statements, (4) will be read as something like 'every event which consists of *x*'s satisfying *S* is identical with some event which consists of *x*'s satisfying some or other predicate belonging to the disjunction '$P_1 \vee P_2 \vee \ldots \vee P_n$'.'

Now, in cases of reduction where what corresponds to (2) is not a law, what corresponds to (3) will not be either, and for the same reason. Namely, the predicates appearing in the antecedent or consequent will, by hypothesis, not be natural kind predicates. Rather, what we will have is something that looks like (5) (see next page).

That is, the antecedent and consequent of the reduced law will each be connected with a disjunction of predicates in the reducing science, and, if the reduced law is exceptionless, there will be laws of the reducing science which connect the satisfaction of each member of the disjunction associated with the antecedent to the satisfaction of some member of the disjunction associated with the consequent. That is, if $S_1x \to S_2x$ is

(5) Law of special science X:

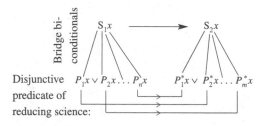

exceptionless, then there must be some proper law of the reducing science which either states or entails that $P_1x \to P^*$ for some P^*, and similarly for P_2x through P_nx. Since there must be such laws, it follows that each disjunct of '$P_1 \vee P_2 \vee \ldots \vee P_n$' is a natural kind predicate, as is each disjunct of '$P_1^* \vee P_2^* \vee \ldots \vee P_n^*$'.

This, however, is where push comes to shove. For, it might be argued that if each disjunct of the P disjunction is lawfully connected to some disjunct of the P^* disjunction, it follows that (6) is itself a law.

(6) $P_1x \vee P_2x \vee \ldots \vee P_nx \to P_1^* x \vee P_2^*x \vee \ldots \vee P_n^*x.$

The point would be that (5) gives us $P_1x \to P_2^*x$, $P_2x \to P_m^*x$, etc., and the argument from a premise of the form $(P \supset R)$ and $(Q \supset S)$ to a conclusion of the form $(P \vee Q) \supset (R \vee S)$ is valid.

What I am inclined to say about this is that it just shows that 'it's a law that — ' defines a nontruth functional context (or, equivalently for these purposes, that not all truth functions of natural kind predicates are themselves natural kind predicates). In particular, that one may not argue from 'it's a law that P brings about R' and 'it's a law that Q brings about S' to 'it's a law that P or Q brings about R or S'. (Though, of course, the argument from those premises to 'P or Q brings about R or S' *simpliciter* is fine.) I think, for example, that it is a law that the irradiation of green plants by sunlight causes carbohydrate synthesis, and I think that it is a law that

friction causes heat, but I do not think that it is a law that (either the irradiation of green plants by sunlight or friction) causes (either carbohydrate synthesis or heat). Correspondingly, I doubt that 'is either carbohydrate synthesis or heat' is plausibly taken to be a natural kind predicate.

It is not strictly mandatory that one should agree with all this, but one denies it at a price. In particular, if one allows the full range of truth functional arguments inside the context 'it's a law that — ', then one gives up the possibility of identifying the natural kind predicates of a science with those predicates which appear as the antecedents or the consequents of its proper laws. (Thus (6) would be a proper law of physics which fails to satisfy that condition.) One thus inherits the need for an alternative construal of the notion of a natural kind, and I don't know what that alternative might be like.

The upshot seems to be this. If we do not require that bridge statements must be laws, then either some of the generalizations to which the laws of special sciences reduce are not themselves lawlike, or some laws are not formulable in terms of natural kinds. Whichever way one takes (5), the important point is that it is weaker than standard reductivism: it does not require correspondences between the natural kinds of the reduced and the reducing science. Yet it is physicalistic on the same assumption that makes standard reductivism physicalistic (namely, that the bridge statements express true token identities). But these are precisely the properties that we wanted a revised account of the unity of science to exhibit.

I now want to give two reasons for thinking that this construal of the unity of science is right. First, it allows us to see how the laws of the special sciences could reasonably have exceptions, and, second, it allows us to see why there are special sciences at all. These points in turn.

Consider, again, the model of reduction implicit in (2) and (3). I assume that the laws of basic science are strictly exceptionless, and I assume that it is common knowledge that the laws of the special sciences are not. But now we have a painful dilemma. Since '$\to$' expresses a relation (or relations) which must be transitive, (1) can have exceptions only if the bridge laws do. But if the bridge laws have exceptions, reductivism loses its ontological bite, since we can no longer say that every event which consists of the instantiation of an S predicate is identical with some event which consists of the instantiation of a P predicate. In short, given the reductionist model, we cannot consistently assume that the bridge laws and the basic laws are exceptionless while assuming that the special laws are not. But we cannot accept the violation of the bridge laws unless we are willing to vitiate the ontological claim that is the main point of the reductivist program.

We can get out of this (*salve* the model) in one of two ways. We can give up the claim that the special laws have exceptions or we can give up the claim that the basic laws are exceptionless. I suggest that both alternatives are undesirable. The first because it flies in the face of fact. There is just no chance at all that the true, counterfactual supporting generalizations of, say, psychology, will turn out to hold in strictly each and every condition where their antecedents are satisfied. Even where the spirit is willing, the flesh is often weak. There are always going to be behavioral lapses which are physiologically explicable but which are uninteresting from the point of view of psychological theory. The second alternative is only slightly better. It may, after all, turn out that the laws of basic science have exceptions. But the question arises whether one wants the unity of science to depend upon the assumption that they do.

On the account summarized in (5), however, everything works out satisfactorily. A nomologically sufficient condition for an exception to $S_1x \rightarrow S_2x$ is that the bridge statements should identify some occurrence of the satisfaction of S_1 with an occurrence of the satisfaction of a P predicate which is not itself lawfully connected to the satisfaction of any P^* predicate. (I.e., suppose S_1 is connected to a P' such that there is no law which connects P' to any predicate which bridge statements associate with S_2. Then any instantiation of S_1 which is contingently identical to an instantiation of P' will be an event which constitutes an exception to $S_1x \rightarrow S_2x$.) Notice that, in this case, we need assume no exceptions to the laws of the *reducing* science since, by hypothesis, (6) *is not a law*.

In fact, strictly speaking, (6) has no status in the reduction at all. It is simply what one gets when one universally quantifies a formula whose antecedent is the physical disjunction corresponding to S_1 and whose consequent is the physical disjunction corresponding to S_2. As such, it will be true when $S_1 \rightarrow S_2$ is exceptionless and false otherwise. What does the work of expressing the physical mechanisms whereby n-tuples of events conform, or fail to conform, to $S_1 \rightarrow S_2$ is not (6) but the laws

which severally relate elements of the disjunction $P_1 \vee P_2 \vee \ldots \vee P_n$ to elements of the disjunction $P_1^* \vee P_2^* \vee \ldots \vee P_n^*$. When there *is* a law which relates an event that satisfies one of the P disjuncts to an event which satisfies one of the P^* disjuncts, the pair of events so related conforms to $S_1 \rightarrow S_2$. When an event which satisfies a P predicate is *not* related by law to an event which satisfies a P^* predicate, that event will constitute an exception to $S_1 \rightarrow S_2$. The point is that none of the laws which effect these several connections need themselves have exceptions in order that $S_1 \rightarrow S_2$ should do so.

To put this discussion less technically: we could, if we liked, *require* the taxonomies of the special sciences to correspond to the taxonomy of physics by insisting upon distinctions between the natural kinds postulated by the former wherever they turn out to correspond to distinct natural kinds in the latter. This would *make* the laws of the special sciences exceptionless if the laws of basic science are. But it would also loose us precisely the generalizations which we want the special sciences to express. (If economics were to posit as many *kinds* of monetary systems as there are kinds of physical realizations of monetary systems, then the generalizations of economics *would* be exceptionless. But, presumably, only vacuously so, since there would be no generalizations left to state. Graham's law, for example, would have to be formulated as a vast, open disjunction about what happens in monetary system$_1$ or monetary system$_n$ under conditions which would themselves defy uniform characterization. We would not be able to say what happens in monetary systems *tourt court* since, by hypothesis, 'is a monetary system' corresponds to no natural kind predicate of physics.)

In fact, what we do is precisely the reverse. We allow the generalizations of the special sciences to *have* exceptions, thus preserving the natural kinds to which the generalizations apply. But since we know that the *physical* descriptions of the natural kinds may be quite heterogeneous, and since we know that the physical mechanisms which connect the satisfaction of the antecedents of such generalizations to the satisfaction of their consequents may be equally diverse, we expect both that there will be exceptions to the generalizations and that these exceptions will be 'explained away' at the level of the reducing science. This is one of the respects in which physics really is assumed to be bedrock science; exceptions to *its* generalizations (if there are any) had better be random, because there is nowhere 'further down' to go in explaining the mechanism whereby the exceptions occur.

This brings us to why there are special sciences at all. Reducitivism as we remarked at the outset, flies in the face of the facts about the scientific institution: the existence of a vast and interleaved conglomerate of special scientific disciplines which often appear to proceed with only the most token acknowledgment of the constraint that their theories must turn out to be physics 'in the long run.' I mean that the acceptance of this constraint, *in practice,* often plays little or no role in the validation of theories. Why is this so? Presumably, the reductivist answer must be *entirely* epistemological. If only physical particles weren't so small (if only brains were on the *out*side, where one can get a look at them), *then* we would do physics instead of palentology (neurology instead of psychology; psychology instead of economics; and so on down). There is an epistemological reply; namely, that even if brains were out where they can be looked *at,* as things now stand, we wouldn't know what to look *for:* we lack the appropriate theoretical apparatus for the psychological taxonomy of neurological events.

If it turns out that the functional decomposition of the nervous system corresponds to its neurological (anatomical, biochemical, physical) decomposition, then there are only epistemological reasons for studying the former instead of the latter. But suppose there is no such correspondence? Suppose the functional organization of the nervous system cross-cuts its neurological organization (so that quite different neurological structures can subserve identical psychological functions across times or across organisms). Then the existence of psychology depends not on the fact that neurons are so sadly small, but rather on the fact that neurology does not posit the natural kinds that psychology requires.

I am suggesting, roughly, that there are special sciences not because of the nature of our epistemic relation to the world, but because of the way the world is put together: not all natural kinds (not all the classes of things and events about which there are important, counterfactual supporting generalizations to make) are, or correspond to, physical natural kinds. A way of stating the classical reductionist view is that things which belong to different physical kinds ipso facto can have no projectible descriptions in common; that if x and y differ in those descriptions by virtue of which they fall under the proper laws of physics, they must differ in those descriptions by virtue of which they fall under any laws at all. But why should we believe that this is so? Any pair of entities, however different their physical structure, must nevertheless converge in indefinitely many of their properties. Why should there not be, among those convergent properties, some whose lawful interrelations support the generalizations of the special sciences? Why, in short, should not the natural kind predicates of the special sciences *cross-classify* the physical natural kinds?[6]

Physics develops the taxonomy of its subject-matter which best suits its purposes: the formulation of exceptionless laws which are basic in the several senses discussed above. But this is not the only taxonomy which may be required if the purposes of science in general are to be served: e.g., if we are to state such true, counterfactual supporting generalizations as there are to state. So, there are special sciences, with their specialized taxonomies, in the business of stating some of these generalizations. If science is to be unified, then all such taxonomies must apply *to the same things.* If physics is to be basic science, then each of these things had better be a physical thing. But it is not further required that the taxonomies which the special sciences employ must themselves reduce to the taxonomy of physics. It is not required, and it is probably not true.

NOTES

I wish to express my gratitude to Ned Block for having read a version of this paper and for the very useful comments he made.

1. I shall usually assume that sciences are about events, in at least the sense that it is the occurrence of events that makes the laws of a science true. But I shall be pretty free with the relation between events, states, things and properties. I shall even permit myself some latitude in construing the relation between properties and predicates. I realize that all these relations are problems, but they aren't my problem in this paper. Explanation has to *start* somewhere, too.

2. The version of reductionism I shall be concerned with is a stronger one than many philosophers of science hold; a point worth emphasizing since my argument will be precisely that it is too strong to get

away with. Still, I think that what I shall be attacking is what many people have in mind when they refer to the unity of science, and I suspect (though I shan't try to prove it) that many of the liberalized versions suffer from the same basic defect as what I take to be the classical form of the doctrine.

3. There is an implicit assumption that a science simply *is* a formulation of a set of laws. I think this assumption is implausible, but it is usually made when the unity of science is discussed, and it is neutral so far as the main argument of this paper is concerned.

4. I shall sometimes refer to 'the predicate which constitutes the antecedent or consequent of a law.' This is shorthand for 'the predicate such that the an-

tecedent or consequent of a law consists of that predicate, together with its bound variables and the quantifiers which bind them.' (Truth functions of elementary predicates are, of course, themselves predicates in this usage.)

5. I don't think there is any chance at all that this is true. What is more likely is that type-identification for psychological states can be carried out in terms of the 'total states' of an abstract automaton which models the organism. For discussion, see Block and Fodor (1972).

6. As, by the way, the predicates of natural languages quite certainly do. For discussion, see Chomsky (1965).

BIBLIOGRAPHY

Block, N. and Fodor, J., 'What Psychological States Are Not,' *Philosophical Review* 81 (1972) 159–81.

Chomsky, N., *Aspects of the Theory of Syntax*, MIT Press, Cambridge, 1965.

19 | Multiple Realization and the Metaphysics of Reduction

Jaegwon Kim

I. Introduction

It is part of today's conventional wisdom in philosophy of mind that psychological states are "multiply realizable," and are in fact so realized, in a variety of structures and organisms. We are constantly reminded that any mental state, say pain, is capable of "realization," "instantiation," or "implementation" in widely diverse neural-biological structures in humans, felines, reptiles, mollusks, and perhaps other organisms further removed from us. Sometimes we are asked to contemplate the possibility that extra-terrestrial creatures with a biochemistry radically different from the earthlings', or even electro-mechanical devices, can "realize the same psychology" that characterizes humans. This claim, to be called hereafter "the Multiple Realization Thesis" ("MR,"[1] for short), is widely accepted by philosophers, especially those who are inclined to favor the functionalist line on mentality. I will not here dispute the truth of

MR, although what I will say may prompt a reassessment of the considerations that have led to its nearly universal acceptance.

And there is an influential and virtually uncontested view about the philosophical significance of MR. This is the belief that MR refutes psychophysical reductionism once and for all. In particular, the classic psychoneural identity theory of Feigl and Smart, the so-called "type physicalism", is standardly thought to have been definitively dispatched by MR to the heap of obsolete philosophical theories of mind. At any rate, it is this claim, that MR proves the physical irreducibility of the mental, that will be the starting point of my discussion.

Evidently, the current popularity of antireductionist physicalism is owed, for the most part, to the influence of the MR-based antireductionist argument originally developed by Hilary Putnam and elaborated further by Jerry Fodor[2]—rather more so than to the "anomalist" argument associated with Donald Davidson.[3]

From *Philosophy and Phenomenological Research* 52:1–26, 1992. Reprinted with permission of the publisher.

For example, in their elegant paper on nonreductive physicalism,[4] Geoffrey Hellman and Frank Thompson motivate their project in the following way:

> Traditionally, physicalism has taken the form of reductionism—roughly, that all scientific terms can be given explicit definitions in physical terms. Of late there has been growing awareness, however, that reductionism is an unreasonably strong claim.

But why is reductionism "unreasonably strong"? In a footnote Hellman and Thompson explain, citing Fodor's "Special Sciences":

> Doubts have arisen especially in connection with functional explanation in the higher-level sciences (psychology, linguistics, social theory, etc.). Functional predicates may be physically realizable in heterogeneous ways, so as to elude physical definition.

And Ernest LePore and Barry Loewer tell us this:[5]

> It is practically received wisdom among philosophers of mind that psychological properties (including content properties) are not identical to neurophysiological or other physical properties. The relationship between psychological and neurophysiological properties is that the latter *realize* the former. Furthermore, a single psychological property might (in the sense of conceptual possibility) be realized by a large number, perhaps an infinitely many, of different physical properties and even by non-physical properties.

They then go on to sketch the reason why MR, on their view, leads to the rejection of mind–body reduction:[6]

> If there are infinitely many physical (and perhaps nonphysical) properties which can realize *F* then *F* will not be reducible to a basic physical property. Even if *F* can only be realized by finitely many basic physical properties it might not be reducible to a basic physical property since the disjunction of these properties might not itself be a basic physical property (i.e., occur in a fundamental physical law). We will understand 'multiple realizability' as involving such irreducibility.

This antireductionist reading of MR continues to this day; in a recent paper, Ned Block writes:[7]

> Whatever the merits of physiological reductionism, it is not available to the cognitive science point of view assumed here. According to cognitive science, the essence of the mental is computational, and any computational state is 'multiply realizable' by physiological or electronic states that are not identical with one another, and so content cannot be identified with any one of them.

Considerations of these sorts have succeeded in persuading a large majority of philosophers of mind[8] to reject reductionism and type physicalism. The upshot of all this has been impressive: MR has not only ushered in "nonreductive physicalism" as the new orthodoxy on the mind–body problem, but in the process has put the very word "reductionism" in disrepute, making reductionisms of all stripes an easy target of disdain and curt dismissals.

I believe a reappraisal of MR is overdue. There is something right and instructive in the antireductionist claim based on MR and the basic argument in its support, but I believe that we have failed to follow out the implications of MR far enough, and have as a result failed to appreciate its full significance. One specific point that I will argue is this: the popular view that psychology constitutes an *autonomous special science,* a doctrine heavily promoted in the wake of the MR-inspired antireductionist dialectic, may in fact be inconsistent with the real implications of MR. Our discussion will show that MR, when combined with certain plausible metaphysical and methodological assumptions, leads to some surprising conclusions about the status of the mental and the nature of psychology as a science. I hope it will become clear that the fate of type physicalism is not among the more interesting consequences of MR.

II. Multiple Realization

It was Putnam, in a paper published in 1967,[9] who first injected MR into debates on the mind–body problem. According to him, the classic reductive theories of mind presupposed the following naive picture of how psychological kinds (properties, event and state types, etc.) are correlated with physical kinds:

> For each psychological kind *M* there is a unique physical (presumably, neurobiological) kind *P* that is *nomologically coextensive* with it (i.e., as a matter of law, any system instantiates *M* at *t* iff that system instantiates *P* at *t*).

(We may call this "the Correlation Thesis.") So take pain: the Correlation Thesis has it that pain as an event kind has a neural substrate, perhaps as yet not fully and precisely identified, that, as a matter of law, always co-occurs with it in all pain-capable organisms and structures. Here there is no mention of species or types of organisms or structures: the neural correlate of pain is invariant across biological species and structure types. In his 1967 paper, Putnam pointed out something that, in retrospect, seems all too obvious:[10]

Consider what the brain-state theorist has to do to make good his claims. He has to specify a physical-chemical state such that any organism (not just a mammal) is in pain if and only if (a) it possesses a brain of a suitable physical-chemical structure; and (b) its brain is in that physical-chemical state. This means that the physical-chemical state in question must be a possible state of a mammalian brain, a reptilian brain, a mollusc's brain (octopuses are mollusca, and certainly feel pain), etc. At the same time, it must not be a possible brain of any physically possible creature that cannot feel pain.

Putnam went on to argue that the Correlation Thesis was *empirically false*. Later writers, however, have stressed the multiple realizability of the mental as a *conceptual* point: it is an a priori, conceptual fact about psychological properties that they are "second-order" physical properties, and that their specification does not include constraints on the manner of their physical implementation.[11] Many proponents of the functionalist account of psychological terms and properties hold such a view.

Thus, on the new, improved picture, the relationship between psychological and physical kinds is something like this: there is no single neural kind N that "realizes" pain, across all types of organisms or physical systems; rather, there is a multiplicity of neural-physical kinds, $N_h, N_r, N_m, \ldots$ such that N_h realizes pain in humans, N_r realizes pain in reptiles, N_m realizes pain in Martians, etc. Perhaps, biological species as standardly understood are too broad to yield unique physical-biological realization bases; the neural basis of pain could perhaps change even in a single organism over time. But the main point is clear: any system capable of psychological states (that is, any system that "has a psychology") falls under some structure type T such that systems with structure T share the same physical base for each mental state-kind that they are capable of instantiating (we should regard this as relativized with respect to time to allow for the possibility that an individual may fall under different structure types at different times). Thus physical realization bases for mental states must be relativized to species or, better, physical structure-types. We thus have the following thesis:

If anything has mental property M at time t, there is some physical structure type T and physical property P such that it is a system of type T at t and has P at t, and it holds as a matter of law that all systems of type T have M at a time just in case they have P at the time.

We may call this "the Structure-Restricted Correlation Thesis" (or "the Restricted Correlation Thesis" for short).

It may have been noticed that neither this nor the correlation thesis speaks of "realization."[12] The talk of "realization" is not metaphysically neutral: the idea that mental properties are "realized" or "implemented" by physical properties carries with it a certain ontological picture of mental properties as derivative and dependent. There is the suggestion that when we look at concrete reality there is nothing over and beyond instantiations of physical properties and relations, and that the instantiation on a given occasion of an appropriate physical property in the right contextual (often causal) setting simply *counts as,* or *constitutes,* an instantiation of a mental property on that occasion. An idea like this is evident in the functionalist conception of a mental property as *extrinsically* characterized in terms of its "causal role," where what fills this role is a physical (or, at any rate, nonmental) property (the latter property will then be said to "realize" the mental property in question). The same idea can be seen in the related functionalist proposal to construe a mental property as a "second-order property" consisting in the having of a physical property satisfying certain extrinsic specifications. We will recur to this topic later; however, we should note that someone who accepts either of the two correlation theses need not espouse the "realization" idiom. That is, it is prima facie a coherent position to think of mental properties as "first-order properties" in their own right, characterized by their intrinsic natures (e.g., phenomenal feel), which, as it happens, turn out to have nomological correlates in neural properties. (In fact, anyone interested in defending a serious dualist position on the mental should eschew the realization talk altogether and consider mental properties as first-order properties on a par with physical properties.) The main point of MR that is relevant to the antireductionist argument it has generated is just this: *mental properties do not have nomically coextensive physical properties, when the latter are appropriately individuated.* It may be that properties that are candidates for reduction must be thought of as being realized, or implemented, by properties in the prospective reduction base;[13] that is, if we think of certain properties as having their own intrinsic characterizations that are entirely independent of another set of properties, there is no hope of *reducing* the former to the latter. But this point needs to be argued, and will, in any case, not play a role in what follows.

Assume that property M is realized by property P. How are M and P related to each other and, in particular, how do they covary with each other? LePore and Loewer say this:[14]

> The usual conception is that e's being P realizes e's being F if e is P and there is a strong connection of some sort between P and F. We propose to understand this connection as a necessary connection which is *explanatory*. The existence of an explanatory connection between two properties is stronger than the claim that $P \rightarrow F$ is physically necessary since not every physically necessary connection is explanatory.

Thus, LePore and Loewer require only that the realization base of M be *sufficient* for M, not both necessary and sufficient. This presumably is in response to MR: if pain is multiply realized in three ways as above, each of N_h, N_r, and N_m will be sufficient for pain, and none necessary for it. This I believe is not a correct response, however; the correct response is not to weaken the joint necessity and sufficiency of the physical base, but rather to *relativize* it, as in the Restricted Correlation Thesis, with respect to species or structure types. For suppose we are designing a physical system that will instantiate a certain psychology, and let $M_1, \ldots, M_n$ be the psychological properties required by this psychology. The design process must involve the specification of an n-tuple of physical properties, $P_1, \ldots, P_n$, all of them instantiable by the system, such that for each i, P_i constitutes a *necessary and sufficient* condition *in this system* (and others of relevantly similar physical structure), not merely a sufficient one, for the occurrence of M_i. (Each such n-tuple of physical properties can be called a "physical realization" of the psychology in question.[15]) That is, for each psychological state we must design into the system a nomologically coextensive physical state. We must do this *if we are to control both the occurrence and nonoccurrence of the psychological states involved,* and control of this kind necessary if we are to ensure that the

physical device will properly instantiate the psychology. (This is especially clear if we think of building a computer; computer analogies loom large in our thoughts about "realization".)

But isn't it possible for multiple realization to occur "locally" as well? That is, we may want to avail ourselves of the flexibility of allowing a psychological state, or function, to be instantiated by alternative mechanisms within a single system. This means that P_i can be a *disjunction* of physical properties; thus, M_i is instantiated in the system in question at a time if and only if at least one of the disjuncts of P_i is instantiated at that time. The upshot of all this is that LePore and Loewer's condition that $P \rightarrow M$ holds as a matter of law needs to be upgraded to the condition that, *relative to the species or structure-type in question (and allowing P to be disjunctive), $P \leftrightarrow M$ holds as a matter of law.*[16]

For simplicity let us suppose that pain is realized in three ways as above, by N_h in humans, N_r in reptiles, and N_m in Martians. The finitude assumption is not essential to any of my arguments: if the list is not finite, we will have an infinite disjunction rather than a finite one (alternatively, we can talk in terms of "sets" of such properties instead of their disjunctions). If the list is "open-ended," that's all right, too; it will not affect the metaphysics of the situation. We allowed above the possibility of a realization base of a psychological property itself being disjunctive; to get the discussion going, though, we will assume that these Ns, the three imagined physical realization bases of pain, are not themselves disjunctive—or, at any rate, that their status as properties is not in dispute. The propriety and significance of "disjunctive properties" is precisely one of the principal issues we will be dealing with below, and it will make little difference just at what stage this issue is faced.

III. Disjunctive Properties and Fodor's Argument

An obvious initial response to the MR-based argument against reducibility is "the disjunction move": Why not take the disjunction, N_h v N_r v N_m, as the single physical substrate of pain? In his 1967 paper, Putnam considers such a move but dismisses it out of hand: "Granted, in such a case the brain-state theorist can save himself by ad hoc assumptions (e.g., defining the disjunction of two states to be a single 'physical-chemical state'), but this does not have to be taken seriously."[17] Putnam gives no hint as to why he thinks the disjunction strategy does not merit serious consideration.

If there is something deeply wrong with disjunctions of the sort involved here, that surely isn't obvious; we need to go beyond a sense of unease with such disjunctions and develop an intelligible rationale for banning them. Here is where Fodor steps in, for he appears to have an argument for disallowing disjunctions. As I see it, Fodor's argument in "Special Sciences" depends crucially on the following two assumptions:

1. To reduce a special-science theory T_M to physical theory T_P, each "kind" in T_M (presumably, represented by a basic predicate of T_M) must have a nomologically coextensive "kind" in T_P;
2. A disjunction of heterogeneous kinds is not itself a kind.

Point (1) is apparently prompted by the derivational model of intertheoretic reduction due to Ernest Nagel:[18] the reduction of T_2 to T_1 consists in the derivation of laws of T_2 from the laws of T_1, in conjunction with "bridge" laws or principles connecting T_2-terms with T_1-terms. Although this characterization does not in general require that each T_2-term be correlated with a *coextensive* T_1-term, the natural thought is that the existence of T_1-coextensions for T_2-terms would in effect give us definitions of T_2-terms in T_1-terms, enabling us to rewrite T_2-laws exclusively in the vocabulary of T_1; we could then derive these rewrites of T_2-laws from the laws of T_1 (if they cannot be so derived, we can add them as additional T_1-laws—assuming both theories to be true).

Another thought that again leads us to look for T_1-coextensions for T_2-terms is this: for genuine reduction, the bridge laws must be construed as *property identities,* not mere *property correlations*—namely, we must be in a position to identify the property expressed by a given T_2-term (say, water-solubility) with a property expressed by a term in the reduction base (say, having a certain molecular structure). This of course requires that each T_2-term have a nomic (or otherwise suitably modalized) coextension in the vocabulary of the reduction base. To put it another way, ontologically significant reduction requires the reduction of higher-level *properties,* and this in turn requires (unless one takes an eliminativist stance) that they be identified

with complexes of lower-level properties. Identity of properties of course requires, at a minimum, an appropriately modalized coextensivity.[19]

So assume M is a psychological kind, and let us agree that to reduce $M,$ or to reduce the psychological theory containing $M,$ we need a physical coextension, $P,$ for $M.$ But why should we suppose that P must be a physical "kind"? But what is a "kind," anyway? Fodor explains this notion in terms of *law,* saying that a given predicate P is a "kind predicate" of a science just in case the science contains a law with P as its antecedent or consequent.[20] There are various problems with Fodor's characterization, but we don't need to take its exact wording seriously; the main idea is that kinds, or kind predicates, of a science are those that figure in the laws of that science.

To return to our question, why should "bridge laws" connect kinds to kinds, in this special sense of "kind"? To say that bridge laws are "laws" and that, by definition, only kind predicates can occur in laws is not much of an answer. For that only invites the further question why "bridge laws" ought to be "laws"—what would be lacking in a reductive derivation if bridge laws were replaced by "bridge principles" which do not necessarily connect kinds to kinds.[21] But what of the consideration that these principles must represent property identities? Does this force on us the requirement that each reduced kind must find a coextensive kind in the reduction base? No; for it isn't obvious why it isn't perfectly proper to reduce kinds by identifying them with properties expressed by nonkind (disjunctive) predicates in the reduction base.

There is the following possible argument for insisting on kinds: if M is identified with nonkind Q (or M is reduced via a biconditional bridge principle "$M \leftrightarrow Q$", where Q is a nonkind), M could no longer figure in special science laws; e.g., the law, "$M \rightarrow R$", would in effect reduce to "$Q \rightarrow R$", and therefore loses its status as a law on account of containing $Q,$ a non-kind.

I think this is a plausible response—at least, the beginning of one. As it stands, though, it smacks of circularity: "$Q \rightarrow R$" is not a law because a non-kind, $Q,$ occurs in it, and Q is a non-kind because it cannot occur in a law and "$Q \rightarrow R$", in particular, is not a law. What we need is an *independent* reason for the claim that the sort of Q we are dealing with under MR, namely a badly heterogeneous disjunction, is unsuited for laws.

This means that point (1) really reduces to point (2) above. For, given Fodor's notion of a kind, (2) comes to this: disjunctions of heterogeneous kinds are unfit for laws. What we now need is an *argument* for this claim; to dismiss such disjunctions as "wildly disjunctive" or "heterogeneous and unsystematic" is to label a problem, not to offer a diagnosis of it.[22] In the sections to follow, I hope to take some steps toward such a diagnosis and draw some implications which I believe are significant for the status of mentality.

IV. Jade, Jadeite, and Nephrite

Let me begin with an analogy that will guide us in our thinking about multiply realizable kinds.

Consider *jade:* we are told that jade, as it turns out, is not a mineral kind, contrary to what was once believed; rather, jade is comprised of two distinct minerals with dissimilar molecular structures, *jadeite* and *nephrite*. Consider the following generalization:

(L) Jade is green

We may have thought, before the discovery of the dual nature of jade, that (L) was a law, a law about jade; and we may have thought, with reason, that (L) had been strongly confirmed by all the millions of jade samples that had been observed to be green (and none that had been observed not to be green). We now know better: (L) is really a conjunction of these two laws:

(L_1) Jadeite is green
(L_2) Nephrite is green

But (L) itself might still be a law as well; is that possible? It has the standard basic form of a law, and it apparently has the power to support counterfactuals: if anything were jade—that is, if anything were a sample of jadeite or of nephrite—then, in either case, it would follow, by law, that it was green. No problem here.

But there is another standard mark of lawlikeness that is often cited, and this is "projectibility," the ability to be confirmed by observation of "positive instances." Any generalized conditional of the form "All Fs are G" can be confirmed by the *exhaustion* of the class of Fs—that is, by eliminating all of its potential falsifiers. It is in this sense that we can verify such general-

izations as "All the coins in my pockets are copper" and "Everyone in this room is either first-born or an only child." Lawlike generalizations, however, are thought to have the following further property: observation of positive instances, Fs that are Gs, can strengthen our credence in the next F's being G. It is this kind of instance-to-instance accretion of confirmation that is supposed to be the hallmark of lawlikeness; it is what explains the possibility of confirming a generalization about an indefinitely large class of items on the basis of a finite number of favorable observations. This rough characterization of projectibility should suffice for our purposes.

Does (L), "Jade is green," pass the projectibility test? Here we seem to have a problem.[23] For we can imagine this: on re-examining the records of past observations, we find, to our dismay, that all the positive instances of (L), that is, all the millions of observed samples of green jade, turn out to have been samples of jadeite, and none of nephrite! If this should happen, we clearly would not, and should not, continue to think of (L) as well confirmed. All we have is evidence strongly confirming (L_1), and none having anything to do with (L_2). (L) is merely a conjunction of two laws, one well confirmed and the other with its epistemic status wholly up in the air. But all the millions of green jadeite samples *are* positive instances of (L): they satisfy both the antecedent and the consequent of (L). As we have just seen, however, (L) is not confirmed by them, at least not in the standard way we expect. And the reason, I suggest, is that jade is a true disjunctive kind, a disjunction of two heterogeneous nomic kinds which, however, is not itself a nomic kind.[24]

That disjunction is implicated in this failure of projectibility can be seen in the following way: inductive projection of generalizations like (L) with disjunctive antecedents would sanction a cheap, and illegitimate, confirmation procedure. For assume that "All Fs are G" is a law that has been confirmed by the observation of appropriately numerous positive instances, things that are both F and G. But these are also positive instances of the generalization "All things that are F or H are G," for any H you please. So, if you in general permit projection of generalizations with a disjunctive antecedent, this latter generalization is also well confirmed. But "All things that are F or H are G" logically implies "All Hs are G." Any statement implied by a well confirmed statement must itself be well confirmed.[25] So "All Hs are G" is well confirmed—in fact, it is confirmed by the observation of Fs that are Gs!

One might protest: "Look, the very same strategy can be applied to something that is a genuine law. We can think of any nomic kind—say, being an emerald—as a disjunction, being an African emerald or a non-African emerald. This would make 'All emeralds are green' a conjunction of two laws, 'All African emeralds are green' and 'All non-African emeralds are green.' But surely this doesn't show there is anything wrong with the lawlikeness of 'All emeralds are green.'" Our reply is obvious: the disjunction, "being an African emerald or non-African emerald," does not denote some heterogeneously disjunctive, nonnomic kind; it denotes a perfectly well-behaved nomic kind, that of being an emerald! There is nothing wrong with disjunctive predicates as such; the trouble arises when the kinds denoted by the disjoined predicates are heterogeneous, "wildly disjunctive," so that instances falling under them do not show the kind of "similarity," or unity, that we expect of instances falling under a single kind.

The phenomenon under discussion, therefore, is related to the simple maxim sometimes claimed to underlie inductive inference: "similar things behave in similar ways," "same cause, same effect," and so on. The source of the trouble we saw with instantial confirmation of "All jade is green" is the fact, or belief, that samples of jadeite and sample of nephrite do not exhibit an appropriate "similarity" with respect to each other to warrant inductive projections from the observed samples of jadeite to unobserved samples of nephrite. But similarity of the required sort presumably holds for African emeralds and non-African emeralds—at least, that is what we believe, and that is what makes the "disjunctive kind," being an African emerald or a non-African emerald, a single nomic kind. More generally, the phenomenon is related to the point often made about disjunctive properties: disjunctive properties, unlike conjunctive properties, do not guarantee similarity for instances falling under them. And similarity, it is said, is the core of our idea of a property. If that is your idea of a property, you will believe that there are no such things as disjunctive properties (or "negative properties"). More precisely, though, we should remember that properties are not inherently disjunctive or conjunctive any more than classes are inherently unions or intersections, and that any property can be expressed by a disjunctive predicate. Properties of course can be conjunctions, or disjunctions, *of* other properties. The point about disjunctive properties is best put as a closure condition on properties: the class of properties is not closed under disjunction (presumably, nor under negation). Thus, there may well be properties P and Q such that P *or* Q is so a property, but its being so doesn't follow from the mere fact that P and Q are properties.[26]

V. Jade and Pain

Let us now return to pain and its multiple realization bases, N_h, N_r, and N_m. I believe the situation here is instructively parallel to the case of jade in relation to jadeite and nephrite. It seems that we think of jadeite and nephrite as distinct kinds (and of jade not as a kind) because they are different chemical kinds. But why is their being distinct as chemical kinds relevant here? Because many important properties of minerals, we think, are supervenient on, and explainable in terms of, their microstructure, and chemical kinds constitute a microstructural taxonomy that is explanatorily rich and powerful. Microstructure is important, in short, because macrophysical properties of substances are determined by microstructure. These ideas make up our "metaphysics" of microdetermination for properties of minerals and other substances, a background of partly empirical and partly metaphysical assumptions that regulate our inductive and explanatory practices.

The parallel metaphysical underpinnings for pain, and other mental states in general, are, first, the belief, expressed by the Restricted Correlation Thesis, that pain, or any other mental state, occurs in a system when, and only when, appropriate physical conditions are present in the system, and, second, the corollary belief that significant properties of mental states, in particular nomic relationships amongst them, are due to, and explainable in terms of, the properties and causal-nomic connections among their physical "substrates." I will call the conjunction of these two beliefs "the Physical Realization Thesis."[27] Whether or not the micro-explanation of the sort indicated in the second half of the thesis amounts to a "reduction" is a question we will take up later. Apart from this question, though, the Physical Realization Thesis is widely accepted by philosophers who talk of "physical realization", and this includes most functionalists; it is all but explicit in LePore and Loewer, for example, and in Fodor.[28]

Define a property, N, by disjoining N_h, N_r, and N_m, that is, N has a disjunctive definition, N_h v N_r v N_m. If we assume, with those who endorse the MR-based antireductionist argument, that N_h, N_r, and N_m are a heterogeneous lot, we cannot make the heterogeneity go away merely by introducing a simpler expression, "N"; if there is a problem with certain disjunctive properties, it is not a *linguistic* problem about the form of expressions used to refer to them.

Now, we put the following question to Fodor and like-minded philosophers: If pain is nomically equivalent to N, the property claimed to be wildly disjunctive and obviously nonnomic, *why isn't pain itself equally heterogeneous and nonnomic as a kind?* Why isn't pain's relationship to its realization bases, N_h, N_r, and N_m analogous to jade's relationship to jadeite and nephrite? If jade turns out to be nonnomic on account of its dual "realizations" in distinct microstructures, why doesn't the same fate befall pain? After all, the group of actual and nomologically possible realizations of pain, as they are described by the MR enthusiasts with such imagination, is far more motley than the two chemical kinds comprising jade.

I believe we should insist on answers to these questions from those functionalists who view mental properties as "second-order" properties, i.e., properties that consist in having a property with a certain functional specification.[29] Thus, pain is said to be a second-order property in that it is the *property of having some property with a certain specification* in terms of its typical causes and effects and its relation to other mental properties; call this "specification H." The point of MR, on this view, is that there is more than one property that meets specification H—in fact, an open-ended set of such properties, it will be said. But pain itself, it is argued, is a more abstract but well-behaved property at a higher level, namely the property of having one of these properties meeting specification H. It should be clear why a position like this is vulnerable to the questions that have been raised. For the property of having property P is exactly identical with P, and the property of having *one* of the properties, $P_1, P_2, \ldots, P_n$, is exactly identical with the disjunctive property, P_1 v P_2 v $\ldots$ v P_n. On the assumption that N_h, N_r, and N_m are all the properties satisfying specification H, the property of having a property with H, namely pain, is none other than the property of having

either N_h or N_r or N_m[30]—namely, the *disjunctive* property, N_h v N_r v N_m! We cannot hide the disjunctive character of pain behind the second-order *expression*, "the property of having a property with specification H." Thus, on the construal of mental properties as second-order properties, mental properties will in general turn out to be disjunctions of their physical realization bases. It is difficult to see how one could have it both ways–that is, to castigate N_h v N_r v N_m as unacceptably disjunctive while insisting on the integrity of pain as a scientific kind.

Moreover, when we think about making projections over pain, very much the same worry should arise about their propriety as did for jade. Consider a possible law: "Sharp pains administered at random intervals cause anxiety reactions." Suppose this generalization has been well confirmed for humans. Should we expect *on that basis* that it will hold also for Martians whose psychology is implemented (we assume) by a vastly different physical mechanism? Not if we accept the Physical Realization Thesis, fundamental to functionalism, that psychological regularities hold, to the extent that they do, in virtue of the causal-nomological regularities at the physical implementation level. The reason the law is true for humans is due to the way the human brain is "wired"; the Martians have a brain with a different wiring plan, and we certainly should not expect the regularity to hold for them just because it does for humans.[31] "Pains cause anxiety reactions" may turn out to possess no more unity as a scientific law than does "Jade is green."

Suppose that in spite of all this Fodor insists on defending pain as a nomic kind. It isn't clear that that would be a viable strategy. For he would then owe us an explanation of why the "wildly disjunctive" N, which after all is equivalent to pain, is not a nomic kind. If a predicate is nomically equivalent to a well-behaved predicate, why isn't that enough to show that it, too, is well behaved, and expresses a well-behaved property? To say, as Fodor does,[32] that "it is a law that . . ." is "intensional" and does not permit substitution of equivalent expressions ("equivalent" in various appropriate senses) is merely to locate a potential problem, not to resolve it.

Thus, the nomicity of pain may lead to the nomicity of N; but this isn't very interesting. For given the Physical Realization Thesis, and the priority of the physical implicit in it, our earlier line of argument, leading from the nonnomicity of N to the nonnomicity of pain, is more compelling. We must, I think, take seriously the reasoning leading to the conclusion that pain, and other mental states, might turn out to be nonnomic. If this turns out to be the case, it puts in serious jeopardy Fodor's contention that its physical irreducibility renders psychology an autonomous special science. If pain fails to be nomic, it is not the sort of property in terms of which laws can be formulated; and "pain" is not a predicate that can enter into a scientific theory that seeks to formulate causal laws and causal explanations. And the same goes for all multiply realizable psychological kinds—which, according to MR, means *all* psychological kinds. There are no scientific theories of jade, and we don't need any; if you insist on having one, you can help yourself with the *conjunction* of the theory of jadeite and the theory of nephrite. In the same way, there will be theories about human pains (instances of N_h), reptilian pains (instances of N_r), and so on; but there will be no unified, integrated theory encompassing all pains in all pain-capable organisms, only a conjunction of pain theories for appropriately individuated biological species and physical structure-types. Scientific psychology, like the theory of jade, gives way to a conjunction of structure-specific theories. If this is right, the correct conclusion to be drawn from the MR-inspired antireductionist argument is not the claim that psychology is an irreducible and autononomous science, but something that contradicts it, namely that it cannot be a science with a unified subject matter. This is the picture that is beginning to emerge from MR when combined with the Physical Realization Thesis.

These reflections have been prompted by the analogy with the case of jade; it is a strong and instructive analogy, I think, and suggests the possibility of a general argument. In the following section I will develop a direct argument, with explicit premises and assumptions.

VI. Causal Powers and Mental Kinds

One crucial premise we need for a direct argument is a constraint on concept formation, or kind individuation, in science that has been around for many years; it has lately been resurrected by Fodor in connection with content externalism.[33] A precise statement of the constraint may be difficult and controversial, but its main idea can be put as follows:

> [Principle of Causal Individuation of Kinds] Kinds in science are individuated on the basis of causal powers; that is, objects and events fall under a kind, or share in a property, insofar as they have similar causal powers.

I believe this is a plausible principle, and it is, in any case, widely accepted.

We can see that this principle enables us to give a specific interpretation to the claim that N_h, N_r, and N_m are *heterogeneous* as kinds: the claim must mean that they are *heterogeneous as causal powers*—that is, they are diverse as causal powers and enter into diverse causal laws. This must mean, given the Physical Realization Thesis, that pain itself can show no more unity as a causal power than the disjunction, N_h v N_r v N_m. This becomes especially clear if we set forth the following principle, which arguably is implied by the Physical Realization Thesis (but we need not make an issue of this here):

> [The Causal Inheritance Principle] If mental property M is realized in a system at t in virtue of physical realization base P, the causal powers of *this instance* of M are identical with the causal powers of P.[34]

It is important to bear in mind that this principle only concerns the causal powers of *individual instances* of M; it does not identify the causal powers of mental property M *in general* with the causal powers of some physical property P; such identification is precluded by the multiple physical realizability of M.

Why should we accept this principle? Let us just note that to deny it would be to accept *emergent* causal powers: causal powers that magically emerge at a higher-level and of which there is no accounting in terms of lower-level properties and their causal powers and nomic connections. This leads to the notorious problem of "downward causation" and the attendant violation of the causal closure of the physical domain.[35] I believe that a serious physicalist would find these consequences intolerable.

It is clear that the Causal Inheritance Principle, in conjunction with the Physical Realization Thesis, has the consequence that mental kinds cannot satisfy the Causal Individuation Principle, and this effectively rules out mental kinds as scientific kinds. The reasoning is simple: instances of M that are realized by the same physical base must be grouped under one kind, since *ex hypothesi* the physical base is a causal kind; and instances of *M* with different realization bases must be grouped under distinct kinds, since, again *ex hypothesi,* these realization bases are distinct as causal kinds. Given that mental kinds are realized by diverse physical causal kinds, therefore, it follows that mental kinds are not causal kinds, and hence are disqualified as proper scientific kinds. Each mental kind is sundered into as many kinds as there are physical realization bases for it, and the psychology as a science with disciplinary unity turns out to be an impossible project.

What is the relationship between this argument and the argument adumbrated in our reflections based on the jade analogy? At first blush, the two arguments might seem unrelated: the earlier argument depended chiefly on epistemological considerations, considerations on inductive projectibility of certain predicates, whereas the crucial premise of the second argument is the Causal Kind Individuation Principle, a broadly metaphysical and methodological principle about science. I think, though, that the two arguments are closely related, and the key to seeing the relationship is this: causal powers involve laws, and laws are regularities that are projectible. Thus, if pain (or jade) is not a kind over which inductive projections can be made, it cannot enter into laws, and therefore cannot qualify as a causal kind; and this disqualifies it as a scientific kind. If this is right, the jade-inspired reflections provide a possible rationale for the Causal Individuation Principle. Fleshing out this rough chain of reasoning in precise terms, however, goes beyond what I can attempt in this paper.

VII. The Status of Psychology: Local Reductions

Our conclusion at this point, therefore, is this: If MR is true, psychological kinds are not scientific kinds. What does this imply about the status of psychology as a science? Do our considerations show that psychology is a pseudo-science like astrology and alchemy? Of course not. The crucial difference, from the metaphysical point of view, is that psychology has physical realizations, but alchemy does not. To have a physical realization is to be physically grounded and explainable in terms of the processes at an underlying level. In fact, if each of the psychological kinds posited in a psychological theory has a

physical realization for a fixed species, the theory can be "locally reduced" to the physical theory of that species, in the following sense. Let *S* be the species involved; for each law L_m of psychological theory T_m, $S \to L_m$ (the proposition that L_m holds for members of *S*) is the "*S*-restricted" version of L_m; and $S \to T_m$ is the *S*-restricted version of T_m, the set of all *S*-restricted laws of T_m. We can then say that T_m is "locally reduced" for species *S* to an underlying theory, T_p, just in case $S \to T_m$ is reduced to T_p. And the latter obtains just in case each *S*-restricted law of T_m, $S \to L_m$,[36] is derivable from the laws of the reducing theory T_p, taken together with bridge laws. What bridge laws suffice to guarantee the derivation? Obviously, an array of *S*-restricted bridge laws of the form, $S \to (M_i \leftrightarrow P_i)$, for each mental kind M_i. Just as unrestricted psychophysical bridge laws can underwrite a "global" or "uniform" reduction of psychology, species- or structure-restricted bridge laws sanction its "local" reduction.

If the same psychological theory is true of humans, reptiles, and Martians, the psychological kinds posited by that theory must have realizations in human, reptilian, and Martian physiologies. This implies that the theory is locally reducible in three ways, for humans, reptiles, and Martians. If the dependence of the mental on the physical means anything, it must mean that the regularities posited by this common psychology must have divergent physical explanations for the three species. The very idea of physical realization involves the possibility of physically explaining psychological properties and regularities, and the supposition of multiple such realizations, namely MR, involves a commitment to the possibility of multiple explanatory reductions of psychology.[37] The important moral of MR we need to keep in mind is this: *if psychological properties are multiply realized, so is psychology itself.* If physical realizations of psychological properties are a "wildly heterogeneous" and "unsystematic" lot, psychological theory itself must be realized by an equally heterogeneous and unsystematic lot of physical theories.

I am inclined to think that multiple local reductions, rather than global reductions, are the rule, even in areas in which we standardly suppose reductions are possible. I will now deal with a possible objection to the idea of local reduction, at least as it is applied to psychology. The objection goes like this: given what we know about the differences among members of a single species, even species are too wide to yield determinate realization bases for psychological states, and given what we know about the phenomena of maturation and development, brain injuries, and the like, the physical bases of mentality may change even for a single individual. This throws into serious doubt, continues the objection, the availability of species-restricted bridge laws needed for local reductions.

The point of this objection may well be correct as a matter of empirical fact. Two points can be made in reply, however. First, neurophysiological research goes on because there is a shared, and probably well grounded, belief among the workers that there are not huge individual differences within a species in the way psychological kinds are realized. Conspecifics must show important physical-physiological similarities, and there probably is good reason for thinking that they share physical realization bases to a sufficient degree to make search for species-wide neural substrates for mental states feasible and rewarding. Researchers in this area evidently aim for neurobiological explanations of psychological capacities and processes that are generalizable over all or most ("normal") members of a given species.

Second, even if there are huge individual differences among conspecifics as to how their psychology is realized, that does not touch the metaphysical point: as long as you believe in the Physical Realization Thesis, you must believe that every organism or system with mentality falls under a physical structure-type such that its mental states are realized by determinate physical states of organisms with that structure. It may be that these structures are so finely individuated and so few *actual* individuals fall under them that research into the neural bases of mental states in these structures is no longer worthwhile, theoretically or practically. What we need to recognize here is that the scientific possibility of, say, human psychology is a contingent fact (assuming it is a fact); it depends on the fortunate fact that individual humans do not show huge physiological-biological differences that are psychologically relevant. But if they did, that would not change the metaphysics of the situation one bit; it would remain true that the psychology of each of us was determined by, and locally reducible to, his neurobiology.

Realistically, there are going to be psychological differences among individual humans: it is a commonsense platitude that no two persons are exactly alike—either physically or psycho-

logically. And individual differences may be manifested not only in particular psychological facts but in psychological regularities. If we believe in the Physical Realization Thesis, we must believe that our psychological differences are rooted in, and explainable by, our physical differences, just as we expect our psychological similarities to be so explainable. Humans probably are less alike among themselves than, say, tokens of a Chevrolet model.[38] And psychological laws for humans, at a certain level of specificity, must be expected to be statistical in character, not deterministic—or, if you prefer, "ceteris paribus laws" rather than "strict laws." But this is nothing peculiar to psychology; these remarks surely apply to human physiology and anatomy as much as human psychology. In any case, none of this affects the metaphysical point being argued here concerning microdetermination and microreductive explanation.

VIII. Metaphysical Implications

But does local reduction have any interesting philosophical significance, especially in regard to the status of mental properties? If a psychological property has been multiply locally reduced, does that mean that the property itself has been reduced? Ned Block has raised just such a point, arguing that species-restricted reductionism (or species-restricted type physicalism) "sidesteps the main metaphysical question: 'What is common to the pains of dogs and people (and all other species) in virtue of which they are pains?' "[39]

Pereboom and Kornblith elaborate on Block's point as follows:

> . . . even if there is a single type of physical state that normally realizes pain in each type of organism, or in each structure type, this does not show that pain, *as a type of mental state,* is reducible to physical states. Reduction, in the present debate, must be understood as reduction of types, since the primary object of reductive strategies is explanations and theories, and explanations and theories quantify over types. . . . The suggestion that there are species-specific reductions of pain results in the claim that pains in different species have nothing in common. But this is just a form of eliminativism.[40]

There are several related but separable issues raised here. But first we should ask: Must all pains have "something in common" in virtue of which they are pains?

According to the phenomenological conception of pain, all pains do have something in common: they all *hurt*. But as I take it, those who hold this view of pain would reject any reductionist program, independently of the issues presently on hand. Even if there were a species-invariant uniform bridge law correlating pains with a single physical substrate across all species and structures, they would claim that the correlation holds as a brute, unexplainable matter of fact, and that pain as a qualitative event, a "raw feel," would remain irreducibly distinct from its neural substrate. Many emergentists apparently held a view of this kind.

I presume that Block, and Pereboom and Kornblith, are speaking not from a phenomenological viewpoint of this kind but from a broadly functionalist one. But from a functionalist perspective, it is by no means clear how we should understand the question "What do all pains have in common in virtue of which they are all pains?" Why should all pains have "something in common"? As I understand it, at the core of the functionalist program is the attempt to explain the meanings of mental terms *relationally,* in terms of inputs, outputs, and connections with other mental states. And on the view, discussed briefly earlier, that mental properties are second-order properties, pain is the property of having a property with a certain functional specification *H* (in terms of inputs, outputs, etc.). This yields a short answer to Block's question: what all pains have in common is the pattern of connections as specified by *H*. The local reductionist is entitled to that answer as much as the functionalist is. Compare two pains, an instance of N_h and one of N_m: what they have in common is that each is an instance of a property that realizes pain—that is, they exhibit the same pattern of input-output-other internal state connections, namely the pattern specified by *H*.

But some will say: "But *H* is only an *extrinsic* characterization; what do these instances of pain have in common that is *intrinsic* to them?" The local reductionist must grant that on his view there is nothing intrinsic that all pains have in common in virtue of which they are pains (assuming that N_h, N_r, and N_m "have nothing intrinsic in common"). But that is also precisely the consequence of the functionalist view. That, one might say, is the whole point of functionalism: the functionalist, especially one who believes in MR, would not, and should not, look for something common to all pains over and above *H* (the heart of functionalism, one might say, is the belief that mental states have no "intrinsic essence").

But there is a further question raised by Block et al.: What happens to properties that have been locally reduced? Are they still with us, distinct and separate from the underlying physical-biological properties? Granted: human pain is reduced to N_h, Martian pain to N_m, and so forth, but what of *pain itself?* It remains unreduced. Are we still stuck with the dualism of mental and physical properties?

I will sketch two possible ways of meeting this challenge. First, recall my earlier remarks about the functionalist conception of mental properties as second-order properties: pain is *the property of having a property with specification H,* and, given that N_h, N_r, and N_m are the properties meeting *H,* pain turns to be the disjunctive property, N_h v N_r v N_m. If you hold the second-order property view of mental properties, pain has been reduced to, and survives as, this disjunctive physical kind. Quite apart from considerations of local reduction, the very conception of pain you hold commits you to the conclusion that pain is a disjunctive kind, and if you accept any form of respectable physicalism (in particular, the Physical Realization Thesis), it is a disjunctive *physical* kind. And even if you don't accept the view of mental properties as second-order properties, as long as you are comfortable with disjunctive kinds and properties, you can, in the aftermath of local reduction, identify pain with the disjunction of its realization bases. On this approach, then, you have another, more direct, answer to Block's question: what all pains have in common is that they all fall under the disjunctive kind, N_h v N_r v N_m.

If you are averse to disjunctive kinds, there is another more radical, and in some ways more satisfying, approach. The starting point of this approach is the frank acknowledgement that MR leads to the conclusion that pain as a property or kind must go. Local reduction after all is reduction, and to be reduced is to be eliminated as an *independent* entity. You might say: global reduction is different in that it is also *conservative*—if pain is globally reduced to physical property *P,* pain survives as *P.* But it is also true that under local reduction, pain survives as N_h in humans, as N_r in reptiles, and so on. It must be admitted, however, that pain as a kind does not survive multiple local reduction. But is this so bad?

Let us return to jade once again. Is jade a *kind?* We know it is not a mineral kind; but is it any kind of a kind? That of course depends on what we mean by "kind." There are certain shared criteria, largely based on observable macroproperties of mineral samples (e.g., hardness, color, etc.), that determine whether something is a sample of jade, or whether the predicate "is jade" is correctly applicable to it. What all samples of jade have in common is just these observable macrophysical properties that define the applicability of the predicate "is jade." In this sense, speakers of English who have "jade" in their repertoire associate the same *concept* with "jade"; and we can recognize the existence of the concept of jade and at the same time acknowledge that the concept does not pick out, or answer to, a property or kind in the natural world.

I think we can say something similar about pain and "pain": there are shared criteria for the application of the predicate "pain" or "is in pain," and these criteria may well be for the most part functionalist ones. These criteria generate for us a *concept of pain,* a concept whose clarity and determinacy depend, we may assume, on certain characteristics (such as explicitness, coherence, and completeness) of the criteria governing the application of "pain". But the concept of pain, on this construal, need not pick out an objective kind any more than the concept of jade does.

All this presupposes a distinction between concepts and properties (or kinds). Do we have such a distinction? I believe we do. Roughly, concepts are in the same ball park as predicates, meanings (perhaps, something like Fregean *Sinnen*), ideas, and the like; Putnam has suggested that concepts be identified with "synonymy classes of predicates,"[41] and that comes close enough to what I have in mind. Properties and relations, on the other hand, are "out there in the world"; they are features and characteristics of things and events in the world. They include fundamental physical magnitudes and quantities, like mass, energy, size, and shape, and are part of the causal structure of the world. The property of being water is arguably identical with the property of being H_2O, but evidently the concept of water is distinct from the concept of H_2O (Socrates had the former but not the latter). Most of us would agree that ethical predicates are meaningful, and that we have the concepts of "good," "right," etc.; however, it is a debatable issue, and has lately been much debated, whether there are such properties as goodness and rightness.[42] If you find that most of these remarks make sense, you understand the concept-property distinction that I have in mind. Admittedly, this is all a little vague and programmatic, and we clearly need a better articulated theory of properties and concepts; but the distinction is there, supported by an impressively systematic set of intuitions and philosophical requirements.[43]

But is this second approach a form of mental eliminativism? In a sense it is: as I said, on this approach no properties in the world answer to general, species-unrestricted mental concepts. But remember: there still are pains, and we sometimes are in pain, just as there still are samples of jade. We must also keep in mind that the present approach is not, in its ontological implications, a form of the standard mental eliminativism currently on the scene.[44] Without elaborating on what the differences are, let us just note a few important points. First, the present view does not take away species-restricted mental properties, e.g., human pain, Martian pain, canine pain, and the rest, although it takes away "pain as such." Second, while the standard eliminativism consigns mentality to the same ontological limbo to which phlogiston, witches, and magnetic effluvia, have been dispatched, the position I have been sketching views it on a par with jade, tables, and adding machines. To see jade as a nonkind is not to question the existence of jade, or the legitimacy and utility of the concept of jade. Tables do not constitute a scientific kind; there are no laws about tables as such, and being a table is not a causal-explanatory kind. But that must be sharply distinguished from the false claim that there are no tables. The same goes for pains. These points suggest the following difference in regard to the status of psychology: the present view allows, and in fact encourages, "species-specific psychologies," but the standard eliminativism would do away with all things psychological—species-specific psychologies as well as global psychology.[45]

To summarize, then, the two metaphysical schemes I have sketched offer these choices: either we allow disjunctive kinds and construe pain and other mental properties as such kinds, or else we must acknowledge that our general mental terms and concepts do not pick out properties and kinds in the world (we may call this "mental property irrealism"). I should add that I am not interested in promoting either disjunctive kinds or mental irrealism, a troubling set of choices to most of us. Rather, my main interest has been to follow out the consequences of MR and try to come to terms with them within a reasonable metaphysical scheme.

I have already commented on the status of psychology as a science under MR. As I argued, MR seriously compromises the disciplinary unity and autonomy of psychology as a science. But that does not have to be taken as a negative message. In particular, the claim does not imply that a scientific study of psychological phenomena is not possible or useful; on the contrary, MR says that psychological processes have a foundation in the biological and physical processes

and regularities, and it opens the possibility of enlightening explanations of psychological processes at a more basic level. It is only that at a deeper level, psychology becomes sundered by being multiply locally reduced. However, species-specific psychologies, e.g., human psychology, Martian psychology, etc., can all flourish as scientific theories. Psychology remains *scientific,* though perhaps not *a science.* If you insist on having a global psychology valid for all species and structures, you can help yourself with that, too; but you must think of it as a *conjunction* of species-restricted psychologies and be careful, above all, with your inductions.[46]

NOTES

1. On occasion, "MR" will refer to the *phenomenon* of multiple realization rather than the *claim* that such a phenomenon exists; there should be no danger of confusion.
2. Jerry Fodor, "Special Sciences, or the Disunity of Science as a Working Hypothesis" (hereafter, "Special Sciences"), *Synthese* 28 (1974): 97–115; reprinted in *Representations* (MIT Press: Cambridge, 1981), and as the introductory chapter in Fodor, *The Language of Thought* (New York: Crowell, 1975).
3. Donald Davidson, "Mental Events" reprinted in *Essays on Actions and Events* (Oxford: Oxford University Press, 1980).
4. "Physicalism: Ontology, Determination, and Reduction," *Journal of Philosophy* 72 (1975): 551–64. The two quotations below are from p. 551.
5. "More on Making Mind Matter," *Philosophical Topics* 17 (1989): 175–92. The quotation is from p. 179.
6. "More on Making Mind Matter," p. 180.
7. In "Can the Mind Change the World?", *Meaning and Method: Essays in Honor of Hilary Putnam,* ed. George Boolos (Cambridge University Press: Cambridge, 1990), p. 146.
8. They include Richard Boyd, "Materialism without Reductionism: What Physicalism Does Not Entail," in Block, *Readings in Philosophy of Psychology,* vol. 1; Block, in "Introduction: What is Functionalism?" in his anthology just cited, pp. 178–79; John Post, *The Faces of Existence* (Ithaca: Cornell University Press, 1987); Derk Pereboom and Hilary Kornblith, "The Metaphysics of Irreducibility," (*Philosophical Studies*) 63 (1991): 125–45. One philosopher who is not impressed by the received view of MR is David Lewis; see his "Review of Putnam" in Block, *Readings in Philosophy of Psychology,* vol. 1.
9. Hilary Putnam, "Psychological Predicates," in W. H. Capitan and D. D. Merrill, eds., *Art, Mind, and Religion* (Pittsburgh: University of Pittsburgh, 1967); reprinted with a new title, "The Nature of Mental States," in Ned Block, ed., *Readings in Philosophy of Psychology,* vol. 1 (Cambridge: Harvard University Press, 1980).
10. "The Nature of Mental States," p. 228 (in the Block volume).
11. Thus, Post says, "Functional and intentional states are defined without regard to their physical or other

realizations," *The Faces of Existence,* p. 161. Also compare the earlier quotation from Block.
12. As far as I know, the term "realization" was first used in something like its present sense by Hilary Putnam in "Minds and Machines," in Sydney Hook, ed., *Dimensions of Mind* (New York: New York University Press, 1960).
13. On this point see Robert Van Gulick, "Nonreductive Materialism and Intertheoretic Constraints," in *Emergence or Reduction?,* ed. Ansgar Beckermann, Hans Flohr, and Jaegwon Kim (Berlin and New York: De Gruyter, 1992).
14. "More on Making Mind Matter," p. 179.
15. Cf. Hartry Field, "Mental Representation," in Block, *Readings in Philosophy of Psychology* (Cambridge: Harvard University Press, 1981), vol. 2.
16. What of LePore and Loewer's condition (ii), the requirement that the realization basis "explain" the realized property? Something like this explanatory relation may well be entailed by the realization relation; however, I do not believe it should be part of the definition of "realization"; that such an explanatory relation holds should be a consequence of the realization relation, not constitutive of it.
17. "The Nature of Mental States," p. 228 (in the Block volume).
18. *The Structure of Science* (New York: Harcourt, Brace & World, 1961), chap. 11.
19. My remarks here and the preceding paragraph assume that the higher-level theory requires no "correction" in relation to the base theory. With appropriate caveats and qualifications, they should apply to models of reduction that allow such corrections, or models that only require the deduction of a suitable analogue, or "image", in the reduction base—as long as the departures are not so extreme as to warrant talk of replacement or elimination rather than reduction. Cf. Patricia Churchland, *Neurophilosophy* (Cambridge: The MIT Press, 1986), chap. 7.
20. See "Special Sciences," pp. 132–33 (in *Representations*).
21. Fodor appears to assume that the requirement that bridge laws must connect "kinds" to "kinds" is part of the classic positivist conception of reduction. I don't believe there is any warrant for this assumption, however.

22. See Pereboom and Kornblith, "The Metaphysics of Irreducibility" in which it is suggested that laws with disjunctive predicates are not "explanatory." I think, though, that this suggestion is not fully developed there.

23. The points to follow concerning disjunctive predicates were developed about a decade ago; however, I have just come across some related and, in some respects similar, points in David Owens's interesting paper "Disjunctive Laws," *Analysis* 49 (1989): 197–202. See also William Seager, "Disjunctive Laws and Supervenience," *Analysis* 51 (1991): 93–98.

24. This can be taken to define one useful sense of kind heterogeneity: two kinds are heterogeneous with respect to each other just in case their disjunction is not a kind.

25. Note: this doesn't say that for any *e*, if *e* is "positive evidence" for *h* and *h* logically implies *j*, then *e* is positive evidence for *j*. About the latter principle there is some dispute; see Carl G. Hempel, "Studies in the Logic of Confirmation", reprinted in Hempel, *Aspects of Scientific Explanation* (New York: The Free Press, 1965), especially pp. 30–35; Rudolf Carnap, *Logical Foundations of Probability* (Chicago: University of Chicago Press, 1950), pp. 471–76.

26. On issues concerning properties, kinds, similarity, and lawlikeness, see W. V. Quine, "Natural Kinds" in *Ontological Relativity and Other Essays* (New York: Columbia University Press, 1969); David Lewis, "New Work for a Theory of Universals," *Australasian Journal of Philosophy* 61 (1983): 347–77; D. M. Armstrong, *Universals* (Boulder, Colorado: Westview Press, 1989).

27. This term is a little misleading since the two subtheses have been stated without the term "realization" and may be acceptable to those who would reject the "realization" idiom in connection with the mental. I use the term since we are chiefly addressing philosophers (mainly functionalists) who construe the psychophysical relation in terms of realization, rather than, say, emergence or brute correlation.

28. See "Special Sciences," and "Making Mind Matter More," *Philosophical Topics* 17 (1989): 59–79.

29. See, e.g., Block, "Can the Mind Change the World?," p. 155.

30. We might keep in mind the close relationship between disjunction and the existential quantifier standardly noted in logic textbooks.

31. It may be a complicated affair to formulate this argument within certain functionalist schemes; if, for example, mental properties are functionally defined by Ramseyfying a total psychological theory, it will turn out that humans and Martians cannot share any psychological state unless the same total psychology (including the putative law in question) is true (or held to be true) for both.

32. "Special Sciences," p. 140 (in *Representations*).

33. See, e.g., Carl G. Hempel, *Fundamentals of Concept Formation in Empirical Science* (Chicago: University of Chicago Press, 1952); W. Q. Quine, "Natural Kinds." Fodor gives it an explicit statement in *Psychosemantics* (Cambridge: MIT Press, 1988), chap. 2. A principle like this is often invoked in the current externalism/internalism debate about content; most principal participants in this debate seem to accept it.

34. A principle like this is sometimes put in terms of "supervenience" and "supervenience base" rather than "realization" and "realization base." See my "Epiphenomenal and Supervenient Causation," *Midwest Studies in Philosophy* 9 (1984): 257–70. Fodor appears to accept just such a principle of supervenient causation for mental properties in chap. 2 of his *Psychosemantics*. In "The Metaphysics of Irreducibility" Pereboom and Kornblith appear to reject it.

35. For more details see my "'Downward Causation' in Emergentism and Nonreductive Physicalism," in *Emergence or Reduction?*, ed. Beckermann, Flohr, and Kim, and "The Nonreductivist's Troubles with Mental Causation", in *Mental Causation*, ed. John Heil and Alfred Mele (New York: Oxford University Press, 1992).

36. Or an appropriately corrected version thereof (this qualification applies to the bridge laws as well).

37. In "Special Sciences" and "Making Mind Matter More" Fodor appears to accept the local reducibility of psychology and other special sciences. But he uses the terminology of local *explanation*, rather than reduction, of psychological regularities in terms of underlying microstructure. I think this is because his preoccupation with Nagelian uniform reduction prevents him from seeing that this is a form of intertheoretic reduction if anything is.

38. Compare J. J. C. Smart's instructive analogy between biological organisms and superheterodyne radios, in *Philosophy and Scientific Realism* (London: Routledge & Kegan Paul, 1963), pp. 56–57. Smart's conception of the relation between physics and the special sciences, such as biology and psychology, is similar in some respects to the position I am defending here.

39. "Introduction: What Is Functionalism?" in *Readings in Philosophy of Psychology*, pp. 178–79.

40. In their "The Metaphysics of Irreducibility." See also Ronald Endicott, "The Species-Specific Strategy," forthcoming. In personal correspondence Earl Conee and Joe Mendola have raised similar points. There is a useful discussion of various metaphysical issues relating to MR in Cynthia Macdonald, *Mind–Body Identity Theories* (London and New York: Routledge, 1989).

41. In "The Nature of Mental States."

42. I of course have in mind the controversy concerning moral realism; see essays in Geoffrey Sayre-McCord, ed., *Essays on Moral Realism* (Ithaca: Cornell University Press, 1988).

43. On concepts and properties, see, e.g., Hilary Putnam, "On Properties," *Mathematics, Matter and Method* (Cambridge: Cambridge University Press, 1975); Mark Wilson, "Predicate Meets Property," *Philosophical Review* 91 (1982): 549–90, especially, section III.

44. Such as the versions favored by W. V. Quine, Stephen Stich, and Paul Churchland.

45. The approach to the mind–body problem being adumbrated here is elaborated in my "Functionalism as Mental Irrealism" (in preparation).

46. This paper is descended from an unpublished paper, "The Disunity of Psychology as a Working Hypothesis?," which was circulated in the early 1980s. I am indebted to the following persons, among others, for helpful comments: Fred Feldman, Hilary Kornblith, Barry Loewer, Brian McLaughlin, Joe Mendola, Marcelo Sabates, and James Van Cleve.

From Supervenience to Superdupervenience

20

Meeting the Demands of a Material World

Terence Horgan

Supervenience is a determination relation between properties or characteristics of objects. The basic idea is this: properties of type A are supervenient on properties of type B if and only if two objects cannot differ with respect to their A-properties without also differing in their B-properties. For example, *being healthy,* a property instantiable by humans, plausibly is supervenient on physical features such as percentage of body fat, level of cholesterol in the bloodstream, absence of cancerous tissue, and the like: i.e., if one human being is healthy and another is not, then they must also differ in some of these physical features.

The term in its current philosophical usage evidently entered the analytic philosophy literature in a classic work of 20th century metaethics, Hare (1952):

> Let me illustrate one of the most characteristic features of value-words in terms of a particular example. It is a feature sometimes described by saying that 'good' and other such words are names of 'supervenient' or 'consequential' properties. Suppose that a picture is hanging upon the wall and we are discussing whether it is a good picture; that is to say, we are debating whether to assent to, or dissent from, the judgment 'P is a good picture'. . . . Suppose that there is another picture next to P in the gallery (I will call it Q). . . . Now there is one thing that we cannot say; we cannot say 'P is exactly like Q in all respects save this one, that P is a good picture and Q not'. . . . There must be some *further* difference between them to make one good and the other not. (1952, pp. 80–81).

Professor Hare has recently written, however, that this use of the term was already current in Oxford, and did not originate with him (Hare 1984, p. 1). And the concept we currently express by "supervenience," although not the word itself, had already been invoked in moral philosophy by G. E. Moore (1922), who held that intrinsic value is (as we would now say) supervenient on non-normative properties. Moore wrote:

> [I]f a given thing possesses any kind of intrinsic value in a certain degree, then not only must that same thing possess it, under all circumstances, in the same degree, but also anything *exactly like it,* must, under all circumstances, possess it in exactly the same degree. Or, to put it in the corresponding negative form: It is not *possible* that of two exactly similar things one should possess it and the other not, or that one should possess it in one degree, and the other in a different one. (1922, pp. 261)

Supervenience, then, is a modal notion. As David Lewis (1986) puts it, "Supervenience means that there *could* be no difference of one sort without difference of the other sort" (p. 15).

Although the concept of supervenience has been employed for a variety of purposes in recent philosophy, a rather dominant tendency since the early 1970s has been to invoke it in efforts to articulate a broadly materialistic, or physicalistic, position in philosophy of mind or in metaphysics generally. Often it has been invoked with the goal of articulating a materialistic metaphysical picture that eschews various strictures on inter-level connections that were sometimes built into earlier formulations of materialism—in particular, the requirement that psychological and other "higher-order" properties be *reducible* to physico-chemical properties.

Lately, however, the wave of relative enthusiasm about supervenience theses has begun to subside. There now seems to be emerging (e.g., Kim 1990; 1993b, ch. 9) an attitude of sober reassessment, accompanied by a suspicion that supervenience theses per se do less work philosophically than some had hoped they would.

I think this change of mood was in many ways inevitable, given certain ironic facts about the history of the notion of supervenience in philosophical thought during the 20th century. There is much to be learned from this history about both the uses and the limitations of supervenience theses, especially with respect to materialism. So the first half of this paper, sections

Excerpted from *Mind* 102:555–86, 1993. Reprinted with minor changes by permission of publisher and author.

1–4, will be a historical overview, aimed at highlighting some key ironies and drawing some important lessons for materialist metaphysics. The principal moral will be that supervenience relations, in order to figure in a broadly materialistic worldview, must be explainable rather than sui generis.

I will next take up some issues that have figured prominently in recent philosophical discussions of supervenience[1]: how to formulate supervenience theses (section 5); supervenience and the causal/explanatory efficacy of higher-order properties (section 6); supervenience and inter-theoretic reduction (section 7). Finally (section 8) I will return to the issue whose importance is the central moral of sections 1–4, but which has so far gone largely unnoticed in the philosophical literature: the explainability of supervenience relations.

Let me make several preliminary points. First, I take it that the question of what constitutes a broadly materialistic, or physicalistic, worldview is itself a philosophical question.[2] Although many philosophers, myself included, are disposed toward some sort of materialistic metaphysics, it is no simple matter to articulate such a view. Much of the philosophical interest of the notion of supervenience lies in its potential usefulness in this respect.

Second, for reasons of simplicity I will generally talk in terms of the basic physical level of description (the level of physics per se) vis-à-vis other levels of description—and often in terms of the physical vis-à-vis the mental. But much of what I will say presumably can be extended to inter-level supervenience relations more generally.

Third, for reasons of simplicity I will conduct the discussion in a way that presupposes an ontology of properties and facts. The language of properties and facts allows for perspicuous formulation of the central theses and issues I will be concerned with. But analogous theses and issues presumably would arise even under a more nominalistic ontology, although nominalists might seek to reformulate them or might deny that talk of facts and properties carries genuine ontological commitment to these putative entities.[3]

1. British Emergentism

It will be instructive to begin by considering supervenience in relation to an account of the special sciences that has been dubbed "British emergentism" in a splendid and fascinating recent paper, McLaughlin (1992). The British emergentist tradition began in the middle of the nineteenth century and flourished in the first quarter of this century. It began with John Stuart Mill's *System of Logic* (1843), then traced through Alexander Bain's *Logic* (1870), George Henry Lewes's *Problems of Life and Mind* (1875), Samuel Alexander's *Space, Time, and Deity* (1920), Lloyd Morgan's *Emergent Evolution* (1923), and finally C. D. Broad's *The Mind and Its Place in Nature* (1925). The latter was the last major work in this tradition, although the tradition continues even today in the work of a few authors, notably the neurophysiologist Roger Sperry.

The British emergentists were not substance-dualists; they held that all particulars are physical entities wholly constituted out of physical entities as their parts. But they were not full-fledged materialists either, because they denied that physics is a causally complete science. They maintained that at various junctures in the course of evolution, complex physical entities came into being that had certain non-physical, "emergent," properties. These properties, they claimed, are fundamental force-generating properties, over and above the force-generating properties of physics; when such a property is instantiated by an individual, the *total* causal forces operative within the individual are a combination of physical and non-physical forces, and the resulting behavior of the individual is different from what it would have been had the emergent force(s) not been operative alongside the lower-level forces.[4] Furthermore, there is no explanation for why emergent properties come into being, or why they generate the specific non-physical forces they do. These facts are metaphysically and scientifically basic, in much the same way that fundamental laws of physics are basic; they are unexplained explainers, which must be accepted (in Samuel Alexander's striking phrase) "with natural piety." Putative examples of emergent properties included (i) chemical-bonding properties of molecules, which were held to be emergent from physical properties of atoms or their constituents; (ii) self-maintenance and reproductive properties of living things, emergent from physical and chemical properties; and (iii) mental properties of creatures with consciousness, emergent from physical, chemical, and biological properties.[5] . . .

Could the British emergentists have held, consistently with their other principal doctrines, that emergent properties are *supervenient* (in the contemporary philosophical sense) on lower level properties—i.e., that individuals cannot differ in their emergent properties without also differing in their lower-order properties? . . . The answer to this question, as far as I can see, is affirmative. Certain higher-level properties could be supervenient on lower-level ones (ultimately on physical ones) and also possess the two key features the emergentists stressed: (i) the supervenient higher-order properties could be fundamental causal properties, generating causal forces over and above physical causal forces; and (ii) the connections between lower-order and higher-order properties—supervenience connections—could be metaphysically fundamental, hence unexplainable.

There are important lessons in the fact that the thesis of physical supervenience is consistent with the central doctrines of British emergentism, because those doctrines should surely be repudiated by anyone who advocates a broadly materialistic metaphysics. A materialist position should surely assert, contrary to emergentism, (i) that physics is causally complete (i.e., all fundamental causal forces are physical forces, and the laws of physics are never violated); and (ii) that any metaphysically basic facts or laws—any unexplained explainers, so to speak—are facts or laws within physics itself.

So the two principal lessons of British emergentism are these:

(L1) All properties and facts could be supervenient on physical properties and facts even if physics is not causally complete; for, certain non-physical properties could be supervenient on physical properties and yet causally basic (in the sense that they generate fundamental causal forces over and above physical forces). Yet a materialistic metaphysical position should assert the causal completeness of physics.

(L2) All properties and facts could be supervenient on physical properties and facts even if certain supervenience facts are metaphysically sui generis, unexplainable in more fundamental terms. Yet a materialistic metaphysical position should assert that all supervenience facts are explainable—indeed, explainable in some materialistically acceptable way.

I take it that any supervenient properties whose supervenience is materialistically explainable would not be causally basic properties in the sense of (L1). On the other hand, a metaphysical position affirming that there are supervenient properties whose supervenience is not materialistically explainable would not deserve the label "materialism," not even if it did affirm the causal completeness of physics. . . .

3. Hare and Meta-ethical Non-cognitivism

Although supervenience is typically regarded nowadays as an inter-level relation between properties or facts, it was not so regarded by the analytic philosopher who first used the term in print, Professor Hare. Hare was one of the principal advocates in this century of the meta-ethical position commonly called non-cognitivism; and on this view, there *are* no moral properties or moral facts. For Hare, supervenience in morals is a conceptual/semantic constraint on moral discourse and moral judgment; it is part of the "logic" of value-words (as was said in Oxford in the 1950s). Thus, if one uses moral language in a way that violates the supervenience constraint, one thereby abuses the very meaning of moral terms; and if one professes moral beliefs whose linguistic expression would violate the supervenience constraint, then either one misunderstands what one claims to believe, or else one's moral beliefs manifest a certain sort of inconsistency. . . .

So not all manifestations of supervenience need necessarily involve genuine higher-order properties or facts; and in general, explaining supervenience relations where there *are* such facts can be a substantially more demanding task than explaining supervenience as a mere constraint on discourse or judgment. For some kinds of discourse, it might turn out that only the less demanding kind of explanation is possible; for such cases, the proper *metaphysical* account of the discourse is likely to be an irrealist account. So here are two further morals concerning supervenience and metaphysics, in addition to those stated in section 1:

(L3) A metaphysical position, materialistic or otherwise, can combine supervenience as a doctrine about the terms and concepts in a given body of discourse with ontological irrealism about the discourse.

(L4) For some forms of discourse, it might turn out that although a materialistically acceptable explanation can be given for supervenience as a conceptual/semantic constraint on the discourse, no materialistically acceptable explanation can be given for putative in-the-world supervenience relations between lower-order properties and putative higher-order properties seemingly posited by the discourse.

Let us say that supervenience is *ontological* if it is an objective relation between lower-order properties and facts and genuine, objective, higher-order properties and facts; cf. Klagge (1988). Let us say that supervenience for a given mode of discourse is *robustly* explainable if it is explainable as ontological—i.e., explainable not merely as a conceptual/semantic constraint, but as an objective necessitation relation between lower-order and higher-order properties and facts. The general moral we obtain from lessons (L1)–(L4), then, is this: any genuinely materialistic metaphysics should countenance inter-level supervenience connections only if they are explainable in a materialistically acceptable way, and should countenance *ontological* inter-level supervenience relations only if they are *robustly* explainable in a materialistically acceptable way.

4. Davidson and the Materialist Appropriation of Supervenience

The notion of supervenience made its entrance into discussions of materialism in a seminal paper in the philosophy of mind, Davidson (1970). Here Davidson articulated and defended his 'anomalous monism,' a position with these key contentions: (i) every concrete, spatio-temporally located, mental event is identical to a concrete physical event; (ii) mental properties (event-types) are not identical to physical properties, and are not reducible to them via definition or law. The claim that physics is causally complete figured explicitly as a premise in his overall argument for this position; so did the claim that there are no strict psycho-physical laws, for which he gave a well-known subsidiary argument appealing largely to the allegedly holistic nature of propositional-attitude attribution.

The invocation of supervenience entered, briefly, in the context of emphasizing his rejection of psychophysical type-type identity and reducibility, and also by way of saying something positive about relations between physical and mental characteristics. Here is the key passage, frequently quoted:

> Although the position I describe denies there are psychophysical laws, it is consistent with the view that mental characteristics are in some sense dependent, or supervenient, on physical characteristics. Such supervenience might be taken to mean that there cannot be two events exactly alike in all physical respects but differing in some mental respect, or that an object cannot alter in some mental respect without altering in some physical respect. Dependence or supervenience of this kind does not entail reducibility through law or definition. . . . (1970, p. 88)

In another paper Davidson not only claimed that the supervenience of the mental on the physical is consistent with anomalous monism, but he went on to explicitly advocate such a dependence thesis. Concerning the theme of "the relation between psychological descriptions and characterizations of events, and physical (or biological or physiological) descriptions," he said:

> Although, as I am urging, psychological characteristics cannot be reduced to the others, nevertheless they may be (and I think are) strongly supervenient on them. Indeed, there is a sense in which the physical characteristics of an event (or object or state) *determine* the psychological characteristics: in G. E. Moore's word, psychological concepts are *supervenient* on physical concepts. Moore's way of explaining this relation (which he maintained held between evaluative and descriptive characteristics) is this: it is impossible for two events (objects, states) to agree in all their physical characteristics (in Moore's case, their descriptive characteristics) and to differ in their psychological characteristics (evaluative). (Davidson 1973, pp. 716–17)

Although Davidson was mistaken in attributing the *word* "supervenient" to Moore, he was of course correct in attributing to him the concept. (Note too the *modal* characterization of supervenience in both passages, and the similarity to Moore's own formulation I quoted at the outset.)

Davidson's invocation of supervenience in connection with the mind/body problem resonated strongly among philosophers working in philosophy of mind and metaphysics; there commenced a rapid and fairly widespread appropriation of supervenience into these branches of philosophy.[6] Two features of the above-quoted remarks are especially striking, and both evidently contributed to the subsequent popularity of supervenience among materialistically minded philosophers. First is Davidson's firm and explicit rejection of the *reducibility* of psychological characteristics to physical ones. In embracing a version of materialism that does not assert either the identity or the nomic equivalence of mental properties with physical properties, Davidson was evidently loosening the requirements for inter-level "fit" between different levels of description, in particular the physical and mental levels. Many philosophers were attracted by the thought that a broadly materialistic metaphysics can eschew reductionism, and supervenience seemed to hold out the promise of being a non-reductive inter-level relation that could figure centrally in a non-reductive materialism.

Second (and closely related), the passages implicitly suggest that psychophysical supervenience is an inter-level metaphysical determination-relation that renders mental properties *materialistically respectable,* as it were. The idea is that a reasonable materialism need only claim that physical facts and properties are the ontically *basic* ones, the ones that fix or determine all the facts. And supervenience of higher-order properties and facts on physical facts, it seemed, is just this sort of determination.

In light of the lessons we have drawn in earlier sections, however, it should be clear that mere supervenience of higher-order properties and facts on physical properties and facts cannot be enough to confer materialistic respectability. Moore in particular comes to mind—which is strikingly ironic, since Davidson actually *cites* Moore when he invokes supervenience. So it is not really surprising that doubts have now begun to emerge about whether supervenience, by itself, can carry as much weight in explicating a plausible materialism as some philosophers initially thought it could. Stephen Schiffer (1987) nicely expresses the reasons for scepticism, and the related irony:

> Tough-minded physicalist types (including many Logical Positivists) agreed [with Moore] that moral properties could not be reduced to natural properties . . . but had no sympathy at all with Moore's positive thesis, which postulated a realm of non-natural properties and facts. These properties, it was felt, could not be made sense of within a scientific world view: they were ob-

scurantist and produced more problems than they solved. At the same time, philosophers who abhorred Moore's irreducibly non-natural properties knew he also held this thesis about them: that it was not possible for two things or events to be alike in all physical respects while differing in some moral property. . . . No one thought that Moore's positive theory of moral properties was in any way mitigated by this further supervenience thesis. How *could* being told that non-natural moral properties stood in the supervenience relation to physical properties make them any more palatable? On the contrary, invoking a special primitive metaphysical relation of supervenience to explain how non-natural moral properties were related to physical properties was just to add mystery to mystery, to cover one obscurantist move with another. I therefore find it more than a little ironic, and puzzling, that supervenience is nowadays being heralded as a way of making non-pleonastic, irreducibly non-natural mental properties cohere with an acceptably naturalistic solution to the mind-body problem. (1987, pp. 153–54)

These remarks reinforce and underscore the negative moral that already emerged in sections 1–3. The moral is not that supervenience cannot be an important part of a broadly materialistic metaphysics, but rather this: putative supervenience relations that are themselves unexplainable and *sui generis* cannot play such a role. The corresponding positive moral is that the sort of inter-level relation needed by the materialist who is also a realist about a given mode of discourse (e.g., mental discourse) is not bare supervenience, but rather what I hereby dub *superdupervenience:* viz., ontological supervenience that is robustly explainable in a materialistically explainable way.[7] Superdupervenience would indeed constitute a kind of ontic determination which is itself materialistically kosher, and which thereby confers materialistic respectability on higher-order properties and facts. . . .

5. Versions of Supervenience: Weak, Strong, Global, and Regional

As philosophers began to turn in the 1970s to the notion of supervenience in attempts to articulate broadly materialist positions in philosophy of mind and metaphysics, there began to emerge a bewildering panoply of alternative ways of articulating supervenience theses themselves (cf. Teller 1984).

One parameter that can vary from one supervenience thesis to another is the class of possible worlds that fall within the scope of a given thesis. Some, e.g., Moore's thesis that intrinsic value is supervenient on natural properties, are plausibly construed as involving all possible worlds. Supervenience theses of interest to materialists, however, seem more plausibly construed as involving all *physically* possible worlds.

An orthogonal distinction is that between what Kim (1984a) calls "weak" and "strong" supervenience. Let A and B be two sets of properties, where we think of the A properties as supervenient on the B properties. The two kinds of supervenience can be expressed as follows:

Weak Supervenience: Necessarily, if something has an A-property F, then there exists a B-property G in B such that the thing has G, and everything that has G has F.
Strong Supervenience: Necessarily, if anything has property F in A, there exists a property G in B such that the thing has G, and *necessarily* everything that has G has F.

Here the B-property can be a conjunction of more basic B-properties. Weak supervenience pertains only to things that occupy the same possible world; it says that *within* any world, all things that are B-indiscernible are also A-indiscernible. Strong supervenience pertains across possible worlds; it says that for any worlds w and w′ and any things x and y (in w and w′ respectively), if x in w is B-indiscernible from y in w′, then x in w is A-indiscernible from y in w′. It is sometimes alleged that ordinary-language formulations of supervenience theses, like those of Moore, Hare, and Davidson I quoted earlier, only express weak supervenience; and it is often urged that strong supervenience better reflects the kind of inter-level dependence relation that supervenience theses are intended to capture. But my own view is that the traditional natural-language formulations really express strong supervenience—and that the formalizations expressing mere weak supervenience are mistranslations.[8]

Another issue in formulating supervenience theses arises from the fact that traditional formulations are what might be called *co-instantiation* theses: they are worded in a way that requires supervenient properties and subvenient properties to be instantiated by the *same individual.* This requirement creates at least two kinds of concern. For one thing, there seem to be numerous higher-order properties of individuals that depend for their instantiation not merely on the lower-order properties of the individual itself, but also on a wider range of lower-order properties and relations involving various other individuals too. For instance, the property *being a bank,* instantiated by the brick building on Main Street, is not supervenient on (intrinsic) physical properties of the bank itself; rather, the building's having this social-institutional property depends on a considerably broader range of physical facts and features, some of which are involved in subserving the social practice of banking. In addition, it is not obvious that materialism requires that high-level entities (such as universities and corporations) be identical to the entities that instantiate low-level properties.

One suggestion for accommodating these kinds of considerations is to formulate supervenience theses in terms of entire possible worlds. Kim (1984a, 1987) calls this *global* supervenience, a phrase now widely used. Standardly the idea of global *physical* supervenience, for instance, is expressed in some such way as this:

Global Physical Supervenience: There are no two physically possible worlds that are exactly alike in all physical respects but different in some other respect.

As is often pointed out, however (e.g., Horgan 1982; Kim 1984a, 1987), purely global supervenience seems too weak to fully capture the idea that the physical facts determine all the facts. For, the global thesis does not exclude the possibility that there are two spatio-temporal regions, within either the same physically possible world or two different ones, that are exactly alike in all intrinsic physical respects but different in some intrinsic non-physical respect—say, different in the respect that mental properties are instantiated by individuals in one region, but not by their physical duplicates in the other.

A natural strategy for accommodating this problem, proposed in Horgan (1982), is to strengthen global supervenience into what I will here dub *regional* supervenience. The thesis of regional *physical* supervenience may be expressed this way:

Regional Physical Supervenience: There are no two physically possible spatiotemporal regions that are exactly alike in all intrinsic physical respects but different in some other intrinsic respect.[9] . . .

7. Supervenience and Inter-level Reduction

I remarked in section 4 that one reason why the notion of supervenience caught on, in attempts to formulate a broadly materialistic position in philosophy of mind and metaphysics, was the feeling among many philosophers that traditional formulations of materialism posited an unduly tight, reductive, connection between the facts and properties posited by physics and higher-order facts and properties. The thought was that inter-level supervenience connections can be looser, and thus that supervenience-based materialism could be a *non-reductive* materialism.

But even among those who have embraced supervenience in connection with materialist metaphysics, there has been an ongoing debate about whether a viable materialism can really be non-reductive. The most ardent defender of the negative position is the philosopher who has perhaps been most active and influential in exploring and advocating supervenience in metaphysics and philosophy of mind, Jaegwon Kim. . . .

Let me turn briefly to Kim's position, as I understand it. Kim rejects the contention that mental properties in particular, and special-science properties in general, are identical to physical properties; he maintains instead that in general, higher-order theoretical properties are supervenient on lower-level properties, and ultimately on physical properties. He affirms the causal/explanatory efficacy of mental properties, and of special-science properties in general; as already noted in section 6, he maintains that supervenience transmits causal/explanatory efficacy from physical properties to higher-order properties that supervene on them. . . . As regards inter-theoretic reduction, he denies that genuine reductions must involve inter-level property-identities. He maintains instead that full-fledged reductions can be effected by inter-theoretic "bridge laws" expressing the nomic equivalence of lower-level and higher-level properties, provided that the laws of the higher-level theory are derivable from those of the lower-level theory plus the bridge laws. Finally, and with these other views as backdrop, he contends that a viable non-eliminativist position in philosophy of mind will inevitably end up committed to the reducibility of mentalistic psychology to natural science, and ultimately to physics.

Although I cannot here canvas the various arguments that Kim and others have employed in support of this contention, let me focus on one key argument. Concerning strong supervenience (as characterized in section 5 above) he writes:

> [I]t says that whenever a supervening property P is instantiated by an object, there is a subvenient property Q such that the instantiating object has it and the following conditional holds: necessarily if anything has Q, then it has P. So the picture we have is that for supervenient property P, there is a set of properties, $Q_1, Q_2, \ldots$ in the subvenient set such that each Q_i is necessarily sufficient for P. Assume this list contains all the subvenient properties each of which is sufficient for P. Consider their disjunction. . . . This disjunction . . . is necessarily coextensive with P. . . . So P and UQ_i are necessarily coextensive, and whether the modality here is metaphysical, logical, or nomological, it should be strong enough to give us a serviceable "bridge law" for reduction. . . . Some philosophers will resist this inference. . . . There are two questions, and only two as far as I can see, that can be raised here: (1) Is disjunction a proper way of forming properties out of properties? (2) Given that disjunction is a permissible property-forming operation, is it proper to form infinite disjunctions? (Kim 1990, pp. 19–20)

He then takes up arguments that have been given supporting negative answers to questions (1) and (2), and explains why he does not find them compelling.

Let me enter the dialectic at this point, by posing a third question: Are radically disjunctive properties *causal/explanatory* properties? Arguably, in general they are not; rather, on any given occasion when a higher-order theoretical property P is instantiated, the underlying physical causal/explanatory property that is operative (on that occasion) will be whichever specific *disjunct* Q_i, from the disjunctive property UQ_i, is instantiated (on that occasion)—and not the property UQ_i itself. Furthermore, a very plausible-looking condition on genuine reduction is that each higher-order causal/explanatory property be nomically coextensive with not just with any old lower-order property, but with some lower-order *causal/explanatory* property. For, if this condition is not met, then the higher-order causal/explanatory properties will cross-classify the lower-order ones, and thus will figure in higher-order causal/explanatory generalizations that are not directly mirrored at the lower theoretical level. In paradigmatic inter-theoretic reductions, by contrast, higher-order theoretical properties are not multiply realizable in this way; rather, higher-order theoretical laws *are* directly mirrored by lower-level causal/explanatory generalizations. (The Boyle/Charles law of thermodynamics, which links a gas's temperature, pressure, and volume, is directly mirrored by the law of statistical mechanics linking a gas's mean kinetic energy, mean surface pressure, and volume). Arguably, this kind of inter-level mirroring is the very essence of genuine inter-theoretic reduction.

Considerations involving multiple realization, along the lines just sketched, are among the reasons why many materialistically minded philosophers, myself included, deny that reductive materialism is the only viable alternative to eliminativism. But the reductionists remain unconvinced by multiple-realization arguments (e.g., Bickle 1992, Kim 1992b), and meanwhile maintain an active dialectical siege against nonreductive materialism.

8. Superdupervenience

Our conclusion at the end of section 4 was that the sort of inter-level relation that would confer materialistic "respectability" on higher-order properties and facts would be not bare ontological supervenience, but superdupervenience—ontological supervenience that is robustly explainable in a materialistically acceptable way. (Recall that *ontological* supervenience is an objective relation between lower-order properties and facts and genuine, objective, higher-order properties and facts; it is not merely a conceptual/semantic constraint on higher-order discourse. And, to give a robust explanation of supervenience is to explain it qua ontological, rather than explaining it merely as a feature of the "logic" of the higher-order terms and concepts.) Hereafter, unless I indicate otherwise, when I speak of explaining supervenience I will mean robustly explaining ontological supervenience in a materialistically acceptable way.

Although the task of explaining supervenience has been little appreciated and little discussed in the philosophical literature, it is time for that to change. I will conclude this essay with some brief remarks on the matter, set forth in a fairly staccato fashion.

In considering how inter-level supervenience relations might be materialistically explained, three interrelated questions arise:

The Standpoint Question: What sorts of facts, over and above physical facts and physical laws, could combine with physical facts and laws to yield materialistically kosher explanations of inter-level supervenience relations, and why would it be kosher to cite such facts in these explanations?

The Target Question: What facts specifically need explaining in order to explain a given inter-level supervenience relation, and why would a materialistic explanation of *these* facts constitute an explanation of that supervenience relation?

The Resource Question: Do there exist adequate explanatory resources to provide such explanations?

In order to get explanation off the ground, it seems we need to know *something* about the higher-order properties whose supervenience on physical properties is the target of explanation. The standpoint question and the target question, which are largely complementary, both arise from this apparent need for information about higher-order properties. The standpoint question (cf. Horgan 1984) arises because apparently we need *some* facts other than those of basic physics. It is hard to see how one could possibly explain an inter-level necessitation relation without employing, as part of one's explanans, *some* sorts of "connecting statements" in which purely physical properties and facts somehow get linked to higher-order properties. But which such facts are kosher, and why? The target question involves the explanandum: the to-be-explained facts. We need to know which facts are such that explaining *these* facts materialistically would constitute explaining why the higher-order properties supervene on the physical the way they do, and we need to know *why* these facts are the crucial ones. Philosophers need to get clearer about the standpoint and target questions. And they also need to ask, for any given domain of putative higher-order properties, whether there really exist adequate explanatory resources to yield materialistically kosher explanations of specific inter-level supervenience relations involving these properties; this is the resource question.

The problem of explaining supervenience does not go away if the generalizations of a higher-level theory or explanatory framework happen to be derivable from physics plus some set of "bridge laws" expressing the nomic coextensiveness of higher-order properties with physical properties. For, there remains the need to explain why these bridge laws *themselves* are true in all physically possible worlds (cf. Horgan 1978, Beckermann 1992b, McLaughlin 1992). Bridge laws, after all, are not part of physics; they should not be scientifically and metaphysically rock-bottom, sui generis and unexplainable. Further-more, even if the inter-theoretic bridge laws real-ly express property identities (rather than the mere nomic coextensiveness of higher-order properties and physical ones), an analogous ex-planatory task arises anyway—although now the key questions are about inter-level linkages be-tween terms and/or concepts. In virtue of what does such-and-such physical property, rather than various other candidate physical properties, count as the property expressed by a given high-er-order theoretical predicate?

For at least *some* kinds of properties we seem to have a fairly good idea about what would count as a materialistically acceptable explana-tion of why such a property is supervenient on a given configuration of physical properties. Con-sider, for instance, the property *liquidity*. We un-derstand well enough the essential features, or defining conditions, of liquidity: if a quantity of stuff is liquid, then it will neither spontaneously dissipate into the atmosphere nor retain a rigid shape when unconstrained, but instead will tend to flow, and to assume the shape of a vessel that contains it. Thus, explaining why liquidity su-pervenes on certain microphysical properties is essentially a matter of explaining why any quantity of stuff with these microphysical prop-erties will exhibit those macro-features. (As re-gards the target question, this suffices to explain the supervenience of liquidity because those macro-features are *definitive* of liquidity. As re-gards the standpoint problem, it seems explana-torily kosher to assume a "connecting principle" linking the macro-features to liquidity, precise-ly because those features *are* definitive; the con-necting principle expresses a fact about what liquidity *is*.)

A variety of recent so-called "naturalizing" projects, in philosophy of mind and elsewhere in philosophy, can be regarded as being, in effect, attempts to articulate the essential or definitive characteristics of certain higher-order properties (e.g., mental properties) in such a way that these properties, as so characterized, are susceptible to materialistic explanations of their supervenience. Functionalism in the philosophy of mind provides an example: if mental proper-ties as a family were identical with certain func-tional properties whose definitive causal roles involve typical-cause relations to sensory stimu-lation, bodily motion, and one another, then spe-cific physical/mental supervenience relations presumably would be materialistically explain-able in terms of causal/dispositional roles of categorial physical properties. Co-variance ac-counts of intentional content (e.g., Fodor 1987, 1990; Dretske 1981) provide another example: if the instantiating of a given intentional property, with content "that p," were essentially a matter of instantiating some physical property whose occurrence systematically co-varies with the cir-cumstance that p, then the supervenience of the content-property could be explained by citing the fact that the realizing physical property P co-varies with the circumstance that p.

Naturalizing projects are thus *reductive* in a certain sense, even though they are not commit-ted to the kinds of type-type inter-level connec-tions that make for inter-theoretic reduction in science. Their goal is to give a tractable specifi-cation, in non-intentional and non-mental vo-cabulary (although not necessarily in the vocab-ulary of physics), of sufficient conditions (or sufficient and necessary conditions) for the in-stantiation of mental properties. To the extent that this could be done, it would pave the way for physicalistic explanations of supervenience connections.

But there are a variety of reasons for being sceptical about such naturalizing projects. For one thing, reductive accounts of this kind usual-ly end up susceptible to counterexamples of one sort of another; inductive evidence, based on past failures both in this arena and in other philosophical arenas where attempts at reduc-tive analyses have been pursued, suggests that there always *will* be counterexamples to such proposals. In addition, it seems likely that hu-man concepts of mental states, and indeed most human concepts, just don't have reductive suffi-cient conditions at all (or reductive sufficient and necessary conditions), not even vague ones; this general claim about the structure of human concepts is strongly suggested by work in cog-nitive science on concepts and categories.[10]

So it makes sense to rethink what might count as philosophical "naturalization" of higher-order properties. Maybe there are ways of con-struing higher-order properties which (i) do not provide reductive sufficient conditions, but nev-ertheless (ii) render the physical supervenience of these properties materialistically explainable anyway. If so, then such accounts would still make room for the higher-order properties as part of the physical world, and thereby would naturalize them. (Rethinking naturalization would go hand in hand with investigating the standpoint, target, and resource questions mentioned above.)

But we should be sensitive to the possibility that for many kinds of higher-order discourse, it will not be possible to give an account of putative higher-order properties under which their ontological supervenience on the physical could be successfully explained. Consider mental properties, for example. With respect to the target problem, a fairly plausible-looking contention is that for any creature that instantiates mental properties, the generalizations of common-sense intentional psychology must be by-and-large true of that creature. With respect to the standpoint problem, it seems fairly plausible that the constraint just mentioned reflects the very *nature* of mental properties, and thus can be legitimately cited in explaining psychophysical supervenience relations. But now the resource problem arises: Since there evidently will always be vastly many incompatible ways of assigning propositional attitudes to someone over the course of his lifetime, all of which satisfy the given constraint, it appears that the constraint does not suffice to yield *determinate* supervenience connections between physical properties and facts and mental ones (cf. Quine 1960).[11]

We should also keep well in mind the reasons for metaphysical scepticism about in-the-world *normative* facts, a kind of scepticism which after all has been very prominent in meta-ethics throughout this century. One important reason is the difficulty of seeing how one could possibly give materialistic or naturalistic explanations for putative ontological supervenience-relations between natural properties and facts and putative normative properties and facts. Objective moral values do not appear to be part of the natural order.

But certain important supervenience relations, including but not limited to those that figure in ethics, evidently involve normativity— and thus an is-ought gap. In particular, there is arguably a normative element involved in intentional content—both the content of public-language expressions and the content of intentional mental properties. The "Kripkenstein problem" (Kripke 1982), for instance, can be seen as a sceptical challenge about whether there are any objective facts or properties, there in the world, that could ground semantic *correctness* (like the putative correctness of answering "125" to the query "68 + 57"). And a parallel problem can be raised about the objective groundability of the correct/incorrect distinction for the putative intentional content of people's mental states. The task of explaining supervenience facts, including perhaps psychological supervenience facts, therefore apparently includes the task of explaining how certain objective, in-the-world, is-ought gaps get bridged. Metaphysical scepticism about in-the-world normative facts now threatens to spill over into philosophy of mind and philosophy of language (not to mention epistemology, since *epistemic warrant* is a normative concept too).

Given the apparent difficulty of materialistically explaining ontological supervenience connections in a way that simultaneously handles the target, standpoint, and resource problems, and given that the challenge becomes all the greater insofar as normativity is involved, materialistically minded philosophers should be exploring *irrealist* ways of accommodating higher-order discourse. They should keep in mind that one can be an irrealist about a given body of discourse (e.g., moral discourse, or mental discourse) without being an eliminativist—someone who regards the discourse as defective, and needing replacement or elimination. Another broad option is *preservative* irrealism, which would treat higher-order discourse as quite legitimate and perhaps indispensable, while also repudiating its apparent ontological commitments. Instrumentalism, of course, is one form of preservative irrealism; instrumentalist views typically attribute utility to the given body of discourse, but deny that it expresses genuine truths. But the intellectual landscape includes other possible versions of preservative irrealism too— for instance, versions that treat truth itself as a normative notion, and which allow for higher-order discourse to be genuinely true even in the absence of any corresponding properties or facts (cf. Horwich 1990; Horgan 1991, forthcoming; Wright 1992; Horgan and Timmons 1993).

Superdupervenience would render higher-order properties metaphysically respectable. But it is not a relation that comes cheap. Explaining ontological supervenience relations in a materialistically acceptable way looks to be a very daunting task, whose difficulty suggests the need for materialists to take seriously the prospects for preservative irrealism about much of our higher-order discourse. It is not easy formulating a metaphysical position that meets the demands of a material world; there is still a lot of philosophical work to do.[12]

NOTES

1. Several other papers that usefully overview recent issues and discussions are Teller (1984), Kim (1990), and Beckermann (1992a, 1992b).
2. It is also a philosophical question what constitutes a broadly *naturalistic* worldview, and how (if at all) metaphysical naturalism might differ from materialism.
3. I will occasionally employ talk of possible worlds, in connection with modal locutions used to express supervenience theses. The remarks just made about properties and facts apply, mutatis mutandis, to possible worlds too.
4. Does this mean that the laws of physics are abrogated when emergent properties are instantiated? According to the emergentists, no. For, the laws of physics do not actually assert that physical forces are always the *only* operative forces in a physical system. So the laws of physics remain true when an emergent property is instantiated: the usual physical forces are present, and these physical forces are still additive in the usual way. It's just that the physical forces are not the only forces present, and hence the total net force in the system is not identical to the net *physical* force.
5. When Broad wrote, "Nothing that we know about Oxygen by itself or in its combinations with anything but Hydrogen would give us the least reason to suppose that it would combine with Hydrogen at all. Nothing that we know about Hydrogen by itself or in its combinations with anything but Oxygen would give us the least reason to expect that it would combine with Oxygen at all" (1925, pp. 62–63), his claim was true. Classical physics could not explain chemical bonding. But the claim didn't stay true for long: by the end of the decade quantum mechanics had come into being, and quantum-mechanical explanations of chemical bonding were in sight. Within another two decades, James Watson and Francis Crick, drawing upon the work of Linus Pauling and others on chemical bonding, explained the information-coding and self-replicating properties of the DNA molecule, thereby ushering in physical explanations of biological phenomena in general. (These kinds of advances in science itself, rather than any internal conceptual difficulties, were what led to the downfall of British emergentism—as McLaughlin [1992] persuasively argues.)
6. E.g., Hellman and Thompson (1975, 1977), Haugeland (1982), Horgan (1981, 1982), Kim (1978, 1979, 1981), Lewis (1983), and the papers collected in Horgan (1984). Although much of this subsequent literature was influenced, directly or indirectly, by Davidson on supervenience, this may not be so for Hellman and Thompson (1975, 1977), who used the word "determination" rather than "supervenience."
7. Although the definition is mine, the word is borrowed, with kind permission, from Bill Lycan (1986, p. 92). I thank him for it.
8. See Lewis (1986) pp. 15–17, and also Section 5 of the original version of the present paper.
9. For reasons of simplicity and brevity, this formulation of regional physical supervenience ignores certain niceties built into the formulation in the original version of the present paper.
10. For further adumbration of these kinds of considerations, including discussions of relevant psychological literature, see Stich (1992), Tye (1992), and Stich and Laurence (1994).
11. There are also the "phenomenal" or "what-it's-like" mental properties to deal with, the so-called "qualia." Prima facie, it is enormously hard to see how one could possibly explain why any particular physical or neurobiological property always gets co-instantiated with (or why it *necessarily* always gets co-instantiated with) a particular phenomenal property—or with any phenomenal property at all. (Appeals to type/type identity seem only to shift the mystery, rather than eliminating it: Why should any given physical or neurobiological property be identical to a particular experiential what-it's-like property—e.g., the property *experiencing phenomenal redness*—rather than to some other phenomenal property or to none at all?) This "explanatory gap" problem is well described, specifically in relation to type-identity treatments of qualia, by Levine (1983). The supervenience version of the problem is given a thorough and detailed treatment by Chalmers (1993); he argues that the explanatory gap cannot be bridged, and he defends a positive theory of consciousness which in some ways resembles Broad's emergentism.
12. I thank David Henderson, Jaegwon Kim, John Tienson, and Mark Timmons for helpful comments and discussion.

REFERENCES

Alexander, Samuel 1920: *Space, Time, and Deity,* 2 Volumes. London: Macmillan.

Bain, Alexander 1870: *Logic,* Books II and III.

Beckermann, Ansgar 1992a: "Reductive and Nonreductive Physicalism," in Beckermann et. al. 1992, pp. 1–21.

———— 1992b: "Supervenience, Emergence, and Reduction," in Beckermann et. al. 1992, pp. 94–118.

Beckermann, Ansgar, Flohr, Hans, and Kim, Jaegwon, eds. 1992: *Emergence or Reduction? Essays on the Prospects of Nonreductive Physicalism.* Berlin: Walter de Gruyter.

Bickle, John 1992: "Multiple Realizability and Psychophysical Reduction," *Behavior and Philosophy,* 20, 1, pp. 47–58.

Blackburn, Simon, 1971: "Moral Realism," in J. Casey, ed., *Morality and Moral Reasoning.* London: Methuen, pp. 101–24.

———— 1984: *Spreading the Word.* Oxford: Oxford University Press.

———— 1985: "Supervenience Revisited," in I. Hacking, ed., *Exercises in Analysis: Essays by Students of Casimir Levy.* Cambridge: Cambridge University Press, pp. 47–67.

Brink, David 1984: "Moral Realism and Skeptical Arguments from Disagreement and Queerness," *Australasian Journal of Philosophy, 62,* 2, pp. 111–25.

Broad, C. D. 1925: *The Mind and Its Place in Nature.* London: Routledge and Kegan Paul.

Chalmers, David 1993: *Toward a Theory of Consciousness.* Center for Research on Concepts and Cognition, Indiana University.

Churchland, Patricia Smith 1986: *Neurophilosophy.* Cambridge MA: MIT Press.

Davidson, Donald 1970: "Mental Events," in Foster, L. and Swanson, J. W., eds., *Experience and Theory.* Amherst: University of Massachusetts Press, 1970, pp. 79–101. Reprinted in Davidson 1980.

——— 1973: "The Material Mind," in P. Suppes et al., eds., *Logic, Methodology, and the Philosophy of Science.* Amsterdam: North-Holland, 1973, pp. 709–22. Reprinted in Davidson 1980.

——— 1980: *Essays on Actions and Events.* Oxford: Clarendon Press.

——— 1985: "Replies to Essays X–XII," in Bruce Vermazen and Merrill B. Hintikka, eds., *Essays on Davidson: Actions and Events.* Oxford: Clarendon Press, pp. 242–52.

Dretske, Fred 1981: *Knowledge and the Flow of Information.* Cambridge MA: MIT Press.

Dreier, James 1992: "The Supervenience Argument against Moral Realism," *Southern Journal of Philosophy,* 30, 3, pp. 13–38.

Fodor, Jerry 1981: "Special Sciences," in his *Representations.* Cambridge MA: MIT Press, pp. 127–43.

——— 1987: *Psychosemantics: The Problem of Meaning in the Philosophy of Mind.* Cambridge MA: MIT Press.

——— 1990: *A Theory of Content and Other Essays.* Cambridge MA: MIT Press.

——— 1991: "A Modal Argument for Narrow Content," *Journal of Philosophy,* 88, 1, pp. 5–26.

Hare, R. M. 1952: *The Language of Morals.* Oxford: Clarendon Press.

——— 1984: "Supervenience," *The Aristotelian Society Supplementary Volume,* 58, pp. 1–16.

Haugeland, John 1982: "Weak Supervenience," *American Philosophical Quarterly,* 19, 1, pp. 93–101.

Hellman, Geoffrey, and Thompson, Frank 1975: "Physicalism: Ontology, Determination, and Reduction," *Journal of Philosophy,* 72, 17, pp. 551–64.

——— 1977: "Physicalist Materialism," *Nous,* 11, 4, pp. 309–45.

Horgan, Terence 1978: "Supervenient Bridge Laws," *Philosophy of Science,* 45, 2, pp. 227–49.

——— 1981: "Token Physicalism, Supervenience, and the Generality of Physics," *Synthese,* 49, 3, pp. 395–413.

——— 1982: "Supervenience and Microphysics," *Pacific Philosophical Quarterly,* 63, 1, pp. 29–43.

——— 1984: "Supervenience and Cosmic Hermeneutics," in Horgan 1984, pp. 19–38.

——— 1991: "Metaphysical Realism and Psychologistic Semantics," *Erkenntnis,* 34, 3, pp. 297–322.

Horgan, Terence, ed. 1984: *The Concept of Supervenience in Contemporary Philosophy.* Spindel Conference Supplement, *Southern Journal of Philosophy,* 22.

Horgan, Terence, and Timmons, Mark 1993: "Metaphysical Naturalism, Semantic Normativity, and Meta-Semantic Irrealism," *Philosophical Issues,* 4, pp. 180–204.

Horwich, Paul 1990: *Truth.* Oxford: Basil Blackwell.

Kim, Jaegwon 1978: "Supervenience and Nomological Incommensurables," *American Philosophical Quarterly,* 15, 2, pp. 149–56.

——— 1979: "Causality, Identity, and Supervenience in the Mind-Body Problem," *Midwest Studies in Philosophy,* 4, pp. 31–49.

——— 1982: "Psychophysical Supervenience," *Philosophical Studies,* 41, 1, pp. 51–70.

——— 1984a: "Concepts of Supervenience," *Philosophy and Phenomenological Research,* 45, 2, pp. 153–76.

——— 1984b: "Epiphenomenal and Supervenient Causation," *Midwest Studies in Philosophy,* 9, pp. 257–70.

——— 1984c: "Supervenience and Supervenient Causation," in Horgan 1984, pp. 45–56.

——— 1987: "'Strong' and 'Global' Supervenience Revisited," *Philosophy and Phenomenological Research,* 10, 7, pp. 315–26.

——— 1989: "The Myth of Nonreductive Materialism," *Proceedings and Addresses of the American Philosophical Association,* 63, 3, pp. 31–47.

——— 1990: "Supervenience as a Philosophical Concept," *Metaphilosophy,* 21, 1 & 2, pp. 1–27.

——— 1992a: "'Downward Causation' in Emergentism and Nonreductive Physicalism," in Beckermann et al. 1992, pp. 119–38.

——— 1992b: "Multiple Realization and the Metaphysics of Reduction," *Philosophy and Phenomenological Research,* 70, 1, pp. 1–26.

——— 1993a: "The Non-Reductivist's Troubles with Mental Causation," in John Heil and Alfred Mele, eds., *Mental Causation.* Oxford: Clarendon Press, pp. 189–210.

——— 1993b: *Supervenience and Mind.* Cambridge: Cambridge University Press.

Klagge, James 1988: "Supervenience: Ontological and Ascriptive," *Australasian Journal of Philosophy,* 66, 4, pp. 461–70.

Kripke, Saul 1982: *Wittgenstein on Rules and Private Language.* Cambridge MA: Harvard University Press.

Levine, Joseph 1993: "Materialism and Qualia: The Explanatory Gap," *Pacific Philosophical Quarterly,* 64, 4, pp. 354–61.

Lewes, George Henry 1875: *Problems of Life and Mind,* Volume 2. London: Kegan Paul, Trench, Turbner, & Co.

Lewis, David 1979: "Counterfactual Dependence and Time's Arrow," *Nous,* 13, 4, pp. 455–76.

——— 1983: "New Work for a Theory of Universals," *Australasian Journal of Philosophy,* 61, 4, pp. 343–77.

——— 1986: *On the Plurality of Worlds.* Oxford: Basil Blackwell.

Lycan, William 1986: "Moral Facts and Moral Knowledge," in N. Gillespie, ed., *Moral Realism.* Spindel Conference Supplement, *Southern Journal of Philosophy,* 24, pp. 79–94.

Mackie, J. L. 1977: *Ethics: Inventing Right and Wrong.* New York: Penguin Books.

Marras, Ausonio 1993a: "Psychophysical Supervenience and Nonreductive Materialism," *Synthese,* 95, pp. 275–304.

——— 1993b: "Supervenience and Reducibility: An Odd Couple," *Philosophical Quarterly,* 43, 171, pp. 215–22.

McLaughlin, Brian 1989: "Type Epiphenomenalism, Type Dualism, and the Causal Priority of the Physical," *Philosophical Perspectives,* 3, pp. 109–35.

——— 1992: "The Rise and Fall of British Emergentism," in Beckermann et al. 1992, pp. 49–93.

Melnyk, Andrew 1991: "Physicalism: From Supervenience to Elimination," *Philosophy and Phenomenological Research,* 51, 3, pp. 573–87.

Mill, John Stuart 1843: *System of Logic.* London: Longmans, Green, Reader, and Dyer. Eighth edition, 1872.

Moore, G. E. 1922: "The Conception of Instrinsic Value," in his *Philosophical Studies.* New York: Harcourt, Brace, and Co., pp. 253–75.

Morgan, C. Lloyd 1923: *Emergent Evolution.* London: Williams & Norgate.

Quine, W. V. O. 1960: *Word and Object.* Cambridge MA: MIT Press.

Schiffer, Stephen 1987: *Remnants of Meaning.* Cambridge, MA: MIT Press.

Stich, Stephen 1978: "Autonomous Psychology and the Belief-Desire Thesis," *Monist,* 61, 4, pp. 573–91.

——— 1992: "What Is a Theory of Mental Representation?" *Mind,* 101, 402, pp. 243–61.

Stich, Stephen, and Laurence, Stephen 1994: "Intentionality and Naturalism," *Midwest Studies in Philosophy,* 19, pp. 159–82.

Teller, Paul 1984: "A Poor Man's Guide to Supervenience and Determination," in Horgan 1984, pp. 137–62.

Tye, Michael 1992: "Naturalism and the Mental," *Mind,* 101, 403, pp. 421–41.

Van Gulick, Robert 1992: "Nonreductive Materialism and the Nature of the Intertheoretical Constraint," in Beckermann et al. 1992, pp. 157–79.

Wright, Crispin 1992: *Truth and Objectivity.* Cambridge MA: Harvard University Press

21 | Finding the Mind in the Natural World

Frank Jackson

Conceptual analysis played a prominent role in the defence of materialism mounted by the Australian materialists and their American ally David Lewis. It was how they found a place for the mind within the material world. The leading idea is encapsulated in the following argument schema:

1. Mental state M = occupant of functional role F.   (By conceptual analysis)
2. Occupant of role F = brain state B.
                                           (By science)
3. Therefore, $M = B$.   (By transitivity)

This schema gives the role of conceptual analysis in the Australian defence. But it does not tell us why conceptual analysis had to have a role in the defence. Indeed, the schema positively invites the thought that conceptual analysis was not needed. For to get the conclusion that $M = B$, all that is needed is the truth of the two premises. It is not necessary that one of them be a conceptual truth. And I think, speaking more generally, that the Australian materialists left it unclear why materialists need to do some conceptual analysis. Nevertheless, I think that they were right that materialists need to do

From R. Casati, B. Smith, and G. White, eds., *Philosophy and the Cognitive Sciences* (Holder-Pichler-Tempsky, 1994). Reprinted with permission of the author.

some conceptual analysis. This paper is a defence of this view. In a nutshell my argument will be that only by doing some conceptual analysis can materialists find a place for the mind in their naturalistic picture of the world. In a final section we will note the implications of our discussion for the knowledge argument.

In arguing for the necessity of conceptual analysis I am swimming against the tide. Current orthodoxy repudiates the role of conceptual analysis in the defence of materialism for at least three reasons. First, materialism is a doctrine in speculative metaphysics. And, runs the first reason, though conceptual analysis has a role in the philosophy of language and the study of concepts, it has no essential role when our subject is what the world is, at bottom, like. The second reason is that the history of conceptual analysis is the history of failure. For any proffered analysis someone clever always finds a counterexample. The final reason turns on the claim that we have learnt from Hilary Putnam and Saul Kripke about the necessary a posteriori, and that tells us that there can be necessary connections that, precisely by virtue of being a posteriori, are not revealed by or answerable to conceptual analysis. The materialist should, according to this line of thought, hold that the connection between the mental and the material or physical is a necessary a posteriori one, and so not a matter accessible via conceptual analysis. During the course of the discussion we will see how to reply to each of these objections to the need for conceptual analysis in the defence of materialism.

The first step in our defence of the materialists' need for conceptual analysis is to note that materialism is a piece of what I will call serious metaphysics, and that, like any piece of serious metaphysics, it faces the location problem.

1. The Location Problem

Metaphysics is about what there is and what it is like. But it is concerned not with any old shopping list of what there is and what it is like. Metaphysicians seek a comprehensive account of some subject matter—the mind, the semantic, or, most ambitiously, everything—in terms of a limited number of more or less fundamental notions. Some who discuss the debate in the philosophy of mind between dualism and monism complain that *each* position is equally absurd. We should be *pluralists*. Of course we should be

pluralists in some sense or other. However, if the thought is that any attempt to explain it all, or to explain it all as far as the mind is concerned, in terms of some limited set of fundamental ingredients is mistaken in principle, then it seems to me that we are being, in effect, invited to abandon serious metaphysics in favour of drawing up big lists. And we know we can do better than that. At least some of the diversity in our world conceals an underlying identity of ingredients. The diversity is a matter of the same elements differently selected and arranged. But if metaphysics seeks comprehension in terms of limited ingredients, it is continually going to be faced with the problem of location. Because the ingredients *are* limited, some putative features of the world are not going to appear explicitly in the story told in the favoured terms. The question then will be whether the features nevertheless figure *implicitly* in the story. Serious metaphysics is simultaneously discriminatory and putatively complete, and the combination of these two facts means that there is bound to be a whole range of putative features of our world up for either elimination or location.

What then is it for some putative feature to have a place in the story some metaphysic tells in its favoured terms? One answer is for the feature to be entailed by the story told in the favoured terms. Perhaps the story includes information about mass and volume in so many words, but nowhere mentions density by name. No matter—density facts are entailed by mass and volume facts. Or perhaps the story in the favoured terms says that many of the objects around us are nothing but aggregations of molecules held in a lattice-like array by various inter-molecular forces. Nowhere in the story in the favoured terms is there any mention of solidity. Should we then infer that nothing is solid, or at any rate that this particular metaphysic is committed to nothing being solid? Obviously not. The story in the favoured terms will, we may suppose, tell us that these lattice-like arrays of molecules exclude each other, the inter-molecular forces being such as to prevent the lattices encroaching on each others' spaces. And *that* is what we understand by solidity. That's what it takes, according to our concept, to be solid. Or at least it is near enough. Perhaps pre-scientifically we might have been tempted to insist that being solid required being everywhere dense in addition to resisting encroachment. But resisting encroachment explains the stubbing of toes quite well enough for it to be pedantic to insist on anything more in order to be solid. Hence, solidity gets a location or place in the molecular story about our world by being entailed by that story, and we see this by asking ourselves about our concept of solidity in the sense of asking what it takes to be solid.

Thus, one way materialists can show that the psychological has a place in their world view is by showing that the psychological story is entailed by the story about the world told in the materialists' favoured terms. We will see, however, that it is not just one way; it is the one and only way.

2. Completeness and Supervenience

Materialism is the very opposite of a 'big list' metaphysics. It is highly discriminatory, operating in terms of a small set of favoured particulars, properties and relations, typically dubbed 'physical'—hence its other name, 'physicalism'; and it claims that a complete story, or anyway a complete story of everything contingent, including everything psychological, about our world can in principle be told in terms of these physical particulars, properties and relations alone. Only then is materialism interestingly different from dual attribute theories of mind.

Now what, precisely, is a complete story? We can make a start by noting that one particularly clear way of showing *incompleteness* is by appeal to independent variation. What shows that three co-ordinates do not provide a complete account of location in space-time is that we can vary position in space-time while keeping any three co-ordinates constant. Hence, an obvious way to approach completeness is in terms of the lack of independent variation. But, of course, lack of independent variation is supervenience: position in space-time supervenes on the four co-ordinates. So the place to look when looking for illumination regarding the sense in which materialism claims to be complete, and, in particular, to be complete with respect to the psychological, is at various supervenience theses.[1]

Now materialism is not just a claim about the completeness of the physical story concerning certain individuals or particulars in our world. It claims completeness concerning the world itself, concerning, that is, the total way things are. Accordingly, we need to think of the supervenience base as consisting of possible worlds—complete ways things might be. We need, ac-

cordingly, to look to global supervenience theses, an example of which is

(I)   Any two possible worlds that are physical duplicates (physical property, particular and relation for physical property, particular and relation identical) are duplicates *simpliciter.*

But (I) does not capture what the materialists have in mind. Materialism is a claim about our world, the actual world, to the effect that its physical nature exhausts all its nature, whereas (I) is a claim about worlds in general. A more restricted supervenience thesis in which our world is explicitly mentioned is:

(II) Any world that is a physical duplicate of our world is a duplicate *simpliciter* of our world.

However, materialists can surely grant that there is a possible world physically exactly like ours but which contains as an addition a lot of mental life sustained in non-physical stuff, as long as they insist that this world is not our world. Consider the view of those theists that hold that materialism is the correct account of earthly existence but it leaves out of account the after-life. When we die our purely material psychology is reinstated in purely non-physical stuff. Surely materialists can grant that these theists are right about some world, some way things might be, as long as they insist that it is *not* our world, not the way things actually are. Hence, materialists are not committed to (II).

The trouble with (II) is that it represents materialists' claims as more wide ranging than they in fact are. What we need is something like (II) but that limits itself to worlds more nearly like ours, or at least more nearly like ours on the materialists' conception of what our world is like. I suggest.

(III) Any world that is a *minimal* physical duplicate of our world is a duplicate *simpliciter* of our world.

What is a minimal physical duplicate? Think of a recipe for making scones. It tells you what to do, but not what *not* to do. It tells you to add butter to the flour but does not tell you not to add whole peppercorns to the flour. Why doesn't it? Part of the reason is that no one would think to add them unless explicitly told to. But part of the reason is logical. It is impossible to list all the things *not* to do. There are indefinitely many of them. Of necessity the writers of recipes rely on an intuitive understanding of an implicitly included 'stop' clause in their recipes. A minimal physical duplicate of our world is what you would get if you used the physical nature of our world (including of course its physical laws) as a recipe in this sense for making a world.

We arrived at (III) by eliminating alternatives. But we can give a positive argument for the conclusion that the materialist is committed to (III). Suppose that (III) is false; then there is a difference in nature between our world and some minimal physical duplicate of it. But then either our world contains some nature that the minimal physical duplicate does not, or the minimal physical duplicate contains some nature that our world does not. The second is impossible because the extra nature would have to be non-physical (as our world and the duplicate are physically identical), and the minimal physical duplicate contains no non-physical nature by definition. But if our world contains some nature that the duplicate does not, this nature must be non-physical (as our world and the duplicate are physically identical). But then materialism would be false, for our world would contain some non-physical nature. Hence, if (III) is false, materialism is false—that is to say, materialism is committed to (III).

3. From (III) to Entry by Entailment

Given that (III) follows from materialism, there is a straightforward and familiar argument to show that if materialism is true, then the psychological story about our world is entailed by the physical story about our world.

We can think of a statement as telling a story about the way the world is, and as being true inasmuch as the world is the way the story says it is. Let Φ be the statement which tells the rich, complex and detailed physical story that is true at the actual world and all and only the minimal physical duplicates of the actual world, and false elsewhere. Let Π be any true statement entirely about the psychological nature of our world: Π is true at our world, and every world at which Π is false differs in some psychological way from our world. If (III) is true, every world at which Φ is true is a duplicate *simpliciter* of our world, and so a fortiori a psychological duplicate of our world. But then every world at which Π is true is a world at which Π is true—that is, Φ entails Π.

We have thus derived what we might call the *entry by entailment thesis:* a putative psychological fact has a place in the materialists' world view if and only if it is entailed by the physical story about the world. The one and only way of getting a place is by entailment.

4. From Entry by Entailment to Conceptual Analysis

How does entry by entailment show the importance of conceptual analysis? If Φ entails Π, what makes Φ true also makes Π true (at least when Φ and Π are contingent). But what makes Φ true is the physical way our world is. Hence, the materialist is committed to each and every psychological statement being made true by a purely physical way our world is. But it is the very business of conceptual analysis to address which matters framed in terms of one set of terms and concepts are made true by which matters framed in a different set of terms and concepts. For instance, when we seek an analysis of knowledge in terms of truth, belief, justification, causation and so on, we seek an account of how matters described in terms of the latter notions make true matters described in terms of the former. When we seek an account of reference, we seek an account of the kinds of causal and descriptive facts which make it true that a term names an object. When and if we succeed, we will have an account of what makes it true that 'Moses' names Moses in terms of, among other things, causal links between uses of the word and Moses himself. And so on and so forth.

How could the a priori reflections on, and intuitions about, possible cases so distinctive of conceptual analysis be relevant to, for instance, the causal theory of reference? Well, the causal theory of reference is a theory about the conditions under which, say, 'Moses' refers to a certain person. But that is nothing other than a theory about the possible situations in which 'Moses' refers to that person, and the possible situations in which 'Moses' does not refer to that person. Hence, intuitions about various possible situations—the meat and potatoes of conceptual analysis—are bound to hold centre stage. (This is particularly true when the test situations cannot be realised. We cannot, for instance, make twin earth to check empirically what we would say about whether XYZ is water.)

The alternative is to *invent* our answers. Faced with the question, say, of whether the physical way things are makes true the belief way things are, we *could* stipulate the conditions under which something counts as a belief in such a way as to ensure that there are beliefs, or, if we preferred, that there are no beliefs. But that would not bear on whether beliefs according to *our* concept have a place in the materialists' picture of things, only on whether beliefs according to the stipulated concept have a place. In order to address the question of whether beliefs as we understand them have a place, what else can we do but consult and be guided by our honed intuitions about what counts as a belief? Would it be better to invent, or to go by what seems counter-intuitive?

I should emphasise, though, that a sensible use of conceptual analysis will allow a limited but significant place for a posteriori stipulation. We mentioned earlier the example of finding a place for solidity in the molecular picture of our world, and the fact that what the molecular picture vindicates is the existence of solid bodies according to a conception of solidity cashed out in terms of mutual exclusion rather than in terms of the conjunction of mutual exclusion and being everywhere dense. For our day to day traffic with objects, it is the mutual exclusion that matters, and accordingly it is entirely reasonable to rule that mutual exclusion is enough for solidity. The role of conceptual analysis of *K*-hood is not always to settle on a nice, neat, *totally* a priori list of necessary and sufficient conditions for being a *K*—indeed, that is the task that has so often been beyond us. It is rather to guide us in dividing up the cases that clearly are not cases of a *K,* from the cases that a principle of charity might lead us to allow as cases of a *K.* Then, armed with this information, we are in a position to address the question of whether some inventory of fundamental ingredients does, or does not, have a place for *K*s.

I should also emphasise that the contention is not that a priori reflection on possible cases gives us new information, let alone some sort of infallible new information, about what the world is like. The reflection is a priori in the sense that we are not consulting our intuitions about what would *happen* in certain possible cases—it is not like the famous thought experiments in science—rather we are consulting our intuitions about how to *describe* certain possible cases. And what we learn (in the sense of making explicit) is not something new about what the world is like, but something about how, given what the world is like as described in one set of terms, it should be described in some other set of terms. Perhaps the point is clearest in the example about finding solidity in the molecular account of the objects around us. Reflection on our concept of solidity tells us that the molecular account includes solidity, but it does not tell us that solidity is an addition to what appears in the molecular account of objects, let alone an infallible one.

5. The Objection from the Necessary a Posteriori

It might well be urged that the argument given above from (III) to the conclusion that Φ entails Π is undermined by the existence of necessary a posteriori truths. The objection can be put in two different ways. Consider

Over 60% of the Earth is covered by H_2O.

Therefore, over 60% of the Earth is covered by water.

One way of putting the objection is that although every world where the premise is true is a world where the conclusion is true, the argument is not valid because the premise does not entail the conclusion in the relevant sense. It is not possible to move a priori from the premise to the conclusion. The premise fixes the conclusion without entailing it, as it is sometimes put. Likewise, for all we have shown by the considerations based on (III), Φ fixes Π but does not entail it.

This way of putting the objection makes it sound like a quarrel over terminology. It invites the response of distinguishing entailment *simpliciter,* the notion cashed out simply in terms of being necessarily truth-preserving, from a priori or, as it is sometimes called, conceptual, entailment, the latter being the notion tied to a priori deducibility. But the real objection, of course, is that the necessarily truth-preserving nature of the passage from 'Over 60% of the Earth is covered by H_2O' to 'Over 60% of the Earth is covered by water' is not one that can in principle be revealed by conceptual analysis. Reflection on, and intuitions about, possible cases and concepts, unless supplemented by the a posteriori information that water is H_2O, will get you nowhere. Materialists, it seems, can allow that (III) forces them to admit a necessarily truth-preserving passage from Φ to Π, without allowing a role for conceptual analysis. They can simply insist that the entailment from Φ to Π is an a posteriori one.

We will see, however, that acknowledging the necessary a posteriori does not alter matters in any essential respects as far as the importance of conceptual analysis goes. The argument to this conclusion turns on a negative claim about the nature of the necessity possessed by the necessary a posteriori, and a consequent view about the role of conceptual analysis, in the sense of intuitions about possibilities, in the detection of the necessary a posteriori.

6. The Necessity of the Necessary A Posteriori

There are two different ways of looking at the distinction between necessary a posteriori statements like 'Water = H_2O' and necessary a priori ones like '$H_2O = H_2O$' (all necessary modulo worlds where there is no water, of course). You might say that the latter are analytically or conceptually or logically (in some wide sense not tied to provability in a formal system) necessary, whereas the former are metaphysically necessary, meaning by the terminology that we are dealing with two senses of 'necessary' in somewhat the way that we are when we contrast logical necessity with nomic necessity. On this approach, the reason the necessity of water's being H_2O is not available a priori is that its necessity is not the kind that is available a priori.

I think, as against this view, that it is a mistake to hold that the necessity possessed by 'Water = H_2O' and 'If over 60% of the Earth is covered by H_2O, then over 60% of the Earth is covered by water' is different from that possessed by 'Water = water' and 'If over 60% of the Earth is covered by H_2O, then over 60% of the Earth is covered by H_2O.' Just as Quine insists that numbers and tables exist in the very same sense, I think that we should insist that water's being H_2O and water's being water are necessary in the very same sense.

My reason for holding that there is one sense of necessity here relates to what it was that convinced us that 'Water = H_2O' is necessarily true. What convinced us were the arguments of Saul Kripke and Hilary Putnam about how to *describe* certain possibilities, rather than arguments about what is possible per se. Kripke and Putnam convinced us that a world where XYZ plays the water role—that is, satisfies enough of (but how much is enough is vague): filling the oceans, being necessary for life, being colourless, being called 'water' by experts, being of a kind with the exemplars we are acquainted with,

and so on—did not warrant the description 'world where water is XYZ', and the stuff correctly described as water in a counterfactual world is the stuff—H_2O—which fills the water role in the actual world. The key point is that the right way to describe a counterfactual world sometimes depends in part on how the actual world is, and not solely on how the counterfactual world is in itself. The point is not one about the space of possible worlds in some newly recognised sense of 'possible', but instead one about the role of the actual possible world in determining the correct way to describe certain counterfactual possible worlds—in the sense of 'possible' already recognised.

All this was, it seems to me, an exercise in conceptual analysis. We had an old theory about the meaning of 'water,' namely, that it meant 'that which fills the water role,' a theory that was refuted by appealing to our intuitions about how to describe possible worlds in which something different from that which actually fills the water role fills the water role. We became convinced of a new theory—again by reflection on possible cases, the meat and potatoes of conceptual analysis—according to which 'water' is a rigid designator of the stuff that fills the water role in the actual world. At no time did we have to recognise a new sort of possibility, only a new way for something in some counterfactual situation to count as a *K,* namely, by virtue not solely of how things are in that counterfactual situation, but in part in virtue of how things actually are.

If this is right, the inference

Over 60% of the Earth is covered by H_2O.

Therefore, over 60% of the Earth is covered by water.

is not an example of an a posteriori entailment that shows the irrelevance of conceptual analysis to the question of whether an a posteriori entailment holds. For it is conceptual analysis that tells us, in light of the fact that H_2O fills the water role, that the entailment holds.

7. Two-Dimensionalism and the Knowledge Argument

I have argued that materialists must hold that the complete story about the physical nature of our world given by Φ entails everything about our psychology, and that such a position cannot be maintained independently of the results of conceptual analysis. But it is quite another question whether they must hold that Φ a priori entails everything about our psychology, including its phenomenal side, and so quite another question whether they must hold that it is in principle possible to deduce from the full physical story alone what it is like to see red or smell a rose—the key assumption in the knowledge argument that materialism leaves out qualia. I will conclude by noting how the two dimensional treatment of the necessary a posteriori—the obvious treatment of the necessary a posteriori for anyone sympathetic to the view that such necessity is not a new sort of necessity—means that materialists are committed to the a priori deducibility of the phenomenal from the physical.

If the explanation of the a posteriori nature of the necessary a posteriori does not lie in the special necessity possessed, where does it lie? Two dimensionalists insist that the issue is an issue about sentences, and not about propositions, or at least not propositions thought of as sets of possible worlds. For, by the conclusion that we are not dealing with a new sort of necessity, the set of worlds where water is water is the very same set as the set where water is H_2O, and so, by Leibnitz's Law, there is no question of the proposition that water is water differing from the proposition that water is H_2O in that one is, and one is not, necessary a posteriori. Their contention is that there are sentences such that the proposition expressed by them depends on the context of utterance.[2] We understand them in that we know how the proposition expressed depends on the context, but if we do not know the relevant fact about the context, we will not know the proposition expressed. (In Robert Stalnaker's terminology, we know the propositional concept but not the proposition; in David Kaplan's, we know the character but not the content.[3]) Consider 'Over 60% of the Earth is covered by water.' Because 'water' is a rigid designator whose reference is fixed by 'the stuff that fills the water role,' someone who does not know what that stuff is does not know which proposition the sentence expresses, but they understand the sentence by virtue of knowing how the proposition expressed depends on how things actually are, and, in particular, this being the relevant contextual matter in this case, on what actually fills the water role. The explanation of the necessary a posteriori status of 'If over 60% of the Earth is covered by H_2O, then over 60% of the Earth is covered by water' then runs as follows. The proposition expressed by the sentence 'Over 60% of the Earth is covered

by H_2O,' is the same as the proposition expressed by 'Over 60% of the Earth is covered by water,' and so the proposition expressed by the conditional sentence is a priori and necessary. But consistent with what is required to count as understanding the conditional sentence, it is contingent and a posteriori that it expresses a necessary a priori proposition.

I should emphasise that this does not mean that people who fully understand a sentence like 'Over 60% of the Earth is covered by water' but do not know that water is H_2O do not, in some perfectly natural sense, know the conditions under which what they are saying is true.[4] True, full understanding of the sentence does not in itself yield which proposition is expressed by the sentence, but knowledge of the way in which the proposition expressed depends on context, combined with knowledge of the truth conditions of the various propositions, does enable them to say when the sentence they produce is true. For their knowledge about how the proposition expressed depends on context together with the conditions under which the various propositions are true is given in the following array:

If H_2O fills the water role, then 'Over 60% of the Earth is covered by water' expresses a proposition that is true iff over 60% of the Earth is covered by H_2O.

If XYZ fills the water role, then 'Over 60% of the Earth is covered by water' expresses a proposition that is true iff over 60% of the Earth is covered by XYZ.

If — fills the water role, then 'Over 60% of the Earth is covered by water' expresses a proposition that is true iff over 60% of the Earth is covered by —.

For each distinct, context-giving, antecedent, a distinct proposition is expressed by the sentence. Nevertheless, simple inspection of the array shows that the sentence is true iff over 60% of the Earth is covered by the stuff that fills the water role. That is the sense in which the fully understanding producer of the sentence knows when the sentence is true.[5]

Now, to return to the main plot, although understanding alone does not necessarily give the proposition expressed by certain sentences—that is how they can be necessary and yet this fact be in principle not accessible to understanding plus acumen alone, that is how they can be necessary a posteriori—understanding alone does give us the way the proposition expressed depends on context; and that fact is enough for us to move a priori from, for example, sentences about the distribution of H_2O combined with the right context-giving sentences, to information about the distribution of water. Consider, for instance, a supplementation of our earlier inference:

(1) Over 60% of the Earth is covered by H_2O.

(2) H_2O fills the water role.

(3) Therefore, over 60% of the Earth is covered by water.

Although, as noted earlier, the passage from (1) to (3) is necessarily truth-preserving but a posteriori being an a posteriori entailment, the passage from (1) and (2), to (3) is a priori. And it is so because, although our understanding of 'Over 60% of the Earth is covered by H_2O' does not in itself yield the proposition expressed by the sentence, it yields how the proposition depends on context, and (2) gives that context. (2) gives the relevant fact about how things are "outside the head." We did not know that (1) entailed (3) until we learnt (2), because we did not, and could not, have known that (1) and (3) express the same proposition until we learnt (2). But as soon as we learn (2), we have the wherewithal, if we are smart enough, to move a priori to (3).

The point, then, is that the necessary a posteriori nature of 'Water = H_2O' does not mean that the fact that the H_2O way things are entails the water way things are is not answerable to our grasp of the relevant concepts plus acumen. It means, rather, that we need to tell a rich enough story about the H_2O way things are, a story that includes the crucial contextual information, before we can move from the H_2O way things are to the water way they are using our grasp of the concepts alone.

More generally, the two-dimensional way of looking at the necessary a posteriori means that even if the entailment the materialist is committed to from some physical story about the world to the full psychological story is a posteriori, there is still an a priori story tellable about how the story in physical terms about our world makes true the story in psychological terms about our world. Although understanding may not, even in principle, be enough to yield the proposition expressed by the physical story, understanding and logical acumen is enough to yield how the proposition expressed depends on context. But, of course, the context is, according to the materialist, entirely physical. The context concerns various matters about the nature of the actual world, and that nature is capturable in entirely physical terms according to the materialist. Hence, the materialist is committed to there being an a priori story to tell about how the physical way things are makes true the psychological way things are. But the story may come in two parts. It may be that one part of the story says which physical way things are, Φ_1, makes some psychological statement true, and the other part of the story, the part that tells the context, says which different physical way things are, Φ_2, makes it the case that it is Φ_1 that makes the psychological statement true. What will be a priori accessible is that Φ_1 and Φ_2 together make the psychological statement true.[6]

NOTES

1. What follows is one version of a familiar story. See, for example, T. Horgan 1982 and D. Lewis 1983.
2. I take it that what follows is a sketch of the approach suggested by the version of two-dimensionalism in Stalnaker 1978.
3. Stalnaker 1978 and Kaplan 1978.
4. I am indebted here to David Lewis and David Chalmers.
5. This observation bears on the dispute about whether Earthians and Twin Earthians believe alike. Although the sentence 'Water is plentiful' expresses different propositions in the mouths of the Earthians and the Twin Earthians, they agree about when the sentence is true, and so in *that* sense agree in belief.
6. I am indebted to Lloyd Humberstone, David Chalmers, David Lewis, Michael Smith, and Philip Pettit.

REFERENCES

Terence Horgan 1982 "Supervenience and Microphysics," *Pacific Philosophical Quarterly* 63, 29–43.

David Kaplan 1978 "Dthat," in P. Cole (ed.), *Syntax and Semantics* Vol. 9, New York: Academic Press.

David Lewis 1983 "New Work for a Theory of Universals," *Australasian Journal of Philosophy* 61, 343–377.

Robert C. Stalnaker 1978 "Assertion" in P. Cole (ed.), *Syntax and Semantics* Vol. 9, New York: Academic Press, pp. 315–32.

F. Mental Causation

22 | The Many Problems of Mental Causation

Jaegwon Kim

Giving an account of mental causation—in particular, explaining how it is possible for the mental to exercise causal influences in the physical world—has been one of the main preoccupations in the philosophy of mind over the past two decades. The problem of course is not new: as we learn early in our philosophy classes, Descartes was confronted forcefully by his contemporaries on this issue,[1] to explain how there could be causal transactions between minds and bodies. But this does not mean that Descartes' problem is our problem. His problem, as his contemporaries saw, was to show just how his all-too-commonsensical thesis of mind–body interaction was tenable within his ontology of two radically diverse domains of substances, minds and bodies. In his replies, Descartes hemmed and hawed, and was ultimately unable to produce an effective response. Many of his contemporaries, like Leibniz and Malebranche, chose to abandon mental causation in favor of substantival dualism. In staying with mental causation to the end, however, Descartes showed a healthy and commendable respect for philosophical commonsense—more so than many of his major philosophical rivals who opted for radical and implausible solutions—and I believe we should remember him for this as well as for his much publicized failure to reconcile mental causation with his ontology. In any case substance dualism is not the source of our current worries about mental causation; substantival minds are no longer a live philosophical option for most of us.

Philosophical problems do not arise in a vacuum. Typically they emerge when we come to see a conflict among the assumptions and presumptions that we explicitly or tacitly accept, or commitments that command our presumptive respect. The seriousness of a philosophical problem therefore depends on two related questions: First, how deep is our attachment to the assumptions and commitments that give rise to the apparent conflict? Second, how easy or difficult is it to bring the conflicting assumptions into an acceptable reconciliation? The process of reconciliation may require serious modifications to our original commitments. Short of abandoning the entire framework of the existing commitments, compromises must be negotiated. There are no free lunches in philosophy any more than in real life.

In this lecture I want to set out, in what to my mind is the simplest and starkest way, how our principal current problem of mental causation arises. In saying this, I do not want to imply that there is a single problem of mental causation. In fact, as we will shortly see, several different sets of assumptions and principles that many of us find plausible can make trouble for mental causation. I will first describe three sources that seem to generate difficulties for mental causation. This means that we are faced with at least three distinct problems of mental causation. However, in the rest of this lecture, I will focus on one particular version of the third of these problems ("the exclusion problem"). This problem arises from what I will call "the supervenience argument." This, I claim, is our principal problem of mental causation. In referring to this as "our" problem of mental causation, what I mean to suggest is that it is a problem that arises for anyone with the kind of broadly physicalist outlook that many philosophers, including myself, find compelling or, at least, plausible and attractive. In contrast, the other two problems (the mental anomaly problem and the extrinsicness problem) are not essentially tied to physicalism. They are largely independent of physicalist commitments and can arise outside the physicalist framework. As we will see, the exclusion problem is distinctive in that it strikes at the very heart of physicalism, and I believe that the supervenience argument captures the essence of the difficulties involved. The fundamental problem of mental causation for us, then, is to answer this question: How is it possible for the mind to exercise its causal powers in a world that is fundamentally physical?

Let me begin with some reasons for wanting to save mental causation—why it is important to us that mental causation is real (some will say that its existence is an ultimate, nonnegotiable commitment). First, the possibility of human agency evidently requires that our mental states—our beliefs, desires, and intentions—have causal effects in the physical world: in voluntary actions our beliefs and desires, or intentions and decisions, must somehow cause our limbs to move in appropriate ways, thereby causing the objects around us to be rearranged. That is how we manage to cope with our surroundings, write philosophy papers, build bridges and cities, and make holes in the ozone layers. Second, the possibility of human knowledge presupposes the reality of mental causation: perception, our sole window on the world, requires the causation of perceptual experiences and beliefs by physical objects and events around us. Reasoning, by which we acquire new knowledge and belief from the existing fund of what we already know or believe, involves the causation of new belief by old belief; more generally, causation arguably is essential to the transmission of evidential groundedness. Memory is a complex causal process involving interactions between experiences, their physical storage, and retrieval in the form of belief. If you take away perception, memory, and reasoning, you pretty much take away all of human knowledge. To move on, it seems plain that the possibility of psychology as a theoretical science capable of generating law-based explanations of human behavior depends on the reality of mental causation: mental phenomena must be capable of functioning as indispensable links in causal chains leading to physical behavior. A science that invokes mental phenomena in its explanations is presumptively committed to their causal efficacy; for any phenomenon to have an explanatory role, its presence or absence in a given situation must make a difference—a *causal difference.*

It is no wonder then that for most philosophers the causal efficacy of the mental is something that absolutely cannot be given away no matter how great the pressures are from other quarters. Jerry Fodor is among these philosophers; he writes:

... if it isn't literally true that my wanting is causally responsible for my reaching, and my itching is causally responsible for my scratching, and my believing is causally responsible for my saying ... , if none of that is literally true, then practically everything I believe about anything is false and it's the end of the world.[2]

If mental causation is only an illusion, that perhaps is not the end of the world, but it surely seems like the end of a world that includes Fodor and the rest of us as agents and cognizers. The problem of determinism threatens human agency, and the challenge of skepticism threatens human knowledge. The stakes seem even higher with the problem of mental causation, for this problem threatens to take away both agency and cognition.

Three Problems of Mental Causation

What then are the assumptions and presumptions that make trouble for mental causation, prompting us to attempt its "vindication"? I believe there are three doctrines currently on the scene each of which poses prima facie difficulties for mental causation. The first two have been with us for some time; the third, though not new, has begun to receive serious new considerations. One is "mental anomalism," the claim that there are no causal laws about psychological phenomena. The second source of the problem is computationalism and content externalism. The third I call "causal exclusion." Each of these generates a distinct problem of mental causation, though the problems are to some extent interconnected. A truly comprehensive theory of mental causation must provide a solution to each problem, a solution that simultaneously satisfies the demands of all three problems.

The Problem of Anomalous Mental Properties

Let us begin with mental anomalism. Davidson's version of this doctrine holds that there are no causal laws (or, in Davidson's terms, "strict" laws) about psychological phenomena—no such laws connecting mental events with physical events and no such laws connecting mental events with other mental events.[3] But why does mental anomalism pose a difficulty for mental causation? The initial difficulty arises when anomalism is combined with the widely accepted nomological requirement on causal relations,[4] the condition that events standing in a causal relation must instantiate a causal law. But this seems to make mental causation impossible: mental causation requires mental events to instantiate laws, but mental anomalism says there are no laws about mental events.

Davidson's own proposal is well-known; he calls it "anomalous monism." We have already considered it as a mind–body theory and found it wanting; but here our interest lies in Davidson's ingenious argument leading to his physical monism. True, says Davidson, mental events in causal relations must instantiate laws but since there aren't any psychological laws, that can only mean that they instantiate physical laws. This shows that mental events fall under physical kinds (or have true physical descriptions), from which it further follows, argues Davidson, that they are physical events. This is the monism in his anomalous monism. The general upshot of the argument is that for any event to enter into a causal relation, it must be covered by a physical law and hence be part of the physical domain. Causal relations can obtain only between physical events covered by physical laws, although of course some of these events are also mental events. The causal structure of this world—the total set of causal relations that hold in this world—is entirely due to the prevailing physical laws. Mental events are causally efficacious therefore only because they are identical with causally efficacious physical events.

But this ingenious solution has failed to satisfy very many philosophers. On the contrary, there has been an impressive unanimity among Davidson's commentators on just why anomalous monism falls short as an account of mental causation.[5] Take any mental event m that stands in a causal relation, say as a cause of event e. According to Davidson, this causal relation obtains just in case m and e instantiate a physical law. Thus m falls under a certain physical (perhaps, neural) kind N, e falls under a physical kind P, and an appropriate causal law connects events of kind N with events of kind P. But this apparently threatens the causal relevance of mentality: the fact that m is a mental event—that it is the kind of mental event it is—appears to have no role in determining what causal relations it enters into. Event m's causal relations are fixed, wholly and exclusively, by the totality of its physical properties, and there is in this picture no causal work that m's mental properties can, or need to, contribute.[6] If mental properties were arbitrarily redistributed over the events of this world, or even if mentality were wholly removed from this world—possibilities apparently left open by Davidson's mental anomalism—that would not affect a single causal relation between events of this world, leaving the causal structure of the world entirely untouched. This seems to consign mental properties to the status of epiphenomena.[7] Thus the problem of mental causation arising out of mental anomalism is to answer this question: *How can anomalous properties be causal properties?* A solution to this problem would have to show either that contrary to Davidson, mental properties are not in reality anomalous, or that being anomalous in Davidson's sense is no barrier to their having causal relevance or being causally efficacious.

There have been several attempts to rehabilitate the causal status of mental properties within the constraint of mental anomalism. Most of these attempts have taken the tack of relaxing, or somehow circumventing, the nomological requirement on causal relations. This is usually done in one of three ways. First, you may want to allow laws that are less than "strict," perhaps laws tacitly qualified by "ceteris paribus" clauses, to subsume individual events in causal relations, and argue that there are nonstrict laws of this kind involving mental properties. Second, you look to some form of counterfactual dependency, rather than subsumptive causal laws, to generate causal relations. Fodor's approach[8] is an example of the first strategy; those of LePore and Loewer's[9] and of Horgan's[10] are examples of the second. A third approach (which is consistent with the second) is to define a notion of causal relevance or efficacy weaker than causation regulated by strict laws. A version of this approach, recently embraced by Davidson,[11] attempts to invoke supervenience of the mental on the physical to explain the causal relevance of the mental. But, as we will see, mind–body supervenience itself can be seen to lead to difficulties for mental causation.

The Problem of Extrinsic Mental Properties

Let us begin with syntacticalism, the view that only "syntactic" properties of mental states, not their "semantic" (or "content" or "representational") properties, can be causally relevant—in particular, to behavior causation.[12] Given the further assumption that the mentality of an important class of mental states, like beliefs and desires, consists in their semantic or representational character, syntacticalism appears to force upon us the conclusion that the intentional properties of mental states, the properties that are constitutive of their mentality, are causally irrelevant. But what persuades us to take syntacticalism seriously?

Syntacticalism most naturally arises in the context of computationalism, an approach that urges us to view mental processes as computational processes on internal representations, on the model of information processing in digital computers. It is apparent that computational processes—that is, causal processes that constitute computation—are sensitive to the syntax, not semantics, of the representations or data structures that are being manipulated; it is the shapes, not meanings, of symbols that determine the course of computation. It matters none to computation whether a given string of 1s and 0s means the inventory count of toothpaste at the local supermarket, the atmospheric pressure in Providence at noon today, the altitude of an airplane on a landing approach, or nothing at all. Similarly, if mental activities are computational processes on beliefs, desires, and such, it would seem that it is the syntactic shapes of these states, not their representational contents, that are causally relevant.[13]

The essential problem here is easily divorced from computationalism and talk of an inner mental language with a syntax and semantics. The internal cause of physical behavior must be supervenient on the total internal state of the agent or organism at the time.[14] For it seems highly plausible to assume that if two organisms are in an identical total internal state at a given time, they will emit identical motor output. However, semantic properties of internal states are not in general supervenient on their *synchronous internal* properties, for as a rule they involve facts about the organism's history and ecological conditions.[15] Thus two organisms whose total states at a given time have identical intrinsic properties can differ in respect of the semantical properties they instantiate; they can differ in the contents of their beliefs and desires, the extensions of their homophonic predicates, and the truth conditions of their homophonic sentences. But prima facie these semantical differences should make no difference to behavior

output. The realization that ordinary content ascriptions have this extrinsic/relational dimension is one of the more notable developments in the philosophy of mind and language during the past two decades.[16] You on this earth have the belief that water is wet; yet, as the story goes, your exact physical duplicate on Twin Earth believes that XYZ is wet, not that water is wet. Frogs on the earth, when appropriately stimulated optically, have the "belief" that a fly is flitting across its visual field (or, at any rate, "sees" a fly); frogs on another planet without flies, when identically stimulated, don't have a belief about flies, or at any rate are not in a state that represent flies—they "believe" that a "schmy" is flitting across its visual field (schmies are tiny black bats which the frogs of this other planet feed on). Thus, that a given intentional state of an organism instantiates a certain semantic property is a *relational* fact, a fact that essentially involves the organism's relationship to various external environmental and historical factors. This makes semantic properties relational, or extrinsic, whereas we expect causative properties involved in behavior production to be nonrelational, or intrinsic, properties of the organism. If inner states are implicated in behavior causation, it seems that all the causal work is done by their "syntactic," or at any rate internal/intrinsic, properties, leaving their semantic properties causally otiose. The problem of mental causation generated by syntacticalism therefore is to answer the following question: *How can extrinsic, relational properties be causally efficacious in behavior production?*

So the crux of the problem lies in the supposed fact that mental properties, in particular, content properties (e.g., being a belief that *P*), are relational properties, extrinsic to the organisms instantiating them, whereas we expect the causative properties of behavior to be intrinsic and internal.[17]

The Problem of Causal Exclusion

The third, and final, problem about mental causation I have in mind arises as follows: suppose that we have somehow put together an account of how mental events can be causes of physical events, an account that meets the requirements of the problems of anomalous mental properties and of syntacticalism. Suppose then that mental event *m*, occurring at time *t*, causes physical event p, and let us suppose that this causal relation holds in virtue of the fact that m is an event of mental kind M and p an event of physical kind P. Does p also have a physical cause at t, an event of some physical kind N?

To acknowledge mental event m (occurring at t) as a cause of physical event p but deny that p has a physical cause at t would be a clear violation of the causal closure of the physical domain, a relapse into Cartesian interactionist dualism which mixes physical and nonphysical events in a single causal chain. But to acknowledge that p has also a physical cause, p^*, at t is to invite the question: Given that p has a physical cause p^*, what causal work is left for m to contribute? The physical cause therefore threatens to exclude, and preempt, the mental cause. This is the problem of causal exclusion. The antireductive physicalist who wants to remain a mental realist, therefore, must give an account of how the mental cause and the physical cause of one and the same event are related to each other. Token physicalism, like Davidson's anomalous monism, is not enough, since the question ultimately involves the causal efficacy of mental *properties,* and antireductionism precludes their reductive identification with physical properties. Thus the problem of causal exclusion is to answer this question: *Given that every physical event that has a cause has a physical cause, how is a mental cause also possible?*

These then are the three principal ways in which I believe the problem of mental causation arises in current debates in philosophy of mind. This means that there really are three separable problems, although of course this does not preclude their resolution by a single unified approach. Here I will not deal directly with the first two problems; as I said at the outset of this talk, what I want to do is to develop the third problem—the exclusion problem—in a more concrete and detailed way by focusing on the two theses we discussed in my first lecture, namely the claim that the mental supervenes on the physical and the claim that the mental is realized in the physical. I hope to show how both mind-body supervenience and physical realizationism can be seen to lead to prima facie difficulties for mental causation. In a later lecture I will discuss how physical realizationism, via a functional reduction of mental properties, presents an opening for a possible accommodation of mentality within the causal structure of the physical world, although the opening may well turn out to be not wide enough to let in all mental properties.

The Supervenience Argument, or Descartes' Revenge

In my first lecture I argued that mind–body supervenience could usefully be thought of as defining minimal physicalism—that it is the minimal commitment that anyone who calls herself a physicalist should be willing to accept. We saw also that mind–body supervenience is entailed by physical realizationism, the thesis that mental properties are instantiated in virtue of being realized by physical properties in physical systems. Moreover emergentism, too, is arguably committed to mind–body supervenience: if two systems are wholly alike physically, we should expect the same mental properties to emerge, or fail to emerge, in each.

Let us now turn to an argument designed to show that mind–body supervenience itself leads to apparent difficulties with mental causation. If we take the supervenience thesis to define minimal physicalism, as I earlier suggested, the argument will show that these difficulties will beset physicalism in general—that is, even the weakest form of physicalism must come to terms with this argument one way or another. If this is right, abandoning the substantival dualism of Descartes doesn't get us out of the woods as far as mental causation is concerned. Indeed one notable development in the recent philosophy of mind is the return of the problem of mental causation as a serious challenge to mainstream physicalism, a phenomenon that would have amused Descartes.

I will now proceed to construct a dilemma-style argument that apparently leads to the conclusion that mental causation is unintelligible. In essence the argument to be presented is the result of superimposing mind–body supervenience on the causal exclusion problem. We begin by setting forth the two horns of the dilemma:

(i) Either mind–body supervenience holds or it fails.

But what does mind–body supervenience assert? Let me restate the mind–body supervenience thesis:

Mind-body supervenience Mental properties supervene on physical properties in the sense that if something instantiates any mental property M

at t, there is a physical base property P such that the thing has P at t, and necessarily anything with P at a time has M at that time.

Note that a base property is *necessarily* sufficient for the supervenient property; the necessity involved here is standardly taken to be at least *nomological necessity*—so that if mind–body supervenience holds, it holds in all worlds that share with our world the same fundamental laws of nature.

Returning to (i), we briefly pursue the second horn first:

(ii) If mind-body supervenience fails, there is no visible way of understanding the possibility of mental causation.

According to Jerry Fodor, "If mind/body supervenience goes, the intelligibility of mental causation goes with it."[18] To my knowledge he has never explained why he has said this (and not just once!). Fodor is not alone in tying the fate of mental causation to supervenience: Horgan, for example, has argued for the physical supervenience of qualia on the ground that it is needed to make qualia causally efficacious.[19] But what exactly is the connection between supervenience and mental causation? The simplest and most obvious reason for the physicalist to accept (ii) lies, I think, in her commitment to *the causal closure of the physical domain,* an idea that has already made a brief appearance above. One way of stating the principle of physical causal closure is this: If you pick any physical event and trace out its causal ancestry or posterity, that will never take you outside the physical domain. That is, no causal chain will ever cross the boundary between the physical and the nonphysical. The interactionist dualism of Descartes is in clear contravention of this principle. If you reject this principle, you are ipso facto rejecting the in-principle completability of physics—that is, the possibility of a complete and comprehensive physical theory of all physical phenomena. For you would be saying that any complete explanatory theory of the physical domain must invoke nonphysical causal agents. Never mind a complete physical explanation of everything there is; there couldn't even be a complete physical explanation of everything physical. It is safe to assume that no serious physicalist could accept such a prospect.

Now if mind–body supervenience fails—that is, if the mental domain floats freely, unanchored in the physical domain, causation from the mental to the physical would obviously breach the physical causal closure. Mind–body supervenience grounds each mental phenomenon in the physical domain by providing for it a set of physical conditions that are (at least) nomologically sufficient for it and on which its occurrence depends. A corollary is the thesis that no mental phenomenon can occur, and no mental property can be instantiated, unless an appropriate physical base condition is present. Every mental event, be it a sensation like pain or itch, or an intentional state like belief and desire, must have a physical basis: it occurs because an appropriate physical basis is present, and it would not occur if such a basis was absent.[20] These comments hold true if you wish to speak in terms of realization. If any mental property gets instantiated because, and only because, one of its physical realizers is instantiated, there is a similar dependence of mental occurrences on physical occurrences.

In any case mind–body supervenience brings mental phenomena within the ambit of the physical: the physical determines the mental, and in that sense the mental does not constitute an ontologically independent domain that injects causal influences into the physical domain from the outside. Now it is another question whether or not mind–body supervenience brings the mental *close enough* to the physical to allow mental causation to circumvent the constraint of the physical causal closure.[21] But we can skirt this question here, for if the answer is no, that would only show that mind–body supervenience isn't enough to give us a solution to the problem of causal exclusion of the mental by the physical. But there is a potentially more serious problem with supervenience: mind–body supervenience may itself be a source of the problem. That is, mind–body supervenience, far from being part of the solution, as hoped for by Fodor, Horgan, and others, may turn out to be part of the problem. Let us now look into this possibility.

(iii) Suppose that an instance of mental property M causes another mental property M^* to be instantiated.

So this is a case of mental-to-mental causation, one in which an instance of a mental property causes an instance of another mental property. We may take "instances" or "instantiations" of properties as events, states, or phenomena. For brevity, I will often speak of one property causing another property; this is to be understood to mean that an *instance* of the first causes an *instance* of the second.[22] Returning to our argument, we see that (ii), the supervenience premise, yields:

(iv) $M*$ has a physical supervenience base $P*$.

We now ask the following critical question: *Where does this instance of $M*$ come from? How does $M*$ get instantiated on this occasion?* There apparently are two possible answers to consider:

(v) $M*$ is instantiated on this occasion: (a) because, ex hypothesi, M caused $M*$ to be instantiated; (b) because $P*$, the physical supervenience base of $M*$, is instantiated on this occasion.

I hope that you are like me in seeing a real tension between these two answers: Under the assumption of mind–body supervenience, $M*$ occurs because its supervenience base $P*$ occurs, and as long as $P*$ occurs, $M*$ must occur no matter what other events preceded this instance of $M*$—in particular, regardless of whether or not an instance of M preceded it. This puts the claim of M to be a cause of $M*$ in jeopardy: $P*$ alone seems fully responsible for, and capable of accounting for, the occurrence of $M*$.[23] As long as $P*$, or another base property of $M*$, is present, that absolutely guarantees the presence of $M*$, and unless such a base is there on this occasion, $M*$ can't be there either. Given this, the only way anything can have a role in the causation of $M*$ would have to be via its relationship to $M*$'s supervenience base $P*$, and as far as I can see, the only way of reconciling the claim of M to be a cause of $M*$ with the fact that $M*$ has $P*$ as its supervenience base is to accept this:

(vi) M caused $M*$ *by causing* $P*$. That is how this instance of M caused $M*$ to be instantiated on this occasion.

There may be a plausible general principle involved here, which is by itself sufficient to justify (vi) even if you do not see the tension in (v), and it is this: *To cause a supervenient property to be instantiated, you must cause its base property (or one of its base properties) to be instantiated.* To relieve a headache, you take aspirin: that is, you causally intervene in the brain process on which the headache supervenes. That's the only way we can do anything about our headaches. To make your painting more beautiful, more expressive, or more dramatic, you must do physical work on the painting and

thereby alter the physical supervenience base of the aesthetic properties you want to improve. There is no direct way of making your painting more beautiful or less beautiful; you must change it physically if you want to change it aesthetically—there is no other way.

But note what (vi) asserts: it says that a mental property M causes a physical property $P*$ to be instantiated. This of course is a case of mental-to-physical causation. So what our argument has shown so far is this: *Under the mind-body supervenience assumption, mental-to-mental causation implies, or presupposes, mental-to-physical causation.* So the question that we now face is whether we can make sense of mental-to-physical causation—that is, under the premise of mind–body supervenience.[24]

Going back to (vi): we see that on the assumption of mind–body supervenience, it follows:

(vii) M itself has a physical supervenience base P.

We must now compare M and P in regard to their causal status with respect to $P*$. When we reflect on this point, I believe, we begin to see reasons for taking P as preempting the claim of M as a cause of $P*$. If you take causation as grounded in nomological sufficiency, P qualifies as a cause of $P*$, for, since P is sufficient for M and M is sufficient for $P*$, P is sufficient for $P*$. If you choose to understand causation in terms of counterfactuals, again there is good reason to think that P qualifies: if P hadn't occurred M would not have occurred (we may assume, without prejudice, that no alternative physical base of M would have been available on this occasion), and given that if M had not occurred $P*$ would not have occurred, we may reasonably conclude that if P had not occurred, $P*$ would not have either.[25]

It seems then that we are now blessed with an overabundance of causes: both M and P seem severally eligible as a sufficient cause of $P*$. And it is not possible to escape the threat of causal overdetermination by thinking of the situation as involving a causal chain from P to M and then to $P*$, with M as an intermediate causal link. For the relation from P to M is not happily thought of as a causal relation; in general, the relation between base properties and supervenient properties is not happily construed as causal.[26] For one thing, the instantiations of the related properties are wholly simultaneous, whereas causes are standardly thought to precede their effects; second, it is difficult, perhaps incoherent, to imagine a causal chain, with intermediate links, between the subvenient and the supervenient properties. What intermediate stages could link the beauty of a painting to its physical properties? What intermediary events could causally connect a mental event with its subvenient physical base? Would such intermediaries themselves be mental or physical? Moreover, for the present case, the causal chain approach, in taking M to be a nonphysical cause of P^*, would violate the causal closure of the physical domain, an option foreclosed to the physicalist.

Nor does it seem plausible to take M and P together to constitute a single sufficient cause of P^*. There are two reasons for this. First, P alone is causally sufficient for P^*, and so is M. It is difficult to see how M and P together can pack any more causal power than M alone or P alone. Second, this approach is plausible only if it claims M to be a necessary component in the causation of P^*, and this means that, as with the causal chain proposal, it involves a violation of the physical causal closure. For a complete causal explanation of why P^* was instantiated on this occasion would have to advert to the presence of a nonphysical causal agent, $M,$ in addition to $P.$

And, finally, it is not possible to take this simply as a case of causal overdetermination—that the instance of P^* is causally overdetermined by two sufficient causes, P and M. Apart from the implausible consequence that it makes every case of mental causation a case of overdetermination, this approach encounters two difficulties: first, in making a physical cause available to substitute for every mental cause, it appears to make mental causes dispensable in any case; second, the approach may come into conflict with the physical causal closure. For consider a world in which the physical cause does not occur and which in other respects is as much like our world as possible. The overdetermination approach says that in such a world, the mental cause causes a physical event—namely that the principle of causal closure of the physical domain no longer holds. I do not think we can accept this consequence: that a minimal counterfactual supposition like that can lead to a major change in the world.

It seems to me that the most natural way of viewing the situation is this:

(viii) P caused P^*, and M supervenes on P and M^* supervenes on P^*.

This explains the observed regularities between M-instances and M^*-instances, and those between M-instances and P^*-instances.[27] These regularities are by no means accidental; in a clear sense they are law-based, and may even be able to support appropriate counterfactuals. However, if we understand the difference between genuine, productive and generative causal processes, on the one hand, and the noncausal regularities that are observed because they are parasitic on real causal processes, we are in a position to understand the picture recommended by (viii). In the case of supposed M-M^* causation, the situation is rather like a series of shadows cast by a moving car: there is no causal connection between the shadow of the car at one instant and its shadow an instant later, each being an effect of the moving car. The moving car represents a genuine causal process, but the series of shadows it casts, however regular and lawlike it may be, does not constitute a causal process.[28] Hence we have:

(ix) The M-to-M^* and M-to-P^* causal relations are only apparent, arising out of a genuine causal process from P to P^*.

Whence a dilemma:

(x) If mind–body supervenience fails, mental causation is unintelligible; if it holds, mental causation is again unintelligible. Hence mental causation is unintelligible.

That then is the supervenience argument against mental causation, or Descartes' revenge against the physicalists. I believe it poses a serious challenge to physicalism by casting doubts on the possibility of mental causation within the parameters it sets for itself. Descartes' difficulties arose from the duality of mental and material substances. Current mainstream physicalism, which calls itself "nonreductive physicalism," runs into parallel difficulties on account of its commitment to the duality of psychological and physical properties—or its failure to make a reductionist commitment for psychological properties. For it is clear that the tacit assumption that gets the supervenience argument going is mind–body antireductionism; if the mental properties are viewed as reducible to physical properties in an appropriate way, we should expect to be able to disarm the argument (although of course the details will need to be worked out).

One good question to raise about the foregoing argument is this: Wouldn't the same argument show that all properties that supervene on basic physical properties are epiphenomenal, and that their causal efficacy is unintelligible? However, there seems to be more than ample reason to think that geological properties, say, are supervenient on fundamental physical properties, and if mind–body supervenience could be shown to put mental causation in jeopardy, wouldn't the very same considerations do the same for geological properties? But no one seems to worry about geological causation, and there evidently seems no reason to start worrying. If so, shouldn't we conclude that there must be something wrong with the argument of the preceding section?[29]

I will deal with this question in detail in my two remaining lectures. As I see it, however, the heart of the issue here is this: with properties like geological and biological properties, we are much more willing, intuitively, to accept a reductionist picture in relation to basic physical properties. I believe that this is true even for philosophers who are vocal in their claim that antireductionism holds across the board, at all levels in relation to their lower levels, and that geological and biological properties are no more reducible to basic physical properties than mental properties. Clearly it is possible that their antireductionism is more correct about mental properties than about these other "higher-level" physical properties. . . .

NOTES

1. For Pierre Gassendi's vigorous challenge to Descartes, see René Descartes, *The Philosophical Writings of Descartes,* vol. 2, ed. John Cottingham, Robert Stoothoff, and Dugald Murdoch (Cambridge: Cambridge University Press, 1985), p. 238.
2. "Making Mind Matter More," reprinted in *A Theory of Content and Other Essays* (Cambridge: MIT Press, 1990), p. 156.
3. Davidson, "Mental Events," reprinted in *Essays on Actions and Events* (Oxford: Oxford University Press, 1980). For wholly different considerations in favor of mental anomalism, see Norman Malcolm, *Memory and Mind* (Ithaca: Cornell University Press, 1977), and Bruce Goldberg, "The Correspondence Hypothesis," *Philosophical Review 77* (1968): 439–454.
4. This condition is not as widely accepted as it used to be. All known alternatives have their own difficulties, however, and it is fair to say that the nomological conception of causation, in its many variants, is still "the received view."
5. To cite a few of the papers in which this issue has been raised, Frederick Stoutland, "Oblique Causation and Reasons for Action," *Synthese* 43 (1980): 351–367; Ted Honderich, "The Argument for Anomalous Monism," *Analysis* 42 (1982): 59–64; Ernest Sosa, "Mind-Body Interaction and Supervenient Causation," *Midwest Studies in Philosophy* 9 (1984): 271–281; Jaegwon Kim, "Self-understanding and Rationalizing Explanations," *Philosophia Naturalis* 82 (1984): 309–320; Louise Antony, "Anomalous Monism and the Problem of Explanatory Force," *Philosophical Review* 98 (1989): 153–187. Davidson defends his position in "Thinking Causes," in *Mental Causation,* ed. John Heil and Alfred Mele (Oxford: Clarendon, 1993). This volume also includes rejoinders to Davidson by Kim, Sosa, and Brian McLaughlin.
6. This remains true even if Davidson's "strict law" requirement on causation is weakened so that nonstrict laws (or *ceteris paribus* laws)—including nonstrict psychophysical laws—are allowed to support causal

relations. For suppose that *m* falls under mental kind *M* and that there is a nonstrict law connecting *M* with *P* (or another physical kind *P** under which *p* falls). Might this show *M* to be efficacious in *m*'s causation of *p?* Hardly, for given that *m*'s causation of *p* is covered by the strict law connecting *N* and *P,* what *further* causal work is left for *M,* or the law connecting *M* and *P?* This is a form of "the exclusion problem"; see below for further discussion.
7. Brian McLaughlin calls this "type epiphenomenalism" in "Type Epiphenomenalism, Type Dualism, and the Causal Priority of the Physical," *Philosophical Perspectives* 3 (1989): 109–135.
8. Jerry A. Fodor, "Making Mind Matter More," *Philosophical Topics* 17 (1989): 59–80. In his "Thinking Causes" (in *Mental Causation,* ed. Heil and Mele), Davidson seems to buy into Fodor's proposal. To see why this won't work, at least for Davidson, see note 6 above.
9. Ernest LePore and Barry Loewer, "Mind Matters," *Journal of Philosophy* 93 (1987): 630–642.
10. Terence Horgan, "Mental Quausation," *Philosophical Perspectives,* 3 (1989): 47–76.
11. Davidson, "Thinking Causes," in *Mental Causation,* ed. Heil and Mele. For an earlier attempt to make use of supervenience to explain mental causation, see my "Epiphenomenal and Supervenient Causation," *Midwest Studies in Philosophy* 9 (1984): 257–270; reprinted in *Supervenience and Mind.* I explain why I now think this approach to be inadequate in *Supervenience and Mind,* pp. 358–362.
12. See Stephen P. Stich, *From Folk Psychology to Cognitive Science* (Cambridge: MIT Press, 1983).
13. For a clear development of these issues, see Ned Block, "Can Mind Change the World?" in *Meaning and Method,* ed. George Boolos (Cambridge: Cambridge University Press, 1990).
14. For a more detailed statement of this argument, see Stephen P. Stich, "Autonomous Psychology and the Belief-Desire Thesis," *The Monist* 61 (1978): 573–591.
15. There are well-known considerations supporting a

view of this kind; see, for example, Hilary Putnam, "The Meaning of 'Meaning'," in *Philosophical Papers,* vol. 2 (Cambridge: Cambridge University Press, 1975); Tyler Burge, "Individualism and the Mental," *Midwest Studies in Philosophy* 4 (1979): 73–121; Stich, "Autonomous Psychology and the Belief-Desire Thesis;" Kim, "Psychophysical Supervenience," *Philosophical Studies* 41 (1982): 51–70.

16. Due to the works by Hilary Putnam, Saul Kripke, Tyler Burge, and others.

17. For instructive and helpful discussion of issues concerning the causal/explanatory efficacy of contentful mental states, see Lynne Rudder Baker, *Explaining Attitudes* (Cambridge: Cambridge University Press, 1995), and Pierre Jacob, *What Minds Can Do* (Cambridge: Cambridge University Press, 1997).

18. *Psychosemantics* (Cambridge: MIT Press, 1987), p. 42.

19. Terence Horgan, "Supervenient Qualia," *Philosophical Review* 96 (1987): 491–520.

20. On content externalism, wide-content states will not supervene on internal physical properties of the subject, but physicalists will not deny that they supervene on the subject's extrinsic/relational physical properties. For the present paper, we will ignore the issues that arise from content externalism. But see the works by Baker and Jacob cited in note 17.

21. On this issue see my "Postscripts on Mental Causation" in *Supervenience and Mind* (Cambridge: Cambridge University Press, 1993).

22. Strictly speaking, this doesn't go far enough: it must further be the case that one instance causes another instance *in virtue of the fact that the first is an F-instance and the second is a G-instance.*

23. This argument is based on what I have called "the principle of causal/explanatory exclusion"; see, for example, my "Mechanism, Purpose, and Explanatory Exclusion," reprinted in *Supervenience and Mind.*

24. We could have begun with (vi) as our initial premise of mental causation. The point of starting with (iii) is to show that the argument applies to mental-mental causation as well as to mental-physical causation. On the assumption of mind-body supervenience, the former is as problematic, in my view, as the latter.

25. This of course is not to assume transitivity for counterfactuals in general.

26. One philosopher who holds the unorthodox view that the base properties "cause" the supervenient properties is John Searle, in his *The Rediscovery of the Mind* (Cambridge: MIT Press, 1992).

27. Note, however, that these regularities are likely to be restricted in generality. The reason is that M's alternative supervenience bases cannot be counted on to cause P^* and hence M^*.

28. On the distinction between "causal process" and "pseudo-process," see Wesley Salmon, *Scientific Explanation and the Causal Structure of the World* (Princeton: Princeton University Press, 1984).

29. Several philosophers have raised exactly these questions (though not necessarily directed against our first argument); for example, Lynne Rudder Baker, "Metaphysics and Mental Causation," in *Mental Causation,* ed. Heil and Mele (Oxford: Clarendon Press, 1993); Robert Van Gulick, "Three Bad Arguments for Intentional Property Epiphenomenalism," *Erkenntnis* 36 (1992); Louise M. Antony, "The Inadequacy of Anomalous Monism as a Realist Theory of Mind," in *Language, Mind, and Epistemology,* ed. G. Preyer, F. Siebelt, and A. Ulfig (Dordrecht: Kluwer, 1994).

23 | # Mental Causation
Stephen Yablo

1

Writing to Descartes in 1643, Princess Elisabeth of Bohemia requests an explanation of "how man's soul, being only a thinking substance, can determine animal spirits so as to cause voluntary actions."[1] Agreeing that "the question which your Highness raises [is] one which can most reasonably be asked," Descartes launches with his reply a grand tradition of dualist apologetics about mind–body causation that has disappointed ever since. Apologetics are in order because, as Descartes appreciates, his conception of mental and physical as metaphysically separate invites the question, "how, in that case, does the one manage to affect the other?"; and because having invited the question, he seems unable to answer it. Much as the Cartesian epistemology breeds skepticism, then, the metaphysics breeds epiphenomenalism: the theory that our mental lives exercise no causal influence whatever over the progress of physical events.

That was the price Descartes paid for his dualism, someone might say. Why should epiphenomenalism concern anyone today? Part of the answer is that dualism is not dead, only evolved. Immaterial minds are gone, it is true, but mental *phenomena* (facts, properties, events) remain. And although the latter are admitted to be physically *realized,* and physically *necessitated,* their literal numerical *identity* with their physical bases is roundly denied.[2]

Surely, though, it is hard to imagine a dualism more congenial to mental causation than this! So it would seem. But epiphenomenalism has been evolving too; and in its latest and boldest manifestation, this is all the dualism it asks for. As a result we find ourselves in a somewhat paradoxical situation. Just when the conditions for accommodating mental causation have become little short of ideal, epiphenomenalist anxiety rages higher than ever. Nor is this a pretended anxiety, put on for dialectical purposes but posing no genuine danger to established views. Some say we must simply make our peace with the fact that "the mental does not enjoy its own independent causal powers."[3] Others would renounce (distinctively) mental phenomena altogether, rather than see them causally disabled.[4] Radical as these proposals are, they are backed by a straightforward line of reasoning.

"How can mental phenomena affect what happens physically? Every physical outcome is causally assured already by preexisting physical circumstances; its mental antecedents are therefore left with nothing further to contribute." This is the *exclusion argument* for epiphenomenalism. Here is the argument as it applies to mental events; for the version which applies to properties, replace 'event *x*' with 'property *X*':[5]

1. If an event x is causally sufficient for an event y, then no event x^* distinct from x is causally relevant to y (*exclusion*).[6]
2. For every physical event y, some physical event x is causally sufficient for y (*physical determinism*).[7]
3. For every physical event x and mental event x^*, x is distinct from x^* (*dualism*).
4. So: for every physical event y, no mental event x^* is causally relevant to y (*epiphenomenalism*).

This is bad enough—as Malcolm says in "The Conceivability of Mechanism," it means that no one ever speaks or acts—but a simple extension

of the argument promises to deprive mental phenomena of all causal influence whatsoever. Every event z of whatever type is metaphysically necessitated by some underlying physical event y, whose causally sufficient physical antecedents are presumably sufficient for z as well. But then by the exclusion principle, z's mental antecedents are irrelevant to its occurrence. So, mental phenomena are *absolutely* causally inert. And now it is not only speech and action that are chimerical but also thinking.

Note well that the exclusion argument raises *two* problems for mental causation, one about mental particulars (events), the other about mental properties.[8] Strangely, philosophers have tended to treat these problems in isolation and to favor different strategies of solution.[9] In Malcolm's original presentation, he emphasizes problem one. Given a neurophysiological theory rich enough to

> provide sufficient causal conditions for every human movement, . . . there would be no cases at all in which [the] movement would not have occurred if the person had not had [the] desire or intention . . . [thus] desires and intentions would not be causes of human movements.[10]

Here the mystery is how mental *events,* desires for example, can be making a causal difference when their unsupplemented neurophysiological underpinnings are already sufficient to the task at hand. To reply with the majority that mental events just *are* certain physical events, whose causal powers they therefore share,[11] only relocates the problem from the particulars to their universal features:

> the being of a desire by my desire has no causal relevance to my extending my hand . . . if the event that is in fact my desire had not been my desire but had remained a neurological event of a certain sort, then it would have caused my extending my hand just the same.[12]

Mental events are effective, maybe, but not by way of their mental *properties;* any causal role that the latter might have hoped to play is occupied already by their physical rivals.[13] Although someone *could,* following the line above, attempt to *identify* mental properties with (certain) physical properties, say, being a desire with instantiating such and such a neurophysiological type, this approach is now discredited, because of the well-known multiple realizability objection.[14] Properties are identical only if each necessitates the other; but any physical property specific enough to necessitate a mental property is inevitably *so* specific that the converse necessitation fails. Since (as I'll maintain) the objection applies, *mutatis mutandis,* to mental *particulars,* the identity response is unworkable in either case.[15]

So I find no fault with dualism, or with the associated picture of mental phenomena as necessitated by physical phenomena which they are possible without. Rather than objecting, in fact, to the asymmetric necessitation picture, I propose to go it one better. Traditionally, the paradigm of one-way necessitation was the relation of *determinate* to *determinable* (sections 2 and 5). What if mental phenomena are determinables of physical phenomena in something like the traditional sense (sections 3 and 6)? Then since a determinate cannot preempt its own determinable, mental events and properties lose nothing in causal relevance to their physical bases (sections 4 and 7).[16] If anything, it is the other way around. Overladen as they frequently are with physical details far beyond the effect's causal requirements, it is the *physical* phenomena which are liable to disqualification on grounds of superfluity (section 8).

2

Before asking what determinates and determinables might be, consider the "easier" question of when properties are identical. Probably no one would quarrel with

(**I**) *P* is identical to *Q* iff: for a thing to be *P* is for it to be *Q,*

on at least some interpretation. But, apart from its possible circularity, (**I**) explains one obscurity with another; and it has become customary to seek relief from both complaints in the modal idiom. That idiom permits no sufficient condition for property identity, unfortunately; so something is sacrificed. But we're repaid with the necessary condition that

(I) $P = Q$ only if: necessarily, for all x, x has P iff x has Q.[17]

Properties are identical, in other words, only if it is impossible for a thing to possess either without possessing the other.

Among (I)'s attractions is that we *know* it is true since it follows from Leibniz's Law, the indiscernibility of identicals. Or better: it follows if the modality is read as *metaphysical.* Whether because they conflated conceptual with meta-

physical necessity, or because they construed the properties themselves as concepts, philosophers *used* to think that properties were the same only if it was *conceptually* or a priori[18] true that their instances could not differ.[19] (Thus they felt justified in arguing from purely conceptual considerations to a distinction between, say, being salt and being sodium chloride.) This stronger condition can of course claim no support from Leibniz's Law.[20] But that isn't what led to its rejection: it was rejected because it proved unable to cope with the discovery of identical properties, such as the ones just mentioned, whose necessary coextensiveness was knowable only a posteriori.[21] So the mutual conceptual necessitation requirement is now defunct; its metaphysical kernel (I), although insufficient for property identity, is the only game in town.

According to a still reputable traditional doctrine, some properties stand to others as *determinate* to *determinable*–for example, *crimson* is a determinate of the determinable *red, red* is a determinate of *colored,* and so on.[22] Since the distinction is relative, one does better to speak of a determination *relation* among properties, where

(Δ) *P* determines *Q* iff: for a thing to be *P* is for it to be *Q,* not *simpliciter,* but in a specific way.

Except for the 'not *simpliciter . . .*', (Δ) would describe identity; and like identity, determination as traditionally understood involves conceptual and metaphysical elements jumbled confusingly together. Metaphysically, the central idea is that

(Δ) *P* determines *Q* ($P > Q$) only if:
(i) necessarily, for all *x,* if *x* has *P* then *x* has *Q;* and
(ii) possibly, for some *x, x* has *Q* but lacks *P.*

Not always distinguished from this is a requirement of asymmetric conceptual entailment: there is no conceptual difficulty about a world in which some *Q* lacks *P,* but the converse scenario is excludable on a priori grounds.

Now, just as the discovery of a posteriori necessities upset the traditional presumption of a conceptual equivalence condition on property *identity,* it also makes trouble for the conceptual entailment condition on *determination.* Take the property of being at temperature 95°C, and some highly specific micromechanical property K chosen so that necessarily whatever has K has the temperature property, though not conversely. Since Ks which are warmer than 95°C cannot be ruled out on a priori grounds alone, traditional determination fails. Yet the relevance of this to the properties' strictly *metaphysical* relations is obscure; and since it is only the metaphysics that matters to causation, we should discount the traditional doctrine's conceptual component and reconceive determination in wholly metaphysical terms.[23] What justifies the continued use of the word 'determine' is that (Δ) holds essentially as before. To be in the micromechanical condition of this steaming tea, for instance, is to be at temperature 95°C *in a certain micromechanical way.*

3

As I write, I am in a certain overall physical condition, and I am also thinking; presumably the one fact about me has quite a lot to do with the other. Suppose the pertinent aspects of my physical condition to be encoded in some physical property P. Could it be that P is a *determinate* of thinking? Barring some unsuspected conceptual entailment from physics to thought, the full-scale traditional doctrine answers in the negative. On the other hand, traditional determination incorporates elements visibly irrelevant to how the properties are related in themselves; so the interesting question is whether P determines thinking in the *metaphysical* sense.[24] I say that it does. And I hold further that there is this sort of physical determination whenever a mental property is exemplified.

Such a view is in fact implicit in the reigning orthodoxy about mind–body relations, namely, that the mental is *supervenient* on, but *multiply realizable* in, the physical.[25] Because neither thesis concerns determination directly, the point is easily missed that in combination their effect is to portray mental properties as determinables of their physical realizations. Take supervenience first, the claim that a thing's mental properties are fixed by how it is physically:

(S) Necessarily, for every x and every mental property M of x, x has some physical property P such that necessarily all Ps are Ms.[26]

Now, thinking is a mental property, and I possess it. By supervenience, then, I have a physi-

cal property P given which thinking is metaphysically guaranteed. Of course, P can be considered a determination of thinking only if it is possible to think *without P,* which is to say otherwise than by way of the physical property that *does* realize my thinking; and this is where the official story's second element comes in.

When philosophers abandoned the hope of finding for every mental property an identical physical property, the reason was that mental properties seemed intuitively to be multiply realizable in the physical.[27] However, some care should be taken about what this means. Is the claim that for *any* pair of properties, one mental and the other physical, something could have the first without the second? Really, this is stronger than intended, or needed. Imagine someone who holds that necessarily every thinker is spatially extended. Surely such a person could accept multiple realization, intuitively understood, without falling into inconsistency; yet since the necessitation of extension by thinking is the necessitation of a physical property by a mental one, her view actually runs contrary to multiple realization as just explained. Provided that they are suitably unspecific, then, physical properties *can* be necessitated by mental properties compatibly with multiple realization—which suggests as the thesis's proper formulation that M necessitates no physical P that is *specific enough to necessitate M in return:*

(M) Necessarily, for every mental property M, and every physical property P which necessitates M, possibly something possesses M but not P.[28]

For purposes of refuting the identity theory, note, (M) is all that's required. If M were P, then P would necessitate it. But then by (M), it could not necessitate P in return, contrary to their assumed identity.

Together, (M) and (S) make it a matter of necessity that something has a mental property if it has a physical property by which that mental property is asymmetrically necessitated. But this is extremely suggestive, for with 'determines' substituted for 'asymmetrically necessitates', it becomes

(D) Necessarily, something has a mental property iff it has also a physical determination of that mental property;

and (D) is an instance of the standard equation for determinables and determinates generally, namely, that something has a determinable property iff it has some determinate falling thereunder. This calls out for explanation, and the one that comes first to mind is that mental/physical relations are a species of determinable/determinate relations. "Can you really be saying that mental properties stand to their physical realizations in the relation that rectangularity bears to squareness, or that colors bear to their shades?"[29] Yes. At least that is my conjecture, to be evaluated like any other by the evidence for it and by its theoretical fruitfulness. The evidence is as just described; its consequences for mental causation are considered next.

4

Imagine a pigeon, Sophie, conditioned to peck at red to the exclusion of other colors; a red triangle is presented, and Sophie pecks. Most people would say that the redness was causally relevant to her pecking, even that this was a paradigm case of causal relevance. But wait! I forgot to mention that the triangle in question was a specific shade of red: scarlet. Assuming that the scarlet was causally sufficient for the pecking, we can conclude by the exclusion principle that every *other* property was irrelevant. Apparently, then, the redness, although it looked to be *precisely* what Sophie was responding to, makes in reality no causal contribution whatever. Another example concerns properties of events. Suppose that the structures in a certain region, though built to withstand lesser earthquakes, are in the event of a *violent* earthquake—one registering over five on the Richter scale—causally guaranteed to fall. When one unexpectedly hits, and the buildings collapse, one property of the earthquake that seems relevant to their doing so is that it was violent. Or so you might think, until I add that this particular earthquake was *barely* violent (its Richter magnitude was over five but less than six). What with the earthquake's *bare* violence being *already* causally sufficient for the effect, that it was *violent* made no causal difference.

Surprising results! To the untrained eye, the redness and the violence are *paradigm cases* of causal relevance, but only a little philosophy is needed to set matters straight. Now, though, one begins to wonder: if even paradigm cases of causal relevance fail the exclusion test, what passes it? Not much, it turns out. Almost whenever a property Q is prima facie relevant to an effect, a causally sufficient determination Q' of Q can be found to expose it as irrelevant after all.[30] Applying the argument to Q', Q'', etc. in turn, it appears that only ultimate determinates—properties unamenable to further determination—can hope to retain their causal standing.

Or, on second thought, maybe not them either. Not everything about a cause contributes to its effect; and even where a property does contribute, it need not do so in all its aspects. From the examples it is clear that such irrelevancies do indeed creep in, as we pass from determinable to determinate (e.g., registering less than six); and if the determination process is continued ad finem, they may be expected to accumulate significantly. So any ultimate determinate seems likely to incoorate causally extraneous detail. But then, abstracting some or all of this detail away should leave a determinable which, since it falls short of the original only in irrelevant respects, is no less sufficient for the effect.[31] By the exclusion principle, this robs even ultimate determinates of their causal powers. And now it begins to look as though no property ever makes any causal difference.

At least as it applies to properties, then, the exclusion principle is badly overdrawn. Not that there is nothing right about it. In *some* sense of 'separate,' it stands to reason, separate properties *are* causal rivals as the principle says. Then what if someone identifies the appropriate notion of separateness and reformulates the exclusion principle accordingly? Suppose it done. Even without hearing the details, we *know* that the corrected principle does not apply to determinates and their determinables—for we know that they are not causal rivals. This kind of position is of course familiar from other contexts. Take for example the claim that a space completely filled by one object can contain no other. Then are even the object's *parts* crowded out? No. In this competition wholes and parts are not on opposing teams; hence any principle that puts them there needs rethinking. Likewise any credible reconstruction of the exclusion principle must respect the truism that determinates do not contend with their determinables for causal influence.[32]

With the exclusion principle neutralized, the application to mental causation is anticlimactic. As a rule, determinates are tolerant, indeed supportive, of the causal aspirations of their determinables. Why should it be different, if the determinate is physical and the determinable mental? Inferring the causal irrelevance of, say, my *dizziness,* from the causal sufficiency of its physical basis, is not appreciably better than rejecting the redness as irrelevant on the ground that all the causal work is accomplished already by its determinate scarlet. Or, if someone thinks it *is* better, then she owes us an explanation of what the metaphysically important difference is between the cases. That there is a conceptual difference is granted, but it is not to the point; there is no conceptual entailment either from the tea's micromechanical condition to its high temperature, yet this occasions little skepticism about the role of the tea's temperature in its burning my tongue. If there is a metaphysical difference, then someone should say what it is, and why it matters to causation.

5

According to our guiding principle (Δ) for property determination, P determines Q iff to possess the one is to possess the other, not *simpliciter,* but in a certain way. But this way of putting things comes naturally, too, in connection with particulars, and especially events. If p is the bolt's *suddenly* snapping, for example, and q is its snapping per se, then for p to occur is for q to occur in a certain way, namely suddenly; and my *slamming* the door consists in my shutting it, not *simpliciter,* but with significant force.[33] This suggests the possibility of a determination relation for events:

> (δ) p determines q iff: for p to occur (in a possible world) is for q to occur (there), not *simpliciter,* but in a certain way.[34]

If the relation can be made out, then in addition to the examples mentioned, Icarus's flying too near the sun determines his flying per se, Brutus's killing Caesar determines his stabbing Caesar,[35] Gödel's discovering the incompleteness of arithmetic determines his realizing that arithmetic was incomplete, and so on indefinitely.

There is a complication. Determination involves the idea that the requirements associated with one thing include the requirements associated with another; and although properties are requiremental on their face, particulars are not. Hence the need for a notion of individual essence.

By a thing's *essential* properties, I mean those it cannot exist without. And its *essence* is a certain selection of its essential properties. But which essential properties does it make sense to

include? The simplest proposal, obviously, would be to include *all* of them. For two related reasons, though, that won't do. Naively, the "what-it-is" of a thing—its identity and kind—should be *in virtue of* its essence. Yet if identity- and kind-properties are allowed into essences, this requirement becomes quickly trivialized: a thing does not get to be identical to Brutus's stabbing Caesar, or of the kind *stabbing,* by having the property of so being, but by having certain *other* properties and by their dividing along appropriate lines between essential and accidental. Second, the essence of a thing is supposed to be a measure of what is *required* in order to be that thing. Thus if more is required to be y than to be $x,$ this should be reflected in an inclusion relation between their essences. The problem is that identity-properties, kind-properties, and the like are liable to disrupt these inclusion relations. Allowing *identity-with-x* into x's essence precludes the possibility of a y whose essence includes everything in x's essence, and more besides; and the effect of allowing x's kind into its essence is to kill the chances for a thing y whose essence exceeds x's by properties which things of that kind possess at best accidentally.[36]

Both problems have the same solution: essences are to be drawn from a pool of properties such that any particular such property's modal status—essential or accidental—is without undue prejudice to the modal status of the others. Dubbing these the *cumulative* properties, x's *essence* will be the set of cumulative properties that it possesses essentially. When q's essence is a subset of p's essence, p is said to subsume q ($p \geqslant q$); and p *determines* q ($p > q$) when the inclusion is strict.[37]

Explaining determination by essence has three points in its favor: it fits the intuitive examples; it supports the analogy with property determination; and it predicts the principle that p determines q only if for p to occur is for q to occur in a certain way. Take the example of Gödel's *discovering,* versus his simply *realizing,* that arithmetic was incomplete. Though identical on some accounts, there is in fact a subtle difference between them. Speaking first of Gödel's *realizing* that arithmetic was incomplete, this *could* have been the realization of a result already widely known (in that case, it would not have made Gödel famous). To Gödel's *discovering* arithmetic's incompleteness, though, some degree of priority is essential. Otherwise one could ask, would it still have made Gödel famous, if incompleteness had been common knowledge? But this is like asking, of Brutus killing Caesar, what Caesar would have done to Brutus if he had not died of it. So the essence of Gödel's discovering that arithmetic was incomplete *adds* something to the essence of his realizing that it was.

For the analogy with property determination, we need a distinction: a property is *categorical* if its possession by a thing x at a possible world is strictly a matter of x's condition in that world, without regard to how it would or could have been; other properties, for example counterfactual and modal properties, are *hypothetical*.[38] This gives the idea of categoricity, but as a definition it would be circular. To see why, suppose it is a categorical property of this piece of wax to be spherical. How can this depend on the wax's condition in other worlds? In a way, though, it does, for the wax cannot be spherical in this world without being possibly spherical in every other world it inhabits. More generally, sensitivity to its possessors' *hypothetical* characteristics in other worlds should not make a property noncategorical, or *no* properties will be categorical. What we *meant* to say, it seems, is that a property is categorical iff it attaches to its objects regardless of how they would or could have been in *categorical* respects. And now the circularity is apparent.

Luckily the categorical properties can be approached from another direction. When p *subsumes q,* their difference (if any) comes down ultimately to the fact that they possess different of their shared properties essentially. Such a difference is *merely* hypothetical if any difference is; so

(γ) C is categorical only if: necessarily, for all p and q such that $p \geqslant q$, p has C iff q does.

This, although only a necessary condition on categoricity, is all that the announced analogy requires.[39] For it entails that in worlds where both exist, the subsuming particular p and the subsumed q are categorically indiscernible, or as I will say *coincident*. And since p cannot exist *without q*[40] (the bolt's suddenly snapping is impossible without its snapping) we have:

(μ) $p \geqslant q$ only if: necessarily, if p exists, then q exists and is coincident with p.

This divides into two subconditions, according to whether p is identical to q or determines it.[41]

By Leibniz's Law, or a double application of (μ),

(ι) $p = q$ only if: necessarily, p exists iff q exists, and if existent, they are coincident.

When p determines q, the condition holds in one direction only:

(δ) $p > q$ only if:
    (i)   necessarily, if p exists, then q exists and is coincident with p;
    (ii) possibly, q exists and p does not exist.[42]

That we get these analogues for particulars of **(I)** and **(Δ)** is the second attraction of using essence to explain determination.

Now for the fact that reflects most favorably on the essence approach: that it predicts (δ)'s intuitive description of determination. From (δ) we know that a determinate p exists in some, though not all, of the worlds where its determinable q is found. But how does p decide in *which* of these q-worlds to put in its appearances? For instance, what separates the worlds in which the bolt's suddenly snapping accompanies its snapping per se from those in which it does not? In the former worlds, presumably, the snapping is sudden; and as it turns out, this answer holds good in general:

(ε) $p > q$ only if: necessarily, p exists iff q (both) exists and exemplifies the difference S between its own essence and p's larger essence.[43]

Mirabile dictu, this is just what (δ) *says* about determinates and their determinables: for p to occur is for q to occur, not *simpliciter,* but S-ly.

6

Identicals are indiscernible; so an argument that mental events have different essential properties from physical events is an argument that they are not identical. According to one popular line of thought, this essential difference can be established in the following simple form: only mental events possess mental properties (e.g., phenomenal and content properties) essentially. Thus Kripke:

> Let 's' name a particular pain sensation, and let 'b' name the corresponding brain state, or the brain state some identity theorist wishes to identify with s. *Prima facie,* it would seem that it is at least logically possible that b should have ex-

isted (Jones's brain could have been in exactly that state at the time in question) without Jones feeling any pain at all, and thus without the presence of s.[44]

Prima facie, Kripke says, b could have occurred without there being any pain, and presumably he would say the same about other physical events p and mental properties. Unless these prima facie appearances can be overcome, mental properties are at best accidental to physical events.

Are these really the prima facie appearances, though? Remember that all it takes for p to have a mental characteristic essentially is for its essential physical properties to necessitate one— and that the dominant modal intuition in recent years has been that mental properties *supervene* on physical properties and so are necessitated by them *all the time*.[45] Someone might of course ask why any physical p should have the mentally consequential *kind* of physical property, but this is easily explained. Consider the bearing of supervenience on *mental* events: for each of m's mental properties, supervenience assigns it a necessitating physical property. But it is hard to think what m's physical properties could be if not those of some physical event p which subserved it. Thus, among p's physical properties are some with m's mental properties as necessary consequences. Only if p somehow managed to have *all* of these physical properties contingently could it avoid having at least some mental properties essentially.

Instead of insisting that p has *no* essential mental properties, perhaps the token dualist should say that it doesn't have *all* the essential mental properties of its alleged mental identical. Here is a bad way to argue for that result: since no mental event is physical, p lacks mental kind-properties, for example, being of the kind *after-image, sensation,* or indeed *mental;* therefore it doesn't have these properties essentially. Dialectically, of course, this begs the question against the token identity theory. But there is a deeper problem: it says nothing about what *makes* a mental event m different from a physical event p, to be told that only the former is (essentially) mental, or of some specific mental kind. Mental events are mental rather than physical not because mentality is essential to them alone, but because of some *prior* fact about them—the sort of fact that essences were designed to capture. Thus m's essential mental advantage over p, if it exists, should be that its *essence* contains mental properties beyond those in p's essence.

Yet supervenience opposes this weakening of the essential mental advantage view as much as the original. The reason is this. Every mental property M_k in m's essence is backed by a necessitating physical property P_k; and as before, these physical properties attach also to some realizing physical event (this time called q). Even if some or all of the P_ks are only accidental to q, we can imagine a more determinate physical event p to which they are all essential. But then p has essential physical properties to necessitate every mental property in m's essence; and it follows that these mental properties are in p's essence too. Not only does this rule out an essential mental advantage for mental events, it puts us in sight of an intriguing parallel between the ways that mental events and properties relate to their physical underpinnings. For assuming that p can be chosen determinate enough to essentially possess such few *non*mental properties as might be found in m's essence, we have

(s) Whenever a mental event m occurs, there occurs also a subsuming physical event p, that is, a physical event whose essence includes m's essence[46]

—an analogue for events of the supervenience thesis.

From (s) it is clear that if there is an essential difference between mental events and physical ones, it is *not* that physical events' essences are mentally impoverished. Instead, I suggest, it is the other way around: the essences of *mental* events are *physically* impoverished. For those who believe, with Descartes, that their mental lives could have proceeded just the same in a wholly immaterial world, this hardly requires argument.[47] Events which can occur in such a world presumably have *none* of their physical properties essentially. But Cartesian dualism is only the most dramatic expression of a thought which seems probable in any case, namely, that in comparison with their physical bases, mental phenomena are exceedingly modally elastic.[48]

Take for example the pain sensation s, and the underlying brain event b whose identity with s is in question; and grant the identity theorist that b at least subsumes s and so necessitates it. The problem is that as b takes on the degree of essential physical detail that this requires, it becomes intuitively irresistible that the pain is possible even in b's absence. Something like this is Kripke's second argument against the identity theory:

[B]eing a brain state is evidently an essential property of *b* (the brain state). Indeed, even more is true: not only being a brain state, but even being a brain state of a specific type is essential to *b*. The configuration of brain cells whose presence at a given time constitutes the presence of *b* at that time is essential to *b*, and in its absence *b* would not have existed. Thus someone who wishes to claim that the brain state and the pain are identical must argue that the pain could not have existed without a quite specific type of configuration of molecules.[49]

Prima facie, it seems obvious that the pain could still have occurred, even if that specific arrangement of molecules hadn't, and as Kripke says, the prima facie appearances aren't easily defeated.[50] But if the molecular arrangement is essential to *b* alone, then *b*'s essence is physically richer than *s*'s essence. Therefore *b* subsumes *s* *properly;* and this, extended across mental events in general, gives an analogue for particulars of the multiple realizability thesis:

(m) For every mental event *m,* and every physical event *p* which subsumes *m, p* subsumes *m* properly and so determines it.

Token dualism follows: if *m* were identical to *p,* then *p* would subsume *m;* hence by (m) it would determine *m,* contrary to their assumed identity.

Drawing these various threads together, we find that the relation between mental and physical events effectively duplicates that of mental to physical properties. Whenever a mental event *m* occurs, (s) guarantees a subsuming physical event *p,* which by (m) is not identical to *m* but determines it. Thus with every mental *m* comes a determining physical *p.*[51] Since for *p* to occur is just for *m* to occur in a certain physical way, the converse is trivial; so we can say that

(d) A mental event *m* occurs iff some physical determination *p* of *m* occurs.

This is our analogue for events of the mental/physical determination thesis for properties.

7

Haven't we now made mental events causally irrelevant? By the exclusion principle, *m* can influence an outcome only to the extent that *p* leaves that outcome causally undecided. Results which *p* causally guarantees, therefore, it renders insusceptible to causal influence from any other source, *m* included. Assuming, for example, that all it took for me to wince, clutch my brow, and so on, was my antecedent physical condition, everything else was strictly by the way. Since my headache is a different thing from its determining physical basis, it is not a *bona fide* causal factor in my headache behavior.

By now the deficiencies of this line of argument must be apparent. Suppose that we think of the exclusion principle as saying that for every irreflexive relation *R* (every "form of nonidentity"), and every *R*-related pair *x* and *x*, x*'s causal sufficiency for an effect entails *x**'s causal irrelevance. Though there may be irreflexive relations *R* whose relata *do* contend for causal influence as the principle says, for many *R*s this competition arises only sometimes, and for others it *never* arises. Ironically, *R* = causation is a case in point. Let *x* be causally sufficient for *y*. Then taken at its word, the exclusion principle predicts that *y* owes nothing to the causal intermediaries by which *x* brings *y* about. When *R* is causation's converse, the prediction is different but still absurd: events causally antecedent to *x* can claim no role in *y*'s production.[52] Of course, the case that interests us is *R* = the determination relation. Remember Archimedes' excited outburst on discovering the principle of displacement in his bath. Assuming that his shouting "Eureka!!" was causally sufficient for his cat's startled flight, nobody would think that this disqualified his (simply) shouting from being causally relevant as well. And it would be incredible to treat Socrates' *drinking* the poison as irrelevant to his death, on the ground that his *guzzling* it was causally sufficient.

Thinking of causal influence as something that an effect's would-be causal antecedents compete over in a zero-sum game, the exclusion principle looks not unreasonable. If the causally sufficient antecedent monopolizes *all* the influence, then the others are left with none. To judge by the examples, though, causation is not like that: rather than competing for causal honors, determinables and their determinates seem likelier to share in one another's success. Again the application to mental and physical events is anticlimactic. Unless an arbitrary exception is to be made of them, it is no argument at all for the causal irrelevance of, say, a sensation that its occurring in some specific physical way was causally sufficient.[53] With events as with properties, physical determinates cannot defeat the causal pretensions of their mental determinables.[54]

8

To this point our position is wholly negative: for all that the exclusion argument shows, mental phenomena *can* be causally relevant compatibly with the causal sufficiency of their physical bases. It is a further question whether they *will* be in any particular case. And even if some mental antecedent *is* causally relevant, it is a further question yet whether it actually *causes* the effect.

Notice some important differences between causal relevance and sufficiency, on the one hand, and causation, on the other: x can be causally sufficient for y even though it incorporates enormous amounts of causally extraneous detail, and it can be causally relevant to y even though it omits factors critical to y's occurrence. What distinguishes causation from these other relations is that causes are expected to be *commensurate* with their effects: roughly, they should incorporate a good deal of causally important material but not too much that is causally unimportant. And this makes causation special in another way. Although determinables and determinates do not compete for causal *influence,* broadly conceived as encompassing everything from causal relevance to causal sufficiency, they *do* compete for the role of *cause,* with the more commensurate candidate prevailing. Now I argue that the effect's mental antecedents often fare *better* in this competition than their more determinate physical bases.[55]

Inspiring the commensuration constraint is a certain platitude: the cause was the thing that "made the difference" between the effect's occurring and its not. Had the cause been absent, the platitude seems to say, then (i) the effect would have been absent too, but (ii) it *would* have occurred if the cause had. Thus effects are *contingent* on their causes:

(C) If x had not occurred, then y would not have occurred either;[56]

and causes are *adequate* for their effects:

(A) If x had not occurred, then *if it had, y* would have occurred as well.[57]

Without mentioning determination explicitly, these conditions do nevertheless discover causal differences between unequally determinate events. Suppose we stipulate that it contributed nothing to Socrates' demise that he guzzled the hemlock rather than simply drinking it. Then Xanthippe is mistaken when, disgusted at Socrates' sloppy habits, she complains that his *guzzling* the hemlock caused his death. Assuming that the drinking would still have occurred, if the guzzling hadn't, (C) explains the error nicely. Even without the guzzling, the death would still have followed on the drinking. So while Socrates' death may have been contingent on his drinking the hemlock, it was *not* contingent on his guzzling it.[58]

Here the contingency condition exposes an overly determinate pretender; sometimes, though, the pretender's problem is that it is not determinate enough. Safety valves are designed to open quickly under extreme pressure, thus easing the burden on the equipment upstream. This particular valve has begun to operate as advertised when a freak molecular misalignment stiffens the mechanism; this decelerates the opening to just past the point of endurance and the boiler explodes. Assuming that the explosion does *not* result from the valve's opening per se, I ask why not. Because the contingency condition is violated? But we can arrange it so that the explosion *was* contingent on the opening, say, by stipulating that if the opening had not occurred, rather than the boiler's exploding the connecting pipe would have burst. Adequacy does better: given the unlikelihood of the molecular mishap, had the opening failed to occur, it might easily have been quicker if it had.[59] Speaking then of how things *would* have been if not for the opening, it cannot be said that, *were* it to have occurred, it would still have brought the explosion in its wake.

Important as they are, contingency and adequacy capture the commensuration intuition only partly. Imagine that Socrates, always a sloppy eater, had difficulty drinking without guzzling, to such a degree that if the guzzling hadn't occurred, the drinking wouldn't have either. Then Socrates' death *was* contingent on his guzzling the hemlock; and so more than contingency is needed to explain why it was not the effect of his doing so. Intuitively, it appears that not *all* of the guzzling was needed, because there occurred also a lesser event, the drinking, which would still have done the job even in the guzzling's absence. By hypothesis, of course, without the guzzling this lesser event would not have taken place; but that doesn't stop us from asking what would have happened if it had, and evaluating the guzzling on that basis. Suppose we call x *required* for y just in case

(R) For all $x^- < x$, if x^- had occurred without x, then y would not have occurred.

Then what disqualifies the guzzling is that, given the drinking, the death did not require it.

Symmetry considerations suggest the possibility of a condition complementary to (R), and a variation on the valve example shows that one is in fact needed. Imagine that the mechanism stiffens, not extemporaneously as above, but because of a preexisting structural defect that would have decelerated the opening in any case. Presumably this means that if the opening had not occurred, it would still have been protracted if it had, and the explosion would still have ensued. Since now the opening *is* adequate for the effect, the problem with taking it for the cause lies elsewhere; and the obvious thought is that the effect required something more. Thus define x as *enough* for y iff no more than x was required:

(E) For all $x^+ > x$, x^+ was not required for y.

Because the valve's *slowly* opening was required for the explosion, its opening per se was not enough; and that is why it was not the cause.

When all of the conditions are met—that is, y is contingent on x, and requires it, and x is adequate, and enough, for y—x will be called *proportional* to y. Without claiming that proportionality is strictly necessary for causation,[60] it seems clear that faced with a choice between two candidate causes, normally the more proportional candidate is to be preferred. Which of the contenders proportionality favors depends, of course, on the effect in view; Socrates' drinking the hemlock is better positioned than his guzzling it to cause his death, but relative to other effects proportionality may back the guzzling over the drinking.

More to the present point is the following example: I arrive on your doorstep and, rather than knocking, decide to press the buzzer. Epiphenomenalist neuroscientists are monitoring my brain activity from a remote location, and an event e in their neurometer indicates my neural condition to be such and such. Now, like any mental event, my decision m has a physical determination p, and the question arises to which of these the neurometer reading e is due. The scientists reason as follows: Because the neurometer is keyed to the precise condition of his brain, e would not have occurred if the decision had been taken in a different neural way, in particular if it had occurred in p's absence. So m was not enough for e;[61] p on the other hand looks *roughly* proportional to e and so has the better claim to cause it. Another triumph for epiphenomenalism!

Everything is all right except for the last step. What is true is that *this* mental event did not cause *that* effect. But who would have thought otherwise? When an effect depends not simply on an event's occurring, but on its occurring in some specific manner, one rightly hesitates to attribute causation. Taking the meter reading to result from my decision would be like attributing Zsa Zsa's speeding citation to her driving through the police radar per se, or the officer's abrasions to her touching his face.

Then when *do* we attribute effects to mental causes? Only when we believe, I can only suppose rightly, that the effect is relatively insensitive to the finer details of m's physical implementation. Having decided to push the button, I do so, and the doorbell rings. Most people would say, and I agree, that my decision had the ringing as one of its effects. Of course, the decision had a physical determination p; but, most people would also say, and I agree again, that it would still have been succeeded by the ringing, if it had occurred in a different physical way, that is, if its physical determination had been not p but some other physical event. And this is just to say that p was not *required* for the effect.

Remember that this makes no prediction about what would have happened if the decision had occurred in *whatever* physical way, but speaks only of what transpires in the *nearest* world where its physical implementation was not as actually—the world in which it undergoes only the minimum physical distortion required to put its actual implementation out of existence. Maybe, of course, we were wrong to think that the ringing would still have occurred in that world; if so, then let us hurry to withdraw the assertion that the decision caused it (the real cause is some physically more determinate event). But if not, then our conclusions should be these (where r = the doorbell's ringing):

(i)   m is a counterexample to r's requiring p (for r would still have occurred, if m had occurred without p);

(ii) p is not proportional to r (since r does not require it);

(iii) p does not cause r (since it is not proportional to r);

(iv) p is not a counterexample to m's

enoughness for r (it could be a counterexample only if r required it);

(v) p is not a counterexample to m's proportionality with r (by inspection of the remaining conditions);

(vi) p poses no evident threat to the hypothesis that m caused r.

Here are the beginnings, at least, of a story
wherein a mental event emerges as better qualified than its physical basis for the role of cause.
I believe that this *kind* of story is enacted virtually wherever common sense finds mental causation.

9

Indeterministic scruples aside, everything that
happens is in strict causal consequence of its
physical antecedents. But causally necessitating
is a different thing from causing, and the physical has no monopoly on causation. Among causation's prerequisites is that the cause should be,
as far as possible, commensurate with its effect;
and part of commensuration is that nothing causes an effect which is essentially overladen with
materials to which the effect is in no way be-

holden. This, though, is a condition of which
would-be physical causes often fall afoul, thus
opening up the market to less determinate events
with essences better attuned to the effect's causal
requirements. Sometimes, these events are mental; and that is how mental causation happens.

In a "Concluding Unscientific Postscript" to
"The Conceivability of Mechanism," Malcolm
remarks that

it is true for me (and for others, too) that a sequence of sounds tends to lose the aspect of
speech (language) when we conceive of those
sounds as being caused neurologically. . . .
Likewise, a sequence of movements loses the
aspect of action . . . ;

and he asks, "Is this tendency due to a false picture or misleading analogy?"[62] Many philosophers, anxious to defend the possibility of
speech and action, have struggled to articulate
what the analogy is which so misleads us. But
maybe we are *not* misled to think that outcomes
effected by their physical antecedents are neither speech nor action, nor expressions of any
sort of human agency. Maybe the mistake was
to think that outcomes of the kind normally
credited to human agency are caused by their
physical antecedents.[63]

NOTES

Thanks to Louise Antony, Simon Blackburn, Paul
Boghossian, Donald Davidson, Graeme Forbes, Sally
Haslanger, Jaegwon Kim, Vann McGee, Sarah Patterson,
Gideon Rosen, Larry Sklar, William Taschek, David
Velleman, Ken Walton, Catherine Wright, Crispin
Wright, and two anonymous readers for reactions and ad-
vice. Versions of the paper were read at Chicago Circle,
the University of North Carolina at Chapel Hill, and the
University of Western Ontario; discussions there were
extremely useful and I'm grateful to all who took part.
Research was supported by the National Endowment for
the Humanities and the Social Sciences and Humanities
Research Council of Canada.

1. *The Essential Descartes,* ed. M. Wilson (New York:
New American Library, 1969), 373. In the "Fifth
Objections," Gassendi puts a similar question: "How
can there be effort directed against anything, or motion set up in it, unless there is mutual contact between what moves and what is moved? And how can
there be contact without a body . . . ?" (*The Philosophical Writings of Descartes,* vol. 2, ed. J. Cottingham, R. Stoothoff, and D. Murdoch [Cambridge:
Cambridge University Press, 1984], 236ff.).

2. In case it seems odd to describe the picture just outlined as dualist, bear in mind that all I mean by the
term is that mental and physical phenomena are,
contrary to the identity theory, *distinct,* and contrary
to eliminativism, *existents.* That this much dualism

is acceptable even to many materialists is in a way
the point: having broken with dualism's Cartesian
version over its vulnerability to epiphenomenalism,
they find to their horror that epiphenomenalism lives
equally happily on the lesser dualism latent in their
own view.

3. Kim, "Supervenience and Supervenient Causation,"
Southern Journal of Philosophy, supp. vol. 22
(1983): 54. Kim does allow the mental a role in what
he calls *epiphenomenal* causal relations, and he says
that macrophysical causation is epiphenomenal in
the same sense. My position is that neither sort
of causation is epiphenomenal in any interesting
sense.

4. This is particularly clear in Schiffer, who rejects
mental *properties* on the ground that they would be
causally superfluous, and makes mental *events* a
subspecies of physical events on the theory that they
would *otherwise* be causally superfluous (*Remnants
of Meaning* [Cambridge: MIT Press, 1989], chap. 6).

5. So 'x' and '$x*$' become 'X' and '$X*$', and where either is prefixed by 'event', this becomes 'property';
'event y' and 'event z' are unaffected. Although causes and effects are events, properties as well as events
can be causally relevant or sufficient. I try to remain
neutral about what exactly causal sufficiency and
relevance amount to (e.g., causal sufficiency could
be sufficiency-in-the-circumstances, or it could be

absolute). Versions of the exclusion argument are found in H. Feigl, "Mind–Body, Not a Pseudo-Problem," in *The Mind-Brain Identity Theory,* ed. C. V. Borst (New York: St. Martin's Press, 1970), 33–41; N. Malcolm, "The Conceivability of Mechanism," in *Free Will,* ed. G. Watson (Oxford: Oxford University Press, 1982), 127–49; A. Goldman, "The Compatibility of Mechanism and Purpose," *Philosophical Review* 78 (1969): 468–82; K. Campbell, *Body and Mind* (New York: Macmillan, 1970); J. Kim, "Causality, Identity, and Supervenience in the Mind-Body Problem," *Midwest Studies in Philosophy* 4 (1979): 31–50, and "Mechanism, Purpose, and Explanatory Exclusion," *Philosophical Perspectives* 3 (1989): 77–108; E. Sosa, "Mind–Body Interaction and Supervenient Causation," *Midwest Studies in Philosophy* 9 (1984): 271–81; T. Honderich, *Mind and Brain: A Theory of Determinism* (Oxford: Oxford University Press, 1988); and C. Macdonald and G. Macdonald, "Mental Causation and Explanation of Action," in *Mind, Causation, and Action,* ed. L. Stevenson, R. Squires, and J. Haldane (Oxford: Basil Blackwell, 1986), 35–48. Objections similar in spirit to the exclusion argument are sometimes raised against the causal claims of other phenomena apparently unneeded in fundamental physical explanation (e.g., macroscopic and color phenomena). This paper offers a potentially general strategy of response.

6. Some authors use a slightly weaker premise: if x is causally sufficient for y, then unless y is causally overdetermined, every distinct event x^* is causally irrelevant (see note 53).

7. (2) could obviously be questioned, but I take it that physical determinism isn't the issue. For one thing, the conviction that mind makes a causal difference is not beholden to the contemporary opinion that determinism is false, and would remain if that opinion were reversed. Second, nothing essential is lost if 'x is causally sufficient for y' is replaced throughout by 'x determines y's objective probability'. So unless the argument can be faulted on other grounds, mental causation is problematic under indeterminism too.

8. C. D. Broad was perhaps the first to emphasize epiphenomenalism's double-sidedness: "[it] asserts . . . that mental events either (a) do not function at all as cause-factors; or (b) that, if they do, they do so in virtue of their physiological characteristics and not in virtue of their mental characteristics" (*Mind and Its Place in Nature* [London: Routledge and Kegan Paul, 1925], 473).

9. Kim, "Epiphenomenal and Supervenient Causation" (*Midwest Studies in Philosophy* 9 [1984]: 257–70) is an important exception.

10. Malcolm, "The Conceivability of Mechanism," 136.

11. See Feigl, "Mind–Body, Not a Pseudo-Problem," 36ff.; J. Smart, "Sensations and Brain Processes," in Borst, *The Mind-Brain Identity Theory,* 54, 65–66; and Davidson, "Mental Events," in *Essays on Actions and Events* (Oxford: Oxford University Press, 1980), 207–24. Note that Davidson advances the token identity theory in response to a slightly different problem. His aim is to reconcile the following assumptions: singular causal claims need always to be backed by strict causal laws; strict laws are physical laws; every event subsumable under a physical law

is a physical event; and mental events are efficacious.

12. Sosa, "Mind–Body Interaction," 278.

13. Again, this needs to be distinguished from a somewhat different worry directed primarily at Davidson's anomalous monism: singular causal claims need always to be backed by strict causal laws; x's causally relevant properties vis-à-vis y are those figuring in the antecedent of some such backing law; strict causal laws never involve mental properties; so x's mental properties are causally irrelevant. For discussion, see Stoutland, "Oblique Causation and Reasons for Action," *Synthese* 43 (1980): 351–67; Honderich, "The Argument for Anomalous Monism," *Analysis* 42 (1982): 59–64; Sosa, "Mind–Body Interaction"; Loewer and Lepore, "Mind Matters," *Journal of Philosophy* 84 (1987):30–42; Fodor, "Making Mind Matter More," *Philosophical Topics* 17 (1989): 59–79; Loewer and Lepore, "More on Making Mind Matter More," same volume: 175–91; Cynthia Macdonald and Graham Macdonald, "Mental Causation and Explanation of Action"; and Brian McLaughlin, "Type Epiphenomenalism, Type Dualism, and the Causal Priority of the Physical," *Philosophical Perspectives* 3 (1989): 109–35 (some of these papers discuss the exclusion objection also). Note that the exclusion objection, the subject of the present paper, assumes nothing about the role of laws in causation or in the characterization of causally relevant properties.

14. See, for example, H. Putnam, "The Nature of Mental States," and N. Block and J. Fodor, "What Psychological States Are Not," both in *Readings in Philosophy of Psychology,* vol. 1, ed. Block (Cambridge: Cambridge University Press, 1980).

15. This is hardly a cause for regret. Identifying mental phenomena with physical phenomena, we saddle the former with the causal properties of the latter; but common sense sees mental phenomena as possessed of *distinctive* causal properties (see sections 8 and 9).

16. About mental and physical *properties,* the Macdonalds ("Mental Causation and Explanation of Action") reach a similar conclusion; however, their argument depends on treating mental *events* as identical to, rather than determinables of, physical events (see note 32 for the problems this causes).

17. Treating necessary coextensiveness as also *sufficient* for property identity would lead to various unwanted results, for instance, that there is only one universally necessary property.

18. I lump these two together not out of conviction but just as an expedient.

19. This, the condition (I_1) that properties are identical only if their *necessary* coextensiveness is conceptually guaranteed, entails (I) trivially; (I) does not entail (I_1) conversely because some necessary coextensiveness claims are not a priori knowable, for example, that necessarily, the extension of identity-with-Hesperus is the same as that of identity-with-Phosphorus. Note the contrast between (I_1) and the weaker condition (I_2) that $P = Q$ only if their *actual* coextensiveness is knowable a priori. (I_1) and (I_2) fail for essentially similar reasons (see note 21), but it is (I_1) that I have in mind in the text.

20. Reason: 'it is a priori that . . .', like 'Jones believes that . . .', generates an opaque context.

21. Kripke, *Naming and Necessity* (Cambridge: Harvard University Press, 1980). Likewise, the weaker condition (I_2) cited in note 19 was overturned by the discovery of identical properties whose *actual* coextensiveness was not knowable a priori (e.g., identity-with-Hesperus and identity-with-Phosphorus).

22. Two classic discussions are W. E. Johnson, *Logic* (New York: Dover, 1964), vol. 1, chap. 11, and Arthur Prior, "Determinables, Determinates and Determinants (I, II)," *Mind* 58 (1949): 1–20, 178–94.

23. So *P* determines *Q* just in case the traditional relation's first, metaphysical component is in place, where this consists primarily in the fact that *P* necessitates *Q* asymmetrically. Probably it goes too far to identify determination with asymmetric necessitation outright; otherwise, for example, conjunctive properties determine their conjuncts and universally impossible properties are all-determining. For dialectical reasons, I try to remain as neutral as I can about where determination leaves off and "mere" asymmetric necessitation begins (Prior, "Determinables, Determinates and Determinants," reviews some of the fascinating history of this problem).

24. "But if there is no conceptual entailment from *P* to thinking, then unthinking *P*s are conceivable, and to that extent possible; thus *P* doesn't determine thinking in the metaphysical sense either." I grant that the conceivability of a proposition ϕ is prima facie evidence of its possibility. But this prima facie evidence is defeated if there is not improbably a proposition ψ such that (a) ϕ is true, (b) if ψ is true, then ϕ is impossible, and (c) ϕ is conceivable only because one was unaware of (a) and/or (b). The ancients, for instance, were able to conceive Hesperus as existing without Phosphorus only because they were unaware of their identity; and if I find it conceivable that something should be in the micromechanical condition of this steaming tea but with a different temperature, that is for ignorance of the temperature's microphysical explanation. But I take it that there may also be an explanation of how thinking arises out of neurophysiology, such that if I knew it, then I would find it *in*conceivable, and consider it impossible, that something should be *P* without thinking. What's more, the prospect of such an explanation makes the hypothesis of an unthinking *P* only dubiously conceivable *today*. So the complaint is questionable on two counts. First, from a proposition's conceptual coherence, from the fact that its denial is not conceptually false, its conceivability does not follow—witness the Hesperus/Phosphorus example. Even where conceptual difficulties are absent, conceivability can be inhibited by the knowledge or suspicion of a defeater; and this is how it is, for many of us, with the proposition that there could be *P*s that did not think. Second, any conceivability intuition I *might* muster in this area I regard as unreliable, because liable to defeat by the progress of science. (For the (a), (b), (c) model of modal error, see Yablo, "The Real Distinction between Mind and Body," *Canadian Journal of Philosophy,* supp. vol. 16 [1990]: 149–201, and "Is Conceivability a Guide to Possibility?" *Philosophy and Phenomenological Research* [1993].)

25. "All but explicit" would not be much of an exaggeration; determination lies so near the surface and so

neatly organizes received opinion that one wonders why it is not already a standard theme.

26. This is Kim's "strong supervenience" ("Concepts of Supervenience," *Philosophy and Phenomenological Research* 45 [1984]: 153–76). Perhaps not everyone accepts supervenience in quite this strong a form; perhaps I don't myself (Yablo, "The Real Distinction between Mind and Body"). Yet for two reasons I have thought it better to formulate the thesis as in the text: (i) strong supervenience is seen nowadays not as the *answer* to epiphenomenalism but rather as the context in which the problem as currently discussed arises (avoiding epiphenomenalism may indeed have been part of the original impulse behind (S), but that is what makes its reappearance *under* (S) all the more troubling); (ii) it focuses the essential line of thought to work within relatively strong assumptions. How much supervenience the approach really needs, and whether that much is plausible, are questions for another paper. For now I just state my hope of getting by with a form of supervenience that allows for the possibility of nonphysical thinkers (see note 47).

27. See Putnam, "The Nature of Mental States," and Block and Fodor, "What Psychological States Are Not."

28. "Now you contradict yourself, for (M) is incompatible with supervenience. Let $\vee P_i$ be the disjunction of all *M*-necessitating physical properties (alternatively, the second-order property of possessing some P_i or other); then (S) entails that *M* and $\vee P_i$ necessitate each other, contrary to (M)'s claim that physical properties necessitate mental properties only asymmetrically." To respond by denying the reality of disjunctive properties, on the principle that co-possessors of *real* properties are thereby similar, forgets that the $\vee P_i$s *are* similar in that they have *M* in common. However, a related point still holds good: sharing of *physical* properties should make for *physical* similarity, and unless the multiple realizability thesis can be faulted on other grounds, the $\vee P_i$s are only mentally alike. (The tendency to think of the physical properties as closed under disjunction may owe something to a confusion of wide- and narrow-scope readings of '*x* exemplifies a P_i'. What is true is that for each P_i, whether *x* possesses *it* is a physical question; this does not make it a physical question whether *x* has some P_i or other.)

29. "There is a crucial difference: My mental properties *result* from my physical condition, but in no sense does a thing's redness result from its being scarlet." Actually this raises a subtle interpretive question about supervenience. On the *emergence* interpretation, a thing's physical properties are metaphysically prior to its mental properties and bring them into being. To caricature emergentism just slightly, supervenience is a kind of "supercausation" which improves on the original in that supercauses act *immediately* and metaphysically *guarantee* their supereffects (the supervenience/causation analogy is common; see, e.g., Kim, "Concepts of Supervenience"). Another view is that the supervening mental properties are *immanent* in their physical bases; rather than giving rise to thought by some obscure metaphysical motion, certain material conditions are inherently conditions of thinking. Now, as the objector suggests, immanentism is clearly correct in stan-

dard cases of conceptual entailment, for example, scarlet and red, squareness and rectangularity. Surely, though, this ought to make us suspicious about emergentism as an interpretation of the other cases—for how can the properties' conceptual relations bear on the metaphysical character of the supervenience? That the emergentist thinks they do hints at an unconscious appeal to the neo-Humean prejudice that regularities divide into the conceptual and the causal, or causal-like. But the dilemma is unreal: 'whatever is in the micromechanical condition of this tea is at temperature 95°C' fits into neither category, and I see no reason to treat 'whatever is in the physical condition of this person is thinking' differently. On the immanence model, of course, the alleged disanalogy with colors and their shades evaporates.

30. Depending on what exactly the exclusion principle demands in the way of causal sufficiency, Q' might be a determination of Q only in a fairly relaxed sense (see notes 5 and 23). Those uncomfortable about this should remember the dialectical context: we are trying to show that the assumption needed to disempower mental properties—namely, that determinates are causally competitive with their determinables—would, if true, disempower virtually *all* properties. But if they are causally competitive on a *strict* reading of the determination relation, then when it is *loosely* construed they should be competitive also; and the argument in the text, with determination read the second way, shows that this results in a basically unmeetable standard of causal relevance.

31. Although it contributed nothing to the earthquake's destructiveness that it registered under Richter six, a determinate of its violence that omitted this would ipso facto not be ultimate. Hence the ultimate determinate, whatever exactly it may be, sets a causally idle upper bound on the earthquake's violence; abstracting this upper bound away, we arrive at a determinable still sufficient for the buildings' collapse. (Again, in some cases, this might be a determinable of the ultimate determinate only in a fairly relaxed sense—but see the previous note.)

32. This is the Macdonalds' view also, but I question their rationale. Sometimes they seem to be arguing as follows: properties derive their causal powers from their instances; if one property determines another, an instance of the first is an instance of the second; so whenever a determinate is efficacious, its determinables are too. However, the conclusion is much too strong. Imagine a glass which shatters if Ella sings at 70 decibels or more. Tonight, as it happens, she sang at 80 db, with predictable results. Although it was relevant to the glass's shattering that the volume was *80* db, it contributed nothing that it was *under 90* db. Therefore, an efficacious determinate can have an irrelevant determinable. Another reading of the Macdonalds' position might be that the determinate's instances are instances of the determinable only *sometimes,* and that it is only in *these* cases that the determinable is efficacious if the determinate is. But notice what this requires: Ella's singing at 80 db is *identical* to her singing at over 70 db, but *distinct* from her singing at under 90 db. Apart from its intrinsic implausibility, such a view is untenable for logical reasons. P and its determinable Q are efficacious not absolutely, but only relative to

some specified effect; whether their instantiations are identical, though, has to be decided once and for all. So the strategy of identifying the P- and Q-events iff both P and Q are efficacious leads to inconsistent results: they *can't* be the same event, because there are effects (the glass's shattering) to which only P is relevant; at the same time they *must* be, to accommodate effects (the neighbor's turning up her hearing aid) to which Q is relevant too.

33. Here and throughout 'events' are event tokens, not types; my slamming the door is something that happens at a specific time, in a specific place, and in a particular way.

34. Where this is understood fairly generally, so that, for example, Poindexter's lying to Congress is his speaking to Congress in a certain way, to wit falsely.

35. Killings need not be stabbings, and Brutus could have killed Caesar without stabbing him; but this *particular* killing, I assume, could not have occurred except by way of the associated stabbing (this is important if the killing is to be a determination of the stabbing).

36. For example, to *stabbings,* unlike *killings,* it is not essential that someone die.

37. Here is the basic condition on cumulative properties stated more formally: (κ) for all x, for all possible worlds w, for all sets S of cumulative properties [x exists in w and possesses there every member of $S \leftrightarrow$ there exists in w an $x^+ \geq x$ to which every member of S belongs essentially]. To see how this works to exclude identity properties, suppose that x possesses some cumulative P accidentally in some world w where it exists. If *identity-with-x* were cumulative, by (κ) there would be an x^+ in w to which *identity-with-x* and P were both essential—a contradiction, since nothing can be both identical to x and essentially possessed of a property which x possesses only accidentally. Likewise for kind-properties: if x is accidentally P and of such and such a kind, it will normally be impossible to strengthen x into an x^+ still of that kind but possessing P essentially. Thus, no *person* is *essentially* born on a certain day, no *stabbing* is *essentially* fatal, no *landslide* is *essentially* between nine and ten seconds long, and so on. (Terminological note: subsumption is called 'refinement' in "Identity, Essence, and Indiscernibility," *Journal of Philosophy* 84 [1987]: 293–314, and 'strengthening' in "Cause and Essence," *Synthese* [1992].)

38. More familiar are the notions of an *occurrent* property: one whose possession by a thing at a time is insensitive to how matters stand at other times; and an *intrinsic* property: one which a thing possesses wholly in virtue of how it is in itself, irrespective of what goes on around it. Within limits we can think of categoricity as standing to the modal dimension as occurrence stands to time and intrinsicness to space (see "Identity, Essence, and Indiscernibility," and "Intrinsic, Occurrent, Categorical," manuscript).

39. Assuming that the logical space of particulars is *full* in a sense I discuss elsewhere, the stated condition is sufficient also ("Identity, Essence, and Indiscernibility," secs. 4 and 5). Fullness is a sort of plenitude principle whose point is to ensure that there are particulars enough to witness the hypotheticality of every hypothetical property; that is, that for each hypothetical H, there exist in some possible world $\geq$-related p and q such that H attaches to exactly one

of them. To illustrate, part of the assumption is that for any particular q and any non-empty set W of worlds in which it exists, there is a $p \geqslant q$ which exists in the W-worlds exactly. Now suppose we agree that to be, say, flexible, a thing must be at least capable of flexing, that is, it needs to flex in at least some worlds. By fullness, any flexible q, provided only that there are worlds in which it never flexes, will have a determination p which metaphysically *cannot* flex. This shows that flexibility is hypothetical. (Some say that if dispositional properties are hypothetical, then *all* properties are, for it is essential to every property, however categorical it might otherwise seem, to confer on its possessors correlative causal dispositions, for instance, flexibility, corrosiveness, visibility. But the idea that even seemingly categorical properties are essentially disposition-conferring is, in the context of the fullness assumption, quite implausible. For instance, it detracts not at all from a thing's actual-world *roundness* to restrict or otherwise adjust its counterfactual career, but its dispositions can be varied almost at will by the same operation. What *might* be essential to roundness is to confer appropriate dispositions on particulars meeting *further hypothetical conditions,* conditions aimed at ruling out unusual hypothetical coloration such as we saw above. Yet since roundness "entails" these dispositions only over its hypothetically *ordinary* possessors, the objection is analogous to the following: no *ordinary* thing moves discontinuously; so being at such and such a location at a given time "entails" the non-occurrent property of not being at every *other* time a million miles away; so, location properties are not occurrent!)

40. That is, if $p \geqslant q$, then necessarily if p exists then so does q. *Proof:* Run (κ) from right to left with $S =$ the empty set. (Another proof uses the assumption that x exists in w iff x's essence is satisfied there, that is, something possesses there all its member properties: w contains p only if p's essence is satisfied in w only if q's smaller essence is satisfied in w only if w contains q.)

41. That these exhaust the possibilities is not trivial; but it can be proven from (μ) and the assumption (σ) that distinct particulars either exist in different worlds or are noncoincident in some world where they exist together. *Proof:* It suffices to show that $p = q$ if they have the same essence. Suppose they do. Then each subsumes the other. By (μ), they exist in the same worlds and are coincident in all of them. By (σ), $p = q$.

42. *Proof:* (i) is immediate from (μ) and the fact that determination entails subsumption. (ii) If p existed in every world in which q did, then by (μ) and (i) they would exist in the same worlds and be coincident in all of them. Given (σ) that would make them identical, contrary to the assumption that p determines q.

43. *Proof:* Suppose that q exists in a world w and exemplifies S there. By (κ)'s left-to-right direction, there exists in w a $q^+ \geqslant p$; it follows from (μ) that p exists in w. For the converse, run (κ) from right to left with S as before.

44. *Naming and Necessity,* 146, with inessential relettering. Note that if "logically possible" is taken literally, as covering everything permitted by logic, then even identicals can differ in what is logically possible for them—for example, it is logically possible

that Hesperus, but not that Phosphorus, should exist in Phosphorus's absence. Obviously this would make logical possibility useless in applications of Leibniz's Law; so I assume that Kripke is using "logical possibility" for metaphysical possibility.

45. Two remarks. First, the point of calling this an *intuition* is that Kripke's argument might be read as objecting to supervenience itself (*Naming and Necessity,* 155). So read, the argument assumes that the weight of modal intuition favors the antisupervenience position. This I deny; there are many reasons for supervenience's popularity, but one, surely, is its enormous modal intuitiveness. (Such antisupervenience intuitions as may exist I would hope to explain away in the manner of note 24.) Second, someone might complain that "the dominant intuition" is only that the mental characteristics of *objects,* or perhaps *worlds,* are necessitated by their physical properties; *events* are another story. Otherwise supervenience entails, as it surely should not, that every mental event is a physical event. But the objection assumes that events with mental properties are thereby mental events; and I am in the process of questioning whether even *essential* mental properties are enough to make an event mental. (For the idea that strong supervenience presupposes token identity, see Haugeland, "Weak Supervenience," *American Philosophical Quarterly* 19 [1982]: 93–103, and Kim, "Supervenience for Multiple Domains," *Philosophical Topics* 16 [1988]: 129–50.)

46. Notice what (s) doesn't say: that every property *essential* to m is essential to p. For all we know so far, no mental event is physical; in that case m's mental identity- and kind-properties are not properties of p at all.

47. Of course, whoever accepts supervenience in form (S) will find the Cartesian hypothesis hard to swallow, for (S) implies that in, and across, immaterial worlds, everyone is thinking exactly the same thing! This has led some authors (e.g., David Lewis) to seek more permissive interpretations of supervenience.

48. This is a particular theme of Richard Boyd, "Materialism without Reductionism," in *Readings in the Philosophy of Psychology,* vol. 1, ed. N. Block (Cambridge: Harvard University Press, 1980), 67–106.

49. *Naming and Necessity,* with inessential relettering.

50. "Granted that a pain could still have occurred in the absence of that molecular configuration, what makes you think that it is the same pain that occurred actually?" Among the lessons of *Naming and Necessity* is that to find a thing x capable of existing in some counterfactual condition, one imagines this *directly*—as opposed to imagining something y in that condition whose transworld identity with x must then be established. This is crucial if imaginability is to be a source of knowledge about *de re* possibility. For (i) having imagined y in the indicated condition, verifying that y is x requires appeal to transworld identity criteria which, if they are available at all, are typically *more* controversial than the *de re* attributions they are called on to support; and (ii) without reliance on direct *de re* imagination there would be no way to justify these criteria in the first place. Stripped then of its reference to transworld identity, the question is, Is m really imaginable in the absence of b, or is the only

imaginable scenario one in which a distinct if similar pain occurs in *b*'s absence? Here I can do no more than echo Kripke in claiming the former intuition. Such intuitions are of course defeasible by reference to unnoticed complications, but they are prima facie credible and the burden of proof is on the critic (see Boyd, "Materialism without Reductionism," for pertinent thought experiments, and note 24 for the defeasibility of modal intuition). On a deeper level, perhaps the objection reflects not any particular attachment to a picture of mental events as bound to their physical underpinnings, but a more general malaise attending *all* modal thinking about events. Whereas objects fall into more or less settled kinds, which then guide us in our assessment of what counterfactual changes they will tolerate, with events our commonsense sortal apparatus is relatively primitive and modally inarticulate; that something is a pain, or an explosion, tells us enormously less about its possibilities than that it is a person or a ship. Hence our admitted squeamishness about events' potential for contrary-to-fact behavior—which hardens all too easily into the positive thesis that potential is extremely limited (i.e., that events are inherently modally inflexible). This last, though, is surely an overreaction. What the squeamishness really signifies is the inadequacy of everyday event-sortals to the task of identifying just which of various coincident-but-hypothetically-different items one has in mind. Small wonder, then, if the identificatory task falls partly to the *de re* modal attributions themselves; and some of the more dogmatic-sounding attributions in the text may seem less so when understood in this spirit: as partial specifications of their subject matter rather than as attempts to describe an already singled-out particular.

51. This may seem doubtful, if one insists on seeing *p* as (i) a localized brain event, (ii) capable of occurring in isolation from anything like its actual neural context. Imagine a C-fiber stimulation, *b,* and a pain sensation, *s,* with the following properties. First, they are both occurring in me right now; second, *b could* have occurred in isolated C-fibers afloat in agar jelly; third, had *b* occurred in the latter environment, *s* would not have accompanied it. Then since determination entails necessitation, *b* does not determine *s*. The moral is that (i) and (ii) ask too much. Most mental events *m* seem not to be localizable in any specific portion of the brain; determination entailing coincidence, their physical determinations *p* will not be localizable either (thus *p* might be the event of my falling into a certain overall neural condition). Perhaps no mental event is localizable, but if *m* is an exception, its physical determination *p* will have a partly extrinsic essence (thus *p* might be my C-fibers' firing in normal neural surroundings). So-called "wide content" mental events raise related but different problems which I don't discuss. Possibly they will have to be allowed as exceptions to the physical/mental determination thesis; in that case, the paper should be read as defending the causal potency of *other*-than-"wide content" mental events. Two remarks, though, to put this in perspective: First, it is controversial how often such events are genuinely efficacious, in particular because their "narrow" counterparts seem ordinarily to be more commensurate, in the sense of section 8, with their supposed effects (see J. Fodor, *Psychosemantics* [Cambridge: MIT Press, 1987], chap. 2 and "A Modal Argument for Narrow Content," *Journal of Philosophy* 88 [1991]: 5–26). Second, determination is only the most obvious of a number of intimate identity-like relations equally unsupportive of the "x_1 was sufficient, so x_2 was irrelevant" reflex. Neither of Beamon's outjumping the competition and his jumping 29′ 2¹⁄4″ determines the other; but nobody would think the latter irrelevant to his being awarded the gold medal because the former was sufficient (see J. Heil and A. Mele, "Mental Causes," *American Philosophical Quarterly* 28 [1991]: 49–59).

52. Goldman, "The Compatibility of Mechanism and Purpose," and Kim, "Mechanism, Purpose, and Explanatory Exclusion," make related observations.

53. Lately there has been a tendency to argue that *p*'s causal sufficiency for an effect, though it does not *directly* entail *m*'s irrelevance, limits *m*'s role to that of a causal overdeterminant at best (see note 6); that *m* is indeed irrelevant then emerges from the fact that the effect is not overdetermined. With as much or little plausibility, one could argue that Ella's singing at over 70 db was irrelevant to the glass's breaking, since the latter was causally guaranteed, but not overdetermined, by her singing at 80 db exactly.

54. Suppose that causal sufficiency is read in some fairly demanding way, say, as requiring the strict nomological impossibility of *x*'s occurring without *y*'s doing so. Then no physical event *p* with hopes of determining a mental event *m* is likely to be itself causally sufficient for *m*'s apparent effect *y*. For *p* can determine *m* only if they are the same size, and nothing that small—assuming anyway that its essence is not unconscionably extrinsic—can nomologically guarantee any but the most trifling and immediate results. Let it be granted, then, that *p* is not causally sufficient for *y;* that honor falls instead to a spatially more extensive physical event *p′*, whose occurrence essentially requires, in addition to *p*'s occurring, that the surrounding physical conditions be approximately as they are in fact. This affects the question of *m*'s causal potency, *only* if there is more causal rivalry between *m* and *p′* than we found between *m* and *p* (namely, none). But, how could there be? What dispelled the illusion of rivalry between *m* and *p* was that *p*'s occurrence consisted, in part, in *m*'s occurrence, and that is as true of *m* and *p′* as it was of *m* and *p:* for *p′* to occur is for *m* to occur in a certain physical way, and in a certain physical environment. So *p′* poses no greater threat than *p* to *m*'s causal aspirations.

55. To keep things simple, I'll focus on mental events; there is a related story about mental properties.

56. For definiteness, we interpret would-counterfactuals Stalnaker's way: 'if it had been that *P,* then it would have been that *Q*' is true iff *Q* is true in the *P*-world best resembling actuality; where it is indeterminate which *P*-world that is, the condition must hold on all admissible ways of resolving the indeterminacy. Might-counterfactuals, 'if it had been that *P,* then it might have been that *Q*', are true just in case their associated would-counterfactuals, 'if it had been that *P,* it would have been that not-*Q*', are *not* true. Equivalently, a might-counterfactual holds iff on at least one admissible selection of closest *P*-world, the

closest *P*-world is a *Q*-world. (See Lewis, "Counter-factuals and Comparative Possibility," and Stal-naker, "A Theory of Conditionals" and "A Defense of Conditional Excluded Middle," all in *Ifs,* ed. W. L. Harper, R. Stalnaker, and G. Pearce [Dordrecht, The Netherlands: D. Reidel, 1981].)

57. Rasmussen, "Ruben on Lewis and Causal Sufficien-cy" (*Analysis* 42 [1982]: 207–11) contains the only explicit reference to (A) that I have seen. There it is argued, fallaciously I think, that (A) follows from (C) on the assumption that *x* and *y* actually occur. Another erroneous criticism, encountered mostly in conversation, is that (A) is trivial given just the oc-currence of *x* and *y:* (A) is true iff *y* occurs in the nearest *x*-containing world *w* to the nearest *x*-omit-ting world *v* to actuality; but since *x* actually occurs, the nearest *x*-containing world *w* to *v* is the actual world, which contains *y* by hypothesis. This forgets that *w* is the actual world only if no *x*-containing worlds are nearer to *v* than the actual world is, and that some are bound to be if, as seems likely, the ac-tual world sits in the interior of a neighborhood of *x*-containing worlds. (What *does* follow trivially from the occurrence of *x* and *y* is the condition that if *x* had occurred, so would have *y;* this is why we use (A) despite its greater complexity.)

58. David Lewis puts contingency to similar use in his "Events," in *Philosophical Papers,* vol. 2 (Oxford: Oxford University Press, 1986).

59. I emphasize that the decelerating stiffness sets in only *after* the opening gets under way because I want it to be clear that *that very opening* could have been less protracted (as opposed to: a slower open-ing could have occurred in its place). To deny this would be to hold that the opening, once begun, *could not* have continued apace, that is, that the approach-ing deceleration was essential to it. As for the further claim that it *might* have been less protracted, sup-pose if you like that indeterminism holds, and that the misalignment's objective probability, condition-al on preceding events, was extremely low. (The re-lation between 'would' and 'might' is described in note 56.)

60. Because of the problems of preemption, overdeter-mination, and so on, strictly necessary conditions on causation are extremely hard to find. As far as I know, philosophers have not succeeded in turning up even a single one, beyond the trivialities that cause and effect should both occur and be suitably distinct (see Lewis, "Causation," with "Postscripts," in *Philosophical Papers,* vol. 2).

61. Strictly speaking this assumes that *p* was required for *e*—in other words, that *each* of *p*'s deter-minables, not just *m,* is such that if it had occurred in *p*'s absence, *e* would not have ensued. (For the inter-pretation of (R) and (E)'s event-quantifiers see "Cause and Essence," sec. 11.)

62. Malcolm, "The Conceivability of Mechanism," 149.

63. Obviously these remarks cannot hope to resolve *all* the problems that physical determinism has been thought to raise for agency; they are directed only at the outright contradiction between agency and deter-minism's alleged consequence epiphenomenalism. There my solution is: deny epiphenomenalism.

2 Consciousness

Consciousness poses arguably the most difficult problems in the philosophy and science of the mind. What is consciousness? Can consciousness be explained in physical terms? Is consciousness itself something physical? How can we have a theory of consciousness? These questions have been central in the history of the philosophy of mind. Many of the foundational papers in Part I were concerned at least in part with questions about consciousness, but in recent years, these questions have received particularly close attention. Some of this discussion is represented by the chapters in this part.

A. General

The term "consciousness" can be used with many different meanings, so at the start it is helpful to get these meanings clear. Ned Block's contribution to this section (chapter 24) is particularly useful here. Block distinguishes a number of senses of "consciousness." The central sort of consciousness is *phenomenal consciousness*. We can say that a subject is phenomenally conscious when there is *something it is like* to be that subject, and a mental state is phenomenally conscious when there is something it is like to be in that state. Phenomenally conscious mental states include the experience of seeing colors, feeling pains, and experiencing mental images and emotions. All of these involve a certain qualitative, experiential character. Block distinguishes phenomenal consciousness from *access consciousness* (which involves a certain sort of access to information), *self-consciousness* (which involves representation of oneself), and *monitoring consciousness* (which involves representation of one's own mental states). All of these notions of consciousness are important, but phenomenal consciousness is by far the most puzzling, and it is the central focus of most of the papers here.

Block's characterization of phenomenal consciousness in terms of "what it is like" is taken from Thomas Nagel's influential 1974 paper, "What Is It Like to Be a Bat?" (chapter 25). Here, Nagel focuses attention on this aspect of consciousness and argues that it is particularly difficult to explain. A major source of the difficulty is that standard explanations in science and philosophy are cast in objective terms, but consciousness is subjective by its nature. We might know all about the objective functioning in a bat's brain, but we still would not know what it is like to be the bat, from its own subjective viewpoint. Nagel does not rule out an eventual understanding of consciousness in physical terms, but suggests that it may require conceptual developments that are as yet quite beyond us.

A quite different perspective is given by Daniel Dennett's paper "Quining Qualia" (chapter 26). The term "qualia," as standardly used, refers to the properties of mental states that characterize what it is like to have them; so qualia and phenomenal consciousness are tightly bound together. Dennett argues that there is no reason to believe that qualia exist. He suggests that qualia are standardly taken to be ineffable, intrinsic, private, and directly apprehensible; and he argues through a series of thought-experiments that there is no reason to believe that mental states have properties of this sort. Dennett suggests that the notion of "qualia" reflects a confusion and refers to no properties at all.

Finally, my paper (chapter 27) gives an overview of issues about the metaphysics of consciousness. (As such it can be used to complement this introduction.) It distinguishes the "hard" and "easy" problems of consciousness and summarizes the three main sorts of arguments against materialism about consciousness: conceivability arguments, knowledge arguments, and explanatory arguments. It divides the theoretical landscape of views according to how they react to these arguments, all of which proceed by establishing an *epistemic gap* between physical processes and consciousness and inferring an *ontological gap*. The paper distinguishes three sorts of broadly materialist views: type-A materialism (which denies the epistemic gap), type-B materialism (which accepts the epistemic gap but denies the ontological gap), and type-C materialism (which accepts the epistemic gap but holds that it can be closed in principle). It also distinguishes three sorts of broadly nonreductive views: type-D dualism (interactionism), type-E dualism (epiphenomenalism), and type-F monism (a sort of "panprotopsychism" locating the grounds of experience in the unknown intrinsic qualities of the physical world). In addition to taxonomy, the paper argues against the first three views and defends the last three views. As such it can be seen as an extended argument against materialism about consciousness and an exploration of the alternative options.

FURTHER READING

Block, Flanagan, and Güzeldere (1997) is an excellent collection of important philosophical articles on consciousness. Baars, Banks, and Newman (forthcoming) does the same for scientific articles. Nagel (1986), Dennett (1991), and Chalmers (1996) give book-length statements of their respective views. Numerous responses to Block's article are contained in the 1995 issue of *Behavioral and Brain Sciences* in which Block's article was published; some of these are included in the Block, Flanagan, and Güzeldere volume. That volume also contains a number of papers commenting on Nagel, as does this volume; see also Akins (1993) for an account of the phenomenology of bats, based on empirical studies. Seager (1999) contains an extensive discussion of Dennett's views, while also giving a general introduction to philosophical issues about consciousness. A number of responses to Chalmers are collected in Shear (1997).

Akins, K. 1993. What is it like to be boring and myopic? In B. Dahlbom (ed.), *Dennett and His Critics*. Blackwell.

Baars, B. J., Banks, W. F., and Newman, J. forthcoming. *Essential Sources in the Scientific Study of Consciousness*. MIT Press.

Block, N., Flanagan, O., and Güzeldere, G. (eds.). 1997. *The Nature of Consciousness: Philosophical Debates*. MIT Press.

Chalmers, D. J. 1996. *The Conscious Mind: In Search of a Fundamental Theory*. Oxford University Press.

Dennett, D. C. 1991. *Consciousness Explained*. Little, Brown.

Nagel, T. 1986. *The View from Nowhere*. Oxford University Press.

Seager, W. E. 1999. *Theories of Consciousness: An Introduction and Assessment*. Routledge.

Shear, J. (ed.). 1997. *Explaining Consciousness: The Hard Problem*. MIT Press.

B. The Knowledge Argument

The most widely debated question in the philosophy of consciousness is whether consciousness is physical or nonphysical. The majority of contemporary philosophers of mind are materialists, but there have been a number of important arguments against materialism. Of these, perhaps the two most important are the *knowledge argument* and the *modal argument.*

The knowledge argument argues that there are truths about consciousness that cannot be deduced from physical truths and infers that consciousness is nonphysical. Aspects of the knowledge argument are present in Broad (chapter 16) and Nagel (chapter 25), but its classic statement is given by Frank Jackson's paper in this section (chapter 28). Jackson imagines a future neuroscientist, Mary, who has been brought up in a black-and-white room, but who knows all the physical truths about the brain. Jackson argues that although Mary knows all the physical facts, she does not know all the facts about consciousness: In particular, she does not know what it is like to see red. This can be seen by noting that she gains knowledge of what it is like to see red when she leaves the room. He infers that facts about consciousness are nonphysical facts and that materialism is false and epiphenomenalism about consciousness is true. This paper is supplemented by an excerpt from Jackson's 1987 paper "What Mary Didn't Know," which gives a formalization of the knowledge argument.

Materialists have responded to this argument in a number of different ways. Almost everyone agrees that Mary learns *something* when she leaves the room, but materialists argue that this new knowledge does not threaten materialism. One important strategy (taken by type-A materialists) argues that Mary does not gain any new *factual* knowledge, but merely gains an ability, analogous to the ability to ride a bicycle (which arguably goes beyond knowledge of facts). David Lewis (chapter 29) takes this strategy (the so-called "ability analysis"), holding that Mary lacked no factual knowledge when inside her black-and-white room, so that her physical knowledge was complete.

The ability analysis offers a neat solution to the materialist's problem, but even many materialists find its central claim intuitively difficult to accept. A more common materialist strategy (taken by type-B materialists) has been to argue that Mary gains factual knowledge, but this is knowledge of an old fact seen in a new way. Mary's situation might be held to be analogous to someone who knew that Superman could fly and who discovers that Clark Kent can fly. Arguably this is knowledge of the same fact through a different mode of presentation. A sophisticated version of this strategy is taken by Brian Loar (chapter 30). Loar recognizes that for the strategy to work, it must go beyond analogies with standard cases such as the above (since in these cases, the new knowledge always involves knowledge of new associated facts connecting the modes of presentation), and puts forward a detailed analysis based on the claim that phenomenal concepts (concepts of experience) are recognitional concepts that pick out physical properties, without doing so via a distinct property as a mode of presentation. If this strategy succeeds, the materialist can acknowledge a gap between physical and phenomenal *concepts,* while denying any gap between physical and phenomenal *properties* in the world.

A third, quite different strategy is taken by Daniel Stoljar (chapter 31). Stoljar rejects Lewis's and Loar's strategies, but holds that materialism can be saved by distinguishing between two different notions of the physical. On the first, physical truths involve the truths of physical *theory;* on the second, physical truths involve truths about physical *objects.* Stoljar argues that Mary has complete knowledge of physical truths in the first sense but not the second, and he argues that physicalism should be understood to require the completeness of physical truths in the second sense but not the first. If so, the argument has no force against materialism, as long as we acknowledge that truths about physical objects go beyond the truths of physical theory. Stoljar argues that this result is independently plausible, since fundamental physical entities must have an intrinsic nature about which physical theory is silent. The resulting view is a sort of type-F monism on which the intrinsic aspects of physical entities are partly responsible for constituting consciousness.

FURTHER READING

Versions of the knowledge argument are discussed by Broad (chapter 16), Nagel (chapter 25), and Chalmers (chapter 27). Ludlow, Stoljar, and Nagasawa (forthcoming) is a collection of articles on the knowledge argument. The ability hypothesis was first put forward by Nemirow (1990) and is argued against by Lycan (1995). Versions of the type-B response are put forward by Churchland (1985), Horgan (1984), Lycan (1995), and others. Jackson (chapter 21) can be seen as a rejoinder to this sort of response. Jackson (1998) rejects the conclusion of the argument and embraces a sort of type-A view. Nordby (1990) is a real-life exemplar of the Mary situation.

Churchland, P. M. 1985. Reduction, qualia and the direct introspection of brain states. Journal of Philosophy 82:8–28. Reprinted in *A Neurocomputational Perspective* (MIT Press, 1989).

Horgan, T. 1984. Jackson on physical information and qualia. *Philosophical Quarterly* 34:147–83.

Jackson, F. 1998. Postscript to "What Mary didn't know." In *Mind, Method, and Conditionals.* Cambridge University Press.

Ludlow, P., Stoljar, D., and Nagasawa, Y. (eds.). forthcoming. *There's Something about Mary.* MIT Press.

Lycan, W. G. 1995. A limited defense of phenomenal information. In T. Metzinger (ed.), *Conscious Experience.* Imprint Academic.

Nemirow, L. 1990. Physicalism and the cognitive role of acquaintance. In W. Lycan (ed.), *Mind and Cognition.* Blackwell.

Nordby, K. 1990. Vision in a complete achromat: A personal account. In R. Hess, L. Sharpe, and K. Nordby (eds.), *Night Vision: Basic, Clinical, and Applied Aspects.* Cambridge University Press.

C.   Modal Arguments

Another important group of arguments exploit the *modal* notions of possibility and necessity to argue against materialism. The classic argument of this sort is Descartes' argument in the Sixth Meditation (chapter 1) that he can imagine himself existing without a body, so it is possible that he could exist without a body, so he is not physical. Contemporary modal arguments do not embrace exactly this reasoning, but like Descartes' argument, they often proceed from the *conceivability* (or imaginability, or apparent possibility) of a dissociation between consciousness and physical processes to the possibility of such a dissociation, and so to the falsity of materialism. One argument of this sort (see Chalmers, chapter 27) appeals to the conceivability of *zombies:* creatures that are physically identical to conscious beings, but that are not conscious. From here, the argument infers the possibility of zombies, and so the falsity of materialism.

At the end of his book *Naming and Necessity,* Saul Kripke gives a somewhat more intricate modal argument. Earlier in the book, Kripke has argued that true identities (such as "heat is the motion of molecules") are necessary and hold in all possible worlds. He argues that when it seems that we can imagine that heat is not the motion of molecules, what we are really imagining is that something other than molecular motion could have the *appearance* of heat. In the selection reproduced here (chapter 32), Kripke argues that for any mental state (e.g., pain) and any physical state (e.g., C-fiber firing), we can imagine the mental state without the physical state and vice versa. Further, he argues that this cannot be explained away as merely involving the appearance of the mental state, since the appearance of pain is itself pain. So he argues that it is possible that the mental state can exist without the physical state and vice versa. If so, and if true identities are necessary, mental states cannot be identical to physical states. Kripke uses this as an argument against (type- and token-) identity theories, but related arguments can be made against materialism more generally.

Christopher Hill (chapter 33) explores a way of responding to Kripke's argument, as well as to related modal arguments. Developing a suggestion of Nagel's, he suggests that the imaginability of physical states without conscious mental states can be explained away by a strategy different to Kripke's. He argues that this imaginability can be explained by the fact that imagining physical states and imagining mental states involve quite different cognitive faculties, so one should expect that these acts of imagination should come apart, even if mental states and physical states are the same in reality. In effect, this is an instance of the type-B materialist strategy of appealing to deep differences in mental and physical *concepts,* while holding that these concepts refer to the same properties in the world.

Grover Maxwell (chapter 34) gives a quite different analysis of modal arguments. While he agrees with Kripke that modal intuitions cannot be explained away as involving the mere appearance of mental states, he suggests that they can be explained away as involving the mere appearance of *physical* states. That is, when we imagine a physical state without a mental state, we are merely imagining a system with the same structure and effects as the original physical state, but not the same intrinsic nature. On this view, physical terms rigidly designate underlying intrinsic properties, and these intrinsic properties may necessitate mental properties. This leads to what Maxwell calls "nonmaterialist physicalism" (it should be noted that Maxwell uses "materialist" in a nonstandard way). This is a sort of type-F monism that is somewhat similar in spirit to the view put forward by Stoljar (chapter 31).

FURTHER READING

Chalmers (chapter 27) gives a related modal argument against materialism, supplemented by an analysis using two-dimensional semantics. Jackson (chapter 21) discusses some closely related issues involving modality and materialism. Levine (chapter 35) addresses Kripke's argument, while Loar (chapter 30) addresses modal arguments in a manner broadly compatible with Hill's approach. In the literature, modal arguments involving zombies are put forward by Campbell (1970) and Kirk (1974) and are developed by Chalmers (1996). Chalmers (1999) responds to Hill's and Loar's analyses. Gendler and Hawthorne (2002) contains a number of recent papers discussing modal arguments. Maxwell's view is grounded in some ideas of Russell (1927), which are developed in more depth by Lockwood (1989), and criticized by Foster (1991).

Campbell, K. K. 1970. *Body and Mind.* Doubleday.

Chalmers, D. J. 1996. *The Conscious Mind.* Oxford University Press.

Chalmers, D. J. 1999. Materialism and the metaphysics of modality. *Philosophy and Phenomenological Research.* http://consc.net/papers/modality.html.

Foster, J. 1991. *The Immaterial Self: A Defense of the Cartesian Dualist Conception of Mind.* Routledge.

Gendler, T., and Hawthorne, J. 2002. *Imaginability, Conceivability, and Possibility.* Oxford University Press.

Kirk, R. 1974. Zombies vs materialists. *Proceedings of the Aristotelian Society, Supplementary Volume* 48:135–52.

Lockwood, M. 1989. *Mind, Brain, and the Quantum.* Oxford University Press.

Russell, B. 1927. *The Analysis of Matter.* London: Kegan Paul.

D. The Explanatory Gap

The issue of whether consciousness is itself physical is sometimes distinguished from the question of whether consciousness can be *explained* in physical terms. Where the first question concerns the ontological connection between physical processes and consciousness, the second concerns the epistemic connection. Some philosophers hold that even if consciousness is physical, there is a deep and perhaps unanswerable problem of giving an explanation of consciousness. So the question of whether and how consciousness might be physically explained can be seen as an important question that raises distinct issues of its own.

Joseph Levine (chapter 35) argues that while epistemic considerations such as Kripke's may not refute materialism, they suggest a deep *explanatory gap* between physical processes and consciousness. The mere fact that we can conceive any given physical process without consciousness suggests that we cannot have a fully satisfying explanation of consciousness in physical terms. In an addendum from his later paper "On Leaving Out What It Is Like," Levine fleshes out the roots of this problem by arguing that reductive explanation of the sort found elsewhere requires a conceptual connection of a broadly a priori sort between low-level descriptions and high-level descriptions. There appears to be no such connection in the case of consciousness, so the explanatory gap remains wide open.

Paul Churchland (chapter 36) argues that there is no in-principle gap between physical processes and consciousness. Some of Churchland's discussion is aimed at questions about materialism, but it can be seen as mostly centrally concerned with problems about explanation. Churchland argues for his conclusion indirectly, by paralleling arguments about consciousness with a series of parallel arguments that *light* is irreducible and cannot be explained in physical terms. Churchland suggests that these arguments are fallacious and concludes that the parallel arguments about consciousness are equally fallacious. If so, just as the explanatory gap was closed for light, we can expect that it will be closed for consciousness.

Ned Block and Robert Stalnaker (chapter 37) argue against Levine's viewpoint, as well as against related views of Jackson and Chalmers. They argue that reductive explanation does not require a priori entailments between low-level descriptions and high-level descriptions, and they argue that most high-level concepts cannot be analyzed in such a way to support such an entailment. If this is so, then the absence of such analyses and entailments in the case of consciousness is no obstacle to reductive explanation. This leaves the door open for a type-B materialist view according to which (as Levine holds) consciousness is physical, and (as Levine denies) consciousness can be fully explained in physical terms.

Finally, Colin McGinn (chapter 38) argues that we may never have an adequate theory of consciousness. This is not because no explanation exists, but because our limited human minds may be *cognitively closed* to the correct explanation—that is, it may be beyond our limited powers of understanding. On this view (which has much in common with the type-C materialism discussed earlier, although it may also have elements of type-F monism), consciousness may be grounded in physical properties, but these properties are inaccessible to us, since we can grasp them neither by perception or introspection. If this is right, then although some possible beings might be able to solve the mind–body problem, it will remain forever closed to us.

FURTHER READING

Churchland (1995), Levine (2000), and McGinn (1991, 1999) are book-length treatments of their respective views about consciousness. Churchland's paper is in part a response to the views of Searle (1992; see also chapter 63). Van Gulick (1993) addresses

Levine's and McGinn's arguments. Chalmers and Jackson (2001) is a reply to Block and Stalnaker. The papers in Shear (1997) address the explanatory gap from many different perspectives.

Chalmers, D. J., and Jackson, F. 2001. Conceptual analysis and reductive explanation. *Philosophical Review* 110:315–61. http://consc.net/papers/analysis.html.

Churchland, P. M. 1995. *The Engine of Reason, the Seat of the Soul: A Philosophical Journey into the Brain.* MIT Press.

Levine, J. 2000. *Purple Haze: The Puzzle of Conscious Experience.* MIT Press.

McGinn, C. 1991. *The Problem of Consciousness: Essays toward a Resolution.* Blackwell.

McGinn, C. 1999. *The Mysterious Flame: Conscious Minds in a Material World.* Basic Books.

Searle, J. R. 1992. *The Rediscovery of the Mind.* MIT Press.

Shear, J. (ed.) 1997. *Explaining Consciousness: The Hard Problem.* MIT Press.

van Gulick, R. 1993. Understanding the phenomenal mind: Are we all just armadillos? In M. Davies and G. Humphreys (eds.), *Consciousness: Psychological and Philosophical Essays.* Blackwell.

E.   Higher-Order Thought and Representationalism

If consciousness can be explained in simpler terms, how can it be explained? Some such theories of consciousness are scientific theories, cast in terms of neural and/or computional mechanisms. Other such theories are philosophical theories, explaining consciousness in terms of other concepts that do not presuppose consciousness. The papers in this section discuss two of the most important such theories: *higher-order thought* theories and *representationalist* theories.

Higher-order theories of consciousness explain conscious states in terms of the existence of a higher-order mental state that is directed at the original state. These theories can be divided into *higher-order perception* theories and *higher-order thought* theories, of which the latter are the more popular. David Rosenthal (chapter 39) has developed a detailed account of this sort, holding that a mental state is conscious when it is the object of an appropriate sort of higher-order thought. Rosenthal argues for this conclusion from the premise that conscious states are states that we are conscious of, develops the view in some depth, and draws out consequences.

Fred Dretske (chapter 40) distinguishes a number of different aspects of consciousness, including consciousness of facts and of things. Dretske goes on to argue, by appeal to examples concerning visual experience, that there can be features of a subject's conscious experience such that the subject is not conscious of these features (either through consciousness of facts or things). From here, Dretske argues that higher-order thought theories of consciousness are incorrect. He suggests that conscious states do not turn on our being conscious of those states, but rather turn on those states making us conscious of the world.

Representationalist theories hold that consciousness is reducible to a sort of representation: To a first approximation, the nature of a conscious state is exhausted by the way in which it represents the world. This suggestion is discussed and rebutted by Christopher Peacocke (chapter 41). Peacocke formulates a version of representationalism as the "Adequacy Thesis" and argues that this thesis is false, since there are cases where experiences have features that are irrelevant to representational content. Peacocke calls these *sensational* features of experience, over and above the representational properties of experience.

Michael Tye (chapter 42) argues for representationalism, holding that perceptual consciousness is exhausted by its representational content. Tye denies that there are perceptual "Qualia" (Peacocke's sensational features of experience); he accepts that there are "qualia," corresponding to what it is like to experience the world, but holds that these are equivalent to representational properties. Tye argues for this conclusion in part by considering the "transparent" world-directed nature of conscious experience. Tye rebuts various objections, including Peacocke's arguments, and draws out a number of consequences of his view, including the consequence that the character of experience is not fully determined by the internal state of the subject.

Sydney Shoemaker (chapter 43) argues for a sort of representationalism intermediate in strength between Peacocke's and Tye's views. Like Tye, Shoemaker argues that qualia are equivalent to representational properties, but unlike Tye, Shoemaker argues that the content of these representational properties involve qualia themselves (so like Peacocke, he denies the Adequacy Thesis): Roughly, a qualitative state represents the world as standing in a certain relation to that state. This aspect of Shoemaker's view is nonreductive, in the contents are characterized in terms of qualia (it is worth noting that representationalism alone does not entail a reductive view of consciousness); he combines this with an additional functionalist claim to yield a reductive view. This view also differs from Tye's in that the relevant representational properties are determined by the internal state of the subject. Shoemaker develops the view by considering a number of subtle questions about the contents of perception and applies the view to the analysis of introspection.

FURTHER READING

The views of the authors in this section are developed at book length in Rosenthal (2002), Dretske (1995), Peacocke (1983), Tye (1995, 2000), and Shoemaker (1996). Another important higher-order thought view, on which consciousness involves *potential* higher-order thoughts, is set out by Carruthers (2000). Armstrong (1968) and Lycan (1995) develop higher-order perception views. Dretske's objections to higher-order views are developed further in Dretske (1995), and addressed by Rosenthal (chapter 39). Block (chapter 24), Byrne (1997), Güzeldere (1995), and Siewert (1998) present further objections. Other representationalist views are laid out by Byrne (2001), Dretske (1995), Harman (1990), Lycan (1996), and Siewert (1998). Criticisms are developed by Block (1990), Neander (1998), and Warfield (1999). Tye (2000) argues against Shoemaker's view. Crane (1992) contains many interesting papers on the contents of perceptual experience.

Armstrong, D. M. 1968. *A Materialist Theory of the Mind.* Routledge.

Block, N. 1990. Inverted earth. *Philosophical Perspectives* 4:53–79.

Byrne, A. 1997. Some like it HOT: Consciousness and higher-order thoughts. *Philosophical Studies* 2:103–29.

Byrne, A. 2001. Intentionalism defended. *Philosophical Review* 110:199–240.

Carruthers, P. 2000. *Phenomenal Consciousness: A Naturalistic Theory.* Cambridge University Press.

Crane, T. 1992. *The Contents of Experience: Essays on Perception.* Cambridge University Press.

Dretske, F. 1995. *Naturalizing the Mind.* MIT Press.

Güzeldere, G. 1995. Is consciousness the perception of what passes in one's own mind? In T. Metzinger (ed.), *Conscious Experience.* Imprint Academic.

Harman, G. 1990. The intrinsic quality of experience. *Philosophical Perspectives* 4:31–52. Reprinted in Block, Flanagan, and Güzeldere 1997.

Lycan, W. G. 1995. Consciousness as internal monitoring, I. *Philosophical Perspectives* 9:1–14. Reprinted in Block, Flanagan, and Güzeldere 1997.

Lycan, W. G. 1996. *Consciousness and Experience.* MIT Press.

Neander, K. 1998. The division of phenomenal labor: A problem for representationalist theories of consciousness. *Philosophical Perspectives* 12:411–34.

Peacocke, C. 1983. *Sense and Content: Experience, Thought, and Their Relations.* Oxford University Press.

Rosenthal, D. 2002. *Consciousness and Mind.* Oxford University Press.

Shoemaker, S. 1996. *The First-Person Perspective and other Essays.* Cambridge University Press.

Siewert, C. 1998. *The Significance of Consciousness.* Princeton University Press.

Tye, M. 1995. *Ten Problems of Consciousness: A Representational Theory of the Phenomenal Mind.* MIT Press.

Tye, M. 2000. *Consciousness, Color, and Content.* MIT Press.

Warfield, T. 1999. Against representational theories of consciousness. *Journal of Consciousness Studies* 6:66–69.

A. General

24 | Concepts of Consciousness[1]
Ned Block

The concept of consciousness is a hybrid or better, a mongrel concept: the word 'consciousness' connotes a number of different concepts and denotes a number of different phenomena. We reason about "consciousness" using some premises that apply to one of the phenomena that fall under "consciousness," other premises that apply to other "consciousness" and we end up with trouble. There are many parallels in the history of science. Aristotle used 'velocity' sometimes to mean average velocity and sometimes to mean instantaneous velocity; his failure to see the distinction caused confusion. The Florentine Experimenters of the 17th Century used a single word (roughly translatable as "degree of heat") for temperature and for heat, generating paradoxes. For example, when they measured "degree of heat" by whether various heat sources could melt paraffin, heat source A came out hotter than B, but when they measured "degree of heat" by how much ice a heat source could melt in a given time, B was hotter than A.[2] These are very different cases, but there is a similarity, one that they share with the case of 'consciousness.' The similarity is: very different concepts are treated as a single concept. I think we all have some tendency to make this mistake in the case of "consciousness."

Phenomenal Consciousness

First, consider phenomenal consciousness, or P-consciousness, as I will call it. Phenomenal consciousness is experience; what makes a state phenomenally conscious is that there is something "it is like" (Nagel, 1974) to be in that state. Let me acknowledge at the outset that I cannot define P-consciousness in any remotely noncircular way. I don't consider this an embarrassment. The history of reductive definitions in philosophy should lead one not to expect a reductive definition of anything. But the best one can do for P-consciousness is in some respects worse than for many other things because really all one can do is *point* to the phenomenon (cf. Goldman, 1993a). Nonetheless, it is important to point properly. John Searle, acknowledging that consciousness cannot be defined non-circularly, defines it as follows:

> By consciousness I simply mean those subjective states of awareness or sentience that begin when one wakes in the morning and continue throughout the period that one is awake until one falls into a dreamless sleep, into a coma, or dies or is otherwise, as they say, unconscious. [This comes from Searle 1990; there is a much longer attempt along the same lines in his 1992, p. 83ff.]

I will argue that this sort of pointing is flawed because it points to too many things, too many different consciousnesses.

So how should we point to P-consciousness? Well, one way is via rough synonyms. As I said, P-consciousness is experience. P-conscious properties are experiential properties. P-conscious states are experiential states; that is, a state is P-conscious just in case it has experiential properties. The totality of the experiential properties of a state are "what it is like" to have it. Moving from synonyms to examples, we have P-conscious states when we see, hear, smell, taste and have pains. P-conscious properties include the experiential properties of sensations, feelings and perceptions, but I would also include thoughts, wants and emotions.[3] An important feature of P-consciousness is that differences in intentional content often make a P-conscious difference. What it is like to hear a sound as coming from the left differs from what it is like to hear a sound as coming from the right.

Abridged and revised from "On a Confusion about a Function of Consciousness," *Behavioral and Brain Sciences* 18:227–47, 1995, with the permission of Cambridge University Press.

Further, P-conscious differences often make an intentional difference. And this is partially explained by the fact that P-consciousness is often—perhaps even always—representational. (See Jackendoff, 1987; van Gulick, 1989; McGinn, 1991, Ch 2; Flanagan, 1992, Ch 4; Goldman, 1993b.) So far, I don't take myself to have said anything terribly controversial. The controversial part is that I take P-conscious properties to be distinct from any cognitive, intentional, or functional property. At least, no such reduction of P-consciousness to the cognitive, intentional or functional can be known in the armchair manner of recent deflationist approaches. (Cognitive = essentially involving thought; intentional properties = properties in virtue of which a representation or state is about something; functional properties = e.g., properties definable in terms of a computer program. See Searle, 1983 on intentionality; See Block, 1980, 1994, for better characterizations of a functional property.) But I am trying hard to limit the controversiality of my assumptions. Though I will be assuming that functionalism about P-consciousness is false, I will be pointing out that limited versions of many of the points I will be making can be acceptable to the functionalist.[4]

By way of homing in on P-consciousness, it is useful to appeal to what may be a contingent property of it, namely the famous "explanatory gap." To quote T. H. Huxley (1866), "How it is that anything so remarkable as a state of consciousness comes about as a result of irritating nervous tissue, is just as unaccountable as the appearance of Djin when Aladdin rubbed his lamp." Consider a famous neurophysiological theory of P-consciousness offered by Francis Crick and Christof Koch: namely, that a synchronized 35–75 hertz neural oscillation in the sensory areas of the cortex is at the heart of phenomenal consciousness. Assuming for the moment that such neural oscillations are the neural basis of sensory consciousness, no one has produced the concepts that would allow us to explain why such oscillations are the neural basis of one phenomenally conscious state rather than another or why the oscillations are the neural basis of a phenomenally conscious state rather than a phenomenally unconscious state.

However, Crick and Koch have offered a sketch of an account of how the 35–75 hertz oscillation might contribute to a solution to the "binding problem." Suppose one simultaneously sees a red square moving to the right and a blue circle moving to the left. Different areas of the visual cortex are differentially sensitive to color, shape, motion, etc. so what binds together redness, squareness and rightward motion? That is, why don't you see redness and blueness without seeing them as belonging with particular shapes and particular motions? And why aren't the colors normally seen as bound to the wrong shapes and motions? Representations of colors, shapes and motions of a single object are supposed to involve oscillations that are in phase with one another but not with representations of other objects. But even if the oscillation hypothesis deals with the informational aspect of the binding problem (and there is some evidence against it), how does it explain *what it is like to see something as red in the first place*— or for that matter, as square or as moving to the right? Why couldn't there be brains functionally or physiologically just like ours, including oscillation patterns, whose owners' experience was different from ours or who had no experience at all? (Note that I don't say that there *could be* such brains. I just want to know *why not*.) No one has a clue how to answer these questions.

The explanatory gap in the case of P-consciousness contrasts with our better (though still not very good) understanding of the scientific basis of cognition. We have two serious research programs into the nature of cognition, the classical "language of thought" paradigm, and the connectionist research program. Both assume that the scientific basis of cognition is computational. If this idea is right—and it seems increasingly promising—it gives us a better grip on why the neural basis of a thought state is the neural basis of that thought rather than some other thought or none at all than we have about the analogous issue for consciousness.

What I've been saying about P-consciousness is of course controversial in a variety of ways, both for some advocates and some opponents of some notion of P-consciousness. I have tried to steer clear of some controversies, e.g., controversies over inverted and absent qualia; over Jackson's (1986) Mary, the woman who is raised in a black and white room, learning all the physiological and functional facts about the brain and color vision, but nonetheless discovers a new fact when she goes outside the room for the first time and learns what it is like to see red; and even Nagel's view that we cannot know what it is like to be a bat.[5] Even if you think that

P-consciousness as I have described it is an incoherent notion, you may be able to agree with the main point of this paper, which is that a great deal of confusion arises as a result of confusing P-consciousness with something else. Not even the concept of what time it is now on the sun is so confused that it cannot itself be confused with something else.

Access-Consciousness

I now turn to the non-phenomenal notion of consciousness that is most easily and dangerously conflated with P-consciousness: access-consciousness. I will characterize access-consciousness, give some examples of how it makes sense for someone to have access-consciousness without phenomenal consciousness and vice versa, and then go on to the main theme of the paper, the damage done by conflating the two.

A-consciousness is access-consciousness. A representation is A-conscious if it is broadcast for free use in reasoning and for direct "rational" control of action (including reporting). An A-state is one that consists in having an A-representation. I see A-consciousness as a cluster concept in which reportability is the element of the cluster that has the smallest weight even though it is often the best practical guide to A-consciousness.

The 'rational' is meant to rule out the kind of automatic control that obtains in blindsight. (Blindsight is a syndrome involving patients who have brain damage in the first stage of visual processing, primary visual cortex. These patients seem to have "holes" in their visual fields. If the experimenter flashes stimuli in these holes and asks the patient what was flashed, the patient claims to see nothing but can often guess at high levels of accuracy, choosing between two locations or directions or whether what was flashed was an 'X' or an 'O'.)

I will suggest that A-consciousness plays a deep role in our ordinary 'consciousness' talk and thought. However, I must admit at the outset that this role allows for substantial indeterminacy in the concept itself. In addition, there are some loose ends in the characterization of the concept which cannot be tied up without deciding about certain controversial issues, to be mentioned below.[6] My guide in making precise the notion of A-consciousness is to formulate an information processing correlate of P-con-

sciousness that is not ad hoc and mirrors P-consciousness as well as a non–ad hoc information processing notion can.

In the original version of this paper, I defined 'A-consciousness' as (roughly) 'poised for control of speech, reasoning and action.'[7] In a comment on the original version of this paper, David Chalmers (1997) suggested defining 'A-consciousness' instead as 'directly available for global control.' Chalmers' definition has the advantage of avoiding enumerating the kinds of control. That makes the notion more general, applying to creatures who have kinds of control that differ from ours. But it has the disadvantage of that advantage, counting simple organisms as having A-consciousness if they have representations that are directly available for global control of whatever resources they happen to have. If the idea of A-consciousness is to be an information processing image of P-consciousness, it would not do to count a slug as having A-conscious states simply because there is some machinery of control of the resources that a slug happens to command.

As I noted, my goal in precisifying the ordinary notion of access as it is used in thinking about consciousness is to formulate a non–ad hoc notion that is close to an information processing image of P-consciousness. A flaw in both my definition and Chalmers' definition is that they make A-consciousness dispositional whereas P-consciousness is occurrent. As noted in the critique by Atkinson and Davies (1995), that makes the relation between P-consciousness and A-consciousness the relation between the ground of a disposition and the disposition itself. (See also Burge, 1997.) This has long been one ground of criticism of both functionalism and behaviorism (Block and Fodor, 1972), but there is no real need for an information-processing notion of consciousness to be saddled with a category mistake of this sort. I have dealt with the issue here by using the term 'broadcast,' as in Baars' (1988) theory that conscious representations are ones that are broadcast in a global workspace. A-consciousness is similar to that notion and to Dennett's (1993) notion of consciousness as cerebral celebrity.[8]

The interest in the A/P distinction arises from the battle between two different conceptions of the mind, the biological and the computational. The computational approach supposes that all of the mind (including consciousness) can be captured with notions of information processing, computation and function in a system. According to this view (often called functionalism by philosophers), the level of abstraction for understanding the mind is one that allows multiple realizations, just as one computer can be realized electrically or hydraulically. Their bet is that the different realizations don't matter to the mind, generally, and to consciousness specifically. The biological approach bets that the realization does matter. If P = A, the information processing side is right. But if the biological nature of experience is crucial, then realizations *do* matter, and we can expect that P and A will diverge.[9]

Although I make a distinction between A-consciousness and P-consciousness, I also want to insist that they interact. For example, what perceptual information is being accessed can change figure to ground and conversely, and a figure-ground switch can affect one's phenomenal state. For example, attending to the feel of the shirt on your neck, accessing those perceptual contents, switches what was in the background to the foreground, thereby changing one's phenomenal state. (See Hill, 1991, 118–26; Searle, 1992.)

Of course, there are notions of access in which the blindsight patient's guesses count as access. There is no right or wrong here. Access comes in various degrees and kinds, and my choice here is mainly determined by the desideratum of finding a notion of A-consciousness that mirrors P-consciousness. If the blindsight patient's perceptual representations are not P-conscious, it would not do to count them as A-conscious. (I also happen to think that the notion I characterize is more or less one that plays a big role in our thought, but that won't be a major factor here.)

I will mention three main differences between P-consciousness and A-consciousness. The first point, *put crudely,* is that P-conscious content is phenomenal, whereas A-conscious content is representational. It is of the essence of A-conscious content to play a role in reasoning, and only representational content can figure in reasoning. The reason this way of putting the point is crude is that many (perhaps even all) phenomenal contents are *also* representational. And some of the representational contents of a P-conscious state may be intrinsic to those P-contents.[10]

(In the last paragraph, I used the notion of P-conscious *content.* The P-conscious content of a state is the totality of the state's experiential properties, what it is like to be in that state. One

can think of the P-conscious content of a state as the state's experiential "value" by analogy to the representational content as the state's representational "value." In my view, the content of an experience can be both P-conscious and A-conscious; the former in virtue of its phenomenal feel and the latter in virtue of its representational properties.)

A closely related point: A-conscious states are necessarily transitive: A-conscious states must always be states of consciousness *of.* P-conscious states, by contrast, sometimes are and sometimes are not transitive. P-consciousness, as such, is not consciousness of. (I'll return to this point in a few paragraphs.)

Second, A-consciousness is a functional notion, and so A-conscious content is system-relative: what makes a state A-conscious is what a representation of its content does in a system. P-consciousness is not a functional notion.[11] In terms of Schacter's model of the mind (see the original version of this paper Block [1995]), content gets to be P-conscious because of what happens *inside* the P-consciousness module. But what makes content A-conscious is not anything that could go on *inside* a module, but rather informational relations *among* modules. Content is A-conscious in virtue of (a representation with that content) reaching the Executive system, the system that is in charge of rational control of action and speech, and to that extent, we could regard the Executive module as the A-consciousness module. But to regard *anything* as an A-consciousness module is misleading, because what makes a typical A-conscious representation A-conscious is what getting to the Executive module sets it up to *do,* namely affect reasoning and action.

A third difference is that there is such a thing as a P-conscious *type* or *kind* of state. For example the feel of pain is a P-conscious type—every pain must have that feel. But any particular token thought that is A-conscious at a given time could fail to be accessible at some other time, just as my car is accessible now, but will not be later when my wife has it. A state whose content is informationally promiscuous now may not be so later.

The paradigm P-conscious states are sensations, whereas the paradigm A-conscious states are "propositional attitude" states like thoughts, beliefs and desires, states with representational content expressed by "that" clauses. (E.g., the thought that grass is green.) What, then, gets broadcast when a P-conscious state is also

A-conscious? The most straightforward answer is: the P-content itself. However, exactly what this comes to depends on what exactly P-content is. If P-content is non-conceptual, it may be said that P contents are not the right sort of thing to play a role in inference and guiding action. However, even with non-humans, pain plays a rational role in guiding action. Different actions are appropriate responses to pains in different locations. Since the contents of pain do in fact play a rational role, either their contents are conceptualized *enough,* or else nonconceptual or not very conceptual content can play a rational role.

There is a familiar distinction, alluded to above, between 'consciousness' in the sense in which we speak of a state as being a conscious state (intransitive consciousness) and consciousness *of* something (transitive consciousness). (The transitive/intransitive terminology seems to have appeared first in Malcolm [1984], but see also Rosenthal [1997]. Humphrey [1992] mentions that the intransitive usage is much more recent, only 200 years old.) It is easy to fall into an identification of P-consciousness with intransitive consciousness and a corresponding identification of access-consciousness with transitive consciousness. Such an identification is over simple. As I mentioned earlier, P-conscious contents can be representational. Consider a perceptual state of seeing a square. This state has a P-conscious content that represents something, a square, and thus it is a state of P-consciousness *of* the square. It is a state of P-consciousness of the square even if it doesn't represent the square *as* a square, as would be the case if the perceptual state is a state of an animal that doesn't have the concept of a square. Since there can be P-consciousness *of* something, P-consciousness is not to be identified with intransitive consciousness.

Here is a second reason why the transitive/intransitive distinction cannot be identified with the P-consciousness/A-consciousness distinction: The *of*-ness required for transitivity does not guarantee that a content be utilizable by a **consuming** system, a system that uses the representations for reasoning or planning or control of action at the level required for A-consciousness. For example, a perceptual state of a brain-damaged creature might be a state of P-consciousness of, say, motion, even though connections to reasoning and rational control of action are damaged so that the state is not A-conscious. In sum, P-consciousness can be

consciousness of, and consciousness of need not be A-consciousness.

Those who are uncomfortable with P-consciousness should pay close attention to A-consciousness because it is a good candidate for a reductionist identification with P-consciousness.[12]

Many of my critics (Searle, 1992, Burge, 1997) have noted that if there can be "zombies," cases of A without P, they are not conscious in any sense of the term. I am sympathetic, but I don't agree with the conclusion that some have drawn that the A-sense is not a sense of "consciousness" and that A is not a kind of consciousness. A-consciousness can be a kind of consciousness even if it is parasitic on a core notion of P-consciousness. A parquet floor is a floor even though it requires another floor beneath it. A-consciousness can come and go against a background of P-consciousness.

The rationale for calling A-consciousness a kind of consciousness is first that it fits a certain kind of quasi-ordinary usage. Suppose one has a vivid mental image that is repressed. Repression need not make the image go away or make it non-phenomenal. One might realize after psychoanalysis that one had the image all along, but that one could not cope with it. It is "unconscious" in the Freudian sense—which is A-unconsciousness. Second, A-consciousness is typically the kind of consciousness that is relevant to use of words like "conscious" and "aware" in cognitive neuroscience. This point is made in detail in my comment on a special issue of the journal *Cognition* (Block, 2001) This issue summarizes the "state of the art" and some of the writers are clearly talking about A-consciousness (or one or another version of monitoring consciousness—see below) whereas others are usually talking about P-consciousness. The A notion of consciousness is the most prominent one in the discussion in that issue and in much of the rest of cognitive neuroscience. (See the article by Dehaene and Naccache in that volume which is very explicit about the use of A-consciousness.) Finally, recall that my purpose in framing the notion of A-consciousness is to get a functional notion of consciousness that is not ad hoc and comes as close to matching P-consciousness as a purely functional notion can. I hope to show that nonetheless there are cracks between P and A. In this context, I prefer to be liberal with terminology, allowing that A is a form of consciousness but not identical to phenomenal consciousness.

A-Consciousness without P-Consciousness

The main point of this paper is that these two concepts of consciousness are distinct and quite likely have different extensions yet are easily confused. Let us consider conceptually possible cases of one without the other. Actual cases will be more controversial.

First, I will give some putative examples of A-consciousness without P-consciousness. If there could be a full-fledged phenomenal zombie, say a robot computationally identical to a person, but whose silicon brain did not support P-consciousness, that would do the trick. I think such cases conceptually possible, but this is very controversial. (See Shoemaker, 1975, 1981.)

But there is a less controversial kind of case, a very limited sort of partial zombie. Consider the blindsight patient who "guesses" that there is an 'X' rather than an 'O' in his blind field. Taking his word for it (for the moment), I am assuming that he has no P-consciousness of the 'X'. The blindsight patient also has no 'X'-representing A-conscious content, because although the information that there is an 'X' affects his "guess," it is not available as a premise in reasoning (until he has the quite distinct state of hearing and believing his own guess), or for rational control of action or speech. Marcel (1986) points out that the thirsty blindsight patient would not reach for a glass of water in the blind field. So the blindsight patient's perceptual or quasi-perceptual state is unconscious in the phenomenal *and* access senses (*and* in the monitoring senses to be mentioned below too).

Now imagine something that may not exist, what we might call *superblindsight*. A real blindsight patient can only guess when given a choice from a small set of alternatives ('X'/'O'; horizontal/vertical, etc.). But suppose—interestingly, apparently contrary to fact—that a blindsight patient could be trained to prompt himself at will, guessing what is in the blind field without being told to guess. The superblindsighter spontaneously says "Now I know that there is a horizontal line in my blind field even though I don't actually see it." Visual information of a certain limited sort (excluding color and complicated shapes) from his blind field simply pops into his thoughts in the way that solutions to problems we've been worrying about pop into our thoughts, or in the way some people just know the time or which way is North without having any perceptual experience of it. He

knows there is an 'X' in his blind field, but he doesn't know the type font of the 'X'. The superblindsighter himself contrasts what it is like to know visually about an 'X' in his blind field and an 'X' in his sighted field. There is something it is like to experience the latter, but not the former he says. It is the difference between *just knowing* and knowing via a visual experience. Taking his word for it, here is the point: the perceptual content that there is an 'X' in his visual field is A-conscious but not P-conscious. The superblindsight case is a very limited partial zombie.

Of course, the superblindsighter has a *thought* that there is an 'X' in his blind field that is *both* A-conscious and P-conscious. But I am not talking about the thought. Rather, I am talking about the state of his perceptual system that gives rise to the thought. It is this state that is A-conscious without being P-conscious.[13]

The (apparent) non-existence of superblindsight is a striking fact, one that a number of writers have noticed, more or less. What Marcel was in effect pointing out was that the blindsight patients, in not reaching for a glass of water, are not superblindsighters. (See also Farah [1994].) Blind perception is never super blind perception.[14]

Notice that the superblindsighter I have described is just a little bit different (though in a crucial way) from the ordinary blindsight patient. In particular, I am *not relying* on what might be thought of as a full-fledged *quasi-zombie*, a super-*duper*-blindsighter whose blindsight is *every bit* as good, functionally speaking, as his sight. In the case of the super-duper blindsighter, the *only* difference between vision in the blind and sighted fields, functionally speaking, is that the quasi-zombie himself regards them differently. Such an example will be regarded by some (though not me) as incoherent—see Dennett, 1991, for example. But we can avoid disagreement about the super-duper-blindsighter by illustrating the idea of A-consciousness without P-consciousness by appealing only to the superblindsighter. Functionalists may want to know why the superblindsight case counts as A-conscious without P-consciousness. After all, they may say, if we have *really high quality access* in mind, the superblindsighter that I have described does not have it, so he lacks *both* P-consciousness and really high quality A-consciousness. The super-duper-blindsighter, on the other hand, *has* both, according to the functionalist, so in neither case, according to the objection, is there A-consciousness without P-consciousness.

One could put the point by distinguishing three types of access: (1) really high quality access, (2) medium access and (3) poor access. The *actual* blindsight patient has poor access (he has to be prompted to guess), the superblindsight patient has medium access and the super-duper blindsight patient—as well as most of us—has really high quality access. The functionalist objector I am talking about identifies P-consciousness with A-consciousness of the really high quality kind, whereas I am allowing A-consciousness with only medium access. (We agree in excluding low quality access.) The issue, then, is whether the functionalist can get away with restricting access to high quality access. I think not. I believe that in some cases, normal phenomenal vision involves only medium access. The easiest case to see for yourself with is peripheral vision. If you wave a colored object near your ear, you will find that in the right location you can see the movement without having the kind of rich access that you have in foveal vision. For example, your ability to recover shape and color is poor.

Why isn't peripheral vision a case of A without P? In peripheral vision, we are both A and P conscious of the same features—e.g., motion but not color. But in superblindsight—so the story goes—there is no P-consciousness of the horizontal line. (He just knows.) I conclude that A without P is conceptually possible even if not actual.

P-Consciousness without A-Consciousness

Consider an animal that you are happy to think of as having P-consciousness for which brain damage has destroyed centers of reasoning and rational control of action, thus preventing A-consciousness. It certainly seems *conceptually possible* that the neural bases of P-consciousness systems and A-consciousness systems be distinct, and if they are distinct, then it is possible, at least conceptually possible, for one to be damaged while the other is working well. Evidence has been accumulating for twenty-five years that the primate visual system has distinct dorsal and ventral subsystems. Though there is much disagreement about the specializations of the two systems, it does appear that much of the information in the ventral system is much more closely connected to P-consciousness than information in the dorsal system (Goodale and Milner, 1992). So it may actually be possible to damage A-consciousness without P-consciousness and perhaps even conversely.[15]

Further, one might suppose (Rey, 1983, 1988; White, 1987) that some of our own subsystems—say each of the two hemispheres of the brain—might themselves be separately P-conscious. Some of these subsystems might also be A-consciousness, but other subsystems might not have sufficient machinery for reasoning or reporting or rational control of action to allow their P-conscious states to be A-conscious; so if those states are not accessible to another system that does have adequate machinery, they will be P-conscious but not A-conscious.

Here is another reason to believe in P-consciousness without A-consciousness: Suppose that you are engaged in intense conversation when suddenly at noon you realize that right outside your window, there is—and has been for some time—a pneumatic drill digging up the street. You were aware of the noise all along, one might say, but only at noon are you *consciously aware* of it. That is, you were P-conscious of the noise all along, but at noon you are both P-conscious *and* A-conscious of it. Of course, there is a very similar string of events in which the crucial event at noon is a bit more intellectual. In this alternative scenario, at noon you realize not just that there is and has been a noise, but also that *you are now and have been hearing* the noise. In this alternative scenario, you get "higher order thought" as well as A-consciousness at noon. So on the first scenario, the belief that is acquired at noon is that there is and has been a noise, and on the second scenario, the beliefs that are acquired at noon are the first one plus the belief that you are and have been hearing the noise. But it is the first scenario, not the second that interests me. It is a good case of P-consciousness without A-consciousness. Only at noon is the content of your representation of the drill *broadcast* for use in rational control of action and speech. (Note that A-consciousness requires being broadcast, not merely being available for use.)

In addition, this case involves a natural use of 'conscious' and 'aware' for A-consciousness and P-consciousness. 'Conscious' and 'aware' are more or less synonymous, so when we have one of them we might think of it as awareness, but when we have both it is natural to call that conscious awareness. This case of P-consciousness without A-consciousness exploits what William James (1890) called "secondary consciousness" (at least I think it does; James scholars may know better), a category that he may have meant to include cases of P-consciousness without attention.

I have found that the argument of the last paragraph makes those who are distrustful of introspection uncomfortable. I agree that introspection is not the last word, but it is the first word, when it comes to P-consciousness. The example shows the conceptual distinctness of P-consciousness from A-consciousness and it also puts the burden of proof on anyone who would argue that as a matter of empirical fact they come to the same thing.

A-consciousness and P-consciousness very often occur together. When one or the other is missing, we can often speak of unconscious states (when the context is right). Thus, in virtue of missing A-consciousness, we think of Freudian states as unconscious. And in virtue of missing P-consciousness, it is natural to describe the superblindsighter or the unfeeling robot or computer as unconscious. Lack of monitoring-consciousness in the presence of A and P is also sometimes described as unconsciousness. Thus Julian Jaynes describes Greeks as becoming conscious when—in between the time of the Iliad and the Odyssey, they become more reflective.

Flanagan (1992) criticizes my notion of A-consciousness, suggesting that we replace it with a more liberal notion of informational sensitivity that counts the blindsight patient as having access-consciousness of the stimuli in his blind field. The idea is that the blindsight patient has **some** access to the information about the stimuli in the blind field, and that amount of access is enough for access consciousness. Of course, as I keep saying, the notion of A-consciousness that I have framed is just one of a family of access notions. But there is more than a verbal issue here. The real question is what good is A-consciousness as I have framed it in relation to the blindsight issue? The answer is that in blindsight, the patient is supposed to **lack** "consciousness" of the stimuli in the blind field. My point is that the blindsight lacks both P-consciousness and a kind of access (both medium and high level access in the terminology used earlier), and that these are easily confused. This point is not challenged by pointing out that the blindsight patient also has a lower level of access to this information.

The kind of access that I have built into A-consciousness plays a role in theory outside of this issue and in daily life. Consider the Freudian unconscious. Suppose I have a Freudian unconscious desire to kill my father and marry my mother. Nothing in Freudian theory requires that this desire be P-unconscious; for all Freudians should care, it might be P-conscious. What is the key to the desire being Freudianly unconscious is that it come out in slips, dreams, and the like, but *not* be freely available as a premise in reasoning (in virtue of having the unconscious desire) and that it not be freely available to guide action and reporting. Coming out in slips and dreams *makes it conscious in Flanagan's sense,* so that sense of access is no good for capturing the Freudian idea. But it is unconscious in my A-sense. If I can just tell you that I have a desire to kill my father and marry my mother (and not as a result of therapy) then it isn't an unconscious state in either Freud's sense or my A sense. Similar points can be made about a number of the syndromes that are often regarded as disorders of consciousness. For example, consider prosopagnosia, a syndrome in which someone who can see noses, eyes, etc., cannot recognize faces. Prosopagnosia is a disorder of A-consciousness, not P-consciousness and not Flanagan's informational sensitivity. We count someone as a prosopagnosic even when they are able to guess at better than a chance level who the face belongs to, so that excludes Flanagan's notion. Further, P-consciousness is irrelevant, and that excludes P-consciousness as a criterion. It isn't the presence or absence of a feeling of familiarity that defines prosopagnosia, but rather the patient not knowing who the person is whose face he is seeing or whether he knows that person.

I am finished sketching the contrast between P-consciousness and A-consciousness. In the remainder of this section, I will briefly discuss two cognitive notions of consciousness, so that they are firmly distinguished from both P-consciousness and A-consciousness.

Self-Consciousness

By this term, I mean the possession of the concept of the self and the ability to use this concept in thinking about oneself. A number of higher primates show signs of recognizing that they see themselves in mirrors. They display interest in correspondences between their own actions and the movements of their mirror images. By contrast, dogs treat their mirror images as strangers at first, slowly habituating. In one experimental paradigm, experimenters painted colored spots on the foreheads and ears of anesthetized primates, watching what happened. Chimps between ages 7 and 15 usually try to wipe the spot off (Povinelli, 1994; Gallup, 1982). Monkeys do not do this, according to published reports as of 1994. (Since then, Hauser et al., 1995, have shown that monkeys can pass the test if the mark is salient enough.) Human babies don't show similar behavior until the last half of their second year. Perhaps this is a test for self-consciousness. (Or perhaps it is only a test for understanding mirrors; but what is involved in understanding mirrors if not that it is oneself one is seeing?) But even if monkeys and dogs have no self-consciousness, no one should deny that they have P-conscious pains, or that there is something it is like for them to see their reflections in the mirror. P-conscious states often seem to have a "me-ishness" about them, the phenomenal content often represents the state as a state of me. But this fact does not at all suggest that we can reduce P-consciousness to self-consciousness, since such "me-ishness" is the same in states whose P-conscious content is different. For example, the experience as of red is the same as the experience as of green in self-orientation, but the two states are different in phenomenal feel.[16]

Monitoring-Consciousness

The idea of consciousness as some sort of internal monitoring takes many forms. One notion is that of some sort of inner perception. This could be a form of P-consciousness, namely P-consciousness of one's own states or of the self. Another notion is often put in information-processing terms: internal scanning. And a third, metacognitive notion, is that of a conscious state as one that is accompanied by a thought to the effect that one is in that state.[17] Let us lump these together as one or another form of monitoring-consciousness. Given my liberal terminological policy, I have no objection to monitoring-consciousness as a notion of consciousness. Where I balk is at the idea that P-consciousness just is one or another form of monitoring-consciousness.

To identify P-consciousness with internal scanning is just to grease the slide to eliminativism about P-consciousness. Indeed, as Georges Rey (1983) has pointed out, ordinary laptop computers are capable of various types of self-scanning, but as he also points out, no one would think of their laptop computer as "conscious" (using the term in the ordinary way, without making any of the distinctions I've introduced). Since, according to Rey, internal scanning is essential to consciousness, he concludes that the concept of consciousness is incoherent. If one regards the various elements of the mongrel concept that I have been delineating as elements of a single concept, then that concept is indeed incoherent and needs repair by making distinctions along the lines I have been suggesting. I doubt that the ordinary concept of consciousness is sufficiently determinate for it to be incoherent, though whether or not this is so is an empirical question about how people use words that it is not my job to decide. However that inquiry turns out, Rey's mistake is to trumpet the putative incoherence of the concept of consciousness as if it showed the incoherence of the concept of *phenomenal* consciousness.[18]

Rosenthal (1997) defines reflexive consciousness as follows: S is a reflexively conscious state of mine ↔ S is accompanied by a thought—arrived at non-inferentially and non-observationally—to the effect that I am in S. He offers this "higher order thought" (HOT) theory as a theory of phenomenal consciousness. It is obvious that phenomenal consciousness without HOT and HOT without phenomenal consciousness are both *conceptually* possible. For examples, perhaps dogs and infants have phenomenally conscious pains without higher order thoughts about them. For the converse case, imagine that by bio-feedback and imaging techniques of the distant future, I learn to detect the state in myself of having the Freudian unconscious thought that it would be nice to kill my father and marry my mother. I could come to know—non-inferentially and non-observationally—that I have this Freudian thought even though the thought is not phenomenally conscious.

Rosenthal sometimes talks as if it is supposed to be a basic law of nature that phenomenal states and HOTs about them co-occur. That is a very adventurous claim. But even if it is true, then there must be a mechanism that explains the correlation, as the fact that both heat and electricity are carried by free electrons explains the correlation of electrical and thermal conductivity. But any mechanism breaks down under extreme conditions, as does the corrrelation of electrical and thermal conductivity at extremely high temperatures. So the correlation between phenomenality and HOT would break down too, showing that higher order thought does not yield the basic scientific nature of phenomenality.

Rosenthal's definition of his version of monitoring-consciousness has a number of ad hoc features. "Non-observationally" is required to rule out (e.g.) a case in which I know about a thought I have repressed by observing my own behavior. "Non-inferentially" is needed to avoid a somewhat different case in which I appreciate (non-observationally) my own pain and infer a repressed thought from it. Further, Rosenthal's definition involves a stipulation that the possessor of the monitoring-conscious state is the same as the thinker of the thought—otherwise *my* thinking about *your* pain would make *it* a conscious pain. All these ad hoc features can be eliminated by moving to the following definition of monitoring-consciousness: S is a monitoring-conscious state ↔ S is phenomenally presented in a thought about S. This definition uses the notion of phenomenality, but this is no disadvantage unless one holds that there is no such thing apart from monitoring itself. The new definition, requiring phenomenality as it does, has the additional advantage of making it clear why monitoring-consciousness is a kind of *consciousness*.

There is an element of plausibility to the collapse of P-consciousness into monitoring-consciousness. Consider two dogs, one of which has a perceptual state whereas the other has a similar perceptual state plus a representation of it. Surely the latter dog has a conscious state even if the former dog does not. Quite right, because *consciousness of* plausibly brings consciousness with it. (I'm only endorsing the plausibility of this idea, not its truth.) But the *converse* is more problematic. If I am conscious of a pain or a thought, then, plausibly, that pain or thought has some P-conscious aspect. But even if consciousness of entails P-consciousness, that gives us no reason to believe that P-consciousness entails consciousness of, and it is the implausibility of this converse proposition that is pointed to by the dog problem. The first dog can have a P-conscious state too, even if it is not conscious of it.

Perhaps you are wondering why I am being so terminologically liberal, counting P-consciousness, A-consciousness, monitoring consciousness and self-consciousness all as types of consciousness. Oddly, I find that many critics wonder why I would count *phenomenal* consciousness as consciousness, whereas many others wonder why I would count access or monitoring or *self* consciousness as consciousness. In fact two reviewers of this paper complained about my terminological liberalism, but for incompatible reasons. One reviewer said: "While what he uses ['P-consciousness'] to refer to—the 'what it is like' aspect of mentality—seems to me interesting and important, I suspect that the discussion of it under the heading 'consciousness' is a source of confusion . . . he is right to distinguish access-consciousness (which is what I think deserves the name 'consciousness') from this." Another reviewer said: "I really still can't see why access is called . . . access-consciousness? Why isn't access just . . . a purely information processing (functionalist) analysis?" This is not a merely verbal matter. In my view, all of us, despite our explicit verbal preferences, have some tendency to use 'conscious' and related words in both ways, and our failure to see this causes a good deal of difficulty in thinking about "consciousness."

I've been talking about different concepts of "consciousness" and I've also said that *the* concept of consciousness is a mongrel concept. Perhaps, you are thinking, I should make up my mind. My view is that 'consciousness' is actually an ambiguous word, though the ambiguity I have in mind is not one that I've found in any dictionary. I started the paper with an analogy between 'consciousness' and 'velocity,' and I think there is an important similarity. One important difference, however, is that in the case of 'velocity,' it is easy to get rid of the temptation to conflate the two senses, even though for many purposes the distinction is not very useful. With 'consciousness,' there is a tendency towards "now you see it, now you don't." I think the main reason for this is that P-consciousness presents itself to us in a way that makes it hard to imagine how a conscious state could fail to be accessible and self-reflective, so it is easy to fall into habits of thought that do not distinguish these concepts.[19]

The chief alternative to the ambiguity hypothesis is that there is a single concept of consciousness that is a *cluster concept*. For example, a prototypical religion involves belief in supernatural beings, sacred and profane objects, rituals, a moral code, religious feelings, prayer, a worldview, an organization of life based on the world view and a social group bound together by the previous items (Alston, 1967). But for all of these items, there are actual or possible religions that lack them. For example, some forms of Buddhism do not involve belief in a supreme being and Quakers have no sacred objects. It is convenient for us to use a concept of religion that binds together a number of disparate concepts whose referents are often found together.

The distinction between ambiguity and cluster concept can be drawn in a number of equally legitimate ways that classify some cases differently. That is, there is some indeterminacy in the distinction. Some might even say that *velocity* is a cluster concept because for many purposes it is convenient to group average and instantaneous velocity together. I favor tying the distinction to the clear and present danger of conflation, especially in the form of equivocation in an argument. Of course, this is no analysis, since equivocation is definable in terms of ambiguity. My point, rather, is that one can make up one's mind about whether there is ambiguity by finding equivocation hard to deny. In Block (1995), the longer paper from which this paper derives, I give some examples of conflations.

When I called *consciousness* a mongrel concept I was not declaring allegiance to the cluster theory. Rather, what I had in mind was that an ambiguous word often corresponds to an ambiguous mental representation, one that functions in thought as a unitary entity and thereby misleads. These are mongrels. I would also describe *velocity* and *degree of heat* (as used by the Florentine Experiments of the 17th Century) as mongrel concepts. This is the grain of truth in the cluster-concept theory.

Note the distinction between the claim that the concept of consciousness is a mongrel concept and the claim that consciousness is not a natural kind (Churchland, 1983, 1986). The former is a claim about the concept, one that can be verified by reflection alone. The latter is like the claim that dirt or cancer are not natural kinds, claims that require empirical investigation.[20]

NOTES

1. Abridged (with changes by the author). I have changed only what seems mistaken even from the point of view of my former position. No attempt has been made to systematically update the references.
2. See Kuhn (1964) on velocity, and Block and Dworkin (1974) and Wiser and Covey (1983) on heat.
3. But what is it about thoughts that makes them P-conscious? One possibility is that it is just a series of mental images or sub vocalizations that make thoughts P-conscious. Another possibility is that the contents themselves have a P-conscious aspect independently of their vehicles. See Lormand, forthcoming and Burge, 1997.
4. My view is that although P-conscious content cannot be *reduced to* or identified with intentional content (at least not on relatively apriori grounds), P-conscious contents often—maybe always—have an intentional aspect, representing in a primitive nonintentional way.
5. I know some will think that I invoked inverted and absent qualia a few paragraphs above when I described the explanatory gap as involving the question of why a creature with a brain which has a physiological and functional nature like ours couldn't have different experience or none at all. But the spirit of the question as I asked it allows for an answer that explains why such creatures cannot exist, and thus there is no presupposition that these are real possibilities.
6. I have been using the P-consciousness/A-consciousness distinction in my lectures for many years, but it only found its way into print in my "Consciousness and Accessibility" (1990), and my (1991, 1992, 1993). My claims about the distinction have been criticized in Searle (1990, 1992) and Flanagan (1992)—I reply to Flanagan below; and there is an illuminating discussion in Davies and Humphreys (1993b), a point of which will be taken up in a footnote to follow. See also Levine's (1994) review of Flanagan which discusses Flanagan's critique of the distinction. See also Kirk (1992) for an identification of P-consciousness with something like A-consciousness.
7. The full definition was: A state is access-conscious if, in virtue of one's having the state, a representation of its content is (1) inferentially promiscuous, that is, poised for use as a premise in reasoning, (2) poised for rational control of action, and (3) poised for rational control of speech.
8. Dennett (1991) and Dennett and Kinsbourne (1992) advocate the "multiple drafts" account of consciousness. Dennett switched to the cerebral celebrity view in his 1993 paper.
9. See Dennett (2001) and Block (2001) for a more sophisticated treatment of this dialectic.
10. Some may say that only fully conceptualized content can play a role in reasoning, be reportable, and rationally control action. Such a view should not be adopted in isolation from views about which contents are personal and which are sub-personal.
11. The concept of P-consciousness is not a functional concept, however, I acknowledge the empirical possibility that the scientific nature of P-consciousness has something to do with information processing. We can ill afford to close off empirical possibilities given the difficulty of solving the mystery of P-consciousness.
12. The distinction has some similarity to the sensation/perception distinction; I won't take the space to

lay out the differences. See Humphrey (1992) for an interesting discussion of the latter distinction.

13. If you are tempted to deny the existence of these states of the perceptual system, you should think back to the total zombie just mentioned. Putting aside the issue of the possibility of this zombie, note that on a computational notion of cognition, the zombie has *all* the same A-conscious contents that you have (if he is your computational duplicate). A-consciousness is an informational notion. The states of the superblindsighter's perceptual system are A-conscious for the same reason as the zombie's.

14. Farah claims that blindsight is more degraded than sight. But Weiskrantz (1988) notes that his patient DB had better acuity in some areas of the blind field (in some circumstances) than in his sighted field. It would be better to understand her "degraded" in terms of lack of access.

15. Thus, there is a conflict between this physiological claim and the Schacter model which dictates that destroying the P-consciousness module will prevent A-consciousness.

16. See White (1987) for an account of why self-consciousness should be firmly distinguished from P-consciousness, and why self-consciousness is more relevant to certain issues of value.

17. The pioneer of these ideas in the philosophical literature is David Armstrong (1968, 1980). William Lycan (1987) has energetically pursued self-scanning, and David Rosenthal (1986, 1993), Peter Carruthers (1989, 1992) and Norton Nelkin (1993) have championed higher order thought. See also Natsoulas (1993). Lormand (forthcoming) makes some powerful criticisms of Rosenthal.

18. To be fair to Rey, his argument is more like a dilemma: for any supposed feature of consciousness, either a laptop of the sort we have today has it or else you can't be sure you have it yourself. In the case of P-consciousness, laptops don't have it, and we are sure we do, so once we make these distinctions, his argument loses plausibility.

19. This represents a change of view from Block, 1994, wherein I said that 'consciousness' ought to be ambiguous rather than saying it is now ambiguous.

20. I would like to thank Tyler Burge, Susan Carey, David Chalmers, Martin Davies, Wayne Davis, Bert Dreyfus, Guven Guzeldere, Paul Horwich, Jerry Katz, Leonard Katz, Joe Levine, David Rosenthal, Jerome Schaffer, Sydney Shoemaker, Stephen White and Andrew Young for their very helpful comments on earlier versions of this paper. I have been giving this paper at colloquia and meetings since the fall of 1990, and I am grateful to the many audiences which have made interesting and useful comments, especially the audience at the conference on my work at the University of Barcelona in June, 1993.

REFERENCES

Alston, W. (1967) Religion. In *The Encyclopedia of Philosophy*. Macmillan/Free Press, 140–145.

Armstrong, D. M. (1968) *A Materialist Theory of Mind*. Humanities Press.

———. What is consciousness? In *The Nature of Mind*. Cornell University Press.

Atkinson, A. and Davies, M. (1995) Consciousness without conflation. *The Behavioral and Brain Sciences* 18, 2, 248–249.

Baars, B. J. (1988) *A Cognitive Theory of Consciousness*. Cambridge University Press.

Block, N. (1980) What is functionalism? In N. Block (ed) *Readings in the Philosophy of Psychology* vol 1. Harvard University Press.

———. (1990) Consciousness and accessibility. *Behavioral and Brain Sciences* 13, 596–598.

———. (1991) Evidence against epiphenomenalism. *Behavioral and Brain Sciences* 14, 4, 670–72.

———. (1992) Begging the question against phenomenal consciousness. *Behavioral and Brain Sciences* 15, 205–6.

———. (1993) Review of D. Dennett, *Consciousness Explained, The Journal of Philosophy* XC, 4, 181–193.

———. (1994) "Consciousness," "Functionalism," "Qualia." In S. Guttenplan (ed) *A Companion to Philosophy of Mind*. Blackwell.

———. (1995) "On a Confusion about a function of consciousness." *The Behavioral and Brain Sciences*. 18, 227–47.

———. (2001) Paradox and cross purposes in recent work on consciousness. *Cognition* 79, 1–2, 197–219.

Block, N. and Dworkin, G. (1974) "IQ, heritability and inequality," Part I, *Philosophy and Public Affairs*, 3, 4, 331–409.

Burge, Tyler (1997) Two kinds of consciousness. In N. Block et al. (eds) *The Nature of Consciousness: Philosophical Debates*. MIT Press.

Carruthers, P. (1989) Brute experience. *Journal of Philosophy* 86, 258–69.

———. (1992) Consciousness and concepts. *Proceedings of the Aristotelian Society, Supplementary Volume LXVI*, 40–59.

Chalmers, D. J. (1997) Availability: The cognitive basis of experience? In N. Block et al. (eds) *The Nature of Consciousness*. MIT Press.

Churchland, P. S. (1983) Consciousness: The transmutation of a concept. *Pacific Philosophical Quarterly* 64, 80–93.

Crick, F. and Koch, C. (1990) Towards a neurobiological theory of consciousness. *Seminars in the Neurosciences* 2, 263–275.

Crick, F. (1994). *The Astonishing Hypothesis*. Scribners.

Davies, M. and Humphreys, G. (1993a) *Consciousness*. Blackwell.

———. (1993b) Introduction. In Davies and Humphreys (1993a).

Dennett, D. (1991) *Consciousness Explained*. Little, Brown.

———. (1993) The message is: There is no medium. *Philosophy and Phenomenological Research* III, 4.

———. (2001) "Are we explaining consciousness yet? *Cognition* 79, 1–2, 221–37.

Dennett, D. and Kinsbourne, M. (1992a) Time and the observer: The where and when of consciousness in the brain *Behavioral and Brain Sciences* 15, 183–200.

———. (1992b) Escape from the Cartesian theater. *Behavioral and Brain Sciences* 15, 234–48.

Farah, M. (1994) Visual perception and visual awareness after brain damage: A tutorial overview. In Umilta and Moscovitch (1994).

Flanagan, O. (1992) *Consciousness Reconsidered.* MIT Press.

Gallup, G. (1982) Self-awareness and the emergence of mind in primates. *American Journal of Primatology* 2, 237–48.

Goldman, A. (1993a) The psychology of folk psychology. *Behavioral and Brain Sciences* 16, 1, 15–28.

Goldman, A. (1993b) Consciousness, folk psychology and cognitive science. *Consciousness and Cognition* II, 3.

Goodale, M. and Milner, D. (1992) Separate visual pathways for perception and action. *Trends in Neuroscience* 15, 20–25.

Hauser, M. D., Kralik, J., Botto, C., Garrett, M., and Oser, J. (1995). Self-recognition in primates: Phylogeny and the salience of species-typical traits. *Proc. Nat. Acad. Sci.* 92, 10811–10814.

Hill, C. (1991) *Sensations; A Defense of Type Materialism.* Cambridge.

Humphrey, N. (1992) *A History of the Mind.* Simon & Schuster.

Huxley, T. H. (1866) *Lessons in Elementary Psychology* 8, p. 210. Quoted in Humphrey, 1992.

Jackendoff, R. (1987) *Consciousness and the Computational Mind.* MIT Press.

Jackson, F. (1986) What Mary didn't know. *Journal of Philosophy* 83, 291–95.

Kirk, R. (1992) Consciousness and concepts. *Proceedings of the Aristotelian Society, Supplementary Volume LXVI,* 23–40.

Kuhn, T. (1964) A function for thought experiments. In *Melanges Alexandre Koyre* Vol. 1. Hermann, 307–334.

Levine, J. (1994) Review of Owen Flanagan's *Consciousness Reconsidered. Philosophical Review* 103, 353–56.

Loar, B. (1990) Phenomenal properties. In J. Tomberlin (ed.) *Philosophical Perspectives: Action Theory and Philosophy of Mind.* Ridgeview.

Lormand, E. (forthcoming) What qualitative consciousness is like.

Lycan, W. (1987) *Consciousness.* MIT Press.

McGinn, C. (1991) *The Problem of Consciousness.* Blackwell.

Malcolm, N. (1984) Consciousness and causality. In D. M. Armstrong and N. Malcolm, *Consciousness and Causality.* Blackwell.

Marcel, A. J. (1986) Consciousness and processing: Choosing and testing a null hypothesis. *The Behavioral and Brain Sciences* 9, 40–41.

Nagel, T. (1974) What is it like to be a bat? *Philosophical Review.* 83, 435–50.

———. (1979) *Mortal Questions.* Cambridge University Press.

Natsoulas, T. (1993) What is wrong with the appendage theory of consciousness? Philosophical Psychology VI, 2, 137–154.

Nelkin, N. The connection between intentionality and consciousness. In Davies and Humphreys (1993a).

Povinelli, D. (1994) What chimpanzees know about the mind. In *Behavioral Diversity in Chimpanzees.* Harvard University Press.

Rey, G. (1983) A reason for doubting the existence of consciousness. In R. Davidson et al. (eds), *Consciousness and Self-Regulation,* vol 3. Plenum.

———. (1988) A question about consciousness. In H. Otto and J. Tuedio (eds), *Perspectives on Mind.* Reidel.

Rosenthal, David (1986) Two concepts of consciousness. *Philosophical Studies* 49, 329–59.

———. (1997) A theory of consciousness. in N. Block et al. (eds), *The Nature of Consciousness: Philosophical Debates.* MIT Press.

Schacter, D. (1989) On the relation between memory and consciousness: Dissociable interactions and conscious experience. In H. Roediger and F. Craik (eds), *Varieties of Memory and Consciousness: Essays in Honour of Endel Tulving.* Erlbaum.

Searle, J. (1983) *Intentionality.* Cambridge.

———. (1990) Who is computing with the brain? *Behavioral and Brain Sciences* 13, 4, 632–642.

———. (1992) *The Rediscovery of the Mind.* MIT Press.

Shoemaker, S. (1975) Functionalism and qualia. *Philosophical Studies,* 27, 291–315.

———. (1981) The inverted spectrum. *The Journal of Philosophy* 74, 7, 357–81.

Stich, S. (1978) Autonomous psychology and the belief-desire thesis. *The Monist* 61: 573–91.

Van Gulick, R. (1989) What difference does consciousness make? *Philosophical Topics* 17, 1, 211–230.

———. (1993) Understanding the phenomenal mind: Are we all just armadillos? In Davies and Humphreys (1993a).

Weiskrantz, L. (1988) Some contributions of neuropsychology of vision and memory to the problem of consciousness. In Marcel and Bisiach (1988).

White, S. L. (1987) What is it like to be an homunculus? *Pacific Philosophical Quarterly* 68, 148–174.

Wiser, M. and Carey, S. (1983) When heat and temperature were one. In D. Gentner and A. Stevens (eds) *Mental Models.* Lawrence Erlbaum.

25 | What Is It Like to Be a Bat?

Thomas Nagel

Consciousness is what makes the mind–body problem really intractable. Perhaps that is why current discussions of the problem give it little attention or get it obviously wrong. The recent wave of reductionist euphoria has produced several analyses of mental phenomena and mental concepts designed to explain the possibility of some variety of materialism, psychophysical identification, or reduction.[1] But the problems dealt with are those common to this type of reduction and other types, and what makes the mind–body problem unique, and unlike the water–H_2O problem or the Turing machine–IBM machine problem or the lightning–electrical discharge problem or the gene–DNA problem or the oak tree–hydrocarbon problem, is ignored.

Every reductionist has his favorite analogy from modern science. It is most unlikely that any of these unrelated examples of successful reduction will shed light on the relation of mind to brain. But philosophers share the general human weakness for explanations of what is incomprehensible in terms suited for what is familiar and well understood, though entirely different. This has led to the acceptance of implausible accounts of the mental largely because they would permit familiar kinds of reduction. I shall try to explain why the usual examples do not help us to understand the relation between mind and body—why, indeed, we have at present no conception of what an explanation of the physical nature of a mental phenomenon would be. Without consciousness the mind–body problem would be much less interesting. With consciousness it seems hopeless. The most important and characteristic feature of conscious mental phenomena is very poorly understood. Most reductionist theories do not even try to explain it. And careful examination will show that no currently available concept of reduction is applicable to it. Perhaps a new theoretical form can be devised for the purpose, but such a solution, if it exists, lies in the distant intellectual future.

Conscious experience is a widespread phenomenon. It occurs at many levels of animal life, though we cannot be sure of its presence in the simpler organisms, and it is very difficult to say in general what provides evidence of it. (Some extremists have been prepared to deny it even of mammals other than man.) No doubt it occurs in countless forms totally unimaginable to us, on other planets in other solar systems throughout the universe. But no matter how the form may vary, the fact that an organism has conscious experience *at all* means, basically, that there is something it is like to *be* that organism. There may be further implications about the form of the experience; there may even (though I doubt it) be implications about the behavior of the organism. But fundamentally an organism has conscious mental states if and only if there is something that it is like to *be* that organism—something it is like *for* the organism.

We may call this the subjective character of experience. It is not captured by any of the familiar, recently devised reductive analyses of the mental, for all of them are logically compatible with its absence. It is not analyzable in terms of any explanatory system of functional states, or intentional states, since these could be ascribed to robots or automata that behaved like people though they experienced nothing.[2] It is not analyzable in terms of the causal role of experiences in relation to typical human behavior—for similar reasons.[3] I do not deny that conscious mental states and events cause behavior, nor that they may be given functional characterizations. I deny only that this kind of thing exhausts their analysis. Any reductionist program has to be based on an analysis of what is to be reduced. If the analysis leaves something out, the problem will be falsely posed. It is useless to base the defense of materialism on any analysis of mental phenomena that fails to deal explicitly with their subjective character. For there is no reason to suppose that a reduction which seems plausible when no attempt is made to account for consciousness can be extended to include consciousness. Without some idea,

From *Philosophical Review* 83:435–50, 1974. Copyright © 1974 Cornell University Press. Reprinted with permission of the publisher.

therefore, of what the subjective character of experience is, we cannot know what is required of a physicalist theory.

While an account of the physical basis of mind must explain many things, this appears to be the most difficult. It is impossible to exclude the phenomenological features of experience from a reduction in the same way that one excludes the phenomenal features of an ordinary substance from a physical or chemical reduction of it—namely, by explaining them as effects on the minds of human observers.[4] If physicalism is to be defended, the phenomenological features must themselves be given a physical account. But when we examine their subjective character it seems that such a result is impossible. The reason is that every subjective phenomenon is essentially connected with a single point of view, and it seems inevitable that an objective, physical theory will abandon that point of view.

Let me first try to state the issue somewhat more fully than by referring to the relation between the subjective and the objective, or between the *pour-soi* and the *en-soi*. This is far from easy. Facts about what it is like to be an *X* are very peculiar, so peculiar that some may be inclined to doubt their reality, or the significance of claims about them. To illustrate the connection between subjectivity and a point of view, and to make evident the importance of subjective features, it will help to explore the matter in relation to an example that brings out clearly the divergence between the two types of conception, subjective and objective.

I assume we all believe that bats have experience. After all, they are mammals, and there is no more doubt that they have experience than that mice or pigeons or whales have experience. I have chosen bats instead of wasps or flounders because if one travels too far down the phylogenetic tree, people gradually shed their faith that there is experience there at all. Bats, although more closely related to us than those other species, nevertheless present a range of activity and a sensory apparatus so different from ours that the problem I want to pose is exceptionally vivid (though it certainly could be raised with other species). Even without the benefit of philosophical reflection, anyone who has spent some time in an enclosed space with an excited bat knows what it is to encounter a fundamentally *alien* form of life.

I have said that the essence of the belief that bats have experience is that there is something

that it is like to be a bat. Now we know that most bats (the microchiroptera, to be precise) perceive the external world primarily by sonar, or echolocation, detecting the reflections, from objects within range, of their own rapid, subtly modulated, high-frequency shrieks. Their brains are designed to correlate the outgoing impulses with the subsequent echoes, and the information thus acquired enables bats to make precise discriminations of distance, size, shape, motion, and texture comparable to those we make by vision. But bat sonar, though clearly a form of perception, is not similar in its operation to any sense that we possess, and there is no reason to suppose that it is subjectively like anything we can experience or imagine. This appears to create difficulties for the notion of what it is like to be a bat. We must consider whether any method will permit us to extrapolate to the inner life of the bat from our own case,[5] and if not, what alternative methods there may be for understanding the notion.

Our own experience provides the basic material for our imagination, whose range is therefore limited. It will not help to try to imagine that one has webbing on one's arms, which enables one to fly around at dusk and dawn catching insects in one's mouth; that one has very poor vision, and perceives the surrounding world by a system of reflected high-frequency sound signals; and that one spends the day hanging upside down by one's feet in an attic. In so far as I can imagine this (which is not very far), it tells me only what it would be like for *me* to behave as a bat behaves. But that is not the question. I want to know what it is like for a *bat* to be a bat. Yet if I try to imagine this, I am restricted to the resources of my own mind, and those resources are inadequate to the task. I cannot perform it either by imagining additions to my present experience, or by imagining segments gradually subtracted from it, or by imagining some combination of additions, subtractions, and modifications.

To the extent that I could look and behave like a wasp or a bat without changing my fundamental structure, my experiences would not be anything like the experiences of those animals. On the other hand, it is doubtful that any meaning can be attached to the supposition that I should possess the internal neurophysiological constitution of a bat. Even if I could by gradual degrees be transformed into a bat, nothing in my present constitution enables me to imagine what the experiences of such a future stage of myself thus metamorphosed would be like. The best evidence would come from the experiences of bats, if we only knew what they were like.

So if extrapolation from our own case is involved in the idea of what it is like to be a bat, the extrapolation must be incompletable. We cannot form more than a schematic conception of what it *is* like. For example, we may ascribe general *types* of experience on the basis of the animal's structure and behavior. Thus we describe bat sonar as a form of three-dimensional forward perception; we believe that bats feel some versions of pain, fear, hunger, and lust, and that they have other, more familiar types of perception besides sonar. But we believe that these experiences also have in each case a specific subjective character, which it is beyond our ability to conceive. And if there is conscious life elsewhere in the universe, it is likely that some of it will not be describable even in the most general experiential terms available to us.[6] (The problem is not confined to exotic cases, however, for it exists between one person and another. The subjective character of the experience of a person deaf and blind from birth is not accessible to me, for example, nor presumably is mine to him. This does not prevent us each from believing that the other's experience has such a subjective character.)

If anyone is inclined to deny that we can believe in the existence of facts like this whose exact nature we cannot possibly conceive, he should reflect that in contemplating the bats we are in much the same position that intelligent bats or Martians[7] would occupy if they tried to form a conception of what it was like to be us. The structure of their own minds might make it impossible for them to succeed, but we know they would be wrong to conclude that there is not anything precise that it is like to be us: that only certain general types of mental state could be ascribed to us (perhaps perception and appetite would be concepts common to us both; perhaps not). We know they would be wrong to draw such a skeptical conclusion because we know what it is like to be us. And we know that while it includes an enormous amount of variation and complexity, and while we do not possess the vocabulary to describe it adequately, its subjective character is highly specific, and in some respects describable in terms that can be understood only by creatures like us. The fact that we cannot expect ever to accommodate in our language a detailed description of Martian or bat phenomenology should not lead us to dismiss as meaningless the claim that bats and Martians have experiences fully comparable in richness of detail to our own. It would be fine if someone were to develop concepts and a theory that enabled us to think about those things; but such an understanding may be permanently denied to us by the limits of our nature. And to deny the reality or logical significance of what we can never describe or understand is the crudest form of cognitive dissonance.

This brings us to the edge of a topic that requires much more discussion than I can give it here: namely, the relation between facts on the one hand and conceptual schemes or systems of representation on the other. My realism about the subjective domain in all its forms implies a belief in the existence of facts beyond the reach of human concepts. Certainly it is possible for a human being to believe that there are facts which humans never *will* possess the requisite concepts to represent or comprehend. Indeed, it would be foolish to doubt this, given the finiteness of humanity's expectations. After all, there would have been transfinite numbers even if everyone had been wiped out by the Black Death before Cantor discovered them. But one might also believe that there are facts which *could* not ever be represented or comprehended by human beings, even if the species lasted forever—simply because our structure does not permit us to operate with concepts of the requisite type. This impossibility might even be observed by other beings, but it is not clear that the existence of such beings, or the possibility of their existence, is a precondition of the significance of the hypothesis that there are humanly inaccessible facts. (After all, the nature of beings with access to humanly inaccessible facts is presumably itself a humanly inaccessible fact.) Reflection on what it is like to be a bat seems to lead us, therefore, to the conclusion that there are facts that do not consist in the truth of propositions expressible in a human language. We can be compelled to recognize the existence of such facts without being able to state or comprehend them.

I shall not pursue this subject, however. Its bearing on the topic before us (namely, the mind–body problem) is that it enables us to make a general observation about the subjective character of experience. Whatever may be the status of facts about what it is like to be a human being, or a bat, or a Martian, these appear to be facts that embody a particular point of view.

I am not adverting here to the alleged privacy

of experience to its possessor. The point of view in question is not one accessible only to a single individual. Rather it is a *type*. It is often possible to take up a point of view other than one's own, so the comprehension of such facts is not limited to one's own case. There is a sense in which phenomenological facts are perfectly objective: one person can know or say of another what the quality of the other's experience is. They are subjective, however, in the sense that even this objective ascription of experience is possible only for someone sufficiently similar to the object of ascription to be able to adopt his point of view—to understand the ascription in the first person as well as in the third, so to speak. The more different from oneself the other experiencer is, the less success one can expect with this enterprise. In our own case we occupy the relevant point of view, but we will have as much difficulty understanding our own experience properly if we approach it from another point of view as we would if we tried to understand the experience of another species without taking up *its* point of view.[8]

This bears directly on the mind–body problem. For if the facts of experience—facts about what it is like *for* the experiencing organism—are accessible only from one point of view, then it is a mystery how the true character of experiences could be revealed in the physical operation of that organism. The latter is a domain of objective facts *par excellence*—the kind that can be observed and understood from many points of view and by individuals with differing perceptual systems. There are no comparable imaginative obstacles to the acquisition of knowledge about bat neurophysiology by human scientists, and intelligent bats or Martians might learn more about the human brain than we ever will.

This is not by itself an argument against reduction. A Martian scientist with no understanding of visual perception could understand the rainbow, or lightning, or clouds as physical phenomena, though he would never be able to understand the human concepts of rainbow, lightning, or cloud, or the place these things occupy in our phenomenal world. The objective nature of the things picked out by these concepts could be apprehended by him because, although the concepts themselves are connected with a particular point of view and a particular visual phenomenology, the things apprehended from that point of view are not: they are observable from the point of view but external to it; hence they can be comprehended from other

points of view also, either by the same organisms or by others. Lightning has an objective character that is not exhausted by its visual appearance, and this can be investigated by a Martian without vision. To be precise, it has a *more* objective character than is revealed in its visual appearance. In speaking of the move from subjective to objective characterization, I wish to remain noncommittal about the existence of an end point, the completely objective intrinsic nature of the thing, which one might or might not be able to reach. It may be more accurate to think of objectivity as a direction in which the understanding can travel. And in understanding a phenomenon like lightning, it is legitimate to go as far away as one can from a strictly human viewpoint.[9]

In the case of experience, on the other hand, the connection with a particular point of view seems much closer. It is difficult to understand what could be meant by the *objective* character of an experience, apart from the particular point of view from which its subject apprehends it. After all, what would be left of what it was like to be a bat if one removed the viewpoint of the bat? But if experience does not have, in addition to its subjective character, an objective nature that can be apprehended from many different points of view, then how can it be supposed that a Martian investigating my brain might be observing physical processes which were my mental processes (as he might observe physical processes which were bolts of lightning), only from a different point of view? How, for that matter, could a human physiologist observe them from another point of view?[10]

We appear to be faced with a general difficulty about psychophysical reduction. In other areas the process of reduction is a move in the direction of greater objectivity, toward a more accurate view of the real nature of things. This is accomplished by reducing our dependence on individual or species-specific points of view toward the object of investigation. We describe it not in terms of the impressions it makes on our senses, but in terms of its more general effects and of properties detectable by means other than the human senses. The less it depends on a specifically human viewpoint, the more objective is our description. It is possible to follow this path because although the concepts and ideas we employ in thinking about the external world are initially applied from a point of view that involves our perceptual apparatus, they are used by us to refer to things beyond themselves—toward which we *have* the phenomenal point of view. Therefore we can abandon it in favor of another, and still be thinking about the same things.

Experience itself, however, does not seem to fit the pattern. The idea of moving from appearance to reality seems to make no sense here. What is the analogue in this case to pursuing a more objective understanding of the same phenomena by abandoning the initial subjective viewpoint toward them in favor of another that is more objective but concerns the same thing? Certainly it *appears* unlikely that we will get closer to the real nature of human experience by leaving behind the particularity of our human point of view and striving for a description in terms accessible to beings that could not imagine what it was like to be us. If the subjective character of experience is fully comprehensible only from one point of view, then any shift to greater objectivity—that is, less attachment to a specific viewpoint—does not take us nearer to the real nature of the phenomenon: it takes us farther away from it.

In a sense, the seeds of this objection to the reducibility of experience are already detectable in successful cases of reduction; for in discovering sound to be, in reality, a wave phenomenon in air or other media, we leave behind one viewpoint to take up another, and the auditory, human or animal viewpoint that we leave behind remains unreduced. Members of radically different species may both understand the same physical events in objective terms, and this does not require that they understand the phenomenal forms in which those events appear to the senses of members of the other species. Thus it is a condition of their referring to a common reality that their more particular viewpoints are not part of the common reality that they both apprehend. The reduction can succeed only if the species-specific viewpoint is omitted from what is to be reduced.

But while we are right to leave this point of view aside in seeking a fuller understanding of the external world, we cannot ignore it permanently, since it is the essence of the internal world, and not merely a point of view on it. Most of the neobehaviorism of recent philosophical psychology results from the effort to substitute an objective concept of mind for the real thing, in order to have nothing left over which cannot be reduced. If we acknowledge that a physical theory of mind must account for the subjective character of experience, we must

admit that no presently available conception gives us a clue how this could be done. The problem is unique. If mental processes are indeed physical processes, then there is something it is like, intrinsically,[11] to undergo certain physical processes. What it is for such a thing to be the case remains a mystery.

What moral should be drawn from these reflections, and what should be done next? It would be a mistake to conclude that physicalism must be false. Nothing is proved by the inadequacy of physicalist hypotheses that assume a faulty objective analysis of mind. It would be truer to say that physicalism is a position we cannot understand because we do not at present have any conception of how it might be true. Perhaps it will be thought unreasonable to require such a conception as a condition of understanding. After all, it might be said, the meaning of physicalism is clear enough: mental states are states of the body; mental events are physical events. We do not know *which* physical states and events they are, but that should not prevent us from understanding the hypothesis. What could be clearer than the words "is" and "are"?

But I believe it is precisely this apparent clarity of the word "is" that is deceptive. Usually, when we are told that X is Y we know *how* it is supposed to be true, but that depends on a conceptual or theoretical background and is not conveyed by the "is" alone. We know how both "*X*" and "*Y*" refer, and the kinds of things to which they refer, and we have a rough idea how the two referential paths might converge on a single thing, be it an object, a person, a process, an event, or whatever. But when the two terms of the identification are very disparate it may not be so clear how it could be true. We may not have even a rough idea of how the two referential paths could converge, or what kind of things they might converge on, and a theoretical framework may have to be supplied to enable us to understand this. Without the framework, an air of mysticism surrounds the identification.

This explains the magical flavor of popular presentations of fundamental scientific discoveries, given out as propositions to which one must subscribe without really understanding them. For example, people are now told at an early age that all matter is really energy. But despite the fact that they know what "is" means, most of them never form a conception of what makes this claim true, because they lack the theoretical background.

At the present time the status of physicalism

is similar to that which the hypothesis that matter is energy would have had if uttered by a pre-Socratic philosopher. We do not have the beginnings of a conception of how it might be true. In order to understand the hypothesis that a mental event is a physical event, we require more than an understanding of the word "is." The idea of how a mental and a physical term might refer to the same thing is lacking, and the usual analogies with theoretical identification in other fields fail to supply it. They fail because if we construe the reference of mental terms to physical events on the usual model, we either get a reappearance of separate subjective events as the effects through which mental reference to physical events is secured, or else we get a false account of how mental terms refer (for example, a causal behaviorist one).

Strangely enough, we may have evidence for the truth of something we cannot really understand. Suppose a caterpillar is locked in a sterile safe by someone unfamiliar with insect metamorphosis, and weeks later the safe is reopened, revealing a butterfly. If the person knows that the safe has been shut the whole time, he has reason to believe that the butterfly is or was once the caterpillar, without having any idea in what sense this might be so. (One possibility is that the caterpillar contained a tiny winged parasite that devoured it and grew into the butterfly.)

It is conceivable that we are in such a position with regard to physicalism. Donald Davidson has argued that if mental events have physical causes and effects, they must have physical descriptions. He holds that we have reason to believe this even though we do not—and in fact *could* not—have a general psychophysical theory.[12] His argument applies to intentional mental events, but I think we also have some reason to believe that sensations are physical processes, without being in a position to understand how. Davidson's position is that certain physical events have irreducibly mental properties, and perhaps some view describable in this way is correct. But nothing of which we can now form a conception corresponds to it; nor have we any idea what a theory would be like that enabled us to conceive of it.[13]

Very little work has been done on the basic question (from which mention of the brain can be entirely omitted) whether any sense can be made of experiences' having an objective character at all. Does it make sense, in other words, to ask what my experiences are *really* like, as opposed to how they appear to me? We cannot

genuinely understand the hypothesis that their nature is captured in a physical description unless we understand the more fundamental idea that they *have* an objective nature (or that objective processes can have a subjective nature).[14]

I should like to close with a speculative proposal. It may be possible to approach the gap between subjective and objective from another direction. Setting aside temporarily the relation between the mind and the brain, we can pursue a more objective understanding of the mental in its own right. At present we are completely unequipped to think about the subjective character of experience without relying on the imagination—without taking up the point of view of the experiential subject. This should be regarded as a challenge to form new concepts and devise a new method—an objective phenomenology not dependent on empathy or the imagination. Though presumably it would not capture everything, its goal would be to describe, at least in part, the subjective character of experiences in a form comprehensible to beings incapable of having those experiences.

We would have to develop such a phenomenology to describe the sonar experiences of bats; but it would also be possible to begin with humans. One might try, for example, to develop concepts that could be used to explain to a person blind from birth what it was like to see. One would reach a blank wall eventually, but it should be possible to devise a method of expressing in objective terms much more than we can at present, and with much greater precision. The loose intermodal analogies—for example, "Red is like the sound of a trumpet"—which crop up in discussions of this subject are of little use. That should be clear to anyone who has both heard a trumpet and seen red. But structural features of perception might be more accessible to objective description, even though something would be left out. And concepts alternative to those we learn in the first person may enable us to arrive at a kind of understanding even of our own experience which is denied us by the very ease of description and lack of distance that subjective concepts afford.

Apart from its own interest, a phenomenology that is in this sense objective may permit questions about the physical[15] basis of experience to assume a more intelligible form. Aspects of subjective experience that admitted this kind of objective description might be better candidates for objective explanations of a more familiar sort. But whether or not this guess is correct, it seems unlikely that any physical theory of mind can be contemplated until more thought has been given to the general problem of subjective and objective. Otherwise we cannot even pose the mind–body problem without sidestepping it.[16]

NOTES

1. Examples are J. J. C. Smart, *Philosophy and Scientific Realism* (London, 1963); David K. Lewis, "An Argument for the Identity Theory," *Journal of Philosophy,* LXIII (1966), reprinted with addenda in David M. Rosenthal, *Materialism & the Mind-Body Problem* (Englewood Cliffs, N.J., 1971); Hilary Putnam, "Psychological Predicates" in Capitan and Merrill, *Art, Mind, & Religion* (Pittsburgh, 1967), reprinted in Rosenthal, op. cit., as "The Nature of Mental States"; D. M. Armstrong, *A Materialist Theory of the Mind* (London, 1968); D. C. Dennett, *Content and Consciousness* (London, 1969). I have expressed earlier doubts in "Armstrong on the Mind," *Philosophical Review,* LXXIX (1970), 394–403; "Brain Bisection and the Unity of Consciousness," *Synthèse,* 22 (1971); and a review of Dennett, *Journal of Philosophy,* LXIX (1972). See also Saul Kripke, "Naming and Necessity" in Davidson and Harman, *Semantics of Natural Language* (Dordrecht, 1972), esp. pp. 334–42; and M. T. Thornton, "Ostensive Terms and Materialism," *The Monist,* 56 (1972).

2. Perhaps there could not actually be such robots. Perhaps anything complex enough to behave like a person would have experiences. But that, if true, is a fact which cannot be discovered merely by analyzing the concept of experience.

3. It is not equivalent to that about which we are incorrigible, both because we are not incorrigible about experience and because experience is present in animals lacking language and thought, who have no beliefs at all about their experiences.

4. Cf. Richard Rorty, "Mind–Body Identity, Privacy, and Categories," *The Review of Metaphysics,* XIX (1965), esp. 37–38.

5. By "our own case" I do not mean just "my own case," but rather the mentalistic ideas that we apply unproblematically to ourselves and other human beings.

6. Therefore the analogical form of the English expression "what it is *like*" is misleading. It does not mean "what (in our experience) it *resembles,*" but rather "how it is for the subject himself."

7. Any intelligent extraterrestrial beings totally different from us.

8. It may be easier than I suppose to transcend interspecies barriers with the aid of the imagination. For example, blind people are able to detect objects near them by a form of sonar, using vocal clicks or taps of a cane. Perhaps if one knew what that was like, one could by extension imagine roughly what it was like to possess the much more refined sonar of a bat. The distance between oneself and other persons and other species can fall anywhere on a continuum. Even for other persons the understanding of what it is like to be them is only partial, and when one moves to species very different from oneself, a lesser degree of partial understanding may still be available. The imagination is remarkably flexible. My point, however, is not that we cannot *know* what it is like to be a bat. I am not raising that epistemological problem. My point is rather that even to form a *conception* of what it is like to be a bat (and a fortiori to know what it is like to be a bat) one must take up the bat's point of view. If one can take it up roughly, or partially, then one's conception will also be rough or partial. Or so it seems in our present state of understanding.

9. The problem I am going to raise can therefore be posed even if the distinction between more subjective and more objective descriptions or viewpoints can itself be made only within a larger human point of view. I do not accept this kind of conceptual relativism, but it need not be refuted to make the point that psychophysical reduction cannot be accommodated by the subjective-to-objective model familiar from other cases.

10. The problem is not just that when I look at the "Mona Lisa," my visual experience has a certain quality, no trace of which is to be found by someone looking into my brain. For even if he did observe there a tiny image of the "Mona Lisa," he would have no reason to identify it with the experience.

11. The relation would therefore not be a contingent one, like that of a cause and its distinct effect. It would be necessarily true that a certain physical state felt a certain way. Saul Kripke (op. cit.) argues that causal behaviorist and related analyses of the mental fail because they construe, e.g., "pain" as a merely contingent name of pains. The subjective character of an experience ("its immediate phenomenological quality" Kripke calls it [p. 340]) is the essential property left out by such analyses, and the one in virtue of which it is, necessarily, the experience it is. My view is closely related to his. Like Kripke, I find the hypothesis that a certain brain state should *necessarily* have a certain subjective character incomprehensible without further explanation. No such explanation emerges from theories which view the mind–brain relation as contingent, but perhaps there are other alternatives, not yet discovered.

A theory that explained how the mind–brain relation was necessary would still leave us with Kripke's problem of explaining why it nevertheless appears contingent. That difficulty seems to me surmountable, in the following way. We may imagine something by representing it to ourselves either perceptually, sympathetically, or symbolically. I shall not try to say how symbolic imagination works, but part of what happens in the other two cases is this. To imagine something perceptually, we put ourselves in a conscious state resembling the state we would be in if we perceived it. To imagine something sympathetically, we put ourselves in a conscious state resembling the thing itself. (This method can be used only to imagine mental events and states—our own or another's.) When we try to imagine a mental state occurring without its associated brain state, we first sympathetically imagine the occurrence of the mental state: that is, we put ourselves into a state that resembles it mentally. At the same time, we attempt to perceptually imagine the non-occurrence of the associated physical state, by putting ourselves into another state unconnected with the first: one resembling that which we would be in if we perceived the non-occurrence of the physical state. Where the imagination of physical features is perceptual and the imagination of mental features is sympathetic, it appears to us that we can imagine any experience occurring without its associated brain state, and vice versa. The relation between them will appear contingent even if it is necessary, because of the independence of the disparate types of imagination.

(Solipsism, incidentally, results if one misinterprets sympathetic imagination as if it worked like perceptual imagination: it then seems impossible to imagine any experience that is not one's own.)

12. See "Mental Events" in Foster and Swanson, *Experience and Theory* (Amherst, 1970); though I don't understand the argument against psychophysical laws.

13. Similar remarks apply to my paper "Physicalism," *Philosophical Review* LXXIV (1965), 339–56, re-

printed with postscript in John O'Connor, *Modern Materialism* (New York, 1969).

14. This question also lies at the heart of the problem of other minds, whose close connection with the mind–body problem is often overlooked. If one understood how subjective experience could have an objective nature, one would understand the existence of subjects other than oneself.

15. I have not defined the term "physical." Obviously it does not apply just to what can be described by the concepts of contemporary physics, since we expect further developments. Some may think there is nothing to prevent mental phenomena from eventually being recognized as physical in their own right. But whatever else may be said of the physical, it has to be objective. So if our idea of the physical ever expands to include mental phenomena, it will have to assign them an objective character—whether or not this is done by analyzing them in terms of other phenomena already regarded as physical. It seems to me more likely, however, that mental–physical relations will eventually be expressed in a theory whose fundamental terms cannot be placed clearly in either category.

16. I have read versions of this paper to a number of audiences, and am indebted to many people for their comments.

26 | Quining Qualia
Daniel C. Dennett

1. Corralling the Quicksilver

"Qualia" is an unfamiliar term for something that could not be more familiar to each of us: the *ways things seem to us*. As is so often the case with philosophical jargon, it is easier to give examples than to give a definition of the term. Look at a glass of milk at sunset; *the way it looks to you*—the particular, personal, subjective visual quality of the glass of milk is the *quale* of your visual experience at the moment. The *way the milk tastes to you then* is another, gustatory, *quale,* and *how it sounds to you* as you swallow is an auditory *quale*. These various "properties of conscious experience" are prime examples of *qualia*. Nothing, it seems, could you know more intimately than your own

qualia; let the entire universe be some vast illusion, some mere figment of Descartes's evil demon, and yet what the figment is *made of* (for you) will be the *qualia* of your hallucinatory experiences. Descartes claimed to doubt everything that could be doubted, but he never doubted that his conscious experiences had qualia, the properties by which he knew or apprehended them.

The verb "to quine" is even more esoteric. It comes from *The Philosophical Lexicon* (Dennett 1978c, 8th edn 1987), a satirical dictionary of eponyms: "quine, *v.* To deny resolutely the existence or importance of something real or significant." At first blush it would be hard to imagine a more quixotic quest than trying to convince people that there are no such properties as qualia; hence the ironic title of this chapter. But I am not kidding.

My goal is subversive. I am out to overthrow an idea that, in one form or another, is "obvious" to most people—to scientists, philosophers, lay people. My quarry is frustratingly elusive; no sooner does it retreat in the face of one argument than "it" reappears, apparently innocent of all charges, in a new guise.

Which idea of qualia am I trying to extirpate? Everything real has properties, and since I don't deny the reality of conscious experience, I grant that conscious experience has properties. I grant moreover that each person's states of consciousness have properties in virtue of which those states have the experiential content that they do. That is to say, whenever someone experiences something as being one way rather than another, this is true in virtue of some property of something happening in them at the time, but these properties are so unlike the properties traditionally imputed to consciousness that it would be grossly misleading to call any of them the long-sought qualia. Qualia are supposed to be *special* properties, in some hard-to-define way. My claim—which can only come into focus as we proceed—is that conscious experience has *no* properties that are special in *any* of the ways qualia have been supposed to be special.

The standard reaction to this claim is the complacent acknowledgment that while some people may indeed have succumbed to one confusion or fanaticism or another, one's own appeal to a modest, innocent notion of properties of subjective experience is surely safe. It is just that presumption of innocence I want to overthrow. I want to shift the burden of proof, so that anyone who wants to appeal to private, subjective properties has to prove first that in so doing they are *not* making a mistake. This status of *guilty until proven innocent* is neither unprecedented nor indefensible (so long as we restrict ourselves to concepts). Today, no biologist would dream of supposing that it was quite all right to appeal to some innocent concept of *élan vital*. Of course one *could* use the term to mean something in good standing; one could use *élan vital* as one's name for DNA, for instance, but this would be foolish nomenclature, considering the deserved suspicion with which the term is nowadays burdened. I want to make it just as uncomfortable for anyone to talk of qualia–or "raw feels" or "phenomenal properties" or "subjective and intrinsic properties" or "the qualitative character" of experience–with the standard presumption that they, and everyone else, knows what on earth they are talking about.[1]

What are qualia, *exactly?* This obstreperous query is dismissed by one author ("only half in jest") by invoking Louis Armstrong's legendary reply when asked what jazz was: "If you got to ask, you ain't never gonna get to know." (Block 1978 p. 281). This amusing tactic perfectly illustrates the presumption that is my target. If I succeed in my task, this move, which passes muster in most circles today, will look as quaint and insupportable as a jocular appeal to the ludicrousness of a living thing—a living thing, mind you!—doubting the existence of *élan vital.*

My claim, then, is not just that the various technical or theoretical concepts of qualia are vague or equivocal, but that the source concept, the "pretheoretical" notion of which the former are presumed to be refinements, is so thoroughly confused that even if we undertook to salvage some "lowest common denominator" from the theoreticians' proposals, any acceptable version would have to be so radically unlike the ill-formed notions that are commonly appealed to that it would be tactically obtuse–not to say Pickwickian—to cling to the term. Far better, tactically, to declare that there simply are no qualia at all.[2]

Rigorous arguments only work on well-defined materials, and since my goal is to destroy our faith in the pretheoretical or "intuitive" concept, the right tools for my task are intuition pumps, not formal arguments. What follows is a series of fifteen intuition pumps, posed in a sequence designed to flush out—and then flush away—the offending intuitions. In section 2, I will use the first two intuition pumps to focus attention on the traditional notion. It will be the burden of the rest of the paper to convince you that these two pumps, for all their effectiveness, mislead us and should be discarded. In section 3, the next four intuition pumps create and refine a "paradox" lurking in the tradition. This is not a formal paradox, but only a very powerful argument pitted against some almost irresistibly attractive ideas. In section 4, six more intuition pumps are arrayed in order to dissipate the attractiveness of those ideas, and section 5 drives this point home by showing how hapless those ideas prove to be when confronted with some real cases of anomalous experience. This will leave something of a vacuum, and in the final section three more intuition pumps are used to introduce and motivate some suitable replacements for the banished notions.

2. The Special Properties of Qualia

Intuition pump #1: watching you eat cauliflower. I see you tucking eagerly into a helping of steaming cauliflower, the merest whiff of which makes me faintly nauseated, and I find myself wondering how you could possibly relish *that taste,* and then it occurs to me that to you, cauliflower probably tastes (must taste?) different. A plausible hypothesis, it seems, especially since I know that the very same food often tastes different to me at different times. For instance, my first sip of breakfast orange juice tastes much sweeter than my second sip if I interpose a bit of pancakes and maple syrup, but after a swallow or two of coffee, the orange juice goes back to tasting (roughly? exactly?) the way it did the first sip. Surely we want to say (or think about) such things, and surely we are not wildly wrong when we do, so . . . surely it is quite OK to talk of *the way the juice tastes to Dennett at time t,* and ask whether it is just the same as or different from *the way the juice tastes to Dennett at time t′* or *the way the juice tastes to Jones at time t.*

This "conclusion" seems innocent, but right here we have already made the big mistake. The final step presumes that we can isolate the qualia from everything else that is going on—at least in principle or for the sake of argument. What counts as *the way the juice tastes to x* can be distinguished, one supposes, from what is a mere accompaniment, contributory cause, or by-product of this "central" way. One dimly imagines taking such cases and stripping them down gradually to the essentials, leaving their common residuum, the way things look, sound, feel, taste, smell to various individuals at various times, independently of how those individuals are stimulated or non-perceptually affected, and independently of how they are subsequently disposed to behave or believe. The mistake is not in supposing that we can in practice ever or always perform this act of purification with certainty, but the more fundamental mistake of supposing that there is such a residual property to take seriously, however uncertain our actual attempts at isolation of instances might be.

The examples that seduce us are abundant in every modality. I cannot imagine, will never

know, could never know, it seems, how Bach sounded to Glenn Gould. (I can barely recover in my memory the way Bach sounded to me when I was a child.) And I cannot know, it seems, what it is like to be a bat (Nagel 1974), or whether you see what I see, colorwise, when we look up at a clear "blue" sky. The homely cases convince us of the reality of these special properties—those subjective tastes, looks, aromas, sounds—that we then apparently isolate for definition by this philosophical distillation.

The specialness of these properties is hard to pin down, but can be seen at work in *intuition pump #2: the wine-tasting machine.* Could Gallo Brothers replace their human wine tasters with a machine? A computer-based "expert system" for quality control and classification is probably within the bounds of existing technology. We now know enough about the relevant chemistry to make the transducers that would replace taste buds and olfactory organs (delicate color vision would perhaps be more problematic), and we can imagine using the output of such transducers as the raw material—the "sense data" in effect—for elaborate evaluations, descriptions, classifications. Pour the sample in the funnel and, in a few minutes or hours, the system would type out a chemical assay, along with commentary: "a flamboyant and velvety Pinot, though lacking in stamina"—or words to such effect. Such a machine might well perform better than human wine tasters on all reasonable tests of accuracy and consistency the winemakers could devise,[3] but *surely* no matter how "sensitive" and "discriminating" such a system becomes, it will never have, and enjoy, what *we* do when we taste a wine: the qualia of conscious experience! Whatever informational, dispositional, functional properties its internal states have, none of them will be special in the way qualia are. If you share that intuition, you believe that there are qualia in the sense I am targeting for demolition.

What is special about qualia? Traditional analyses suggest some fascinating second-order properties of these properties. First, since one *cannot say* to another, no matter how eloquent one is and no matter how cooperative and imaginative one's audience is, exactly what way one is currently seeing, tasting, smelling and so forth, qualia are *ineffable*—in fact the paradigm cases of ineffable items. According to tradition, at least part of the reason why qualia are ineffable is that they are *intrinsic* properties—which seems to imply *inter alia* that they are somehow atomic and unanalyzable. Since they are "simple" or "homogeneous" there is nothing to get hold of when trying to describe such a property to one unacquainted with the particular instance in question.

Moreover, verbal comparisons are not the only cross-checks ruled out. *Any* objective, physiological or "merely behavioral" test—such as those passed by the imaginary wine-tasting system—would of necessity miss the target (one can plausibly argue), so all interpersonal comparisons of these ways-of-appearing are (apparently) systematically impossible. In other words, qualia are essentially *private* properties. And, finally, since they *are* properties of *my experiences* (they're not chopped liver, and they're not properties of, say, my cerebral blood flow—or haven't you been paying attention?), qualia are essentially directly accessible to the consciousness of their experiencer (whatever that means) or qualia are properties of one's experience with which one is intimately or directly acquainted (whatever that means) or "immediate phenomenological qualities" (Block 1978) (whatever that means). They are, after all, the very properties the appreciation of which permits us to identify our conscious states. So, to summarize the tradition, qualia are supposed to be properties of a subject's mental states that are

1. ineffable
2. intrinsic
3. private
4. directly or immediately apprehensible in consciousness

Thus are qualia introduced onto the philosophical stage. They have seemed to be very significant properties to some theorists because they have seemed to provide an insurmountable and unavoidable stumbling block to functionalism, or more broadly, to materialism, or more broadly still, to any purely "third-person" objective viewpoint or approach to the world (Nagel 1986). Theorists of the contrary persuasion have patiently and ingeniously knocked down all the arguments, and said most of the right things, but they have made a tactical error, I am claiming, of saying in one way or another: "We theorists can handle *those qualia* you talk about just fine; we will show that you are just slightly in error about the nature of qualia." What they ought to have said is: "What qualia?"

My challenge strikes some theorists as outrageous or misguided because they think they have a much blander and hence less vulnerable notion of qualia to begin with. They think I am setting up and knocking down a strawman, and ask, in effect: "Who said qualia are ineffable, intrinsic, private, directly apprehensible ways things seem to one?" Since my suggested four-fold essence of qualia may strike many readers as tendentious, it may be instructive to consider, briefly, an apparently milder alternative: qualia are simply "the qualitative or phenomenal features of sense experience[s], in virtue of having which they resemble and differ from each other, qualitatively, in the ways they do" (Shoemaker 1982, p. 367). Surely I do not mean to deny *those* features!

I reply: it all depends on what "qualitative or phenomenal" comes to. Shoemaker contrasts *qualitative* similarity and difference with "intentional" similarity and difference—similarity and difference of the properties an experience represents or is "of". That is clear enough, but what then of "phenomenal"? Among the non-intentional (and hence qualitative?) properties of my visual states are their physiological properties. Might these very properties be the qualia Shoemaker speaks of? It is supposed to be obvious, I take it, that these sorts of features are ruled out, because they are not "accessible to introspection" (Shoemaker, private correspondence). These are features of my visual *state,* perhaps, but not of my visual *experience.* They are not *phenomenal* properties.

But then another non-intentional similarity some of my visual states share is that they tend to make me think about going to bed. I think this feature of them *is* accessible to introspection—on any ordinary, pretheoretical construal. Is that a phenomenal property or not? The term "phenomenal" means nothing obvious and untendentious to me, and looks suspiciously like a gesture in the direction leading back to ineffable, private, directly apprehensible ways things seem to one.[4]

I suspect, in fact, that many are unwilling to take my radical challenge seriously largely because they want so much for qualia to be acknowledged. Qualia seem to many people to be the last ditch defense of the inwardness and elusiveness of our minds, a bulwark against creeping mechanism. They are sure there must be *some* sound path from the homely cases to the redoubtable category of the philosophers, since otherwise their last bastion of specialness will be stormed by science.

This special status for these presumed properties has a long and eminent tradition. I believe it was Einstein who once advised us that science could not give us the *taste* of the soup. Could such a wise man have been wrong? Yes, if he is taken to have been trying to remind us of the qualia that hide forever from objective science in the subjective inner sancta of our minds. There are no such things. Another wise man said so—Wittgenstein (1958, esp. pp. 91–100). Actually, what he said was:

> The thing in the box has no place in the language-game at all; not even as a *something;* for the box might even be empty—No, one can "divide through" by the thing in the box; it cancels out, whatever it is. (p. 100)

and then he went on to hedge his bets by saying "It is not a *something,* but not a *nothing* either! The conclusion was only that a nothing would serve just as well as a something about which nothing could be said" (p. 102). Both Einstein's and Wittgenstein's remarks are endlessly amenable to exegesis, but rather than undertaking to referee this War of the Titans, I choose to take what may well be a more radical stand than Wittgenstein's.[5] Qualia are not even "something about which nothing can be said"; "qualia" is a philosophers' term which fosters[6] nothing but confusion, and refers in the end to no properties or features at all.

3. The Traditional Paradox Regained

Qualia have not always been in good odor among philosophers. Although many have thought, along with Descartes and Locke, that it made sense to talk about private, ineffable properties of minds, others have argued that this is strictly nonsense—however naturally it trips off the tongue. It is worth recalling how qualia were presumably rehabilitated as properties to be taken seriously in the wake of Wittgensteinian and verificationist attacks on them as pseudo-hypotheses. The original version of *intuition pump #3: the inverted spectrum* (Locke 1690: II, xxxii, 15) is a speculation about two people: how do I know that you and I see the same subjective color when we look at something? Since we both learned color words by being shown public colored objects, our verbal behavior will match *even if we experience entirely different subjective colors.* The intuition that this hypothesis is systematically unconfirmable (and undis-

confirmable, of course) has always been quite robust, but some people have always been tempted to think technology could (in principle) bridge the gap.

Suppose, in *intuition pump #4: the Brainstorm machine,* there were some neuroscientific apparatus that fits on your head and feeds your visual experience into my brain (as in the movie, *Brainstorm,* which is not to be confused with the book, *Brainstorms*). With eyes closed I accurately report everything you are looking at, except that I marvel at how the sky is yellow, the grass red, and so forth. Would this not confirm, empirically, that our qualia were different? But suppose the technician then pulls the plug on the connecting cable, inverts it 180 degrees and reinserts it in the socket. Now I report the sky is blue, the grass green, and so forth. Which is the "right" orientation of the plug? Designing and building such a device would require that its "fidelity" be tuned or calibrated by the normalization of the two subjects' reports—so we would be right back at our evidential starting point. The moral of this intuition pump is that no intersubjective comparison of qualia is possible, even with perfect technology.

So matters stood until someone dreamt up the presumably improved version of the thought experiment: the *intra*personal inverted spectrum. The idea seems to have occurred to several people independently (Gert 1965; Putnam 1965; Taylor 1966; Shoemaker 1969, 1975; Lycan 1973). Probably Block and Fodor (1972) have it in mind when they say "It seems to us that the standard verificationist counterarguments against the view that the 'inverted spectrum' hypothesis is conceptually incoherent are not persuasive" (p. 172). In this version, *intuition pump #5: the neurosurgical prank,* the experiences to be compared are all in one mind. You wake up one morning to find that the grass has turned red, the sky yellow, and so forth. No one else notices any color anomalies in the world, so the problem must be in you. You are entitled, it seems, to conclude that you have undergone visual color qualia inversion (and we later discover, if you like, just how the evil neurophysiologists tampered with your neurons to accomplish this).

Here it seems at first—and indeed for quite a while—that qualia are acceptable properties after all, because propositions about them can be justifiably asserted, empirically verified and even explained. After all, in the imagined case, we can tell a tale in which we confirm a detailed neurophysiological account of the precise etiology of the dramatic change you undergo. It is tempting to suppose, then, that neurophysiological evidence, incorporated into a robust and ramifying theory, would have all the resolving power we could cvcr need for determining whether or not someone's qualia have actually shifted.

But this is a mistake. It will take some patient exploration to reveal the mistake in depth, but the conclusion can be reached—if not secured—quickly with the help of *intuition pump #6: alternative neurosurgery.* There are (at least) two different ways the evil neurosurgeon might create the inversion effect described in intuition pump #5:

1. Invert one of the "early" qualia-producing channels, e.g. in the optic nerve, so that all relevant neural events "downstream" are the "opposite" of their original and normal values. *Ex hypothesi* this inverts your qualia.
2. Leave all those early pathways intact and simply invert certain memory-access links—whatever it is that accomplishes your tacit (and even unconscious!) comparison of today's hues with those of yore. *Ex hypothesi* this does *not* invert your qualia at all, but just your memory-anchored dispositions to react to them.

On waking up and finding your visual world highly anomalous, you should exclaim "Egad! *Something* has happened! Either my qualia have been inverted or my memory-linked qualia-reactions have been inverted. I wonder which!"

The intrapersonal inverted spectrum thought experiment was widely supposed to be an improvement, since it moved the needed comparison into one subject's head. But now we can see that this is an illusion, since the link to earlier experiences, the link via memory, is analogous to the imaginary cable that might link two subjects in the original version.

This point is routinely—one might say traditionally—missed by the constructors of "intrasubjective inverted spectrum" thought experiments, who suppose that the subject's *noticing the difference*—surely a vivid experience of discovery by the subject—would have to be an instance of (directly? incorrigibly?) recognizing the difference *as a shift in qualia.* But as my example shows, we could achieve the same startling effect in a subject without tampering with his presumed qualia at all. Since *ex hypothesi*

the two different surgical invasions can produce exactly the same introspective effects while only one operation inverts the qualia, nothing in the subject's experience can favor one of the hypotheses over the other. So unless he seeks outside help, the state of his own qualia must be as unknowable to him as the state of anyone else's qualia. Hardly the privileged access or immediate acquaintance or direct apprehension the friends of qualia had supposed "phenomenal features" to enjoy!

The outcome of this series of thought experiments is an intensification of the "verificationist" argument against qualia. *If* there are qualia, they are even less accessible to our ken than we had thought. Not only are the classical intersubjective comparisons impossible (as the Brainstorm machine shows), but we cannot tell in our own cases whether our qualia have been inverted—at least not by introspection. It is surely tempting at this point—especially to non-philosophers—to decide that this paradoxical result must be an artifact of some philosophical misanalysis or other, the sort of thing that might well happen if you took a perfectly good pretheoretical notion—our everyday notion of qualia—and illicitly stretched it beyond the breaking point. The philosophers have made a mess; let them clean it up; meanwhile we others can get back to work, relying as always on our sober and unmetaphysical acquaintance with qualia.

Overcoming this ubiquitous temptation is the task of the next section, which will seek to establish the unsalvageable incoherence of the hunches that lead to the paradox by looking more closely at their sources and their motivation.

4. Making Mistakes about Qualia

The idea that people might be mistaken about their own qualia is at the heart of the ongoing confusion, and must be explored in more detail, and with somewhat more realistic examples, if we are to see the delicate role it plays.

Intuition pump #7: Chase and Sanborn. Once upon a time there were two coffee tasters, Mr Chase and Mr Sanborn, who worked for Maxwell House.[7] Along with half a dozen other coffee tasters, their job was to ensure that the taste of Maxwell House stayed constant, year after year. One day, about six years after Mr Chase had come to work for Maxwell House, he confessed to Mr Sanborn:

I hate to admit it, but I'm not enjoying this work any more. When I came to Maxwell House six years ago, I thought Maxwell House coffee was the best-tasting coffee in the world. I was proud to have a share in the responsibility for preserving that flavor over the years. And we've done our job well; the coffee tastes just the same today as it tasted when I arrived. But, you know, I no longer like it! My tastes have changed. I've become a more sophisticated coffee drinker. I no longer like *that taste* at all.

Sanborn greeted this revelation with considerable interest. "It's funny you should mention it," he replied, "for something rather similar has happened to me." He went on:

When I arrived here, shortly before you did, I, like you, thought Maxwell House coffee was tops in flavor. And now I, like you, really don't care for the coffee we're making. But *my* tastes haven't changed; my . . . *tasters* have changed. That is, I think something has gone wrong with my taste buds or some other part of my taste-analyzing perceptual machinery. Maxwell House coffee doesn't taste to me the way it used to taste; if only it did, I'd still love it, for I still think *that taste* is the best taste in coffee. Now I'm not saying we haven't done our job well. You other tasters all agree that the taste is the same, and I must admit that on a day-to-day basis I can detect no change either. So it must be my problem alone. I guess I'm no longer cut out for this work.

Chase and Sanborn are alike in one way at least: they both used to like Maxwell House coffee, and now neither likes it. But they claim to be different in another way. Maxwell House tastes to Chase just the way it always did, but not so for Sanborn. But can we take their protestations at face value? Must we? Might one or both of them simply be wrong? Might their predicaments be importantly the same and their apparent disagreement more a difference in manner of expression than in experiential or psychological state? Since both of them make claims that depend on the reliability of their memories, is there any way to check on this reliability?

My reason for introducing two characters in the example is not to set up an interpersonal comparison between how the coffee tastes to Chase and how it tastes to Sanborn, but just to exhibit, side-by-side, two poles between which cases of intrapersonal experiential shift can wander. Such cases of intrapersonal experiential shift, and the possibility of adaptation to them, or interference with memory in them, have

often been discussed in the literature on qualia, but without sufficient attention to the details, in my opinion. Let us look at Chase first. Falling in for the nonce with the received manner of speaking, it appears at first that there are the following possibilities:

(a) Chase's coffee-taste-qualia have stayed constant, while his reactive attitudes to those qualia, devolving on his canons of aesthetic judgment, etc., have shifted—which is what he seems, in his informal, casual way, to be asserting.

(b) Chase is simply wrong about the constancy of his qualia; they have shifted gradually and imperceptibly over the years, while his standards of taste haven't budged—in spite of his delusions about having become more sophisticated. He is in the state Sanborn claims to be in, but just lacks Sanborn's self-knowledge.

(c) Chase is in some predicament intermediate between (a) and (b); his qualia have shifted some *and* his standards of judgment have also slipped.

Sanborn's case seems amenable to three counterpart versions:

(a) Sanborn is right; his qualia have shifted, due to some sort of derangement in his perceptal machinery, but his standards have indeed remained constant.

(b) Sanborn's standards have shifted unbeknownst to him. He is thus misremembering his past experiences, in what we might call a nostalgia effect. Think of the familiar experience of returning to some object from your childhood (a classroom desk, a tree-house) and finding it much smaller than you remember it to have been. Presumably as you grew larger your internal standard for what was large grew with you somehow, but your memories (which are stored as fractions or multiples of that standard) didn't compensate, and hence when you consult your memory, it returns a distorted judgment. Sanborn's nostalgia-tinged memory of good old Maxwell House is similarly distorted. (There are obviously many different ways this impressionistic sketch of a memory mechanism could be implemented, and there is considerable experimental work in cognitive psychology that suggests how different hypotheses about such mechanisms could be tested.)

(c) As before, Sanborn's state is some combination of (a) and (b).

I think that everyone writing about qualia today would agree that there are all these possibilities for Chase and Sanborn. I know of no one these days who is tempted to defend the high line on infallibility or incorrigibility that would declare that alternative (a) is—and must be—the truth in each case, since people just cannot be wrong about such private, subjective matters.[8]

Since quandaries are about to arise, however, it might be wise to review in outline why the attractiveness of the infallibilist position is only superficial, so it won't recover its erstwhile allure when the going gets tough. First, in the wake of Wittgenstein (1958) and Malcolm (1956, 1959) we have seen that one way to buy such infallibility is to acquiesce in the complete evaporation of content (Dennet 1976). "Imagine someone saying: 'But I know how tall I am!' and laying his hand on top of his head to prove *it*" (Wittgenstein 1958, p. 96). By diminishing one's claim until there is nothing left to be right or wrong about, one can achieve a certain empty invincibility, but that will not do in this case. One of the things we want Chase to be right about (if he is right) is that he is not in Sanborn's predicament, so if the claim is to be viewed as infallible, it can hardly be because it declines to assert anything.

There is a strong temptation, I have found, to respond to my claims in this paper more or less as follows: "But after all is said and done, there is still something I know in a special way: I know *how it is with me right now*." But if absolutely nothing follows from this presumed knowledge—nothing, for instance, that would shed any light on the different psychological claims that might be true of Chase or Sanborn—what is the point of asserting that one has it? Perhaps people just want to reaffirm their sense of proprietorship over their own conscious states.

The infallibilist line on qualia treats them as properties of one's experience one cannot in principle misdiscover, and this is a mysterious doctrine (at least as mysterious as papal infallibility) unless we shift the emphasis a little and treat qualia as *logical constructs* out of subjects' qualia-judgments: a subject's experience has the quale *F* if and only if the subject judges his experience to have quale *F*. We can then treat such judgings as constitutive acts, in effect, bringing the quale into existence by the same sort of license as novelists have to determine the hair color of their characters by fiat. We do not ask how Dostoevski knows that Raskolnikov's hair is light brown.

There is a limited use for such interpretations of subjects' protocols, I have argued (Dennett 1978a; 1979, esp. pp. 109–10; 1982), but they will not help the defenders of qualia here. Logical constructs out of judgments must be viewed as akin to theorists' fictions, and the friends of qualia want the existence of a particular quale in any particular case to be an empirical fact in good standing, not a theorists's useful interpretive fiction, else it will not loom as a challenge to functionalism or materialism or third-person, objective science.

It seems easy enough, then, to dream up empirical tests that would tend to confirm Chase and Sanborn's different tales, but if passing such tests could support their authority (that is to say, their reliability), failing the tests would have to undermine it. The price you pay for the possibility of empirically confirming your assertions is the outside chance of being discredited. The friends of qualia are prepared, today, to pay that price, but perhaps only because they haven't reckoned how the bargain they have struck will subvert the concept they want to defend.

Consider how we could shed light on the question of where the truth lies in the particular cases of Chase and Sanborn, even if we might not be able to settle the matter definitively. It is obvious that there might be telling objective support for one extreme version or another of their stories. Thus if Chase is unable to reidentify coffees, teas, and wines in blind tastings in which only minutes intervene between first and second sips, his claim to *know* that Maxwell House tastes just the same to him now as it did six years ago will be seriously undercut. Alternatively, if he does excellently in blind tastings, and exhibits considerable knowledge about the canons of coffee style (if such there be), his claim to have become a more sophisticated taster will be supported. Exploitation of the standard principles of inductive testing—basically Mill's method of differences—can go a long way toward indicating what sort of change has occurred in Chase or Sanborn—a change near the brute perceptual processing end of the spectrum or a change near the ultimate reactive judgment end of the spectrum. And as Shoemaker (1982) and others have noted, physiological measures, suitably interpreted in some larger theoretical framework, could also weight the scales in favor of one extreme or the other. For instance, the well-studied phenomenon of induced illusory boundaries (see figure 26.1) has often been claimed to be a particularly "cognitive" illusion, dependent on "top down" processes, and hence, presumably, near the reactive judgment end of the spectrum, but recent experimental work (Von der Heydt et al. 1984) has revealed that "edge detector" neurons *relatively* low in the visual pathways—in area 18 of the visual cortex—are as responsive to illusory edges as to real light–dark boundaries on the retina, suggesting (but not quite proving, since these might somehow still be "descending effects") that illusory contours are not imposed from on high, but generated quite early in visual processing. One can imagine discovering a similarly "early" anomaly in the pathways leading from taste buds to judgment in Sanborn, for instance, tending to confirm his claim that he has suffered some change in his basic perceptual—as opposed to judgmental—machinery.

But let us not overestimate the resolving power of such empirical testing. The space in each case between the two poles represented by possibility (a) and possibility (b) would be occupied by phenomena that were the product, somehow, of two factors in varying proportion: roughly, dispositions to generate or produce qualia and dispositions to react to the qualia once they are produced. (That is how our intuitive picture of qualia would envisage it.) Qualia are supposed to affect our action or behavior only via the intermediary of our judgments about them, so any behavioral test, such as a discrimination or memory test, since it takes acts based on judgments as its primary data, can give us direct evidence only about the *resultant* of our two factors. In extreme cases we can have indirect evidence to suggest that one factor has varied a great deal, the other factor hardly at all, and we can test the hypothesis further by checking the relative sensitivity of the subject to variations in the conditions that presumably alter the two component factors. But such indirect testing cannot be expected to resolve the issue when the effects are relatively small—when, for instance, our rival hypotheses are Chase's preferred hypothesis (a) and the minor variant to the effect that his qualia have shifted *a little* and his standards *less than he thinks*. This will be true even when we include in our data any unintended or unconscious behavioral effects, for their import will be ambiguous (Would a longer response latency in Chase today be indicative of a process of "attempted qualia renormalization" or "extended aesthetic evaluation"?)

The limited evidential power of neurophysiology comes out particularly clearly if we imagine a case of adaptation. Suppose, in *intuition pump #8: the gradual post-operative recovery,* that we have somehow "surgically inverted"

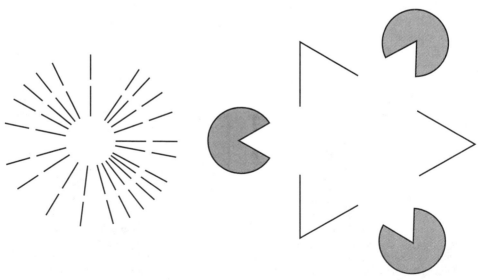

Figure 26.1

Chase's taste bud connections in the standard imaginary way: post-operatively, sugar tastes salty, salt tastes sour, etc. But suppose further—and this is as realistic a supposition as its denial—that Chase has subsequently compensated—as revealed by his behavior. He now *says* that the sugary substance we place on his tongue is sweet, and no longer favors gravy on his ice cream. Let us suppose the compensation is so thorough that on all behavioral and verbal tests his performance is indistinguishable from that of normal subjects—and from his own pre-surgical performance.

If all the internal compensatory adjustment has been accomplished early in the process—intuitively, pre-qualia—then his qualia today are restored to just as they were (relative to external sources of stimulation) before the surgery. If on the other hand some or all of the internal compensatory adjustment is post-qualia, then his qualia have not been renormalized *even if he thinks they have.* But the physiological facts will not in themselves shed any light on where in the stream of physiological process twixt tasting and telling to draw the line at which the putative qualia appear as properties of that phase of the process. The qualia are the "immediate or phenomenal" properties, of course, but this description will not serve to locate the right phase in the physiological stream, for, echoing intuition pump #6, there will always be at least two possible ways of interpreting the neurophysiological theory, however it comes out. Suppose our physiological theory tells us (in as much detail as you like) that the compensatory effect in him has been achieved by an *adjustment in the memory-accessing process* that is required for our victim to compare today's hues to those of yore. There are *still* two stories that might be told:

I. Chase's current qualia are still abnormal, but thanks to the revision in his memory-accessing process, he has in effect adjusted his memories of how things used to taste, so he no longer notices any anomaly.
II. The memory-comparison step occurs just prior to the qualia phase in taste perception; thanks to the revision, it now *yields* the same old qualia for the same stimulation.

In (I) the qualia contribute to the input, in effect, to the memory-comparator. In (II) they are part of the output of the memory-comparator. These seem to be two substantially different hy-potheses, but the physiological evidence, no matter how well developed, will not tell us on which side of memory to put the qualia. Chase's introspective evidence will not settle the issue between (I) and (II) either, since *ex hypothesi* those stories are not reliably distinguishable by him. Remember that it was in order to confirm or disconfirm Chase's opinion that we turned to the neurophysiological evidence in the first place. We can hardly use his opinion in the end to settle the matter between our rival neurophysiological theories. Chase may think that he thinks his experiences are the same as before *because* they really are (and he remembers accurately how it used to be), but he must admit that he has no introspective resources for distinguishing that possibility from alternative (I), on which he thinks things are as they used to be *because* his memory of how they used to be has been distorted by his new compensatory habits.

Faced with their subject's systematic neutrality, the physiologists may have their own reasons for preferring (I) to (II) or vice versa, for they may have *appropriated* the term "qualia" to their own theoretical ends, to denote some family of detectable properties that strike them as playing an important role in their neurophysiological theory of perceptual recognition and memory. Chase or Sanborn might complain—in the company of more than a few philosophical spokesmen—that these properties the neurophysiologists choose to call "qualia" are not the qualia they are speaking of. The scientists' retort is: "If we cannot distinguish (I) from (II), we certainly cannot support either of your claims. If you want our support, you must relinquish your concept of qualia."

What is striking about this is not just that the empirical methods would fall short of distinguishing what seem to be such different claims about qualia, but that they would fall short *in spite of being better evidence than the subject's own introspective convictions.* For the subject's own judgments, like the behaviors or actions that express them, are the resultant of our two postulated factors, and cannot discern the component proportions any better than external behavioral tests can. Indeed, a subject's "introspective" convictions will generally be *worse* evidence than what outside observers can gather. For if our subject is—as most are—a "naive subject," unacquainted with statistical data about his own case or similar cases, his immediate, frank judgments are, evidentially, like any naive observer's perceptual judgments about factors in the outside world. Chase's intuitive judgments about his qualia constancy are no better off, epistemically, than his intuitive judgments about, say, lighting intensity constancy or room temperature constancy— or his own body temperature constancy. Moving to a condition inside his body does not change the intimacy of the epistemic relation in any special way. Is Chase running a fever or just feeling feverish? Unless he has taken steps to calibrate and cross-check his own performance, his opinion that his fever-perception apparatus is undisturbed is no better than a hunch. Similarly, Chase may have a strongly held opinion about the degree to which his taste-perceiving apparatus has maintained its integrity, and the degree to which his judgment has evolved through sophistication, but pending the results of the sort of laborious third-person testing just imagined, he would be a fool to claim to know—especially to know directly or immediately—that his was a pure case (a), closer to (a) than to (b), or a case near (b).

He is on quite firm ground, epistemically, when he reports that *the relation* between his coffee-sipping activity and his judging activity has changed. Recall that this is the factor that Chase and Sanborn have in common: they used to like Maxwell House; now they don't. But unless he carries out on himself the sorts of tests others might carry out on him, his convictions about what has stayed constant (or nearly so) and what has shifted *must be sheer guessing.*

But then qualia—supposing for the time being that we know what we are talking about— must lose one of their "essential" second-order properties: far from being directly or immediately apprehensible properties of our experience, they are properties whose changes or constancies are either entirely beyond our ken, or inferrable (at best) from "third-person" examinations of our behavioral and physiological reaction patterns (if Chase and Sanborn acquiesce in the neurophysiologists' sense of the term). On this view, Chase and Sanborn should be viewed not as introspectors capable of a privileged view of these properties, but as autopsychologists, theorists whose convictions about the properties of their own nervous systems are based not only on their "immediate" or current experiential convictions, but also on their appreciation of the import of events they remember from the recent past.

There are, as we shall see, good reasons for neurophysiologists and other "objective, third-person" theorists to single out such a class of properties to study. But they are not qualia, for the simple reason that one's epistemic relation to them is *exactly* the same as one's epistemic relation to such external, but readily—if fallibly—detectable, properties as room temperature or weight. The idea that one should consult an outside expert, and perform elaborate behavioral tests on oneself in order to confirm what qualia one had, surely takes us too far away from our original idea of qualia as properties with which we have a particularly intimate acquaintance.

So perhaps we have taken a wrong turning. The doctrine that led to this embarrassing result was the doctrine that sharply distinguished qualia from their (normal) effects on reactions. Consider Chase again. He claims that coffee tastes "just the same" as it always did, but he admits—nay insists—that his reaction to "that taste" is not what it used to be. That is, he pretends to be able to divorce his apprehension (or recollection) of the quale—the taste, in ordinary parlance—from his different reactions to the taste. But this apprehension or recollection is itself a reaction to the presumed quale, so some sleight-of-hand is being perpetrated—innocently no doubt—by Chase. So suppose instead that Chase had insisted that precisely *because* his reaction was now different, the taste had changed for him. (When he told his wife his original tale, she said "Don't be silly! Once you add the dislike you change the experience!"—and the more he thought about it, the more he decided she was right.)

Intuition pump #9: the experienced beer drinker. It is familiarly said that beer, for example, is an acquired taste; one gradually trains oneself—or just comes—to enjoy that flavor. What flavor? The flavor of the first sip? No one could like *that* flavor, an experienced beer drinker might retort:

> Beer tastes different to the experienced beer drinker. If beer went on tasting to me the way the first sip tasted, I would never have gone on drinking beer! Or to put the same point the other way around, if my first sip of beer had tasted to me the way my most recent sip just tasted, I would never have had to acquire the taste in the first place! I would have loved the first sip as much as the one I just enjoyed.

If we let this speech pass, we must admit that beer is *not* an acquired taste. No one comes to enjoy *the way the first sip tasted.* Instead, prolonged beer drinking leads people to experience a taste they enjoy, but precisely their enjoying the taste guarantees that it is not the taste they first experienced.[9]

But this conclusion, if it is accepted, wreaks havoc of a different sort with the traditional philosophical view of qualia. For if it is admitted that one's attitudes towards, or reactions to, experiences are in any way and in any degree constitutive of their experiential qualities, so that a change in reactivity *amounts to* or *guarantees* a change in the property, then those properties, those "qualitative or phenomenal features," cease to be "intrinsic" properties, and in fact become paradigmatically extrinsic, relational properties.

Properties that "seem intrinsic" at first often turn out on more careful analysis to be relational. Bennett (1965) is the author of *intuition pump #10: the world-wide eugenics experiment.* He draws our attention to phenol-thio-urea, a substance which tastes very bitter to three-fourths of humanity, and as tasteless as water to the rest. Is it bitter? Since the reactivity to phenol-thio-urea is genetically transmitted, we could make it paradigmatically bitter by performing a large-scale breeding experiment: prevent the people to whom it is tasteless from breeding, and in a few generations phenol would be as bitter as anything to be found in the world. But we could also (in principle!) perform the contrary feat of mass "eugenics'" and thereby make phenol paradigmatically tasteless—as tasteless as water—without ever touching phenol. Clearly, public bitterness or tastelessness is not an intrinsic property of phenol-thio-urea but a relational property, since the property is changed by a change in the reference class of normal detectors.

The public versions of perceptual "qualia" all *seem* intrinsic, in spite of their relationality. They are not alone. Think of the "felt value" of a dollar (or whatever your native currency is). "How much is that in *real* money?" the American tourist is reputed to have asked, hoping to translate a foreign price onto the scale of "intrinsic value" he keeps in his head. As Elster (1985) claims, "there is a tendency to overlook the implicitly relational character of certain monadic predicates." Walzer (1985) points out that " . . . a ten-dollar bill might seem to have a life of its own as a thing of value, but, as Elster suggests, its value implicitly depends on 'other people who are prepared to accept money as payment for goods.' " But even as one concedes this, there is still a tendency to reserve something subjective, felt value, as an "intrinsic"

property of that ten-dollar bill. But as we now see, such intrinsic properties cannot be properties to which a subject's access is in any way privileged.

Which way should Chase go? Should he take his wife's advice and declare that since he can't stand the coffee any more, it no longer tastes the same to him (it used to taste good and now it tastes bad)? Or should he say that really, in a certain sense, it does taste the way it always did or at least it sort of does—when you subtract the fact that it tastes so bad now, of course?

We have now reached the heart of my case. The fact is that we have to ask Chase which way he wants to go, and there really are two drastically different alternatives available to him *if we force the issue.* Which way would *you* go? Which concept of qualia did you "always have in the back of your mind," guiding your imagination as you thought about theories? If you acknowledge that the answer is not obvious, and especially if you complain that this forced choice drives apart two aspects that you had supposed united in your pretheoretic concept, you support my contention that there is no secure foundation in ordinary "folk psychology" for a concept of qualia. We *normally* think in a confused and potentially incoherent way when we think about the ways things seem to us.

When Chase thinks of "that taste" he thinks equivocally or vaguely. He harkens back in memory to earlier experiences but need not try—or be able—to settle whether he is including any or all of his reactions or excluding them from what he intends by "that taste." His state then and his state now are different—*that* he can avow with confidence—but he has no "immediate" resources for making a finer distinction, nor any need to do so.[10]

This suggests that qualia are no more essential to the professional vocabulary of the phenomenologist (or professional coffee taster) than to the vocabulary of the physiologist (Dennett 1978b). To see this, consider again the example of my dislike of cauliflower. Imagine now, in *intuition pump #11: the cauliflower cure,* that someone offers me a pill to cure my loathing for cauliflower. He promises that after I swallow this pill cauliflower will taste exactly the same to me as it always has, but I will like that taste! "Hang on," I might reply. "I think you may have just contradicted yourself." But in any event I take the pill and it works. I become an instant cauliflower-appreciator, but if I am asked which of the two possible effects (Chase-type or

Sanborn-type) the pill has had on me, I will be puzzled, and will find nothing *in my experience* to shed light on the question. Of course I recognize that the taste is (sort of) the same—the pill hasn't made cauliflower taste like chocolate cake, after all—but at the same time my experience is so different now that I resist saying that cauliflower tastes the way it used to taste. There is in any event no reason to be cowed into supposing that my cauliflower experiences have some intrinsic properties behind, or in addition to, their various dispositional, reaction-provoking properties.

"But in principle there has to be a right answer to the question of how it is, intrinsically, with you now, even if you are unable to say with any confidence!" Why? Would one say the same about all other properties of experience? Consider *intuition pump #12: visual field inversion created by wearing inverting spectacles,* a phenomenon which has been empirically studied for years. (G. M. Stratton published the pioneering work in 1896, and J. J. Gibson and Ivo Kohler were among the principal investigators. For an introductory account, see Gregory 1977.) After wearing inverting spectacles for several days subjects make an astonishingly successful adaptation. Suppose we pressed on them this question: "Does your adaptation consist in your re-inverting your visual field, or in your turning the rest of your mind upside-down in a host of compensations?" If they demur, may we insist that there has to be a right answer, even if they cannot say with any confidence which it is? Such an insistence would lead directly to a new version of the old inverted spectrum thought experiment: "How do I know whether some people see things upside-down (but are perfectly used to it), while others see things right-side-up?"

Only a very naive view of visual perception could sustain the idea that one's visual field has a property of right-side-upness or upside-downness *independent of one's dispositions to react to it*—"intrinsic right-side-upness" we could call it. (See my discussion of the properties of the "images" processed by the robot SHAKEY, in Dennett 1982.) So not all properties of conscious experience invite or require treatment as "intrinsic" properties. Is there something distinguishing about a certain subclass of properties (the "qualitative or phenomenal" subclass, presumably) that forces us to treat them—unlike subjective right-side-upness—as intrinsic properties? If not, such properties have

no role to play, in either physiological theories of experience, or in introspective theories.

Some may be inclined to argue this way: I can definitely imagine the experience of "spectrum inversion" from the inside; after all I have actually experienced temporary effects of the same type, such as the "taste displacement" effect of the maple syrup on the orange juice. What is imaginable, or actual, is possible. Therefore spectrum inversion or displacement (in all sensory modalities) is possible. But such phenomena just *are* the inversion or displacement of qualia, or intrinsic subjective properties. Therefore there must be qualia: intrinsic subjective properties.

This is fallacious. What one imagines and what one says one imagines may be two different things. To imagine visual field inversion, of the sort Stratton and Kohler's subjects experienced, is not necessarily to imagine the absolute inversion of a visual field (even if that is what it "feels like" to the subjects). Less obviously, imagining—as vividly as you like—a case of subjective color-perception displacement is not necessarily imagining what that phenomenon is typically called by philosophers: an inverted or displaced spectrum *of qualia.* In so far as that term carries the problematic implications scouted here, there is no support for its use arising simply from the vividness or naturalness of the imagined possibility.

If there are no such properties as qualia, does that mean that "spectrum inversion" is impossible? Yes and no. Spectrum inversion as classically debated is impossible, but something like it is perfectly possible—something that is as like "qualia inversion" as visual field inversion is like the impossible *absolute* visual image inversion we just dismissed.

5. Some Puzzling Real Cases

It is not enough to withhold our theoretical allegiances until the sunny day when the philosophers complete the tricky task of purifying the everyday concept of qualia. Unless we take active steps to shed this source concept, and replace it with better ideas, it will continue to cripple our imaginations and systematically distort our attempts to understand the phenomena already encountered.

What we find, if we look at the actual phenomena of anomalies of color perception, for instance, amply bears out our suspicions about the inadequacy of the traditional notion of qualia. Several varieties of *cerebral achromatopsia* (brain based impairment of color vision) have been reported, and while there remains much that is unsettled about their analysis, there is little doubt that the philosophical thought experiments have underestimated or overlooked the possibilities for counter-intuitive collections of symptoms, as a few very brief excerpts from case histories will reveal.

> Objects to the right of the vertical meridian appeared to be of normal hue, while to the left they were perceived only in shades of gray, though without distortions of form. . . . He was unable to recognize or name any color in any portion of the left field of either eye, including bright reds, blues, greens and yellows. As soon as any portion of the colored object crossed the vertical meridian, he was able to instantly recognize and accurately name its color. (Damasio et al. 1980)

This patient would seem at first to be unproblematically describable as suffering a shift or loss of color qualia in the left hemifield, but there is a problem of interpretation here, brought about by another case:

> The patient failed in all tasks in which he was required to match the seen color with its spoken name. Thus, the patient failed to give the names of colors and failed to choose a color in response to its name. By contrast he succeeded on all tasks where the matching was either purely verbal or purely nonverbal. Thus, he could give verbally the names of colors corresponding to named objects and vice versa. He could match seen colors to each other and to pictures of objects and could sort colors without error. (Geschwind and Fusillo 1966)

This second patient was quite unaware of any deficit. He "never replied with a simple 'I don't know' to the demand for naming a color" (Geschwind and Fusillo 1966, p. 140). There is a striking contrast between these two patients; both have impaired ability to name the colors of things in at least part of their visual field, but whereas the former is acutely aware of his deficit, the latter is not. Does this difference make all the difference about qualia? If so, what on earth should we say about this third patient?

> His other main complaint was that "everything looked black or grey" and this caused him some difficulty in everyday life. . . . He had considerable difficulty recognizing and naming colours. He would, for example, usually describe bright red objects as either red or black, bright green objects as either green, blue or black, and bright

blue objects as black. The difficulty appeared to be perceptual and he would make remarks suggesting this; for example when shown a bright red object he said "a dirty smudgy red, not as red as you would normally see red." Colours of lesser saturation or brightness were described in such terms as "grey" "off-white" or "black," but if told to guess at the colour, he would be correct on about 50 per cent of occasions, being notably less successful with blues and greens than reds. (Meadows 1974)

This man's awareness of his deficit is problematic to say the least. It contrasts rather sharply with yet another case:

> One morning in November 1977, upon awakening, she noted that although she was able to see details of objects and people, colors appeared "drained out" and "not true." She had no other complaint . . . her vision was good, 20/20 in each eye . . . The difficulty in color perception persisted, and she had to seek the advice of her husband to choose what to wear. Eight weeks later she noted that she could no longer recognize the faces of her husband and daughter. . . . [So in] addition to achromatopsia, the patient had prosopagnosia, but her linguistic and cognitive performances were otherwise unaffected. The patient was able to tell her story cogently and to have remarkable insight about her defects. (Damasio et al. 1980)

As Meadows notes, "Some patients thus complain that their vision for colours is defective while others have no spontaneous complaint but show striking abnormalities on testing."

What should one say in these cases? When no complaint is volunteered but the patient shows an impairment in color vision, is this a sign that his qualia are unaffected? ("His capacities to discriminate are terribly impaired, but luckily for him, his inner life is untouched by this merely public loss!") We could line up the qualia this way, but equally we could claim that the patient has simply not noticed the perhaps gradual draining away or inversion or merging of his qualia revealed by his poor performance. ("So slowly did his inner life lose its complexity and variety that he never noticed how impoverished it had become!") What if our last patient described her complaint just as she did above, but performed normally on testing? One hypothesis would be that her qualia had indeed, as she suggested, become washed out. Another would be that in the light of her sterling performance on the color discrimination tests, her qualia were fine; she was suffering from some hysterical or depressive anomaly, a sort of color-vision hypochondria that makes her complain about a loss of color perception. Or perhaps one could claim that her qualia were untouched; her disorder was purely verbal: an anomalous understanding of the words she uses to describe her experience. (Other startlingly specific color-*word* disorders have been reported in the literature.)

The traditional concept leads us to overlook genuine possibilities. Once we have learned of the curious deficit reported by Geschwind and Fusillo, for instance, we realize that our first patient was never tested to see if he could still sort colors seen on the left or pass other non-naming, non-verbal color-blindness tests. Those tests are by no means superfluous. Perhaps he would have passed them; perhaps, *in spite of what he says* his qualia are as intact for the left field as for the right!—if we take the capacity to pass such tests as "criterial." Perhaps his problem is "purely verbal." If your reaction to this hypothesis is that this is impossible, that must mean you are making his verbal, reporting behavior sovereign in settling the issue—but then you must rule out a priori the possibility of the condition I described as color-vision hypochondria.

There is no prospect of *finding* the answers to these brain-teasers in our everyday usage or the intuitions it arouses, but it is of course open to the philosopher to *create* an edifice of theory defending a particular set of interlocking proposals. The problem is that although normally a certain family of stimulus and bodily conditions yields a certain family of effects, any particular effect can be disconnected, and our intuitions do not tell us which effects are "essential" to quale identity or qualia constancy (cf. Dennett 1978a, ch. 11). It seems fairly obvious to me that none of the real problems of interpretation that face us in these curious cases is advanced by any analysis of how the concept of *qualia* is to be applied—unless we wish to propose a novel, technical sense for which the traditional term might be appropriated. But that would be at least a tactical error: the intuitions that surround and *purport* to anchor the current understanding of the term are revealed to be in utter disarray when confronted with these cases.

My informal sampling shows that some philosophers have strong opinions about each case and how it should be described in terms of qualia, but they find they are in strident (and ultimately comic) disagreement with other philosophers about how these "obvious" descriptions should go. Other philosophers discover they really don't know what to say—not because there aren't enough facts presented in the descriptions of the cases, but because it begins to dawn on them that they haven't really known what they were talking about over the years.

6. Filling the Vacuum

If qualia are such a bad idea, why have they seemed to be such a good idea? Why does it seem as if there are these intrinsic, ineffable, private, "qualitative" properties in our experience? A review of the presumptive second-order properties of the properties of our conscious experiences will permit us to diagnose their attractiveness and find suitable substitutes. (For a similar exercise see Kitcher 1979).

Consider "intrinsic" first. It is far from clear what an intrinsic property would be. Although the term has had a certain vogue in philosophy, and often seems to secure an important contrast, there has never been an accepted definition of the second-order property of intrinsicality. If even such a brilliant theory-monger as David Lewis can try and fail, by his own admission, to define the extrinsic/intrinsic distinction coherently, we can begin to wonder if the concept deserves our further attention after all. In fact Lewis (1983) begins his survey of versions of the distinction by listing as one option: "We could Quine the lot, give over the entire family as unintelligible and dispensable," but he dismisses the suggestion immediately: "That would be absurd" (p. 197). In the end, however, his effort to salvage the accounts of Chisholm (1976) and Kim (1982) are stymied, and he conjectures that "if we still want to break in we had best try another window" (p. 200).

Even if we are as loath as Lewis is to abandon the distinction, shouldn't we be suspicious of the following curious fact? If challenged to explain the idea of an intrinsic property to a neophyte, many people would hit on the following sort of example: consider Tom's ball; it has many properties, such as its being made of rubber from India, its belonging to Tom, its having spent the last week in the closet, and its redness. All but the last of these are clearly *relational* or *extrinsic* properties of the ball. Its redness, however, is an intrinsic property. Except this isn't so. Ever since Boyle and Locke we have known better. Redness—public redness—is a quintessentially relational property, as many thought experiments about "secondary qualities" show. (One of the first was Berkeley's [1713] pail of lukewarm water, and one of the best is Bennett's [1965] phenol-thio-urea.) The seductive step, on learning that public redness (like public bitterness, etc.) is a relational property after all, is to cling to intrinsicality ("*something* has to be intrinsic!") and move it into the subject's head. It is often thought, in fact, that if we take a Lockean, relational position on objective bitterness, redness, etc., we *must* complete our account of the relations in question by appeal to non-relational, intrinsic properties. If what it is to be objectively bitter is to produce a certain effect in the members of the class of normal observers, we must be able to specify that effect, and distinguish it from the effect produced by objective sourness and so forth.

What else could distinguish this effect but some intrinsic property? Why not another relational or extrinsic property? The relational treatment of monetary value does not require, for its completion, the supposition of items of intrinsic value (value independent of the valuers' dispositions to react behaviorally). The claim that certain perceptual properties are different is, in the absence of any supporting argument, just question-begging. It will not do to say that it is just obvious that they are intrinsic. It may have seemed obvious to some, but the considerations raised by Chase's quandary show that it is far from obvious that any intrinsic property (whatever that comes to) could play the role of anchor for the Lockean relational treatment of the public perceptual properties.

Why not give up intrinsicality as a second-order property altogether, at least pending resolution of the disarray of philosophical opinion about what intrinsicality might be? Until such time the insistence that qualia are the intrinsic properties of experience is an empty gesture at best; no one could claim that it provides a clear, coherent, understood prerequisite for theory.[11]

What, then, of ineffability? Why does it seem that our conscious experiences have ineffable properties? Because they do have *practically* ineffable properties. Suppose, in *intuition pump #13: the osprey cry,* that I have never heard the cry of an osprey, even in a recording, but know roughly, from reading my bird books, what to listen for: "a series of short, sharp, cheeping whistles, *cheep cheep* or *chewk chewk,* etc; sounds annoyed" (Peterson 1947) (or words to that effect or better). The verbal decription gives me a partial confinement of the logical space of possible bird cries. On its basis I can rule out many bird calls I have heard or might hear, but there is still a broad range of discriminable-by-me possibilities within which the actuality lies hidden from me like a needle in a haystack.

Then one day, armed with both my verbal description and my binoculars, I identify an osprey visually, and then hear its cry. So *that's* what it sounds like, I say to myself, ostending—it seems—a particular mental complex of intrinsic, ineffable qualia. I dub the complex "S" (*pace* Wittgenstein), rehearse it in short term memory, check it against the bird book descriptions, and see that while the verbal descriptions are true, accurate and even poetically evocative—I decide I could not do better with a thousand words—they still fall short of *capturing* the qualia-complex I have called *S.* In fact, that is why I need the neologism "*S*" to refer directly to the ineffable property I cannot pick out by description. My perceptual experience has pinpointed for me the location of the osprey cry in the logical space of possibilities in a way verbal description could not.

But tempting as this view of matters is, it is overstated. First of all, it is obvious that from a single experience of this sort I don't—can't—know how to generalize to other osprey calls. Would a cry that differed only in being half an octave higher also be an osprey call? That is an empirical, ornithological question for which my experience provides scant evidence. But moreover—and this is a psychological, not ornithological, matter—I don't and can't know, from a single such experience, which physical variations and constancies in stimuli would produce an indistinguishable experience in me. Nor can I know whether I would react the same (have the same experience) if I were presented with what was, by all physical measures, a re-stimulation identical to the first. I cannot know the modulating effect, if any, of variations in my body (or psyche).

This inscrutability of projection is surely one of the sources of plausibility for Wittgenstein's skepticism regarding the possibility of a private language.

> Wittgenstein emphasizes that ostensive definitions are always in principle capable of being misunderstood, even the ostensive definition of a color word such as "sepia". How someone understands the word is exhibited in the way someone goes on, "the use that he makes of the word defined". One may go on in the right way given a purely minimal explanation, while on

the other hand one may go on in another way no matter how many clarifications are added, since these too can be misunderstood . . . (Kripke 1982, p. 83; see also pp. 40–6)

But what is inscrutable in a single glance, and somewhat ambiguous after limited testing, can come to be justifiably seen as the deliverance of a highly specific, reliable, and projectible property-detector, once it has been field-tested under a suitably wide variety of circumstances.

In other words, when first I hear the osprey cry, I may have identified a property-detector in myself, but I have no idea (yet) what property my new-found property-detector detects. It might seem then that I know nothing new at all—that my novel experience has not improved my epistemic predicament in the slightest. But of course this is not so. I may not be able to describe the property or identify it relative to any readily usable public landmarks (yet), but I am acquainted with it in a modest way: I can refer to the property I detected: it is the property I detected in *that* event. My experience of the osprey cry has given me a new way of thinking about osprey cries (an unavoidably inflated way of saying something very simple) which is practically ineffable both because it has (as yet for me) an untested profile in response to perceptual circumstances, and because it is—as the poverty of the bird-book description attests—such a highly informative way of thinking: a deliverance of an informationally very sensitive portion of my nervous system.

In this instance I mean information in the formal information theory sense of the term. Consider (*intuition pump #14: the Jello box*) the old spy trick, most famously encountered in the case of Julius and Ethel Rosenberg, of improving on a password system by tearing something in two (a Jello box, in the Rosenberg's case), and giving half to each of the two parties who must be careful about identifying each other. Why does it work? Because tearing the paper in two produces an edge of such informational complexity that it would be virtually impossible to reproduce by deliberate construction. (Cutting the Jello box with straight edge and razor would entirely defeat the purpose.) The particular jagged edge of one piece becomes a *practically* unique pattern-recognition device for its mate; it is an apparatus for detecting the shape property M, where M is uniquely instantiated by its mate. It is of the essence of the trick that we cannot replace our dummy predicate "M" with a longer, more complex, but accurate and exhaustive de-

scription of the property, for if we could, we could use the description as a recipe or feasible algorithm for producing another instance of M or another M detector. The only *readily available* way of saying what property M is is just to point to our M-detector and say that M is the shape property detected by this thing here.

And that is just what we do when we seem to ostend, with the mental finger of inter intention, a quale or qualia-complex in our experience. We refer to a property—a public property of uncharted boundaries—via reference to our personal and idiosyncratic capacity to respond to it. That idiosyncrasy is the extent of our privacy. If I wonder whether your blue is my blue, your middle-C is my middle-C, I can coherently be wondering whether our discrimination profiles over a wide variation in conditions will be approximately the same. And they may not be; people experience the world quite differently. But that is empirically discoverable by all the usual objective testing procedures.[12]

Peter Bieri has pointed out to me that there is a natural way of exploiting Dretske's (1981) sense of information in a reformulation of my first three second-order properties of qualia: intrinsicality, ineffability, and privacy. (There are problems with Dretske's attempt to harness information theory in this way—see my discussion in "Evolution, error and intentionality" (Dennett 1987)—but they are not relevant to this point.) We could speak of what Bieri would call "phenomenal information properties" of psychological events. Consider the information—what Dretske would call the *natural meaning*—that a type of internal perceptual event might carry. That it carries that information is an objective (and hence, in a loose sense, intrinsic) matter since it is independent of what information (if any) the subject *takes* the event type to carry. Exactly what information is carried is (practically) ineffable, for the reasons just given. And it is private in the sense just given: proprietary and potentially idiosyncratic.

Consider how Bieri's proposed "phenomenal information properties" (let's call them *pips*) would apply in the case of Chase and Sanborn. Both Chase and Sanborn ought to wonder whether their pips have changed. Chase's speech shows that he is under the impression that his pips are unchanged (under normal circumstances—all bets are off if he has just eaten horseradish). He believes that the same objective things in the world—in particular, chemically identical caffeine-rich fluids—give rise to his particular types of taste-experiences now as six years ago.

Sanborn is under the impression that his pips are different. He thinks his objective property-detectors are deranged. He no longer has confidence that their deliverances today inform him of what they did six years ago. And what, exactly, did they inform him of then? If Sanborn were an ordinary person, we would not expect him to have an explicit answer, since most of us treat our taste-detectors as mere *M*-detectors, detecting whatever-it-is that they detect. (There are good reasons for this, analyzed by Akins 1987.) But professional coffee-tasters are probaby different. They probably have some pretty good idea of what kind of chemical-analysis transduction machinery they have in their mouths and nervous systems.

So far, so good. We could reinterpret Chase and Sanborn's speeches as hypotheses about the constancies or changes in the outputs of their perceptual information-processing apparatus, and just the sort of empirical testing we imagined before would tend to confirm or disconfirm their opinions thus interpreted. But what would justify calling such an information-bearing property "phenomenal"?

Such a pip has, as the testimony of Chase and Sanborn reveals, the power to provoke in Chase and Sanborn acts of (apparent) re-identification or recognition. This power is of course a Lockean, dispositional property on a par with the power of bitter things to provoke a certain reaction in people. It is this power alone, however it might be realized in the brain, that gives Chase and Sanborn "access" to the deliverances of their individual property-detectors.

We may "point inwardly" to one of the deliverances of our idiosyncratic, proprietary property-detectors, but when we do, what are we pointing *at?* What does that deliverance itself *consist of?* Or what are its consciously apprehensible properties, if not just our banished friends the qualia? We must be careful here, for if we invoke an inner perceptual process in which we observe the deliverance with some inner eye and thereby discern its properties, we will be stepping back into the frying pan of the view according to which qualia are just ordinary properties of our inner states.

But nothing requires us to make such an invocation. We don't have to know how we identify or re-identify or gain access to such internal response types in order to be able so to identify them. This is a point that was forcefully made by

the pioneer functionalists and materialists, and has never been rebutted (Farrell 1950; Smart 1959). The properties of the "thing experienced" are not to be confused with the properties of the event that realizes the experiencing. To put the matter vividly, the physical difference between someone's imagining a purple cow and imagining a green cow *might* be nothing more than the presence or absence of a particular zero or one in one of the brain's "registers." Such a brute physical presence is all that it would take to anchor the sorts of dispositional differences between imagining a purple cow and imagining a green cow that could then flow, causally, from that "intrinsic" fact. (I doubt that this is what the friends of qualia have had in mind when they have insisted that qualia are intrinsic properties.)

Moreover, it is our very inability to expand on, or modify, these brute dispositions so to identify or recognize such states that creates the doctrinal illusion of "homogeneity" or "atomicity to analysis" or "grainlessness" that characterizes the qualia of philosophical tradition.

This putative grainlessness, I hypothesize, is nothing but a sort of functional invariability: it is close kin to what Pylyshyn (1980, 1984) calls *cognitive impenetrability.* Moreover, this functional invariability or impenetrability is not absolute but itself plastic over time. Just as on the efferent side of the nervous system, *basic actions*—in the sense of Danto (1963, 1965) and others (see Goldman 1970)—have been discovered to be variable, and subject under training to decomposition (one can learn with the help of "biofeedback" to will the firing of a particular motor neuron "directly"), so what counts for an individual as the simple or atomic properties of experienced items is subject to variation with training.[13]

Consider the results of "educating" the palate of a wine taster, or "ear training" for musicians. What had been "atomic" or "unanalyzable" becomes noticeably compound and describable; pairs that had been indistinguishable become distinguishable, and when this happens we say *the experience changes.* A swift and striking example of this is illustrated in *intuition pump #15: the guitar string.* Pluck the bass or low E string open, and listen carefully to the sound. Does it have describable parts or is it one and whole and ineffably guitarish? Many will opt for the latter way of talking. Now pluck the open string again and carefully bring a finger down lightly over the octave fret to create a high "harmonic." Suddenly a *new* sound is heard: "purer" somehow and of course an octave higher. Some people insist that this is an entirely novel sound, while others will describe the experience by saying "the bottom fell out of the note"—leaving just the top. But then on a third open plucking one can hear, with surprising distinctness, the harmonic overtone that was isolated in the second plucking. The homogeneity and ineffability of the first experience is gone, replaced by a duality as "directly apprehensible" and clearly describable as that of any chord.

The difference in experience is striking, but the complexity apprehended on the third plucking was *there* all along (being responded to or discriminated). After all, it was by the complex pattern of overtones that you were able to recognize the sound as that of a guitar rather than a lute or harpsichord. In other words, although the subjective experience has changed dramatically, the *pip* hasn't changed; you are still responding, as before, to a complex property so highly informative that it practically defies verbal description.

There is nothing to stop further refinement of one's capacity to describe this heretofore ineffable complexity. At any time, of course, there is one's current horizon of distinguishability—

and that horizon is what sets, if anything does, what we should call the primary or atomic properties of what one consciously experiences (Farrell 1950). But it would be a mistake to transform the fact that inevitably there is a limit to our capacity to describe things we experience into the supposition that there are absolutely indescribable properties in our experience.

So when we look one last time at our original characterization of qualia, as ineffable, intrinsic, private, directly apprehensible properties of experience, we find that there is nothing to fill the bill. In their place are relatively or practically ineffable public properties we can refer to indirectly via reference to our private property-detectors—private only in the sense of idiosyncratic. And in so far as we wish to cling to our subjective authority about the occurrence within us of states of certain types or with certain properties, we can have some authority—not infallibility or incorrigibility, but something better than sheer guessing—but only if we restrict ourselves to relational, extrinsic properties like the power of certain internal states of ours to provoke acts of apparent re-identification. So contrary to what seems obvious at first blush, there simply are no qualia at all.[14]

NOTES

1. A representative sample of the most recent literature on qualia would include Block 1980; Shoemaker 1981, 1982; Davis 1982; White 1985; Armstrong and Malcolm 1984; Churchland 1985; and Conee 1985.

2. The difference between "eliminative materialism"—of which my position on qualia is an instance—and a "reductive" materialism that takes on the burden of identifying the problematic item in terms of the foundational materialistic theory is thus often best seen not so much as a doctrinal issue as a tactical issue: how might we most gracefully or effectively enlighten the confused in this instance? See my discussion of "fatigues" in the Introduction to *Brainstorms* (Dennett 1978a), and earlier, my discussion of what the enlightened ought to say about the metaphysical status of *sakes* and *voices* in *Content and Consciousness* (Dennett 1969), ch. 1.

3. The plausibility of this concession depends less on a high regard for the technology than on a proper skepticism about human powers, now documented in a fascinating study by Lehrer (1983).

4. Shoemaker (1984) seems to be moving reluctantly towards agreement with this conclusion: "So unless we can find some grounds on which we can deny the possibility of the sort of situation envisaged . . . we must apparently choose between rejecting the functionalist account of qualitative similarity and rejecting the standard conception of qualia.
 I would prefer not to have to make this choice; but

if I am forced to make it, I reject the standard conception of qualia" (p. 356).

5. Shoemaker (1982) attributes a view to Wittgenstein (acknowledging that "it is none too clear" that this is actually what Wittgenstein held) which is very close to the view I defend here. But to Shoemaker, "it would seem offhand that Wittgenstein was mistaken" (p. 360), a claim Shoemaker supports with a far from offhand thought experiment—which Shoemaker misanalyzes if the present paper is correct. (There is no good reason, contrary to Shoemaker's declaration, to believe that his subject's *experience* is systematically different from what it was before the inversion.) Smart (1959) expresses guarded and partial approval of Wittgenstein's hard line, but cannot see his way clear to as uncompromising an eliminativism as I maintain here.

6. In 1979, I read an earlier version of this paper in Oxford, with a commentary by John Foster, who defended qualia to the last breath, which was: "qualia should not be quined but fostered!" Symmetry demands, of course, the following definition for the eighth edition of *The Philosophical Lexicon*: "foster, *v.* To acclaim resolutely the existence or importance of something chimerical or insignificant."

7. This example first appeared in print in my "Reflections on Smullyan" in *The Mind's I* (Hofstadter and Dennett 1981), p. 427–28.

8. Kripke (1982) comes close, when he asks rhetorical-

ly "Do I not know, directly, and *with a fair degree of certainty* [emphasis added], that I mean plus [by the function I call "plus"]?" (p. 40) Kripke does not tell us what is implied by "a fair degree of certainty," but presumably he means by this remark to declare his allegiance to what Millikan (1984) attacks under the name of "meaning rationalism."

9. We can save the traditional claim by ignoring presumably private or subjective qualia and talking always of public tastes—such as the public taste of Maxwell House coffee that both Chase and Sanborn agree has remained constant. Individuals can be said to acquire a taste for such a public taste.

10. "I am not so wild as to deny that my sensation of red today is like my sensation of red yesterday. I only say that the similarity can *consist* only in the physiological force behind consciousness—which leads me to say, I recognize this feeling the same as the former one, and so does not consist in a community of sensation." (C. S. Peirce, *Collected Works,* vol. V, p. 172, fn. 2).

11. A heroic (and, to me, baffling) refusal to abandon intrinsicality is Wilfrid Sellars's contemplation over the years of his famous pink ice cube, which leads him to postulate a revolution in microphysics, restoring objective "absolute sensory processes" in the face of Boyle and Locke and almost everybody since them. See Sellars (1981) and my commentary (Dennett 1981).

12. Stich (1983) discusses the implications for psycho-logical theory of incommensurability problems that can arise from such differences in discrimination profiles. See esp chs. 4 and 5.

13. See Churchland 1979, esp. ch 2, for supporting observations on the variability of perceptual properties, and for novel arguments against the use of "intrinsic properties" as determiners of the meaning of perceptual predicates. See also Churchland 1985 for further arguments and observations in support of the position sketched here.

14. The first version of this paper was presented at University College London, in November 1978, and in various revisions at a dozen other universities in 1979 and 1980. It was never published, but was circulated widely as Tufts University Cognitive Science Working Paper #7, December 1979. A second version was presented at the Universities of Adelaide and Sydney in 1984, and in 1985 to psychology department colloquia at Harvard and Brown under the title "Properties of conscious experience." The second version was the basis for my presentation at the workshop on consciousness in modern science, Villa Olmo, Como, Italy, April 1985, and circulated in preprint in 1985, again under the title "Quining qualia." The present version, the fourth, is a substantial revision, thanks to the helpful comments of many peope, including Kathleen Akins, Ned Block, Alan Cowey, Sydney Shoemaker, Peter Bieri, William Lycan, Paul Churchland, Gilbert Harman and the participants at Villa Olmo.

REFERENCES

Akins, K. (1987) *Information and Organisms: Or, Why Nature Doesn't Build Epistemic Engines,* Ph.D. dissertation, Univ. of Michigan Dept of Philosophy.

Armstrong, D. and Malcolm, N. (eds) (1984) *Consciousness and Causality.* Oxford: Basil Blackwell.

Bennett, J. (1965) "Substance, reality and primary qualities," *American Philosophical Quarterly 2,* 1–17.

Berkeley, G. (1713) *Three Dialogues between Hylas and Philonous.*

Block, N. (1978) "Troubles with Functionalism," in W. Savage (ed.) *Perception and Cognition: Minnesota Studies in the Philosophy of Science, Vol. IX* Minneapolis: University of Minnesota Press.

Block, N. (1980) "Are absent qualia impossible?," *Philosophical Review* 89, 257.

Block, N. and Fodor J. (1972) "What psychological states are not," *Philosophical Review* 81, 159–81.

Chisholm, R. (1976) *Person and Object.* La Salle, Illinois: Open Court Press.

Churchland, P. M. (1979) *Scientific Realism and the Plasticity of Mind.* Cambridge, MA: Cambridge University Press.

Churchland, P. M. (1985) "Reduction, qualia and the direct inspection of brain states," *Journal of Philosophy,* LXXXII, 8–28.

Conee, E. (1985) "The possibility of absent qualia," *Philosophical Review* 94, 345–66.

Damasio, A. et al. (1980) "Central Achromatopsia: Behavioral, anatomic, and physiological aspects," *Neurology* 30, 1064–71.

Danto, A. (1963) "What we can do," *Journal of Philosophy,* LX, 435–45.

Danto, A. (1965) "Basic actions," *American Philosophical Quarterly,* 141–48.

Davis, L. (1982) "Functionalism and absent qualia," *Philosophical Studies* 41, 231–51.

Dennett, D. C. (1969) *Content and Consciousness.* London: Routledge & Kegan Paul.

Dennett, D. C. (1976) "Are dreams experiences?," *Philosophical Review* 85, 151–71. (Reprinted in Dennett 1978a.)

Dennett, D. C. (1978a) *Brainstorms.* Bradford Books/ MIT Press.

Dennett, D. C. (1978b) "Two approaches to mental images," in Dennett 1978a.

Dennett, D. C. (1978c) *The Philosophical Lexicon,* 8th edn. (http://www.blackwellpublishers.co.uk/lexicon/

Dennett, D. C. (1979) "On the absence of phenomenology," in D. F. Gustafson and B. L. Tapscott (eds) *Body, Mind, and Method* (Festschrift for Virgil Aldrich). Dordrecht: Reidel, pp. 93–114.

Dennett, D. C. (1981) "Wondering where the yellow went," *Monist* 64, 102–8.

Dennett, D. C. (1982) "How to study human consciousness empirically: Or nothing comes to mind," *Synthese* 53, 159–80.

Dennett, D. C. (1987) *The Intentional Stance.* Cambridge MA: Bradford/MIT.

Dretske, F. (1981) *Knowledge and the Flow of Information.* Cambridge MA: Bradford/MIT.

Elster, J. (1985) *Making Sense of Marx.* Cambridge, England: Cambridge University Press.

Farrell, B. A. (1950) "Experience," *Mind* 59, 170–98.

Gert, B. (1965) "Imagination and verifiability," *Philosophical Studies 16,* 44–47.

Geschwind, N. and Fusillo, M. (1966) "Color-naming defects in association with alexia," *Archives of neurology* 15, 137–46.

Goldman, A. (1970) *A Theory of Human Action.* Englewood Cliffs, NJ: Prentice Hall.

Gregory, R. (1977) *Eye and Brain,* 3rd edn. London: Weidenfeld & Nicolson.

Hofstadter, D. and Dennett, D. C. (1981) *The Mind's I: Fantasies and Reflections on Mind and Soul.* New York: Basic Books.

Kim, J. (1982) "Psychophysical supervenience," *Philosophical Studies* 41, 51–70.

Kitcher, P. (1979) "Phenomenal qualities," *American Philosophical Quarterly* 16, 123–29.

Kripke, S. (1982) *Wittgenstein on Rules and Private Language.* Cambridge, MA: Harvard University Press.

Lehrer, A. (1983) *Wine and Conversation.* Bloomington, Indiana: Univ. of Indiana Press.

Lewis, D. (1983) "Extrinsic properties," *Philosophical Studies* 44, 197–200.

Locke, J. (1690) *An Essay Concerning Human Understanding* (A. C. Fraser edition). New York: Dover, 1959.

Lycan, W. (1973) "Inverted spectrum," *Ratio* XV, 315–19.

Malcolm, N. (1956) "Dreaming and skepticism," *Philosophical Review* 64, 14–37.

Malcolm, N. (1959) *Dreaming.* London: Routledge & Kegan Paul.

Meadows, J. C. (1974) "Disturbed perception of colours associated with localized cerebral lesions," *Brain* 97, 615–32.

Millikan, R. (1984) *Language, Thought and Other Biological Categories.* Cambridge, MA: Bradford/MIT.

Nagel, T. (1974) "What is it like to be a bat?," *Philosophical Review* 83, 435–51.

Nagel, T. (1986) *The View from Nowhere.* Oxford: Oxford University Press.

Peirce, C. (1931–58) C. Hartshorne and P. Weiss (eds), *Collected Works.* Cambridge MA: Harvard University Press.

Peterson, R. T. (1947) *A Field Guide to the Birds,* Boston: Houghton Mifflin.

Putnam, H. (1965) "Brains and behavior," in J. Butler (ed.) *Analytical Philosophy* (second series). Oxford: Basil Blackwell.

Pylyshyn, Z. (1980) "Computation and cognition: Issues in the foundation of cognitive science," *Behavioral and Brain Sciences* 3, 111–32.

Pylyshyn, Z. (1984) *Computation and Cognition: Toward a Foundation for Cognitive Scicnec.* Cambridge, MA: Bradford/MIT Press.

Sellars, W. (1981) "Foundations for a metaphysics of pure process" (the Carus Lectures), *Monist,* 64, 3–90.

Shoemaker, S. (1969) "Time without change," *Journal of Philosophy* 66, 363–81.

Shoemaker, S. (1975) "Functionalism and qualia," *Philosophical Studies* 27, 291–315.

Shoemaker, S. (1981) "Absent qualia are impossible—A Reply to Block," *Philosophical Review* 90, 581–99.

Shoemaker, S. (1982) "The inverted spectrum," *Journal of Philosophy* 79, 357–81.

Shoemaker, S. (1984) "Postscript (1983)," in *Identity, Cause, and Mind.* Cambridge, England: Cambridge Univ. Press, pp. 351–57.

Smart, J. J. C. (1959) "Sensations and brain processes," *Philosophical Review* 68, 141–56. (Reprinted in Chappell 1962).

Stich, S. (1983) *From Folk Psychology to Cognitive Science: The Case against Belief.* Cambridge, MA: Bradford/MIT.

Taylor, D. M. (1966) "The incommunicability of content," *Mind* 75, 527–41.

Von der Heydt, R., Peterhans, E. and Baumgartner, G. (1984) "Illusory contours and cortical neuron response," *Science* 224, 1260–262.

Walzer, M. (1985) "What's left of Marx," *New York Review of Books,* Nov. 21, pp. 43–46.

White, S. (1985) "Professor Shoemaker and so-called 'qualia' of experience," *Philosophical Studies* 47, 369–83.

Wittgenstein, L. (1958) G. E. M. Anscombe (ed.), *Philosophical Investigations.* Oxford: Basil Blackwell.

27 | Consciousness and Its Place in Nature

David J. Chalmers

1. Introduction[1]

Consciousness fits uneasily into our conception of the natural world. On the most common conception of nature, the natural world is the physical world. But on the most common conception of consciousness, it is not easy to see how it could be part of the physical world. So it seems that to find a place for consciousness within the natural order, we must either revise our conception of consciousness, or revise our conception of nature.

In twentieth-century philosophy, this dilemma is posed most acutely in C. D. Broad's *The Mind and its Place in Nature* (Broad 1925). The phenomena of mind, for Broad, are the phenomena of consciousness. The central problem is that of locating mind with respect to the physical world. Broad's exhaustive discussion of the problem culminates in a taxonomy of seventeen different views of the mental-physical relation.[2] On Broad's taxonomy, a view might see the mental as nonexistent ("delusive"), as reducible, as emergent, or as a basic property of a substance (a "differentiating" attribute). The physical might be seen in one of the same four ways. So a four-by-four matrix of views results. (The seventeenth entry arises from Broad's division of the substance/substance view according to whether one substance or two is involved.) At the end, three views are left standing: those on which mentality is an emergent characteristic of either a physical substance or a neutral substance, where in the latter case, the physical might be either emergent or delusive.

In this paper I take my cue from Broad, approaching the problem of consciousness by a strategy of divide-and-conquer. I will not adopt Broad's categories: our understanding of the mind-body problem has advanced in the last 75 years, and it would be nice to think that we have a better understanding of the crucial issues. On my view, the most important views on the metaphysics of consciousness can be divided almost exhaustively into six classes, which I will label "type A" through "type F." Three of these (A

through C) involve broadly reductive views, seeing consciousness as a physical process that requires no expansion of a physical ontology. The other three (D through F) involve broadly nonreductive views, on which consciousness involves something irreducible in nature, and requires expansion or reconception of a physical ontology.

The discussion will be cast at an abstract level, giving an overview of the metaphysical landscape. Rather than engaging the empirical science of consciousness, or detailed philosophical theories of consciousness, I will be examining some general classes into which theories of consciousness might fall. I will not pretend to be neutral in this discussion. I think that each of the reductive views is incorrect, while each of the nonreductive views holds some promise. So the first part of this paper can be seen as an extended argument against reductive views of consciousness, while the second part can be seen as an investigation of where we go from there.

2. The Problem

The word 'consciousness' is used in many different ways. It is sometimes used for the ability to discriminate stimuli, or to report information, or to monitor internal states, or to control behavior. We can think of these phenomena as posing the "easy problems" of consciousness. These are important phenomena, and there is much that is not understood about them, but the problems of explaining them have the character of puzzles rather than mysteries. There seems to be no deep problem in principle with the idea that a physical system could be "conscious" in these senses, and there is no obvious obstacle to an eventual explanation of these phenomena in neurobiological or computational terms.

The hard problem of consciousness is the problem of experience. Human beings have subjective experience: there is something it is like to be them. We can say that a being is conscious in this sense—or is phenomenally conscious, as it is sometimes put—when there is something it is like to be that being. A mental state is conscious when there is something it is like to be in that state. Conscious states include states of perceptual experience, bodily sensation, mental imagery, emotional experience, occurrent thought, and more. There is something it is like to see a vivid green, to feel a sharp pain, to visualize the Eiffel tower, to feel a deep regret, and to think that one is late. Each of these states has a *phenomenal character*, with *phenomenal properties* (or *qualia*) characterizing what it is like to be in the state.[3]

There is no question that experience is closely associated with physical processes in systems such as brains. It seems that physical processes give rise to experience, at least in the sense that producing a physical system (such as a brain) with the right physical properties inevitably yields corresponding states of experience. But how and why do physical processes give rise to experience? Why do not these processes take place "in the dark," without any accompanying states of experience? This is the central mystery of consciousness.

What makes the easy problems easy? For these problems, the task is to explain certain behavioral or cognitive functions: that is, to explain how some causal role is played in the cognitive system, ultimately in the production of behavior. To explain the performance of such a function, one need only specify a mechanism that plays the relevant role. And there is good reason to believe that neural or computational mechanisms can play those roles.

What makes the hard problem hard? Here, the task is not to explain behavioral and cognitive functions: even once one has an explanation of all the relevant functions in the vicinity of consciousness—discrimination, integration, access, report, control—there may still remain a further question: why is the performance of these functions accompanied by experience? Because of this, the hard problem seems to be a different sort of problem, requiring a different sort of solution.

A solution to the hard problem would involve an account of the relation between physical processes and consciousness, explaining on the basis of natural principles how and why it is that physical processes are associated with states of experience. A *reductive explanation* of consciousness will explain this wholly on the basis of physical principles that do not themselves make any appeal to consciousness.[4] A *materialist* (or physicalist) solution will be a solution on which consciousness is itself seen as a physical process. A *nonmaterialist* (or nonphysicalist) solution will be a solution on which consciousness is seen as nonphysical (even if closely associated with physical processes). A *nonreductive* solution will be one on which consciousness (or principles involving consciousness) is admitted as a basic part of the explanation.

It is natural to hope that there will be a materialist solution to the hard problem and a reductive explanation of consciousness, just as there have been reductive explanations of many other phenomena in many other domains. But consciousness seems to resist materialist explanation in a way that other phenomena do not. This resistance can be encapsulated in three related arguments against materialism, summarized in what follows.

3. Arguments against Materialism

3.1. The Explanatory Argument[5]

The first argument is grounded in the difference between the easy problems and the hard problem, as characterized above: the easy problems concern the explanation of behavioral and cognitive functions, but the hard problem does not. One can argue that by the character of physical explanation, physical accounts explain *only* structure and function, where the relevant structures are spatiotemporal structures, and the relevant functions are causal roles in the production of a system's behavior. And one can argue as above that explaining structures and functions does not suffice to explain consciousness. If so, no physical account can explain consciousness.

We can call this the *explanatory argument:*

(1) Physical accounts explain at most structure and function.

(2) Explaining structure and function does not suffice to explain consciousness

———————

(3) No physical account can explain consciousness.

If this is right, then while physical accounts can solve the easy problems (which involve only explaining functions), something more is needed to solve the hard problem. It would seem that no reductive explanation of consciousness could succeed. And if we add the premise that what cannot be physically explained is not itself physical (this can be considered an additional final step of the explanatory argument), then materialism about consciousness is false, and the natural world contains more than the physical world.

Of course this sort of argument is controversial. But before examining various ways of responding, it is useful to examine two closely related arguments that also aim to establish that materialism about consciousness is false.

3.2. The Conceivability Argument[6]

According to this argument, it is conceivable that there be a system that is physically identical to a conscious being, but that lacks at least some of that being's conscious states. Such a system might be a *zombie:* a system that is physically identical to a conscious being but that lacks consciousness entirely. It might also be an *invert,* with some of the original being's experiences replaced by different experiences, or a *partial zombie,* with some experiences absent, or a combination thereof. These systems will look identical to a normal conscious being from the third-person perspective: in particular, their brain processes will be molecule-for-molecule identical with the original, and their behavior will be indistinguishable. But things will be different from the first-person point of view. What it is like to be an invert or a partial zombie will differ from what it is like to be the original being. And there is nothing it is like to be a zombie.

There is little reason to believe that zombies exist in the actual world. But many hold that they are at least conceivable: we can coherently imagine zombies, and there is no contradiction in the idea that reveals itself even on reflection. As an extension of the idea, many hold that the same goes for a *zombie world:* a universe physically identical to ours, but in which there is no consciousness. Something similar applies to inverts and other duplicates.

From the conceivability of zombies, proponents of the argument infer their *metaphysical possibility.* Zombies are probably not naturally possible: they probably cannot exist in our world, with its laws of nature. But the argument holds that zombies *could have* existed, perhaps in a very different sort of universe. For example, it is sometimes suggested that God could have created a zombie world, if he had so chosen. From here, it is inferred that consciousness must

be nonphysical. If there is a metaphysically possible universe that is physically identical to ours but that lacks consciousness, then consciousness must be a further, nonphysical component of our universe. If God could have created a zombie world, then (as Kripke puts it) after creating the physical processes in our world, he had to do more work to ensure that it contained consciousness.

We can put the argument, in its simplest form, as follows:

(1) It is conceivable that there be zombies
(2) If it is conceivable that there be zombies, it is metaphysically possible that there be zombies.
(3) If it is metaphysically possible that there be zombies, then consciousness is nonphysical.

_____

(4) Consciousness is nonphysical.

A somewhat more general and precise version of the argument appeals to P, the conjunction of all microphysical truths about the universe, and Q, an arbitrary phenomenal truth about the universe. (Here '$\wedge$' represents 'and' and '$\neg$' represents 'not'.)

(1) It is conceivable that $P \wedge \neg Q$.
(2) If it is conceivable that $P \wedge \neg Q$, it is metaphysically possible that $P \wedge \neg Q$.
(3) If it is metaphysically possible that $P \wedge \neg Q$, then materialism is false.

_____

(4) Materialism is false.

3.3. The Knowledge Argument[7]

According to the knowledge argument, there are facts about consciousness that are not deducible from physical facts. Someone could know all the physical facts, be a perfect reasoner, and still be unable to know all the facts about consciousness on that basis.

Frank Jackson's canonical version of the argument provides a vivid illustration. On this version, Mary is a neuroscientist who knows everything there is to know about the physical processes relevant to color vision. But Mary has been brought up in a black-and-white room (on an alternative version, she is colorblind[8]) and has never experienced red. Despite all her knowledge, it seems that there is something very important about color vision that Mary does not know: she does not know what it is like to see red. Even complete physical knowledge and unrestricted powers of deduction do not enable her to know this. Later, if she comes to experience red for the first time, she will learn a new fact of which she was previously ignorant: she will learn what it is like to see red.

Jackson's version of the argument can be put as follows (here the premises concern Mary's knowledge when she has not yet experienced red):

(1) Mary knows all the physical facts.
(2) Mary does not know all the facts

———

(3) The physical facts do not exhaust all the facts.

One can put the knowledge argument more generally:

(1) There are truths about consciousness that are not deducible from physical truths.
(2) If there are truths about consciousness that are not deducible from physical truths, then materialism is false.

———

(3) Materialism is false.

3.4. The Shape of the Arguments

These three sorts of argument are closely related. They all start by establishing an *epistemic gap* between the physical and phenomenal domains. Each denies a certain sort of close epistemic relation between the domains: a relation involving what we can know, or conceive, or explain. In particular, each of them denies a certain sort of *epistemic entailment* from physical truths P to the phenomenal truths Q: deducibility of Q from P, or explainability of Q in terms of P, or conceiving of Q upon reflective conceiving of P.

Perhaps the most basic sort of epistemic entailment is a priori entailment, or *implication*. On this notion, P implies Q when the material conditional $P \supset Q$ is a priori; that is, when a subject can know that if P is the case then Q is the case, with justification independent of experience. All of the three arguments above can be seen as making a case against an a priori entailment of Q by P. If a subject who knows only P cannot deduce that Q (as the knowledge argument suggests), or if one can rationally conceive of P without Q (as the conceivability argument

suggests), then it seems that P does not imply Q. The explanatory argument can be seen as turning on the claim that an implication from P to Q would require a functional analysis of consciousness, and that the concept of consciousness is not a functional concept.

After establishing an epistemic gap, these arguments proceed by inferring an ontological gap, where ontology concerns the nature of things in the world. The conceivability argument infers from conceivability to metaphysical possibility; the knowledge argument infers from failure of deducibility to difference in facts; and the explanatory argument infers from failure of physical explanation to nonphysicality. One might say that these arguments infer from a failure of epistemic entailment to a failure of ontological entailment. The paradigmatic sort of ontological entailment is *necessitation:* P necessitates Q when the material conditional $P \supset Q$ is metaphysically necessary, or when it is metaphysically impossible for P to hold without Q holding. It is widely agreed that materialism requires that P necessitates all truths (perhaps with minor qualifications). So if there are phenomenal truths Q that P does not necessitate, then materialism is false.

We might call of these arguments *epistemic arguments* against materialism. Epistemic arguments arguably descend from Descartes' arguments against materialism (although these have a slightly different form), and are given their first thorough airing in Broad's book, which contains elements of all three arguments above.[9] The general form of an epistemic argument against materialism is as follows:

(1) There is an epistemic gap between physical and phenomenal truths.
(2) If there is an epistemic gap between physical and phenomenal truths, then there is an ontological gap, and materialism is false.

———

(3) Materialism is false.

Of course this way of looking at things oversimplifies matters, and abstracts away from the differences between the arguments.[10] The same goes for the precise analysis in terms of implication and necessitation. Nevertheless, this analysis provides a useful lens through which to see what the arguments have in common, and through which to analyze various responses to the arguments.

There are roughly three ways that a materialist might resist the epistemic arguments. A type-A materialist denies that there is the relevant sort of epistemic gap. A type-B materialist accepts that there is an unclosable epistemic gap, but denies that there is an ontological gap. And a type-C materialist accepts that there is a deep epistemic gap, but holds that it will eventually be closed. In what follows, I discuss all three of these strategies.

4. Type-A Materialism

According to type-A materialism, there is no epistemic gap between physical and phenomenal truths; or at least, any apparent epistemic gap is easily closed. According to this view, it is not conceivable (at least on reflection) that there be duplicates of conscious beings that have absent or inverted conscious states. On this view, there are no phenomenal truths of which Mary is ignorant in principle from inside her black-and-white room (when she leaves the room, she gains at most an ability). And on this view, on reflection there is no "hard problem" of explaining consciousness that remains once one has solved the easy problems of explaining the various cognitive, behavioral, and environmental functions.[11]

Type-A materialism sometimes takes the form of eliminativism, holding that consciousness does not exist, and that there are no phenomenal truths. It sometimes takes the form of analytic functionalism or logical behaviorism, holding that consciousness exists, where the concept of "consciousness" is defined in wholly functional or behavioral terms (e.g., where to be conscious might be to have certain sorts of access to information, and/or certain sorts of dispositions to make verbal reports). For our purposes, the difference between these two views can be seen as terminological. Both agree that we are conscious in the sense of having the functional capacities of access, report, control, and the like; and they agree that we are not conscious in any further (nonfunctionally defined) sense. The analytic functionalist thinks that ordinary terms such as 'conscious' should be used in the first sort of sense (expressing a functional concept), while the eliminativist thinks that it should be used in the second. Beyond this terminological disagreement about the use of existing terms and concepts, the substance of the views is the same.

Some philosophers and scientists who do not explicitly embrace eliminativism, analytic functionalism, and the like are nevertheless recognizably type-A materialists. The characteristic feature of the type-A materialist is the view that on reflection there is nothing in the vicinity of consciousness that needs explaining over and above explaining the various functions: to explain these things is to explain everything in the vicinity that needs to be explained. The relevant functions may be quite subtle and complex, involving fine-grained capacities for access, self-monitoring, report, control, and their interaction, for example. They may also be taken to include all sorts of environmental relations. And the explanation of these functions will probably involve much neurobiological detail. So views that are put forward as rejecting functionalism on the grounds that it neglects biology or neglects the role of the environment may still be type-A views.

One might think that there is room in logical space for a view that denies even this sort of broadly functionalist view of consciousness, but still holds that there is no epistemic gap between physical and phenomenal truths. In practice, there appears to be little room for such a view, for reasons that I will discuss under type C, and there are few examples of such views in practice.[12] So I will take it for granted that a type-A view is one that holds that explaining the functions explains everything, and will class other views that hold that there is no unclosable epistemic gap under type C.

The obvious problem with type-A materialism is that it appears to deny the manifest. It is an uncontested truth that we have the various functional capacities of access, control, report, and the like, and these phenomena pose uncontested explananda (phenomena in need of explanation) for a science of consciousness. But in addition, it seems to be a further truth that we are conscious, and this phenomenon seems to pose a further explanandum. It is this explanandum that raises the interesting problems of consciousness. To flatly deny the further truth, or to deny without argument that there is a hard problem of consciousness over and above the easy problems, would be to make a highly counterintuitive claim that begs the important questions. This is not to say that highly counterintuitive claims are always false, but they need to be supported by extremely strong arguments. So the crucial question is: are there any compelling *arguments* for the claim that on reflection, explaining the functions explains everything?

Type-A materialists often argue by analogy. They point out that in other areas of science, we accept that explaining the various functions explains the phenomena, so we should accept the same here. In response, an opponent may well accept that in other domains, the functions are all we need to explain. In explaining life, for example, the only phenomena that present themselves as needing explanation are phenomena of adaptation, growth, metabolism, reproduction, and so on, and there is nothing else that even calls out for explanation. But the opponent holds that the case of consciousness is different and possibly unique, precisely because there is something else, phenomenal experience, that calls out for explanation. The type-A materialist must either deny even the appearance of a further explanandum, which seems to deny the obvious, or accept the apparent disanalogy and give further substantial arguments for why, contrary to appearances, only the functions need to be explained.

At this point, type-A materialists often press a different sort of analogy, holding that at various points in the past, thinkers held that there was an analogous epistemic gap for other phenomena, but that these turned out to be physically explained. For example, Dennett (1996) suggests that a vitalist might have held that there was a further "hard problem" of life over and above explaining the biological function, but that this would have been misguided.

On examining the cases, however, the analogies do not support the type-A materialist. Vitalists typically *accepted,* implicitly or explicitly, that the biological functions in question were what needed explaining. Their vitalism arose because they thought that the functions (adaptation, growth, reproduction, and so on) would not be physically explained. So this is quite different from the case of consciousness. The disanalogy is very clear in the case of Broad. Broad was a vitalist about life, holding that the functions would require a non-mechanical explanation. But at the same time, he held that in the case of life, unlike the case of consciousness, the only evidence we have for the phenomenon is behavioral, and that "being alive" means exhibiting certain sorts of behavior. Other vitalists were less explicit, but very few of them held that something more than the functions needed explaining (except consciousness itself, in some cases). If a vitalist had held this, the obvious reply would have been that there is no reason to believe in such an explanandum. There is no analogy here.[13]

So these arguments by analogy have no force for the type-A materialist. In other cases, it was always clear that structure and function exhausted the apparent explananda, apart from those tied directly to consciousness itself. So the type-A materialist needs to address the apparent further explanandum in the case of consciousness head on: either flatly denying it, or giving substantial arguments to dissolve it.

Some arguments for type-A materialists proceed indirectly, by pointing out the unsavory metaphysical or epistemological consequences of rejecting the view: e.g., that the rejection leads to dualism, or to problems involving knowledge of consciousness.[14] An opponent will either embrace the consequences or deny that they are consequences. As long as the consequences are not completely untenable, then for the type-A materialist to make progress, this sort of argument needs to be supplemented by a substantial direct argument against the further explanandum.

Such direct arguments are surprisingly hard to find. Many arguments for type-A materialism end up presupposing the conclusion at crucial points. For example, it is sometimes argued (e.g., Rey 1995) that there is no reason to postulate qualia, since they are not needed to explain behavior; but this argument presupposes that only behavior needs explaining. The opponent will hold that qualia are an explanandum in their own right. Similarly, Dennett's use of "heterophenomenology" (verbal reports) as the primary data to ground his theory of consciousness (Dennett 1991) appears to rest on the assumption that these reports are what need explaining, or that the only "seemings" that need explaining are dispositions to react and report.

One way to argue for type-A materialism is to argue that there is some intermediate X such that (i) explaining functions suffices to explain X, and (ii) explaining X suffices to explain consciousness. One possible X here is *representation:* it is often held both that conscious states are representational states, representing things in the world, and that we can explain representation in functional terms. If so, it may seem to follow that we can explain consciousness in functional terms. On examination, though, this argument appeals to an ambiguity in the notion of representation. There is a notion of *functional representation,* on which P is represented roughly when a system responds to P and/or produces behavior appropriate for P. In this sense, explaining functioning may explain representation, but explaining representation does not explain consciousness. There is also a notion of *phenomenal representation,* on which P is represented roughly when a system has a conscious experience as if P. In this sense, explaining representation may explain consciousness, but explaining functioning does not explain representation. Either way, the epistemic gap between the functional and the phenomenal remains as wide as ever. Similar sorts of equivocation can be found with other X's that might be appealed to here, such as "perception" or "information."

Perhaps the most interesting arguments for type-A materialism are those that argue that we can give a physical explanation of our *beliefs* about consciousness, such as the belief that we are conscious, the belief that consciousness is a further explanandum, and the belief that consciousness is nonphysical. From here it is argued that once we have explained the belief, we have done enough to explain, or to explain away, the phenomenon (e.g., Clark 2000, Dennett forthcoming). Here it is worth noting that this only works if the beliefs themselves are functionally analyzable; Chalmers (2002a) gives reason to deny this. But even if one accepts that beliefs are ultimately functional, this claim then reduces to the claim that explaining our dispositions to talk about consciousness (and the like) explains everything. An opponent will deny this claim: explaining the dispositions to report may remove the third-person warrant (based on observation of others) for accepting a further explanandum, but it does not remove the crucial first-person warrant (from one's own case). Still, this is a strategy that deserves extended discussion.

At a certain point, the debate between type-A materialists and their opponents usually comes down to intuition: most centrally, the intuition that consciousness (in a nonfunctionally defined sense) exists, or that there is something that needs to be explained (over and above explaining the functions). This claim does not gain its support from argument, but from a sort of observation, along with rebuttal of counterarguments. The intuition appears to be shared by the large majority of philosophers, scientists, and others; and it is so strong that to deny it, a type-A materialist needs exceptionally powerful arguments. The result is that even among materialists, type-A materialists are a distinct minority.

5. Type-B Materialism[15]

According to type-B materialism, there is an epistemic gap between the physical and phenomenal domains, but there is no ontological gap. According to this view, zombies and the like are conceivable, but they are not metaphysically possible. On this view, Mary is ignorant of some phenomenal truths from inside her room, but nevertheless these truths concern an underlying physical reality (when she leaves the room, she learns old facts in a new way). And on this view, while there is a hard problem distinct from the easy problems, it does not correspond to a distinct ontological domain.

The most common form of type-B materialism holds that phenomenal states can be *identified* with certain physical or functional states. This identity is held to be analogous in certain respects (although perhaps not in all respects) with the identity between water and H_2O, or between genes and DNA.[16] These identities are not derived through conceptual analysis, but are discovered empirically: the concept *water* is different from the concept H_2O, but they are found to refer to the same thing in nature. On the type-B view, something similar applies to consciousness: the concept of consciousness is distinct from any physical or functional concepts, but we may discover empirically that these refer to the same thing in nature. In this way, we can explain why there is an epistemic gap between the physical and phenomenal domains, while denying any ontological gap. This yields the attractive possibility that we can acknowledge the deep epistemic problems of consciousness while retaining a materialist worldview.

Although such a view is attractive, it faces immediate difficulties. These difficulties stem from the fact that the character of the epistemic gap with consciousness seems to differ from that of epistemic gaps in other domains. For a start, there do not seem to be analogs of the epistemic arguments above in the cases of water, genes, and so on. To explain genes, we merely have to explain why systems function a certain way in transmitting hereditary characteristics; to explain water, we have to explain why a substance has a certain objective structure and behavior. Given a complete physical description of the world, Mary would be able to deduce all the relevant truths about water and about genes, by deducing which systems have the appropriate structure and function. Finally, it seems that we cannot coherently conceive of a world physically identical to our own, in which there is no water, or in which there are no genes. So there is no epistemic gap between the *complete* physical truth about the world and the truth about water and genes that is analogous to the epistemic gap with consciousness.

(Except, perhaps, for epistemic gaps that derive from the epistemic gap for consciousness. For example, perhaps Mary could not deduce or explain the perceptual *appearance* of water from the physical truth about the world. But this would just be another instance of the problem we are concerned with, and so cannot help the type-B materialist.)

So it seems that there is something unique about the case of consciousness. We can put this by saying that while the identity between genes and DNA is empirical, it is not *epistemically primitive:* the identity is itself deducible from the complete physical truth about the world. By contrast, the type-B materialist must hold that the identification between consciousness and physical or functional states is epistemically primitive: the identity is not deducible from the complete physical truth. (If it were deducible, type-A materialism would be true instead.) So the identity between consciousness and a physical state will be a sort of primitive principle in one's theory of the world.

Here, one might suggest that something has gone wrong. Elsewhere, the only sort of place that one finds this sort of primitive principle is in the fundamental laws of physics. Indeed, it is often held that this sort of primitiveness—the inability to be deduced from more basic principles—is the mark of a fundamental law of nature. In effect, the type-B materialist recognizes a principle that has the epistemic status of a fundamental law, but gives it the ontological status of an identity. An opponent will hold that this move is more akin to theft than to honest toil: elsewhere, identifications are grounded in explanations, and primitive principles are acknowledged as fundamental laws.

It is natural to suggest that the same should apply here. If one acknowledges the epistemically primitive connection between physical states and consciousness as a fundamental law, it will follow that consciousness is distinct from any physical property, since fundamental laws always connect distinct properties. So the usual standard will lead to one of the nonreductive views discussed in the second half of this paper. By contrast, the type-B materialist takes an observed connection between physical and phenomenal states, unexplainable in more basic terms, and suggests that it is an identity. This suggestion is made largely in order to preserve a prior commitment to materialism. Unless there

is an independent case for primitive identities, the suggestion will seem at best ad hoc and mysterious, and at worst incoherent.

A type-B materialist might respond in various ways. First, some (e.g., Papineau 1993) suggest that identities do not *need* to be explained, so are always primitive. But we have seen that identities in other domains can at least be *deduced* from more basic truths, and so are not primitive in the relevant sense. Second, some (e.g., Block and Stalnaker 1999) suggest that even truths involving water and genes cannot be deduced from underlying physical truths. This matter is too complex to go into here (see Chalmers and Jackson 2001 for a response[17]), but one can note that the epistemic arguments outlined at the beginning suggest a very strong disanalogy between consciousness and other cases. Third, some (e.g., Loar 1990/1997) acknowledge that identities involving consciousness are unlike other identities by being epistemically primitive, but seek to explain this uniqueness by appealing to unique features of the concept of consciousness. This response is perhaps the most interesting, and I will return to it.

There is another line that a type-B materialist can take. One can first note that an *identity* between consciousness and physical states is not strictly required for a materialist position. Rather, one can plausibly hold that materialism about consciousness simply requires that physical states *necessitate* phenomenal states, in that it is metaphysically impossible for the physical states to be present while the phenomenal states are absent or different. That is, materialism requires that entailments $P \supset Q$ be necessary, where P is the complete physical truth about the world and Q is an arbitrary phenomenal truth.

At this point, a type-B materialist can naturally appeal to the work of Kripke (1980), which suggests that some truths are necessarily true without being a priori. For example, Kripke suggests that 'water is H_2O' is necessary—true in all possible worlds—but not knowable a priori. Here, a type-B materialist can suggest that $P \supset Q$ may be a Kripkean a posteriori necessity, like 'water is H_2O' (though it should be noted that Kripke himself denies this claim). If so, then we would *expect* there to be an epistemic gap, since there is no a priori entailment from P to Q, but at the same time there will be no ontological gap. In this way, Kripke's work can seem to be just what the type-B materialist needs.

Here, some of the issues that arose previously arise again. One can argue that in other domains, necessities are not epistemically primitive. The necessary connection between water and H_2O may be a posteriori, but it can itself be deduced from a complete physical description of the world (one can deduce that water is identical to H_2O, from which it follows that water is necessarily H_2O). The same applies to the other necessities that Kripke discusses. By contrast, the type-B materialist must hold that the connection between physical states and consciousness is epistemically primitive, in that it cannot be deduced from the complete physical truth about the world. Again, one can suggest that this sort of primitive necessary connection is mysterious and ad hoc, and that the connection should instead be viewed as a fundamental law of nature.

I will discuss further problems with these necessities in the next section. But here, it is worth noting that there is a sense in which any type-B materialist position gives up on reductive explanation. Even if type-B materialism is true, we cannot give consciousness the same sort of explanation that we give genes and like, in purely physical terms. Rather, our explanation will always require explanatorily primitive principles to bridge the gap from the physical to the phenomenal. The *explanatory* structure of a theory of consciousness, on such a view, will be very much unlike that of a materialist theory in other domains, and very much like the explanatory structure of the nonreductive theories described below. By labeling these principles identities or necessities rather than laws, the view may preserve the letter of materialism; but by requiring primitive bridging principles, it sacrifices much of materialism's spirit.

6. The Two-Dimensional Argument against Type-B Materialism

As discussed above, the type-B materialist holds that zombie worlds and the like are conceivable (there is no contradiction in $P \wedge \neg Q$) but are not metaphysically possible. That is, $P \supset Q$ is held to be an a posteriori necessity, akin to such a posteriori necessities as 'water is H_2O'. We can analyze this position in more depth by taking a closer look at the Kripkean cases of a posteriori necessity. This material is somewhat technical (hence the separate section) and can be skipped if necessary on a first reading.

It is often said that in Kripkean cases, conceivability does not entail possibility: it is conceivable that water is not H_2O (in that it is coherent to suppose that water is not H_2O), but it is not possible that water is not H_2O. But at the same time, it seems that there is *some* possibility in the vicinity of what one conceives. When one conceives that water is not H_2O, one conceives of a world W (the XYZ-world) in which the watery liquid in the oceans is not H_2O, but XYZ, say. There is no reason to doubt that the XYZ-world is metaphysically possible. If Kripke is correct, the XYZ-world is not correctly described as one in which water is XYZ. Nevertheless, this world is relevant to the truth of 'water is XYZ' in a slightly different way, which can be brought out as follows.

One can say that the XYZ-world could *turn out* to be actual, in that for all we know a priori, the actual world is just like the XYZ-world. And one can say that *if* the XYZ-world turns out to be actual, it will turn out that water is XYZ. Similarly: if we hypothesize that the XYZ-world is actual, we should rationally conclude on that basis that water is not H_2O. That is, there is a deep *epistemic* connection between the XYZ-world and 'water is not H_2O'. Even Kripke allows that it is *epistemically possible* that water is not H_2O (in the broad sense that this is not ruled out a priori). It seems that the epistemic possibility that the XYZ-world is actual is a specific instance of the epistemic possibility that water is not H_2O.

Here, we adopt a special attitude to a world W. We think of W as an epistemic possibility: as a way the world might actually be. When we do this, we consider W *as actual*. When we think of W as actual, it may make a given sentence S true or false. For example, when thinking of the XYZ-world as actual, it makes 'water is not H_2O' true. This is brought out in the intuitive judgment that if W turns out to be actual, it will turn out that water is not H_2O, and that the epistemic possibility that W is actual is an instance of the epistemic possibility that water is H_2O.

By contrast, one can also consider a world W *as counterfactual*. When we do this, we acknowledge that the character of the actual world is already fixed, and we think of W as a counterfactual way things might have been but are not. If Kripke is right, then if the watery stuff *had been* XYZ, XYZ would nevertheless not have been water. So when we consider the XYZ-world as counterfactual, it does not make 'water is not H_2O' true. Considered as counterfactual, we describe the XYZ-world in light of the actual-world fact that water is H_2O, and we conclude that XYZ is not water but merely watery stuff. These results do not conflict: they simply involve two different ways of considering and describing possible worlds. Kripke's claims consider *counterfactual* evaluation of worlds, whereas the claims in the previous paragraph concern the *epistemic* evaluation of worlds.

One can formalize this using two-dimensional semantics (see Chalmers [this volume, chapter 56]).[18] We can say that if W considered as actual-world makes S true, then W *verifies* S, and that if W considered as counterfactual makes S true, then W *satisfies* S. Verification involves the epistemic evaluation of worlds, whereas satisfaction involves the counterfactual evaluation of worlds. Correspondingly, we can associate S with different *intensions,* or functions from worlds to truth values. The *primary* (or epistemic) intension of *S* is a function that is true at a world W iff W verifies S, and the *secondary* (or subjunctive) intension is a function that is true at a world W if W satisfies S. For example, where S is 'water is not H_2O', and W is the XYZ-world, we can say that W verifies S but W does not satisfy S; and we can say that the primary intension of S is true at W, but the secondary intension of S is false at W.

With this in mind, one can suggest that when a statement S is conceivable—that is, when its truth cannot be ruled out a priori—then there is some world that verifies S, or equivalently, there is some world at which S's primary intension is true. This makes intuitive sense: when S is conceivable, S represents an epistemic possibility. It is natural to suggest that corresponding to these epistemic possibilities are specific worlds W, such that when these are considered *as* epistemic possibilities, they verify S. That is, W is such that intuitively, if W turns out to be actual, it would turn out that S.

This model seems to fit all of Kripke's cases. For example, Kripke holds that it is an a posteriori necessity that heat is the motion of molecules. So it is conceivable in the relevant sense that heat is not the motion of molecules. Corresponding to this conceivable scenario is a world W in which heat sensations are caused by something other than the motion of molecules. W represents an epistemic possibility: and we can say that if W turns out to be actual, it will turn out that heat is not the motion of molecules. The same goes in many other cases. The moral is that these Kripkean phenomena involve two different ways of thinking of possible worlds, with just one underlying space of worlds.

If this principle is applied to the case of type-B materialism, trouble immediately arises. As before, let P be the complete physical truth about the world, and let Q be a phenomenal truth. Let us say that S is conceivable when the truth of S is not ruled out a priori. Then one can mount an argument as follows.[19]

(1) $P \wedge \neg Q$ is conceivable
(2) If $P \wedge \neg Q$ is conceivable, then a world verifies $P \wedge \neg Q$.
(3) If a world verifies $P \wedge \neg Q$, then a world satisfies $P \wedge \neg Q$ or type-F monism is true.
(4) If a world satisfies $P \wedge \neg Q$, materialism is false.
_____
(5) Materialism is false or type-F monism is true.

The type-B materialist grants premise (1): to deny this would be to deny type-B materialism. Premise (2) is an instance of the general principle discussed above. Premise (4) can be taken as definitive of materialism. As for premise (3): in general one cannot immediately move from a world verifying S to a world satisfying S, as the case of 'water is H_2O' (and the XYZ-world) suggests. But in the case of $P \wedge \neg Q$, a little reflection on the nature of P and Q takes us in that direction, as follows.

First, Q. Here, it is plausible that if W verifies 'there is consciousness', then W satisfies 'there is consciousness', and vice versa. This corresponds to the Kripkean point that in the case of consciousness, there is no distinction analogous to that between water itself and mere watery stuff. To put it intuitively, if W verifies 'there is consciousness', it contains something that at least *feels* conscious, and if something *feels* conscious, it *is* conscious. One can hold more generally that the primary and secondary intensions of our core phenomenal concepts are the same (see Chalmers 2002a). It follows that if world W verifies $\neg Q$, W satisfies $\neg Q$. (This claim is not required for the argument to go through, but it is plausible and makes things more straightforward.)

Second, P. A type-B materialist might seek to evade the argument by arguing that while W verifies P, it does not satisfy P. On reflection, the only way this might work is as follows. If a world verifies P, it must have at least the *structure* of the actual physical world. The only reason why W might not satisfy P is that it lacks the intrinsic properties underlying this structure in the actual world. (On this view, the primary intension of a physical concept picks out whatever property plays a certain role in a given world, and the secondary intension picks out the actual intrinsic property across all worlds.) If this difference in W is responsible for the absence of consciousness in W, it follows that consciousness in the actual world is not necessitated by the structural aspects of physics, but by its underlying intrinsic nature. This is precisely the position I call type-F monism, or "panprotopsychism." Type-F monism is an interesting and important position, but it is much more radical than type-B materialism as usually conceived, and I count it as a different position. I will defer discussion of the reasoning and of the resulting position until then.

It follows that premise (3) is correct. If a world verifies P∧¬Q, then either a world satisfies P∧¬Q, or type-F monism is true. Setting aside type-F monism for now, it follows that the physical truth about our world does not necessitate the phenomenal truth, and materialism is false.

This conclusion is in effect a consequence of (i) the claim that P∧¬Q is conceivable (in the relevant sense), (ii) the claim that when S is conceivable, there is a world that verifies S, and (iii) some straightforward reasoning. A materialist might respond by denying (i), but that is simply to deny the relevant epistemic gap between the physical and the phenomenal, and so to deny type-B materialism. I think there is little promise for the type-B materialist in denying the reasoning involved in (iii). So the only hope for the type-B materialist is to deny the central thesis (ii), and to deny premise (2) above.[20]

To do this, a type-B materialist could deny the coherence of the distinction between verification and satisfaction, or accept that the distinction is coherent but deny that thesis (ii) holds even in the standard Kripkean cases, or accept that thesis (ii) holds in the standard Kripkean cases but deny that it holds in the case of consciousness. The first two options deserve exploration, but I think they are ultimately unpromising, as the distinction and the thesis appear to fit the Kripkean phenomena very well. Ultimately, I think a type-B materialist must hold that the case of consciousness is special, and that the thesis that holds elsewhere fails here.

On this view, the a posteriori necessities connecting the physical and phenomenal domains are much stronger than those in other domains, in that although they are a posteriori they are verified by all worlds. Elsewhere, I have called these unusual a posteriori necessities *strong necessities,* and have argued that there is no good reason to believe they exist. As with explanatorily primitive identities, they appear to be primitive facts postulated in an ad hoc way, largely in order to save a theory, with no support from cases elsewhere. Further, one can argue that this view leads to an underlying *modal dualism,* with independent primitive domains of logical and metaphysical possibility; and one can argue that this is unacceptable.

Perhaps the most interesting response from a type-B materialist is to acknowledge that strong necessities are unique to the case of consciousness, and to try to explain this uniqueness in terms of special features of our conceptual system. For example, Christopher Hill (1997) has argued that one can predict the epistemic gap in the case of consciousness from the fact that physical concepts and phenomenal concepts have different conceptual roles. Brian Loar (1990/1997) has appealed to the claim that phenomenal concepts are recognitional concepts that lack contingent modes of presentation. Joseph Levine (2000) has argued that phenomenal concepts have nonascriptive modes of presentation. In response, I have argued (Chalmers 1999) that these responses do not work, and that there are systematic reasons why they cannot work.[21] But it is likely that further attempts in this direction will be forthcoming. This remains one of the key areas of debate on the metaphysics of consciousness.

Overall, my own view is that there is little reason to think that explanatorily primitive identities or strong necessities exist. There is no good *independent* reason to believe in them: the best reason to postulate them is to save materialism, but in the context of a debate over whether materialism is true this reasoning is uncompelling, especially if there are viable alternatives. Nevertheless, further investigation into the key issues underlying this debate is likely to be philosophically fruitful.

7. Type-C Materialism

According to type-C materialism, there is a deep epistemic gap between the physical and phenomenal domains, but it is closable in principle. On this view, zombies and the like are conceivable for us now, but they will not be conceivable in the limit. On this view, it currently seems that Mary lacks information about the phenomenal, but in the limit there would be no information that she lacks. And on this view, while we cannot see now how to solve the hard problem in physical terms, the problem is solvable in principle.

This view is initially very attractive. It seems to acknowledge the deep explanatory gap with which we seem to be faced, while at the same time allowing that the apparent gap may be due to our own limitations. There are different versions of the view. Nagel (1974) has suggested that just as the pre-Socratics could not have understood how matter could be energy, we cannot understand how consciousness could be physical, but a conceptual revolution might allow the relevant understanding. Churchland (1997) suggests that even if we cannot now imagine how consciousness could be a physical process, that is simply a psychological limitation on our part that further progress in science will overcome. Van Gulick (1993) suggests that conceivability arguments are question-begging, since once we have a good explanation of consciousness, zombies and the like will no longer be conceivable. McGinn (1989) has suggested that the problem may be unsolvable by humans due to deep limitations in our cognitive abilities, but that it nevertheless has a solution in principle.

One way to put the view is as follows. Zombies and the like are *prima facie* conceivable (for us now, with our current cognitive processes), but they are not *ideally* conceivable (under idealized rational reflection). Or we could say: phenomenal truths are deducible in principle from physical truths, but the deducibility is akin to that of a complex truth of mathematics: it is accessible in principle (perhaps accessible a priori), but is not accessible to us now, perhaps because the reasoning required is currently beyond us, or perhaps because we do not currently grasp all the required physical truths. If this is so, then there will appear to us that there is a gap between physical processes and consciousness, but there will be no gap in nature.

Despite its appeal, I think that the type-C view is inherently unstable. Upon examination, it turns out either to be untenable, or to collapse into one of the other views on the table. In particular, it seems that the view must collapse into a version of type-A materialism, type-B materialism, type-D dualism, or type-F monism, and so is not ultimately a distinct option.

One way to hold that the epistemic gap might be closed in the limit is to hold that in the limit, we will see that explaining the functions explains everything, and that there is no further explanandum. It is at least coherent to hold that we currently suffer from some sort of conceptual confusion or unclarity that leads us to believe that there is a further explanandum, and that this situation could be cleared up by better reasoning. I will count this position as a version of type-A materialism, not type-C materialism: it is obviously closely related to standard type-A materialism (the main difference is whether we have yet had the relevant insight), and the same issues arise. Like standard type-A materialism, this view ultimately stands or falls with the strength of (actual and potential) first-order arguments that dissolve any apparent further explanandum.

Once type-A materialism is set aside, the potential options for closing the epistemic gap are highly constrained. These constraints are grounded in the nature of physical concepts, and in the nature of the concept of consciousness. The basic problem has already been mentioned. First: Physical descriptions of the world characterize the world in terms of structure and dynamics. Second: From truths about structure and dynamics, one can deduce only further truths about structure and dynamics. And third: Truths about consciousness are not truths about structure and dynamics. But we can take these steps one at a time.

First: A microphysical description of the world specifies a distribution of particles, fields, and waves in space and time. These basic systems are characterized by their spatiotemporal properties, and properties such as mass, charge, and quantum wavefunction state. These latter properties are ultimately defined in terms of spaces of states that have a certain abstract structure (e.g., the space of continuously varying real quantities, or of Hilbert space states), such that the states play a certain causal role with respect to other states. We can subsume spatiotemporal descriptions and descriptions in terms of properties in these formal spaces under the rubric of *structural* descriptions. The state of these systems can change over time in accord with dynamic principles defined over the relevant properties. The result is a description of the world in terms of its underlying spatiotemporal and formal structure, and dynamic evolution over this structure.

Some type-C materialists hold we do not yet

have a complete physics, so we cannot know what such a physics might explain. But here we do not need to have a complete physics: we simply need the claim that physical descriptions are in terms of structure and dynamics. This point is general across physical theories. Such novel theories as relativity, quantum mechanics, and the like may introduce new structures, and new dynamics over those structures, but the general point (and the gap with consciousness) remains.

A type-C materialist might hold that there could be new physical theories that go beyond structure and dynamics. But given the character of physical explanation, it is unclear what sort of theory this could be. Novel physical properties are postulated for their potential in explaining existing physical phenomena, themselves characterized in terms of structure and dynamics, and it seems that structure and dynamics always suffices here. One possibility is that instead of postulating novel properties, physics might end up appealing to consciousness itself, in the way that some theorists hold that quantum mechanics does. This possibility cannot be excluded, but it leads to a view on which consciousness is itself irreducible, and is therefore to be classed in a nonreductive category (type D or type F).

There is one appeal to a "complete physics" that should be taken seriously. This is the idea that current physics characterizes its underlying properties (such as mass and charge) in terms of abstract structures and relations, but it leaves open their intrinsic natures. On this view, a complete physical description of the world must also characterize the intrinsic properties that ground these structures and relations; and once such intrinsic properties are invoked, physics will go beyond structure and dynamics, in such a way that truths about consciousness may be entailed. The relevant intrinsic properties are unknown to us, but they are knowable in principle. This is an important position, but it is precisely the position discussed under type F, so I defer discussion of it until then.

Second: What can be inferred from this sort of description in terms of structure and dynamics? A low-level microphysical description can entail all sorts of surprising and interesting macroscopic properties, as with the emergence of chemistry from physics, of biology from chemistry, or more generally of complex emergent behaviors in complex systems theory. But in all these cases, the complex properties that are entailed are nevertheless structural and dynamic: they describe complex spatiotemporal structures and complex dynamic patterns of behavior over those structures. So these cases support the general principle that from structure and dynamics, one can infer only structure and dynamics.

A type-C materialist might suggest there are some truths that are not themselves structural-dynamical that are nevertheless implied by a structural-dynamical description. It might be argued, perhaps, that truths about *representation* or *belief* have this character. But as we saw earlier, it seems clear that any sense in which these truths are implied by a structural-dynamic description involves a tacitly functional sense of representation or of belief. This is what we would expect: if claims involving these can be seen (on conceptual grounds) to be true *in virtue* of a structural-dynamic descriptions holding, the notions involved must themselves be structural-dynamic, at some level.

One might hold that there is some intermediate notion X, such that truths about X hold in virtue of structural-dynamic descriptions, and truths about consciousness hold in virtue of X. But as in the case of type-A materialism, either X is functionally analyzable (in the broad sense), in which case the second step fails, or X is not functionally analyzable, in which case the first step fails. This is brought out clearly in the case of representation: for the notion of functional representation, the first step fails, and for the notion of phenomenal representation, the second step fails. So this sort of strategy can only work by equivocation.

Third: Does explaining or deducing complex structure and dynamics suffice to explain or deduce consciousness? It seems clearly not, for the usual reasons. Mary could know from her black-and-white room all about the spatiotemporal structure and dynamics of the world at all levels, but this will not tell her what it is like to see red. For any complex macroscopic structural or dynamic description of a system, one can conceive of that description being instantiated without consciousness. And explaining structure and dynamics of a human system is only to solve the easy problems, while leaving the hard problems untouched. To resist this last step, an opponent would have to hold that explaining structure and dynamics *thereby* suffices to explain consciousness. The only remotely tenable way to do this would be to embrace type-A materialism, which we have set aside.

A type-C materialist might suggest that instead of leaning on dynamics (as a type-A materialist does), one could lean on structure. Here, spatiotemporal structure seems very unpromising: to explain a system's size, shape, position, motion, and so on is clearly not to explain consciousness. A final possibility is leaning on the structure present in conscious states themselves. Conscious states have structure: there is both internal structure within a single complex conscious state, and there are patterns of similarities and differences between conscious states. But this structure is a distinctively *phenomenal* structure, quite different in kind from the spatiotemporal and formal structure present in physics. The structure of a complex phenomenal state is not spatiotemporal structure (although it may involve the representation of spatiotemporal structure), and the similarities and differences between phenomenal states are not formal similarities and differences, but differences between specific phenomenal characters. This is reflected in the fact that one can conceive of any spatiotemporal structure and formal structure without any associated phenomenal structure; one can know about the first without knowing about the second; and so on. So the epistemic gap is as wide as ever.

The basic problem with any type-C materialist strategy is that epistemic implication from A to B requires some sort of *conceptual hook* by virtue of which the condition described in A can satisfy the conceptual requirements for the truth of B. When a physical account implies truths about life, for example, it does so in virtue of implying information about the macroscopic functioning of physical systems, of the sort required for life: here, broadly functional notions provide the conceptual hook. But in the case of consciousness, no such conceptual hook is available, given the structural-dynamic character of physical concepts, and the quite different character of the concept of consciousness.

Ultimately, it seems that any type-C strategy is doomed for familiar reasons. Once we accept that the concept of consciousness is not itself a functional concept, and that physical descriptions of the world are structural-dynamic descriptions, there is simply no conceptual room for it to be implied by a physical description. So the only room left is to hold that consciousness is a broadly functional concept after all (accepting type-A materialism), hold that there is more in physics than structure and dynamics (accepting type-D dualism or type-F monism), or holding that the truth of material-

ism does not require an implication from physics to consciousness (accepting type-B materialism).[22] So in the end, there is no separate space for the type-C materialist.

8. Interlude

Are there any other options for the materialist? One further option is to reject the distinctions on which this taxonomy rests. For example, some philosophers, especially followers of Quine (1951), reject any distinction between conceptual truth and empirical truth, or between the a priori and the a posteriori, or between the contingent and the necessary. One who is sufficiently Quinean might therefore reject the distinction between type-A and type-B materialism, holding that talk of epistemic implication and/or modal entailment is ungrounded, but that materialism is true nevertheless. We might call such a view type-Q materialism. Still, even on this view, similar issues arise. Some Quineans hold that explaining the functions explain everything (Dennett may be an example); if so, all the problems of type-A materialism arise. Others hold that we can postulate identities between physical states and conscious states in virtue of the strong isomorphic connections between them in nature (Paul Churchland may be an example); if so, the problems of type-B materialism arise. Others may appeal to novel future sorts of explanation; if so, the problems of type-C materialism arise. So the Quinean approach cannot avoid the relevant problems.

Leaving this sort of view aside, it looks like the only remotely viable options for the materialist are type-A materialism and type-B materialism. I think that other views are either ultimately unstable, or collapse into one of these (or the three remaining options).[23] It seems to me that the costs of these views—denying the manifest explanandum in the first case, and embracing primitive identities or strong necessities in the second case—suggest very strongly that they are to be avoided unless there are no viable alternatives.

So the residual question is whether there are viable alternatives. If consciousness is not necessitated by physical truths, then it must involve something ontologically novel in the world: to use Kripke's metaphor, after fixing all the physical truths, God had to do more work to fix all the truths about consciousness. That is, there must be ontologically fundamental features of the world over and above the features characterized by physical theory. We are used to the idea that some features of the world are fundamental: in physics, features such as spacetime, mass, and charge, are taken as fundamental and not further explained. If the arguments against materialism are correct, these features from physics do not exhaust the fundamental features of the world: we need to expand our catalog of the world's basic features.

There are two possibilities here. First, it could be that consciousness is itself a fundamental feature of the world, like spacetime and mass. In this case, we can say that phenomenal properties are fundamental. Second, it could be that consciousness is not itself fundamental, but is necessitated by some more primitive fundamental feature X that is not itself necessitated by physics. In this case, we might call X a *protophenomenal* property, and we can say that protophenomenal properties are fundamental. I will typically put things in terms of the first possibility for ease of discussion, but the discussion that follows applies equally to the second. Either way, consciousness involves something novel and fundamental in the world.

The question then arises: how do these novel fundamental properties relate to the already acknowledged fundamental properties of the world, namely those invoked in microphysics? In general, where there are fundamental properties, there are fundamental laws. So we can expect that there will be some sort of fundamental principles—psychophysical laws—connecting physical and phenomenal properties. Like the fundamental laws of relativity or quantum mechanics, these psychophysical laws will not be deducible from more basic principles, but instead will be taken as primitive.

But what is the character of these laws? An immediate worry is that the microphysical aspects of the world are often held to be causally closed, in that every microphysical state has a microphysical sufficient cause. How are fundamental phenomenal properties to be integrated with this causally closed network?

There seem to be three main options for the nonreductionist here. First, one could deny the causal closure of the microphysical, holding that there are causal gaps in microphysical dynamics that are filled by a causal role for distinct phenomenal properties: this is type-D dualism. Second, one could accept the causal closure of the microphysical and hold that phenomenal properties play no causal role with respect to the

physical network: this is type-E dualism. Third, one could accept that the microphysical network is causally closed, but hold that phenomenal properties are nevertheless integrated with it and play a causal role, by virtue of constituting the intrinsic nature of the physical: this is type-F monism.

In what follows, I will discuss each of these views. The discussion is necessarily speculative in certain respects, and I do not claim to establish that any one of the views is true or completely unproblematic. But I do aim to suggest that none of them has obvious fatal flaws, and that each deserves further investigation.

9. Type-D Dualism

Type-D dualism holds that microphysics is not causally closed, and that phenomenal properties play a causal role in affecting the physical world.[24] On this view, usually known as *interactionism,* physical states will cause phenomenal states, and phenomenal states cause physical states. The corresponding psychophysical laws will run in both directions. On this view, the evolution of microphysical states will not be determined by physical principles alone. Psychophysical principles specifying the effect of phenomenal states on physical states will also play an irreducible role.

The most familiar version of this sort of view is Descartes' substance dualism (hence D for Descartes), on which there are separate interacting mental and physical substances or entities. But this sort of view is also compatible with a property dualism, on which there is just one sort of substance or entity with both physical and phenomenal fundamental properties, such that the phenomenal properties play an irreducible role in affecting the physical properties. In particular, the view is compatible with an "emergentist" view such as Broad's, on which phenomenal properties are ontologically novel properties of physical systems (not deducible from microphysical properties alone), and have novel effects on microphysical properties (not deducible from microphysical principles alone). Such a view would involve basic principles of "downward" causation of the mental on the microphysical (hence also D for downward causation).

It is sometimes objected that distinct physical and mental states could not interact, since there is no causal nexus between them. But one lesson from Hume and from modern science is that the same goes for any fundamental causal interactions, including those found in physics. Newtonian science reveals no causal nexus by which gravitation works, for example; rather, the relevant laws are simply fundamental. The same goes for basic laws in other physical theories. And the same, presumably, applies to fundamental psychophysical laws: there is no need for a causal nexus distinct from the physical and mental properties themselves.

By far the most influential objection to interactionism is that it is incompatible with physics. It is widely held that science tells us that the microphysical realm is causally closed, so that there is no room for mental states to have any effects. An interactionist might respond in various ways. For example, it could be suggested that although no experimental studies have revealed these effects, none have ruled them out. It might further be suggested that physical theory allows any number of basic *forces* (four as things stand, but there is always room for more), and that an extra force associated with a mental field would be a reasonable extension of existing physical theory. These suggestions would invoke significant revisions to physical theory, so are not to be made lightly; but one could argue that nothing rules them out.

By far the strongest response to this objection is to suggest that far from ruling out interactionism, contemporary physics is positively encouraging to the possibility. On the standard formulation of quantum mechanics, the state of the world is described by a wave function, according to which physical entities are often in a superposed state (e.g., in a superposition of two different positions), even though superpositions are never directly observed. On the standard dynamics, the wave function can evolve in two ways: linear evolution by the Schrödinger equation (which tends to produce superposed states), and nonlinear *collapses* from superposed states into nonsuperposed states. Schrödinger evolution is deterministic, but collapse is nondeterministic. Schrödinger evolution is constantly ongoing, but on the standard formulation, collapses occur only occasionally, on measurement.

The collapse dynamics leaves a door wide open for an interactionist interpretation. Any physical nondeterminism might be held to leave room for nonphysical effects, but the principles of collapse do much more than that. Collapse is supposed to occur on measurement. There is no

widely agreed definition of what a measurement is, but there is one sort of event that everyone agrees is a measurement: observation by a conscious observer. Further, it seems that no purely physical criterion for a measurement can work, since purely physical systems are governed by the linear Schrödinger dynamics. As such, it is natural to suggest that a measurement is precisely a conscious observation, and that this conscious observation causes a collapse.

The claim should not be too strong: quantum mechanics does not force this interpretation of the situation onto us, and there are alternative interpretations of quantum mechanics on which there are no collapses, or on which measurement has no special role in collapse.[25] Nevertheless, quantum mechanics appears to be quite *compatible* with such an interpretation. In fact, one might argue that if one was to design elegant laws of physics that allow a role for the conscious mind, one could not do much better than the bipartite dynamics of standard quantum mechanics: one principle governing deterministic evolution in normal cases, and one principle governing nondeterministic evolution in special situations that have a prima facie link to the mental.

Of course such an interpretation of quantum mechanics is controversial. Many physicists reject it precisely because it is dualistic, giving a fundamental role to consciousness. This rejection is not surprising, but it carries no force when we have independent reason to hold that consciousness may be fundamental. There is some irony in the fact that philosophers reject interactionism on largely physical grounds[26] (it is incompatible with physical theory), while physicists reject an interactionist interpretation of quantum mechanics on largely philosophical grounds (it is dualistic). Taken conjointly, these reasons carry little force, especially in light of the arguments against materialism elsewhere in this paper.

This sort of interpretation needs to be formulated in detail to be assessed.[27] I think the most promising version of such an interpretation allows conscious states to be correlated with the total quantum state of a system, with the extra constraint that conscious states (unlike physical states) can never be superposed. In a conscious physical system such as a brain, the physical and phenomenal states of the system will be correlated in a (nonsuperposed) quantum state. Upon observation of a superposed external system, Schrödinger evolution at the moment of observation would cause the observed system to become correlated with the brain, yielding a resulting superposition of brain states and so (by psychophysical correlation) a superposition of conscious states. But such a superposition cannot occur, so one of the potential resulting conscious states is somehow selected (presumably by a nondeterministic dynamic principle at the phenomenal level). The result is that (by psychophysical correlation) a definite brain state and a definite state of the observed object are also selected. The same might apply to the connection between consciousness and non-conscious processes in the brain: when superposed non-conscious processes threaten to affect consciousness, there will be some sort of selection. In this way, there is a causal role for consciousness in the physical world.

(Interestingly, such a theory may be empirically testable. In quantum mechanics, collapse theories yield predictions slightly different from no-collapse theories, and different hypotheses about the location of collapse yield predictions that differ from each other, although the differences are extremely subtle and are currently impossible to measure. If the relevant experiments can one day be performed, some outcomes would give us strong reason to accept a collapse theory, and might in turn give us grounds to accept a role for consciousness. As a bonus, this could even yield an empirical criterion for the presence of consciousness.)

There are any number of further questions concerning the precise formulation of such a view, its compatibility with physical theory more generally (e.g., relativity and quantum field theory), and its philosophical tenability (e.g., does this view yield the sort of causal role that we are inclined to think consciousness must have?). But at the very least, it cannot be said that physical theory immediately rules out the possibility of an interactionist theory. Those who make this claim often raise their eyebrows when a specific theory such as quantum mechanics is mentioned; but this is quite clearly an inconsistent set of attitudes. If physics is supposed to rule out interactionism, then careful attention to the detail of physical theory is required.

All this suggests that there is at least room for a viable interactionism to be explored, and that the most common objection to interactionism has little force. Of course it does not entail that interactionism is true. There is much that is attractive about the view of the physical world as causally closed, and there is little direct evi-

dence from cognitive science of the hypothesis that behavior cannot be wholly explained in terms of physical causes. Still, if we have independent reason to think that consciousness is irreducible, and if we wish to retain the intuitive view that consciousness plays a causal role, then this is a view to be taken very seriously.

10. Type-E Dualism

Type-E dualism holds that phenomenal properties are ontologically distinct from physical properties, and that the phenomenal has no effect on the physical.[28] This is the view usually known as *epiphenomenalism* (hence type-E): physical states cause phenomenal states, but not vice versa. On this view, psychophysical laws run in one direction only, from physical to phenomenal. The view is naturally combined with the view that the physical realm is causally closed. This further claim is not essential to type-E dualism, but it provides much of the motivation for the view.

As with type-D dualism, type-E dualism is compatible with a substance dualism with distinct physical and mental substances or entities, and is also compatible with a property dualism with one sort of substance or entity and two sorts of properties. Again, it is compatible with an emergentism such as Broad's, on which mental properties are ontologically novel emergent properties of an underlying entity, but in this case although there are emergent qualities, there is no emergent downward causation.

Type-E dualism is usually put forward as respecting both consciousness and science: it simultaneously accommodates the anti-materialist arguments about consciousness and the causal closure of the physical. At the same time, type-E dualism is frequently rejected as deeply counterintuitive. If type-E dualism is correct, then phenomenal states have no effect on our actions, physically construed. For example, a sensation of pain will play no causal role in my hand's moving away from a flame; my experience of decision will play no causal role in my moving to a new country; and a sensation of red will play no causal role in my producing the utterance 'I am experiencing red now.' These consequences are often held to be obviously false, or at least unacceptable.

Still, the type-E dualist can reply that there is no direct *evidence* that contradicts their view. Our evidence reveals only regular connections between phenomenal states and actions, so that certain sorts of experiences are typically followed by certain sorts of actions. Being exposed to this sort of constant conjunction produces a strong *belief* in a causal connection (as Hume pointed out in another context); but it is nevertheless compatible with the absence of a causal connection. Indeed, it seems that if epiphenomenalism *were* true, we would have exactly the same evidence, and be led to believe that consciousness has a causal role for much the same reasons. So if epiphenomenalism is otherwise coherent and acceptable, it seems that these considerations do not provide strong reasons to reject it.[29]

Another objection holds that if consciousness is epiphenomenal, it could not have evolved by natural selection. The type-E dualist has a straightforward reply, however. On the type-E view, there are fundamental psychophysical laws associating physical and phenomenal properties. If evolution selects appropriate physical properties (perhaps involving physical or informational configurations in the brain), then the psychophysical laws will ensure that phenomenal properties are instantiated, too. If the laws have the right form, one can even expect that as more complex physical systems are selected, more complex states of consciousness will evolve. In this way, physical evolution will carry the evolution of consciousness along with it as a sort of byproduct.

Perhaps the most interesting objections to epiphenomenalism focus on the relation between consciousness and representations of consciousness. It is certainly at least strange to suggest that consciousness plays no causal role in my utterances of 'I am conscious'. Some have suggested more strongly that this rules out any *knowledge* of consciousness. It is often held that if a belief about X is to qualify as knowledge, the belief must be caused in some fashion by X. But if consciousness does not effect physical states, and if beliefs are physically constituted, then consciousness cannot cause beliefs. And even if beliefs are not physically constituted, it is not clear how epiphenomenalism can accommodate a causal connection between consciousness and belief.

In response, an epiphenomenalist can deny that knowledge always requires a causal connection. One can argue on independent grounds that there is a stronger connection between consciousness and beliefs about consciousness: consciousness plays a role in *constituting* phe-nomenal concepts and phenomenal beliefs. A red experience plays a role in constituting a belief that one is having a red experience, for example. If so, there is no causal distance between the experience and the belief. And one can argue that this immediate connection to experience and belief allows for the belief to be justified. If this is right, then epiphenomenalism poses no obstacle to knowledge of consciousness.

A related objection holds that my zombie twin would produce the same reports (e.g., 'I am conscious'), caused by the same mechanisms, and that his reports are unjustified; if so, my own reports are unjustified. In response, one can hold that the true bearers of justification are beliefs, and that my zombie twin and I have *different* beliefs, involving different concepts, because of the role that consciousness plays in constituting my concepts but not the zombie's. Further, the fact that we produce isomorphic reports implies that a third-person observer might not be any more justified in believing that I am conscious than that the zombie is conscious, but it does not imply a difference in first-person justification. The first-person justification for my belief that I am conscious is not grounded in any way in my reports but rather in my experiences themselves, experiences that the zombie lacks.

I think that there is no knockdown objection to epiphenomenalism here. Still, it must be acknowledged that the situation is at least odd and counterintuitive. The oddness of epiphenomenalism is exacerbated by the fact that the relationship between consciousness and reports about consciousness seems to be something of a lucky coincidence, on the epiphenomenalist view. After all, if psychophysical laws are independent of physical evolution, then there will be possible worlds where physical evolution is the same as ours but the psychophysical laws are very different, so that there is a radical mismatch between reports and experiences. It seems lucky that we are in a world whose psychophysical laws match them up so well. In response, an epiphenomenalist might try to make the case that these laws are somehow the most "natural" and are to be expected; but there is at least a significant burden of proof here.

Overall, I think that epiphenomenalism is a coherent view without fatal problems. At the same time, it is an inelegant view, producing a fragmented picture of nature, on which physical and phenomenal properties are only very weakly integrated in the natural world. And of course it is a counterintuitive view that many people find difficult to accept. Inelegance and counter-intuitiveness are better than incoherence; so if good arguments force us to epiphenomenalism as the most coherent view, then we should take it seriously. But at the same time, we have good reason to examine other views very carefully.

11. Type-F Monism

Type-F monism is the view that consciousness is constituted by the intrinsic properties of fundamental physical entities: that is, by the categorical bases of fundamental physical dispositions.[30] On this view, phenomenal or protophenomenal properties are located at the fundamental level of physical reality, and in a certain sense, underlie physical reality itself.

This view takes its cue from Bertrand Russell's discussion of physics in *The Analysis of Matter*. Russell pointed out that physics characterizes physical entities and properties by their relations to one another and to us. For example, a quark is characterized by its relations to other physical entities, and a property such as mass is characterized by an associated dispositional role, such as the tendency to resist acceleration. At the same time, physics says nothing about the intrinsic nature of these entities and properties. Where we have relations and dispositions, we expect some underlying intrinsic properties that ground the dispositions, characterizing the entities that stand in these relations.[31] But physics is silent about the intrinsic nature of a quark, or about the intrinsic properties that play the role associated with mass. So this is one metaphysical problem: what are the intrinsic properties of fundamental physical systems?

At the same time, there is another metaphysical problem: how can phenomenal properties be integrated with the physical world? Phenomenal properties seem to be intrinsic properties that are hard to fit in with the structural/dynamic character of physical theory; and arguably, they are the only intrinsic properties that we have direct knowledge of. Russell's insight was that we might solve both these problems at once. Perhaps the intrinsic properties of the physical world are themselves phenomenal properties. Or perhaps the intrinsic properties of the physical world are not phenomenal properties, but nevertheless constitute phenomenal properties: that is, perhaps they are protophenomenal properties. If so, then consciousness and physical reality are deeply intertwined.

This view holds the promise of integrating phenomenal and physical properties very tightly in the natural world. Here, nature consists of entities with intrinsic (proto)phenomenal qualities standing in causal relations within a spacetime manifold. Physics as we know it emerges from the relations between these entities, whereas consciousness as we know it emerges from their intrinsic nature. As a bonus, this view is perfectly compatible with the causal closure of the microphysical, and indeed with existing physical laws. The view can retain the *structure* of physical theory as it already exists; it simply supplements this structure with an intrinsic nature. And the view acknowledges a clear causal role for consciousness in the physical world: (proto)phenomenal properties serve as the ultimate categorical basis of all physical causation.

This view has elements in common with both materialism and dualism. From one perspective, it can be seen as a sort of materialism. If one holds that physical terms refer not to dispositional properties but the underlying intrinsic properties, then the protophenomenal properties can be seen as physical properties, thus preserving a sort of materialism. From another perspective, it can be seen as a sort of dualism. The view acknowledges phenomenal or protophenomenal properties as ontologically fundamental, and it retains an underlying duality between structural-dispositional properties (those directly characterized in physical theory) and intrinsic protophenomenal properties (those responsible for consciousness). One might suggest that while the view arguably fits the letter of materialism, it shares the spirit of antimaterialism.

In its protophenomenal form, the view can be seen as a sort of neutral monism: there are underlying neutral properties X (the protophenomenal properties), such that the X properties are simultaneously responsible for constituting the physical domain (by their relations) and the phenomenal domain (by their intrinsic nature). In its phenomenal form, the view can be seen as a sort of idealism, such that mental properties constitute physical properties, although these need not be mental properties in the mind of an observer, and they may need to be supplemented by causal and spatiotemporal properties in addition. One could also characterize this form of the view as a sort of panpsychism, with phenomenal properties ubiquitous at the fundamental level. One could give the view in its most general form the name *panprotopsychism*, with either protophenomenal or phenomenal properties underlying all of physical reality.

A type-F monist may have one of a number of attitudes to the zombie argument against materialism. Some type-F monists may hold that a complete physical description must be expanded to include an intrinsic description, and may consequently deny that zombies are conceivable. (We think we are conceiving of a physically identical system only because we overlook intrinsic properties.) Others could maintain that existing physical concepts refer via dispositions to those intrinsic properties that ground the dispositions. If so, these concepts have different primary and secondary intensions, and a type-F monist could correspondingly accept conceivability but deny possibility: we misdescribe the conceived world as physically identical to ours, when in fact it is just structurally identical.[32] Finally, a type-F monist might hold that physical concepts refer to dispositional properties, so that zombies are both conceivable and possible, and the intrinsic properties are not physical properties. The differences between these three attitudes seem to be ultimately terminological rather than substantive.

As for the knowledge argument, a type-F monist might insist that for Mary to have complete physical knowledge, she would have to have a description of the world involving concepts that directly characterize the intrinsic properties; if she had this (as opposed to her impoverished description involving dispositional concepts), she might thereby be in a position to know what it is like to see red. Regarding the explanatory argument, a type-F monist might hold that physical accounts involving intrinsic properties can explain more than structure and function. Alternatively, a type-F monist who sticks to dispositional physical concepts will make responses analogous to one of the other two responses above.

The type-F view is admittedly speculative, and it can sound strange at first hearing. Many find it extremely counterintuitive to suppose that fundamental physical systems have phenomenal properties: e.g., that there is something it is like to be an electron. The protophenomenal version of the view rejects this claim, but retains something of its strangeness: it seems that any properties responsible for constituting consciousness must be strange and unusual properties, of a sort that we might not expect to find in microphysical reality. Still, it is not clear that this strangeness yields any strong objections.

Like epiphenomenalism, the view appears to be compatible with all our evidence, and there is no direct evidence against it. One can argue that if the view were true, things would appear to us just as they in fact appear. And we have learned from modern physics that the world is a strange place: we cannot expect it to obey all the dictates of common sense.

One might also object that we do not have any conception of what protophenomenal properties might be like, or of how they could constitute phenomenal properties. This is true, but one could suggest that this is merely a product of our ignorance. In the case of familiar physical properties, there were principled reasons (based on the character of physical concepts) for denying a constitutive connection to phenomenal properties. Here, there are no such principled reasons. At most, there is ignorance of a connection. Of course it would be very desirable to form a positive conception of protophenomenal properties. Perhaps we can do this indirectly, by some sort of theoretical inference from the character of phenomenal properties to their underlying constituents; or perhaps knowledge of the nature of protophenomenal properties will remain beyond us. Either way, this is no reason to reject the truth of the view.[33]

There is one sort of principled problem in the vicinity, pointed out by James (1890). Our phenomenology has a rich and specific structure: it is unified, bounded, differentiated into many different aspects, but with an underlying homogeneity to many of the aspects, and appears to have a single subject of experience. It is not easy to see how a distribution of a large number of individual microphysical systems, each with their own protophenomenal properties, could somehow add up to this rich and specific structure. Should one not expect something more like a disunified, jagged collection of phenomenal spikes?

This is a version of the *combination problem* for panpsychism (Seager, 1995), or what Stoljar (2001) calls the *structural mismatch* problem for the Russellian view (see also Foster 1991, pp. 119–30). To answer it, it seems that we need a much better understanding of the *compositional* principles of phenomenology: that is, the principles by which phenomenal properties can be composed or constituted from underlying phenomenal properties, or protophenomenal properties. We have a good understanding of the principles of physical composition, but no real understanding of the principles of phenomenal composition. This is an area that deserves much close attention: I think it is easily the most serious problem for the type-F monist view. At this point, it is an open question whether or not the problem can be solved.

Some type-F monists appear to hold that they can avoid the combination problem by holding that phenomenal properties are the intrinsic properties of *high-level* physical dispositions (e.g., those involved in neural states), and need not be constituted by the intrinsic properties of microphysical states (hence they may also deny panprotopsychism). But this seems to be untenable: if the low-level network is causally closed and the high-level intrinsic properties are not constituted by low-level intrinsic properties, the high-level intrinsic properties will be epiphenomenal all over again, for familiar reasons. The only way to embrace this position would seem to be in combination with a denial of microphysical causal closure, holding that there are fundamental dispositions above the microphysical level, which have phenomenal properties as their grounds. But such a view would be indistinguishable from type-D dualism.[34] So a distinctive type-F monism will have to face the combination problem directly.

Overall, type-F monism promises a deeply integrated and elegant view of nature. No-one has yet developed a precise and detailed theory in this class, and it is not yet clear whether such a theory can be developed. But at the same time, there appear to be no strong reasons to reject the view. As such, type-F monism is likely to provide fertile grounds for further investigation, and it may ultimately provide the best integration of the physical and the phenomenal within the natural world.

12. Conclusions

Are there any other options for the nonreductionist? There are two views that may not fit straightforwardly into the categories above.

First, some nonmaterialists hold that phenomenal properties are ontologically wholly distinct from physical properties, that microphysics is causally closed, but that phenomenal properties play a causal role with respect to the physical nevertheless. One way this might happen is by a sort of causal overdetermination: physical states causally determine behavior, but phenomenal states cause behavior at the same time. Another is by causal mediation: it might be that in at least some instances of microphysical causation from physical state P_1 to P_2, there is actually a causal connection from P_1 to the mind to P_2, so that the mind enters the causal nexus without altering the structure of the network. And there may be further strategies here. We might call this class type-O dualism (taking overdetermination as a paradigm case). These views share much of the structure of the type-E view (causally closed physical world, distinct phenomenal properties), but escapes the charge of epiphenomenalism. The special causal setups of these views may be hard to swallow, and they share some of the same problems as the type-E view (e.g., the fragmented view of nature, and the "lucky" psychophysical laws), but this class should nevertheless be put on the table as an option.[35]

Second, some nonmaterialists are *idealists* (in a Berkeleyan sense), holding that the physical world is itself constituted by the conscious states of an observing agent. We might call this view type-I monism. It shares with type-F monism the property that phenomenal states play a role in constituting physical reality, but on the type-I view this happens in a very different way: not by having separate "microscopic" phenomenal states underlying each physical state, but rather by having physical states constituted holistically by a "macroscopic" phenomenal mind. This view seems to be non-naturalistic in a much deeper sense than any of the views above, and in particular seems to suffer from an absence of causal or explanatory closure in nature: once the natural explanation in terms of the external world is removed, highly complex regularities among phenomenal states have to be taken as unexplained in terms of simpler principles. But again, this sort of view should at least be acknowledged.

As I see things, the best options for a nonreductionist are type-D dualism, type-E dualism, or type-F monism: that is, interactionism, epiphenomenalism, or panprotopsychism. If we acknowledge the epistemic gap between the physical and the phenomenal, and we rule out primitive identities and strong necessities, then we are led to a disjunction of these three views. Each of the views has at least some promise, and none have clear fatal flaws. For my part, I give some credence to each of them. I think that in some ways the type-F view is the most appealing, but this sense is largely grounded in aesthetic considerations whose force is unclear.

The choice between these three views may depend in large part on the development of specific theories within these frameworks. Especially for the type-D view and type-F view, further theoretical work is crucial in assessing the theories (e.g., in explicating quantum interactionism, or in understanding phenomenal composition). It may also be that the empirical science of consciousness will give some guidance. As the science progress, we will be led to infer simple principles that underlie correlations between physical and phenomenal states. It may be that these principles turn out to point strongly toward one or the other of these views: e.g., if simple principles connecting microphysical states to phenomenal or protophenomenal states can do the explanatory work, then we may have reason to favor a type-F view, while if the principles latch onto the physical world at a higher level, then we may have reason to favor a type-D or type-E view. And if consciousness has a specific pattern of effects on the physical world, as the type-D view suggests, then empirical studies ought in principle to be able to find these effects, although perhaps only with great difficulty.

Not everyone will agree that each of these views is viable. It may be that further examination will reveal deep problems with some of these views. But this further examination needs to be performed. There has been little critical examination of type-F views to date, for example;

we have seen that the standard arguments against type-D views carry very little weight; and while arguments against type-E views carry some intuitive force, they are far from making a knockdown case against the views. I suspect that even if further examination reveals deep problems for some views in this vicinity, it is very unlikely that all such views will be eliminated.

In any case, this gives us some perspective on the mind–body problem. It is often held that even though it is hard to see how materialism could be true, materialism *must* be true, since the alternatives are unacceptable. As I see it, there are at least three prima facie acceptable alternatives to materialism on the table, each of which is compatible with a broadly naturalistic (even if not materialistic) worldview, and none of which has fatal problems. So given the clear arguments against materialism, it seems to me that we should at least tentatively embrace the conclusion that one of these views is correct. Of course all of the views discussed in this paper need to be developed in much more detail, and examined in light of all relevant scientific and philosophical developments, in order to be comprehensively assessed. But as things stand, I think that we have good reason to suppose that consciousness has a fundamental place in nature.

NOTES

1. This paper is an overview of issues concerning the metaphysics of consciousness. Much of the discussion in this paper (especially the first part) recapitulates discussion in Chalmers (1995; 1996; 1997), although it often takes a different form, and sometimes goes beyond the discussion there. I give a more detailed treatment of many of the issues discussed here in the works cited in the bibliography.

2. The taxonomy is in the final chapter, Chapter 14, of Broad's book (set out on pp. 607–11, and discussed until p. 650). The dramatization of Broad's taxonomy as a 4×4 matrix is illustrated on Andrew Chrucky's website devoted to Broad, at http://www.ditext.com/broad/mpn14.html#t.

3. On my usage, qualia are simply those properties that characterize conscious states according to what it is like to have them. The definition does not build in any further substantive requirements, such as the requirement that qualia are intrinsic or nonintentional. If qualia are intrinsic or nonintentional, this will be a substantive rather than a definitional point (so the claim that the properties of consciousness are non-intrinsic or that they are wholly intentional should not be taken to entail that there are no qualia). Phenomenal properties can also be taken to be properties of individuals (e.g., people) rather than of mental states, characterizing aspects of what it is like to

be them at a given time; the difference will not matter much for present purposes.

4. Note that I use 'reductive' in a broader sense than it is sometimes used. Reductive explanation requires only that a high-level phenomena can be explained wholly in terms of low-level phenomena. This is compatible with the "multiple realizability" of high-level phenomena in low-level phenomena. For example, there may be many different ways in which digestion could be realized in a physiological system, but one can nevertheless reductively explain a system's digestion in terms of underlying physiology. Another subtlety concerns the possibility of a view on which consciousness can be explained in terms of principles which do not make appeal to consciousness but cannot themselves be physically explained. The definitions above count such a view as neither reductive nor nonreductive. It could reasonably be classified either way, but I will generally assimilate it with the nonreductive class.

5. A version of the explanatory argument as formulated here is given in Chalmers 1995. For related considerations about explanation, see Levine 1983 on the "explanatory gap" and Nagel 1974. See also the papers in Shear 1997.

6. Versions of the conceivability argument are put forward by Bealer 1994, Campbell 1970, Chalmers

1996, Kirk 1974, and Kripke 1980, among others. Important predecessors include Descartes' conceivability argument about disembodiment, and Leibniz's "mill" argument.

7. Sources for the knowledge argument include Jackson 1982, Maxwell 1968, Nagel 1974, and others. Predecessors of the argument are present in Broad's discussion of a "mathematical archangel" who cannot deduce the smell of ammonia from physical facts (Broad 1925, pp. 70–71), and Feigl's discussion of a "Martian superscientist" who cannot know what colors look like and what musical tones sound like (Feigl 1958/1967, pp. 64, 68, 140).

8. This version of the thought-experiment has a real life exemplar in Knut Nordby, a Norwegian sensory biologist who is a rod monochromat (lacking cones in his retina for color vision), and who works on the physiology of color vision. See Nordby 1990.

9. For limited versions of the conceivability argument and the explanatory argument, see Broad, pp. 614–15. For the knowledge argument, see pp. 70–72, where Broad argues that even a "mathematical archangel" could not deduce the smell of ammonia from microscopic knowledge of atoms. Broad is arguing against "mechanism", which is roughly equivalently to contemporary materialism. Perhaps the biggest lacuna in Broad's argument, to contemporary eyes, is any consideration of the possibility that there is an epistemic but not an ontological gap.

10. For a discussion of the relationship between the conceivability argument and the knowledge argument, see Chalmers 1996 and Chalmers 2002b.

11. Type-A materialists include Armstrong 1968, Dennett 1991, Dretske 1995, Harman 1990, Lewis 1988, Rey 1995, and Ryle 1949.

12. Two specific views may be worth mentioning. (i) Some views (e.g., Dretske 1995) deny an epistemic gap while at the same time denying functionalism, by holding that consciousness involves not just functional role but also causal and historical relations to objects in the environment. I count these as type-A views: we can view the relevant relations as part of functional role, broadly construed, and exactly the same considerations arise. (ii) Some views (e.g., Stoljar 2001 and Strawson 2000) deny an epistemic gap not by functionally analyzing consciousness but by expanding our view of the physical base to include underlying intrinsic properties. These views are discussed under type F.

13. In another analogy, Churchland (1996) suggests that someone in Goethe's time might have mounted analogous epistemic arguments against the reductive explanation of "luminescence." But on a close look, it is not hard to see that the only further explanandum that could have caused doubts here is the *experience* of seeing light (see Chalmers 1997). This point is no help to the type-A materialist, since this explanandum remains unexplained.

14. For an argument from unsavory metaphysical consequences, see White 1986. For an argument from unsavory epistemological consequences, see Shoemaker 1975. The metaphysical consequences are addressed in the second half of this paper. The epistemological consequences are addressed in Chalmers 2002a.

15. Type-B materialists include Block and Stalnaker 1999, Hill 1997, Levine 1983, Loar 1990/1997,

Lycan 1996, Papineau 1993, Perry 2001, and Tye 1995.

16. In certain respects, where type-A materialism can be seen as deriving from the logical behaviorism of Ryle and Carnap, type-B materialism can be seen as deriving from the identity theory of Place and Smart. The matter is complicated, however, by the fact that the early identity-theorists advocated "topic-neutral" (functional) analyses of phenomenal properties, suggesting an underlying type-A materialism.

17. Block and Stalnaker (1999) argue against deducibility in part by arguing that there is usually no explicit conceptual analysis of high-level terms such as 'water' in microphysical terms, or in any other terms that could ground an a priori entailment from microphysical truths to truths about water. In response, Chalmers and Jackson (2001) argue that explicit conceptual analyses are not required for a priori entailments, and that there is good reason to believe that such entailments exist in these cases.

18. Two-dimensional semantic frameworks originate in work of Kaplan (1989), Stalnaker (1978), and Evans (1979). The version used in these arguments is somewhat different: for discussion of the differences, see Chalmers (forthcoming).

19. This is a slightly more formal version of an argument in Chalmers 1996 (pp. 131–36). It is quite closely related to Kripke's modal argument against the identity theory, though different in some important respects. The central premise 2 can be seen as a way of formalizing Kripke's claim that where there is "apparent contingency", there is some misdescribed possibility in the background. The argument can also be seen as a way of formalizing a version of the "dual property" objection attributed to Max Black by Smart 1959, and developed by Jackson 1979 and White 1986. Related applications of the two-dimensional framework to questions about materialism are given by Jackson 1994 and Lewis 1994.

20. I have passed over a few subtleties here. One concerns the role of indexicals: to handle claims such as 'I am here', primary intensions are defined over *centered worlds:* worlds with a marked individual and time, corresponding to indexical "locating information" about one's position in the world. This change does not help the type-B materialist, however. Even if we supplement P with indexical locating information I (e.g., telling Mary about her location in the world), there is as much of an epistemic gap with Q as ever; so $P \wedge I \wedge \neg Q$ is conceivable. And given that there is a centered world that verifies $P \wedge I \wedge \neg Q$, one can see as above that either there is a world satisfying $P \wedge \neg Q$, or type-F monism is true.

21. Hill (1997) tries to explain away our modal intuitions about consciousness in cognitive terms. Chalmers (1999) responds that any modal intuition might be explained in cognitive terms (a similar argument could "explain away" our intuition that there might be red squares), but that this has no tendency to suggest that the intuition is incorrect. If such an account tells us that modal intuitions about consciousness are unreliable, the same goes for all modal intuitions. What is really needed is not an explanation of our modal intuitions about consciousness, but an explanation of why these intuitions in particular should be unreliable.

Loar (1990/1997) attempts to provide such an explanation in terms of the unique features of phenomenal concepts. He suggests that (1) phenomenal concepts are recognitional concepts (*"that* sort of thing"); that (2) like other recognitional concepts, they can corefer with physical concepts that are cognitively distinct; and that (3) unlike other recognitional concepts, they lack contingent modes of presentation (i.e., their primary and secondary intensions coincide). If (2) and (3) both hold (and if we assume that physical concepts also lack contingent modes of presentation), then a phenomenal-physical identity will be a strong necessity in the sense above. In response, Chalmers (1999) argues that (2) and (3) cannot both hold. The coreference of other recognitional concepts with theoretical concepts is *grounded* in their contingent modes of presentation; in the absence of such modes of presentation, there is no reason to think that these concepts can corefer. So accepting (3) undercuts any support for (2): Chalmers (1999) also argues that by assuming that physical properties can have phenomenal modes of presentation noncontingently, Loar's account is in effect presupposing rather than explaining the relevant strong necessities.

22. Of those mentioned above as apparently sympathetic with type-C materialism, I think McGinn is ultimately a type-F monist, Nagel is either a type-B materialist or a type-F monist, and Churchland is either a type-B materialist or a type-Q materialist (below).

23. One might ask about specific reductive views, such as representationalism (which identifies consciousness with certain representational states), and higher-order thought theory (which identifies consciousness with the objects of higher-order thoughts). How these views are classified depends on how a given theorist regards the representational or higher-order states (e.g., functionally definable or not) and their connection to consciousness (e.g., conceptual or empirical). Among representationalists, I think that Dretske 1995 and Harman 1990 are type-A materialists, while Lycan 1996 and Tye 1995 are type-B materialists. Among higher-order thought theorists, Carruthers 2000 is clearly a type-B materialist, while Rosenthal 1997 is either type-A or type-B. One could also in principle hold nonmaterialist versions of each of these views.

24. Type-D dualists include Foster 1991, Hodgson 1991, Popper and Eccles 1977, Sellars 1981, Stapp 1993, and Swinburne 1986.

25. No-collapse interpretations include Bohm's "hidden-variable" interpretations, and Everett's "many-worlds" (or "many-minds") interpretation. A collapse interpretation that does not invoke measurement is the Ghirardi-Rimini-Weber interpretation (with random occasional collapses). Each of these interpretations requires a significant revision to the standard dynamics of quantum mechanics, and each is controversial, although each has its benefits. (See Albert 1993 for discussion of these and other interpretations.) It is notable that there seems to be no remotely tenable interpretation that preserves the standard claim that collapses occur upon measurement, except for the interpretation involving consciousness.

26. I have been as guilty of this as anyone, setting aside interactionism in Chalmers 1996 partly for reasons of compatibility with physics. I am still not especially inclined to endorse interactionism, but I now think that the argument from physics is much too glib. Three further reasons for rejecting the view are mentioned in Chalmers 1996. First, if consciousness is to make an interesting qualitative difference to behavior, this requires that it act nonrandomly, in violation of the probabilistic requirements of quantum mechanics. I think there is something to this, but one could bite the bullet on nonrandomness in response, or one could hold that even a random causal role for consciousness is good enough. Second, I argued that denying causal closure yields no special advantage, as a view with causal closure can achieve much the same effect via type-F monism. Again there is something to this, but the type-D view does have the significant advantage of avoiding the type-F view's "combination problem." Third, it is not clear that the collapse interpretation yields the *sort* of causal role for consciousness that we expect it to have. I think that this is an important open question that requires detailed investigation.

27. Consciousness-collapse interpretations of quantum mechanics have been put forward by Wigner (1961), Hodgson (1991), and Stapp (1993). Only Stapp goes into much detail, with an interesting but somewhat idiosyncratic account that goes in a direction different from that suggested above.

28. Type-E dualists include Campbell 1970, Huxley 1874, Jackson 1982, and Robinson 1988.

29. Some accuse the epiphenomenalist of a double standard: relying on intuition in making the case against materialism, but going counter to intuition in denying a causal role for consciousness. But intuitions must be assessed against the background of reasons and evidence. To deny the relevant intuitions in the anti-materialist argument (in particular, the intuition of a further explanandum) appears to contradict the available first-person evidence; but denying a causal role for consciousness appears to be compatible on reflection with all our evidence, including first-person evidence.

30. Versions of type-F monism have been put forward by Russell 1927, Feigl 1958/1967, Maxwell 1979, Lockwood 1989, Chalmers 1996, Rosenberg 1997, Griffin 1998, Strawson 2000, and Stoljar 2001.

31. There is philosophical debate over the thesis that all dispositions have a categorical basis. If the thesis is accepted, the case for type-F monism is particularly strong, since microphysical dispositional must have a categorical basis, and we have no independent characterization of that basis. But even if the thesis is rejected, type-F monism is still viable. We need only the thesis that microphysical dispositions *may* have a categorical basis to open room for intrinsic properties here. (Some distinguish intrinsic properties from categorical properties, holding that even dispositional properties are intrinsic. On this view, references to intrinsic properties can be understood as invoking intrinsic categorical properties.)

32. Hence type-F monism is the sort of "physicalism" that emerges from the loophole mentioned in the two-dimensional argument against type-B materialism. The only way a "zombie world" W could satisfy the primary intension but not the secondary intension of P is for it to share the dispositional structure of our world but not the underlying intrinsic microphysical properties. If this difference is responsible for the lack of consciousness in W, then the intrinsic microphysical properties in our world are responsible for constituting consciousness. Maxwell (1979)

exploits this sort of loophole in replying to Kripke's argument.

Note that such a W must involve either a different corpus of intrinsic properties from those in our world, or no intrinsic properties at all. A type-F monist who holds that the only coherent intrinsic properties are protophenomenal properties might end up denying the conceivability of zombies, even under a structural-functional description of their physical state—for reasons very different from those of the type-A materialist.

33. McGinn (1991) can be read as advocating a type-F view, while denying that we can know the nature of the protophenomenal properties. His arguments rests on the claim that these properties cannot be known either through perception of through introspection. But this does not rule out the possibility that they might be known through some sort of inference to the best explanation of (introspected) phenomenology, subject to the additional constraints of (perceived) physical structure.

34. In this way, we can see that type-D views and type-F views are quite closely related. We can imagine that if a type-D view is true and there are microphysical causal gaps, we could be led through physical observation alone to postulate higher-level entities to fill these gaps—"psychons", say—where these are characterized in wholly structural/dispositional terms. The type-D view adds to this the suggestion that psychons have an intrinsic phenomenal nature. The main difference between the type-D view and the type-F view is that the type-D view involves fundamental causation above the microphysical level. This will involve a more radical view of physics, but it might have the advantage of avoiding the combination problem.

35. Type-O positions are advocated by Bealer (forthcoming), Lowe 1996, and Mills 1996.

BIBLIOGRAPHY

Armstrong, D. M. 1968. *A Materialist Theory of the Mind.* Routledge.

Albert, D. Z. 1993. *Quantum Mechanics and Experience.* Harvard University Press.

Bealer, G. 1994. Mental properties. *Journal of Philosophy* 91:185–208.

Bealer, G. (forthcoming). Mental causation.

Block, N., and Stalnaker, R. 1999. Conceptual analysis, dualism, and the explanatory gap. *Philosophical Review* 108:1–46.

Broad, C. D. 1925. *The Mind and its Place in Nature.* Routledge and Kegan Paul.

Campbell, K. K. 1970. *Body and Mind.* Doubleday.

Carruthers, P. 2000. *Phenomenal Consciousness: A Naturalistic Theory.* Cambridge University Press.

Chalmers, D. J. 1995. Facing up to the problem of consciousness. *Journal of Consciousness Studies* 2: 200–19. Reprinted in Shear 1997. http://consc.net/papers/facing.html.

Chalmers, D. J. 1996. *The Conscious Mind: In Search of a Fundamental Theory.* Oxford University Press.

Chalmers, D. J. 1997. Moving forward on the problem of consciousness. *Journal of Consciousness Studies* 4:3–46. Reprinted in Shear 1997. http://consc.net/papers/moving.html.

Chalmers, D. J. 1999. Materialism and the metaphysics of modality. *Philosophy and Phenomenological Research* 59:473–93. http://consc.net/papers/modality.html.

Chalmers, D. J. 2002a. The content and epistemology of phenomenal belief. In Q. Smith and A. Jokic (eds.), *Consciousness: New Philosophical Essays.* Oxford University Press. http://consc.net/papers/belief.html.

Chalmers, D. J. 2002b. Does conceivability entail possibility? In T. Gendler and J. Hawthorne (eds.), *Conceivability and Possibility.* Oxford University Press. http://consc.net/papers/conceivability.html.

Chalmers, D. J. (this volume). The components of content.

Chalmers, D. J., and Jackson, F. 2001. Conceptual analysis and reductive explanation. *Philosophical Review* 110:315–61. http://consc.net/papers/analysis.html.

Churchland, P. M. 1996. The rediscovery of light. *Journal of Philosophy* 93:211–28.

Churchland, P. S. 1997. The hornswoggle problem. In Shear 1997.

Clark, A. 2000. A case where access implies qualia? *Analysis* 60:30–38.

Dennett, D. C. 1991. *Consciousness Explained.* Little-Brown.

Dennett, D. C. 1996. Facing backward on the problem of consciousness. *Journal of Consciousness Studies* 3:4–6.

Dennett, D. C. forthcoming. The fantasy of first-person science. http://ase.tufts.edu/cogstud/papers/chalmersdeb3dft.htm.

Dretske, F. 1995. *Naturalizing the Mind.* MIT Press.

Evans, G. 1979. Reference and contingency. *The Monist* 62:161–89.

Feigl, H. 1958/1967. The 'mental' and the 'physical.' *Minnesota Studies in the Philosophy of Science* 2: 370–497. Reprinted (with a postscript) as *The 'Mental' and the 'Physical.'* University of Minnesota Press.

Foster, J. 1991. *The Immaterial Self: A Defence of the Cartesian Dualist Conception of the Mind.* Oxford University Press.

Griffin, D. R. 1998. *Unsnarling the World-Knot: Consciousness, Freedom, and the Mind–Body Problem.* University of California Press.

Harman, G. 1990. The intrinsic quality of experience. *Philosophical Perspectives* 4:31–52.

Hill, C. S. 1997. Imaginability, conceivability, possibility, and the mind–body problem. *Philosophical Studies* 87:61–85.

Hodgson, D. 1991. *The Mind Matters: Consciousness and Choice in a Quantum World.* Oxford University Press.

Huxley, T. 1874. On the hypothesis that animals are automata, and its history. *Fortnightly Review* 95: 555–80. Reprinted in *Collected Essays*. London, 1893.

Jackson, F. 1979. A note on physicalism and heat. *Australasian Journal of Philosophy* 58:26–34.

Jackson, F. 1982. Epiphenomenal qualia. *Philosophical Quarterly* 32:127–136.

Jackson, F. 1994. Finding the mind in the natural world. In R. Casati, B. Smith, and G. White (eds.), *Philosophy and the Cognitive Sciences*. Vienna: Holder-Pichler-Tempsky.

James, W. 1890. *The Principles of Psychology*. Henry Holt and Co.

Kaplan, D. 1989. Demonstratives. In J. Almog, J. Perry, and H. Wettstein (eds.), *Themes from Kaplan*. New York: Oxford University Press.

Kirk, R. 1974. Zombies vs materialists. *Proceedings of the Aristotelian Society (Supplementary Volume)* 48:135–52.

Kripke, S. A. 1980. *Naming and Necessity*. Harvard Univerty Press.

Levine, J. 1983. Materialism and qualia: The explanatory gap. *Pacific Philosophical Quarterly* 64:354–61.

Levine, J. 2000. *Purple Haze: The Puzzle of Conscious Experience*. MIT Press.

Lewis, D. 1988. What experience teaches. *Proceedings of the Russellian Society* (University of Sydney).

Lewis, D. 1994. Reduction of mind. In S. Guttenplan (ed.), *Companion to the Philosophy of Mind*. Blackwell.

Loar, B. 1990/1997. Phenomenal states. *Philosophical Perspectives* 4:81–108. Revised edition in (N. Block, O. Flanagan, and G. Güzeldere, eds.) *The Nature of Consciousness*. MIT Press.

Lockwood, M. 1989. *Mind, Brain, and the Quantum*. Oxford University Press.

Lowe, E. J. 1996. *Subjects of Experience*. Cambridge University Press.

Lycan, W. G. 1996. *Consciousness and Experience*. MIT Press.

Maxwell, N. 1968. Understanding sensations. *Australasian Journal of Philosophy* 46:127–45.

Maxwell, G. 1979. Rigid designators and mind-brain identity. *Minnesota Studies in the Philosophy of Science* 9:365–403.

McGinn, C. 1989. Can we solve the mind-body problem? *Mind* 98:349–66.

Mills, E. 1996. Interactionism and overdetermination. *American Philosophical Quarterly* 33:105–15.

Nagel, T. 1974. What is it like to be a bat? *Philosophical Review* 83:435–50.

Nordby, K. 1990. Vision in a complete achromat: A personal account. In R. Hess, L, Sharpe, and K. Nordby (eds.), *Night Vision: Basic, Clinical, and Applied Aspects*. Cambridge University Press.

Papineau, D. 1993. Physicalism, consciousness, and the antipathetic fallacy. *Australasian Journal of Philosophy* 71:169–83.

Perry, J. 2001. *Knowledge, Possibility, and Consciousness*. MIT Press.

Popper, K. and Eccles, J. 1977. *The Self and Its Brain: An Argument for Interactionism*. Springer.

Quine, W. V. 1951. Two dogmas of empiricism. *Philosophical Review* 60:20–43.

Rey, G. 1995. Toward a projectivist account of conscious experience. In T. Metzinger (ed.), *Conscious Experience*. Ferdinand Schoningh.

Robinson, W. S. 1988. *Brains and People: An Essay on Mentality and its Causal Conditions*. Temple University Press.

Rosenberg, G. H. 1997. A Place for Consciousness: Probing the Deep Structure of the Natural World. Ph.D. dissertation, Indiana University. http://www.ai.uga.edu/~ghrosenb/book.html.

Rosenthal, D. M. 1997. A theory of consciousness. In N. Block, O. Flanagan, and G. Güzeldere (eds.), *The Nature of Consciousness*. MIT Press.

Russell, B. 1927. *The Analysis of Matter*. London: Kegan Paul.

Ryle, G. 1949. *The Concept of Mind*. Hutchinson and Co.

Seager, W. 1995. Consciousness, information and panpsychism. *Journal of Consciousness Studies* 2:272–88.

Sellars, W. 1981. Is consciousness physical? *The Monist* 64:66–90.

Shear, J. (ed.), 1997. *Explaining Consciousness: The Hard Problem*. MIT Press.

Shoemaker, S. 1975. Functionalism and qualia. *Philosophical Studies* 27:291–315.

Smart, J. J. C. 1959. Sensations and brain processes. *Philosophical Review* 68:141–56.

Stalnaker, R. 1978. Assertion. In P. Cole (ed.), *Syntax and Semantics: Pragmatics, Vol. 9*. New York: Academic Press.

Stapp, H. 1993. *Mind, Matter, and Quantum Mechanics*. Springer-Verlag.

Stoljar, D. 2001. Two conceptions of the physical. *Philosophy and Phenomenological Research* 62:253–81.

Strawson, G. 2000. Realistic materialist monism. In S. Hameroff, A. Kaszniak, and D. Chalmers (eds.), *Toward a Science of Consciousness III*. MIT Press.

Swinburne, R. 1986. *The Evolution of the Soul*. Oxford University Press.

Tye, M. 1995. *Ten Problems of Consciousness: A Representational Theory of the Phenomenal Mind*. MIT Press.

Van Gulick, R. 1993. Understanding the phenomenal mind: Are we all just armadillos? In M. Davies and G. Humphreys (eds.) *Consciousness: Philosophical and Psychological Aspects*. Blackwell.

White, S. 1986. Curse of the qualia. *Synthese* 68:333–68.

Wigner, E. P. 1961. Remarks on the mind-body question. In I. J. Good (ed.), *The Scientist Speculates*. Basic Books.

28 | Epiphenomenal Qualia

Frank Jackson

It is undeniable that the physical, chemical and biological sciences have provided a great deal of information about the world we live in and about ourselves. I will use the label 'physical information' for this kind of information, and also for information that automatically comes along with it. For example, if a medical scientist tells me enough about the processes that go on in my nervous system, and about how they relate to happenings in the world around me, to what has happened in the past and is likely to happen in the future, to what happens to other similar and dissimilar organisms, and the like, he or she tells me—if I am clever enough to fit it together appropriately—about what is often called the functional role of those states in me (and in organisms in general in similar cases). This information, and its kin, I also label 'physical'.

I do not mean these sketchy remarks to constitute a definition of 'physical information', and of the correlative notions of physical property, process, and so on, but to indicate what I have in mind here. It is well known that there are problems with giving a precise definition of these notions, and so of the thesis of Physicalism that all (correct) information is physical information.[1] But—unlike some—I take the question of definition to cut across the central problems I want to discuss in this paper.

I am what is sometimes known as a "qualia freak." I think that there are certain features of the bodily sensations especially, but also of certain perceptual experiences, which no amount of purely physical information includes. Tell me everything physical there is to tell about what is going on in a living brain, the kind of states, their functional role, their relation to what goes on at other times and in other brains, and so on and so forth, and be I as clever as can be in fitting it all together, you won't have told me about the hurtfulness of pains, the itchiness of itches, pangs of jealousy, or about the characteristic experience of tasting a lemon, smelling a rose, hearing a loud noise or seeing the sky.

There are many qualia freaks, and some of them say that their rejection of Physicalism is an unargued intuition.[2] I think that they are being unfair to themselves. They have the following argument. Nothing you could tell of a physical sort captures the smell of a rose, for instance. Therefore, Physicalism is false. By our lights this is a perfectly good argument. It is obviously not to the point to question its validity, and the premise is intuitively obviously true both to them and to me.

I must, however, admit that it is weak from a polemical point of view. There are, unfortunately for us, many who do not find the premise intuitively obvious. The task then is to present an argument whose premises are obvious to all, or at least to as many as possible. This I try to do in §I with what I will call "the Knowledge argument." In §II I contrast the Knowledge argument with the Modal argument and in §III with the "What is it like to be" argument. In §IV I tackle the question of the causal role of qualia. The major factor in stopping people from admitting qualia is the belief that they would have to be given a causal role with respect to the physical world and especially the brain;[3] and it is hard to do this without sounding like someone who believes in fairies. I seek in §IV to turn this objection by arguing that the view that qualia are epiphenomenal is a perfectly possible one.

From *Philosophical Quarterly* 32:127–136, 1982. Reprinted with permission of the publisher. Addendum excerpted from "What Mary Didn't Know," *Journal of Philosophy* 83:291–95, 1986, with permission of author and publisher.

I. The Knowledge Argument for Qualia

People vary considerably in their ability to discriminate colours. Suppose that in an experiment to catalogue this variation Fred is discovered. Fred has better colour vision than anyone else on record; he makes every discrimination that anyone has ever made, and moreover he makes one that we cannot even begin to make. Show him a batch of ripe tomatoes and he sorts them into two roughly equal groups and does so with complete consistency. That is, if you blindfold him, shuffle the tomatoes up, and then remove the blindfold and ask him to sort them out again, he sorts them into exactly the same two groups.

We ask Fred how he does it. He explains that all ripe tomatoes do not look the same colour to him, and in fact that this is true of a great many objects that we classify together as red. He sees two colours where we see one, and he has in consequence developed for his own use two words 'red$_1$' and 'red$_2$' to mark the difference. Perhaps he tells us that he has often tried to teach the difference between red$_1$ and red$_2$ to his friends but has got nowhere and has concluded that the rest of the world is red$_1$-red$_2$ colour-blind—or perhaps he has had partial success with his children, it doesn't matter. In any case he explains to us that it would be quite wrong to think that because 'red' appears in both 'red$_1$' and 'red$_2$' that the two colours are shades of the one colour. He only uses the common term 'red' to fit more easily into our restricted usage. To him red$_1$ and red$_2$ are as different from each other and all the other colours as yellow is from blue. And his discriminatory behaviour bears this out: he sorts red$_1$ from red$_2$ tomatoes with the greatest of ease in a wide variety of viewing circumstances. Moreover, an investigation of the physiological basis of Fred's exceptional ability reveals that Fred's optical system is able to separate out two groups of wavelengths in the red spectrum as sharply as we are able to sort out yellow from blue.[4]

I think that we should admit that Fred can see, really see, at least one more colour than we can; red$_1$ is a different colour from red$_2$. We are to Fred as a totally red-green colour-blind person is to us. H. G. Wells' story "The Country of the Blind" is about a sighted person in a totally blind community.[5] This person never manages to convince them that he can see, that he has an extra sense. They ridicule this sense as quite inconceivable, and treat his capacity to avoid falling into ditches, to win fights and so on as precisely that capacity and nothing more. We would be making their mistake if we refused to allow that Fred can see one more colour than we can.

What kind of experience does Fred have when he sees red$_1$ and red$_2$? What is the new colour or colours like? We would dearly like to know but do not; and it seems that no amount of physical information about Fred's brain and optical system tells us. We find out perhaps that Fred's cones respond differentially to certain light waves in the red section of the spectrum that make no difference to ours (or perhaps he has an extra cone) and that this leads in Fred to a wider range of those brain states responsible for visual discriminatory behaviour. But none of this tells us what we really want to know about his colour experience. There is something about it we don't know. But we know, we may suppose, everything about Fred's body, his behaviour and dispositions to behaviour and about his internal physiology, and everything about his history and relation to others that can be given in physical accounts of persons. We have all the physical information. Therefore, knowing all this is *not* knowing everything about Fred. It follows that Physicalism leaves something out.

To reinforce this conclusion, imagine that as a result of our investigations into the internal workings of Fred we find out how to make everyone's physiology like Fred's in the relevant respects; or perhaps Fred donates his body to science and on his death we are able to transplant his optical system into someone else—again the fine detail doesn't matter. The important point is that such a happening would create enormous interest. People would say, "At last we will know what it is like to see the extra colour, at last we will know how Fred has differed from us in the way he has struggled to tell us about for so long." Then it cannot be that we knew all along all about Fred. But *ex hypothesi* we did know all along everything about Fred that features in the physicalist scheme; hence the physicalist scheme leaves something out.

Put it this way. *After* the operation, we will know *more* about Fred and especially about his colour experiences. But beforehand we had all the physical information we could desire about his body and brain, and indeed everything that has ever featured in physicalist accounts of mind and consciousness. Hence there is more to know than all that. Hence Physicalism is incomplete.

Fred and the new colour(s) are of course essentially rhetorical devices. The same point can be made with normal people and familiar colours. Mary is a brilliant scientist who is, for whatever reason, forced to investigate the world from a black and white room *via* a black and white television monitor. She specialises in the neurophysiology of vision and acquires, let us suppose, all the physical information there is to obtain about what goes on when we see ripe tomatoes, or the sky, and use terms like 'red', 'blue', and so on. She discovers, for example, just which wave-length combinations from the sky stimulate the retina, and exactly how this produces *via* the central nervous system the contraction of the vocal chords and expulsion of air from the lungs that results in the uttering of the sentence 'The sky is blue.' (It can hardly be denied that it is in principle possible to obtain all this physical information from black and white television, otherwise the Open University would *of necessity* need to use colour television.)

What will happen when Mary is released from her black and white room or is given a colour television monitor? Will she *learn* anything or not? It seems just obvious that she will learn something about the world and our visual experience of it. But then it is inescapable that her previous knowledge was incomplete. But she had *all* the physical information. Ergo there is more to have than that, and Physicalism is false.

Clearly the same style of Knowledge argument could be deployed for taste, hearing, the bodily sensations and generally speaking for the various mental states which are said to have (as it is variously put) raw feels, phenomenal features or qualia. The conclusion in each case is that the qualia are left out of the physicalist story. And the polemical strength of the Knowledge argument is that it is so hard to deny the central claim that one can have all the physical information without having all the information there is to have.

II. The Modal Argument

By the Modal Argument I mean an argument of the following style.[6] Sceptics about other minds are not making a mistake in deductive logic, whatever else may be wrong with their position. No amount of physical information about another *logically entails* that he or she is conscious or feels anything at all. Consequently there is a possible world with organisms exactly like us in every physical respect (and remember that in-

cludes functional states, physical history, et al.) but which differ from us profoundly in that they have no conscious mental life at all. But then what is it that we have and they lack? Not anything physical ex hypothesi. In all physical regards we and they are exactly alike. Consequently there is more to us than the purely physical. Thus Physicalism is false.[7]

It is sometimes objected that the Modal argument misconceives Physicalism on the ground that that doctrine is advanced as a *contingent* truth.[8] But to say this is only to say that physicalists restrict their claim to *some* possible worlds, including especially ours; and the Modal argument is only directed against this lesser claim. If we in *our* world, let alone beings in any others, have features additional to those of our physical replicas in other possible worlds, then we have non-physical features or qualia.

The trouble rather with the Modal argument is that it rests on a disputable modal intuition. Disputable because it is disputed. Some sincerely deny that there can be physical replicas of us in other possible worlds which nevertheless lack consciousness. Moreover, at least one person who once had the intuition now has doubts.[9]

Head-counting may seem a poor approach to a discussion of the Modal argument. But frequently we can do no better when modal intuitions are in question, and remember our initial goal was to find the argument with the greatest polemical utility.

Of course, qua protagonists of the Knowledge argument we may well accept the modal intuition in question; but this will be a *consequence* of our already having an argument to the conclusion that qualia are left out of the physicalist story, not our ground for that conclusion. Moreover, the matter is complicated by the possibility that the connection between matters physical and qualia is like that sometimes held to obtain between aesthetic qualities and natural ones. Two possible worlds which agree in all "natural" respects (including the experiences of sentient creatures) must agree in all aesthetic qualities also, but it is plausibly held that the aesthetic qualities cannot be reduced to the natural.

III. The "What Is It Like to Be" Argument

In "What is it like to be a bat?" Thomas Nagel argues that no amount of physical information can tell us what it is like to be a bat, and indeed that we, human beings, cannot imagine what it is like to be a bat.[10] His reason is that what this is like can only be understood from a bat's point of view, which is not our point of view and is not something capturable in physical terms which are essentially terms understandable equally from many points of view.

It is important to distinguish this argument from the Knowledge argument. When I complained that all the physical knowledge about Fred was not enough to tell us what his special colour experience was like, I was not complaining that we weren't finding out what it is like to *be* Fred. I was complaining that there is something *about* his experience, a property of it, of which we were left ignorant. And if and when we come to know what this property is we still will not know what it is like to *be* Fred, but we will know more *about* him. No amount of knowledge about Fred, be it physical or not, amounts to knowledge "from the inside" concerning Fred. We are not Fred. There is thus a whole set of items of knowledge expressed by forms of words like 'that it is *I myself* who is . . .' which Fred has and we simply cannot have because we are not him.[11]

When Fred sees the colour he alone can see, one thing he knows is the way his experience of it differs from his experience of seeing red and so on, *another* is that he himself is seeing it. Physicalist and qualia freaks alike should acknowledge that no amount of information of whatever kind that *others* have *about* Fred amounts to knowledge of the second. My complaint though concerned the first and was that the special quality of his experience is certainly a fact about it, and one which Physicalism leaves out because no amount of physical information told us what it is.

Nagel speaks as if the problem he is raising is one of extrapolating from knowledge of one experience to another, of imagining what an unfamiliar experience would be like on the basis of familiar ones. In terms of Hume's example, from knowledge of some shades of blue we can work out what it would be like to see other shades of blue. Nagel argues that the trouble with bats et al. is that they are too unlike us. It is hard to see an objection to Physicalism here. Physicalism makes no special claims about the imaginative or extrapolative powers of human beings, and it is hard to see why it need do so.[12]

Anyway, our Knowledge argument makes no assumptions on this point. If Physicalism were true, enough physical information about Fred

would obviate any need to extrapolate or to perform special feats of imagination or understanding in order to know all about his special colour experience. *The information would already be in our possession.* But it clearly isn't. That was the nub of the argument.

IV. The Bogey of Epiphenomenalism

Is there any really *good* reason for refusing to countenance the idea that qualia are causally impotent with respect to the physical world? I will argue for the answer no, but in doing this I will say nothing about two views associated with the classical epiphenomenalist position. The first is that mental *states* are inefficacious with respect to the physical world. All I will be concerned to defend is that it is possible to hold that certain *properties* of certain mental states, namely those I've called qualia, are such that their possession or absence makes no difference to the physical world. The second is that the mental is *totally* causally inefficacious. For all I will say it may be that you have to hold that the instantiation of *qualia* makes a difference to *other mental states* though not to anything physical. Indeed general considerations to do with how you could come to be aware of the instantiation of qualia suggest such a position.[13]

Three reasons are standardly given for holding that a quale like the hurtfulness of a pain must be causally efficacious in the physical world, and so, for instance, that its instantiation must sometimes make a difference to what happens in the brain. None, I will argue, has any real force. (I am much indebted to Alec Hyslop and John Lucas for convincing me of this.)

(i) It is supposed to be just obvious that the hurtfulness of pain is partly responsible for the subject seeking to avoid pain, saying 'It hurts' and so on. But, to reverse Hume, anything can fail to cause anything. No matter how often *B* follows *A,* and no matter how initially obvious the causality of the connection seems, the hypothesis that *A* causes *B* can be overturned by an over-arching theory which shows the two as distinct effects of a common underlying causal process.

To the untutored the image on the screen of Lee Marvin's fist moving from left to right immediately followed by the image of John Wayne's head moving in the same general direction looks as causal as anything.[14] And of course throughout countless Westerns images similar to the first are followed by images similar to the second. All this counts for precisely nothing when we know the over-arching theory concerning how the relevant images are both effects of an underlying causal process involving the projector and the film. The epiphenomenalist can say exactly the same about the connection between, for example, hurtfulness and behaviour. It is simply a consequence of the fact that certain happenings in the brain cause both.

(ii) The second objection relates to Darwin's Theory of Evolution. According to natural selection the traits that evolve over time are those conducive to physical survival. We may assume that qualia evolved over time—we have them, the earliest forms of life do not—and so we should expect qualia to be conducive to survival. The objection is that they could hardly help us to survive if they do nothing to the physical world.

The appeal of this argument is undeniable, but there is a good reply to it. Polar bears have particularly thick, warm coats. The Theory of Evolution explains this (we suppose) by pointing out that having a thick, warm coat is conducive to survival in the Arctic. But having a thick coat goes along with having a heavy coat, and having a heavy coat is *not* conducive to survival. It slows the animal down.

Does this mean that we have refuted Darwin because we have found an evolved trait—having a heavy coat—which is not conducive to survival? Clearly not. Having a heavy coat is an unavoidable concomitant of having a warm coat (in the context, modern insulation was not available), and the advantages for survival of having a warm coat outweighed the disadvantages of having a heavy one. The point is that all we can extract from Darwin's theory is that we should expect any evolved characteristic to be *either* conducive to survival *or* a by-product of one that is so conducive. The epiphenomenalist holds that qualia fall into the latter category. They are a by-product of certain brain processes that are highly conducive to survival.

(iii) The third objection is based on a point about how we come to know about other minds. We know about other minds by knowing about other behaviour, at least in part. The nature of the inference is a matter of some controversy, but it is not a matter of controversy that it proceeds from behaviour. That is why we think that stones do not feel and dogs do feel. But, runs the objection, how can a person's behaviour pro-

vide any reason for believing he has qualia like mine, or indeed any qualia at all, unless this behaviour can be regarded as the *outcome* of the qualia. Man Friday's footprint was evidence of Man Friday because footprints are causal outcomes of feet attached to people. And an epiphenomenalist cannot regard behaviour, or indeed anything physical, as an outcome of qualia.

But consider my reading in *The Times* that Spurs won. This provides excellent evidence that *The Telegraph* has also reported that Spurs won, despite the fact that (I trust) *The Telegraph* does not get the results from *The Times*. They each send their own reporters to the game. *The Telegraph*'s report is in no sense an outcome of *The Times*', but the latter provides good evidence for the former nevertheless.

The reasoning involved can be reconstructed thus. I read in *The Times* that Spurs won. This gives me reason to think that Spurs won because I know that Spurs' winning is the most likely candidate to be what caused the report in *The Times*. But I also know that Spurs' winning would have had many effects, including almost certainly a report in *The Telegraph*.

I am arguing from one effect back to its cause and out again to another effect. The fact that neither effect causes the other is irrelevant. Now the epiphenomenalist allows that qualia are effects of what goes on in the brain. Qualia cause nothing physical but are caused by something physical. Hence the epiphenomenalist can argue from the behaviour of others to the qualia of others by arguing from the behaviour of others back to its causes in the brains of others and out again to their qualia.

You may well feel for one reason or another that this is a more dubious chain of reasoning than its model in the case of newspaper reports. You are right. The problem of other minds is a major philosophical problem, the problem of other newspaper reports is not. But there is no special problem of Epiphenomenalism as opposed to, say, Interactionism here.

There is a very understandable response to the three replies I have just made. "All right, there is no knockdown refutation of the existence of epiphenomenal qualia. But the fact remains that they are an excrescence. They *do* nothing, they *explain* nothing, they serve merely to soothe the intuitions of dualists, and it is left a total mystery how they fit into the world view of science. In short we do not and cannot understand the how and why of them."

This is perfectly true; but is no objection to qualia, for it rests on an overly optimistic view of the human animal, and its powers. We are the products of Evolution. We understand and sense what we need to understand and sense in order to survive. Epiphenomenal qualia are totally irrelevant to survival. At no stage of our evolution did natural selection favour those who could make sense of how they are caused and the laws governing them, or in fact why they exist at all. And that is why we can't.

It is not sufficiently appreciated that Physicalism is an extremely optimistic view of our powers. If it is true, we have, in very broad outline admittedly, a grasp of our place in the scheme of things. Certain matters of sheer complexity defeat us—there are an awful lot of neurons—but in principle we have it all. But consider the antecedent probability that everything in the Universe be of a kind that is relevant in some way or other to the survival of *homo sapiens.* It is very low surely. But then one must admit that it is very likely that there is a part of the whole scheme of things, maybe a big part, which no amount of evolution will ever bring us near to knowledge about or understanding. For the simple reason that such knowledge and understanding is irrelevant to survival.

Physicalists typically emphasise that we are a part of nature on their view, which is fair enough. But if we are a part of nature, we are as nature has left us after however many years of evolution it is, and each step in that evolutionary progression has been a matter of chance constrained just by the need to preserve or increase survival value. The wonder is that we understand as much as we do, and there is no wonder that there should be matters which fall quite outside our comprehension. Perhaps exactly how

epiphenomenal qualia fit into the scheme of things is one such.

This may seem an unduly pessimistic view of our capacity to articulate a truly comprehensive picture of our world and our place in it. But suppose we discovered living on the bottom of the deepest oceans a sort of sea slug which manifested intelligence. Perhaps survival in the conditions required rational powers. Despite their intelligence, these sea slugs have only a very restricted conception of the world by comparison with ours, the explanation for this being the nature of their immediate environment. Nevertheless they have developed sciences which work surprisingly well in these restricted terms. They also have philosophers, called slugists. Some call themselves tough-minded slugists, others confess to being soft-minded slugists.

The tough-minded slugists hold that the restricted terms (or ones pretty like them which may be introduced as their sciences progress) suffice in principle to describe everything without remainder. These tough-minded slugists admit in moments of weakness to a feeling that their theory leaves something out. They resist this feeling and their opponents, the soft-minded slugists, by pointing out—absolutely correctly—that no slugist has ever succeeded in spelling out how this mysterious residue fits into the highly successful view that their sciences have and are developing of how their world works.

Our sea slugs don't exist, but they might. And there might also exist super beings which stand to us as we stand to the sea slugs. We cannot adopt the perspective of these super beings, because we are not them, but the possibility of such a perspective is, I think, an antidote to excessive optimism.[15]

ADDENDUM: FROM "WHAT MARY DIDN'T KNOW"

I. Three Clarifications

The knowledge argument does not rest on the dubious claim that logically you cannot imagine what sensing red is like unless you have sensed red. Powers of imagination are not to the point. The contention about Mary is not that, despite her fantastic grasp of neurophysiology and everything else physical, she *could not imagine* what it is like to sense red; it is that, as a matter of fact, she *would not know.* But if physicalism

is true, she would know; and no great powers of imagination would be called for. Imagination is a faculty that those who *lack* knowledge need to fall back on.

Secondly, the intensionality of knowledge is not to the point. The argument does not rest on assuming falsely that, if S knows that a is F and if $a = b$, then S knows that b is F. It is concerned with the nature of Mary's total body of knowledge before she is released: is it complete, or do some facts escape it? What is to the point is that

S may know that a is F and *know* that $a = b$, yet arguably not know that b is F, by virtue of not being sufficiently logically alert to follow the consequences through. If Mary's lack of knowledge were at all like this, there would be no threat to physicalism in it. But it is very hard to believe that her lack of knowledge could be remedied merely by her explicitly following through enough logical consequences of her vast physical knowledge. Endowing her with great logical acumen and persistence is not in itself enough to fill in the gaps in her knowledge. On being let out, she will not say "I could have worked all this out before by making some more purely logical inferences."

Thirdly, the knowledge Mary lacked which is of particular point for the knowledge argument against physicalism is *knowledge about the experiences of others,* not about her own. When she is let out, she has new experiences, color experiences she has never had before. It is not, therefore, an objection to physicalism that she learns *something* on being let out. Before she was let out, she could not have known facts about her experience of red, for there were no such facts to know. That physicalist and nonphysicalist alike can agree on. After she is let out, things change; and physicalism can happily admit that she learns this; after all, some physical things will change, for instance, her brain states and their functional roles. The trouble for physicalism is that, after Mary sees her first ripe tomato, she will realize how impoverished her conception of the mental life of *others* has been *all along.* She will realize that there was, all the time she was carrying out her laborious investigations into the neurophysiologies of others and into the functional roles of their internal states, something about these people she was quite unaware of. All along their experiences (or many of them, those got from tomatoes, the sky, . . .) had a feature conspicuous to them but until now hidden from her (in fact, not in logic). But she knew all the physical facts about them all along; hence, what she did not know until her release is not a physical fact about their experiences. But it is a fact about them. That is the trouble for physicalism.

II. Churchland's Three Objections[16]

(i) Churchland's first objection is that the knowledge argument contains a defect that "is simplicity itself" (23). The argument equivocates on the sense of 'knows about.' How so? Churchland suggests that the following is "a conveniently tightened version" of the knowledge argument:

(1) Mary knows everything there is to know about brain states and their properties.
(2) It is not the case that Mary knows everything there is to know about sensations and their properties.

Therefore, by Leibniz's law,

(3) Sensations and their properties ≠ brain states and their properties (23).

Churchland observes, plausibly enough, that the type or kind of knowledge involved in premise 1 is distinct from the kind of knowledge involved in premise 2. We might follow his lead and tag the first 'knowledge by description,' and the second 'knowledge by acquaintance'; but, whatever the tags, he is right that the displayed argument involves a highly dubious use of Leibniz's law.

My reply is that the displayed argument may be convenient, but it is not accurate. It is not the knowledge argument. Take, for instance, premise 1. The whole thrust of the knowledge argument is that Mary (before her release) does *not* know everything there is to know about brain states and their properties, because she does not know about certain qualia associated with them. What is complete, according to the argument, is her knowledge of matters physical. A convenient and accurate way of displaying the argument is:

(1)′ Mary (before her release) knows everything physical there is to know about other people.
(2)′ Mary (before her release) does not know everything there is to know about other people (because she *learns* something about them on her release).

Therefore,

(3)′ There are truths about other people (and herself) which escape the physicalist story.

What is immediately to the point is not the kind, manner, or type of knowledge Mary has, but *what* she knows. What she knows beforehand is *ex hypothesi* everything physical there is to know, but is it everything there is to know? That is the crucial question.

NOTES

1. See, e.g., D. H. Mellor, "Materialism and Phenomenal Qualities," *Aristotelian Society Supp. Vol.* 47 (1973), 107–19; and J. W. Cornman, *Materialism and Sensations* (New Haven and London, 1971).

2. Particularly in discussion, but see, e.g., Keith Campbell, *Metaphysics* (Belmont, 1976), p. 67.

3. See, e.g., D. C. Dennett, "Current Issues in the Philosophy of Mind," *American Philosophical Quarterly,* 15 (1978), 249–61.

4. Put this, and similar simplifications below, in terms of Land's theory if you prefer. See, e.g., Edwin H. Land, "Experiments in Color Vision," *Scientific American,* 200 (5 May 1959), 84–99.

5. H. G. Wells, *The Country of the Blind and Other Stories* (London, n.d.).

6. See, e.g., Keith Campbell, *Body and Mind* (New York, 1970); and Robert Kirk, "Sentience and Behaviour," *Mind,* 83 (1974), 43–60.

7. I have presented the argument in an inter-world rather than the more usual intra-world fashion to avoid inessential complications to do with supervenience, causal anomalies and the like.

8. See, e.g., W. G. Lycan, "A New Lilliputian Argument against Machine Functionalism," *Philosophical Studies,* 35 (1979), 279–87, p. 280; and Don Locke, "Zombies, Schizophrenics and Purely Physical Objects," *Mind,* 85 (1976), 97–99.

9. See R. Kirk, "From Physical Explicability to Full-Blooded Materialism," *The Philosophical Quarterly,* 29 (1979), 229–37. See also the arguments against the modal intuition in, e.g., Sydney Shoemaker, "Functionalism and Qualia," *Philosophical Studies,* 27 (1975), 291–315.

10. *The Philosophical Review,* 83 (1974), 435–50. Two things need to be said about this article. One is that, despite my dissociations to come, I am much indebted to it. The other is that the emphasis changes through the article, and by the end Nagel is objecting not so much to Physicalism as to all extant theories of mind for ignoring points of view, including those that admit (irreducible) qualia.

11. Knowledge *de se* in the terms of David Lewis, "Attitudes De Dicto and De Se," *The Philosophical Review,* 88 (1979), 513–43.

12. See Laurence Nemirow's comments on "What is it . . ." in his review of T. Nagel, *Mortal Questions,* in *The Philosophical Review,* 89 (1980), 473–77. I am indebted here in particular to a discussion with David Lewis.

13. See my review of K. Campbell, *Body and Mind,* in *Australasian Journal of Philosophy,* 50 (1972), 77–80.

14. Cf. Jean Piaget, "The Child's Conception of Physical Causality," reprinted in *The Essential Piaget* (London, 1977).

15. I am indebted to Robert Pargetter for a number of comments and, despite his dissent, to §IV of Paul E. Meehl, "The Compleat Autocerebroscopist" in *Mind, Matter, and Method,* ed. Paul Feyerabend and Grover Maxwell (Minneapolis, 1966).

16. Paul M. Churchland, "Reduction, Qualia, and the Direct Introspection of Brain States," *The Journal of Philosophy,* LXXXII, 1 (January 1985): 8–28. Unless otherwise stated, future page references are to this paper.

29 What Experience Teaches

David Lewis

Experience the Best Teacher

They say that experience is the best teacher, and the classroom is no substitute for Real Life. There's truth to this. If you want to know what some new and different experience is like, you can learn it by going out and really *having* that experience. You can't learn it by being told about the experience, however thorough your lessons may be.

Does this prove much of anything about the metaphysics of mind and the limits of science? I think not.

Example: Skunks and Vegemite

I have smelled skunks, so I know what it's like to smell skunks. But skunks live only in some parts of the world, so you may never have smelled a skunk. If you haven't smelled a skunk, then you don't know what it's like. You never will, unless someday you smell a skunk for yourself. On the other hand, you may have tasted Vegemite, that famous Australian substance; and I never have. So you may know what it's like to taste Vegemite. I don't, and unless I taste Vegemite (what, and spoil a good example!), I never will. It won't help at all to take lessons on the chemical composition of skunk scent or Vegemite, the physiology of the nostrils or the taste-buds, and the neurophysiology of the sensory nerves and the brain.

Example: The Captive Scientist[1]

Mary, a brilliant scientist, has lived from birth in a cell where everything is black or white. (Even she herself is painted all over.) She views the world on black-and-white television. By television she reads books, she joins in discussion, she watches the results of experiments done under her direction. In this way she becomes the world's leading expert on color and color vision and the brain states produced by exposure to colors. But she doesn't know what it's like to see color. And she never will, unless she escapes from her cell.

Example: The Bat[2]

The bat is an alien creature, with a sonar sense quite unlike any sense of ours. We can never have the experiences of a bat; because we could not become bat-like enough to have those experiences and still be ourselves. We will never know what it's like to be a bat. Not even if we come to know all the facts there are about the bat's behavior and behavioral dispositions, about the bat's physical structure and processes, about the bat's functional organization. Not even if we come to know all the same sort of physical facts about all the other bats, or about other creatures, or about ourselves. Not even if we come to possess all physical facts whatever. Not even if we become able to recognize all the mathematical and logical implications of all these facts, no matter how complicated and how far beyond the reach of finite deduction.

Experience is the best teacher, in this sense: having an experience is the best way or perhaps the only way, of coming to know what that experience is like. No amount of scientific information about the stimuli that produce that experience and the process that goes on in you when you have that experience will enable you to know what it's like to have the experience.

. . . But Not Necessarily

Having an experience is surely one good way, and surely the only practical way, of coming to know what that experience is like. Can we say, flatly, that it is the only *possible* way? Probably not. There is a change that takes place in you when you have the experience and thereby come to know what it's like. Perhaps the exact same change could in principle be produced in you by precise neurosurgery, very far beyond the limits of present-day technique. Or it could possibly be produced in you by magic. If we ignore the laws of nature, which are after all contingent, then there is no necessary connection between cause and effect: anything could cause anything. For instance, the casting of a spell

Reprinted from *Proceedings of the Russellian Society* (University of Sydney), 1988, with permission of the author's estate and the publisher.

could do to you exactly what your first smell of skunk would do. We might quibble about whether a state produced in this artificial fashion would deserve the *name* "knowing what it's like to smell a skunk," but we can imagine that so far as what goes on within you is concerned, it would differ not at all.[3]

Just as we can imagine that a spell might produce the same change as a smell, so likewise we can imagine that science lessons might cause that same change. Even that is possible, in the broadest sense of the word. If we ignored all we know about how the world really works, we could not say what might happen to someone if he were taught about the chemistry of scent and the physiology of the nose. There might have been a causal mechanism that transforms science lessons into whatever it is that experience gives us. But there isn't. It is not an absolutely necessary truth that experience is the best teacher about what a new experience is like. It's a contingent truth. But we have good reason to think it's true.

We have good reason to think that something of this kind is true, anyway, but less reason to be sure exactly what. Maybe some way of giving the lessons that hasn't yet been invented, and some way of taking them in that hasn't yet been practiced, could give us a big surprise. Consider sight-reading: a trained musician can read the score and know what it would be like to hear the music. If I'd never heard that some people can sight-read, I would never have thought it humanly possible. Of course the moral is that new music isn't altogether new—the big new experience is a rearrangement of lots of little old experiences. It just might turn out the same for new smells and tastes vis-à-vis old ones; or even for color vision vis-à-vis black and white;[4] or even for sonar sense experience vis-à-vis the sort we enjoy. The thing we can say with some confidence is that we have no faculty for knowing on the basis of mere science lessons what some *new enough* experience would be like. But how new is "new enough"?—There, we just might be in for surprises.

Three Ways to Miss the Point

The First Way

A literalist might see the phrase "know what it's like" and take that to mean: "know what it resembles." Then he might ask: what's so hard about that? Why can't you just be told which ex-

periences resemble one another? You needn't have had the experiences—all you need, to be taught your lessons, is some way of referring to them. You could be told: the smell of skunk somewhat resembles the smell of burning rubber. I have been told: the taste of Vegemite somewhat resembles that of Marmite. Black-and-white Mary might know more than most of us about the resemblances among color-experiences. She might know which ones are spontaneously called "similar" by subjects who have them; which gradual changes from one to another tend to escape notice; which ones get conflated with which in memory; which ones involve roughly the same neurons firing in similar rhythms; and so forth. We could even know what the bat's sonar experiences resemble just by knowing that they do not at all resemble any experiences of humans, but do resemble—as it might be—certain experiences that occur in certain fish. This misses the point. Pace the literalist, "know what it's like" does not mean "know what it resembles." The most that's true is that knowing what it resembles *may* help you to know what it's like. If you are taught that experience A resembles B and C closely, D less, E not at all, that will help you know what A is like—*if* you know already what B and C and D and E are like. Otherwise, it helps you not at all. I don't know any better what it's like to taste Vegemite when I'm told that it tastes like Marmite, because I don't know what Marmite tastes like either. (Nor do I know any better what Marmite tastes like for being told it tastes like Vegemite.) Maybe Mary knows enough to triangulate each color experience exactly in a network of resemblances, or in many networks of resemblance in different respects, while never knowing what any node of any network is like. Maybe we could do the same for bat experiences. But no amount of information about resemblances, just by itself, does anything to help us know what an experience is like.

The Second Way

In so far as I don't know what it would be like to drive a steam locomotive fast on a cold, stormy night, part of my problem is just that I don't know what experiences I would have. The firebox puts out a lot of heat, especially when the fireman opens the door to throw on more coal; on the other hand, the cab is drafty and gives poor protection from the weather. Would I be too hot or too cold? Or both by turns? Or would it be chilled face and scorched legs? If I knew the answers to such questions, I'd know much better what it would be like to drive the locomotive. So maybe "know what it's like" just means "know what experiences one has." Then again: what's the problem? Why can't you just be told what experiences you would have if, say, you tasted Vegemite? Again, you needn't have had the experiences—all you need, to be taught your lessons, is some way of referring to them. We have ways to refer to experiences we haven't had. We can refer to them in terms of their causes: the experience one has upon tasting Vegemite, the experience one has upon tasting a substance of such-and-such chemical composition. Or we can refer to them in terms of their effects: the experience that just caused Fred to say "Yeeuch!" Or we can refer to them in terms of the physical states of the nervous system that mediate between those causes and effects: the experience one has when one's nerves are firing in such-and-such pattern. (According to some materialists, I myself for one, this means the experience which is identical with such-and-such firing pattern. According to other materialists it means the experience which is realized by such-and-such firing pattern. According to many dualists, it means the experience which is merely the lawful companion of such-and-such firing pattern. But whichever it is, we get a way of referring to the experience.) Black-and-white Mary is in a position to refer to color-experiences in all these ways. Therefore you should have no problem in telling her exactly what experiences one has upon seeing the colors. Or rather, your only problem is that you'd be telling her what she knows very well already! In general, to know what is the X is to know that the X is the Y, where it's not too obvious that the X is the Y. (Just knowing that the X is the X won't do, of course, because it is too obvious.) If Mary knows that the experience of seeing green is the experience associated with such-and-such pattern of nerve firings, then she knows the right sort of unobvious identity. So she knows what experience one has upon seeing green.

(Sometimes it's suggested that you need a "rigid designator": you know what is the X by knowing that the X is the Y only if "the Y" is a term whose referent does not depend on any contingent matter of fact. In the first place, this suggestion is false. You can know who is the man on the balcony by knowing that the man on the balcony is the Prime Minister even if neither "the Prime Minister" nor any other phrase available to you rigidly designates the man who is, in fact, the Prime Minister. In the second place, according to one version of Materialism [the one I accept] a description of the form "the state of having nerves firing in such-and-such a pattern" *is* a rigid designator, and what it designates is in fact an experience; and according to another version of Materialism, a description of the form "having some or other state which occupies so-and-so functional role" is a rigid designator of an experience. So even if the false suggestion were granted, still it hasn't been shown, without begging the question against Materialism, that Mary could not know what experience one has upon seeing red.)

Since Mary *does* know what experiences she would have if she saw the colors, but she *doesn't* know what it would be like to see the colors, we'd better conclude that "know what it's like" does not after all mean "know what experiences one has." The locomotive example was misleading. Yes, by learning what experiences the driver would have, I can know what driving the locomotive would be like; but only because I already know what those experiences are like. (It matters that I know what they're like under the appropriate descriptions—as it might be, the description "chilled face and scorched legs." This is something we'll return to later.) Mary may know as well as I do that when the driver leans out into the storm to watch the signals, he will have the experience of seeing sometimes green lights and sometimes red. She knows better than I what experiences he has when signals come into view. She can give many more unobviously equivalent descriptions of those experiences than I can. But knowing what color-experiences the driver has won't help Mary to know what his job is like. It will help me.

The Third Way

Until Mary sees green, here is one thing she will never know: she will never know that she is seeing green. The reason why is just that until she sees green, it will never be true that she is seeing green. Some knowledge is irreducibly egocentric, or *de se*.[5] It is not just knowledge about what goes on in the world; it is knowledge of who and when in the world one is. Knowledge of what goes on in the world will be true alike for all who live in that world; whereas egocentric knowledge may be true for one and false for another, or true for one at one time and false for the same one at another time. Maybe Mary knows in advance, as she plots her escape, that 9 A.M. on the 13th of May, 1997, is the moment when someone previously confined in a black-and-white cell sees color for the first time. But until that moment comes, she will never know that she herself is then seeing color—because she isn't. What isn't true isn't knowledge. This goes as much for egocentric knowledge as for the rest. So only those of whom an egocentric proposition is true can know it, and only at times when it is true of them can they know it. That one is then seeing color is an egocentric proposition. So we've found a proposition which Mary can never know until she sees color—which, as it happens, is the very moment when she will first know what it's like to see color! Have we discovered the reason why experience is the best teacher? And not contingently after all, but as a necessary consequence of the logic of egocentric knowledge?

No; we have two separate phenomena here, and only some bewitchment about the "first-person perspective" could make us miss the difference. In the first place, Mary will probably go on knowing what it's like to see green after she stops knowing the egocentric proposition that she's then seeing green. Since what isn't true isn't known she must stop knowing that proposition the moment she stops seeing green. (Does that only mean that we should have taken a different egocentric proposition: that one *has* seen green? No; for in that case Mary could go on knowing the proposition even after she forgets what it's like to see green, as might happen if she were soon recaptured.) In the second place, Mary might come to know what it's like to see green even if she didn't know the egocentric proposition. She might not have known in advance that her escape route would take her across a green meadow, and it might take her a little while to recognize grass by its shape. So at first she might know only that she was seeing some colors or other, and thereby finding out what some color-experiences or other were like, without being able to put a name either to the colors or to the experiences. She would then know what it was like to see green, though not under that description, indeed not under any description more useful than "the color-experience I'm having now"; but she would not know the egocentric proposition that she is then seeing green, since she wouldn't know which color she was seeing. In the third place, the gaining of egocentric knowledge may have prerequisites that have nothing to do with experience. Just as

Mary can't know she's seeing green until she *does* see green, she can't know she's turning 50 until she *does* turn 50. But—I hope!—turning 50 does not involve some special experience. In short, though indeed one can gain egocentric knowledge that one is in some situation only when one is in it, that is not the same as finding out what an experience is like only when one has that experience.

We've just rejected two suggestions that don't work separately, and we may note that they don't work any better when put together. One knows what is the X by knowing that the X is the Y, where the identity is not too obvious; and "the Y" might be an egocentric description. So knowledge that the X is the Y might be irreducibly egocentric knowledge, therefore knowledge that cannot be had until it is true of one that the X is the Y. So one way of knowing what is the X will remain unavailable until it comes true of one that the X is the Y. One way that I could gain an unobvious identity concerning the taste of Vegemite would be for it to come true that the taste of Vegemite was the taste I was having at that very moment—and that would come true at the very moment I tasted Vegemite and found out what it was like! Is this why experience is the best teacher?—No; cases of gaining an unobvious egocentric identity are a dime a dozen, and most of them do not result in finding out what an experience is like. Suppose I plan ahead that I will finally break down and taste Vegemite next Thursday noon. Then on Wednesday noon, if I watch the clock, I first gain the unobvious egocentric knowledge that the taste of Vegemite is the taste I shall be having in exactly 24 hours, and thereby I have a new way of knowing what is the taste of Vegemite. But on Wednesday noon I don't yet know what it's like. Another example: from time to time I find myself next to a Vegemite-taster. On those occasions, and only those, I know what is the taste of Vegemite by knowing that it is the taste being had by the person next to me. But on no such occasion has it ever yet happened that I knew what it was like to taste Vegemite.

The Hypothesis of Phenomenal Information

No amount of the physical information that black-and-white Mary gathers could help her know what it was like see colors; no amount of the physical information that we might gather about bats could help us know what it's like to have their experiences; and likewise in other cases. There is a natural and tempting explanation of why physical information does not help. That is the hypothesis that besides physical information there is an irreducibly different kind of information to be had: *phenomenal information*. The two are independent. Two possible cases might be exactly alike physically, yet differ phenomenally. When we get physical information we narrow down the physical possibilities, and perhaps we narrow them down all the way to one, but we leave open a range of phenomenal possibilities. When we have an experience, on the other hand, we acquire phenomenal information; possibilities previously open are eliminated; and that is what it is to learn what the experience is like.

(Analogy. Suppose the question concerned the location of a point within a certain region of the *x-y* plane. We might be told that its *x*-coordinate lies in certain intervals, and outside certain others. We might even get enough of this information to fix the *x*-coordinate exactly. But no amount of *x*-information would tell us anything about the *y*-coordinate; any amount of *x*-information leaves open all the *y*-possibilities. But when at last we make a *y*-measurement, we acquire a new kind of information; possibilities previously open are eliminated; and that is how we learn where the point is in the *y*-direction.)

What might the subject matter of phenomenal information be? *If* the Hypothesis of Phenomenal Information is true, then you have an easy answer: it is information about experience. More specifically, it is information about a certain part or aspect or feature of experience. But if the Hypothesis is false, then there is still experience (complete with all its parts and aspects and features) and yet no information about experience is phenomenal information. So it cannot be said in a neutral way, without presupposing the Hypothesis, that information about experience is phenomenal information. For if the Hypothesis is false and Materialism is true, it may be that all the information there is about experience is physical information, and can very well be presented in lessons for the inexperienced.

It makes no difference to put some fashionable new phrase in place of "experience." If instead of "experience" you say "raw feel" (or just "feeling"), or "way it feels," or "what it's like," then I submit that you mean nothing different. Is there anything it's like to be this robot? Does

this robot have experiences?—I can tell no difference between the new question and the old. Does sunburn feel the same way to you that it does to me? Do we have the same raw feel? Do we have the same experience when sunburned?—Again, same question. "Know the feeling," "know what it's like"—interchangeable. (Except that the former may hint at an alternative to the Hypothesis of Phenomenal Information.) So if the friend of phenomenal information says that its subject matter is raw feels, or ways to feel, or what it's like, then I respond just as I do if he says that the subject matter is experience. Maybe so, *if* the Hypothesis of Phenomenal Information is true; but if the Hypothesis is false and Materialism is true, nevertheless there is still information about raw feels, ways to feel or what it's like; but in that case it is physical information and can be conveyed in lessons.

We might get a candidate for the subject matter of phenomenal information that is not just experience renamed, but is still tendentious. For instance, we might be told that phenomenal information concerns the intrinsic character of experience. A friend of phenomenal information might indeed believe that it reveals certain special, non-physical intrinsic properties of experience. He might even believe that it reveals the existence of some special non-physical thing or process, *all* of whose intrinsic properties are non-physical. But he is by no means alone in saying that experience has an intrinsic character. Plenty of us materialists say so too. We say that a certain color-experience is whatever state occupies a certain functional role. So if the occupant of that role (universally, or in the case of humans, or in the case of certain humans) is a certain pattern of neural firing, then that pattern of firing *is* the experience (in the case in question). Therefore the intrinsic character of the experience is the intrinsic character of the firing pattern. For instance, a frequency of firing is part of the intrinsic character of the experience. If we materialists are right about what experience is, then black-and-white Mary knows all about the intrinsic character of color-experience; whereas most people who know what color-experience is like remain totally ignorant about its intrinsic character.[6]

To say that phenomenal information concerns "qualia" would be tendentious in much the same way. For how was this notion introduced? Often thus. We are told to imagine someone who, when he sees red things, has just the sort of experiences that we have when we see green things, and vice versa; and we are told to call this a case of "inverted qualia". And then we are told to imagine someone queerer still, who sees red and responds to it appropriately, and indeed has entirely the same functional organization of inner states as we do and yet has no experiences at all; and we are told to call this a case of "absent qualia." Now a friend of phenomenal information might well think that these deficiencies have something to do with the non-physical subject matter of phenomenal information. But others can understand them otherwise. Some materialists will reject the cases outright, but others, and I for one, will make sense of them as best we can. Maybe the point is that the states that occupy the roles of experiences, and therefore *are* the experiences, in normal people are inverted or absent in victims of inverted or absent qualia. (This presupposes, what might be false, that most people are enough alike). Experience of red—the state that occupies that role in normal people—occurs also in the victim of "inverted qualia," but in him it occupies the role of experience of green; whereas the state that occupies in him the role of experience of red is the state that occupies in normal people the role of experience of green. Experience of red and of green—that is, the occupants of those roles for normal people—do not occur at all in the victim of "absent qualia"; the occupants of those roles for him are states that don't occur at all in the normal. Thus we make good sense of inverted and absent qualia; but in such a way that "qualia" is just the word for role-occupying states taken *per se* rather than *qua* occupants of roles. Qualia, so understood, could not be the subject matter of phenomenal information. Mary knows all about them. We who have them mostly don't.[7]

It is best to rest content with an unhelpful name and a *via negativa*. Stipulate that "the phenomenal aspect of the world" is to name whatever is the subject matter of phenomenal information, if there is any such thing; the phenomenal aspect, if such there be, is that which we can become informed about by having new experiences but never by taking lessons. Having said this, it will be safe to say that information about the phenomenal aspect of the world can only be phenomenal information. But all we really know, after thus closing the circle, is that phenomenal information is supposed to reveal the presence of some sort of non-physical things or processes within experience, or else it is supposed to reveal that certain physical things or processes within experience have some sort of nonphysical properties.

The Knowledge Argument

If we invoke the Hypothesis of Phenomenal Information to explain why no amount of physical information suffices to teach us what a new experience is like, then we have a powerful argument to refute any materialist theory of the mind. Frank Jackson (see note 1) calls it the "Knowledge Argument." Arguments against one materialist theory or another are never very conclusive. It is always possible to adjust the details. But the Knowledge Argument, if it worked, would directly refute the bare minimum that is common to *all* materialist theories.

It goes as follows. First in a simplified form; afterward we'll do it properly. Minimal Materialism is a supervenience thesis: no difference without physical difference. That is: any two possibilities that are just alike physically are just alike *simpliciter.* If two possibilities are just alike physically, then no physical information can eliminate one but not both of them. If two possibilities are just alike *simpliciter* (if that is possible) then no information whatsoever can eliminate one but not both of them. So if there is a kind of information—namely, phenomenal information—that can eliminate possibilities that any amount of physical information leaves open, then there must be possibilities that are just alike physically, but not just alike *simpliciter.* That is just what minimal Materialism denies.

(Analogy. If two possible locations in our region agree in their x-coordinate, then no amount of x-information can eliminate one but not both. If, *per impossibile,* two possible locations agreed in all their coordinates, then no information whatsoever could eliminate one but not both. So if there is a kind of information—namely, y-information—that can eliminate locations that any amount of x-information leaves open, then there must be locations in the region that agree in their x-coordinate but not in all their coordinates.)

Now to remove the simplification. What we saw so far was the Knowledge Argument against Materialism taken as a necessary truth, applying unrestrictedly to all possible worlds. But we materialists usually think that Materialism is a contingent truth. We grant that there are spooky possible worlds where Materialism is false, but we insist that our actual world isn't one of them. If so, then there might after all be two possibilities that are alike physically but not alike *simpliciter;* but one or both of the two would have to be possibilities where Materialism was false. Spooky worlds could differ with respect to their spooks without differing physically. Our minimal Materialism must be a *restricted* supervenience thesis: within a certain class of worlds, which includes our actual world, there is no difference without physical difference. Within that class, any two possibilities just alike physically are just alike *simpliciter.* But what delineates the relevant class? (It is trivial that our world belongs to *some* class wherein there is no difference without physical difference. That will be so however spooky our world may be. The unit class of our world is one such class, for instance. And so is any class that contains our world, and contains no two physical duplicates.) I think the relevant class should consist of the worlds that have nothing wholly alien to this world. The inhabitants of such a non-alien world could be made from the inhabitants of ours, so to speak, by a process of division and recombination. That will make no wholly different kinds of things, and no wholly different fundamental properties of things.[8] Our restricted materialist supervenience thesis should go as follows: throughout the non-alien worlds, there is no difference without physical difference.

If the Hypothesis of Phenomenal Information be granted, then the Knowledge Argument refutes this restricted supervenience nearly as decisively as it refutes the unrestricted version. Consider a possibility that is eliminated by phenomenal information, but not by any amount of physical information. There are two cases. Maybe this possibility has nothing that is alien to our world. In that case the argument goes as before: actuality and the eliminated possibility are just alike physically, they are not just alike *simpliciter;* furthermore, both of them fall within the restriction to non-alien worlds, so we have a counterexample even to restricted supervenience. Or maybe instead the eliminated possibility does have something X which is alien to this world—an alien kind of thing, or maybe an alien fundamental property of non-alien things. Then the phenomenal information gained by having a new experience has revealed something negative: at least in part, it is the information that X is *not* present. How can that be? If there is such a thing as phenomenal information, presumably what it reveals is positive: the presence of something hitherto unknown. Not, of course, something alien from actuality itself; but something alien from actuality as it is inadequately represented by the inexperienced and by the materialists. If Mary learns something when she finds out what it's like to see the colors, presumably she learns that there's *more* to the world than she knew before—not *less.* It's easy to think that phenomenal information might eliminate possibilities that are impoverished by comparison with actuality, but that would make a counterexample to the restricted supervenience thesis. To eliminate possibilities without making a counterexample, phenomenal information would have to eliminate possibilities less impoverished than actuality. And how can phenomenal information do that? Compare ordinary perceptual information. Maybe Jean-Paul can just *see* that Pierre is absent from the café, at least if it's a small café. But how can he just see that Pierre is absent from Paris, let alone from the whole of actuality?

(Is there a third case? What if the eliminated possibility is in one respect richer than actuality, in another respect poorer? Suppose the eliminated possibility has X, which is alien from actuality, but also it lacks Y. Then phenomenal information might eliminate it by revealing the actual presence of Y, without having to reveal the actual absence of X—But then I say there ought to be a third possibility, one with neither X nor Y, poorer and in no respect richer than actuality, and again without any physical difference from actuality. For why should taking away X automatically restore Y? Why can't they vary independently?[9] But this third possibility differs *simpliciter* from actuality without differing physically. Further, it has nothing alien from actuality. So we regain a counterexample to the restricted supervenience thesis.)

The Knowledge Argument works. There is no way to grant the Hypothesis of Phenomenal Information and still uphold Materialism. Therefore I deny the Hypothesis. I cannot refute it outright. But later I shall argue, first, that it is more peculiar, and therefore less tempting, that it may at first seem; and, second, that we are not forced to accept it, since an alternative hypothesis does justice to the way experience best teaches us what it's like.

Three More Ways to Miss the Point

The Hypothesis of Phenomenal Information characterizes information in terms of eliminated possibilities. But there are other conceptions of "information." Therefore the Hypothesis has look-alikes: hypotheses which say that experience produces "information" which could not be gained otherwise, but do not characterize this "information" in terms of eliminated possibilities. These look-alikes do not work as premises for the Knowledge Argument. They do not say that phenomenal information eliminates possibilities that differ, but do not differ physically, from uneliminated possibilities. The look-alike hypotheses of phenomenal "information" are consistent with Materialism, and may very well be true. But they don't make the Knowledge Argument go away. Whatever harmless look-alikes may or may not be true, and whatever conception may or may not deserve the name "information," the only way to save Materialism is fix our attention squarely on the genuine Hypothesis of Phenomenal Information, and deny it. To avert our eyes, and attend to something else, is no substitute for that denial.

Might a look-alike help at least to this extent: by giving us something true that well might have been confused with the genuine Hypothesis, thereby explaining how we might have believed the Hypothesis although it was false? I think not. Each of the look-alikes turns out to imply not only that experience can give us "information" that no amount of lessons can give, but also that lessons in Russian can give us "information" that no amount of lessons in English can give (and vice versa). I doubt that any friend of phenomenal information ever thought that the special role of experience in teaching what it's like was on a par with the special role of Russian! I will have to say before I'm done that phenomenal information is an illusion, but I think I must look elsewhere for a credible hypothesis about what sort of illusion it might be.

The Fourth Way

If a hidden camera takes photographs of a room, the film ends up bearing traces of what went on in the room. The traces are distinctive: that is, the details of the traces depend on the details of what went on, and if what went on had been different in any of many ways, the traces would have been correspondingly different. So we can say that the traces bear information, and that he who has the film has the information. That might be said because the traces, plus the way they depend on what went on, suffice to eliminate possibilities; but instead we might say "in-

formation" and just mean "distinctive traces." If so, it's certainly true that new experience imparts "information" unlike any that can be gained from lessons. Experience and lessons leave different kinds of traces. That is so whether or not the experience eliminates possibilities that the lessons leave open. It is equally true, of course, that lessons in Russian leave traces unlike any that are left by lessons in English, regardless of whether the lessons cover the same ground and eliminate the same possibilities.

The Fifth Way

When we speak of transmission of "information," we often mean transmission of text. Repositories of "information," such as libraries, are storehouses of text. Whether the text is empty verbiage or highly informative is beside the point. Maybe we too contain information by being storehouses of text. Maybe there is a language of thought, and maybe the way we believe things is to store sentences of this language in some special way, or in some special part of our brains. In that case, we could say that storing away a new sentence was storing away a new piece of "information," whether or not that new piece eliminated any possibilities not already eliminated by the sentences stored previously. Maybe, also, the language of thought is not fixed once and for all, but can gain new words. Maybe, for instance, it borrows words from public language. And maybe, when one has a new experience, that causes one's language of thought to gain a new word which denotes that experience—a word which could not have been added to the language by any other means. If all this is so, then when Mary sees colors, her language of thought gains new words, allowing her to store away new sentences and thereby gain "information." All this about the language of thought, the storing of sentences, and the gaining of words is speculation. But it is plausible speculation, even if no longer the only game in town. If it is all true, then we have another look-alike hypothesis of phenomenal "information." When Mary gains new words and stores new sentences, that is "information" that she never had before, regardless of whether it eliminates any possibilities that she had not eliminated already.

But again, the special role of experience turns out to be on a par with the special role of Russian. If the language of thought picks up new words by borrowing from public language, then lessons in Russian add new words, and result in the storing of new sentences, and thereby impart "information" that never could have been had from lessons in English. (You might say that the new Russian words are mere synonyms of old words, or at least old phrases, that were there already; and synonyms don't count. But no reason has been given why the new inner words created by experience may not also be synonyms of old phrases, perhaps of long descriptions in the language of neurophysiology.)

The Sixth Way

A philosopher who is skeptical about possibility, as so many are, may wish to replace possibilities themselves with linguistic ersatz possibilities: maximal consistent sets of sentences. And he may be content to take "consistent" in a narrowly logical sense, so that a set with "Fred is married" and "Fred is a bachelor" may count as consistent, and only an overt contradiction like "Fred is married" and "Fred is not married" will be ruled out.[10] The ersatz possibilities might also be taken as sets of sentences of the language of thought, if the philosopher believes in it. Then if someone's language of thought gains new words, whether as a result of new experience or as a result of being taught in Russian, the ersatz possibilities become richer and more numerous. The sets of sentences that were maximal before are no longer maximal after new words are added. So when Mary sees colors and her language of thought gains new words, there are new ersatz possibilities; and she can straightway eliminate some of them. Suppose she knows beforehand that she is about to see green, and that the experience of seeing green is associated with neural firing pattern F. So when she sees green and gains the new word G for her experience, then straightway there are new, enriched ersatz possibilities with sentences saying that she has G without F, and straightway she knows enough to eliminate these ersatz possibilities. (Even if she does not know beforehand what she is about to see, straightway she can eliminate at least those of her new-found ersatz possibilities with sentences denying that she then has G.) Just as we can characterize information in terms of elimination of possibilities, so we can characterize ersatz "information" in terms of elimination of ersatz "possibilities." So here we have the closest look-alike hypothesis of all, provided that language-of-thoughtism is

true. But we still do not have the genuine Hypothesis of Phenomenal Information, since the eliminated ersatz possibility of G without F may not have been a genuine possibility at all. It may have been like the ersatz possibility of married bachelors.

Curiouser and Curiouser

The Hypothesis of Phenomenal Information is more peculiar than it may at first seem. For one thing, because it is opposed to more than just Materialism. Some of you may have welcomed the Knowledge Argument because you thought all along that physical information was inadequate to explain the phenomena of mind. You may have been convinced all along that the mind could do things that no physical system could do: bend spoons, invent new jokes, demonstrate the consistency of arithmetic, reduce the wave packet, or what have you. You may have been convinced that the full causal story of how the deeds of mind are accomplished involves the causal interactions not only of material bodies but also of astral bodies; not only the vibrations of the electromagnetic field but also the good or bad vibes of the psionic field; not only protoplasm but ectoplasm. I doubt it, but never mind. It's irrelevant to our topic. The Knowledge Argument is targeted against you no less than it is against Materialism itself.

Let *parapsychology* be the science of all the non-physical things, properties, causal processes, laws of nature, and so forth that may be required to explain the things we do. Let us suppose that we learn ever so much parapsychology. It will make no difference. Black-and-white Mary may study all the parapsychology as well as all the psychophysics of color vision, but she still won't know what it's like. Lessons on the aura of Vegemite will do no more for us than lessons on its chemical composition. And so it goes. Our intuitive starting point wasn't just that *physics* lessons couldn't help the inexperienced to know what it's like. It was that *lessons* couldn't help. If there is such a thing as phenomenal information, it isn't just independent of physical information. It's independent of every sort of information that could be served up in lessons for the inexperienced. For it is supposed to eliminate possibilities that any amount of lessons leave open. Therefore phenomenal information is not just parapsychological information, if such there be. It's something very much stranger.

The genuine Hypothesis of Phenomenal Information, as distinguished from its look-alikes, treats information in terms of the elimination of possibilities. When we lack information, several alternative possibilities are open, when we get the information some of the alternatives are excluded. But a second peculiar thing about phenomenal information is that it resists this treatment. (So does logical or mathematical "information." However, phenomenal information cannot be logical or mathematical, because lessons in logic and mathematics no more teach us what a new experience is like than lessons in physics or parapsychology do.) When someone doesn't know what it's like to have an experience, where are the alternative open possibilities? I cannot present to myself in thought a range of alternative possibilities about what it might be like to taste Vegemite. That is because I cannot imagine either what it *is* like to taste Vegemite, or any alternative way that it *might* be like but in fact isn't. (I could perfectly well imagine that Vegemite tastes just like peanut butter, or something else familiar to me, but let's suppose I've been told authoritatively that this isn't so.) I can't even pose the question that phenomenal information is supposed to answer: is it this way or that? It seems that the alternative possibilities must be unthinkable beforehand; and afterward too, except for the one that turns out to be actualized. I don't say there's anything altogether impossible about a range of unthinkable alternatives; only something peculiar. But it's peculiar enough to suggest that we may somehow have gone astray.

From Phenomenal to Epiphenomenal

A third peculiar thing about phenomenal information is that it is strangely isolated from all other sorts of information; and this is so regardless of whether the mind works on physical or parapsychological principles. The phenomenal aspect of the world has nothing to do with explaining why people seemingly talk about the phenomenal aspect of the world. For instance, it plays no part in explaining the movements of the pens of philosophers writing treatises about phenomenal information and the way experience has provided them with it.

When Mary gets out of her black-and-white

cell, her jaw drops. She says "At last! So this is what it's like to see colors!" Afterward she does things she couldn't do before, such as recognizing a new sample of the first color she ever saw. She may also do other things she didn't do before: unfortunate things, like writing about phenomenal information and the poverty of Materialism. One might think she said what she said and did what she did because she came to know what it's like to see colors. Not so, if the Hypothesis of Phenomenal Information is right. For suppose the phenomenal aspect of the world had been otherwise, so that she gained different phenomenal information. Or suppose the phenomenal aspect of the world had been absent altogether, as we materialists think it is. Would that have made the slightest difference to what she did or said then or later? I think not. Making a difference to what she does or says means, at least in part, making a difference to the motions of the particles of which she is composed. (Or better: making a difference to the spatiotemporal shape of the wave-function of those particles. But let that pass.) For how could she do or say anything different, if none of her particles moved any differently? But if something non-physical sometimes makes a difference to the motions of physical particles, then physics as we know it is wrong. Not just silent, not just incomplete—wrong. Either the particles are caused to change their motion without benefit of any force, or else there is some extra force that works very differently from the usual four. To believe in the phenomenal aspect of the world, but deny that it is epiphenomenal, is to bet against the truth of physics. Given the success of physics hitherto, and even with due allowance for the foundational ailments of quantum mechanics, such betting is rash! A friend of the phenomenal aspect would be safer to join Jackson in defense of *epiphenomenal qualia*.

But there is more to the case than just an empirical bet in favor of physics. Suppose there is a phenomenal aspect of the world, and suppose it does make some difference to the motions of Mary's jaw or the noises out of her mouth. Then we can describe the phenomenal aspect, if we know enough, in terms of its physical effects. It is that on which physical phenomena depend in such-and-such way. This descriptive handle will enable us to give lessons on it to the inexperienced. But in so far as we can give lessons on it, what we have is just parapsychology. That whereof we cannot learn except by having the experience still eludes us. I do not argue that *everything* about the alleged distinctive subject matter of phenomenal information must be epiphenomenal. Part of it may be parapsychological instead. But I insist that *some* aspect of it must be epiphenomenal.

Suppose that the Hypothesis of Phenomenal Information is true and suppose that V_1 and V_2 are all of the maximally specific phenomenal possibilities concerning what it's like to taste Vegemite; anyone who tastes Vegemite will find out which one obtains, and no one else can. And suppose that P_1 and P_2 are all the maximally specific physical possibilities. (Of course we really need far more than two Ps, and maybe a friend of phenomenal information would want more than two Vs, but absurdly small numbers will do for an example.) Then we have four alternative hypotheses about the causal independence or dependence of the Ps on the Vs. Each one can be expressed as a pair of counterfactual conditionals. Two hypotheses are patterns of dependence.

K_1: if V_1 then P_1, if V_2 then P_2
K_2: if V_1 then P_2, if V_2 then P_1

The other two are patterns of independence.

K_3: if V_1 then P_1, if V_2 then P_1
K_4: if V_1 then P_2, if V_2 then P_2

These dependency hypotheses are, I take it, contingent propositions. They are made true, if they are, by some contingent feature of the world, though it's indeed a vexed question what sort of feature it is.[11] Now we have eight joint possibilities.

$K_1V_1P_1$ $K_3V_1P_1$ $K_3V_2P_1$ $K_2V_2P_1$
$K_2V_1P_2$ $K_4V_1P_2$ $K_4V_2P_2$ $K_1V_2P_2$

Between the four on the top row and the four on the bottom row, there is the physical difference between P_1 and P_2. Between the four on the left and the four on the right, there is the phenomenal difference between V_1 and V_2. And between the four on the edges and the four in the middle there is a parapsychological difference. It is the difference between dependence and independence of the physical on the phenomenal; between efficacy and epiphenomenalism, so far as this one example is concerned. There's nothing ineffable about that. Whether or not you've tasted Vegemite, and whether or not you can conceive of the alleged difference between V_1 and V_2, you can still be told whether the physical difference between P_1 and P_2 does or doesn't depend on some part of the phenomenal aspect of the world.

Lessons can teach the inexperienced which parapsychological possibility obtains, dependence or independence. Let it be dependence: we have either K_1 or K_2. For if we had independence, then already we would have found our epiphenomenal difference: namely, the difference between V_1 and V_2. And lessons can teach the inexperienced which of the two physical possibilities obtains. Without loss of generality let it be P_1. Now two of our original eight joint possibilities remain open: $K_1V_1P_1$ and $K_2V_2P_1$. The difference between those is not at all physical, and not at all parapsychological: it's P_1, and it's dependence, in both cases. The difference is entirely phenomenal. And also it is entirely epiphenomenal. Nothing physical, and nothing parapsychological, depends on the difference between $K_1V_1P_1$ and $K_2V_2P_1$. We have the same sort of pattern of dependence either way; it's just that the phenomenal possibilities have been swapped. Whether it's independence or whether it's dependence, therefore, we have found an epiphenomenal part of the phenomenal aspect of the world. It is the residue left behind when we remove the parapsychological part.

Suppose that someday I taste Vegemite, and hold forth about how I know at last what it's like. The sound of my holding forth is a physical effect, part of the realized physical possibility P_1. This physical effect is exactly the same whether it's part of the joint possibility $K_1V_1P_1$ or part of its alternative $K_2V_2P_1$. It may be caused by V_1 in accordance with K_1, or it may instead be caused by V_2 in accordance with K_2, but it's the same either way. So it does not occur because we have K_1V_1 rather than K_2V_2, or vice versa. The alleged difference between these two possibilities does nothing to explain the alleged physical manifestation of my finding out which one of them is realized. It is in that way that the difference is epiphenomenal. That makes it very queer, and repugnant to good sense.

The Ability Hypothesis

So the Hypothesis of Phenomenal Information turns out to be very peculiar indeed. It would be nice, and not only for materialists, if we could reject it. For materialists, it is essential to reject it. And we can. There is an alternative hypothesis about what it is to learn what an experience is like: the *Ability Hypothesis*. Laurence Nemirow summarizes it thus:

> some modes of understanding consist, not in the grasping of facts, but in the acquisition of abilities. . . . As for understanding an experience, we may construe that as an ability to place oneself, at will, in a state representative of the experience. I understand the experience of seeing red if I can at will visualize red. Now it is perfectly clear why there must be a special connection between the ability to place oneself in a state representative of a given experience and the point of view of experiencer: exercising the ability just *is* what we call "adopting the point of view of experiencer." . . . We can, then, come to terms with the subjectivity of our understanding of experience without positing subjective facts as the objects of our understanding. This account explains, incidentally, the linguistic incommunicability of our subjective understanding of experience (a phenomenon which might seem to support the hypothesis of subjective facts). The latter is explained as a special case of the linguistic incommunicability of abilities to place oneself at will in a given state, such as the state of having lowered blood pressure, and the state of having wiggling ears.[12]

If you have a new experience, you gain abilities to remember and to imagine. After you taste Vegemite, and you learn what it's like, you can afterward remember the experience you had. By remembering how it once was, you can afterward imagine such an experience. Indeed, even if you eventually forget the occasion itself, you will very likely retain your ability to imagine such an experience.

Further, you gain an ability to recognize the same experience if it comes again. If you taste Vegemite on another day, you will probably know that you have met the taste once before. And if, while tasting Vegemite, you know that it is Vegemite you are tasting, then you will be able to put the name to the experience if you have it again. Or if you are told nothing at the time, but later you somehow know that it is Vegemite that you are then remembering or imagining tasting, again you can put the name to the experience, or to the memory, or to the experience of imagining, if it comes again. Here, the ability you gain is an ability to gain information if given other information. Nevertheless, the information gained is not phenomenal, and the ability to gain information is not the same thing as information itself.

Earlier, I mentioned "knowing what an experience is like under a description." Now I can say that what I meant by this was having the ability to remember or imagine an experience while also knowing the egocentric proposition that what one is then imagining is the experience of such-and-such description. One might well know what an experience is like under one description, but not under another. One might even know what some experience is like, but not under any description whatever—unless it be some rather trivial description like "that queer taste that I'm imagining right now." That is what would happen if you slipped a dab of Vegemite into my food without telling me what it was: afterward, I would know what it was like to taste Vegemite, but not under that description, and not under any other non-trivial description. It might be suggested that "knowing what it's like to taste Vegemite" really means what I'd call "knowing what it's like to taste Vegemite under the description 'tasting Vegemite' "; and if so, knowing what it's like would involve both ability and information. I disagree. For surely it would make sense to say: "I know this experience well, I've long known what it's like, but only today have I found out that it's the experience of tasting Vegemite." But this verbal question is unimportant. For the information involved in knowing what it's like under a description, and allegedly involved in knowing what it's like, is anyhow not the queer phenomenal information that needs rejecting.

(Is there a problem here for the friend of phenomenal information? Suppose he says that knowing what it's like to taste Vegemite means knowing that the taste of Vegemite has a certain "phenomenal character." This requires putting the name to the taste, so clearly it corresponds to our notion of knowing what it's like to taste Vegemite under the description "tasting Vegemite." But we also have our notion of knowing what it's like *simpliciter,* and what can he offer that corresponds to that? Perhaps he should answer by appeal to a trivial description, as follows: knowing what it's like *simpliciter* means knowing what it's like under the trivial description "taste I'm imagining now," and that means knowing that the taste one is imagining now has a certain phenomenal character.)

As well as gaining the ability to remember and imagine the experience you had, you also gain the ability to imagine related experiences that you never had. After tasting Vegemite, you might for instance become able to imagine tasting Vegemite ice cream. By performing imaginative experiments, you can predict with some confidence what you would do in circumstances that have never arisen—whether you'd ask for a second helping of Vegemite ice cream, for example.

These abilities to remember and imagine and recognize are abilities you cannot gain (unless by super-neurosurgery, or by magic) except by tasting Vegemite and learning what it's like. You can't get them by taking lessons on the physics or the parapsychology of the experience, or even by taking comprehensive lessons that cover the whole of physics and parapsychology. The Ability Hypothesis says that knowing what an experience is like just *is* the possession of these abilities to remember, imagine, and recognize. It isn't the possession of any kind of information, ordinary or peculiar. It isn't knowing that certain possibilities aren't actualized. It isn't knowing-that. It's knowing-how. Therefore it should be no surprise that lessons won't teach you what an experience is like. Lessons impart information; ability is something else. Knowledge-that does not automatically provide know-how.

There are parallel cases. Some know how to wiggle their ears; others don't. If you can't do it, no amount of information will help. Some know how to eat with chopsticks, others don't. Information will help up to a point—for instance, if your trouble is that you hold one chopstick in each hand—but no amount of information, by itself, will bring you to a very high level of know-how. Some know how to recognize a C-38 locomotive by sight, others don't. If you don't, it won't much help if you memorize a detailed geometrical description of its shape, even though that does all the eliminating of possibilities that there is to be done. (Conversely, knowing the shape by sight doesn't enable you to write down the geometrical description.) Information very often contributes to know-how, but often it doesn't contribute enough. That's why music students have to practice.

Know-how is ability. But of course some aspects of ability are in no sense knowledge: strength, sufficient funds. Other aspects of ability are, purely and simply, a matter of information. If you want to know how to open the combination lock on the bank vault, information is all you need. It remains that there are aspects of ability that do *not* consist simply of possession of information, and that we *do* call knowledge. The Ability Hypothesis holds that knowing what an experience is like is that sort of knowledge.

If the Ability Hypothesis is the correct analysis of knowing what an experience is like, then phenomenal information is an illusion. We ought to explain that illusion. It would be feeble, I think, just to say that we're fooled by the ambiguity of the word "know": we confuse ability with information because we confuse knowledge in the sense of knowing-how with knowledge in the sense of knowing-that. There may be two senses of the word "know," but they are well and truly entangled. They mark the two pure endpoints of a range of mixed cases. The usual thing is that we gain information and ability together. If so, it should be no surprise if we apply to pure cases of gaining ability, or to pure cases of gaining information, the same word "know" that we apply to all the mixed cases.

Along with information and ability, acquaintance is a third element of the mixture. If Lloyd George died too soon, there's a sense in which Father never can know him. Information won't do it, even if Father is a most thorough biographer and the archives are very complete. (And the trouble isn't that there's some very special information about someone that you can only get by being in his presence.) Know-how won't do it either, no matter how good Father may be at imagining Lloyd George, seemingly remembering him, and recognizing him. (Father may be able to recognize Lloyd George even if there's no longer any Lloyd George to recognize—if *per impossible* he did turn up, Father could tell it was him.) Again, what we have is not just a third separate sense of "know." Meeting someone, gaining a lot of information about him that would be hard to gain otherwise, and gaining abilities regarding him usually go together. The pure cases are exceptions.

A friend of phenomenal information will agree, of course, that when we learn what an experience is like, we gain abilities to remember, imagine, and recognize. But he will say that it is because we gain phenomenal information that we gain the abilities. He might even say the same about other cases of gaining know-how: you can recognize the C-38 when you have phenomenal information about what it's like to see that shape, you can eat with chopsticks or wiggle your ears when you gain phenomenal information about the experience of doing so, and so on. What should friends of the Ability Hypothesis make of this? Is he offering a conjecture, which we must reject, about the causal origin of abilities? I think not. He thinks, as we do, that experiences leave distinctive traces in people, and that these traces enable us to do things. Likewise being taught to recognize a C-38 or to eat with chopsticks, or whatever happens on first wiggling the ears, leave traces that enable us to do things afterward. That much is common ground. He also interprets these enabling traces as representations that bear information about their causes. (If the same traces had been caused in some deviant way they might perhaps have carried misinformation.) We might even be able to accept that too. The time for us to quarrel comes only when he says that these traces represent special phenomenal facts, facts which cannot be represented in any other way, and therefore which cannot be taught in physics lessons or even in parapsychology lessons. That is the part, and the *only* part, which we must reject. But that is no part of his psychological story about how we gain abilities. It is just a gratuitous metaphysical gloss on that story.

We say that learning what an experience is like means gaining certain abilities. If the causal basis for those abilities turns out also to be a special kind of representation of some sort of information, so be it. We need only deny that it represents a special kind of information about a special subject matter. Apart from that it's up for grabs what, if anything, it may represent. The details of stimuli: the chemical composition of Vegemite, reflectances of surfaces, the motions of well-handled chopsticks or of ears? The details of inner states produced by those stimuli: patterns of firings of nerves? We could agree to either, so long as we did not confuse 'having information' represented in this special way with having the same information in the form of knowledge or belief. Or we could disagree. Treating the ability-conferring trace as a representation is optional. What's essential is that when we learn what an experience is like by having it, we gain abilities to remember, imagine, and recognize.

NOTES

Part of this paper derives from a lecture at LaTrobe University in 1981. I thank LaTrobe for support in 1981, Harvard University for support under a Santayana Fellowship in 1988, and Frank Jackson for very helpful discussion.

1. See Frank Jackson, "Epiphenomenal qualia," *Philosophical Quarterly* 32 (1982), pp. 127–36, and reprinted in this volume; "What Mary didn't know," *Journal of Philosophy* 83 (1986), pp. 291–95.
2. See B. A. Farrell, "Experience," *Mind* 59 (1950), pp. 170–98; and Thomas Nagel, "What is it like to be a bat?" *Philosophical Review* 83 (1974), pp. 435–50, also in Thomas Nagel, *Mortal Questions* (Cambridge: Cambridge University Press, 1979).
3. See Peter Unger, "On experience and the development of the understanding," *American Philosophical Quarterly* 3 (1966), pp. 1–9.
4. For such speculation, see Paul M. Churchland, "Reduction, qualia, and the direct introspection of brain states," *Journal of Philosophy* 82 (1985), pp. 8–28.
5. See my "Attitudes *de dicto* and *de se*," *Philosophical Review* 88 (1979), pp. 513–43, also in my *Philosophical Papers*, vol. I (New York: Oxford University Press, 1983); and Roderick Chisholm, *The First Person: An Essay on Reference and Intentionality* (Minneapolis: University of Minnesota Press, 1981).
6. See Gilbert Harman, "The intrinsic quality of experience," *Philosophical Perspectives* 4 (1990).
7. See Ned Block and Jerry A. Fodor, "What psychological states are not," *Philosophical Review* 81 (1972), pp. 159–81 and my "Mad pain and Martian pain," in *Readings in Philosophy of Psychology*, vol. I, and in my *Philosophical Papers*, vol. I.
8. See my "New work for a theory of universals," *Australasian Journal of Philosophy* 61 (1983), pp. 343–77, especially pp. 361–64. For a different view about how to state minimal Materialism, see Terence Horgan, "Supervenience and microphysics," *Pacific Philosophical Quarterly* 63 (1982), pp. 29–43.
9. On recombination of possibilities, see my *On the Plurality of Worlds* (Oxford: Blackwell, 1986), pp. 87–92. The present argument may call for a principle that also allows recombination of properties; I now think that would not necessarily require treating properties as non-spatiotemporal parts of their instances. On recombination of properties, see also D. M. Armstrong, *A Combinatorial Theory of Possibility* (Cambridge: Cambridge University Press 1989).
10. See *On the Plurality of Worlds*, pp. 142–65, on linguistic ersatz possibilities.
11. On dependency hypotheses, see my "Causal decision theory," *Australasian Journal of Philosophy* 59 (1981), pp. 5–30, reprinted in *Philosophical Papers*, vol. II (New York: Oxford University Press, 1986).
12. Laurence Nemirow, review of Nagel's *Mortal Questions*, *Philosophical Review* 89 (1980), pp. 475–76. For a fuller statement, see Nemirow, "Physicalism and the cognitive role of acquaintance," in W. Lycan (ed.), *Mind and Cognition* (Oxford: Blackwell, 1990); and *Functionalism and the Subjective Quality of Experience* (doctoral dissertation, Stanford, 1979). See also Michael Tye, "The subjective qualities of experience," *Mind* 95 (1986), pp. 1–17.

   I should record a disagreement with Nemirow on one very small point. We agree that the phrase "what experience E is like" does not denote some "subjective quality" of E, something which supposedly would be part of the subject matter of the phenomenal information gained by having E. But whereas I have taken the phrase to denote E itself, Nemirow takes it to be a syncategorematic part of the expression "know what experience E is like." See "Physicalism and the cognitive role of acquaintance" section III.

30 | Phenomenal States

Brian Loar

On a natural view of ourselves, we introspectively discriminate our own experiences and thereby form conceptions of their qualities, both salient and subtle. These discriminations are of various degrees of generality, from small differences in tactual and color experience to broad differences of sensory modality, for example, those among smell, hearing, and pain. What we apparently discern are ways experiences differ and resemble each other with respect to *what it is like to have them.* Following common usage, I will call these experiential resemblances *phenomenal qualities,* and the conceptions we have of them, *phenomenal concepts.* Phenomenal concepts are formed "from one's own case." They are *type-demonstratives* that derive their reference from a first-person perspective: 'that type of sensation,' 'that feature of visual experience.' And so third-person ascriptions of phenomenal qualities are projective ascriptions of what one has grasped in one's own case: 'she has an experience of that type.'

'Phenomenal quality' can have a different sense, namely, how the *object* of a perceptual experience appears. In this sense, a phenomenal quality is ascribed to an object and not directly to an experience. Some have argued that all we discern phenomenologically are phenomenal qualities in this sense; they deny that experiences themselves have introspectible qualities that are not ascribed primarily to their objects (Harman 1990; Block 1990). I will not pursue the issue here, but will assume a certain view of it. For the present objective is to engage antiphysicalist arguments and entrenched intuitions to the effect that conscious mental qualities cannot be identical with ordinary physical properties, or at least that it is problematic to suppose that they are so. Antiphysicalists typically suppose that such mental properties are not relational—that is, that they present themselves as not intrinsically involving relations to things outside the mind. They may allow that, say, visual experiences are in some sense intrinsically representational.

That is hard to deny because, as regards ordinary visual experiences, we cannot apparently conceive them phenomenally in a way that abstracts from their *purporting* to represent things in a certain way. The antiphysicalist intuition is compatible with visual experiences' having (some sort of) internally determined intentional structure, so that it is an introspectable and nonrelational feature of a visual experience that it represents things visually as being thus and so. Antiphysicalists suppose that we have conceptions of how visual experiences differ and resemble each other with respect to what it is like to have those experiences. These conceptions then are of qualities of experiences, whatever allowances one may also make for the apparent qualities of the intrinsic objects of those experiences. I will assume that the antiphysicalists' phenomenological and internalist intuitions are correct. The idea is to engage them over the central point, that is, whether those aspects of the mental that we both count as phenomenologically compelling raise substantive difficulties for the thesis that phenomenal qualities (thus understood) are physical properties of the brain that lie within the scope of current science.

We have to distinguish between *concepts* and *properties,* and this chapter turns on that distinction. Antiphysicalist arguments and intuitions take off from a sound intuition about concepts. Phenomenal concepts are conceptually irreducible in this sense: they neither a priori imply, nor are implied by, physical-functional concepts. Although that is denied by analytical functionalists (Levin 1983, 1986), many other physicalists, including me, find it intuitively appealing. The antiphysicalist takes this conceptual intuition a good deal further, to the conclusion that phenomenal qualities are themselves irreducible, are not physical-functional properties, at least not of the ordinary sort. The upshot is a range of antireductionist views: that consciousness and phenomenal qualities are unreal because irreducible;[1] that they are irreducibly

Original version published in J. Tomberlin, ed., *Philosophical Perspectives 4, Action Theory and the Philosophy of Mind*, pp. 81–108, 1990. Copyright © Ridgeview Publishing Company 1990. Revised version published in N. Block, O. Flanagan, & G. Güzeldere, *The Nature of Consciousness* (MIT Press), 1997. Reprinted with permission of Ridgeview Publishing Company.

non-physical-functional facts;[2] that they are forever mysterious, or pose an intellectual problem
different from other empirical problems, or require new conceptions of the physical.[3]

It is my view that we can have it both ways.
We may take the phenomenological intuition at
face value, accepting introspective concepts and
their conceptual irreducibility, and at the same
time take phenomenal qualities to be identical
with physical-functional properties of the sort
envisaged by contemporary brain science. As I
see it, there is no persuasive philosophically articulated argument to the contrary.

This is not to deny the power of raw metaphysical intuition. Thoughtful people compare
phenomenal qualities and kinds of physical-
functional property, say the activation of neural
assemblies. It appears to them to be an evident
and unmediated truth, independent of further
premises, that phenomenal qualities cannot be
identical with properties of those types or perhaps of any physical-functional type. This intuition is so compelling that it is tempting to regard
antiphysicalist arguments as rationalizations of
an intuition whose independent force masks
their tendentiousness. It is the point of this chapter to consider the arguments. But I will also
present a positive account of the relation between phenomenal concepts and physical properties that may provide some relief, or at least
some distance, from the illusory metaphysical
intuition.

In recent years the central problem with physicalism has been thought by many to be "the explanatory gap." This is the idea that we cannot
explain, in terms of physical-functional properties, what makes a certain experience 'feel like
this,' in the way we can explain what makes a
certain substance a liquid, say. It is concluded
that physicalism is defective in some respect,
that there cannot be a (proper) reduction of the
mental to the physical. Before we consider this
explanatory gap, we must first examine, in some
detail, a more basic antiphysicalist line of reasoning that goes back to Leibniz and beyond, a
leading version of which is now called the
knowledge argument. Answering this argument
will generate a framework in which to address
antiphysicalist concerns in general.

1. The Knowledge Argument and Its Semantic Premise

The knowledge argument is straightforward on
the face of it. Consider any phenomenal quality

and any physical property however complex. We
can know that a person has the physical property
without knowing that she experiences the phenomenal quality. And no amount of a priori
reasoning or construction can bridge this conceptual gap. That is the intuitive premise. The
conclusion is drawn that the phenomenal quality
cannot be identical with the physical property.
The argument is equivalent to this: since physical and phenomenal conceptions can be connected only a posteriori, physical properties must be
distinct from phenomenal properties.

The best known and liveliest version of the
knowledge argument is Frank Jackson's, which
features the physiologically omniscient Mary,
who has never seen color and so does not know
what it is like for us to see red, despite her
knowing all the physical-functional facts about
us.[4] She later sees colors, and thus learns what it
has been like all along for us to see red. She
learns a new fact about us. Jackson concludes
that this fact is not among the physical facts,
since Mary already knew them. It is not difficult
to see that this argument depends on a more or
less technical premise.

In my view, the physicalist should accept
Jackson's intuitive description of Mary: she
fails to know that we have certain color experiences even though she knows all relevant physical facts about us. And when she acquires color
experience, she does learn something new about
us—if you like, learns a new fact or truth. But
this is to be granted, of course, only on an
opaque reading of 'Mary learns that we have
such and such color experiences,' and on corresponding readings of 'learns a new fact or truth
about us.' For as regards the transparent versions of those ascriptions of what Mary did not
know and then learned, they would beg the
question, amounting to this: 'as for the property
of having such and such color experiences,
Mary did not know, but then learned, of that
property that we have it.' Physicalists reject this,
for according to us those experiential properties
are physical properties, and Mary already knew
of all our physical properties that we have
them—under their physical descriptions. What
she lacked and then acquired, rather, was
knowledge of certain such properties couched
in experiential terms.

Drawing metaphysical conclusions from
opaque contexts is risky. And in fact inferences
of Jackson's form, without additional premises,
are open to straightforward counterexamples of
a familiar sort. Let me describe two cases.

(1) Max learns that the bottle before him con-

tains CH_3CH_2OH. But he does not know that the bottle contains alcohol. This holds on an opaque reading: he would not assert that there's stuff called alcohol in the bottle, or that the bottle contains the intoxicating component of beer and wine. Let sheltered Max even lack the ordinary concept 'alcohol.' After he acquires that ordinary concept, he learns something new—that the bottle contained alcohol. If the knowledge argument has a generally valid form, we could then infer from Max's epistemic situation that alcohol is not identical with CH_3CH_2OH. Evidently this does not follow.

(2) Margot learns about the element Au and reads that people decorate themselves with alloys of Au. But she has never seen gold and cannot visually identify it: she lacks an adequate visual conception. She later is shown some gold and forms a visual conception of it, "that stuff," and she acquires a new piece of information—individuated opaquely—to the effect that those previously read about embellishments are made of that stuff. Again, if the knowledge argument were unrestrictedly valid, it would follow that that stuff is not identical with Au. This case differs from the case of Max by involving not a descriptive mode of presentation but (as we might say) a perceptual mode of presentation.

It is not difficult to find a difference between both these cases and the case of Mary. Max lacks knowledge of the bottle's contents under a contingent description of it—"ingredient of wine and beer that makes you intoxicated." What Margot lacks is a certain visual conception of Au, which is to say gold. This typically would not be a descriptive conception; it would not self-consciously take the form "the stuff that occasions this type of visual experience." Still on the face of it such a concept implicates a visual-experience type. For it picks out the kind it picks out by virtue of that kind's occasioning experiences of that type. And that is a crucial *contingency* in how the concept that Margot lacks is related to its reference. I hope I will be understood, then, if I say that the visual take on Au that Margot lacks would have conceived Au 'under a contingent mode of presentation.'

This brings us back to Mary, whose acquired conception of what it is like to see red does not conceive it under a contingent mode of presentation. She is not conceiving of a property that presents itself *contingently* thus: it is like such and such to experience *P*. Being experienced like that is essential to the property Mary conceives. She conceives it directly. When Mary

later acquires new information about us (construed opaquely), the novelty of this information cannot be explained—as in the case of Margot—as her acquiring a new contingent mode of presentation of something she has otherwise known of all along. She has a *direct* grasp of the property involved in the new information; she conceives of it somehow, but not under a contingent mode of presentation. Proponents of the knowledge argument will say that is why it is valid on an opaque reading: there is no contingency in Mary's conception of the new phenomenal information that explains it as a novel take on old facts. She learns new facts simpliciter and not new conceptions of old facts.

Notice how close this comes to Saul Kripke's well-known antiphysicalist argument (1980). Kripke assumes that a phenomenal concept such as 'pain' cannot be a priori linked with a physical concept such as that of the stimulation of C-fibers. The case of Mary is a vivid way of making the same point. Kripke points out that property identities can be true even if not a priori, for example, 'heat = such and such molecular property.' It seems fair to represent the next step in his argument as follows. 'Heat' has a contingent higher-order mode of presentation that connotes the property 'feeling like this.' That is what accounts for the a posteriori status of the identity. But, as Kripke points out, this cannot be how 'pain' works: the phenomenal concept 'pain' does not pick out its referent via a contingent mode of presentation; it conceives pain directly and essentially. Kripke concludes that pain is not identical with a physical property.

The two arguments then turn on the same implicit assumption. The only way to account for the a posteriori status of a true property identity is this: one of the terms expresses a contingent mode of presentation. This ought to be given a place of prominence.

(Semantic premise) A statement of property identity that links conceptually independent concepts is true only if at least one concept picks out the property it refers to by connoting a contingent property of that property.

The knowledge argument and Kripke's argument then depend on two assumptions: the conceptual independence of phenomenal concepts and physical-functional concepts, which I accept, and the semantic premise, which I deny.

The antiphysicalist intuition that links concept-individuation and property-individuation (more closely than is in my view correct) is perhaps this. Phenomenal concepts and theoretical expressions of physical properties both conceive their references essentially. But if two concepts conceive a given property essentially, neither mediated by contingent modes of presentation, one ought to be able to see a priori—at least after optimal reflection—that they pick out the same property. Such concepts' connections cannot be a posteriori; that they pick out the same property would have to be transparent.

But as against this, if a phenomenal concept can pick out a physical property directly or essentially, not via a contingent mode of presentation, and yet be *conceptually independent* of all physical-functional concepts, so that Mary's history is coherent, then Jackson's and Kripke's arguments are ineffectual. We could have two conceptually independent conceptions of a property, neither of which connote contingent modes of presentation, such that substituting one for the other in an opaquely interpreted epistemic context does not preserve truth. Even granting that our conception of phenomenal qualities is direct, physicalism would not entail that knowing the physical-functional facts implies knowing, on an opaque construal, the phenomenal facts; and so the failure of this implication would be quite compatible with physicalism. The next few sections give an account of phenomenal concepts and properties that would justify this claim.

2. Recognitional Concepts

Phenomenal concepts belong to a wide class of concepts that I will call recognitional concepts. They have the form 'x is one of *that* kind'; they are type-demonstratives. These type-demonstratives are grounded in dispositions to classify, by way of perceptual discriminations, certain objects, events, situations. Suppose you go into the California desert and spot a succulent never seen before. You become adept at recognizing instances, and gain a recognitional command of their kind, without a name for it; you are disposed to identify positive and negative instances and thereby pick out a kind. These dispositions are typically linked with capacities to form images, whose conceptual role seems to be to focus thoughts about an identifiable kind in the absence of currently perceived instances. An image is presumably 'of' a given kind by virtue of both past recognitions and current dispositions.

Recognitional concepts are generally formed against a further conceptual background. In identifying a thing as of a recognized kind, we almost always presuppose a more general type to which the kind belongs: four-legged animal, plant, physical thing, perceptible event. A recognitional concept will then have the form 'physical thing of that (perceived) kind' or 'internal state of that kind,' and so forth.[5]

Here are some basic features of recognitional concepts that it will help to have in mind in connection with the account of phenomenal concepts that follows.

1. You can understand 'porcelain' from a technical description and only later learn visually, tactually, and aurally to recognize instances. By contrast, in the phenomenon I mean the concept is recognitional at its core; the original concept is recognitional.

2. A recognitional concept need involve no reference to a past instance, or have the form 'is of the same type as that (remembered) one.' You can forget particular instances and still judge 'another one of those.'

3. Recognitional abilities depend on no consciously accessible analysis into component features; they can be irreducibly gestalt.

4. Recognitional concepts are perspectival. Suppose you see certain creatures up close and form a recognitional concept—'those creatures$_1$'; and suppose you see others at a distance, not being able to tell that they are of the same kind (even when they are), and form another recognitional concept—'those creatures$_2$.' These concepts will be a priori independent. Now the respect in which they differ is *perspectival,* in some intuitive sense. A recognitional concept is in part individuated by its constitutive perspective. Here is the important point: a recognitional concept can be ascribed outside its constitutive perspective; 'that thing (seen at distance) is one of those creatures$_1$ (seen up close)' makes perfectly good sense. This plays a key role below in the account of third-person ascriptions of phenomenal concepts.

(This casual invoking of reference-determining dispositions will be a red flag for many who are aware of the vexing foundations of the theory of reference. Problems about referential scrutability, rule-following, naturalizing intentionality—however one wishes to put it—are as frustrating as any in contemporary philosophy. I do not propose to address them here. The idea rather is to appeal to unanalyzed common sense concerning a natural group of concepts and apparent conceptual abilities. The apparent irreducibility of phenomenal qualities itself arises from appeal to intuitions independent of the theory of reference; and it seems reasonable that we should, in resolving that issue, appeal to notions that arise at the same intuitive level. That we *appear* to have recognitional concepts and identifying dispositions that are more or less determinate in their reference is hard to deny. My conception of 'those hedges' [seen around the neighborhood] may unambiguously pick out a variety of eugenia. An example closer to the present topic is this. We can imagine an experiment in which the experimenter tries to determine which internal property is the focus of her subject's identifications: 'again,' . . . 'there it is again.' There seems no commonsensical implausibility—putting aside foundational worries about the inscrutability of reference—in the idea that there is a best possible answer to the experimenter's question, in the scientific long run.[6])

3. Phenomenal Concepts as Recognitional Concepts

Here is the view to be defended. Phenomenal concepts are recognitional concepts that pick out certain internal properties; these are physical-functional properties of the brain. They are the concepts we deploy in our phenomenological reflections; and there is no good philosophical reason to deny that, odd though it may sound, the properties these conceptions *phenomenologically reveal* are physical-functional properties—but not of course under physical-functional descriptions. Granted that brain research might discover that (what we take to be) our phenomenal concepts do not in fact discriminate unified physical-functional properties. Failing that, it is quite coherent for a physicalist to take the phenomenology at face value: the property of *its being like this* to have a certain experience is nothing over and above a certain physical-functional property of the brain.

Phenomenal concepts are conceptually independent of physical-functional descriptions, and yet pairs of such concepts may converge on, pick out, the same properties. Rebutting the semantic premise of the knowledge argument requires making sense of the idea that phenomenal concepts conceive physical-functional properties 'directly,' that is, not by way of contingent modes of presentation. The objective is

to show that the knowledge argument fails for the same reason in the case of Mary as in the case of Max: both arguments require substitution in opaque contexts of terms that are conceptually independent. In the case of Max, the conceptual independence appears to derive from 'alcohol''s connoting a contingent mode of presentation that is metaphysically independent of the property referred to by the chemical concept. In the case of Mary it has a different source.

What then accounts for the conceptual independence of phenomenal and physical-functional concepts? The simple answer is that recognitional concepts and theoretical concepts are in general conceptually independent. It is true that recognitional concepts other than phenomenal concepts connote contingent modes of presentation that are metaphysically independent of the natural kinds they pick out, and hence independent of the kind referred to by the theoretical term of the pair. But we need not count this metaphysical independence as essential to the conceptual independence of coreferring recognitional and theoretical concepts. Concepts of the two sorts have quite different conceptual roles. It is hardly surprising that a recognitional conception of a physical property should discriminate it without analyzing it in scientific terms. Nor should it be surprising that, if there are recognitional concepts that pick out physical properties *not* via contingent modes of presentation, they do not discriminate their references by analyzing them (even implicitly) in scientific terms. Basic recognitional abilities do not depend on or get triggered by conscious scientific analysis. If phenomenal concepts reflect basic recognitions of internal physical-functional states, they *should* be conceptually independent of theoretical physical-functional descriptions. That is what you expect quite apart from issues concerning physicalism.

An antireductionist may reply that the physicalist view depends on an ad hoc assumption and that it is tendentious to suppose that phenomenal concepts differ from all other recognitional concepts in not having contingent modes of presentation.

But this is not fair. Even on the antiphysicalist view, phenomenal concepts are recognitional concepts, and we have 'direct' recognitional conceptions of phenomenal qualities, that is, conceptions unmediated by contingent modes of presentation. Evidently it would be absurd to insist that the antiphysicalist hold that we conceive of a phenomenal quality of one kind via a phenomenal mode of presentation of a distinct kind. And why should the physicalist not agree that phenomenal recognitional concepts are structured in whatever simple way the antiphysicalist requires? That is after all the intuitive situation, and the physicalist simply claims that the intuitive facts about phenomenal qualities are compatible with physicalism. The physicalist makes the additional claim that the phenomenal quality thus directly conceived is a physical-functional property. On both metaphysical views, phenomenal concepts differ from other recognitional concepts; phenomenal concepts are a peculiar sort of recognitional concept on any account, and that can hardly count against physicalism. The two views agree about conceptual structure and disagree about the nature of phenomenal qualities. To insist that physicalism implies, absurdly, that phenomenal concepts could pick out physical properties only via metaphysically distinct phenomenal modes of presentation is unmotivated. There is, though, still more to be said about whether phenomenal concepts should be regarded as having modes of presentation of some sort, and we continue the account in section 5.

Suppose this account of how phenomenal concepts refer is true. Here is a semantic consequence. The physicalist thesis implies that the judgments "the state *a* feels like that" and "the state *a* has physical-functional property *P*" can have the same truth condition even though their joint truth or falsity can be known only a posteriori. I mean, same condition of truth in a possible world. For truth conditions are determined in part by the possible world satisfaction conditions of predicates; and if a phenomenal predicate directly refers to a physical property, that property constitutes its satisfaction condition.

On this account, a phenomenal concept rigidly designates the property it picks out. But then it rigidly designates the same property that some theoretical physical concept rigidly designates. This could seem problematic, for if a concept rigidly designates a property not via a contingent mode of presentation, must that concept not capture the *essence* of the designated property? And if two concepts capture the essence of the same property, must we not be able to know this a priori? These are equivocating uses of 'capture the essence of.' On one use, it expresses a referential notion that comes to no more than 'directly rigidly designate.' On the other, it means something like 'be conceptually inter-

derivable with some theoretical predicate that reveals the internal structure of' the designated property. But the first does not imply the second. What is correct in the observation about rigid designation has no tendency to imply that the two concepts must be a priori interderivable.

4. The Concept 'Phenomenal Concept'

Not all self-directed recognitional concepts are phenomenal concepts, as may be seen in these two cases.

(1) Cramps have a characteristic feel, but they are not feelings. Cramps are certain muscle contractions, while feelings of cramp are, if physical, brain states. (Witness phantom-limb sufferers.) One has a recognitional concept that picks out certain muscle contractions in the having of them. This is not a phenomenal concept, for it does not purport to pick out a phenomenal quality. But of course, in exercising this concept, one often conceives its reference by way of a phenomenal mode of presentation, a cramp feeling or a cramp-feeling image.

(2) A more fanciful self-directed nonphenomenal concept can be conceived. To begin with, consider blindsight. Some cortically damaged people are phenomenally blind in restricted retinal regions; and yet when a vertical or horizontal line (say) is presented to those regions, they can, when prompted, guess what is there with a somewhat high degree of correctness. We can extend the example by imagining a blindsight that is exercised spontaneously and accurately. At this point we shift the focus to internal properties and conceive of a self-directed recognitional ability, which is like the previous ability in being phenomenally blank and spontaneous but which discriminates an internal property of one's own. If this recognitional ability were suitably governed by the concept 'that state,' the resulting concept would be a self-directed recognitional concept that is phenomenally blank.

The two examples show that 'phenomenal concept' cannot mean 'self-directed recognitional concept.' This is compatible with my proposal. For it implies neither (a) that we can reductively explicate the concept 'phenomenal quality' as 'property picked out by a self-directed discriminative ability,' or (b) that we can reductively explicate the concept 'phenomenal concept' as 'self-directed recognitional concept.' Phenomenal concepts are certain self-directed recognitional concepts. Our higher-order concept 'phenomenal concept' cannot be reductively explicated, any more than can our concept 'phenomenal quality.' The higher-order concept 'phenomenal concept' is as irreducibly demonstrative as phenomenal concepts themselves.

5. Phenomenal Modes of Presentation

Self-directed recognitional concepts of the blindsight type might appear to raise a problem for the claim that phenomenal concepts pick out physical-functional properties directly. Here is a way to put the point.

> The difference between a self-directed blindsight recognitional concept and a phenomenal concept appears to be that the latter involves a phenomenal mode of presentation while the former conceives its referent in some other, odd, way. So, if the phenomenal concept is taken to discriminate some physical property, it then does so via a phenomenal mode of presentation. But that conflicts with your assertion that phenomenal concepts refer directly, with no contingent mode of presentation. A similar point arises concerning recognitional concepts of cramps and of cramp feelings. Both concepts must presumably have modes of presentation. It is far-fetched to suppose that one of them has and the other lacks a mode of presentation; the phenomenal concept does not pick out a physical state *nakedly*. The 'cramp' concept connotes a mode of presentation of the form 'the physical state that causes such and such phenomenal state.' If we attempt to capture the phenomenal concept analogously, its mode of presentation would have the form 'the state that has such and such phenomenal aspect.' But then, contrary to what the physicalist must say, phenomenal concepts point to physical states only by way of phenomenal modes of presentation.

What might an antiphysicalist say about these various self-directed recognitional concepts? Let me make a good-faith attempt to present a reasonable version.

(1) A cramp concept picks out a muscular property indirectly, by way of a causal chain that is mediated by the phenomenal quality associated with the concept. In addition to this mode of presentation type—the phenomenal quality—we can also note the role of, as we might say, "token modes of presentation." One and the same cramp concept (type) can on different occasions be focussed differently: by an actual cramp feeling, by a cramp-feeling image, or by an imageless inclination to identify cramp feelings when they occur (with a cramp-feeling image on the tip of one's imagination.)

(2) We turn from cramp concepts to cramp-feeling concepts. These do not refer (i.e., to cramp feelings) by way of contingent modes of presentation. But they can mimic the working of cramp concepts as regards "token modes of presentation." If one can focus attention on the bodily property of cramp by way of a token cramp feeling, surely one can focus attention on the phenomenal quality cramp-feeling by way of a token cramp feeling. The same goes for cramp-feeling images and those gossamer identifying inclinations. Should antiphysicalists say that cramp-feeling concepts have 'noncontingent' modes of presentation? We might say that a phenomenal concept has as its mode of presentation the very phenomenal quality that it picks out. We might also say that phenomenal concepts have "token modes of presentation" that are noncontingently tied to the phenomenal qualities to which those concepts point: particular cramp feelings and images can focus one's conception of the phenomenal quality of cramp feeling.

(3) As for self-directed blindsight concepts, the antiphysicalist then ought to say, they differ from phenomenal concepts in the obvious way, whether one puts it by saying that they lack the noncontingent phenomenal modes of presentation (types) that phenomenal qualities have, or that they lack their phenomenal "token modes of presentation."

The main point is by now more than obvious. Whatever the antiphysicalist has said about these cases the physicalist may say as well. The idea that one picks out the phenomenal quality of cramp feeling by way of a particular feeling of cramp (or image, etc.) is hardly incompatible with holding that that phenomenal quality is a physical property. The contrast between phenomenal concepts and self-directed blindsight concepts and cramp concepts finds physicalist and antiphysicalist equally able to say something sensible.

A phenomenal concept exercised in the absence of the phenomenal quality it stands for often involves not merely a recognitional disposition but also an image. And so, as a psychological state in its own right, a phenomenal concept—given its intimate connection with imaging—bears a phenomenological affinity to a phenomenal state that neither state bears to the entertaining of a physical-theoretical concept. When we then bring phenomenal and physical-theoretical concepts together in our philosophical ruminations, those cognitive states are phenomenologically so different that the illusion may be created that their references must be different. It is as though antiphysicalist intuitions rest on a resemblance theory of mental representation, as though we conclude from the lack of resemblance in our phenomenal and physical-functional conceptions a lack of sameness in the properties to which they refer.

6. Third-Person Ascriptions

Ascriptions of phenomenal qualities to others ostensibly refer to properties that others may have independently of our ascribing them:[7] we have realist conceptions of the phenomenal states of others. But at the same time they are projections from one's own case; they have the form 'x has a state of this sort,' where the demonstrative gets its reference from an actual or possible state of one's own.

Can phenomenal concepts as we predicate them of others be identified with the recognitional concepts we have characterized? A question naturally arises how essentially self-directed recognitional concepts can be applied in cases where it makes no sense to say that one can directly apply these concepts. This is a question that exercised Wittgensteinians.

As we have already pointed out, recognitional concepts are perspectival, in the sense that their reference is determined from a certain constitutive perspective (depending on the concept). The above concept 'those creatures$_1$' (seen up close) picks out a creature-kind that one discriminates on close sightings. But nothing prevents ascribing the recognitional concept 'one of those creatures$_1$' to something observed from a different perspective, seen in the distance or heard in the dark. We have to distinguish the perspective from which reference is determined and the far broader range of contexts in which the referentially fixed concept can be ascribed. The former perspective hardly restricts the latter contexts. This holds also for phenomenal concepts. We acquire them from a first-person perspective, by discriminating a property in the having of it. Assuming that we successfully pick out a more or less determinate physical property, the extraperspectival ascription 'she is in a state of *this* kind' makes complete sense. And so it is not easy to see that Wittgensteinians succeeded in raising a philosophical problem that survives the observation that we can discriminate physical properties and so fix the reference of phenomenal concepts from a first-person perspective, and then go on to ascribe those concepts third-personally.

There is though a more up-to-date worry about the interpersonal ascribability of first-person concepts, however physical we suppose their references to be. Evidently there will be vagueness, and indeterminacy, concerning whether another person—whose neural assemblies will presumably always differ from mine in various respects—has a certain physical property that I discriminate phenomenally. And this on the face of it poses a problem, which may be framed as follows:

> The question whether another person's phenomenal states resemble yours can hardly consist in their neural assemblies' resembling yours. Any physical similarity you choose will be arbitrarily related to a given phenomenal similarity. Suppose there is a small physical difference between a neural state of yours and another person's state. What makes it the case that this small neural difference constitutes a small phenomenal difference or a large one or no phenomenal difference at all? It appears that there cannot be a fact of the matter.

But this objection appears to me to overlook a crucial element of the physicalist view we have presented—that phenomenal concepts are (type) demonstrative concepts that pick out physical properties and relations. A first step in answering it is to consider the connection between interpersonal and intrapersonal phenomenal similarity. It appears that one's phenomenological conception of how others' phenomenal states resemble one's own has to be drawn from one's idea of how one's own phenomenal states resemble each other. A person's quality space of interpersonal similarity must derive from her quality space of intrapersonal similarity. How else is one to get a conceptual grip on interpersonal phenomenal similarity? This seems inevitable on any account—physicalist or antiphysicalist—on which phenomenal concepts are formed from one's own case.

But conceptions of phenomenal similarity relations are as much type-demonstrative concepts as those of phenomenal qualities. All one can apparently mean by "that spectrum of phenomenal similarity" is "*that ordering* among my phenomenal states." Physicalism implies that if such a type-demonstrative refers, it picks out a physical ordering. And there is no obvious philosophical difficulty (if we put aside scepticism in the theory of reference) in the idea that discriminations of resemblances and differences among one's own phenomenal properties pick out reasonably well defined physical relations.

Now I have to confess some uneasiness about extending this to interpersonal similarity without qualification; but the implications of the foregoing remarks are clear enough. If they are correct, whatever physical ordering relations are picked out by one's personal notions of phenomenal similarity must also constitute (what one thinks of as) interpersonal phenomenal similarity. It is easy to see that there still is room here for further trouble. But the difficulty the objection raises seems considerably diminished if one insists on the demonstrative nature of all phenomenal concepts, however relational and of whatever order. For the objection then becomes, "Suppose there is a small physical difference between a neural state of yours and another person's state. What makes it the case that this small neural difference constitutes a small difference of *that* type, or a large one, or no difference of *that* type at all?" If "that type" picks out a physical relation, then the question answers itself, and there seems no gloomy philosophical threat of phenomenal incommensurability.

Naturally there is the risk that physical investigation will not deliver the right physical properties and relations. Even if the risk is increased by bringing in interpersonal similarities, the nature of the risk is the same as in one's own case: the phenomenal might turn out to be not adequately embodied.

It goes without saying that one can coherently conceive that another person has *P*, conceived in physical-functional terms, and doubt that she has any given phenomenal quality; that has been central to this chapter. But one cannot coherently wonder whether another person in a *P* state has a state with *this* phenomenal quality if one acknowledges that one's concept 'this quality' refers to the property the concept discriminates in oneself (what else?) and that moreover it discriminates *P*.

Why then is there an apparent problem of other minds? It is as if one wishes to do to others as one does to oneself—namely, apply phenomenal concepts directly, apply phenomenal recognitional capacities to others from a first-person perspective. The impossibility of this can present itself as an epistemological barrier, as something that makes it impossible to know certain facts. Doubtless more can be said in explanation of the naturalness of the conflation of the innocuous conceptual fact with a severe epistemological disability. It is not easy to shake the grip of that conflation or therefore easy to dispel the problem of other minds. The cognitive remedy, the fortification against the illusion, is the idea of recognitional concepts that can be ascribed beyond their constitutive perspective, coupled with the reflection that there is no reason to doubt that it is physical-functional properties that those recognitional concepts discriminate.

7. Knowing How versus Knowing That

Consider a different physicalist reply, to an antiphysicalist argument posed in this form: "knowledge of physical-functional facts does not yield knowledge of the phenomenal facts; therefore phenomenal facts are not physical-functional." Laurence Nemirow and David Lewis have replied in effect that the premise is true only if you equivocate on "knowledge."[8] The first occurrence means theoretical knowledge, the second the ability to discriminate introspectively or to imagine certain properties. But theoretical knowledge of physical-functional properties that are identical with phenomenal qualities does not yield the other sort of knowledge of the same properties, that is, the ability to discriminate them in introspection or to imagine them. There are two epistemic relations to one class of properties.

Now this suggests something significantly different from my account. On the Nemirow-Lewis proposal, the only knowledge "that such and such" is knowledge couched in physical-functional terms, while what corresponds to (what we have been calling) phenomenal concepts is knowing how to identify or to imagine certain states. What I have proposed is evidently different. Knowing that a state feels a certain way is having distinctive information about it, couched in phenomenal conceptions. There is of course a central role for recognitional abilities, but that is in the constitution of phenomenal concepts. Antiphysicalists are right to count phenomenal knowledge as the possession of distinctive information, for it involves genuinely predicative components of judgment, whose association with physical-functional concepts is straightforwardly a posteriori.

Physicalists are forced into the Nemirow-Lewis reply if they individuate pieces of knowledge or cognitive information in terms of possible-world truth-conditions, that is, hold that 'knowing that p' and 'knowing that q' ascribe distinct pieces of knowledge just in case 'that-p' and 'that-q' denote distinct sets of possible worlds. Then knowing that x's phenomenal qualities are such and such will be distinct from knowing that x's physical properties are so and so only if the former qualities are distinct from the latter properties. So then a physicalist who counts the basic antiphysicalist premise as true on some interpretation must deny either that knowledge, cognitive information, is individuated in terms of possible-world truth-conditions or deny that knowing the phenomenal facts (in the sense that makes the basic antiphysicalist premise true) is knowing that such and such or having distinctive information about it. Nemirow and Lewis deny the latter. Of course I deny the former; there are ample independent reasons to deny it, and it seems otherwise unmotivated to deny the latter.

There are straightforward reasons to prefer the phenomenal concept view.

1. A person can have thoughts not only of the form "coconuts have *this* taste" but also of the form "if coconuts did not have *this* taste, then Q." You may get away with saying that the former expresses (not a genuine judgment but) the mere possession of recognitional know-how. But there is no comparable way to account for the embedded occurrence of "coconuts have this taste"; it occurs as a predicate with a distinctive content.

2. We entertain thoughts about the phenomenal states of other people—"she has a state of that type"; this clearly calls for a predicative concept. It does of course involve a recognitional ability, but one that contributes to the formation of a distinctive concept.

3. For many conceptions of phenomenal qualities, there is no candidate for an independently mastered term that one then learns how to apply: thinking of a peculiar way my left knee feels when I run (a conception that occurs predicatively in various judgments) is not knowing how to apply an independently understood term. I suppose a functionalist might say that, in such cases, one implicitly individuates the state in terms of some functional description that is

fashioned on the spot, but this appears psychologically implausible.

8. The Explanatory Gap

Can we *explain* how a certain phenomenal property might be identical with a certain physical-functional property? The answer is no, and then again, yes.

First, the no. When we explain, say, liquidity in physical-functional terms, the explanation is in crucial part a priori. You may find this surprising; but what we in effect do is analyze liquidity (or more precisely those aspects of liquidity that we count as explained[9]) in terms of a functional description, and then show that the physical theory of water implies, a priori, that the functional description is realized. But given the conceptual independence of phenomenal concepts and physical-functional concepts, we cannot have such an a priori explanation of phenomenal qualities in physical-functional terms.

Does this matter? The explanatory gap, as it appears to me, is an epistemic or conceptual phenomenon, without metaphysical consequences,[10] and it is predictable from the physicalist account we have proposed. But this may seem somewhat glib. As Georges Rey points out (Rey 1995), the mere fact of conceptual inequivalence for recognitional type-demonstratives and descriptive terms does not generate an explanatory gap. Many examples would make the point. We do not find a troubling explanatory gap in judgments of the form "that stuff is CH_3CH_2OH," even though this does not hold a priori.

Now what is it that needs accounting for? This seems to me to be it: how identity statements that connect phenomenal concepts and physical-functional concepts can be true despite our sense that, if true, they *ought to be* explanatory and yet are not. We can explain how such identity statements fail to be both explanatory (conceptual independence) and true; but this does not account for the thought that something that ought to be there is missing. We have to explain away the intuition that such identity statements ought to be explanatory.

There must be something special about phenomenal concepts that creates the expectation and the consequent puzzle. We have already seen a significant difference between phenomenal concepts and all other phenomenally mediated recognitional concepts. Might this make the difference here as well? That is what I will try to show.

Perhaps this is why we think that true phenomenal-physical identity judgments ought to be explanatory. It is natural to regard our conceptions of phenomenal qualities as conceiving them as they are in themselves, that is, to suppose we have a direct grasp of their essence. So in this respect there is a parallel with liquidity: the phenomenal concept and the concept 'liquid' both pick out properties directly, that is, not via contingent modes of presentation. And of course the physical-functional theoretical term of the identity, couched in fundamental theoretical terms, also reveals the essence of the property it picks out. Since both conceptions reveal this essence, then, if the psychophysical identity judgment is true, the sameness of that property, it might seem, ought to be evident from those conceptions, as in the liquidity case. The physical-functional concept structurally analyzes the property, and so we expect *it* to explain, asymmetrically, the phenomenal quality, much as physics explains liquidity, on the basis of an a priori analysis. The fact that this is not so makes it then difficult to understand how there can be just one property here.

If this is what makes the explanatory gap troubling, then the idea that phenomenal concepts are recognitional concepts of a certain sort does account for the explanatory gap in a way compatible with physicalism. Phenomenal concepts, as we have seen, do not conceive their reference via contingent modes of presentation. And so they can be counted as conceiving phenomenal qualities directly. Calling this a grasp of essence seems to me all right, for phenomenal concepts do not conceive their references by way of their accidental properties. But this is quite a different grasp of essence than we have in the term "liquid": for that term (or what there is in it that we count as functionally explained) is conceptually equivalent to some functional description that is entailed by the theoretical term of the identity.

The problem of the explanatory gap stems then from an illusion. What generates the problem is not appreciating that there can be two conceptually independent "direct grasps" of a single essence, that is, grasping it demonstratively by experiencing it, and grasping it in theoretical terms. The illusion is of *expected transparency:* a direct grasp of a property ought to reveal how it is internally constituted, and if it is not revealed as physically constituted, then it is

not so. The mistake is the thought that a direct grasp of essence ought to be a transparent grasp, and it is a natural enough expectation.

The explanatory gap has led many philosophers of mind seriously astray into mistaken arguments for epiphenomenalism, for mystery, for eliminativism. At the root of almost all weird positions in the philosophy of mind lies this rather elementary and unremarkable conceptual fact, blown up into a metaphysical problem that appears to require an extreme solution. But it is a mistake to think that, if physicalism is true, consciousness as we conceive it at first hand needs explaining in the way that liquidity as we ordinarily conceive it gets explained.

There is another interpretation of "can we understand how physicalism might be true?," for which the answer is clearly yes. For we can explain, and indeed we have explained, how a given phenomenal concept can manage to pick out a particular physical-functional property without remainder: the concept discriminates the property but not via a contingent mode of presentation. This in its way closes the explanatory gap between the phenomenal and the physical. We understand how "such and such phenomenal quality" could pick out physical property P, even though "such and such phenomenal quality = P" does not provide an (a priori) explanation in physical terms of why a given phenomenal quality feels as it does. Since the former, when generalized, would entail that physicalism about phenomenal qualities is true, and since we understand both of these things, we thereby understand how physicalism can be true.

9. Subjective Concepts and Subjective Properties

You can ascribe an objective property—one completely expressable in the objective terms of natural science—under a subjective conception: 'x's state has *this* quality.' Thomas Nagel writes that mental facts are "accessible only from one point of view."[11] This does reflect something about phenomenal concepts; they are in some intuitive sense "from a point of view" and moreover subjective. Phenomenal concepts are subjective because they are essentially self-directed, involving capacities to discriminate certain states in the having of them and also involve imaginative capacities anchored in such recognitional capacities. If that is it, then Nagel takes a correct observation about concepts and draws a wrong conclusion about facts and properties. For concepts can in that sense be "from a point of view" and subjective, and still introduce properties that are exhaustively captured in objective science.

But we can go further. Let us grant even that the *property* of experiencing such and such is aptly counted as subjective, as intrinsically involving a point of view. Why should this subjectivity not itself be identical with a physical-functional property, and therefore completely objectively conceivable under its physical-functional description? There is no contradiction in supposing that a property that is subjective—in the sense of being individuated in a way that invokes a relation to a mind—is also conceivable under an objective mode of presentation. There is no incoherence in the thought that the "subjectivity" of a phenomenal quality is identical with an objective physical-functional aspect of that property.

Does a fully objective description of reality not still leave something out, viz. the subjective conceptions? This is a play on 'leave something out.' A complete objective description leaves out subjective conceptions, not because it cannot fully characterize the properties they discriminate or fully account for the concepts themselves as psychological states but simply because it does not employ them.

10. Phenomenal Structure, and Exotic Others

Some functionalists might think this account ignores a major feature of our conceptions of the mental, namely, their systematic structure. We have conceptions of different sensory modalities, and of intramodality comparisons along various spectra, of pitch, timbre, hue, brightness, shape, size, texture, acidity, acridity, and so on. These could be seen as subsidiary functional organizations within a theory of the mental. Antiphysicalists may share something of the point, wanting to speak of phenomenological structures. My account could seem to imply that phenomenal concepts are atomistic, unstructured, unsystematic, for are these recognitional dispositions not in principle independent of each other?

We have phenomenal recognitional concepts of various degrees of generality. Some are of highly determinate qualities, and others are of

phenomenal determinables: crimson, dark red, red, warm colored, colored, visual. The last is the recognitional conception of a whole sensory modality. And there is the most general of all, the recognitional concept *phenomenal* (state, quality), the highest ranking phenomenal determinable. (This is a recognitional concept. One discriminates phenomenal states from nonphenomenal states, feeling a twinge from having a bruise, hearing a chirp from jerking a knee, and that highly general discriminative capacity is the basis of the concept of a phenomenal quality.)

There are also relational concepts: quality x is a determinate of quality y; quality x is more like quality y than like quality z; quality x is of a different modality from quality y. These are also recognitional concepts: dispositions to classify together, on phenomenal grounds, certain pairs and triples of phenomenal qualities. Combining them yields complex conceptions of abstract phenomenal structures, for example, of a structured sensory modality. One's general conception of such a structure is in effect one's ability to exercise in concert a group of such general phenomenal concepts.

Now it is important that our conceptions of such phenomenal structures, while abstract, are yet phenomenal conceptions. No purely functional conception of a complex structure, however isomorphic to a phenomenal-structure conception it may be, will be cognitively equivalent to it; purely functional conceptions ignore that the structures are of phenomenal similarity relations, of phenomenal determinateness, and so on.

But given the falsity of the semantic minor premise, that is no impediment to holding that those abstract phenomenal conceptions can have purely functional or physical-functional structures as their references. For such structures may well be what these abstract phenomenal recognitional capacities in fact discriminate. Indeed we may go on to say that, if our phenomenal conceptions are to be fully vindicated by brain science, then the brain must have a certain functional structure; any possible totality of (as it were) semantic values for our phenomenal conceptions must have certain functional structures. This perhaps explains the strong intuition of some commonsense functionalists that phenomenal concepts are functional concepts, without our having to accept that counterintuitive view.

"Can your projection analysis accommodate the thought that a bat has highly specific, determinate, phenomenal states that are not like anything I can experience or imagine? It seems to me that your program will require you to bring in the bat's own recognitional-imaginative capacities, such as they are."[12]

When one thinks about a bat's sonar phenomenal states, one thinks about them as phenomenal, that is, as having in common with my phenomenal states what I discriminate them all as having in common, and that may be something physical-functional. One also thinks of them as of a distinctive phenomenal kind or modality, different from one's own states, of roughly that order of determinateness at which one's visual states are marked off from one's auditory states. One has such a general concept from one's own case, and one can project it. Again, that concept—'distinctive phenomenal modality'—may denote a physical-functional property of sets of phenomenal states. And one thinks of the bat's sonar states as exhibiting phenomenal variation of different degrees of specificity. These conceptions of general phenomenal structure, determinable-determinate relations, resemblance relations, and so on, we have, as I have said, from our own case.

Now nothing in the foregoing requires that a necessary condition of having certain phenomenal qualities is having the capacity to discriminate them. (See, however, the discussion below of transparency.) We ascribe to bats not phenomenal concepts but phenomenal states; and we do that by projection, in the manner characterized above. Other-directed phenomenal conceptions are of others' states, and not as such of their conceptions.

Nagel proposes that we can achieve objectivity about the mental by abstracting from subjective conceptions of our own psychology, fashioning objective mental conceptions that are neither physical nor functional.[13] This would enable us to conceive abstractly of mental lives of which we have no subjective, projective, understanding whatever. Now that is evidentially at odds with my proposal. It appears to me that all mental concepts that are not functional concepts (where the latter include concepts of theoretical psychology) are subjective-projective concepts, however general and abstract they may be. The reason is simple: as far as I can determine, I have no objective nonfunctional mental concepts. If I try to conceive an alien mind in nonfunctional mental terms, I rely on concepts like 'sensory modality' and other general conceptions of phenomenological structure of the

sort mentioned above, and I understand them from my own case. They are abstract conceptions; but, it appears to me, they are still recognitional concepts and hence as subjective as the highly specific phenomenal concept of having an itch in the left ankle.

11. Transparency

The following could appear possible on my account: another person is in the state that in me amounts to feeling such and such but sincerely denies feeling anything relevant. It apparently has been left open that others have phenomenal states that are not introspectable at will, for no requirement of transparency has been mentioned. Then the property that is the referent of my concept of feeling like *that* could, even if it occurs transparently in me, occur nontransparently in you. But (the objection continues) denying transparency is tantamount to allowing unconscious experiences; and it would not be unreasonable to say that the topic of phenomenal states is the topic of certain conscious states.

There really is no issue here. Suppose that any phenomenal quality must be essentially transparent, and that no property I correctly identify as phenomenal can be realized in another nontransparently. If cognitive integration is essential to the intuitive property of transparency, so be it; there is no reason to think that such integration itself is not a physical-functional property, as it were implicated by each phenomenal property.

But it is not obvious that phenomenal properties must be transparent in such a reflexive cognitive sense. What about infants and bats? There has always been a philosophical puzzle about how subtracting reflexive cognitive awareness from phenomenal or conscious states leaves something that is still phenomenal or conscious. But that puzzle is independent of the present account. All that is implied here is that if I have a conception of a phenomenal quality that is shared by me and an infant, my conception of it involves a recognitional concept, and there is no reason why that phenomenal quality itself should not be a physical-functional property. Whatever indefinable, elusive aspect of phenomenal qualities might constitute their being conscious—transparent in some appropriately minimal sense—without requiring reflexive conceptualizability, there would be no reason to doubt it is a physical-functional property.

12. Incorrigibility

Physicalism, it may be said, cannot acknowledge the incorrigibility of phenomenal judgments of the form 'it feels like that.' For surely there is no guarantee that a capacity for recognizing a given physical property does not at times misfire; and perhaps even more to the point, there can be no guarantee that to a given recognitional disposition there corresponds a repeatable physical property. Perhaps an antiphysicalist will grant that certain kinds of mistake about phenomenal qualities are possible;[14] but the antiphysicalist will insist that we cannot be wrong in thinking that *there are* phenomenal qualities.

Now suppose it turns out that no system of physical-functional properties corresponds to the system of our phenomenal concepts. Would a physicalist not then have to say there are no phenomenal qualities? And is the fact that physicalism leaves this open not a serious problem?

But that very possibility ought to make us dubious about the incorrigibility of the judgment that there are real phenomenal repeatables. What reason have we to think that our phenomenal judgments discriminate real properties? Memory, one might say, cannot be that mistaken: we can hardly deny that present inner states resemble past states in ways we would recognize again. Despite this conviction, however, if no system of physical-functional properties corresponded to one's putative phenomenal discriminations, an alternative to nonphysical qualities would be this: memory radically deceives us into thinking we discriminate internal features and nonrandomly classify our own states. Strong evidence that no suitable physical-functional properties exist might amaze and stagger one. It would then have emerged that we are subject to a powerful illusion, a cognitive rather than a phenomenal illusion; we would be judging falsely that we thereby discriminate real properties.

It does seem likely that we genuinely discriminate internal physical-functional states in introspection.[15] But with that said, positing nonphysical properties to forestall the *possibility* of radical error, however theoretically adventurous (even reckless) this may be, would in something like a moral sense still be rather faint-hearted. The whole point about the phenomenal is how it appears. And that means there is no introspective guarantee of *anything* beyond mere appearance, even of discriminations of genuine repeatables. The dualist balks at the implications and invents a realm of properties to ensure that the appearances are facts, but this does not respect the truly phenomenal nature of what is revealed by introspection at its least theoretical.

I have to grant that, if it were to turn out that no brain properties are suitably correlated with our ascriptions of phenomenal qualities, one might well feel some justification in questioning physicalism. But that does not imply that one now has such a justification. There is no good reason for prophylactic dualism.

13. Functionalism

There are two functionalist theses: that all concepts of mental states are functional concepts, and that all mental properties are functional properties. The first I rejected in accepting the antiphysicalist intuition. I agree with the antiphysicalist that phenomenal concepts cannot be captured in purely functional terms. But nothing in philosophy prevents phenomenal properties from being functional properties. There are two possibilities: they are commonsense-functional properties or they are psychofunctional, and I take the latter to be the interesting one.[16] Might the phenomenal quality of seeing red be identical with a property captured by a detailed psychological theory? This would be so if the repeatable that triggers one's phenomenal concept 'seeing red' has psychofunctional rather than say biochemical identity conditions. That this is possible has been denied by antifunctionalist physicalists on the grounds of inverted qualia and absent qualia possibilities, but I do not find these arguments persuasive.

The inverted qualia argument is commonly advanced against identifying phenomenal qualities with commonsense functional properties and also against the psychofunctional identification. The position I espouse is agnostic: for all philosophers know, phenomenal qualities are psychofunctional, neurofunctional, or some other fine-grained functional properties. The opposing argument is that it is possible that the functional role that seeing red has in me is had in you by, as I would think of it, seeing green. If this is, as they say, metaphysically possible, then of course phenomenal qualities are not functional properties.

But it seems the only argument for the possibility is the coherent conceivability of inverted qualia. One cannot presuppose that inverted qualia are *nomologically* possible. There seems to be no philosophical reason to assert that, apart from the coherent conceivability of inverted qualia. If there is empirical reason to assert that nomological possibility, then of course we should retreat from agnosticism. The present point is that nothing about the idea of inverted qualia provides philosophical reason to reject functionalism about qualia. For that would require another version of the antiphysicalist argument: it is conceivable that any given functional state can occur without the seeing of green and with the seeing of red, say; therefore the psychofunctional role and the phenomenal quality involve distinct properties. Clearly one cannot accept this argument against functionalism without also accepting the analogous argument against physicalism itself; the philosophical antifunctionalist argument requires a premise that implies antiphysicalism.

There is a well-known absent qualia argument against functionalism by Ned Block (1978). Suppose the Chinese nation were organized so as to realize the psychofunctional organization of a person seeing green. Evidently the Chinese nation would not collectively be seeing green or having any other sensation. Any psychofunctional property could in this way be realized without a given phenomenal quality and hence cannot be identical with one. Now this argument might appear dialectically more telling than the inverted qualia argument, for it apparently rests on more than a conceptual possibility. It seems a plain truth that the Chinese people would not thereby be having a collective sensation. Surely it is barmy to be agnostic about that. Block suggests a principle. "If a doctrine has an absurd conclusion which there is no independent reason to believe, and if there is no way of explaining away the absurdity or showing it to be misleading or irrelevant, and if there is no good reason to believe the doctrine that leads to the absurdity in the first place, then don't accept the doctrine."[17]

While we doubtless find an absurdity in ascribing phenomenal qualities to the Chinese nation as a whole, the matter is not so simple. It is hard to see how such a judgment of absurdity can be *justified* except by our having some intuitive knowledge of the nature of phenomenal qualities whereby we can say that the Chinese nation cannot have them collectively. Have I a special insight into my physical states whereby I can say: the repeatable that I reidentify whenever I attend to my seeing green is not a functional property? One feels sceptical that introspection can yield such knowledge. If the argument is not 'they do not collectively have, by virtue of their functional organization, however fine-grained, what I have when *this* occurs,' then what is it? Is a further philosophical argument in the offing? It is difficult to see whence chest-beating to the contrary derives its credibility. Perhaps a dualist conception of Platonic insight into mental essences might help. But, on a naturalist view of human nature, one ought to find it puzzling that we have such a first-person insight into the nature of our mental properties. Perhaps there is reason to suppose that what one introspects and reidentifies is a categorical and not a dispositional property. That has an intuitive ring to it, but it is not that easy to produce a decent argument for it. We are left with this question: how might we know short of detailed brain research that what we reidentify in ourselves when we see green is not a fine-grained functional property? But if we cannot know this by sheer insight into the essence of our own properties, or by philosophical argument, then we cannot know that the Chinese nation lacks what we have. Our ignorance concerns the nature of our own properties, and that ignorance would appear to prevent drawing substantive conclusions from thought experiments of this type.

There is no question that ordinary intuition counts strongly against applying phenomenal concepts to things that are not single organisms, and one cannot deny that the reply just given makes one uncomfortable, at the very least. And yet the alternative appears to be Platonism about mental essences, and that sits awkwardly with naturalism. It is possible that phenomenal qualities are biochemical properties: and yet again it is difficult to see that philosophers know anything that implies that they are not fine-grained functional, or neurofunctional, properties.[18]

NOTES

1. Cf. Rey (1995) and Dennett (1991).
2. Jackson (1982, 1986).
3. Nagel (1974, 1986); McGinn (1993).
4. Jackson (1982, 1986).

5. How such background concepts themselves arise is not my topic; but we might think of them variously as deriving from more general recognitional capacities, or as functions of complex inferential roles, or

as socially deferential; or they may be components of innate structures. Background concepts are not always presupposed. Someone may be extremely good at telling stars from other objects (e.g., lightning bugs, airplanes, comets, planets) without having any real idea of what they are.

6. For more on recognitional concepts and on the determinacy of reference, see Loar (1990; 1991, 1995).

7. The earlier version of this chapter made heavy weather of third-person ascription of phenomenal concepts. General considerations about the perspectival nature of recognitional concepts permit a far neater account, which I here present.

8. Nemirow (1980); Lewis (1983).

9. This leaves open the possibility of twin-Earth cases in which the apparently defining properties of liquidity—those that are functionally explained—are kept constant across worlds even though the underlying kind changes. The defining properties then turn out to be merely reference-fixing.

10. For illuminating accounts of the explanatory gap and its significance see Levine (1983, 1993). Levine's diagnosis of the significance of the explanatory gap is different from mine.

11. Nagel (1974).

12. Thomas Nagel, in a note commenting on an earlier draft.

13. Nagel (1974).

14. See Warner (1986).

15. When I see a ripe lemon in daylight and attend to my visual experience, I form the memory belief that what I introspect is what I introspected (phenomenologically inclined as I am) the last time I saw a ripe lemon in daylight. It seems a reasonable empirical inference that probably ripe lemons in such circumstances cause in me states that my memory accurately records as the same. But this inference is, I take it, not reasonable on introspective grounds alone; it presupposes much about how the world works.

16. It is empirically unlikely that phenomenal qualities are identical with commonsense functional properties. Here is one way to see this. We know sensations can be produced by nonstandard means, that is, by poking around in the brain; but this of course is no part of the commonsense functional role of the property of seeing red. Now suppose this property is produced in me by a brain probe. What constitutes its being a sensation of red? If it is its commonsense functional role, then that property would be the sensation of red by virtue of (something like) its *normally* having such and such causes and effects (it doesn't have them here). But this makes sense only if the property in question is itself a *distinct* lower-order property about which it is contingently true that normally it has such and such causes and effects although it lacks them here. That lower-order property would then be a far better candidate (than the commonsense functional property) for being the property one's phenomenal conception discriminates. For this reason, such brain probes turn out to be strong and perhaps even conclusive evidence that phenomenal qualities, the ones we discriminate in applying phenomenal concepts, are not identical with commonsense functional properties. There are other ways of reaching the same conclusion.

17. Block 1978.

18. (Original version) For pointing out a substantial error in an ancestor of the paper, I am indebted to George Myro, whose correction put me on the right track as I now see it. I have learned much from conversations on phenomenal qualities with Janet Levin and Richard Warner. Stephen Schiffer made several valuable suggestions about the structure of the paper and got me to clarify certain arguments. I am also grateful for comments on the mentioned ancestor to Kent Bach, Hartry Field, Andreas Kemmerling, Dugald Owen, Thomas Ricketts, Hans Sluga, Stephen Stich, and Bruce Vermazen.

(Revised version) Many thanks to Ned Block for raising questions about modes of presentation and the blindsight case, to Georges Rey for making me see that more needed to be said about the explanatory gap, and to Kent Bach for helpful remarks on a number of points.

REFERENCES

Block, N. (1978). "Troubles with Functionalism," in C. Wade Savage, ed., *Perception and Cognition: Issues in the Foundations of Psychology.* Vol. 9, *Minnesota Studies in the Philosophy of Science.* Minneapolis: University of Minnesota Press.

———. (1990). "Inverted Earth." *Philosophical Perspectives* 4, 53–79.

Dennett, Daniel (1991). *Consciousness Explained.* Boston: Little, Brown.

Harman, Gilbert (1990). "The Intrinsic Quality of Experience," *Philosophical Perspectives* 4, 31–52.

Jackson, Frank (1982). "Epiphenomenal Qualia," *Philosophical Quarterly* 1982, 127–36.

———. (1986). "What Mary Didn't Know," *Journal of Philosophy* 83: 291–95.

———. (1994). "Armchair Metaphysics," in M. Michael ed., *Philosophy in Mind.* Norwell, MA: Kluwer.

Kripke, Saul (1980). *Naming and Necessity.* Cambridge, MA: Harvard University Press.

Levin, Janet (1983). "Functionalism and the Argument from Conceivability," *Canadian Journal of Philosophy,* Supplementary Volume 11.

———. (1986). "Could Love Be Like a Heatwave?" *Philosophical Studies,* 49: 245–61.

Levine, Joseph (1983). "Materialism and Qualia: The Explanatory Gap," *Pacific Philosophical Quarterly,* 64: 354–61.

———. (1993). "On Leaving Out What It Is Like," in M. Davies and G. Humphreys, eds., *Consciousness.* Oxford: Blackwell.

Lewis, David (1983a). "Mad Pain and Martian Pain," in *Philosophical Papers,* Vol. 1. Oxford: Oxford University Press.

———. (1983b). "Postscript" to the foregoing.

Loar, Brian (1990). "Personal References," in E. Villanueva, ed., *Information, Semantics and Epistemology.* Oxford: Blackwell.

———. (1991). "Can We Explain Intentionality?," in G. Rey and B. Loewer, eds., *Meaning in Mind.* Oxford: Blackwell.

———. (1995). "Reference from the First-Person Perspective," in *Philosophical Issues* vol. 5.

McGinn, Colin (1993). "Consciousness and Cosmology: Hyperdualism Ventilated," in M. Davies and G. Humphreys, eds., *Consciousness.* Oxford: Blackwell.

Nagel, Thomas (1974). "What Is It Like to Be a Bat?" *Philosophical Review,* 1974: 435–50.

———. (1986). *The View from Nowhere.* Oxford: Oxford University Press.

Nemirow, Laurence (1980). Review of Nagel's *Mortal Questions, Philosophical Review,* July 1980.

Rey, Georges (1995). "Towards a Projectivist Account of Conscious Experience," in T. Metzinger, ed., *Essays on Consciousness.*

Warner, Richard (1986). "A Challenge to Physicalism," *Australasian Journal of Philosophy,* 64; 249–65.

———. (1993). "Incorrigibility," in H. Robinson, ed., *Objections to Physicalism,* Oxford: Oxford University Press.

31 Two Conceptions of the Physical
Daniel Stoljar

The debate over physicalism in philosophy of mind can be seen as concerning an inconsistent tetrad of theses: (1) if physicalism is true, a priori physicalism is true; (2) a priori physicalism is false; (3) if physicalism is false, epiphenomenalism is true; (4) epiphenomenalism is false. This paper argues that one may resolve the debate by distinguishing two conceptions of the physical: on the *theory-based conception,* it is plausible that (2) is true and (3) is false; on the *object-based conception,* it is plausible that (3) is true and (2) is false. The paper also defends and explores the version of physicalism that results from this strategy.

1

One way to view the contemporary debate in philosophy of mind over physicalism is to see it as being organized around an inconsistent tetrad of theses. These are:

(1) If physicalism is true, a priori physicalism is true.

(2) A priori physicalism is false.

(3) If physicalism is false, epiphenomenalism is true.

(4) Epiphenomenalism is false.

It is obvious of course that these theses *are* inconsistent: (1) and (2) entail that physicalism is false, while (3) and (4) entail that it is true. Barring ambiguity, therefore, one thing we know is that one of the theses if false.

On the other hand, each of the theses has powerful considerations, or at least what seem initially to be powerful considerations, in its favor.[1] In support of (1) are considerations of supervenience, articulated most clearly in recent times by Frank Jackson and David Chalmers. A priori physicalism is a thesis with two parts. The first part—the physicalist part—is that the mental supervenes with metaphysical necessity on the physical. The second part—the a priori part—is that mental truths are a priori entailed by physical truths. Many philosophers hold that supervenience stands in need of justification or explanation; Jackson and Chalmers argue that the project of justifying or explaining supervenience *just is* the project of making it plausible that there is an a priori entailment of the mental by the physical. This suggests that the first part of a priori physicalism inevitably involves the second. By considerations of supervenience, therefore, (1) is true: if physicalism is true, a priori physicalism is true.[2]

In support of (2) are considerations of the apparent epistemic distinctness of qualia from

From *Philosophy and Phenomenological Research* 62:253–81, 2001. Reprinted with permission of the publisher.

anything physical. According to many philosophers, knowledge of every physical property a person has cannot by itself suffice to know which qualia, if any, his or her experiences instantiate.[3] The conclusion drawn from this is that a priori physicalism is false; for if physical truths a priori entail mental truths, one could know qualia merely on the basis of physical knowledge. By considerations of epistemic distinctness, therefore, (2) is true: a priori physicalism is false.[4]

In support of (3) are considerations of the causal closure of the physical. Causal closure is the conjunction of two distinct theses. The first is a thesis about events; it is that for all physical events e, if there is an event e* such that e* causes e, then e* is a physical event. The second is a thesis about properties; it is that if any property is causally efficacious in one physical event's causing another, that property is a physical property. Of course, neither these theses nor their conjunction implies that there are no irreducibly mental events or properties. What causal closure does plausibly imply however is that irreducibly mental events and properties can play no causal role in the production of physical events, and so, of behavior. But the thesis that the mental has no causal work to do in the production of behavior *just is* epiphenomenalism. By considerations of causal closure, therefore, (3) is true: if physicalism is false, epiphenomenalism is true.[5]

In support of (4) are considerations of evidence, and, in particular, considerations of what constitutes evidence for the existence and instantiation of qualia. In both ourselves and others, we come to know about qualia via systems of memory, introspection and perception. According to one natural approach to these systems, however, they provide evidence of aspects of the world only if those aspects stand in an appropriately direct causal link to us. But if epiphenomenalism is true, it is hard to see how qualia might stand in any such link, and thus it is hard to see our reason for saying there are qualia in the first place. By considerations of evidence, therefore, (4) is true: epiphenomenalism is false.[6]

Of course, the fact that each of (1–4) has arguments in its favor does not affect the possibility that, on reflection, one of them might turn out to be false. Indeed, interpreted in the simplest possible way, most recent contributions to the debate (and in fact most classical contributions) are arguments to the effect that, despite initial plausibility, one or more of the theses is

false. Thus, a posteriori physicalists reject (1): according to them, it is not the case that the only way of justifying or explaining the supervenience thesis implied by physicalism is by making plausible the a priori entailment of the mental by the physical. A priori physicalists reject (2): according to them, either physical knowledge can suffice for qualitative knowledge after all, or else the sense in which it cannot poses no threat to a priori physicalism. Interactionist dualists reject (3): according to them, physical closure is false, either because some physical events are caused by irreducibly mental events, or else because the properties which are efficacious in the production of some physical events are irreducibly mental. And epiphenomenalists reject (4): according to them, one thing can be evidence for another even if no direct causal relation obtains between them.

Certainly the rational weight behind each of these options might in the end be such that we ought to endorse it. But it is important to see that rejecting one or more of its constituent theses is only one way of resolving the physicalism debate. Another possibility is to argue for some kind of ambiguity. If we can discern an ambiguity in (1–4) then it would seem possible to believe *all* the theses that make up the debate, rather than rejecting one of them.[7]

My aim in this paper is to suggest that it *is* plausible to discern an ambiguity in (1–4), and to defend a version of physicalism on that basis. There are, I think, two rather different conceptions of the physical, and hence of physicalism, at play in the physicalism debate. What I want to suggest is that if these two conceptions are distinguished, the apparent inconsistency of (1–4) disappears. More particularly, if the two conceptions are distinguished, it becomes clear that there is no *one* notion of the physical according to which it is plausible to believe both (2) and (3): the sense of 'physical' in which a priori physicalism is false is not the sense in which the rejection of physicalism inevitably leads to epiphenomenalism.

This possibility will of course recommend itself to those who find each of (1–4) attractive. But it is also of interest for another reason. Much of the recent discussion in philosophy of mind has had physicalists either denying that one can have propositional knowledge concerning qualia or else appealing to what Chalmers (1996) calls 'strong necessities'—necessities which are a posteriori but are totally unlike the sort of a posteriori necessities discussed by

Kripke (1980). Perhaps it will turn out that one cannot have propositional knowledge of qualia, or that there are strong necessities, but it would be helpful if we had a way of defending physicalism that did not require taking a stand on such issues.[8]

My approach is as follows. In §2, I set out the two conceptions of the physical I will be interested in. In §§3 and 4, I suggest that distinguishing the two conceptions resolves the contemporary debate. In §5, I defend this suggestion against some objections, with a particular focus on the sort of physicalism one is left with if the suggestion is adopted—as we will see, the position that emerges is similar in important respects to Russell's neutral monism, and to modern versions of that view. Finally, in §6, I close the paper by providing some positive reasons for endorsing the strategy I propose.

2

According to the first conception of the physical—which I will call *the theory-based conception*—a physical property is a property which *either* is the sort of property that physical theory tells us about *or* else is a property which metaphysically (or logically) supervenes on the sort of property that physical theory tells us about. According to this conception, for example, if physical theory tells us about the property of having mass, then having mass is a physical property. Similarly, if physical theory tells us about the property of being a rock—or, what is perhaps more likely, if the property of being a rock supervenes on properties which physical theory tell us about—then it too is a physical property. Let us say that any property which is physical by the lights of the theory-based conception is a *t-physical property*.[9]

According to the second conception of the physical—which I will call *the object-based conception*—a physical property is a property which *either* is the sort of property required by a complete account of the intrinsic nature of paradigmatic physical objects and their constituents *or* else is a property which metaphysically (or logically) supervenes on the sort of property required by a complete account of the intrinsic nature of paradigmatic physical objects and their constituents.[10] According to this conception, for example, if rocks, trees, planets and so on are paradigmatic physical objects, then the property of being a rock, tree or planet is a physical prop-

erty. Similarly, if the property of having mass is required in a complete account of the intrinsic nature of physical objects and their constituents, then having mass is a physical property. Let us say that any property which is physical by the lights of the object-based conception is an *o-physical property*.

Since it is one of the more central and difficult notions that we have, many issues will arise whenever one is discussing *any* notion of the physical. However, the issue I want to focus on here is the sense in which the two conceptions I have described are distinct.[11] Of course, it is obvious that they are distinct in some sense: one concerns theories, the other objects. But what is of interest to me is whether the class of properties characterized by both is co-extensive. I will argue that they are not co-extensive for the following reason: some o-physicals are not t-physical.

The point emerges most clearly if we have two theses before us. The first is that physical theory tells us only about the *dispositional* properties of physical objects and so does not tell us about the *categorical* properties, if any, that they have. A thesis of this sort has been held (at least implicitly) by many philosophers, but the following passage from Blackburn provides an effective illustration:

> When we think of categorical grounds, we are apt to think of spatial configurations of things—hard, massy, shaped things, resisting penetration and displacement by others of their kind. But the categorical credentials of any item in this list are poor. Resistance is *par excellence* dispositional; extension is only of use, as Leibniz insisted, if there is some other property whose instancing defines the boundaries; hardness goes with resistance, and mass is knowable only by its dynamical effects. Turn up the magnification and we find things like an electrical charge at a point, or rather varying over a region, but the magnitude of a field at a region is known only through its effects on other things in spatial relations to that region. A region with charge is very different from a region without. . . . It differs precisely in its dispositions or powers. But science finds only dispositions all the way down. (1992, pp. 62–63)

What Blackburn is saying here is that when we consider both the properties of physical objects we normally think of as primary qualities—such as resistance—and the physical properties we normally think of as being associated with modern physics—such as having a certain charge—we find that such properties are dispositional. His final remark suggests that something more general is true and that in scientific theory—Blackburn means, I think, *physical* scientific theory—one only "finds" dispositional properties. It seems reasonable to summarize this by saying that physical theory tells us only about dispositional properties.[12]

The second thesis we need to consider is that the dispositional properties of physical objects *do* require categorical grounds, i.e. for all dispositional properties, there must be a non-dispositional property, or non-dispositional properties, such that the instantiation of the latter is metaphysically sufficient for the instantiation of the former. For example, if a vase is fragile, there must be a non-dispositional property, or non-dispositional properties, whose instantiation makes it the case that the vase is fragile; and if a chair is uncomfortable, there must be a non-dispositional property, or non-dispositional properties, whose instantiation makes it the case that the chair is uncomfortable.[13] It might perhaps be thought that there is some conflict between this thesis and the first. But there is certainly no *logical* inconsistency here. And indeed, many (but not all) philosophers who hold the first thesis also hold the second. A prominent example is D.M. Armstrong, who in *A Materialist Theory of the Mind,* holds that, since physical theory only characterizes the dispositional or relational nature of physical objects, it therefore "does not tell us"—as Armstrong (1968, p. 282) says—about their categorical or non-relational nature.

With these two theses in place it is easy to argue that the theory-based conception is distinct from the object-based conception. Suppose a physical object x has a dispositional physical property F. From the thesis that dispositional properties require categorical grounds, it follows that x (or its constituents) must also have a further non-dispositional property, which we may call G. But now let us ask: is G a physical property or not? If we are operating with the theory-based conception, it would seem that G is *not* physical. For from the thesis that physical theory tells us only about dispositions, it follows that t-physical properties are either dispositional or else supervene on dispositional properties. But neither is true in the case of G; so G itself is not t-physical. On the other hand, if we are operating with the object-based conception, there is no reason at all to deny that G is a physical property. After all, G is—or at least could perfectly well be—the kind of property required in a complete account of the intrinsic nature of

paradigmatic physical objects and their constituents. In sum, properties such as G—the properties which are the categorical grounds of the dispositional properties that physical theory tells us about—serve to show that the two conceptions of the physical are distinct. By the lights of the theory-based conception, G and its ilk are not physical; but by the lights of the object-based conception, G and its ilk are.

The chief complication with this argument—apart of course from the issues that we have already set aside (cf. fns 12 and 13)—derives from the fact that there are two different senses in which physical theory might fail to tell us about the categorical properties of physical objects. In the first sense, physical theory fails to tell us about a property just in case no expression of the theory *refers* to that property. Now, in this sense, the argument we just considered will not go through. For even if dispositional properties do require categorical grounds, it is still perfectly possible that the expressions of physical theory might refer to those grounds inter alia. But then G and its ilk will count as t-physical as well as o-physical, and there is no reason for supposing that the two conceptions of the physical are distinct.

But there is also is a second sense in which physical theory might fail to tell us about categorical grounds. In this sense, physical theory fails to tell us about categorical grounds just in case there might be two possible worlds w and w^* such that (i) they are exactly alike in terms of their distribution of dispositional properties—in both w and w^*, x has F; but (ii) they are different in terms of their categorical properties—in w, x has G but in w^*, x has a quite distinct categorical property G^*; and (iii) they are from the point of view of the theory epistemically indiscernible—the two worlds are (in Kripke's famous phrase) epistemically and qualitatively identical, though they might nevertheless be semantically different in the sense that in w, an expression of physical theory refers to G while in w^* the counterpart expression refers to G^*. It is this idea that Blackburn and Armstrong are appealing to when they (respectively) say that science finds dispositions all the way down, and that physical theory does not tell us about the categorical nature of physical objects. Similarly, it is this idea that is required by the argument we just considered that some o-physical properties are not t-physical.[14]

The right response to this complication is to acknowledge it and set it aside. Suppose there *are* two senses of what it is for a theory to tell us about a property. Then we will of course have *two* different versions of the theory-based conception of the physical. Moreover, only one of these versions is distinct from the object-based conception. On the other hand, the two different versions of the theory-based conception will *themselves* determine two different classes of properties: according to the version which employs the first sense of 'tells us about,' the theory-based conception of the physical will acknowledge both dispositional and categorical properties as physical; according to the version which employs the second sense, the theory-based conception will acknowledge only dispositional properties as physical. And thus our basic point remains the same: there is distinction between two conceptions of the physical and these two conceptions determine two classes of physical properties, the first of which is limited to the dispositional properties of physical objects, the second of which includes both the dispositional and categorical properties of physical objects. More generally, one could run the following discussion in one of two ways: either one could operate with the two versions of the theory-based conception, or else one could operate with the object-based conception and the version of the theory-based conception which employs the second sense of 'tells us about.' I will here adopt the latter course—and thus I will continue to contrast o-physical properties and t-physical properties—but it is important to notice that the former course is also available.

3

So far, I have introduced two conceptions of the physical, and argued that they characterize distinct classes of properties. I turn now to the suggestion that distinguishing the two conceptions provides a way of believing all the constituent theses in the physicalism debate.

The first thing to say is that the issue of the interpretation of the notion of the physical does not seem to affect the reasons for believing either thesis (1) or thesis (4). The arguments that support (1)—viz., the claim that if physicalism is true a priori physicalism is—are arguments of a very general nature about supervenience, and whether or not the defence of supervenience will in the end involve an a priori entailment of the mental by the physical. These arguments are

of course highly controversial. But, however things turn out with these arguments, it seems plain that the issues they raise are orthogonal to the issues having to do with the conceptions of the physical.

The same thing applies to the arguments one might adduce in support of (4)—viz., the claim that epiphenomenalism is false. These are arguments to the conclusion that if epiphenomenalism is true, the systems by which we gather evidence of qualia break down. But once again, while these arguments are controversial, I think we can set them aside. However things turn out with these arguments, it seems plain that the issues they raise are irrelevant to the issues with which we are concerned.

However, while the issue of interpretation does not affect the reasons for (1) and (4), it *does* affect the reasons for (2) and (3).

Let us consider first (2), the claim that a priori physicalism is false. Given our distinction between the theory-based and the object-based conceptions, we can distinguish two interpretations of (2). According to the first, (2) asserts that it is not the case that qualia supervene on t-physical properties *and* that t-physical truths a priori entail qualitative truths. We might express this by rendering (2) as:

(2-t) A priori t-physicalism is false.

According to the second interpretation, (2) asserts that it is not the case that qualia supervene on o-physical properties *and* that o-physical truths a priori entail qualitative truths. We might express this by rendering (2) as:

(2-o) A priori o-physicalism is false.

It is obvious that (2-t) and (2-o) are, given our assumptions, distinct. After all, if there are properties which are o-physical but not t-physical, it follows that even if t-physicalism is false, o-physicalism might still be true.[15]

Now, earlier I said that what supports (2)—and so counts against a priori physicalism—are considerations of epistemic distinctness. Given that (2) can be disambiguated into (2-t) and (2-o), what we need to ask is whether these considerations support both disambiguations. I think it can be argued, however, that while the considerations of epistemic distinctness do support (2-t), they do not likewise support (2-o). And this means that we can maintain a priori o-physicalism in the face of the considerations of epistemic distinctness even while we cannot maintain a priori t-physicalism.

While there are a number of different kinds of consideration of epistemic distinctness, we will focus here on what is perhaps the clearest and most notorious of them, Frank Jackson's (1982) knowledge argument.[16] As is extremely well-known, this argument asks us to imagine Mary, a famous neuroscientist confined to a black and white room. Mary is forced to learn about the world via black and white television and computers. However, despite these hardships Mary learns (and therefore knows) all that physical theory can teach her. Now, if a priori physicalism were true, it is plausible to suppose that Mary knows everything about the world. And yet—and here is Jackson's point—it seems she does not know everything. For, upon being released into the world of color, it will become obvious that, inside her room, she did not know what it is like for both herself and others to see colors—that is, she did not know about the qualia instantiated by particular experiences of seeing colors. Following Jackson (1986), we may summarize the argument as follows:

(5) Mary (before her release) knows everything physical there is to know about other people.

(6) Mary (before her release) does not know everything there is to know about other people (because she learns something about them on being released).

Therefore,

(7) There are truths about other people (and herself) that escape the physicalist story.

And of course, the truth of (7) entails (2), the thesis that a priori physicalism is false; for, if a priori physicalism were true, there would be no truths about anybody (or anything) that escape the physicalist story. For our purposes, therefore, it is reasonable to by-pass (7) and interpret the knowledge argument simply as urging that (5) and (6) entail (2).

Given our distinction between the theory-based and the object-based conceptions of the physical, however, it is clear that the first premise of this argument is subject to interpretation in either of two ways. We might express these as (5-t) and (5-o):

(5-t) Mary (before her release) knows everything t-physical there is to know about other people.

(5-o) Mary (before her release) knows everything o-physical there is to know about other people.

Moreover, it is clear that (5-t) and (5-o) differ both in plausibility and in what conclusions they support. (5-t) is certainly very plausible given the story of Mary. After all, if Mary knows all of physical theory, and if physical theory tells us about t-physical properties, she presumably will know everything t-physical there is to know about other people. But the trouble here is that, when combined with (6), (5-t) only yields the falsity of a priori t-physicalism, not a priori o-physicalism, i.e., it only yields (2-t), not (2-o). If some o-physical properties are not t-physical, from the fact that Mary knows everything t-physical about the world, it does not follow that she knows everything o-physical, and it therefore does not follow that when she learns something about the world she has learnt something non-physical. The truth of (5-t) and (6), then, leaves us free to endorse a priori o-physicalism, and therefore free to reject (2-o).

But what if we operate with (5-o) rather than (5-t)? It is obvious that the conjunction of (5-o) and (6), unlike the conjunction of (5-t) and (6), *does* entail the falsity of a priori o-physicalism, i.e., does entail (2-o). But the trouble now is that the story of Mary gives us no reason at all to endorse (5-o). The reason for this is that, on the construal that we have adopted, physical theory *will not tell us* about certain of the o-physical properties. After all, if the physical theory does not tell us about the categorical properties of physical objects, and if some o-physical properties are categorical, it would seem that, no matter how much physical theory one knows, one will still not know about certain o-physical properties. But then no matter how much physical theory *Mary* knows, she will still not know about certain of the o-physical properties. Nothing she knows, therefore, rules out the possibility that the truths about herself and others are entirely o-physical. More generally, while (5-o) and (6) certainly provide premises from which one might validly argue to the falsehood of a priori o-physicalism, the argument is a failure nevertheless, because we have no reason to believe its first premise.

In sum, the distinction between the theory-based conception and the object-based conception provides a way in which we might defeat the knowledge argument and at the same time concede the central intuition that motivates it.[17] In consequence, we can both accept and deny thesis (2). On one interpretation, (2) is equivalent to (2-t), and we have seen that the knowledge argument gives us very good reason to grant this. On the other interpretation, (2) is equivalent to (2-o), and we have seen that the knowledge argument gives us no good reason to grant this. To that extent then, we can with good conscience accept (2) if it is interpreted as (2-t), and reject it if it is interpreted as (2-o).

4

The suggestion that one might reject (2) on one interpretation and accept it on another is an important step in resolving the puzzle posed by the inconsistency of (1–4). But this alone does not complete the resolution. For I have conceded that (2) is very plausible on the theory-based conception of the physical; that is, that (2-t) is very plausible. And I have also suggested that the truth of (1) and (4) remains untouched by any issue about how to interpret the physical. But this means that if (3)—viz., the claim that if physicalism is false, epiphenomenalism is true—is plausible on the theory-based conception, we are back where we started. To complete the resolution of the puzzle, therefore, it needs to be argued that (3) is implausible if interpreted from the standpoint of the theory-based conception.

However, (3) *is* implausible if interpreted from the standpoint of the theory-based conception.

Let us first distinguish the two interpretations of (3) just as we did for (2). On the first interpretation, (3) asserts that if qualia do not supervene on t-physical properties, the inevitable result is epiphenomenalism. We might express this by rendering (3) as:

(3-t) If t-physicalism is false, epiphenomenalism is true.

On the second interpretation, (3) asserts that if qualia do not supervene on o-physical properties, the inevitable result is epiphenomenalism. We might express this by rendering (3) as:

(3-o) If o-physicalism is false, epiphenomenalism is true.

Once again, it is clear that (3-t) and (3-o) are, given our assumptions, distinct. If there are o-physical properties which are not t-physical, it is clear that we might have grounds for rejecting (3-t) but no grounds at all for rejecting (3-o).

Now, earlier I said that the considerations in favor of (3) are considerations of causal closure. And we also saw that causal closure is the conjunction of two theses, one about events, the other about properties. We might summarize these theses as (8) and (9):

(8) For all physical events e, if there is an event e* such that e* causes e, then e* is a physical event.

(9) For all physical events e and e*, if there is a property F such that F is causally efficacious in e's causing e*, then F is a physical property.

Now, (8) can from our point of view be set aside. The reason is that the conceptions of the physical with which we are operating apply in the first instance to *properties,* and do not obviously extend to items of other ontological categories. More particularly, neither conception as it stands says anything about what it is to be a physical event. But this means that the conceptions are silent on the plausibility of (8).

On the other hand, the conceptions are not silent on the plausibility of (9). If we interpret (9) in accordance with the theory-based conception, it asserts that the only properties that are causally efficacious are *t-physical* properties, a thesis we might call (9-t):

(9-t) For all physical events e and e*, if there is a property F such that F is causally efficacious in e's causing e*, then F is a t-physical property.

If we interpret (9) in accordance with the object-based conception, by contrast, it asserts that the only properties that are causally efficacious are *o-physical* properties, a thesis we might call (9-o):

(9-o) For all physical events e and e*, if there is a property F such that F is causally efficacious in e's causing e*, then F is an o-physical property.

And once again, it is clear that (9-t) and (9-o) are, given our assumptions, distinct. The first implies that only t-physical properties are causally efficacious, while the second allows that some causally efficacious properties are not t-physical, i.e., those properties which are o-physical but not t-physical.

Now, I think we should concede that *if* (9-t) is true, we have a very good argument for (3-t). Similarly, we should concede that *if* (9-o) is true, we have a very good argument for (3-o).

For consider: if (9-t) is true, the only causally efficacious properties in the production of physical events, and therefore of behavioral events, are t-physical; but if t-physicalism is false, qualia are not t-physical. It follows that qualia are not efficacious in the production of behavior. *Mutatis mutandis* for (9-o): if (9-o) is true, the only causally efficacious properties in the production of physical events, and therefore of behavioral events, are o-physical; but if o-physicalism is false, qualia are not o-physical. It again follows that qualia are not efficacious in the production of behavior.

On the other hand, there is an important difference between (9-t) and (9-o), and this is that it is far from obvious that (9-t) is *true*. For let us consider more directly what (9-t) says. (9-t) says that in the realm of physical causation, the only causally efficacious properties are t-physical. In general, however, this seems to be quite mistaken. The reason is that it is very implausible to suppose that the efficacy of dispositional properties has nothing whatsoever to do with the efficacy of their categorical grounds.

To illustrate this point, consider Ned Block's famous example of the bull and the bull-fighter. Block writes:

> Consider the bull-fighter's cape. The myth (which we will accept, ignoring the inconvenient color-blindness of bulls) is that its red color provoked the bull, i.e., redness is causally relevant to the bull's anger. The cape also has the second order property of being provocative, of having some property or other that provokes the bull, of having some property or other that is causally relevant to the bull's anger. But does the provocativeness of the cape provoke the bull? Is the provocativeness causally relevant to the bull's anger? It would seem not. The bull is too stupid for that. The provocativeness of the cape might provoke the ASPCA, but not the bull. (1990, p. 155)

The moral that Block wants to draw from this example is the contentious one that provocativeness and similar properties are in a large class of cases not causally efficacious ("causally relevant") while properties such as redness are. For our purposes, it is sufficient to draw the less contentious moral that while dispositional properties are causally efficacious—for of course provocativeness is a dispositional property—they are only efficacious if their categorical grounds are—for of course redness is (or anyway may be taken to be for the purposes of the example) the categorical ground of provocative-

ness. As Mark Johnston puts it in a related context, if dispositional properties are efficacious, they are so "at one remove and by courtesy" (1992; p. 235). But this means that (9-t) is false. (9-t) tells us that the only properties which are causally efficacious are dispositional, i.e., properties similar to provocativeness. But it seems clear that, if dispositional properties *are* causally efficacious, so too are their categorical grounds. And, if categorical grounds are, as we are assuming, non-dispositional, then, contrary to (9-t), dispositional properties are not the only properties that are causally efficacious.

On the other hand, examples such a Block's do nothing whatsoever to undermine (9-o). (9-o), after all, does not restrict itself to dispositional properties, and so is not subject to the criticism that (9-t) is. More generally, if we interpret (9) in accordance with the theory-based conception, we can reasonably regard it as false and therefore as providing no support for (3). On the other hand, if we interpret (9) in accordance with the object-based conception, we can reasonably regard it as true and therefore as providing support for (3). In summary, (9-o) provides support for (3-o), but (9-t) provides no support for (3-t).

How does this bear on the resolution of (1–4)? Well, earlier we saw that thesis (2) has two versions—viz., the version expressed by (2-t) and the version expressed by (2-o)—and that only the *first* of these receives support from considerations of epistemic distinctness; that is, considerations of epistemic distinctness leave us free to reject (2-o). What we have just seen is that thesis (3) also has two versions—viz., the version expressed by (3-t) and the version expressed by (3-o)—and that only the *second* of these receives support from considerations of closure; that is, considerations of closure leave us free to reject (3-t). But this suggests that the predicament which in fact confronts us is not quite the predicament we originally imagined ourselves to be in.

Originally, we imagined ourselves to be confronted with four inconsistent theses (1–4) each of which we had powerful reason to believe:

(1) If physicalism is true, a priori physicalism is true.
(2) A priori physicalism is false.
(3) If physicalism is false, epiphenomenalism is true.
(4) Epiphenomenalism is false.

If we distinguish between the two conceptions of the physical, however, it is plain that (1–4) fail to articulate *precisely* the theses we have reason to believe. What we in fact have reason to believe is not (1–4) but rather:

(1)   If physicalism is true, a priori physicalism is true.

(2-t)   A priori t-physicalism is false.

(3-o)   If o-physicalism is false, epiphenomenalism is true.

(4)   Epiphenomenalism is false.

But this second tetrad is importantly different from first. The first is inconsistent, the second is not. As a consequence, if you find the considerations of supervenience, epistemic distinctness, closure and evidence compelling, you may believe the second tetrad without fear of contradiction. And our original puzzle is solved.

5

My strategy so far has been to distinguish two conceptions of the physical, and to suggest that, if these conceptions can be kept apart, the appearance of inconsistency of (1–4) is resolved. If we adopt the object-based conception, we can reasonably regard (2) as true and (3) as false. But if we adopt the theory-based conception, we can reasonably regard (3) as true and (2) as false. I turn now to some objections to this strategy.

Broadly speaking, there are two classes of objection to consider. The first class raises questions about the assumptions I required in order to argue that, properly understood, (1–4) do not present a contradiction: the thesis that dispositions require categorical grounds, and the thesis that physical theory tells us only about dispositional properties. The second class raises questions about the outline of the position that one is left with if one pursues our strategy. Obviously, it is no good to resolve the inconsistency of (1–4) only to be forced into an even more unpalatable position. I have already noted that I will set aside the first class of objection, and so here I will concentrate on the second class.

What sort of position is one left with if one accepts (1), (2-t), (3-o), (4) and rejects (2-o) and (3-t)? The answer is that one is left with a view that bears a close resemblance to Russell's in *The Analysis of Matter,* and even closer resemblance to the view discussed by contemporary defenders of a Russell-inspired physicalism such as Maxwell (1978) and Lockwood (1989, 1992).[18]

The broad contours of the position may be brought out by considering the following analogy. Imagine a mosaic constituted by two basic shapes, triangles and pieces of pie, as well as a large number of shapes obtained by a transparent combination of these: squares, half-moons, circles, rhombuses etc. Imagine also that our access to the mosaic is limited to two shape-detecting systems: the first scans the mosaic and detects triangles; the second scans it and detects circles. For one reason or another we spontaneously assume that the triangle-detector tells us everything about the nature of the mosaic—we become trianglists, i.e., those who believe that triangles are the fundamental shape and that all other shapes supervene. The problem of the circle then stares us in the face: the circle-detector tells us the mosaic contains circles, but there is apparently no place for circles in a mosaic totally constituted by triangles. Different people respond to the problem in different ways: some say the circle-detecting system leads us astray, and that properly understood it provides no propositional knowledge of circles; others declare circles a posteriori identical with triangles; still others decide that circles are irreducible, and postulate contingent laws linking them and triangles. Of course all these responses are mistaken, and moreover they make a common mistake. The mistake is that the triangle-detector does not tell us everything about the mosaic: it is selective and only tells us about triangles when in addition there are pieces of pie. Of course the pieces of pie are not themselves circles. But in combination they may constitute circles. When God created the mosaic, all he had to do was to create triangles and pieces of pie, and arrange them in just the way he wanted; in doing so, he created everything else including circles.

As it is with triangles, pieces of pie, and circles so (largely) it is with t-physical, o-physical and qualia, according to the Russell-inspired view. Physical theory tells us about the physical world, and introspection tells us about qualia. For one reason or another we spontaneously assume that physical theory tells us everything about the nature of the world—we become t-physicalists, i.e., those who believe that t-physical properties, properties that physical theory tells us about, are fundamental and all other properties supervene. The problem of qualia then stares us in the face: introspection tells us there are qualia, but there is apparently no place for qualia in a world totally constituted by t-physical properties. Different people respond to the problem in different ways: some say introspection leads us astray, and that properly understood it provides no propositional knowledge of qualia; others declare qualia a posteriori identical with t-physical properties; still others decide that qualia are irreducible, and postulate contingent laws linking them and t-physical properties. Of course all these responses are mistaken, and moreover they make a common mistake. The mistake is that physical theory does not tell us everything about the physical world: it is selective and only tells us about dispositional t-physical properties when in addition there are categorical o-physical properties. Of course, the categorical o-physical properties are not themselves qualia. But in combination—perhaps also in combination with the t-physicals—they may constitute qualia. When God created the world, all he had to do was create the fundamental physical properties—o-physical and t-physical—and arrange them in just the way he wanted; in doing so, he created everything else including qualia.

To put things less picturesquely, the Russell-inspired position as I will understand it here has two parts. The first part—the physicalist part—is that qualia supervene not on the class of properties that physical theory tells us about—the t-physical properties, as I have called them—but on a larger class that includes both the t-physicals and categorical bases of such properties—o-physical properties, as I have called them. The second part—the a priori part—is that mental truths (in particular, qualitative truths) are a priori entailed by physical truths. In considering the following objections, then, I will be interested in the nature and plausibility of this Russell-inspired view, which I will continue to call a priori o-physicalism, or, more simply, o-physicalism.[19]

Objection #1: Is This Really Physicalism?

The first objection is whether o-physicalism is really physicalism. An objection of this sort is in effect mentioned by Chalmers. In the course of providing an otherwise extremely sympathetic discussion of the view I have been discussing, Chalmers says that "there is a sense in which this view can be seen as a monism rather than a dualism, but it is not a materialist monism" (1996; p. 155).[20] Rather, he says, the view is either panpsychism or neutral monism, depending on how it is developed. If correct, this seems to constitute a major reason to doubt our claim

to have found a resolution of the debate over physicalism: for we would have resolved the debate simply by giving up physicalism.

The general response to this objection is that it misses the distinction between the theory-based and the object-based conception of the physical. If one operates *only* with the theory-based conception—as Chalmers in effect does (1996; p. 33)—then any property which is not a t-physical property will need to be excluded from the class of physical properties, and thus must be classed as either a mental property or a neutral property, i.e., a property which is neither mental nor physical. But if one accepts that there are more physical properties than the t-physicals, the landscape looks somewhat different.

To illustrate this, let us examine first the question of whether o-physicalism is a version of neutral monism. The crucial consideration here is that neutral monism as usually defined *presupposes* the theory-based conception of the physical: neutral properties are properties which are neither mental nor t-physical; and neutral monism is the thesis—to put it in modern terms—that mental and t-physical properties metaphysically supervene on neutral properties. Now, if this is what neutral monism is, there is certainly some plausibility in supposing that o-physicalism is a version of neutral monism. Since some o-physical properties are neither mental nor t-physical, those o-physical properties will be neutral in this sense. On the other hand, it is less clear that this feature of the view compromises its status as physicalism. If one accepts that there are physical properties which are not t-physical, then one way to hold this first version of neutral monism is to adopt o-physicalism. So the charge that o-physicalism is not a version of physicalism rests on a failure to distinguish the two conceptions of the physical.

One might be tempted at this point to reject the object-based conception of the physical and to operate only with the theory-based conception. Of course, if one operates only with the theory-based conception, one may draw a clear distinction between neutral monism and physicalism. However, on the assumption that dispositions require categorical grounds, this option is not available to physicalists. For suppose you are a physicalist who believes that dispositional properties require categorical grounds. If you in addition believe that only dispositional properties are physical, it follows that for every dispositional physical property that is instantiated, a non-physical categorical property is instantiated also. But then physicalism is false—and for reasons that have nothing to do with philosophy of mind. In sum, if a physicalist wants a version of physicalism according to which the doctrine can be true compatibly with certain metaphysical assumptions about dispositions, it is necessary that he or she operates with a conception of the physical broader than simply the theory-based conception. In the context of our argument, this means that physicalists must adopt the object-based conception.[21]

So there seems little reason to be concerned that o-physicalism is a form of neutral monism—but what then of panpsychism? According to panpsychism, the categorical properties which underlie dispositional t-physical properties are in every case qualia. It follows from panpsychism therefore that all the physical objects of our acquaintance—computers, trees, planets etc.—all instantiate qualia just as I do. Now, while this view is somewhat startling, it can be given a motivation. Part of its motivation is once again the idea that (dispositional) t-physical properties exhaust the class of physical properties. But in part also its motivation is that we seem to glean the concept of a categorical property from our concepts of qualia—as Blackburn (1992; p. 65) puts it, "categoricity comes with the subjective view." Putting these two ideas together, it becomes tempting to suppose that, in general, physical properties require categorical bases, and that these categorical bases are simply qualia. The result is panpsychism.

Now of course the first part of this motivation will be rejected by someone who accepts the object-based conception of the physical. But the second part of the motivation is also open to objection. For even if one derives one's concept of a categorical property from one's concept of qualia—and this is something we can remain neutral on—it does not follow that all categorical properties are qualitative properties. In Kripke's (1982; p. 118) example, even if one derives one's concept of a duck from the ducks in Central Park, it does not follow that the concept so derived does not apply to ducks not in Central Park. And this means that one can at least imagine a range of categorical properties which are both physical and non-qualitative: these are the properties which make up the categorical nature of physical objects, the properties we have called o-physical. If o-physicalism is right, then some of these properties will in combination be the supervenience base for qualitative proper-

ties. Unless there is something incoherent in the very idea of such a class of properties, we have no reason to suppose that o-physicalism will collapse into panpsychism.

Objection #2: Concepts Unattainable?

The second objection I will consider concerns the a priori part of o-physicalism: the thesis that the qualitative truths are a priori entailed by physical truths.

It needs to be appreciated that in committing itself to such physical truths o-physicalism is committing itself to a class of truths which cannot be expressed in a language we currently understand, or, to put it in another idiom, cannot be formulated using concepts we currently possess. For consider: what could the relevant concepts be? They cannot be (what we might call) *t-concepts*, i.e., concepts which tell us about t-physical properties—for in our discussion of the knowledge argument we in effect conceded that such t-concepts are not a priori equivalent to concepts of qualia. And nor can they be concepts of qualia—for the position is precisely that the concepts in question are physical not qualitative. So o-physicalism requires the postulation of a third class of concept, which me might call *o-concepts:* these are concepts which tell us about the categorical o-physical properties of physical objects, just as qualitative concepts tell us about qualia, and t-concepts tell us about the dispositional t-physical properties of physical objects.

Now, the mere fact that o-physicalism is committed to a class of concepts which we do not currently possess is not by itself an objection against the view. For one thing, any sober assessment of our epistemic achievements must always acknowledge the possibility that our conceptual repertoire is in various respects limited. Moreover, the concepts at issue here are concepts which for most practical purposes do not matter, and so the fact that we lack them is not going to disrupt our usual epistemic engagement with the world. Those philosophers who hold that it is dispositions 'all the way down,' and thus that there are no categorical properties, are in my view mistaken. But the grain of truth in their position is that the distinction between categorical and dispositional does not seem to matter much to the main business of science.

Nevertheless, one might try to develop this feature of our account—that it requires a new class of concept—into an objection against it in a number of ways. One suggestion is that, not only do we not possess o-concepts, no possible being *could* possess them. However, while it is difficult to argue against this suggestion it is also difficult to see the motivation for it. In general we *know* that one can possess concepts relevantly like o-concepts. As Blackburn (1992) points out, concepts of qualia are precisely such concepts, at least in the sense that these are concepts of non-dispositional properties. Why then, on an analogy with such concepts, can we not imagine a being who possessed concepts of the categorical properties of physical objects? The claim that no possible being could possess these concepts might have some force if we did not possess concepts of qualia. But the trouble is that we *do* possess such concepts.

Alternatively, one might argue that the idea of a class of o-concepts is incoherent, on the ground, for example, that it is simply incoherent to suppose that physical truths could a priori entail qualitative truths. However, the problem with this suggestion is that we have at present no argument for it (even if such an argument could be developed in the future). One of the lessons of the knowledge argument is that t-concepts are not a priori equivalent to concepts of qualia. But it does not follow from this that o-concepts are not so equivalent. Again: what the knowledge argument shows is that a priori t-physicalism is false. But it does not show that a priori o-physicalism is false.

Of course, it remains an interesting and open question whether the contingent facts about our history or environment or psychology will allow us to develop the concepts at issue. One possibility is that we could develop such concepts, perhaps by undergoing an intellectual or scientific revolution akin to the revolutions of the 17th century. If that were true, our position would be similar to that represented by Nagel's (1974) famous presocratic philosopher who does not understand the identification of matter and energy. Another possibility is that our contingent psychological nature is such that we will never attain the o-concepts. If that were true, our position becomes a species of the position defended by McGinn (1989; see also Jackson 1982)—though we have arrived at the position from another direction. On this view, there are a class of concepts which would tell us about the categorical properties of physical objects, and which are required to formulate the physical truths which a priori entail the qualitative truths. But our contingent psychological nature is such

that we shall never develop such concepts: we can develop concepts of the dispositional properties of physical objects; and we can develop concepts of qualia, but we cannot develop concepts of the categorical properties. Hence we are epistemically bounded with respect to what McGinn thinks of as 'the solution to the mind–body problem.'

It is not important for our purposes to decide between these possibilities. What is more important is to see the o-concepts as a kind of epistemic ideal. In general, we can imagine a kind of inquiry which would tell us about the categorical properties of physical objects—categorical inquiry, as we might call it. What our position predicts is that in order to have an priori physicalist theory of qualia and their place in the world—one which provides an a priori analysis of the nature of the world in terms of a relatively small list of physical concepts—one would need to complete the categorical inquiry. Whether we will ever be able to achieve this aim is an open question, but the goal remains as something to which we can aspire.

One might object that an account of the metaphysics of mind should not postulate epistemic goals and then offer no constructive suggestions about how that goal is to be reached. I agree that this is a drawback, and something that needs to be taken into consideration when one compares the present proposal with others. But it is possible also to take a somewhat more positive view of the situation. For one thing, the issue of epistemic goals needs to be sharply distinguished from the issue of the truth of physicalism. We are no longer debating whether qualia supervene on the physical or not, we are debating whether we ourselves can attain a certain epistemic goal, viz., come to possess a class of physical concepts from which the concepts of qualia would a priori follow. For another, a pleasing aspect of our position is that it allows us to characterize the epistemic problem that faces us with relative precision. All that remains to be seen is if we can solve the problem

Objection #3: The Grain Problem

Finally, I consider the grain problem. This problem was originally raised by Sellars as a problem for physicalism in general, but many who have discussed or defended the Russell-inspired view have thought it the central problem that the doctrine faces—"certainly the hardest problem for any sort of Russellian View" (Chalmers

1996: 307). The reason the problem is pressing is because it threatens to show that, in principle, a (potentially huge and extremely complicated) collection of o-physical properties cannot constitute qualia. If this is right, regardless of its status as a version of physicalism, and regardless of the nature of the epistemic goals it envisions, our position is false. So no discussion of the Russell-inspired view can fail to address the grain problem.

While there are a number of statements of the grain problem in the literature, I will concentrate on Maxwell's. He writes:

The objection asks, for example, how it is that the occurrence of a smooth continuous expanse of red in our visual experience can be identical with a brain process that must, it would seem, involve particulate, discontinuous affairs such as transfers of or interactions among large numbers of electrons or the like. Surely being smooth is a structural property, and being particulate or discontinuous is also a structural property, one moreover that is incompatible with being smooth and continuous. This strongly, suggests, the objection continues, that at least some mental events exemplify structural properties that are not exemplified by any brain event. ... It follows that the mental event and the brain event do not share all of their (structural) properties, and thus, the objector concludes, they cannot be identical (1978, p. 398).

Here Maxwell is concentrating on identity, and thus one might be tempted to argue that his objection does not threaten o-physicalism. For of course our claim is that qualia *supervene* on o-physical properties, not that they are identical with them. However, I don't think this reply is going to carry much weight with a proponent of the grain objection. For the question can be stated without appealing to identity, as follows: how could a potentially noncontinuous and unsmooth myriad of o-physical properties combine together to entail a smooth continuous expanse of red? Unless we can answer this more general question, the grain problem remains unsolved.

If the grain problem cannot be answered by distinguishing between identity and supervenience, how *can* it be answered? My own view[22] is that the answer emerges when we focus on what precisely it is in Maxwell's example that is supposed to be smooth and continuous. It seems plausible to say that it is the *expanse* that is smooth and continuous, and also that the expanse is something that we represent in visual experience, i.e., Maxwell's example is an example in which we are having an experience which represents an expanse as being smooth and continuous. But of course, it does not follow from this that the experience *itself* is smooth and continuous. Consider: an experience of red represents something as being red, but it itself is not red. So the answer to the grain problem is that it gets the phenomenology wrong and mislocates the absence of grain: absence of grain is not a feature of experiences, but a feature of something that experiences represent.

One might object that it is obvious in introspection that one's experience of a red expanse is *itself* smooth and continuous and not simply that it represents an expanse as being so. However, this is not obvious at all. As many philosophers have emphasized, many acts or states of experiencing seem in a certain respect "diaphanous" to introspection: introspection reveals the intentional objects of experiences to us, but not the experiences themselves. As Moore put it: "when we try to introspect the sensation of blue, all we can see is the blue: the other element is as if it were diaphanous" (1922; p. 25). To apply this to the case at hand, if we try to introspect the experience of a smooth and continuous expanse, all we see is the the smoothness and continuity of the expanse: the other element—i.e., the experience itself—is as if it were diaphanous. If this account of the phenomenology of introspection is correct, it is by no means obvious that introspection reveals experiences to be smooth at all. What it reveals rather is that we often have experiences which represent things as being smooth and continuous. But that is a different matter.

Alternatively, one might object that to appeal to Moore's point about diaphanousness, and perhaps also to the difference between properties of experiences and properties represented by experiences, is to undercut the idea that there are qualia in the first place. However, while some philosophers—e.g., Harman (1990)—have argued in this way, there is no certainly necessary connection here. As Shoemaker (1994) argues, it is perfectly possible to develop a theory of experience which honours the phenomenological point that Moore was making, and at the same time postulates qualia. On Shoemaker's preferred version of such a theory, an experience of a red expanse represents the expanse has having two properties—the property of being red (which Shoemaker thinks of as some physical property) and what he calls a *phenomenal property,* the property of causing an associated r-quale, where an r-quale is the type of quale typically produced by red things. One way (not the only way) of developing Shoemaker's theory to handle the grain problem would be to argue that the experience of a smooth expanse represents the expanse has having two properties— smoothness (which we might think of as some physical property of a surface) and the phenomenal property of causing an associated s-quale, where an s-quale is the type of quale typically produced by smooth things. Since the s-quale it not itself smooth—just as the r-quale is not itself red—it will not be the case that the experience or the quale have structural properties that the o-physical properties lack; at any rate, this is something that might well be denied by a proponent of o-physicalism. But to deny this is to deny the central premise of the grain problem.

Of course, providing this sort of answer to the grain problem makes no progress at all on what one might suspect is really lying behind the grain problem, viz., whether we can *in fact* articulate a body of physical truths which a priori entail truths about r-qualia (or s-qualia, if such there be). I have already admitted that our account makes no progress on this question beyond formulating in general terms what an answer to it would be like. The grain problem shows how hard this question is to answer, but it does not show that it is impossible to answer in principle.

6

I began by suggesting that the contemporary debate in philosophy of mind over physicalism might be viewed as involving an inconsistent tetrad of theses. Then I suggested that one plausible way of resolving the debate is by distinguishing between two conceptions of the physical, the object-based conception and the theory-based conception. What I have just done is defend the resulting version of physicalism against some objections.

Of course, even if my argument is right, it has only been shown that this is one way of resolving the debate. It has not been shown that this is the best or the only way. In order to provide anything approaching a full-dress defence of the proposal then, one would need to consider all the other attempts at resolving the puzzle presented by (1–4), and to demonstrate that these attempts are unsatisfactory, or at any rate less satisfactory than the proposal I have been considering. Obviously, there is no chance of my doing anything of the sort here. What I will do

instead, however, is close the paper by making three points which are designed to show the prima facie plausibility of a proposal along the lines we have been considering.

The first point simply reiterates something from my discussion of physicalism and neutral monism. If one operates *only* with the theory-based conception of the physical, one ends up with a version of physicalism (and physical closure—cf. fn 19) that, given certain metaphysical assumptions about dispositions and their categorical bases, is false. One is thus forced to introduce both the object-based conception of the physical and o-physicalism in order that one has a viable version of these theses at all. Hence if you want to be a physicalist—and if you accept those metaphysical assumptions—you had better be an o-physicalist.

The second point concerns the problem of other minds. Whether or not we are sceptics about other minds, we should all agree with the modal premise that sets the problem up. A version of that premise is:

(10) No amount of information of the sort presented in visual and sensory experience concerning another person *P* by itself entails that *P*'s experiences instantiate qualia.

Now, one sort of criticism of traditional formulations of physicalism—made, e.g., by Nagel (1970)—is that, on those formulations, the truth of physicalism makes it hard to see why the problem of other minds is a problem in the first place. I take this to mean that it is hard to see how physicalism and (10) could be true together: on the assumption that physical information can in principle be presented as visual and sensory information (at least if the latter is enriched with causal and counterfactual notions), physicalism will entail that (10) is false. When taken as a criticism of t-physicalism, this objection seems to have some force. After all, when enriched with causal and counterfactual notions, the sort of information presented in visual and sensory experience might well amount to t-physical information; but if qualitative truths a priori follow from t-physical information, then (10) would be false. On the other hand, when taken as a criticism of o-physicalism, this criticism has no force. For the object-conception of the physical precisely allows two situations to be epistemically indiscernible but physically distinct: hence o-physicalism allows (10) to be true. Since the problem of other minds is a hard philosophical problem, and not simply an empirical concern, we have reason to prefer o-physicalism to t-physicalism.

The final point turns on a distinction between two kinds of strategies. A *rejectionist* strategy (as I will call it) is a strategy according to which we reject one or more of the theses (1–4) with which we began. An *accommodationist* strategy (as I will call it) is a strategy according to which we attempt to show, despite appearances, that (1–4) are jointly consistent. Now, other things being equal, it would seem that any accommodationist strategy is to be preferred over any rejectionist strategy. After all, as we saw in §1, it

is not difficult to articulate reasons for believing each of (1–4). The disadvantage common to all rejectionist strategies is that they involve giving up something that we believe. As we saw at the outset, however, most contributions to the contemporary debate are (as usually interpreted) rejectionist: a posteriori physicalists reject (1); a priori physicalists reject (2); interactionist dualists reject (3); and epiphenomenalists reject (4). On the other hand, the strategy that we have been considering is obviously accommodationist—in fact it is the only accommodationist proposal currently on the table—and this gives us a strong prima facie reason to prefer it to any rejectionist strategy.[23]

NOTES

1. It is important to note that I am merely trying to state the considerations in favor of (1) here, not defend them. Likewise, the considerations in favor of (2–4) I consider in a moment.

2. For a statement of this argument, and for an analysis of the notion of a priori entailment, see Jackson 1998, and Chalmers (1996, 1999); for criticism, see Block and Stalnaker 1999, Byrne 1999, Loar (1997, 1999), and Yablo 1999. One should perhaps talk more correctly of mental truths being a priori entailed by physical and *topic neutral* truths, but I will leave this extension largely implicit in what follows.

3. By 'qualia,' I mean the properties of experiences in virtue of which there is something it is like (in the phrase made famous by Nagel) to have those experiences.

4. For a recent statement of this argument, see Braddon-Mitchell and Jackson 1996 and Chalmers 1996. Of course, there are other reasons for resisting a priori physicalism—for example, reasons having to do with intentionality—but I will limit my discussion here to qualia.

5. For a recent statement of this argument, see Kim 1999; for criticism, see Yablo 1992. The question of what the relation is between the two parts of causal closure—the thesis about events and the thesis about properties—is a question about the metaphysics of causation, and in particular about the metaphysics of causal relata, which I will set aside here. It is worth noting also that causal closure as I have defined it rules out the possibility of overdetermination—I will set aside this issue also.

6. For a recent statement of this sort of argument, see Shoemaker 1999 and Chalmers 1996; for criticism, see Jackson 1982 and Chalmers 1996, 1998.

7. It is interesting to note that Gilbert Harman's 1986 sharp distinction between what follows from what and what one ought to believe provides yet another possibility here. More particularly, in Harmanesque fashion, one might suppose that, even if (1–4) *are* contradictory, it is nevertheless a rational strategy to resolve to believe all of them so long as one also resolves not to exploit this contradiction in one's rea-

soning. This suggestion seems to me to present not a resolution of the puzzle posed by (1–4) so much as a way in which one might live with oneself in the absence of such a resolution, but in any event I will set it aside here.

8. For examples of those who deny that one can have propositional knowledge of qualia, see Lewis 1994, and references therein; for strong necessities, see Yablo 1999 and Loar 1999.

9. The theory-based conception bears some relation to the notion of physical$_1$ discussed in Meehl and Sellars 1956 and in Feigl 1965; more explicit defense is found in Smart 1978, Lewis 1994, Braddon-Mitchell and Jackson 1996, and Chalmers 1996. There is of course the threat that a formulation of physicalism which utilizes the theory-based conception will be trivial: if the notion of a physical theory is sufficiently unconstrained, any property including irreducibly mental properties might be such that physical theory tells us about them. (For this sort of criticism, see Crane and Mellor 1990, and Chomsky 1995.) There are a number of ways in which one might seek to constrain the notion to meet this threat: by speaking of physical theory sufficiently similar to current physical theory; by speaking of physical theory sufficiently similar to commonsense physical theory; or by speaking of physical theory as constrained by the methodology of physics. I will assume here that some such strategy is available, but it will not matter for our purposes to decide which is the best.

10. The best examples of philosophers who operate with the object-conception of the physical are Meehl and Sellars 1956 and Feigl 1965; it is also a position that one encounters regularly in discussion. There is of course the threat that a formulation of physicalism which utilizes the object-based conception will be trivial: if the notion of a paradigm physical object is sufficiently unconstrained, any property including irreducibly mental properties might be such that paradigm physical objects have them. There are a number of ways in which one might seek to constrain the notion to meet this threat: by speaking of physical objects-as-we-currently-conceive-them; by insisting

that the notion of a physical object presupposes that such objects cannot turn out to be irreducibly mental; by operating with the notion of a purely physical object, where a purely physical object is something completely non-mental. As with the theory-based conception, I will assume here that some such strategy is available, but it will not matter for our purposes to decide which is best.

11. Two other issues deserve to be mentioned briefly. First, one might object that both conceptions are inadequate because they are circular, i.e., both appeal to the notion of something physical (a theory or an object) to characterize a physical property. The response to this is that circularity is only a problem if the conceptions are interpreted as providing a reductive analysis of the notion of the physical rather than simply an understanding of it. But there is no reason why they should be interpreted in the former way. Second, it might be thought that notion of an o-physical property is open to the following objection discussed by Ned Block: "it is conceivable that there are physical laws that 'come into play' in brains of a certain size and complexity, but that nonetheless these laws are 'translatable' into physical language, and that, so translated, they are clearly physical laws (though irreducible to other physical laws). Arguably, in this situation, physicalism could be true—though not according to [this] account of 'physical property' " (1980, n. 4). However, at least as developed here, the object-based conception does not face this objection because the properties and laws that Block is describing *supervene* on properties required in an account of paradigmatic physical objects, and so o-physicalism *would* be true in the case he is envisaging.

12. There is of course a large literature in support of the thesis that physical theory tells us only about dispositional properties, a literature which has at least three sources: Russell's (1927) discussion of the nature of physical theory; the approach to the structure of scientific theories and theoretical terms due to Ramsey, Carnap and Lewis (see, e.g. Lewis 1970); and an epistemological thesis that, in perception, we are acquainted only with dispositional properties of physical objects (see, e.g. Armstrong 1961, 1968). I will not in this paper be able to explore this literature or defend the thesis in any detail. My reason is partly space and partly that the contemporary exponents of the anti-physicalist position (or related positions) agree with the thesis, so there is nothing problematic about making this assumption in the course of defending physicalism; see, e.g., Chalmers 1996, pp. 153–54.

It is worth noting also that it is an oversimplification to say that physical theory tells us only about dispositional properties: physical theory also tells us about what might be called structural properties, i.e., geometrical, spatiotemporal or causal properties. But this complication does not matter for our purposes. The crucial point for our purposes is that there are categorical or non-dispositional properties of physical objects which physical theory does not tell us about.

13. There is of course a large literature concerning the thesis that dispositions require categorical grounds, but I will not here explore this literature or defend the thesis in any detail. (For a recent defence, see Smith and Stoljar 1997.) Once again my reason is partly space and partly that contemporary defenders of the anti-physicalists position agree with the thesis; see, e.g., Chalmers 1996, n. 29 on p. 375. To avoid confusion, however, it is worth noting two points: (i) The thesis does not require that if a thing has a dispositional property then there must be a non-dispositional property of *that very thing* such that the latter is metaphysically sufficient for the instantiation of the former, i.e., it is perfectly consistent with the thesis that the categorical properties on which the dispositional properties supervene might be properties of constituents of the thing in question rather than the thing itself. (ii) The thesis is a metaphysical thesis, rather than an explanatory one, i.e., it is perfectly consistent with the thesis that to explain the presence of a certain dispositional property one might cite a further dispositional property. All that is being urged is the metaphysical claim that the dispositional supervenes on the non-dispositional.

14. For a very similar notion, see the discussion of 'Kantian Physicalism' in Jackson 1998.

15. While I will for the most part speak of 'o-physical properties which are not t-physical,' I will sometimes speak only of 'o-physical properties.' It will be clear from context whether what is intended is the class of o-physical properties *tout court*—i.e., a class which includes t-physicals—or the class of o-physicals which are not t-physicals.

16. The other main argument against a priori physicalism is the conceivability argument. I think the strategy of this paper also holds good against this argument but I will not discuss this issue here.

17. For a catalogue and criticisms of the other main attempts to defeat the knowledge argument, see Braddon-Mitchell and Jackson 1996. They do not consider the kind of proposal that we are considering here.

18. It is important to emphasize that the views at issue here are Russell-*inspired* rather than Russell's. The question of what Russell's actual views are is a difficult scholarly one that I will not address here. Similarly, it is important to emphasize that while there is much similarity between the position discussed in the text and that of Maxwell and Lockwood—for example, Maxwell describes his position as 'nonmaterialist physicalism' (1978; p. 365) which echoes the distinction I have drawn between the theory-based and objectbased conception of the physical—neither of these writers develop or defend the position in the way I will do here. For further discussion of Russell-inspired views and related matters, see Chalmers 1996, Foster (1982, 1994) and Unger 1998.

19. It is worth emphasis that the first part of o-physicalism is neutral on the issue of whether qualia supervene on o-physical properties which *exclude* t-physical properties or on o-physical properties which *include* t-physical properties. The general question of the role of t-physical properties in o-physicalism is an interesting question, but it is not a question that I will decide here.

20. Indeed, it is for this reason that Chalmers takes himself to have argued *against* physicalism in *The Conscious Mind*. As far as the metaphysics of mind goes, the overall conclusion of that book is disjunctive: either epiphenomenalism is true, or interactionist dualism is true, or the Russell-inspired position is true. Given Chalmers' assumption that the third disjunct

is not a version of physicalism, *The Conscious Mind* is an anti-physicalist book. However, if the argument of this paper is correct, there is no reason to suppose that the Russell-inspired position *must* be non-physicalist. It follows—contrary to what I take to be Chalmers' aim—that there is a version of physicalism which is compatible with *The Conscious Mind.*

21. It is easy to see that an extension of this argument would show that if a proponent of causal closure wants to defend a thesis that is compatible with the idea that we discussed in §4—that if dispositional properties are causally efficacious, their categorical grounds are—he or she must likewise adopt the object-based conception of the physical, or some equivalent conception.

22. For very different responses to the grain problem, see Maxwell 1978, Lockwood 1992 and Chalmers 1996.

23. Material drawn from this paper was presented to the philosophy department at the University of Colorado at Boulder, and to the Consciousness and Metaphysics in Philosophy of Mind Conference, Chateau Hotel, Sydney. I am very much indebted to all who took part on those occasions. I would also like to thank the following for comments, discussion and advice: George Bealer, Helen Beebee, Andrew Botterell, David Braddon-Mitchell, Alex Byrne, David Chalmers, Cian Dorr, John Fisher, Frank Jackson, Michael Griffin, Benj Hellie, Jakob Hohwy, Stephen Leeds, Michael Martin, Daniel Nolan, Graham Oddie, Philip Pettit, Kieran Setiya, Michael Smith, Sheldon Smith, Robert Stainton, Jason Stanley, Zoltan Szabo, and Adam Vinueza. Particular thanks to David Chalmers for many extremely enjoyable and helpful discussions about the topic of this paper.

REFERENCES

Armstrong, D. M. 1961. *Perception and the Physical World.* London: Routledge.

Armstrong, D. M. 1968. *A Materialist Theory of the Mind.* London: Routledge.

Blackburn, S. 1992. 'Filling in Space,' *Analysis,* 52: 60–65.

Block, N. 1980. 'Troubles with Functionalism.' In Block, N. (ed.) *Readings in the Philosophy of Psychology, Vol. I.* Cambridge, MA: Harvard University Press.

Block, N. 1990. 'Can the Mind Change the World?' In Boolos, G. (ed.) *Meaning and Method: Essays in Honor of Hilary Putnam.* Cambridge: Cambridge University Press.

Block, N. and Robert Stalnaker, 1999. 'Conceptual Analysis, Dualism and the Explanatory Gap,' *The Philosophical Review,* 108: 1–46.

Byrne, A. 1999. 'Cosmic Hermeneutics,' *Philosophical Perspectives,* 13: 347–83.

Braddon-Mitchell D. and Jackson F. 1996. *Philosophy of Mind and Cognition.* Oxford: Blackwell.

Chalmers, D. 1996. *The Conscious Mind.* New York: Oxford University Press.

Chalmers, D. 1999. 'Materialism and the Metaphysics of Modality,' *Philosophy and Phenomenological Research,* 59: 473–96.

Chomsky, N. 1995. 'Language and Nature,' *Mind,* 104: 1–61.

Crane, T. and Mellor, D. H. 1990. 'There Is No Question of Physicalism,' *Mind,* 99: 185–206.

Feigl, H. 1967. 'The "Mental" and the "Physical" ' (Minneapolis: University of Minnesota Press. Original Publication: 1958).

Foster, J. 1982. *The Case or Idealism.* London: Routledge.

Foster, J. 1991. *The Immaterial Self: A Defence of the Cartesian Dualist Conception of Mind.* London: Routledge.

Harman, G. 1986. *Change in View.* Cambridge, MA: MIT Press.

Harman, G. 1990. 'The Intrinsic Quality of Experience,' *Philosophical Perspectives,* 4: 31–52.

Jackson, F. 1982. 'Epiphenomenal Qualia,' *Philosophical Quarterly,* 32: 127–36.

Jackson, F. 1986. 'What Mary Didn't Know,' *Journal of Philosophy,* 83: 291–95.

Jackson, F. 1998. *From Metaphysics to Ethics: A Defense of Conceptual Analysis.* Oxford: Clarendon.

Johnston, M. 1992. 'How to Speak of the Colors,' *Philosophical Studies,* 68: 221–63.

Kim, J. 1993. *Mind and Supervenience.* Cambridge: Cambridge University Press.

Kim, J. 1998. *Mind in a Physical World.* Cambridge: Cambridge University Press.

Kripke, S. 1980. *Naming and Necessity.* Cambridge, MA: Harvard University Press.

Kripke, S. 1982. *Wittgenstein on Rules and Private Language: An Elementary Exposition.* Oxford: Blackwell.

Lewis, D. 1970. 'How to Define Theoretical Terms,' *Journal of Philosophy,* 67: 427–46.

Lewis, D. 1994. 'Reduction of Mind.' In Guttenplan, S. (ed.) *A Companion to the Philosophy of Mind.* Oxford: Blackwell.

Loar, B. 1997. 'Phenomenal States.' In Block et al. (eds.) *The Nature of Consciousness: Philosophical Debates.* Cambridge, MA: MIT Press.

Loar, B. 1999. 'David Chalmers' *The Conscious Mind, Philosophy and Phenomenological Research,* 59: 465–72.

Lockwood, M. 1989. *Mind, Brain and Quantum.* Oxford: Blackwell.

Lockwood, M. 1992. 'The Grain Problem.' In Robinson, H. (ed.) *Objections to Physicalism.* Oxford: Oxford University Press.

Maxwell, G. 1978. 'Rigid Designators and Mind-Brain Identity.' In Savage, C. (ed.) *Perception and Cognition: Minnesota Studies in the Philosophy of Science Vol. 9.* Minneapolis: Minnesota University Press.

McGinn, C. 1989. 'Can We Solve the Mind-Body Problem?' *Mind,* 98: 349–66.

Moore, G. E. 1922. *Philosophical Studies.* Routledge: London.

Nagel, T. 1970. 'Armstrong on the Mind,' *The Philosophical Review,* 79: 394–403.

Nagel, T. 1974. 'What Is It Like to Be a Bat?,' *The Philosophical Review,* 83: 435–50.

Russell, B. 1927. *The Analysis of Matter.* London: Kegan Paul.

Shoemaker, S. 1994. 'Phenomenal Character,' *Noûs,* 28: 21–38.

Shoemaker, S. 1999. 'On David Chalmers' *The Conscious Mind,' Philosophy and Phenomenological Research,* 59: 439–44.

Smart, J. J. C. 1978. 'The Content of Physicalism,' *Philosophical Quarterly,* 28: 239–41.

Smith, M. and Stoljar, D. 1998. 'Global Response-Dependence and Noumenal Realism,' *The Monist,* 81: 85–111.

Unger, P. 1998. 'The Mystery of the Physical and the Matter of Qualities,' *Midwest Studies in Philosophy,* Vol. 22.

Yablo, S. 1992. 'Mental Causation,' *The Philosophical Review,* 101: 245–80.

Yablo, S. 1999. 'Concepts and Consciousness,' *Philosophy and Phenomenological Research,* 59: 455–63.

C. Modal Arguments

32 | Naming and Necessity
Saul A. Kripke

. . . I finally turn to an all too cursory discussion of the application of the foregoing considerations to the identity thesis. Identity theorists have been concerned with several distinct types of identifications: of a person with his body, of a particular sensation (or event or state of having the sensation) with a particular brain state (Jones's pain at 06:00 was his C-fiber stimulation at that time), and of *types* of mental states with the corresponding *types* of physical states (pain is the stimulation of C-fibers). Each of these, and other types of identifications in the literature, present analytical problems, rightly raised by Cartesian critics, which cannot be avoided by a simple appeal to an alleged confusion of synonymy with identity. I should mention that there is of course no obvious bar, at least (I say cautiously) none which should occur to any intelligent thinker on a first reflection just before bedtime, to advocacy of some identity theses while doubting or denying others. For example, some philosophers have accepted the identity of particular sensations with particular brain states while denying the possibility of identities between mental and physical *types*.[1] I will concern myself primarily with the type-type identities, and the philosophers in question will thus be immune to much of the discussion; but I will mention the other kinds of identities briefly.

Descartes, and others following him, argued that a person or mind is distinct from his body, since the mind could exist without the body. He might equally well have argued the same conclusion from the premise that the body could have existed without the mind.[2] Now the one response which I regard as plainly inadmissible is the response which cheerfully accepts the Cartesian premise while denying the Cartesian conclusion, Let 'Descartes' be a name, or rigid designator, of a certain person, and let '*B*' be a rigid designator of his body. Then if Descartes were indeed identical to *B*, the supposed identity, being an identity between two rigid designators, would be necessary, and Descartes could not exist without *B* and *B* could not exist without Descartes. The case is not at all comparable to the alleged analogue, the identity of the first Postmaster General with the inventor of bifocals. True, this identity obtains despite the fact that there could have been a first Postmaster General even though bifocals had never been invented. The reason is that 'the inventor of bifocals' is not a rigid designator; a world in which no one invented bifocals is not *ipso facto* a world in which Franklin did not exist. The alleged analogy therefore collapses; a philosopher who wishes to refute the Cartesian conclusion must refute the Cartesian premise, and the latter task is not trivial.

Let '*A*' name a particular pain sensation, and let '*B*' name the corresponding brain state, or the brain state some identity theorist wishes to identify with *A*. Prima facie, it would seem that it is at least logically possible that *B* should have existed (Jones's brain could have been in exactly that state at the time in question) without Jones feeling any pain at all, and thus without the presence of *A*. Once again, the identity theorist cannot admit the possibility cheerfully and proceed from there; consistency, and the principle of the necessity of identities using rigid designators, disallows any such course. If *A* and *B* were identical, the identity would have to be necessary. The difficulty can hardly be evaded by arguing that although *B* could not exist without *A*, *being a pain* is merely a contingent property of *A*, and that therefore the presence of *B* without pain does not imply the presence of *B* without *A*. Can any case of essence be more obvious than the fact that *being a pain* is a neces-

From *Naming and Necessity*, pp. 144–55. Harvard University Press, 1980. Copyright © 1972, 1980 Saul A. Kripke. Reprinted with permission of the publisher.

sary property of each pain? The identity theorist who wishes to adopt the strategy in question must even argue that *being a sensation* is a contingent property of *A,* for prima facie it would seem logically possible that *B* could exist without any sensation with which it might plausibly be identified. Consider a particular pain, or other sensation, that you once had. Do you find it at all plausible that *that very sensation* could have existed without being a sensation, the way a certain inventor (Franklin) could have existed without being an inventor?

I mention this strategy because it seems to me to be adopted by a large number of identity theorists. These theorists, believing as they do that the supposed identity of a brain state with the corresponding mental state is to be analyzed on the paradigm of the contingent identity of Benjamin Franklin with the inventor of bifocals, realize that just as his contingent activity made Benjamin Franklin into the inventor of bifocals, so some contingent property of the brain state must make it into a pain. Generally they wish this property to be one statable in physical or at least 'topic-neutral' language, so that the materialist cannot be accused of positing irreducible nonphysical properties. A typical view is that *being a pain,* as a property of a physical state, is to be analyzed in terms of the 'causal role' of the state,[3] in terms of the characteristic stimuli (e.g., pinpricks) which cause it and the characteristic behavior it causes. I will not go into the details of such analyses, even though I usually find them faulty on specific grounds in addition to the general modal considerations I argue here. All I need to observe here is that the 'causal role' of the physical state is regarded by the theorists in question as a contingent property of the state, and thus it is supposed to be a contingent property of the state that it is a mental state at all, let alone that it is something as specific as a pain. To repeat, this notion seems to me self-evidently absurd. It amounts to the view that the *very pain I now have* could have existed without being a mental state at all.

I have not discussed the converse problem, which is closer to the original Cartesian consideration—namely, that just as it seems that the brain state could have existed without any pain, so it seems that the pain could have existed without the corresponding brain state. Note that *being a brain state* is evidently an essential property of *B* (the brain state). Indeed, even more is true: not only being a brain state, but even being a brain state of a specific type is an

essential property of *B*. The configuration of brain cells whose presence at a given time constitutes the presence of *B* at that time is essential to *B,* and in its absence *B* would not have existed. Thus someone who wishes to claim that the brain state and the pain are identical must argue that the pain *A* could not have existed without a quite specific type of configuration of molecules. If *A = B,* then the identity of *A* with *B* is necessary, and any essential property of one must be an essential property of the other. Someone who wishes to maintain an identity thesis cannot simply *accept* the Cartesian intuitions that *A* can exist without *B,* that *B* can exist without *A,* that the correlative presence of anything with mental properties is merely contingent to *B,* and that the correlative presence of any specific physical properties is merely contingent to *A.* He must explain these intuitions away, showing how they are illusory. This task may not be impossible; we have seen above how some things which appear to be contingent turn out, on closer examination, to be necessary. The task, however, is obviously not child's play, and we shall see below how difficult it is.

The final kind of identity, the one which I said would get the closest attention, is the type-type sort of identity exemplified by the identification of pain with the stimulation of C-fibers. These identifications are supposed to be analogous with such scientific type-type identifications as the identity of heat with molecular motion, of water with hydrogen hydroxide, and the like. Let us consider, as an example, the analogy supposed to hold between the materialist identification and that of heat with molecular motion; both identifications identify two types of phenomena. The usual view holds that the identification of heat with molecular motion and of pain with the stimulation of C-fibers are both contingent. We have seen above that since 'heat' and 'molecular motion' are both rigid designators, the identification of the phenomena they name is necessary. What about 'pain' and 'C-fiber stimulation'? It should be clear from the previous discussion that 'pain' is a rigid designator of the type, or phenomenon, it designates: if something is a pain it is essentially so, and it seems absurd to suppose that pain could have been some phenomenon other than the one it is. The same holds for the term 'C-fiber stimulation,' provided that 'C-fibers' is a rigid designator, as I will suppose here. (The supposition is somewhat risky, since I know virtually nothing about C-fibers, except that the stimulation of them is said to be correlated with pain.[4] The point is unimportant; if 'C-fibers' is not a rigid designator, simply replace it by one which is, or suppose it used as a rigid designator in the present context.) Thus the identity of pain with the stimulation of C-fibers, if true, must be *necessary.*

So far the analogy between the identification of heat with molecular motion and pain with the stimulation of C-fibers has not failed; it has merely turned out to be the opposite of what is usually thought—both, if true, must be necessary. This means that the identity theorist is committed to the view that there could not be a C-fiber stimulation which was not a pain nor a pain which was not a C-fiber stimulation. These consequences are certainly surprising and counterintuitive, but let us not dismiss the identity theorist too quickly. Can he perhaps show that the apparent possibility of pain not having turned out to be C-fiber stimulation, or of there being an instance of one of the phenomena which is not an instance of the other, is an illusion of the same sort as the illusion that water might not have been hydrogen hydroxide, or that heat might not have been molecular motion? If so, he will have rebutted the Cartesian, not, as in the conventional analysis, by accepting his premise while exposing the fallacy of his argument, but rather by the reverse—while the Cartesian argument, given its premise of the contingency of the identification, is granted to yield its conclusion, the premise is to be exposed as superficially plausible but false.

Now I do not think it likely that the identity theorist will succeed in such an endeavor. I want to argue that, at least, the case cannot be interpreted as analogous to that of scientific identification of the usual sort, as exemplified by the identity of heat and molecular motion. What was the strategy used above to handle the apparent contingency of certain cases of the necessary *a posteriori?* The strategy was to argue that although the statement itself is necessary, someone could, *qualitatively* speaking, be in the same epistemic situation as the original, and in such a situation a *qualitatively* analogous statement could be false. In the case of identities between two rigid designators, the strategy can be approximated by a simpler one: Consider how the references of the designators are determined; if these coincide only contingently, it is this fact which gives the original statement its illusion of contingency. In the case of heat and molecular motion, the way these two paradigms work out is simple. When someone says, inac-

curately, that heat might have turned out not to be molecular motion, what is true in what he says is that someone could have sensed a phenomenon in the same way we sense heat, that is, feels it by means of its production of the sensation we call 'the sensation of heat' (call it '*S*'), even though that phenomenon was not molecular motion. He means, additionally, that the planet might have been inhabited by creatures who did not get *S* when they were in the presence of molecular motion, though perhaps getting it in the presence of something else. Such creatures would be, in some qualitative sense, in the same epistemic situation as we are, they could use a rigid designator for the phenomenon that causes sensation *S* in them (the rigid designator could even be 'heat'), yet it would not be molecular motion (and therefore not heat!), which was causing the sensation.

Now can something be said analogously to explain away the feeling that the identity of pain and the stimulation of C-fibers, if it is a scientific discovery, could have turned out otherwise? I do not see that such an analogy is possible. In the case of the apparent possibility that molecular motion might have existed in the absence of heat, what seemed really possible is that molecular motion should have existed without being *felt as heat,* that is, it might have existed without producing the sensation *S,* the sensation of heat. In the appropriate sentient beings is it analogously possible that a stimulation of C-fibers should have existed without being felt as pain? If this is possible, then the stimulation of C-fibers can itself exist without pain, since for it to exist without being *felt as pain* is for it to exist without there *being any* pain. Such a situation would be in flat out contradiction with the supposed necessary identity of pain and the corresponding physical state, and the analogue holds for any physical state which might be identified with a corresponding mental state. The trouble is that the identity theorist does not hold that the physical state merely *produces* the mental state, rather he wishes the two to be identical and thus a fortiori necessarily co-occurrent. In the case of molecular motion and heat there is something, namely, the sensation of heat, which is an intermediary between the external phenomenon and the observer. In the mental-physical case no such intermediary is possible, since here the physical phenomenon is supposed to be identical with the internal phenomenon itself. Someone can be in the same epistemic situation as he would be if there were heat, even in the absence of heat, simply by feeling the sensation of heat; and even in the presence of heat, he can have the same evidence as he would have in the absence of heat simply by lacking the sensation *S*. No such possibility exists in the case of pain and other mental phenomena. To be in the same epistemic situation that would obtain if one had a pain *is* to have a pain; to be in the same epistemic situation that would obtain in the absence of a pain *is* not to have a pain. The apparent contingency of the connection between the mental state and the corresponding brain state thus cannot be explained by some sort of qualitative analogue as in the case of heat.

We have just analyzed the situation in terms of the notion of a qualitatively identical epistemic situation. The trouble is that the notion of an epistemic situation qualitatively identical to one in which the observer had a sensation *S* simply *is* one in which the observer had that sensation. The same point can be made in terms of the notion of what picks out the reference of a rigid designator. In the case of the identity of heat with molecular motion the important consideration was that although 'heat' is a rigid designator, the reference of that designator was determined by an accidental property of the referent, namely the property of producing in us the sensation *S*. It is thus possible that a phenomenon should have been rigidly designated in the same way as a phenomenon of heat, with its reference also picked out by means of the sensation *S,* without that phenomenon being heat and therefore without its being molecular motion. Pain, on the other hand, is not picked out by one of its accidental properties; rather it is picked out by the property of being pain itself, by its immediate phenomenological quality. Thus pain, unlike heat, is not only rigidly designated by 'pain' but the reference of the designator is determined by an essential property of the referent. Thus it is not possible to say that although pain is necessarily identical with a certain physical state, a certain phenomenon can be picked out in the same way we pick out pain without being correlated with that physical state. If any phenomenon is picked out in exactly the same way that we pick out pain, then that phenomenon *is* pain.

Perhaps the same point can be made more vivid without such specific reference to the technical apparatus in these lectures. Suppose we imagine God creating the world; what does He need to do to make the identity of heat and molecular motion obtain? Here it would seem that all He needs to do is to create the heat, that is, the molecular motion itself. If the air molecules on this earth are sufficiently agitated, if there is a burning fire, then the earth will be hot even if there are no observers to see it. God created light (and thus created streams of photons, according to present scientific doctrine) before He created human and animal observers; and the same presumably holds for heat. How then does it appear to us that the identity of molecular motion with heat is a substantive scientific fact, that the mere creation of molecular motion still leaves God with the additional task of making molecular motion into heat? This feeling is indeed illusory, but what *is* a substantive task for the Deity is the task of making molecular motion felt as heat. To do this He must create some sentient beings to insure that the molecular motion produces the sensation *S* in them. Only after he has done this will there be beings who can learn that the sentence 'Heat is the motion of molecules' expresses an a posteriori truth in precisely the same way that we do.

What about the case of the stimulation of C-fibers? To create this phenomenon, it would seem that God need only create beings with C-fibers capable of the appropriate type of physical stimulation; whether the beings are conscious or not is irrelevant here. It would seem, though, that to make the C-fiber stimulation correspond to pain, or be felt as pain, God must do something in addition to the mere creation of the C-fiber stimulation; He must let the creatures feel the C-fiber stimulation as *pain,* and not as a tickle, or as warmth, or as nothing, as apparently would also have been within His powers. If these things in fact are within His powers, the relation between the pain God creates and the stimulation of C-fibers cannot be identity. For if so, the stimulation could exist without the pain; and since 'pain' and 'C-fiber stimulation' are rigid, this fact implies that the relation between the two phenomena is not that of identity. God had to do some work, in addition to making the man himself, to make a certain man be the inventor of bifocals; the man could well exist without inventing any such thing. The same cannot be said for pain; if the phenomenon exists at all, no further work should be required to make it into pain.

In sum, the correspondence between a brain state and a mental state seems to have a certain obvious element of contingency. We have seen that identity is not a relation which can hold contingently between objects. Therefore, if the identity thesis were correct, the element of contingency would not lie in the relation between the mental and physical states. It cannot lie, as in the case of heat and molecular motion, in the relation between the phenomenon (= heat = molecular motion) and the way it is felt or appears (sensation *S*), since in the case of mental phenomena there is no 'appearance' beyond the mental phenomenon itself.

Here I have been emphasizing the possibility, or apparent possibility, of a physical state without the corresponding mental state. The reverse possibility, the mental state (pain) without the physical state (C-fiber stimulation) also presents problems for the identity theorists which cannot be resolved by appeal to the analogy of heat and molecular motion.

I have discussed similar problems more briefly for views equating the self with the body, and particular mental events with particular physical events, without discussing possible countermoves in the same detail as in the type-type case. Suffice it to say that I suspect that the considerations given indicate that the theorist who wishes to identify various particular mental and physical events will have to face problems fairly similar to those of the type-type theorist; he too will be unable to appeal to the standard alleged analogues.

That the usual moves and analogies are not available to solve the problems of the identity theorist is, of course, no proof that no moves are available. I certainly cannot discuss all the possibilities here. I suspect, however, that the present considerations tell heavily against the usual forms of materialism. Materialism, I think, must hold that a physical description of the world is a *complete* description of it, that any mental facts are 'ontologically dependent' on physical facts in the straight-forward sense of following from them by necessity. No identity theorist seems to me to have made a convincing argument against the intuitive view that this is not the case.[5]

NOTES

1. Thomas Nagel and Donald Davidson are notable examples. Their views are very interesting, and I wish I could discuss them in further detail. It is doubtful that such philosophers wish to call themselves 'materialists'. Davidson, in particular, bases his case for his version of the identity theory on the supposed *impossibility* of correlating psychological properties with physical ones.

    The argument against token-token identification in the text *does* apply to these views.

2. Of course, the body *does* exist without the mind and presumably without the person, when the body is a corpse. This consideration, if accepted, would already show that a person and his body are distinct. (See David Wiggins, 'On Being at the Same Place at the Same Time.' *Philosophical Review,* Vol. 77 (1968), pp. 90–95.) Similarly, it can be argued that a statue is not the hunk of matter of which it is composed. In the latter case, however, one might say instead that the former is 'nothing over and above' the latter; and the same device might be tried for the relation of the person and the body. The difficulties in the text would not then arise in the same form, but analogous difficulties would appear. A theory that a person is nothing over and above his body in the way that a statue is nothing over and above the matter of which it is composed, would have to hold that (necessarily) a person exists if and only if his body exists and has a certain additional physical organization. Such a thesis would be subject to modal difficulties similar to those besetting the ordinary identity thesis, and the same would apply to suggested analogues replacing the identification of mental states with physical states. A further discussion of this matter must be left for another place. Another view which I will not discuss, although I have little tendency to accept it and am not even certain that it has been set out with genuine clarity, is the so-called functional state view of psychological concepts.

3. For example, David Armstrong, A Materialist Theory of the Mind, London and New York, 1968, see the discussion review by Thomas Nagel, Philosophical Review 79 (1970), pp. 394–403; and David Lewis, 'An Argument for the Identity Theory,' The Journal of Philosophy, pp. 17–25.

4. I have been surprised to find that at least one able listener took my use of such terms as 'correlated with,' 'corresponding to,' and the like as already begging the question against the identity thesis. The identity thesis, so he said, is not the thesis that pains and brain states are correlated, but rather that they are identical. Thus my entire discussion presupposes the anti-materialist position that I set out to prove. Although I was surprised to hear an objection which concedes so little intelligence to the argument, I have tried especially to avoid the term 'correlated' which seems to give rise to the objection. Nevertheless, to obviate misunderstanding, I shall explain my usage. Assuming, at least *arguendo,* that scientific discoveries have turned out so as not to refute materialism from the beginning, both the dualist and the identity theorist agree that there is a correlation or correspondence between mental states and physical states. The dualist holds that the 'correlation' relation in question is irreflexive; the identity theorist holds that it is simply a special case of the identity relation. Such terms as 'correlation' and 'correspondence' can be used neutrally without prejudging which side is correct.

5. Having expressed these doubts about the identity theory in the text, I should emphasize two things:

first, identity theorists have presented positive arguments for their view, which I certainly have not answered here. Some of these arguments seem to me to be weak or based on ideological prejudices, but others strike me as highly compelling arguments which I am at present unable to answer convincingly. Second, rejection of the identity thesis does not imply acceptance of Cartesian dualism. In fact, my view above that a person could not have come from a different sperm and egg from the ones from which he actually originated implicitly suggests a rejection of the Cartesian picture. If we had a clear idea of the soul or the mind as an independent, susbsistent, spiritual entity, why should it have to have any necessary connection with particular material objects such as a particular sperm or a particular egg? A convinced dualist may think that my views on sperms and eggs beg the question against Descartes. I would tend to argue the other way; the fact that it is hard to imagine me coming from a sperm and egg different from my actual origins seems to me to indicate that we have no such clear conception of a soul or self. In any event, Descartes' notion seems to have been rendered dubious ever since Hume's critique of the notion of a Cartesian self. I regard the mind-body problem as wide open and extremely confusing.

Imaginability, Conceivability, Possibility, and the Mind–Body Problem

33

Christopher S. Hill

In the early seventies Kripke unveiled a line of thought that was designed to resuscitate dualistic philosophies of mind.[1] This line of thought was greeted with a chorus of objections, some of which have helped considerably to bring the relevant issues into sharper focus. Still, despite the number and philosophical value of these replies, the line of thought has continued to attract sympathetic attention. Indeed, it figures prominently in three of the most original and provocative contributions to the contemporary literature on the mind–body problem—W. D. Hart's *Engines of the Soul,* Stephen Yablo's "The Real Distinction between Mind and Body" (as amplified in its companion piece "Is Conceivability a Guide to Possibility?"), and David Chalmers's *The Conscious Mind.*[2]

In addition to being provocative, Kripke's line of thought was characterized by broad relevance. In one version it challenged token-materialism, and in another, type-materialism. Both versions continue to attract admirers. (Token-materialism asserts that each concrete psychological particular, such as the pain I experienced at 10:00 last night, is identical with a concrete physical particular, such as the firing of my C-fibers at 10:00 last night. Type-materialism comes in more than one variety. The strongest version claims that every type of psychological state is identical with some type of physical state. A much weaker version, which is substantially more plausible, claims that every type of *sensory* state is identical with some type of physical state.)

In this paper I will try to show that those who continue to be favorably impressed by Kripke's line of thought have underestimated the resources that are available to materialists. Specifically, I will maintain that the most widely accepted part of that line of thought, the argument against type materialism, admits of an answer that is fully satisfactory.

Two last preliminary comments. First, I will be concerned only to defend type-materialism about qualitative states, that is, type-materialism about states that are like *being a pain* in that they are forms of sentience. Second, although it is of course my intention to carry the discussion forward, I will not be aiming at radical originality. Thus, I will be relying heavily on ideas that are found in earlier papers by Thomas Nagel and myself. My aims are to clarify these ideas, to develop and supplement them in certain ways, and to show that it is possible to embrace

Excerpted from *Philosophical Studies* 87:61–85, 1997, with permission from the author and Kluwer Academic Publishers.

them without incurring any questionable philosophical commitments.

I

I will begin with a brief review of the portion of Kripke's line of thought that counts directly against type-materialism. (I will follow Kripke in focussing on pain and the physical state which in fact accompanies pain in the human brain. [As is usual, I will refer to this brain state as "C-fiber stimulation."] But the argument should be seen as implicitly general: according to Kripke, what the argument claims about pain and its accompanying brain state could also be claimed, with equal legitimacy, about any other pair consisting of a type of sensation and its corresponding brain state.)

Kripke's Argument

First premise: It appears to be possible for there to be instances of the property *being a pain* that are not instances of the property *being a case of C-fiber stimulation.* For we can easily imagine, and easily conceive of, a disembodied person who is experiencing pain.

Second premise: It appears to be possible for there to be instances of *being a case of C-fiber stimulation* that are not instances of *being a pain.* For we can easily imagine, and easily conceive of, a zombie whose C-fibers are undergoing a high degree of electro-chemical activity.

Third premise: Where X and Y are any two properties, if it seems to be the case that X and Y are *separable,* in the sense that it seems to be possible for there to be instances of X that are not instances of Y, then, unless this appearance of separability can be explained away, it really is the case that X and Y are separable.

Fourth premise: Where X and Y are any two properties, if X and Y are separable, then it is not the case that X and Y are identical.

Fifth premise: In general, if X is a commonsense natural kind and Y is a scientific kind that can plausibly be identified with X, then there is a tendency for it to appear to us that X is separable from Y. However, it is possible in most cases to explain away the apparent separability of X and Y by attributing it to a tendency to confuse X with a different property—a property that normally guides us in recognizing instances of X, but that is only contingently connected with X. (To elaborate: In most cases, if X is a com-

monsense natural kind, then there exists a property Z such that (a) instances of Z are normally instances of X, (b) this connection between Z and X is contingent, and (c) we normally recognize instances of X by identifying thcm as instances of Z [i.e., Z is the property that guides us in "picking out" instances of X]. When X is associated with a property Z that meets this condition, it is possible to explain away X's apparent separability from an associated scientific kind Y by saying that the appearance of separability is due in part to a tendency to misconstrue possible situations that contain instances of Z as situations that contain instances of X, and in part also to a tendency to misconstrue possible situations that lack instances of Z as situations that lack instances of X. To be more specific, when it appears to a subject that it is possible for there to be an instance of X that is not an instance of the associated scientific kind Y, it is possible to explain this appearance away by saying that the subject has (i) imagined or conceived of a possible situation that contains an instance of Z that is not an instance of Y and (ii) misconstrued this situation as one in which there is an instance of X that is not an instance of Y. Equally, when it appears to a subject that it is possible for there to be an instance of Y that is not an instance of X, it is possible to explain this appearance away by saying that the subject has (i) imagined or conceived of a possible situation that contains an instance of Y that is not an instance of Z and (ii) misconstrued this situation as one in which there is an instance of Y that is not an instance of X.)

Sixth premise: The apparent separability of *being a pain* and *being a case of C-fiber stimulation* cannot be explained away in the way indicated in the fifth premise. (Thus, there is no property Z such that (a) instances of Z are normally instances of *being a pain,* (b) this connection between Z and *being a pain* is contingent, and (c) we normally recognize instances of *being a pain* by identifying them as instances of Z. *Being a pain* is *itself* the property that guides us in recognizing instances of *being a pain.* [Kripke puts the point in the following way: "Pain, on the other hand, is not picked out by one of its accidental properties; rather it is picked out by the property of being pain itself, by its immediate phenomenological quality."[3]])

Seventh premise: The paradigm described in the fifth premise is the *only* model for explaining appearances of separability away.

Lemma: By the fifth, sixth, and seventh premises, it is not possible to explain away the apparent separability of *being a pain* and *being a case of C-fiber stimulation.*

Conclusion: By the first premise, the second premise, the third premise, the fourth premise, and the lemma, *being a pain* is not identical to *being a case of C-fiber stimulation.*

In addition to sketching this argument, Kripke takes pains to illustrate the paradigm of explanation that is described in the fifth premise. Kripke begins this part of his discussion by pointing out that, despite the fact that the commonsense natural kind heat is known to be identical with the scientific kind molecular kinetic energy, it seems possible for heat to exist without being accompanied by molecular motion. Kripke then maintains that we are normally guided in recognizing heat by the property *being the external phenomenon that causes the sensation S,* where "S" names the sensation that heat normally produces in human observers in the actual world. Next, he says that when it seems to us that heat can exist without being accompanied by molecular motion, this is because we are misconstruing a situation that we are imagining or conceiving of. In particular, he says, when we have an impression of possibility of the sort in question, we have it because (a) we are imagining or conceiving of a situation in which *being the external phenomenon that causes the sensation S* is exemplified but there is no molecular motion, and (b) we are misconstruing this situation as one in which heat is present but molecular motion is not. That is to say, as Kripke sees it, we are confusing a situation in which the property by which we normally identify heat is exemplified with a situation in which heat itself is present.

Before concluding this review of Kripke's line of thought, we should recall that Kripke nowhere provides any defense of the assumption that I have listed as the seventh premise, the assumption that the explanatory paradigm illustrated by the heat example is the *only* paradigm for explaining appearances of possibility away.[4] As we will see, this premise is false. Indeed, it is irredeemably false, in the sense that there is no true claim, or set of true claims, that is capable of taking its place in the argument.

II

I will now sketch an explanation of the apparent separability of pain and C-fiber stimulation that does not conform to the paradigm we have just been considering. Instead of exploiting the distinction between a property and its mode of presentation (that is, the distinction between a property X and the property that guides us in recognizing instances of X), this alternative explanation exploits a distinction between two types of imagination.

The explanatory strategy I have in mind is set forth in a little-noticed footnote in Thomas Nagel's wonderful "What Is It Like to Be a Bat?"[5] The relevant part of the footnote runs as follows:

> A theory that explained how the mind-brain relation was necessary would still leave us with Kripke's problem of explaining why it nevertheless appears contingent. That difficulty seems to me surmountable, in the following way. We may imagine something by representing it to ourselves either perceptually, sympathetically, or symbolically. I shall not try to say how symbolic imagination works, but part of what happens in the other two cases is this. To imagine something perceptually, we put ourselves in a conscious state resembling the state we would be in if we perceived it. To imagine something sympathetically, we put ourselves in a conscious state resembling the thing itself. (This method can only be used to imagine mental events and states—our own or another's.) When we try to imagine a mental state occurring without its associated brain state, we first sympathetically imagine the occurrence of the mental state: that is, we put ourselves in a state that resembles it mentally. At the same time, we attempt to perceptually imagine the non-occurrence of the associated physical state, by putting ourselves into another state unconnected with the first: one resembling that which we would be in if we perceived the non-occurrence of the physical state. Where the imagination of physical features is perceptual and the imagination of mental features is sympathetic, it appears to us that we can imagine any experience occurring without its associated brain state, and vice versa. The relation between them will appear contingent even if it is necessary, because of the independence of the disparate types of imagination.[6]

According to Nagel, then, there are three different types of imagination; the symbolic, the sympathetic, and the perceptual. We use the sympathetic imagination in imagining mental states and the perceptual imagination in imagining brain processes. It is also part of Nagel's story that we can use the perceptual imagination to form images of the *absence* of brain processes, that is, images that represent situations in which no brain processes exist. Nagel uses this story as the foundation of an account of how we are able to imagine disembodiment. According to Nagel's account, when we imagine a mental state that is not accompanied by a brain process, what we do is to splice together a sympathetic image of a situation that contains a mental state and a perceptual image of a situation in which no brain process is present. The fact that we can do this without incoherence has no tendency to show that it is objectively possible for the imagined mental state to exist without being accompanied by a brain process. Rather our ability to do it is due to the fact that there are two types of imagination that operate independently of one another.

The key element of this explanation is a claim that can be expressed as follows: If P is a property of which one can be introspectively or perceptually aware, then, when one imagines an instance of P, what one does is to put oneself into a state which is similar to the state one is in when one is experientially aware of an instance of P. This claim is intuitively plausible, and it also seems to be supported by the beautiful experimental results about images and the imagination that psychologists obtained in the seventies and eighties. Thus, there are many results, such as the classic experiments by Roger Shepherd and his colleagues concerning the processes by which we determine congruence and incongruence relations between geometric forms, which strongly suggest that visual images of objects and situations have many of the same properties as the corresponding perceptual states.[7] Moreover, Nagel's claim receives additional support from the results which indicate that imagination can facilitate perceptual tasks. Ronald A. Finke summarizes these results in the following passage:

> [T]he process of forming a visual image can serve a perceptual anticipatory function: it can prepare a person to receive information about imagined objects. Mental imagery may therefore enhance the perception of an object by causing the selective priming of mechanisms in the visual system.[8]

As Finke points out, this priming hypothesis provides strong support for the view that the process of forming a mental image involves many of the neural mechanisms that underlie visual perception.[9]

This brings us to the question of whether Nagel's explanation is genuinely compatible with materialism. At first sight, at least, the answer appears to be "yes." Consider, for example, the doctrine that pain is the very same thing as an electrochemical process in one's C-fibers. If this doctrine is true, one might ask, then how is it possible for experiences that count as imaginative presentations of pains to be quite different in character from experiences that count as imaginative presentations of cases of C-fiber stimulation? Nagel can respond by saying that the experiences are different because they are produced by different psychological mechanisms: experiences that count as imaginative presentations of pains are produced by mechanisms that serve the sympathetic imagination, and experiences that count as imaginative presentations of C-fiber stimulation are produced by mechanisms that serve the perceptual imagination. But is it possible for psychological mechanisms to produce radically different experiences if those experiences are in fact presentations of the same property? Well, yes; this happens all of the time in the case of perceptual presentations. Compare a visual presentation of the surface of a piece of sandpaper with a tactual presentation of the same surface. Any two such presentations will be quite different in point of intrinsic character; but still, the properties that are presented by the former will overlap with the properties that are presented by the latter.

This answer is plausible; but it seems that there is an aspect of the worry about the compatibility of Nagel's explanation with materialism that it fails to address. Let us trade our hypothesis about pain in for the slightly more concrete hypothesis that pain is the very same thing as electrochemical activity in a network of C-fibers that is essentially G-shaped, where G is a certain geometric structure. Now it can seem that if this hypothesis is true, then any presentation of pain, whether a genuine case of awareness or an imaginative construction, should have features which indicate that what is presented is activity in a network that essentially exemplifies G. In other words, it can seem that there should be something G-ish about both real and imagined pains, something that would present a foothold for the concept of G. If G-ishness is part of the very essence of pain, shouldn't we be able to detect at least a hint of G-ishness by inspecting a presentation of pain?

I think that this intuition is quite natural, but I also think that it is due to a confusion. If presentations of pain do not present a foothold for the concept of G, this is because the mechanisms that control the applicability of the concept are exclusively perceptual, in the sense that they are exclusively responsive to features of perceptual presentations. Thus, like all other concepts with spatial significance, the concept of G owes its existence to our need to have concepts that make it possible for us to classify extramental entities that are given to us perceptually; and, as a result, the presentations that are capable of triggering the concept of G are limited to veridical presentations of instances of G and to other mental states that are similar to such presentations. Presentations of pain, whether genuine states of awareness or imaginative constructions, are quite different from veridical presentations of instances of G. Hence, when we examine such presentations with a view to detecting a hint of G-ishness, it is inevitable that we will come up empty handed.

It appears, then, that Nagel's account of how we are able to imagine disembodiment has a couple of important virtues. Unfortunately, it is also true that it has a flaw. Nagel's account presupposes that it is possible for us to perceive brain processes, and this presupposition is highly questionable. To be sure, we are able to use the naked eye to perceive whole brains and various parts of brains. Further, by focussing microscopes on preparations of dead tissue, we are able to perceive certain aspects of the structure of individual brain cells. But neither of these things count as perceiving electrochemical activity in living neurons. Accordingly, it seems reasonable to say that brain processes lie on the theoretical side of the fuzzy line that divides theoretical entities from observable entities. Our access to brain processes is mediated by theories. We cannot be said to perceive them.

If it is wrong to say that one can perceive a brain process, then it must also be wrong to say that one imagines a brain process by putting oneself into a state which resembles the state one is in when one perceives a brain process. So Nagel's account of what is involved in imagining a brain process is mistaken. We must replace it with a more realistic picture.

Reflection suggests that there are two ways of imagining a brain process. First, it is possible to do so by putting oneself into a state which resembles the state one is in when one *indirectly* perceives a brain process, that is, by putting oneself into a state which resembles the state one is in when the following conditions are satisfied: (a) one is perceiving a piece of apparatus whose function it is to detect the presence of various kinds of brain process; (b) the apparatus indicates that a brain process of a certain type T

is currently occurring; and (c) one is aware that the apparatus indicates that a process of type T is occurring. Second, it is possible to imagine a brain process by putting oneself into a state which resembles the state one is in when one is perceiving a *model* of a brain process and one is perceiving it *as* a model, that is, by putting oneself into a state which resembles the state one is in when the following conditions are satisfied: (d) one is perceiving a series of events that are more accessible to the senses than brain processes; (e) there is a structural isomorphism between the series of events and the segments of a certain brain process; (f) one is aware of this isomorphism; and (g) in perceiving the series, one makes use of one's awareness of the isomorphism, that is, one thinks of the series as a representation of the brain process in question.

Assuming that this account is more or less correct, we can explain what is involved in imagining the *absence* of a brain process by saying that one does this by putting oneself in an imaginative state that fails to satisfy conditions (a)–(c) and that also fails to satisfy conditions (d)–(g). (If it should turn out that this account is inadequate, we can improve it by adding that requirement that the state must include the *thought* that the situation one is imagining is devoid of brain processes.)

At this point, we should take note of the fact that the explanatory paradigm that is developed above can be applied not only to explain intuitions about disembodiment, but also to explain intuitions about the possibility of zombies. Just as intuitions of the first kind can be explained as due to one's sympathetically imagining the presence of pain while "perceptually" imagining the absence of C-fiber stimulation, so also intuitions of the second kind can be explained as due to one's sympathetically imagining the absence of pain while "perceptually" imagining the presence of C-fiber stimulation. (I put "perceptually" in scare quotes to remind the reader of the need for qualifications of the sort described two paragraphs back—that is, qualifications based on conditions like (a)–(c) and (d)–(g).) It is clear, I think, that the possibility of forming imaginative representations of the latter sort is no less compatible with type-materialism than the possibility of forming imaginative representations of the former sort.

Before concluding these Nagelian reflections, we must consider one further issue. Although I have tried to show that Nagel's footnote offers us an adequate explanation of certain of our intuitions about disembodiment and zombiehood, I have not yet indicated how it might be true that our Nagelian account explains these intuitions *away*. One explains a set of intuitions by describing the mechanisms that produce them. To explain the members of the set *away* one must in addition provide evidence which calls the reliability of the relevant mechanisms into question, i.e., one must produce evidence which makes it reasonable to doubt that the intuitions produced by these mechanisms are quite likely to be true.

To see that there are grounds for doubting the reliability of intuitions about the possibility of disembodiment and zombiehood, we should first take note of the fact that other intuitions about separability can plausibly be claimed to be due to mechanisms of the same sort as the mechanisms I have claimed to be responsible for these "Cartesian" intuitions. Here is a description of one of the "Cartesian" mechanisms: it produces intuitions to the effect that pain can occur without being accompanied by C-fiber stimulation by splicing together images of the presence of pain and images of the absence of C-fiber stimulation. Now consider intuitions to the effect that heat can occur without being accompanied by molecular motion. It is plausible, I think, to attribute such intuitions to a mechanism that operates by splicing together images of the presence of heat and images of the absence of molecular motion. Or consider intuitions to the effect that water can exist without being accompanied by H_2O. It is plausible to attribute such intuitions to a mechanism that operates by splicing together images of the presence of water and images of the absence of H_2O.

Summarizing, we can say that the mechanisms that are responsible for intuitions about the possibility of disembodiment and zombiehood are members of a family F of mechanisms that can be described as follows: where M is any psychological mechanism, M is a member of F if M operates by splicing together images of the presence (or absence) of a commonsense phenomenon (i.e., a phenomenon to which we have access by a commonsense faculty of awareness, such as introspection or visual perception) and images of the absence (or presence) of a theoretical phenomenon (i.e., a phenomenon to which we have access only via theory-construction and laboratory apparatus). Just as it is plausible to say that intuitions about the possibility of disembodiment and zombiehood are due to the Nagelian mechanisms that I have described above, so also, I wish to claim, it is

plausible to say that our other intuitions about the separability of commonsense phenomena and theoretical phenomena are due, or at least tend to be due, to other members of F.[10,11]

We are in a position to assess the reliability of many of the members of F without begging any questions concerning the mind–body problem, and when we make such assessments, we find that the results are quite negative. Intuitions to the effect that heat is separable from molecular motion are false, as are intuitions to the effect that water is separable from H_2O, as are intuitions to the effect that light is separable from electromagnetic radiation. And so on. Since it is plausible to say that the Nagelian mechanisms that are responsible for intuitions about disembodiment and zombiehood are fundamentally akin to the mechanisms that are responsible for other intuitions about the separability of commonsense and theoretical kinds, and since we know that the latter mechanisms are fundamentally unreliable, the type-materialist can claim to be in possession of an argument which makes it rational to doubt the reliability of Nagelian mechanisms.

To be sure, there is a significant difference between Nagelian mechanisms and the other members of F—Nagelian mechanisms make use of the sympathetic imagination as well as the perceptual imagination, but presumably this is not true, for example, of the mechanisms that are responsible for intuitions about heat and molecular motion. (Perhaps we could describe the non-Nagelian members of F as mechanisms that splice together images provided by the perceptual imagination and images provided by the "perceptual" imagination.) It would be implausible to maintain, however, that this difference makes the Nagelian mechanisms more reliable that the other members of F. . . .

V

There is an important issue that has not yet been addressed. I have maintained that the mechanisms that are responsible for a number of our modal intuitions are unreliable. This might be taken to show that the line of thought in the present paper presupposes a general scepticism about our ability to obtain knowledge of modal facts. And, by the same token, it might be taken to show that the line of thought in question suffers from a disabling flaw. No argument that calls the general run of our claims to have modal knowledge into question can be fully satisfactory, for we feel sure that we possess a fairly large amount of such knowledge.

Fortunately, there are two features of the argument that prevent it from leading to a radical modal scepticism. First, my claims about unreliability have been restricted to intuitions that have implications concerning a posteriori questions about matters of fact. (Hereafter I will call such intuitions *a posteriori modal intuitions*.) Thus, consider the intuition that heat is separable from molecular motion. When it is combined with the true thesis that properties are necessarily identical if they are identical at all, this intuition leads to a negative answer to the question of whether heat and molecular motion are identical—a question that is a paradigm of a posteriority. Accordingly, the intuition is an a posteriori modal intuition. Second, I have not assumed that we are *incapable* of forming a posteriori modal intuitions that are correct, but only that our a posteriori modal intuitions tend to be incorrect when we form them without being fully apprised of the relevant empirical facts. Thus, for example, in my account of conceivability-based intuitions concerning the separability of heat and molecular motion, I claimed that the mechanisms that are responsible for such intuitions operate only when we lack the scientific information which indicates that the concepts of heat and molecular motion are necessarily coextensive.

In sum, while it is true that the lines of thought in earlier sections call a class of modal intuitions into question, this class is highly restricted, consisting as it does only of a posteriori modal intuitions that are formed independently of information concerning the relevant empirical matters. Accordingly, the foregoing lines of thought have no tendency to promote a *general* scepticism about the possibility of obtaining modal knowledge. Moreover, it seems to me to be *good* to be sceptical about the intuitions that belong to the given restricted class; for as I see it, it follows from their description that such intuitions could not possibly be worthy of our trust![12]

NOTES

This is an expanded version of a section of a paper that was read at the 1994 meetings of the Pacific Division of the American Philosophical Association. I thank W.D. Hart and Stephen Yablo for extremely useful comments on that earlier paper. In writing the present paper I have benefitted substantially from criticism and encouragement from David Chalmers, Ivan Fox, and Stephen Yablo.

1. See Saul A. Kripke, *Naming and Necessity* (Cambridge, MA: Harvard University Press, 1980). See also Kripke's "Identity and Necessity" in Stephen P. Schwartz (ed.), *Naming, Necessity, and Natural Kinds* (Ithaca, NY: Cornell University Press, 1977), 66–101.

2. W.D. Hart, *Engines of the Soul* (Cambridge: Cambridge University Press, 1988); Stephen Yablo, "The Real Distinction Between Mind and Body," *Canadian Journal of Philosophy*, Supplementary Volume 16 (1990), 149–201; Stephen Yablo, "Is Conceivability a Guide to Possibility?" *Philosophy and Phenomenological Research* 53 (1993), 1–42; David Chalmers, *The Conscious Mind: In Search of a Theory of Consciousness* (Oxford: Oxford University Press, forthcoming).

3. Kripke, *Naming and Necessity*, p. 152.

4. Kripke says that the model illustrated by the heat example is "the only model [he] can think of." See Kripke, "Identity and Necessity," p. 101.

5. Thomas Nagel, "What Is It Like to Be a Bat?" *The Philosophical Review* 83 (1974), 435–50.

6. Quoted from Nagel, ibid., footnote 11. Oddly, the ideas in this footnote have not received any attention from the contemporary defenders of Kripke's argument, nor, as far as I know, from any of Kripke's other commentators.

7. See, e.g., the papers collected in Roger N. Shepherd and Lynn Cooper (eds.), *Mental Images and Their Transformations* (Cambridge, MA: MIT Press, 1982).

   Of course, the interpretation of Shepherd's results is a matter of controversy. Not everyone would agree with the assessment offered above. For a quite different view, see Zenon Pylyshyn, "The Imagery Debate: Analog Media versus Tacit Knowledge," in Ned. Block (ed.), *Imagery* (Cambridge, MA: MIT Press, 1981), 151–205.

8. Ronald A. Finke, "Mental Imagery and the Visual System," *The Scientific American* 1986, 88–95. The quoted passage is on p. 92.

9. Ibid., p. 88.

10. In effect, I am here proposing a new explanation of such intuitions as the intuition that heat is separable from molecular motion—that is, an explanation that is quite different than Kripke's explanation. According to Kripke, it seems to us that heat is separable from molecular motion because we take ourselves to be imagining a situation in which heat is present but molecular motion is absent when we are actually imagining a situation in which the *sensation* of heat is present but molecular motion is absent (or because we take ourselves to be imaging a situation in which molecular motion is present but heat is absent when we are actually imagining a situation in which molecular motion is present but the *sensation* of heat is absent). As I see it, this explanation is fundamentally misguided; for as I see it, in non-pathological cir-

cumstances introspection gives us pretty accurate access to the contents of our own states of imagination. Accordingly, I prefer to explain the intuition about the separability of heat and molecular motion, and all related intuitions, such as the intuition that water is separable from H_2O, by saying that they are due to image-splicing mechanisms of the sort described in the text.

11. As indicated in the previous note, I here mean to be proposing an explanation of imagination-based intuitions of separability. There is one respect in which the present sketch of the explanation is incomplete. As I see it, the "splicing" mechanisms operate to produce an intuition to the effect that it is possible that p only when a subject is not already in possession of a "defeater" for that intuition—that is, only when a subject is not already in possession of rea-

sons for believing that it is necessary that not-p. Nothing is said about the inhibiting effects of such defeaters in the text.

I am abstracting from considerations having to do with defeaters in the present section because I want there to be one place in the paper in which the main idea is presented without being accompanied by a forest of qualifications. However, when we consider conceivability-based intuitions of separability in section III, I will be at pains to acknowledge the role of defeaters in inhibiting intuitions of separability. See especially the penultimate and ante-penultimate paragraphs of Section III.

12. The question broached in this final section deserves a great deal more attention than I am able to give it in a paper that is primarily concerned with other matters. I hope to return to it on another occasion.

34 | Rigid Designators and Mind–Brain Identity

Grover Maxwell

A kind of mind–brain identity theory that is immune to recent objections by Kripke (1971 and 1972)[1] is outlined and defended in this paper. For reasons, the details of which will be given later, I have characterized the view as a *nonmaterialist physicalism*. It is nonmaterialist in that it does not attempt to eliminate or in any way deemphasize the importance of the "truly mental." On the contrary, it accords central roles to *consciousness,* "private experience," subjectivity, "raw feels," "what it's like to be something,"[2] thoughts, pains, feelings, emotions, etc., as we live through them in all of their qualitative richness. The theory also claims, however, that all of these genuinely mental entities are also genuinely physical, from which it follows that some genuinely physical entities are genuinely mental. This should occasion no shock, for it is a consequence of any authentic mental–physical identity thesis. Of course, some call themselves identity theorists and, at the same time, deny the existence of the genuinely mental (in my sense); but the result of this is always some kind of physical–physical identity thesis rather than a genuine mental–physical identity claim. One of

the main reasons that Kripke's arguments do not hold against this theory is that it incorporates a significant revision of our basic beliefs about the nature of "the physical." The revision, however, is by no means ad hoc. It is virtually forced upon us, quite independently of Kripke's argument—indeed, quite apart from the mind–brain issue—by contemporary physics, physiology, neurophychology, and psychophysiology. It will turn out that Kripke's arguments *do* reveal, in a novel and cogent manner, the inadequacies of materialism. At the same time they provide valuable considerations that can be used to bolster the case for nonmaterialist physicalism.

All of this will become more clear later, I hope, when more detail is given. But, even at this point, perhaps I should attempt a crude and somewhat inaccurate characterization of "the physical." *The physical* is, very roughly, the subject matter of physics. By 'subject matter' I mean *not* the *theories, laws, principles,* etc., of physics, but rather what the theories and laws are about. *The physical* thus includes tables, stars, human bodies and brains, and whatever the constituents of these may be. The crucial contention is that contemporary science gives us good reason to suppose that these constituents are quite different from what common sense *and* traditional materialism believe them to be. While "the dematerialization of matter" has perhaps been overplayed in some quarters, its advocates do make an important point (see, e.g., Hanson, 1962 and Feigl, 1962); and this point is crucial for the mind–body problem. A nonmaterialist physicalism is one that rejects those erroneous prescientific beliefs about physical entities that I shall argue are endemic to common sense and are carried over, to a great extent, into traditional *and* contemporary materialism. The elimination of these beliefs clears the way for a mind–brain identity theory that avoids the antimentalist reductionism of materialism, behaviorism, and similar views. (No contempt of common sense is involved here at all. Science, at best, is modified and improved common sense. Often the improvement is minimal; but, if it is genuine, surely it ought to be preferred to the unimproved version.)

Before considering Kripke's argument against mind–brain identity, I should remark that I am assuming that his ("quasi-technical") system of "rigid designation," "reference-fixing," etc., is a viable system. This is not to assume that it provides, necessarily, an account that is in perfect accord with our customary modes of conceptualization, inference, ascription of necessity, etc. Kripke, I think, intends and believes that it does, but many disagree. This explains, no doubt, why they feel that some of his conclusions are wrong or at best highly counterintuitive or based on eccentric terminology. Be this as it may, I believe that his terminology is clear and consistent and that his system provides, if not an "analysis," at least a tenable alternative "reconstruction" of conceptualization, reasoning, etc., both in everyday and in scientific contexts. (I am *not* so sure about his *essentialism*. However, for the sake of argument—that is, for the purpose of defending the identity thesis against his objections—I shall accept his essentialism insofar as I am able to understand it.)

Let me now introduce the elements of Kripke's system that are needed for the argument in question. A *rigid designator* is a symbol the referent of which remains the same in our discourse about all possible worlds *provided two conditions obtain*. The first is the rather trivial one that the language must remain the same. Obviously if we change the meaning or the conventional (*or* stipulated) use of a term, its referent will not nec-

essarily remain constant. The second condition is that the referent exist in the possible world in question, and this condition will, of course, fail to obtain in many possible worlds. Another way of stating the matter is to say that the referent of a rigid designator either remains constant or becomes null as our discourse ranges over different possible worlds. Proper names are, for Kripke, paradigm examples of rigid designators. As long as the term 'Richard Nixon' has its standard and established role in our language, it refers to the same entity, namely Nixon, no matter what possible world we may be talking about, *unless*, of course, we happen to be talking about a possible world in which Nixon does not exist. (Instead of using the "possible worlds" terminology, we could say that a rigid designator has the same referent in every occurrence no matter whether the statement in which it occurs is about an actual or a counterfactual state of affairs.) The most common instances of nonrigid or "accidental" designators are descriptive phrases. To use an example of Kripke, the phrase 'the inventor of bifocals' refers to Benjamin Franklin; but obviously the phrase is not a rigid designator. There are many possible worlds in which bifocals were invented by someone else—or we can easily imagine counterfactual situations such that bifocals were invented, say, by Thomas Paine. In discourse about the latter situation the referent of the phrase 'the inventor of bifocals' would be Thomas Paine instead of Benjamin Franklin.

We come now to a crucial juncture in Kripke's system. In attempting to make it as clear as possible, I shall use an example of different form and somewhat simpler than those employed by Kripke. Suppose we are convinced that one and only one man invented the incandescent electric light bulb but that we do not know who he was. Nevertheless, suppose that we stipulate that the term 'Oscar' is to be used to *rigidly designate* this so far unidentified inventor. What does this mean? It means that 'Oscar' always refers to the man who invented, as a contingent matter of fact in this the actual world, the incandescent bulb. And this referential relation holds whether or not our discourse is about the actual world or about other possible worlds—whether it is about actual or counterfactual states of affairs. There are, of course, many possible worlds in which Oscar did not invent the bulb, worlds in which someone else invented it or in which it was not invented at all. This is just to say that there are possible worlds in which the bulb was not invented by the man who actually did invent it (in this, the actual world—to be redundant). Nevertheless, in our discourse about these worlds 'Oscar' still refers to the same man—the man who invented the bulb in this, the actual world. . . .

Before proceeding to the mind–brain identity thesis, it will be helpful to continue examination of the "Oscar" example in order to understand better Kripke's views about identity in general. Suppose that, after fixing the referent of 'Oscar' as we did above, we make the (contingent) discovery that Thomas A. Edison invented the incandescent electric light bulb. It follows, obviously, that Oscar and Edison are identical—that "they" are one and the same person. It also follows, given the Kripkean system, that Edison and Oscar are *necessarily* identical. This follows simply because both 'Oscar' and 'Thomas A. Edison' are rigid designators. This means that 'Oscar' *always* refers to the same man and that, of course, the referent of 'Thomas A. Edison' *always* remains constant, whether our discourse is about the actual world (or about actual situations) or about any other possible world or any counterfactual situation. It follows that, if Edison and Oscar are identical in any possible world (including the actual world, of course), then "they" are identical in all possible worlds (in all actual and counterfactual situations). Therefore, "They" are *necessarily* identical, since something holds *necessarily* if and only if it holds in all possible worlds—in all actual and counterfactual situations. . . .

This is a good point at which to give a somewhat truncated but forceful sketch of Kripke's argument against the mind–brain identity thesis. The sketch follows:

(1) There seems to be *no way* for a brain state (or brain event) to be *necessarily* identical with a mental state (or a mental event). So, (1′) if mind–brain identities exist, they are contingent identities. But (as we have seen above) (2) there *are no* contingent identities. Therefore, there are no mind–brain identities.

Obviously the argument is valid; if we are to reject the conclusion, we must reject at least one premise. Many—probably most—mind–brain identity theorists accept the first premise. Indeed, they emphasize and insist that mental-physical identities are contingent identities. They then proceed, either explicitly or tacitly, to reject premise (2). Needless to say, I accept (2) and shall argue that (1) and therefore (1′) are false.

Kripke emphasizes that this is just what the identity theorist *must* do if he is to retain any hope of rejecting the argument's conclusion. He then argues at some length that the first premise seems quite invulnerable. I shall argue that the first premise is false.

Kripke notes and indeed emphasizes that his apparatus provides what might seem to offer an escape route for the identity theorist, and we have already touched upon the matter earlier. If we could show that the apparent truth of premise (1) is due entirely to an *illusion of contingency,* we would have produced conclusive grounds for rejecting the premise. In order to do this we would need to indicate how there could be a *contingent associated fact* that is responsible for this "illusion of contingency." Kripke argues that the existence of such a fact seems out of the question. Before examining these arguments, it will be helpful to continue our discussion of identity and necessity. . . .

Returning now to the mind–brain identity thesis, consider a claim that, say, a certain *determinate* kind of pain, call it 'pain$_{39}$' is identical with a certain *determinate* kind of brain state b_{76}.[3] Rather than speaking of *states,* it is much better, I believe, to (attempt to) identify mental *events* with physical *events.* So let us change the matter a little and take 'pain$_{39}$' to refer to the *occurrence* of a certain determinate kind of pain and let 'b_{76}' refer to a certain determinate kind of brain event. (This is actually more in line with Kripke's main example. In it, the physical entity is *C*-fiber stimulation, which is a process or an event.) Let us suppose further that 'b_{76}' is the genuine rigid designator for the relevant physical event that Kripke suggests we use just in case '*C*-fiber stimulation' is not a rigid designator.

Now, since 'pain$_{39}$' and 'b_{76}' are both rigid designators, it follows that, if pain$_{39}$ and b_{76} are identical, they are necessarily identical. So, if the identity does hold, there must be some contingent associated fact involved in fixing the reference either of 'pain$_{39}$' or of 'b_{76},' a fact, moreover, that would explain the all but overwhelming "illusion of contingency" about the claim of identity. Kripke argues convincingly and, in my opinion, conclusively that no such fact can exist for a designator such as 'pain$_{39}$.' He says that the referent of 'pain' is picked out by a *necessary* (or "essential") property of pain, by, indeed, the property of *being pain.* This precludes the existence of a contingent reference-fixing fact for 'pain' (and for 'pain$_{39}$'); for the reference of 'pain' (and 'pain$_{39}$') is fixed *ontologically without* any reference fixing fact. It is fixed *solely* by virtue of conventional linguistic practice. In contrast, fixing the reference of 'Oscar' and 'heat' involved contingent facts *in addition* to the linguistic factors. Finally, and equally importantly, language alone not only fixes ontologically the reference of 'pain,' it also *epistemically determines* what its referent *is;* in this case no contingent associated fact is involved.

So the referent of 'pain' is picked out by a necessary truth about pain, namely, the truth that pain is necessarily pain. It is *not possible* that pain (or pain$_{39}$) could have been something that was not pain. This necessary truth may seem quite trivial, and in a sense it is. Note, however, that is is not a necessary truth about the inventor of the incandescent bulb that he invented the incandescent bulb. Under the appropriate arrangement of Russell's "scope operator," we can even say truthfully that it is not necessarily true that the inventor of the bulb was the inventor of the bulb; i.e., the man who *did* invent it *might* not have (cf. Kripke, p. 279). Someone other than Edison might have done it. (Or more than one person might have invented it, or it might not have been invented at all.) Or, to say it in still another manner; the man who in this, the actual, world invented the bulb did not invent it in every possible world. Or, returning to the essentialist framework, being the inventor of the bulb is not an *essential* property of the inventor of the bulb. (Or course, however, being the inventor of the bulb *is* an essential property of *being* the inventor of the bulb [as is the property of being an inventor, etc.].) Consider another example. Neither being red nor being crimson is an essential property of my sweater, which *is,* as a matter of contingent fact, crimson. But being red is of course an essential property of being crimson. Being red, therefore, is an essential property of an "accidental" property of my sweater. So we see that there are not only "illusions of contingency" but, as in the case of the inventor being the inventor, "illusions of necessity" as well. Something which, prima facie, seems necessary may turn out on closer examination to be contingent. . . .

Returning once again to Kripke's arguments, I have agreed very strongly with him that the referent of the *word* 'pain' (and the referent of the word 'pain$_{39}$') is picked out by a necessary fact about (or an "essential" property of) the referent; i.e., the word 'pain$_{39}$' rigidly designates the event *pain*$_{39}$ by virtue of the necessity of pain$_{39}$'s

being pain$_{39}$. This precludes the possibility of fixing the reference of the term 'pain$_{39}$' by means of any contingent fact. But we have seen above that this by no means precludes the existence of another, different word, say 'factor *a*' that rigidly designates the *event* pain$_{39}$ and *that,* moreover, *rigidly designates it by virtue of a contingent fact.* It seems to me that such a possibility is overlooked by Kripke. However this may be, I claim that *terms referring to certain kinds of brain events,* properly construed,—terms such as 'b_{76}'—*do rigidly refer to mental events* (events such as pain$_{39}$). *Such reference is accomplished,* moreover, *by means of the (contingent) neurophysiological causal roles of the relevant events.* These "accidental" causal properties of the events *fix their reference ontologically.* However, due to our lack of neurological, psycho-physiological, and neuropsychological knowledge about the details of these causal properties, the reference has *not* been, so far, *epistemically determined.* Nevertheless, the identity theorist speculates that it is mental events that are the real actors in *some* of these neurophysiological causal roles. More specifically, he speculates that there is a certain brain event, call it 'b_{76},' which plays, contingently, a certain neurophysiological causal role. Moreover, the referent of 'b_{76}' can, in principle, be fixed by means of this (contingent) role; i.e., the relevant neurophysiological details, if only we knew them, could pick out the referent of 'b_{76}' ontologically. Next, he continues, the relevant (contingent) psychophysiological or neuropsychological details, if only we knew them, could epistemically determine that it is pain$_{39}$ that plays the neurophysiological role in question.

Kripke stresses the disanalogies between claiming that heat (or an instance of heat) is identical with molecular motion, on the one hand, and claiming that a brain event is identical with a pain, on the other. He concludes that, although heat and molecular motion are necessarily identical, these disanalogies preclude the possibility of a brain event and a pain's being necessarily identical and therefore preclude their being identical at all. He is correct about the existence of the disanalogies but wrong, I believe, in inferring that they preclude the necessity of mind-brain identities. He summarizes his argument on this matter (p. 340) as follows:

> Thus pain, unlike heat, is not only rigidly designated by 'pain' but the reference of the designator is determined by an essential property of the referent. Thus it is not possible to say that although pain is necessarily identical with a cer-

tain physical state, a certain phenomenon can be picked out in the same way we pick out pain without being correlated with that physical state. If any phenomenon is picked out in exactly the same way we pick out pain, then that phenomenon is pain.

This is certainly correct. However, it does not preclude mind–brain identities. For what we *can* say is that, although $pain_{39}$ is necessarily identical with a certain brain event (call it 'b_{76}'), a (different!) brain event could, in some possible worlds, be picked out in the same way that we (in the actual world) pick out b_{76} without being identical with or even correlated with pain. This is true because the referent of 'b_{76}' is fixed as being the event that plays such and such a neurophysiological causal role *in this world*. In some other possible worlds *that role* will be played by entities other than b_{76}. The identity theorist maintains, of course, that the role in question is played by $pain_{39}$ *in this world,* although it could be played by another event (which might not even be a mental event) in some other possible world. This is what is responsible for *the illusion of contingency* concerning the necessary identity of $pain_{39}$ and b_{76}.

It seems that Kripke assumes, tacitly at least, that designators such as '$pain_{39}$' correspond to the designator 'heat' and thus that those such as 'b_{76}' correspond to 'molecular motion.' I contend that the relevant analogies are rather between 'heat' and 'b_{76}' on the one hand and 'molecular motion' and '$pain_{39}$' on the other. For the reference of 'heat' and the reference of 'b_{76}' are fixed by contingent facts (by "accidental properties" of the referents). And it is the contingent associated discoveries that molecular motion causes heat sensations and that $pain_{39}$ plays such and such a neurophysiological causal role that account for, respectively, the illusions of contingency about the necessary identity of heat and molecular motion and the necessary identity of $pain_{39}$ and the brain event b_{76}.

Now it may seem that Kripke has protected his flank on this score, for he does contend (p. 336) that "*being a brain state* is evidently an essential property of B (the brain state)." In other words, he would claim that every brain state of necessity *had* to be a brain state (and surely he would make the analogous claim about brain events). He goes on to say, "even being a brain state of a specific type is an essential property of [the brain state] B." If the same *is* true of brain *events* (whether Kripke so contends or not), then my counterargument *would* be unsound; for this would entail that the reference of 'b_{76}' is

fixed by means of a necessary truth (i.e., that an "essential property" of b_{76} fixes it as the referent of 'b_{76}'). This would preclude fixing the reference of 'b_{76}' by means of one of the "accidental properties" of the referent, and therefore there could not exist any contingent associated fact to account for the apparent contingency of the correlation between b_{76} and $pain_{39}$. Following Kripke (p. 336), the difficulty may also be put: "If $A = B$, then the identity of A with B is necessary, and any essential property of one must be an essential property of the other." Now suppose that being a brain event *is* an essential property of b_{76}. Since being a brain event is *not* an essential property of $pain_{39}$, it would follow that b_{76} and $pain_{39}$ do not share all of their essential properties and thus cannot be identical.

It is time now for one of the central and, perhaps, one of the most counterintuitive contentions of this paper: *being a brain event* is not, in general, an essential property of brain events. (Although, of course, *being a brain event* is an essential property of *being* a brain event.) Again, this is a matter of *scope* (in Russell's sense of "scope"). Just as Russell pointed out long ago how it is that we can say that a given inventor might not have been an inventor (e.g., Edison might have spent his life writing mystery novels, never inventing even a mouse trap), we are now in a position to understand how *a given brain event might not have been a brain event.* For, I claim, to be a brain event is to play a neurophysiological causal role of an appropriate, broadly specifiable ("determin*able*") kind; and to be a brain event of a specific ("determi*nate*") kind is to play a specific, determinate kind of neurophysiological causal role (e.g., of the kind we are supposing b_{76} to play), and if we assume (in agreement with Hume) that *to say of a given event (or kind of event) that it plays a certain kind of causal role is to say something contingent,* then we see immediately that *to say of a given event (or kind of event) that it is a brain event is to say something contingent.* This follows, of course, because to say of an event that it is a brain event is merely to say that it plays a certain kind of causal role. And to say that this very brain event might not have been a brain event is merely to say that although this event, as a matter of contingent fact, plays a certain causal role, it is possible that it might not have played such a role; in some possible worlds it plays a very different role. As to the case at hand, although $pain_{39}$ (alias b_{76}) plays a certain specific neurophysiological causal role and is thereby (contingently) a brain event (of a certain kind), it *might not* have played such a role. It might not even have played any kind of neurological role, and thus it might not have been a brain event. Exactly the same holds for b_{76}—which is, in effect, to say the same thing again, for b_{76} and pain$_{39}$ are necessarily identical; 'b_{76}' and 'pain$_{39}$' refer to one and the same event. Moreover and *obviously* by now, *being a brain event is not* an essential property of *the brain event b_{76}*; but *being a pain is* an essential property of *the brain event b_{76}*. And, of course, being a brain event is *not* an essential property of the *brain* (!) *event,* pain$_{39}$; but being a pain *is* an essential property of the brain event,[4] pain$_{39}$. Pain$_{39}$ and b_{76} *do* share all of "their" properties, including all of "their" essential properties; they are one and the same event. To paraphrase Russell, there is no more difficulty about a pain being both a sensation and a brain event than there is about a man being both a rational animal and a barber. . . .

What I want to do next is to argue directly that, when God made the relevant kind of brain event, say b_{76}, this very act of creation was the creation of (the mental event—the sensation) pain$_{39}$. After God created b_{76}, there did *not* remain for Him the substantive task of creating pain$_{39}$ (nor the task of then correlating it with b_{76}). The creation of b_{76} *was* the creation of pain$_{39}$, for "they" are one and the same event. What *was* a substantive task for the Deity was to give pain$_{39}$ (alias b_{76}) the kind of (contingent) neurophysiological causal role that it has. He *could* have decided to give it a different neurophysiological role or even not to give it *any neurophysiological* role at all (just as He *could* have decided not to give mo-

lecular motion the causal role of producing "heat sensations"). Our implicit recognition that the Deity had to make this contingent decision about the causal role of b_{76} is responsible for our *mistaken* feeling that the creation of b_{76} was a different act from the act of creation of pain$_{39}$ and thus for the *illusion of contingency* about the *actual necessity* of the identity of (the mental event) pain$_{39}$ and (the brain event)b_{76}. . . .

To consider these questions we shall need to develop a small amount of "quasi technical" apparatus of our own. We need the notion of *causal structure* and the notion of a *causal network.* The accompanying greatly oversimplified sketch will serve both to explain these notions and to help answer the questions at issue. In the diagram, the circles represent events, and the arrows connecting them represent causal connections. A lower-case letter indicates that an event is a brain event. If the letter is from the beginning portion of the alphabet, the brain event is (also) a mental event; letters toward the end of the alphabet indicate brain events (or other neurological events) that are not mental events. Capital letters indicate "input" and "output" events—input into the neurological network and output from the network. For example, the event, A, might be light striking the eyes and B sound waves entering the ears, while X and Y might be lifting an arm and uttering a word, respectively. Dots and arrows with no circles at their heads or no circles at their tails indicate that large portions of (indeed, most of) the network is not shown in the diagram.

The entire diagram represents a *causal network,* and every item shown is an essential part

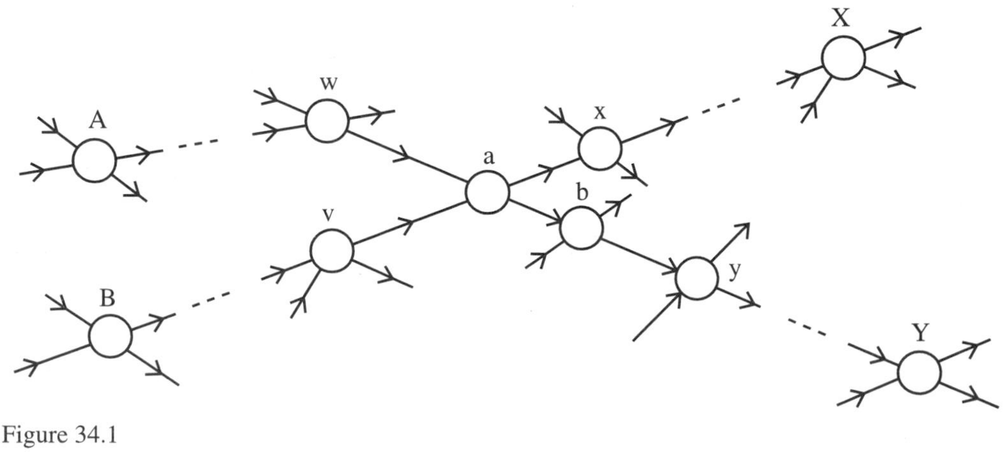

Figure 34.1

of the particular network that is illustrated. In other words, a causal network consists of a number of (causally connected) events and of the causal connections among them. The *causal structure* of the network consists entirely of the causal connections and the positions or loci of the events in the network. For example, if in the diagram event B were replaced by another event or even by an event of another *kind,* the result would be a *different* causal *network,* but the causal *structure* would remain *exactly the same.* The same holds for event a, event y, or any and all other events.

Let us now suppose that the events represented in the central part of the diagram occur in the C-fiber regions of the brain and that the event labeled 'a' is pain$_{39}$ (alias b_{76}). Pain$_{39}$ is, thus, a part of the activity taking place in this region of the C-fibers. Its immediate causal ancestors u and v are also a part of this activity, although, unlike a (alias pain$_{39}$, alias b_{76}), they are not mental events. Among pain$_{39}$'s causal descendants are b, a brain event that is also a mental event (anger$_{64}$, perhaps), and y, a brain event and perhaps a C-fiber event that is *not* a mental event. . . .

If we recognize that C-fiber activity is a complex causal network in which at least some of the events are pure events and that neurophysiology, physics, chemistry, etc., provide us *only* with knowledge of the *causal structure* of the network, the way is left entirely open for the neuropsychologist to theorize that some of the events in the network *just are pains* (in all of their qualitative, experiential, mentalistic richness).

Let us now return to Kripke's claim that, in order to create C-fiber stimulation (C-fiber activity, in our terms), "it would seem that God need only to create beings with C-fibers capable of the appropriate type of *physical* . . . [activity]; whether the beings are conscious or not is irrelevant" [my italics]. Interpreted in one way, this claim is true; but under this interpretation, it in no way counts against the identity thesis. Interpreted in another way, the claim is inconsistent with the identity thesis; however, under this second interpretation, I contend, it becomes false. Under the first interpretation, 'C-fiber activity' refers to a *causal structure;* more specifically, it refers to a certain kind of causal structure of a complex of events in the C-fiber regions of the brain. Now, quite obviously, it is (logically) possible for one and the same causal structure to be exemplified by many different complexes of events (by many different causal networks). So in order for God to create C-fiber activity *in this sense,* all He has to do is create a complex of events that has the appropriate causal structure. *The nature of the events in the complex* is *irrelevant;* some or all of them may be tickles, feelings of warmth, or, even, pain; or, on the other hand, every one of them could be entirely nonmental. In this sense of 'C-fiber activity,' Kripke is entirely correct in his claim that whether or not conscious beings are involved is irrelevant. However, the identity thesis, properly formulated, does *not* attempt to identify mental activity with C-fiber activity *in this sense;* i.e., it does *not* identify pain with the *causal structure of the complex of events—just as Kripke does not identify heat with the causal structure of heat-sensation production.* What is identified with (a specific kind of) pain is a (specific kind of) event, or complex of events, in the causal *network*—a (kind of) event, moreover, that has the position it has in the network *in this, the actual, world.* (Analogously, what is identified with heat is a [specific kind of] event, or complex of events, that causes the heat sensations in this, the actual world.) If the term 'C-fiber activity' is used to refer to such events (or complexes of events)—events that have the appropriate position in the causal network in this, the actual world—then, according to the identity thesis, 'C-fiber activity' *in this* (second) *sense* refers to pain and *does so rigidly.* If Kripke's claim is interpreted according to this sense of 'C-fiber activity,' then it must be denied; for, in this sense, 'C-fiber activity' rigidly designates pain, and the existence of sentient beings is necessarily involved with the existence of pain and, therefore, necessarily involved with the existence of C-fiber activity *in this sense* (just as the existence of mobile molecules is necessarily involved with the existence of heat). . . .

Returning to the main point, let us examine again the term 'C-fiber activity'—or, better and less subject to ambiguity, the rigid designator that I, in response to Kripke's suggestion, have been using in its stead, 'b_{76}'. Once more we must emphasize that the referent of this rigid designator is *epistemically undetermined* as far as neurophysiology and other "purely physical" sciences are concerned. Physical science leaves us completely ignorant as to *what* the referent of 'C-fiber activity' (or better, 'b_{76}') *is;* it provides us *only* with knowledge about the locus of the referent in the causal network. Or, stated without the quasi-technical, rigid-designator terminology, physical science leaves us entirely ignorant as to *what* C-fiber activity *is* and provides us *only* with knowledge about its causal structure (including, of course, its causal connections to the rest of the neurophysiological causal network).

We see now that when God created the C-fiber event, pain$_{39}$ (alias a, alias b_{76}), the existence of an essentially involved conscious being was *not* irrelevant; it was *necessarily* required. The creation of *this* particular bit of C-fiber activity *just was* the creation of pain$_{39}$ (alias a, alias b_{76}). Nothing *else* had to be done in order to make it be *felt* as pain; its "essence" *is* being *felt as pain*. And, of course, it would *not* be in God's powers to make pain$_{39}$ (alias a and b_{76}) be felt as a tickle, or as warmth, or as nothing, rather than felt as pain. Feeling a certain determinate kind of pain is one and the same event *as* pain$_{39}$. (To *be* pain is to be *felt* as pain.) On the other hand, in addition to creating pain$_{39}$ (alias b_{76}, alias a), God did do *something* else; He made the contingent decision to give pain$_{39}$ the causal role that is indicated in the diagram. He *could* have decided to give it an entirely different neurophysiological causal role or even to give it no neurophysiological role at all; for example, He might have decided to cast the world in a Cartesian mold. Analogously, God could have decided to give molecular motion (alias heat) a different causal role from the one that it has; He might, for example, have decided *not* to have it cause heat sensations. And, just as He could have decided to have events of a different kind, say low-frequency radio waves, be the principal and proximal cause of heat sensations, he also could have decided to have an event of a quite different kind play the neurophysiological causal role that, as a matter of contingent fact, is played by pain$_{39}$. In particular, he could have decided to have this role played by a nonmental event.

The points illustrated by these examples follow from the more general principle: *it is* (logically) *possible for different causal networks to have the same causal structure;* or, in other words, one and the same causal structure may be realized in a number of different ways, i.e., may be exemplified by a number of different causal networks. Thus God could have created a causal network such that it differed from the one in the diagram only in that the positions occupied by a and b were occupied by different events—perhaps by events that were nonmental. This creation would have been a different causal network, but it would have been the same causal structure. Or, giving the Deity a rest, *in some possible worlds, mental events are* (some of the) *elements of C-fiber activity,* and, *in other possible worlds, none of the elements of C-fiber activity are mental events.* More generally, *in some possible worlds, mental events are brain events,* and, *in other possible worlds, no mental events are brain events.* This is true, I claim, because to be a brain event is to occupy a position in an appropriate portion of the neurophysiological causal network, and it is a contingent matter as to what kind of events occupy any such position. *With this understanding,* we may take the *identity thesis* to be *the thesis that all mental events are brain events. Such a thesis is contingent,* as we have just seen. But *this,* of course, *does not by any means entail that there are contingent identities.* A fortiori, it is entirely consistent with what, indeed, *must* be the case: *all the identities* that hold between mental events and brain events *hold necessarily. . . .*

Unfortunately, the strongest objection to the identity thesis is, in my opinion, yet to come. Just how it is related to Kripke's objections remains to be seen. Given what physiology and physics tell us about C-fibers and their activity, is it reasonable or even coherent to suppose that mental events comprise (a portion of) such activity? A prime—perhaps *the* prime—ingredient of this activity seems to be neuronal activity, which, let us assume, consists of chemical and (the associated) electrical activity. Chemical and electrical events, in turn, involve the transfer and transportation of electrons, ions, etc. How can one claim that (some of) the goings-on of these tiny charged particles of matter are identical with pains, joys, sorrows, thoughts that two plus two equals four, etc.? Surely, it may seem, such a claim is absurd! I once heard Benson Mates remark that it makes no more sense to identify a mental event with a brain event than it does to identify a quadratic equation with a billy goat. It is not difficult to empathize with his sentiments. Let us state the objection in a more general manner: (1) We know from common sense, from physics, from neurophysiology, etc., what brain events are like. (2) We know ("by acquaintance"—and perhaps better than we know anything else) what mental events are like. (3) This knowledge reveals that brain events differ radically from mental events; more specifically, it reveals that mental events have properties that brain events lack and that brain events have properties that mental events lack.

Therefore, the objection concludes, no mental events are brain events.[5]

This, in my opinion, is *the* argument against the identity thesis, and the most important specific objections to the thesis, including Kripke's, depend upon it in one way or another. The details of the dependence need not concern us. What should be done, rather, is to acknowledge the obvious: premise (or, rather, intermediate conclusion) number (3) above must be denied if the identity thesis is to be maintained; if the thesis is to be plausible, it must be plausible to contend that some brain events share *all* of their properties, both "essential" and "accidental" ones, with mental events. . . .

The typical materialist move is to deny premise (2) above. Materialists tend to hold that knowledge of mental events, if it exists at all, is at best second or third rate knowledge. The belief that we are directly acquainted with the (ingredients of) mental events that comprise our very being is, according to them, at least partly and perhaps totally mistaken. Some go on to maintain that knowledge claims about our mental events (about "private experience," etc.) are so defective that they should, in principle, be abandoned entirely—that, as our knowledge from physics, physiology, etc. increases, we shall see that talk about (allegedly) mental events, private experience, etc., is on a par with talk about witches, demons, or perhaps phlogiston and epicycles. When that happy day arrives, they tell us, we shall talk only about brain events, molecules and electrons, and other "scientifically respectable" entities. This position has been called the *replacement* or the *disappearance* version of the identity thesis (see, e.g., Feyerabend, 1963, and Rorty, 1965). Quite obviously, however, it is not an identity thesis at all; it purports to eliminate mental entities altogether rather than to identify them with brain events. This is not the place to give detailed arguments against such a view. I *will* say more about it later, but now I just want to remark that this position is certainly rejected by Kripke. It is fair to say, I believe, that both he and I find it "self-evidently absurd." . . .

This failure of materialism results from the fact that it must attack the objection at its strongest point, premise (2). I say this *not* because I believe that knowledge about our mental events is certain, infallible, or complete (I do not so believe), but rather because it provides us with the best (perhaps the only) knowledge that we have of the *intrinsic* properties of individual

events (as opposed to *causal* and other *structural* properties). Moreover, if the objection is to retain anything at all of its great intuitive potency, premises (1) and (2) as well as intermediate conclusion (3) must be taken to refer to knowledge about *intrinsic* properties.

There is a widespread tendency to identify[6] the mind–body identity thesis with materialism. To do so, however, is to miss the point *entirely* of any genuine mind-brain identity claim. Materialism, as it is typically proposed and defended, seeks to eliminate the *genuinely mental* realm, to deny that genuinely mental events exist. But, if there *are* no mental events, then the thesis that all mental events are brain events is either nonsensical or vacuously true. A *genuine mind*–brain identity thesis must hold that there are both mental events and brain events, that all mental events are brain events, and that therefore *some brain events are mental events*—in the most full-blown "mentalistic" sense of 'mental.' Such a view I have called *nonmaterialist physicalism*[7] (see, e.g., Maxwell, 1976).

As should be apparent by now, I propose to defend the identity thesis against the prime objection by denying premise (1). More specifically: although physics, neurophysiology, etc., *do* provide us with the best knowledge we have of the *structure* of the neurophysiological causal networks that comprise the brain, they provide us with *no knowledge* (or precious little) about the *intrinsic* properties of individual brain events.[8] *Thus the possibility is entirely open that some of these brain events* just are *our twinges of pain, our feelings of joy and sorrow, our thoughts that two plus two equals four, etc.* Such a brain event would, of course, "share"[9] all of its properties with the mental event which it *is*—all "essential" properties and all "accidental" properties, all intrinsic properties and all causal properties, etc., etc. By now, I hope, this is no more mysterious than the fact that the 51-year-old brother of Billy Carter "shares" all of his properties, be they accidental, essential, intrinsic, relational, etc., with the present (February 1977) president of the United States.

Well, perhaps it *is somewhat* more mysterious, for reasons to be discussed in a moment. But first it should be emphasized that the materialist has the matter entirely backwards and reversed: there is no need whatever to replace mentalistic terms with "topic-neutral" ones. For, I hold, premise (2) is correct: we *do* know (*by acquaintance*) the intrinsic nature of our mental events, i.e., we know *what* the "topic" of discourse about mental events *is.* On the other hand, we do not have this kind of knowledge about anything in the nonmental realm, i.e., we reject premise (1) insofar as it pertains to the intrinsic nature of the entities involved. Therefore, with one kind of exception, we *must* refer to physical events in a *topic-neutral* manner, unless we are willing to introduce a certain amount of confusion and unnecessary puzzlement.[10] We can refer to such physical events only with descriptions or with terms whose reference has been fixed by means of descriptions or by other *topic-neutral,* nonostensive means.[11] This is not, of course, a "disappearance" or "replacement" view of the physical. It is just that our references to physical events by means of *topic-neutral designators* is an explicit signal of our ignorance of their intrinsic nature—our ignorance as to *what* such physical entities *are.* It is a reminder that our knowledge of them is limited to their causal and other structural properties. The kind of exception to all this mentioned above is comprised by those physical events that are mental events.

I have been trying to remove, layer by layer, the obstacles that stand in the way of maintaining a mind–brain identity thesis—emphasizing along the way the untenability of accomplishing this by means of antimentalist stratagems such as materialism. So far the task has been relatively easy, if somewhat tedious and repetitive due to the fact that layers tend to overlap each other. We approach now what is perhaps the last and certainly the thickest and most formidable layer. This difficulty arises from our rejection, or, rather from our *qualified* acceptance, of premise (1). We agreed that (physical[12]) science provides us with the best information that we have about the structure of the physical realm, including the structure of the brain. But, we insist, science is in the main completely silent about the intrinsic, qualitative properties exemplified by physical events.[13] The difficulty is two-fold: (a) Science does seem, sometimes, to deal explicitly with intrinsic properties. For example, we certainly seem to be dealing directly with intrinsic properties when we say that electrons are negatively charged—indeed, that each electron has a charge of 4.8×10^{-10} e.s.u. It would appear that having a negative electrical charge of 4.8×10^{-10} e.s.u. is an intrinsic property of an electron; moreover, *being an electron* seems to be an intrinsic property. (b) The structures exemplified in our (private) experience, i.e., the structures we know by "acquaintance," are prima

facie quite different from any known *or* hypothesized brain structures—from any structures exemplified in brain events. If these differences are actual rather than merely apparent, then the identity thesis is refuted: *unless each mental event "shares" all of its properties, both intrinsic and structural with some brain event, identity cannot hold.*

The first difficulty is not serious. *To be an electron* is to play a certain kind of *causal* (and/or otherwise *structural*) role: or more precisely, the reference of the term 'electron' is fixed (ontologically) by specifying the positions that electrons occupy in causal-structural networks. Similarly the reference of 'having a negative charge of 4.8×10^{-10} e.s.u.' is (ontologically) fixed by the causal-structural role played by such charges. However, the reference of such terms is not (to this date) *epistemically determined.* The terms *do* refer to intrinsic properties, but we do not know *what* the referents *are,* e.g., we do not know what a negative electrical charge *is*—just as we did not know what heat *was* until we discovered that molecular motion caused heat sensation. (Actually, just as we do not know what an electron *is,* we *still* don't know what heat [alias molecular motion] *is.* We just know more about its causal roles than we used to.) Our earlier statement that physical science provides us with knowledge of structural properties but not with knowledge of intrinsic properties was an oversimplification: science *does* assert the *existence* of instances of a variety of intrinsic properties; moreover, it provides information about the various causal-structural roles that such instances play. However, it *does* leave us completely ignorant as to *what* these intrinsic properties *are.* This crucial matter calls for repeated emphasis: physics, chemistry, physiology, etc., leave us entirely ignorant about the intrinsic nature of physical entities in general and of brain events in particular; the physical sciences, properly construed, do refer to intrinsic properties, but they do so via *topic-neutral* designators—designators that leave us entirely in the dark as to *what* their referents *are;* their referents remain epistemically *unde*termined. This disposes of the first difficulty, (a). For it leaves entirely open the possibility that some brain events just *are* events such as the occurrence of a twinge of pain, the occurrence of a red expanse in the visual field, thinking that two plus two equals four, and exemplification of other intrinsic properties that characterize our experience (our "mental processes"). This consequence that (at least) *a portion of the physical realm may be intrinsically mental* must be entertained in complete literalness by anyone who wishes to entertain seriously a genuine mind–brain identity thesis.

What the statement of the second difficulty, (b), amounts to is a somewhat more precise statement of the "grain objection" referred to in footnote 5. The objection asks, for example, how is it that the occurrence of a smooth, continuous expanse of red in our visual experience can be identical with a brain process that must, it would seem, involve particulate, discontinuous affairs such as transfers of or interactions among large numbers of electrons, ions, or the like? Surely being smooth or continuous is a *structural* property, and being particulate or discontinuous is also a structural property, one moreover that is incompatible with being smooth and continuous. This strongly suggests, the objection continues, that at least some mental events exemplify structural properties that are not exemplified by any brain event, or, at any rate, not in any brain event that is an otherwise feasible candidate for being identical with the mental event. It follows that the mental event and the brain event do not share all of their (structural) properties, and thus, the objector concludes, they cannot be identical.

The difficulty is genuine and crucial. Unless there is good reason to hope that it can be overcome, there is no good reason to hope that mind–brain identity is possible. This difficulty is not, however, the one that has been the main concern of this paper, which has been the difficulty posed by Kripke. Nevertheless our answer to Kripke's challenge has emphasized the indirectness, the abstractness, and the incompleteness of our knowledge of the physical realm, and reflection upon this makes the "grain objection" appear—to me, at least—somewhat less formidable. It is true that we have not, in principle, set any limits on the scope of our knowledge about the structure of the physical realm; but the indirect, highly theoretical nature of such knowledge strongly suggests that it *is* quite incomplete and imperfect. There are also strong independent grounds for the same conclusion. Surely very few historians, philosophers, and practitioners of the physical sciences believe that our knowledge of the structure of the manifold of physical events is nearing perfection or completeness. For example, what many consider to be the unsatisfactory status of the foundations of quantum theory may well be due to crucial gaps in our knowledge of structure at the micro-level; and perhaps it is not too fanciful to suspect that the failure to integrate quantum theory and general relativity is due in part to a lack of knowledge of structures of causal networks that are somewhere between the very small ones and the very large ones. Perhaps it is precisely this "middle-sized" realm that provides the relevant context for investigation of mind–brain identities. In sum, as our knowledge grows about the various manifolds of events that constitute the physical realm, perhaps we shall discover that some of the structures that are exemplified by them *are* entirely isomorphic and quite possibly identical with instances of the structures with which we are acquainted in our "private" experience.

Even within the bounds of present physical theory, we might consider a fanciful but logically coherent possibility. Fields—electrical, magnetic, or gravitational—and fluctuations in fields are, *as far as their structures are concerned,* viable candidates for identification with (some kinds of) mental states or mental events. There are, no doubt, strong objections against supposing that, say a fluctuation in an electrical field could be a mental event (such as a twinge of pain). However, such objections could not be based on a difference in structure or "grain"; as far as I can see, such a fluctuation could be entirely isomorphic in all respects with a twinge of pain. The identity theorist must hope that continued developments in physics, neurophysiology, etc., will make manifest the existence of physical entities that have such appropriate structures and that are also otherwise more feasible candidates for being identified with mental entities.

Fortunately some neurophysiologists and neuropsychologists are devoting detailed attention to these problems. For example, the holographic theories of Pribram and others represent attempts to incorporate the structural features of mental functions (e.g., memory) and the structural features of brain processes into *one* (self-identical!) model (Pribram, Baron, & Nuwer, 1974). More accurately, they attempt to describe models in which the structural properties that characterize brain processes are ("also") structural properties of mental functions, and conversely. In other words, they are searching for a model such that, in any given case, there is only *one* process (or function), and it is both a brain process and a mental process.

Whether or not the holographic approach will

survive long-range investigation is not a matter about which I would care to forecast, even if I felt competent about its details. It does seem clear that this general *kind* of approach is a necessary condition for significant future development and progress in dealing with mind–body problems. A model such as the holographic one should, obviously, warm the heart of an identity theorist. If it turned out to be "successful"—if it stood up to experimental testing, successfully predicted startling new experimental outcomes, etc.—this would provide a considerable degree of confirmation (by no means conclusive, of course) of the identity thesis.

Let us suppose the holographic model turned out to be unsuccessful. Would this refute or "falsify" the identity thesis? Would it even count very strongly against it (strongly disconfirm it)? Both questions must be answered, I believe, in the negative. This seems to me an instance of a kind of methodological situation that frequently obtains in scientific inquiry, a situation such that positive experimental results would strongly confirm the hypothesis being tested but such that negative results, far from refuting the hypothesis (pace Popper), would disconfirm it only very slightly. (For discussion of a notorious example, the experimental "detection" of the neutrino, see Maxwell, 1974.) It is true that, if there followed *repeated* failures of *other* various identity theoretic models in addition to failure of the holographic model, then the identity thesis would begin to be appreciably, perhaps strongly, disconfirmed, especially if all of this were accom-

panied by impressive successes of dualistic models. I mention this matter to illustrate the complexity of the relationships between experimental evidence and contingent scientific (cum philosophical) problems *such as the mind–body problem!* I have discussed this in some detail in Maxwell 1976; and I argue there that it leads to the conclusion that, in several of the traditional problem areas, the mind–body problem being a prime example, there is no sharp line or very helpful distinction between scientific inquiry and philosophical inquiry. In other words, philosophical investigation is *not* exhausted without remainder by logical, conceptual, and linguistic considerations however important, difficult, and interesting these may be. For this very general reason coupled with more specific ones such as the "grain" problem just discussed, I do not believe that philosophers are going to contribute a great deal more to the "solutions" of mind–brain issues until they attain something close to specialists' competence in neurophysiology, neuropsychology, etc. I am willing to go one step further and predict that the next important breakthrough, if it comes at all, will come from the neurosciences. On the other hand, the neuroscientists will probably not contribute much either unless they understand and appreciate the logical, conceptual and, *yes* (!), the contingent components of the "mind–body problem" that have concerned philosophers over the centuries. The work of Kripke that we have been considering provides valuable, fresh perspectives on these crucial components.

NOTES

This research was supported in part by the National Science Foundation and the Minnesota Center for Philosophy of Science of the University of Minnesota.

1. In subsequent references to Kripke, page numbers refer to his 1972 essay.
2. Cf. Thomas Nagel, 1974.
3. Kripke directs his arguments mainly against "type-type" mental–physical identities and says that advocates of "token-token" identities are perhaps partially immune to his criticism. The reason for the immunity is not clear to me. However, I shall also consider, in the main, type-type identities. Absolving them of Kripke's charges will also absolve token-token identities, since these are entailed by the type-type ones.
4. Although, as indicated earlier, being a brain event *is* an essential property of *being* a brain event; and being a brain event *is* an essential property of *being* a brain event of a specific kind. Also, being a pain is *never* an essential property of *being* a specific kind

of brain event. Again, all of this is true simply because it is *necessarily* true that all neurophysiological roles are neurophysiological roles, but it is not necessarily true that pain plays any neurophysiological role at all.

5. The "grain" objection, attributed to Wilfrid Sellars (1965) and elaborated by Paul E. Meehl (1966), is a special case of this objection.
6. You should pardon the expression!
7. *Physicalism* because to be a physical event is to have a locus in the spatio-temporal causal network.
8. The claim is a general one, holding out only for the brain but for all physical systems. See, e.g., Russell, 1948, and Maxwell, 1970.
9. The word 'share' is put in "shudder quotes" because what we are talking about, of course, is a thing "sharing" all of its properties with itself. This seems to be a somewhat atypical way of talking. The same is true of saying that if "two [!] things" are identical, "they" "share" all of "their" properties, etc. All of

this results, does it not, because reflexive relations, especially identities, are somewhat atypical?

10. In most of our practical, everyday discourse, such confusion does not, of course, arise. In such contexts, there is no more need to reform our customary beliefs and modes of reference than there would be to replace, in most of its uses, the word 'salt' with the words 'sodium chloride' on the grounds that common table salt, sodium chloride, is just one out of thousands of kinds of salts, most of which are inedible and poisonous.

11. In a full-scale program, such reference-fixing can be accomplished systematically by using either Ram-

sey sentences or model-theoretic techniques. See Maxwell, 1970.

12. Psychology and some social sciences, properly conducted, do deal explicitly with intrinsic as well as structural properties.

13. This paper cannot provide a systematic account of the distinction between intrinsic and structural properties. I *have* made preliminary efforts in this direction in Maxwell, 1970. I believe that the examples used here, however, coupled with our commonsense grasp of the distinction, will be sufficient for the purposes of this paper.

REFERENCES

Carnap, R. Meaning postulates. *Philosophical Studies,* 1952, 3, 65–73.

Carnap, R. Beobachtungsprache und theoretische sprache. *Dialectica,* 1957, 12, 236–48.

Feigl, H. Matter still largely material. *Philosophy of Science,* 1962, 29, 39–46.

Feyerabend, P. K. Materialism and the mind-body problem. *Review of Metaphysics,* 1963, 17, 46–64.

Hanson, N. R. The dematerialization of matter. *Philosophy of Science,* 1962, 29, 27–38.

Kripke, S. Naming and necessity. In D. Davidson & G. Harman (Eds.), *Semantics of natural language.* Boston and Dordrecht: Reidel, 1972.

Kripke, S. Identity and necessity. In M. Munitz (Ed.), *Identity and individuation.* New York: New York University Press, 1971.

Maxwell, G. Meaning postulates in scientific theories. In H. Feigl & G. Maxwell (Eds.), *Current issues in the philosophy of science.* New York: Holt, Rinehart, & Winston, 1961.

Maxwell, G. Structural realism and the meaning of theoretical terms. In M. Radner & S. Winokur (Eds.), *Analyses of theories and methods of physics and psychology: Minnesota studies in the philosophy of science* (Vol. 4). Minneapolis: University of Minnesota Press, 1970.

Maxwell, G. Russell on perception: A study in philosophical method. In D. Pears (Ed.), *Bertrand Russell: A collection of critical essays.* New York: Doubleday (Anchor Paperbacks), 1972.

Maxwell, G. Corroboration with demarcation. In P. A. Schlipp (Ed.), *The philosophy of Karl Popper.* LaSalle, Ill.: Open Court, 1974.

Maxwell, G. Scientific results and the mind–brain issue:

Some afterthoughts. In G. Globus, G. Maxwell, & I. Savodnik (Eds.), *Consciousness and the brain: A scientific and philosophical inquiry.* New York: Plenum Press, 1976.

Meehl, P. E. The compleat autocerebroscopists: A thought experiment on Professor Feigl's mind-body identity thesis. In P. K. Feyerabend & G. Maxwell (Eds.), *Mind, matter, and method: Essays in philosophy and science in honor of Herbert Feigl.* Minneapolis: University of Minnesota Press, 1966.

Nagel, T. What is it like to be a bat? *Philosophical Review,* 1974, 83, 435–50.

Pribram, K. H., Baron, R., & Nuwer, M. The holographic hypothesis of memory in brain function and perception. In R. C. Atkinson, D. H. Krantz, R. C. Luce, & P. Suppes, (Eds.), *Contemporary developments in mathematical psychology.* San Francisco: W. H. Freeman, 1974.

Rorty, R. Mind-body identity, privacy, and categories. *Review of Metaphysics,* 1965, 19, 24–54.

Russell, B. *Human knowledge: Its scope and limits.* New York: Simon & Schuster, 1948.

Russell, B. *Portraits from memory.* New York: Simon & Schuster, 1956.

Schlick, M. *General theory of knowledge* (Albert E. Blumberg, trans.). Vienna and New York: Springer-Verlag, 1974.

Sellars, W. S. The identity approach to the mind–body problem. *Review of Metaphysics,* 1965, 18, 430–51.

Shaffer, J. Could mental states be brain processes? *Journal of Philosophy,* 1961, 58, 812–22.

Smart, J. J. C. Sensations and brain processes. *Philosophical Review,* 1959, 68, 141–56.

D. The Explanatory Gap

Materialism and Qualia
35 | The Explanatory Gap

Joseph Levine

In "Naming and Necessity"[1] and "Identity and Necessity,"[2] Kripke presents a version of the Cartesian argument against materialism. His argument involves two central claims: first, that all identity statements using rigid designators on both sides of the identity sign are, if true at all, true in all possible worlds where the terms refer; second, that psycho-physical identity statements are conceivably false, and therefore, by the first claim, actually false.

My purpose in this paper is to transform Kripke's argument from a metaphysical one into an epistemological one. My general point is this. Kripke relies upon a particular intuition regarding conscious experience to support his second claim. I find this intuition important, not least because of its stubborn resistance to philosophical dissolution. But I don't believe this intuition supports the meta-physical thesis Kripke defends—namely, that psycho-physical identity statements must be false. Rather, I think it supports a closely related epistemological thesis—namely, that psycho-physical identity statements leave a significant *explanatory gap,* and, as a corollary, that we don't have any way of determining exactly which psycho-physical identity statements are true.[3] One cannot conclude from my version of the argument that materialism is false, which makes my version a weaker attack than Kripke's. Nevertheless, it does, if correct, constitute a problem for materialism, and one that I think better captures the uneasiness many philosophers feel regarding that doctrine.

I will present this epistemological argument by starting with Kripke's own argument and extracting the underlying intuition. For brevity's sake, I am going to assume knowledge of Kripke's general position concerning necessity and the theory of reference, and concentrate only on the argument against materialism. To begin with, let us assume that we are dealing with a physicalist type-identity theory. That is, our materialist is committed to statements like:

(1) Pain is the firing of C-fibers.

On Kripke's general theory, if (1) is true at all it is necessarily true. The same of course, is the case with the following statement:

(2) Heat is the motion of molecules.

That is, if (2) is true at all it is necessarily true. So far so good.

The problem arises when we note that, with both (1) and (2), there is a felt contingency about them. That is, it seems conceivable that they be false. If they are necessarily true, however, that means there is no possible world in which they are false. Thus, imagining heat without the motion of molecules, or pain without the firing of C-fibers, must be to imagine a logically impossible world. Yet these suppositions *seem* coherent enough. Kripke responds that the felt contingency of (2) can be satisfactorily explained away, but that this can't be done for (1). Thus, there is an important difference between psycho-physical identities and other theoretical identities, and this difference makes belief in the former implausible.

The difference between the two cases is this. When it seems plausible that (2) is contingent, one can become disabused of this notion by noting that instead of imagining *heat* without the motion of molecules, one is really imagining there being some phenomenon that affects our senses the way heat in fact does, but is not the motion of molecules. The truly contingent statement is not (2) but

From *Pacific Philosophical Quarterly* 64:354–61, 1983. Reprinted with permission of author and publisher. Addendum excerpted from "On Leaving Out What It's Like," in M. Davies & G. Humphreys, eds., *Consciousness* (Blackwell, 1993), with permission of author and publisher.

(2′) The phenomenon we experience through the sensations of warmth and cold, which is responsible for the expansion and contraction of mercury in thermometers, which causes some gases to rise and others to sink, etc., is the motion of molecules.

However, this sort of explanation will not work for (1). When we imagine a possible world in which a phenomenon is experienced as pain but we have no C-fibers, that is a possible world in which there *is* pain without there being any C-fibers. This is so, argues Kripke, for the simple reason that the experience of pain, the sensation of pain, counts as pain itself. We cannot make the distinction here, as we can with heat, between the way it appears to us and the phenomenon itself. Thus, we have no good account of our intuition that (1) is contingent, unless we give up the truth of (1) altogether.

Now, there are several responses available to the materialist. First of all, the most popular materialist view nowadays is functionalism, which is not committed to even the contingent truth of statements like (1). Rather than identifying types of mental states with types of physical states, functionalists identify the former with types of functional, or what Boyd calls "configurational" states.[4] Functional states are more abstract than physical states, and are capable of realization in a wide variety of physical constitutions. In terms of the computer metaphor, which is behind many functionalist views, our mentality is a matter of the way we are "programmed," our "software," whereas our physiology is a matter of our "hardware." On this view, the intuition that pain could exist without C-fibers is explained in terms of the multiple realizability of mental states. This particular dilemma, then, doesn't appear to arise for functionalist materialists.

However, this reply won't work. First of all, a Kripke-style argument can be mounted against functionalist identity statements as well. Ned Block, in "Troubles with Functionalism,"[5] actually makes the argument. He asks us to imagine any complete functionalist description of pain (embedded, of course, in a relatively complete functionalist psychological theory). Though we have no idea as yet exactly what this description would be, insofar as it is a *functionalist* description, we know roughly what form it would take. Call this functionalist description "F." Then functionalism entails the following statement:

(3) To be in pain is to be in state F.

Again, on Kripke's theory of reference, (3) is necessarily true if true at all. Again, it seems imaginable that in some possible world (perhaps even in the actual world) (3) is false. Block attempts to persuade us of this by describing a situation where some object is in F but it is doubtful that it is in pain. For instance, suppose F were satisfied by the entire nation of China—which, given the nature of functional descriptions, is logically possible. Note that all the argument requires is that it should be *possible* that the entire nation of China, while realizing F, not be in pain. This certainly does seem possible.

Furthermore, some adherents of functionalism have moved back toward physicalist reductionism for qualia, largely in response to considerations like those put forward by Block. The idea is this. What Block's example seems to indicate is that functional descriptions are just *too* abstract to capture the essential features of qualitative sensory experiences. The so-called "inverted spectrum" argument—which involves the hypothesis that two people could share functional descriptions yet experience different visual qualia when viewing the same object—also points up the excessive abstractness of functional descriptions. Now one way some functionalists propose to deal with this problem is to return to a physicalist type-identity theory for sensory qualia, or at least for particular kinds of sensory qualia.[6] The gist of the latter proposal is this. While it's sufficient for being conscious (for having qualia at all) that an entity realize the appropriate functional description, the particular way a qualitative state is experienced is determined by the nature of the physical realization. So if, while looking at a ripe McIntosh apple, I experience the visual quality normally associated with looking at ripe McIntosh apples, and my inverted friend experiences the quality normally associated with looking at ripe cucumbers, this has to do with the difference in our physical realizations of the same functional state. Obviously, if we adopt this position Kripke's original argument applies.

So far, then, we see that the move to functionalism doesn't provide materialists with a way to avoid the dilemma Kripke poses: either bite the bullet and deny that (1), or (3), is contingent, or give up materialism. Well, what about biting the bullet? Why not just say that, intuition notwithstanding, statements like (1) and (3) are not contingent? In fact, Kripke himself, by emphasizing the gulf between epistemological possibility and metaphysical possibility, might even seem to give the materialist the ammunition she needs to attack the legitimacy of the appeal to this intuition. For what seems intuitively to be the case is, if anything, merely an epistemological matter. Since epistemological possibility is not sufficient for metaphysical possibility, the fact that what is intuitively contingent turns out to be metaphysically necessary should not bother us terribly. It's to be expected.

In the end, of course, one can just stand pat and say that. This is why I don't think Kripke's argument is entirely successful. However, I do think the intuitive resistance to materialism brought out by Kripke (and Block) should not be shrugged off as *merely* a matter of epistemology. Though clearly an epistemological matter, I think this intuitive resistance to materialism should bother us a lot. But before I can defend this claim, the intuition in question requires some clarification.

First of all, let's return to our list of statements. What I want to do is look more closely at the difference between statement (2) on the one hand, and statements (1) and (3) on the other. One difference between them, already noted, was the fact that the felt contingency of (2) could be explained away while the felt contingency of the others could not. But I want to focus on another difference, one which I think underlies the first one. Statement (2), I want to say, expresses an identity that is *fully explanatory,* with nothing crucial left out. On the other hand, statements (1) and (3) do seem to leave something crucial unexplained, there is a "gap" in the explanatory import of these statements. It is this explanatory gap, I claim, which is responsible for their vulnerability to Kripke-type objections. Let me explain what I mean by an "explanatory gap."

What is explanatory about (2)? (2) states that heat is the motion of molecules. The explanatory force of this statement is captured in statements like (2′) above. (2′) tells us by what mechanism the causal functions we associate with heat are effected. It is explanatory in the sense that our knowledge of chemistry and physics makes intelligible how it is that something like the motion of molecules could play the causal role we associate with heat. Furthermore, antecedent to our discovery of the essential nature of heat, its causal role, captured in statements like (2′), exhausts our notion of it. Once we understand how this causal role is carried out there is nothing more we need to understand.

Now, what is the situation with (1)? What is explained by learning that pain is the firing of C-fibers? Well, one might say that in fact quite a bit is explained. If we believe that part of the concept expressed by the term "pain" is that of a state which plays a certain causal role in our interaction with the environment (e.g. it warns us of damage, it causes us to attempt to avoid situations we believe will result in it, etc.), (2) explains the mechanisms underlying the performance of these functions. So, for instance, if penetration of the skin by a sharp metallic object excites certain nerve endings, which in turn excite the C-fibers, which then causes various avoidance mechanisms to go into effect, the causal role of pain has been explained.

Of course, the above is precisely the functionalist story. Obviously, there is something right about it. Indeed, we do feel that the causal role of pain is crucial to our concept of it, and that discovering the physical mechanism by which this causal role is effected explains an important facet of what there is to be explained about pain. However, there is more to our concept of pain than its causal role, there is its qualitative character, how it feels; and what is left unexplained by the discovery of C-fiber firing is *why pain should feel the way it does!* For there seems to be nothing about C-fiber firing which makes it naturally "fit" the phenomenal properties of pain, any more than it would fit some other set of phenomenal properties. Unlike its functional role, the identification of the qualitative side of pain with C-fiber firing (or some property of C-fiber firing) leaves the connection between it and what we identify it with completely mysterious. One might say, it makes the way pain feels into merely a brute fact.

Perhaps my point is easier to see with the example above involving vision. Let's consider again what it is to see green and red. The physical story involves talk about the various wavelengths detectable by the retina, and the receptors and processors that discriminate among them. Let's call the physical story for seeing red "R" and the physical story for seeing green "G." My claim is this. When we consider the qualitative character of our visual experiences when looking at ripe McIntosh apples, as opposed to looking at ripe cucumbers, the difference is not explained by appeal to G and R. For R doesn't really explain why I have the one kind of qualitative experience—the kind I have when looking at McIntosh apples—and not the other. As evidence for this, note that it seems just as easy to imagine G as it is to imagine R underlying the qualitative experience that is in fact associated with R. The reverse, of course, also seems quite imaginable.

It should be clear from what's been said that it doesn't help if we actually identify qualia with their functional roles. First of all, as I mentioned above, some functionalists resist this and prefer to adopt some form of type-physicalism for qualia. So when seeking the essence of how it feels to be in a certain functional state, they claim we must look to the essence of the physical realization. Secondly, even if we don't take this route, it still seems that we can ask why the kind of state that performs the function performed by pain, whatever its physical basis, should *feel* the way pain does. The analogous question regarding heat doesn't feel compelling. If someone asks why the motion of molecules plays the physical role it does, one can properly reply that an understanding of chemistry and physics is all that is needed to answer that question. If one objects that the phenomenal properties we associate with heat are not explained by identifying it with the motion of molecules, since being the motion of molecules seems compatible with all sorts of phenomenal properties, this just reduces to the problem under discussion. For it is precisely phenomenal properties—how it is for us to be in certain mental (including perceptual) states— which seem to resist physical (including functional) explanations.

Of course, the claim that (1) and (3) leave an explanatory gap in a way that (2) doesn't cannot be made more precise than the notion of explanation itself. Obviously, the D-N model of explanation is not sufficient for my purposes, since (1) and (3) presumably support counterfactuals and could be used, along with other premises, to deduce all sorts of particular facts.[7] What we need is an account of what it is for a phenomenon to be made *intelligible,* along with rules which determine when the demand for further intelligibility is inappropriate. For instance, I presume that the laws of gravity explain, in the sense at issue here, the phenomena of falling bodies. There doesn't seem to be anything "left out." Yet I am told that the value of G, the gravitational constant, is not derived from any basic laws. It is a given, a primitive, brute fact about the universe. Does this leave us with a feeling that something which ought to be explained is not? Or do we expect that some facts of nature should appear arbitrary in this way? I am inclined to take the latter attitude with respect to G. So, one may ask, why does the connection between what it's like to be in a particular functional (or physical) state and the state itself demand explanation, to be made intelligible?

Without a theoretical account of the notion of intelligibility I have in mind, I can't provide a really adequate answer to this question. Yet I think there are ways to at least indicate why it is reasonable to seek such an explanation. First of all, the phenomenon of consciousness arises on the macroscopic level. That is, it is only highly organized physical systems which exhibit mentality. This is of course what one would expect if mentality were a matter of functional organization. Now, it just seems odd that primitive facts of the sort apparently presented by statements like (1) and (3) should arise at this level of organization. Materialism, as I understand it, implies explanatory reductionism of at least this minimal sort: that for every phenomenon not describable in terms of the fundamental physical magnitudes (whatever they turn out to be), there is a mechanism that is describable in terms of the fundamental physical magnitudes such that occurrences of the former are intelligible in terms of occurrences of the latter. While this minimal reductionism does not imply anything about the reducibility of theories like psychology to physics, it does imply that brute facts—of the sort exemplified by the value of G—will not arise in the domain of theories like psychology.

Furthermore, to return to my original point, the claim that statements (1) and (3) leave an explanatory gap accounts for their apparent contingency, and, more importantly, for the failure to explain away their apparent contingency in the standard way. After all, why is it that we can account for the apparent contingency of (2) in a theoretically and intuitively satisfactory manner, but not for that of (1) and (3)? Even if one believes that we don't have to take this intuitive resistance seriously, it is still legitimate to ask why the problem arises in these particular cases. As I claimed above, I think the difference in this regard between (2) on the one hand, and (1) and (3) on the other, is accounted for by the explanatory gap left by the latter as opposed to the former. Since this is the crucial connection between Kripke's argument and mine, let me belabor this point for a bit.

The idea is this. If there is nothing we can determine about C-fiber firing that explains why having one's C-fibers fire has the qualitative character that it does—or, to put it another way, if what it's particularly like to have one's C-fibers fire is not explained, or made intelligible, by understanding the physical or functional properties of C-fiber firings—it immediately becomes imaginable that there be C-fiber firings without the feeling of pain, and vice versa. We don't have the corresponding intuition in the case of heat and the motion of molecules—once we get clear about the right way to characterize what we imagine—because whatever there is to explain about heat is explained by its being the motion of molecules. So, how could it be anything else?

The point I am trying to make was captured by Locke[8] in his discussion of the relation between primary and secondary qualities. He states that the simple ideas which we experience in response to impingements from the external world bear no intelligible relation to the corpuscular processes underlying impingement and response. Rather, the two sets of phenomena—corpuscular processes and simple ideas—are stuck together in an arbitrary manner. The simple ideas go with their respective corpuscular configurations because God chose to so attach them. He could have chosen to do it differently. Now, so long as the two states of affairs seem arbitrarily stuck together in this way, imagination will pry them apart. Thus it is the non-intelligibility of the connection between the feeling of pain and its physical correlate that underlies the apparent contingency of that connection.

Another way to support my contention that psycho-physical (or psycho-functional) identity statements leave an explanatory gap will also serve to establish the corollary I mentioned at the beginning of this paper; namely, that even if some psycho-physical identity statements are true, we can't determine exactly which ones are true. The two claims, that there is an explanatory gap and that such identities are, in a sense, unknowable, are interdependent and mutually supporting. First I will show why there is a significant problem about our ever coming to know that statements like (1) are true, then I will show how this is connected to the problem of the explanatory gap.

So suppose, as a matter of fact, that having the feeling of pain is identical with being in a particular kind of physical state. Well, which physical state? Suppose we believed it to be the firing of C-fibers because that was the state we found to be correlated with the feeling of pain in ourselves. Now imagine we come across alien life which gives every behavioral and functional sign of sharing our qualitative states. Do they have the feeling of pain we have? Well, if we believed that to have that feeling is to have one's C-fibers fire, and if the aliens don't have firing C-fibers, then we must suppose that they can't have this feeling. But the problem is, even if it is true that creatures with physical constitutions radically different from ours do not share our qualitative states, how do we determine what measure of physical similarity/dissimilarity to use? That is, the fact that the feeling of pain is a kind of physical state, if it is, doesn't itself tell us how thickly or thinly to slice our physical kinds when determining which physical state it is identical to. For all we know, pain is identical to the disjunctive state, the firing of C-fibers *or* the opening of D-valves (the latter disjunct realizing pain [say] in creatures with a hydraulic nervous system).[9]

This objection may seem like the standard argument for functionalism. However, I am actually making a quite different argument. First of all, the same objection can be made against various forms of functionalist identity statements. That is, if we believe that to have the feeling of pain is to be in some functional state, what measure of functional similarity/dissimilarity do we use in judging whether or not some alien creature shares our qualitative states? Now, the more inclusive we make this measure, the more pressure we feel about questions of inverted qualia, and therefore the more reason we have to adopt a physicalist-reductionist position concerning particular kinds of qualia. This just brings us back where we started. That is, if having a radically different physical constitution is sufficient for having different qualia, there must be some fact of the matter about *how* different the physical constitution must be. But what possible evidence could tell between the hypothesis that the qualitative character of our pain is a matter of having firing C-fibers, and the hypothesis that it is a matter of having either firing C-fibers or opening D-valves?[10]

Now, if there were some intrinsic connection discernible between having one's C-fibers firing (or being in functional state F) and what it's like to be in pain, by which I mean that experiencing the latter was intelligible in terms of the properties of the former, then we could derive our measure of similarity from the nature of the explanation. Whatever properties of the firing of C-fibers (or being in state F) that explained the feel of pain would determine the properties a kind of physical (or functional) state had to have in order to count as feeling like our pain. But without this explanatory gap filled in, facts about the kind or the existence of phenomenal experiences of pain in creatures physically (or functionally) different from us become impossible to determine. This, in turn, entails that the truth or falsity of (1), while perhaps metaphysically factual, is nevertheless epistemologically inaccessible. This seems to be a very undesirable consequence of materialism.

There is only one way in the end that I can see to escape this dilemma and remain a materialist. One must either deny, or dissolve, the intuition which lies at the foundation of the argument. This would involve, I believe, taking more of an climinationist line with respect to qualia than many materialist philosophers are prepared to take. As I said earlier, this kind of intuition about our qualitative experience seems surprisingly resistant to philosophical attempts to eliminate it. As long as it remains, the mind/body problem will remain.[11]

ADDENDUM: FROM "ON LEAVING OUT WHAT IT'S LIKE"

. . . This difference between the two cases reflects an important epistemological difference between the purported reductions of water to H_2O and pain to the firing of C-fibres: namely, that the chemical theory of water explains what needs to be explained, whereas a physicalist theory of qualia still 'leaves something out.' It is because the qualitative character itself is left *unexplained* by the physicalist or functionalist theory that it remains conceivable that a creature should occupy the relevant physical or functional state and yet not experience qualitative character.

The basic idea is that a reduction should explain what is reduced, and the way we tell whether this has been accomplished is to see whether the phenomenon to be reduced is epistemologically necessitated by the reducing phenomenon, i.e. whether we can see why, given the facts cited in the reduction, things must be the way they seem on the surface. I claim that we have this with the chemical theory of water but not with a physical or functional theory of qualia. The robustness of the absent and inverted qualia intuitions is testimony to this lack of explanatory import.

Let me make the contrast between the reduction of water to H_2O and a physico-functional reduction of qualia more vivid. What is explained by the theory that water is H_2O? Well, as an instance of something that's explained by the reduction of water to H_2O, let's take its boiling point at sea level. The story goes something like this. Molecules of H_2O move about at various speeds. Some fast-moving molecules that happen to be near the surface of the liquid have sufficient kinetic energy to escape the intermolecular attractive forces that keep the liquid intact. These molecules enter the atmosphere. That's evaporation. The precise value of the intermolecular attractive forces of H_2O molecules determines the vapour pressure of liquid masses of H_2O, the pressure exerted by molecules attempting to escape into saturated air. As the average kinetic energy of the molecules increases, so does the vapour pressure. When the vapour pressure reaches the point where it is equal to atmospheric pressure, large bubbles form within the liquid and burst forth at the liquid's surface. The water boils.

I claim that given a sufficiently rich elaboration of the story above, it is inconceivable that H_2O should not boil at 212°F at sea level (assuming, again, that we keep the rest of the chemical world constant). But now contrast this situation with a physical or functional reduction of some conscious sensory state. No matter how rich the information processing or the neurophysiological story gets, it still seems quite coherent to imagine that all that should be going on without there being anything it's like to undergo the states in question. Yet, if the physical or functional story really explained the qualitative character, it would not be so clearly imaginable that the qualia should be missing. For, we would say to ourselves something like the following:

> Suppose creature X satisfies functional (or physical) description F. I understand—from my functional (or physical) theory of consciousness—what it is about instantiating F that is responsible for its being a conscious experience. So how could X occupy a state with those very features and yet *not* be having a conscious experience?

The Conceptual Basis of the Explanatory Gap

I have argued that there is an important difference between the identification of water with

H_2O, on the one hand, and the identification of qualitative character with a physico-functional property on the other. In the former case the identification affords a deeper understanding of what water is by explaining its behaviour. Whereas, in the case of qualia, the subjective character of qualitative experience is left unexplained, and therefore we are left with an incomplete understanding of that experience. The basis of my argument for the existence of this explanatory gap was the conceivability of a creature's instantiating the physico-functional property in question while not undergoing an experience with the qualitative character in question, or any qualitative character at all.

In order fully to appreciate the nature and scope of the problem, however, it is necessary to explore in more detail the basis of the explanatory adequacy of theoretical reductions such as that of water to H_2O, as well as the difference between these cases and the case of qualitative character. I can only begin that project here, with the following admittedly sketchy account. We will see that an adequate account must confront deep problems in the theory of conceptual content, thus drawing a connection between the issue of intentionality and the issue of consciousness.

Explanation and Reduction

To begin with, it seems clear that theoretical reduction is justified principally on the basis of its explanatory power. For instance, what justifies the claim that water is H_2O anyway? Well, we might say that we find a preponderance of H_2O molecules in our lakes and oceans, but of course that can't be the whole story. First of all, given all the impurities in most samples of water, this may not be true. Second, if we found that everything in the world had a lot of H_2O in it—suppose H_2O were as ubiquitous as protons—we wouldn't identify *water* with H_2O. Rather, we justify the claim that water is H_2O by tracing the causal responsibility for, and the explicability of, the various superficial properties by which we identify water—its liquidity at room temperature, its freezing and boiling points etc.—to H_2O.

But suppose someone pressed further, asking why being causally responsible for this particular syndrome of superficial properties should be so crucial.[12] Well, we would say, *what else* could it take to count as water? But the source of this 'what else' is obscure. In fact, I think we have to recognize an a priori element in our jus-

tification. That is, what justifies us in basing the identification of water with H_2O on the causal responsibility of H_2O for the typical behaviour of water is the fact that our very concept of water is of a substance that plays such-and-such a causal role. To adopt Kripke's terminology, we might say that our pretheoretic concept of water is characterizable in terms of a 'reference-fixing' description that roughly carves out a causal role. When we find the structure that in this world occupies that role, then we have the referent of our concept.

But now how is it that we get an explanation of these superficial properties from the chemical theory? Remember, explanation is supposed to involve a deductive relation between explanans and explanandum. The problem is that chemical theory and folk theory don't have an identical vocabulary, so somewhere one is going to have to introduce bridge principles. For instance, suppose I want to explain why water boils, or freezes, at the temperatures it does. In order to get an explanation of these facts, we need a definition of 'boiling' and 'freezing' that brings these terms into the proprietary vocabularies of the theories appealed to in the explanation.

Well, the obvious way to obtain the requisite bridge principles is to provide theoretical reductions of these properties as well.[13] To take another example, we say that one of water's superficial properties is that it is colourless. But being colourless is not a chemical property, so before we can explain why water is colourless in terms of the molecular structure of water and the way that such structures interact with light waves, we need to reduce colourlessness to a property like having a particular spectral reflectance function. Of course, the justification for this reduction will, like the reduction of water to H_2O, have to be justified on grounds of explanatory enrichment as well. That is, there are certain central phenomena we associate with colour, by means of which we pick it out, such that explaining those phenomena is a principal criterion for our acceptance of a theoretical reduction of colour.

The picture of theoretical reduction and explanation that emerges is of roughly the following form. Our concepts of substances and properties like water and liquidity can be thought of as representations of nodes in a network of causal relations, each node itself capable of further reduction to yet another network, until we get down to the fundamental causal determinants of nature. We get bottom-up necessity, and thereby explanatory force, from the identification of the macroproperties with the microproperties because the network of causal relations constitutive of the micro level realizes the network of causal relations constitutive of the macro level. Any concept that can be analysed in this way will yield to explanatory reduction.

Notice that on this view explanatory reduc-tion is, in a way, a two-stage process. Stage 1 involves the (relatively? quasi?) a priori process of working the concept of the property to be re-duced 'into shape' for reduction by identifying the causal role for which we are seeking the un-derlying mechanisms. Stage 2 involves the em-pirical work of discovering just what those un-derlying mechanisms are.[14] . . .

NOTES

1. Saul Kripke, "Naming and Necessity," reprinted in *Semantics of Natural Language,* second edition, ed-ited by Donald Davidson and Gilbert Harman, D. Reidel Publishing Co., 1972.
2. Saul Kripke, "Identity and Necessity," reprinted in *Naming, Necessity, and Natural Kinds,* edited by Stephen Schwartz, Cornell U. Press, 1977.
3. My argument in this paper is influenced by Thomas Nagel's in his paper "What Is It Like to Be a Bat?" (reprinted in *Readings in the Philosophy of Psychology,* volume 1, edited by Ned Block, Har-vard U. Press, 1980), as readers who are familiar with Nagel's paper will notice as it develops.
4. Richard Boyd, "Materialism without Reduction-ism," reprinted in *Readings in the Philosophy of Psychology,* volume 1.
5. Ned Block, "Troubles with Functionalism," reprint-ed in *Readings in the Philosophy of Psychology,* volume 1.
6. Cf. Sydney Shoemaker, "The Inverted Spectrum," *The Journal of Philosophy,* volume LXXIX, no. 7, July 1982.
7. To elaborate a bit, on the D-N model of explanation, a particular event *e* is explained when it is shown to be deducible from general laws together with what-ever description of the particular situation is rele-vant. Statements (1) and (3) could obviously be em-ployed as premises in a deduction concerning (say) someone's psychological state. Cf. Carl Hempel, "Aspects of Scientific Explanation," reprinted in Hempel, *Aspects of Scientific Explanation,* Free Press, 1968.
8. Cf. Locke, *An Essay Concerning Human Under-standing,* edited by J. Yolton, Everyman's Library, 1971 (originally published 1690); Bk. II, Ch. VIII, sec. 13, and Bk. IV, Ch. III, secs. 12 and 13.
9. This point is similar to an argument of Putnam's in the chapter of *Reason, Truth, and History* (Cam-bridge U. Press, 1981) entitled "Mind and Body." Putnam uses the argument to serve a different pur-pose from mine, however. The example of the hy-draulic nervous system is from David Lewis, "Mad Pain and Martian Pain," reprinted in *Readings in the Philosophy of Psychology,* volume 1.
10. Shoemaker, in "The Inverted Spectrum," op. cit. ex-plicitly tries to deal with this problem. He proposes a fairly complicated principle according to which dis-junctive states like the one mentioned in the text do not qualify for identification with (or realization of) qualitative states. I cannot discuss his principle in detail here. However, the main idea is that we look to the causal role of a quale for its individuation condi-tions. That is, if the causal effects of pain in human beings are explained by their C-fiber firings *alone,* then the state of having one's C-fibers fire *or* having one's D-valves open is not a legitimate candidate for the physical realization of pain. Viewed from the standpoint of my argument in this paper, Shoemak-er's principle begs the very question at issue; name-ly, whether the qualitative character of pain is ex-plained by its causal role. For if it isn't, there is no reason to presume that the identity conditions of the physical state causally responsible for pain's func-tional role would determine the presence or absence of a particular kind of qualitative character. So long as the nature of that qualitative character is not ex-plained by anything peculiar to any particular physi-cal realization of pain, we have no way of knowing whether or not a different physical realization of pain, in a different creature, is associated with the same qualitative character.
11. An earlier version of this paper, under the title "Qualia, Materialism, and the Explanatory Gap," was delivered at the APA Eastern Division meetings, 1982. I would like to thank Carolyn McMullen for her comments on that occasion. I would also like to thank Louise Antony, Hilary Putnam, and Susan Wolf for their helpful comments on even earlier versions.
12. Of course, it's possible to imagine situations in which we would accept a theory of water that never-theless left many of its superficial properties unex-plained. However, unless the theory explained at least some of these properties, it would be hard to say why we consider this a theory of *water.*
13. In some cases, for instance with properties such as liquidity and mass, it might be better to think of their theoretical articulations in physical and chemical theory more as a matter of incorporating and refining folk theoretic concepts than as a matter of reducing them. But this is not an idea I can pursue here.
14. To a certain extent my argument here is similar to Alan Sidelle's defence of conventionalism in *Neces-sity, Essence, and Individuation* (Cornell University Press, 1989) though I don't believe our positions co-incide completely.

36 | The Rediscovery of Light
Paul M. Churchland

There is a family of seven arguments advanced by John Searle urging the ontologically distinct and physically irreducible nature of conscious phenomena. These are joined by three arguments from Frank Jackson and David Chalmers which tend to the same conclusion. My aim in what follows is to construct systematic and unitary analogs of all ten arguments, analogs that support a parallel family of antireductive conclusions about the nature of light. Since those analogous conclusions are already known to be false in the case of light (its physicalist reduction is one of the many triumphs of electromagnetic theory), it becomes problematic whether the integrity of the original family of antireductionist arguments is any greater than the purely specious integrity of their deliberately constructed analogs.

I. A Searle-like Family of Arguments Concerning the Nature of Light

(A) A fundamental distinction:

original (intrinsic) visibility versus derivative (secondary) visibility

Only light itself has original visibility; for light alone is visible, when directed into the eyes, without the causal intervention of any mediating agent. By contrast, any physical object, physical configuration, or physical event is visible only when and only because light is somehow reflected from or emitted by that object, configuration, or event. Such physical items have at most *derivative* visibility, because they are utterly and forever *in*visible, save as they interact appropriately with the one thing that has *original* visibility, namely, light itself.

These conclusions reflect the obvious fact that, if the universe contained no light at all, then absolutely nothing would be visible, neither intrinsically nor derivatively.[1]

(B) The original visibility of light marks it off as belonging to a *unique ontological category,* distinct in its essential nature from the essential nature of any physical phenomenon, which must always *lack* original visibility. In other words, for any physical object, configuration, or event, it is always a contingent matter whether or not it happens to be visible on this occasion (it is a matter of whether or not it happens somehow to be illuminated). By contrast, light itself is always and essentially visible. The ontology of light is an ontology of things and features that are uniquely accessible from the visual point of view.

This means that the phenomenon of light must be *irreducible* to any complex of purely physical or not-essentially-visible phenomena. You simply cannot get *original* visibility from things that have, at most, derivative visibility.[2]

(C) The consequence just reached is denied by a celebrated research program called *Strong EM*. This program claims not only that light can be "instructively simulated" by the behavior of interacting electric and magnetic fields (to which all may agree); it makes the stronger claim that light is actually *identical with* electromagnetic (EM) waves. The folly of Strong EM can be seen in the following obviously sound argument.

1. Electricity and magnetism are physical forces.
2. The essential nature of light is original visibility.
3. Physical forces, no matter how they are deployed, are neither identical with, nor sufficient for, original visibility.

Therefore,

4. Electricity and magnetism are neither identical with, nor sufficient for, light.

Premises (1) and (2) are obvious. That premise (3) is obvious can be seen by the following thought experiment. According to EM theory, an oscillating magnet or charged particle will generate an expanding sphere of oscillating EM fields: an EM wavefront. And by the same theo-

From *Journal of Philosophy* 93:211–28, 1996. Reprinted with permission of author and publisher.

ry, this is strictly sufficient for the existence of light. But imagine a man in a pitch-black room who begins to pump a bar magnet back and forth. Clearly, it will do nothing to illuminate the room. The room will remain wholly devoid of light.[3]

(D) The ontologically distinct nature of light is further reflected in the fact that the distinction between (visual) appearance and reality, which holds for any broadly physical phenomenon, cannot be drawn in the case of light itself. It there disappears. For while light is an agent that typically *represents* the physical objects, configurations, or events from which it has been differentially reflected or emitted, light does not represent *itself.* It is neither reflected nor emitted from itself. It thus cannot possibly *mis*represent itself, as it may occasionally misrepresent things other than itself from which it has been reflected or emitted. Accordingly, where the reality at issue is light itself (as opposed to any and all physical phenomena), the appearance just *is* the reality.[4]

(E) The irreducibility here claimed can be further seen as follows. Suppose we tried to say that the redness or blueness of light was *nothing but* a specific wavelength of EM waves. Well, if we tried such an ontological reduction, the essential features of the light would be left out. No description of the extrinsic wavelengths of EM waves could possibly convey the intrinsic character of (objective) visible redness and visible blueness, for the simple reason that the *visible* properties of light are distinct from the *physical* properties of EM waves. This argument is ludicrously simple and quite decisive.[5]

(F) Light is always and necessarily visible: there can be no such thing as *invisible* light. Granted, not all light is visible at any given time or place: light can be "shallowly" invisible to me simply because its path does not lead into my eyes. But if light exists at all, then there is some perspective from which it will be directly visible. Let us call this *the connection principle,* since it unites (*i*) being light and (*ii*) being accessible-from-the-visual-point-of-view.[6]

(G) Considerations (A)–(F) indicate that light is a phenomenon that is ontologically distinct from and irreducible to any purely physical phenomena. And yet, while nonphysical in itself, light is plainly *caused* by certain special physical phenomena, such as very high temperatures or the electrical stimulation of gases. Let us call our position here *nonreductive physical naturalism:* it holds that light is a natural (but irre-

ducible) phenomenon caused to occur within certain special kinds of physical systems—specifically, within *self-luminous* objects, such as the sun, fires, and incandescent filaments. The aim of a scientific account of light should be to explain how such a nonphysical phenomenon is *caused* to occur within such highly special physical systems as stars and light bulbs.[7]

II. Three Jackson/Chalmers-like Arguments Concerning the Nature of Light

(H) In the study of the nature of light, there is a distinction to be drawn between the "easy" problems and "the hard problem." The first class concerns such problems as the emission, propagation, and absorption of light, its reflection and refraction, its velocity, its carrying energy, its self-interference, and so forth. These are all causal, relational, functional, and in general *extrinsic* features of light, features variously accessible by a wide variety of physical instruments and techniques; and it may well be that someday they will all be satisfactorily explained in terms of, for example, the propagation and interactions of EM fields.

But there remains a highly special *intrinsic* feature of light whose explanation must be found along some other path. This intrinsic feature is *luminance,* and it is what is responsible for the "original visibility" that is unique to light. Unlike all of the extrinsic (that is, physical) features of light listed above, luminance is unique in being epistemically accessible only from "the visual point of view."[8]

(I) We can illustrate and reinforce the contrast just drawn with a thought experiment about a physicist named Mary who is completely blind, but comes to know everything physical there is to know about EM waves, about their internal structure and their causal behavior. And yet, because she is blind and thus has no access at all to "the visual point of view," she cannot know about, she must remain ignorant of, the special intrinsic feature of light—luminance—which is accessible from that point of view alone. Evidently, even complete knowledge of the physical facts must still leave her ignorant of the nature of luminance. Luminance must therefore be, in some way, *non*physical.[9]

(J) As just illustrated, any possible physicalist story about the structure and causal functions of EM waves must still leave open an "explanatory gap" between the physical processes and luminance. In particular, it leaves unanswered the following question: Why should mutually-inducing electric and magnetic fields (for example) oscillating at a million billion Hertz and propagating at 300,000 km/sec ever give rise to the intrinsic feature of *luminance?* After all, we can easily imagine a universe that is filled with oscillating EM fields propagating back and forth all over the place, a universe that is nonetheless utterly *dark,* because it is devoid of the additional feature of luminance. We need to know how, when, and why oscillating EM fields *cause* the ontologically distinct feature of intrinsic luminance. Until we understand *that* mysterious causal relation, we shall never understand the ground and real nature of light.[10]

III. Critical Commentary

Concerning (A). As an exercise in term introduction ("original" visibility, and so on), this is strictly harmless, perhaps. But it falsely elevates an extremely peripheral feature of light—namely, its capacity to stimulate the idiosyncratic rods and cones of terrestrial animals—into a deep and presumptively defining feature of light. This is thrice problematic. First, it is arbitrarily selective. Second, it is strictly false that *only* light will stimulate rods and cones (charged particles of suitable energy will also do it, though at some cost to the retina). And third, infrared and ultraviolet light is quite *in*visible to terrestrial eyes. Our eyes evolved to exploit a narrow window of EM transparency in the earth's idiosyncratic atmosphere and oceans. Nothing of ontological importance need correspond to what makes our rods and cones sing.

Concerning (B). The dubious distinction legislated in (A) is here deployed to consign all physical phenomena to a class (things with merely derivative visibility) that *excludes* the phenomenon of light. This division certainly appeals to our default stereotype of a physical object (a tree, or a stone, has merely derivative visibility), but it begs the question against the research program of physicalism, because some unfamiliar physical things may indeed have original visibility, our common-sense expectations notwithstanding. As it turns out, EM waves with a wavelength between .4 and .7 μm are capable of stimulating the retina all by themselves, and thus have original visibility as defined in (A). The argument of (B) is thus a ques-

tion-begging exploitation of superficial stereotypes and EM ignorance.

Concerning (C). The crucial premise of this argument (premise 3) may seem highly plausible to those who have a common-sense prototype of forces and who are ignorant of the details of EM theory, but it plainly begs the central question against physicalism. (Premise 3 is the direct denial of the basic physicalist claim.) Moreover, it is false. As mentioned in the preceding paragraph, EM waves of suitable wavelength *are* sufficient for original visibility. The "Luminous Room" thought experiment, concerning the oscillating bar magnet in the pitch-black parlor, is designed specifically to make premise 3 plausible, but that prejudicial story illegitimately exploits the fact that some forms of EM radiation have wavelengths that are simply too long to *interact* effectively with the rods and cones of terrestrial retinas. The darkened parlor may *look* to be devoid of light, but, thanks to the oscillating magnet, a very weak form of light is there regardless.

Concerning (D). While superficially plausible, perhaps, this argument refuses to take into account the many ways in which we can be mistaken or misled about the character of the light entering our eyes (for example, the light from a cinema screen appears continuous, but is really discontinuous at 36 frames/sec; the light of an incandescent automobile headlight, while really yellowish, looks white at night; and so forth). Its brief plausibility is a reflection of nothing more than our unfamiliarity with how light is perceptually apprehended and with how that intricate process can occasionally produce false perceptual beliefs. It is a reflection of our own ignorance, rather than of any unique ontological status had by light.

Concerning (E). This argument is sheer question-begging assertion rather than instructive argument. Whether objective properties of light such as spectral redness or spectral blueness are identical with, or distinct from, specific wavelengths of EM radiation is precisely what is at issue. And in this case, it has been plain for a century that these properties are identical. It is also plain that spectral redness, spectral blueness, and their various causal properties—their refractive and absorptive behavior, their velocity and interference effects—are positively *explained*, rather than impotently "left out," by their smooth reduction to EM features.

The point about what an EM vocabulary can or cannot "convey" about certain perceptual properties is a distinct point (and a red herring) to be dealt with below in "*Concerning* (I)."

Concerning (F). This argument also would be found plausible by someone still imprisoned by prescientific prototypes of light. *Invisible light* may well be a conceptual impossibility against the assumptions of the story just told, but we now know better. Indeed, we have learned that *most* light is invisible—and not just "shallowly" invisible, but permanently beyond human visual apprehension. Once again, we find ignorance being paraded as positive knowledge.

Concerning (G). This summary attempts to find a proper place in nature for the phenomenon touted as ontologically distinct and physically irreducible in arguments (A)–(F). The place suggested is that of a nonphysical *causal* consequence of certain special but purely physical events.

Such a move threatens to violate well-established laws concerning the conservation of both energy and momentum, at least if light is presumed to have any causal powers of its own. But we need not enter into these matters here, for as the critical commentary to this point shows, there is no significant motivation for any such antireductionist research program in the first place. And in the second place, the proper place in nature of light has already been made clear: it has been smoothly and systematically reduced to EM waves.

Concerning (H). Light is here conceded to have a wide variety of physical features—its so-called "extrinsic" or "structural/functional" features—to which some sort of physical explanation is deemed appropriate. But light is also assigned an allegedly special or "intrinsic" feature, a feature that is epistemically accessible through vision, but not through the "structural/functional" stories to which current physical science (alas) is limited.

Once again, our prescientific noninferential epistemic access (namely, vision) to certain entirely physical properties is portrayed as a unique window onto an ontologically special domain. And to compound the felony further, the potential reach of physical explanation is restricted, by arbitrary fiat at the outset (rather than by any empirical failures revealed during the course of ongoing research), so as inevitably to fall short of the so-called "intrinsic" features within the "special" domain at issue.

The "hard problem" is thus *made* transcendently hard at the outset by presumptive and question-begging fiat, rather than by any sub-stantive considerations. As EM theory has taught us, *there is no* "hard problem" here at all, and no defensible ontological distinction between intrinsic and extrinsic features. "Luminance"—if we concede the integrity of this notion at all—is just the normal and entirely physical capacity of EM waves to excite our own rods and cones (and to induce chemical changes in photographic film, to free electrons in a television camera, and so forth).

Concerning (I). This "knowledge" argument equivocates on 'knows about.' It elevates two distinct modes of epistemic access to light into a false dichotomy of distinct phenomena thereby accessed—physical features by scientific description, and a special range of nonphysical features by normal human vision. But for light, at least, we know perfectly well that there is only one thing here rather than two, only one class of objective features rather than two.

What Blind Mary is missing is one common *form* of knowledge about light: she lacks perceptual/discriminative knowledge of light. And yet, people who have such knowledge are accessing the very same features of reality that she is obliged to access in other ways. The difference lies in the manner of the knowing, not in the nature of the thing(s) known. It is true that no amount of propositional knowledge of light will ever *constitute* the visual apprehension of light, but that is entirely to be expected. They are different forms of knowledge; they operate with different representational "palettes" inside Mary's brain. But they both represent, each in their own distinct way, one and the same entirely physical thing: light.

Our contemporary scientific knowledge about light aside, one can see immediately that the crucial divergence here is merely epistemic rather than ontological (as the argument pretends). For while it is indeed true that Blind Mary does not know what it is like to *see* spectral-red light, it is equally true, and for exactly the same reasons, that she does not know what it is like to *see* EM waves at .65 μm. The deficit here evidently lies with Mary and her epistemic failings, not with EM waves and their ontological shortcomings vis-à-vis light. For Mary would continue to have her deficit even if light *were* (as it is) identical with EM waves. Her deficit, therefore, can hardly weigh against that identity.

Concerning (J). This "open question" argument begs the question in favor of the ontological distinctness of "luminance," and then insists on our providing a *causal* account of how EM waves might produce it. This gets everything backward. We no longer have need for an account of how EM waves might "cause" the various phenomena associated with light, because the systematic reconstruction of optical phenomena within EM theory leads us to believe that light is simply identical with EM waves, and that the assembled properties of light are identical with, rather than caused by, the corresponding properties of EM waves.

The conceivability of a dark universe filled with EM waves shows only that the various cross-theoretic identities motivated by the EM reduction are, as they should be, contingent rather than necessary identities. It should also be pointed out that such an "open question" argument will be maximally appealing to one who is minimally instructed in EM theory. This is because the more one learns about EM waves, about their effects on matter in general and on our eyes in particular, the *harder* it becomes to imagine a consistent scenario in which a universe abuzz with EM waves of all wavelengths remains dark even so. Here, as in so many of the earlier arguments, the audience's presumed ignorance is once more a lubricant that smooths the path of a worthless argument.

This concludes my attempt to construct, and to deflate, a systematic analog for the family of arguments currently so influential in the philosophy of mind. My point, of course, is that the family of arguments on which they are modeled is just as empty of real virtue.

IV. A Final Nagel/Searle Argument for Irreducibility

A question will inevitably arise over the fairness of the global analogy deployed above. In particular, it will be complained that the global analogy is faulty in placing the *objective* properties of "original visibility" and "luminance" in the role played by the *subjective* properties of original intentionality and inner qualia in the arguments under attack.

The analogy deployed does indeed proceed in precisely this fashion, but this assimilation is the central point of the exercise. It should at least give us pause that the original family of arguments can be collectively and successfully mirrored in a ten-dimensional analogy that deliberately and self-consciously concerns "objective" features. After all, if the analog arguments are at all compelling—and to the electromagnetically uninformed, they will be—then the essential appeal of both families of arguments presumably derives from something other than the unique status of the "subjective."

Second, there is no mystery about what drives the plausibility of the analog arguments. It is the ignorance-fueled appeal of the idea that the epistemic modality of vision is or might be a unique window onto an ontologically distinct class of properties. But in the case of light it is also plain, at least in retrospect, that nothing substantive motivates that repeated insistence. We have to wonder if the same failure might be true of the original family of arguments. After all, and whatever else it might be, introspection *is* an epistemic modality, or perhaps a family of them. And while it may have its own quirks and distinguishing profile, it is entirely unclear whether it, alone among all of our epistemic modalities, constitutes a window onto a unique *ontological* domain of nonphysical properties. None of our other epistemic modalities has any such distinction: they all access some aspect or other of the purely physical world. Why should introspection be any different?

Searle has a further argument, unaddressed to this point, whose burden is to illustrate the ontological cleft he sees between the domain of "outer sense" and the domain of "inner sense," as Immanuel Kant called them. Searle's argument here appeals, uncharacteristically, to the history of science. The argument originally appeared, very briefly, in Thomas Nagel,[11] but Searle has more recently developed it in detail.

Premise (1). We must draw a distinction between the real and objective properties of objects and the contingent subjective effects those properties happen to have on the conscious processes of humans. For example, objective heat (molecular KE) is one thing; the subjective feeling of warmth in humans *produced by* objective heat is quite another.

Premise (2). The scientific reduction of observable phenomena typically ignores or "carves off" their contingent subjective effects on the conscious processes of humans, and reduces only the nonsubjective aspects of the phenomena. (For example, kinetic theory successfully reduces objective heat to molecular KE, but leaves its *subjective conscious effects* on humans aside. EM theory successfully reduces objective spectral colors to different wavelengths of EM radiation, but leaves their *subjective conscious effects* on humans aside. And so forth.)

Premise (3). When we attempt to provide a physicalistic reduction of those subjective conscious effects themselves, we must realize that here we *cannot* "carve off" their subjective-effects-on-us from their objective properties, and reduce only the latter, because it is precisely those subjective-effects-on-us which we wish to understand. Here, inside the mind, there is no longer any meaningful or defensible distinction between the "objective" and the "subjective" which would allow us to repeat the pattern of reduction described above. The subjective phenomena are exclusively and *essentially* subjective. Any alleged "reduction" would simply leave out what is essential to their nature.

Therefore, mental phenomena are irreducible to physical phenomena. The proper pattern of a physicalist reduction (an "objective"-to-"objective" mapping) uniquely precludes any reduction of the subjective.[12]

What is going on here? Simply this. The Nagel/Searle argument treats a contingent, minor, and remediable feature (of a handful of historical examples of reductions) as if it were a necessary, central, and permanent feature of any possible physicalistic reduction. Specifically, the merely contingent feature that is paraded as essential is the feature: *leaves aside the-effects-on-human-consciousness* (the "C-effects," for short). The argument then points out that this "essential" feature of physicalistic reduction precludes any such reduction in the unique case of C-effects themselves, since "leaving the C-effects aside" is here not an option.

It is indeed true that historical property reductions pay little or no attention to, or provide us with little or no insight into, the C-effects of the various phenomena being reduced. Searle and Nagel seem antecedently convinced that this historical fact is the inevitable reflection of an ontological gulf already fixed between "objective" phenomena and "subjective" phenomena.

That is one (distant) possibility. But there is an obvious alternative explanation of why physicalistic reductions so regularly leave out any account of the human C-effects of the phenomena being reduced, as the historical reduction of heat to molecular energy made no attempt to account for the subjective sensation of warmth, or as the historical reduction of light to EM waves made no attempt to account for the subjective sensation of redness.

The obvious alternative explanation is that *such C-effects are the proper province of a distinct science,* a science such as cognitive neuro-

biology or computational neuroscience. Searle is wrongly demanding that the kinetic theory of heat do, all by itself, something that clearly requires, in addition, an adequate theory of the brain. The fact is, during the late nineteenth century, we were too ignorant about neurobiology for the kinetic theory to suggest any worthwhile hypotheses about the human C-effects of molecular energy. It is no surprise, then, that physicists simply walked past that arcane problem, if it ever occurred to them to address it in the first place. The same is true for the EM theory of light and the problem of our subjective sensations of redness.

Accordingly, this incidental "leaving-aside" need have no metaphysical or ontological significance. This deflationary view is further encouraged by the fact that physicalistic reductions such as the kinetic theory also "leave aside" any explanatory account of millions of other phenomena, so there is no automatic reason to find any special significance in its ignoring of human C-effects in particular. If I may give several examples, historical reductions of heat typically leave aside any attempt to account for:

heat's effect on Antarctic anchovy production
heat's effect on bluebird-egg cholesterol
    levels
heat's effect on pneumonial infections
heat's effect on the Gross National Product
    of Peru
heat's effect on the rotting of vegetable
    matter
heat's effect on the conscious states of
    humans
(this list is extendible indefinitely)

The great reductions of classical and modern physics *typically* leave out any account of heat's (or light's, or sound's) effect on all of these things, and of millions more, because no reduction all by itself can presume to account for the ever-more-distant causal effects of its proprietary phenomena as they are progressively articulated into all possible causal domains. There are far too many domains, and causal understanding of the phenomena within those other domains will typically require the resources of further theories in addition to the theory that achieves the local reduction at issue.

It is in no way noteworthy or ontologically significant, then, that the kinetic theory of heat, all by itself, provides no account of any of the arcane phenomena listed above, nor of millions of others as well. In particular, it is neither note-worthy nor ontologically significant that the ki-netic theory of heat provides no account of the human conscious response to heat. This margin-al and idiosyncratic phenomenon has no more ontological significance than any of the other arcane phenomena just listed. And they all re-quire the resources of theories beyond the kinet-ic theory of heat to address them adequately. Specifically, heat's effect on

anchovy production needs ecology

egg cholesterol levels needs metabolic chemistry

pneumonia needs immunology and bacteriology

Peru's Gross National Product needs biology and economics

vegetable rotting needs bacteriology and cell chemistry

human conscious experience needs cognitive neurobiology

My counterclaim, then, against Nagel and Searle, is that it is *not* an essential feature of physicalistic reductions that they always "leave aside" human C-effects, or any of the many other effects cited. It is a merely contingent and wholly explicable fact that historical reductions have so far done so. It is not an essential pattern that all physicalistic reductions are doomed-by-nature to follow; nor is it a self-imposed defini-tional stipulation on what counts as a reduction, as Searle[13] at one point inexplicably suggests. Once we begin to address human C-effects with some appropriately focused science—as neu-ronal vector-coding theories are already doing, with striking success[14]—then that earlier "pat-tern" will be well and truly broken. For that pat-tern reflected only our own scientific ignorance, not some ontological division in nature.

In sum, human conscious experience has no quicksilver history of darting off to one side each time our reductive scientific thumb has tried to pin it down. There have *been* no significant re-ductive attempts at that target, not, at least, with-in the grand historical reductions of physics and chemistry. Instead, the phenomena of human conscious experience have quite properly been waiting, patiently and at the sidelines, for the maturation of the only theory that has any realis-tic hope of providing such a reductive account, namely, an adequate theory of the brain. If and when *that* approach has been fully tried, and proves a failure, *then,* perhaps, it will be time to insist on nonphysical approaches.

Both the appeal to ignorance and the ques-tion-begging nature of the Nagel-Searle argu-ment become finally vivid if one plays at con-structing a series of parallel arguments to "establish" the physicalistic irreducibility of whatever arcane, complex, and puzzling phe-nomenon one might choose to consider (some-thing from the preceding list, for example). Simply note that historical reductions of various important phenomena have invariably left that particular phenomenon aside as an unaddressed mystery; pretend that this is an essential pattern, a reflection of an antecedent metaphysical divi-sion, or the result of some appropriately exclu-sive definition of "reduction"; note that said leave-aside pattern (surprise!) precludes any similar reduction of *exactly* the phenomenon at issue; and you are home free. You will then have performed for us the same empty service that Nagel and Searle have performed.

V. Some Diagnostic Remarks on Qualia

There is a chronic temptation among philoso-phers to assign a special epistemological, se-mantical, or ontological status to those features or properties which form the "discriminational simples" within each of our several sensory or epistemic modalities, such as brightness and colors in the case of vision, sweetness and sour-ness in the case of taste, and so on. These are the features of the world where one is unable to *say* how it is that one discriminates one such feature from another; one simply can. As well, one is unable to *say* how the meaning of 'red' differs from the meaning of 'green'; one simply has to point to appropriate exemplars.

Such discriminational simples are typically contrasted with properties, such as "being a horse," where one can usually articulate the more elemental constituting features that make up the type in question: size, shapes, configura-tion, color, texture, and so forth, which more el-emental features lead us stepwise back toward the discriminational simples.

Too much has been made of these "simples," for the existence of such discriminable but inar-ticulable features is entirely inevitable. Such features must exist, if only to prevent an infinite regress of features discriminated by constituting subfeatures discriminated by constituting *sub*-subfeatures, and so on.[15] And their existence is inevitable even on wholly physicalist concep-tions of cognition. It simply cannot be the case that *all* conscious feature discriminations are made on the basis of distinct conscious (sub) feature discriminations. Given any person at any time, there must be some set of features whose spontaneous or noninferential discrimination is currently basic for that person, a set of features whose discrimination does not depend on the conscious discrimination of any more elemental perceptual features. In short, there must be something that counts, for that person, as a set of inarticulable qualia.

Accordingly, we should not be tempted to find anything physically irreducible or ontologically special about such inarticulable features. They need reflect nothing more than the current and perhaps changeable limits of the person's capacity for epistemic and semantic articulation, the current limits, that is, of the person's *knowledge* of the world's fine structure and his own epistemic access to it. Most importantly, there is no reason to expect that the current limits of the typical person's knowledge must mark the boundary of a distinct ontological domain. This is just as true, note, for the epistemic modalities that underwrite (what we loosely call) "introspection" as it is for the epistemic modalities of vision, taste, and audition.

And yet, philosophers have regularly been tempted here, some beyond redemption. Bishop Berkeley rejected the identification of sound with atmospheric compression waves; William Blake and Johann Wolfgang Goethe rejected the identification of light with Isaac Newton's ballistic particles; and Nagel, Jackson, Searle, and Chalmers reject the proposed reduction of inner qualia to physical states of the brain.

There is an important factor here that may help to explain why such features have so frequently been held to be beyond the reach of any physicalist reduction. Specifically, any reduction succeeds by reconstructing, within the resources of the new theory, the antecedently known nature, structure, and causal properties of the target phenomena. That is what intertheoretic reduction is. But if the target phenomena, such as sensory qualia, are features whose internal structure (if any) we are currently unable to articulate, and whose causal properties (if any) are largely unknown to us, then the target phenomena will inevitably seem to offer *the minimum purchase possible* for any aspirant reducing theory. They will display no structure worth reconstructing. They will present themselves as smooth-walled mystery. They will appear to be irreducible to any "structural/functional" theory from conventional science.

But the appearance of seamless simplicity need reflect nothing more than our own ignorance, an ignorance, we should note, that already holds promise of repair. In sum, we should not be too quickly impressed by qualia, whether outer or inner. If cognitive creatures exist at all, then the existence of inarticulable qualia is inevitable, even in a purely physical universe.

If ultimately they are physical, then inner qualia ought to be epistemically accessible from more than just the first-person or "subjective" point of view; they ought to be accessible as well from one or more "objective" points of view, via some appropriate instruments that scan brain activity, for example.

Some will continue to find this implausible on its face. That is mainly because the terms 'objective' and 'subjective' are commonly used in mutually *exclusive* contrast. But the default implication of mutual exclusivity may well be inappropriate in precisely the case at issue. After all, we know that the two epistemic modalities of vision and touch, for example, are not mutually exclusive in the phenomena that they access—one can both see and feel the shape of an object, see and feel that the sun is out, see and feel that rain is falling, and so forth. Why should it be impossible a priori that the epistemic modality we call "introspection" have some similar overlap with one or more of our other epistemic modalities?

Indeed, such overlap appears actual, even by the standards of common sense. One can tell by introspection that one's own bladder is full, but an ultrasound image will tell anyone the same thing. One can tell by introspection that and where one's retinal cells are photo-fatigued (we call it an "after image"), but that too is accessible by nonsubjective means. One can tell by introspection that the cochlear cells of one's inner ear are firing randomly (the condition is called "tinnitus"), but others can access their behavior instrumentally. There are, of course, thousands more such examples.

It would seem, then, that the "subjective" and the "objective" are not mutually exclusive after all. In at least some cases, one and the same (physical) state can be known both subjectively *and* objectively, from both the first-person perspective *and* the third-person perspective. Further, it would seem that the extent and location of the overlap is somewhat fluid, and that it varies as a function of how much background knowledge, conceptual sophistication, and recognitional skill the person has acquired. The process is called "coming to understand explicitly what was hitherto inarticulate," and it is entirely to be encouraged. The more epistemic modalities we can bring to bear on any puzzling phenomenon, the deeper our understanding will become. To insist, in *advance* of real understanding, that a given phenomenon is locked forever within its own epistemic box serves only to block the very research that might dissolve such a prejudicial conception.

VI. A Final Point about Light

In closing, let me return to the opening family of arguments concerning the irreducibility of light. Someone may remark that, with light, I have used an example that is antithetical to my own reductive inclinations in the philosophy of mind. For while light reduces cleanly to EM waves, light is still famous for having escaped the various *mechanical* reductions (ballistic particle theories, elastic media theories) that everyone in the nineteenth century expected. And it is still famous for having thus emerged as one incarnation of a fundamental and nonmechanical aspect of reality: electromagnetism.

This is quite true, and more than a little instructive. But in the present context it is also instructive (1) that while nonmechanical, light remains an entirely physical phenomenon, and, (2) more importantly, that the modestly special status that light eventually discovered had *absolutely nothing to do* with any of the considerations urged in the family of antireductive arguments in my opening parody. Light's nonmechanical status emerged primarily as a consequence of Special Relativity, as a consequence of the unity of space-time and the impossibility of a universal elastic aether. It was not a consequence or reflection of any of the arguments offered above. It is ironic that, even though light did turn out, unexpectedly, to be a rather special kind of physical phenomenon, the parody-arguments (A)–(J) did nothing whatever to herald it, and they are, after the fact, quite irrelevant to it.

The parallel lesson about mental states is that, even if conscious phenomena are ontologically special in some way, roughly analogous to the case of light, there is no reason to think that the arguments of Searle, Jackson, and Chalmers do anything to illustrate or establish it. Those arguments are no more instructive about the ultimate nature of mental phenomena than arguments (A)–(J) are instructive about the ultimate nature of light.

NOTES

1. Cf. Searle, "Intrinsic Intentionality: Reply to Criticisms of Minds, Brains, and Programs," *Behavioral and Brain Sciences,* III (1980): 450–56, and *The Rediscovery of the Mind* (Cambridge: MIT, 1992), pp. 78–82.
2. Cf. Searle, "Is the Brain's Mind a Computer Program?" *Scientific American,* CCLXII, 1 (January 1990): 26–31, here pp. 26–27; and *The Rediscovery of Mind,* pp. 93–95.
3. Cf. Searle, "Intrinsic Intentionality," pp. 417–57, and "Is the Brain's Mind a Computer Program?" pp. 26–31. This analogy was earlier deployed in Paul Churchland and Patricia Churchland, "Could a Machine Think?" in *Scientific American,* CCLXII, 1 (January 1990): 32–37. We did not then appreciate that the analogy was a member of a systematic and much larger family.
4. Cf. Searle, *The Rediscovery of Mind,* p. 122, and "The Mystery of Consciousness: Part II," *The New York Review of Books,* XLII, 18 (November 16, 1995): 54–61, here p. 58.
5. Cf. *The Rediscovery of Mind.,* pp. 117–18.
6. Cf. ibid., pp. 132, 151–56.
7. Cf. ibid, pp. 1, 89–93, 124–26; also Searle, "The Mystery of Consciousness: Part II," pp. 55–56.
8. Cf. Chalmers, "The Puzzle of Conscious Experi-

ence," *Scientific American,* CCLXXIII, 6 (December 1995): 80–86, here pp. 81–82.
9. Cf. Jackson, "Epiphenomenal Qualia," *Philosophical Quarterly,* XXXII, 127 (1982): 127–36, here p. 130; and Chalmers, "The Puzzle of Conscious Experience," pp. 81–82.
10. Cf. Chalmers, "The Puzzle of Conscious Experience," pp. 82–83; also Searle, "The Mystery of Consciousness: Part II," pp. 55–56.
11. "What Is It Like to Be a Bat?" *Philosophical Review,* LXXXIII, 4 (1974): 435–50.
12. Cf. ibid. p. 437; also Searle, *The Rediscovery of Mind,* pp. 116–24.
13. *The Rediscovery of Mind,* pp. 124, 112–16. Though here is not the place to mount a systematic criticism, it must be said that Searle's 1992 sketch of the nature and varieties of reduction muddies far more than it clarifies. First, it wrongly assimilates ontological reduction to ontological elimination. Second, there simply is no further category or "half-way house"— Searle's so-called "causal reduction"—distinct from ontological reduction. And third, as we just saw, the account attempts to stipulate the closure of certain empirically open questions. To a neutral philosopher of science, Searle's account will appear more as a reflection of his peculiar intuitions in the philosophy

of mind rather than as an independently motivated attempt to account for the full range of cases throughout the history of science.

14. See Austen Clark, *Sensory Qualities* (New York: Oxford, 1994).

15. See Mary Hesse, "Is There an Independent Observation Language?" in Robert Colodny, ed., *The Nature and Function of Scientific Theories* (Pittsburgh: University Press, 1970), pp. 35–77.

37 | Conceptual Analysis, Dualism, and the Explanatory Gap

Ned Block and Robert Stalnaker

1. Introduction

One point of view on consciousness is constituted by two claims:

The explanatory gap. Consciousness is a mystery. No one has ever given an account, even a highly speculative, hypothetical, and incomplete account of how a physical thing could have phenomenal states (Nagel 1974, Levine 1983). Suppose that consciousness is identical to a property of the brain—say, activity in the pyramidal cells of layer 5 of the cortex involving reverberatory circuits from cortical layer 6 to the thalamus and back to layers 4 and 6—as Crick and Koch have suggested for visual consciousness (Crick 1994). Still, that identity itself calls out for explanation! Proponents of an explanatory gap disagree about whether the gap is permanent. Some (e.g., Nagel 1974) say that we are like the scientifically naive person who is told that matter = energy, but does not have the concepts required to make sense of the idea. If we can acquire these concepts, the gap is closable. Others say the gap is unclosable because of our cognitive limitations (McGinn 1991). Still others say that the gap is a consequence of the fundamental nature of consciousness.

No conceptual analysis. Some concepts are analyzable functionally, or in terms of the concepts of physics. Perhaps even some mental concepts can be given functional or physi-

cal analyses. But consciousness is not one of these analyzable concepts. Further, this unanalyzability is no accident: any putative functional or physical analysis would leave out the fundamental nature of consciousness. Because there is no conceptual analysis of consciousness in physical or functional terms, there is no contradiction in the notion of a zombie that is a functional duplicate—or even a microphysical duplicate—of one of us, but that has no consciousness at all.

Our main concern is with the relation between these two claims: specifically, with the relation between the claim that there is an unclosable explanatory gap as a result of the fundamental nature of consciousness and the claim that there is no conceptual analysis of consciousness in functional or physical terms. It should be uncontroversial that the first entails the second, for if the concept of consciousness were functionally analyzable, we could close the explanatory gap by showing how that functional role could be physically implemented. What is more controversial is whether the claim that there is no conceptual analysis of consciousness entails that there is an explanatory gap that can never be closed. We will call this position—that conceptual analysis is *necessary* to close the explanatory gap—the *conceptual analysis thesis*. It is shared by a number of philosophers whose overall responses to the problem of consciousness is otherwise quite different. For example, Joseph Levine differs on the metaphysical consequences of the explanatory gap from Frank Jackson and David Chalmers. Levine argues that the gap is an epistemological one that is compatible with the thesis that facts about consciousness supervene on the physical facts, while Jackson and Chalmers argue that the fact that there can be no conceptual analysis of consciousness supports metaphysical dualism: consciousness is neither identical with nor supervenient on the physical. We will be criticizing the conceptual analysis thesis and the further claim that the lack of a conceptual analysis of consciousness entails dualism. We will be paying more attention to the views shared by the proponents of these theses than to their differences.[1]

2. The Epistemic Version

The arguments for the existence of an explanatory gap between the mental and the physical standardly rely on thought experiments that purport to show that certain situations (for example, the existence of a mind just like mine without a body, or of a body in the same physical state as mine when I am feeling pain, but without anyone feeling pain) are possible. But Levine emphasizes that the metaphysical intuitions on which such conclusions rest are controversial. His strategy is to argue for an explanatory gap on more cautious assumptions—assumptions that are compatible with the truth of physicalism. The explanatory gap, he argues, is epistemological rather than metaphysical: it is a gap in our understanding of *how* the physical facts make the mental facts true, a gap that would not be closed even if we accepted the thesis that the mental facts *are* made true by the physical facts. Levine's argument makes use of the same kinds of thought experiments, but it takes them to be about what is merely conceivable or imaginable rather than about what is metaphysically possible. He claims that conceivability arguments, even if insufficient to establish a metaphysical conclusion, can still show that a certain kind of explanation of mental phenomena in terms of the physical is unavailable.

After sketching Levine's argument, we will look closely at just what is meant by conceivability, at the relation between conceivability and possibility, and at the relation between what is conceivable and what is compatible with conceptual truths. We will contrast two ways of understanding conceivability. On one, intuitions about what is conceivable are at least as prob-

lematic and controversial as intuitions about what is metaphysically possible. On the other, we will grant that the case has been made for a conceivability gap between the mental and the physical, but argue that conceivability in this sense is insufficient for an explanatory gap.

Both Levine and Jackson recognize and are responding to the distinction brought out in Kripke 1972 between what is metaphysically necessary and what is a priori. Some necessary truths, such as that water = H_2O, are not a priori truths, and so despite their necessity, their truth cannot be established by analysis of the relevant concepts. We can imagine discovering that water is something other than H_2O, and so in a sense it is conceivable, even though impossible, that water is not H_2O. The existence of necessary a posteriori truths shows that there is no simple and direct path from the conceptual independence of consciousness and the physical to their metaphysical independence. As Kripke emphasized, a posteriori necessities give rise to an illusion of contingency that needs to be explained away, but as Levine emphasizes, the fact that the appearance of contingency is sometimes an illusion shows the fragility of intuitions about metaphysical possibilities. Levine in fact rejects the assumption that our intuitions give us access to metaphysical reality, arguing that "one's ideas can be as clear and distinct as you like, and nevertheless not correspond to what is in fact possible" (1993, 123). It is for this reason that he wants his argument to remain neutral on metaphysical questions, such as whether consciousness is in fact identical to pyramidal cell activity. But it is essential to his argument that it bring out an asymmetry between the water/H_2O case and the consciousness/pyramidal cell activity case, since the point is to show that physical theory cannot explain the phenomena of consciousness in the way that it can explain the behavior of water.

Levine's argument rests on an account of how the explanatory gap is closed in the paradigm cases of satisfactory explanation. Consider the question, Why does water boil when it is heated? Here is a rough sketch of an answer: The molecular kinetic energy of the H_2O molecules increases, causing more and more molecules to escape from the liquid, forming bubbles within the liquid. The average momentum of these molecules is a kind of pressure ("vapor pressure"), which increases as the temperature increases at a rate dependent on the strength of the bonds between molecules. When the vapor pressure = the atmospheric pressure, bonds break throughout the water, causing H_2O vapor to escape from the surface and to form globules that bubble up.

According to Levine, this is a sketch of an adequate explanation of why water boils under certain conditions because it shows how it can be deduced from microphysics and chemistry that water boils in certain conditions. But since the word 'boil' is not a term of the microphysical and chemical theories, how is this to be done? "The problem," Levine says, "is that chemical theory and folk theory don't have an identical vocabulary, so somewhere one is going to have to introduce bridge principles. . . . We need a definition of 'boiling' and 'freezing' that brings these terms into the proprietary vocabularies of the theories appealed to in the explanation" (1993, 131). With the help of such definitions we can deduce from chemistry and physics answers to questions stated in our ordinary folk vocabulary. "On this view, explanatory reduction is, in a way, a two-stage process. Stage 1 involves the (relatively? quasi?) *a priori* process of working the concept of the property to be reduced 'into shape' for reduction by identifying the causal role for which we are seeking the underlying mechanisms. Stage 2 involves the empirical work of discovering just what those underlying mechanisms are" (1993, 132).[2]

Levine of course recognizes that many of the required bridge principles connecting folk with scientific vocabulary (such as that water is H_2O, and that boiling is the particular microphysical process that it is) will not be analytic definitions: very often, what is needed are the notorious necessary a posteriori truths. But Levine's original point was that metaphysical necessity alone would not suffice to close an explanatory gap; his claim is that for explanation, we need a *deduction* of the phenomenon to be explained from a lower level explanatory science, with the help of bridge principles that are provided by a priori conceptual analysis—the kind of conceptual analysis that cannot be given for consciousness. We need to show, not just that it is *impossible* (given our scientific theory) for water not to boil in the relevant circumstances, but that it is *inconceivable* that it not boil in those circumstances.

It is clear enough that the kind of explanation sketched above removes any mystery about why water boils, but what reason is there to think that conceptual analyses of 'water' and 'boiling' are implicit in the story? It may be necessary that boiling is the particular physical process with which the explanation identifies it, but if so, it is clearly necessary a posteriori. The stuff they call 'water' on Twin Earth does something Twin Earthians call 'boiling,' but XYZ does not therefore do what *we* call 'boiling.' Levine grants that we cannot reason a priori from the existence of boiling water to the existence of H_2O undergoing the particular physical process that constitutes boiling, but he argues that we *can* reason a priori in the other direction—from microphysical theory and fact to the presence of water and the realization of the property of boiling—and that this reasoning reveals a contrast with the case of conscious states and brain processes.

Levine does not provide an actual analysis of boiling that would support this claim, but instead appeals to intuitions about conceivability. "While it is conceivable that something other than H_2O should manifest the superficial macro properties of water, as Kripke suggests, it is not conceivable, I contend, that H_2O should fail to manifest these properties (assuming of course that we keep the rest of chemistry constant)" (1993, 128). Nothing (holding our chemistry and physics constant) could conceivably be H_2O and not, for example, boil under the appropriate conditions. Moreover, nothing could conceivably instantiate the molecular motions that are actually characteristic of water boiling (vapor molecules bubbling off the surface of liquid H_2O) without being *boiling*. However, according to Levine, one cannot say the analogous thing about conscious states and their neural correlates. Even if pain turns out to be perfectly correlated with pyramidal cell activity, and even if we decide that pain *is* (necessarily) pyramidal cell activity, it will remain possible (Levine contends) to conceive of pyramidal cell activity without pain.

But such claims about conceivability seem at least as fragile and fallible as intuitions about what is metaphysically possible. What exactly does it mean to say that we can conceive of something even if it may in fact be impossible? The intuition that we can make sense of this is fueled by Kripke's cases of necessary a posteriori truths: it is conceivable (even if impossible) that water should turn out not to be H_2O, or that Queen Elizabeth II should be the daughter of Bess and Harry Truman (Kripke 1972). But as Kripke's discussion makes clear, these are cases of misdescribed possibilities. What we imagine, or conceive of, in these cases are genuine metaphysical possibilities—they are not just the possibilities that water is something other than H_2O, or that Elizabeth herself has different parents. What lies behind Kripke's cases is the fact that the meaning and reference of our terms depend on empirical facts, facts that we might be ignorant or mistaken about. What we conceive of when we conceive of a possibility we describe as one in which water is something other than H_2O is a genuine possibility, a possible world in which as speakers *there* use the term 'water' it refers to something other than H_2O—and so something other than water. (This is the first of our two notions of conceivability.) Now if, in describing a possible world, we stipulate that all the facts on which the meaning and reference of certain terms depend are the same as they are in the actual world, then the possibility we are describing will of course be one in which those terms, as speakers use them *there,* refer to the same things they refer to when we use them. (We shall be making use of this point later.) So if we hold physics and chemistry, and the relevant particular facts fixed, we can be sure we have a possible situation in which the expression 'water is boiling' (as used by us, or by them) expresses a truth. Perhaps this fact shows a sense in which it is inconceivable that (holding physics and chemistry fixed) water should not boil in the relevant circumstances, but this has nothing to do with conceptual analysis, and it will not show that there is any asymmetry between the H_2O/boiling case and the pain/pyramidal cell case. Grant, for the moment, the metaphysical thesis that pain is (necessarily) identical to pca. Now consider a possible world in which the relevant physical theories and circumstances are held fixed (that is, are stipulated to be the same as in the actual world). 'Pain,' as we use the term, obviously applies to pca in this possible world, but what about 'pain,' as used by the people in this counterfactual world? Can we consistently say about such a possible world that the people in it, who are physically just like us, refer with 'pain' to something other than what we call 'pain'? It is not clear that we can, and if we cannot, then this way of thinking about conceivability without possibility does not show that pca without pain is conceivable, and so does not show any asymmetry.

Here is a different way of trying to make sense of conceivability without possibility, one that ties conceivability explicitly to what is compatible with concepts: One might say that P without Q is conceivable if it is not possible to deduce Q from P, using only logic and conceptual truths (such as truths that follow from conceptual

analyses). Water in the bathtub without H_2O in the bathtub is conceivable because one cannot deduce from a correct conceptual analysis of water that it is H_2O. This is a purely negative conception of conceivability (and so the term is somewhat misleading). One might, for example, conclude that it is conceivable that Bill Clinton is identical with Newt Gingrich simply on the ground that there are no analytic truths involving the proper names from which 'Bill Clinton is not Newt Gingrich' can be deduced.

Now on this account of conceivability, we think it will be right to say that even if pain is in fact pca, pca without pain is still conceivable, but on this account, Levine's argument about the water boiling example won't work. Let C be a complete description, in microphysical terms, of a situation in which water (H_2O) is boiling, and let T be a complete theory of physics. Can one deduce from T, supplemented with analytic definitions, that H_2O would boil in circumstances C? To see that one cannot, suppose that the deduction is taking place on Twin Earth. The stuff they call 'water' is XYZ, and the process they call 'boiling' is a process that superficially resembles boiling, but that involves a different physical process. Just as they would say (truly), "Water is XYZ, and not H_2O (and if there were H_2O, it wouldn't be water)," so they would say (truly), "If there were H_2O, and it were behaving like that, it wouldn't be boiling." They could hardly deduce 'H_2O would boil in circumstances C' if on their meaning of 'boil,' H_2O can't boil at all. (We assume that boiling is a natural kind concept. If you don't agree, substitute some other process term that does express a natural kind concept.)

We don't really need a Twin Earth story to make our point. Consider a person on actual Earth, who does not know the story about how water boils—perhaps she doesn't even know that water is made up of molecules. One presents her with the theory T, and a description (in microphysical terms) of a water boiling situation. Can she then deduce that if T is true and a situation met conditions C, then the H_2O would be boiling? No, since for all she knows the actual situation is like the one on Twin Earth. Perhaps, if she were told, or could figure out, that the theory was actually true of the relevant stuff in her environment, she could then conclude (using her knowledge of the observable behavior of the things in her environment) that H_2O is water, and that the relevant microphysical description is a description of boiling, but the additional information is of course not a priori, and the inference from her experience would be inductive.

So we are not persuaded by Levine's argument, but we agree, nevertheless, with his sketch of the kind of explanation required for facts such as that water boils. All we reject is the a priori, purely conceptual status attributed to the bridge principles connecting the ordinary description of the phenomena to be explained with its description in the language of science. What is actually deduced in such an explanation is a description wholly within the language of science of the phenomenon to be explained. For this to answer the original explanatory question, posed in so-called folk vocabulary, all we need to add is the claim that the phenomenon described in scientific language is the same ordinary phenomenon described in a different way. But if the closing of an explanatory gap does not require an a priori deduction of the folk description of the phenomena, then it has not been shown that unavailability of a conceptual analysis of consciousness need be an obstacle to the closing of the explanatory gap between consciousness and the physical.

3. The Metaphysical Version

Levine's argument tries to use the conceptual analysis thesis to *bypass* the metaphysical question about whether the mental supervenes on the physical. Frank Jackson and David Chalmers, in contrast, want to use the conceptual analysis thesis to *support* the claim that there is a metaphysical gap between mental and physical; it is part of an argument for a kind of dualism, for the conclusion that the facts about consciousness do not supervene on the physical facts. Like Levine, Jackson and Chalmers are concerned with the relation between ordinary pre-scientific terms—such as 'water,' 'heat,' and 'boiling'—and the terms of chemistry and microphysics, and with the role of the latter in the explanation of phenomena described in ordinary terms. Like Levine, they recognize that statements connecting the terms of the two kinds (such as that water is H_2O) are often both necessary and a posteriori, and so are not claims that can be justified on purely conceptual grounds. Thus, they agree with Levine that there is not in general any simple and direct inference from the conceptual independence of terms to the metaphysical independence of the properties expressed by the terms. It is agreed that the concepts expressed by 'water' and 'H_2O' are independent even though they name the same thing. But they argue that even with a posteriori necessities, the justification for the claim of necessity must be grounded in conceptual analysis. They argue that one can give conceptual analyses of terms like 'water' and 'heat,' analyses that when conjoined with contingent empirical microphysical claims are sufficient to deduce the a posteriori necessities, and so to connect folk descriptions of phenomena with their scientific explanations. Since the kind of conceptual analysis that is available for terms like 'water' and 'heat' is not available for the terms expressing phenomenal concepts, we can conclude that physicalism is false: there is no metaphysically necessary connection between phenomenal consciousness and the physical, and no possibility of an explanation of phenomenal consciousness in physical terms.

The metaphysical thesis of physicalism, according to Jackson, can be defined as follows: any possible world that is a *minimal* physical duplicate of our world is a duplicate *simpliciter* of our world. A minimal physical duplicate of a world is one that is indiscernible from that world with respect to all physical objects, properties, and relations, and in addition contains nothing "extra," nothing that is not required in order to be a physical duplicate. The reason for the minimality requirement is this: physicalists may grant the metaphysical possibility of non-physical stuff—ghostly ectoplasm for example—and so may grant the possibility of worlds that are physical duplicates of ours, but contain some nonphysical stuff as well. Since the thesis the physicalist wants to defend will be false in such possible worlds, the thesis must be formulated to as to exclude them.

Jackson claims that it follows from physicalism, understood this way, that "any psychological fact about our world is *entailed* by the physical nature of our world" (1993, 131; our emphasis). Entailment, as Jackson uses the term, is to be understood as a metaphysical rather than a logical relation: a set of premises entails a conclusion if and only if it is metaphysically necessary that if all propositions in the premise set are true, then the proposition expressed in the conclusion is true. Since some entailments are not a priori, Jackson recognizes that he needs additional argument to show that conceptual analysis of the mental in physical terms is required for a defense of physicalism. As Jackson says, "Conceptual analysis in the traditional sense . . . is constituted by *a priori* reflection on concepts and possible cases with an aim to elucidating connections between different ways of describing matters. Hence, it might be objected, if we allow that some entailments are *a posteriori,* to demonstrate an entailment is conspicuously not to demonstrate the importance of conceptual analysis" (1993, 136). The main burden of Jackson's case is to provide this additional argument.

Jackson's central example will help to explain both the problem and his solution to it, and we will keep coming back to it. Consider the fact that the earth is covered 60 percent by water. We should be able to show, Jackson contends, that this fact is entailed a priori by the microphysical facts, which means that we should be able to deduce the statement that the earth is covered 60 percent by water from truths statable in the vocabulary of microphysics, together with truths knowable by a priori reflection. Suppose we can deduce "the earth is covered 60 percent by H_2O" from the microphysical facts. Then we can conclude that the fact about water is *entailed* (in Jackson's sense) by the microphysical facts (since it is metaphysically necessary that water is H_2O), but not that the entailment is a priori. To draw this further conclusion, we need a conceptual analysis that will mediate between claims about H_2O and claims about water. To illustrate the sort of conceptual analysis that might do this, Jackson invites us to "suppose that the right account of the semantics of 'water' is that it is a rigidified definite description meaning roughly 'stuff which actually falls from the sky, fills the oceans, is odourless and colourless, is essential for life, is called "water" by experts, . . . , or which satisfies enough of the foregoing' " (1993, 39). We will label the appropriate description, however the details are filled out, 'the waterish stuff', though in the context of the idea that the analyses are supposed to be functional (in terms of roles), we will use the terminology 'the water role.' Using this abbreviation and an "actual" operator that rigidifies a description, the definition of 'water' is as follows: water $=_{df}$ the actual waterish stuff.[3] Now, the statement 'H_2O = the waterish stuff' is a *contingent* a posteriori truth. Let us assume for the moment that it can be deduced a priori from microphysics (with the help of other such definitions for the terms that occur in the definition—a complication we will also ignore for the moment). Given the definition, the statement 'water is the waterish stuff' is contingent, but a priori, since if we replace 'water' with its definition in this statement, the

result will have the form *the actual F = the F.* (The reason 'the actual F = the F' is contingent is that it has a rigid designator on one side and a definite description on the other. In this it is like 'Grandma = the local bald thing.' Unlike the latter, however, the rigid designator is formed from the very definite description that appears on the other side, and that is what makes the identity a priori.)

From H_2O = the waterish stuff (microphysical truth) and water = the waterish stuff (a priori truth), it follows by logic alone that water = H_2O. So we can derive a priori from the two contingent premises

(a) the earth is covered 60 percent by H_2O

(b) H_2O = the waterish stuff

the contingent conclusion

(d) the earth is covered 60 percent by water.

The key is the a priori

(c) Water = the waterish stuff.

The strategy, in effect, is to factor the necessary a posteriori statement that water = H_2O into two parts, a contingent statement about H_2O that is (assumed to be) derivable from microphysics (H_2O = the odorless, etc. stuff) and a contingent a priori statement that can be justified by conceptual analysis (water = the odorless, etc. stuff).

Why can't the consciousness facts be shown to follow a priori from the microphysical facts in a parallel way? Both Jackson and Chalmers, like Levine, rely on conceivability arguments to cast doubt on the hypothesis that there could be analytic definitions, in physical terms, of the expressions we use to describe our phenomenal experience. There is, for example, Jackson's famous thought experiment about Mary, a neuroscientist who has been raised in a black and white room, and so has had no visual experience of colors such as red. She has learned all the relevant physical facts about color and about the physiology of color vision, but is still ignorant of what it is like to see red. It would be highly implausible to suppose that she might come to know what it is like to see red by engaging in some conceptual analysis and logical deduction. Then there are the philosophical zombies. Chalmers and others argue that there does not seem to be any contradiction in the concept of a zombie—a creature that is functionally and physically just like us, but that has no consciousness.

The considerations that Jackson and Chalmers appeal to can be used to argue directly for the metaphysical possibility of zombies, and so for the falsity of physicalism, bypassing any consideration of conceptual analysis or reductive explanation. But as Levine emphasized, the metaphysical intuitions are controversial. It is much less controversial to break the argument into two steps: first, to use the intuitions to support only the judgment that the concept of consciousness cannot be given an analytic definition in functional or physical terms, and second, to argue from this to the metaphysical conclusion, using the general thesis that conceptual independence implies metaphysical independence. We agree that, independently of this kind of argument, the hypothesis that zombies are metaphysically possible has considerable prima facie plausibility that needs to be explained away if the hypothesis is to be rejected. (See Nagel 1974 and Hill 1997 for attempts to explain it away that seem to us promising.) But our project here is not to explain away this controversial intuition, but to rebut the second stage of the argument that attempts to derive the hypothesis from the unanalyzability of the concept of consciousness.

4. A Reason for Doubting the Premise about A Priori Analysis

Jackson and Chalmers argue that a priori conceptual analysis in terms of basic physics (microphysics, in the terms that Chalmers uses and we will adopt) is required for a defense of the thesis of physicalism, and for the possibility of a physicalist explanation that closes the explanatory gap. Since the concept of consciousness cannot be given such an analysis, the explanatory gap cannot be closed. But what is their *argument* that a priori conceptual analysis is required to close such a gap? What is offered is not an argument for this, but *examples* that show that *if* a conceptual analysis of a certain kind were always available, then we could use these conceptual analyses to account for the necessary a posteriori truths of reductive explanation. We have no quarrel with this conditional. What we doubt is that these conceptual analyses are very often available. They show that their model of reductive explanation *might* be right, not that it *must* be right.

Might a real explanatory gap be closed with-

out a conceptual analysis of the terms in which the explanatory problem is posed? Consider how the explanatory gap was closed in the case of life. Famously, it was once thought that the explanation of life required appeal to some kind of vital force. How was this idea rejected? One might try to analyze life a priori in terms of reproduction, locomotion, digestion, excretion, respiration, and the like, and then give further analyses of these terms, eventually grounding the functions in microphysical terms. But one doesn't have to be a Quinean who rejects all a priori analyses to see that this one is hopeless. Note first that 'digestion,' etc. are not terms of microphysics. In fact, not a single example of an analysis of a non-microphysical term in terms of microphysics is given by either Jackson or Chalmers. The most plausible candidates for a priori analyses are ones in which analysand and analysandum involve the same "family" of terms. Further, nothing in the concept of life rules out the possibility that there could be living beings that are immortal, and don't reproduce, that are tree-like (so don't locomote), get their energy by electromagnetic induction (so don't digest or excrete), and have no need for any substance in the air (so don't respire). Perhaps such possible beings take in chemicals from the soil but use all that they absorb so don't excrete any residue. Perhaps the definition will be of the reference-fixing kind: life = $_{df}$ the actual process that realizes the relevant cluster of functions. But is it really plausibly a priori that actual living things reproduce, locomote, digest, excrete, and respire (or any sufficiently large set of these)? For example, can't we imagine an alternative history in which physiologists discover that the humans don't do any digestion themselves—rather, our stomachs contain insects that digest our food for us, excreting waste products which are exactly what we need to live.

More relevantly, it is doubtful that fulfilling any set of functions is conceptually *sufficient* for life. A moving van locomotes, processes fuel and oxygen, and excretes waste gasses. If one adds a miniaturized moving van factory in the rear, it reproduces. Add a TV camera, a computer, and a sophisticated self-guiding computer program, and the whole system could be made to have more sophistication, on many measures, than lots of living creatures.

These examples suggest that no a priori functional analysis has much to do with the closing of the explanatory gap in the case of life. Still, the explanation of how living creatures can carry out the functions used to characterize life is part of the story of how the gap was closed. For example, the discovery of the physical machinery of reproduction by Watson and Crick no doubt was a gap narrower. More generally, it seems reasonable to think that the story of the closing of the explanatory gap about life takes something like this form: There are some paradigm cases of living things, including some that are quite simple. (We need not assume that it is a *conceptual* truth that even the paradigm cases of living things are alive.) We understand completely how some of the simpler forms of life work. We have reason to think that more complicated living things work by similar principles, and see no bar, in principle, to our extending our explanations of simple living things to all forms of life. This particular model may not apply very well to consciousness, but the example of life does seem to us to illustrate how an explanatory gap can be closed without the sort of conceptual analysis that Jackson and Chalmers argue is required. Closing the explanatory gap in the case of life has nothing to do with any analytic definition of 'life,' but rather is a matter of showing how living things around here work.

Jackson's and Chalmers's examples of conceptual analyses fall into two categories. Chalmers gives an example of reproduction as the production of a certain kind of copy. Perhaps a correct a priori functional analysis can be constructed along these lines. Chalmers does not fill in "certain kind," so we are given no reason to expect an analysis. But we very much doubt that any *analysis in microphysical terms* will be forthcoming.

The second category is that of a priori reference-fixing definitions, as with the example of 'water.' The functional analysis does not give the meaning of the term in the ordinary sense, but is nevertheless supposed to be a priori and part of the "semantics" of the term and the concept, recoverable by anyone who understands the term, or possesses the concept. To rehearse Gareth Evans's example (1982, 31), to illustrate the pattern, we might use 'Julius' as an abbreviation for the actual inventor of the zipper. A conceptual analysis of the term 'Julius' that is available in principle to anyone who understands that term will reveal that Julius, if he exists, invented the zipper.

'Julius,' of course, is a highly contrived example, as are all clear examples of such reference-fixing definitions. Even if descriptions play an essential role in fixing the reference of a name, there is no reason why they must become part of the semantics of the name in this way. The point has long been a familiar one; it was the main thesis of Kripke 1972 that ordinary proper names are *not* like 'Julius.' All of the examples of the second of Kripke's three lectures are directed at the refutation of a reference-fixing version of the description theory of names. Suppose we consider, not 'Julius,' but 'Kevin.' This name was introduced—acquired its reference—in an act of dubbing that involved a definite description. The proud but pedantic new parent said, "Let 'Kevin' be the name of the baby in the third crib from the right." One might argue that Kevin's parent, at the moment of the act of dubbing, had a priori knowledge that Kevin was the baby in the third crib from the right (though we think even this is doubtful), but it is clear that the information is quickly lost, and is not something that can be extracted by competent users of the name from their understanding of it. Perhaps the semantics of 'water' is more like 'Kevin' than it is like 'Julius,' in which case there is no way to fill in the details of 'the water role' so that it is a conceptual truth that water occupies the water role. And of course it is even more doubtful that any such analysis of the water role would be both a conceptual truth and be an analysis in *microphysical* terms.

In sum, we have strong reason to doubt that reductive explanations that close explanatory gaps depend on the kind of a priori conceptual analyses that Levine, Jackson, and Chalmers appeal to.

5. Uniqueness

Let us look a bit more closely at the supposed conceptual truth that water = the waterish stuff. Recall that 'the waterish stuff' abbreviates an appropriate cluster of descriptions of the superficial properties of water by which it is commonly identified by competent users of the term, something like "the stuff that falls from the sky, fills the oceans, is odourless and colourless, is essential for life, is called 'water' by experts . . . or which satisfies enough of the foregoing." Now the assumption that H_2O is *a* waterish stuff is not enough to ensure that H_2O = water, for there might be other waterish stuffs too. For Jackson's pattern of argument to go through, H_2O must be *the* unique waterish stuff. But we don't want our definition to rule out the possibility that there are other waterish stuffs elsewhere that are unrelated to our applications of the concept of water, for example, XYZ on twin earth (where here, twin earth is not regarded as a counterfactual possibility, but as a distant part of our universe). So the water role must include an indexical element, which we can specify by adding 'around here.' Then our definition of 'water' is: water = the actual (unique) waterish stuff around here. (The indexical condition is independent of the rigidifying operator.) And the relevant conceptual truth will be a version of (c):

(c) water = the (unique) waterish stuff around here.

Then the overall argument says that the two microphysical facts, (a) that H_2O covers 60 percent of the globe, and (b) that H_2O = the waterish stuff around here, together with the conceptual truth (c), logically imply (d) that water covers 60 percent of the globe. Since (c) is a conceptual truth, the entailment of (d) by (a) and (b) can be established a priori. That is, since it is a conceptual truth that water = the actual waterish stuff around here, it is also a conceptual truth that water = the waterish stuff around here. So from (b) we can move a priori to: water = H_2O, and from (a) and (b), we can move a priori to (d).

We doubt that there is a way to spell out 'waterish' so that (c) is a conceptual truth, and we doubt further that any remotely plausible analysis would get to first base when substituted in (b) as a truth of microphysics; but even if we set this issue aside, there is an additional problem with the argument: Even if 'water' can be given such a definition, the uniqueness assumption in the description throws doubt on the claim that premise (b) of the argument is a microphysical fact.

If 'waterish' is spelled out so that it is a conceptual truth that only a physical stuff can be waterish, then it will perhaps be a microphysical fact that there is only one waterish stuff around here. But for at least some names for substances or properties that are in fact physical, the reference-fixing definition might be a functional one that did not exclude on conceptual grounds the possibility that the substance or property be nonphysical. Consider a different example: at one time, heat was thought to be a fluid substance, caloric. Imagine an alternative scientific history in which the caloric theory coexisted with the observation that molecular kinetic energy goes up and down, covarying with influx and outflow of heat. The theory might have aris-

en that what we might ahistorically call "ghost heat" was correlated with but not identical to molecular kinetic energy. Let us define 'heatish' by analogy to 'waterish'. A heatish stuff satisfies most of a list of properties such as: produces sensations of warmth,[4] makes water boil when added, makes water freeze when taken away, is called 'heat' by experts. Then the comparable claim to the one being discussed would be: the (unique) heatish stuff around here is mean molecular kinetic energy. But the claim that mean molecular kinetic energy = the (unique) heatish stuff around here is not a purely microphysical claim, since it rules out the possibility that ghost heat is also a heatish stuff around here.

Applying this point to Jackson's argument, we can't move a priori from microphysics to the claim that water covers 60 percent of the earth because there is a world (considered as actual) in which some of what counts as water is ghost water, so even if H_2O covers 60 percent of the earth in that world, what they call 'water' will cover more. Further, we can't move a priori to 'H_2O covers *at least* 60 percent of the earth' because ghost substances could increase the surface area of the earth, or alternatively, cover some of the H_2O, putting it below the surface.[5]

Recall that Jackson's definition of physicalism recognized the possibility of a world that is a microphysical duplicate of the actual world, while also containing some additional nonphysical substances and properties. In response, a "nothing but" condition is built into the definition of physicalism by requiring for the truth of physicalism only that *minimal* physical duplicates of the actual world be duplicates *simpliciter.* But the need for this qualification presupposes that the "nothing but" condition is not something that is entailed by microphysics *itself,* that is, *it is not a claim of microphysics that our world is a minimal physical duplicate of itself.* To take the "nothing but" condition to be an implicit claim of microphysics would be *to build the thesis of physicalism into microphysics,* which philosophers such as Jackson and Chalmers, who reject physicalism, should be reluctant to do. They reject physicalism, not microphysics. The truth of what physicists write in textbooks does not depend on the mind-body problem. Even if it is a microphysical fact that H_2O is *a* waterish stuff around here, it is not a microphysical fact that it is *the* waterish stuff around here.

Reacting to this point, Jackson remarked (personal communication) that the medical profession would be outraged at the idea that they have failed to show that fairies don't cause cancer. True enough. We also think that the physics profession has sufficient reason to rule out the existence of ghost heat. But we are making a point, not about what it is reasonable for scientists to believe, but about what can be deduced a priori from their theories. The kind of causal overdetermination that one would have to hypothesize to reconcile either ghost heat or fairies that could cause cancer with accepted theories would have not a shred of scientific plausibility, but this judgment is quite compatible with the claim that there is no logical derivation from medical science (or thermodynamics), together with conceptual truths, of the absence of such nonphysical overdetermining causes.

Our hypotheses about "ghost" properties— redundant nonphysical phenomena—are obviously contrived, but they are relevant to the issue, since on the dualist view of consciousness that Jackson and Chalmers support, consciousness is a kind of ghost property—something that is either epiphenomenal or a property with redundant overdetermining influence on the physical world. We argue that hypotheses about ghost properties are ruled out on empirical methodological grounds, rather than by conceptual analysis. The same kind of methodological considerations might be used to argue against dualism about consciousness.

In section 1, we noted the distinction between what can be deduced a priori from microphysics alone and what can be deduced a priori from microphysics augmented by the claim that certain microphysical entities are the referents of *our* words. We noted that one cannot move a priori from microphysics alone to the conclusion that H_2O boils, since one might not know that water is H_2O. If one's 'water' picked out XYZ instead of H_2O, then one's 'boil' would pick out a kind of thing that happens to XYZ when it is heated enough rather than the superficially similar behavior of sufficiently heated H_2O. This point also applies in the current context. One cannot move a priori from microphysics alone to the claim that there is water around here. The problem cannot be evaded by appeal to the formula "Add indexicals to microphysics." There might be both H_2O *and* XYZ around here. What has to be added to microphysics is something that has the upshot that our term 'water' refers to H_2O, and it is not clear that this can be done without simply assuming that the microphysical facts determine the referential facts, an assumption that is no part of microphysics.

We have argued that the assumption that there is at most one waterish stuff around here is essential to the argument, and that it cannot be extracted from microphysics. The argument might still work if we could deduce this proposition instead from the alleged conceptual truth (c) water = *the* waterish stuff around here. As noted above, when 'water' is replaced by its definition, (c) is seen to have the form 'the actual F = the F,' a form of a statement that is said to be knowable a priori, but nevertheless to express a contingent proposition. Consider the analogy mentioned earlier to 'Grandma = the local bald thing.' This is obviously contingent, since Grandma might not have been bald and someone else might have been the local bald thing. But 'the actual local bald thing,' like 'Grandma,' is a rigid designator naming Grandma. So it is just as contingent that the actual local bald thing = the local bald thing. Though contingent, it is also a priori, since the rigid designator is formed from the same definite description that appears on both sides of the identity sign. If it designates anything, both occurrences designate the same thing. But what if, in fact, there is no unique local bald thing? Then the reference fixing fails, and no contingent proposition is expressed. In this case, what is the status of the statement? We might say that when uniqueness in fact fails, the statement that the actual F = the F is not true, since it expresses no proposition at all. All that is really a priori is this: *if* there is a unique F, then the actual F = the F. Alternatively, we might stipulate that 'the actual F = the F' (and therefore (c)) shall be true anyway in this case. But then, although the statement can be known a priori, it doesn't imply that there is a unique F. The upshot is that if, in Jackson's derivation, we replace (b), which we have argued is not a microphysical claim, with the weaker claim that H_2O is *a* waterish stuff around here, then there will be no way to derive the conclusion from the premises. Even if it is a priori that water, *if there is such a thing,* is the unique waterish stuff around here, that won't suffice to get out of microphysics the conclusion that water covers 60 percent of the earth.

The possibility of additional waterish stuff that is nonphysical is not, perhaps, to be taken too seriously, but it is not so implausible to imagine the discovery that even though water was believed to be the unique waterish stuff, in fact there turn out to be two or more different (physical) kinds of waterish stuff. What should we say in such a case? If it is a definitional truth that water = the actual unique waterish stuff around here, then we should have to conclude that there is no such thing as water, and set about to construct a new definition. This is one possible response, but there are others, and choosing between them seems to be a decision that will be driven by empirical and theoretical considerations. We might decide that the kind term partially denotes both occupants (see Field 1973 on 'mass'). Another possibility is that we should regard the term as a non-kind term denoting a disjunctive property, the disjunction of the two items. A third possibility is that we should regard the kind term as denoting the *role* property shared by the two items rather than the *fillers* of the role. In any actual case, the matter may be decided by the relevant details. It is a part of the semantics of natural kind terms that they are natural kinds, but it may also be part of the semantics of these terms that this is a defeasible condition. What is not plausibly part of the semantics, something we all know in virtue of knowing our language alone, is what to say in all the myriad cases in which the defeasible condition is defeated. In these cases, what we should say will no doubt be dictated by principles of "simplicity," conservativeness, etc.

These issues often arise in medicine where disease names are used to denote the filler of a role on the assumption that there is a single filler. Then it is discovered that there are many fillers. For example, the term 'rheumatism' was once used to mean a disease characterized by pain in the joints or muscles that was caused by the flow of an evil fluid which flowed from the brain to the affected parts of the body. The term comes from the Greek 'rheuma,' meaning a watery discharge, but the use of the term described here dates from the seventeenth century. The term was used for very different diseases, including rheumatic fever, arthrosis, and arthritis (which is itself a term that covers different diseases, some caused by infection, some by autoimmune problems, and another by wear and tear). As it slowly dawned on the medical community that the cases lumped under that term had nothing in common but the symptoms, the name was used to denote the syndrome itself. Many disease names—'lumbago,' for example—follow this course.

The contrast mentioned above between a disjunctive kind and a role property is important to the point we are making about uniqueness. If we took 'jade' to denote a disjunctive non-kind, we would take it to denote the disjunction of jadeite and nephrite, the two types of jade. If instead we took 'jade' to denote a role property, we would take it to denote a cluster of superficial properties such as a certain color, weight, hardness, shapeability, and the like. Or perhaps it should be constructed as the property of having most of the elements of the cluster. What is it for something to be jade? Is it to have the property of being either jadeite or nephrite? Or is it to have a certain color (greenish whitish), etc.? We are not sure. If we discovered a new substance that had those superficial properties, wouldn't that be a new kind of jade? If so, or if it is indeterminate, then the disjunctive analysis is not right.

Our point doesn't require making up our minds about jade or disease names. All we need is these two assumptions: first, there is a real distinction between disjunctive properties, such as the property of being either jadeite or nephrite, and superficial cluster properties, such as the property of having a certain weight, hardness, color, etc.; second, in some cases in which the paradigm examples of some putative natural kind term turn out to be members of two or more quite different natural kinds, it would be right to take the term to denote the superficial property, or to have indeterminate reference. If it could, for all that is built into the concept, have turned out that 'water' referred to any waterish stuff, or that 'water' had indeterminate reference, then this is enough to show that we should not regard it as a piece of conceptual analysis that water is the actual waterish stuff around here.

We have been criticizing the idea that there is any way to specify an appropriate meaning for 'waterish' or 'heatish' so that it is a conceptual truth that water = the actual unique waterish stuff around here or that heat = the actual unique heatish stuff around here. The criticism has depended on the issue of what we should think if there turns out to be two different role fillers. But the fact that these are not conceptual truths can be seen another way, by a consideration of *why* we usually think that there is only one filler. The supposition that it is a conceptual truth that heat = the actual unique heatish stuff around here is incompatible with the actual practice of scientific reduction. The claim that heat and molecular kinetic energy are dual occupants of the same role is not false because it falls afoul of the concept of heat. The view that heat and molecular kinetic energy are two rather than one is not contradictory or conceptually incoherent. It is false, and can be shown to be false by attention to certain methodological principles whose power and importance are widely acknowledged even if no one has ever been able to formulate them precisely. We refer to the set of methodological principles that are usually invoked with the misleading name 'simplicity.'

6. Digression on "Simplicity"

Levine, Jackson, and Chalmers suppose that the gap between descriptions in terms of microphysics and descriptions in terms of, for example, 'water' and 'heat' is filled by conceptual analysis. A deep inadequacy in this view is revealed by the role of methodological considerations in our actual decisions about such matters. Why do we suppose that heat = molecular kinetic energy? Consider the explanation given above of why heating water makes it boil. Suppose that heat = molecular kinetic energy, pressure = molecular momentum transfer, and boiling = a certain kind of molecular motion. (We are alluding to an empirical identity claim, not the a priori behavioral analysis considered earlier.) Then we have an account of how heating water produces boiling. If we were to accept mere correlations instead of identities, we would only have an account of how something correlated with heating causes something correlated with boiling. Further, we may wish to know how it is that increasing the molecular kinetic energy of a packet of water causes boiling. Identities allow a transfer of explanatory and causal force not allowed by mere correlations. Assuming that heat = mke, that pressure = molecular momentum transfer, etc. allows us to explain facts that we could not otherwise explain. Thus, we are justified by the principle of inference to the best explanation in inferring that these identities are true.

If we believe that heat is correlated with but not identical to molecular kinetic energy, we should regard as legitimate the question of why the correlation exists and what its mechanism is. But once we realize that heat *is* molecular kinetic energy, questions like this will be seen as wrongheaded.

Suppose one group of historians of the distant future studies Mark Twain and another studies Samuel Clemens. They happen to sit at the same table at a meeting of the American Historical Association. A briefcase falls open, a list of the events in the life of Mark Twain tumbles out and is picked up by a student of the life of Samuel Clemens. "My Lord," he says, "the events in the life of Mark Twain are exactly the same as the events in the life of Samuel Clemens. What could explain this amazing coincidence?" The answer, someone observes, is that Mark Twain = Samuel Clemens.[6] Note that it makes sense to ask for an explanation of the correlation between the two sets of events. But it does not make the same kind of sense to ask for an explanation of the identity. Identities don't *have* explanations (though of course there are explanations of how the two terms can denote the same thing). The role of identities is to disallow some questions and allow others.

This point about identities is relevant not only to identity theorists, such as Smart, who identify mental properties with physiological properties of the brain, but also to functionalists who identify mental properties with functional properties, arguing that they are realized by, rather than identical with, physiological or (ultimately) microphysical properties. The functionalist makes identity claims too—that mental properties are functional properties—and we argue that such claims might be a posteriori claims that are justified on methodological rather than conceptual grounds.

Smart (1959) asked the question of what shows that pain is identical to a brain process as opposed to merely correlated with it. He invoked methodological considerations of the sort mentioned above (avoiding "nomological danglers," he said). Let's lump such methodological considerations together under the unfortunate heading 'simplicity.' In a paper that inspired Jackson and Chalmers, Lewis (1966) argued that simplicity was not needed—our concepts are enough. The considerations mentioned here favor Smart over Lewis.

7. A Different Kind of Analysis?

We have been arguing against the plausibility of a certain kind of conceptual analysis of terms like 'water' and 'heat.' Jackson and Chalmers would reply, we suspect, that they have no commitment to any particular conceptual analysis, and so their general point is not affected by arguments against the plausibility of any particular analysis, or pattern of analysis. But, they would insist, there *must* be some kind of analysis. "Of course any view about how 'water' gets to pick out what it does will be controversial. But it is incredible that there is *no* story to tell. It is not a bit of magic that 'water' picks out what it does" (Jackson 1993, 42 n. 25). Our reply is that of course there must be a story to be told (whether physicalism is true or not) about how 'water' comes to refer to water, but we need not assume that the story involves a conceptual analysis in microphysical terms, or that the story is one that is available a priori to all competent users of the word 'water.' We suggested above that the story to be told might be the kind of account that Kripke argued should be given for proper names; Jackson suggests, at one point, that his argument could accommodate such a story—that it is just another kind of conceptual analysis. "If you prefer a causal-historical theory," he says, "you would have to replace [the second premise, (b), of the argument] by something like 'It is H_2O that was (the right kind of) causal origin of our use of the word "water"' " (1993, 42 n. 25).

According to this suggestion, the argument pattern would now be something like this:

(a) 60 percent of the earth is covered with H_2O.

(b′) H_2O is the stuff that plays the right kind of causal role in explaining our use of the word 'water.'

(d) Therefore, 60 percent of the earth is covered with water.

The assumption must be that the inference from (a) and (b′) to (d) is now mediated by the following conceptual analysis:

(c′) Water is the stuff that plays the right kind of causal role in explaining our use of the word 'water.'

Even granting, for the moment, that (b′) is a truth of microphysics, there is a problem: (c′), of course, is not a conceptual analysis of 'water.' It conveys no information about the meaning of the word 'water' that distinguishes that word from any other that names a liquid. If there is a gesture toward a conceptual analysis of anything in the allegedly a priori (c′), it is an analysis of reference, or meaning, and it would be this only if the phrase "the right kind of causal role" is taken (as we assume Jackson intends) as shorthand to be filled in with a substantive account of what the right kind of causal role is. But what reason is there to think that the story to be told about the relation that constitutes reference or meaning is a conceptual analysis (in microphysical terms), or is true a priori?[7]

Suppose we were to grant that there must be an a priori conceptual analysis of reference in physical terms to be found. Then consider the following argument pattern:

[A] Pyramidal cell activity is taking place in Jones at time t.

[B] Pyramidal cell activity is the process that plays the right kind of causal role in explaining our use of the word 'pain.'

[D] Therefore, pain is taking place in Jones at time t.

The inference from [A] and [B] to [D] is justified by the following quite trivial instantiation of our account of reference:

[C] Pain is the process that plays the right kind of causal role in our use of the word 'pain.'

Of course, the defender of physicalism must defend the crucial premise [B], but this is a purely contingent, entirely physicalist claim—at least, it is if (b′) is. The fact, if it is a fact, that we can imagine pain without pyramidal cell activity or pyramidal cell activity without pain, seems quite irrelevant to the defense of [B], and since the conceptual analysis is an analysis of reference, it is not clear that these possibilities are relevant to the truth of [C] either. It may be said that epiphenomenalism shows that [C] is not an a priori truth, but has no such impact on (c′). But if epiphenomenalism is coherent, we don't see why the comparable doctrine with respect to water or heat is not coherent. Suppose, for example, that we refer to pains via a "causal fork"—a brain state causes both the pain and our uses of the word 'pain.' Why should an analogous claim for 'water' be ruled out a priori? [C] and (c′) stand or fall together.

So while we agree with Jackson that there must be some nonmagical story to be told about how our words manage to refer, we don't agree that such a story will drive a wedge between reductionism about water and reductionism about pain.

8. Can Jackson and Chalmers Make Do with Approximate Conceptual Analyses?

Jackson emphasizes that there is an element of stipulation involved in the a priori entailments from physics of everything outside of consciousness. In discussing the example of the entailment of the facts of solidity from physics, he says, "That's what it takes, according to our concept, to be solid. Or at least it is near enough" (1993, 103). Near enough for what? His answer is: near enough for practical purposes. "For our day to day traffic with objects, it is the mutual exclusion that matters [as opposed to being everywhere dense], and accordingly it is entirely reasonable to rule that mutual exclusion is enough for solidity" (107).

But it can hardly be assumed that what matters for practical purposes is a priori. What matters for practical purposes depends on the facts of psychology and economics (for example). That is why the agents in Rawls's "original position" need to know basic facts of psychology and economics. Introducing such a notion of approximation does not seem a promising way to avoid the problems we have been raising for the a priori entailment from physics of everything outside consciousness.

9. The Upshot

To sum up, we have argued:

> There is no reason to believe that reductive explanation of facts about phenomena described in our ordinary folk vocabulary requires conceptual analyses of the terms of that vocabulary in microphysical terms, and there is no reason to believe that there are often such analyses to be found.

> Even if one had such an analysis (of the form "water is the unique waterish stuff"), another assumption of the argument would still fail, since the claim that H_2O is *the* unique waterish stuff would not be a microphysical claim. Given the possibility of ghost water that covers part of the earth not covered by physical water, it cannot follow from microphysics that water covers 60 percent of the earth. (Note that the ghost water point is not directed at the claim that there are a priori conceptual analyses of ordinary folk terms in microphysical terms. Chalmers and Jackson say little to support that claim and we have given some reason to doubt it. We use the ghost examples to show that even accepting the conceptual analyses, the water facts do not follow a priori.)

> It cannot be a priori that water = the occupant of the such and such role, since in some cir-

cumstances the right thing to say is that a term picks out the role itself—or is indeterminate between the role and its occupant. And it remains to be shown that there is some more complicated analysis (for example, a set of conditionals) that is really a priori.

The claim that water is *a* waterish stuff might be a microphysical claim, but if Jackson and Chalmers try to make do with this weaker premise, their argument faces the following dilemma: the allegedly a priori conceptual truth that water is the unique waterish stuff either has an existential presupposition (that there is a unique waterish stuff), in which case it is sufficient for the argument, but not knowable a priori, or else it does not imply the existential claim, in which case it may be a priori, but will be insufficient for the argument.

Suppose it were agreed that no conceptual analyses for natural kind terms like 'water' and 'heat' are available, and so that there is no a priori entailment of statements about water by microphysical theory and fact. What would the significance of this be? Why would it matter for dualism and the explanatory gap? Does it really challenge the overall drift of the Levine-Jackson-Chalmers point of view?

The point of view that we are criticizing depends on two claims that we are accepting: first, that Jackson's Mary cannot deduce the facts about what it is like to see red from the microphysical and functional facts; second, that there is no contradiction or incoherence in the extreme zombie hypothesis, the idea of a microphysical duplicate of one of us but with no consciousness—that is, even with a full knowledge of microphysics and the microphysical state of a conscious human being, one could not come to know, by reasoning from these facts, that the person was conscious. These ideas are supposed to show that the facts of consciousness are not *a priori* entailed by the microphysical facts. But we have been arguing that the facts about *water are not a priori entailed by the microphysical facts either*. To derive 'The earth is 60 percent covered by water' from microphysics, we need the a posteriori (necessary) truth that water = H_2O. But now we can see that even if Jackson's and Chalmers's thought experiments show something about what can be extracted a priori from microphysics, they don't show any disanalogy between the concept of consciousness and the concept of water. In particular, they don't show that an identity claim connecting consciousness with a kind of neurophysiological process cannot be true, and cannot play a role in closing an explanatory gap. (Note that we are not saying that the identity closes the gap all by itself.) Suppose that there is an a posteriori truth of the form consciousness = brain state B. Recall the suggestion by Crick and Koch, mentioned earlier, that consciousness is pyramidal cell activity. Then the facts of consciousness are necessitated by the microphysical facts (though not entailed a priori). The fact that the notion of an unconscious zombie is not a contradiction cuts no ice.

Without the help of a conceptual analysis, how might such an identity claim be justified? By using the kinds of methodological consideration sketched in our discussion of simplicity above—the same kinds of considerations that are used to justify the claim that water = H_2O. We said that simplicity considerations are not a priori, but this is not really necessary to the argument. Let simplicity be as a priori as you like. Whatever a priori status simplicity has will apply as well to reductive explanation of consciousness as to reductive explanation of water.

After making the microphysical world, did God have to add consciousness? Not if the identity claim is true, and we might have reason to believe that it is, even without the help of a conceptual analysis.

10. The Two-Dimensional Framework

The conceptual analysis thesis, in the form that we have been discussing it, requires explicit a priori verbal analyses in microphysical terms (or at least a priori sufficient conditions in microphysical terms) of all concepts that do not involve consciousness. This is an incredible claim. The best candidates for a priori conceptual analyses have been ones in which the terms of the analysis are in the same "family" as the term analyzed—for example, one mentalistic, epistemic, and normative concept is analyzed in terms of others. But the conceptual analyses we are criticizing would analyze ordinary terms in terms of a language (that of microphysics) that is unknown to ordinary people.

However, there is no real commitment on the part of the philosophers whose views we are criticizing to any such analyses. The official view stated by Jackson and Chalmers is not that the relevant concepts can really be given verbal

analyses but that they have meanings or intensions of a particular kind. To spell out their account, they appeal to the well-known two-dimensional framework. We will argue that this appeal misfires. The two-dimensional account does nothing at all to motivate the claim that there is an a priori accessible conceptual component of content. If there is such a component, it can be represented in terms of the two-dimensional apparatus, but that apparatus provides not the slightest reason to believe in it. Further, even if there is such a component, it cannot be used to drive a wedge between consciousness and realms where physicalism is not controversial.

To motivate the two-dimensional apparatus, we will begin by considering some familiar externalist objections to the kind of specification of *the water role* that we have been considering. It is argued that we are not guaranteed a priori that water is the—or even *an*—odorless drinkable liquid in rivers and lakes that we have been calling 'water,' since it is not even guaranteed a priori that water is a liquid. There is a twin earth in which the stuff that they call 'water' is H_2O, as here, but the stuff that they call 'liquid' is virtually all a slippery granular solid (White 1982). According to this story, water is an exception, one that the residents of Twin Earth would not call 'a liquid' if they knew the scientific facts. (Imagine that on Twin Earth, water is rare.) Because (the argument goes) the counterfactual situation in which this story is true is a twin of ours, an utterance is actually a priori only if the counterpart utterance in that situation is a priori there. Since the counterpart of "water is a liquid" is false there, it cannot be a priori true.

Note that the uses of 'liquid,' 'solid,' etc. that are assumed here are "natural kind" uses. There are nonnatural kind uses which for lack of a better term we will call "superficial" uses of these terms according to which on the twin earth specified above, water is correctly called 'a liquid.' This fact may be used to motivate a reply, namely that the sense of 'liquid' assumed in the reference-fixing definition is the superficial sense. What is this superficial sense? The idea is that just as 'water' is associated with a cluster of superficial properties that some other stuff could possibly have, so 'liquid' is associated with superficial manifestations (which we might abbreviate with 'liquidish,' or 'the liquid role'). A spelling out of the liquid role can be expected to reveal further terms that have an externalist dimension, since as Tyler Burge and others have persuasively argued, the dependence of meaning and content on an external environment is not restricted just to natural kind terms, but is pervasive, extending even to color terms (Burge 1978). The issue about how deep externalism goes is controversial, and familiar from the extensive literature on narrow content. We will not try to settle it here, since our point is just to motivate a strategy for bypassing the question by trying to give a general method for abstracting away from the external component of content without giving any particular conceptual analyses, yielding a general representation of the information that can be extracted from concepts by understanding alone.

Grant that the meaning of a word, or of a concept,[8] has an external dimension; that is, grant that the fact that a word or concept *has* a certain meaning is not a fact wholly about the internal state of the speaker or thinker, and is not a fact that is available a priori to everyone who understands the word or possesses the concept. This implies that the extension of one's concepts, and the truth values of one's thoughts, may depend on external facts in two different ways. First, external facts contribute to determining what their content is, and second, they contribute to determining whether and where a concept with that content is instantiated. That is, first there are the facts, whatever they are, that make it true that 'water' refers to water (H_2O), and second, there are facts such as that there is water (H_2O) covering the basement floor. Together, these facts imply that the thought that one would express with the sentence 'There is water all over the basement floor' is true. Now even if the externalist disputes the possibility of conceptual analysis, he cannot dispute that extensions and truth values depend on the facts in these two different ways. The strategy of the two-dimensional analysis is to use this distinction to separate out the purely conceptual component of content.

The world is all that is the case, and a possible world is all that would be the case if that world were actual. So whatever external (or internal) facts are relevant to the determination of the content of an expression or a concept, a specification of a possible world will include a specification of those facts. So we can identify the purely internal, purely conceptual component of content with a function from possible worlds (or possible worlds centered on a speaker or thinker and a time) to contents. The value of the function—the content in the ordinary sense of the relevant concept or expression—may itself

be identified with a function from possible worlds to extensions, so the conceptual component of content will be a *two-dimensional intension*—a function from (centered) possible worlds to functions from possible worlds to extensions (truth values, in the case of sentences). Or equivalently, it will be a function taking two arguments—a centered world and a world—into an extension.

The reason that the first argument of the function is a centered world is that one and the same utterance type can occur in different contexts within the same possible world. For example, water and twin water can exist in the same world; 'water' in one mouth can pick out water and in another mouth pick out twin water. So the two-dimensional intensions must be functions whose arguments are more fine-grained than possible worlds: a centered world is a world plus a designated spatiotemporal location in the world.[9]

Given the two-dimensional intension, we can define two other kinds of intensions, which in Chalmers's terminology are called the primary and secondary intensions. The secondary intension is the ordinary intension, the one to which the externalist arguments apply. It is the function from worlds to extensions that are the values of the two-dimensional function. The primary intension, like the secondary intension, takes just one argument into extensions, though in this case the argument is a centered world. The value of the primary intension for a given centered world as argument is defined to be the same as the value of the two-dimensional intension for the pair of arguments consisting of the centered world and the same world, uncentered. Slightly more intuitively, to get the value of the primary intension in a given world, ask what the extension would be in that world considered as actual—what the words *as used in that world* refer to in that world. If on counterfactual twin earth, there is XYZ (but no H_2O) in the relevant bathtub, then we say (speaking in the actual world) that it is false that in that counterfactual world there is water in the tub. But our twin there truly says, "There is water in the tub." And if we associate the same two-dimensional intension with their utterance as with ours, then using Chalmers's terminology, we say that the secondary intension (determined in the actual world) is a proposition that is false on counterfactual twin earth, while the primary intension is a proposition that is true there.

A speaker or thinker who knows what the two-dimensional intension of some expression

Worlds considered as counterfactual (uncentered)

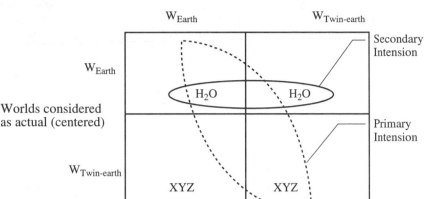

Figure 37.1. 2-D intension of 'water'

is, and so who knows what the primary intension is, might still be ignorant of the secondary intension, which unlike the primary intension may vary from world to world. It is this variation that represents the dependence on external facts to which the externalist points. But the primary intension is determined (by the two-dimensional intension) independently of any particular possible world, and is supposed to represent the internal component of content, the component that can be determined a priori.[10]

So without worrying about how to specify its details, we can represent the water role simply by identifying it with the primary intension of 'water.' All the problems that we have raised for conceptual analysis may now seem to disappear. First, recall our example of a counterfactual twin earth in which our duplicates use 'water' to pick out water, but use 'liquid' to pick out a type of substance (a slippery granular solid) that doesn't include water. This is a counterexample to any definition of water that includes the requirement that it be a liquid, and to the assumption that it is knowable a priori that water is a liquid. But the fact that water is not correctly called 'a liquid' in this possible world does not prevent the primary intension of 'water' from picking out water there. All it shows is that the primary intension of 'liquid' may fail to apply to something to which the primary intension of 'water' applies. A similar point can be made in response to the type of consideration advanced by Burge (1978). Imagine a twin earth in which you exist just as you are internally but in which the words 'colorless,' 'odorless,' 'river,' 'lake,'

and 'thirst-quenching' are all used differently by your language community so as to make all of these words fail to apply to water. Any of the familiar reference-fixing definitions would be false (showing that they are not really a priori), but that needn't keep your word 'water' from picking out water. If it does, then the (actual) primary intension of 'water' still picks out water in that counterfactual world. The coherence of such twin earth scenarios might be disputed, but with the two-dimensional apparatus, one can bypass that issue. The proposal that we identify the contents of concepts with primary intensions avoids the problem of the rigidified description theory by not *defining* 'water' in words. The primary intension is just a function from centered worlds to extensions. So the primary intension for our term 'water' maps each world into the right stuff, whether or not it is a liquid, and whether or not the linguistic community uses words differently from the way the utterer of 'water = H_2O' uses them. The right stuff is the stuff that is properly related to our uses and those of our language community. In any world in which our word 'water' actually picks out something, the primary intension will yield that very value (cf. White 1982).

Further, the primary intension apparatus appears to get around the problems of uniqueness that we discussed above. If in fact there is one thing that satisfies the primary intension for (our actual word) 'water' in the actual world, it is water. That is an a priori conceptual truth, for after all the primary intension is simply defined to ensure that this is true. Of course, some worlds have no water at all, and some worlds have a number of different substances that have an equal claim to the water role, as with jade in the actual world. As we suggested above, in some of the worlds in which it is discovered that there are several kinds of stuff to which the term 'water' has been applied, it would be decided by rational and knowledgeable speakers that there was no such thing as water; in other such worlds, they would decide that water was a disjunctive kind; and in still others, they would decide that water, despite what was previously thought, was really a superficial kind, the term applying to whatever has certain superficial properties commonly associated with water. Since the primary intension (of *our* word 'water' in the actual world) is determined by what rational and appropriately informed speakers would say in the different possible worlds, this intension will therefore, by definition, account for any of these possibilities.

So, it seems, none of the objections we have raised to reference-fixing conceptual analyses apply to primary intensions. So let us just identify the water role with the primary intension of 'water,' and use that as our definition in Jackson's pattern of argument. Reflection on the primary intension together with the microphysical facts about this world is enough to determine that H_2O satisfies that primary intension, that is, that H_2O = the unique waterish stuff. So we have achieved the Holy Grail: it is an a priori conceptual truth that if H_2O covers 60 percent of the globe and H_2O satisfies the 'water'-primary intension, then water covers 60 percent of the globe!

We hope that the reader is by now a little suspicious. How can so little do so much? Have we really succeeded, by this simple and perfectly general abstract maneuver, in identifying and isolating, for any expression, a component of its content that both is accessible a priori to anyone who understands the expression and will do the required work in Jackson's argument? We will argue that this apparatus contributes nothing to the identification of a purely conceptual or a priori knowable component of the content of a concept, or to the support of a claim that there is such a thing to be identified. At best, it provides a *framework for representing such a component,* should there be one to be represented. And we will also argue that even if it is granted, for the sake of the argument, that terms such as 'water' have primary intensions that are available a priori, that will not suffice to support Jackson's form of argument.

Second point first: suppose 'water' has a primary intension—say X—and that it is knowable a priori that water has this primary intension. Consider the paradigm argument, put in terms of primary intensions:

(a) 60 percent of the globe is covered by H_2O.
(b) H_2O = the satisfier of X (the primary intension of 'water').
(c) Water = the satisfier of X.

Therefore,

(d) 60 percent of the globe is covered by water.

For the argument to succeed in showing that (d) is entailed on conceptual grounds by the microphysical facts, it is required that (c) be a conceptual truth, and that (b) be a microphysical truth. The first we are granting for the moment, but it should be immediately obvious that the apparatus of primary intensions does nothing to show the second. What (b) says is that the primary intension of 'water' maps the actual world onto exactly one item, H_2O. But we can conclude that this is a microphysical fact only if it is *assumed* that microphysical facts determine or include all the facts. The primary intension of 'water' is a function that takes W_{Earth} to water, $W_{Twin\ Earth}$ to twin water, etc. But we can't, without begging the question, take for granted that the *microphysical* description of W_{Earth} describes only W_{Earth}. Suppose there are two microphysically indiscernible possible worlds, W_{Earth} and $W_{Super\ Twin\ Earth}$. Suppose further that there are primary intensions that take W_{Earth} to H_2O, but $W_{Super\ Twin\ Earth}$ to something else. (Primary intensions are just functions, and given any difference in inputs, there will be some functions that yield a difference in outputs.) If this is true for the primary intension of 'water,' then (b) will be a fact, but not a microphysical fact, or even supervenient on the microphysical facts. Unless we assume that the microphysical facts determine all the facts, or at least that the value of the primary intension for 'water' depends only on microphysical facts in the worlds that are the arguments to the function, the argument won't work. If our candidate conceptual analysis were an explicit verbal definition, in the vocabulary of microphysics, then we could be sure that the analogue of premise (b) was a microphysical truth, but once we move to the more abstract and unconstrained representation of meaning given by the two-dimensional intensional framework, we can no longer assume that this premise is necessitated by microphysical theory, and even if we could assume this, it is not clear what it would mean to say that this premise is deducible a priori from microphysics. In any case, if we do allow ourselves to assume that it is a microphysical truth that H_2O is the satisfier of the primary intension of 'water,' why do we not have equal justification to assume that it might be a microphysical truth about the actual world that pyramidal cell activity is the satisfier of the primary intension of 'consciousness'?

Earlier (in section 5) we discussed Jackson's remark that the medical profession would be outraged at the claim that they have not shown that fairies don't cause cancer. Our response was that although doctors can certainly rule out fairies as a cause of cancer, the claim that fairies don't cause cancer should not be regarded as literally a part of or deducible a priori from their theories. The discussion of the last paragraph shows that there is some value in translating the discussion into two-dimensional terms, since doing so reveals more starkly that the microphysical premise in Jackson's argument depends on the hidden assumption that the microphysical facts determine all the facts.

Let us now move to the other question: whether the two-dimensional apparatus provides a reason to believe that anything with the form of (c) is a conceptual truth. One might be tempted to think that the two-dimensional framework provides a recipe for determining the primary intension of any expression in the following way: Everyone can agree that *the world*—all that is the case—contains enough information to determine the semantic values (intensions of whatever kind, extensions, senses, contents, or whatever semantic values happen to be) of any expression that has a semantic value. So everyone can agree that if we are given an expression and a set of possible worlds in each of which the expression has some semantic value, this will determine a function taking the possible worlds into the semantic values, whatever they are, that the expression has in that world. If the values are secondary intensions, then this function will be a two-dimensional intension that will determine a primary intension. But is this the *relevant* two-dimensional intension? We doubt that it is, since this function is not itself a kind of meaning that the expression has, but is a representation of the *possible* meanings that it might have. Primary intensions, understood this

way, are like the primary weights of physical objects. Ordinary weight, which we might call 'secondary weight,' is an empirical property of physical objects, but we can also define the primary weight of a thing in the following way: Primary weight is a property of a physical object that is knowable a priori: it is a function that takes any possible world and time into the secondary weight of the thing at that time. So, for example, you know the primary weight of Alexander the Great if you could infer his weight at any time in any possible world in which he exists from a complete description of that possible world. There is a world in which he is a giant of 500 pounds, and the value of the function for that world is 500 pounds. There is another in which he is a skinny 120 pounds, and the value for that world is 120 pounds. And so forth. Obviously, this is not something you need empirical information to be able to do.

Now consider the English word 'coumarone.' Do you know what it means?[11] Perhaps not, but if primary intensions are determined in the way we have suggested, then you know its primary intension. That is, if you were told enough about *the world,* or about any possible world, then without leaving your armchair you would be able to tell what that word meant and referred to in that world. Suppose that for all you know, our world might be one in which 'coumarone' refers to an extinct flightless bird. There is surely a possible world in which the word (or at least one orthographically like it) has such a meaning, and there is a two-dimensional intension that takes the actual world into the actual meaning of 'coumarone' and this counterfactual world into the meaning that it has there. Functions are cheap—there are lots of different two-dimensional intensions that could be defined—but is this the relevant one for that word?

One might reply that the relevant two-dimensional intensions are fixed by the dispositions that the speaker has in virtue of understanding, or being a competent user of, the term in question, and so the reference of the word 'coumarone' in possible worlds which are compatible with the beliefs only of speakers who don't understand the word are not relevant. But this reply requires an account of how two-dimensional intensions are determined that is different from the one we are considering, an account that has not been provided. What exactly does one have to know to be a competent user of the term 'coumarone'? Is there any reason to believe that one can isolate a purely conceptual component of the knowledge of competent users of the term? The abstract two-dimensional framework itself is silent on these questions.

Alternatively, it may be suggested that the coumarone example is illicit because we are imagining speakers whose dispositions to use the word 'coumarone' are different from ours, or, better, for whom the functional role of 'coumarone' is different from ours. But this condition smuggles in a functionalist theory of concepts (via a functionalist theory of concept possession), and if we are prepared to buy that, it is unclear why we also need the primary intension theory. If the functionalist theory of concepts presupposes that there are analytic inferences that provide a purely conceptual component of the knowledge of competent users, that presupposition would have to be justified. If it does not suppose this, we will have to deal with the familiar holism problem of nonanalytic functionalism. How, and in what ways, can people differ in roles for a word while still expressing the same concept by that word?

If the relevant two-dimensional intension is the one determined in the way we have been suggesting, then it may, in a trivial sense, be knowable a priori, but it won't do the work that needs to be done in the paradigm argument. Why not? The reason is that since it is not a kind of meaning, intuitions such as those appealed to in thought experiments about Jackson's Mary, or about Chalmers's zombies, are not relevant to the limits of this primary intension for 'con-

sciousness.' No one will deny that the word 'consciousness,' or at least a word that is phonologically and orthographically indistinguishable from it, might have referred to some brain process (or to a flightless bird, for that matter). But is a possible world in which 'consciousness' refers to a brain process a world in which the primary intension of *our* word 'consciousness' has a secondary intensions that picks out a brain process, or is it a world in which the word 'consciousness' has a different primary intension from the one it has in our world?

The primary intensions defined by the procedure we have outlined are *derivative* from the actual and possible secondary intensions that a word has. To get the value of the primary intension at a given world, just find the secondary intension that the word has in that world, and the extension that it determines. But Chalmers insists that the primary intensions he is talking about are not derivative in this way. To determine the primary intension of some concept, it is just irrelevant what meaning the concept *would* have if used in some other possible world. It is *our* concept, as used in the actual world, that determines the referent in other possible worlds. "Given an individual's concept in thought, we can assign a primary intension corresponding to what it will pick out depending on how the actual world turns out" (Chalmers 1996, 65). "We can retain the concept from our own world, and consider how it applies to other worlds considered as actual" (366). Recall that, for Chalmers,

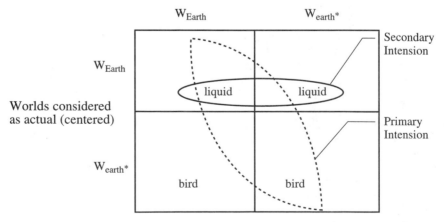

Figure 37.2.   2-D intension of 'coumarone'

a concept is something like a mental word—a syntactic or quasi-syntactic object. It is not a meaning, but something that has a meaning. But of course a word (or a concept, in this sense) will "pick out" or refer to something in a world only in virtue of its semantic properties—its meaning. So when we consider how a concept from our own world applies in other worlds, we are considering the interpreted concept—the concept with its actual meaning. On the interpretation of primary intensions that Chalmers is rejecting, the meaning used to "pick out" an extension for the concept in a given possible world was the meaning that it had in that world. On Chalmers's intended interpretation, we "retain" the meaning the concept has in the actual world, asking what extension it determined in a given counterfactual possible world "considered as actual." But now we can see a dilemma: to get the primary intension, we carry our concept around from world to world, taking its actual meaning with it, to see what it picks out. In the case of our 'water' concept, the result is supposed to be that it picks out water on Earth, twin water on Twin Earth, etc. But what is it exactly that we carry, or "retain," from world to world? If it is the meaning in the ordinary sense (the "wide" meaning, or secondary intension), then it does *not* pick out twin water on Twin Earth, since as Putnam taught us 'water' refers to *water* (H_2O) everywhere (or to nothing in situations where there is no water). So it must be the narrow meaning—the purely conceptual content—that is retained. But the primary intension (or perhaps the two-dimensional intension) is supposed to be the explication of narrow, or purely conceptual, content. So this answer is of no help in explaining what the primary intension of a concept is. All that is being said is that the primary intension of a concept is the function that yields, for each possible world, the value of its primary intension for that world.

We can agree that *if* a word has a conceptual content that is available to anyone who understands the word, then this content might be usefully represented by a two-dimensional intension, but the apparatus by itself gives no support to the hypothesis that there is such a content. The apparatus *presupposes, rather than explains or justifies,* the distinctions that are required to factor the content of a concept into a priori and external components.

Chalmers does say some things about how to think about the primary intensions of our concepts, and so about what the facts are that give a concept its primary intension: we should reflect on what we should (not would, but would if rational) say if we were to find out certain things about the actual world. If we were to find out that the colorless odorless drinkable (more or less) stuff in rivers and lakes is XYZ, we would conclude that water is (necessarily) XYZ. If we found that such stuff is not really a liquid, we would have found out, and we should say, that water is not a liquid. (But isn't it also true that if we were to learn that the word 'coumarone' referred to an extinct flightless bird, we would conclude that coumarones—as we would put it—are extinct flightless birds?) This seems to be armchair reasoning, reflection that does not include any obvious reference to real experiments, so it is tempting to conclude that this reflection just unfolds our concepts in a totally a priori way. But what this conclusion misses is that our reasoning about the proper epistemic response in various counterfactual situations is informed not only by our concepts, but by implicit and explicit theories and general methodological principles that we have absorbed through our scientific culture—by everything that the "we" who are performing these thought experiments believe. What people should rationally say in response to various hypothesized discoveries will vary depending on their experience, commitments and epistemic priorities.

We need not, however, put any weight on the claim that the methodological principles and priorities that we use to answer such questions are not a priori, or on any assumptions about what is or is not properly said to be part of conceptual content. The crucial question, for the issue we have been discussing in this paper, is whether a relevant contrast can be shown between the relation between water and H_2O on the one hand and the relation between consciousness and some brain process on the other.

Suppose, to try to get at the primary intension of the word 'consciousness,' in the way suggested by Chalmers, we ask how "we" should respond if the neurophysiological and behavioral evidence were to provide dramatic support for the conclusion that there is (at least) a strong correlation between phenomenal consciousness and a certain very specific kind of brain process (for example, the kind suggested in the work of Crick and Koch discussed above). Further, suppose that the cluster of properties that a functionalist might be inclined to use to define phenomenal consciousness (the consciousness role) could be explained in terms of this brain process. A philosopher with physicalist leanings in such a possible world might reasonably conclude that these facts would justify identifying consciousness with the brain process. So an actual philosopher with such inclinations might reasonably conclude that the value of the function that is the primary intension of our word 'consciousness' for this possible scenario is this brain process, just as the value of the 'water' primary intension for our world is H_2O. Jackson and Chalmers would presumably disagree with this conclusion. Is this dispute a purely conceptual or semantic one, a dispute that shows that these different philosophers use the word 'consciousness' with different primary intensions? We doubt it, but however the disagreement is characterized, the issue does not seem to be different in principle from issues about the kind of scientific reduction and explanation that Levine, Jackson, and Chalmers are trying to contrast with the issue about the explanation of consciousness.

Consider once again an analogue of the paradigm argument for the case of a conscious state.

(a*) Pyramidal cell activity was rampant in medieval prisons.
(b*) Pyramidal cell activity = the satisfier of the primary intension of 'pain.'
(c*) Pain = the satisfier of the primary intension of 'pain.'

Therefore,

(d*) Pain was rampant in medieval prisons.

Our point is that there could be compelling motivation for (b*) and that (c*) has whatever a priori status (c) above has.

In the first nine sections of this paper, we discussed physicalism and reductive explanation in the context of putative explicit verbal analyses in microphysical terms of such ordinary concepts as *life* and *water*. We expressed skepticism about whether such concepts are a priori analyzable in microphysical terms (or whether there are microphysical sufficient conditions for their application). But Jackson and Chalmers are skeptical too, regarding every such analysis that they mention as only an approximation. To go beyond approximation, they recommend the two-dimensional framework that we have been discussing in this section. But as we have pointed out here, the two-dimensional apparatus does not in any way help to isolate an a priori conceptual component of content, but—at least as used by Jackson and Chalmers—merely presupposes that there is such a thing.

We have made three major points in this section

1. We argued earlier that there is no reason to believe reductive explanation requires conceptual analyses of the sort "Water is the odorless, colorless liquid that. . . ." The move to primary intensions does not get around these considerations.

2. The claim that H_2O is the (or even a) satisfier of the primary intension of 'water' is not a microphysical claim.

3. The a priori status of the claim that water is the satisfier of the primary intension of 'water' does not escape the main criticisms applied to its less technical predecessor. And whatever a priori status it does have applies equally to the claim that pain is the satisfier of the primary intension of 'pain.'

NOTES

We are grateful to the following persons for their helpful comments on previous drafts of this paper: Alex Byrne, David Chalmers, Frank Jackson, Joe Levine, Barry Lower, and the editors and referees for the *Philosophical Review*.

1. Horgan 1984 (building on Lewis 1983) argues that a Laplacean demon could figure out all the facts from the microphysical facts and meaning constraints. Versions of the view that facts that don't involve consciousness follow a priori from physics appear in Jackson 1993, 1994, 1995; Levine 1983, 1993; and Chalmers 1996. (Important precursors are to be found in Lewis 1966 and Nagel 1974.) Jackson 1994

is a variant of Jackson 1993. Jackson 1995 is a brief and lucid summary of the same points in the context of Jackson's "Mary" argument against physicalism. Two Ph. D. theses, Byrne 1993 and Chalmers 1993, cover much the same ground.

2. As is clear from this quotation, and also from other passages in this paper, Levine has some reservations about the conceptual analysis thesis. If one concedes that the analyses that result from the process of working ordinary concepts into shape for reduction are only relatively or quasi a priori, then (depending on how the qualifications are developed) it may be more plausible to assume that terms like 'water' and

'boiling' have analyses. But it may at the same time become more plausible to say that consciousness has an analysis of this kind in physical terms.

3. The rigidifying operator works as follows: the extension of 'the actual F,' in any possible world w, is the thing that is the unique F in the actual world. In an earlier draft, we used some jargon from David Kaplan's work on demonstratives to represent rigidified descriptions: "dthat[the F]" instead of "the actual F." Kaplan's device is often interpreted as a rigidifying operator, but as Jim Pryor and Alex Byrne reminded us, this misrepresents Kaplan's original intentions in a way that is subtle, but important for the general issue we are discussing. As Kaplan first explained it, 'dthat' is not an operator on definite descriptions that turns them into rigid designators of the denotation of the description, but instead a semantically complete but context-dependent referring term. It is like a demonstrative 'that' whose use is accompanied by a pointing gesture, or a 'she' used in a context that somehow makes salient one particular female. The description in brackets following the 'dthat' should be understood, not as a constituent of the sentence, but as a substitute for the contextual features that do the job of fixing the reference—a bit of stage direction rather than a part of the dialogue. See Kaplan 1989, 578ff. for a discussion of the contrast between these two interpretations of 'dthat.'

4. We will ignore the fact that reference-fixing definitions of terms like 'heat' might be expected to contain such a reference to sensations.

5. Chalmers acknowledges a "minor complication" (1996, 40), that "negative facts" do not follow a priori from microphysics. A positive fact in W is defined as a fact that holds in every world that contains W as a proper part. We are skeptical about the use of 'proper part' as a relation between worlds. We understand possible worlds as ways things might be. What is a proper part of a way things might be? To the extent that we get a grip on the notion, we doubt that there are any positive facts.

6. One of us heard this story somewhere, but we don't know where (see Block 1978).

7. Cf. Kripke 1972, 88 n. 38, where Kripke comments on a point made by Robert Nozick that, in a sense, a description theory of names would be trivially true if there were a reductive analysis of reference of any kind. But Kripke disclaims any attempt to give such a reductive analysis, and expresses doubt that there is one to be had.

8. It is a familiar point that the word 'concept' is ambiguous, and we think that equivocation on it is implicated in some of the confusions in the application of the two-dimensional apparatus. Sometimes 'concept' refers to something abstract like a meaning. Concepts are what predicates are used to express, as propositions are what sentences are used to say. Propositions are also the contents of thoughts (acts of thinking, states of believing); concepts, in this semantic sense, are perhaps components of what is said and thought. Other times, by 'concept' one is attempting to refer to a mental analogue of a predicate—a mental word rather than what the mental word expresses. If one applies the type-token distinction to concepts, or if one talks about the content of a concept, one is using the word in this sense. It is controversial whether there are concepts in this latter sense and whether if there are, they play any significant role in thought, but we will go along for the ride, following Chalmers in using 'concept' in this sense.

9. In other applications of this kind of framework, this complication is not necessary since if it is a particular token utterance, rather than an utterance type, that is associated with a two-dimensional intension, then both arguments of the function can be simply possible worlds.

10. The abstract two-dimensional semantic apparatus has its origin in work by Hans Kamp and Frank Vlach, extended and applied by David Kaplan in his theory of demonstratives. An important purely abstract development of two-dimensional semantics is Segerberg 1973. Stalnaker 1978 is a more general application of the framework to semantic and pragmatic phenomena, including the use of it to represent Kripke's distinctions between a priori/a posteriori and necessary/contingent. Davies and Humberstone 1980, another application of the apparatus, is the source of the terminology "world considered as actual" versus "world considered as counterfactual." White 1982 applies a version of Kaplan's content/character distinction to the language of thought. Stalnaker 1990 and Block 1991 consider the use of the apparatus to define a notion of narrow content.

11. In case you are curious, it is another colorless liquid, not H_2O, but C_6H_4OCHCH. But of course it is not knowable a priori that that is what it is.

REFERENCES

Block, N. 1978. "Reductionism." In *Encyclopedia of Bioethics,* ed. Warren T. Reich, 1419–24. London: Macmillan.

——. 1991. "What Narrow Content Is Not." In *Meaning in Mind: Fodor and His Critics,* ed. B. Loewer and G. Rey. Oxford: Blackwell.

Burge, T. 1979. "Individualism and the Mental." *Midwest Studies in Philosophy* 4:73–122.

Byrne, A. 1993. "The Emergent Mind." Ph.D. diss., Princeton University.

Chalmers, D. 1993. "Toward a Theory of Consciousness." Ph.D. diss., Indiana University.

——. 1996. *The Conscious Mind.* New York: Oxford University Press.

Crick, F. 1994. *The Astonishing Hypothesis.* New York: Scribner.

Crick, F., and C. Koch. 1990. "Towards a Neurobiological Theory of Consciousness." *Seminars in the Neurosciences* 2:263–75.

Davies, M., and L. Humberstone. 1980. "Two Notions of Necessity." *Philosophical Studies* 38:1–30.

Davies, M., and G. Humphreys. 1993. *Consciousness: Psychological and Philosophical Essays.* Oxford: Blackwell.

Evans, G. 1982. *The Varieties of Reference.* Oxford: Oxford University Press.

Field, H. 1973. "Theory Change and the Indeterminacy of Reference." *Journal of Philosophy* 70.

Hill, C. 1997. "Imaginability, Conceivability, Possibility and the Mind-Body Problem." *Philosophical Studies* 87:61–85.

Horgan, T. 1984. "Supervenience and Cosmic Hermeneutics." *Southern Journal of Philosophy* 22 (supp.): 19–38.

Jackson, F 1982. "Epiphenomenal Qualia." *Philosophical Quarterly* 32:127–36.

———. "Armchair Metaphysics." In *Philosophy in Mind,* ed. J. O'Leary-Hawthorne and M. Michael. Dordrecht: Kluwer.

———. 1994. "Finding the Mind in the Natural World." In *Philosophy and the Cognitive Sciences,* ed. R. Casati, B. Smith, G. White, 100–12. Vienna:Verlag Hölder-Pichler-Tempsky. Reprinted in *The Nature of Consciousness: Philosophical Debates,* ed. N. Block, O. Flanagan, and G. Güzeldere (Cambridge: MIT, 1997).

———. 1995. "Postscript to 'What Mary Didn't Know.' " In *Contemporary Materialism,* ed. P. K. Moser and J. D. Trout. London: Routledge.

Kaplan, D. 1978. "Dthat." In *Pragmatics, Syntax and Semantics,* vol. 9: *Pragmatics,* ed. P. Cole. New York: Academic Press.

———. 1989. "Afterthoughts." In *Themes From Kaplan,* ed. J. Almog, J. Perry, and H. Wettstein, 565–614. Oxford: Oxford University Press.

Levine, J. 1983. "Materialism and qualia: The explanatory gap." *Pacific Philosophical Quarterly* 64:354–61.

———. 1993. "On Leaving Out What It Is Like." In Davies and Humphreys 1993.

Lewis, D. 1966. "An Argument for the Identity Theory." *Journal of Philosophy* 63:17–25.

———. 1983. "New Work for a Theory of Universals." *Australasian Journal of Philosophy* 61:343–77.

Loar, B. 1990. "Phenomenal Properties." In *Philosophical Perspectives: Action Theory and Philosophy of Mind,* ed. J. Tomberlin. Atascadero, Calif.: Ridgeview.

McGinn, C. 1991. *The Problem of Consciousness.* Oxford: Blackwell.

Nagel, T. 1974. "What Is It Like to Be a Bat?" *Philosophical Review* 83:435–50.

Segerberg, K. 1973. "Two-dimensional modal logic." *Journal of Philosophical Logic* 2:77–96.

Smart, J.J. C. 1959. "Sensations and Brain Processes." *Philosophical Review* 68:141–56.

Stalnaker, R. 1978. "Assertion." In *Syntax and Semantics,* vol. 9: *Pragmatics,* ed. P. Cole. New York: Academic Press.

———. 1990. "Narrow Content." In *Propositional Attitudes: The Role of Content in Logic, Language and Mind,* ed. C. A. Anderson and J. Owens, 131–46. Stanford: CSLI.

White, S. 1982. "Partial Character and the Language of Thought." *Pacific Philosophical Quarterly* 63:347–65.

38 | Can We Solve the Mind–Body Problem?

Colin McGinn

> How it is that anything so remarkable as a state of consciousness comes about as a result of initiating nerve tissue, is just as unaccountable as the appearance of the Djin, where Aladdin rubbed his lamp in the story . . .
>
> (Julian Huxley)

We have been trying for a long time to solve the mind–body problem. It has stubbornly resisted our best efforts. The mystery persists. I think the time has come to admit candidly that we cannot resolve the mystery. But I also think that this very insolubility—or the reason for it—removes the philosophical problem. In this paper I explain why I say these outrageous things.

The specific problem I want to discuss concerns consciousness, the hard nut of the mind–body problem. How is it possible for conscious states to depend upon brain states? How can technicolour phenomenology arise from soggy grey matter? What makes the bodily organ we call the brain so radically different from other bodily organs, say the kidneys—the body parts without a trace of consciousness? How could the aggregation of millions of indi-

From *Mind* 98:349–66, 1989. Reprinted with permission of author and publisher.

vidually insentient neurons generate subjective awareness? We know that brains are the de facto causal basis of consciousness, but we have, it seems, no understanding whatever of how this can be so. It strikes us as miraculous, eerie, even faintly comic. Somehow, we feel, the water of the physical brain is turned into the wine of consciousness, but we draw a total blank on the nature of this conversion. Neural transmissions just seem like the wrong kind of materials with which to bring consciousness into the world, but it appears that in some way they perform this mysterious feat. The mind–body problem is the problem of understanding how the miracle is wrought, thus removing the sense of deep mystery. We want to take the magic out of the link between consciousness and the brain.[1]

Purported solutions to the problem have tended to assume one of two forms. One form, which we may call constructive, attempts to specify some natural property of the brain (or body) which explains how consciousness can be elicited from it. Thus functionalism, for example, suggests a property—namely, causal role—which is held to be satisfied by both brain states and mental states; this property is supposed to explain how conscious states can come from brain states.[2] The other form, which has been historically dominant, frankly admits that nothing merely natural could do the job, and suggests instead that we invoke supernatural entities or divine interventions. Thus we have Cartesian dualism and Leibnizian pre-established harmony. These 'solutions' at least recognize that something pretty remarkable is needed if the mind–body relation is to be made sense of; they are as extreme as the problem. The approach I favour is naturalistic but not constructive: I do not believe we can ever specify what it is about the brain that is responsible for consciousness, but I am sure that whatever it is it is not inherently miraculous. The problem arises, I want to suggest, because we are cut off by our very cognitive constitution from achieving a conception of that natural property of the brain (or of consciousness) that accounts for the psychophysical link. This is a kind of causal nexus that we are precluded from ever understanding, given the way we have to form our concepts and develop our theories. No wonder we find the problem so difficult!

Before I can hope to make this view plausible, I need to sketch the general conception of cognitive competence that underlies my position. Let me introduce the idea of *cognitive clo-*

sure. A type of mind M is cognitively closed with respect to a property P (or theory T) if and only if the concept-forming procedures at M's disposal cannot extend to a grasp of P (or an understanding of T). Conceiving minds come in different kinds, equipped with varying powers and limitations, biases and blindspots, so that properties (or theories) may be accessible to some minds but not to others. What is closed to the mind of a rat may be open to the mind of a monkey, and what is open to us may be closed to the monkey. Representational power is not all or nothing. Minds are biological products like bodies, and like bodies they come in different shapes and sizes, more or less capacious, more or less suited to certain cognitive tasks.[3] This is particularly clear for perceptual faculties, of course: perceptual closure is hardly to be denied. Different species are capable of perceiving different properties of the world, and no species can perceive every property things may instantiate (without artificial instrumentation anyway). But such closure does not reflect adversely on the reality of the properties that lie outside the representational capacities in question; a property is no less real for not being reachable from a certain kind of perceiving and conceiving mind. The invisible parts of the electromagnetic spectrum are just as real as the visible parts, and whether a specific kind of creature can form conceptual representations of these imperceptible parts does not determine whether they exist. Thus cognitive closure with respect to P does not imply irrealism about P. That P is (as we might say) *noumenal* for M does not show that P does not occur in some naturalistic scientific theory T—it shows only that T is not cognitively accessible to M. Presumably monkey minds and the property of being an electron illustrate this possibility. And the question must arise as to whether human minds are closed with respect to certain true explanatory theories. Nothing, at least, in the concept of reality shows that everything real is open to the human concept-forming faculty—if, that is, we are realists about reality.[4]

Consider a mind constructed according to the principles of classical empiricism, a Humean mind. Hume mistakenly thought that human minds were Humean, but we can at least conceive of such a mind (perhaps dogs and monkeys have Humean minds). A Humean mind is such that perceptual closure determines cognitive closure, since 'ideas' must always be copies of 'impressions'; therefore the concept-forming system cannot transcend what can be perceptually presented to the subject. Such a mind will be closed with respect to unobservables; the properties of atoms, say, will not be representable by a mind constructed in this way. This implies that explanatory theories in which these properties are essentially mentioned will not be accessible to a Humean mind.[5] And hence the observable phenomena that are explained by allusion to unobservables will be inexplicable by a mind thus limited. But notice: the incapacity to explain certain phenomena does not carry with it a lack of recognition of the theoretical problems the phenomena pose. You might be able to appreciate a problem without being able to formulate (even in principle) the solution to that problem (I suppose human children are often in this position, at least for a while). A Humean mind cannot solve the problems that our physics solves, yet it might be able to have an inkling of what needs to be explained. We would expect, then, that a moderately intelligent enquiring Humean mind will feel permanently perplexed and mystified by the physical world, since the correct science is forever beyond its cognitive reach. Indeed, something like this was precisely the view of Locke. He thought that our ideas of matter are quite sharply constrained by our perceptions and so concluded that the true science of matter is eternally beyond us—that we could never remove our perplexities about (say) what solidity ultimately is.[6] But it does not follow for Locke that nature is itself inherently mysterious; the felt mystery comes from our own cognitive limitations, not from any objective eeriness in the world. It looks today as if Locke was wrong about our capacity to fathom the nature of the physical world, but we can still learn from his fundamental thought—the insistence that our cognitive faculties may not be up to solving every problem that confronts us. To put the point more generally: the human mind may not conform to empiricist principles, but it must conform to *some* principles—and it is a substantive claim that these principles permit the solution of every problem we can formulate or sense. Total cognitive openness is not guaranteed for human beings and it should not be expected. Yet what is noumenal for us may not be miraculous in itself. We should therefore be alert to the possibility that a problem that strikes us as deeply intractable, as utterly baffling, may arise from an area of cognitive closure in our ways of representing the world.[7] That is what I now want to argue is the case with our sense of the mysterious nature of the connection be-

tween consciousness and the brain. We are biased away from arriving at the correct explanatory theory of the psychophysical nexus. And this makes us prone to an illusion of objective mystery. Appreciating this should remove the philosophical problem: consciousness does not, in reality, arise from the brain in the miraculous way in which the Djin arises from the lamp.

I now need to establish three things: (i) there exists some property of the brain that accounts naturalistically for consciousness; (ii) we are cognitively closed with respect to that property; but (iii) there is no philosophical (as opposed to scientific) mind–body problem. Most of the work will go into establishing (ii).

Resolutely shunning the supernatural, I think it is undeniable that it must be in virtue of *some* natural property of the brain that organisms are conscious. There just *has* to be some explanation for how brains subserve minds. If we are not to be eliminativists about consciousness, then some theory must exist which accounts for the psychophysical correlations we observe. It is implausible to take these correlations as ultimate and inexplicable facts, as simply brute. And we do not want to acknowledge radical emergence of the conscious with respect to the cerebral: that is too much like accepting miracles *de re*. Brain states cause conscious states, we know, and this causal nexus must proceed through necessary connections of some kind— the kind that would make the nexus intelligible *if* they were understood.[8] Consciousness is like life in this respect. We know that life evolved from inorganic matter, so we expect there to be some explanation of this process. We cannot plausibly take the arrival of life as a primitive brute fact, nor can we accept that life arose by some form of miraculous emergence. Rather, there must be some natural account of how life comes from matter, whether or not we can know it. Eschewing vitalism and the magic touch of God's finger, we rightly insist that it must be in virtue of some natural property of (organized) matter that parcels of it get to be alive. But consciousness itself is just a further biological development, and so it too must be susceptible of some natural explanation—whether or not human beings are capable of arriving at this explanation. Presumably there exist objective natural laws that somehow account for the upsurge of consciousness. Consciousness, in short, must be a natural phenomenon, naturally arising from certain organizations of matter. Let us then say that there exists some property *P*, instantiated by the brain, in virtue of which the brain is the basis of consciousness. Equivalently, there exists some theory T, referring to P, which fully explains the dependence of conscious states on brain states. If we knew T, then we would have a constructive solution to the mind–body problem. The question then is whether we can ever come to know T and grasp the nature of P.

Let me first observe that it is surely *possible* that we could never arrive at a grasp of P; there is, as I said, no guarantee that our cognitive powers permit the solution of every problem we can recognize. Only a misplaced idealism about the natural world could warrant the dogmatic claim that everything is knowable by the human species at this stage of its evolutionary development (consider the same claim made on behalf of the intellect of cro-Magnon man). It *may* be that every property for which we can form a concept is such that *it* could never solve the mind–body problem. We *could* be like five-year old children trying to understand Relativity Theory. Still, so far this is just a possibility claim: what reason do we have for asserting, positively, that our minds are closed with respect to P?

Longstanding historical failure is suggestive, but scarcely conclusive. Maybe, it will be said, the solution is just around the corner, or it has to wait upon the completion of the physical sciences? Perhaps we simply have yet to produce the Einstein-like genius who will restructure the problem in some clever way and then present an astonished world with the solution?[9] However, I think that our deep bafflement about the problem, amounting to a vertiginous sense of ultimate mystery, which resists even articulate formulation, should at least encourage us to explore the idea that there is something terminal about our perplexity. Rather as traditional theologians found themselves conceding cognitive closure with respect to certain of the properties of God, so we should look seriously at the idea that the mind–body problem brings us bang up against the limits of our capacity to understand the world. That is what I shall do now.

There seem to be two possible avenues open to us in our aspiration to identify P: we could try to get to P by investigating consciousness directly, or we could look to the study of the brain for P. Let us consider these in turn, starting with consciousness. Our acquaintance with consciousness could hardly be more direct; phenomenological description thus comes (relatively) easily. 'Introspection' is the name of the faculty through which we catch consciousness in all its vivid nakedness. By virtue of possessing this cognitive faculty we ascribe concepts of consciousness to ourselves; we thus have 'immediate access' to the properties of consciousness. But does the introspective faculty reveal property P? Can we tell just by introspecting what the solution to the mind–body problem is? Clearly not. We have direct cognitive access to one term of the mind–brain relation, but we do not have such access to the nature of the link. Introspection does not present conscious states *as* depending upon the brain in some intelligible way. We cannot therefore introspect P. Moreover, it seems impossible that we should ever augment our stock of introspectively ascribed concepts with the concept P—that is, we could not acquire this concept simply on the basis of sustained and careful introspection. Pure phenomenology will never provide the solution to the mind–body problem. Neither does it seem feasible to try to extract P from the concepts of consciousness we now have by some procedure of conceptual analysis—any more than we could solve the life–matter problem simply by reflecting on the concept *life*.[10] P has to lie outside the field of the introspectable, and it is not implicitly contained in the concepts we bring to bear in our first-person ascriptions. Thus the faculty of introspection, as a concept-forming capacity, is cognitively closed with respect to P; which is not surprising in view of its highly limited domain of operation (*most* properties of the world are closed to introspection).

But there is a further point to be made about P and consciousness, which concerns our restricted access to the concepts of consciousness themselves. It is a familiar point that the range of concepts of consciousness attainable by a mind M is constrained by the specific forms of consciousness possessed by M. Crudely, you cannot form concepts of conscious properties unless you yourself instantiate those properties. The man born blind cannot grasp the concept of a visual experience of red, and human beings cannot conceive of the echolocatory experiences of bats.[11] These are cases of cognitive closure within the class of conscious properties. But now this kind of closure will, it seems, affect our hopes of access to P. For suppose that we were cognitively open with respect to P; suppose, that is, that we had the solution to the problem of how specific forms of consciousness depend upon different kinds of physiological structure. Then, of course, we would understand how the brain of a bat subserves the subjective experiences of bats. Call this type of experience *B*, and call the explanatory property that links *B* to the bat's brain P_1. By grasping P_1 it would be perfectly intelligible to us how the bat's brain generates *B*-experiences; we would have an explanatory theory of the causal nexus in question. We would be in possession of the same kind of understanding we would have of our own experiences if we had the correct psychophysical theory of them. But then it seems to follow that grasp of the theory that explains *B*-experiences would *confer* a grasp of the nature of those experiences: for how could we understand that theory without understanding the concept *B* that occurs in it? How could we grasp the *nature* of *B*-experiences without grasping the *character* of those experiences? The true psychophysical theory would seem to provide a route to a grasp of the subjective form of the bat's experiences. But now we face a dilemma, a dilemma which threatens to become a reductio: either we *can* grasp this theory, in which case the property *B* becomes open to us; or we *cannot* grasp the theory, simply because property *B* is *not* open to us. It seems to me that the looming reductio here is compelling: our concepts of consciousness just *are* inherently constrained by our own form of consciousness, so that any theory the understanding of which required us to transcend these constraints would ipso facto be inaccessible to us. Similarly, I think, any theory that required us to transcend the finiteness of our cognitive capacities would ipso facto be a theory we could not grasp—and this despite the fact that it might be needed to explain something we can see needs explaining. We cannot simply stipulate that our concept-forming abilities are indefinitely plastic and unlimited just because they would have to be to enable us to grasp the truth about the world. We constitutionally lack the concept-forming capacity to encompass all possible types of conscious state, and this obstructs our path to a general solution to the mind–body problem. Even if we could solve it for our own case, we could not solve it for bats and Martians. *P* is, as it were, too close to the different forms of subjectivity for it to be accessible to all such forms, given that one's form of subjectivity restricts one's concepts of subjectivity.[12]

I suspect that most optimists about constructively solving the mind–body problem will prefer to place their bets on the brain side of the relation. Neuroscience is the place to look for property *P*, they will say. My question then is whether there is any conceivable way in which we might come to introduce *P* in the course of our empirical investigations of the brain. New concepts have been introduced in the effort to understand the workings of the brain, certainly: could not *P* then occur in conceivable extensions of this manner of introduction? So far, indeed, the theoretical concepts we ascribe to the brain seem as remote from consciousness as any ordinary physical properties are, but perhaps we might reach *P* by diligent application of essentially the same procedures: so it is tempting to think. I want to suggest, to the contrary, that such procedures are inherently closed with respect to *P*. The fundamental reason for this, I think, is the role of *perception* in shaping our understanding of the brain—the way that our perception of the brain constrains the concepts we can apply to it. A point whose significance it would be hard to overstress here is this: the property of consciousness itself (or specific conscious states) is not an observable or perceptible property of the brain. You can stare into a living conscious brain, your own or someone else's, and see there a wide variety of unstantiated properties—its shape, colour, texture, etc.—but you will not thereby *see* what the subject is experiencing, the conscious state itself. Conscious states are simply not potential objects of perception: they depend upon the brain but they cannot be observed by directing the senses onto the brain. In other words, consciousness is noumenal with respect to perception of the brain.[13] I take it this is obvious. So we know there *are* properties of the brain that are necessarily closed to perception of the brain; the question now is whether *P* is likewise closed to perception.

My argument will proceed as follows. I shall first argue that *P* is indeed perceptually closed; then I shall complete the argument to full cognitive closure by insisting that no form of *inference* from what is perceived can lead us to *P*. The argument for perceptual closure starts from the thought that nothing we can imagine perceiving in the brain would ever convince us that we have located the intelligible nexus we seek. No matter what recondite property we could see to be instantiated in the brain we would always be baffled about how it could give rise to consciousness. I hereby invite you to try to conceive of a perceptible property of the brain that might allay the feeling of mystery that attends our contemplation of the brain–mind link: I do not think you will be able to do it. It is like trying to conceive of a perceptible property of a rock that would render it perspicuous that the rock was conscious. In fact, I think it is the very impossibility of this that lies at the root of the felt mind–body problem. But why is this? Basically, I think, it is because the senses are geared to representing a spatial world; they essentially present things in space with spatially defined properties. But it is precisely *such* properties that seem inherently incapable of resolving the mind–body problem: we cannot link consciousness to the brain in virtue of spatial properties of the brain. There the brain is, an object of perception, laid out in space, containing spatially distributed processes; but consciousness defies explanation in such terms. Consciousness does not seem made up out of smaller spatial processes; yet perception of the brain seems limited to revealing such processes.[14] The senses are responsive to certain *kinds* of properties—those that are essentially bound up with space—but these properties are of the wrong sort (the wrong *category*) to constitute *P*. Kant was right, the form of outer sensibility is spatial; but if so, then *P* will be noumenal with respect to the senses, since no spatial property will ever deliver a satisfying answer to the mind–body problem. We simply do not understand the idea that conscious states might intelligibly arise from spatial configurations of the kind disclosed by perception of the world.

I take it this claim will not seem terribly controversial. After all, we do not generally expect that every property referred to in our theories should be a potential object of human perception: consider quantum theory and cosmology. Unrestricted perceptual openness is a dogma of empiricism if ever there was one. And there is no compelling reason to suppose that the property needed to explain the mind–brain relation should be in principle perceptible; it might be essentially 'theoretical,' an object of thought not sensory experience. Looking harder at nature is not the only (or the best) way of discovering its theoretically significant properties. Perceptual closure does not entail cognitive closure, since we have available the procedure of hypothesis formation, in which *un*observables come to be conceptualized.

I readily agree with these sentiments, but I think there are reasons for believing that no coherent method of concept introduction will ever lead us to *P*. This is because a certain principle of *homogeneity* operates in our introduction of theoretical concepts on the basis of observation. Let me first note that consciousness itself could not be introduced simply on the basis of what we observe about the brain and its physical effects. If our data, arrived at by perception of the brain, do not include anything that brings in conscious states, then the theoretical properties we need to explain these data will not include conscious states either. Inference to the best explanation of purely physical data will never take us outside the realm of the physical, forcing us to introduce concepts of consciousness.[15] Everything physical has a purely physical explanation. So the property of consciousness is cognitively closed with respect to the introduction of concepts by means of inference to the best explanation of perceptual data about the brain.

Now the question is whether *P* could ever be arrived at by this kind of inference. Here we must be careful to guard against a form of magical emergentism with respect to concept formation. Suppose we try out a relatively clear theory of how theoretical concepts are formed: we get them by a sort of analogical extension of what we observe. Thus, for example, we arrive at the concept of a molecule by taking our perceptual representations of macroscopic objects and conceiving of smaller scale objects of the same general kind. This method seems to work well enough for unobservable material objects, but it will not help in arriving at *P*, since analogical extensions of the entities we observe in the brain are precisely as hopeless as the original entities were as solutions to the mind–body problem. We would need a method that left the base of observational properties behind in a much more radical way. But it seems to me that even a more unconstrained conception of inference to the best explanation would still not do what is required: it would no more serve to introduce *P* than it serves to introduce the property of consciousness itself. To explain the observed physical data we need only such theoretical properties as bear upon those data, not the property that explains consciousness, which does not occur in the data. Since we do not need consciousness to explain those data, we do not need the property that explains consciousness. We will never get as far away from the perceptual data in our explanations of those data as we need to get in order to connect up explanatorily with consciousness. This is, indeed, why it seems that consciousness is theoretically epiphenomenal in the task of accounting for physical events. No concept needed to explain the workings of the physical world will suffice to explain how the physical world produces consciousness. So if *P* is perceptually noumenal, then it will be noumenal with respect to perception-based explanatory inferences. Accordingly, I do not think that P could be arrived at by empirical studies of the brain alone. Nevertheless, the brain *has* this property, as it has the property of consciousness. Only a magical idea of how we come by concepts could lead one to think that we can reach P by first perceiving the brain and then asking what is needed to explain what we perceive.[16] (The mind–body problem tempts us to magic in more ways than one.)

It will help elucidate the position I am driving towards if I contrast it with another view of the source of the perplexity we feel about the mind–brain nexus. I have argued that we cannot know which property of the brain accounts for consciousness, and so we find the mind–brain link unintelligible. But, it may be said, there is another account of our sense of irremediable mystery, which does not require positing properties our minds cannot represent. This alternative view claims that, even if we *now* had a grasp of P, we would *still* feel that there is something mysterious about the link, because of a special epistemological feature of the situation. Namely this: our acquaintance with the brain and our acquaintance with consciousness are necessarily mediated by distinct cognitive faculties, namely perception and introspection. Thus the faculty through which we apprehend one term of the relation is necessarily distinct from the faculty through which we apprehend the other. In consequence, it is not possible for us to use one of these faculties to apprehend the nature of the psychophysical nexus. No single faculty will enable us ever to apprehend the fact that consciousness depends upon the brain in virtue of property P. Neither perception alone nor introspection alone will ever enable us to witness the dependence. And this, my objector insists, is the real reason we find the link baffling: we cannot make sense of it in terms of the deliverances of a single cognitive faculty. So, even if we now had concepts for the properties of the brain that explain consciousness, we would still feel a residual sense of unintelligibility; we would still take there to be something mysterious going on. The necessity to shift from one faculty to the other produces in us an illusion of inexplicability. We might in fact have the explanation right now but be under the illusion that we do not. The right diagnosis, then, is that we should recognize the peculiarity of the epistemological situation and stop trying to make sense of the psychophysical nexus in the way

we make sense of other sorts of nexus. It only *seems* to us that we can never discover a property that will render the nexus intelligible.

I think this line of thought deserves to be taken seriously, but I doubt that it correctly diagnoses our predicament. It is true enough that the problematic nexus is essentially apprehended by distinct faculties, so that it will never reveal its secrets to a single faculty; but I doubt that our intuitive sense of intelligibility is so rigidly governed by the 'single-faculty condition.' Why *should* facts only seem intelligible to us if we can conceive of apprehending them by one (sort of) cognitive faculty? Why not allow that we can recognize intelligible connections between concepts (or properties) even when those concepts (or properties) are necessarily ascribed using different faculties? Is it not suspiciously empiricist to insist that a causal nexus can only be made sense of by us if we can conceive of its being an object of a single faculty of apprehension? Would we think this of a nexus that called for touch and sight to apprehend each term of the relation? Suppose (*per impossibile*) that we were offered P on a plate, as a gift from God: would we still shake our heads and wonder how that could resolve the mystery, being still the victims of the illusion of mystery generated by the epistemological duality in question? No, I think this suggestion is not enough to account for the miraculous appearance of the link: it is better to suppose that we are permanently blocked from forming a concept of what accounts for that link.

How strong is the thesis I am urging? Let me distinguish *absolute* from *relative* claims of cognitive closure. A problem is absolutely cognitively closed if no possible mind could resolve it; a problem is relatively closed if minds of some sorts can in principle solve it while minds of other sorts cannot. Most problems we may safely suppose, are only relatively closed: armadillo minds cannot solve problems of elementary arithmetic but human minds can. Should we say that the mind–body problem is only relatively closed or is the closure absolute? This depends on what we allow as a possible concept-forming mind, which is not an easy question. If we allow for minds that form their concepts of the brain and consciousness in ways that are quite independent of perception and introspection, then there may be room for the idea that there are possible minds for which the mind–body problem is soluble, and easily so. But if we suppose that *all* concept formation is tied to perception and introspection, however loosely, then *no* mind will be capable of understanding how it relates to its own body—the insolubility will be absolute. I think we can just about make sense of the former kind of mind, by exploiting our own faculty of a priori reasoning. Our mathematical concepts (say) do not seem tied either to perception or to introspection, so there does seem to be a mode of concept formation that operates without the constraints I identified earlier. The suggestion might then be that a mind that formed all of its concepts in this way—including its concepts of the brain and consciousness—would be free of the biases that prevent *us* from coming up with the right theory of how the two connect. Such a mind would have to be able to think of the brain and consciousness in ways that utterly prescind from the perceptual and the introspective—in somewhat the way we now (it seems) think about numbers. This mind would conceive of the psychophysical link in totally a priori terms. Perhaps this is how we should think of God's mind, and God's understanding of the mind–body relation. At any rate, something pretty radical is going to be needed if we are to devise a mind that can escape the kinds of closure that make the problem insoluble for us—if I am right in my diagnosis of our difficulty. *If* the problem is only relatively insoluble, then the type of mind that can solve it is going to be very different from ours and the kinds of mind we can readily make sense of (there may, of course, be cognitive closure here too). It certainly seems to me to be at least an open question whether the problem is absolutely insoluble; I would not be surprised if it were.[17]

My position is both pessimistic and optimistic at the same time. It is pessimistic about the prospects for arriving at a constructive solution to the mind–body problem, but it is optimistic about our hopes of removing the philosophical perplexity. The central point here is that I do not think we need to do the former in order to achieve the latter. This depends on a rather special understanding of what the philosophical problem consists in. What I want to suggest is that the nature of the psychophysical connection has a full and non-mysterious explanation in a certain science, but that this science is inaccessible to us as a matter of principle. Call this explanatory scientific theory *T: T* is as natural and prosaic and devoid of miracle as any theory of nature; it describes the link between consciousness and the brain in a way that is no

more remarkable (or alarming) than the way we now describe the link between the liver and bile.[18] According to *T,* there is nothing eerie going on in the world when an event in my visual cortex causes me to have an experience of yellow—however much it seems to *us* that there is. In other words, there is no intrinsic conceptual or metaphysical difficulty about how consciousness depends on the brain. It is not that the correct science is compelled to postulate miracles *de re;* it is rather that the correct science lies in the dark part of the world for us. We confuse our own cognitive limitations with objective eeriness. We are like a Humean mind trying to understand the physical world, or a creature without spatial concepts trying to understand the possibility of motion. This removes the philosophical problem because it assures us that the entities *themselves* pose no inherent philosophical difficulty. The case is unlike, for example, the problem of how the abstract world of numbers might be intelligibly related to the world of concrete knowing subjects: here the mystery seems intrinsic to the entities, not a mere artefact of our cognitive limitations or biases in trying to understand the relation.[19] It would not be plausible to suggest that there exists a science, whose theoretical concepts we cannot grasp, which completely resolves any sense of mystery that surrounds the question how the abstract becomes an object of knowledge for us. In this case, then, eliminativism seems a live option. The *philosophical* problem about consciousness and the brain arises from a sense that we are compelled to accept that nature contains miracles—as if the merely metallic lamp of the brain could really spirit into existence the Djin of consciousness. But we do not need to accept this: we can rest secure in the knowledge that some (unknowable) property of the brain makes everything fall into place. What creates the philosophical puzzlement is the assumption that the problem must somehow be scientific but that any science *we* can come up with will represent things as utterly miraculous. And the solution is to recognize that the sense of miracle comes from us and not from the world. There is, in reality, nothing mysterious about how the brain generates consciousness. There is no *metaphysical* problem.[20]

So far that deflationary claim has been justified by a general naturalism and certain considerations about cognitive closure and the illusions it can give rise to. Now I want to marshall some reasons for thinking that consciousness is actually a rather simple natural fact; objectively, consciousness is nothing very special. We should now be comfortable with the idea that our own sense of difficulty is a fallible guide to objective complexity: what is hard for us to grasp may not be very fancy in itself. The grain of our thinking is not a mirror held up to the facts of nature.[21] In particular, it may be that the extent of our understanding of facts about the mind is not commensurate with some objective estimate of their intrinsic complexity: we may be good at understanding the mind in some of its aspects but hopeless with respect to others, in a way that cuts across objective differences in what the aspects involve. Thus we are adept at understanding action in terms of the folk psychology of belief and desire, and we seem not entirely out of our depth when it comes to devising theories of language. But our understanding of how consciousness develops from the organization of matter is nonexistent. But now, think of these various aspects of mind from the point of view of evolutionary biology. Surely language and the propositional attitudes are more complex and advanced evolutionary achievements than the mere possession of consciousness by a physical organism. Thus it seems that we are better at understanding some of the more complex aspects of mind than the simpler ones. Consciousness arises early in evolutionary history and is found right across the animal kingdom. In some respects it seems that the biological engineering required for consciousness is less fancy than that needed for certain kinds of complex motor behaviour. Yet we can come to understand the latter while drawing a total blank with respect to the former. Conscious states seem biologically quite primitive, comparatively speaking. So the theory T that explains the occurrence of consciousness in a physical world is very probably less objectively complex (by some standard) than a range of other theories that do not defy our intellects. If only we could know the psychophysical mechanism it might surprise us with its simplicity, its utter naturalness. In the manual that God consulted when he made the earth and all the beasts that dwell thereon the chapter about how to engineer consciousness from matter occurs fairly early on, well before the really difficult later chapters on mammalian reproduction and speech. It is not the *size* of the problem but its *type* that makes the mind–body problem so hard for us. This reflection should make us receptive to the idea that it is something about the tracks of our thought that prevents us from achieving a

science that relates consciousness to its physical basis: the enemy lies within the gates.[22]

The position I have reached has implications for a tangle of intuitions it is natural to have regarding the mind–body relation. On the one hand, there are intuitions, pressed from Descartes to Kripke, to the effect that the relation between conscious states and bodily states is fundamentally contingent.[23] It can easily seem to us that there is no necessitation involved in the dependence of the mind on the brain. But, on the other hand, it looks absurd to try to dissociate the two entirely, to let the mind float completely free of the body. Disembodiment is a dubious possibility at best, and some kind of necessary supervenience of the mental on the physical has seemed undeniable to many. It is not my aim here to adjudicate this longstanding dispute; I want simply to offer a diagnosis of what is going on when one finds oneself assailed with this flurry of conflicting intuitions. The reason we feel the tug of contingency, pulling consciousness loose from its physical moorings, may be that we do not and cannot grasp the nature of the property that intelligibly links them. The brain has physical properties we can grasp, and variations in these correlate with changes in consciousness, but we cannot draw the veil that conceals the manner of their connection. Not grasping the nature of the connection, it strikes us as deeply contingent; we cannot make the assertion of a necessary connection intelligible to ourselves. There *may* then be a real necessary connection; it is just that it will always strike us as curiously brute and unperspicuous. We may thus, as upholders of intrinsic contingency, be the dupes of our own cognitive blindness. On the other hand, we are scarcely in a position to assert that there *is* a necessary connection between the properties of the brain we can grasp and states of consciousness, since we are so ignorant (and irremediably so) about the character of the connection. For all we know, the connection may be contingent, as access to P would reveal if we could have such access. The link between consciousness and property P is not, to be sure, contingent—virtually by definition—but we are not in a position to say exactly how P is related to the 'ordinary' properties of the brain. It may be necessary or it may be contingent. Thus it is that we tend to vacillate between contingency and necessity; for we lack the conceptual resources to decide the question—or to understand the answer we are inclined to give. The indicated conclusion appears to be that we can never really know whether disembodiment is metaphysically possible, or whether necessary supervenience is the case, or whether spectrum inversion could occur. For these all involve claims about the modal connections between properties of consciousness and the ordinary properties of the body and brain that we can conceptualize; and the real nature of these connections is not accessible to us. Perhaps *P* makes the relation between C-fibre firing and pain necessary or perhaps it does not: we are simply not equipped to know. We are like a Humean mind wondering whether the observed link between the temperature of a gas and its pressure (at a constant volume) is necessary or contingent. To know the answer to that you need to grasp atomic (or molecular) theory, and a Humean mind just is not up to attaining the requisite theoretical understanding. Similarly, we are constitutionally ignorant at precisely the spot where the answer exists.

I predict that many readers of this paper will find its main thesis utterly incredible, even ludicrous. Let me remark that I sympathize with such readers: the thesis is not easily digestible. But I would say this: if the thesis *is* actually true, it will still strike us as hard to believe. For the idea of an explanatory property (or set of properties) that is noumenal for us, yet is essential for the (constructive) solution of a problem we face, offends a kind of natural idealism that tends to dominate our thinking. We find it taxing to conceive of the existence of a real property, under our noses as it were, which we are built not to grasp—a property that is responsible for phenomena that we observe in the most direct way

possible. This kind of realism, which brings cognitive closure so close to home, is apt to seem both an affront to our intellects and impossible to get our minds around. We try to think of this unthinkable property and understandably fail in the effort; so we rush to infer that the very supposition of such a property is nonsensical. Realism of the kind I am presupposing thus seems difficult to hold in focus, and any philosophical theory that depends upon it will also seem to rest on something systematically elusive.[24] My response to such misgivings, however, is unconcessive: the limits of our minds are just not the limits of reality. It is deplorably anthropocentric to insist that reality be constrained by what the human mind can conceive. We need to cultivate a vision of reality (a metaphysics) that makes it truly independent of our given cognitive powers, a conception that includes these powers as a proper part. It is just that, in the case of the mind–body problem, the bit of reality that systematically eludes our cognitive grasp is an aspect of our own nature. Indeed, it is an aspect that makes it possible for us to have minds at all and to think about how they are related to our bodies. This particular transcendent tract of reality happens to lie within our own heads. A deep fact about our own nature as a form of embodied consciousness is thus necessarily hidden from us. Yet there is nothing inherently eerie or bizarre about this embodiment. We are much more straightforward than we seem. Our weirdness lies in the eye of the beholder.

The answer to the question that forms my title is therefore 'No and Yes.'[25]

NOTES

1. One of the peculiarities of the mind–body problem is the difficulty of formulating it in a rigorous way. We have a sense of the problem that outruns our capacity to articulate it clearly. Thus we quickly find ourselves resorting to invitations to look inward, instead of specifying precisely *what* it is about consciousness that makes it inexplicable in terms of ordinary physical properties. And this can make it seem that the problem is spurious. A creature without consciousness would not properly appreciate the problem (assuming such a creature could appreciate other problems). I think an adequate treatment of the mind–body problem should explain why it is so hard to state the problem explicitly. My treatment locates our difficulty in our inadequate conceptions of the nature of the brain and consciousness. In fact, if we knew their natures fully we would already have solved the problem. This should become clear later.

2. I would also classify panpsychism as a constructive

solution, since it attempts to explain consciousness in terms of properties of the brain that are as natural as consciousness itself. Attributing specks of proto-consciousness to the constituents of matter is not supernatural in the way postulating immaterial substances or divine interventions is; it is merely extravagant. I shall here be assuming that panpsychism, like all other extant constructive solutions, is inadequate as an answer to the mind–body problem—as (of course) are the supernatural 'solutions.' I am speaking to those who still feel perplexed (almost everyone, I would think, at least in their heart).

3. This kind of view of cognitive capacity is forcefully advocated by Noam Chomsky in *Reflections on Language,* Patheon Books, 1975, and by Jerry Fodor in *The Modularity of Mind,* Cambridge, Mass., MIT Press, 1983. Chomsky distinguishes between 'problems', which human minds are in principle equipped to solve, and 'mysteries', which systematically elude

our understanding; and he envisages a study of our cognitive systems that would chart these powers and limitations. I am here engaged in such a study, citing the mind–body problem as falling on the side of the mysteries.

4. See Thomas Nagel's discussion of realism in *The View from Nowhere,* Oxford, Oxford University Press, 1986, ch. VI. He argues there for the possibility of properties we can never grasp. Combining Nagel's realism with Chomsky–Fodor cognitive closure gives a position looking very much like Locke's in the *Essay Concerning Human Understanding:* the idea that our God-given faculties do not equip us to fathom the deep truth about reality. In fact, Locke held precisely this about the relation between mind and brain: only divine revelation could enable us to understand how 'perceptions' are produced in our minds by material objects.

5. Hume, of course, argued, in effect, that no theory essentially employing a notion of objective causal necessitation could be grasped by our minds—and likewise for the notion of objective persistence. We might compare the frustrations of the Humean mind to the conceptual travails of the pure sound beings discussed in Ch. II of P. F. Strawson's *Individuals,* London, Methuen, 1959; both are types of mind whose constitution puts various concepts beyond them. We can do a lot better than these truncated minds, but we also have our constitutional limitations.

6. See the *Essay,* Book II, ch. IV. Locke compares the project of saying what solidity ultimately is to trying to clear up a blind man's vision by talking to him.

7. Some of the more arcane aspects of cosmology and quantum theory might be thought to lie just within the bounds of human intelligibility. Chomsky suggests that the causation of behaviour might be necessarily mysterious to human investigators: see *Reflections on Language,* p. 156. I myself believe that the mind–body problem exhibits a qualitatively different level of mystery from this case (unless it is taken as an aspect of that problem).

8. Cf. Nagel's discussion of emergence in 'Panpsychism,' in *Mortal Questions,* Cambridge, Cambridge University Press, 1979. I agree with him that the apparent radical emergence of mind from matter has to be epistemic only, on pain of accepting inexplicable miracles in the world.

9. Despite his reputation for pessimism over the mind–body problem, a careful reading of Nagel reveals an optimistic strain in his thought (by the standards of the present paper): see, in particular, the closing remarks of 'What Is It Like to Be a Bat?' in *Mortal Questions.* Nagel speculates that we might be able to devise an 'objective phenomenology' that made conscious states more amenable to physical analysis. Unlike me, he does not regard the problem as inherently beyond us.

10. This is perhaps the most remarkably optimistic view of all—the expectation that reflecting on the ordinary concept of pain (say) will reveal the manner of pain's dependence on the brain. If I am not mistaken, this is in effect the view of common-sense functionalists: they think that *P* consists in causal role, and that this can be inferred analytically from the concepts of conscious states. This would make it truly amazing that we should ever have felt there to be a mind–body

problem at all, since the solution is already contained in our mental concepts. What optimism!

11. See Nagel, 'What Is It Like to Be a Bat?' Notice that the fugitive character of such properties with respect to our concepts has nothing to do with their 'complexity'; like fugitive colour properties, such experiential properties are 'simple'. Note too that such properties provide counter-examples to the claim that (somehow) rationality is a faculty that, once possessed, can be extended to encompass all concepts, so that if *any* concept can be possessed then *every* concept can.

12. It might be suggested that we borrow Nagel's idea of 'objective phenomenology' in order to get around this problem. Instead of representing experiences under subjective descriptions, we should describe them in entirely objective terms, thus bringing them within our conceptual ken. My problem with this is that, even allowing that there could be such a form of description, it would not permit us to understand how the subjective aspects of experience depend upon the brain—which is really the problem we are trying to solve. In fact, I doubt that the notion of objective phenomenology is any more coherent than the notion of subjective physiology. Both involve trying to bridge the psychophysical gap by a sort of stipulation. The lesson here is that the gap cannot be bridged just by applying concepts drawn from one side to items that belong on the other side; and this is because neither sort of concept could ever do what is needed.

13. We should distinguish two claims about the imperceptibility of consciousness: (i) consciousness is not perceivable by directing the senses onto the brain; (ii) consciousness is not perceivable by directing the senses anywhere, even towards the behaviour that 'expresses' conscious states. I believe both theses, but my present point requires only (i). I am assuming, of course, that perception cannot be unrestrictedly theory-laden; or that if it can, the infusions of theory cannot have been originally derived simply by looking at things or tasting them or touching them or . . .

14. Nagel discusses the difficulty of thinking of conscious processes in the spatial terms that apply to the brain in *The View from Nowhere,* pp. 50–51, but he does not draw my despairing conclusion. The case is exactly *un*like (say) the dependence of liquidity on the properties of molecules, since here we do think of both terms of the relation as spatial in character; so we can simply employ the idea of spatial composition.

15. Cf. Nagel: 'it will never be legitimate to infer, as a theoretical explanation of physical phenomena alone, a property that includes or implies the consciousness of its subject,' 'Panpsychism,' p. 183.

16. It is surely a striking fact that the microprocesses that have been discovered in the brain by the usual methods seem no nearer to consciousness than the gross properties of the brain open to casual inspection. Neither do more abstract 'holistic' features of brain function seem to be on the right lines to tell us the nature of consciousness. The deeper science probes into the brain the more remote it seems to get from consciousness. Greater knowledge of the brain thus destroys our illusions about the kinds of properties that might be discovered by travelling along this path. Advanced neurophysiological theory seems only to deepen the miracle.

17. The kind of limitation I have identified is therefore not the kind that could be remedied simply by a large increase in general intelligence. No matter how large the frontal lobes of our biological descendants may become, they will still be stumped by the mind–body problem, so long as they form their (empirical) concepts on the basis of perception and introspection.

18. Or again, no more miraculous than the theory of evolution. Creationism is an understandable response to the theoretical problem posed by the existence of complex organisms; fortunately, we now have a theory that renders this response unnecessary, and so undermines the theism required by the creationist thesis. In the case of consciousness, the appearance of miracle might also tempt us in a 'creationist' direction, with God required to perform the alchemy necessary to transform matter into experience. Thus the mind–body problem might similarly be used to prove the existence of God (no miracle without a miracle-maker). We cannot, I think, refute this argument in the way we can the original creationist argument, namely by actually producing a non-miraculous explanatory theory, but we can refute it by arguing that such a naturalistic theory must *exist*. (It is a condition of adequacy upon any account of the mind–body relation that it avoid assuming theism.)

19. See Paul Benacerraf, 'Mathematical Truth,' *Journal of Philosophy*, 1973, for a statement of this problem about abstract entities. Another problem that seems to me to differ from the mind–body problem is the problem of free will. I do not believe that there is some unknowable property Q which reconciles free will with determinism (or indeterminism); rather, the concept of free will contains internal incoherencies—as the concept of consciousness does not. This is why it is much more reasonable to be an eliminativist about free will than about consciousness.

20. A test of whether a proposed solution to the mind–body problem is adequate is whether it relieves the pressure towards eliminativism. If the data can only be explained by postulating a miracle (i.e. not explained), then we must repudiate the data—this is the principle behind the impulse to deny that conscious states exist. My proposal passes this test because it allows us to resist the postulation of miracles; it interprets the eeriness as merely epistemic, though deeply so. Constructive solutions are not the only way to relieve the pressure.

21. Chomsky suggests that the very faculties of mind that make us good at some cognitive tasks may make us poor at others; see *Reflections on Language,* pp. 155–56. It seems to me possible that what makes us good at the science of the purely physical world is what skews us away from developing a science of consciousness. Our faculties bias us towards understanding matter in motion, but it is precisely this kind of understanding that is inapplicable to the mind–body problem. Perhaps, then, the price of being good at understanding matter is that we cannot understand mind. Certainly our notorious tendency to think of everything in spatial terms does not help us in understanding the mind.

22. I get this phrase from Fodor, *The Modularity of Mind,* p. 121. The intended contrast is with kinds of cognitive closure that stem from exogenous factors—as, say, in astronomy. Our problem with P is not that it is too distant or too small or too large or too complex; rather, the very structure of our concept-forming apparatus points us away from P.

23. Saul Kripke, *Naming and Necessity*, Oxford, Blackwell, 1980. Of course, Descartes explicitly argued from (what he took to be) the essential natures of the body and mind to the contingency of their connection. If we abandon the assumption that we know these natures, then agnosticism about the modality of the connection seems the indicated conclusion.

24. This is the kind of realism defended by Nagel in ch. VI of *The View from Nowhere:* to be is not to be conceivable by us. I would say that the mind–body problem provides a demonstration that there *are* such concept-transcending properties—not merely that there *could* be. I would also say that realism of this kind should be accepted precisely because it helps solve the mind–body problem; it is a metaphysical thesis that pulls its weight in coping with a problem that looks hopeless otherwise. There is thus nothing 'epiphenomenal' about such radical realism: the existence of a reality we cannot know can yet have intellectual significance for us.

25. Discussions with the following people have helped me work out the ideas of this paper: Anita Avramides, Jerry Katz, Ernie Lepore, Michael Levin, Thomas Nagel, Galen Strawson, Peter Unger. My large debt to Nagel's work should be obvious throughout the paper: I would not have tried to face the mind–body problem down had he not first faced up to it.

39 | Explaining Consciousness

David M. Rosenthal

Among mental phenomena, none seems so thoroughly to resist informative explanation as does consciousness. Part of the difficulty is due to our using the term 'conscious' and its cognates to cover several distinct phenomena, whose connections with one another are not always clear. And that often leads us to run these distinct phenomena together. Any attempt to explain consciousness, therefore, must begin by distinguishing the various things we call consciousness.

One such phenomenon is closely related to simply being awake. We describe people, and other creatures, as being conscious when they are awake and their sensory systems are receptive in the way normal for a waking state. I call this phenomenon *creature consciousness*. Consciousness in this sense is a biological matter, consisting in a creature's not being unconscious—that is, roughly, in its not being asleep or knocked out.

But we also use the term 'consciousness' for other phenomena that seem a lot less tractable to understanding and explanation. Not only do we distinguish between conscious and unconscious creatures; we also distinguish between mental states that are conscious and those which are not. I'll call this second property *state consciousness*. It's widely recognized that not all mental states are conscious. Intentional states such as beliefs and desires plainly occur without being conscious.[1] And, despite some division of opinion on the matter, I shall argue that the same is true of sensory states, such as pains and sensations of color. Such states not only can, but often do occur nonconsciously.[2]

Though creature consciousness and state consciousness are distinct properties, they are very likely related in various ways. Perhaps, for example, creatures must themselves be conscious for any of their mental states to be conscious, though if ordinary dreams are ever conscious states they are counterexamples to this generalization.[3]

Whatever the case about that, the property of creature consciousness is relatively unproblematic. We can see this by considering creatures mentally less well-endowed than we are whose mental states are never conscious, even when they are awake.[4] Their mental states are all like the nonconscious mental states we are in when we are awake. Doubtless some creatures are actually like this, say, frogs or turtles. And it's plain that when none of a creature's mental states is conscious, there is nothing puzzling about what it is for the creature to be conscious. Some theorists might deny that such a case is possible, urging that no creature counts as conscious unless some of the mental states it is in are conscious states. But this seems little more than an unwarranted extrapolation of the normal human waking state to the case of all creatures. Even if their view were correct, moreover, it would be state consciousness that introduces the apparent mystery.

What is puzzling about consciousness must therefore be a matter not of creature consciousness, but of the consciousness of a creature's mental states. Because creature consciousness involves being responsive to sensory stimuli, if sensory states were all conscious, every conscious creature would perforce be in some conscious states. But it would still, then, be the consciousness of the states, not of the creature, which seems to induce some mystery.

For this reason, I shall focus here on state consciousness. After laying some groundwork in section I, I go on in section II to develop a hypothesis about what it is for a mental state to be conscious. On this hypothesis, a mental state is conscious if it is accompanied by a specific type

This paper is published here for the first time.

of thought. This is so whether the state that is conscious is itself an intentional state or a sensory state. Section III, then, supports this hypothesis with an argument that appeals to the ability creatures like ourselves have to report noninferentially about their own conscious states.

Sections IV and V take up the special case of conscious qualitative states. I argue in section IV that such sensory consciousness is just a special case of state consciousness and poses no additional problems of its own. And section V gives reasons for thinking that an accompanying intentional state can actually result in there being something it's like for one to be in a conscious sensory state. Section VI, finally, considers two general questions about state consciousness: What function it might have and whether consciousness can misrepresent what mental states we are in.

I. State Consciousness and Transitive Consciousness

Whatever else we may discover about consciousness, it's clear that, if one is totally unaware of some mental state, that state is not a conscious state. A state may of course be conscious without one's paying conscious attention to it and, indeed, even without one's being conscious of every mental aspect of the state. But if one is not at all aware of a state, that state is not a conscious state. This observation provides a useful start toward a theory of state consciousness. Because it is sufficient for a state not to be conscious that one be completely unaware of it, being aware of a state is perforce a necessary condition for that state to be a conscious state.

Being aware of a mental state, however, is not also a sufficient condition for the state to be conscious. There are ways we can be aware of our mental states even when those states are not conscious states. So, if we can rule out those ways, we'll be left with the particular way in which we are aware of our mental states when those states are conscious states. And this would give us a condition that's both necessary and sufficient for a mental state to be conscious.

For present purposes, I'll speak interchangeably of being aware of something and being conscious of that thing. So my strategy is to explain a state's being a conscious state in terms of our being conscious of that state in some particular way. No circle is involved here, since we are ex-

plaining one phenomenon in terms of another. It is one thing for us to be conscious *of* something—what we may call *transitive consciousness*—and another for a state to be a conscious state—what I'm calling state consciousness. And we understand transitive consciousness— our being conscious *of* things—independently of understanding what it is for mental states to be conscious states. We are transitively conscious of something by virtue of being either in an intentional or a sensory state whose content is directed upon that thing. And a state's having a certain content is a distinct property from that of a state's being conscious.[5]

It seems relatively uncontroversial that a state of which one is in no way transitively conscious could not be a conscious state. Even Descartes' usage, which still strongly influences our own, conforms to this commonsense observation, since he invariably describes the states we call conscious as states we are immediately conscious of. Nonetheless, Fred Dretske has recently challenged the observation that we are conscious of all our conscious states. According to Dretske, a state's being conscious does not consist in one's being conscious of the state; rather, a state is conscious if, in virtue of being in that state, one is conscious of something or conscious that something is the case. But every mental state satisfies this condition; so Dretske must hold that all mental states are conscious states. Accordingly, he urges that alleged cases of nonconscious mental states are unconvincing. Thus it is often said that a long-distance driver whose attention lapses perceives the road unconsciously,[6] but Dretske rightly notes that perceiving can be inattentive without failing to be conscious.[7]

Many other examples of nonconscious mental states, however, are far more decisive. We often consciously puzzle over a question about what to do or how to solve a problem, only to have the answer occur to us later, without the matter having in the meantime been in any way consciously before our mind. Though it doesn't seem, from a first-person point of view, that we were thinking about the issue, it's clear that we must have been. And unlike the case of the long-distance driver, here no shift of attention would change things. Also we often take in sensory information without being at all aware of doing so, again no matter what we're paying attention to. Since, from a first-person perspective, we seem not to be in any relevant sensory states, those states are not conscious states.

Dretske also argues, however, that there are actual counterexamples to the idea that we are transitively conscious of all our conscious states. To adapt his argument slightly, consider two scenes, one of ten trees and the other just like it, but with one tree missing. And suppose that I consciously see both scenes, and indeed that I consciously see all the trees in each scene. But suppose, finally, that despite all this I do not notice any difference between the two scenes.

Dretske sensibly assumes that in this case I have conscious experiences of both scenes, including all the trees in each. Moreover, there is some part of the conscious experience of ten trees that is not part of the conscious experience of nine trees. That part is itself a conscious experience—a conscious experience of a tree. But, because I am not transitively conscious of the difference between the two scenes, Dretske concludes that I will not be transitively conscious of the experience of that extra tree. If so, the experience of the extra tree is a conscious experience of which I am not transitively conscious.[8]

This sort of thing is hardly an esoteric occurrence. Indeed, it happens all the time; let one scene be a slightly later version of the other, such that the later scene is altered in some small, unnoticed way. So, if Dretske's argument is sound, we often fail to be conscious of our conscious experiences.[9]

But the argument isn't sound. One can be conscious of an experience in one respect while not being conscious of it in another. For example, one may be conscious of a visual experience as an experience of a blurry patch, but not as an experience of a particular kind of object. Similarly, one could be conscious of the experience of the extra tree as an experience of a tree, or even just as part of one's overall experience, without being at all conscious of it as the thing that makes the difference between the experiences of the two scenes. Presumably this is just what happens in the case Dretske constructs. Dretske has not described a conscious state of which one is not transitively conscious.

There is a complication in Dretske's discussion that is worth noting. Dretske insists that being conscious of a difference, unlike being conscious of concrete objects and events, always amounts to being conscious "that such a difference exists."[10] So he might urge that being conscious of a difference is always being conscious of it as a difference. But this won't help. The experience of the extra tree is that in virtue of which the two overall experiences differ.

Still, one can be conscious of the thing in virtue of which they happen to differ without being conscious that they do differ. As Dretske would put it, one can be conscious of that in virtue of which they differ but not of the difference between them;[11] indeed, he explicitly acknowledges that this very thing can happen.[12] Dretske's argument does not, therefore, undermine the commonsense observation that we are transitively conscious of all our conscious states.[13]

II. The Hypothesis

Let us turn, then, to the question of what it is that is special about the way we are transitively conscious of our mental states when those states are conscious states. Perhaps the most obvious thing is that, when a state is conscious, we are conscious of it in a way that seems immediate. Descartes emphasized this intuitive immediacy,[14] which many have thought points toward a Cartesian theory of mind, on which a mental state's being conscious is an intrinsic property of that state. If nothing mediates between a state and one's being transitively conscious of it, perhaps that transitive consciousness is something internal to the state itself.

But the intuition about immediacy does not show that a mental state's being conscious is internal to the state. It does seem, from a first-person point of view, that nothing mediates between the conscious states we are conscious of and our transitive consciousness of them. But all that shows is that, if anything does mediate between a conscious state and our transitive consciousness of it, the mediating factor is not one we are conscious of. And the absence of conscious mediation is no reason to think that nonconscious mediation does not occur.[15] Failure to appreciate this has led some to hold that we are conscious of our conscious states in a way wholly unlike the way we are conscious of everything else.

Even when something mediates between a conscious mental state and our being conscious of it, we can be conscious of the mediating factor; we just cannot be conscious of it as mediating. Compare what happens in perceiving. When we consciously perceive things, our conscious sensory states mediate between our perceptions and the objects we perceive, and since those states are conscious, we are conscious of them. Still, nothing in these cases seems intuitively to mediate. That's because we aren't conscious of anything as mediating. And the best explanation of that, in turn, is that the conscious sensory states that do in fact mediate do not figure in any conscious inference on which our perceiving is based. Similarly with the way we are conscious of our conscious mental states. Our being conscious of them seems unmediated because we are conscious of them in a way that relies on no conscious inference, no inference, that is, of which we are aware.[16]

Consider a case. I am annoyed, but unaware of it. Though my annoyance is not conscious, you observe my annoyed behavior and tell me I am annoyed. There are two ways I might react. I might accept what you tell me, but still feel no conscious annoyance. My belief that I'm annoyed would be the result of a conscious inference based on your remark, and possibly also a conscious inference from my coming to notice my own relevant behavior.[17] But there is another possibility; your remark might cause me to become conscious of my annoyance independently of any such conscious inference. In that case my annoyance would have become a conscious state.

A state's being conscious involves one's being noninferentially conscious of that state. Can we pin down any further the way we are transitively conscious of our conscious states? There are two broad ways of being transitively conscious of things. We are conscious of something when we see it or hear it, or perceive it in some other way. And we are conscious of something when we have a thought about it. Which kind of transitive consciousness is relevant here? When our mental states are conscious, do we somehow sense those states or do we have thoughts about them?

The perceptual model may seem inviting. When we perceive things, we seem intuitively to be directly conscious of them; nothing seems to mediate between our perceptions and the objects we perceive.[18] So perhaps the perceptual model can explain the apparent immediacy of the way we are conscious of our conscious states. But this advantage of the perceptual model won't help us decide between that model and the alternative view that we are conscious of our conscious states by having thoughts about them. Even though our thoughts do often rely on conscious inferences involving perceptions or other thoughts, they often don't.

There is, however, another consideration that seems to favor the perceptual model. A theory of consciousness must explain the qualitative

dimension of our conscious sensory states. And sensing always involves some sensory quality. So if we are conscious of our conscious states by sensing them, perhaps we can explain the qualitative dimension of consciousness as due to that higher-order sensing. Such an explanation, however, would at best just put off the problem, since the qualitative aspect of this higher-order perceiving would itself need to be explained in turn.

Not only do the considerations favoring the perceptual model fail to hold up; there is also reason to reject the model. Higher-order sensing would have to exhibit characteristic mental qualities; what qualities might those be? One possibility is that the higher-order perception and the state we perceive would both exhibit the same sensory quality. But this is theoretically unmotivated. When we perceive something, the quality of our perceptual state is distinct from any property of the object we perceive. When we see a tomato, for example, the redness of our sensation is not the same property as the redness of the tomato.[19] So we have no reason to think that the higher-order qualities would be the same as those of our lower-order states.

If the higher- and lower-order qualities were distinct, however, it's a mystery what those higher-order qualities could be. What mental qualities are there in our mental lives other than those which characterize our first-order sensory states? And if the higher-order qualities are neither the same as nor distinct from our first-order qualities, the higher-order states in virtue of which we are conscious of our conscious states cannot have qualities at all. But if those higher-order states have no qualitative properties, they can only be higher-order intentional states of some sort.[20]

We must therefore reject the perceptual model of how we are transitively conscious of our conscious states. The only alternative is that we are conscious of our conscious states by virtue of having thoughts about them. Since these thoughts are about other mental states, I shall refer to them as *higher-order thoughts* (HOTs).

This narrows down somewhat the way we are transitively conscious of our mental states when those states are conscious. But we can narrow things down even more. When a mental state is conscious, we are conscious of being in that state; so the content of our HOT must be, roughly, that one is in that very state.[21] And, since merely being disposed to have a thought about something does not make one conscious of that thing, the HOT must be an occurrent thought, rather than just a disposition to think that one is in the target state. Moreover, when we are conscious of something by being in an intentional state that's about that thing, the intentional state is normally assertoric. Indeed, it's likely that being in an intentional state whose mental attitude is not assertoric does not result in one's being conscious of the thing the intentional state is about.[22] So we should require that the HOT has an assertoric mental attitude.[23] Finally, to capture the intuition about immediacy, we have seen that our HOTs must be independent of any inference of which we are aware. Our hypothesis, therefore, is that a mental state is conscious just in case it is accompanied by a noninferential, nondispositional, assertoric thought to the effect that one is in that very state.[24]

One problem that seems to face this hypothesis is that, even when we are in many conscious states, we are typically unaware of having any such HOTs. But this is not a difficulty; we are conscious of our HOTs only when those thoughts are themselves conscious, and it's rare that they are. Moreover, the hypothesis readily explains why this should be so. The HOTs it posits are conscious thoughts only when they are accompanied, in turn, by yet higher-order thoughts about them, and that seldom happens. Not having conscious HOTs, moreover, does nothing at all to show that we do not have HOTs that fail to be conscious.

There is another reason it's useful to distinguish cases in which HOTs are conscious from cases in which they are not. The way we are ordinarily conscious of our conscious states differs from the way we are conscious of mental states of which we are introspectively conscious. Being introspectively conscious of a mental state involves, roughly, our deliberately focusing on that state, and very few of our conscious states are the subjects of any such introspective scrutiny. If being conscious of a mental state were the same as being introspectively conscious of it, it would be rare that we are conscious of our conscious states, and we would be unable to explain state consciousness in terms of transitive consciousness. Not distinguishing the two, moreover, would lead one mistakenly to see the HOT hypothesis as providing a theory only of introspective consciousness, and not of state consciousness generally.[25] But the present hypothesis actually allows us to explain what is distinctive about introspective consciousness. A state is introspectively conscious when the ac-

companying HOT is a conscious thought. Ordinary, nonintrospective state consciousness, by contrast, occurs instead when the HOT is not itself conscious.

The HOT model is a hypothesis about the nature of state consciousness, not an analysis of that concept. So it doesn't count against the hypothesis simply that one can imagine its not holding; one can always imagine things being different from the way they are.

There is an especially interesting argument that supports the appeal to HOTs. When a mental state is conscious, one can noninferentially report being in that state, whereas one cannot report one's nonconscious mental states. Every speech act, moreover, expresses an intentional state with the same content as that of the speech act and a mental attitude that corresponds to its illocutionary force. So a noninferential report that one is in a mental state will express a noninferential thought that one is in that state, that is, a HOT about the state. We can best explain this ability noninferentially to report our conscious states by supposing that the relevant HOT is there to be expressed. Correspondingly, the best explanation of our inability to report nonconscious states is that no HOTs accompany them.[26]

One might reply that the ability to report conscious states shows only that there is a disposition for these states to be accompanied by HOTs, not that any HOTs actually accompany them.[27] Indeed, Peter Carruthers has extensively developed and supported the view that conscious states are simply those disposed to be accompanied by HOTs, and no actual HOT need occur. This, he argues, avoids having to posit the overwhelming computational capacity and cognitive space required for actual HOTs.[28]

But this concern is not compelling. Neural implementation is not a problem, since ample cortical resources exist to accommodate actual HOTs. And, though introspection seems to suggest that the mind cannot accommodate very many actual HOTs at a time, that worry is also groundless. Introspection can tell us only about our conscious states, and by hypothesis HOTs are seldom conscious.

In any case, the dispositional model cannot explain what it is for states to be conscious. A mental state's being conscious consists in one's being conscious of that state in some suitable way, and simply being disposed to have a thought about something cannot make one conscious of it. Carruthers urges that we can get around this difficulty if we understand a state's intentional content in terms of what other intentional states it is disposed to cause. A state's being disposed to cause a HOT might then confer suitable higher-order content on that state itself. But, if a state's being disposed to cause a HOT were a function of its intentional content, we could no longer explain how a state with some particular content is sometimes conscious and sometimes not.

III. Sensory Consciousness

On this argument, sensory consciousness is simply a special case of state consciousness—the special case in which the state that's conscious is a sensory state. Sensory states are states with sensory quality. So sensory consciousness occurs when a mental state has two properties: sensory quality and the property of state consciousness.

Moreover, these two properties are distinct and can occur independently of one another. State consciousness can of course occur without sensory quality, since nonsensory, intentional states are often conscious. But the converse is possible as well; sensory qualities can occur without state consciousness. Sensory qualities are just whatever properties sensory states have on the basis of which we distinguish among them and sort them into types. Since state consciousness consists in our being conscious of a mental state in some suitable way, these properties are independent of state consciousness. We would need some special reason to think that the properties on the basis of which we distinguish among sensations cannot occur except when we're conscious of the states that have those properties. It's hard to see what special reason there could be.

This conclusion conflicts with the familiar contention that sensory quality cannot occur nonconsciously. On that view, state consciousness is intrinsic, or essential, to sensory quality. But it's far from clear that this view is correct. Subliminal perception and peripheral vision both involve perceptual sensations of which we're wholly unaware, and the same is very likely true of such dissociative phenomena as blindsight.[29] Bodily sensations such as pains can also occur without being conscious. For example, we often have a headache or other pain throughout an extended period even when distractions intermittently make us wholly unaware of the pain.

One could of course simply dig in one's heels and insist that these phenomena are mere physiological occurrences that instantiate no sensory quality, and therefore that they are not mental phenomena at all. But without independent argument, that move amounts simply to saving a view by verbal fiat.

In any case there is good reason to resist that claim. The relevant nonconscious phenomena occur as essential parts of distinctively mental processes, and that suggests that they are themselves mental phenomena.[30] More specifically, conscious sensory states play the same roles in mental processing when their sensory qualities are the same, and correspondingly different roles when the qualities differ. And the nonconscious states in subliminal perception, peripheral vision, and blindsight play roles that in some respects at least parallel the roles played by conscious sensory states.

When bodily and perceptual sensations occur consciously, we taxonomize them by way of the sensory qualities we are conscious of. What is it, then, in virtue of which we taxonomize the nonconscious states that occur in these cases? Since many of the same qualitative distinctions figure in the nonconscious cases as figure in conscious sensing, we must assume that the nonconscious cases have the very same qualitative properties.[31] Sensory qualities are the distinguishing properties of sensory states, the properties in virtue of which we classify those states. We use the properties we are conscious of to taxonomize sensory states generally, whether they are conscious or not. It's just that in the nonconscious cases we are not conscious of those properties. And, since there is nothing problematic about these distinguishing properties when the states that have them are not conscious, there can be no reason to find those properties puzzling when we are conscious of them. Sensory qualities will seem mysterious only if we assume that they cannot occur without being conscious. These considerations make the claim that sensory quality must be conscious seem less like a compelling commonsense intuition than a question-begging theoretical doctrine.

There is, of course, nothing it's like to have a pain or a sensation of red unless the sensation in question is conscious. And some have argued from this to the conclusion that sensory quality simply cannot exist unless there's something it's like to have it.[32] But what it's like for one to have a pain, in the relevant sense of that idiom, is simply what it's like for one to be conscious of having that pain. So there won't be anything it's like to have a pain unless the pain is conscious. Of course, if nonconscious pains were impossible, there would be no difference between a pain's existing and its being conscious, and its sensory quality would then exist only when there is something it's like to have it. But it begs the question simply to assume that pains, or other sensations, cannot exist nonconsciously. Moreover, the intuition that sensory states cannot exist nonconsciously gets whatever force it has from our first-person point of view. And it's unreasonable to rely on consciousness to tell us whether some phenomenon can exist outside of consciousness.

In a useful series of papers, Ned Block has urged that there are two distinct properties of mental states, both of which we call consciousness. One is captured by the notion of there being something it's like for one to be in a particular mental state; Block calls this property *phenomenal consciousness*. A state has the other property when its content is "poised to be used as a premise in reasoning, . . . [and] for [the] *rational* control of action and . . . speech."[33] This second property Block calls *access consciousness*. And he maintains that the two properties are, conceptually at least, independent. If Block is right, there is no single property of state consciousness, and the kind of consciousness that is characteristic of sensory states is, conceptually at least, distinct from the kind exhibited by many nonsensory states.

The idea behind Block's account of access consciousness is that a state's playing various executive, inferential, and reporting roles involves one's having access to that state, and having access to a state makes it conscious. But that's not always the case. States often play executive, inferential, and even certain reporting roles[34] without being conscious in any intuitive sense whatever. So, for a state to be access conscious, one must have access to that state, presumably by being transitively conscious of it in an intuitively immediate way.[35]

Block's appeal to states' playing these roles doubtless reflects a desire to account for this kind of consciousness in computationally inspired functional terms, by providing a kind of flow chart that charts the connections a state has with various relevant systems. But for any such attempt to succeed, it must reflect an initial account of such consciousness in ordinary folk-psychological terms. Going straight to a subper-

sonal account is unlikely to give even an extensionally adequate account.

Block is doubtless right that access consciousness often occurs without phenomenal consciousness. We frequently have access to our mental states in the relevant way without there being anything it's like for us to be in them. Indeed, that's typically how it is with our thoughts and other intentional states. But the converse is far less clear. A state is access conscious only if one is transitively conscious of it. And if one is in no way transitively conscious of a mental state, there is nothing it's like for one to be in that state. It's not enough for the state just to have the distinguishing properties characteristic of some type of sensory state; for there to be something it's like for one to be in a state, one must be conscious of those distinguishing properties. So phenomenal consciousness cannot occur without access consciousness. Block's distinction does not, after all, show that sensory states are conscious in a way distinct from other types of mental state, nor that sensory states are in some special way invariably conscious.[36]

IV. HOTs and What It's Like

Nonetheless, there does seem to be a serious problem about what it is for sensory states to be conscious. When a sensory state is conscious, there is something it's like for us to be in that state. When it's not conscious, we do not consciously experience any of its qualitative properties; so then there is nothing it's like for us to be in that state. How can we explain this difference? A sensory state's being conscious means that we are transitively conscious of that state in some suitable way. So being transitively conscious of a sensory state, in that particular way, must result in there being something it's like to be in that state. But how can being transitively conscious of a sensory state have this result? What way of being transitively conscious of our sensory states could, by itself, give rise to there being something it's like for us to be in those states? Perhaps, after all, Block is right that a sensory state's being conscious is not a matter of one's having suitable access to it.

The difficulty seems particularly pressing for the HOT hypothesis. An attraction of the perceptual model was that it might help explain the qualitative dimension of our conscious sensory states. Since perceiving involves sensory qualities, if a state's being conscious consisted in our perceiving it, perhaps we could explain the way we are conscious of the qualities of our conscious sensations. As we saw, that explanation fails, since the higher-order qualities it appeals to would themselves need to be explained. But the HOT hypothesis may seem even less well-suited to deal with this problem. How can one's being in an intentional state, of whatever sort, result in there being something it's like for one to be in a conscious sensory state?

There are two ways the HOT theorist might try to show that being in a suitable intentional state can have this result. One would be to show that it's evident, from a first-person point of view, that one has a suitable HOT when, and only when, there is something it's like for one to be in some sensory state. We could then argue that one's having that HOT is responsible for there being something it's like for one to be in that state.

But if the HOT hypothesis is correct, we cannot expect to find any such first-person correlations. That's because, on that hypothesis, the HOTs in virtue of which our sensory states are conscious are seldom conscious thoughts. And when a thought is not conscious, it will seem, from a first-person point of view, that one does not have it.

So if the HOT hypothesis is correct, it will rarely seem, from a first-person point of view, that HOTs accompany one's conscious sensory states. Our first-person access reveals correlations only with conscious HOTs, not HOTs generally. And HOTs are conscious only in those rare cases in which one has a third-order thought about the HOT. But on the HOT hypothesis, HOTs need not be conscious for there to be something it's like to be in the target sensory states. So we cannot hope to test the hypothesis by correlating in a first-person way the occurrence of HOTs with there being something it's like to be in conscious sensory states.

But we need not rely solely on first-person considerations; there are other factors that help establish the correlation between having HOTs and there being something it's like for one to be in conscious sensory states. In particular, there is a striking connection between what HOTs we are able to have and what sensory qualities we are able to be aware of. And the best explanation of this connection is that accompanying HOTs do result in there being something it's like for one to be in states with those sensory qualities.

Consider wine tasting. Learning new concepts for our experiences of the gustatory and olfactory properties of wines typically leads to our being conscious of more fine-grained differences among the qualities of our sensory states. Similarly with other sensory modalities; acquiring new concepts for specific musical and artistic experiences, for example, enables us to have conscious experiences with more finely differentiated sensory qualities. Somehow, the new concepts appear to generate new conscious sensory qualities.

There are two ways this might happen. One is that coming to have new concepts results in our sensory states' coming to have distinguishing properties that they did not previously have. This is highly implausible. How could merely having new concepts give rise to our sensory states' having new properties? On a widespread view, concepts are abilities to think certain things; how could having a new ability change the properties of the sensory states that result from the same type of stimulus?

But there is another possibility. The new concepts might result in new conscious qualities not by generating those properties, but by making us conscious of properties that were already there. The new concepts would enable us to be conscious of sensory qualities we already had, but had not been conscious of.[37]

Possessing a concept allows us to form intentional states that have a certain range of contents. So which contents our intentional states can have must somehow make a difference to which sensory qualities can occur consciously. Moreover, the new concepts, which make possible conscious experiences with qualities that seem new to us, are the concepts of those very qualities.[38] So being able to form intentional states about certain sensory qualities must somehow result in our being able to experience those qualities consciously. It must result, that is, in there being something specific that it's like for us to be in the relevant sensory states.

How could this happen? The only plausible explanation is that a sensory quality's being conscious does actually consist in our having a HOT about that quality. This is true not only of the relatively finely differentiated qualities we have just now been considering. We can extrapolate to any sensory quality, however crudely individuated, and extrapolate even to whether or not we are conscious of any quality at all.

Take the conscious experience of hearing the sound of an oboe. If one's HOTs couldn't classify one's sensations in terms of the sound of an oboe but only that of some undifferentiated woodwind, having that sensation could not be for one like hearing an oboe. And if one also lacked any concept of the sound of a woodwind, what it would be like for one to have that sensation would then be correspondingly more generic. If one lacked even the concept of a sensation's being of a sound as against being of some other type of stimulus, having the sensation would for one be like merely having some indiscriminate sensory experience or other. This sequence makes it plausible that peeling away that weakest HOT would result, finally, in its no longer being like anything at all to have that sensation. Even though HOTs are just intentional states, and so have no qualitative properties, having HOTs does make the difference between whether there is or is not something it's like for one to have particular sensations.

Because HOTs seldom occur consciously, we cannot, from a first-person point of view, note the occurrence of HOTs when, and only when, we are in conscious sensory states. Still, the argument from wine tasting does draw on first-person considerations. We know in a first-person way that learning new concepts for sensory qualities is enough for us to come to be conscious of our sensory states as having those qualities. And on that basis, we can infer that nonconscious HOTs are responsible for there being something it's like for one to be conscious of our sensory states in that way. It's just that the direct correlation between nonconscious HOTs and conscious sensory states is unavailable from a first-person point of view.

Is it enough to have correlations inferred from first-person considerations? Or must we work completely within a first-person point of view if we are to show that HOTs are responsible for there being something it's like for one to be in conscious sensory states?

A theory of consciousness must explain the first-person aspects of our conscious states. But the explanation need not itself rely only on first-person aspects. Indeed, to demand otherwise is to make any such explanation viciously circular. So the factor responsible for there being something it's like to be in a sensory state need not itself be a first-person aspect of that state, nor even something available from a first-person point of view. The HOTs in virtue of which our mental states are conscious need not, themselves, be conscious thoughts.

Compare the causal relations conscious sensory states have to stimuli, behavior, and other mental states. These relations are typically unavailable from a first-person point of view; we must infer them from other considerations, both first- and third-person. Similarly, we may expect that whatever is responsible for there being something it's like for one to be in conscious sensory states is not directly accessible from a first-person point of view, but must instead be learned about by way of theoretical inference.

Some theorists have insisted that no correlations or theoretical developments could ever enable us to understand fully how physiological occurrences give rise to there being something it's like for one to be in conscious qualitative states. If so, perhaps we also cannot fully understand how HOTs could give rise to conscious qualities.

Joseph Levine calls this difficulty the "explanatory gap" and argues that it results from our being able to conceive of physiological occurrences without conscious qualities. By contrast, he claims, it's inconceivable that water could boil at a different temperature, at least holding constant the rest of chemistry.[39] But our ability to understand things and the apparent limits on what we can conceive are always relative to prevailing theory, whether scientific or folk theory, as Levine's holding chemistry constant illustrates.

Since the appearance of an explanatory gap simply attests our current lack of a well-developed, suitable theory, theoretical advances pertaining to conscious qualitative states should substantially narrow whatever gap seems now to obtain. And, though we may never fully eliminate that gap, we seldom if ever have a complete understanding of how any commonsense, macroscopic phenomenon arises.[40]

The HOT model proceeds independently of physiology, but a similar explanatory gap seems to arise, since we need to understand how nonconscious HOTs can result in conscious qualities. Causal connections are irrelevant here, since there need be no causal tie between a HOT and its target. Rather, HOTs result in conscious qualities because they make us *conscious of ourselves as being in certain qualitative states,* which results in the subjective impression of conscious mental qualities. And the considerations raised earlier in this section provide reason to hold that HOTs can actually do this.

V. Consciousness, Confabulation, and Function

In closing I turn briefly to two unexpected implications of the HOT hypothesis, indeed, of any theory on which a mental state's being conscious consists, as I've argued it must, in one's being transitively conscious of that state.

As we have seen, the HOTs in virtue of which mental states are conscious represent those states in more or less fine-grained ways. And the way our HOTs represent the states they are about influences what those states are like from a first-person point of view. What it's like for me to have a particular gustatory sensation of wine depends on how much detail and differentiation goes into the HOT in virtue of which that sensation is conscious. Given any particular sensory state, different HOTs would yield different ways it's like for one thing one to be in that state.

Since the HOT that accompanies any particular sensory state can be more or less fine-grained, it is not the sensory state alone that determines what HOT one will have. That will depend also on such additional factors as the size of one's repertoire of concepts, one's current interests, how attentive one is, and how experienced one is in making the relevant sensory discriminations.

This raises an interesting question. Since the sensation itself does not determine what HOT one has, why can't the HOT misrepresent the sensory state one is in? Why can't one be in a sensory state of one type, but have a HOT that represents one as being in a sensory state of some different sort? The HOT one has, moreover, determines what it's like for one to be in the relevant sensory state. So why wouldn't an erroneous HOT make it seem, from a first-person point of view, as though one were in a sensory state that one is not in fact in?

There is reason to believe that this actually happens. Dental patients sometimes seem, from a first-person point of view, to experience pain even when nerve damage or local anesthetic makes it indisputable that no such pain could be occurring. The usual hypothesis is that the patient experiences fear or anxiety along with vibration from the drill, and consciously reacts as though in pain. Explaining this to the patient typically results in a corresponding change in what it's like for the patient when drilling resumes, but the patient's sense of what the earlier experience was like generally remains unaltered. The prior, nonveridical appearance of pain is indistinguishable, subjectively, from the real thing.

Other striking examples occur in connection with our perceptual sensations. As Daniel Dennett notes in *Consciousness Explained,* parafoveal vision can produce only low-

resolution sensations of most of the Marilyns in Warhol's famous painting,[41] but we are aware of them all as clear and focused. What it's like for us is a function not of the character of our sensations, but of how we're conscious of those sensations.

There is a also well-known tendency people have to confabulate being in various intentional states, often in ways that seem to make *ex post facto* sense of their behavior;[42] here it's plain that HOTs misrepresent the states that subjects are in. Similarly, it is very likely that repressed beliefs and desires are often actually conscious beliefs and desires whose content one radically misrepresents. Thus one might experience one's desire for some unacceptable thing as a desire for something else instead. In such a case, the desire is not literally unconscious; it is a conscious desire whose character is distorted by inaccurate HOTs. What it's like for one to have that desire fails accurately to reflect its actual content.[43]

The HOT hypothesis is not the only theory to make room for these things; any theory on which a mental state's being conscious consists in one's being transitively conscious of that state will do so. As long as a conscious state is distinct from one's transitive consciousness of it, the content of that transitive consciousness may misrepresent the state. Conscious states are states *we are conscious of ourselves as being in,* whether or not we are actually in them.

The idea that what it's like for one to be in a state is determined not by that state's intrinsic properties but by the way one's HOT represents it enables us to understand certain cases that seem otherwise intractable to explanation. Suppose you're walking through the woods, stepping over branches as needed, but so deeply engrossed in conversation that you pay no conscious attention whatever to the branches. From a first-person point of view, you appear to have no thoughts about the branches; any thoughts about them you do have are not conscious thoughts.

To negotiate through the branches, however, you presumably need more than just thoughts about them; you must also have sensations of the branches. But from a first-person point of view, it may well also seem as though you have no such sensations. Unlike your thoughts, however, there is reason to doubt that your sensations of the branches literally fail to be conscious. It's not that there are no conscious sensations where one would expect sensations of branches to occur in one's visual field; the visual field does not seem to have gaps where the relevant sensations would be. Rather, the sensations that seem to you to be there are, roughly, just sensations of the undifferentiated rustic environment.

Why, then, are you unaware of your sensations of the branches? Plainly you have such sensations; that's how you manage to negotiate through the branches. And the sensations you have of the relevant part of the environment are all conscious; that's why your visual field doesn't seem to contain gaps. So it must be that the sensations are conscious not as sensations of branches, but only as sensations of the undiscriminated environment. We can explain this kind of occurrence only if the way one is transitively conscious of our sensations determines what it's like for one to have them. Compare Dennett's vivid example of looking straight at a thimble but failing to see it as a thimble. It's clear that one's sensation of the thimble is conscious, but one is conscious of it not as a sensation of a thimble but only, say, as a sensation of part of the clutter on a shelf.[44]

In the thimble and branches cases, what it's like for one to be in particular sensory states is informationally less rich than the states themselves. But the opposite also happens, as when we experience our low-resolution sensations of the parafoveal Marilyns as though they were clear and focused. The best explanation is that our HOTs about our blurry parafoveal sensations represent them as having high resolution; the way we are conscious of our sensations actually corrects them by, as it were, bringing them into focus and touching them up.[45] Indeed, this drives home the need to posit occurrent higher-order states, since the high-resolution information must be embodied in some occurrent state.

This disparity between the properties of our sensations and the way we're conscious of them has important implications. For an example, consider Wilfrid Sellars' well-known argument that the sensory qualities of sensations exhibit an "ultimate homogeneity" that sets them apart from the particulate character of ordinary physical properties.[46] Sellars holds that this ultimate homogeneity derives from the way we conceive, in commonsense terms, of the perceptible properties of physical objects. Whatever the case about that, it is likely that those sensory qualities of sensations are themselves particulate. Being neurally based, the relevant sensory information will occur in the form of particular pixels that represent color, shape, motion, and the like. We experience such information, however, as ultimately homogeneous simply because that is how we are conscious of the relevant informational states. The way we are conscious of our sensations smooths them out, so to speak, and elides the details of their particulate, bit-map nature.

Dretske has noted that theories on which a state's being conscious consists in one's being transitively conscious of the state seem unable to explain how a mental state's being conscious could have any function.[47] Being transitively conscious of a state, on these theories, makes no difference to the state's nonrelational properties. So the state's being conscious will make no difference to its causal role nor, therefore, to its function.

It's easy to overestimate the degree to which a state's being conscious does actually play any role. It's inviting to think, for example, that a state's being conscious somehow enhances any planning or reasoning in which that state figures. But the role a state plays in planning and reasoning is due to the content the state has, and that content will be invariant whether or not the state is conscious. So whether or not a state is conscious will not affect the state's role in planning and reasoning. We find it tempting to insist that a state's being conscious affects planning and reasoning when we consider actual cases in which the planning and reasoning are conscious. But those cases tell us nothing unless we compare them to nonconscious cases, to which we have no first-person access. Intuitions cannot help here.

In any event, Dretske has misdescribed the situation. On the HOT hypothesis, a conscious state is a compound state, consisting of the state one is conscious of together with a HOT. So the causal role a conscious state plays is actually the interaction of two causal roles: that played by the state itself and that played by the HOT.[48] This explains how a state's being conscious may to some extent matter to its causal role. Moreover, the way one is conscious of a conscious state may not fully match the target state one is actually in. In those cases, the causal role played by the HOT will matter even more. State consciousness does, after all, make some small difference to the function mental states have.[49]

But what, then, of the compelling intuition that a mental state's being conscious does make a large and significant difference to its mental functioning? That intuition is very likely due to the sense we have that our conscious thoughts, desires, and intentions occur freely and that this apparent freedom enhances our ability to reason and make rational choices. But our sense that these states occur freely itself arguably results from the way we are conscious of those states. Because we are seldom if ever conscious of anything as causing our conscious thoughts and desires, we have the subjective impression that they are uncaused, and hence free. So it seems that just being conscious of these states makes a significant difference to the role they can play in our lives. It is because the way we are conscious

of our intentional states presents them as free and uncaused that their being conscious seems to matter to our ability to reason and make rational choices.

I have argued that the HOT hypothesis explains how conscious states differ from nonconscious mental states, and why, to the extent that it does, state consciousness has a function. Moreover, the hypothesis squares well with there being something it's like to be in conscious sensory states. We can provisionally conclude that the hypothesis deals satisfactorily with the phenomenon of state consciousness, even for the special case of sensory states.

NOTES

1. *Pace* John R. Searle, *The Rediscovery of the Mind,* Cambridge, Massachusetts: MIT Press, 1992; see note 8, below.

   I use 'intentional state' here to refer to states, like beliefs and desires, that exhibit propositional content along with some mental attitude.
2. For some related observations about different uses of 'consciousness' see Edmund Husserl, *Logical Investigations,* London: Routledge & Kegan Paul, 1970, II, pp. 535–36.
3. 'Ordinary' is to exclude so-called hypnogogic dreams, which occur in a semi-waking state.

   Intuitions here are in any case hardly decisive. Are very vivid dream states conscious states? Must we be conscious when we're in them? Since it's far from clear what to say about these matters, it may well be that conscious states can occur without the creature itself being conscious.
4. There is, of course, nothing it's *like* for such a creature to be conscious—nothing it's like *for* the creature. But that doesn't mean there's nothing it *is* to be conscious.
5. Even if all sensations were conscious, what it is for a sensation to be *of* something would be a function not of its being conscious, but rather of the ways it qualitatively resembles and differs from other comparable sensations.

   Strictly speaking, mental states aren't conscious of things; rather, it's creatures that are conscious of things in virtue of their being in mental states.
6. The best known version of the example is due to D. M. Armstrong, "What Is Consciousness?" in his *The Nature of Mind,* St. Lucia, Queensland: University of Queensland Press, 1980: 55–67, p. 59. See Dretske's *Naturalizing the Mind,* Cambridge, Massachusetts: MIT Press/Bradford Books, 1995, pp. 104–5.
7. "Conscious Experience," *Mind* 102, 406 (April 1993): 263–83; reprinted in Dretske, *Perception, Knowledge, and Belief: Selected Essays,* Cambridge: Cambridge University Press, 2000, 113–37, p. 123; *Naturalizing the Mind,* chapter 4.
8. "Conscious Experience," pp. 125–28; cf. *Naturalizing the Mind,* pp. 112–3.
9. One might object that we are, in any case, conscious

of our conscious states when we are introspectively aware of them. To forestall this objection, Dretske has recently argued that introspection resembles what he calls displaced perception. Just as we come to know how full the gas tank is by looking at the gauge, so we come to know what mental state we're in by noticing what we're seeing. We thereby come to be conscious *that* we're in some particular mental state, but not conscious *of* that state. (Dretske, "Introspection," *Proceedings of the Aristotelian Society,* CXV [1994/95]: 263–78, and *Naturalizing the Mind,* ch. 2.)

   On this ingenious proposal, introspection is a matter of coming to know how one represents things (274–75). But introspection is better construed as knowing what mental state one is in, independently of how that state represents nonmental reality. But even if Dretske's right about what introspection is, just seeing that I represent things as being a certain way won't yield introspection unless I see this consciously. So either the argument rests on Dretske's assumption that all mental states are conscious, or he must give a different account of what it is for states to be conscious.
10. "Conscious Experience," 128; cf. 117–18.
11. In his useful "Dretske on HOT Theories of Consciousness," William Seager independently gives a similar account of how Dretske's argument fails to undermine the HOT hypothesis (*Analysis* 54, 1 [January 1994]: 270–76, esp. pp. 275–76).
12. "But readers who were only thing-aware of the difference between Alpha and Beta [the two arrays in Dretske's example] were not fact-conscious of the difference between Alpha and Beta." ("Conscious Experience," p. 128.)
13. John R. Searle also denies that we are conscious of our conscious mental states, though for reasons different from Dretske's. "[W]here conscious subjectivity is concerned, there is no distinction between the observation and the thing observed" (*The Rediscovery of the Mind,* p. 97). The context makes clear that Searle is denying not just that we can observe our conscious states, but that we are conscious of them at all, in the way we're conscious of other

things: "We cannot get at the reality of consciousness in the way that, using consciousness, we can get
at the reality of other phenomena" (96–97). This is
because "where conscious subjectivity is concerned,
there is no distinction between the observation and
the thing observed" (97).

Searle argues for this by appeal to the idea that we
can describe consciousness only in terms of what it's
consciousness *of* (96). But even if that's so, there
will be states in virtue of which we are conscious of
things. So it doesn't follow that there aren't states in
virtue of which we are conscious of our conscious
states.

14. "[T]he word 'thought' applies to all that exists in us
in such a way that we are immediately conscious of
it" (Geometrical Exposition of the *Second Replies,
Oeuvres de Descartes,* ed. Charles Adam and Paul
Tannery, Paris: J. Vrin, 1964–75, VII, 160).

15. Nonconscious mediation, moreover, might well
occur; factors of which we're in no way conscious
often causally mediate among distinct mental states,
even when we're aware of them from a first-person
point of view.

Our intuitive sense that we're not conscious of our
conscious states in any way that's mediated may be
what leads Searle to claim that there's no way in
which we're conscious *of* our conscious states (see n.
13). It also distinguishes this case from the way
we're perceptually conscious of things, in which we
are sometimes conscious of the intervening medium.

16. A slight adjustment to this is needed. One might
hold a theory on which an inference mediates between our being conscious of our conscious states
and the states themselves, though we're conscious of
that inference only by another inference based on the
theory. (I thank Eric Lormand for raising this possibility.) We would still count as conscious the same
states, even though the theory makes us conscious of
the inferential mediations. We can provide for this
by stipulating that if a state is conscious, we're conscious of it in a way that does not require that we be
conscious of any inference that may occur. Our
being conscious of the state may rely on some inference, but not on our being conscious of it.

This handles a related possibility as well. Suppose
that inferences of which we're not conscious normally mediate between our being conscious of our
conscious states and those states. Even if we somehow became conscious of some of those inferences
without benefit of theory, we'd count the same states
as conscious. The adjusted stipulation provides for
this. Since nothing in what follows hinges on this
sort of thing, I'll omit this qualification.

If the way we're conscious of our conscious states
were sometimes based on conscious inference, we'd
then know how we come to be conscious of those
states. Though we're conscious of our conscious
states, we generally don't, from a first-person point
of view, have any idea how we come to be conscious
of them. That ignorance helps explain the air of mystery that surrounds state consciousness.

17. The inference that consciously mediates between
mental states and one's being conscious of them
need not begin with the mental state to one's being
conscious of it; typically, the conscious inference
would start, instead, from noticing one's behavior or
from the remarks of others. And because those

things are causally due to one's mental state, such an
inference counts as mediating between a mental
state and one's being conscious of it.

We need not independently preclude reliance on
observation. Intuitively, one's being conscious of a
mental state can be immediate even if it relies on observation, so long as one is not aware of its doing so.
And that will be so if there's no reliance on any conscious inference. E.g., if one observes one's happy
gait and so, without any inference of which one is
aware, takes oneself to be happy, the way one is conscious of being happy is intuitively immediate.

18. Although we recognize on reflection that mediation
does in fact occur, no conscious inference normally
mediates, and as we've seen, that's what matters for
the intuition of immediacy.

19. On this, see David M. Rosenthal, "The Colors and
Shapes of Visual Experiences," in *Consciousness and
Intentionality: Models and Modalities of Attribution,*
ed. Denis Fisette, Dordrecht: Kluwer Academic Publishers, 1998, pp. 137–69; and "The Independence
of Consciousness and Sensory Quality," in *Consciousness: Philosophical Issues, 1, 1991,* ed. En-
rique Villanueva, Atascadero, California: Ridgeview
Publishing Company, 1991, pp. 15–36, reprinted in
Consciousness and Mind, Oxford: Clarendon Press,
forthcoming.

20. These considerations are reminiscent of an argument
of Aristotle's at *de Anima* III, 2, 425b12–14, though
Aristotle also held that the redness of our perceptions is the very same quality as the redness of physical objects (e.g., *de Anima* II, 5, 418a4; II, 11,
423b31; II, 12, 424a18; III, 2, 425b23).

Perhaps the qualities of the higher-order states are
those our sensory states seem to have, and the lower-
order qualities do not figure in what it's like for us to
be in sensory states. But locating the qualities that
figure in what it's like to be in sensory states at the
higher level doesn't help explain the qualitative dimension of those states.

21. The concern that nonlinguistic creatures can't be in
intentional states with such sophisticated content
may also motivate preference for the perceptual
model, since perceiving is a less sophisticated mental phenomenon. But little conceptual richness is
needed to be in such intentional states. The concept
of self, e.g., need involve no more than the distinction between oneself and everything else. And the
state itself can be conceptualized in a relatively minimal way, say, just as some way the creature is.

22. So HOTs are not simply about intentional contents,
but about full-fledged intentional states: contents
plus mental attitudes.

If I doubt or wonder whether a particular physical
object is red, I'm conscious of that object; similarly
if I expect, hope, or desire that it is. But it's not the
doubt, wonder, hope, or desire that makes me conscious of the object. Rather, if I doubt whether the
object is red or desire or suspect that it is, I must also
think assertorically that the object is there, or exists,
and I'm conscious of the object in virtue of my having that assertoric thought. This is evident because,
in such a case, I wouldn't be conscious of the object
as red, but just as something that exists. The content
of my consciousness is determined not by the content of my nonassertoric intentional state, but by the
assertoric state. Similarly with intentional states

about our own mental states; being in nonassertoric intentional states about one's mental states make one conscious of being in those states only if they require one also to have the assertoric thought that one is in that state.

It's worth noting an argument of Robert M. Gordon that many emotions must be accompanied by corresponding beliefs; being angry that *p,* e.g., requires believing that *p.* (*The Structure of Emotions: Investigations in Cognitive Philosophy,* Cambridge: Cambridge University Press, 1987, pp. 47ff.) If so, the required belief would explain why, when one's angry that *p,* one is conscious of whatever ⌜*p*⌝ is about. In any case, this result depends on describing the emotion in terms of its intentional content. Thus, if one describes a person not as being angry that *p,* e.g., but as being angry because *p,* no corresponding belief is implied.

23. This helps deal with an interesting objection. Freudian theory may seem to posit states that are nonconscious despite their being accompanied by suitable HOTs. (This idea has been pressed by Georges Rey and Stephen Schiffer.) But it's not easy to come up with convincing examples. Pleasure or guilt about repressed states won't do because pleasure and guilt aren't assertoric; so we often aren't conscious of the objects of our pleasure or guilt—even when those states are conscious.

Even if we could come up with plausible examples, moreover, it is far from obvious that Freudian theory requires that we describe the situation as involving nonconscious states accompanied by HOTs, since there typically are several equally good explanations for any such phenomenon. It's also important to note that repressed states are seldom nonconscious states. Rather, they're typically states we disguise by radically misrepresenting their content, or distract ourselves from by creating elaborate mental noise. See p. 29, below.

24. According to Searle, the intentional content of perceptual states always refers to those very states; if I see a yellow station wagon, the content of my visual perception is "that there is a yellow station wagon there and that there is a yellow station wagon there is causing this visual experience" (*Intentionality: An Essay in the Philosophy of Mind,* Cambridge: Cambridge University Press, 1983, p. 48). If the content of every perceptual state were partly that one is in that state, then on the HOT hypothesis, just being in the state would make one conscious of it, and nonconscious perceptions would be impossible. (I am grateful to Gilbert Harman for raising this concern.) Moreover, perceiving something does presumably make one conscious of that thing, arguably because the mental attitude of perceiving is assertoric.

Searle's argument for this claim appeals to the truth conditions of perceptions; a state's intentional content "determines under what conditions it is satisfied" (p. 48), and one perceives a thing only if it causes one's perception. But the conditions under which the perception is satisfied are simply that there's a yellow station wagon there, not also that the perception is caused by there being a yellow station wagon there. The causal condition is relevant not to the truth of what I perceive, but of whether I perceive it.

These considerations do, however, point toward an explanation of how many perceptual states do come to be conscious. We assume as a general belief about about the world that the states of affairs we perceive normally cause the relevant perceptual states. When one has the (typically nonconscious) thought that a perceived state of affairs has caused the perceptual state, that thought results in a HOT that one is in the perceptual state, and thus results in that state's being conscious.

25. See, e.g., Dretske, "Conscious Experience," esp. Section 4; also Ned Block, review of Daniel C. Dennett, *Consciousness Explained, The Journal of Philosophy* XC, 4 (April 1993): 181–93, who alludes on p. 182 to the HOT hypothesis.

26. This argument is developed in detail in my "Thinking That One Thinks," in *Consciousness: Psychological and Philosophical Essays,* ed. Martin Davies and Glyn W. Humphreys, Oxford: Basil Blackwell, 1993, pp. 197–223. On the connection between thought and genuine speech, see my "Intentionality," *Midwest Studies in Philosophy,* X (1986): 151–84. Both will be reprinted in *Consciousness and Mind.*

The argument relies on creatures that can describe their mental states. But noninferential reportability simply helps fix the extension of 'conscious state'; many nonlinguistic creatures are also in conscious states.

Special issues arise about qualitative states, since there is no such thing as verbally expressing a perceptual sensation. We can express perceptions, but only because perceptions, unlike sensations, have an intentional aspect and it's that intentional component that we can verbally express. The same may also hold for bodily sensations; though we can express a pain by uttering 'ouch,' it's unclear that 'ouch' counts as a verbal, as opposed to nonverbal, form of expressing. And, though saying 'It hurts' is linguistic, that reports the pain, rather than expressing it. Still, creatures with suitable linguistic ability can noninferentially report their conscious states, whether the states are intentional or sensory.

These considerations have a bearing on the perceptual model. When a state is conscious, creatures with the relevant linguistic ability can express their transitive consciousness of the state. If there were a higher-order perception of the state, one's report would verbally express only the intentional component of that higher-order perception. But that's in effect just to express a HOT. So the argument from reporting and expressing shows that if the transitive consciousness of a conscious state did have a sensory aspect, that sensory aspect would be irrelevant to the state's being intransitively conscious.

27. Dennett and Harman have independently pressed this reply in conversation, and it receives tacit expression in Dennett's view that "[c]onsciousness is cerebral celebrity" ("The Message Is: There is no Medium," *Philosophy and Phenomenological Research* LIII, 4 [December 1993]: 919–31, p. 929). See also Dennett, *Consciousness Explained,* ch. 10 and esp. p. 315.

28. Peter Carruthers, *Language, Thought, and Consciousness: An Essay in Philosophical Psychology,* Cambridge: Cambridge University Press, 1996, and *Phenomenal Consciousness: A Naturalistic Theory,* Cambridge: Cambridge University Press, 2000.

29. See Lawrence Weiskrantz, *Blindsight,* Oxford: Oxford University Press, 1986, and *Consciousness Lost*

and Found: A Neuropsychological Exploration, Oxford: Oxford University Press, 1997.

There is reason to think that discrimination of stimuli with different form may be due to discrimination of orientation, rather than of form itself (*Blindsight,* 84). Van Gulick has argued that this shows that blindsight does not involve states with phenomenal properties like those of conscious visual sensations. ("Deficit Studies and the Function of Phenomenal Consciousness," in *Philosophical Psychopathology,* ed. George Graham and G. Lynn Stephens, Cambridge, Massachusetts: MIT, 1994.) But that conclusion follows only if one assumes that sensory qualities must be integrated in just the way they are in normal conscious cases.

30. A classical example is the so-called cocktail-party effect. We typically screen out the sounds of conversations other than our own, though mention of one's name in a screened-out conversation normally causes one's attention suddenly to shift to that conversation.

31. Compare parallel arguments that certain nonconscious states have mental properties because of the roles they play in mental processes; e.g., J. A. Fodor, "Methodological Solipsism Considered as a Research Strategy in Cognitive Psychology," *The Behavioral and Brain Sciences* III, 1 (March 1980): 63–73.

32. See Thomas Nagel's "What Is It Like to Be a Bat?," *The Philosophical Review* LXXXIII, 4 (October 1974): 435–50; "Panpsychism," in *Mortal Questions,* Cambridge: Cambridge University Press, 1979, pp. 181–95; and *The View from Nowhere,* New York: Oxford University Press, 1986, chapters 1–4.

33. "On a Confusion about a Function of Consciousness," *The Behavioral and Brain Sciences,* 18, 2 (June 1995): 227–47, p. 231; emphasis Block's. See also Block, review of Dennett's *Consciousness Explained,* p. 184; "Begging the Question against Phenomenal Consciousness," *The Behavioral and Brain Sciences* 15, 2 (June 1992): 205–6; "Consciousness and Accessibility," *The Behavioral and Brain Sciences* XIII, 4 (December 1990): 596–98.

34. It's not that the states we report are nonconscious, but nonconscious states influence what we report and how we do it.

35. Block's definition of access consciousness in terms of a state's being "poised" for certain things gives a dispositional mark of such consciousness. (In the review of Dennett's book he uses the phrase 'freely available' [p. 182].) That is compatible with access consciousness's consisting in a subject's being transitively conscious of a mental state, rather than simply being disposed to be conscious of it. States we are transitively conscious of have many dispositional properties, among them being reportable and introspectible.

36. Block distinguishes a third concept of consciousness, which he calls reflective consciousness (review of Dennett, p. 182) or monitoring consciousness ("On a Confusion," p. 235). According to Block, a state is conscious in this way if one has a HOT about it. But the states he counts as reflectively or monitoring conscious are states that we're introspectively conscious of: states that we're conscious of being conscious of. This is a distinct notion of consciousness, but Block is mistaken to define it in terms of

having HOTs. Rather a state has monitoring consciousness, in his terms, only if one has a *conscious* HOT about it. See n. 25.

For more on Block, see Rosenthal, "Phenomenal Consciousness and What It's Like," *The Behavioral and Brain Sciences,* 20, 1 (March 1997), pp. 64–65, "The Kinds of Consciousness," MS, and "How Many Kinds of Consciousness," MS.

37. Of course, the relevant sensory states will often have been conscious before one acquired the more finegrained concepts, but conscious only with respect to qualities individuated in a more course-grained way. E.g., one might initially be conscious of a particular type of olfactory sensation solely as being winelike, and subsequently become conscious of it in terms of more fine-grained sensory qualities.

38. One might argue that the new concepts pertain not to the distinguishing properties of our conscious sensory experiences, but rather to the perceptible properties of the perceived physical objects and processes, e.g., the wine or the musical performance. (See Harman, "The Intrinsic Quality of Experience," *Philosophical Perspectives, 4: Action Theory and Philosophy of Mind,* 1990, pp. 31–52.) But it's clear that in the cases just imagined we also focus introspectively on the distinguishing properties of our conscious sensory states. So those cases involve new concepts of the distinguishing properties of sensory states.

39. "On Leaving Out What It's Like," in *Consciousness: Psychological and Philosophical Essays,* ed. Martin Davies and Glyn W. Humphreys, Oxford: Basil Blackwell, 1993, 121–36, p. 134, and *Purple Haze: The Puzzle of Consciousness,* New York: Oxford University Press, 2001, pp. 79. See also "Materialism and Qualia: The Explanatory Gap," *Pacific Philosophical Quarterly* LXIV, 4 (October 1983): 354–61. For related arguments see David J. Chalmers, *The Conscious Mind: In Search of a Fundamental Theory,* New York: Oxford University Press, 1996.

Similarly, Nagel claims we have a purely rational understanding of why "heat caus[es] water to boil, rocks caus[e] glass to break, magnets induc[e] electric current, [and] the wind mak[es] waves" ("Panpsychism," 186), but currently lack any understanding of how physical heat, e.g., or a brain process, could causally necessitate a pain or other sensation ("Panpsychism," 187).

40. See my "Reductionism and Knowledge," in *How Many Questions?,* ed. Leigh S. Cauman, Isaac Levi, Charles Parsons, and Robert Schwartz, Indianapolis: Hackett Publishing Co., 1983, 276–300.

41. Daniel C. Dennett, *Consciousness Explained,* Boston: Little, Brown and Company, 1991, p. 354. See pp. 53–54 for Dennett's striking illustration of these limits in attempting to discern the color of playing cards seen parafoveally at arm's length.

42. For a classic study, see Richard E. Nisbett and Timothy DeCamp Wilson, "Telling More Than We Can Know: Verbal Reports on Mental Processes," *Psychological Review* LXXXIV, 3 [May 1977]: 231–59.) Nisbett and Wilson's influential study focused not only on cases in which subjects confabulate stories about the causes of their being in particular cognitive states, but also on cases in which they confabulate accounts about what states they're actually in.

43. Perhaps such erroneous HOTs might figure also in apparent self-deception.

It may sometimes be difficult to tell whether a HOT misrepresents an actual target or the HOT has only a notional target, and there is an actual state that simply isn't conscious. Indeed, it may well be arbitrary within a certain range of cases which way we describe a case.

44. *Consciousness Explained,* p. 336.

Similarly, in the cocktail-party effect, one's attention shifts to a previously unattended conversation in which one's name was mentioned. So one must have been hearing the articulated words in that conversation, though to consciousness it seemed just to be background din.

Robust experimental findings, e.g., those involving masked priming, also provide compelling evidence that what it's like to have a sensation sometimes diverges from the properties of the sensation itself. In masked priming, subjects report being unaware of qualitative input whose presence is evident from its effect on subsequent cognitive behavior. For a classic study, see Anthony J. Marcel, "Conscious and Unconscious Perception: Experiments on Visual Masking and Word Recognition," *Cognitive Psychology* 15 (1983): 197–237.

Experimental work on change blindness also provides vivid evidence for divergence of how we're conscious of our sensations from their actual properties. Subjects here fail consciously to register visible changes so salient that it's overwhelmingly likely that corresponding changes do occur in their visual sensations. So subjects' sensations diverge from how they're aware of them. Moreover, the compelling impression we all have of being continuously conscious of salient qualitative detail is evidently erroneous. See John Grimes, "On the Failure to Detect Changes in Scenes across Saccades," in *Perception,* ed. Kathleen Akins, New York: Oxford University Press, 1996, pp. 89–110; Daniel J. Simons, "Current Approaches to Change Blindness," *Visual Cognition* 7 (2000): 1–16; and Ronald A. Rensink, "The Dynamic Representation of Scenes," *Visual Cognition,* 7, 1/2/3 (January 2000): 17–42, and "Seeing, Sensing, and Scrutinizing," *Vision Research,* 40, 10–12 (2000): 1469–87.

45. In aesthetic experience, also, how we are conscious of a sensation presumably outstrips that sensation's qualitative character.

For more on sensations' diverging from the way we are conscious of of them and the way HOTs function in that connection, see "Sensory Qualities, Consciousness, and Perception," forthcoming in *Consciousness and Mind,* and "Consciousness and Metacognition," in *Metarepresentation: Proceedings of the Tenth Vancouver Cognitive Science Conference,* ed. Daniel Sperber, New York: Oxford University Press, 2000, 265–95.

46. Often referred to as Sellars' "grain argument." Wilfrid Sellars, "Philosophy and the Scientific Image of Man," in *Frontiers of Science and Philosophy,* ed. Robert G. Colodny, Pittsburgh: University of Pittsburgh Press, 1962, pp. 35–78; reprinted in *Science, Perception and Reality,* 1–40, p. 36; also p. 35, and "Phenomenalism," also in *Science, Perception and Reality,* 60–105, pp. 103–5.

Cf. Peter Carruthers' claim that "perceptual information is *analogue* (that is, 'filled in' and continuous)," and "the subjective aspect of an experience just *is* analogue information about [physical] red, presented to a cognitive apparatus having the power classify states as information carriers, as well as to classify the information carried" (Peter Carruthers, *Language, Thought, and Consciousness: An Essay in Philosophical Psychology,* Cambridge: Cambridge University Press, 1996, pp. 167, 214).

47. *Naturalizing the Mind,* p. 117.

48. The interaction of the two roles may not be additive; the causal properties of the HOT may interact with those of the state in such a way that the original causal properties of the state are modified, or even blocked altogether.

49. So conscious inessentialism, on which every intelligent activity we perform consciously could be performed without its being conscious, is mistaken. The label is due to Owen Flanagan, who rejects the thesis (*Consciousness Reconsidered,* Cambridge, Massachusetts: MIT Press/Bradford Books, 1992, pp. 5, 129ff.).

40 | Conscious Experience[1]
Fred Dretske

There is a difference between hearing Clyde play the piano and seeing him play the piano. The difference consists in a difference in the kind of experience caused by Clyde's piano playing. Clyde's performance can also cause a belief—the belief that he is playing the piano. A perceptual belief that he is playing the piano must be distinguished from a perceptual experience of this same event. A person (or an animal, for that matter) can hear or see a piano being played without knowing, believing, or judging that a piano is being played. Conversely, a person (I do not know about animals) can come to believe that Clyde is playing the piano without seeing or hearing him do it—without experiencing the performance for themselves.

This distinction between a perceptual experience of x and a perceptual belief about x is, I hope, obvious enough. I will spend some time enlarging upon it, but only for the sake of sorting out relevant interconnections (or lack thereof). My primary interest is not in this distinction, but, rather, in what it reveals about the nature of conscious experience and, thus, consciousness itself. For unless one understands the difference between a consciousness of things (Clyde playing the piano) and a consciousness of facts (that he is playing the piano), and the way this difference depends, in turn, on a difference between a concept-free mental state (e.g., an experience) and a concept-charged mental state (e.g., a belief), one will fail to understand how one can have conscious experiences without being aware that one is having them. One will fail to understand, therefore, how an experience can be conscious without anyone—including the person having it—being conscious of having it. Failure to understand how this is possible constitutes a failure to understand what makes something conscious and, hence, what consciousness is.

The possibility of a person's having a conscious experience she is not conscious of having will certainly sound odd, perhaps even contradictory, to those philosophers who (consciously or not) embrace an inner spotlight view of consciousness according to which a mental state is conscious in so far as the light of consciousness shines *on* it—thus making one conscious *of* it.[2] It will also sound confused to those like Dennett (1991) who, though rejecting theatre metaphors (and the spotlight images they encourage), espouse a kind of first person operationalism about mental phenomena that links conscious mental states to those that can be reported and of which, therefore, the reporter is necessarily aware of having.

There is, however, nothing confused or contradictory about the idea of a conscious experience that one is not conscious of having. The first step in understanding the nature of conscious experience is understanding why this is so.

1. Awareness of Facts and Awareness of Things[3]

For purposes of this discussion I regard "conscious" and "aware" as synonyms. Being conscious of a thing (or fact) is being aware of it. Accordingly, "conscious awareness" and "consciously aware" are redundancies.

A. White (1964) describes interesting differences between the ordinary use of "aware" and "conscious." He also describes the different liaisons they have to noticing, attending, and realizing. Though my treatment of these expressions (for the purposes of this inquiry) as synonymous blurs some of these ordinary distinctions, even (occasionally) violating some of the strictures White records, nothing essential to my project is lost by ignoring the niceties. No useful theory of consciousness can hope (nor, I think, should it even aspire) to capture all the subtle nuances of ordinary usage.

By contrasting our awareness of things (x) with our awareness of facts (that P) I mean to be distinguishing particular (spatial) objects and (temporal) events[4] on the one hand from facts involving these things on the other. Clyde (a physical object), his piano (another object), and Clyde's playing his piano (an event) are all things as I am using the word "thing"; that he is

From *Mind* 102:263–283, 1993. Reprinted with permission of author and publisher.

playing his piano is a fact. Things are neither true nor false though, in the case of events, states of affairs, and conditions, we sometimes speak of them as what makes a statement true. Facts are what we express in making true statements about things. We describe our awareness of facts by using a factive complement, a that-clause, after the verb; we describe our awareness of things by using a (concrete) noun or noun phrase as direct object of the verb. We are aware of Clyde, his piano, and of Clyde's playing his piano (things); we are also aware that he is playing the piano (a fact).

Seeing, hearing, and smelling x are ways of being conscious of x.[5] Seeing a tree, smelling a rose, and feeling a wrinkle is to be (perceptually) aware (conscious) of the tree, the rose, and the wrinkle. There may be other ways of being conscious of objects and events. It may be that thinking or dreaming about Clyde is a way of being aware of Clyde without perceiving him.[6] I do not deny it (though I think it stretches usage). I affirm, only, the converse: that to see and feel a thing is to be (perceptually) conscious of it. And the same is true of facts: to see, smell, or feel that P is to be (or become) aware that P. Hence,

(1) S sees (hears, etc.) x (or that P) $\Rightarrow$ S is conscious of x (that P)[7]

In this essay I shall be mainly concerned with *perceptual* forms of consciousness. So when I speak of S's being conscious (or aware) of something I will have in mind S's seeing, hearing, smelling, or in some way sensing a thing (or fact).

Consciousness of facts implies a deployment of concepts. If S is aware that x is F, then S has the concept F and uses (applies) it in his awareness of x.[8] If a person smells that the toast is burning, thus becoming aware that the toast is burning, this person applies the concept *burning* (perhaps also the concept *toast*) to what he smells. One cannot be conscious that the toast is burning unless one understands what toast is and what it means to burn—unless, that is, one has the concepts needed to classify objects and events in this way. I will follow the practice of supposing that our awareness of facts takes the form of a belief. Thus, to smell that the toast is burning is to be aware that the toast is burning is to believe that the toast is burning. It is conventional in epistemology to assume that when perceptual verbs take factive nominals as complements, what is being described is not just belief but knowledge. Seeing or smelling that the toast

is burning is a way of coming to *know* (or, at least, verifying the knowledge) that the toast is burning. It will be enough for present purposes if we operate with a weaker claim: that perceptual awareness of facts is a mental state or attitude that involves the possession and use of concepts, the sort of cognitive or intellectual capacity involved in thought and belief. I will, for convenience, take belief (that P) as the normal realization of an awareness that P.

Perceptual awareness of facts has a close tie with behaviour—with, in particular (for those who have language), an ability to *say* what one is aware of. This is not so with a consciousness of things. One can smell or see (hence, be conscious of) burning toast while having little or no understanding of what toast is or what it means to burn. "What is that strange smell?" might well be the remark of someone who smells burning toast but is ignorant of what toast is or what it means to burn something. The cat can smell, and thus be aware of, burning toast as well as the cook, but only the cook will be aware that the toast is burning (or that it is the toast that is burning).

The first time I became aware of an armadillo (I saw it on a Texas road), I did not know what it was. I did not even know what armadillos were, much less what they looked like. My ignorance did not impair my eyesight, of course. I saw the animal. I was aware of it ahead of me on the road. That is why I swerved. Ignorance of what armadillos are or how they look can prevent someone from being conscious of certain facts (that the object crossing the road is an armadillo) without impairing in the slightest one's awareness of the things—the armadillos crossing roads—that (so to speak) constitute these facts. This suggests the following important result. For all things (as specified above) x and properties F,

(2) S is conscious of $x \not\Rightarrow$ S is conscious that x is F.

Though (2) strikes me as self-evident, I have discovered, over the years, that it does not strike everyone that way. The reason it does not (I have also found) is usually connected with a failure to appreciate or apply one or more of the following distinctions. The first two are, I hope, more or less obvious. I will be brief. The third will take a little longer.

(a) *Not Implying vs. Implying Not.* There is a big difference between denying that A implies B and affirming that A implies not-B. (2) does not affirm, it denies, an implication. It does not say that one can only be aware of a thing by *not* being aware of what it is.

(b) *Implication vs. Implicature.* The implication (2) denies is a logical implication, not a Gricean (1989) implicature. *Saying* you are aware of an *F* (i.e., a thing, *x*, which is *F*) implies (as a conversational implication) that you are aware that *x* is *F*. Anyone who said he was conscious of (e.g., saw or smelled) an armadillo would (normally) imply that he thought it was an armadillo. This is true, but irrelevant.

(c) *Concrete Objects vs. Abstract Objects.* When perceptual verbs (including the generic "aware of" and "conscious of") are followed by abstract nouns (the difference, the number, the answer, the problem, the size, the colour) and interrogative nominals (where the cat is, who he is talking to, when they left), what is being described is normally an awareness of some (unspecified) fact. The abstract noun phrase or interrogative nominal stands in for some factive clause. Thus, seeing (being conscious of) the difference between *A* and *B* is to see (be conscious) *that* they differ. If the problem is the clogged drain, then to be aware of the problem is to be aware that the drain is clogged. To be aware of the problem it isn't enough to be aware of (e.g., to see) the thing that is the problem (the clogged drain). One has to see (the fact) *that* it is clogged. Until one becomes aware of this fact, one hasn't become aware of the problem. Likewise, to see where the cat is hiding is to see that it is hiding *there,* for some value of "there."

This can get tricky, and is often the source of confusion in discussing what can be observed. This is not the place for gory details, but I must mention one instance of this problem since it will come up again when we discuss which aspects of experience are conscious when we are perceiving a complicated scene. To use a traditional philosophical example, suppose S sees a speckled hen on which there are (on the facing side) 27 speckles. Each speckle is clearly visible. Not troubling to count, S does not realize that (hence, is not aware that) there are 27 speckles. Nonetheless, we assume that S looked long enough, and carefully enough, to see each speckle. In such a case, although S is aware of all 27 speckles (things), he is not aware of the number of speckles because being aware of the number of speckles requires being aware that there is that number of speckles (a fact), and S is not aware of this fact.[9] For epistemological purposes, abstract objects are disguised facts; you

cannot be conscious of these objects without being conscious of a fact.

(2) is a thesis about concrete objects. The values of *x* are *things* as this was defined above. Abstract objects do not count as things for purposes of (2). Hence, even though one cannot see the difference between *A* and *B* without seeing that they differ, cannot be aware of the number of speckles on the hen without being aware that there are 27, and cannot be conscious of an object's irregular shape without being conscious that it has an irregular shape, this is irrelevant to the truth of (2).

As linguists (e.g., Lees, 1963, p. 14) observe, however, abstract nouns may appear in copula sentences opposite both factive (that) clauses and concrete nominals. We can say that the problem is *that his tonsils are inflamed* (a fact); but we can also say that the problem is, simply, *his* (inflamed) *tonsils* (a thing). This can give rise to an ambiguity when the abstract noun is the object of a perceptual verb. Though it is, I think, normal to interpret the abstract noun as referring to a fact in perceptual contexts, there exists the possibility of interpreting it as referring to a thing. Thus, suppose that Tom at time t_1 differs (perceptibly) from Tom at t_2 only in having a moustache at t_2. S sees Tom at both times but does not notice the moustache—is not, therefore, aware that he has grown a moustache. Since, however, S spends twenty minutes talking to Tom in broad daylight, it is reasonable to say that although S did not notice the moustache, he (must) nonetheless have seen it.[10] If S did see Tom's moustache without (as we say) registering it at the time, can we describe S as seeing, and thus (in this sense) being aware of, a difference in Tom's appearance between t_1 and t_2? In the factive sense of awareness (the normal interpretation, I think), no; S was not aware that there was a difference. S was not aware at t_2 that Tom had a moustache. In the thing sense of awareness, however, the answer is: yes. S was aware of the moustache at t_2, something he was not aware of at t_1, and the moustache is a difference in Tom's appearance.

If, as in this example, "the difference between *A* and *B*" is taken to refer, not to the fact that *A* and *B* differ, but to a particular element or condition of *A* and *B* that constitutes their difference, then seeing the difference between *A* and *B* would be seeing this element or condition—a thing, not a fact. In this thing sense of "the difference" a person or animal who had not yet learned to discriminate (in any behaviourally relevant way) between (say) two forms might nonetheless be said to see (and in this sense be aware of) the difference between them if it saw the parts of one that distinguished it from the other. When two objects differ in this perceptible way, one can be conscious of the thing (speckle, line, star, stripe) that is the difference without being conscious of the difference (= conscious *that* they differ). In order to avoid confusion about this critical (for my purposes) point, I will, when speaking of our awareness or consciousness of something designated by an abstract noun or phrase (the colour, the size, the difference, the number, etc.), always specify whether I mean thing-awareness or fact-awareness. To be thing-aware of a difference is to be aware of the thing (some object, event, or condition, x) that makes the difference. To be fact-aware of the difference is to be aware of the fact that there is a difference (not necessarily the fact that x is the difference). In the above example, S was thing-aware, but not fact-aware, of the difference between Tom at t_1 and t_2. He was (at t_2) aware of the thing that made the difference, but not fact-aware (at t_2 or later) of this difference.

So much by way of clarifying (2). What can be said in its support? I have already given several examples of properties or kinds, F, which are such that one can be aware of a thing which is F without being aware that it is F (an armadillo, burning toast, a moustache). But (2) says something stronger. It says that there is no property F which is such that an awareness of a thing which is F requires an awareness of the fact that it is F. It may be felt that this is much too strong. One can, to be sure, see armadillos without seeing that they are armadillos, but perhaps one must, in order to see them, see that they are (say) animals of some sort. To see x (which is an animal) is to see that it is an animal. If this sounds implausible (one can surely mistake an animal for a rock or a bush) maybe one must, in seeing an object, at least see that it is an object of some sort. To be aware of a thing is at least be aware that it is . . . how shall we say it? . . . a thing. *Something or other.* Whether or not this is true depends, of course, on what is involved in being aware that a thing is a thing. Since we can certainly see a physical object without being aware that it is a physical object (we can think we are hallucinating), the required concept F (required to be aware that x is F) cannot be much of a concept. It seems most implausible to suppose infants and animals (presumably, conscious of things) have con-

cepts of this sort. If the concept one must have to be aware of something is a concept that applies to *everything* one can be aware of, what is the point of insisting that one must have it to be aware?

I therefore conclude that awareness of things (x) requires no fact-awareness (that x is F, for any F) of those things.[11] Those who feel that this conclusion has too little support are welcome to substitute a weaker version of (2): namely, there is no *reasonably specific property* F which is such that awareness of a thing which is F requires fact-awareness that it is F. This will not affect my use of (2).

2. Conscious Beings and Conscious States

Agents are said to be conscious in an intransitive sense of this word (he regained consciousness) and in a transitive sense (he was conscious of her). I will follow Rosenthal (1990) and refer to both as *creature* consciousness. Creature consciousness (whether transitive or intransitive) is to be contrasted with what Rosenthal calls *state* consciousness—the (always intransitive) sense in which certain internal states, processes, events and attitudes (typically in or of conscious beings) are said to be conscious.

For purposes of being explicit about my own (standard, I hope) way of using these words, I assume that for any x and P,

(3) S is conscious of x or that $P \Rightarrow$ S is conscious (a conscious being).

That is, transitive (creature) consciousness implies intransitive (creature) consciousness. You cannot see or hear, taste or smell, a thing without (thereby) being conscious.[12] You cannot be aware that your cheque-book doesn't balance or conscious that you are late for an appointment (a fact) without being a conscious being.[13]

The converse of (3) is more problematic. Perhaps one can be conscious with out being conscious of anything. Some philosophers think that during hallucination, for example, one might be fully conscious but (*qua* hallucinator) not conscious of anything. To suppose that hallucination (involving intransitive consciousness) is a consciousness of something would (or so it is feared) commit one to objectionable mental particulars—the sense data that one hallucinates. Whether or not this is so I will not try to say. I leave the issue open. (3) only endorses the innocent idea that beings who are conscious of something are conscious; it does not say that conscious beings must be conscious of something.

By way of interconnecting creature and state consciousness I also posit:

(4) S is conscious of x or that $P \Rightarrow$ S is in a
     conscious state of some sort.

Transitive creature consciousness requires state (of the creature) consciousness. S's consciousness of x or that P is a relational state of affairs; it involves both the agent, S, and the object (or fact) S is conscious of. The conscious state which (according to (4)) S must be in when he is conscious of x or that P, however, is not the sort of state the existence of which logically requires x or the condition described by P. Tokens of this state type may be caused by x or the condition described by "P" (and when they are, they may qualify as experiences of x or knowledge that P), but to qualify as a token of this type, x and the condition described by "P" are not necessary.

Thus, according to (4), when I see or hear Clyde playing the piano (or that he is playing the piano) and (thus) am conscious of him playing the piano (or that he is playing the piano), I am in a conscious state of some kind. When hallucinating (or simply when listening to a recording) I can be in the same kind of conscious state even if Clyde is not playing the piano (or I do not perceive him playing the piano). When Clyde is not playing the piano (or I am not perceiving him play the piano), we speak of the conscious state in question not as knowledge (that he is playing the piano) but as belief, not as perception (of Clyde playing the piano) but as hallucination (or perception of something else).[14]

I do not know how to argue for (4). I would like to say that it states the obvious and leave it at that. I know, however, that nothing is obvious in this area. Not even the obvious. (4) says that our perceptual awareness of both things (smelling the burning toast) and facts (becoming aware that it is burning) involves, in some essential way, conscious subjective (i.e., non-relational and, in this sense, internal or subjective) states of the perceiver—beliefs (in the case of awareness of facts) and experiences (in the awareness of things). Not everything that happens in or to us when we become conscious of some external object or fact is conscious, of course. Certain events, processes, and states involved in the processing of sensory information

are presumably not conscious. But *something,* some state or other of S, either an experience or a belief, has to be conscious in order for S to be made conscious of the things and facts around him. If the state of S caused by x is not a conscious state, then the causation will not make S conscious of x. This is why one can *contract* poison ivy without ever becoming aware of the plant that poisons one. The plant causes one to occupy an internal state of some sort, yes, but this internal state is not a conscious state. Hence, one is not (at least not in contracting poison ivy) conscious of the plant.

David Armstrong (1980, p. 59) has a favourite example that he uses to illustrate differences in consciousness. Some may think it tells against (4). I think it does not. Armstrong asks one to imagine a long-distance truck driver:

> After driving for long periods of time, particularly at night, it is possible to "come to" and realize that for some time past one has been driving without being aware of what one has been doing. The coming-to is an alarming experience. It is natural to describe what went on before one came to by saying that during that time one lacked consciousness. Yet it seems clear that, in the two senses of the word that we have so far isolated, consciousness was present. There was mental activity, and as part of that mental activity, there was perception. That is to say, there was minimal consciousness and perceptual consciousness. If there is an inclination to doubt this, then consider the extraordinary sophistication of the activities successfully undertaken during the period of "unconsciousness." (p. 59)

Armstrong thinks it plausible to say that the driver is conscious (perceptually) of the road, the curves, the stop signs, etc. He *sees* the road. I agree. There is transitive creature consciousness of both things (the roads, the stop signs) and facts (that the road curves left, that the stop sign is red, etc.). How else explain the extraordinary performance?

But does the driver thereby have, in accordance with (4), conscious experiences of the road? Armstrong thinks there is a form of consciousness that the driver lacks. I agree. He thinks what the driver lacks is an introspective awareness, a perception-like awareness, of the current states and activities of his own mind. Once again, I agree. The driver is neither thing-aware nor fact-aware of his own mental states (including whatever experiences he is having of the road). I am not sure that normal people have this in normal circumstances, but I'm certainly willing to agree that the truck driver lacks it. But where does this leave us? Armstrong says (p. 61) that if one is not introspectively aware of a mental state (e.g., an experience), then it (the experience) is "in one good sense of the word" unconscious. I disagree. The only sense in which it is unconscious is that the person whose state it is is not conscious of having it. But from this it does not follow that the state itself is unconscious. Not unless one accepts a higher-order theory according to which state-consciousness is analysed in terms of creature-consciousness of the state. Such a theory may be true, but it is by no means obvious. I shall, in fact, argue that it is false. At any rate, such a theory cannot be invoked at this stage of the proceedings as an objection to (4). (4) is, as it should be, neutral about what makes the state of a person (who is transitively conscious of x or that P) a conscious state.

I therefore accept Armstrong's example, his description of what forms of consciousness the driver has, and the fact that the driver lacks an important type of higher level (introspective) consciousness of his own mental states. What we disagree about is whether any of this implies that the driver's experiences of the road (whatever it is *in* the driver that is required to make him conscious *of* the road) are themselves unconscious. We will return to that question in the final section.

Many investigators take perceptual experience and belief to be paradigmatic conscious phenomena.[15] *If* one chooses to talk about state consciousness (in addition to creature consciousness) at all, the clearest and most compelling instance of it is in the domain of sensory experience and belief. My present visual experience of the screen in front of me and my present perceptual beliefs about what is on that screen are internal states that deserve classification as conscious if anything does. (4) merely records a decision to regard such perceptual phenomena as central (but by no means the only) instances of conscious mental states.

Such is my justification for accepting (4). I will continue to refer to the conscious states associated with our consciousness of things (hearing Clyde playing the piano) as experiences and our consciousness of facts (that he is playing the piano) as beliefs. This is, I think, fairly standard usage. I have not, of course, said what an experience or a belief is. I won't try. That is not my project. I am trying to say what makes (or doesn't make) an experience conscious, not what makes it an experience.

Consciousness of things—e.g., seeing a stoplight turn green—requires a conscious experience of that thing. Consciousness of a fact—that the stop light is turning green—requires a conscious belief that this is a fact. And we can have the first without the second—an awareness of the stoplight's turning green without an awareness that it is turning green—hence a conscious experience (of the light's turning green) without a conscious belief (that it is turning green). Likewise, we can have the second without the first—a conscious belief about the stoplight, that it is turning green, without an experience of it. Someone I trust tells me (and I believe her) that the stoplight is turning green. So much by way of summary of the relationships between the forms of consciousness codified in (1) through (4).

We are, I think, now in a position to answer some preliminary questions. First: can one have conscious experiences without being conscious that one is having them? Can there, in other words, be conscious states without the person in whom they occur being fact-aware of their occurrence? Second: can there be conscious states in a person who is not thing-aware of them?

Alpha   **Beta**

Figure 40.1

These are important preliminary questions because important theories of what makes a mental state conscious, including what passes as
orthodox theory today, depend on negative answers to one (or, in some cases both) of these
questions. If, as I believe, the answers to both
questions are affirmative, then these theories are
simply wrong.

3. Experienced Differences Require Different Experiences

Glance at Figure 40.1 long enough to assure
yourself that you have seen all the elements
composing constellation Alpha (on the left) and
constellation Beta (on the right). It may be necessary to change fixation points in order to
foveate (focus on the sensitive part of the retina)
all parts of Alpha and Beta. If the figure is being
held at arm's length, though, this should not be
necessary though it may occur anyway via the
frequent involuntary saccades the eyes make. A
second or two should suffice.

During this brief interval some readers may
have noticed the difference between Alpha and
Beta. For expository purposes, I will assume no
one did. The difference is indicated in Figure
40.2. Call the spot, the one that occurs in Alpha
but not Beta, Spot.

According to my assumptions, then, everyone (when looking at Figure 40.1) saw Spot.
Hence, according to (1), everyone was aware of
the thing that constitutes the difference between
Alpha and Beta. According to (4), then, everyone consciously experienced (i.e., had a conscious experience of) the thing that distinguishes Alpha from Beta. Everyone, therefore, was
thing-aware, but not fact-aware, of the difference between Alpha and Beta. Spot, if you like,
is Alpha's moustache.

Let E(Alpha) and E(Beta) stand for one's
experience of Alpha and one's experience of
Beta respectively. Alpha and Beta differ; Alpha
has Spot as a part, Beta does not. E(Alpha)
and E(Beta) must also differ. E(Alpha) has an
element corresponding to (caused by) Spot.
E(Beta) does not. E(Alpha) contains or embodies, as a part, an E(Spot), an experience of Spot,
while E(Beta) does not. If it did not, then one's
experience of Alpha would have been the same
as one's experience of Beta and, hence, contrary
to (4), one would not have seen Spot when looking at Alpha.[16]

One can, of course, be conscious of things

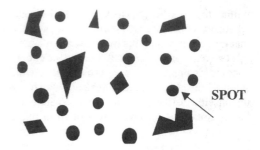

Figure 40.2

that differ without one's experience of them differing in any intrinsic way. Think of seeing visually indistinguishable objects—similar looking thumb tacks, say. One sees (experiences)
numerically different things, but one's experience of them is the same. Both experiences are
conscious, and they are experiences of different
things, but the differences in the experiences are
not conscious differences. The differences are
extrinsic to the experience itself. It is like having an experience in Chicago and another one in
New York. The numerically different experiences may be qualitatively identical even
though they have different (relational) properties—one occurs in Chicago, the other in New
York. The perception of (visually) indistinguishable thumb tacks is like that.

The experiences of Alpha and Beta, however,
are not like that. They are qualitatively different.
They differ in their relational properties, yes, as
all numerically different objects do, but they
also differ in their intrinsic properties. These
two experiences are not only experiences of
qualitatively different objects (Alpha and Beta),
they are experiences of the qualitative differences. The respects in which Alpha and Beta
differ are not only visible, they are (by hypothesis) seen. One is, after all, thing-aware of Spot,
the difference between Alpha and Beta. The experiences are not distinguished in terms of their
intrinsic qualities by the person who has the experiences, of course, but that is merely to say
that there is, on the part of this person, no fact-
awareness of any differences in his experience
of Alpha and his experience of Beta. That,
though, is not the issue. The question is one
about differences in a person's conscious experiences, not a question about a person's awareness of differences in his experiences. It is a
question about *state* consciousness, not a question about *creature* consciousness.

Once one makes the distinction between state and creature consciousness and embraces the distinction between fact- and thing-awareness, there is no reason to suppose that a person must be able to distinguish (i.e., tell the difference between) his conscious experiences. Qualitative differences in conscious experiences are *state* differences; distinguishing these differences, on the other hand, is a fact about the *creature* consciousness of the person in whom these experiences occur.

The argument assumes, of course, that if one is thing-aware of the difference between Alpha and Beta (i.e., thing-aware of Spot), then E(Alpha) and E(Beta) must differ. It assumes, that is, that *experienced* differences require different experiences. What else could experienced differences be? The difference between E(Alpha) and E(Beta), then, is being taken to be the same as the difference between seeing, in broad daylight, directly in front of your eyes, one finger raised and two fingers raised. Seeing the two fingers is not like seeing a flock of geese (from a distance) where individual geese are "fused" into a whole and not seen. In the case of the fingers, one sees both the finger on the left and the finger on the right. Quite a different experience from seeing only the finger on the left. When the numbers get larger, as they do with Alpha and Beta, the experiences are no longer discernibly different to the person having them. Given that each spot is seen, however, the experiences *are,* nonetheless, different. Large numbers merely make it harder to achieve fact-awareness of the differences on the part of the person experiencing the differences. E(Spot) is really no different than the difference between experiencing one finger and two fingers in broad daylight. The only difference is that in the case of Alpha and Beta there is no fact-awareness of the thing that makes the difference.[17]

Since the point is critical to my argument, let me emphasize the last point. In speaking of conscious differences in experience it is important to remember that one need not be conscious of the difference (= conscious that such a difference exists) in order for such differences to exist. Readers who noticed a difference between Alpha and Beta were, thereby, fact-aware of the difference between Alpha and Beta. Such readers may also have become fact-aware (by inference?) of the difference between their experience of Alpha and their experience of Beta—i.e., the difference between E(Alpha) and E(Beta). But readers who were only thing-aware of the difference between Alpha and Beta were not fact-conscious of the difference between Alpha and Beta. They were not, therefore, fact-conscious of any difference between E(Alpha) and E(Beta)—their conscious experience of Alpha and Beta. These are conscious differences of which no one is conscious.

In saying that the reader was conscious of Spot—and, hence, in this sense, the difference between Alpha and Beta—without being conscious of the fact that they differed, we commit ourselves to the possibility of differences in conscious experience that are not reflected in conscious belief. Consciousness of Spot requires a conscious experience of Spot, a conscious E(Spot); yet, there is nothing in one's conscious beliefs—either about Spot, about the difference between Alpha and Beta, or about the difference between E(Alpha) and E(Beta)—that registers this difference. What we have in such cases is internal *state* consciousness with no corresponding (transitive) *creature* consciousness of the conscious state.[18] With no creature consciousness we lack any way of discovering, *even in our own case,* that there exists this difference in conscious state. To regard this as a contradiction is merely to confuse the way an internal state like an experience can be conscious with the way the person who is in that state can be, or fail to be, conscious of it.

It may be supposed that my conclusion rests on the special character of my example. Alpha contains a numerically distinct element, Spot, and our intuitions about what is required to see a (distinct) thing are, perhaps, shaping our intuitions about the character of the experience needed to see it. Let me, therefore, borrow an example from Irvin Rock (1983). Once again, the reader is asked to view Figure 40.3 (after Rock 1983, p. 54) for a second and then say which, Alpha or Beta at the bottom, is the same as the figure shown at the top.

As closer inspection reveals, the upper left part of Alpha contains a few wiggles found in the original but not in Beta. Experimental subjects asked to identify which form it was they had seen did no better than chance. Many of them did not notice that there were wiggles on the figure they were shown. At least they could not remember having seen them. As Rock (1983, p. 55) observes:

> Taken together, these results imply that when a given region of a figure is a nonconsequential part of the whole, something is lacking in the

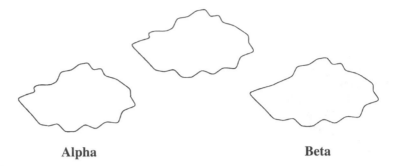

Alpha   **Beta**

Figure 40.3

perception of it, with the result that no adequate memory of it seems to be established.

No adequate *memory* of it is established because, I submit, at the time the figure is seen there is no fact-awareness of the wiggles. You cannot remember *that* there are wiggles on the left if you were never aware that there were wiggles on the left.[19] Subjects were (or may well have been) aware (thing-aware) of the wiggles (they saw them), but never became aware that they were there. The wiggles are what Spot (or Tom's moustache) is: a thing one is thing-aware of but never notices. What is lacking in the subject's perception of the figure, then, is an awareness of certain facts (that there are wiggles on the upper left), not (at least not necessarily) an awareness of the things (the wiggles) on the left.

In some minds the second example may suffer from the same defects as the first: it exploits subtle (at least not easily noticeable) differences in detail of the object being perceived. The differences are out there in the objects, yes, but who can say whether these differences are registered in here, in our experience of the objects? Perhaps our conviction (or *my* conviction) that we do see (and, hence, consciously experience) these points of detail, *despite* not noticing them, is simply a result of the fact that we see figures (Alpha and Beta, for instance) between which there are visible differences, differences that *could* be identified (noticed) by an appropriate shift of attention. But just because the details are visible does not mean that we see them or, if we do, that there must be some intrinsic (conscious) difference in the experience of the figures that differ in these points of detail.

This is a way of saying that conscious experiences, the sort of experiences you have when looking around the room, cannot differ unless one is consciously aware that they differ. Nothing mental is to count as conscious (no state

consciousness) unless one is conscious of it (without creature consciousness). This objection smacks of verificationism, but calling it names does nothing to blunt its appeal. So I offer one final example. It will, of necessity, come at the same point in a more indirect way. I turn to perceptually salient conditions, conditions it is hard to believe are not consciously experienced. In order to break the connection between experience and belief, between thing-awareness and factawareness, then, I turn to creatures with a diminished capacity for fact-awareness.[20]

Eleanor Gibson (1969, p. 284), in reporting Kluver's studies with monkeys, describes a case in which the animals are trained to the larger of two rectangles. When the rectangles are altered in size, the monkeys continue to respond to the larger of the two—whatever their absolute size happens to be. In Kluver's words, they "abstract" the LARGER THAN relation. After they succeed in abstracting this relation, and when responding appropriately to the larger (A) of two presented rectangles (A and B), we can say that they are aware of A, aware of B (thing-awareness), and aware that A is larger than B (fact awareness). Some philosophers may be a little uncomfortable about assigning beliefs to monkeys in these situations, uncomfortable about saying that the monkey is aware *that* A is larger than B, but let that pass. The monkeys at least exhibit a differential response, and that is enough. How shall we describe the monkeys' perceptual situation *before* they learned to abstract this relation? Did the rectangles *look* different to the monkeys? Was there any difference in their experience of A and B *before* they became aware that A was larger than B? We can imagine the difference in size to be as great as we please. They were not fact-aware of the difference, not aware that A is larger than B, to be sure. But that isn't the question. The question is: were they conscious of the condition of A and B that, so to speak, makes it true that A is larger than B?[21] Does their experience of objects change when, presented with two objects the same size, one of these objects expands making it much larger than the other? If not, how could these animals ever learn to do what they are being trained to do—distinguish between A's being larger than B and A's not being larger than B?

It seems reasonable to suppose that, prior to learning, the monkeys were thing-aware of a difference which only became fact-aware of after learning was complete. Their experience of A and B was different, consciously so, before they were capable of exhibiting this difference in behaviour. Learning of this sort is simply the development of fact-awareness from thing-awareness.

The situation becomes even more compelling if we present the monkeys with three rectangles and try to get them to abstract the INTERMEDIATE IN SIZE relation. This more difficult problem proves capable of solution by chimpanzees, but monkeys find it extremely difficult. Suppose monkey M cannot solve it. What shall we say about M's perceptual condition when he sees three rectangles, A, B and C of descending size. If we use behavioural criteria for what kind of facts M is conscious of and assume that M has already mastered the first abstraction (the LARGER THAN relation), M is aware of the three rectangles, A, B and C. M is also aware that A is larger than B, that B is larger than C, and that A is larger than C. M is not, however, aware that B is INTERMEDIATE IN SIZE even though this is logically implied by the facts he is aware of. Clearly, although M is not (and, apparently, cannot be made) aware of the fact that B is intermediate in size, he is nonetheless aware of the differences (A's being larger than B, B's being larger than C) that logically constitute the fact that he is not aware of. B's being intermediate in size is a condition the monkey is thing-aware of but cannot be made fact-aware of. There are conscious features of the animal's experiences that are not registered in the animal's fact-awareness and, hence, not evinced in the animal's deliberate behaviour.

4. What, Then, Makes Experiences Conscious?

We have just concluded that there can be conscious differences in a person's experience of the world—and, in this sense, conscious features of his experience—of which that person is not conscious. If this is true, then it cannot be a person's awareness of a mental state that makes that state conscious. E(Spot) is conscious, and it constitutes a conscious difference between E(Alpha) and E(Beta) even though no one, including the person in whom it occurs, being conscious of it. It follows, therefore, that what *makes* a mental state conscious cannot be our consciousness of it. If we have conscious experiences, beliefs, desires, and fears, it cannot be our introspective awareness of them that makes them conscious.

This conclusion is a bit premature. The argument mounted in §3 was primarily directed at higher-order-thought (HOT) theories that take an experience or a belief (mental states) to be conscious in virtue of their being the object of some higher-order-thought-like entity, a higher-order mental state that (like a thought) involves the deployment of concepts. My concern in §3, therefore, was to show that conscious experience required no fact-awareness—either of facts related to what one experiences (e.g., Spot) or of facts related to the experience itself (e.g., E(Spot)). One does not have to be fact-aware of E(Spot) in order for E(Spot) to be conscious.

This leaves the possibility, however, that in order for one's experience of Spot to be conscious, one must be thing-aware of it. Perhaps, that is, E(Spot) is conscious, not because there is some higher order *thought* (involving concepts) about E(Spot), but rather because there is a higher-order *experience* (a non-conceptual mental state) of E(Spot), something that makes one thing-aware of E(Spot) in the same way one is thing-aware (perceptually) of Spot. This is a form of the HOT theory that Lycan (1992, p. 216) describes as Locke's "inner sense" account of state-consciousness. What makes an experience conscious is not one's (fact) awareness that one is having it, but one's (thing) awareness of it.

To my mind, Rosenthal (1990, pp. 34ff.) makes a convincing case against this "inner sense" version of state consciousness. He points out, for example, that one of the respects in which experiences are unlike thoughts is in having a sensory quality to them. E(Alpha), for instance, has visual, not auditory or tactile qualities. If what made E(Alpha) into a conscious experience was some higher order experience of E(Alpha), one would expect some distinctive qualia of this higher-order experience to intrude. But all one finds are the qualia associated with E(Alpha), the lower-order experience. For this reason (among others) Rosenthal himself prefers a version of the inner spotlight theory of consciousness in which the spotlight is something in the nature of a fact-awareness, not thing-awareness, of the lower order mental state or activity.

Aside, though, from the merits of such specific objections, I think the "inner sense" approach loses all its attraction once the distinction between thing-awareness and fact-awareness is firmly in place. Notice, first, that if it is thing-awareness of a mental state that is supposed to make that mental state conscious, then the "inner sense" theory has no grounds for saying that E(Spot) is not conscious. For a person might well be thing-aware of E(Spot)—thus making E(Spot) conscious—just as he is thing-aware of Spot, without ever being fact-aware of it. So on this version of the spotlight theory, a failure to realize, a total unawareness of the fact *that* there is a difference between E(Alpha) and E(Beta), is irrelevant to whether there is a conscious difference between these two experiences. This being so, the "inner sense" theory of what makes a mental state conscious does nothing to *improve* one's epistemic access to one's own conscious states. *As far as one can tell,* E(Spot) (just like Spot) may as well not exist. What good is an inner spotlight, an introspective awareness of mental events, if it doesn't give one epistemic access to the events on which it shines? The "inner sense" theory does nothing to solve the problem of what makes E(Spot) conscious. On the contrary, it multiplies the problems by multiplying the facts of which we are not aware. We started with E(Spot) and gave arguments in support of the view that E(Spot) was conscious even though the person in whom it occurred was not fact-aware of it. We are now being asked to explain this fact by another fact of which we are not fact-aware: namely, the fact that we are thing-aware of E(Spot). Neither E(Spot) nor the thing-awareness of E(Spot) makes any *discernible* difference to the person in whom they occur. This, surely, is a job for Occam's Razor.

If we do not have to be conscious of a mental state (like an experience) for the mental state to be conscious, then, it seems, consciousness of something cannot be what it is that makes a thing conscious. Creature consciousness (of either the factive or thing form) is not necessary

for state consciousness.[22] What, then, makes a mental state conscious? When S smells, and thereby becomes aware of, the burning toast, what makes his experience of the burning toast a conscious experience? When S becomes aware that the light has turned green, what makes his belief that the light has turned green a conscious belief?

This is the big question, of course, and I am not confronting it in this paper. I am concerned only with a preliminary issue—a question about the relationship (or lack thereof) between creature consciousness and state consciousness. For it is the absence of this relation (in the right form) that undermines the orthodox view that what makes certain mental states conscious is one's awareness of them. Nonetheless, though I lack the space (and, at this stage, the theory) to answer the big question, I would like to indicate, if only briefly, the direction in which these considerations lead.

What makes an internal state or process conscious is the role it plays in making one (intransitively) conscious—normally, the role it plays in making one (transitively) conscious of some thing or fact. An experience of *x* is conscious, not because one is aware of the experience, or aware that one is having it, but because, being a certain sort of representation, it makes one aware of the properties (of *x*) and objects (*x* itself) of which it is a (sensory) representation. My visual experience of a barn is conscious, not because I am introspectively aware of it (or introspectively aware that I am having it), but because it (when brought about in the right way) makes me aware of the barn. It enables me to perceive the barn. For the same reason, a certain belief is conscious, not because the believer is conscious of *it* (or conscious of having it[23]), but because it is a representation that makes one conscious of the fact (that *P*) that it is a belief about. Experiences and beliefs are conscious, not because you are conscious of them, but because, so to speak, you are conscious *with* them.

This is not to deny that one may, in fact, be conscious of one's own experiences in the way one is, in ordinary perception, conscious of barns and other people. Perhaps we are equipped with an introspective faculty, some special internal scanner, that takes as its objects (the *x*s it is an awareness of), one's experiences of barns and people. Perhaps this is so. Perhaps introspection is a form of metaspectation—a sensing of one's own sensing of the world. I doubt this. I think introspection is best understood, not as thing-awareness, but as fact-awareness—an awareness that one has certain beliefs, thoughts, desires and experiences *without* a corresponding awareness of the things (the beliefs, thoughts, experiences and desires) themselves. Introspection is more like coming to know (be aware) that one has a virus than it is like coming to see, hear, or feel (i.e., be aware of) the virus (the thing) itself.

Whether these speculations on the nature of introspection are true or not, however, is, independent of the present thesis about consciousness. The claim is not that we are unaware of our own conscious beliefs and experiences (or unaware that we have them). It is, instead, that our being aware of them, or that we have them, is not what makes them conscious. What make them conscious is the way they make us conscious of something else—the world we live in and (in proprioception) the condition of our own bodies.

Saying just what the special status is that makes certain internal representations conscious while other internal states (lacking this status) remain unconscious is, of course, the job for a fully developed theory of consciousness. I haven't supplied that. All I have tried to do is to indicate where not to look for it.

NOTES

1. I am grateful to Berent Enc, Güven Güzeldere, Lydia Sanchez, Ken Norman, David Robb and Bill Lycan for critical feedback. I would also like to thank the Editor and anonymous referees of *Mind* for a number of very helpful suggestions.
2. I am thinking here of those who subscribe to what are called higher order thought (HOT) theories of consciousness, theories that hold that what makes an experience conscious is its being an object of some higher-order thought or experience. See Rosenthal (1986, 1990, 1991), Armstrong (1968, 1980, especially Ch. 4, "What Is Consciousness?") and Lycan (1987, 1992). I return to these theories in §4.
3. This section is a summary and minor extension of points I have made elsewhere; see especially Dretske 1969, 1978, 1979.
4. When I speak of events I should be understood to be including any of a large assortment of entities that occupy temporal positions (or duration): happenings, occurrences, states, states-of-affairs, processes, conditions, situations, and so on. In speaking of these as temporal entities, I do not mean to deny that they have spatial attributes—only that they do so in a way that is derived from the objects to which they happen. Games occur in stadiums because that is where the players are when they play the game. Movements (of a passenger, say) occur in a vehicle because that is where the person is when she moves.
5. White (1964, p. 42) calls "aware" a polymorphous concept (p. 6); it takes many forms. What it is to become or be aware of something depends on what one is aware of. To become aware of a perceptual object takes the form of seeing for hearing or smelling or tasting or feeling it.
6. One must distinguish Clyde from such things as Clyde's location, virtues, etc. One can be aware of Clyde's location and virtues without, at the time, perceiving them. But unlike Clyde, his virtues and location are not what I am calling things. See the discussion of abstract objects below.
7. I will not try to distinguish direct from indirect forms of perception (and, thus, awareness). We speak of seeing Michael Jordan on TV. If this counts as seeing Michael Jordan, then (for purposes of this essay), it also counts as being aware or conscious of Michael Jordan (on TV). Likewise, if one has philosophical scruples about saying one smells a rose or hears a bell—thinking, perhaps, that it is really only scents and sounds (not the objects that give off those scents or make those sounds) that one smells and hears—then, when I speak of being conscious of a flower (by smelling) or bell (by hearing), one can translate this as being indirectly conscious of the flower via its scent and the bell via the sound it makes.
8. Generally speaking, the concepts necessary for awareness of facts are those corresponding to terms occurring obliquely in the clause (the that-clause) describing the fact one is aware of.
9. I am here indebted to Perkins' (1983, pp. 295–305) insightful discussion.
10. If it helps, the reader may suppose that later, at t_3, S remembers having seen Tom's moustache at t_2 while being completely unaware at the time (i.e., at t_2) that Tom had a moustache. Such later memories are not essential (S may see the moustache and *never* realise he saw it), but they may, at this point in the discussion, help calm verificationists' anxieties about the example.
11. For further arguments see Dretske (1969, Ch. 2; 1979; 1981, Ch. 6; and my reply to Heil in McLaughlin, 1991, pp. 180–185).
12. White (1964, p. 59): "Being conscious or unconscious *of* so and so is not the same as simply being conscious or unconscious. If there is anything of which a man is conscious, it follows that he is conscious; to lose consciousness is to cease to be conscious of anything."
13. One might mention dreams as a possible exception to (3): one is (in a dream) aware of certain things (images?) while being asleep and, therefore, unconscious in the intransitive sense. I think this is not a genuine exception to (3), but since I do not want to get sidetracked arguing about it, I let the possibility stand as a "possible" exception. Nothing will depend on how the matter is decided.
14. For purposes of illustrating distinctions I use a simple causal theory of knowledge (to know that *P* is to be caused to believe that *P* by the fact that *P*) and

perception (to perceive x is to be caused to have an experience by x). Though sympathetic to certain versions of these theories, I wish to remain neutral here.

15. E.g., Baars (1988), Velmans (1991), Humphrey (1992).

16. I do not think it necessary to speculate about how E(Spot) is realized or about its exact relation to E(Alpha). I certainly do not think E(Spot) must literally be a *spatial* part of E(Alpha) in the way Spot is a spatial part of Alpha. The argument is that there is an intrinsic *difference* between E(Alpha) and E(Beta). E(Spot) is just a convenient way of referring to this difference.

17. Speaking of large numbers, Elizabeth, a remarkable eidetiker (a person who can maintain visual images for a long time) studied by Stromeyer and Psotka (1970), was tested with computer-generated random-dot stereograms. She looked at a 10,000 dot pattern for one minute with one eye. Then she looked at another 10,000 dot pattern with the other eye. Some of the individual dots in the second pattern were systematically offset so that a figure in depth would emerge (as in using a stereoscope) if the patterns from the two eyes were fused. Elizabeth succeeded in superimposing the eidetic image that she retained from the first pattern over the second pattern. She saw the figure that normal subjects can only see by viewing the two patterns (one with each eye) simultaneously.

I note here that to fuse the two patterns the *individual dots* seen with one eye must somehow be paired with those retained by the brain (*not* the eye; this is not an after-image) from the other eye.

18. I return, in the next section, to the question of whether we might not have thingawareness of E(Spot)—that is, the same kind of awareness of the difference between E(Alpha) and E(Beta) as we have of the difference between Alpha and Beta.

19. Though there may be other ways of remembering the wiggles. To use an earlier example, one might remember seeing Tom's moustache without (at the time) noticing it (being fact-aware of it). Even if one cannot remember *that* Tom had a moustache (since one never knew this), one can, I think, remember *seeing* Tom's moustache. This is the kind of memory (episodic vs. declarative) involved in a well-known example: remembering how many windows there are in a familiar house (e.g., the house one grew up in) by imagining oneself walking through the house and counting the windows. One does not, in this case, remember that there were 23 windows although one comes to know that there were 23 windows by using one's memory.

20. The following is an adaptation of the discussion in Dretske (1981, p. 151–52).

21. *Conditions,* recall, are things in my sense of this word. One can be aware of an object's condition (its movement, for instance) without being aware that it is moving. This is what happens when one sees an adjacent vehicle's movement *as* one's own movement or an object's movement as an expansion or contraction. It is also what occurs in infants and, perhaps, animals who do not have the concept of movement: they are aware of O's movement, but not aware that O is moving.

22. Neither is it sufficient. We are conscious of a great many internal states and activities that are not themselves conscious (heart beats, a loose tooth, hiccoughs of a fetus, a cinder in the eye).

23. If fact-awareness was what made a belief conscious, it would be very hard for young children (those under the age of 3 or 4 years, say) to have conscious beliefs. They don't yet have a firm grasp of the concept of a belief and are, therefore, unaware of the fact that they have beliefs. See Flavell (1988), Wellman (1990).

REFERENCES

Armstrong, D. M. 1968: *A Materialist Theory of the Mind.* London: Routledge and Kegan Paul.

———. 1980: *The Nature of Mind and Other Essays.* Ithaca, New York: Cornell University Press.

Astington, J., P. Harris, and D. Olson, eds. 1988: *Developing Theories of the Mind.* New York: Cambridge University Press.

Baars, B. 1988: *A Cognitive Theory of Consciousness.* Cambridge: Cambridge University Press.

Dennett, D. C. 1991: *Consciousness Explained.* Boston: Little Brown.

Dretske, F. 1969: *Seeing and Knowing.* Chicago: University of Chicago Press.

———. 1978: "The role of the percept in visual cognition," in Savage 1978, pp. 107–27.

———. 1979: "Simple seeing," in Gustafson and Tapscott 1979, pp. 1–15.

———. 1981: *Knowledge and the Flow of Information.* Cambridge, Massachusetts: MIT Press/A Bradford Book.

———. 1990: "Seeing, believing and knowing," in Osherson, Kosslyn and Hollerbach 1990.

Flavell, J. H. 1988: "The development of children's knowledge about the mind: From cognitive connections to mental representations," in Astington, Harris, and Olson 1988.

Gibson, E. 1969: *Principles of Perceptual Learning and Development.* New York: Appleton Century & Crofts.

Grice, P. 1989: *Studies in the Way of Words.* Cambridge, Massachusetts: Harvard University Press.

Gustafson, D. F. and B. L. Tapscott, eds. 1979: *Body, Mind and Method: Essays in Honor of Virgil Aldrich.* Dordrecht, Holland: Reidel.

Humphrey, N. 1992: *A History of the Mind: Evolution and the Birth of Consciousness.* New York: Simon and Schuster.

Lees, R. B. 1963: *The Grammar of English Nominalizations.* Bloomington, Indiana: Indiana University Press.

Lycan, W. 1987: *Consciousness.* Cambridge, Massachusetts: MIT Press.

——— . 1992: "Uncertain Materialism and Lockean introspection." *Behavioral and Brain Sciences* 15.2, pp. 216–17.

McLaughlin, B., ed. 1991: *Critical Essays on the Philosophy of Fred Dretske.* Oxford: Basil Blackwell.

Milner, A. D. & M. D. Rugg, eds. 1992: *The Neuropsychology of Consciousness.* London: Academic Press.

Osherson, D., S. Kosslyn and J. Hollerback, eds. 1990: *An Invitation to Cognitive Science, Volume 2, Visual Cognition and Action.* Cambridge, Massachusetts: MIT Press.

Perkins, M. 1983: *Sensing the World.* Indianapolis, Indiana: Hackett Publishing Company.

Rock, I. 1983: *The Logic of Perception.* Cambridge, Massachusetts: MIT Press/A Bradford Book.

Rosenthal, D. 1986: "Two concepts of consciousness." *Philosophical Studies* 94.3, pp. 329–59.

——— . 1990: "A theory of consciousness." Report No. 40, Research Group on Mind and Brain, ZiF, University of Bielefeld.

——— . 1991: "The independence of consciousness and sensory quality," in Villanueva (1991), pp. 15–36.

Savage, W. ed. 1978: *Minnesota Studies in the Philosophy of Science: Perception and Cognition,* Vol IX. Minneapolis, Minnesota: University of Minnesota Press.

Stromeyer, C. F. & J. Psotka 1970: "The detailed texture of eidetic images." *Nature,* 225, pp. 346–349.

Velmans, M. 1991: "Is human information processing conscious?" *Behavioral and Brain Sciences* 14.4, pp. 651–668.

Villanueva, E., ed. 1991: *Consciousness.* Atascadero, CA: Ridgeview Publishing Company.

Wellman, H. M. 1990: *The Child's Theory of the Mind.* Cambridge, Massachusetts; MIT Press/A Bradford Book.

White, A. R. 1964: *Attention.* Oxford: Basil Blackwell.

41 | Sensation and the Content of Experience
A Distinction

Christopher Peacocke

. . . My claim in this chapter will be that concepts of sensation are indispensable to the description of the nature of any experience. This claim stands in opposition to the view that, while sensations may occur when a subject is asked to concentrate in a particular way on his own experience, or may occur as by-products of perception, they are not to be found in the mainstream of normal human experience, and certainly not in visual experience. But first we need to clarify the issues.

Historically, the distinction between putative perceptual experiences and sensations has been the distinction between those experiences which do in themselves represent the environment of the experiencer as being a certain way, and those experiences which have no such representational content. A visual perceptual experience enjoyed by someone sitting at a desk may represent various writing implements and items of furniture as having particular spatial relations to one another and to the experiencer, and as themselves having various qualities; a sensation of small, by contrast, may have no representational content of any sort, though of course the sensation will be of a distinctive kind. The representational content of a perceptual experience has to be given by a proposition, or set of propositions, which specifies the way the experience represents the world to be. To avoid any ambiguity, I will use the phrase 'content of experience' only for the representational content of an experience, and never for a type of sensation: many past writers followed the opposite practice and used 'object' or 'meaning' for representational content. Corresponding to the historical distinction between sensation and perception, we can draw a distinction between sensational

Reprinted from *Sense and Content: Experience, Thought, and Their Relations* (Oxford University Press, 1983), Chapter 1, with permission of Oxford University Press.

and representational properties of experience. Representational properties will be properties an experience has in virtue of features of its representational content; while sensational properties will be properties an experience has in virtue of some aspect—other than its representational content—of what it is like to have that experience.[1]

The content of an experience is to be distinguished from the content of a judgement caused by the experience. A man may be familiar with a perfect *trompe l'œil* violin painted on a door, and be sure from his past experience that it is a *trompe l'œil:* nevertheless his experience may continue to represent a violin as hanging on the door in front of him. The possibility of such independence is one of the marks of the content of experience as opposed to the content of judgement. One of the earliest writers to state a distinction between sensation and perceptual experience, Thomas Reid, introduced it in terms which require that perceptual experience implies belief in the content of the experience.[2] In fact, we need a threefold distinction between sensation, perception, and judgement, to formulate the issues precisely.

This independence of the contents of judgement and experience does not mean that judgements cannot causally influence the content of experiences. In some cases they do. You may walk into your sitting-room and seem to hear rain falling outside. Then you notice that someone has left the stereo system on, and realize that the sound you hear is that of applause at the end of a concert. It happens to many people that after realizing this, the sound comes to be heard as applause: the content of experience is influenced by that of judgement. All the independence claim means is that this need not happen.

Among the many current uses of the term 'information,' there is one in particular from which the present notion of representational content should be distinguished. There is a sense in which a footprint contains the information that a person with a foot of such-and-such shape and size was at the location of the footprint earlier; and in which a fossil may contain the information that there was an organism of a certain kind at its location in the past. This is a clear and important use of 'informational content,' and it seems that it is, very roughly, to be explained along these lines (the details will not matter for us): x's being F at t has the informational content that there was something standing in R to x at some earlier time t' and which was then G, iff in normal circumstances an object's being F at some particular time is causally, and perhaps differentially, explained by there existing at some earlier time an object standing in R to it and which was then G.[3] An experience, or more strictly the occurrence to someone of an experience of a certain type at a certain time, will certainly have informational content in this sense. But informational content differs from representational content in at least four respects. First, the informational content of a visual experience will include the proposition that a bundle of light rays with such-and-such physical properties struck the retina; nothing like this will be in the representational content of the experience. Second, there are cases in which the representational content and the informational content of an experience are incompatible. This will be so for experiences of geometrical illusions. Such experiences are normally differentially explained by the presence of objects with properties incompatible with those they are represented by the experience as having. Third, though both informational content and representational content are specified by 'that'-clauses, the contents are of different kinds. A specification of informational content is completely referentially transparent in genuine singular term position: this property it inherits from the corresponding transparency of 'causally explains.' In the representational content of an experience, on the other hand, objects are presented under perceptual modes of presentation. (This contrast applies not only to singular term position, but also to predicate position. We shall later wish to distinguish properties from modes of presentation of properties, and when that distinction is drawn, it will appear that only the properties themselves, and not properties under modes of presentation, enter causal explanations.) Finally, it is in the nature of representational content that it cannot be built up from concepts unless the subject of the experience himself has those concepts: the representational content is the way the experience presents the world as being, and it can hardly present the world as being that way if the subject is incapable of appreciating what that way is. Only those with the concept of a sphere can have an experience as of a sphere in front of them, and only those with spatial concepts can have experiences which represent things as distributed in depth in space.

By emphasizing these differences, I do not mean to exclude the possibility that possession of representational content can be analysed in terms of informational content (whether this is so is a complex and difficult matter). The present point is just that any such analysis would not consist in an identity. So when I argue that all experiences have nonrepresentational properties, this is *not* a claim to the effect that the intrinsic properties of experience are not determined by their informational content. It is rather a claim about the range of intrinsic properties themselves.

Those who say that sensation has almost no role to play in normal, mature human experience, or at least in normal human visual experience, commonly cite as their ground the fact that all visual experiences have some representational content. If this is indeed a fact, it shows that no human visual experience is a pure sensation. But it does not follow that such experiences do not have sensational properties. It is one thing to say that all mature visual experiences have representational content, another thing to say that no such experience has intrinsic properties (properties which help to specify what it is like to have the experience) explicable without reference to representational content. To assert that all experiences have sensational properties is not necessarily to return to the views of Wundt and his followers.[4] My aim is just to argue that every experience has some sensational properties, and I will concentrate on visual experience as the most challenging case. We can label those who dispute this view, and hold that all intrinsic properties of mature human visual experiences are possessed in virtue of their representational content, 'extreme perceptual theorists.'

Again, we need to sharpen the dispute. One way to do so is to introduce for consideration what I will call the *Adequacy Thesis* (AT). The AT states that a complete intrinsic characterization of an experience can be given by embedding within an operator like 'it visually appears to the subject that . . .' some complex condition concerning physical objects. One component of the condition might be that there is a black telephone in front of oneself and a bookshelf a certain distance and direction to one's left, above and behind which is a window. Such contents can equally be the contents of perceptual or hallucinatory experiences.[5] The content need not be restricted to the qualitative properties of objects, their spatial relations to one another and to the location of the experiencer. It can also concern the relations of the objects and the experiencer to some environmental dimension: the ex-

perience of being in a tilted room is different from that of being in the same room when it is upright and the experiencer's body is tilted. Or again, a visual experience as of everything around one swinging to one's left can be distinguished from the visual experience as of oneself revolving rightwards on one's vertical axis. The specification of content may also need in some way to make reference to individuals whom the subject of the experience can recognize: a visual experience can represent Nixon as giving a speech in front of one. The representational content of a visual experience seems always to contain the indexical notions 'now' and 'I,' and almost always 'here' and 'there.' It should be emphasized that the propositional contents available to the defender of the AT are not all restricted to those features of experience which do not result from unconscious cognitive processing. If there are indeed unconscious mechanisms analogous, say, to inference in the production of experience, then certainly many features of the representational content of an experience will result from the operation of these mechanisms. The important point about representational content, as the notion is used here, is not its freedom from processing but its simultaneous possession of two features. The first is that the representational content concerns the world external to the experiencer, and as such is assessable as true or false. The second feature is that this content is something intrinsic to the experience itself—any experience which does not represent to the subject the world as being the way that this content specifies is phenomenologically different, an experience of a different type. It is quite consistent with these two features that the presence of experiences with a given representational content has been caused by past experience and learning. What one must not do is to suppose that such explanations show that representational content is a matter of judgement caused by some purer experience: even when an experience has a rich representational content, the judgement of the subject may still endorse or reject this content.

The extreme perceptual theorist is committed to the AT. For if the AT is false, there are intrinsic features of visual experience which are not captured by representational content. My initial strategy in opposition to the extreme perceptual theorist will be to argue against the AT by counterexamples. There is no obvious defender of the AT whose views one can take as a stalking horse, no doubt partly because the sensational/representational distinction seems not to have been sufficiently sharply formulated. There are, though, strong hints of the thesis in Hintikka. He writes 'The appropriate way of speaking of our spontaneous perceptions is to use the same vocabulary and the same syntax as we apply to the objects of perception . . . *all* there is (in principle) to perception (at this level of analysis) is a specification of the information in question' (Hintikka's emphasis). He is not here using 'information' in the sense of informational content, for he writes of the information that our perceptual systems give *us*.[6]

There are at least three types of example which are prima facie evidence against the AT. I will give all three before discussing ways in which the extreme perceptual theorist might try to account for each type; for any satisfactory account must accommodate all three types. The point in giving these examples is not to cite newly discovered phenomena—on the contrary, all the phenomena are familiar. The point is rather to consider their bearing on the correct conception of the representational and sensational properties of experience. Any novelty lies in claims about this bearing.

Since I shall be arguing by counterexample, the extreme perceptualist's reasons for his view will not initially affect the argument. But his views do not come from nowhere, and if the counterexamples are sound, the extreme perceptualist's reasons for his views must be insufficient: in so far as there are true beliefs amongst his reasons, those beliefs cannot carry him all the way to his extreme perceptualism. The extreme perceptualist's main motivation is likely to be the thought that if the AT is false, then there are intrinsic features of an experience which are unknowable by anyone not actually having that experience. This thought may be backed by the following superficially plausible argument. We can tell what kind of experience someone has if we know his desires and intentions, and find that he is disposed to act in such-and-such ways when he takes his experience at face value. If, for instance, he wants to travel to a certain place, and takes the shortest available route even though this is not on a straight line, we can come to have reason to believe that he perceives an obstacle on the most direct route: this hypothesis could be inductively confirmed. But it seems that techniques of this sort could only ever reveal representational properties of the subject's experience: for the technique consists in checking that he acts in ways appropri-

ate to the world being as his experience represents it. If this is the only way in which we could come to know the intrinsic properties or another's experiences, the nonrepresentational properties of another's experiences would be unknowable. If the counterexamples below are correct, there must be a gap in this argument. Though the massive general topic of our understanding of consciousness in others is beyond the scope of this book, I will try to indicate at suitable points how we might know of the sensational properties of others' experiences.

There is one last preliminary. Our perceptual experience is always of a more determinate character than our observational concepts which we might use in characterizing it. A normal person does not, and possibly could not, have observational concepts of every possible shade of colour, where shades are individuated by Goodman's identity condition for qualia.[7] Even concepts like 'yellow ochre' and 'burnt sienna' will not distinguish every such shade; and in any case not everyone has such concepts. Thus if the extreme perceptualist is not to be mistaken for trivial reasons, the most that he can maintain is this: the intrinsic properties of a visual experience are exhausted by a specification of its representational content together with some more specific determination of the properties mentioned in that content. I will not trade on this qualification.

Here then are the examples:

(1) Suppose you are standing on a road which stretches from you in a straight line to the horizon. There are two trees at the roadside, one a hundred yards from you, the other two hundred. Your experience represents these objects as being of the same physical height and other dimensions; that is, taking your experience at face value you would judge that the trees are roughly the same physical size, just as in the *trompe l'œil* example, without countervailing beliefs you would judge that there is a violin on the door; and in this case we can suppose that the experience is a perception of the scene around you. Yet there is also some sense in which the nearer tree occupies more of your visual field than the more distant tree. This is as much a feature of your experience itself as is its representing the trees as being the same height. The experience can possess this feature without your having any concept of the feature or of the visual field: you simply enjoy an experience which has the feature. It is a feature which makes Rock say that the greater size of the retinal image of

the nearer tree is not without some reflection in consciousness, and may be what earlier writers such as Ward meant when they wrote of differences in extensity.[8] It presents an initial challenge to the Adequacy Thesis, since no veridical experience can represent one tree as larger than another and also as the same size as the other. The challenge to the extreme perceptual theorist is to account for these facts about size in the visual field without abandoning the AT. We can label this problem 'the problem of the additional characterization'.

The problem of the additional characterization does not arise only for size in the visual field, or for properties such as speed of movement in the visual field which are defined in terms of it. It can arise for colours and sounds. Imagine you are in a room looking at a corner formed by two of its walls. The walls are covered with paper of a uniform hue, brightness and saturation. But one wall is more brightly illuminated than the other. In these circumstances, your experience can represent both walls as being the same colour: it does not look to you as if one of the walls is painted with brighter paint than the other. Yet it is equally an aspect of your visual experience itself that the region of the visual field in which one wall is presented is brighter than that in which the other is presented. An example of the same type of phenomenon involving hearing might be this. You see two cars at different distances from yourself, both with their engines running. Your experience can represent the engines as running equally loudly (if you are searching for a quiet car, your experience gives you no reason to prefer one over the other); but again it seems undeniable that in some sense the nearer car sounds louder.

(2) All these illustrations of the problem of the additional characterization were in some way related to the duality of representational properties and properties of the two-dimensional visual field, but they were not cases in which the additional characterization apparently omitted by representational properties was something which could vary even though representational content is held constant. Yet there are also examples of this, examples in which a pair of experiences in the same sense-modality have the same representational content, but differ in some other intrinsic respect. Suppose you look at an array of pieces of furniture with one eye closed. Some of the pieces of furniture may be represented by your experience as being in front of others. Imagine now that you look at the same scene with both eyes. The experience is different. It may be tempting to try to express this difference by saying that some chairs now appear to be in front of others, but this cannot suffice: for the monocular experience also represented certain objects as being in front of others. Taking your monocular experience at face value, you would judge that some pieces of furniture are in front of others: objects do not suddenly seem to be at no distance from you when you close one eye. The experiential difference between monocular and binocular vision is independent of the double images of unfocussed objects produced by binocular vision. The extra way depth is indicated in binocular vision is present when you look into a child's stereoscope, and there need not be any double images when you do.[9] (There are not many examples of this phenomenon with the other senses, but one such might be this. A stereophonic recording of a wave breaking sounds quite different from a monaural recording, even if one cannot locate aurally the various directions of the components of the whole sound.)

The situation in the visual example is more complex than it may at first seem. The complexity can be brought out by reflecting that there are pairs of experiences which differ in the way in which the experiences of monocular and binocular vision of an ordinary scene differ, and in which only the binocular experience contains any dimension of depth. Consider two arrays of dots, one a random array and the other random except in some region in which the dots are arranged as they are in the corresponding region of the first array, but slightly displaced to take account of binocular disparity. These are the Julesz random-dot patterns.[10] When viewed with two eyes, some dots are seen as being in front of others: when the arrays are seen with only one eye, there is no impression of depth. There are two different attitudes one could take to this example. One, incompatible with what we have so far said, would be that the example shows that though there is indeed an additional way in which depth is represented in binocular as opposed to monocular vision, the extra feature is purely representational; and it is this additional purely representational feature which is present in binocular vision of the random-dot patterns. The second attitude is that even in the random-dot case, the difference between monocular and binocular vision is both sensational and representational. This is the attitude for which I shall argue.

On the second attitude, there is a sensational property which in normal human experience is indeed associated with the representation of depth. If it is granted that visual field properties are sensational, we already have other examples of such association, since in normal humans perceiving an ordinary scene, the visual field properties are associated with a representational content. The difference between the two attitudes lies in the fact that according to the first, it ought to be impossible to conceive of cases in which the alleged sensational property is present, but in which a representation of certain objects as being behind others in the environment is absent. According to the second attitude, this ought to be conceivable.

But it does seem to be conceivable. It could be that there is a being for whom visual experience is in certain respects like the experience enjoyed by a congenitally blind user of a tactile-vision substitution system (TVSS).[11] A TVSS consists of a television camera, the output of which is connected to a two-dimensional array of vibrating rods on the user's back. After using the TVSS for a short time, the congenitally blind subject has intrinsically spatial sensations resulting from the vibrations, sensations which are not those of pressure or vibration on his back, and which are reported to be quite unlike those of touch. These sensations are arranged in a two-dimensional space, and they do not seem to the experiencer to be of objects in the space around him. That is, the space of the sensations is not experienced as bearing any spatial relations to the physical space in which the experiencer is located.[12] The subjects report that the sensations are not as of anything 'out there.' Now it seems that we can also conceive, at least as a logical possibility, of such sensations (perhaps resulting from the output of two cameras) existing in a three-dimensional space, which is nevertheless still not experienced as the space around the perceiver. Finally, it seems that we can conceive of someone's visual experience being like that of the subject in his hypothetical three-dimensional case: someone with tactile experience of the world around him and suddenly given stereoscopic vision of unfamiliar objects (such as small blobs randomly distributed in three-dimensional space) could conceivably be so. Here then a sensational third dimension would be present; but there would be no representation of depth in the sense that the experience itself represents some things as being further away than others in the forward direction in the phys-

ical space in which the experiencer is located. There is, then, a dangerous ambiguity in the term 'depth.' It is indeed true that whenever the extra feature which distinguishes binocular from monocular vision is present, there will be an impression of depth; but since on the sense in which this must be so, depth is a sensational property, the point cannot be used to argue that the difference between monocular and binocular vision is purely representational.[13]

(3) The third type of problem is illustrated by the switching of aspects under which some object or array of objects is seen. Consider an example in which a wire framework in the shape of a cube is viewed with one eye and is seen first with one of its faces in front, the face parallel to this face being seen as behind it, and is then suddenly seen, without any change in the cube or alteration of its position, with that former face now behind the other. The successive experiences have different representational contents. The first experience represents a face ABCD as nearer oneself than the face EFGH, the later experience represents the presence of a state of affairs incompatible with its being nearer. Yet there seems to be some additional level of classification at which the successive experiences fall under the same type; indeed that something like this is so seems to be a feature of the experience of a switch in aspect—as Wittgenstein writes, 'I *see* that it has not changed.'[14] We have here another example of apparently nonrepresentational similarities between experiences.

The challenge to the extreme perceptual theorist is to explain how there can be nonrepresentational similarities between experiences without giving up the AT. He might propose simply to introduce a new classification of visual experience by means of a content which still conforms to the spirit of the AT, but which relates to some time just before the occurrence of the experience: the content would presumably be that the scene around oneself has not altered. But this view ignores the fact that, in normal circumstances, with memory errors aside, the presence of the impression that the scene has or has not altered surely depends on the character of the successive experiences. If we just added this new type of experience to our characterizations, we would still have to say on what properties of successive experiences its presence or absence depends. This suggestion also fails to cope with an aspect switch accompanied by loss of memory of the earlier experience: for here there need be no impression that the scene has not altered. Finally, the suggestion does not capture the nonrepresentational similarity between the experiences of two different subjects looking at the cube, one seeing a certain face in front, the other seeing it as behind. It is not only between successive experiences of a single person that there are nonrepresentational similarities. We do then have a third type of problem for the extreme perceptual theorist.

Why have I chosen to use the example of monocular vision of a three-dimensional wire frame to make these points, rather than the traditional duck–rabbit figure? The reason lies in this: when a subject undergoes an aspect switch while looking at that figure, there is nothing which is seen first as a duck, and then as a rabbit—rather, something is seen first as a representation of a duck, and then is seen as a representation of a rabbit. But then what is so seen, an arrangement of lines on paper, remains constant in the representational content of the successive experiences. So the example does not serve the purpose of showing that there can be nonrepresentational similarities between experiences, since someone who denies that could simply say that in this example the component of representational content concerning the arrangement of the lines on paper remains constant, and accounts for the similarity. In the example of the wire cube, this reply is not available: for after the aspect switch, the wires do not all seem to be in the same relative positions as before.[15]

A natural reaction of the extreme perceptual theorist to examples of these three types is to claim that all the statements whose truth seems to conflict with the Adequacy Thesis can be translated into statements which do not attribute to experiences any features going beyond those countenanced by the AT.[16] Let us consider this translational response as applied to size in the visual field and the two trees on the road. It might be suggested that the statement 'The nearer tree takes up more of the visual field' could be approximately translated by the counterfactual 'For any plane perpendicular to the subject's line of sight and lying between him and the two trees, a larger area of that place would have to be made opaque precisely to obscure the nearer tree than would have to be made opaque precisely to obscure the more distant tree.' It is not clear how the translational response could be implemented in the second kind of example; but does it succeed even for the first kind?

Of what is this translational suggestion offered as an explanation? A first possibility is that it might be offered as an explanation of why we use the same spatial vocabulary as applies to extended objects in space in connection with the visual field. As an explanation of this it is satisfying, and can be extended to such relations as *above* and *next to* in the visual field. But the defender of the AT needs more than this. If this account of the content of experience is to be adequate, he needs this suggestion to supply an account of what it means to say that one object is larger than another in the subject's visual field. This is the second possibility. As a meaning-giving account, the suggestion seems quite inadequate. When we reflect on the possibility that light rays might bend locally, or that the experiencer might have astigmatism, it seems clear that the counterfactual which is alleged to translate the statement 'The nearer tree takes up more of the visual field than the further tree' is in general neither necessary nor sufficient for the truth of that statement. There is also an objection of principle to a counterfactual analysis of an intrinsic property of experience. Whether one object is larger than another in the subject's visual field is a property of his experience in the actual world, be counterfactual circumstances as they may. An account of size in the visual field should make it dependent only upon the actual properties of the experience itself.

The distinction between the acceptable and the unacceptable components of the translational view can be explained in terms of a partial parallel with Kripke's distinction between fixing the referent of an expression and giving its meaning.[17] Kripke noted that though one may fix the reference of a proper name 'Bright' by stipulating that it is to refer to the man who invented the wheel, nevertheless the sentence 'It might have been that Bright never invented the wheel' is true. Now to understand this last sentence, we have to have some grasp of the possibility of a person who actually meets a condition failing to meet it. Similarly, experiences of such a type that the nearer tree is larger in the visual field than the further do actually meet the condition that more of the previously mentioned plane must be obscured precisely to block perception of the nearer tree. This condition fixes the type of the experience, but this type might have failed to meet that condition, just as it might have been that Bright was less inventive. What the translational defender of the extreme perceptual view fails to supply is any account of sameness of experience which allows for the possibility that the type of experience which in fact meets his translational condition fails to do so.

A different strategy in defence of the Adequacy Thesis would be to expand the range of representational contents. It would be conceded that the three types of example make trouble for the AT if we confine ourselves to representational contents of the sorts already considered; but there would be no difficulty, it may be said, if for instance we included in representational content the angle subtended by an object. Such is the view of Rock, who regards perceived visual angle and perceived objective size as simply different aspects of perception. He follows the practice of calling experiences of the former type 'proximal mode experiences' and writes 'Proximal mode experiences are best thought of as perceptions rather than sensations.'[18] Despite his important contributions on the issues of this section, Rock's views here are open to criticism. As we emphasized, it is a conceptual truth that no one can have an experience with a given representational content unless he possesses the concepts from which that content is built up: an experience cannot represent the world to the subject of experience as being a certain way if he is not capable of grasping what that way is. This conceptual point entails that adding contents concerning the visual angle to representational content to save the AT is illegitimate: for an unsophisticated perceiver who does not have the concept of subtended angle it is nevertheless true that one object takes up more of his visual field than another, just as it does for a more sophisticated theorist.[19] This criticism would equally apply to a view once endorsed by Boring, who, after asking what 'observation would demonstrate' that a subject is perceiving the size of his own retinal image, continued: 'For a man to perceive the size of his own retinal images his perception of size must remain invariant under all transformations that leave the size of the retinal images invariant.'[20] If this is a sufficient condition, it is one that can be met by a man who has never heard of a retina. It would also involve a fundamental overdeterminacy of the representational content of experience, since transformations that leave the size of the retinal image invariant will equally leave suitable cross-sections of the light rays in a given plane within the eye unaltered in area, and by Boring's lights this could equally be taken as the content of the perception. These problems result from trying to construe a sensational property, size in the visual field, as a representational property.

It will help at this point if we introduce a simple piece of notation. If a particular experience e has the familiar sensational property which in normal circumstances is produced by a white object (such as a tilted plate) which would be precisely obscured by an opaque elliptical region (r, say) of the imagined interposed plane, let us express this fact in the notation 'elliptical$'$ (r,e) and white$'$ (r,e)'. These primed predicates 'elliptical$'$' and 'white$'$' should not be confused with their unprimed homonyms. In using the notation, we are not thereby saying that experiences have colour properties or spatial properties. With this apparatus we can express what would more traditionally have been expressed by saying 'There is a yellow elliptical region of the visual field next to a white square region.' Thus, using logical notation:

$$\exists r \exists s \, (\text{elliptical}' \, (r,e) \, \& \, \text{yellow}'(r,e) \, \& \, \text{square}' \, (s,e) \, \& \, \text{white}' \, (s,e) \, \& \, \text{next}' \, (r,s)).[21]$$

We said earlier that the means by which these expressions containing primes have been introduced serves only to fix which properties they pick out. The point of invoking Kripke's distinction between fixing the referent and giving the meaning was to emphasize a modal point: that we can conceive of circumstances in which, for example, a tilted plate does not produce an elliptical region of the visual field. But the phrase 'it fixes the referent rather than gives the meaning' is potentially misleading: it may suggest that there is more to understanding 'red$'$' than knowing that it is the sensational property of the visual field in which a red thing is presented in normal circumstances. But there is not more than this. Anyone who knows what it is like to have an experience as of something red and has the concept of the visual field knows what it is like to have an experience which is red$'$ (relative to some region). In this respect the means by which we have fixed which property 'red$'$' refers to does indeed play a special role in understanding that primed predicate. It would be equally true to say that the property of being red$'$ is that property of the visual field normally produced by the presence of an object with such-and-such physical reflectance properties. This description would not convey understanding of 'red$'$,' except in the presence of additional knowledge of which sensational property it is that meets the physically specified condition.

The sensational properties of an experience, like its representational properties, have reliable and publicly identifiable causes. We argued that the property of being presented in a large region of the visual field cannot be identified with the property of being represented as subtending a large visual angle: but nevertheless the fact that an object does subtend a large visual angle does causally explain its presentation in a large region of the visual field. This explanatory fact is one which concerns the physical spatial relations of the perceiver to the physical objects in his environment. Nor is it true that the sensational properties of an experience cannot explain a subject's behaviour. We can conceive of someone who does indeed want to obscure precisely certain objects by attaching opaque surfaces to a glass plane which is perpendicular to his line of sight. At first, he may have to learn from experience with several particular objects what shape of surface to place on the plane. But it seems clear that we can also imagine that his learning successfully transfers to shapes quite different from those cases in which he learned which shape to choose, and that he comes to need no more than his ordinary visual experience in order to make a selection of the shape. At this stage, the sensational properties of his experience would have to be cited in the explanation of why he chooses one shape rather than another to obscure precisely some particular kind of object seen for the first time behind the glass. It is not clear that the sensational properties of experience are in principle any more problematic epistemologically than are the representational properties (which are, certainly, problematic enough).

These points about sensational properties have been tailored to the first type of example offered against the Adequacy Thesis. But they apply equally to the second: they apply *pari passu* if we introduce a primed relation 'behind'' and fix its reference in terms of the physical conditions which normally produce the sensational property it stands for—the conditions for binocular vision of objects at different depths. I suggest that in the third kind of case, nonrepresentational similarity of experiences consists in sameness or similarity of sensational properties. In all the standard cases of switches of aspect, the successive experiences have the same primed sensational properties, those fixed in terms of the imagined interposed plane. Such identity of sensational properties is also not confined to successive experiences of one individ-

ual. This explanation of the third type of case also generalizes to an example with which it is hard to reconcile the AT. A person can have the experience of waking up in an unfamiliar position or place, and his experience initially has a minimal representational content. The content may be just that there are surfaces at various angles to him, without even a rough specification of distances. Suddenly, everything falls into place, and he has an experience with a rich representational content: he sees that nothing has altered in the scene in the sense in which one sees this when experiencing an aspect switch with the wire cube. Again, the primed sensational properties of the successive experiences are identical.

If this treatment of the examples is correct, then neither one of representational content and sensational properties determines the other. The cases of change of aspect show that sensational properties do not determine representational content, while the case of binocular vision of depth shows that representational content in a given sense-modality does not determine sensational properties. Concepts of both types are needed for a full description.[22]

Sensational properties are ubiquitous features of visual experiences: indeed it seems impossible to conceive of an experience devoid of all sensational properties. This is one reason why the visual properties which have been argued here to be sensational should be distinguished from the early Gibsonian conception of the visual field. Concepts of the Gibsonian visual field apply not to ordinary visual experience, but only to a special kind of experience we can have when we adopt the attitude a painter adopts to his experience. 'By adopting the appropriate attitude, one can have either kind of visual experience . . . The visual field is a product of the chronic habit of civilized men of seeing the world as a picture . . . The visual field is a picture-like phenomenal experience at a presumptive phenomenal distance from the eyes, consisting of perspective size-impressions.'[23] Gibsonian visual field experiences can occur only to those who have the concept of a planar representation of the environment. It would perhaps be open to a Gibsonian to hold that the pictorial attitude and the special experiences it produces merely emphasize features already present in ordinary visual experience. This is indeed the position I have been defending, but on such a defence the account of the nature of these features cannot make essential reference to pictorial representation.

Where do the phenomena to which the Gestalt psychologists referred with the label 'grouping' fall within this classification? One such phenomenon is given by the fact that we see the array

as three columns of dots rather than as four rows. Two points make it plausible to classify grouping phenomena as generally sensational properties of experience. One is that it is manifested simply in the exercise of experientially-based discriminative capacities. Someone who perceives the array grouped into three columns will find this array subjectively more similar to

than to

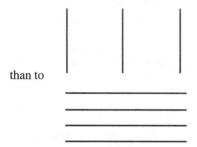

Instances of a three-place relation of comparative subjective similarity can be manifested in experientially-based discriminative reactions. Quine emphasized this point in *The Roots of Reference*,[24] and in this he was in agreement with the experimental techniques of the Gestalt psychologists themselves.[25] A second reason for saying that grouping properties are sensational rather than representational is that they are found in experiences which have no representational properties. In listening to the rhythms produced by a solo drum player, each sound is grouped with some but not with other sounds.[26] It is true that in our initial example, the very description of the case 'seen as three columns rather than four rows' seems to suggest that we are concerned with a representational, not a sensational, property: the concept of a column enters the content. But this is because experiences with a particular sensational property also have, in normal mature humans, a certain representational property. Many of the examples given by Gestalt psychologists are ones in which there are distinctive grouping properties, groupings in particular curves and shapes, and in which the subject of the experience has no concept in advance

with which to pick out the curve or shape in question.[27]

Grouping phenomena do however raise two closely related problems for what I have so far said about the category of sensational properties. In some cases we can perceive one and the same array as differently grouped in successive experiences. This array

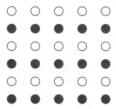

[after Rock, *Introduction to Perception*]

can be seen as either rows or columns. The first problem now is this: we earlier said that in switches of aspect the sensational properties of the successive experiences remained constant. But now, in the case of switches of grouping, we are distinguishing switches *within* the class of sensational properties of experience according to the account so far given. No doubt aspect—and grouping—switches are to be distinguished, but the impression after a switch of either type that nothing has altered seems to have a similar basis; yet the account seems to leave no room for saying that it does. That is the first problem. The second problem, now that grouping is included as a sensational property, is how the particular sensational properties an experience may possess are to be explained. For the primed properties of the successive experiences, for someone who views our most recent array and undergoes a switch of grouping, may be identical; and yet their sensational properties are different.

A full treatment of these problems would give a detailed theory of the types of sensational properties and the relations between them. Here I will just note a distinction which can be applied to the problem. The facts about grouping show that many different types of experience may be produced in normal circumstances by a given pattern of light on the imagined frontal glass plane. We can capture the nonrepresentational differences between these types by using again the fact that if an experience has a particular grouping, it will be subjectively more similar to a second experience with different primed properties than it is to a third. There are at least two levels of classification of visual experience in sensational terms: a basic level, at which terms for the properties have their references fixed by means of the imagined frontal glass plane; and a second level, determined by different possible patterns of comparative subjective similarity between experiences falling under these basic types. The difference between the case in which a given array is seen to be grouped in columns and the case in which it is seen to be grouped in rows is captured at this second level. The difference remains a difference within the class of sensational properties.

NOTES

1. Brian O'Shaughnessy in *The Will: A Dual Aspect Theory* (Cambridge: CUP, 1980) says that experiences with content are the causal consequences of sensations (vol. 1, pp. 172–73; vol. 2, pp. 68–74 and 139–42). I have set up the issues in such a way that sensational properties, if they exist, are properties of the very same thing, the experience, which has representational properties. That some properties of the experience are causally responsible for others would be an empirical psychological hypothesis, and one which involves simultaneous causation. O'Shaughnessy also writes, as I do not, of seeing sensations. Despite these differences and others noted later, much of what O'Shaughnessy says about sensation is congenial and complementary to the main theses of this chapter, in particular his emphasis on the inseparability of sensation from experience and on the nonconceptual character of sensation.

2. Essay II (ch. XVI) of *Essays on the Intellectual Powers of Man* (Edinburgh: Thin, 1895), p. 312: 'sensation, taken by itself, implies neither the conception nor the belief of any external object . . . Perception implies an immediate conviction and belief of something external—something different both from the mind that perceives, and from the act of perception.'

3. For differential explanation, see Ch. 2 of my *Holistic Explanation* (Oxford: OUP, 1979).

4. W. Wundt, *Outlines of Psychology* (Leipzig: Engelmann, 1907).

5. If we are to be strict, the attribution of a common existential content to perceptual and hallucinatory experience is too crude. There is a sense in which, as one incompetently says, a hallucination presents a *particular* nonexistent object, and so has more than a general existential content. (This can be important in explaining such sentences as 'He hallucinated a cup; he believed it to be medieval, and tried to pick it up; later he came to think it a fake.') To capture this the common content of perception and hallucination could be given by perceptual *types* of modes of presentation of objects, types which do not in every context determine an object.

6. 'Information, Causality and the Logic of Perception,' in *The Intentions of Intentionality and Other New Models for Modality* (Dordrecht: Reidel, 1975), pp. 60–62.

7. *The Structure of Appearance* (Indianapolis: Bobbs-Merrill, 1966), p. 290.

8. I. Rock, 'In Defense of Unconscious Inference,' in *Stability and Constancy in Visual Perception* (New York: Wiley, 1977), ed. W. Epstein; J. Ward *Psychological Principles* (Cambridge: CUP, 1920).

9. In *The Perception of the Visual World* (Boston: Houghton Mifflin, 1950); J. J. Gibson says of the impression of distance in depth in binocular vision that 'You can reduce the distance somewhat by closing one eye' (p. 42). Even if this is in fact true in all cases, it cannot be definitional of the distinctive impression produced by depth in binocular vision: one can imagine that closing one eye eliminates this impression even though as a result nothing looks closer than it did before.

10. B. Julesz, 'Texture and visual perception,' *Scientific American*, February 1965.

11. P. Bach-y-Rita et al., 'Vision Substitution by Tactile Image Projection,' *Nature* 221 (1969), 963–64; G. Guarniero, 'Experience of tactile vision,' *Perception* 3 (1974), 101–4.

12. Cp. Guarniero, p. 104: 'By this time objects had come to have a top and a bottom; a right side and a left; but no depth—they existed in an ordered two-dimensional space, the precise location of which has not yet been determined.'

13. My position here is incompatible with that of O'Shaughnessy, *The Will,* vol. 1, pp. 171–73, where he argues that (in my terminology) depth is never a sensational property. He offers three reasons, the first two of which aim to show that 'concepts play a causal role in the genesis of visual depth experience.' The first reason is that '*any* visual depth experience depends upon one's seeing one's visual depth sensations *as* contributing the colour of physical items situated at some distance from one.' This begs the question by presuming that the third dimension in the space of the sensations must represent to the experiencer depth in the physical space around him. The text above gives an imagined counterexample to this claim of necessary coincidence. The second reason given is that 'two visual fields of sensations could be internally indistinguishable and yet thanks to the diverse concepts and beliefs of their owners cause different *veridical* visual depth impressions.' But when there are stereoscopic depth impressions resulting from binocular vision, the three-dimensional visual field properties are not compatible with different depth impressions, at least in respect of the distribution in three dimensions of the surface actually seen. O'Shaughnessy's third reason is that his view is corroborated by the optical facts: but he considers only the bundle of light rays reaching a single eye. In the nature of the case, monocular vision is insufficient for stereopsis; and the optical facts when we consider binocular vision not only make depth as a sensational property intelligible, but also explain why the property should peter out at greater distances.

14. *Philosophical Investigations* (Oxford: Blackwell, 1958), p. 193; cp. also *Remarks on the Philosophy of Psychology* (Oxford: Blackwell, 1980), vol. 1, section 33.

15. The possibility of the notion of representation itself

entering the content of an experience would allow
one to give this explanation of the difference between seeing one area as figure and another as
ground: the whole is seen as a representation in
which the former area is represented as being in
front of the latter.

16. In effect, some philosophers reacted this way to Gibson's use in his earlier writings of the concept of the
visual field; D. W. Hamlyn for instance wrote '. . . the
properties which Gibson ascribes to the visual field
are all logically derivative from those ascribable to
the visual world'. See 'The Visual Field and Perception.' *Proceedings of the Aristotelian Society,* supplementary volume 31 (1957) at p. 121. (I should add
that Hamlyn later changed his mind on this question.)

17. *Naming and Necessity* (Oxford: Blackwell, 1980).

18. 'In Defense of Unconscious Inference,' p. 349, and
also in his *Introduction to Perception* (New York:
Macmillan, 1975), pp. 39, 47, 56.

19. Even if the perceiver does have the concept of the
subtended angle and it enters the representational
content of his experience, it is not clear that the suggestion works. For it would rule out a priori the following possibility. There is someone who suffers
from unsystematic distortion in a particular region of
his visual field. He knows this, and after a time objects presented in that region of his visual field are no
longer presented as being as determinate in size in
the way those presented elsewhere are so represented. If this is possible, then an object may be presented outside the distorting region, and be presented as
subtending a certain angle, and it may occupy the
same size of region of the visual field as an object in
the distorting region which is not presented as subtending any particular angle.

20. 'Visual Perception and Invariance,' *Psychological
Review* 59 (1952), 141–48, at p. 145.

21. The visual field sensational properties caused by an
object can of course be influenced by the properties
of the other objects perceived: geometrical illusions
again illustrate the point. A more complex means of
introducing the primed properties would take account of this relativity.

22. A listener hearing an earlier version of this chapter
drew my attention to David Lewis's unduly neglect-
ed 'Percepts and Color Mosaics in Visual Experience,' *Philosophical Review* 75 (1966), 357–68.
Lewis's notion of experiences which are modifica-
tion-equivalent and his claims concerning it are
clearly close to what I would call the relation of having the same sensational properties and the claim
that sensational properties are distinct from representational properties. But readers wishing to compare his views with those of this chapter should note
that Lewis's percept and my representational content
are not to be identified. He writes of percepts which
are pure percepts of colour mosaic and nothing else
(p. 363): such experiences do not in my sense have
representational content. Like the early experiences
of the TVSS user, they do not represent the world in
the environment of the subject as being a particular
way. Correspondingly they are not directly assessable as veridical or otherwise. (Less direct relations
of correspondence could though be defined.)

23. J. J. Gibson, 'The Visual Field and the Visual World,'
Psychological Review 59 (1952), 149–51.

24. La Salle, Illinois: Open Court, 1974.

25. W. Köhler, *Gestalt Psychology* (New York: Liveright, 1947), Ch. 5.

26. Compare also hearing a chord as an augmented
fourth rather than as a diminished fifth. Someone can
have this experience without having the concept of
an augmented fourth. His hearing it that way is necessarily linked to the resolutions of that chord which
sound right to him. If it is true that different groupings are sensational properties, any proposal to include both grouping phenomena and switches in the
aspect under which an object is perceived under the
common label of 'organization in experience,' needs
some positive justification. Note also that the fact
that there seems to be a conceptual distinction between grouping and seeing something as an instance
of a particular concept may underlie Wittgenstein's
otherwise somewhat obscure remark in his discussion of seeing-as—that one has to distinguish 'purely optical' aspects from those '*mainly* determined by
thoughts and associations': see *Remarks on the Philosophy of Psychology* vol. 1, sections 970, 1017.

27. For sample illustrations, see Köhler, op. cit. and
Rock, *Introduction to Perception.*

42 Visual Qualia and Visual Content Revisited

Michael Tye

Experiences vary widely. For example, I run my fingers over sandpaper, smell a skunk, feel a sharp pain in my finger, seem to see bright purple, become extremely angry. In each of these cases, I am the subject of a mental state with a very distinctive subjective character. There is something it is *like* for me to undergo each state, some phenomenology that it has. Philosophers often use the term 'qualia' to refer to the introspectively accessible properties of experiences that characterize what it is like to have them. In this standard, broad sense of the term, it is very difficult to deny that there are qualia. There is another, more restricted use of the term 'qualia,' under which qualia are intrinsic, introspectively accessible, nonrepresentational qualities of experiences. In my view, there are no qualia, conceived of in this way. They are a philosophical myth.

Elsewhere (Tye 1995, 2000) I have argued that all experiences have representational content and that what it is like to undergo an experience is a matter of a certain sort of representational content the experience has. This view has come to be known as representationalism. In this paper, I shall not try to defend representationalism generally. My concern here is exclusively with the case of visual experience and visual qualia. I shall try to show not only that no good reasons have been adduced for believing in visual qualia in the second sense (hereafter Qualia) but also that, upon proper reflection, the most natural view, is that there are none.

The paper is divided into three sections. In Section I, I say some more about what sorts of properties of visual experience visual Qualia are supposed to be and what it is that I am committed to in denying their existence. In Section II, I discuss a variety of arguments and examples that purport to show that there are visual Qualia. Finally, in Section III, I make some brief comments about representationalism with respect to visual experience and also about the overall significance of my attempt to account for visual experience without Qualia.

I

Consider a painting of a tiger. Viewers of the painting can apprehend not only its content (i.e., its representing a tiger) but also the colors, shapes, and spatial relations obtaining among blobs of paint partly by virtue of which it has that content. It has sometimes been supposed that being aware or conscious of a visual experience is like viewing an inner picture. So, for example, on this conception of vision, if I train my eyes on a tiger in good light, I am subject to a mental picture-like representation of a tiger, introspection of which reveals to me both its content and its intrinsic, nonintentional features partly by virtue of which it has that content. These intrinsic, nonintentional features are not literally colors and shapes of parts of my mental quasi-picture, as in the case of a real picture. After all, it would obviously be absurd to suppose that parts of my brain are orange and black striped when I see a tiger, and it is surely no less absurd to suppose that parts of my soul are. So, whether visual experiences are physical or not, even on a pictorial conception, their introspectible, intrinsic properties are not colors and shapes.

Anyone who believes that there are visual Qualia must at least believe that visual experiences are like pictures to the extent that they (or a mental object they involve) have intrinsic, nonintentional or nonrepresentational features which are accessible to introspection and partly by virtue of which the experiences represent what they do.[1] It is Qualia, so conceived, that are my target. In opposing Qualia, I am not denying, of course, that the contents of visual experiences are introspectible. Nor am I denying that visual experiences have intrinsic, nonintentional or nonrepresentational features. If, as is widely believed, visual experiences are neural items, they will certainly have intrinsic physico-chemical properties.

To emphasize: the rejection of visual Qualia is *not* tantamount to a rejection of the view that there is something it is like for the subjects of visual experiences. On the contrary, as I noted in the introduction, the view I accept is that what it is like to have a visual experience (what is sometimes called 'the phenomenal character of the experience') is a matter of a certain sort of representational content that the experience has.[2] A consequence of this position is that necessarily any two visual experiences that are exactly alike in their representational contents are exactly alike in their phenomenal character. To refute my position, it suffices to specify a clear counter-example to this generalization. I know of no such counter-example. In the next section, I shall consider a variety of putative counter-examples together with a number of other objections.

II

The Argument from Introspection

Standing on the beach in Santa Barbara a number of summers ago on a bright sunny day, I found myself transfixed by the intense blue of the Pacific Ocean. Was I not here delighting in the phenomenal aspects of my visual experience? And if I was, doesn't this show that there are visual Qualia?

I am not convinced. It seems to me that what I found so pleasing in the above instance, what I was focusing on, as it were, were a certain shade and intensity of the colour blue. I experienced blue as a property of the ocean not as a property of my experience. My experience itself certainly wasn't blue. Rather it was an experience that represented the ocean as blue. What I was really delighting in, then, was a quality *represented* by the experience, not a quality *of* the experience. It was the color, blue, not anything else that was immediately accessible to my consciousness and that I found so pleasing. This point, I might note, seems to be the sort of thing G. E. Moore had in mind when he remarked that the sensation of blue is diaphanous (see Moore 1922, p. 22). When one tries to focus on it in introspection one cannot help but see right through it so that what one actually ends up attending to is the real colour blue.

There is another rather different way in which a straightforward appeal to introspection might be made on behalf of Qualia. The visual experience I had that day in Santa Barbara, as I stood entranced by the colour of the sea, was, to my consciousness, very similar to a colour photograph I might have taken of the same scene. My

experience, then, was a picture-like representation of the sea, and my awareness of it was something like my viewing a picture. Since, as I noted in the last section, pictures evidently have accessible intrinsic qualities partly by virtue of which they represent the world, so too, by analogy, do visual experiences.

The most obvious problem with this appeal is that it is not at all clear that my visual experience, while viewing the ocean, was *really* similar to a colour photograph of the ocean. The only undeniable similarity here is between my experience and the experience I would have undergone had I viewed an appropriate photograph. The fact that these experiences are similar shows nothing about the way in which their contents are encoded. What I deny, then, is that the *format* of visual representations—the way in which they encode their contents—is given in introspection. What introspection reveals are simply aspects of the contents themselves.

The second objection I have is simply that even if visual experiences are, in an important sense, picture-like, it evidently does not follow that they have Qualia. One could hold, e.g., that visual experiences have intrinsic qualities partly by virtue of which they represent while denying that these qualities are introspectively accessible (see Harman 1990). Such a position still permits the possibility that visual experiences are picture-like, e.g., with respect to the representation of spatial relations.[3] But it leaves no room for Qualia.

The Argument from Hallucination

Suppose that Paul hallucinates a pink square object. Then there is something that Paul hallucinates. But what Paul hallucinates is not a real pink, square, physical object—Paul, after all, is hallucinating not seeing. So what Paul hallucinates must be a mental object, an idea or an appearance. Now mental objects are not literally coloured nor do they literally have shape. So the terms 'pink' and 'square' in application to what Paul hallucinates must pick out special properties of which Paul is directly aware. These properties are Qualia. Since seeing can be indistinguishable from hallucinating, such properties are present in cases of veridical perception too.

I lack the space to comment on all that is wrong with this argument. When Paul hallucinates in the above case he has an experience *of* a pink square object. *There is,* then, a definite content to Paul's hallucinatory experience. But there is no object, mental or otherwise, that Paul hallucinates. Furthermore the fact that Paul's experience has a certain content no more requires that there really be a pink square object than a picture's representing a three-headed monster, say, requires that there really be any monsters.

Consider the following parallel. Paul wants a blue emerald to give to his wife. There are no blue emeralds. It does not follow that Paul wants the idea of a blue emerald to give to his wife. That he already has. What he wants is that his wife be given a blue emerald (by him). His desire, then, is the desire it is in virtue of its having specific content. When Paul reflects upon or introspects his desire what he is aware of is this content rather than any peculiar qualities of a special mental particular upon which his desire is directed. Likewise when Paul hallucinates a pink square what he introspects, I maintain, is the content of his hallucinatory experience. The qualities of which he is introspectively aware enter into this content (color and shape qualities, among others), and, given that Paul is hallucinating, they belong to nothing before Paul at all. This, it seems to me, is the common-sense view. The idea that the terms 'pink' and 'square' in the context 'Paul hallucinates a pink square' stand for special, phenomenal qualities of which Paul is aware and hence have entirely different meanings from those they have in, say, 'The piece of glass is pink and square' is, on the face of it, very strange indeed. The argument from hallucination does nothing to make this idea palatable.

Visual Qualia without Visual Content

Here is a related argument. Suppose you look at a bright light and turn away. You have an after-image that is red and round, say. In this case you are subject to a visual experience but your experience has no representational content. What it is like for you, then, cannot be a matter of the content of your experience. Rather it must be due to visual Qualia[4] (see Jackson 1977).

It seems to me no more plausible to take the terms 'red' and 'round,' as they apply to an after image, as denoting intrinsic qualities of the image than it is to take the terms 'loud' and 'high-pitched,' as they are employed in connection with the graphical representations of sounds, as denoting intrinsic qualities of oscilloscope readings. People who work with such readings frequently use terms like 'loud' and 'high-pitched'

in application to the readings themselves. (This example is due to Ned Block 1983, pp. 516–17.) It is obvious that in this usage what the terms really pick out are features of sounds *represented* by the readings (loudness and high pitch respectively). Analogously it seems to me that what the terms 'red' and 'round' signify, in application to an after-image, are properties represented by the after-image experience. In my view, there is no after-image that is the mental object of the experience. One who has a red, round after-image is subject to a visual experience, produced by looking at a bright light, the representational content of which is (very crudely) that something red, round and filmy is hovering in space. Since there is no such thing hovering in space, the experience is illusory. There is, then, I claim, a definite content to the visual experience after all.

The fuzziness of most after-images, I might add, is most easily accounted for by supposing that it is a straightforward reflection of the representational impoverishment of the relevant visual experiences. If I have a red, round, fuzzy after-image, my experience does not 'say' exactly where the boundaries of the nonexistent red, round thing lie.

Experienceless 'Sight'

Albert is a very remarkable man. He is blind and he has been so since birth. Nevertheless when he faces objects and concentrates fiercely, thoughts pop into his head—he knows not where they come from—about the visual properties and relations of the objects. These thoughts are so detailed that *content-wise* they are just as rich as the visual experiences sighted people have in the same circumstances. Indeed were one to pay attention merely to the contents of Albert's thoughts, as expressed in his verbal descriptions of what is before him, one would be convinced that he is seeing. But Albert has no visual experiences. For Albert there is experientially no difference between his thoughts on such occasions and his thoughts when he ruminates on mathematics or art or life in general. In each case thoughts just occur and he is introspectively aware of no more than the contents of his thoughts. There is, then, an enormous felt difference between Albert and his sighted fellows at the times at which Albert seems to be seeing. This difference is one that Albert himself would come to appreciate in detail were he to gain sight. It is a difference that can only be explained on the assumption that Albert's inner states lack visual Qualia.[5]

Not so. There is another explanation. Intuitively, the content of visual experience goes far beyond any concepts the subject of the experience may have. Consider, for example, my visual experience of a determinate color hue—red_{19}, say. This does not demand possession of the concept, red_{19}. For I certainly cannot recognize that hue as such when it comes again. I cannot later reliably pick it out from other closely related hues. My ordinary color judgements, of necessity, abstract away from the myriad of details in my experiences of color. The reason presumably is that without some constraints on what can be cognitively extracted, there would be information overload.

Likewise, the representation of viewpoint-relative shape properties is naturally taken to be nonconceptual in some cases. Presented with an unusual shape, I will have an experience of that shape, as seen from my viewpoint. But I need have no concept for the presented shape. I need have no ability to recognize that particular viewer-relative shape when I experience it again. Arguably, even the representation of viewpoint-independent shapes is sometimes nonconceptual.[6] But clearly some representation in visual experience is a conceptual matter (e.g., the representation of object types such as car, ball and telescope).

Some seek to explain the richness of visual experience conceptually by noting that even though the subject often has no appropriate non-indexical concept, he or she is at least aware of the pertinent feature, e.g., red_{19}, as *that* color or *that* shade or *that* shade of red (McDowell 1994). This seems to me unsatisfactory. Intuitively, one can have a visual experience without having such general concepts as *color, shade,* or *shade of red.* Indeed, one can have a visual experience without attending to it or its content at all. Moreover when one does attend, it seems that the explanation of one's awareness of the relevant feature as *that* feature is, in part, that one is having an experience that represents it. But no such explanation is possible if the content of the experience is already conceptual.

If this is correct, then Albert's thoughts cannot possibly have the same content as the visual experiences of his sighted fellows. Albert's thoughts of color and shape are conceptual representations. They have conceptual content. Content-wise, they may *overlap* with the content of visual experiences, since, as noted above, visual experience typically has some partly conceptual content. But there will be no identity. The nonconceptual content of visual experiences is content that cannot be captured in words. For where words enter, so do concepts.[7]

The Inverted Spectrum

Tom has a very peculiar visual system. His visual experiences are systematically inverted with respect to those of his fellows. When Tom looks at red objects, for example, what it is like for him is the same as what it is like for other people when they look at green objects and vice versa. This peculiarity is one of which neither he nor others are aware. Tom has learnt the meanings of colour words in the usual way and he applies these words correctly. Moreover his nonlinguistic behaviour is standard.

Now when Tom views a tomato, say, in good light his experience is phenomenally, subjectively different from the experiences you and I undergo. But his experience has the same representational content as ours. For his experience is the sort that is usually produced in him by viewing red objects and that usually leads him to believe that a red object is present. So he, like you and me, in viewing the tomato has an experience that represents the tomato as *red* (see Shoemaker 1975). The only way that Tom's experience can be subjectively different from yours and mine, then, is if it has a different visual Quale. This intrinsic phenomenal quality partly in virtue of which his experience represents the tomato as red cannot be the one partly in virtue of which our experiences represent it as red. Rather his is the one partly in virtue of which other experiences of ours represent grass and leaves, for example, as green.

One might respond to this argument by denying that a behaviourally undetectable inverted spectrum is possible.[8] There is another response available, however, that seems to me intuitively very satisfying. Contrary to what is claimed above, I believe that the difference between Tom and the rest of us when he views a tomato is that his experience, unlike ours, represents it as *green.* How is this possible? After all, the content of Tom's experience must be given to him, for the difference is a subjective one. But if the content is given to him then he must be introspectively aware that his experience represents the tomato as green. Unfortunately he is aware of no such thing. He sincerely asserts that the tomato is red and even that it looks red to him. Moreover, as was noted above, his experience is the sort that in him is typically produced by viewing red objects.

The answer, I maintain, is as follows: Introspection leads Tom astray. He forms a false belief about the content of his experience.[9] This content is certainly something *of* which he is introspectively aware but it is a content which he misclassifies. He takes it to be the content *red* and so he believes, on the basis of introspection, that he is undergoing an experience that represents red. In reality his experience represents green. *This* representational difference is what is responsible for the subjective difference between his experience and ours. Tom's mistake is due, of course, to the fact that he is unaware of his peculiarity. He does not know that his visual system is producing experiences with atypical contents; he thinks he is normal and he knows that the experience he undergoes viewing the tomato is subjectively like those he undergoes viewing other red objects. So he thinks that his experience represents red.

Perhaps it will be said that I haven't explained how Tom's experience can represent green when it is an experience of the subjective sort that is normally produced in him by viewing red objects and which normally produces in him the belief that something red is present. My reply is that Tom's experience certainly represents red, at the conceptual level. Tomatoes look to him *to be* red. They look to him *as if* they are red. Moreover, tomatoes look to Tom *like* other red things. But that is compatible with holding that, at the nonconceptual level, tomatoes look green to him. As Roderick Chisholm (1957) and Frank Jackson (1977) forcefully argued some years ago, a distinction needs to be drawn between locutions of the form "X looks F to S" and "X appears F to S," where 'F' expresses a sensory property, that is, a property of which one is directly aware via introspection, as one undergoes a visual experience, and the other 'looks' locutions noted above.

In my view, "X looks F to S," given an appropriate "F," is a paradigm of phenomenal talk, and it is best taken to express how S's visual experience represents X, namely as having F. This is reflected in the intensionality of such talk in two ways. First, it can be true that X looks F to S, even if there is no X. Suppose, for example, that I bang my head and I see stars.[10] Here there are no stars, but it can still be true that the stars look bright to me. Secondly, it can be true that X looks F to S without X's looking G to S, even if 'F' and 'G' are co-extensive. Suppose that, as it happens, everything purple is poisonous and everything poisonous is purple. Still, intuitively something, in looking purple to me, does not look poisonous. This example also illustrates the point about different 'looks' locutions. If I am aware of the connection between being purple and being poisonous, upon noting the apparent color of a given object before me, I may see it *as* poisonous; it may look to me *to be* poisonous. But it does not look poisonous, in the phenomenal sense of the term 'looks.'

Even though phenomenal 'looks' talk is intensional, in my view, it is not intensional to the same degree as propositional attitude contexts. And this is because, to repeat, basic visual experience is nonconceptual, as is experience generally. It seems plausible to suppose that for creatures like us, creatures with an evolutionary history, the phenomenal character of states like feeling pain or having a visual sensation of red is phylogenetically fixed. On this view, through learning we can change our beliefs, our thoughts, our judgements, but not (by and large) how things look and feel (in the phenomenal sense of these terms). Having acquired the concept microscope, say, we can come to see something as a microscope, but we do not need concepts simply to see. Once the receptor cells are matured, it suffices to open the eyes. No learning or training is involved. The phenomenal appearances are nonconceptual. Small children see pretty much what the rest of us see. Things look phenomenally to them pretty much as they do to adults, assuming no inverted spectra. They differ in *how* they see things, in what they see things *as*. They do not see that the kettle is boiling, the house as being dilapidated, the computer as malfunctioning.

In the case of Tom, given his visual abnormality, there are striking phenomenal differences from the rest of us. His visual system nonconceptually represents red things as green while conceptually representing them as red. The concept red Tom has is one he shares with you and me, notwithstanding these phenomenal differences (a concept that enables him to recognize red things and to discriminate them from things of other colors directly by sight on the basis of how they appear phenomenally).

Of course, this view entails that Tom is constantly misperceiving at the nonconceptual level, even though his color *judgements* are as accurate as the rest of us. And that, it may be urged, is impossible. But why? So-called "normal misperceptions" occur with respect to shape, length, orientation. For example, in the Muller-Lyer illusion, two parallel lines of the same length look different lengths to normal perceivers in normal viewing conditions. Why not, then, in the case of Tom and color?

Suppose, however, Tom is not a lone invert. Color-qualia inversions are rife. Who now gets to undergo accurate color experiences? Who experiences ripe tomatoes as red, grass as green, and so on, at the nonconceptual level? It may seem that there is no nonarbitrary way of picking out a subpopulation of normal perceivers whose color experiences do not misrepresent. Any choice of a subpopulation may seem as good as any other. Unfortunately, if that is the case, then there is no fact of the matter about who is misrepresenting. So, it may seem, the example of rife phenomenal inversions shows that the attempt to do away with visual Qualia is misguided.

I grant that in the case of rife inversions, without further information, we all have an equal right to accurate color experiences. But this establishes nothing. Only if no further story is available under which some humans could end up being in the wrong while others remain in the right is there any problem here for the representationalist approach to visual qualia.

Such a story can be given in teleological terms.[11] Suppose, for example, there is a genetic defect in certain humans that are alive today, the result of which is that wires are crossed in their visual system, thereby inducing in them color experiences opposite to those that were present (in the same conditions) in most of their ancestors. Originally only a small subpopulation of the human species had the given defect, but now it has spread so that a sizeable number of us have it. These people have an experience of red when they see green things in daylight. They have an experience of green when they see red things in daylight, and so on. Their experiences are now tracking colors that are opposite on the hue circle to those tracked by their biologically normal ancestors. Since the visual systems of the members of this human subpopulation are not functioning as they were designed to do, the colors their sensory states *would* track, *were* they discharging their biological

function, are not the colors they actually track. This is how misrepresentation arises. The nonconceptual visual states of these humans are not tracking the colors they were designed to track. So, error enters. Likewise, for other possible subpopulations. No obvious difficulty, then, for the rejection of visual Qualia.

Twin Earth

Jones is watching a cat. On Putnam's planet, Twin Earth, Jones' doppelganger is watching a creature that looks just like a cat but is genetically and biologically very different (see Putman 1975). Jones and Twin Jones are subject to retinal images that exactly match and their brains are in exactly the same physico-chemical states. Intuitively, then, it may be urged, their visual sensations are phenomenally identical. But the contents of their experiences are different. Since Twin Jones has never seen or heard of cats (there aren't any cats on Twin Earth, only twin cats) and the beliefs he forms on the basis of his visual experiences are never of the type 'This is a cat,' Twin Jones' experience represents not that there is a cat but rather that there is a twin cat present. So the phenomenal sameness obtaining between Jones' and Twin Jones' visual experiences cannot be grounded in a sameness of content. Rather it must be grounded in the experiences sharing identical Qualia.

This argument forgets that Twin Jones' visual experience represents much more than just that a twin cat is present; it also represents the location of the twin cat relative to the viewer, its shape, colour, orientation, and a myriad of other surface details. These aspects of the content of Twin Jones' visual experience will also be found in the content of Jones' experience. I maintain that the phenomenal sameness obtaining between their visual experiences is traceable to these shared aspects.

Still, might not Jones and Twin-Jones differ with respect to their visual representation of color, even though they are microphysical duplicates? If inverted spectrum cases really are possible, then it certainly seems that Jones and Twin-Jones, given their different settings and (let us suppose) evolutionary histories, could differ with respect to their nonconceptual representation of color. So, if our account of the phenomenal is one which ties it to aspects of representational content, and nonconceptual content in particular, then we must reject the widely held view that subjective, phenomenal states of consciousness supervene on brain activity (as is implicitly supposed in the Twin earth argument above).

Why should that disturb us? Those who insist on such supervenience have no strong arguments for their view. The fact that Jones and Twin-Jones' phenomenal states are caused by the same brain states certainly does not show that their phenomenal states must be the same any more than does the fact that their beliefs are caused by the same brain states shows that their beliefs must be the same. Internal supervenience for the phenomenal is no more than a dogma. And sleeping dogmas should not be left undisturbed. Its origin is the Cartesian view of experience as involving inner conscious ideas or pictures. Fix the neurophysiology and you fix the mental paint. Fix that and you fix the phenomenal. Not so, I claim. Phenomenology ain't in the head.

Peacocke's Puzzle Cases

In *Sense and Content* (Peacocke 1983), Christopher Peacocke presents a number of ingenious cases designed to show that sensory experiences have Qualia or, as he calls them, 'sensational properties.'[12] Peacocke's first case is as follows: Two trees of the same size are viewed, one twice as close as the other. Here, if the situation is normal, the visual experience represents the two trees as being of the same size. They look to the viewer the same size. But there is a sense in which the trees look different: the closer tree occupies a larger region in the visual field, and this, according to Peacocke, can only be accounted for nonrepresentationally via a sensational quality or Quale.

There is another possibility. The reason that the trees look different is, I believe, that the experience represents the nearer tree as having a facing surface that differs in its viewpoint-relative size from the facing surface of the further tree, even though it also represents the two trees as having the same viewpoint-independent size. The nearer tree (or its facing surface) is represented as being *larger from here,* while also being represented as being the same objective size as the further tree. There really are two different sorts of feature being represented, then, although they both are concerned with physical objects (or surfaces).

But what exactly is involved in one of two items being larger from here? The obvious answer is that the one item subtends a larger visual angle relative to the eyes of the viewer.[13]

Peacocke rejects this proposal on the grounds that experiences like mine can be had by people who lack the concept of a visual angle. My reply is that the perceptual experience represents the feature, being larger from here, nonconceptually. For a person to undergo an experience that represents one thing as larger relative to his viewing point than another, it suffices that the encoding feature of the experience (larger number of filled array cells, if the representational vehicle has an array-like structure) suitably track or causally covary with the instantiation of the viewpoint-relative relation. The person does not need to have any cognitive grasp of subtended angles.

The key claims I want to make, then, with respect to the tree case are these: (1) the nearer tree looks the same objective size as the further away tree while also looking larger from the given viewing position. (2) X looks F to P only if P undergoes a visual experience with respect to X that represents F. (3) Where the sense of 'looks' in (2) is phenomenal, the representation involved is nonconceptual. (4) The relevant nonconceptual, representational relation is a backward-looking tracking relation. Note that, on this account, the perceiver of the two trees is not the subject of any illusion or error: the nearer tree is just as it looks—both larger from here, the viewing position, and the same viewer-independent size as the further away tree.

Peacocke's second case appeals to a contrast between binocular and monocular vision. If I view a situation with both eyes and then close an eye, things will appear different to me. This difference, according to Peacocke, is not representational. Things are represented in just the same ways in both experiences. So, the difference must be due to a difference in Qualia.

The claim I reject here (not surprisingly) is the claim that there is no representational difference. When I view the situation with both eyes, I see a little more at the periphery of my visual field and there is an increase in how determinately my experience represents object depth. An appeal to Qualia is not required.

Peacocke's third example is a case in which a wire cube is seen first as having one face in front of the other and then with the relative positions of the two faces reversed (see Figure 42.1). Although there is a change in the experience here, something in the experience remains the same. This constant feature of the experience is, Peacocke maintains, a sensational quality.

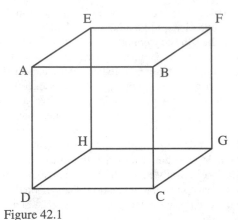

Figure 42.1

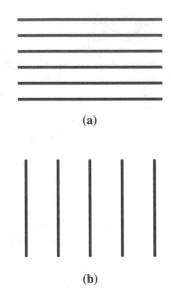

Figure 42.3

The obvious response to this example is to concede the point that something in the experience remains the same but to explain this fact representationally by holding that both before and after the 'aspect' switch, the experience represents the cube as having various unchanging spatial properties relative to the given point of view. For example, both before and after the switch, side ABCD is represented as being lower than and somewhat to the left of side EFGH, side AEHD is represented as being level with and wholly to the left of side BFGC, and so on.

Other aspect switches are no more problematic for my position, I might add. Consider, for example, the pattern in Figure 42.2 (which Peacocke mentions a little later). We may see this pattern either with the dots running from the bottom to the top or from the left to the right. How is this to be accounted for? Answer: The pattern looks composed of columns of dots in the one case and it looks composed of rows of dots in the other. In the former case, the experience represents the pattern as composed of columns; in the latter, rows. The experiences are phenomenally different, then, because they represent different groups of dots. This representational difference explains why the perceiver will

judge the pattern similar to Figure 42.3(a) in the former instance and similar to Figure 42.3(b) in the latter. The overall conclusion I reach, then, is that there is no need to postulate visual QUALIA in order to account for the subjective aspects of our visual experiences.

III

Consider again the hypothesis that necessarily visual experiences with the same representational contents have the same phenomenal character or 'feel.' If this hypothesis is true, as I am claiming, it seems implausible to suppose that its truth is just a brute fact. The natural explanation is that phenomenal 'feel' is itself representational content of a certain sort, representational content that meets certain further conditions.

In Tye 1995 and 2000, I argue that phenomenal content, as we might call it, is PANIC: poised, abstract, nonconceptual, intentional (or representational) content. The requirement that phenomenal content be nonconceptual is compatible with the well established thesis that the way in which one conceives of a scene may causally influence the phenomenal character of one's visual experience of it. In such cases, there is always a difference in the features nonconceptually represented by the experience.[14] So, it is not necessary, to concede that concepts are integral to the 'feel' of the experience. As far as the

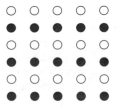

Figure 42.2

'feel' goes, the relevant represented features are not ones for which the subject need possess corresponding concepts at all.

In saying that phenomenal content must be *abstract,* I mean that it must be content into which no particular concrete objects or surfaces enter. This is required by the case of hallucinatory experiences, for which no concrete objects need be present at all; and it is also demanded by cases in which different objects look exactly alike phenomenally. What is crucial to phenomenal character is, I claim, the representation of general features or properties.

The requirement that phenomenal content be (suitably) *poised* is essentially a functional role one. The key idea is that experiences, qua bearers of phenomenal character, play a certain distinctive functional role. They arise at the interface of the nonconceptual and conceptual domains, and they stand ready and available to make a direct impact on beliefs and/or desires. For example, how things phenomenally look typically cause beliefs as to how they are, if attention is properly focused. States with nonconceptual content that are not so poised lack phenomenal character. Consider, for example, states generated in vision that nonconceptually represent changes in light intensity. These states are not appropriately poised. They arise too early, as it were, in the information processing. The information they carry is not directly accessible to the relevant cognitive centers.[15]

Why does it matter whether visual Qualia can be avoided? One answer, I suggest, is that with the rejection of visual Qualia certain aspects of visual experience become less puzzling. Let me explain.

Any adequate account of the subjective or phenomenal aspects of our visual states ought to yield an understanding of why those states have those aspects. Why, for example, does having a visual experience of blue 'feel' the way it does and not some other way? It is hard to see how any satisfying answer can be given to this question if the phenomenal aspects of such experiences derive from visual Qualia.

Suppose, for example, that there are visual Qualia and that such Qualia are nonphysical and irreducible. Then the 'felt' aspect of the visual experience of blue is a matter of its having a special, nonphysical property. It is the presence of this property that gives the visual experience its distinctive 'feel'. Does this really offer us any enlightenment? Apart from the usual concerns about the emergence and causal role of such properties we may still wonder why the visual experience that has the content blue is associated with this irreducible felt quality rather than some other—why, for example, it does not have the felt quality of experiences that represent red. This surely is an impenetrable mystery.

Suppose now that visual Qualia are physically reducible. Then the 'felt' aspect of the visual sensation of blue is a matter of its having a certain physio-chemical property. That is, I think, an improvement on the above alternative—it dissolves the worry about the causal role of Qualia, for example—but again it does not begin to explain why the visual experience that represents blue should 'feel' as it does.

On the proposal I have made there is a simple explanation. Introspection tells us that the visual experience that represents blue differs phenomenally from the visual experience that represents red. This 'felt' difference is, I claim, solely a matter of content. Since the colours represented by the two experiences are different, the experiences themselves are introspectively distinguishable. The reason, then, that the visual experience of blue 'feels' as it does is that it could not 'feel' any other way. The 'felt' aspect simply cannot be divorced from the representational aspect.

The onus now lies with the advocate of Qualia. I have tried to show that the rejection of visual Qualia is defensible against a variety of objections and that it is not only intuitively satisfying but also well motivated.[16]

NOTES

1. If they represent anything at all. Some defenders of Qualia deny that after-image experiences are representational. See Section II.
2. For more here, see Section III.
3. In something like the manner suggested by Stephen Kosslyn for mental images. For a summary of Kosslyn's views here, see Tye 1988 and Tye 1991.
4. Attaching to an image that is the mental object of the experience.

5. A case like that of Albert was suggested to me in conversation by Stephen Stich.
6. See here Peacocke 1992 for some plausible examples.
7. In giving this reply, I am not supposing that a state whose nonconceptual content duplicates the nonconceptual content of a given visual experience *v* is thereby a state whose phenomenology duplicates that of *v* or even that it is a state for which there is

anything it is like to undergo it at all. In my view, a
necessary condition of a state's content endowing it
with phenomenal character is that the content be
nonconceptual. Having nonconceptual content is not
sufficient, however. The content must also be abstract and suitably poised. See here Section III.

8. This is the line taken by Gilbert Harman 1990. One
problem that confronts such a line is that even if
Tom's peculiarity is ultimately behaviourally detectable, it appears that some possible inversions are
not, e.g., inversions pertaining to the experiences of
creatures who see the world in black, white, and
varying shades of grey. See here Shoemaker 1975.
For a reply, see Tye 1995.

9. This position, together with an internalist conception of knowledge which requires Tom to cite the belief that his experience represents a red object in any
adequate justification of the claim that the tomato
before him is red, entails that he does not know that
the tomato is red. Indeed, more generally, it entails
that he does not know the colour of anything on the
basis of vision despite his excellent performance. (I
owe this point to Sydney Shoemaker.) Since the conclusion reached here is obviously false, I maintain
that the above internalist conception of knowledge
must be rejected.

10. This is the phenomenological use of the term 'see,'
not the success use. See Tye 2000, Chapter 4.

11. I endorse such a view only for creatures with an evolutionary history. See here Tye 2000. For an unqual-
ified endorsement of the view, see Dretske 1995.

12. The replies I give below to Peacocke's examples are
influenced by DeBellis 1991 and Harman 1990.

13. For more here, see Tye 1996. For an alternative
reply, see Lycan, 1996. This reply is criticized in Tye
1996.

14. For more here, see Tye 1995, pp. 140–41; Tye 2000.

15. Inclusion of the 'poised' condition in the account of
phenomenal character entails that people with the
real world psychological impairment of blindsight
(not to be confused with Albert's condition) do not
have visual states with phenomenal character with
respect to the blind portions of their visual fields.

16. 1992 version: I am grateful especially for comments
by Chris Peacocke and Sydney Shoemaker. Revised
version: The current essay differs substantially in a
number of places from the original one. In this connection, I am indebted to David Chalmers for some
helpful suggestions. The revisions bring the paper
more in line with my current view (Tye 2000), but in
an attempt to increase accessibility for the present
collection, many subtleties and qualifications have
been passed over. For a detailed and careful statement of the appeal to the transparency or diaphanousness of experience on behalf of representationalism, see Tye 2002.

REFERENCES

Block, N. 1983 "The Photographic Fallacy in the Debate
about Mental Imagery," *Nous,* 83, 654–64.

Chisholm, R. 1957 *Perceiving: A Philosophical Study,*
Ithaca: Cornell University Press.

DeBellis, M. 1991 "The Representational Content of
Musical Experience," *Philosophy and Phenomenological Research,* 51, 303–24.

Dretske, F. 1995 *Naturalizing the Mind* (Cambridge,
Mass: The MIT Press, Bradford Books).

Harman, G. 1990 "The Intrinsic Quality of Experience,"
in *Philosophical Perspectives,* 4, J. Tomberlin, ed.
(Northridge: Ridgeview Publishing Company).

Jackson, F. 1977 *Perception,* Cambridge: Cambridge
University Press.

Lycan, W. 1996 "Layered Perceptual Representation,"
Philosophical Issues, 7, E. Villeneuva, Northridge:
Ridgeview Publishing Company.

McDowell, J. 1994 "The Content of Perceptual Experience," *Philosophical Quarterly.*

Moore, G. 1922 "The Refutation of Idealism," in *Philosophical Studies,* London: Routledge and Kegan
Paul.

Peacocke, C. 1983 *Sense and Content,* Oxford: Oxford
University Press.

Peacocke, C. 1992 "Scenarios, Concepts, and Percep-
tion," in *The Contents of Experience: Essays on
Perception,* T. Crane, ed., Cambridge: Cambridge
University Press, 105–35.

Putnam, H. 1975 "The Meaning of 'Meaning,' " in *Language, Mind and Knowledge: Minnesota Studies in
the Philosophy of Science,* Vol. VII, ed. Keith Gunderson, Minneapolis: University of Minnesota
Press.

Shoemaker, S. 1975 "Functionalism and Qualia," *Philosophical Studies,* 27, 291–315.

Tye, M. 1988 "The Picture Theory of Mental Images,"
Philosophical Review, 88, 497–520.

Tye, M. 1991 *The Imagery Debate,* Cambridge, Mass:
The MIT Press, Bradford Books.

Tye, M. 1995 *Ten Problems of Consciousness,* Cambridge, Mass: The MIT Press, Bradford Books.

Tye, M. 1996 "Perceptual Experience Is a Many-Layered
Thing," *Philosophical Issues,* 7, E. Villeneuva,
Northridge: Ridgeview Publishing Company.

Tye, M. 2000 *Consciousness, Color, and Content,* Cambridge, Mass: The MIT Press, Bradford Books.

Tye, M. 2002. "Representationalism and the Transparency of Experience," *Nous.*

43 | Introspection and Phenomenal Character

Sydney Shoemaker

I

... One view I hold about the nature of phenomenal character, which is also a view about the relation between phenomenal character and the introspective belief about it, is that phenomenal character is "self-intimating." This means that it is of the essence of a state's having a certain phenomenal character that this issues in the subject's being introspectively aware of that character, or does so if the subject reflects. Part of my aim is to give an account which makes it intelligible that this should be so.

A more substantive view I hold about phenomenal character is that a perceptual state's having a certain phenomenal character is a matter of its having a certain sort of representational content. This much I hold in common with a number of recent writers, including Gil Harman, Michael Tye, Bill Lycan, and Fred Dretske. But representationalism about phenomenal character often goes with the rejection of "qualia," and with the rejection of the possibility of spectrum inversion and other sorts of "qualia inversion." My version of representationalism embraces what other versions reject. It assigns an essential role to qualia, and accepts the possibility of qualia-inversion. A central aim of the present paper is to present a version of this view which is free of the defects I now see in my earlier versions of it.

II

As I have said, one of my aims in this paper is to give an account of phenomenal states, and our awareness of them, that is compatible with the possibility of spectrum inversion. But what I mean by the possibility of spectrum inversion is something more modest than what is commonly meant. What is often at issue in discussions of spectrum inversion is the possibility of a state of affairs in which the phenomenal character of the visual experiences of two subjects is systematically different when they are in the same circumstances and viewing objects alike in color, and in which the phenomenal character of the

subjects' visual experiences is sometimes the same when the objects they are viewing are different in color, and yet there is no behavioral difference between those subjects—they make the same color discriminations, apply color words in the same way, and so on. Such a case would be a case of behaviorally undetectable spectrum inversion. One reason why the discussion has fastened on the possibility of such cases is that the supposition that they are possible can seem to aggravate the problem of knowledge of other minds. Another reason is that it is the possibility of such cases that seems to imply that qualia, the properties that give experiences their phenomenal character, are not functionally definable. It seems a short step from holding that there can be behaviorally undetectable spectrum inversion to holding that two subjects who are functionally indistinguishable, at the psychological level, can be spectrum inverted relative to each other—and if this is possible, there can be a psychological difference where there is no corresponding functional difference.[1] It is of course the claim that behaviorally undetectable spectrum inversion is possible that has raised verificationist objections. It is also this claim that has been the target of the empirical objection that our color quality space is asymmetrical in ways that preclude a mapping of determinate shades of color onto other determinate shades of color in a way that preserves the similarity relationships between different shades, preserves boundaries between color categories, and maps unique hues onto unique hues.[2] For some purposes the empirical objection can be finessed by construing the claim about behaviorally undetectable spectrum inversion as saying, not that there could be such inversion in the case of creatures whose color quality space is like our own, but that there could be creatures who perceive colors and whose color quality space is such that for them such inversion is possible.[3] But for my present purposes it is unnecessary for me to claim even this; the claim that behaviorally undetectable inversion is possible plays no role in my argument. All that I need claim is that it is possible for the visual experiences different creatures

Excerpted from *Philosophical Topics*, 2001, with permission of the author and the publisher.

have of objects of certain colors to differ in their phenomenal character without any of these creatures thereby misperceiving the colors, and for the visual experiences of two creatures to be alike in phenomenal character when they are viewing things of different colors, again without either of the creatures misperceiving the colors.

If there were creatures whose color qualia were "alien" relative to ours, so that no color experience of theirs was phenomenally like any color experience of ours, and if these creatures were equivalent to us in their ability to perceive colors, then the relation of their color experience to ours would realize the first of the possibilities but not the second. This would be a case of "alien qualia" but not "inverted qualia."[4] What is true if there can be either alien color qualia or inverted color qualia is that no phenomenal character is such that an experience's having that phenomenal character is a necessary condition of its representing a certain color. What additionally is true if there can be inverted color qualia is that no phenomenal character is such that an experience's having that phenomenal character is sufficient for its representing a certain color.

Anyone who makes the inverted qualia and alien qualia claims about color experience will presumably make the corresponding claims about the perception of other "secondary qualities"—sounds, smells, tastes, and tactile properties like warmth and coldness. Such claims have been made as long as the perception of such properties has been discussed. They are motivated in part by the idea that the phenomenal character of perceptual experiences should be a function not only of the objective states of affairs being perceived but also of the nature of the perceptual system of the perceiver. That idea, taken as completely general, would imply that such claims should be made about the perception of "primary qualities" as well. But in the case of secondary qualities the idea derives much of its plausibility from the fact that there seems to be an "explanatory gap" between the phenomenal character of the experiences and what we know independently of this character about the objective properties of the things that cause them. If we ask why something with a certain molecular structure should taste the way bitter things taste to us, or why something with a certain surface spectral reflectance should look the way blue things look to us, it seems clear that at least part of the answer must have to do with the nature of the perceptual system involved in our perception of these properties. It may indeed seem that an explanatory gap remains even when we bring in the nature of the perceiver.[5] But this remaining gap is an aspect of the mind–body problem, having to do with the relation between states of the brain and the phenomenal character of experiences, and is one that we cannot even formulate without assuming that the phenomenal character of our experiences of things having certain objective properties is fixed by physical states of ours that are caused by things having those properties, and is only contingently related to those properties.

This assumption is supported by what we know about the mechanisms involved in the perception of such properties. We know that what shades of color are perceived as "unique hues" is determined by the rates at which lights of various wavelengths are absorbed by pigments in the cones on the retina, and that because the amount of these pigments varies slightly from one individual to another there are individual differences among normal observers as to what shades are perceived as unique hues—e.g., as to whether something is a unique green or a slightly bluish green.[6] There is no good reason to say that some of these observers are getting it right and the others are misperceiving. So this can count as a case of behaviorally detectable spectrum inversion. We know that because of the way our perceptual system operates many different combinations of wavelengths are visually indistinguishable (such indistinguishable combinations of wavelengths are called "metamers"), and thus that what we perceive as sameness of color and difference of color is determined in part by the nature of our visual system. If whether things look the same or different with respect to color is determined in part by the nature of our visual system, it would seem that how things look must be determined in part by the nature of our visual system.

III

If the phenomenal character of perceptual experiences consisted in their representational content, and if this content consisted entirely in the representation of "objective" properties, then experiences that have the same objective representational content would be alike in phenomenal character, whether the perceptual mechanisms of the subjects of these experiences were the same or different. In that case inverted qualia and absent qualia would be impossible. The way I reconcile the claim that inverted qualia and absent qualia are possible with representationalism about phenomenal character is by holding that among the properties represented by perceptual experiences are what I call "phenomenal properties," and that the phenomenal content of experiences consists in their representation of these.[7] These properties are perceiver relative, in such a way that perceivers can differ in what phenomenal properties they are perceiving the same objects to have while veridically perceiving these objects to have the same objective properties, and in such a way that different perceivers can, when veridically perceiving different objects, perceive the same phenomenal properties even though the objective properties they perceive are different. The idea is that we perceive the colors and other secondary qualities of things *by* perceiving phenomenal properties that are associated with them, and that individuals can differ with respect to what phenomenal properties are associated in their experience with the same objective secondary properties. Originally I held that phenomenal properties are relational properties that things have only when perceived—so, for example, the "color-like" phenomenal property I perceive when I see something red is a property something has just in case it produces an experience of a certain sort in the creature perceiving it.[8] More recently I have suggested that phenomenal properties are instead dispositional properties of a certain kind—dispositions things have to produce experiences of certain sorts in one or more sorts of creatures.[9] The role of qualia in the account is to determine the types of experiences in terms of which the phenomenal properties are individuated, and, what goes with this, to bestow on experiences their phenomenal character, i.e., the part of their content that consists in the representation of phenomenal properties.

One needs such an account if one is to combine representationalism about the phenomenal character of experiences with the view that qualia inversion is possible—more generally, with the view that to some extent the phenomenal character of experiences and their objective representational content can vary independently of one another. If phenomenal character is representational content, phenomenal character can vary independently of *objective* representational content only if there is another sort of representational content that can vary independently of objective representational content.

There is a view about what the phenomenal properties are that makes them aptly called "subjective," and makes the experiential contents in which they are represented aptly called subjective representational contents. This is the projectivist view that they are in fact properties of our experiences themselves, which the experiences falsely represent as instantiated in objects of outer perception—so one's experiences (correctly) represent the tomato as red by (falsely) representing it as having a certain property that is in fact instantiated in the experience itself and is never instantiated except in experiences. This sort of error theory I am anxious to avoid. On my view, the phenomenal properties, although relational and individuated with respect to kinds of experiences, really do belong to the external things in which we perceive them as being instantiated. So while it seems right to say that the representation of these is not part of the objective representational content of experiences, I am reluctant to speak of it as subjective representational content.

I said that one needs a view of this sort if one is to reconcile representationalism about experience with the possibility of spectrum inversion and the like. So if one already accepts both representationalism and the possibility of spectrum inversion, one has a reason to hold such a view. But it seems offhand that if one already accepts the possibility of spectrum inversion, there is a consideration that gives one a reason to hold this view even if one does not already accept representationalism—and which by giving one a way of reconciling the possibility of spectrum inversion with representationalism, gives one a reason to hold representationalism. It is this I want to look at next.

IV

Earlier I characterized the possibility of qualia inversion as the possibility that the phenomenal character of experience and the objective representational content of experience can, to some extent, vary independently of one another, without this resulting in misperception. So, for example, one might characterize a case of spectrum inversion as one in which one person's experiences of red are phenomenally like another person's experiences of green, and vice versa. This should not be put by saying that to one of the people red things look red and green things look green, while to the other red things look green and green things look red. For that of course would imply that one of them systematically misperceives the colors of things. But there is a way of putting this in terms of how things "look" which is not defective in this way—one can say that the way red things look to one of them is the way green things look to the other, and the way green things look to the first is the way red things look to the second. This formulation has the advantage that it does not employ notions—such as those of an experience, of the phenomenal character of experiences, and of the objective representational content of experiences—which might be held to be loaded with questionable philosophical theory. But this way of putting the possibility can seem to lead immediately to the conclusion that the possibility of spectrum inversion requires that our experiences represent phenomenal properties that are distinct from colors. If red and green things look different to the two people, and yet red things look red to both and green things look green to both, and they don't differ in what other objective properties the things look to them to have, it would seem that there must be a kind of properties other than these colors, and other than any kind of objective properties, such that one of the persons perceives red things to have one property of this kind and green things another, while the other perceives green things to have the first of these properties and red things to have the second. The guiding idea here is that if something looks a certain way to a person, there is, corresponding to that "certain way," a certain property that thing looks to the person to have. It is this idea I shall be examining and developing in the remainder of this section and in the one that follows.

If this idea is right, it would seem that we can get to phenomenal properties without invoking anything as controversial as the claim that spectrum inversion is possible. For it is absolutely commonplace for things to look different (either to the same person, or to different persons) without there being any misperception and without there being any difference in the objective representational content of the experiences of them. Consider a case in which I look at a table surface that is partly in shadow, or on which there is a highlight. Different parts of the surface will look different to me. There is no misperception here—indeed, given the circumstances, only a malfunctioning of the visual system could result in the parts of the surface not looking different. Supposing that the table surface is in fact uniform in color, and that I am not misperceiving, this is not a case in which the ob-

jective representational content of my experience of one part of the surface differs from the objective representational content of my experience of another part of the surface. This will be a case of "color constancy"; the part in shadow, although it looks different from the part not in shadow, does not look to have a different color. Of course, it may look to me as if the one part has, while the other lacks, the objective property of being in shadow. But it would get things backwards if we said that it is because of this that the two parts look different to me. Things can look different to one in the way these parts do when one is in doubt whether this is due to a difference in color or a difference in illumination, and if in the present case one part looks to be in shadow and the other doesn't, this is partly because they look different in the way they do (and partly because of clues about illumination provided by the context). If their looking different to me in this way consists in there being different properties they appear to have, these won't be objective properties. They will be candidates for being phenomenal properties in my sense of the term.

What properties might these be? One sort of property that is certainly instantiated in such case is the property something has just in case it is currently looking a certain way to someone. I would construe this as the property of causing, in a certain way, an experience of a certain sort. Call such a property an "occurrent appearance property." This is the sort of property I first took phenomenal properties to be. But a thing's having such a property is bound to be an exercise of a dispositional property it has—the property it has of being apt to produce experiences of a certain sort in some kinds of observers when those observers are related to it in a certain way. Call such a property a "dispositional appearance property." This is the sort of property I took phenomenal properties to be in a more recent discussion.

It should be noted that any object will have a vast number of dispositional properties of the sort indicated—even if we put aside the possibility of spectrum inversion, which entails that the object may be apt to appear differently to different observers because of differences in their perceptual systems. For it will be disposed to appear in different ways depending on the illumination conditions, the distance of the observer from it, the way in which the observer is oriented relative to it, and so forth.[10]

In earlier discussions I have written as if for any sort of observer, each shade of color is associated with a single phenomenal property, in such a way that for an observer of that sort perceiving something to be of that shade of color involves perceiving it to have that phenomenal property. It is clear that if phenomenal properties are any of the "appearance" properties just mentioned, this is a gross oversimplification. Plainly, for any shade of color there will be a large number of different occurrent appearance properties such that, given the right circumstances, perceiving a thing having one of those appearance properties will be sufficient for perceiving it to have that shade. The same is true of the dispositional appearance properties. As noted, an object will have a large number of such properties, and a perceiver will perceive one of these only if she is the right sort of observer and is related to the object in the right sort of way and in the right sort of circumstances. The exercise of these dispositions will always be an instantiation of an occurrent appearance property. And associated with a given shade of color there will be at least as many dispositional properties of this sort as there are occurrent appearance properties associated with it. In fact, there are bound to be more, since sometimes it is one and the same occurrent appearance property that is instantiated in the exercise of the dispositions associated with a number of different dispositional appearance properties.

Among the occurrent appearance properties associated with a color, some will have an especially close relationship to it—relative to a certain sort of observer. It is one or another of these that a thing will have when viewed (by an observer of the relevant sort) under normal or standard viewing conditions. When one speaks of something as looking a particular shade of blue, one is likely to have in mind a way of appearing that belongs to this privileged subset. Call this a "canonical" way of appearing associated with blue. But expressions like "looks blue" seem to be ambiguous. In saying that something looks blue, one may be indicating that if one took one's experience at face value one would judge that the thing is blue. Following Fred Dretske, call this the "doxastic" sense of "looks blue."[11] But saying that something looks blue in this sense is in a certain way unspecific about how it looks. It is unspecific about what occurrent appearance property it has, for the statement could be true even if the way the thing looks is not a canonical way for blue things to look—it is enough if the way the thing looks is such that, given the circumstances, the thing's looking that way indicates that it is blue (and the perceiver is

sensitive to this fact). In a different sense of "looks blue," call it (again following Dretske) the "phenomenal" sense, saying that something looks blue is saying that the way it looks belongs to the privileged subset, i.e., is a canonical way for blue things to look (relative to observers like oneself). And one could say that something looks blue in this sense, $looks_p$ blue, even if taking one's experience at face value would not lead one to judge that it is blue. Under certain circumstances snow $looks_p$ blue (or at any rate bluish). This is not a case of misperception, and it is not a case in which one is disposed to think that the snow is blue. If there is a highlight on the table, one might say that part of its surface $looks_p$ white—but one is not thereby judging, or even disposed to judge, that it is white, and one also will not think one is misperceiving. On the other hand, it is quite common for white things not to $look_p$ white, i.e., not look the way white things look in normal or standard viewing conditions, even though they do look white in the doxastic sense (do $look_d$ white). Roughly speaking, if F is a color then something looks F in the phenomenal sense if a painter would use F pigment to represent how it looks.

We see here that there is an understanding of "ways of looking" such that a thing's looking a certain way (namely $looking_p$ that way) is not in and of itself a matter of its appearing to have certain objective properties. Of course, things appearing to have certain objective properties (appearing$_d$ certain ways) is grounded in their looking phenomenally ($looking_p$) certain ways. But the transition from the ways things appear phenomenally to what objective properties they have, and what objective properties they appear to have, rests on certain contingencies. These include facts about illumination conditions and the spatial relation of the perceiver to the object, and facts about how these combine with the objective properties of a thing to determine how it will $look_p$. The observer needn't have explicit knowledge of these facts, but she must show an appropriate sensitivity to them. And there is a further contingency: how things with certain objective properties appear$_p$, given illumination conditions and the relation of the observer to the object, depends on what sort of visual system the observer has. This is the point that is dramatized by inverted qualia and alien qualia scenarios.

If the way something $looks_p$ to one does not itself amount to one's experience representing the thing as having certain objective properties, does it amount to representing the thing as having any properties at all? In particular, does it amount to representing the instantiation of any of the properties mentioned earlier as candidates for being phenomenal properties? That there *are* what I have called occurrent appearance properties and dispositional appearance properties seems to me beyond question.[12] The question is whether any of these can be properties our experiences represent. For unless some of them are, we cannot characterize the phenomenal character of experience in the way I proposed earlier—namely by saying that an experience's having a certain phenomenal character is a matter of its representing something as having certain phenomenal properties.

V

If one has a perceptual experience in which one is "appeared$_p$-to" in a certain way, an experience "as of" something appearing$_p$ a certain way, then unless one is hallucinating there is something that does appear$_p$ to one that way—something that has the occurrent appearance property of so appearing. For such an experience to be veridical, there must be something that has that property, and if there is something having that property, the experience is to that extent veridical. This does not of course exclude its failing to be veridical in other ways. One's first thought is that it fails to be veridical if the thing fails to be the way it appears to be—e.g., if it looks blue but is not blue. But remember the different senses of "looks blue" distinguished earlier. If something appears$_d$ blue, appears blue in the doxastic sense, then its not being blue would be a failure of veridicality. But if the thing appears$_p$ blue, appears blue in the phenomenal sense, then its not being blue is not sufficient for its failing to be veridical—for it may be that while it is not blue, the circumstances are such that something with its intrinsic properties should look$_p$ blue to an observer like oneself. So the requirement of veridicality could be put as follows: for an experience of a thing to be veridical, the way the thing appears$_p$ must be such that a thing's appearing$_p$ that way to an observer of that sort in those circumstances would not count as misperception. And this amounts to saying that the thing must have a dispositional appearance property of a certain sort. It must be such that in circumstances of this sort it appears$_p$ this way, or can appear$_p$ this way, to an observer of this sort with a normally functioning perceptual system who is related to it as this observer is related to it.[13]

So the veridicality of an experience as of something that appears$_p$ a certain way requires that there be something that has the occurrent appearance property of appearing$_p$ that way and also the dispositional appearance property of appearing$_p$ that way to observers of a certain kind who view it under certain conditions. This seems a reason for saying that such an experience represents the instantiation of properties of both sorts. It is of course not true in general that if something's having a certain property is a necessary condition of an experience's being veridical then that property is represented by the experience. If an experience is of a glass of water, it is a necessary condition of its being veridical that the glass in front of the subject contains hydrogen atoms, but we would not want to say that the experience represents the property of containing hydrogen atoms. But whereas the experience of the glass of water does not, by itself, put the subject in a position to judge that there are hydrogen atoms in front of him, the experience in which something looks$_p$ blue does put the subject in a position to judge both that the thing has the occurrent appearance property of looking$_p$ blue and that it has the, or rather a, dispositional property of looking$_p$ blue. And that makes it plausible to say that these are properties of the thing thing that are represented.

There is a difficulty with this that is indicated by my shift from "the" to "a" a couple of sentences back. Presumably the dispositional appearance property a subject perceives on a particular occasion should be one whose associated disposition is exercised on that occasion by the instantiation of an occurrent appearance property. But when something has the occurrent appearance property of appearing$_p$ F, there will be any number of different dispositional appearance properties of which this could be the manifestation, and the nature of the experience will not in general indicate of which of these it is in fact the manifestation—for the nature of the experience will not reveal all of the relevant details about the circumstances under which the thing is observed. So the experience will not put the observer in a position to judge that the observed thing has any specific appearance dispositional property—and that seems a reason for saying that it does not represent any such property.

But for any way a thing can appear, there will be the higher order property shared by all things that are disposed, under some circumstances or other, to appear that way to normal observers of one or more sorts situated in one or another way with respect to them.[14] This will be the higher order property of having one or another of the dispositional appearance properties which can manifest themselves in an instantiation of a given occurrent appearance property, and will be a property that a perceived thing will have just in case it has that occurrent appearance property. Call this a higher-order dispositional appearance property. If one has an experience as of something that appears$_p$ F, it is a condition of the experience being veridical that the thing have the higher-order dispositional appearance property of appearing$_p$F. And having such an experience does put one in a position to judge that the object perceived does have that property. There seems a good case for saying that such properties are represented by experiences. And these, and the associated occurrent appearance properties, seem good candidates for being the phenomenal properties my account requires.

VI

But suppose we deny that any of these appearance properties are perceived and represented in our perceptual experiences. It will still be true that it is because things appear$_p$ to us in certain ways that we perceive them as having certain properties. And it will still be true that the nature of our experiences, and what we are introspectively aware of in having them, will reflect the ways things appear to us. If anything deserves to be called the phenomenal character of our experiences, it is the part of their introspectable nature that reflects how things look, feel, taste, smell, or sound to us. If this is part of the representational content of our experiences, the appearance properties I have mentioned seem the only candidates for being the properties that are represented. And if this is not part of the representational content of our experience, then representationalism about phenomenal character is false.

But how could this *not* be part of the representational content of our experience? It could be so only if what we are introspectively aware of here, in being aware of the look, feel, etc. of things, are features of our experiences that are not themselves representational. But how could awareness of intrinsic, non-representational features of experience constitute awareness of the look, feel, etc. of things? One view would be that the features we are introspective-

ly aware of are related to the appearance of things in something like the way the paint we see on a canvas is related to what the painting represents—that our awareness of how things appear is grounded on our awareness of non-representational features of the experience in something like the way our perceptual awareness of what the painting represents is grounded on our perceptual awareness of the lines, shapes and colors on the canvas.[15] This view seems to me false to the phenomenology, and to be avoided for all the reasons that have led to the demise of the sense-datum theory.

But my aim in the present paper is not so much to argue for representationalism about phenomenal content as to argue, first, that if representationalism is to be acceptable it must allow that the properties whose representation bestows phenomenal character are phenomenal properties in my sense, which I now claim to be appearance properties of the sort I have characterized, and, second, that in allowing this a representationalist must allow something that representationalists have usually been unwilling to allow—that the phenomenal character of experiences is independent of their *objective* representational content (their representation of objective properties) in a way that allows for the possibility of cases of inverted qualia and alien qualia. To complete the case for this I need to say more about how qualia figure in my account. But before I do this I want to say something about how the account applies to the case of pains and other bodily sensations.

VII

One of my claims about introspective awareness is that it is fact awareness unmediated by thing awareness—awareness *that* which does not involve awareness of any *object*. One source of resistance to this is the awareness we have in cases of after-imaging and the like. It is certainly very natural to say that my awareness that I see a yellowish-orange after image is grounded on an awareness of an object, namely the after-image. Here I follow the lead of J. J. C. Smart, in his seminal paper "Sensations and Brain Processes"; I affirm the existence of "experiences of after-imaging" while denying the existence of after-images.[16] This is the rejection of the "act-object" conception of sensation. In my view, to hold that "seeing a yellowish-orange after-image" involves the existence in one's mind of something that is yellowish-orange is to hold a view that can be adhered to consistently only by someone who embraces a sense-datum theory of perception. So I hold that we should not "reify" after-images.

But it is one thing to hold that we should not reify after-images, and another thing to say that we should not reify pains. Intuitively, a more serious obstacle to holding that introspective awareness is fact awareness unmediated by thing awareness is the overwhelming naturalness of saying that pains, itches, tingles, etc. are particular items of which we are introspectively aware, and that it is by being aware of these items—these "objects"—that one is aware of such facts as that one has a pain in one's foot. It is common to take pains and the like as paradigms of sensations, and sensations as paradigms of experiences—and then it is no wonder that we fall into thinking of experiences as objects that we are aware of in a quasi-perceptual way when we introspect.

This way of thinking is extremely natural, but I think that it is confused. I think that when, as we say, a person has a pain in his foot and feels it, there are two sorts of awareness occurring that need to be distinguished, and which ordinary ways of talking encourage us to conflate. There is perceptual awareness of the condition of some part of one's body. This involves awareness of the instantiation of a phenomenal property—in the sense discussed above—in that part of one's body. By perceiving the instantiation of such a property one may also perceive that there is damage of some sort in that part of one's body—no doubt the biological function of pain and pain awareness intimately involves the perception of bodily damage.[17] Here one can properly be said to be aware of some particular, a region of one's body, as having one or more properties. This awareness is not simply *awareness that;* it is, if you like, awareness of an object. But also, this is not *introspective* awareness; it is *perceptual* awareness. Now, having this perceptual awareness involves being in a perceptual state, a somatic perceptual state, which represents some part of one's body as being a certain way. And of this state one can, and normally will, have introspective awareness. This awareness will be like the introspective awareness one has of one's visual, auditory, tactile, etc. sense-experiences. It is best thought of as *awareness that*—awareness that one is in a certain somatic perceptual state. The content of this awareness will embed the content of the

perceptual state, in the same way that the content of an introspective belief about visual experience will embed the content of the visual experience. The somatic experience is no more in the part of one's body it represents than the visual experience is in the portion of one's visual field it represents. And it no more has the phenomenal property it represents as instantiated in a certain part of one's body than the visual experience has the phenomenal property it represents as instantiated in in some object in front of one—at any rate, this is so unless some projectivist view of phenomenal properties is correct. But in the same sense in which the visual experience has a phenomenal character, the somatic experience has a phenomenal character; its phenomenal character is fixed by what phenomenal properties it represents.

Supposing this account is right, how do we map it onto our ordinary talk of pains and itches, and of feeling pains and itches? I think there is no neat way to do so. We speak of pains and itches as located in parts of our bodies. And we speak of them as felt, which seems to make them objects of some kind of perception. But we also speak of them as mental entities. And the instantiation in some part of one's body of a phenomenal property that can be felt is no more a mental state of affairs than is an apple's having a phenomenal property that is detectable by sight. The somatic experience of pain is mental, and to that extent is a better candidate for being pain than the phenomenal property instantiation. And it seems to be what we are averse to, which also makes it a better candidate. We are as averse to "hallucinatory" somatic experiences of this sort as we are to veridical ones. But the somatic experiences are not located in the parts of our bodies where we are said to feel pains—if they are located anywhere, they are located in the brain. And the somatic experiences are not felt, just as visual experiences are not seen. So nothing there is seems an ideal candidate for being pain as we ordinarily talk about it. Similarly for itches and tingles. This doesn't prevent there being quite definite truth conditions for statements about pains, or about itches and tingles. A person counts as being in pain if she has a somatic experience having a certain phenomenal character, i.e., representing the instantiation of a certain phenomenal property at some point in the person's body. And someone counts as having a pain in a certain location if she has a somatic experience which represents an instantiation of that phenomenal property in that location—even if, as in the case of "referred pains," the organic cause of the pain is in some other part of the body. Because these truth conditions concern the somatic experiences, these may seem the best candidates for being pains. But if we take them to be the pains, we must allow that it is only in what G. E. Moore called a Pickwickean sense that pains have location, and are felt. And we must be careful not to confuse the introspective awareness of pains so understood, i.e., the introspective awareness of this class of somatic sense experiences, with the perceptual awareness that normally accompanies it, viz the perception of conditions of one's body.

The confusion we are apt to fall into here has a parallel in the case of other sorts of sensory experience. It is certainly not unheard of for philosophers to confuse our introspective awareness of visual sense experiences with perceptual awareness of phenomenal properties represented in such experience. This happens in sensedatum accounts. What probably makes the confusion harder to resist in the case of bodily sensations is a fact about our interests. Whereas in the case of other sorts of perception our primary interest is not in experiences but in the things they represent, in the case of pains and itches we have at least as direct an interest in the experiences themselves, namely in avoiding or eliminating them. Being in the habit of taking the items of primary interest to be objects of perception, as they are in other cases, we are prone to do this here, thereby blurring the distinction between perceptual experience and item perceived. So we are apt to accept a sense-datum view about bodily sensation even when we have abandoned it elsewhere. But, as I suggested earlier, taking bodily sensations as our paradigms of experiences can lead one to think that even in the case of vision and hearing our experiences are objects which we can be introspectively aware of as having certain properties—and this is a sort of residue of the sense-datum view. At any rate, that is how I would diagnose my own past thinking about these matters.

VIII

I said above that the instantiation in some part of one's body of a phenomenal property, e.g., in a case of pain, is "no more a mental state of affairs than is an apple's having a phenomenal property that is detectable by sight." But does this mean that it is not a mental state of affairs at all? Recall that my earlier discussion settled on two sorts of properties as the best candidates for being phenomenal properties—higher order dispositional appearance properties, and the occurrent appearance properties in which these are manifested. I see no reason not to count both of these as phenomenal properties. The instantiation of a phenomenal property of the first sort is a "mental" state of affairs only in the very thin sense that the instantiation of such properties requires that there be minded creatures capable of perceiving such instantiations. But the instantiation of a phenomenal property of the second sort, an occurrent appearance property, is a mental state of affairs in a much more robust sense—for it requires that the thing having it be actually perceived.

So it is perhaps not out of the question that pains can be held to be both located where we say they are and mental—or at least partly mental. They will be so if they are instantiations of phenomenal properties of the second sort, occurrent appearance properties. Such a view would not save everything we want to say about pain. For it would allow for the possibility of pain hallucinations, and would imply, contrary to ordinary ways of speaking, that a "referred pain in the arm" is not really in the arm. But then, neither does the view that pains are somatic experiences of (i.e., representing) such property instantiations save everything we want to say about pain.

But I think it is useful to reflect on the fact that insofar as our perceptual experiences represent instantiations of occurrent appearance properties, they represent states of affairs that are in part mental. For this raises a question about the relation between perceptual awareness and the introspective awareness of perceptual experiences. If the properties represented by perceptual experiences were exclusively objective properties, ones whose instantiation was in no way a state of affairs that involves the existence of minds, then the contents of perceptual awarenesses and introspective awarenesses would be logically independent of each other. But if the properties represented by a perceptual experience include occurrent appearance properties, then part of the content of the perceptual experience seems closely related to the content of an introspective awareness the subject might have. Let it be that I am perceptually aware that something has the occurrent appearance property of looking$_p$ blue, and am introspectively aware that I am "appeared$_p$ blue to," i.e., that I am having an experience as of something that looks$_p$ blue. The relation of "That looks$_p$ blue to me" to "I am having an experience as of something that looks$_p$ blue" seems to be one of conceptual entailment. So the introspective awareness expressed by the second proposition seems implicit in the perceptual awareness expressed by the first.

Now of course one can have a perceptual experience that represents that a thing has a certain property without judging that the thing has that property. This can happen when one's attention is not on the thing in question, or when the experience of it is just a momentary glimpse. And it can happen when the property is an occurrent appearance property. So it would be wrong to say that whenever one's experience represents such a property, one is in a position to make the introspective judgment that it does. What seems to be true, however, is that whenever one is in a position to make the perceptual judgment that something has such a property, one is in a position to make the introspective judgment that one's experience represents the property.

In earlier discussions of phenomenal properties I have insisted that while such properties are in fact relational, we are not normally aware of them *as* relational. I now want to qualify this. It is true, I think, of the case where one perceives something to have a phenomenal property but does not judge that the thing has it. But the situation is more complicated in the case where one does judge that a thing has a phenomenal property. One thing that remains true is that while the property is relational, only one of the relata, namely the external object, is perceived—so perceiving the property is not a matter of perceiving a relation between two things. And in some cases the judgement one makes is not relational in form; one judges simply "It looks blue." It may not occur to the person making this judgment that the thing's looking blue is a matter of its looking blue *to her.* For one thing, the person very likely is not distinguishing the occurrent appearance property of looking$_p$ blue and the dispositional appearance property of looking$_p$ blue, and of course the thing's having the latter is not a matter of its standing in a relation to the subject. However, insofar as the subject is ascribing to the thing the occurrent appearance property of looking$_p$ blue, nothing more than reflection on what having this property amounts to should be needed for the person to realize that "looks blue" here means "looks blue

to me," and that the property is relational. And, as suggested above, nothing more than reflection on the content of the latter realization should be needed for the person to realize that she is "appeared blue to," i.e., has an experience that represents something as looking$_p$ blue.

This gives us one way of cashing out the claim that the phenomenal character of perceptual experiences is "self-intimating." It is obvious that insofar as perception is a source of knowledge of the environment, it requires the subject to have at least a sensitivity, which may be only subpersonal, to the contents of perceptual experiences—only so can these give rise to perceptual beliefs with corresponding contents. If it is further the case that perceptual experiences must represent occurrent appearance properties, this sensitivity extends to the representation of these. It would be rash to claim that in general this sensitivity amounts to introspective awareness. But in the case of the representation of occurrent appearance properties, it is arguable that it grounds such awareness. Insofar as experiences representing such properties put one in a position to judge that such properties are instantiated in perceived objects, they put one in a position to judge that they are represented in one's experience—assuming, of course, that one has the concepts such judgment requires.

IX

As I said earlier, my version of representationalism about phenomenal character differs from other versions in assigning a central role to qualia. I must now try to make clear what that role is.

There is a way of putting my view which on first pass does not involve introducing qualia, and seems to be in line with ordinary ways of thinking. We start by saying that we are perceptually aware of the way things appear, and that this involves being aware of the instantiation of appearance properties, both occurrent and dispositional, where the instantiation of the occurrent ones are manifestations of the dispositional ones. The instantiations of the occurrent ones involve the occurrence of states of being-appeared-to on the part of observers, and can be construed as the causing of such states by observed objects; so the dispositional ones can be thought of as dispositions to produce such states under certain circumstances. The states of being-appeared-to are states that represent the appearance properties that cause them or are disposed to cause them.

Here it looks as though the appearance properties are individuated in terms of the states of being appeared to, and that the ways of being appeared to are individuated in terms of the appearance properties. How do we break out of this seeming circle? Could we take the appearance properties as primitive and define the states of being appeared to in terms of them? That obviously will not do. It would not enable us to make sense of the fact that differently constituted observers observe different appearance properties when they perceive the same objects—that what appearance properties a creature observes when viewing a thing is a function of the nature of the perceiver as well as the nature of the thing. Could we take the states of being appeared to as primitive, and define the appearance properties in terms of them? This won't do, given that the states of being appeared to are states that have to be specified in terms of their representational contents, namely in terms of what appearance properties they represent.

Could there be a "package deal" definition, say one involving the Ramsey-Lewis technique, which simultaneously defines both the appearance properties and the states of being appeared to? As a first stab we might try to define a particular state/property pair by saying that the state of being appeared$_p$ blue to and the property of appearing$_p$ blue are the unique state S and the unique property P, such that S represents P and something has P just in case it is producing (or has the disposition to produce in some sort of observers) a state of type S, and in the case of creatures like us something is P only if it looks the way blue things look under optimal conditions. This does not, as it stands, tell us how to apply "is appeared$_p$ blue to" to creatures of kinds other than our own. And, what goes with this, it does not provide a way of distinguishing the appearance property in question from the property that realizes it in the case of observers like ourselves—it doesn't distinguish the dispositional appearance property from the intrinsic surface property that is its categorical base in the case of observers like ourselves, and doesn't distinguish the occurrent appearance property from the property something has when it is instantiating that intrinsic surface property. It should be noted that it invokes the notion of "looking the way . . . ," i.e., the notion of sameness of appearance properties. We would need to be able to apply this notion intrasubjectively

in order to apply the definition at all. And we would need to be able to apply this notion intersubjectively in order to extend the definition so as to apply to creatures in whose experience the phenomenal property in question is associated with a different color. Supposing we could do this, we could revise the account as follows: The state of being appeared$_p$ blue to and the property of appearing$_p$ blue are the unique state S and the unique property P such that S represents P, someone is in state S just in case the way something looks to him is the way blue things look to us under optimal conditions, and something is P just in case it is producing state S in some observer (in a way that does not involve misperception), or is disposed to produce S in some sort of observer. This is still rough and in need of refinement. But plainly any account of these properties and states needs an account of sameness of state of being appeared to.

Here is where qualia come in. We need a kind of sameness, applicable to states of being appeared to, that is not simply defined as sameness with respect to what property is represented. The only thing that will do is sameness with respect to qualitative character, which I think has to be a functionally defined sort of sameness. Qualia will be the properties of perceptual states in virtue of which they stand in relations of qualitative similarity and difference. In the first instance, the relations of qualitative similarity and difference will be defined in terms of the role they play when they hold intrasubjectively. An important part of this role has to do with what sorts of perceptual beliefs experiences related by these relations are apt to cause, and this is of course intimately related to their role in affecting the discriminatory and recognitional behavior of the creature. Discrimination will require qualitatively different experiences, and recognition will require qualitative similarity between experiences occurring in the same subject at different times. Different experiences to the same objective property may be qualitatively different; but once illumination conditions and the relation of the perceiver to the object are fixed, sameness of objective property represented will go with qualitative sameness. And, of course, sameness of phenomenal property represented will go with qualitative similarity, independently of viewing conditions.

I believe that in order to apply the notion of qualitative similarity and difference intersubjectively one must (assuming physicalism) have recourse to the notion of the physical realization of qualia. Supposing that qualia are multiply realizable, each quale will be associated with a set of properties that can be said to be realizers of it in virtue of the way instantiations of them in the same subject are related—i.e., are such that experiences in which different ones of them are instantiated, but are otherwise the same (at the appropriate functional level of description), are qualitatively alike. If two creatures are alike with respect to what physical properties of their brain states serve as realizers of the qualia involved in their experiences, then an experience of one of them is qualitatively similar to an experience of the other to the extent that the qualia realizers they instantiate are ones whose instantiation would yield qualitatively similar experiences if instantiated in the same subject. While it is the intrasubjective functional role of a property that makes it a quale realizer, its being a realizer means that it realizes the same quale in whatever creature it is instantiated in—so if the same realizer is instantiated in the experiences of two different subjects, or two different qualia realizers are instantiated in them but these are ones that realize the same quale when instantiated in the same subject, the experiences of the two subjects will be to that extent the same.[18]

Qualia can be thought of as the vehicles of the representation of properties of perceived objects. As such, they can be said to represent such properties. In the case of objective properties, it will be only contingently that a given quale will represent a particular property—e.g., that a particular quale represents red (or red as viewed under certain conditions). Any view which holds that perceptual experiences represent what they do in virtue of causal correlations between types of experiences and features of the environment, or in virtue of an evolutionary history that bestowed on certain types of experiences the function of indicating certain features of the environment, requires a way of typing experiences that makes it a contingent fact that experiences of a given type represent the particular features of the environment they do. It may be thought that all this requires is that the experiences belong to *physical* types, which physicalist representationalists who reject qualia can readily allow. But I think it is clear that the typing must be functional rather than physical. The types must be so related to each other, and to the rest of the subject's psychology, as to determine its "quality space," and so must play an appropriate role in determining its discriminatory and recognitional capacities, and in generating beliefs about its

environment. What must be true of different tokens of the same type is that they share a certain causal role; this allows for "multiple realization," and so for the possibility that tokens of an experiential type might be physically heterogeneous. Spelling out the conditions for type membership requires a functional account of qualitative similarity and difference, and qualia are the properties of sensory states, presumably physically realizable properties, in virtue of which they stand in these relationships. Thus it is that it is qualia that type the experiences, and thus it is that qualia contingently represent the objective environmental features they do.

But it is necessary, not contingent, that qualia represent the phenomenal properties they do. Phenomenal properties are individuated in terms of the types of experiences they produce, and these experiences are typed by their qualitative character. The qualitative character of an experience, what qualia are instantiated in it, thus fixes its phenomenal character, i.e., what phenomenal properties it represents.

As a representationalist, I hold that our introspective awareness of the phenomenal character of our experience is an awareness of an aspect of their representational content, namely their representation of phenomenal properties. In earlier discussions of this I have maintained that this awareness should not be construed as awareness of qualia, and that qualia are known "only by description." I now think that this was a mistake.[19]

One source of my former view was the idea that I would be involved in vicious circularity if I both typed experiences by their phenomenal character, i.e., what phenomenal properties they represent, and defined phenomenal properties in terms of what types of experiences they produce—and that typing the experiences in terms of qualia would not avoid the circularity if the qualitative character of experience and the phenomenal character of experience turned out to be the same. But as I think the discussion in the earlier part of this section shows, what is needed in order to avoid circularity is a "package deal" account which defines phenomenal properties and phenomenal character together in a way that essentially involves a functional account of sameness of appearance properties and ways of being appeared to—or what comes to the same thing, a functional account of qualitative similarity and difference. And it is compatible with this that qualia, thought of as the properties in virtue of which experiences are qualitatively similar and different, should turn out to be the same as the properties of experiences which are essentially representative of phenomenal properties, and so the same as the properties of experiences we are introspectively aware of when we are aware of that part of the representational content of our experiences which is the representation of phenomenal properties.

No doubt another source of my former view was my taking for granted that qualia are "intrinsic" and non-representational features of experiences—that being, of course, a common way of characterizing them. It is, I think, less than clear what it means to speak of intrinsic features of experiences, given that experiences themselves are states of persons. But it is part of my view that having an experience with a certain qualitative character—one having certain qualia—is an intrinsic feature of a person. If the only properties of things represented by perceptual experiences were objective properties, and if, as I think, we need an externalist account of the representation of objective properties, it would follow that qualia are non-representational—that while they can be "vehicles" of representation, they can be only contingently the vehicles of the representation of particular objective properties. But of course I hold that in addition to representing objective properties, our experiences represent phenomenal properties—occurrent and dispositional appearance properties. About the representation of these my view is internalist rather than externalist. And it is compatible with this that qualia, although internally determined, are essentially representative of such properties.

So I now think that in being introspectively aware of the phenomenal character of one's experience, being aware of how one is appeared$_p$-to, one can be said to be introspectively aware of the qualitative character of the experience, and of the qualia that make up that character. But I should emphasize again that this awareness should not be thought of as a matter of introspectively singling out an experience and noticing that it has certain features. For there is, I think, no such thing as introspectively singling out an experience and noticing something about it. Experiences are states of persons, not quasi-substances to which their subjects have quasi-perceptual access. What one does have in introspective awareness is awareness *that* one has an experience with a certain phenomenal character, which is an awareness one has in being aware that one is "appeared to" in a certain way

in a certain sense modality. Again, introspective awareness is *awareness that.*

X

Part of what I have to say about the belief involved in introspective awareness of phenomenal character is derivative from what I have to say about phenomenal character. Given that phenomenal character is not a matter of mental objects, sense-data or the like, having certain properties, the beliefs this gives rise to are not about such objects. They are beliefs about how things look, feel, smell, etc.—about how one is "appeared to."

But there is a puzzle here. Given that phenomenal character is an aspect of representational content, beliefs about it should be to the effect that one is in a state having such and such representational content. It is natural to suppose that if the introspective belief is true then its content embeds the content, or part of the content, of the perceptual state; and that in any case it embeds what could be the content, or part of the content, of a perceptual state. The way the perceptual content is embedded should be like the way the content of the belief that it is raining is embedded in the content of the belief that one believes that it is raining. But it has recently been urged, with considerable plausibility, that the content of perceptual states is, at least in part, nonconceptual content.[20] If this is true, it seems plausible that the part that is nonconceptual includes the part that determines the phenomenal character of the state. On the other hand, it is widely held that the content of beliefs is, of necessity, conceptual. And how can a content that is conceptual embed a content that is nonconceptual?

Let the state be one of being visually appeared to in a certain way. The introspective belief will simply be the belief that one is visually appeared to in that way. The content of this belief will certainly be partly conceptual—it will involve the concept of being visually appeared to, or of things looking some way. No one who lacks this concept can have the belief that things look a certain way to her, or that she is visually appeared to in a certain way. What is held to be nonconceptual is the "certain way" one is appeared to, the "certain way" things look—or at least some part or aspect of this certain way. If this is nonconceptual, and is embedded in the content of the perceptual belief, then that content will be in part nonconceptual.

I have nothing much, and certainly nothing new, to offer by way of a characterization of nonconceptual content. What I have in mind is similar to what Christopher Peacocke calls "scenario content"—a content "individuated by specifying which ways of filling out the space around the perceiver are consistent with the representational content being correct."[21] On the account I have offered, the "ways of filling out the space" would have to be ways phenomenal properties are distributed in that space. For a person's experience to have such a content it is not required that the person have the concepts such a specification would require. And even if she does, the content is not in any sense composed of those concepts, in the way the content of the belief that rollerblading is dangerous can be thought of as composed of the concepts of rollerblading and danger.

If one thinks that the content of perceptual experience is nonconceptual, and that the contents of beliefs are conceptual, one might offer an account of introspective beliefs about perceptual experience along the lines of one Richard Heck has recently offered as an interpretation of what Gareth Evans had to say about this.[22] Heck's proposal is about how we should understand a person's awareness that things appear a certain way to her. Roughly, it is an awareness, based on an exercise of the conceptualizing capacity that the person uses in making ordinary perceptual judgments about the world, of what one would judge in the absence of certain "extraneous" information—information that bears on whether the experience is veridical. The content of this awareness, and the associated belief, is conceptual. But it "tracks" the nonconceptual content of the experience in question—that to which the conceptualizing ability is applied. As I understand this view, it is never the case that we have a perceptual belief that actually embeds the nonconceptual content of the perceptual experience; the closest we come to this is having a perceptual belief whose content embeds a conceptual content that "tracks" that nonconceptual content.

The awareness of how things "appear" that this view is designed to explain seems to be awareness of how they appear in what I have called, following Dretske, the doxastic sense—the sense in which the way things appear is the way one would take them to be if one took one's experience at face value. How, along these lines, could one explain awareness of how things appear$_p$, i.e., appear in the phenomenal sense? As noted earlier, something can appear$_p$ white without appearing$_d$ white—the highlighted part of a

table surface may look the way white things look under standard or normal conditions, without its being true that one would judge that it is white if one took one's experience at face value. In dim light many things look$_p$ black without looking$_d$ black. If one describes something as looking$_p$ F, where F is a color word, one is of course conceptualizing the content of one's experience in a way. Assuming the possibility of spectrum inversion, an expression like "looks$_p$ blue" may stand for different ways of looking in the mouths of observers with different sorts of perceptual systems—so either it expresses a different concept for different sets of perceivers, or it expresses a concept that picks out a particular way of looking only if indexed to a particular sort of perceiver. And it would seem that in order to employ such a concept a perceiver must know, independently of having it, how blue things appear$_p$ to her under normal viewing conditions and that this is the same as the way a particular thing appears$_p$ to her. This knowledge involves a representation of a way of appearing$_p$; and if this representation is by way of a concept, it is not a concept standardly expressed by any natural language expressions. John McDowell, who thinks that the content of perceptual experience is always conceptual, holds that the concepts involved in this content are often "demonstrative" concepts.[23] And no doubt one can have a demonstrative concept of a particular way of appearing$_p$—a particular phenomenal property. Such a concept might be expressed on a given occasion by a phrase of the form "The way this looks$_p$ to me now." If, as I think, it is implausible to suppose we have enough such concepts to capture the rich content of our perceptual experience at a particular time, that is a reason for rejecting the view that the representational content of perceptual experience is always conceptual. And if, as I am also inclined to believe, it is implausible to suppose that we have enough such concepts to capture the content of our awareness of the content of our perceptual experience, that is a reason for questioning the view that the embedded content of such awareness is always conceptual—and so for questioning the view that the contents of beliefs is always conceptual.

We certainly have introspective beliefs about how things appear that conform to the Evans/Heck account, and whose contents are entirely conceptual. But I am attracted by the idea that we also have introspective beliefs whose embedded content is nonconceptual, and that these are, or include, beliefs about the phenomenal character of our experience. This idea goes nicely with a view which if true would explain the self-intimation of phenomenal character, and permit some introspective beliefs to be infallible. On this view, there is just one tokening of the content that is both the phenomenal character of the perceptual state and the embedded content of the introspective belief about the phenomenal character of that state. Part of the perceptual state is literally included in the perceptual belief, making it impossible to have the belief without having that part of the perceptual state. While this would make introspective beliefs infallible when their content embeds the part of the content of a perceptual state that is the nonconceptual representation of phenomenal properties, it is compatible with it that all beliefs whose content is entirely conceptual are fallible. The self-intimation of phenomenal content would consist in the fact that we are such that when in a perceptual state having a certain phenomenal character, a certain sort of reflective act results in that state, or part of it, being included in a larger state that plays the functional role of a belief embedding the phenomenal part of the content of that state.

While I am attracted by this view, and think that it is worth developing, I am not at all sure it is correct. The single-tokening view faces the difficulty that an introspective belief about the phenomenal character of an experience can be retained in memory after the experience has ceased to exist; the tokening of the embedded content of the memory belief obviously cannot be identical with the no longer existing tokening of the content of the perceptual experience, and

it is unclear how a belief could start by sharing a content tokening with an experience and then come to token that same content in an entirely different way.[24] And any defense of the view that the contents of beliefs can embed nonconceptual contents must take account of the powerful considerations in support of the view that belief content is always conceptual.[25]

XI

What is central to the view advanced in this paper is the claim that the contents of perceptual experiences include representations of properties of external objects (or parts of our bodies) which things have in virtue of appearing to us, or being disposed to appear to us, in certain ways, these being what I call phenomenal properties, and that the phenomenal character of experiences that we are introspectively aware of is this part of their representational content. I think that this view is recommended by the fact that it reconciles representationalism about perceptual content, and the avoidance of phenomenal objects (such as sense-data), with the view that phenomenal character is bestowed by qualia and that inverted qualia and alien qualia are at least conceptually possible. On the present version of this view, unlike the versions in earlier work of mine, our introspective access to the phenomenal character of experiences is equally an access to the qualia that bestow this content, which I hope is a further recommendation of it.[26]

<h2 style="text-align:center">NOTES</h2>

1. See Block and Fodor 1972, and Shoemaker 1975.
2. See Hardin 1988 and Hardin 1997.
3. See Shoemaker 1975 and Shoemaker 1982.
4. The term "alien qualia" comes from Van Gulick 1993.
5. See Levine 1984.
6. See Hardin 1988, and Block 1999.
7. This was perhaps an unfortunate choice of terminology, since the term "phenomenal property" is sometimes used to refer to properties of experiences, i.e., as a synonym of "quale," whereas I am using to to refer to properties of external things. But having made the choice, I will stick with it.
8. See Shoemaker 1994a, and Lecture III of Shoemaker 1994b.
9. See Shoemaker 2000.
10. If we think of the dispositional properties as ones the thing has in virtue of its intrinsic properties, then the specification of the exercise of the disposition will be in conditional terms—it is disposed to appear a

certain way to an observer if the observer is of a certain sort and related in such and such ways to it, and if the illumination conditions are such and such. We can also speak of a dispositional property the object has in virtue of its intrinsic properties plus its current situation, minus any facts about observers. Then the disposition is simply a disposition to appear a certain way to an observer of a certain sort related to it in a certain way. Here the dispositional property will be in part relational—having it will involve being in certain lighting conditions, and perhaps being adjacent or proximal to other objects having thus and such intrinsic properties. Dispositional properties of both kinds will be properties the object can have when not perceived; but while a thing can lose a dispositional property of the first kind only by undergoing an intrinsic change, a thing can lose a dispositional property of the second kind without undergoing any intrinsic change, namely by undergoing of change of situation.

11. See Dretske 1995.
12. Well, beyond question unless one has a very austere view about what it takes to be a genuine property.
13. If a temporary defect in my perceptual system makes something look$_p$ blue, my experience will fail to be veridical, according to the principle stated here. But since the thing does look$_p$ blue to me, won't it have the occurrent appearance property of looking$_p$ blue? One could define "occurrent appearance property" in such a way that this is true; but I think it is better to make it a requirement of something's having such a property that the way it appears$_p$ is not due to a defect in the perceiver's perceptual system.
14. The reason for saying "one or more sorts" rather than "some sort" is that I want to allow that the same appearance property can be observed by observers of different sorts. This must be so if spectrum inversion and the like are possible—for individuals who are spectrum inverted relative to each other will have to be of (at least slightly) different sorts.
15. For the idea of mental "paint" see Harman 1996. Compare Block 1996.
16. Smart 1962.
17. It is quite common to hold that pains can be thought as experiences of bodily damage. But it does not seem right to say that the primary content of these experiences is a proposition having to do with bodi-

ly damage. What these experiences, are, in the first instance, is perceptions representing some part of one's body as instantiating a phenomenal property, e.g., achiness, which is a sign of bodily damage.
18. See Shoemaker 1982 and Shoemaker 1996.
19. I am grateful to many people for helping to persuade me that this is so, including Ned Block, Tyler Burge, David Copp, and Tom Nagel.
20. See Evans 1982, and Peacocke 1992.
21. See Peacocke 1992, p. 61.
22. See Heck forthcoming.
23. McDowell 1994.
24. I am indebted to Jason Stanley and Tyler Burge for objections along these lines.
25. For one argument in support of that view, see Bermundez 1998.
26. This paper is a descendent of a paper I presented at Bowling Green University, the University of Colorado, New York University, and UCLA in the Spring of 2000. I am grateful to the audiences at these places, and in particular to David Copp, George Bealer, Daniel Stoljar, Michael Tooley, Ned Block, Tom Nagel, Tyler Burge, Andrew Hsu, and Michael Thau for comments and criticisms that led me to rethink and extensively revise the paper. Thanks also to Carl Ginet and Benjamin Hellie for comments on the penultimate draft of the present version.

REFERENCES

Bermundez, Jose 1998: *The Pardox of Self-Consciousness.* Cambridge, MA: Bradford-MIT.

Block, N. 1996: "Mental Paint and Mental Latex." *Philosophical Issues,* 7, 19–49.

Block, N. 1999: "Sexism, Racism, Ageism, and the Nature of Consciousness." *Philosophical Topics,* 26, 1&2, 71–88.

Block, N. and Fodor, J. 1972, "What Psychological States Are Not." *The Philosophical Review,* 81, 2, 159–81.

Dretske, F, 1993: "Conscious Experience." *Mind,* 102:406, 263–83.

Dretske, F. 1995: *Naturalizing the Mind.* Cambridge, MA:Bradford-MIT.

Evans, G. 1982: *The Varieties of Reference.* Oxford: The Clarendon Press.

Hardin, C. L. 1988:*Color for Philosophers: Unweaving the Rainbow.* Indianapolis, Indiana: Hackett Publishing Company.

Hardin, C. L. 1997, "Reinverting the Spectrum," in A. Byrne and D. Hilbert, eds., *Readings on Color, Vol. I, The Philosophy of Color.* Cambridge, MA: Bradford-MIT.

Harman, G. 1996: "Explaining Objective Color in Terms of Subjective Experience," *Philosophical Issues,* 7, 1–17.

Heck, R. forthcoming: "Non-Conceptual Content and the 'Space of Reasons.' " *The Philosophical Review.*

Levine, J. 1984: "Materialism and Qualia: The Explanatory Gap." *Pacific Philosophy Quarterly,* 64, 354–61.

McDowell, J. 1994: *Mind and World.* Cambridge, MA: Harvard University Press.

Peacocke, C. 1992: *A Study of Concepts.* Cambridge, MA: Bradford-MIT.

Shoemaker, S. 1975: "Functionalism and Qualia." *Philosophical Studies,* 27, 291–315.

Shoemaker, S. 1982: "The Inverted Spectrum." *Journal of Philosophy,* 79, 7, 357–81.

Shoemaker, S. 1994a: "Phenomenal Character." *Nous,* 28, 21–38.

Shoemaker, S. 1994b: "Introspection and 'Inner Sense.' " *Philosophy and Phenomenological Research,* LIV, 249–314.

Shoemaker, S. 1996: "Intrasubjective/Intersubjective." In S. Shoemaker, *The First-Person Perspective and Other Essays.* Cambridge: Cambridge University Press.

Shoemaker, S. 2000: "Phenomenal Character Revisited." *Philosophy and Phenomenological Research,* LX, 2, 465–68.

Smart, J. J. C. 1962: "Sensations and Brain Processes." In *The Philosophy of Mind,* ed. V. C. Chappell, Englewood Cliffs, N. J.: Prentice Hall. This is a slightly revised version of a paper originally published in *The Philosophical Review,* 68, 1959, 141–56.

Van Gulick, R. 1993: "Understanding the Phenomenal Mind: Are We All Just Armadillos?" in *Consciousness,* ed. M. Davies and G. Humphrey (Oxford: Blackwell), pp. 137–49.

3 Content

A ubiquitous feature of mental states is that they have *content:* that is, they represent features of the world. When I see a tree, my perceptual state represents the tree. When I believe that the Earth is round, my belief represents a state of the Earth. This feature of mental states is often called *intentionality,* or *aboutness.* A belief that Russell was a philosopher is about Russell, a desire to go to heaven is about heaven, and so on. A central feature of this sort of representation is that it can be assessed for *correctness:* my perception of water on the road ahead may be accurate or inaccurate; my belief that it is hot outside may be true or false; my desire for happiness may be satisfied or unsatisfied.

Mental content immediately raises a number of problems. How is it possible for one state of the world to represent another? How can a feature of the world be correct or incorrect? Is it possible to account for mental content in physical terms, and if so how? What is the nature of the states by which we represent the world, especially beliefs and desires? How is the content of our mental states determined? Does this content depend on features internal to the subject, in the environment, or both?

A. The Nature of Intentionality

Franz Brentano, in his 1874 book *Psychology from an Empirical Standpoint,* famously held that intentionality is the mark of the mental. In the selection reproduced here (chapter 44), he raises the question of what distinguishes mental from physical phenomena. He canvases a number of possible answers—that mental phenomena are nonspatial, that they are objects of awareness, and so on—and settles on the claim that mental phenomena exhibit *intentional inexistence:* that is, they contain an *intentional object* within themselves, an object at which they are directed. Physical phenomena are never directed at an intentional object, according to Brentano, but mental phenomena are always directed at such an object.

Roderick Chisholm (chapter 45) takes his cue from Brentano, aiming to to explore the idea of intentional inexistence in more detail. He focuses especially on the idea that the intentional object of a state may not actually exist, as when one believes that there are unicorns, and also on the idea that it is possible for two different states to be directed at the same object. This characterization goes beyond Brentano's, but Chisholm expresses a Brentano-like thesis by saying that descriptions of psychological phenomena involve object-directedness with these features, but descriptions of nonpsychological phenomena do not. He considers three ways in which intentionality might be accounted for in simpler terms—by appeal to linguistic behavior, sign behavior, and expectation—and argues that each of these either presupposes psychological intentionality, or cannot account for the phenomena at issue. The conclusion seems to be that intentionality cannot be explained in nonpsychological, nonintentional terms.

Fred Dretske's paper (chapter 46) can be seen as responding to the Brentano/ Chisholm challenge, examining a way in which the intentionality of mental states might be grounded in the simple nonpsychological phenomena. Dretske argues that the central features of intentionality are present in a system as simple as a compass, which indicates the direction of the North Pole. He uses this sort of example to support a *causal theory* of content, on which a system represents features of its environment when it is causally connected to those features in the right sort of way. One question for such a theory is how a system can *misrepresent* a feature of its environment, but Dretske argues that an appeal to the natural function of the system (grounded in the system's history) can solve this problem. At the end of this paper, he discusses how this sort of intentionality can be extended into the sort of intentionality exhibited by thought.

Ruth Garrett Millikan (chapter 47) responds to the challenge in a different but related way, giving an account of representation that is grounded in the evolutionary functioning of cognitive systems. On this account, the content of a representation is determined by *normal conditions* for proper use of that representation by cognitive systems. Here the normal conditions are grounded in the history of the species as the conditions responsible (via natural selection) for the system's presence in later members of the species. On this account, representation is grounded in evolutionary *teleology,* in combination with the way a representation is used by cognitive systems.

The last two papers explore quite different accounts of the roots of intentionality. Robert Brandom (chapter 48) gives an account on which propositional content is grounded in *reasoning* and *inference:* To a first approximation, a contentful state is one that plays the right sort of role in inference. The specific representational content of these states is grounded in the *social* dimension, through inferential practices involving communication, such as the undertaking of commitment to the judgments of others. Brandom argues that these practices underlie our talk of the truth of mental states, and also underlie our talk of their representational content. He spells out how this works in a specific case, involving attributions of reference through ascriptions of propositional attitudes.

Finally, Terence Horgan and John Tienson (chapter 49) suggest that intentional content is grounded in *phenomenology:* that is, in the character of conscious experience. In a way, this is the reverse of the representationalist claim that phenomenology is grounded in representation. Horgan and Tienson begin by examining the intimate connections between intentionality and phenomenology in both perception and belief. They go on to argue that much intentional content is determined by phenomenology, since any two beings with the same phenomenology will share a great deal of intentional content, irrespective of their other properties. This leads to a very different perspective on intentionality: They conclude that theories on which intentionality is grounded in connections to the environment are fundamentally incorrect, and they suggest that a reductive account of intentionality will be at least as hard as a reductive account of phenomenology.

FURTHER READING

Chisholm's interpretation of Brentano is criticized by McAlister (1974). Dretske (1981, 1991), Millikan (1983, 1995), and Brandom (1994, 2000) elaborate their accounts at book length. The huge literature on theories of content is well represented in Stich and Warfield (1994), which includes criticisms of Dretske's and Millikan's accounts and alternative accounts of content by Fodor (causal), Block (conceptual-role), and Cummins (interpretational). Causal accounts are explored at length by Fodor (1990). Searle (1991) also argues that intentionality requires phenomenology, and Siewert (1998) gives detailed arguments for the claim that phenomenology determines intentional content in both perception and belief.

Brandom, R. 1994. *Making It Explicit.* Harvard University Press.

Brandom, R. 2000. *Articulating Reasons.* Harvard University Press.

Dretske, F. 1981. *Knowledge and the Flow of Information.* MIT Press.

Dretske, F. 1991. *Explaining Behavior.* MIT Press.

Fodor, J. A. 1990. *A Theory of Content and Other Essays.* MIT Press.

McAlister, L. 1974. Chisholm and Brentano on intentionality. *Review of Metaphysics* 28:328–38. Reprinted in L. McAlister (ed.), *The Philosophy of Brentano.* Duckworth, 1976.

Millikan, R. 1983. *Language, Thought, and Other Biological Categories.* MIT Press.

Millikan, R. 1995. *White Queen Psychology and Other Essays for Alice.* MIT Press.

Searle, J. R. 1991. *The Rediscovery of the Mind.* MIT Press.

Siewert, C. 1998. *The Significance of Consciousness.* Princeton University Press.

Stich, S. P., & Warfield, F. (eds.). 1994. *Mental Representation.* Blackwell.

B. Propositional Attitudes

What is the nature of the mental states by which we represent the world? Arguably the most important mental states of this sort are *propositional attitudes,* such as beliefs and desires. These states involve different attitudes to propositions such as the proposition that it is raining outside: One might believe this proposition, or desire that it be true, or hope that it be true, and so on. Propositional attitudes (especially beliefs and related states) are also known as *thoughts.* The papers in this section give various perspectives on the nature of thoughts.

In his important paper "Empiricism and the Philosophy of Mind," Wilfrid Sellars puts forward many key ideas that have been influential in later philosophy. In the first part of the article, he criticizes the "Myth of the Given": roughly, the idea that knowledge of mental states is given to us in some direct and immediate way. In a later part of the article (excerpted here as chapter 50), he suggests that we attribute thoughts to each other as part of a *theory* devised to explain others' behavior. He puts forward this idea in the form of a "myth" about how the notion of thoughts could have become useful to ancestors who did not possess it. He also suggests that thoughts are broadly *linguistic* entities, akin to statements in a language.

Jerry Fodor (chapter 51) pursues this last idea of Sellars' further, arguing that there is a *language of thought*—a sort of internal mental language—and that thoughts are relations to sentences in this mental language. Fodor first sets out a number of conditions that a theory of propositional attitudes should meet, and he then discusses Carnap's idea that thoughts might be relations to sentences of English (or of the thinker's language in general). He argues that English itself will not work for this purpose, but that a distinct mental language might work. This suggestion is put forward as an empirical hypothesis; if it is correct, then there is a very close analogy between thought and language.

Daniel Dennett (chapter 52) offers a very different perspective on the nature of propositional attitudes, and in particular beliefs. Dennett argues that for a system to be a believer, and to have a belief, is for the system to be interpretable in a certain way by someone who adopts the "intentional stance," the stance of predicting a system's behavior using beliefs and desires. On this view, to have a belief is closely tied to exhibiting certain patterns of behavior that allow for the right sort of predictability. Dennett discusses the question of whether beliefs "really" exist on this view, and opts for an intermediate view: There are objective patterns in behavior, but they are sometimes susceptible to multiple interpretations.

Finally, Paul Churchland (chapter 53) gives reasons to hold that propositional attitudes might not exist at all. Like Sellars, Churchland holds that beliefs and desires are entities postulated by a theory used to explain behavior: the commonsense theory known as *folk psychology.* Churchland canvases some reasons to think that this theory may be radically *false:* There are many things it cannot explain, and it may be replaced entirely by a better scientific theory. When a theory is radically false, the entities it postulates are eliminated (as with the phlogiston theory of fire). So if folk psychology is radically false, beliefs and desires do not exist. The resulting view is *eliminativism,* or *eliminative materialism.*

FURTHER READING

Sellars' paper is reprinted in book form (with notes by Brandom) in Sellars (1999), and also (with more extensive notes) in deVries and Triplett (2000). Book-length developments of some of the ideas in this section are given by Fodor (1975, 1987), Dennett (1978, 1987), and Churchland (1990). These ideas are criticized in the respective collections Loewer and Rey (1990), Dahlberg (1993), and McCauley (1996). Field (1978) and Harman (1973) present alternative versions of the language of thought view. A different eliminativist view is outlined by Stich (1983). The question of whether folk psychology is a theory (to be discussed further in the companion volume on philosophy of cognitive science) is addressed by the papers in Davies and Stone (1995) and Greenwood (1991).

Churchland, P. M. 1990. *A Neurocomputational Perspective.* MIT Press.

Dahlberg, B. (ed.). 1993. *Dennett and His Critics.* Blackwell.

Davies, M., and Stone, T. (eds.). 1995. *Folk Psychology: The Theory of Mind Debate.* Blackwell.

Dennett, D. C. 1978. *Brainstorms.* MIT Press.

Dennett, D. C. 1987. *The Intentional Stance.* MIT Press.

deVries, W., and Triplett, T. 2000. *Knowledge, Mind, and the Given.* Hackett.

Field, H. 1978. Mental representation. *Erkenntnis* 13:9–18. Reprinted in Stich and Warfield (1994).

Fodor, J. A. 1975. *The Language of Thought.* Harvard University Press.

Fodor, J. A. 1987. *Psychosemantics.* MIT Press.

Greenwood, J. D. (ed.). 1991. *The Future of Folk Psychology: Intentionality and Cognitive Science.* Cambridge University Press.

Harman, G. 1973. *Thought.* Princeton University Press.

Loewer, B., and Rey, G. 1990. *Meaning in Mind: Fodor and His Critics.* Blackwell.

McCauley, R. 1996. *The Churchlands and Their Critics.* Blackwell.

Sellars, W. 1999. *Empiricism and the Philosophy of Mind.* Harvard University Press.

Stich, S. P. 1983. *From Folk Psychology to Cognitive Science.* MIT Press.

C. Internalism and Externalism

Is the content of our thoughts determined by the internal properties of a subject, by the environment, or both? Almost everyone agrees that our thoughts refer to objects in the world, and that they are affected by the state of the world. Still, the traditional view has been a sort of *internalism,* holding that the *content* of our thoughts is determined by factors internal to the subject, so that any two subjects who are internal duplicates will have thoughts with the same content. More recently, a number of philosophers have argued for *externalism,* holding that the content of our thoughts is often determined by the state of the environment, so that two internally identical subjects may have different thoughts if they are in different environments. This issue has given rise to much fertile debate.

Hilary Putnam's "The Meaning of 'Meaning' " (chapter 54) has provided much of the stimulus for this debate. In this paper, Putnam argues that the meaning of many of our words is not "in the head," but depends on the environment. He introduces the important *Twin Earth* thought-experiment, involving two duplicate subjects living on planets that are superficially identical but that contain different liquids in the oceans and lakes. One (Earth) contains H_2O, and the other (Twin Earth) contains XYZ. Putnam argues that XYZ is not water but something else (twin water), and that when these subjects say 'water,' they mean quite different things. If this is right, then meaning depends directly on the environment. Putnam restricts his conclusion to language, but it is easily extended to the contents of thought. For example, one can argue that one subject *believes* that there is water in the ocean, and the other does not (he believes that there is twin water in the environment). If this is right, it seems to follow that the contents of our thoughts depend on external factors.

Tyler Burge (chapter 55) argues for externalism in a related but different way. He considers duplicate subjects who live in different *social* environments, in which words (such as 'arthritis') are used differently. He argues that as a result, the subjects have different beliefs: One has beliefs about arthritis, and the other has beliefs about a different disease. The result is a kind of *social externalism,* according to which what we think depends on the character of our social community.

Putnam's and Burge's arguments have been highly influential, and many philosophers have accepted their conclusions. Some have argued in response that even if some aspects of content depend on the environment, there is an important aspect of content that is determined wholly internally. My paper in this section (chapter 56) develops this sort of response, arguing for a two-dimensional view of content on which the most important dimension, *epistemic content,* is independent of the environment. On this sort of view, while there is some truth in externalism (one dimension of content depends on the environment), there is still much truth in internalism.

If externalism is true, it has important consequences. There has been considerable debate about just what these consequences are. Michael McKinsey (chapter 57) argues that if externalism is true, it follows that we cannot know the contents of our thoughts simply by reflecting, since we cannot know the state of the environment by reflecting. Both internalists and externalists often find this consequence unacceptable. Anthony Brueckner (chapter 58) argues that it is not in fact a consequence of externalism: He argues that McKinsey's argument fails and that externalism is fully compatible with reflective self-knowledge.

Finally, Andy Clark and David Chalmers (chapter 59) make a case for a very different sort of externalism, involving the active coupling of an organism with its environment. In cases where parts of the environment are fully integrated with a cognitive system (as with a notebook that serves as a memory), those parts of the environment count as part of the cognitive system, and help to constitute the mental states of the subject in question. Clark and Chalmers call this view *active externalism,* as opposed to the "passive externalism" of Putnam and Burge, and argue that it coheres well with a recent body of work in cognitive science.

FURTHER READING

Many important papers on internalism and externalism are collected in Pessin and Goldberg (1996). Burge (1982) extends Putnam's thought experiment to the mental realm. Internalist responses to these are presented by Fodor (1987), Loar (1987), Searle (1983), and Segal (2000), while externalist positions are elaborated by Stalnaker (1999) and

Wilson (1995). Horgan and Tienson (chapter 49) argue for a sort of internalism based on phenomenological considerations; Tye (chapter 42) gives an externalist view of the contents of phenomenology. Block and Stalnaker (chapter 37, section 10) address a version of the two-dimensional view presented by Chalmers. Ludlow and Martin (1998) is a collection of articles on externalism and self-knowledge, developing the themes addressed by McKinsey and Brueckner. Active externalist views are elaborated by Clark (1996), Haugeland (1995), and Hurley (1998) and are criticized by Adams and Aizawa (2001).

Adams, F. & Aizawa, K. 2001. The bounds of cognition. *Philosophical Psychology* 14:43–64.

Burge, T. 1982. Other bodies. In A. Woodfield (ed.), *Thought and Object.* Oxford University Press.

Clark, A. 1996. *Being There: Putting Brain, Body, and World Together Again.* MIT Press.

Fodor, J. 1987. *Psychosemantics.* MIT Press.

Haugeland, J. 1995. Mind embodied and embedded. In Y. Houng and J. Ho (eds.), *Mind and Cognition.* Taipei: Academia Sinica. Reprinted in Haugeland, *Having Thought.* Harvard University Press.

Hurley, S. 1998. *Consciousness in Action.* Harvard University Press.

Loar, B. 1987. Social content and psychological content. In R. Grimm and D. Merrill (eds.), *Contents of Thought.* University of Arizona Press. Reprinted in Pessin and Goldberg (1996).

Ludlow, P., and Martin, N. 1998. *Externalism and Self-Knowledge.* CSLI Press.

Pessin, A., and Goldberg. S. 1996. *The Twin Earth Chronicles: Twenty Years of Reflection on Putnam's 'The Meaning of Meaning.'* M.E. Sharpe, Inc.

Searle, J. R. 1983. *Intentionality.* Cambridge University Press.

Segal, G. 2000. *A Slim Book about Narrow Content.* MIT Press.

Stalnaker, R. 1999. *Context and Content.* Oxford University Press.

Wilson, R. A. 1995. *Cartesian Psychology and Physical Minds: Individualism and the Sciences of the Mind.* Cambridge University Press.

The Distinction between Mental and Physical Phenomena

44

Franz Brentano

1. All the data of our consciousness are divided into two great classes—the class of physical and the class of mental phenomena. We spoke of this distinction earlier when we established the concept of psychology, and we returned to it again in our discussion of psychological method. But what we have said is still not sufficient. We must now establish more firmly and more exactly what was only mentioned in passing before.

This seems all the more necessary since neither agreement nor complete clarity has been achieved regarding the delimitation of the two classes. We have already seen how physical phenomena which appear in the imagination are sometimes taken for mental phenomena. There are many other such instances of confusion. And even important psychologists may be hard pressed to defend themselves against the charge of self-contradiction. For instance, we encounter statements like the following: sensation and imagination are distinguished by the fact that one occurs as the result of a physical phenomenon, while the other is evoked by a mental phenomenon according to the laws of association. But then the same psychologists admit that what appears in sensation does not correspond to its efficient cause. Thus it turns out that the so-called physical phenomenon does not actually appear to us, and, indeed, that we have no presentation of it whatsoever—certainly a curious misuse of the term "phenomenon"! Given such a state of affairs, we cannot avoid going into the question in somewhat greater detail.

2. The explanation we are seeking is not a definition according to the traditional rules of logic. These rules have recently been the object of impartial criticism, and much could be added to what has already been said. Our aim is to clarify the meaning of the two terms *"physical phenomenon"* and *"mental phenomenon,"* removing all misunderstanding and confusion concerning them. And it does not matter to us what means we use, as long as they really serve to clarify these terms.

To this end, it is not sufficient merely to specify more general, more inclusive definitions. Just as deduction is opposed to induction when we speak of kinds of proof, in this case explanation by means of subsumption under a general term is opposed to explanation by means of particulars, through examples. And the latter kind of explanation is appropriate whenever the particular terms are clearer than the general ones. Thus it is probably a more effective procedure to explain the term "color" by saying that it designates the class which contains red, blue, green and yellow, than to do the opposite and attempt to explain "red" by saying it is a particular kind of color. Moreover, explanation through particular definitions will be of even greater use when we are dealing, as in our case, with terms which are not common in ordinary life, while those for the individual phenomena included under them are frequently used. So let us first of all try to clarify the concepts by means of examples.

Every idea or presentation which we acquire either through sense perception or imagination is an example of a mental phenomenon. By presentation I do not mean that which is presented, but rather the act of presentation. Thus, hearing a sound, seeing a colored object, feeling warmth or cold, as well as similar states of imagination are examples of what I mean by this term. I also mean by it the thinking of a general concept, provided such a thing actually does occur. Furthermore, every judgement, every recollection, every expectation, every inference, every conviction or opinion, every doubt, is a mental phenomenon. Also to be in-

Excerpted from D. Terrell, A. Rancurello, and L. McAlister, trans.; L. McAlister, ed., *Psychology from an Empirical Standpoint* (Routledge, 1995). Reprinted with permission of the publisher.

cluded under this term is every emotion: joy, sorrow, fear, hope, courage, despair, anger, love, hate, desire, act of will, intention, astonishment, admiration, contempt, etc.

Examples of physical phenomena, on the other hand, are a color, a figure, a landscape which I see, a chord which I hear, warmth, cold, odor which I sense; as well as similar images which appear in the imagination.

These examples may suffice to illustrate the differences between the two classes of phenomena.

3. Yet we still want to try to find a different and a more unified way of explaining mental phenomena. For this purpose we make use of a definition we used earlier when we said that the term "mental phenomena" applies to presentations as well as to all the phenomena which are based upon presentations. It is hardly necessary to mention again that by "presentation" we do not mean that which is presented, but rather the presenting of it. This act of presentation forms the foundation not merely of the act of judging, but also of desiring and of every other mental act. Nothing can be judged, desired, hoped or feared, unless one has a presentation of that thing. Thus the definition given includes all the examples of mental phenomena which we listed above, and in general all the phenomena belonging to this domain.

It is a sign of the immature state of psychology that we can scarcely utter a single sentence about mental phenomena which will not be disputed by many people. Nevertheless, most psychologists agree with what we have just said, namely, that presentations are the foundation for the other mental phenomena. Thus Herbart asserts quite rightly, "Every time we have a feeling, there will be something or other presented in consciousness, even though it may be something very diversified, confused and varied, so that this particular presentation is included in this particular feeling. Likewise, whenever we desire something . . . we have before our minds that which we desire."[1] . . .

Accordingly, we may consider the following definition of mental phenomena as indubitably correct: they are either presentations or they are based upon presentations in the sense described above. Such a definition offers a second, more simple explanation of this concept. This explanation, of course, is not completely unified because it separates mental phenomena into two groups.

4. People have tried to formulate a complete-ly unified definition which distinguishes all mental phenomena from physical phenomena by means of negation. All physical phenomena, it is said, have extension and spatial location, whether they are phenomena of vision or of some other sense, or products of the imagination, which presents similar objects to us. The opposite, however, is true of mental phenomena; thinking, willing and the like appear without extension and without spatial location.

According to this view, it would be possible for us to characterize physical phenomena easily and exactly in contrast to mental phenomena by saying that they are those phenomena which appear extended and localized in space. Mental phenomena would then be definable with equal exactness as those phenomena which do not have extension or spatial location. Descartes and Spinoza could be cited in support of such a distinction. The chief advocate of this view, however, is Kant, who explains space as the form of the intuition of the external sense. . . .

But even on this point there is no unanimity among psychologists, and we hear it denied for contradictory reasons that extension and lack of extension are characteristics which distinguish physical and mental phenomena.

Many declare that this definition is false because not only mental phenomena, but also many physical phenomena appear to be without extension. A large number of not unimportant psychologists, for example, teach that the phenomena of some, or even of all of our senses originally appear apart from all extension and spatial location. In particular, this view is quite generally held with respect to sounds and olfactory phenomena. . . .

Others, as we said, will reject this definition for the opposite reason. It is not so much the assertion that all physical phenomena appear extended that provokes them, but rather the assertion that all mental phenomena lack extension. According to them, certain mental phenomena also appear to be extended. Aristotle seems to have been of this opinion when, in the first chapter of this treatise on sense and sense objects he considers it immediately evident, without any prior proof, that sense perception is the act of a bodily organ.[2] Modern psychologists and physiologists sometimes express themselves in the same way regarding certain affects. They speak of feelings of pleasure or pain which appear in the external organs, sometimes even after the amputation of the limb and yet, feeling, like perception, is a mental phenomenon. Some authors even maintain that sensory appetites appear localized. This view is shared by the poet when he speaks, not, to be sure, of thought, but of rapture and longing which suffuse the heart and all parts of the body.

Thus we see that the distinction under discussion is disputed from the point of view of both physical and mental phenomena. Perhaps both of these objections are equally unjustified.[3] At any rate, another definition common to all mental phenomena is still desirable. Whether certain mental and physical phenomena appear extended or not, the controversy proves that the criterion given for a clear separation is not adequate. Furthermore, this criterion gives us only a negative definition of mental phenomena.

5. What positive criterion shall we now be able to provide? Or is there perhaps no positive definition which holds true of all mental phenomena generally? Bain thinks that in fact there is none.[4] Nevertheless, psychologists in earlier times have already pointed out that there is a special affinity and analogy which exists among all mental phenomena, and which physical phenomena do not share.

Every mental phenomenon is characterized by what the Scholastics of the Middle Ages called the intentional (or mental)[5] inexistence of an object, and what we might call, though not wholly unambiguously, reference to a content, direction toward an object (which is not to be understood here as meaning a thing), or immanent objectivity. Every mental phenomenon includes something as object within itself, although they do not all do so in the same way. In presentation something is presented, in judgement something is affirmed or denied, in love loved, in hate hated, in desire desired and so on.[6]

This intentional in-existence is characteristic exclusively of mental phenomena. No physical phenomenon exhibits anything like it. We can, therefore, define mental phenomena by saying that they are those phenomena which contain an object intentionally within themselves.

But here, too, we come upon controversies and contradiction. Hamilton, in particular, denies this characteristic to a whole broad class of mental phenomena, namely, to all those which he characterizes as feelings, to pleasure and pain in all their most diverse shades and varieties. With respect to the phenomena of thought and desire he is in agreement with us. Obviously there is no act of thinking without an object that is thought, nor a desire without an object that is desired. "In the phenomena of Feelings—

the phenomena of Pleasure and Pain—on the contrary, consciousness does not place the mental modification or state before itself; it does not contemplate it apart—as separate from itself—but is, as it were, fused into one. The peculiarity of Feeling, therefore, is that there is nothing but what is subjectively subjective; there is no object different from the self—no objectification of any mode of self."[7] In the first instance there would be something which, according to Hamilton's terminology, is "objective," in the second instance something which is "objectively subjective," as in self-awareness, the object of which Hamilton consequently calls the "subject-object." By denying both concerning feelings, Hamilton rejects unequivocally all intentional in-existence of these phenomena.

In reality, what Hamilton says is not entirely correct, since certain feelings undeniably refer to objects. Our language itself indicates this through the expressions it employs. We say that we are pleased with or about something, that we feel sorrow or grieve about something. Likewise, we say: that pleases me, that hurts me, that makes me feel sorry, etc. Joy and sorrow, like affirmation and negation, love and hate, desire and aversion, clearly follow upon a presentation and are related to that which is presented.

One is most inclined to agree with Hamilton in those cases in which, as we saw earlier, it is most easy to fall into the error that feeling is not based upon any presentation: the case of pain caused by a cut or a burn, for example. But the reason is simply the same temptation toward this, as we have seen, erroneous assumption. Even Hamilton recognizes with us the fact that presentations occur without exception and thus even here they form the basis of the feeling. Thus his denial that feelings have an object seems all the more striking.

One thing certainly has to be admitted; the object to which a feeling refers is not always an external object. Even in cases where I hear a harmonious sound, the pleasure which I feel is not actually pleasure in the sound but pleasure in the hearing. In fact you could say, not incorrectly, that in a certain sense it even refers to itself, and this introduces, more or less, what Hamilton was talking about, namely that the feeling and the object are "fused into one." But this is nothing that is not true in the same way of many phenomena of thought and knowledge, as we will see when we come to the investigation of inner consciousness. Still they retain a mental inexistence, a Subject-Object, to use Hamilton's mode of speech, and the same thing is true of these feelings. Hamilton is wrong when he says that with regard to feelings everything is "subjectively subjective"—an expression which is actually self-contradictory, for where you cannot speak of an object, you cannot speak of a subject either. Also, Hamilton spoke of a fusing into one of the feeling with the mental impression, but when carefully considered it can be seen that he is bearing witness against himself here. Every fusion is a unification of several things; and thus the pictorial expression which is intended to make us concretely aware of the distinctive character of feeling still points to a certain duality in the unity.

We may, therefore, consider the intentional inexistence of an object to be a general characteristic of mental phenomena which distinguishes this class of phenomena from the class of physical phenomena.

6. Another characteristic which all mental phenomena have in common is the fact that they are only perceived in inner consciousness, while in the case of physical phenomena only external perception is possible. This distinguishing characteristic is emphasized by Hamilton.[8]

It could be argued that such a definition is not very meaningful. In fact, it seems much more natural to define the act according to the object, and therefore to state that inner perception, in contrast to every other kind, is the perception of mental phenomena. However, besides the fact that it has a special object, inner perception possesses another distinguishing characteristic: its immediate, infallible self-evidence. Of all the types of knowledge of the objects of experience, inner perception alone possesses this characteristic. Consequently, when we say that mental phenomena are those which are apprehended by means of inner perception, we say that their perception is immediately evident.

Moreover, inner perception is not merely the only kind of perception which is immediately evident; it is really the only perception in the strict sense of the word.[9] As we have seen, the phenomena of the so-called external perception cannot be proved true and real even by means of indirect demonstration. For this reason, anyone who in good faith has taken them for what they seem to be is being misled by the manner in which the phenomena are connected. Therefore, strictly speaking, so-called external perception is not perception. Mental phenomena, therefore, may be described as the only phenomena of which perception in the strict sense of the word is possible.

This definition, too, is an adequate characterization of mental phenomena. That is not to say that all mental phenomena are internally perceivable by all men, and so all those which someone cannot perceive are to be included by him among physical phenomena. On the contrary, as we have already expressly noted above, it is obvious that no mental phenomenon is perceived by more than one individual. At the same time, however, we also saw that every type of mental phenomenon is present in every fully developed human mental life. For this reason, the reference to the phenomena which constitute the realm of inner perception serves our purpose satisfactorily.

7. We said that mental phenomena are those phenomena which alone can be perceived in the strict sense of the word. We could just as well say that they are those phenomena which alone possess real existence as well as intentional existence. Knowledge, joy and desire really exist. Color, sound and warmth have only a phenomenal and intentional existence.

There are philosophers who go so far as to say that it is self-evident that phenomena such as those which we call physical phenomena *could not* correspond to any reality. . . .

I must confess that I am unable to convince myself of the soundness of this argument. It is undoubtedly true that a color appears to us only when we have a presentation of it. We cannot conclude from this, however, that a color cannot exist without being presented. Only if the state of being presented were contained in the color as one of its elements, as a certain quality and intensity is contained in it, would a color which is not presented imply a contradiction, since a whole without one of its parts is indeed a contradiction. But this is obviously not the case. . . .

It is not correct, therefore, to say that the assumption that there exists a physical phenomenon outside the mind which is just as real as those which we find intentionally in us, implies a contradiction. It is only that, when we compare one with the other we discover conflicts which clearly show that no real existence corresponds to the intentional existence in this case. And even if this applies only to the realm of our own experience, we will nevertheless make no mistake if in general we deny to physical phenomena any existence other than intentional existence.

8. There is still another circumstance which people have said distinguishes between physical and mental phenomena. They say that mental phenomena always manifest themselves serially, while many physical phenomena manifest

themselves simultaneously. But people do not always mean the same thing by this assertion, and not all of the meanings which it has been given are in accord with the truth. . . .

Indeed, we could, with more reason, make the opposite assertion, namely, that very often many mental phenomena are present in consciousness simultaneously, while there can never be more than one physical phenomenon at a time.

What is the only sense, then, in which we might say that a mental phenomenon always appears by itself, while many physical phenomena can appear at the same time? We can say this insofar as the whole multiplicity of mental phenomena which appear to us in our inner perception always appear as a unity, while the same is not true of the physical phenomena which we grasp simultaneously through the so-called external perception. As happens frequently in other cases, so here, too, unity is confused by many psychologists with simplicity; as a result they have maintained that they perceive themselves in inner consciousness as something simple. Others, in contesting with good reason the simplicity of this phenomenon, at the same time denied its unity. The former could not maintain a consistent position because, as soon as they described their inner life, they found that they were mentioning a large variety of different elements; and the latter could not avoid involuntarily testifying to the unity of mental phenomena. They speak, as do others, of an "I" and not of a "we" and sometimes describe this as a "bundle" of phenomena, and at the other times by other names which characterize a fusion into an inner unity. When we perceive color, sound, warmth, odor simultaneously nothing prevents us from assigning each one to a particular thing. On the other hand, we are forced to take the multiplicity of the various acts of sensing, such as seeing, hearing, experiencing warmth and smelling, and the simultaneous acts of willing and feeling and reflecting, as well as the inner perception which provides us with the knowledge of all those, as parts of one single phenomenon in which they are contained, as one single and unified thing. We shall discuss in detail later on what consti-

tutes the basis for this necessity. At that time we shall also present several other points pertaining to the same subject. The topic under discussion, in fact, is nothing other than the so-called unity of consciousness, one of the most important, but still contested, facts of psychology.

9. Let us, in conclusion, summarize the results of the discussion about the difference between mental and physical phenomena. First of all, we illustrated the specific nature of the two classes by means of *examples.* We then defined mental phenomena as *presentations* or as phenomena which are based *upon presentation;* all the other phenomena being physical phenomena. Next we spoke of *extension,* which psychologists have asserted to be the specific characteristic of all physical phenomena, while all mental phenomena are supposed to be unextended. This assertion, however, ran into contradictions which can only be clarified by later investigations. All that can be determined now is that all mental phenomena really appear to be unextended. Further we found that the *intentional inexistence,* the reference to something as an object, is a distinguishing characteristic of all mental phenomena. No physical phenomenon exhibits anything similar. We went on to define mental phenomena as the exclusive *object of inner perception;* they alone, therefore, are perceived with immediate evidence. Indeed, in the strict sense of the word, they alone are perceived. On this basis we proceeded to define them as the only phenomena which possess *actual existence* in addition to intentional existence. Finally, we emphasized as a distinguishing characteristic the fact that the mental phenomena which we perceive, in spite of all their multiplicity, *always* appear to us *as a unity,* while physical phenomena, which we perceive at the same time, do not all appear in the same way as parts of one single phenomenon.

That feature which best characterizes mental phenomena is undoubtedly their intentional inexistence. By means of this and the other characteristics listed above, we may now consider mental phenomena to have been clearly differentiated from physical phenomena. . . .

NOTES

1. *Psychologie als Wissenschaft,* Part II, Sect. 1, Chap. 1, No. 103. Cp. also Drobisch, *Empirische Psychologie,* p. 38, and others of Herbart's school.
2. *De Sensu et Sensibili,* 1, 436, b. 7. Cp. also what he says in *De Anima,* I, 1, 403, 16, about affective states, in particular about fear.
3. The assertion that even mental phenomena appear to be extended rests obviously on a confusion of mental and physical phenomena similar to the confusion which we became convinced of above when we pointed out that a presentation is also the necessary foundation of sensory feelings.

4. *The Senses and the Intellect,* Introduction.

5. They also use the expression "to exist as an object (objectively) in something," which, if we wanted to use it at the present time, would be considered, on the contrary, as a designation of a real existence outside the mind. At least this is what is suggested by the expression "to exist immanently as an object," which is occasionally used in a similar sense, and in which the term "immanent" should obviously rule out the misunderstanding which is to be feared.

6. Aristotle himself spoke of this mental in-existence. In his books on the soul he says that the sensed object, as such, is in the sensing subject; that the sense contains the sensed object without its matter; that the object which is thought is in the thinking intellect. In Philo, likewise, we find the doctrine of mental existence and in-existence. However, since he confuses them with existence in the proper sense of the word, he reaches his contradictory doctrine of the *logos* and Ideas. The same is true of the Neoplatonists. St. Augustine in his doctrine of the *Verbum mentis* and of its inner origin touches upon the same fact. St. Anselm does the same in his famous ontological argument; many people have observed that his consideration of mental existence as a true existence is at the basis of his paralogism (cp. Überweg, *Geschichte der Philosophie,* II). St. Thomas Aquinas teaches that the object which is thought is intentionally in the thinking subject, the object which is loved in the person who loves, the object which is desired in the person desiring, and he uses this for theological purposes.

7. *Lecture on Metaphysics,* I, 432.

8. *Lecture on Metaphysics,* I, 432.

9. [Translators' note: The German word which we translate as "perception" is "*Wahrnehmung*" which literally means taking something to be true. The English word does not reflect this literal meaning so this paragraph only makes sense if we bear in mind the German word.]

"Intentional Inexistence"

Roderick M. Chisholm

1

. . . Psychological phenomena, according to Brentano, are characterized "by what the scholastics of the Middle Ages referred to as the intentional (also the mental) inexistence of the object, and what we, although with not quite unambiguous expressions, would call relation to a content, direction upon an object (which is not here to be understood as a reality), or immanent objectivity."[1] This "intentional inexistence," Brentano added, is peculiar to what is psychical; things which are merely physical show nothing like it.

Assuming, or *accepting,* is one of the phenomena Brentano would have called intentional. I will first try to formulate Brentano's thesis somewhat more exactly; then I will ask whether it is true of assuming.

2

The phenomena most clearly illustrating the concept of "intentional inexistence" are what are sometimes called psychological attitudes; for example, desiring, hoping, wishing, seeking, believing, and assuming. When Brentano said that these attitudes "intentionally contain an object in themselves," he was referring to the fact that they can be truly said to "have objects" even though the objects which they can be said to have do not in fact exist. Diogenes could have looked for an honest man even if there hadn't been any honest men. The horse can desire to be fed even though he won't be fed. James could believe there are tigers in India, and *take* something there to be a tiger, even if there aren't any tigers in India.

But *physical*—or nonpsychological—phenomena, according to Brentano's thesis, cannot thus "intentionally contain objects in themselves." In order for Diogenes to sit in his tub, for example, there must be a tub for him to sit in; in order for the horse to eat his oats, there must be oats for him to eat; and in order for James to shoot a tiger, there must be a tiger there to shoot.

The statements used in these examples seem

From *Perceiving: A Philosophical Study* (Cornell University Press, 1957).

to have the form of relational statements. "Diogenes sits in his tub" is concerned with a relation between Diogenes and his tub. Syntactically, at least, "Diogenes looks for an honest man" is similar: Diogenes' quest seems to relate him in a certain way to honest men. But the relations described in this and in our other psychological statements, if they can properly be called "relations," are of a peculiar sort. They can hold even though one of their terms, if it can properly be called a "term," does not exist. It may seem, therefore, that one can be "intentionally related" to something which does not exist.[2]

These points can be put somewhat more precisely by referring to the language we have used. We may say that, in our language, the expressions "looks for," "expects," and "believes" occur in sentences which are intentional, or are used intentionally, whereas "sits in," "eats," and "shoots" do not. We can formulate a working criterion by means of which we can distinguish sentences that are intentional, or are used intentionally, in a certain language from sentences that are not. It is easy to see, I think, what this criterion would be like, if stated for ordinary English.

First, let us say that a simple declarative sentence is intentional if it uses a substantival expression—a name or a description—in such a way that neither the sentence nor its contradictory implies either that there is or that there isn't anything to which the substantival expression truly applies. "Diogenes looked for an honest man" is intentional by this criterion. Neither "Diogenes looked for an honest man" nor its contradictory—"Diogenes did *not* look for an honest man"—implies either that there are, or that there are not, any honest men. But "Diogenes sits in his tub" is not intentional by this criterion, for it implies that there *is* a tub in which he sits.

Secondly, let us say, of any noncompound sentence which contains a propositional clause, that it is intentional provided that neither the sentence nor its contradictory implies either that the propositional clause is true or that it is false. "James believes there are tigers in India" is intentional by this criterion, because neither it nor its contradictory implies either that there are, or that there are not, any tigers in India. "He succeeded in visiting India," since it implies that he did visit India, is not intentional. "He is able to visit India," although it does not imply that he will visit India, is also not intentional. For its contradictory—"He is not able to visit India"—implies that he does *not* visit India.

A third mark of intentionality may be described in this way. Suppose there are two names or descriptions which designate the same things and that E is a sentence obtained merely by separating these two names or descriptions by means of "is identical with" (or "are identical with" if the first word is plural). Suppose also that A is a sentence using one of those names or descriptions and that B is like A except that, where A uses the one, B uses the other. Let us say that A is intentional if the conjunction of A and E does not imply B.[3] We can now say of certain cognitive sentences—sentences using "know," "see," "perceive," and the like in one of the ways which have interested us here—that they, too, are intentional. Most of us knew in 1944 that Eisenhower was the one in command (A); but although he was (identical with) the man who was to succeed Truman (E), it is not true that we knew in 1944 that the man who was to succeed Truman was the one in command (B).

Let us say that a *compound* sentence is one compounded from two or more sentences by means of propositional connectives, such as "and," "or," "if-then," "although," "because," and the like. The three foregoing marks of intentionality apply to sentences which are *not* compound. We may now say that a compound declarative sentence is intentional if and only if one or more of its component sentences is intentional. Thus the antecedent of "If Parsifal sought the Holy Grail, he was a Christian" enables us to say that the whole statement is intentional.

When we use perception words propositionally, our sentences display the third of the above marks of intentionality. I may see that John is the man in the corner and John may be someone who is ill; but I do not now *see* that John is someone who is ill. Perception sentences, as we have seen, entail sentences about taking and assuming. And sentences about taking and assuming display the second of the above marks of intentionality. "He takes—and therefore assumes—those rocks to be the reef" does not imply that the rocks *are* the reef and it does not imply that they are not. And similarly for its contradiction: "He does not take—or assume—those rocks to be the reef."

We may now re-express Brentano's thesis—or a thesis resembling that of Brentano—by reference to intentional sentences. Let us say (1) that we do not need to use intentional sentences when we describe nonpsychological phenomena; we can express all of our beliefs about what is merely "physical" in sentences which are not intentional.[4] But (2) when we wish to describe perceiving, assuming, believing, knowing, wanting, hoping, and other such attitudes, then either (a) we must use sentences which are intentional or (b) we must use terms we do not need to use when we describe nonpsychological phenomena.

In describing nonpsychological phenomena, we do, on occasion, use sentences which are intentional by one or more of the above criteria. One may say, "This weapon, suitably placed, is capable of causing the destruction of Boston" and "The cash register knows that 7 and 5 are 12." But although these sentences are intentional according to our criteria, we can readily transform them into others which are not: "If this weapon were suitably placed, then Boston would be destroyed" and "If you press the key marked '7' and the one marked '5', the cash register will yield a slip marked '12'."

It would be an easy matter, of course, to invent a psychological terminology enabling us to describe perceiving, taking, and assuming in sentences which are not intentional. Instead of saying, for example, that a man *takes* something to be a deer, we could say "His perceptual environment is deer-inclusive." But in so doing, we are using technical terms—"perceptual environment" and "deer-inclusive"—which, presumably, are not needed for the description of nonpsychological phenomena. And unless we can re-express the deer-sentence once again, this time as a nonintentional sentence containing no such technical terms, what we say about the man and the deer will conform to our present version of Brentano's thesis.

How would we go about showing that Brentano was wrong? I shall consider the three most likely methods. None of them seems to be satisfactory.

3

Some philosophers have tried to describe psychological attitudes in terms of *linguistic* behavior. In his inaugural lecture, *Thinking and Meaning,* Professor Ayer tried to define the locution "thinking of *x*" by reference to the use of symbols which designate *x*. A man is *thinking of* a unicorn, Ayer suggested, if (among other things) the man is disposed to use symbols which *designate* unicorns; he *believes* that there are unicorns if (among other things) he is disposed to utter sentences containing words

which *designate* or *refer* to unicorns.[5] And perhaps one might try to define "taking" and "assuming" in a similar way. But this type of definition leaves us with our problem.

When we talk about what is "designated" or "referred to" by words or sentences, our own sentences are intentional. When we affirm the sentence "In German, *Einhorn* designates, or refers to, unicorns," we do not imply that there are any unicorns and we do not imply that there are not; and similarly when we deny the sentence. If we think of words and sentences as classes of noises and marks, then we may say that words and sentences are "physical" (nonpsychological) phenomena. But we must not suppose the meaning of words and sentences to be a property which they have apart from their relations to the psychological attitudes of the people who *use* them.

For we know, as Schlick once put it, "that meaning does not inhere in a sentence where it might be discovered"; meaning "must be bestowed upon" the sentence.[6] Instead of saying, "In German, *Einhorn* designates, or refers to, unicorns," we could say, less misleadingly, "German-speaking people use the word *Einhorn* in order to designate, or refer to, unicorns." A word or sentence designates so-and-so only if people *use* it to designate so-and-so.

Or can we describe "linguistic behavior" by means of sentences which are not intentional? Can we define such locutions as "the word '*Q*' designates so-and-so" in language which is not intentional? If we can do these things, and if, as Ayer suggested, we can define "believing," or "assuming," in terms of linguistic behavior, then we must reject our version of Brentano's thesis. But I do not believe that we can do these things; I do not believe that we can define such locutions as "The word '*Q*' designates so-and-so" or "The word '*Q*' has such-and-such a *use*" in language which is not intentional.

Let us consider, briefly, the difficulties involved in one attempt to formulate such a definition.

Instead of saying, of a certain word or predicate of "*Q*", that it designates or refers to so-and-so's, we may say that, if there were any so-and-so's, they would satisfy or fulfill the *intension* of the predicate "*Q*", But how are we to define "intension"? Professor Carnap once proposed a behavioristic definition of this use of "intension" which, if it were adequate, might enable us to formulate a behavioristic, nonintentional definition of "believe" and "assume." Although Carnap later conceded that his account was over-simplified, it is instructive, I think, to note the difficulties which stand in the way of defining "intension"—as well as "designates" and "refers to"—in nonintentional terms.[7]

Carnap had suggested that the "intension" of a predicate in a natural language may be defined in essentially this way: "The intension of a predicate 'Q' for a speaker X is the general condition which an object y must fulfill in order for X to be willing to ascribe the predicate 'Q' to y." Carnap did not define the term "ascribe" which appears in this definition, but from his general discussion we can see, I think, that he would have said something very much like this: "A person X ascribes 'Q' to an object y, provided that, in the presence of y, X gives an affirmative response to the question 'Q?'" (Let us assume that the expressions "is willing to," "in the presence of," "affirmative response," and "question" present no difficulties.)

Such a definition of "intension" is adequate only if it allows us to say of Karl, who speaks German, that an object y fulfills the intension of "*Hund*" for Karl if and only if y is a dog. Let us consider, then, a situation in which Karl mistakes something for a dog; he is in the presence of a fox, say, and takes it to be a dog. In this case, Karl would be willing to give an affirmative response to the question "*Hund?*" Hence the fox fulfills the condition which an object must fulfill for Karl to be willing to ascribe "*Hund*" to it. And therefore the definition is inadequate.

Perhaps we can assume that Karl is usually right when he takes something to be a dog. And perhaps, therefore, we can say this: "The intension of '*Hund*' for Karl is the general condition which, more often than not, an object y must fulfill in order for Karl to be willing to ascribe '*Hund*' to y." But if the occasion we have considered is the only one on which Karl has been in the presence of a *fox*, then, according to the present suggestion, we must say, falsely, that the fox does not fulfill the intension of Karl's word "*Fuchs*". Moreover, if Karl believes there are unicorns and, on the sole occasion when he thinks he sees one, mistakes a horse for a unicorn, then the present suggestion would require us to say, falsely, that the horse fulfills the intension, for Karl, of his word "*Einhorn*".

The obvious way to qualify Carnap's definition would be to reintroduce the term "believe" and say something of this sort: "The intension of a predicate 'Q' for a speaker X is the general

condition which X must *believe* an object y to fulfill in order for X to be willing to ascribe the predicate 'Q' to y." And, in general, when we say, "People use such and such a word to refer to so-and-so," at least part of what we mean to say is that people use that word when they wish to express or convey something they *know* or *believe*—or *perceive* or *take*—with respect to so-and-so. But if we define "intension" and "designates" in terms of "believe" and "assume," we can no longer hope, of course, to define "believe" and "assume" in terms of "intension" or "designates."

4

The second way in which we might try to show that Brentano was wrong may be described by reference to a familiar conception of "sign behavior." Many philosophers and psychologists have suggested, in effect, that a man may be said to *perceive* an object x, or to *take* some object x to have a certain property f, provided only that there is something which *signifies* x to him, or which signifies to him that x is f. But what does "signify" mean?

We cannot be satisfied with the traditional descriptions of "sign behavior," for these, almost invariably, define such terms as "sign" by means of intentional concepts. We cannot say, for instance, that an object is a sign provided it causes someone to *believe,* or *expect,* or *think of* something; for sentences using "believe," "expect," and "think of" are clearly intentional. Nor can we say merely that an object is a sign provided it causes someone to be *set for,* or to be *ready for,* or to *behave appropriately to* something, for sentences using "set for," "ready for," and "behave appropriately to," despite their behavioristic overtones, are also intentional. Similar objections apply to such statements as "One object is a sign of another provided it *introduces* the other object *into the behaviorial environment,* as contrasted with the physical environment, of some organism."

If we are to show that Brentano's thesis as applied to *sign* phenomena is mistaken, then we must not introduce any new technical terms into our analysis of sign behavior unless we can show that these terms apply also to nonpsychological situations.

Most attempts at nonintentional definitions of "sign" make use of the concept of *substitute stimulus.* If we use "referent" as short for "what is signified," we may say that, according to such definitions, the sign is described as a substitute for the referent. It is a substitute in the sense that, as stimulus, it has effects upon the subject which are similar to those the referent would have had. Such definitions usually take this form: V is a *sign* of R for a subject S if and only if V affects S in a manner similar to that in which R would have affected S.[8] The bell is a sign of food to the dog, because the bell affects the dog's responses, or his dispositions to respond, in a way similar to that in which the food would have affected them.

This type of definition involves numerous difficulties of which we need mention but one—that of specifying the respect or degree of similarity which must obtain between the effects attributed to the sign and those attributed to the referent. This difficulty is involved in every version of the substitute-stimulus theory. Shall we say that, given the conditions in the above definition, V is a sign of R to a subject S provided only that those responses of S which are stimulated by V are similar in *some* respect to those which have been (or would be) stimulated by R? In other words, should we say that V is a sign of R provided that V has some of the effects which R has had or would have had? This would have the unacceptable consequence that all stimuli signify each other, since any two stimuli have at least some effect in common. Every stimulus causes neural activity, for example; hence, to that extent at least, any two stimuli will have similar effects. Shall we say that V is a sign of R provided that V has *all* the effects which R would have had? If the bell is to have all the effects which the food would have had, then, as Morris notes, the dog must start to eat the bell.[9] Shall we say that V is a sign of R provided that V has the effects which *only* R would have had? If the sign has effects which only the referent can have, then the sign *is* the referent and only food can be a sign of food. The other methods of specifying the degree or respect of similarity required by the substitute-stimulus definition, so far as I can see, have equally unacceptable consequences.

Reichenbach, in his *Elements of Symbolic Logic,* has applied this type of analysis to the concept of taking; but the consequences are similar. To say of a subject S, according to Reichenbach, that S *takes* something to be a dog is to say: "There is a z which is a bodily state of S and which is such that, whenever S is sensibly stimulated by a dog, S is in this bodily state z."[10] In other words, there are certain bodily conditions which S must fulfill in order for S to be sensibly stimulated by a dog; and whenever S satisfies any of these conditions, then S is taking something to be a dog.

But among the many conditions one must fulfill if one is to be sensibly stimulated by a dog is that of being alive. Hence if we know that S is alive, we can say that S is taking something to be a dog. The difficulty is that the bodily state z, of Reichenbach's formula, is not specified strictly enough. And the problem is to find an acceptable modification.

In reply to this objection, Reichenbach suggested, in effect, that "S takes something to be a dog" means that S's bodily state has all those neural properties which it must have—which are "physically necessary" for it to have—whenever S is sensibly stimulated by a dog.[11] But this definition has the unacceptable consequence that, whenever S is sensibly stimulated by a dog, then S *takes* the thing to be a dog. Thus, although we can say that a man may be stimulated by a fox and yet take it to be a dog, we can never say that he may be stimulated by a dog and *not* take it to be a dog.[12]

Similar objections apply to definitions using such expressions as "dog responses," "responses specific to dogs," "responses appropriate to dogs," and the like. For the problem of specifying what a man's "dog responses" might be is essentially that of specifying the bodily state to which Reichenbach referred.

5

Of all intentional phenomena, expectation is one of the most simple and, I think, one which is most likely to be definable in terms which are not intentional. If we could define, in nonintentional terms, what it means to say of a man, or an animal, that he expects something—that he expects some state of affairs to come about— then, perhaps, we could define "believing" and "assuming," nonintentionally, in terms of this sense of "expecting." If we are to show that Brentano is wrong, our hope lies here, I think.

For every expectancy, there is some possible state of affairs which would *fulfill* or *satisfy* it, and another possible state of affairs which would *frustrate* or *disrupt* it. If I expect the car to stop, then, it would seem, I am in a state which would be fulfilled or satisfied if and only if the car were to stop—and which would be frustrated or disrupted if and only if the car were not to stop. Hence we might consider defining "expects" in this way:

> "*S expects E* to occur" means that *S* is in a bodily state *b* such that either (i) *b* would be fulfilled if and only if *E* were to occur or (ii) *b* would be disrupted if and only if *E* were not to occur.

Our problem now becomes that of finding appropriate meanings for "fulfill" and "disrupt."

Perhaps there is a way of defining "fulfill" in terms of the psychological concept of *re-enforcement* and of defining "disrupt" in terms of *disequilibration, surprise,* or *shock.* And perhaps we can then provide an account of the dog and the bell and the food in terms which will show that this elementary situation is not intentional. It is possible that the dog, because of the sound of the bell, is in a state which is such that either (i) his state will be re-enforced if he receives food or (ii) it will be disequilibrated if he does not. And it is possible that this state can be specified in physiological terms. Whether this is so, of course, is a psychological question which no one, apparently, is yet in a position to answer. But even if it is so, there are difficulties in principle which appear when we try to apply this type of definition to human behavior.

If we apply "expects," as defined, to human behavior, then we must say that the appropriate fulfillments or disruptions must be caused by the occurrence, or nonoccurrence, of the "intentional object"—of *what* it is that is expected. But it is easy to think of situations which, antecedently, we should want to describe as instances of expectation, but in which the fulfillments or disruptions do not occur in the manner required. And to accommodate our definition to such cases, we must make qualifications which can be expressed only by reintroducing the intentional concepts we are trying to eliminate.

This difficulty may be illustrated as follows: Jones, let us suppose, *expects* to meet his aunt at the railroad station within twenty-five minutes. Our formulation, as applied to this situation, would yield: "Jones is in a bodily state which would be fulfilled if he were to meet his aunt at the station within twenty-five minutes or which would be disrupted if he were not to meet her there within that time." But what if he were to meet his aunt and yet *take* her to be someone else? Or if he were to meet someone else and yet *take* her to be his aunt? In such cases, the fulfillments and disruptions would not occur in the manner required by our definition.

If we introduce the intentional term "per-

ceives" or "takes" into our definition of "expects," in order to say, in this instance, that Jones *perceives* his aunt, or *takes* someone to be his aunt, then, of course, we can no longer define "assume"—or "perceive" and "take"—in terms of "expects." It is worth noting, moreover, that even if we allow ourselves the intentional term "perceive" our definition will be inadequate. Suppose that Jones were to visit the bus terminal, believing it to be the railroad station, or that he were to visit the railroad station believing it to be the bus terminal. If he met his aunt at the railroad station, believing it to be the bus terminal, then, contrary to our formula, he may be frustrated or surprised, and, if he fails to meet her there, his state may be fulfilled. Hence we must add further qualifications about what he believes or doesn't believe.[13]

If his visit to the station is brief and if he is not concerned about his aunt, the requisite re-enforcement or frustration may still fail to occur. Shall we add ". . . provided he *looks for* his aunt"? But now we have an intentional expression again. And even if we allow him to look for her, the re-enforcement or frustration may fail to occur if he finds himself able to satisfy desires which are more compelling than that of finding his aunt.

We seem to be led back, then, to the intentional language with which we began. In attempting to apply our definition of "expects" to a situation in which "expects" is ordinarily applicable, we find that we must make certain qualifications and that these qualifications can be formulated only by using intentional terms. We have had to introduce qualifications wherein we speak of the subject *perceiving* or *taking* something to be the object expected; hence we cannot now define "perceive" and "assume" in terms of "expect." We have had to add that the subject has certain *beliefs* concerning the nature of the conditions under which he perceives, or fails to perceive, the object. And we have referred to what he is *looking for* and to his other possible *desires.*

It may be that some of the simple "expectancies" we attribute to infants or to animals can be described, nonintentionally, in terms of re-enforcement or frustration. And possibly, as Ogden and Richards intimated, someone may yet find a way of showing that believing, perceiving, and taking are somehow "theoretically analysable" into such expectancies.[14] But until such programs are carried out, there is, I believe, some justification for saying that Brentano's thesis does apply to the concept of *perceiving.*

NOTES

1. Franz Brentano, *Psychologie vom empirischen Standpunkte* (Leipzig, 1924), I, 124–25.

2. But the point of talking about "intentionality" is not that there is a peculiar type of "inexistent" object; it is rather that there is a type of psychological phenomenon which is unlike anything purely physical. In his later writings Brentano explicitly rejected the view that there are "inexistent objects"; see his *Psychologie,* II, 133 ff., and *Wahrheit und Evidenz* (Leipzig, 1930), pp. 87, 89.

3. This third mark is essentially the same as Frege's concept of "indirect reference." See Gottlob Frege, "Über Sinn und Bedeutung," *Zeitschrift für Philosophie und philosophische Kritik,* n.s. C (1892), 25–50, especially 38; reprinted in Herbert Feigl and W. S. Sellars, eds., *Readings in Philosophical Analysis* (New York, 1949), and Peter Geach and Max Black, eds., *Philosophical Writings of Gottlob Frege* (Oxford, 1952).

4. There are sentences describing relations of comparison—for example, "Some lizards look like dragons"—which may constitute an exception to (1). If they are exceptions, then we may qualify (1) to read: "We do not need any intentional sentences, other than those describing relations of comparison, when we describe nonpsychological phenomena." This qualification would not affect any of the points to be made here.

5. A. J. Ayer, *Thinking and Meaning,* p. 13. Compare W. S. Sellars, "Mind, Meaning, and Behavior," *Philosophical Studies,* III (1952) 83–95; "A Semantical Solution of the Mind-Body Problem," *Methodos* (1953), pp. 45–85; and "Empiricism and the Philosophy of Mind," in Herbert Feigl and Michael Scriven, eds., *The Foundations of Science and the Concepts of Psychology and Psychoanalysis* (Minneapolis, 1956). See also Leonard Bloomfield, *Linguistic Aspects of Science* (Chicago, 1939), pp. 17–19.

6. Moritz Schlick, "Meaning and Verification," *Philosophical Review,* XLV (1936), 348; reprinted in Feigl and Sellars, eds., *Readings in Philosophical Analysis.* Compare this analogy, in "Meaning and Free Will," by John Hospers: "Sentences in themselves do not possess meaning; it is misleading to speak of 'the meaning of sentences' at all; meaning being conferred in every case by the speaker, the sentence's meaning is only like the light of the moon: without the sun to give it light, it would possess none. And for an analysis of the light we must go to the sun" (*Philosophy and Phenomenological Research,* X [1950], 308).

7. Carnap's definition appeared on p. 42 of "Meaning and Synonymy in Natural Languages," *Philosophical Studies,* IV (1955), 33–47. In "On Some Concepts of Pragmatics," *Philosophical Studies,* VI, 89–91, he conceded that "designates" should be defined in terms of "believes." The second article was written in reply to my "A Note on Carnap's Meaning Analysis," which appeared in the same issue (pp. 87–89).

8. Compare Charles E. Osgood, *Method and Theory in Experimental Psychology* (New York, 1953), p. 696: "A pattern of stimulation which is not the object is a sign of the object if it evokes in an organism a mediating reaction, this (a) being some fractional part of the total behavior elicited by the object and (b) producing distinctive self-stimulation that mediates responses which would not occur without the previous association of nonobject and object patterns of stimulation. All of these limiting conditions seem necessary. The mediation process must include part of the same behavior made to the object if the sign is to have its representing property." Some of the difficulties of the substitute stimulus concept [qualification (a) in this definition] are met by qualification (b), which implies that the subject must once have perceived the thing signified. But (b) introduces new difficulties. Since I have never seen the President of the United States, no announcement, according to this definition, could signify to me that the President is about to arrive.

9. See Charles Morris, *Signs, Language, and Behavior,* p. 12, and Max Black, "The Limitations of a Behavioristic Semiotic," *Philosophical Review,* LVI (1947), 258–272.

10. This is a paraphrase of what Hans Reichenbach formulated in special symbols on p. 275 of *Elements of Symbolic Logic* (New York, 1947).

11. Reichenbach suggests this modification in "On Observing and Perceiving," *Philosophical Studies,* II (1951), pp. 92–93. This paper was written in reply to my "Reichenbach on Observing and Perceiving" (*Philosophical Studies,* II, 45–48), which contains some of the above criticisms. In these papers, as well as in Reichenbach's original discussion, the word "perceive" was used in the way in which we have been using "take." Reichenbach used the term "immediate existence" in place of Brentano's "intentional inexistence"; see *Elements of Symbolic Logic,* p. 274.

12. This sort of modification may suggest itself: Consider those bodily states which are such that (i) S is in those states whenever he is sensibly stimulated by a dog and (ii) S cannot be in those states whenever he is *not* being stimulated by a dog. Shall we say "S takes something to be a dog" means that S is in this particular class of states? If we define "taking" in this way, then, we must say that, in the present state of psychology and physiology, we have no way of knowing whether anyone ever *does* take anything to be a dog, much less whether people take things to be dogs on just those occasions on which we want to be able to *say* that they take things to be dogs.

13. R. B. Braithwaite in "Belief and Action" (*Aristotelian Society,* suppl. vol. XX [1946] p. 10) suggests that a man may be said to believe a proposition p provided this condition obtains: "If at a time when an occasion arises relevant to p, his springs of action are s, he will perform an action which is such that, if p is true, it will tend to fulfill s, and which is such that, if p is false, it will not tend to satisfy s." But the definition needs qualifications in order to exclude those people who, believing truly (p) that the water is deep at the base of Niagara Falls and wishing (s) to survive a trip over the falls, have yet acted in a way which has not tended to satisfy s. Moreover, if we are to use such a definition to show that Brentano was wrong, we must provide a nonintentional definition of the present use of "wish" or "spring of action."

And, with Braithwaite's definition of "believe," it would be difficult to preserve the distinction which, apparently, we ought to make between *believing* a proposition and *acting upon* it (see Chapter One, Section 2). I have proposed detailed criticisms of a number of such definitions of "believe" in "Sentences about Believing," *Proceedings of the Aristotelian Society*, LVI (1955–1956), 125–48. Some of the difficulties involved in defining *purpose* nonintentionally are pointed out by Richard Taylor in "Comments on a Mechanistic Conception of Purpose," *Philosophy of Science*, XVII (1950), 310–17, and "Purposeful and Nonpurposeful Behavior: A Rejoinder," ibid., 327–32.

14. C. K. Ogden and I. A. Richards, *The Meaning of Meaning*, 5th ed. (London, 1938), p. 71.

46 | A Recipe for Thought
Fred Dretske

1. If You Can't Make One, You Don't Know How It Works

There are things I believe that I don't know how to say—at least not in such a way as to make them come out true. The title of this section is a case in point. I really do believe that, in the relevant sense of all the relevant words, if you can't make one, you don't know how it works. I just don't know how to specify the relevant sense of all the relevant words.

I know, for instance, that a person can understand how something works and, for a variety of reasons, still not be able to build it. The raw materials are not available. She can't afford them. He is too clumsy or not strong enough. The police won't let him. I also know that a person may be able to make one and still not know how it works. He doesn't know how the parts work. I can solder a snaggle to a radzak, and this is all it takes to make a gizmo, but if I do not know what snaggles and radzaks are, or how they work, making one isn't going to tell me much about what a gizmo is. My son once assembled a television set from a kit by carefully following the instruction manual. Understanding next to nothing about electricity, though, he still had no idea of how television worked.

I am not, however, suggesting that being able to build one is sufficient for knowing how it works. Only necessary. And I do not much care about whether you can actually put one together. It is enough if you know how one is put together. But, as I said, I do not know how to make all the right qualifications. So I won't try. All I intend by my provocative claim is that philosophical naturalism is motivated by a constructivist model of understanding. It embodies something like an engineer's ideal, a designer's vision, of what it takes to really understand how something works. You need a blueprint, a recipe, an instruction manual, a program. That goes for the mind as well as anything else. If you want to know what intelligence is, you need a recipe for creating it out of parts you already understand.

In speaking of parts one already understands, I mean, of course, parts that do not already possess the capacity or feature one follows the recipe to create. One cannot have a recipe for a cake that lists a cake, not even a small cake, as an ingredient. One can, I suppose, make a big cake out of small cakes, but recipes of this sort will not help one understand what a cake is (though they might help you understand what a *big* cake is). As a boy, I once tried to make fudge by melting caramels in a frying pan. All I succeeded in doing was ruining the pan. Don't ask me what I was trying to do—change the shape of the candy, I suppose. There are perfectly respectable recipes for cookies that list candy (e.g., gumdrops) as an ingredient, but one cannot have a recipe for *candy* that lists candy as an ingredient. At least it won't be a recipe that tells

Originally published as "If You Can't Make One, You Don't Know How It Works," in P. French, T. Uehling, and H. Wettstein, eds., *Midwest Studies in Philosophy*, vol. 19, pp. 468–82, 1994. Reprinted (with small revisions by the author) with the permission of the publisher.

you how to make candy or helps you understand what candy is. The same is true of minds. That is why recipes for thought can't have interpretive attitudes or explanatory stances among the ingredients—not even the attitudes and stances of others. That is like making candy out of candy—in this case, one person's fudge out of another person's caramels. You can do it, but you still won't know what candy is.

2. Information and Intentionality

In comparing a mind to candy and television, I do not mean to suggest that minds are the sort of thing that can be assembled from kits in your basement or kitchen. There are things, including things one fully understands, things one knows how to make, that cannot be assembled that way. Try making Rembrandts or one hundred dollar bills in your basement. What you produce may look genuine, it may pass as authentic, but it won't be the real thing. You have to be the right person, occupy the right office, or possess the appropriate legal authority in order to make certain objects. There are recipes for making money and Rembrandts, and knowing them is part of knowing what money and Rembrandts are, but these are not recipes you and I can use. Some recipes require a special cook.

This is one (but only one) of the reasons it is wrong to say, as I did above, that if you cannot make one, you do not know how it works. It would be better to say, as I did earlier, that if you do not know *how* to make one, or *how* one is made, you do not fully understand it.

Some objects are constituted, in part, by their relationships to other objects. Rembrandts and one hundred dollar bills are like that. So are cousins and mothers-in-law. That is why you can't build my cousin in your basement while my aunt and uncle can. Though there is a recipe knowledge of which is necessary for understanding what it takes to be my cousin, it is not a recipe *you* can use to build what it enables you to understand. The mind, I think, is like that, and I will return to this important point in a moment.

It is customary to think of naturalistic recipes for the mind as starting with extensional ingredients and, through some magical blending process, producing an intentional product: a thought, an experience, or a purpose. The idea behind this proscription of intentional ingredients seems to be that since what we are trying to

build—a thought—is an intentional entity, our recipe cannot use intentional ingredients.

This, it seems to me, is a mistake, a mistake that has led otherwise sensible philosophers to despair of ever finding a naturalistic recipe for the mind. It is a mistake that has given naturalism an undeserved bad name. The mistake is the same as if we proscribed using, say, copper wire in our instruction manual for building an amplifier because copper wire conducts electricity—exactly what the thing we are trying to build—an amplifier—does. But there is nothing wrong in listing copper wire in one's recipe for building an amplifier. An amplifier recipe is supposed to help you make (and, thus, understand) how things amplify electricity, not how something conducts electricity. That is why you get to use conductors of electricity as components in a recipe for building an amplifier. Conductors are eligible ingredients in amplifier recipes even if one does not know how conductors manage to conduct. An eligible ingredient, once again, is an ingredient, a part, a component, that does not already have the capacity or power one follows the recipe to create. That is why one can know what gumdrop cookies are, know how to make them, without knowing how to make gumdrops or what, exactly, gumdrops are.

The same is true for mental recipes. As long as there is no mystery—at least not the *same* mystery—about how the parts work as how the whole is supposed to work, it is perfectly acceptable to use intentional ingredients in a recipe for thought, purpose, and intelligence. What we are trying to understand, after all, is not intentionality, per se, but the mind. Thought may be intentional, but that isn't the property we are seeking a recipe to understand. As long as the intentionality we use is not itself mental, then we are as free to use intentionality in our recipe for making a mind as we are in using electrical conductors in building an amplifier or gumdrops in making cookies.

Consider a simple artifact—a compass. If it was manufactured properly (don't buy a cheap one), and if it is used in the correct circumstances (the good ones come with directions), it will tell you the direction of the arctic pole.[1] That is what the pointer indicates. But though the pointer indicates the direction of the arctic pole, it does not indicate the whereabouts of polar bears even though polar bears live in the arctic. If you happen to know this fact about polar bears, that they live in the arctic, you could, of course, figure out where the polar bears are by using a compass. But this fact about what you could figure out *if you knew* does not mean that the compass pointer is sensitive to the location of polar bears—thus indicating their whereabouts—in the way it indicates the location of the arctic pole. The pointer on this instrument does not track the bears; it tracks the pole. If there is any doubt about this, watch the compass needle as you move the polar bears around. It won't even wiggle.

Talking about what a compass indicates is a way of talking about what it tracks, what information it carries, and a compass, just like any other measuring instrument, can track one magnitude without tracking another even though these conditions co-occur. Talk about what instruments and gauges indicate or measure creates the same kind of intensional (with an "s") context as does talk about what a person knows or believes. Knowing or believing that *that* is the north pole is not the same as knowing or believing that that is the habitat of polar bears even though the north pole is the habitat of polar bears. If we use intensional (with an "s") discourse, referentially opaque contexts, as a guide to intentional (with a "t") phenomena, then we have, in a cheap compass, something we can buy at the local hardware store, intentionality. Describing what such an instrument indicates is describing it in intensional terms. What one is describing with these intensional terms is, therefore, in this sense, an intentional state of the instrument.

It is worth emphasizing that this is not derived or in any way second-class intentionality. This is the genuine article—*original* intentionality as some philosophers (including this one) like to say. The intentional states a compass occupies do not depend on our explanatory purposes, attitudes, or stances. To say that the compass indicates the direction of the arctic pole is to say that the position of the pointer depends on the whereabouts of the pole. This dependency exists whether or not we know it exists, whether or not anyone ever exploits this fact to build and use compasses. The intentionality of the device is not like the intentionality of words and maps, borrowed or derived from the intentionality (purposes, attitudes, knowledge) of its users. The power of this instrument to indicate north *to* or *for us* may depend on our taking it to be a reliable indicator (and, thus, on what we believe or know about it), but its *being* a reliable indicator does not depend on us.

Intentionality is a much abused word and it means a variety of different things. But one thing it has been used to mean is some state, condition, activity or event, whose description generates an opaque context, a context in which coextensional terms cannot be automatically substituted for one another. This is what Chisholm describes as the third mark of intentionality.[2] Anything exhibiting this mark is about something under an aspect. It has an aspectual shape.[3] The compass needle is about the arctic under one aspect (as the location of the north pole) and not others (as the habitat of polar bears). This is the same way our thoughts can be about a place under one aspect (as where I was born) but not another (as where you were born). If this is, indeed, one thing that is meant by speaking of a state, condition, or activity as intentional, then it seems clear that there is no need to naturalize intentionality. It is already a completely natural phenomenon, a pervasive feature of our physical world. It exists wherever you find dark clouds, smoke, tree rings, shadows, tracks, lightning, flowing water, and countless other natural conditions that indicate something about how the rest of the world is constituted.

Intentional systems, then, are not the problem. They can be picked up for a few dollars at your local hardware store. We can, therefore, include them on our list of ingredients in our recipe for building a mind without fear that we are merely changing the shape of the candy. What we are trying to build when we speak of a recipe for building a mind is not merely a system that exhibits intentional properties. We already have that in systems that are in no way mental. Rather, what we are trying to build is a system that exhibits that peculiar array of intentional properties that characterizes thought. We are, in particular, trying to build systems that exhibit what Chisholm describes as the first mark of intentionality, the power to say that so-and-so is the case when so-and-so is not the case, the power to misrepresent how things stand in the world. Unlike compasses, these fancy items are not to be found on the shelves of hardware stores. For them we need a recipe.

3. Misrepresentation

Let us be clear about what we are looking for, what we seek a recipe to create. If we are trying to build a thought, we are looking for something that can not only say that x is F without saying x is G (despite the co-extensionality of "F" and

"G"[4]), thus being about x under an aspect, we are looking for something that can say this, like a thought can say it, even when x is not F. Without this, we have no naturalistic understanding of what it is we think, no theory of meaning or content. For meaning or content, the what-it-is one thinks, is, like intelligence and rationality, independent of the truth of what one thinks. So a recipe for understanding misrepresentation is, in effect, a recipe for constructing meanings and, therefore, genuinely intelligent systems.

Jerry Fodor has recently focused attention on what he calls the disjunction problem for naturalistic theories of mental representation.[5] The problem is one of explaining how, in broadly causal terms, a structure in the head, call it R, could represent, say, or mean that something was F even though a great many things other than something's being F are capable of causing R. How can the occurrence of R mean that something is F when something's being F is only one of the things capable of causing R?[6] For someone trying to formulate an information-based recipe for thought, this is, indeed, a vexing problem. But I mention the problem here only to point out that this problem is merely another way of describing the problem of misrepresentation. For if one could specify a recipe for building systems capable of misrepresentation—capable, that is, of saying that something was F when it wasn't—then one would have a recipe for meaning, a recipe for constructing structures having a content that was independent of causes. For anything that can misrepresent something as being F is, of necessity, something whose meaning is independent of its causes, something that can mean cow even when it is caused by a horse on a dark night. It is, therefore, something whose meaning is less than the disjunction of conditions capable of causing it, something whose meaning (in the words of Antony and Levine[7]) is "detached" from causes. A naturalistic recipe for misrepresentation, then, is a recipe for solving the disjunction problem.[8] One way of solving problems is to show that two problems are really, at bottom, the same problem. So we are making progress.

For this problem artifacts are of no help. Although clocks, compasses, thermometers, and fire alarms—all readily available at the corner hardware store—can misrepresent the conditions they are designed to deliver information about, they need our help to do it. Their representational successes and failures are underwritten by the purposes and attitudes of their designers and users. As representational devices, as devices exhibiting a causally detached meaning, such instruments are not, therefore, eligible ingredients in a recipe for making thought.

The reason the representational powers of instruments are not, like their indicative (information-carrying) powers, an available ingredient in mental recipes is, I hope, obvious enough. I will, however, take a moment to expand on it in order to set the stage for what follows.

Consider the thermometer. Since the volume of a metal varies lawfully with the temperature, both the mercury in the glass tube and the paper clips in my desk drawer carry information about the local temperature. Both are intentional systems in that minimal, that first, sense already discussed. Their behavior depends on a certain aspect of their environment (on the temperature, not the color or size, of their neighbors) in the same way the orientation of a compass needle depends on one aspect of its environment, not another. The only relevant difference between thermometers and paper clips is that we have given the one volume of metal—the mercury in the glass tube—the job of telling us about temperature. The paper clips have been given a different job. Since it is the thermometer's job to provide information about temperature, it (we say) misrepresents the temperature when it fails to do its assigned job just as (we say) a book or a map might misrepresent the matters about which they purport to inform us. What such artifacts say or mean is what they have the job of indicating, and since you do not lose your job—at least not immediately—merely by failing to successfully perform your job, these instruments continue to mean that a certain condition exists even when something *else* causes them to perform. Meanings are causally detached from causes for the same reason that functions are causally detached from actual functioning. This is why thermometers can, while paper clips cannot, "say" something false about temperature.

But, as I said, thermometers can't do this by themselves. They need our help. We are the source of the job, the function, without which the thermometer could not say anything false. Take us away and all you have is a tube full of mercury being caused to expand and contract by changes in the temperature—a column of metal doing exactly what paper clips, thumb tacks, and flag poles do. Once we change our attitude, once we stop investing informational trust in it, the instrument loses its power to misrepresent.

Its meaning ceases to be detached. It becomes merely a purveyor of information.

4. Natural Functions

Though representational artifacts are thus not available as eligible ingredients in our recipe for the mind, their derived (from us) power to misrepresent is suggestive. If an information-carrying element in a system could somehow acquire the function of carrying information, and acquire this function in a way that did not depend on our intentions, purposes, and attitudes, then it would thereby acquire (just as a thermometer or a compass acquires) the power to misrepresent the conditions it had the function of informing about. Such functions would bring about a detachment of meaning from cause. Furthermore, since the functions would not be derived from us, the meanings (unlike the meaning of thermometers and compasses) would be original, underived, meaning. Instead of just being able to build an instrument that could fool us, the thing we build could, quite literally, itself be fooled.

If, then, we could find naturalistically acceptable functions, we could combine these with natural indicators (the sort used in the manufacture of compasses, thermometers, pressure gauges, and electric eyes) in a naturalistic recipe for thought. If the word "thought" sounds a bit fancy for the contraption we are assembling, we can describe the results in more modest terms. What we would have is a naturalistic recipe for representation, a product that would have, quite apart from its creator's (or anyone else's) purposes, attitudes, or thoughts, a propositional content that could be false. If that isn't quite a recipe for béarnaise sauce, it is at least a recipe for a passable gravy. I'll come back to the béarnaise sauce in a moment.

What we need in the way of another ingredient, then, is some process whereby elements can acquire, on their own, an information-carrying function. Where might we find these natural processes? There are, as I see it, two possible sources: one phylogenic, the other ontogenic.

If the heart and kidneys have a natural function, something they are supposed to be doing independently of our knowledge or understanding of what it is, then it presumably comes from their evolutionary, their selectional, history.[9] If the heart has the function of pumping blood, if that is why it is there,[10] then, by parity of reasoning, the senses (depending on actual selectional history) might have an information-providing function, the job of "telling" the animal in whom they occur what it needs to know in order to find food and mates and avoid danger. If this were so, then, the natural function of sensory systems would be to provide information about an organism's optical, acoustic, and chemical surroundings. There would thus exist, inside the animal, representations of its environment, elements capable of saying something false. Though I have put it quite crudely, this, I take it, is the idea that inspires biologically oriented approaches to mental representation.[11]

There is, however, a second, an ontogenetic, source of usable (in naturalistic recipes) functions. Think of a system with needs, certain things it must have in order to survive.[12] In order to satisfy those needs it has to do A in conditions C. Nature has not equipped this system with a mechanism that will automatically trigger A in conditions C. There is, in other words, no instinct to A in circumstances C. Maybe C is a condition that has only recently appeared in this animal's natural habitat. Think of C as an attractive (to this kind of animal) mushroom that is quite poisonous. The animal has the sensory resources for picking up information about (i.e., registering) the presence of C (it looks distinctive), but it does not have an instinctive, a genetically hard-wired, reaction to C. It can perceive C, but it has not yet learned to avoid C. We could wait for natural selection to solve this problem for the species, for the descendants of this animal, but if the problem—basically a coordination problem—is to be solved at the individual level (if *this* animal is to survive)—learning must occur. Some internal sign or indicator of C—the animal's sensory registration of C—must be made into a cause of A. Control circuits must be reconfigured by inserting this internal sign into the behavioral chain of command. Short of a miracle—the fortuitous occurrence of A whenever C is encountered—this is the only way the coordination problem can be solved. The internal indicators must be harnessed to effector mechanisms so as to coordinate output to the conditions they carry information about. Learning of this kind has the same results for the individual as do the longer-term evolutionary solutions for the species: internal elements that supply needed information acquire the function of supplying it by being drafted into the control loop because they supply it.[13] They are there, doing what they are doing, *because* they supply this information.

Obviously this ingredient, this source of natural functions, cannot be ordered from a spare parts catalog. There is nothing one can squirt on a temperature indicator that will give it the function of indicating temperature, nothing we can rub on photo-sensitive pigment that will give it the job of detecting light. If something is going to get the function, the job, the purpose, of carrying information in this way, it has to get it on its own. We can't give it.[14] If the only natural functions are those provided by evolutionary history and learning, then, no one is going to build a thinker of thoughts, much less a mind, in the laboratory. This would be like building a heart, a real one, in your basement. If hearts are essentially organs of the body having the biological function of pumping blood, you can't build them. You can wait for them to develop, maybe even hurry things along a bit by timely assists, but you can't assemble them out of ready-made parts. These functions are results of the right kind of history, and you cannot, not *now,* give a thing the right kind of history. There is a recipe for building internal representations, but it is not a recipe you or I, or anyone else, can use to build one.

5. The Disjunction Problem

There are reasonable doubts about whether a recipe consisting of information and natural teleology (derived from natural functions—either phylogenic or ontogenic) is capable of yielding a mental product—something with an original power to misrepresent. The doubts exist even with those who share the naturalistic vision. Jerry Fodor, for instance, does not think Darwin (or Skinner, for that matter) can rescue Brentano's chestnuts from the fire.[15] Teleological stories about intentionality, he says, do not solve the disjunction problem. Given the equivalence of the disjunction problem and the problem of misrepresentation, this is a denial, not just a doubt, that evolutionary or learning-theoretic accounts of functions are up to the task of detaching meaning from cause, of making something say COW when it is caused by something other than a cow.[16]

I agree with Fodor about the irrelevance of Darwin for understanding mental representation. I agree, however, not out of a general skepticism about teleological accounts of meaning, but because I think Darwin is the wrong place to look for the functions underlying the kind of *mental* representations (beliefs, thoughts, judg-

ments, preferences, and their ilk) that explain *action*—the sort of voluntary or deliberate behavior for which we typically have reasons. I expect Darwin to help us understand why people blink, reflexively, when someone pokes a finger at their eye, but not why they (deliberately) wink at their friend. There are probably internal representations (of objects approaching the eye) involved in the blink reflex, representations that have an evolutionary origin, but these are not the sort of representations (beliefs, purposes, and intentions) at work in explaining why we wink at a friend or pack for a trip. If we are looking for a naturalized semantics for thought, the sort of representation that helps explain action, we will have to get our teleology from somewhere else. Darwin won't help us because Darwin is concerned with precisely those behaviors the explanatory mechanisms for which are genetically determined—precisely those behaviors that are not voluntary.

Nonetheless, wherever we get the teleology, Fodor thinks it won't solve the disjunction problem and is, therefore, hopeless as an account of thought content. I disagree. I have tried to supply the details in *Explaining Behavior* so I won't repeat myself here. Let me here mention only a crucial point. An historical theory of content is not, as Fodor thinks, restricted to assigning content in terms of the objects or conditions that actually figured in the development of the representation. If R, a COW indicator, gets its function of indicating cows by "exposure" to only Jersey cows, this does not mean that R means (has as its representational content) JERSEY COW. Whether it means COW, JERSEY COW, or, perhaps, simply ANIMAL, will depend (as Fodor likes to say) on the counterfactuals. In indicating that yonder object is a Jersey cow, R also indicates that it is a cow and, therefore, an animal. It indicates all these things. But though R carries all these pieces of information, a developmental theory of content identifies what R has the function of indicating—hence, what R represents—with that particular piece of information that was causally relevant in the selectional process by means of which R was recruited for causal duties. Was it JERSEY COW, COW, or, perhaps, simply, ANIMAL, the indication of which led to R's recruitment as a determinant of system output? The answer to this question is an answer to the question, "What does R represent?" and it requires an evaluation of the counterfactuals that Fodor thinks relevant to a determination of content.

6. The Recipe

What we have, then, is the following recipe for making a thought. It does not give us a very fancy thought—certainly nothing like the thoughts we have every day: that tomorrow is my birthday or that I left my umbrella in the car. But one thing at a time. The recipe will do its job if it yields *something*—call it a "pro-tothought"—that has belief-like features. We can worry about the fancy trimmings later.

RECIPE FOR THOUGHT: Take a system that has a need (see footnote 12) for the information that F, a system whose survival or well-being depends on its doing A in conditions F. Make sure that this system has a means of detecting (i.e., an internal element that indicates) the presence of condition F. Add a natural process, one capable of conferring on the element that carries information F the function of carrying this piece of information. Of course, you don't just "add" this process the way you add spices in a recipe for lasagna. Adding the function is more like *waiting* for dough to rise. There is nothing you can do but sit back and hope things develop in the right way. And just as you cannot put yeast in just anything and expect it to rise (it doesn't work in sand), you cannot put indicators of F in just anything having a need for this information and expect it to spontaneously generate representations of F. You need a system with the capacity to reorganize control circuits so as to exploit this information in achieving coordination of its behavior with the conditions (F) it is getting information about. These are pretty special sorts of systems, to be sure. They are systems capable of learning. I have no doubt that living systems of a certain level of complexity are the only ones able to perform the trick. However special they might be, though, they needn't be systems that already possess powers of representation. In requiring systems of this sort, therefore, we are not using tainted ingredients in our recipe for thought.

If all goes well, when the process is complete, the result will be a system with internal resources for representing (with the associated power of misrepresenting) its surroundings. Furthermore, that this system represents, as well as what it represents, will be independent of what we know or believe about it. For we, the cooks, are not essential parts of this process. The entire process can happen spontaneously and, when it does, the system will have its own cache of *original* intentionality.

7. Rationality: The Functional Role of Thought

Whether this is really enough to have supplied a recipe for thought depends, of course, on just what one demands of thought. What does it take to be a thought? If all it takes is possession of content, then, perhaps, we have supplied a recipe of sorts. But the product is pretty disappointing, a mere shadow of what we know (in ourselves and others) to be the fullest and richest expression of the mind. What I have described might, after all, be realized in a snail. What we want (I expect to hear) is something more, something exhibiting the complex dynamics, both inferential and explanatory, that our thoughts have. To have a thought about cows it isn't enough to have an internal, completely isolated, cow representation. To be a cow thought this representation must actually do what cow thoughts do. It must be involved in reasoning and inference about cows; it must (together with cow-directed desires) explain cow-related behavior. It must, together with cow-desires, rationalize cow-directed attitudes.

There is validity to this complaint. If we are going to make a thought we want the product to both look and behave like a thought. What we have so far devised may have some of the features of thought. At least it has a representational content or the sort we associate with thought. There is, however, nothing to suggest that our product will behave like a thought. Why, then, advertise the recipe as a recipe for thought? I have, after all, already conceded that there may be representations of this sort, mechanisms in the body having an indicator function, that are not *mental* representations at all. When the underlying functions are phylogenetic (e.g., in the processes controlling various reflexes), the representations are not thoughts. They have a content, yes, but they do not behave like thoughts. They do not, for instance, interact with desires and other beliefs to produce intelligent and purposeful actions. Why, then, suppose that when the functions are ontogenetic, when they develop in learning, the results are any better qualified to be classified as mental? As genuine thought? An edge detector in the visual system might have the function of detecting edges and, for this reason, represent edges, but it is not—surely not for this reason alone—a thought about edges.

Since I have addressed this issue elsewhere,[17] I will merely sketch the answer. A system that acquires, in accordance with our recipe, and in its own lifetime, the power to represent the objects in its immediate environment will also, automatically, be an intelligent system, one capable of behaving in a rational way. To see why this is so, consider the process by means of which an indicator of F acquires the function of providing the information that F and, thereby, becomes a representation of F. In order to become the thought that F, this element must acquire the job of providing information about the F-ness of things. The only way it can acquire this function is by doing (i.e., causing) something—e.g., helping to bring about behavior A in condition F—that is beneficial to the organism when it wants or needs to do A. If the things this element causes are not useful or beneficial in some way, if they do not contribute to the satisfaction of the system's needs and desires, why should the element be selected to cause them? To acquire the function of indicating F, to become (thereby) a representation of F, therefore, a structure must play a part in the production of behavior that is rational from the point of view of the organism's well-being. An internal representation of F becomes a representation of F in a process in which what it causes is, in this sense, a *reasonable* response to F. According to this recipe for thought, nothing can become the thought that F without contributing to a rational response to F, a response that is appropriate given the system's needs and/or desires.

Something not only becomes the thought that F by assisting in the production of an intelligent response to F, it assists in the intelligent response to F precisely *because* it is signifies that condition F exists. That is, not only do thoughts that F conspire to produce intelligent reactions to F, they produce these reactions to F because they have an F-content. It is their content, the

fact that they are F (not G, H, or K) indicators that explains why they are causing what they do. Had they been indicators of some other condition, a condition unrelated to a useful outcome, they would not have been selected for producing a response to F. This, it seems to me, vindicates, in one fell swoop, both the explanatory and rationalizing role of content. We do not need independent "rationality constraints" in our theory of content. Rationality emerges as a by-product in the very process in which representations are created.

Our recipe, then, yields a product with the following features:

1. The product has a propositional content that represents the world in an aspectual way (as being F rather than G even when Fs are always G).
2. This content can be either true or false.
3. The product is a "player" in the determination of system output (thus helping to explain system behavior).
4. The propositional content of this product is the property that explains the product's role in determining system output. The system not only does what it does because it has this product inside it, but it is the propositional content of this internal product that explains why the system behaves the way it does.
5. Though the system *can* behave stupidly, the normal role of this product (the role it will play when it is doing the job for which it was created in the conditions in which it was created) will be in the production of intelligent (need and desire satisfaction) behavior.

Our recipe gives us something that is beginning to both look *and behave* like thought.

NOTES

This article originally appeared with the title, "If You Can't Make One, You Don't Know How It Works" in *Midwest Studies in Philosophy* 19 (1994), 468–82. I have made minor changes.

An early version was presented at the annual meeting of the Society for Philosophy and Psychology, Montreal, 1992. I used an enlarged form of it at the NEH Summer Institute on the Nature of Meaning, codirected by Jerry Fodor and Ernie LePore at Rutgers University in the summer of 1993. There were many people who gave me useful feedback and helpful suggestions. I am grateful to them.

1. I leave aside distracting complications having to do with the difference between magnetic and geographic poles.
2. Roderick M. Chisholm, *Perceiving: A Philosophical Study* (Ithaca, NY, 1957).
3. This is Searle's way of putting it in *The Rediscovery of the Mind* (Cambridge, MA; MIT Press, 1992), p. 131, 156). As should be evident, I think Searle is wrong when he says (p. 161) that there are no aspectual shapes at the level of neurons. The sensory indicators in the brain are as much about the world (that we perceive) under an aspect as is the compass about the arctic under an aspect.
4. Despite even the *nomic* co-extensionality of "F" and

"G". That is, a thought that x is F is different than a thought that x is G even if F-ness and G-ness are nomically related in such a way that nothing can be F without being G. This, too, is an aspect of intentionality. In Dretske (1981, p. 173) I called this the 2nd order of intentionality. Although compasses (indeed, all measuring instruments) exhibit the 1st order of intentionality (they indicate that x is F without necessarily indicating that x is G despite the co-extensionality of "F" and "G"), they do not exhibit the 2nd order of intentionality. If (in virtue of natural law) x must be G when it is F, then anything indicating that x is F will thereby indicate that it is G. If polar bears *cannot* live anywhere but the north pole, then compasses, in indicating the whereabouts of the north pole, will indicate the habitat of polar bears. Compasses cannot, while thoughts can, "pry apart" nomically related properties.

My discussion has so far passed over this important dimension of intentionality. It deserves discussion, but the complications are too great to cover in a brief article.

5. *A Theory of Content and Other Essays* (Cambridge, MA; MIT Press, 1990).

6. In some cases, of course, an F will not even be *among* the causes of R since there are no Fs (unicorns, miracles, angels, etc.). This is a problem that, for lack of space, I skip over.

7. Louise Antony and Joseph Levine, "The Nomic and the Robust," in *Meaning in Mind: Fodor and His Critics* (Oxford, 1991), 1–16.

8. Fodor (1990, p. 91) puts it a bit differently, but the point, I think, is the same: "Solving the disjunction problem and making clear how a symbol's meaning could be so insensitive to variability in the causes of its tokenings are really two ways of describing the same undertaking."

9. For the purpose of this essay I ignore skeptics about functions—those who think, for example, that the heart only has the function of pumping blood because this is an effect in which we have a special interest. See Searle's *The Rediscovery of Mind*, p. 238 and Dan Dennett's "Evolution, Error and Intentionality" in *The Intentional Stance* (Cambridge, MA; MIT Press, 1987).

10. This way of putting the point appeals to the view of natural functions advanced by Larry Wright in "Functions," *Philosophical Review* 82 (1973): 139–168, and *Teleological Explanation* (Berkeley, 1976).

11. E.g., Ruth Millikan, *Language, Thought, and Other Biological Categories: New Foundations for Realism* (Cambridge, MA, 1984) and "Biosemantics," *Journal of Philosophy* 86, no. 6 (1989); David Papineau, *Reality and Representation* (New York, 1987) and "Representation and Explanation," *Philosophy of Science* 51, no. 4 (1984); 550–72; Mohan Matthen, "Biological Functions and Perceptual Content," *Journal of Philosophy* 85, no. 1 (1988): 5–27; and Peter Godfrey-Smith, "Misinformation," *Canadian Journal of Philosophy* 19, no. 4 (December 1989): 533–50 and "Signal, Decision, Action," *Journal of Philosophy* 88, no. 12 (December 1991): 709–722.

12. This may sound as though we are smuggling in the back door what we are not allowing in the front: a tainted ingredient, the idea of a *needful* system, a system that, given its needs, has a use for information. I think not. All that is here meant by a need (for system of type S) is some condition or result without which the system could (or would) not exist as a system of type S. Needs, in this minimal sense, are merely necessary conditions for existence. Even plants have needs in this sense. Plants cannot exist (as plants) without water and sunlight (they can, of course, exist as collections of elementary particles without water and sunlight).

13. This is the short and fast version of the story I tell in *Explaining Behavior* (Cambridge, MA; MIT Press, 1988).

14. Though we can encourage its development by artificial selection.

15. Fodor, *A Theory of Content and Other Essays* (Cambridge, MA; MIT Press, 1990), p. 70.

16. I agree with Fodor (ibid., footnote 35, p. 135) that the only normative quality a naturalistic theory of meaning has to explain is the quality of being able to mean something that isn't so. If we can solve the problem of misrepresentation—or, equivalently, the disjunction problem—we will have all the normativity we want.

17. *Explaining Behavior* (Cambridge, MA; MIT Press, 1988).

47 | Biosemantics

Ruth Garrett Millikan

Causal or informational theories of the semantic content of mental states which have had an eye on the problem of false representations have characteristically begun with something like this intuition. There are some circumstances under which an inner representation has its represented as a necessary and/or sufficient cause or condition of production. That is how the content of the representation is fixed. False representations are to be explained as tokens that are produced under other circumstances. The challenge, then, is to tell what defines certain circumstances as the content-fixing ones.

I

Note that the answer cannot be just that these circumstances are *statistically* normal conditions. To gather such statistics, one would need to delimit a reference class of occasions, know how to count its members, and specify description categories. It would not do, for example, just to average over conditions-in-the-universe-any-place-any-time. Nor is it given how to carve out relevant description categories for conditions on occasions. Is it "average" in the summer for it to be (precisely) between 80° and 80.5° Fahrenheit with humidity 87%? And are average conditions those which obtain on at least 50% of the occasions, or is it 90%? Depending on how one sets these parameters, radically different conditions are "statistically normal." But the notion of semantic content clearly is not relative, in this manner, to arbitrary parameters. The content-fixing circumstances must be *nonarbitrarily* determined.

A number of recent writers have made an appeal to teleology here, specifically to conditions of normal function or well-functioning of the systems that produce inner representations. Where the represented is R and its representation is "R," under conditions of well-functioning, we might suppose, only Rs can or are likely to produce "R"s. Or perhaps "R" is a representation of R just in case the system was designed to react to Rs by producing "R"s. But this sort of move yields too many representations. Every state of every functional system has normal causes, things that it is a response to in accordance with design. These causes may be proximate or remote, and many are disjunctive. Thus, a proximate normal cause of dilation of the skin capillaries is certain substances in the blood, more remote causes include muscular effort, sunburn, and being in an overheated environment. To each of these causes the vascular system responds by design, yet the response (a red face), though it may be a natural sign of burn or exertion or overheating, certainly is not a representation of that. If not every state of a system represents its normal causes, which are the states that do?

Jerry Fodor[1] has said that, whereas the content of an inner representation is determined by some sort of causal story, its status *as* a representation is determined by the functional organization of the part of the system which uses it. There is such a thing, it seems, as behaving like a representation without behaving like a representation of anything in particular. What the thing is a representation of is then determined by its cause under content-fixing conditions. It would be interesting to have the character of universal I-am-a-representation behavior spelled out for us. Yet, as Fodor well knows, there would still be the problem of demonstrating that there was only one normal cause per representation type.

A number of writers, including Dennis Stampe,[2] Fred Dretske,[3] and Mohan Matthen,[4] have suggested that what is different about effects that are representations is that their function is, precisely, to represent, "indicate," or "detect." For example, Matthen says of (fullfledged) perceptual states that they are "state[s]that [have]the function of *detecting* the presence of things of a certain type . . ." (ibid., p. 20). It does not help to be told that inner representations are things that have representing (indicating, detecting) as their function, however, unless we are also told what kind of activity representing (indicating, detecting) is. Matthen does not tell us

From *Journal of Philosophy* 86:281–97, 1989. Reprinted with permission of author and publisher.

how to naturalize the notion "detecting." If "detecting" is a function of a representational state, it must be something that the state effects or produces. For example, it cannot be the function of a state to have been produced in response to something. Or does Matthen mean that it is not the representational states themselves, but the part of the system which produces them, which has the function of detecting? It has the function, say, of producing states that correspond to or covary with something in the outside world? But, unfortunately, not every device whose job description includes producing items that vary with the world is a representation producer. The devices in me that produce calluses are supposed to vary their placement according to where the friction is, but calluses are not representations. The pigment arrangers in the skin of a chameleon, the function of which is to vary the chameleon's color with what it sits on, are not representation producers.

Stampe and Dretske do address the question what representing or (Dretske) "detecting" is. Each brings in his own description of what a natural sign or natural representation is, then assimilates *having the function of representing R* to being a natural sign or representer of *R* when the system functions normally. Now, the production of natural signs is undoubtedly an accidental side effect of normal operation of many systems. From my red face you can tell that either I have been exerting myself, or I have been in the heat, or I am burned. But the production of an accidental side effect, no matter how regular, is not one of a system's functions; that goes by definition. More damaging, however, it simply is not true that representations must carry natural information. Consider the signals with which various animals signal danger. Nature knows that it is better to err on the side of caution, and it is likely that many of these signs occur more often in the absence than in the presence of any real danger. Certainly there is nothing incoherent in the idea that this might be so, hence that many of these signals do not carry natural information concerning the dangers they signal.

II

I fully agree, however, that an appeal to teleology, to function, is what is needed to fly a naturalist theory of content. Moreover, what makes a thing into an inner representation is, near enough, that its function is to represent.

But, I shall argue, the way to unpack this insight is to focus on representation *consumption,* rather than representation production. It is the devices that *use* representations which determine these to be representations and, at the same time (contra Fodor), determine their content. If it really is the function of an inner representation to indicate its represented, clearly it is not just a natural sign, a sign that you or I looking on might interpret. It must be one that functions as a sign or representation *for the system itself.* What is it then for a system to use a representation *as* a representation?

The conception of function on which I shall rely was defined in my *Language, Thought, and Other Biological Categories*[5] and defended in "In Defense of Proper Functions"[6] under the label "proper function." Proper functions are determined by the histories of the items possessing them; functions that were "selected for" are paradigm cases.[7] The notions "function" and "design" should not be read, however, as referring only to origin. Natural selection does not slack after the emergence of a structure but actively preserves it by acting against the later emergence of less fit structures. And structures can be preserved due to performance of new functions unrelated to the forces that originally shaped them. Such functions are "proper functions," too, and are "performed in accordance with design."

The notion "design" should not be read—and this is very important—as a reference to innateness. A system may have been designed to be altered by its experience, perhaps to learn from its experience in a prescribed manner. Doing what it has learned to do in this manner is then "behaving in accordance with design" or "functioning properly."[8]

My term 'normal' should be read normatively, historically, and relative to specific function. In the first instance, 'normal' applies to explanations. A "normal explanation" explains the performance of a particular function, telling how it was (typically) historically performed on those (perhaps rare) occasions when it was properly performed. Normal explanations do not tell, say, why it has been common for a function to be performed; they are not statistical explanations. They cover only past times of actual performance, showing how these performances were entailed by natural law, given certain conditions, coupled with the dispositions and structures of the relevant functional devices.[9] In the second instance, 'normal' applies to conditions. A "normal condition for performance of a function" is a condition, the presence of which must be mentioned in giving a full normal explanation for performance of that function. Other functions of the same organism or system may have other normal conditions. For example, normal conditions for discriminating colors are not the same as normal conditions for discriminating tastes, and normal conditions for seeing very large objects are not the same as for seeing very small ones. It follows that 'normal conditions' must not be read as having anything to do with what is typical or average or even, in many cases, at all common. First, many functions are performed only rarely. For example, very few wild seeds land in conditions normal for their growth and development, and the protective colorings of caterpillars seldom actually succeed in preventing them from being eaten. Indeed, normal conditions might almost better be called "historically optimal" conditions. (If normal conditions for proper functioning, hence survival and proliferation, were a statistical norm, imagine how many rabbits there would be in the world.) Second, many proper functions only need to be performed under rare conditions. Consider, for example, the vomiting reflex, the function of which is to prevent (further) toxification of the body. A normal condition for performance of this function is presence, specifically of poison in the stomach, for (I am guessing) it is only under that condition that this reflex has historically had beneficial effects. But poison in the stomach certainly is not an average condition. (Nor, of course, is it a normal condition for other functions of the digestive system.[10])

If it is actually one of a system's functions to produce representations, as we have said, these representations must function as representations for the system itself. Let us view the system, then, as divided into two parts or two aspects, one of which produces representations for the other to consume. What we need to look at is the consumer part, at what it is to use a thing *as* a representation. Indeed, a good look at the consumer part of the system ought to be all that is needed to determine not only representational status but representational content. We argue this as follows. First, the part of the system which consumes representations must understand the representations proffered to it. Suppose, for example, that there were abundant "natural information" (in Dretske's[11] sense) contained in numerous natural signs all present in a certain state of a system. This information could still not serve the system *as* information, unless the signs were understood by the system, and, furthermore, understood as bearers of whatever specific information they, in fact, do bear. (Contrast Fodor's notion that something could function like a representation without functioning like a representation of anything in particular.) So there must be something about the consumer that *constitutes* its taking the signs to indicate, say, *p, q,* and *r* rather than *s, t,* and *u.* But, if we know what constitutes the consumer's *taking* a sign to indicate *p,* what *q,* what *r,* etc., then, granted that the consumer's takings are in some way systematically derived from the structures of the signs so taken, we can construct a semantics for the consumer's language. Anything the signs may indicate qua natural signs or natural information carriers then drops out as entirely irrelevant; the representation-producing side of the system had better pay undivided attention to the language of its consumer. The sign producer's function will be to produce signs that are true *as the consumer reads the language.*

The problem for the naturalist bent on describing intentionality, then, does not concern representation production at all. Although a representation always is something that is produced by a system whose proper function is to make that representation correspond by rule to the world, what the rule of correspondence is, what gives definition to this function, is determined entirely by the representation's consumers.

For a system to use an inner item as a representation, I propose, is for the following two conditions to be met. First, unless the representation accords, *so* (by a certain rule), with a represented, the consumer's normal use of, or response to, the representation will not be able to fulfill all of the consumer's proper functions in so responding—not, at least, in accordance with a normal explanation. (Of course, it might still fulfill these functions by freak accident, but not in the historically normal way.) Putting this more formally, that the representation and the represented accord with one another, so, is a normal condition for proper functioning of the consumer device as it reacts to the representation.[12] Note that the proposal is not that the content of the representation rests on the function of the representation or of the consumer, on what these do. The idea is not that there is such a thing as behaving like a representation of *X* or as being treated like a representation of *X.* The content hangs only on there being a certain condition that would be *normal* for performance of the consumer's functions—namely, that a certain correspondence relation hold between sign and world—whatever those functions may happen to be. For example, suppose the semantic rules for my belief representations are determined by the fact that belief tokens in me will aid the devices that use them to perform certain of their tasks in accordance with a normal explanation for success only under the condition that the forms or "shapes" of these belief tokens correspond, in accordance with said rules, to conditions in the world. Just what these user tasks are need not be mentioned.[13]

Second, represented conditions are conditions that vary, depending on the *form* of the representation, in accordance with specifiable correspondence rules that give the semantics for the relevant *system* of representation. More precisely, representations always admit of significant transformations (in the mathematical sense), which accord with transformations of their corresponding representeds, thus displaying significant articulation into variant and invariant aspects. If an item considered as compounded of certain variant and invariant aspects can be said to be "composed" of these, then we can also say that every representation is, as such, a member of a representational system having a "compositional semantics." For it is not that the represented condition is itself a normal condition for proper operation of the representation consumer. A certain correspondence between the representation and the world is what is normal. Coordinately, there is no such thing as a representation consumer that can understand only one representation. There are always other representations, composed other ways, saying other things, which it could have understood as well, in accordance with the same principles of operation. A couple of very elementary examples should make this clear.[14]

First, consider beavers, who splash the water smartly with their tails to signal danger. This instinctive behavior has the function of causing other beavers to take cover. The splash means danger, because only when it corresponds to danger does the instinctive response to the splash on the part of the interpreter beavers, the consumers, serve a purpose. If there is no danger present, the interpreter beavers interrupt their activities uselessly. Hence, that the splash corresponds to danger is a normal condition for proper functioning of the interpreter beavers' instinctive reaction to the splash. (It does not follow, of course, that it is a usual condition.

Beavers being skittish, most beaver splashes possibly occur in response to things not in fact endangering the beaver.) In the beaver splash semantic system, the time and place of the splash varies with, "corresponds to," the time and place of danger. The representation is articulate: properly speaking, it is not a splash but a splash-at-a-time-and-a-place. Other representations in the same system, splashes at other times and places, indicate other danger locations.

Second, consider honey bees, which perform "dances" to indicate the location of sources of nectar they have discovered. Variations in the tempo of the dance and in the angle of its long axis vary with the distance and direction of the nectar. The interpreter mechanisms in the watching bees—these are the representation consumers—will not perform their full proper functions of aiding the process of nectar collection in accordance with a normal explanation, unless the location of nectar corresponds correctly to the dance. So, the dances are representations of the location of nectar. The full representation here is a dance-at-a-time-in-a-place-at-a-tempo-with-an-orientation.

Notice that, on this account, it is not necessary to assume that most representations are true. Many biological devices perform their proper functions not on the average, but just often enough. The protective coloring of the juveniles of many animal species, for example, is an adaptation passed on because *occasionally* it prevents a juvenile from being eaten, though most of the juveniles of these species get eaten anyway. Similarly, it is conceivable that the devices that fix human beliefs fix true ones not on the average, but just often enough. If the true beliefs are functional and the false beliefs are, for the most part, no worse than having an empty mind, then even very fallible belief-fixing devices might be better than no belief-fixing devices at all. These devices might even be, in a sense, "designed to deliver some falsehoods." Perhaps, given the difficulty of designing highly accurate belief-fixing mechanisms, it is actually advantageous to fix too many beliefs, letting some of these be false, rather than fix too few beliefs. Coordinately, perhaps our belief-consuming mechanisms are carefully designed to tolerate a large proportion of false beliefs. It would not follow, of course, that the belief consumers are designed to *use* false beliefs, certainly not that false beliefs can serve all of the functions that true ones can. Indeed, surely if none of the mechanisms that used beliefs ever cared at all how or whether these beliefs corresponded to anything in the world, beliefs would not be functioning as representations, but in some other capacity.

Shifting our focus from producing devices to consuming devices in our search for naturalized semantic content is important. But the shift from the *function* of consumers to *normal conditions* for proper operation is equally important. Matthen, for example, characterizes what he calls a "quasi-perceptual state" as, roughly, one whose job is to cause the system to do what it must do to perform its function, given that it is in certain circumstances, which are what it represents. Matthen is thus looking pretty squarely at the representation consumers, but at what it is the representation's job to get these consumers to do, rather than at normal conditions for their proper operation. As a result, Matthen now retreats. The description he has given of quasi-perceptual states, he says, cannot cover "real perception such as that which we humans experience. Quite simply, there is no such thing as *the* proper response, or even a range of functionally appropriate responses, to what perception tells us" (op. cit., p. 20).[15] On the contrary, representational content rests not on univocity of consumer function but on sameness of normal conditions for those functions. The same percept of the world may be used to guide any of very many and diverse activities, practical or theoretical. What stays the same is that the percept must correspond to environmental configurations in accordance with the same correspondence rules for each of these activities. For example, if the position of the chair in the room does not correspond, so, to my visual representation of its position, that will hinder me equally in my attempts to avoid the chair when passing through the room, to move the chair, to sit in it, to remove the cat from it, to make judgments about it, etc. Similarly, my belief that New York is large may be turned to any of diverse purposes, but those which require it to be a *representation* require also that New York indeed be large if these purposes are to succeed in accordance with a normal explanation for functioning of my cognitive systems.

III

We have just cleanly bypassed the whole genre of causal/informational accounts of mental content. To illustrate this, we consider an example

of Dretske's. Dretske tells of a certain species of northern hemisphere bacteria which orient themselves away from toxic oxygen-rich surface water by attending to their magnetosomes, tiny inner magnets, which pull toward the magnetic north pole, hence pull down (ibid.). (Southern hemisphere bacteria have their magnetosomes reversed.) The function of the magnetosome thus appears to be to effect that the bacterium moves into oxygen-free water. Correlatively, intuition tells us that what the pull of the magnetosome represents is the whereabouts of oxygen-free water. The direction of oxygen-free water is not, however, a factor in *causing* the direction of pull of the magnetosome. And the most reliable natural information that the magnetosome carries is surely not about oxygen-free water but about distal and proximal causes of the pull, about the direction of geomagnetic or better, just plain magnetic, north. One can, after all, easily deflect the magnetosome away from the direction of lesser oxygen merely by holding a bar magnet overhead. Moreover, it is surely a function of the magnetosome to respond to that magnetic field, that is part of its normal mechanism of operation, whereas responding to oxygen density is not. None of this makes any sense on a causal or informational approach.

But on the biosemantic theory it does make sense. What the magnetosome represents is only what its *consumers* require that it correspond to in order to perform *their* tasks. Ignore, then, how the representation (a pull-in-a-direction-at-a-time) is normally produced. Concentrate, instead, on how the systems that react to the representation work, on what these systems need in order to do their job. What they need is only that the pull be in the direction of oxygen-free water at the time. For example, they care not at all how it came about that the pull is in that direction; the magnetosome that points toward oxygen-free water quite by accident and not in accordance with any normal explanation will do just as well as one that points that way for the normal reasons. (As Socrates concedes in the *Meno,* true opinion is just as good as knowledge so long as it stays put.) What the magnetosome represents then is univocal; it represents only the direction of oxygen-free water. For that is the only thing that corresponds (by a compositional rule) to it, the absence of which would matter—the absence of which would disrupt the function of those mechanisms which rely on the magnetosome for guidance.

It is worth noting that what is represented by the magnetosome is not proximal but distal; no proximal stimulus is represented at all. Nor, of course, does the bacterium perform an inference from the existence of the proximal stimulus (the magnetic field) to the existence of the represented. These are good results for a theory of content to have, for otherwise one needs to introduce a derivative theory of content for mental representations that do not refer, say, to sensory stimulations, and also a foundationalist account of belief fixation. Note also that, on the present view, representations manufactured in identical ways by different species of animal might have different contents. Thus, a certain kind of small swift image on the toad's retina, manufactured by his eye lens, represents a bug, for that is what it must correspond to if the reflex it (invariably) triggers is to perform its proper functions normally, while exactly the same kind of small swift image on the retina of a male hoverfly, manufactured, let us suppose, by a nearly identical lens, represents a passing female hoverfly, for that is what it must correspond to if the female-chasing reflex it (invariably) triggers is to perform its proper functions normally. Turning the coin over, representations with the same content may be normally manufactured in a diversity of ways, even in the same species. How many different ways do you have, for example, of telling a lemon or your spouse? Nor is it necessary that any of the ways one has of manufacturing a given representation be especially reliable ways in order for the representation to have determinate content. These various results cut the biosemantic approach off from all varieties of verificationism and foundationalism with a clean, sharp knife.

IV

But perhaps it will be thought that belief fixation and consumption are not biologically proper activities, hence that there are no normal explanations, in our defined sense, for proper performances of human beliefs. Unlike bee dances, which are all variations on the same simple theme, beliefs in dinosaurs, in quarks, and in the instability of the dollar are recent, novel, and innumerably diverse, as are their possible uses. How could there be anything *biologically* normal or abnormal about the details of the consumption of such beliefs?

But what an organism does in accordance with evolutionary design can be very novel and surprising, for the more complex of nature's creatures are designed to learn. Unlike evolutionary adaptation, learning is not accomplished by *random* generate-and-test procedures. Even when learning involves trial and error (probably the exception rather than the rule), there are principles in accordance with which responses are selected by the system to try, and there are specific principles of generalization and discrimination, etc., which have been built into the system by natural selection. How these principles normally work, that is, how they work given normal (i.e., historically optimal) environments, to produce changes in the learner's nervous system which will effect the furthering of ends of the system has, of course, an explanation—the normal explanation for proper performance of the learning mechanism and of the states of the nervous system it produces.

Using a worn-out comparison, there is an infinity of functions which a modern computer mainframe is capable of performing, depending upon its input and on the program it is running. Each of these things it can do, so long as it is not damaged or broken, "in accordance with design," and to each of these capacities there corresponds an explanation of how it would be activated or fulfilled normally. The human's mainframe takes, roughly, stimulations of the afferent nerves as input, both to program and to run it.[16] It responds, in part, by developing concepts, by acquiring beliefs and desires in accordance with these concepts, by engaging in practical inference leading ultimately to action. Each of these activities may, of course, involve circumscribed sorts of trial and error learning. When conditions are optimal, all this aids survival and proliferation in accordance with an historically normal explanation—one of high generality, of course. When conditions are not optimal, it may yield, among other things, empty or confused concepts, biologically useless desires, and false beliefs. But, even when the desires are biologically useless (though probably not when the concepts expressed in them are empty or confused), there are still biologically normal ways for them to get fulfilled, the most obvious of which require reliance on true beliefs.[17]

Yet how do we know that our contemporary ways of forming concepts, desires, and beliefs do occur in accordance with evolutionary design? Fodor, for example, is ready with the labels "pop Darwinism" and "naive adaptationism" to abuse anyone who supposes that our cognitive systems were actually selected for their belief and desire using capacities.[18] Clearly, to believe that every structure must have a function would be naive. Nor is it wise uncritically to adopt hypotheses about the functions of structures when these functions are obscure. It does not follow that we should balk at the sort of adaptationist who, having found a highly complex structure that quite evidently is currently and effectively performing a highly complex and obviously indispensable function, then concludes, *ceteris paribus,* that this function has been the most recent historical task stabilizing the structure. To suspect that the brain has not been preserved for thinking with or that the eye has not been preserved for seeing with—to suspect this, moreover, in the absence of any alternative hypotheses about causes of the stability of these structures—would be totally irresponsible. Consider: nearly every human behavior is bound up with intentional action. Are we really to suppose that the degree to which our behaviors help to fulfill intentions, and the degree to which intentions result from logically related desires plus beliefs, is a sheer coincidence— that these patterns are irrelevant to survival and proliferation or, though relevant, have had no stabilizing effect on the gene pool? But the only alternative to biological design, in our sense of 'design', is sheer coincidence, freak accident— unless there is a ghost running the machine!

Indeed, it is reasonable to suppose that the brain structures we have recently been using in developing space technology and elementary particle physics have been operating in accordance with the very same general principles as when prehistoric man used them for more primitive ventures. They are no more performing new and different functions or operating in accordance with new and different principles nowadays than are the eyes when what they see is television screens and space shuttles. Compare: the wheel was invented for the purpose of rolling ox carts, and did not come into its own (pulleys, gears, etc.) for several thousand years thereafter, during the industrial revolution. Similarly, it is reasonable that the cognitive structures with which man is endowed were originally nature's solution to some very simple demands made by man's evolutionary niche. But the solution nature stumbled on was elegant, supremely general, and powerful, indeed; I believe it was a solution that cut to the very bone of the ontological structure of the world.

That solution involved the introduction of representations, inner and/or outer, having a subject/predicate structure, and subject to a negation transformation. (Why I believe that that particular development was so radical and so powerful has been explained in depth in LTOBC, chapters 14—19. But see also section v. 6.)

V

One last worry about our sort of position is voiced by Daniel Dennett[19] and discussed at length by Fodor.[20] Is it really plausible that bacteria and paramecia, or even birds and bees, have inner representations in the same sense that we do? Am I really prepared to say that these creatures, too, have mental states, that they think? I am not prepared to say that. On the contrary, the representations that they have must differ from human beliefs in at least six very fundamental ways.[21]

(1) Self-Representing Elements

The representations that the magnetosome produces have three significant variables, each of which refers to itself. The time of the pull refers to the time of the oxygen-free water, the locale of the pull refers to the locale of the oxygen-free water, and the direction of pull refers to the direction of oxygen-free water. The beaver's splash has two self-referring variables: a splash at a certain time and place indicates that there is danger at that same time and place. (There is nothing necessary about this. It might have meant that there would be danger at the nearest beaver dam in five minutes.) Compare the standard color coding on the outsides of colored markers: each color stands for itself. True, it may be that sophisticated indexical representations such as percepts and indexical beliefs also have their time or place or both as significant self-representing elements, but they also have other significant variables that are not self-representing. The magnetosome does not.

(2) Storing Representations

Any representation the time or place of which is a significant variable obviously cannot be stored away, carried about with the organism for use on future occasions. Most beliefs are representations that can be stored away. Clearly this is an important difference.

(3) Indicative and Imperative Representations

The theory I have sketched here of the content of inner representations applies only to indicative representations, representations which are supposed to be determined by the facts, which tell what is the case. It does not apply to imperative representations, representations which are supposed to determine the facts, which tell the interpreter what to do. Neither do causal-informational theories of content apply to the contents of imperative representations. True, some philosophers seem to have assumed that having defined the content of various mental symbols by reference to what causes them to enter the "belief box," then when one finds these same symbols in, say, the "desire box" or the "intention box," one already knows what they mean. But how do we know that the desire box or the intention box use the same representational system as the belief box? To answer that question we would have to know what constitutes a desire box's or an intention box's using one representational system rather than another which, turned around, is the very question at issue. In LTOBC and "Thoughts without Laws; Cognitive Science with Content,"[22] I developed a parallel theory of the content of imperative representations. Very roughly, one of the proper functions of the consumer system for an imperative representation is to help *produce* a correspondence between the representation and the world. (Of course, this proper function often is not performed.) I also argued that desires and intentions are imperative representations.

Consider, then, the beaver's splash. It tells that there is danger here now. Or why not say, instead, that it tells other nearby beavers what to do now, namely, to seek cover? Consider the magnetosome. It tells which is the direction of oxygen-free water. Or why not say, instead, that it tells the bacterium which way to go? Simple animal signals are invariably both indicative and imperative. Even the dance of the honey bee, which is certainly no simple signal, is both indicative and imperative. It tells the worker bees where the nectar is; equally, it tells them where to go. The step from these primitive representations to human beliefs is an enormous one, for it involves the separation of indicative from imperative functions of the representational system. Representations that are undifferentiated between indicative and imperative connect states of affairs directly to actions, to specific things to be done in the face of those states of affairs. Human beliefs are not tied directly to actions. Unless combined with appropriate desires, human beliefs are impotent. And human desires are equally impotent unless combined with suitable beliefs.[23]

(4) Inference

As indicative and imperative functions are separated in the central inner representational systems of humans, they need to be reintegrated. Thus, humans engage in practical inference, combining beliefs and desires in novel ways to yield first intentions and then action. Humans also combine beliefs with beliefs to yield new beliefs. Surely nothing remotely like this takes place inside the bacterium.

(5) Acts of Identifying

Mediate inferences always turn on something like a middle term, which must have the same representational value in both premises for the inference to go through. Indeed, the representation consumers in us perform many functions that require them to use two or more overlapping representations together, and in such a manner that, unless the representeds corresponding to these indeed have a common element, these functions will not be properly performed. Put informally, the consumer device *takes* these represented elements to be the same, thus identifying their representational values. Suppose, for example, that you intend to speak to Henry about something. In order to carry out this intention you must, when the time comes, be able to recognize Henry in perception as the person to whom you intend to speak. You must identify Henry as represented in perception with Henry as represented in your intention. Activities that involve the coordinated use of representations from different sensory modalities, as in the case of eye-hand coordination, visual-tactile coordination, also require that certain objects, contours, places, or directions, etc., be identified as the same through the two modalities. Now, the foundation upon which modern representational theories of thought are built depends upon a denial that what is thought of is ever placed before a naked mind. Clearly, we can never know what an inner representation represents by a direct comparison of representation to represented. Rather, acts of identifying are our ways of "knowing what our representations represent." The bacterium is quite incapable of knowing, in this sense, what its representations are about. This might be a reason to say that it does not understand its own representations, not really.

(6) Negation and Propositional Content

The representational system to which the magnetosome pull belongs does not contain negation. Indeed, it does not even contain contrary representations, for the magnetosome cannot pull in two directions at once. Similarly, if two beavers splash at different times or places, or if two bees dance different dances at the same time, it may well be that there is indeed beaver danger two times or two places and that there is indeed nectar in two different locations.[24] Without contrariety, no conflict, of course and more specifically, no contradiction. If the law of noncontradiction plays as significant a role in the development of human concepts and knowledge as has traditionally been supposed, this is a large difference between us and the bacterium indeed.[25] In LTOBC, I argued that negation, hence explicit contradiction, is dependent upon subject-predicate, that is, propositional, structure and vice versa. Thus, representations that are simpler also do not have propositional content.

In sum, these six differences between our representations and those of the bacterium, or Fodor's paramecia, ought to be enough amply to secure our superiority, to make us feel comfortably more endowed with mind.

NOTES

1. "Banish Discontent," in Jeremy Butterfield, ed., *Language, Mind and Logic* (New York: Cambridge, 1986), pp. 1–23; *Psychosemantics: The Problem of Meaning in the Philosophy of Mind* (Cambridge: MIT, 1987).
2. "Toward a Causal Theory of Representation," in Peter French, Theodore Uehling Jr., Howard Wettstein, eds., *Contemporary Perspectives in the Philosophy of Language* (Minneapolis: Minnesota UP, 1979), pp. 81–102.
3. "Misrepresentation," in Radu Bogdan, ed., *Belief: Form, Content, and Function* (New York: Oxford, 1986), pp. 17–36.
4. "Biological Functions and Perceptual Content," *The Journal of Philosophy*, LXXXV, 1 (January 1988): 5–27.
5. Cambridge: MIT, 1984 (hereafter LTOBC).
6. *Philosophy of Science*, LVI, 2 (June 1989): 288–302.
7. An odd custom exists of identifying this sort of view with Larry Wright, who does not hold it. See my "in Defense of Proper Functions." Natural selection is not the only source of proper functions. See LTOBC, chs. 1 and 2.
8. See LTOBC; and "Truth Rules, Hoverflies, and the Kripke-Wittgenstein Paradox," *The Philosophical Review* 99:323–53, 1990.
9. This last clarification is offered to aid Fodor ("On There Not Being an Evolutionary Theory of Content" [hereafter NETC], unpublished), who uses my term 'Normal' (here I am not capitalizing it but the idea has not changed) in a multiply confused way, making a parody of my views on representation. In this connection, see also fns. 13 and 17.
10. "Normal explanation" and "normal condition for performance of a function," along with "proper function," are defined with considerable detail in LTOBC. The reader may wish, in particular, to consult the discussion of normal explanations for performance of "adapted and derived proper functions" in ch. 2, for these functions cover the functions of states of the nervous system which result in part from learning, such as states of human belief and desire.
11. *Knowledge and the Flow of Information* (Cambridge: MIT, 1981).
12. Strictly, this normal condition must derive from a "most proximate normal explanation" of the consumer's proper functioning. See LTOBC, ch. 6, where a more precise account of what I am here calling "representations" is given under the heading "intentional icons."
13. In this particular case, one task is, surely, contributing, in conformity with certain general principles or rules, to practical inference processes, hence to the fulfillment of current desires. So, if you like, all beliefs have the *same* proper function. Or, since the rules or principles that govern practical inference dictate that a belief's "shape" determines what other inner representations it may properly be combined with to form what products, we could say that each belief has a *different* range of proper functions. Take your pick. Cf. Fodor, "Information and Representation," in Philip Hanson, ed., *Information, Language, and Cognition* (Vancouver: British Columbia UP, 1989); and NETC.
14. These examples are of representations that are not "inner" but out in the open. As in the case of inner representations, however, they are produced and consumed by mechanisms designed to cooperate with one another; each such representation stands intermediate between two parts of a single biological system.
15. Dretske (in "Misrepresentation," p. 28) and David Papineau [in *Reality and Representation* (New York: Blackwell, 1987), p. 67 ff] have similar concerns.
16. This is a broad metaphor. I am not advocating computationalism.
17. A word of caution. The normal conditions for a desire's fulfillment are not necessarily fulfillable conditions. In general, normal conditions for fulfillment of a function are not quite the same as conditions which, when you add them and stir, always effect proper function, because they may well be impossible conditions. For example, Fodor, in "Information

and Representation" and NETC, has questioned me about the normal conditions under which his desire that it should rain tomorrow will perform its proper function of *getting* it to rain. Now, the biologically normal way for such a desire to be fulfilled is exactly the same as for any other desire: one has or acquires true beliefs about how to effect the fulfillment of the desire and acts on them. Biologically normal conditions for fulfillment of the desire for rain thus include the condition that one has true beliefs about how to make it rain. Clearly this is an example in which the biological norm fails to accord with the statistical norm: most desires about the weather are fulfilled, if at all, by biological accident. It may even be that the laws of nature, coupled with my situation, prohibit my having any true beliefs about how to make it rain; the needed general condition cannot be realized in the particular case. Similarly, normal conditions for proper function of beliefs in impossible things are, of course, impossible conditions: these beliefs are such that they cannot correspond, in accordance with the rules of mentalese, to conditions in the world.

18. *Psychosemantics* and NETC.

19. *Brainstorms* (Montgomery, VT: Bradford Books, 1978).
20. "Why Paramecia Don't Have Mental Representations," in P. French, T. Uehling Jr., and H. Wettstein, eds., *Midwest Studies in Philosophy*, x (Minneapolis: Minnesota UP, 1986), pp. 3–23.
21. Accordingly, in LTOBC I did not call these primitive forms "representations" but "intentional signals" and, for items like bee dances, "intentional icons," reserving the term 'representation' for those icons, the representational values of which must be identified if their consumers are to function properly—see section V.5.
22. *The Philosophical Review*, XLV, 1 (1986):47–80.
23. Possibly human intentions are in both indicative and imperative mood, however, functioning simultaneously to represent settled facts about one's future and to direct one's action.
24. On the other hand, the bees cannot go two places at once.
25. In LTOBC, I defend the position that the law of non-contradiction plays a crucial role in allowing us to develop new methods of mapping the world with representations.

48 | Reasoning and Representing

Robert Brandom

I

1

One useful way of dividing up the broadly cognitive capacities that constitute our mindedness is to distinguish between our sentience and our sapience. Sentience is what we share with nonverbal animals such as cats—the capacity to be *aware* in the sense of being *awake*. Sentience, which so far as our understanding yet reaches is an exclusively biological phenomenon, is in turn to be distinguished from the mere reliable differential responsiveness we sentients share with artifacts such as thermostats and land mines. Sapience, on the other hand, concerns *understanding* or intelligence, rather than irritability or arousal. One is treating something as sapient insofar as one explains its behavior by attributing to it intentional states such as belief and desire as constituting *reasons* for that be-

havior. Sapients act as though reasons matter to them. They are rational agents in the sense that their behavior can be made intelligible, at least sometimes, by attributing to them the capacity to make practical inferences concerning how to get what they want, and theoretical inferences concerning what follows from what.

Besides thinking of sapience in terms of reasons and inference, it is natural to think of it in terms of truth. Sapients are believers, and believing is taking-true. Sapients are agents, and acting is making-true. To be sapient is to have states such as belief, desire, and intention, which are contentful in the sense that the question can appropriately be raised under what circumstances what is believed, desired, or intended would be *true*. Understanding such a content is grasping the conditions that are necessary and sufficient for its truth.

These two ways of conceiving sapience, in

From M. Michael and J. O'Leary-Hawthorne, eds., *Philosophy in Mind* (Kluwer, 1994), pp. 159–78. Reprinted with permission of the author and of Kluwer Academic Publishers.

terms of inference and in terms of truth, have as their common explanatory target contents distinguished as intelligible by their *propositional* form. What we can offer as a reason, what we can take or make true, has a propositional content, a content of the sort that we express by the use of declarative sentences and ascribe by the use of 'that' clauses. Propositional contents stand in inferential relations, and they have truth conditions.

Propositional contentfulness is only part of the story about sapience, however. When we try to understand the thought or discourse of others, the task can be divided initially into two parts: understanding what they are thinking or talking about and understanding what they are thinking or saying about it. My primary aim here is to present a view about the relation between what is *said* or *thought* and what it is said or thought *about*. The former is the propositional dimension of thought and talk, and the latter is its *representational* dimension. The question I will address is why any state or utterance that has propositional content also should be understood as having representational content. (For this so much as to be a question, it must be possible to characterize propositional content in nonrepresentational terms.)

The answer I will defend is that the representational dimension of propositional contents should be understood in terms of their *social* articulation—how a propositionally contentful belief or claim can have a different significance from the perspective of the individual believer or claimer, on the one hand, than it does from the perspective of one who attributes that belief or claim to the individual, on the other. The context within which concern with what is thought and talked *about* arises is the assessment of how the judgements of one individual can serve as reasons for another. The representational content of claims and the beliefs they express reflects the social dimension of the game of giving and asking for reasons.

2

It may be remarked at the outset that it will not do just to think of the representational dimension of semantic contentfulness according to a designational paradigm—that is, on the model of the relation between a name and what it is a name of. For that relation is a *semantic* relation only in virtue of what one can go on to *do* with what is picked out by the name—what one can then *say*

about it. Merely picking out an object or a possible state of affairs is not enough. What about it? One must say something about the object, claim that the state of affairs obtains or is a fact.

One of Kant's epoch-making insights, confirmed and secured for us also by Frege and Wittgenstein, is his recognition of the *primacy of the propositional*. The pre-Kantian tradition took it for granted that the proper order of semantic explanation begins with a doctrine of concepts or terms, divided into singular and general, whose meaningfulness can be grasped independently of and prior to the meaningfulness of judgements. Appealing to this basic level of interpretation, a doctrine of judgements then explains the combination of concepts into judgements, and how the correctness of the resulting judgements depends on what is combined and how. Appealing to this derived interpretation of judgements, a doctrine of consequences finally explains the combination of judgements into inferences, and how the correctness of inferences depends on what is combined and how.

Kant rejects this. One of his cardinal innovations is the claim that the fundamental unit of awareness or cognition, the minimum graspable, is the *judgement*. Thus concepts can only be understood as abstractions, in terms of the role they play in judging. A concept just is a predicate of a possible judgement (Critique of Pure Reason, A69/B94) which is why

> The only use which the understanding can make of concepts is to form judgements by them. (Critique of Pure Reason, A68/B93).

For Kant, any discussion of content must start with the contents of judgements, since anything else only has content insofar as it contributes to the contents of judgements. This is why his transcendental logic can investigate the presuppositions of contentfulness in terms of the categories, that is, the 'functions of unity in judgement' (Critique of Pure Reason, A69/B94). This explanatory strategy is taken over by Frege, for whom the semantic notion of conceptual content ultimately has the theoretical task of explaining pragmatic *force*—the paradigmatic variety of which is *assertional* force, which attaches only to declarative sentences. As the later Wittgenstein puts the point, only the utterance of a sentence makes a move in the language game. Applying a concept is to be understood in terms of making a claim or expressing a belief. The concept 'concept' is not intelligible apart from the possibility of such application in *judging*.

The lesson is that the relation between designation and what is designated can only be understood as an aspect of judging or claiming *that* something (expressed by a declarative sentence, not by a singular term or predicate by itself) is so—i.e., is *true*. That is judging, believing, or claiming *that* a proposition or claim is true (expresses or states a fact), *that* something is *true of* an object or collection of objects, *that* a predicate is *true of* something else. Thus one must be concerned with what is said or expressed, as well as what it is said *of* or true *of*—the thought as well as what the thought is *about*.

3

Accordingly we start our story with an approach to propositional contents—what can be *said,* or *believed,* or *thought,* in general what can be *taken* (to be) *true*. The guiding idea is that the essential feature distinguishing what is propositionally contentful is that it can serve both as a premise and as the conclusion of *inferences.* Taking (to be) true is treating as a fit premise for inferences. This is exploiting Frege's semantic principle—that good inferences never lead from true premises to conclusions that are not true—not in order to define good inferences in terms of their preservation of truth, but rather to define truth as what is preserved by good inferences.

On the side of propositionally contentful *intentional states,* paradigmatically *belief,* the essential inferential articulation of the propositional is manifested in the form of intentional interpretation or explanation. Making behavior intelligible according to this model is taking the individual to act for *reasons.* This is what lies behind Dennett's slogan: 'Rationality is the mother of intention.' The role of belief in imputed pieces of practical reasoning, leading from beliefs and desires to the formation of intentions, is essential to intentional explanation—and so is reasoning in which both premise and conclusion have the form of believables.

On the side of propositionally contentful *speech acts,* paradigmatically assertion, the essential inferential articulation of the propositional is manifested in the fact that the core of specifically *linguistic* practice is the game of giving and asking for *reasons.* Claiming or asserting is what one must do in order to give a reason, and it is a speech act that reasons can be demanded for. Claims both serve as and stand in need of reasons or justifications. They have the

contents they have in part in virtue of the role they play in a network of inferences.

Indeed, the *conceptual* should be distinguished precisely by its inferential articulation. This is a point on which traditional empiricism needed instruction by traditional rationalism. What is the difference between a parrot or a thermostat that represents a light as being red or a room as being cold by exercising its reliable differential responsive disposition to utter the noise 'That's red' or to turn on the furnace, on the one hand, and a knower who does so by applying the concepts *red* and *cold,* on the other? What is the knower able to *do* that the parrot and the thermostat cannot? After all, they may respond differentially to *just* the same range of stimuli. The knower is able to *use* the differentially elicited response in *inference.* The knower has the practical knowhow to situate that response in a network of inferential relations—to tell what follows from something being red or cold, what would be evidence for it, what would be incompatible with it, and so on. For the knower, taking something to be red or cold is making a move in the game of giving and asking for reasons—a move that can justify other moves, be justified by still other moves, and that closes off or precludes still further moves. The parrot and the thermostat lack the concepts in spite of their mastery of the corresponding noninferential differential responsive dispositions, precisely because they lack the practical mastery of the inferential articulation in which grasp of conceptual content consists.

The idea, then, is to start with a story about the sayable, thinkable, believable (and so propositional) contents expressed by the use of declarative sentences and 'that' clauses derived from them—a story couched in terms of their roles in *inference.*[1] Conceptual content is in the first instance *inferentially* articulated. To approach the representational dimension of semantic content from this direction, it is necessary to ask about the relation between *inference* and *reference.* This is to ask about the relation between what is said or thought and what it is said or thought *about.* How can the representational dimension of conceptual content be brought into the inferential picture of propositional contents? The thesis to be elaborated here is that the representational dimension of discourse reflects the fact that conceptual content is not only *inferentially* articulated, but *socially* articulated. The game of giving and asking for reasons is an essentially *social* practice.

4

The rationale for such a claim emerges most clearly from consideration of certain very general features of discursive practice. Here it is useful to start with another of Kant's fundamental insights, into the *normative* character of the significance of what is conceptually contentful. His idea is that judgements and actions are above all things that we are *responsible* for. Kant understands concepts as having the form of *rules,* which is to say that they specify how something *ought* (according to the rule) to be done. The understanding, the conceptual faculty, is the faculty of grasping rules, of appreciating the distinction between correct and incorrect application they determine. Judgings and doings are acts that have contents that one can take or make true and for which the demand for reasons is in order. What is distinctive about them is the way they are governed by rules. Being in an intentional state or performing an intentional action has a normative significance. It counts as undertaking (acquiring) an obligation or commitment; the content of the commitment is determined by the rules that are the concepts in terms of which the act or state is articulated. Thus Kant picks us out as distinctively normative or rule-governed creatures.

Descartes inaugurated a new philosophical era by conceiving of what he took to be the ontological distinction between the mental and the physical in epistemological terms, in terms of accessibility to cognition, in terms, ultimately, of certainty. Kant launched a new philosophical epoch by shifting the center of concern from *certainty* to *necessity.* Where Descartes' descriptive conception of intentionality, centering on certainty, picks out as essential our grip on the concepts employed in cognition and action, Kant's normative conception of intentionality, centering on necessity, treats their grip on us as the heart of the matter. The attempt to understand the source, nature, and significance of the norms implicit in our concepts—both those that govern the theoretical employment of concepts in inquiry and knowledge and those that govern their practical employment in deliberation and action—stands at the very center of Kant's philosophical enterprise. The most urgent question for Kant is how to understand the *rulishness* of concepts, how to understand their *authority, bindingness,* or *validity.* It is this normative character that he calls 'Notwendigkeit,' necessity.

The lesson to be learned from this Kantian normative conceptual pragmatics is that judging

and acting are distinguished from other doings by the kind of *commitment* they involve. Judging or claiming is staking a claim—undertaking a commitment. The conceptual articulation of these commitments, their status as distinctively *discursive* commitments, consists in the way they are liable to demands for *justification,* and the way they serve both to justify some further commitments and to preclude the justification of some other commitments. Their propositional contentfulness consists precisely in this inferential articulation of commitments and entitlements to those commitments.

Specifically *linguistic* practices are those in which some performances are accorded the significance of assertions or claimings—the undertaking of inferentially articulated (and so propositionally contentful) commitments.[2] Mastering such linguistic practices is a matter of learning how to keep score on the inferentially articulated commitments and entitlements of various interlocutors, oneself included. Understanding a speech act—grasping its discursive significance—is being able to attribute the right commitments in response. This is knowing how it changes the score of what the performer and the audience are committed and entitled to.

One way of thinking about the claims by which discursive commitments are expressed is in terms of the interaction of inferentially articulated *authority* and *responsibility.* In making an assertion one lends to the asserted content one's *authority,* licensing others to undertake a corresponding commitment. Thus one essential aspect of this model of discursive practice is *communication:* the interpersonal, intracontent inheritance of entitlement to commitments. In making an assertion one also undertakes a *responsibility,* to justify the claim if appropriately challenged, and thereby to redeem one's entitlement to the commitment acknowledged by the claiming. Thus another essential aspect of this model of discursive practice is *justification:* the intrapersonal, intercontent inheritance of entitlement to commitments.

II

1

One can pick out what is *propositionally* contentful to begin with as whatever can serve both as a premise and as a conclusion in *inference*— what can be offered as and itself stand in need of *reasons.* Understanding or grasping such a propositional content is a kind of know-how—practical mastery of the game of giving and asking for reasons, being able to tell what is a reason for what, distinguish good reasons from bad. To play such a game is to keep *score* of what various interlocutors are committed and entitled to. Understanding the content of a speech act or a belief is being able to accord the performance of that speech act or the acquisition of that belief the proper practical significance—knowing how it would change the score in various contexts. Semantic, that is to begin with, inferential, relations are to be understood in terms of this sort of pragmatic scorekeeping. Taking it that the claim expressed by one sentence entails the claim expressed by another is treating anyone who is committed to the first as thereby committed to the second. We typically think about inference solely in terms of the relation between premise and conclusion, that is, as a monological relation among propositional contents. Discursive practice, the giving and asking for reasons, however, involves both inter*content* and inter*personal* relations. The claim is that the representational aspect of the propositional contents that play the inferential roles of premise and conclusion should be understood in terms of the social or dialogical dimension of communicating reasons, of assessing the significance of reasons offered by others.

If whatever plays a suitable role in inference is propositionally contentful, and whatever is propositionally contentful therefore also has representational content, then nothing can deserve to count as specifically *inferential* practice unless it at least implicitly involves a representational dimension. Nonetheless, one can give sufficient conditions for a social practice to qualify as according *inferentially articulated* significances to performances, that is, to be a practice of making claims that can serve as reasons for others, and for which reasons can be demanded, without using any specifically representational vocabulary. That is what the model of discursive practice as keeping score on commitments and entitlements does. The story I want to tell is then how the implicit representational dimension of the inferential contents of claims arises out of the difference in social perspective between *producers* and *consumers* of reasons. The aim is an account in nonrepresentational terms of what is expressed by the use of explicitly representational vocabulary.

The connection between *representation,* on the one hand, and *communication* or the *social* dimension of inferential practice, on the other, is sufficiently unobvious that I want to start with a quick point that may help show why one could so much as think that representation could be understood in these terms. The claim is that assessment of what people are talking and thinking *about,* rather than what they are saying about it, is a feature of the essentially *social* context of *communication.* Talk about representation is talk about what it is to secure communication by being able to use each other's judgements as reasons, as premises in our own inferences, even just hypothetically, to assess their significance in the context of our own collateral commitments.

One way to get a preliminary taste for how one could think that representational semantic talk could be understood as expressing differences in social perspective among interlocutors, consider how assessments of *truth* work. Perhaps the central context in which such assessments classically arise is attributions of *knowledge.* According to the traditional *JTB* account, knowledge is justified true belief. Transposed into a specification of a normative status something could be taken to have by interlocutors who are keeping score of each others commitments and entitlements, this account requires that in order for it to be *knowledge* that a scorekeeper takes another to have, that scorekeeper must adopt three sorts of practical attitude: First, the scorekeeper must *attribute* an inferentially articulated, hence propositionally contentful *commitment.* This corresponds to the *belief* condition on knowledge. Second, the scorekeeper must *attribute* a sort of inferential *entitlement* to that commitment. This corresponds to the *justification* condition on knowledge.

What is it that then corresponds to the *truth* condition on knowledge? For the scorekeeper to take the attributed claim to be true is just for the scorekeeper to endorse that claim. That is, the third condition is that the scorekeeper himself *undertake* the same commitment attributed to the candidate knower.

Undertaking a commitment is adopting a certain *normative stance* with respect to a claim; it is not attributing a property to it. The classical metaphysics of truth properties misconstrues what one is doing in endorsing the claim as *describing* in a special way. It confuses *attributing* and *undertaking* or *acknowledging* commitments, the two fundamental social flavors of deontic practical attitudes that institute normative statuses. It does so by assimilating the third condition on treating someone as having knowledge to the first two. Properly understanding truth talk in fact requires understanding just this difference of social perspective: between *attributing* a normative status to another, and *undertaking* or adopting it oneself.[3] It is the practice of assessing the truth of claims that underlies the idea that propositional contents can be understood in terms of truth conditions. What I want to do is to show how this idea of *truth* claims as expressing differences in social perspective can be extended to representation more generally.

2

The prime explicitly representational locution of natural languages is *de re ascriptions of propositional attitudes*. It is their use in these locutions that make the words 'of' and 'about' express the intentional directedness of thought and talk—as distinct from their use in such phrases as 'the pen of my aunt' and 'weighing about five pounds.' Thus in order to identify vocabulary in alien languages that means what 'of' and 'about' used in this sense do, one must find expressions of de re ascriptions of propositional attitudes. It is these ascriptions that we use to *say* what we are talking and thinking *about.* My strategy here is to address the question of how to understand what is expressed by representational vocabulary by asking how expressions must be *used* in order to qualify as *de re* ascriptions of propositional attitudes.

The tradition distinguishes two readings of or senses that can be associated with propositional attitude ascriptions. Ascriptions *de dicto* attribute belief in a *dictum* or saying, while ascriptions *de re* attribute belief about some *res* or thing. The distinction arises with sentential operators other than 'believes'; consider to begin with the claim:

The President of the United States will be black by the year 2000.

Read *de dicto,* this means that the dictum or sentence

The President of the United States is black.

will be true by the year 2000. Read *de re,* it means that the *res* or thing, the present President of the United States, namely Bill Clinton, will be black by the year 2000. Our concern here is with how this distinction applies to ascriptions of propositional attitude—though it is a criteri-

on of adequacy on the account offered here that it can be extended to deal with these other contexts as well.

In ordinary parlance the distinction between *de dicto* and *de re* readings is the source of systematic ambiguity. Sometimes, as in the case above, one of the readings involves a sufficiently implausible claim that it is easy to disambiguate. It is best, however, to regiment our usage slightly in order to mark the distinction explicitly. This can be done with little strain to our ears by using 'that' and 'of' in a systematic way. Consider:

Henry Adams believed the popularizer of the lightning rod did not popularize the lightning rod.

It is quite unlikely that what is intended is the *de dicto*

Henry Adams believed that the popularizer of the lightning rod did not popularize the lightning rod.

Adams would presumably not have endorsed the *dictum* that follows the 'that.' It is entirely possible, however, that the *de re* claim

Henry Adams believed of the popularizer of the lightning rod that he did not popularize the lightning rod.

is true. For since the popularizer of the lightning rod is the inventor of bifocals (namely Benjamin Franklin), this latter claim could be true if Henry Adams had the belief that would be ascribed *de dicto* as

Henry Adams believed that the inventor of bifocals did not popularize the lightning rod.

Quine emphasizes that the key grammatical difference between these two sorts of ascriptions concerns the propriety of *substitution* for singular terms occurring in them. Expressions occurring in the *de re* portion of an ascription—within the scope of the 'of' operator in the regimented versions—have in his terminology *referentially transparent* uses: coreferential terms can be intersubstituted *salva veritate,* that is, without changing the truth value of the whole ascription. By contrast, such substitution in the *de dicto* portion of an ascription—within the scope of the 'that' operator in the regimented versions—may well change the truth value of the whole ascription. Syntactically, *de re* ascriptions may be thought of as formed from *de dicto* ones by *exporting* a singular term from within

the 'that' clause, prefacing it with 'of,' and putting a pronoun in the original position. Thus the
de dicto form

S believes that Φ (t),

becomes the *de re*

S believes of t that Φ (it).

The significance of Quine's fundamental observation that the key difference between these
two sorts of ascription lies in the circumstances
under which the substitution of coreferential
expressions is permitted was obscured by considerations that are from my point of view
extraneous:

1. Quine's idiosyncratic view that singular
   terms are dispensable in favor of the quan-
   tificational expressions he takes to be the
   genuine locus of referential commitment
   leads him to look only at quantified ascriptions, embroils his discussion in issues of
   existential commitment, and diverts him
   into worries about when 'exportation' is legitimate.
2. This emphasis led in turn—Kaplan bears
   considerable responsibility here—to ignoring the analysis of ordinary de re ascriptions in favor of what I call *epistemically strong de re* ascriptions, which are
   used to attribute a privileged epistemic relation to the object talked or thought about.
   This detour had fruitful consequences for
   our appreciation of special features of the
   behavior of demonstratives (and as a result, of proper name tokenings anaphori-
   cally dependent on them), particularly in
   modal contexts. But from the point of view
   of understanding aboutness in general—
   my topic here—it was a detour and a distraction nonetheless.

The important point is, as the regimentation
reminds us, that it is *de re* propositional attitude
ascribing locutions that we use in everyday life
to express what we are talking and thinking *of* or
about. One way of trying to understand the representational dimension of propositional content is accordingly to ask what is expressed by
this fundamental sort of representational locution. What are we *doing* when we make claims
about what someone is talking or thinking
about? How must vocabulary be used in order
for it to deserve to count as expressing such *de
re* ascriptions? Answering that question in a
way that does not itself employ representational
vocabulary in specifying that use is then a way

of coming to understand representational relations in nonrepresentational terms.

3

The rest of this essay is about the expressive
role of *de re* ascriptions. I'm going to present it
in the technical vocabulary I prefer, which is in
some ways idiosyncratic; but the basic point
about the way the use of this paradigmatic representational locution expresses differences in
social perspective does not depend on the details of that idiom.[4]

Recall that I think we should understand discursive practice in terms of the adoption of
practical attitudes by which interlocutors keep
score on each other's commitments (and entitlements to those commitments, but we can ignore
them here). Claiming (and so, ultimately, judging) is *undertaking* or *acknowledging* a commitment that is propositionally contentful in virtue
of its *inferential* articulation. The large task is to
show what it is about that inferential articulation
in virtue of which claimable contents are therefore also *representational* contents. This is to
move from propositional contents introduced as
potential premises and conclusions of inferences, via the social dimension of inferential articulation that consists of giving and asking for
reasons of each other in communication, to
propositions as talking of or about objects, and
saying of them how they are. [I'll give short
shrift here to the *objectivity* part of the claim,
but think about how assessments of *truth* were
presented above as distinct from assessments of
belief and *justification.*]

Undertaking a commitment is doing something that makes it appropriate for others to *attribute* it. This can happen in two different
ways. First, one may *acknowledge* the commitment, paradigmatically by being disposed to
avow it by an overt assertion. Or one may acknowledge it by employing it as a premise in
one's theoretical or practical reasoning. This
last includes being disposed to *act* on it *practically*—taking account of it as a premise in the
practical reasoning that stands behind one's intentional actions. Second, one may undertake
the commitment *consequentially,* that is, as a
conclusion one is committed to as an inferential
consequence entailed by what one *does* acknowledge. These correspond to two senses of
'believe' that are often not distinguished: the
sense in which one only believes what one takes
oneself to believe, and the sense in which one
believes willy nilly whatever one's beliefs com-

mit one to. [The fact that people often move back and forth between belief in the empirical sense, which does not involve inferential closure, and belief in the logical or ideal sense that does, is one of the reasons that when being careful I prefer to talk in terms of commitments rather than beliefs—I don't officially believe in beliefs.] The second sense is the one in which if I believe Kant revered Hamann, and I believe Hamann was the Magus of the North, then whether the question has ever arisen for me or not, whether I know it or not, I in fact believe Kant revered the Magus of the North.

Attributing beliefs or commitments is a practical attitude that is *implicit* in the scorekeeping practices within which alone anything can have the significance of a claim or a judgement. *Ascribing* beliefs or commitments is making that *implicit* practical attitude *explicit* in the form of a claim. In a language without explicit attitude ascribing locutions such as the 'believes that' or 'claims that' operator, attributing commitments is something one can only *do*. Propositional attitude ascribing locutions make it possible explicitly to *say* that that is what one is doing: to express that practical deontic scorekeeping attitude as a propositional content—that is, as the content of a claim. In this form it can appear as a premise or conclusion of an inference; it becomes something which can be offered as a reason, and for which reasons can be demanded. The paradigm of the genus of *explicitating* vocabulary, of which propositional attitude ascribing locutions are a species, is the conditional. The use of conditionals makes explicit as the content of a claim, and so something one can *say,* the endorsement of an *inference*—an attitude one could otherwise only manifest by what one *does*. Ascriptional vocabulary such as 'believes' or 'claims' makes *attribution* of doxastic commitments explicit in the form of claimable contents.

4

In asserting an ascriptional claim of the form

> S believes (or is committed to the claim) that Φ (t),

one is accordingly doing two things, adopting two different sorts of deontic attitude: one is *attributing* one doxastic commitment, to Φ (*t*), and one is *undertaking* another, namely a commitment to the ascription. The explicitating role of ascriptional locutions means that the content

of the commitment one *undertakes* is to be understood in terms of what one is doing in *attributing* the first commitment.

The ascription above specifies the content of the commitment attributed by using an unmodified 'that' clause, which according to our regimentation corresponds to an ascription *de dicto*. A full telling of my story requires that quite a bit be said about how these ascriptions work, but I'm not going to do that here. Roughly, the ascriber who specifies the content of the attributed commitment in the *de dicto* way is committed to the target being prepared to *acknowledge* the attributed commitment in essentially the terms specified—that is, to endorse the *dictum*.[5]

I want to take an appropriate account of *de dicto* ascriptions of propositional attitudes for granted, and show what is different about *de re* ascriptions, those that are regimented in the form:

> S claims of t that Φ (it).

I think that the beginning of wisdom in this area is the realization that (once what I have called 'epistemically strong de re ascriptions' have been put to one side) the distinction between *de dicto* and *de re* should not be understood to distinguish two kinds of *belief* or belief-contents, but two kinds of *ascription*—in particular two different *styles* in which the *content* of the commitment ascribed can be *specified*.[6] (Dennett is perhaps the most prominent commentator who has taken this line. See Dennett, 1982.)

In specifying the content of the claim that is attributed by an ascription, a question can arise as to who the ascriber takes to be responsible for this being a way of *saying* (that is, making explicit) what is believed, the content of the commitment. Consider the sly prosecutor, who characterizes his opponent's claim by saying:

> The defense attorney believes a pathological liar is a trustworthy witness.

We can imagine that the defense attorney hotly contests this characterization:

> Not so; what I believe is that the man who just testified is a trustworthy witness.

To which the prosecutor might reply:

> Exactly, and I have presented evidence that ought to convince anyone that the man who just testified is a pathological liar.

If the prosecutor were being fastidious in characterizing the other's claim, he would make it clear who is responsible for what: the defense attorney claims that a certain man is a trustworthy witness, and the prosecutor claims that that man is a pathological liar. The disagreement is about whether this guy is a liar, not about whether liars make trustworthy witnesses. Using the regimentation suggested above, the way to make this explicit is with a *de re* specification of the content of the belief ascribed. What the prosecutor *ought* to say (matters of courtroom strategy aside) is:

> The defense attorney claims of a pathological liar that he is a trustworthy witness.

This way of putting things makes explicit the division of responsibility involved in the ascription. That someone is a trustworthy witness is part of the commitment that is *attributed* by the ascriber, that that individual is in fact a pathological liar is part of the commitment that is *undertaken* by the ascriber.

Ascription always involves attributing one doxastic commitment and, since ascriptions are themselves claims or judgements, undertaking another. My suggestion is that the expressive function of *de re* ascriptions of propositional attitude is to make explicit which aspects of what is said express commitments that are being *attributed* and which express commitments that are *undertaken*. The part of the content specification that appears within the *de dicto* 'that' clause is limited to what, according to the ascriber, the one to whom the commitment is ascribed would (or in a strong sense should) *acknowledge* as an expression of what that individual is committed to. The part of the content specification that appears within the scope of the *de re* 'of' includes what, according to the *ascriber* of the commitment (but not necessarily according to the one to whom it is ascribed) is acknowledged as an expression of what the target of the ascription is committed to. (This is what the target should, according to the ascriber, acknowledge only in a much weaker sense of 'should'.) Thus the marking of portions of the content-specification of a propositional attitude ascription into *de dicto* and *de re* portions makes explicit the essential deontic scorekeeping distinction of *social* perspective between commitments attributed and those undertaken.

5

The difference expressed by segregating the content specification of a propositional attitude

ascription into distinct *de re* and *de dicto* regions, marked in our regimentation by 'of' and 'that,' can be thought of in terms of *inferential* and *substitutional* commitments. According to the model I started with, propositional, that is, assertible, contents are inferentially articulated. Grasping such a content is being able to distinguish in practice what should follow from endorsing it, and what such endorsement should follow from. But the consequences of endorsing a given claim depends on what other commitments are available to be employed as auxiliary hypotheses in the inference. The ascriber of a doxastic commitment has got two different perspectives available from which to draw those auxiliary hypotheses in specifying the content of the commitment being ascribed: that of the one to whom it is *ascribed* and that of the one *ascribing* it. Where the specification of the content depends only on auxiliary premises that (according to the ascriber) the target of the ascription *acknowledges* being committed to, though the ascriber may not, it is put in *de dicto* position, within the 'that' clause. Where the specification of the content depends on auxiliary premises that the *ascriber* endorses, but the target of the ascription may not, it is put in *de re* position.

More particularly, the use of expressions as singular terms is governed by *substitution-inferential* commitments.[7] The rule for determining the scorekeeping significance and so the expressive function of *de re* ascriptions that I am proposing is then the following. Suppose that according to A's scorekeeping on commitments, B acknowledges commitment to the claim $\Phi(t)$. Then A can make this attribution of commitment explicit in the form of a claim by saying

> B claims that Φ (t).

If in addition A acknowledges commitment to the identity $t = t'$, then whether or not A takes it that B would acknowledge that commitment, A can also characterize the content of the commitment ascribed to B by saying

> B claims of t' that Φ (it).

Again, the question just is whose substitutional commitments one is permitted to appeal to in specifying the consequences someone is committed to by acknowledging a particular doxastic commitment. Where in characterizing the commitment the ascriber has exfoliated those consequences employing only commitments the ascriptional target would acknowledge, the content specification is *de dicto*. Where the ascriber has employed substitutional commitments he himself, but perhaps not the target, endorses, the content specification is *de re*.

Understood in this way, what is expressed by *de re* specifications of the contents of the beliefs of others are crucial to *communication*. Being able to understand what others are saying, in the sense that makes their remarks available for use as premises in one's own inferences, depends precisely on being able to specify those contents in *de re*, and not merely *de dicto* terms. If the only way I can specify the content of the shaman's belief is by a de dicto ascription

> He believes malaria can be prevented by drinking the liquor distilled from the bark of that kind of tree,

I may not be in a position to assess the truth of his claim. It is otherwise if I can specify that content in the *de re* ascription

> He believes of quinine that malaria can be prevented by drinking it,

for 'quinine' is a term with rich inferential connections to others I know how to employ. If he says that the seventh god has just risen, I may not know what to make of his remark. Clearly he will take it to have consequences that I could not endorse, so nothing in my mouth could *mean* just what his remark does. But if I am told that the seventh god is the sun, then I can specify the content of his report in a more useful form:

> He claims of the sun that it has just risen,

which I can extract *information* from, that is, can use to generate premises that I can reason with. Again, suppose a student claims that

> The largest number that is not the sum of the squares of distinct primes is the sum of at most 27 primes.

He may have no idea what that number is, or may falsely believe it to be extremely large, but if I know that

> 17163 is the largest number that is not the sum of the squares of distinct primes,

then I can characterize the content of his claim in *de re* form as:

> The student claims of 17163 that it is the sum of at most 27 primes,

and can go on to draw inferences from that claim, to assess its plausibility in the light of the rest of my beliefs. (It is true, but only because *all* integers are the sum of at most 27 primes.) Identifying what is being talked about permits me to extract information across a doxastic gap.

We saw originally in the treatment of truth assessments the crucial difference between *attributing* a commitment and *undertaking* or acknowledging one. We now see what is involved in moving from the claim that

> It is true that Benjamin Franklin invented bifocals,

which is the undertaking of a commitment to the effect that Benjamin Franklin invented bifocals, via the undertaking of a commitment to the claim that Benjamin Franklin is the popularizer of the lightning rod, to the claim that

> It is true of the popularizer of the lightning rod that he invented bifocals.

(It is through this 'true of' locution that the earlier remarks about the essentially social structure of truth assessments connects with the account just offered of the social structure that underlies propositional attitude ascriptions *de re*.) Extracting information from the remarks of others requires grasping what is expressed when one offers *de re* characterizations of the contents of their beliefs—that is to be able to tell what their beliefs would be true *of* if they were true. It is to grasp the *representational* content of their claims. The point I have been making is that doing this is just mastering the *social* dimension of their inferential articulation.

Conclusion

I have claimed that the primary representational locution in ordinary language, the one we use to talk about the representational dimension of our thought and talk, to specify what we are thinking and talking *about,* is *de re* ascriptions of propositional attitude. It is the role they play in such ascriptions that gives their meanings to the 'of' or 'about' we use to express intentional directedness. I have also claimed that the expressive role of these locutions is to make explicit the distinction of social perspective involved in keeping our books straight on who is committed to what. The social dimension of inference involved in the communication to others of claims that must be available as reasons both to the speaker and to the audience, in spite of differences in collateral commitments, is what underlies the representational dimension of discourse.

Beliefs and claims that are *propositionally* contentful are necessarily *representationally* contentful because their inferential articulation essentially involves a *social* dimension. That social dimension is unavoidable because the inferential significance of a claim, the appropriate antecedents and consequences of a doxastic commitment, depend on the background of collateral commitments available for service as auxiliary hypotheses. Thus any specification of a propositional content must be made from the perspective of some such set of commitments.

One wants to say that the *correct* inferential role is determined by the collateral claims that are *true*. Just so; that is what *each* interlocutor wants to say—each has an at least slightly different perspective from which to evaluate inferential proprieties. Representational locutions make explicit the sorting of commitments into those attributed and those undertaken—without which communication would be impossible, given those differences of perspective. The *representational* dimension of propositional contents reflects the *social* structure of their *inferential* articulation in the game of giving and asking for reasons.

NOTES

1. This idea is motivated and explored at greater length in Brandom (1988).
2. By this criterion, the 'Slab' Sprachspiel that Wittgenstein describes early in the *Investigations,* for instance, does not qualify as a genuinely *linguistic* practice. For further discussion of why this is a good way to talk, see Brandom (1983).
3. There are a myriad of technical details that need to be cleared up in order to make an analysis of truth talk along these lines work. I've addressed those difficulties elsewhere—that is where the prosentential or anaphoric account of truth comes in. See Brandom (1988A). For present purposes, those details can be put to one side.
4. The approach pursued here (including both a treatment of *de dicto* ascriptions, and of epistemically strong *de re* ascriptions) is presented at length in my

Making It Explicit: Reasoning, Representing, and Discursive Commitment (Brandom 1994), especially in Chapter Eight 'The Social Route From Reasoning to Representing.'
5. Obviously, such an account requires emendation to handle the cases where the one to whom a propositional attitude is ascribed would use indexicals, or a different language, to express that attitude. See *Making It Explicit,* Chapter Eight.
6. One way to see that this is right is that the ascription-forming operators can be *iterated:* S' can claim of that *S* claims of it that Φ(it). Thus there would in any case not be *two* different kinds of belief (*de dicto* and *de re*), but an infinite number.
7. This line of thought is worked out in detail in 'What Are Singular Terms, and Why Are There Any?' which is Chapter Six of *Making It Explicit.*

REFERENCES

Brandom, R. (1983), 'Asserting,' *Nous,* XVII #4 (November), pp. 637–50.

Brandom, R. (1988), 'Inference, Expression, and Induction: Sellarsian Themes,' *Philosophical Studies* 54, pp. 257–85.

Brandom, R. (1988A), 'Pragmatism, Phenomenalism, and Truth Talk,' *Midwest Studies in Philosophy vol. XII: Realism* (University of Minnesota Press), pp. 75–93.

Brandom, R. (1994), *Making It Explicit: Reasoning, Representing and Discursive Commitment* (Harvard University Press).

Dennett. D. (1982), 'Beyond Belief,' in A. Woodfield (ed.), *Thought and Object* (Oxford University Press).

Kant, I. *Critique of Pure Reason.*

49 The Intentionality of Phenomenology and the Phenomenology of Intentionality

Terence Horgan and John Tienson[1]

What is the relationship between phenomenology and intentionality? A common picture in recent philosophy of mind has been that the phenomenal aspects and the intentional aspects of mentality are independent of one another. According to this view, the phenomenal character of certain mental states or processes—states for which there is "something it is like" to undergo them—is not intentional. Examples that are typically given of states with inherent phenomenal character are sensations, such as pains, itches, and color sensations. This view also asserts, on the other hand, that the intentionality of certain mental states and processes—their being about something—is not phenomenal. Beliefs and desires are the paradigm cases of intentional mental states. Although they are intentionally directed—i.e., they have aboutness—these mental states are not inherently phenomenal. There is nothing that it is like to be in such a state by virtue of which it is directed toward what it is about.

We will call this picture *separatism,* because it treats phenomenal aspects of mentality and intentional aspects of mentality as mutually independent, and thus separable. Although there may be complex states that are both phenomenal and intentional, their phenomenal aspects and their intentional aspects are separable. Many philosophers who hold this picture have thought that these two aspects of mentality lead to quite different sorts of problems with respect to the project of "naturalizing the mental." Proponents of separatism often hold that while the problem of naturalizing phenomenology poses great difficulties, the problem of naturalizing intentionality is much more tractable.[2]

Separatism has been very popular in philosophy of mind in recent decades, and is still widely held. Those who oppose it regard it as a view against which they need to characterize their own positions—a common picture that they must explicitly reject. In this paper we argue that separatism is profoundly wrong. We depart from it quite thoroughly, in ways importantly different from other recent departures. We affirm the following theses, both of which are repudiated by separatism:

> *The Intentionality of Phenomenology:* Mental states of the sort commonly cited as paradigmatically phenomenal (e.g., sensory-experiential states such as color-experiences, itches, and smells) have intentional content that is inseparable from their phenomenal character.
>
> *The Phenomenology of Intentionality:* Mental states of the sort commonly cited as paradigmatically intentional (e.g., cognitive states such as beliefs, and conative states such as desires), when conscious, have phenomenal character that is inseparable from their intentional content.

In addition to these two theses (henceforth, IP and PI), we advocate another important claim about the interpenetration of phenomenology and intentionality:

> *Phenomenal Intentionality:* There is a kind of intentionality, pervasive in human mental life, that is constitutively determined by phenomenology alone.

We use the expression 'constitutively determined' to mean that this kind of intentionality is not merely nomically determined; rather, intentional mental states have such intentional content *by virtue of* their phenomenology.

So-called "representationalist" theories of phenomenal properties are a currently influential departure from separatism.[3] Although extant versions of representationalism embrace thesis IP, typically they do not embrace thesis PI. Nor do they embrace the thesis of Phenomenal Intentionality, since they hold that intentionality is prior to phenomenology. So our position differs significantly from standard representationalism.[4]

We argue for the three theses set out above

This paper is published here for the first time.

(sections 1–3), in part by way of introspective description of actual human experience. If you pay attention to your own experience, we think you will come to appreciate their truth.[5] Our position has important consequences, when combined with the plausible thesis (argued for in section 4) that phenomenology is "narrow," i.e., it does not depend—except perhaps causally—upon what goes on "outside the head" of the experiencer. One consequence is that there is a kind of *narrow* intentionality that is pervasive in human mental life—a form of intentional directedness that is built into phenomenology itself, and that is not constitutively dependent on any extrinsic relations between phenomenal character and the experiencer's actual external environment. A further consequence is that theories that ground all intentionality in connections to the external world, such as causal and teleological theories of intentionality, are deeply mistaken.

1. The Intentionality of Phenomenology

The mental states typically cited as paradigmatically phenomenal have intentional content that is inseparable from their phenomenal character. Let us consider some examples: first, experiences of red as we actually have them. You might see, say, a red pen on a nearby table, and a chair with red arms and back a bit behind the table. There is certainly something that the red that you see is like to you.[6] But the red that you see is seen, first, as a property of objects. These objects are seen as located in space relative to your center of visual awareness. And they are experienced as part of a complete three-dimensional scene—not just a pen with table and chair, but a pen, table, and chair in a room with floor, walls, ceiling, and windows. This spatial character is built into the phenomenology of the experience.

Consider too the experience of seeing an apple on the table, picking up the apple, and taking a bite out of it. There is the look and smell of the apple. Then (as you grasp it) there is the feel of the apple, its smoothness, roundishness, and firmness. Then there is its weight (as you pick it up). Finally there is the feel of the apple in your mouth, followed by the crunching sound, taste, and feel of juiciness as you take a bite. We will not attempt to write the small book one could write describing this simple experience. But we need to note some highlights. First, the look, feel, smell, sound, and taste of the apple are experienced as a unity in space, as all belonging to a single object. The taste is in your mouth; the smoothness and roundishness that you feel—with parts of your mouth as well as your hand—are there, too. Second, it is important to notice that what is experienced tactilely are various spatial properties *of the object,* not sensations. One has, of course, tactile sensations as well, though one does not normally attend to them. (The tactile sensations are, when noticed, experienced as the sort of things that can only belong to a sentient being.) The properties of smoothness, firmness, etc. are experienced as the sorts of things that can only belong to an "external" object in space.[7] Third, the apple is encountered as *moving.* The experience is of a *temporal* object, an object that endures. The same is true when you see another person take a bite of an apple. Experience is not of instants; experience is temporally thick. This is obvious in the case of hearing tunes or sentences, where the temporal *pattern* is a palpable feature of the experience. The temporal pattern is also a palpable feature of the seen moving apple, though less frequently noted as such.[8] But it is no less true that stationary objects are *seen as* enduring and as unchanging.[9]

For any experience involving a specific shade of red, one can abstract away from the total experience and focus on the distinctive what-it's-like of that shade of red per se—a phenomenal aspect of this total experience that it has in common with innumerable other total experiences that differ in the perceived location of the experienced red or in the shape of the red surface, etc. But even considered in isolation from any total visual-experiential state, the what-it's-like of experiencing red is already intentional, because it involves red *as the intentional object of one's experience.* Again, redness is not experienced as an introspectible property of one's own experiential state, but rather as a property of visually presented objects.[10]

Of course, in typical cases of experiencing red, the *overall* phenomenal character of one's visual experience is a structurally rich what-it's-like of *experiencing a visually presented scene,* a scene that contains a whole array of apparent enduring objects with various properties and relations—including the property redness instantiated on the surfaces of some of these objects. The total visual experience with this overall phenomenal character is richly intentional, since it presents a temporally extended scene comprising various objects that instantiate various properties and relations at various spatial locations relative to one's center of visual awareness. This total visual experience is also richly *phenomenal,* because there is an overall what-it's-like of experiencing the whole scene. (Any visually noticeable alteration in the visually presented scene would be a *phenomenal* difference in one's total visual experience.)

Another commonly cited example of phenomenal consciousness is the distinctive phenomenal character of pain. Experiences of pain are thoroughly intentional: pain is experienced as a particular feeling *at a certain place in one's own body.* (This is why there can be such a thing as phantom-limb phenomena, in which pain is experienced as located in a limb that has been amputated.)

More generally, the overall phenomenal character of one's experience includes a structurally rich what-it's-like of *tactilely and kinesthetically experiencing one's presented body,* an apparent body containing a whole array of tactilely and kinesthetically distinguishable apparent parts, many of which are experienced as parts that one can voluntarily move. The total tactile/kinesthetic experience with this overall phenomenal character is richly intentional, by virtue of the complexity of the body as presented. This total experience is also richly *phenomenal,* since it has the what-it's-like-ness of tactilely and kinesthetically experiencing one's whole body. (Any tactilely or kinesthetically distinguishable alteration would be a *phenomenal* difference in one's total tactile/kinesthetic experience.)

The full-fledged phenomenal character of sensory experience is an extraordinarily rich synthetic unity that involves complex, richly intentional, total phenomenal characters of visual-mode phenomenology, tactile-mode phenomenology, kinesthetic body-control phenomenology, auditory and olfactory phenomenology, and so forth—each of which can be abstracted (more or less) from the total experience to be the focus of attention. This overall phenomenal character is thoroughly and essentially intentional. It is the what-it's-like of being an embodied agent in an ambient environment—in short, the what-it's-like of being in a world.

2. The Phenomenology of Intentionality

We have been describing the intentionality of sensory-perceptual phenomenal conscious-

ness.[11] Let us now focus on the thesis of the phenomenology of intentionality (PI): consciously occurring intentional states have phenomenal character that is inseparable from their intentional content.

Intentional states have a phenomenal character, and this phenomenal character is precisely the what-it-is-like of experiencing a specific propositional-attitude type vis-à-vis a specific intentional content. Change either the attitude-type (believing, desiring, wondering, hoping, etc.) or the particular intentional content, and the phenomenal character thereby changes too.[12] Eliminate the intentional state, and the phenomenal character is thereby eliminated too. This particular phenomenal character could not be present in experience in the absence of that intentional state itself.

Consider, for example, an occurrent thought about something that is not perceptually presented, e.g., a thought that rabbits have tails. Quine notwithstanding, it seems plainly false—and false for phenomenological reasons—that there is indeterminacy as to whether one is having a thought that rabbits have tails or whether one is instead having a thought that (say) collections of undetached rabbit parts have tail-subsets. It is false because there is something that it is like to have the occurrent thought that rabbits have tails, and what it is like is different from what it would be like to have the occurrent thought that collections of undetached rabbit parts have tail-subsets.[13]

The overall phenomenology of these kinds of intentional states involves abstractable aspects which themselves are distinctively phenomenological. For example, if one contrasts wondering whether rabbits have tails with thinking that rabbits have tails, one realizes that there is something *common* phenomenologically—something that remains the same in consciousness when one passes from, say, believing that rabbits have tails to wondering whether rabbits have tails, or vice versa. It is the distinctive phenomenal character of holding before one's mind the content *rabbits have tails,* apart from the particular attitude type—be it, say, wondering, hoping, or believing. This aspect of the overall phenomenology of intentionality is *the phenomenology of intentional content.*[14]

In addition, there is also a specific what-its-likeness that goes with the attitude type as such. There is a phenomenological *difference* between wondering whether rabbits have tails on one hand and thinking that rabbits have tails on the other. This aspect is *the phenomenology of attitude type.* Attentive introspection reveals that both the phenomenology of intentional content and the phenomenology of attitude type are phenomenal aspects of experience, aspects that you cannot miss if you simply pay attention.

One might reply that although there is indeed a phenomenological difference between thinking that rabbits have tails and thinking that collections of undetached rabbit parts have tail-subsets, this difference merely involves the fact that we often think in language. Thus, the phenomenological difference between the two thinking experiences involves not the different contents, but rather the fact that the auditory imagery that goes with thinking that rabbits have tails is different from the imagery that goes with thinking that collections of undetached rabbit parts have tail-subsets.

However, nonperceptual intentionality in normal humans does not always involve language and/or auditory imagery. For instance, conscious, unverbalized beliefs about the locations of nearby unperceived objects are just as ubiquitous in human life as is the explicit or imagistic verbalization of one's focal train of thought. Think for example, of cooking, cleaning house, or working in a garage or woodshop. In any such activity, you might spontaneously move to retrieve a needed tool that is out of sight. There is something that it is like to think that a certain tool is just there—in that cabinet, say—but such beliefs are typically not verbalized either vocally or subvocally or by way of verbal imagery. (Your verbal energies might all the while be directed toward ongoing philosophical discussion with a companion, uninterrupted by your selection of an appropriate tool.) You also, of course, frequently have unverbalized thoughts about the locations of objects in distant familiar locations.

In any event, the what-it's-likeness of intentionality that we are talking about—even when it is specifically tied to certain words in English or some other natural language—does not attach to those words simply as sequences or patterns of sounds, or even as syntactic structures. It attaches to awareness of those words qua contentful; it is the what-it's-like of hearing or saying those words when they mean just that: that rabbits have tails. So the basic point holds: even if thinking did always involve auditory imagery, the auditory imagery would be intentionally loaded in the experience, not intentionally empty.

This point is illustrated and defended by Galen Strawson (1994). Strawson discusses what he calls "understanding experience." He contends that understanding and other related kinds of occurrent intentional mental states and processes are very commonly, if not always, laden with distinctive what-it's-likeness. He points out, for example, the phenomenological difference between hearing speech in a language that one does not understand and hearing speech in a language that one does understand. Imagine two people side by side hearing the same spoken sequence of sounds, with one of them understanding the language and the other one not. At a certain relatively raw sensory level, their auditory experience is phenomenologically the same; the sounds are the same, and in some cases may be experienced in much the same way *qua sounds.* Yet it is obvious introspectively that there is something phenomenologically very different about what it is like for each of them: one person is having understanding experience with the distinctive phenomenology of understanding the sentence to mean just what it does, and the other is not.

Consider, as a similar example for a single speaker, first hearing "Dogs dogs dog dog dogs," without realizing that it is an English sentence, and then hearing it as the sentence of English that it is. The phenomenal difference between the experiences is palpable. (If you do not grasp the sentencehood of the "dogs" sentence, recall that 'dog' is a verb in English, and compare, "Cats dogs chase catch mice.")

Consider also hearing an ambiguous sentence. One typically hears it as meaning some one thing in particular, often without realizing that it is ambiguous. There is a phenomenological difference, for example, between hearing "Visiting relatives can be boring," as a remark about the people who are visiting, vs. hearing it as a remark about visiting certain people oneself. Again, imagine hearing or saying "Time flies" as a cliché about the passage of time, vs. saying or hearing it as a command at the insect races. The actual sound or auditory imagery may be the same, but the total experiences are phenomenally quite different. The sound may have some role that would make it appropriate to call it a *vehicle* of intentionality, but its meaning what it does, having the intentional content that it does, is an entirely different aspect of the overall phenomenal character of the experience.

In sum: Cognitive intentional states such as consciously occurrent thoughts, and conative intentional states such as consciously occurrent wishes, are phenomenal qua intentional. The overall phenomenal character of such a state comprises both the phenomenology of its specific intentional content and the phenomenology of its specific attitude-type. These are abstractable phenomenal aspects of the state's unified phenomenal character: the what-it's-like of undergoing this specific propositional attitude vis-à-vis that specific intentional content.

3. Phenomenal Intentionality

The intuitive considerations in the last two sections can be developed into an argument for the thesis of phenomenal intentionality: there is a pervasive kind of intentionality that is constitutively determined by phenomenology alone. One way to articulate and sharpen this claim is the following. Let two creatures be *phenomenal duplicates* just in case each creature's total experience, throughout its existence, is phenomenally exactly similar to the other's. We can then state the Phenomenal Intentionality thesis this way:

> There is a kind of intentional content, pervasive in human mental life, such that any two possible phenomenal duplicates have exactly similar intentional states vis-à-vis such content.

We will call this type of content *phenomenal* intentional content. The full range of a creature's phenomenal intentional content is determined and constituted *wholly by phenomenology.*

Consider any creature who is a complete phenomenal duplicate of yourself—its mental life is phenomenally exactly like yours. Assume nothing *else* about this creature. The thought experiment thus builds in an epistemic "veil of ignorance" about this creature, in order to filter out any factors other than phenomenology itself. So for all you know about this arbitrary phenomenal duplicate of yourself, its sensory-perceptual experiences—including its tactile-kinesthetic experiences and its embodied-agency experiences—might be very largely illusory and hallucinatory concerning the real nature of itself and its surroundings. (It may be helpful to imagine the phenomenal duplicate as a brain in a vat or a disembodied Cartesian mind.) We will argue that you and your phenomenal duplicate share a pervasive kind of intentional content—phenomenal intentional content.[15]

As argued in section 1, sensory-phenomenal states and processes have intentional content that is inseparable from their phenomenal character. These states present an apparent world full of apparent objects that apparently instantiate a wide range of properties and relations, and they present oneself as an apparently embodied agent within that apparent world. Since this kind of intentionality is inseparable from phenomenal character, your phenomenal duplicate will have an apparent world presented to it in exactly the same way.

To make the general point with a representative example, suppose that you have the experience of seeing a picture hanging crooked. Each of your phenomenal duplicates has a phenomenally identical experience. Some of these experiences will be accurate and some will be inaccurate. Whether or not a given duplicate's picture-hanging-crooked experience is accurate—that is, whether or not things are as the experience presents things as being—will depend upon the duplicate's actual environment. Thus, the sensory-phenomenal experience, by itself, determines conditions of accuracy: i.e., a class of ways the environment must be in order for the experience to be accurate.[16] In order for such an experience to be accurate, there must be a picture before oneself, and it must be crooked.

That these phenomenally identical experiences all have the same truth conditions is reflected in the fact that each of the experiences is subject in the same way to investigation as to whether it is accurate.[17] For example, you and your phenomenal duplicate each might have the experience of seeing to oneself to be testing one's perceptual experience for accuracy by making measurements or using a level. You and your phenomenal duplicate each might have the subsequent experience of seeming to oneself to discover that the picture merely appears to be crooked because of irregularities of the wall, or tricks of light. Or, you and your phenomenal duplicate might, in the course of seeming to oneself to be attempting to perform these tests, have the experience of seeming to discover that there actually is no picture—say, by seeming to oneself to discover that one has been looking at a clever holographic image cooked up to make it appear that there is a picture hanging on the wall.[18]

There is also, of course, a sense in which these crooked-picture perceptions of you and your duplicate have different truth conditions. You and your duplicate are looking at different pictures. So the accuracy of your own perception depends on the specific picture you yourself are seeing, whereas the accuracy of your duplicate's perception depends on the specific, and different, picture that it is seeing. There are thus two ways of thinking of truth conditions: as determined wholly by phenomenology, and as determined in part by items in the experiencer's environment that satisfy the experiencer's phenomenology. We return to this distinction in section 5.2.

Your phenomenal duplicate accepts the presentations delivered by perceptual experience—accepts, for example, that there is a picture and a wall—just as you do. These "belief-wise" acceptance states have exactly the same phenomenology, the what-it-is-like of occurrently believing that thus-and-so (where one's occurrent sensory experience presents things as being thus-and-so). The states also are phenomenologically integrated with those ongoing, richly intentional, sensory-perceptual experiences in exactly the same way as yours. Thus, they are experienced as having the same belief-specific role: the same apparent input conditions, involving apparent deliverances of the apparent body's apparent senses, and the same apparent effects, involving experiences of *apparently acting appropriately* with regard to the apparent world as presented. It seems intuitively clear that a belief-wise acceptance state with these phenomenological features is a genuine belief. The phenomenal character of these states, which includes the phenomenology of role, constitutively determines that they are genuine beliefs.[19] And as we argued above, the sensory-presentational content of these states is the same for you and your phenomenal duplicate.

So far we have been discussing perceptual experience and perceptual belief. But since the phenomenal consciousness of your phenomenal duplicate would provide very rich perceptual presentations of a world of numerous apparent objects instantiating numerous apparent properties and relations, such presented items would thereby figure in a wide range of propositional-attitude states whose content goes well beyond the presentations of perceptual experience itself. Here the phenomenology of intentionality—the what-it's-like of occurrent propositional attitudes as such—enters in full force, quite apart from the presentational content of one's current sensory-perceptual experience. For your phenomenal duplicate, no less than for you yourself, there would be something that it's like to wonder whether to cook meatloaf for dinner,

something that it's like to have the thought that there's beer in the fridge, something that it's like to hope that one's spouse isn't angry that one is coming home late from the Philosophy Department party. These occurrent states in the phenomenal duplicate have all the same "propositional attitude-ish" phenomenology as they do in you. They are experienced as having exactly the same causal role vis-à-vis the phenomenal duplicate's apparent embodied behavior in its apparent world as you experience them as having. It seems intuitively clear that states with all these features qualify as full-fledged *propositional attitudes* in your phenomenal duplicate, just as they do in you.

In addition, for each such propositional-attitude state in yourself and in your phenomenal duplicate, the two states have the same phenomenal intentional content, i.e., the same phenomenologically determined truth conditions. Consider, for example, two phenomenologically identical belief-states that you and your phenomenal duplicate would both express by the string of words "The picture behind me is crooked." In order for such a belief to be true, there must indeed be an object in a certain relation to oneself—behind, no intervening walls, etc.—that satisfies the phenomenologically determined criteria for being a picture, and that picture must be hanging crooked. Considered in this way, your belief and that of your phenomenological duplicate have exactly the same truth conditions.[20] These occurrent states in the phenomenal duplicate, by virtue of having the same phenomenologically determined truth conditions as yours, are thereby subject to the same methods of accuracy assessment: for instance, you and your phenomenological duplicate might each experience turning around to see if the picture is still crooked. If it still appears crooked, you might then experience going through the tests mentioned above. The possibility of such tests is in some sense understood, if not explicitly phenomenologically given, in having the conscious belief that there is a picture hanging crooked behind oneself.

Since your phenomenal duplicate shares with you all the phenomenal intentionality so far described, it thereby possesses significant conceptual resources to speculate and theorize—for instance, about what is very distant spatio-temporally, about what is very small, about the underlying causes of experience and of the apparent ambient environment. It can reason causally, form abstract theoretical concepts, formulate scientific hypotheses and theories, and experience itself as an apparent embodied agent actively engaged (in apparent cooperation with other apparent embodied agents) in the apparent empirical corroboration or disconfirmation of such hypotheses and theories. It can have experiences as of apparently reading about such matters or apparently hearing lectures about them, and thereby can acquire a body of well warranted scientific beliefs about itself and its world. In these respects too, your phenomenal duplicate is like yourself, even though the experiential basis upon which it bootstraps its way up to well warranted, semantically evaluable, scientific beliefs might be highly (or even completely) nonveridical. Thus, for each of your propositional-attitude states about such theoretical entities, your phenomenal duplicate has a propositional-attitude state of the same kind. And for each pair of corresponding states in you and your duplicate respectively, the two states have the same phenomenal intentional content—i.e., the same phenomenally determined truth conditions, linked via the same phenomenally determined "web of belief" to the same kinds of experiential methods of accuracy-assessment.[21]

Virtually everything we have been saying is really just attentive phenomenological description, just saying what the what-it's-like of experience *is* like. It is just a matter of introspectively attending to the phenomenal character of one's own experience. You and your phenomenal duplicate share a pervasive kind of mental intentionality—viz., phenomenal intentionality.

We take it that this thought-experimental argument supports the idea that each *specific* occurrent intentional state with phenomenal intentional content is constitutively determined by its own distinctive phenomenal character—viz., the what-it's-like of undergoing that particular attitude-type vis-à-vis that particular phenomenal intentional content. That is, specific phenomenal character determines specific intentional states, provided that the experiencing creature has a sufficiently rich network of actual and possible phenomenal/intentional states. Suppose, for example, that you are now undergoing a psychological state with the distinctive phenomenal what-it's-like of believing that a picture is hanging crooked on a wall directly behind you. Then you thereby *believe* that there is a picture hanging crooked on a wall directly behind you; undergoing this phenomenology constitutively determines that you are instantiating that belief-state. Any experiencing creature undergoing this phenomenology would thereby instantiate the belief-state, even if its overall phenomenology is otherwise quite different from your own.

Although each occurrent intentional state with phenomenal intentional content is constitutively determined by its own phenomenal character, at least in the context of a full-fledged cognitive system, it is important to appreciate that this does not mean that phenomenal intentionality somehow guarantees infallible knowledge about what one's first-order intentional states are. Beliefs about one's own intentional states are *second-order* intentional states, and the Phenomenal Intentionality thesis is compatible with the possibility that such beliefs are sometimes mistaken. Indeed, the thesis is compatible with the possibility that some creatures who have phenomenal intentionality—say, certain kinds of nonlinguistic animals—entirely lack any capacity to undergo second-order intentional states at all. What-it's-likeness is one thing; discursive judgments *about* it are another. Such judgments are fallible (as are judgments about most anything), even though humans do possess especially reliable capacities to form accurate introspective discursive/classificatory judgments about their own phenomenology.[22]

4. The Narrowness of Phenomenology and of Phenomenal Intentionality

Phenomenology does not depend constitutively on factors outside the brain. Now, it is obvious enough that in normal humans, phenomenology does depend *causally* on some such factors; but one need only consider how this causal dependence works in order to appreciate the lack of constitutive dependence. First, phenomenology depends causally on factors in the ambient environment that figure as *distal* causes of one's ongoing sensory experience. But second, these distal environmental causes generate experiential effects only by generating more immediate links in the causal chains between themselves and experience, viz., physical stimulations in the body's sensory receptors—in eyes, ears, tongue, surface of the body, and so forth. And third, these states and processes causally generate experiential effects only by generating still more immediate links in the causal chains between themselves and experience—viz., afferent neural impulses, resulting from transduction at the sites of the sensory receptors on the body. Your mental intercourse with the world is mediated by sensory and motor transducers at the periphery of your central nervous system. Your conscious experience would be phenomenally just the same even if the transducer-external causes and effects of your brain's afferent and efferent neural activity were radically different from what they actually are—for instance, even if you were a Brain in a Vat with no body at all, and hence no bodily sense organs whose physical stimulations get transduced into afferent neural inputs.[23] Among your logically possible phenomenal duplicates, then, are beings whose sensory experience is radically illusory, in the manner of the famous Evil Deceiver scenario in Descartes' First Meditation—or its contemporary version, the Brain in a Vat.

Thus, phenomenology is *narrow,* in the sense that it does not depend constitutively on what's outside the skin, or indeed on what's outside of the brain. We can now make the central argument:

(1) There is pervasive intentional content that constitutively depends on phenomenology alone.

(2) Phenomenology constitutively depends only on narrow factors.

So, (3) There is pervasive intentional content that constitutively depends only on narrow factors.

That is, the theses of phenomenal intentionality and the narrowness of phenomenology jointly entail that there is kind of *narrow* intentional content (the kind we have dubbed *phenomenal* intentional content), pervasive in human life, such that any two creatures who are phenomenal duplicates must also have exactly similar intentional states vis-à-vis this kind of narrow content. Phenomenal intentional content is pervasive and narrow. Any adequate philosophical and scientific conception of mind should accommodate this conclusion.[24]

5. Some Philosophical Morals

We now draw some morals from the preceding discussion, first about strong externalist theories of intentionality, second about how phenomenal intentional content is related to mental reference and to wide content, and third about the ex-

tent of the so-called "hard problem" of phenomenal consciousness.

5.1. Strong Externalist Theories of Mental Intentionality Are Wrong

We certainly do not deny that there is such a thing as "wide content" in language and in thought. Important lessons have been learned from Kripke, Putnam, Burge, and others about the relevance of the external environment in contributing both to the meaning of certain terms in natural language (e.g., natural-kind terms like 'water') and to certain aspects of the content of thought (e.g., aspects of thought that one would express verbally by employing the term 'water'). But Putnam's famous slogan that "meaning ain't in the head" is properly construed as asserting that *not all* meaning is in the head; it doesn't begin to follow from this, or from the considerations adduced in support of it, that *no* meaning is in the head. We will return to the topic of wide content presently.

However, a number of current theories of mental intentionality are *strongly* externalist: they assert that all intentionality is grounded in causal connections between states of the cognitive system and states of the external world; there can be no intentionality without some suitable kind of actual connection between what is going on in the head and the wider environment. Strong externalist theories of intentionality include (i) causal theories of content that find the necessary connection in the causal antecedents of the state, (ii) covariational theories that find the connection in certain kinds of systematic correlations between occurrences of an internal state and occurrences of an external state of affairs, (iii) teleosemantic theories that look to environmentally situated proper functions that certain internal states possess in virtue of evolutionary design, and (iv) learning-based theories that invoke internal adaptational changes in the creature's own history.[25]

Given our conclusions in sections 1–4, it follows that strong externalist theories of intentionality are wrong. They are not just slightly wrong, not just wrong in detail. Rather, they are fundamentally mistaken, because they claim to naturalize the entire phenomenon of mental intentionality and yet there is a rich and pervasive kind of narrow intentionality—phenomenal intentionality—that is constitutively independent of external factors. Strong externalist theories therefore cannot successfully naturalize the full phenomenon of mental intentionality, because they utterly fail to aim at one crucial aspect of it. Ideas employed by strong externalists might still have a useful role to play, however, in contributing to philosophical understanding of phenomena like wide content and mental reference, topics to which we now turn.

5.2. Phenomenal Intentionality, Mental Reference, and Wide Content

Suppose Alfred and Bertrand are looking at two different barns, and each of them says, "That's an old barn." Do their statements have the same truth conditions? Yes and no. In one way, they have different truth conditions. Alfred's statement is made true or false by the age of the barn that he is looking at, while Bertrand's statement is made true or false by the age of the distinct barn that *he* is looking at. Following recent usage, we will call such truth conditions, which depend on the actual entities referred to in a statement or thought, *wide truth conditions*. But in another way, Alfred's and Bertrand's statements have the same truth conditions. In each case the truth condition is that there must be an actual barn that he is looking at (and not, for example a papier-mache mock up of a barn, or only the facing side of a stage "barn" on a movie set), and that barn must be old. Such truth conditions are *narrow truth conditions*. They are determined skin-in, so to speak, and are completely determined by phenomenology. In our view, the situation is similar with respect to phenomenologically identical intentional states shared by phenomenal duplicates.

In section 3 we discussed belief-wise acceptance of the deliverances of perceptual experience. Such acceptance is the normal, default attitude. But it can be cancelled. If you have a lump on a finger, then objects that are smooth and flat will feel as though they have a lump where that finger touches them. But you soon learn not to believe that the object is lumpy. There is similar phenomenology of acceptance concerning propositional attitudes. There is a relevant phenomenal difference, for instance, between these two states: (i) believing that Bill Clinton was U.S. President, and (ii) the state you are in when you say (without believing) that Santa Claus brings presents. The salient difference turns on the fact that the phenomenal character of the first state includes the what-it's-like of accepting the existence of Bill Clinton, whereas the phenomenal character of the second state includes the what-it's-like of believing

that Santa Claus does *not* exist. Similarly, suppose you hope or fear that an object of a certain description will be found. There is a clear phenomenal difference between the case in which you know full well that there is such an object and the case in which you do not know whether or not there is such an object.

Phenomenal intentional content presents to consciousness an apparent world that goes far beyond what one is conscious of at any one time; presuming so is itself an aspect of the overall phenomenal character of experience. Phenomenal intentionality thereby determines a complex set of presuppositions concerning the existence of, the persistence of, and various features of, the sorts of entities presented in experience: presuppositions about individuals (including flora, fauna, and other creatures like yourself), kinds, properties, relations, processes, and events of that world. For reasons that will become clear, we call these presuppositions *grounding presuppositions*. They have the phenomenology of acceptance discussed in the previous paragraph. In making a grounding presupposition, one takes it that there *really exists* an entity of a certain sort; and normally, one also presupposes that the (putative) entity in question has certain specific attributes. If there is an actual entity satisfying that presupposition (or satisfying it near enough), then one's thoughts that are intentionally directed toward such a putative entity will *refer* to the actual entity in question; and so the properties of the satisfier will determine whether the beliefs about it are true or false, whether hopes and desires about it are satisfied, and so forth. Thus, *wide* truth conditions for those beliefs are determined by phenomenal intentionality plus the actual satisfiers of the relevant presuppositions. However, what it takes *to be* a satisfier of the presuppositions is determined by phenomenal intentionality alone. So, when these presuppositions are included in truth conditions, we get *narrow* truth conditions that are thereby determined solely by phenomenal intentionality.[26]

Consider, for example, thoughts about individuals.[27] You, your Twin Earth doppelganger, and your Cartesian duplicate all have certain phenomenologically identical thoughts that you each take to be about a person named "Bill Clinton."[28] Hence these thoughts *presuppose* the existence of such a person. Your own thoughts are about the actual Bill Clinton. Your Twin Earth doppelganger's thoughts are about a different person on Twin Earth. You and your Twin Earth doppelganger have thoughts about different individuals, of course, because what a person's thoughts are about—or *refer to*—depends not only on phenomenal intentional content, but also on certain relations between the thinker and the thing the thought is about. Your Cartesian duplicate also has thoughts that purport to be about a person named "Bill Clinton," but since the Cartesian duplicate has not been in the right sort of relations to any such person, the Cartesian duplicate's thoughts are not about anyone—they lack reference.[29] *Referring* to something, mentally or linguistically, requires appropriate relations to that thing; but having thoughts that are *intentionally directed* toward such a thing— thoughts *purporting* to refer to such a thing— does not.

Straightforwardly, your thoughts about Bill Clinton are made true or false by facts about Bill Clinton, and your Twin Earth doppelganger's phenomenologically identical thoughts are made true or false by facts about the person who satisfies your duplicate's corresponding presupposition. There is no person who satisfies your Cartesian duplicate's corresponding presupposition, so there is nothing that can be a truth maker for its thought that would be expressed by, say, "Bill Clinton is a womanizer."[30]

The differing truth conditions just mentioned are wide truth conditions. But again, there are two ways of thinking about the truth conditions of the phenomenologically identical thoughts of you and your duplicates. In one way, the truth conditions depend upon what is actually referred to (if anything) in those thoughts; this makes them "wide." But in another and more fundamental way, the truth conditions are narrow, because what *can be* referred to in those thoughts is determined by phenomenal intentionality—in particular, by the phenomenally given grounding presuppositions. The thought will have wide content only if something in the thinker's environment satisfies the phenomenal intentional grounding presuppositions of that thought. That is, wide content is grounded by phenomenologically determined presuppositions, which are an aspect of phenomenal intentionality and hence are narrow.

As a consequence, the strong externalist theories of intentionality discussed in the previous subsection are not wrong just because they leave out a kind of intentionality—viz, phenomenal intentionality. They are wrong because what they leave out is the *fundamental* kind of intentionality: the narrow, phenomenal kind that is a prerequisite for wide content and wide truth conditions. Because narrow phenomenal content determines wide content, an adequate account of wide content requires a prior account of narrow content.

Because of relevant similarities between singular reference and natural-kind categories, similar observations can be made concerning the narrow and wide truth conditions of thoughts about natural kinds.[31] You, your Twin Earth doppelganger, and your Cartesian duplicate all have phenomenally identical thoughts with the same narrow truth conditions. For all three of you, these thoughts are intentionally directed toward certain small, common furry critters that meow, rub legs, drink milk, etc. For all three of you, these thoughts have the grounding presupposition that there is a natural kind of which these critters are members. But because of differences concerning the satisfiers (if any) of the common grounding presuppositions, these phenomenally identical thoughts have different wide truth conditions. Your own thoughts are made true or false by cats; your Twin Earth doppelganger's phenomenologically identical thoughts are made true or false by cat-like critters of the kind that she or he and others in her or his community have encountered. Suppose that Putnam's story in which cats are spy robots controlled from Mars is true concerning Twin Earth: the critters called "cats" on Twin Earth are robots controlled from Twin Mars. Then your belief that cats are animals is true; your Twin Earth doppelganger's corresponding belief is false. That is, there are wide truth conditions for these thoughts that are partially determined by features in the environment that may be unknown to the thinker. But again: these wide truth conditions, differing as they do for your thoughts and your Twin Earth doppelganger's phenomenally identical thoughts, are grounded on shared *narrow* truth conditions.

Your Cartesian duplicate has thoughts that are phenomenally identical to your cat-thoughts, and that have the same narrow truth conditions as yours do. Your Cartesian duplicate's thoughts, like yours, are intentionally directed toward— and thus presuppose—small furry critters of a certain kind. But there are no such critters that the Cartesian duplicate has encountered, directly or indirectly, so there is no kind to which the Cartesian duplicate's thoughts refer. This being so, those thoughts do not have wide truth conditions. So the Cartesian duplicate's thoughts that are phenomenologically identical to your own cat-thoughts lack the kind of wide content that your own thoughts possess and your Twin Earth doppelganger's thoughts also possess.

5.3. The Whole Hard Problem

We are among those who believe that what David Chalmers (1995, 1996) has called "the hard problem" of phenomenal consciousness is indeed a very hard problem. This is the problem of explaining why it should be that such and such mental state should be *like this*—that is, why it should have the specific what-it's-like aspect it does, rather than having some other phenomenal character or having none at all. Presumably what it is like for you to undergo a particular mental state depends nomologically on what is going on in your brain, inside of the transducers. But why what depends on this brain process should be *like this,* rather than being some other way or being no way at all, seems inexplicable. Standard materialistic treatments of phenomenal consciousness in philosophy and in cognitive science do not close this "explanatory gap" (as it is dubbed by Joseph Levine 1983); rather, they appear to just leave out the intrinsic what-it's-like aspect of mentality.[32]

In our view, the hard problem is a very pressing and very puzzling conundrum. But its scope is considerably broader than it has often been thought to be. If separatism were correct—i.e., if phenomenology were indeed non-intentional, and intentionality were indeed non-phenomenal—then the hard problem would be limited to the what-it-is-like of non-intentional sensory experience, and would not infect the intentional aspects of mentality. Indeed, discussions of the hard problem often presuppose separatism.[33] But the *whole* hard problem incorporates phenomenal intentionality. Phenomenal consciousness is intentional through and through.

This adds a dimension to the hard problem that often goes unrecognized. Conscious intentional states are intrinsically, *by their very nature,* directed toward whatever they are directed toward.[34] Thus, the hard problem includes this: why should a mental state that is grounded in this physical or physical/functional state be *by its intrinsic phenomenal nature* directed in this precise manner? And this is a very hard problem indeed.[35]

NOTES

1. This paper is thoroughly co-authored; order of authorship is alphabetical.
2. For example, Jaegwon Kim (forthcoming) argues, in a way that firmly presupposes the separatist framework, that we can get more than half way to naturalizing the mental, but not all the way. The leading idea is that the intentional aspects of mentality can be naturalized via "functionalization," but that the phenomenal aspects resist naturalization.
3. For instance, Dretske (1995), Tye (1995, 1999), Lycan (1996), and Carruthers (2000).
4. Another serious difference is worth mentioning. Representationalists typically regard the problem of naturalizing intentionality as tractable, and they seek to bring phenomenal character within the purview of this putatively tractable naturalization project by construing it as a species of intentionality. We, on the other hand, regard the problem of naturalizing phenomenal character as presently intractable, and we maintain that because of the interpenetration of phenomenology and intentionality, the scope of this intractability includes mental intentionality. Our reasons for holding this view will emerge as this paper progresses.
5. For several recent treatments of the relation between phenomenology and intentionality that are similar in spirit to what we say here, see the discussions of McGinn (1991), Flanagan (1992), Strawson (1994), Siewert (1998), and Loar (forthcoming).
6. This formulation is more accurate that the usual, "there is something that it is like to see red" because, we take it, the something-that-it-is-like that is referred to is the something-that-it-is-like of the *seen* not of the *seeing*—although, of course, there is something that it is like to see, as opposed, e.g., to hear or imagine.
7. See Thomas Reid, *Inquiry into the Human Mind on the Principles of Common Sense,* Chapter 5.
8. For a recent exception, see Lamb (2001).
9. See Van Gelder (1999) and Varela (1999) for attempts to account for the temporal thickness of experience in cognitive science terms.
10. We think that the right view of these matters is at least very close to that expressed by Laird Addis (1989): "The idea of the mental is exhausted in all interesting aspects by (1) states of consciousness [primary mental entities]; (2) sensations, emotions, and perception-related entities [secondary mental entities]; and (3) dispositional mental states [tertiary mental entities—i.e., beliefs, etc., that are not presently occurrent].... [O]nly states of consciousness are literally intentional entities. On the other hand, what makes the secondary and tertiary mental entities mental is their relation . . . to states of consciousness. Secondary mental entities cannot exist except as objects of states of consciousness. . . ." (p. 7). Thus, sensations and sensory qualities exist as, and only as, objects of conscious intentional states. This is essentially Brentano's view in the famous—but widely unread—chapter of *Psychology from an Empirical Standpoint* in which he introduces the word 'intentional' and distinguishes between mental phenomena and physical phenomena. Brentano's mental phenomena are Addis' primary mental entities. Brentano's physical phenomena are Addis' secondary mental entities, not physical things.

11. We do not know exactly when the phrase "the intentionality of consciousness" first appeared, but one does well to remember that this was *the* phrase that characterized issues concerning intentionality early in the twentieth century.

12. We are talking about psychological changes *discernible to the experiencer*—not changes such as the experiencer's being unknowingly transported to Twin Earth and gradually coming to have 'water'-thoughts about XYZ that are internally indistinguishable from earlier 'water'-thoughts that were about H_2O.

13. See Ross (1992) for a nice discussion, congenial to what we are saying here, that focuses not on Quinean indeterminacy but on the "Kripkenstein" thesis (set forth in Kripke 1982) that there is no fact of the matter whether the symbol '+' means *plus* or *quus*.

14. Part of what makes this aspect of phenomenology essentially a what-it's-like of holding before one's mind a specific *intentional content* is that semantic evaluability is involved: specific *truth* conditions are attached to it. We expand on this important point in section 3.

15. For an excellent discussion that is complementary to what we will say here and that has considerably more detail about phenomenal intentionality, see Siewert (1998), Chapters 7 and 8. For another admirable and pertinent discussion, also complementary to ours, see Silverberg (1995); although phenomenological considerations are less prominent in Silverberg's discussion, note his emphasis on how things *seem,* for each member of a group of beings who in effect are phenomenal duplicates respectively inhabiting a variety of different Twin Earthly environments.

16. Siewert (1998) emphasizes the idea that a creature's intentional features are ones for which the creature is assessible for accuracy, and he argues in detail that both perceptual and cognitive experiences are assessable for accuracy by virtue of their phenomenology.

17. We are not here presupposing verificationism, or "procedural semantics," or anything of the sort. The point is that differences in sensory-phenomenal content normally are reflected by differences in confirmation/disconfirmation procedures. Thus, sameness of confirmation/disconfirmation procedures provides *strong evidence* for sameness of content (even though it certainly does not *constitute* sameness of content).

18. Of course, even if all these first-person tests for accuracy are successfully passed, this does not guarantee that the sensory-phenomenal experience one is testing really *is* accurate; experiential warrant does not guarantee truth. Also, the reason we talk of *seeming to oneself* to be performing tests and observing outcomes is that a given phenomenal duplicate of yourself might be one whose experiences—including its accuracy-assessment experiences—are systematically non-veridical. This would be so, for instance, for a phenomenal duplicate who is a brain in a vat.

19. There are various further default assumptions involving the intentional objects of perceptual experience that would be psychologically operative in your phenomenal duplicate—normally automatically, as

a matter of course—just as they are in you. Examples include default assumptions about experientially presented objects: that these objects have back sides that are not directly presented; that they persist when they are temporarily obscured from view by interposed objects or when one has the experience of looking away from them; that they normally persist when they cease to be presented in experience; and so on.

20. Of course one can also think of the truth conditions of these states as involving the actual, and different, pictures referred to phenomenologically by you and your duplicate, if there are such pictures. There are two kinds of truth conditions for propositional attitudes, just as there are for perceptual states. Truth conditions of one kind are determined phenomenologically, as we have been discussing in the text. And truth conditions of the other kind incorporate the respective objects or kinds (if any) in your own and your phenomenal duplicate's respective ambient environments that are the respective *satisfiers* of the referring concepts in the respective, phenomenologically identical, thoughts. We explore the relationship between these two kinds of truth conditions in section 5.2.

21. The remarks in the preceding footnote apply to these propositional-attitude states too, and to the various components of the relevant web of belief.

22. The fact that there is something epistemically special about first-person introspective access to the phenomenal character of experience is, of course, the basis for the kind of reflective inquiry often called "phenomenology." But being epistemically special does not make such introspective judgments *infallible.* For insightful discussion of this complex issue, see Chapters 1 and 2 of Siewert (1998).

23. Moreover, phenomenology does not depend constitutively on *anything* beyond phenomenology itself. (Of course, phenomenal character presumably does depend *nomically* on certain states whose nature is describable in non-phenomenological language—in humans, certain brain states.) In this sense, phenomenal character is *intrinsic*. We submit that the intrinsicness of phenomenology (as thus understood) is self-evident to reflective introspection. What-it's-like is what phenomenal consciousness *is*. And what-it's-like is what-it's-like no matter what is going on outside of phenomenology itself.

24. At the scientific level, this means that cognitive science should construe the mind as a "control system" for effectively operating a potential body in a potential world, regardless of whether or not the control system is actually embodied or en-worlded in the kind of body and world for which its functional architecture is appropriate. This is a common view among cognitive scientists themselves. Such a scientific enterprise is important and tractable, even though it presupposes intentionality rather than explaining it, and even though it does not address the so-called "hard problem" of phenomenal consciousness (cf. section 5.3).

25. See Stich and Warfield (1994) for a representative sample of such theories. McGinn (1989) distinguishes two kinds of externalism that he calls "strong" and "weak"; he argues against the former, while embracing a teleosemantic approach to the latter." Although the approach to mental intentionality advo-

cated in Fodor (1987) did acknowledge narrow content, and hence was not a form of strong externalism, it also reflected Fodor's separatism about the phenomenal and intentional aspects of mentality. Because of this, by our lights his construal of narrow content was insufficiently robust, and was a step down the garden path toward strong externalism. He has since gone further down that path; see Fodor (1990, 1994, 1998).

26. Our distinction between narrow and wide truth conditions has some kinship to the approach of so-called two-dimensional modal semantics, which also posits two kinds of truth conditions—one kind narrow and the other kind wide. See Davies and Humberstone (1980); Chalmers (1996), section 2.4, especially pp. 63–65; Jackson (1998), chapters 2 and 3, especially pp. 75–77; and Chalmers (this volume, chapter 56).

27. Here and below we talk about *thoughts* for ease of exposition, but our remarks will apply to occurrent propositional attitudes in general. If one person doubts what another believes, then their propositional attitudes have the same truth conditions—the truth conditions for what is believed by one and doubted by the other. Similarly for other propositional attitudes.

28. Your Cartesian duplicate is an exact phenomenal duplicate of you that is in the First Meditation situation, thoroughly deluded. You do not really have an *exact* phenomenal duplicate on Twin Earth, however, because on Earth people sometimes have the occurrent thought that water is H_2O, whereas on Twin Earth they have instead the thought that water is XYZ. But we will use the useful term "Twin Earth doppelganger" for a person who is as much like you as is consistent with this difference.

29. It is very common in philosophy of mind to gloss the "intentional directedness" constitutive of intentionality by saying that intentional states have *aboutness*. (We did so ourselves in the opening paragraph of this paper.) But the word 'about' also is often used to express the relation of *reference*—as we do in the

paragraph to which this note is appended, and as we will continue to do below. Both uses can be appropriate in context, but it is important not to conflate them.

30. There is a longstanding dispute over whether in such a case we should say that the thought is false or that it merely lacks a truth value, but this dispute does not affect the issues we are concerned with in this paper.

31. For a discussion of both similarities and differences between singular reference and natural-kind categories, see Tienson (1986).

32. We ourselves have pressed this concern recently; see Graham and Horgan (2000), and Horgan and Tienson (in press).

33. Chalmers himself, however, has not presupposed separatism and has left open the question of which aspects of mentality are by their nature phenomenal—and in particular, whether this is true for intentional states like occurrent beliefs and desires. See, for instance, section 3.3 of Chalmers (1996), especially pp. 19–22.

34. In "Philosophy as Rigorous Science" Husserl criticizes naturalists for holding that intentional states have natures. Conscious intentional states have *essences,* he says; they are essentially directed toward what they are directed toward. This is, in effect, the point we are making. When we say that intentional states are directed *by their very nature* toward what they are directed toward, we do not mean that intentional states have natures in the way in which chemical and physical, and perhaps biological, kinds have natures. Thus, we concur with Husserl's point, although we do not adopt his terminology.

35. We thank William Lycan, Michael Lynch, Brian McLaughlin, Steve Tammelleo, Mark Timmons, and audiences at the University of Arizona and the 2000 Society for Philosophy and Psychology for comments and discussion. Special thanks to David Chalmers and George Graham for their extensive and especially valuable help.

REFERENCES

Addis, L. (1989). *Natural Signs: A Theory of Intentionality,* Temple University Press.

Brentano, F. (1973). *Psychology from an Empirical Standpoint,* Routledge (original publication 1874, 1924).

Burge, T. (1979). "Individualism and the Mental," *Midwest Studies in Philosophy* 4, 73–121.

Carruthers, P. (2000). *Phenomenal Consciousness: A Naturalistic Theory,* Cambridge University Press.

Chalmers, D. J. (1995). "The Puzzle of Conscious Experience," *Scientific American* 273, 80–86.

Chalmers, D. J. (1996). *The Conscious Mind,* Oxford University Press.

Chalmers, D. J. (this volume). "The Components of Content."

Davies, M., and Humberstone, I. (1980). "Two Notions of Necessity," *Philosophical Studies* 38, 1–30.

Dretske, F. (1995). *Naturalizing the Mind,* MIT Press.

Flanagan, O. (1992). *Consciousness Reconsidered,* MIT Press.

Fodor, J. (1987). *Psychosemantics: The Problem of Meaning in the Philosophy of Mind,* MIT Press.

Fodor, J. (1990). "A Theory of Content, II: The Theory," in his *A Theory of Content and Other Essays,* MIT Press. Reprinted in Stich and Warfield (1994).

Fodor, J. (1994). *The Elm and the Expert: Mentalese and Its Semantics,* MIT Press.

Fodor, J. (1998). *Concepts: Where Cognitive Science Went Wrong,* Oxford University Press.

Graham, G., and Horgan, T. (2000). "Mary Mary, Quite Contrary," *Philosophical Studies* 99, 59–87.

Horgan, T., and Tienson, J. (in press). "Deconstructing New Wave Materialism," in B. Loewer, ed., *Physicalism and Its Discontents,* Cambridge University Press.

Husserl, E. (1965). "Philosophy as Rigorous Science," in *Phenomenology and the Crisis of Philosophy,* Harper and Row (original publication 1910).

Jackson, F. (1998). *From Metaphysics to Ethics: A Defense of Conceptual Analysis,* Oxford University Press.

Kim, J. (forthcoming). "Physicalism—or Near Enough."

Kripke, S. (1982). *Wittgenstein on Rules and Private Language,* Basil Blackwell.

Lamb, Andrew (2001). "Temporal Dynamics: A Phenomenologically Based Alternative to Four-Dimensionalism and 'Point-Endurantist' Views of Time," *Southern Journal of Philosophy* 39, 235–59.

Levine, J. (1983). "Materialism and Qualia: The Explanatory Gap," *Pacific Philosophical Quarterly* 64.

Loar, B. (forthcoming). "Phenomenal Intentionality as the Basis of Mental Content."

Lycan, W. (1996). *Consciousness and Experience,* MIT Press.

McGinn, C. (1989). *Mental Content,* Blackwell.

McGinn, C. (1991). *The Problem of Consciousness: Essays Towards a Resolution,* Blackwell.

Reid, T. (1997). *Inquiry into the Human Mind on the Principles of Common Sense,* D. Brookes, ed. Pennsylvania State University Press (original publication 1764).

Ross, J. (1992). "Immaterial Aspects of Thought," *Journal of Philosophy* 89, 136–50.

Siewert, C. (1998). *The Significance of Consciousness,* Princeton University Press.

Silverberg, A. (1995). "Narrow Content: A Defense," *Southern Journal of Philosophy* 33, 109–27.

Stich, S., and Warfield, T., eds. (1994). *Mental Representations: A Reader,* Blackwell.

Strawson, G. (1994). *Mental Reality,* MIT Press.

Tienson, J. (1986). "An Observation on Common Names and Proper Names," *Analysis* 46, 73–76.

Tye, M. (1995). *Ten Problems of Consciousness,* MIT Press.

Tye, M. (1999). "Phenomenal Consciousness: the Explanatory Gap as a Cognitive Illusion," *Mind,* 101.

Van Gelder, T. (1999). "Wooden Iron? Husserlian Phenomenology Meets Cognitive Science," in J. Petitot, F. Varela, B. Pachoud, and J. Roy, eds., *Naturalizing Phenomenology: Issues in Contemporary Phenomenology and Cognitive Science,* Stanford University Press.

Varela, F. (1999). "The Specious Present: A Neurophenomenology of Time Consciousness," in J. Petitot, F. Varela, B. Pachoud, and J. Roy, eds., *Naturalizing Phenomenology: Issues in Contemporary Phenomenology and Cognitive Science,* Stanford University Press.

50 | Empiricism and the Philosophy of Mind

Wilfrid Sellars

XI. Thoughts: The Classical View

46. Recent empiricism has been of two minds about the status of *thoughts*. On the one hand, it has resonated to the idea that insofar as there are *episodes* which are thoughts, they are *verbal* or *linguistic* episodes. Clearly, however, even if candid overt verbal behaviors by people who had learned a language *were* thoughts, there are not nearly enough of them to account for all the cases in which it would be argued that a person was thinking. Nor can we plausibly suppose that the remainder is accounted for by those inner episodes which are often very clumsily lumped together under the heading "verbal imagery."

On the other hand, they have been tempted to suppose that the *episodes* which are referred to by verbs pertaining to thinking include all forms of "intelligent behavior," verbal as well as non-verbal, and that the "thought episodes" which are supposed to be manifested by these behaviors are not really episodes at all, but rather hypothetical and mongrel hypothetical-categorical facts about these and still other behaviors. This, however, runs into the difficulty that whenever we try to explain what we mean by calling a piece of *nonhabitual* behavior intelligent, we seem to find it necessary to do so in terms of *thinking*. The uncomfortable feeling will not be downed that the dispositional account of thoughts in terms of intelligent behavior is covertly circular.

47. Now the classical tradition claimed that there is a family of episodes, neither overt verbal behavior nor verbal imagery, which are *thoughts*, and that both overt verbal behavior and verbal imagery owe their meaningfulness to the fact that they stand to these *thoughts* in the unique relation of "expressing" them. These episodes are introspectable. Indeed, it was usually believed that they could not occur without being known to occur. But this can be traced to a number of confusions, perhaps the most important of which was the idea that *thoughts* belong in the same general category as sensations, images, tickles, itches, etc. This mis-assimilation of thoughts to sensations and feelings was equally, as we saw in Sections 26 ff. above, a mis-assimilation of sensations and feelings to thoughts, and a falsification of both. The assumption that if there are thought episodes, they must be immediate experiences is common both to those who propounded the classical view and to those who reject it, saying that they "find no such experiences." If we purge the classical tradition of these confusions, it becomes the idea that to each of us belongs a stream of episodes, not themselves immediate experiences, to which we have privileged, but by no means either invariable or infallible, access. These episodes can occur without being "expressed" by overt verbal behavior, though verbal behavior is—in an important sense—their natural fruition. Again, we can "hear ourselves think," but the verbal imagery which enables us to do this is no more the thinking itself than is the overt verbal behavior by which it is expressed and communicated to others. It is a mistake to suppose that we must be having verbal imagery—indeed, any imagery—when we "know what we are thinking"—in short, to suppose that "privileged access" must be construed on a perceptual or quasi-perceptual model.

Now, it is my purpose to defend such a revised classical analysis of our common-sense conception of thoughts, and in the course of doing so I shall develop distinctions which will later contribute to a resolution, in principle, of

Excerpted from H. Feigl and M. Scriven, ed., *Minnesota Studies in the Philosophy of Science*, Vol. 1 (University of Minnesota Press, 1956), pp. 253–329. Reprinted with permission of the publisher.

the puzzle of *immediate experience.* But before I continue, let me hasten to add that it will turn out that the view I am about to expound could, with equal appropriateness, be represented as a modified form of the view that thoughts are *linguistic* episodes.

XII. Our Rylean Ancestors

48. But, the reader may well ask, in what sense can these episodes be "inner" if they are not immediate experiences? and in what sense can they be "linguistic" if they are neither overt linguistic performances, nor verbal imagery *"in foro interno"*? I am going to answer these and the other questions I have been raising by making a myth of my own, or, to give it an air of up-to-date respectability, by writing a piece of science fiction—anthropological science fiction. Imagine a stage in prehistory in which humans are limited to what I shall call a Rylean language, a language of which the fundamental descriptive vocabulary speaks of public properties of public objects located in Space and enduring through Time. Let me hasten to add that it is also Rylean in that although its basic resources are limited (how limited I shall be discussing in a moment), its total expressive power is very great. For it makes subtle use not only of the elementary logical operations of conjunction, disjunction, negation, and quantification, but especially of the subjunctive conditional. Furthermore, I shall suppose it to be characterized by the presence of the looser logical relations typical of ordinary discourse which are referred to by philosophers under the headings "vagueness" and "open texture."

I am beginning my myth *in medias res* with humans who have already mastered a Rylean language, because the philosophical situation it is designed to clarify is one in which we are not puzzled by how people acquire a language for referring to public properties of public objects, but are very puzzled indeed about how we learn to speak of inner episodes and immediate experiences.

There are, I suppose, still some philosophers who are inclined to think that by allowing these mythical ancestors of ours the use *ad libitum* of subjunctive conditionals, we have, in effect, enabled them to say anything that *we* can say when we speak of *thoughts, experiences* (seeing, hearing, etc.), and *immediate experiences.* I doubt that there are many. In any case, the story I am telling is designed to show exactly *how* the idea

that an intersubjective language *must* be Rylean rests on too simple a picture of the relation of intersubjective discourse to public objects.

49. The questions I am, in effect, raising are "What resources would have to be added to the Rylean language of these talking animals in order that they might come to recognize each other and themselves as animals that *think, observe,* and have *feelings* and *sensations,* as we use these terms?" and "How could the addition of these resources be construed as reasonable?" In the first place, the language would have to be enriched with the fundamental resources of semantical discourse—that is to say, the resources necessary for making such characteristically semantical statements as *"'Rot' means red,"* and *"'Der Mond ist rund' is true if and only if the moon is round."* It is sometimes said, e.g., by Carnap (1942), that these resources can be constructed out of the vocabulary of formal logic, and that they would therefore already be contained, in principle, in our Rylean language. I have criticized this idea in another place (1963) and shall not discuss it here. In any event, a decision on this point is not essential to the argument.

Let it be granted, then, that these mythical ancestors of ours are able to characterize each other's verbal behavior in semantical terms; that, in other words, they not only can talk about each other's predictions as causes and effects, and as indicators (with greater or less reliability) of other verbal and nonverbal states of affairs, but can also say of these verbal productions that they *mean* thus and so, that they say that such and such, that they are true, false, etc. And let me emphasize, as was pointed out in Section 31 above, that to make a semantical statement about a verbal event is not a shorthand way of talking about its causes and effects, although there is a sense of "imply" in which semantical statements about verbal productions do *imply* information about the causes and effects of these productions. Thus, when I say *"'Es regnet' means it is raining,"* my statement "implies" that the causes and effects of utterances of *"Es regnet"* beyond the Rhine parallel the causes and effects of utterances of "It is raining" by myself and other members of the English-speaking community. And if it didn't imply this, it couldn't perform its role. But this is not to say that semantical statements are definitional shorthand for statements about the causes and effects of verbal performances.

50. With the resources of semantical discourse, the language of our fictional ancestors

has acquired a dimension which gives considerably more plausibility to the claim that they are in a position to talk about *thoughts* just as we are. For characteristic of thoughts is their *intentionality, reference,* or *aboutness,* and it is clear that semantical talk about the meaning or reference of verbal expressions has the same structure as mentalistic discourse concerning what thoughts are about. It is therefore all the more tempting to suppose that the intentionality of *thoughts* can be traced to the application of semantical categories to overt verbal performances, and to suggest a modified Rylean account according to which talk about so-called "thoughts" is shorthand for hypothetical and mongrel categorical-hypothetical statements about overt verbal and nonverbal behavior, and that talk about the *intentionality* of these "episodes" is correspondingly reducible to semantical talk about the verbal components.

What is the alternative? Classically it has been the idea that not only are there overt verbal episodes which can be characterized in semantical terms, but, *over and above these,* there are certain inner episodes which are properly characterized by the traditional vocabulary of *intentionality.* And, of course, the classical scheme includes the idea that semantical discourse about overt verbal performances is to be analyzed in terms of talk about the intentionality of the mental episodes which are "expressed" by these overt performances. My immediate problem is to see if I can reconcile the classical idea of thoughts as inner episodes which are neither overt behavior nor verbal imagery and which are properly referred to in terms of the vocabulary of intentionality, with the idea that the categories of intentionality are, at bottom, semantical categories pertaining to overt verbal performances.[1]

XIII. Theories and Models

51. But what might these episodes be? And, in terms of our science fiction, how might our ancestors have come to recognize their existence? The answer to these questions is surprisingly straightforward, once the logical space of our discussion is enlarged to include a distinction, central to the philosophy of science, between the language of *theory* and the language of *observation.* Although this distinction is a familiar one, I shall take a few paragraphs to highlight those aspects of the distinction which are of greatest relevance to our problem.

Informally, to construct a theory is, in its most developed or sophisticated form, to postulate a domain of entities which behave in certain ways set down by the fundamental principles of the theory, and to correlate—perhaps, in a certain sense to identify—complexes of these theoretical entities with certain non-theoretical objects or situations; that is to say, with objects or situations which are either matters of observable fact or, in principle at least, describable in observational terms. This "correlation" or "identification" of theoretical with observational states of affairs is a tentative one "until further notice," and amounts, so to speak, to erecting temporary bridges which permit the passage from sentences in observational discourse to sentences in the theory, and vice versa. Thus, for example, in the kinetic theory of gases, empirical statements of the form "Gas g at such and such a place and time has such and such a volume, pressure, and temperature" are correlated with theoretical statements specifying certain statistical measures of populations of molecules. These temporary bridges are so set up that inductively established laws pertaining to gases, formulated in the language of observable fact, are correlated with derived propositions or theorems in the language of the theory, and that no proposition in the theory is correlated with a falsified empirical generalization. Thus, a good theory (at least of the type we are considering) "explains" established empirical laws by deriving theoretical counterparts of these laws from a small set of postulates relating to unobserved entities.

These remarks, of course, barely scratch the surface of the problem of the status of theories in scientific discourse. And no sooner have I made them, than I must hasten to qualify them—almost beyond recognition. For while this by now classical account of the nature of theories (one of the earlier formulations of which is due to Norman Campbell (1920), and which is to be bound more recently in the writings of Carnap (1953), Reichenbach (1928, 1938), Hempel (1952), and Braithwaite (1953)) does throw light on the logical status of theories, it emphasizes certain features at the expense of others. By speaking of the construction of a theory as the elaboration of a postulate system which is tentatively correlated with observational discourse, it gives a highly artificial and unrealistic picture of what scientists have actually done in the process of constructing theories. I don't wish to deny that logically sophisticated scientists today *might* and perhaps, on occasion, do proceed in true logistical style. I do, however, wish to emphasize two points:

(1) The first is that the fundamental assumptions of a theory are usually developed not by constructing uninterpreted calculi which might correlate in the desired manner with observational discourse, but rather by attempting to find a *model*, i.e. to describe a domain of familiar objects behaving in familiar ways such that we can see how the phenomena to be explained would arise if they consisted of this sort of thing. The essential thing about a model is that it is accompanied, so to speak, by a commentary which *qualifies* or *limits*—but not precisely nor in all respects—the analogy between the familiar objects and the entities which are being introduced by the theory. It is the descriptions of the fundamental ways in which the objects in the model domain, thus qualified, behave, which, transferred to the theoretical entities, correspond to the postulates of the logistical picture of theory construction.

(2) But even more important for our purposes is the fact that the logistical picture of theory construction obscures the most important thing of all, namely that the process of devising "theoretical" explanations of observable phenomena did not spring full-blown from the head of modern science. In particular, it obscures the fact that not all common-sense inductive inferences are of the form

All observed A's have been B, *therefore* (*probably*) all A's are B.

or its statistical counterparts, and leads one mistakenly to suppose that so-called "hypothetic-deductive" explanation is limited to the sophisticated stages of science. The truth of the matter, as I shall shortly be illustrating, is that science is continuous with common sense, and the ways in which the scientist seeks to explain empirical phenomena are refinements of the ways in which plain men, however crudely and schematically, have attempted to understand their environment and their fellow men since the dawn of intelligence. It is this point which I wish to stress at the present time, for I am going to argue that the distinction between theoretical and observational discourse is involved in the logic of concepts pertaining to inner episodes. I say "involved in" for it would be paradoxical and, indeed, incorrect, to say that these concepts *are* theoretical concepts.

52. Now I think it fair to say that some light has already been thrown on the expression "inner episodes"; for while it would indeed be a

category mistake to suppose that the inflammability of a piece of wood is, so to speak, a hidden burning which becomes overt or manifest when the wood is placed on the fire, not all the unobservable episodes we suppose to go on in the world are the offspring of category mistakes. Clearly it is by no means an illegitimate use of "in"—though it is a use which has its own logical grammar—to say, for example, that "in" the air around us there are innumerable molecules which, in spite of the observable stodginess of the air, are participating in a veritable turmoil of episodes. Clearly, the sense in which these episodes are "in" the air is to be explicated in terms of the sense in which the air "is" a population of molecules, and this, in turn, in terms of the logic of the relation between theoretical and observational discourse.

I shall have more to say on this topic in a moment. In the meantime, let us return to our mythical ancestors. It will not surprise my readers to learn that the second stage in the enrichment of their Rylean language is the addition of theoretical discourse. Thus we may suppose these language-using animals to elaborate, without methodological sophistication, crude, sketchy, and vague theories to explain why things which are similar in their observable properties differ in their causal properties, and things which are similar in their causal properties differ in their observable properties.

XIV. Methodological versus Philosophical Behaviorism

53. But we are approaching the time for the central episode in our myth. I want you to suppose that in this Neo-Rylean culture there now appears a genius—let us call him Jones—who is an unsung forerunner of the movement in psychology, once revolutionary, now commonplace, known as Behaviorism. Let me emphasize that what I have in mind is Behaviorism as a methodological thesis, which I shall be concerned to formulate. For the central and guiding theme in the historical complex known by this term has been a certain conception, or family of conceptions, of how to go about building a science of psychology.

Philosophers have sometimes supposed that Behaviorists are, as such, committed to the idea that our ordinary mentalistic concepts are *analyzable* in terms of overt behavior. But although behaviorism has often been characterized by a certain metaphysical bias, it is not a thesis about the *analysis* of *existing* psychological concepts, but one which concerns the construction of new concepts. As a methodological thesis, it involves no commitment whatever concerning the logical analysis of common-sense mentalistic discourse, nor does it involve a denial that each of us has a privileged access to our state of mind, nor that these states of mind can properly be described in terms of such common-sense concepts as believing, wondering, doubting, intending, wishing, inferring, etc. If we permit ourselves to speak of this privileged access to our states of mind as "introspection," avoiding the implication that there is a "means" whereby we "see" what is going on "inside," as we see external circumstances by the eye, then we can say that Behaviorism, as I shall use the term, does not deny that there is such a thing as introspection, nor that it is, on some topics, at least, quite reliable. The essential point about 'introspection' from the standpoint of Behaviorism is that *we introspect in terms of common sense mentalistic concepts.* And while the Behaviorist admits, as anyone must, that much knowledge is embodied in common-sense mentalistic discourse, and that still more can be gained in the future by formulating and testing hypotheses in terms of them, and while he admits that it is perfectly legitimate to call such a psychology "scientific," he proposes, for his own part, to make no more than a heuristic use of mentalistic discourse, and to construct his concepts "from scratch" in the course of developing his own scientific account of the observable behavior of human organisms.

54. But while it is quite clear that scientific Behaviorism is *not* the thesis that common-sense psychological concepts are *analyzable* into concepts pertaining to overt behavior—a thesis which has been maintained by some philosophers and which may be called 'analytical' or 'philosophical' Behaviorism—it is often thought that Behaviorism is committed to the idea that the concepts of a behavioristic psychology must be so analyzable, or, to put things right side up, that properly introduced behavioristic concepts must be built by explicit definition—in the broadest sense—from a basic vocabulary pertaining to overt behavior. The Behaviorist would thus be saying "Whether or not the mentalistic concepts of everyday life are definable in terms of overt behavior, I shall ensure that this is true of the concepts that I shall employ." And it must be confessed that many behavioristically oriented psychologists have believed themselves

committed to this austere program of concept formation.

Now I think it reasonable to say that, *thus conceived,* the behavioristic program would be unduly restrictive. Certainly, nothing in the nature of sound scientific procedure requires this self-denial. Physics, the methodological sophistication of which has so impressed—indeed, overly impressed—the other sciences, does not lay down a corresponding restriction on its concepts, nor has chemistry been built in terms of concepts explicitly definable in terms of the observable properties and behavior of chemical substances. The point I am making should now be clear. The behavioristic requirement that all concepts should be *introduced* in terms of a basic vocabulary pertaining to overt behavior is compatible with the idea that some behavioristic concepts are to be introduced as *theoretical* concepts.

55. It is essential to note that the theoretical terms of a behavioristic psychology are not only *not* defined in terms of overt behavior, they are also *not* defined in terms of nerves, synapses, neural impulses, etc., etc. A behavioristic theory of behavior is not, as such, a physiological explanation of behavior. The ability of a framework of theoretical concepts and propositions successfully to explain behavioral phenomena is logically independent of the identification of these theoretical concepts with concepts of neurophysiology. What *is* true—and this is a logical point—is that each special science dealing with some aspect of the human organism operates within the frame of a certain regulative ideal, the ideal of a coherent system in which the achievements of each have an intelligible place. Thus, it is part of the Behaviorist's business to keep an eye on the total picture of the human organism which is beginning to emerge. And if the tendency to premature identification is held in check, there may be considerable heuristic value in speculative attempts at integration; though, until recently, at least, neurophysiological speculations in behavior theory have not been particularly fruitful. And while it is, I suppose, noncontroversial that when the total scientific picture of man and his behavior is in, it will involve *some* identification of concepts in behavior theory with concepts pertaining to the functioning of anatomical structures, it should not be assumed that behavior theory is committed *ab initio* to a physiological identification of *all* its concepts,—that its concepts are, so to speak, physiological from the start.

We have, in effect, been distinguishing between two dimensions of the logic (or 'methodologic') of theoretical terms: (a) their role in explaining the selected phenomena of which the theory is the theory; (b) their role as candidates for integration in what we have called the "total picture." These roles are equally part of the logic, and hence the "meaning," of theoretical terms. Thus, at any one time the terms in a theory will carry with them as part of their logical force that which it is reasonable to envisage—whether schematically or determinately—as the manner of their integration. However, for the purposes of my argument, it will be useful to refer to these two roles as though it were a matter of a distinction between what I shall call *pure theoretical concepts,* and hypotheses concerning the relation of these concepts to concepts in other specialties. What we *can* say is that the less a scientist is in a position to conjecture about the way in which a certain theory can be expected to integrate with other specialties, the more the concepts of his theory approximate to the status of pure theoretical concepts. To illustrate: We can imagine that Chemistry developed a sophisticated and successful theory to explain chemical phenomena before either electrical or magnetic phenomena were noticed; and that chemists developed as pure theoretical concepts, certain concepts which it later became reasonable to identify with concepts belonging to the framework of electromagnetic theory.

XV. The Logic of Private Episodes: Thoughts

56. With these all too sketchy remarks on Methodological Behaviorism under our belts, let us return once again to our fictional ancestors. We are now in a position to characterize the original Rylean language in which they described themselves and their fellows as not only a *behavioristic* language, but a behavioristic language which is restricted to the *non-theoretical* vocabulary of a behavioristic psychology. Suppose, now, that in the attempt to account for the fact that his fellow men behave intelligently not only when their conduct is threaded on a string of overt verbal episodes—that is to say, as we would put it, when they "think out loud"—but also when no detectable verbal output is present, Jones develops a *theory* according to which overt utterances are but the culmination of a process which begins with certain inner episodes. *And let us suppose that his model for these episodes* which initiate the events which culminate in overt verbal behavior *is that of overt verbal behavior itself. In other words, using the language of the model, the theory is to the effect that overt verbal behavior is the culmination of a process which begins with "inner speech."*

It is essential to bear in mind that what Jones means by "inner speech" is not to be confused with *verbal imagery.* As a matter of fact, Jones, like his fellows, does not as yet even have the concept of an image.

It is easy to see the general lines a Jonesean theory will take. According to it the true cause of intelligent nonhabitual behavior is "inner speech." Thus, even when a hungry person overtly says "Here is an edible object" and proceeds to eat it, the true—theoretical—cause of his eating, given his hunger, is not the overt utterance, but the "inner utterance of this sentence."

57. The first thing to note about the Jonesean theory is that, as built on the model of speech episodes, *it carries over to these inner episodes the applicability of semantical categories.* Thus, just as Jones has, like his fellows, been speaking of overt utterances as *meaning* this or that, or being *about* this or that, so he now speaks of these inner episodes as *meaning* this or that, or being *about* this or that.

The second point to remember is that although Jones' theory involves a *model,* it is not identical with it. Like all theories formulated in terms of a model, it also includes a *commentary* on the model; a commentary which places more or less sharply drawn restrictions on the analogy between the theoretical entities and the entities of the model. Thus, while his theory talks of "inner speech," the commentary hastens to add that, of course, the episodes in question are not the wagging of a hidden tongue, nor are any sounds produced by this "inner speech."

58. The general drift of my story should now be clear. I shall therefore proceed to make the essential points quite briefly:

(1) What we must suppose Jones to have developed is the germ of a theory which permits many different developments. We must not pin it down to any of the more sophisticated forms it takes in the hands of classical philosophers. Thus, the theory need not be given a Socratic or Cartesian form, according to which this "inner speech" is a function of a separate substance;

though primitive peoples may have had good reason to suppose that humans consist of two separate things.

(2) Let us suppose Jones to have called these discursive entities *thoughts*. We can admit at once that the framework of thoughts he has introduced is a framework of "unobserved," "nonempirical" "inner" episodes. For we can point out immediately that in these respects they are no worse off than the particles and episodes of physical theory. For these episodes are "in" language-using animals as molecular impacts are "in" gases, not as "ghosts" are in "machines." They are "nonempirical" in the simple sense that they are *theoretical*—not definable in observational terms. Nor does the fact that they are, *as introduced,* unobserved entities imply that Jones could not have good reason for supposing them to exist. Their "purity" is not a *metaphysical* purity, but, so to speak, a *methodological* purity. As we have seen, the fact that they are not introduced as physiological entities does not preclude the possibility that at a later methodological stage, they may, so to speak, "turn out" to be such. Thus, there are many who would say that it is already reasonable to suppose that these *thoughts* are to be "identified" with complex events in the cerebral cortex functioning along the lines of a calculating machine. Jones, of course, has no such idea.

(3) Although the theory postulates that overt discourse is the culmination of a process which begins with "inner discourse," this should not be taken to mean that overt discourse stands to "inner discourse" *as voluntary movements stand to intentions and motives.* True, overt linguistic events *can* be produced as means to ends. But serious errors creep into the interpretation of both language and thought if one interprets the idea that overt linguistic episodes *express* thoughts, on the model of the use of an instrument. Thus, it should be noted that Jones' theory, as I have sketched it, is perfectly compatible with the idea that the ability to have thoughts is acquired in the process of acquiring overt speech and that only after overt speech is well established, can "inner speech" occur without its overt culmination.

(4) Although the occurrence of overt speech episodes which are characterizable in semantical terms is explained by the theory in terms of *thoughts* which are *also* characterized in semantical terms, this does not mean that the idea that overt speech "has meaning" is being *analyzed* in terms of the intentionality of thoughts. It must

not be forgotten that *the semantical characterization of overt verbal episodes is the primary use of semantical terms, and that overt linguistic events as semantically characterized are the model for the inner episodes introduced by the theory.*

(5) One final point before we come to the dénouement of the first episode in the saga of Jones. It cannot be emphasized too much that although these theoretical discursive episodes or *thoughts* are introduced as *inner* episodes—which is merely to repeat that they are introduced as *theoretical* episodes—they are *not* introduced as *immediate experiences.* Let me remind the reader that Jones, like his Neo-Rylean contemporaries, does not as yet have this concept. And even when he, and they, acquire it, by a process which will be the second episode in my myth, it will only be the philosophers among them who will suppose that the inner episodes introduced for one theoretical purpose—thoughts—must be a subset of immediate experiences, inner episodes introduced for another theoretical purpose.

59. Here, then, is the dénouement. I have suggested a number of times that although it would be most misleading to say that concepts pertaining to thinking are theoretical concepts, yet their status might be illuminated by means of the contrast between theoretical and nontheoretical discourse. We are now in a position to see exactly why this is so. For once our fictitious ancestor, Jones, has developed the theory that overt verbal behavior is the expression of thoughts, and taught his compatriots to make use of the theory in interpreting each other's behavior, it is but a short step to the use of this language in self-description. Thus, when Tom, watching Dick, has behavioral evidence which warrants the use of the sentence (in the language of the theory) "Dick is thinking 'p' " (or "Dick is thinking that p"), Dick, using the same behavioral evidence, can say, in the language of the theory, "I am thinking 'p' " (or "I am thinking that p.") And it now turns out—need it have?—that Dick can be trained to give reasonably reliable self-descriptions, using the language of the theory, without having to observe his overt behavior. Jones brings this about, roughly, by applauding utterances by Dick of "I am thinking that p" when the behavioral evidence strongly supports the theoretical statement "Dick is thinking that p"; and by frowning on utterances of "I am thinking that p," when the evidence does not support this theoretical statement. Our

ancestors begin to speak of the privileged access each of us has to his own thoughts. *What began as a language with a purely theoretical use has gained a reporting role.*

As I see it, this story helps us understand that concepts pertaining to such inner episodes as thoughts are primarily and essentially *intersubjective,* as intersubjective as the concept of a positron, and that the reporting role of these concepts—the fact that each of us has a privileged access to his thoughts—constitutes a dimension of the use of these concepts which is *built on* and *presupposes* this intersubjective status. My myth has shown that the fact that language is essentially an *intersubjective* achievement, and is

learned in intersubjective contexts—a fact rightly stressed in modern psychologies of language, thus by B. F. Skinner (1945), and by certain philosophers, e.g. Carnap (1933), Wittgenstein (1953)—is compatible with the "privacy" of "inner episodes." It also makes clear that this privacy is not an "absolute privacy." For if it recognizes that these concepts have a reporting use in which one is not drawing inferences from behavioral evidence, it nevertheless insists that the fact that overt behavior *is* evidence for these episodes *is built into the very logic of these concepts,* just as the fact that the observable behavior of gases is evidence for molecular episodes is built into the very logic of molecule talk. . . .

NOTES

This paper was first presented as the University of London Special Lectures on Philosophy for 1955–56, delivered on March 1, 8, and 15, 1956, under the title "The

Myth of the Given: Three Lectures on Empiricism and the Philosophy of Mind."

1. An earlier attempt along these lines is to be found in my (1952) and (1953).

REFERENCES

Braithwaite, R. B. *Scientific Explanation.* Cambridge: Cambridge Univ. Pr., 1953.

Campbell, Norman. *Physics: The Elements.* Cambridge: Cambridge Univ. Pr., 1920.

Carnap, Rudolf. *Introduction to Semantics.* Chicago: Univ. of Chicago Pr., 1942.

——. *"Psychologie in Physikalischer Sprache,"* *Erkenntnis,* 3:107–42 (1933).

——. "The Interpretation of Physics," in H. Feigl and M. Brodbeck (eds.), *Readings in the Philosophy of Science,* pp. 309–18. New York: Appleton-Century-Crofts, 1953. This selection consists of pp. 59–69 of his *Foundations of Logic and Mathematics.* Chicago: Univ. of Chicago Pr., 1939.

Hempel, C. G. *Fundamentals of Concept Formation in Empirical Science.* Chicago: Univ. of Chicago Pr., 1952.

Reichenbach, H. *Philosophie der Raum-Zeit-Lehre.* Berlin: de Gruyter, 1928.

——. *Experience and Prediction.* Chicago: Univ. of Chicago Pr., 1938.

Sellars, Wilfrid. "Mind, Meaning and Behavior," *Philosophical Studies,* 3:83–94 (1952).

——. "A Semantic Solution of the Mind-Body Problem," *Methodos,* 5:45–84 (1953).

——. "Empiricism and Abstract Entities," in *Paul A. Schlipp* (ed.), *The Philosophy of Rudolf Carnap.* Evanston (Ill.): Library of Living Philosophers (1963), pp. 431–68.

Skinner, B. F. "The Operational Analysis of Psychological Terms," *Psychological Review,* 52:270–77 (1945). Reprinted in H. Feigl and M. Brodbeck (eds.), *Readings in the Philosophy of Science,* pp. 585–94. New York: Appleton-Century-Crofts, 1953.

Wittgenstein, Ludwig. *Philosophical Investigations.* London: Macmillan, 1953.

51 Propositional Attitudes

Jerry A. Fodor

Some philosophers (Dewey, for example, and maybe Austin) hold that philosophy is what you do to a problem until it's clear enough to solve it by doing science. Others (Ryle, for example, and maybe Wittgenstein) hold that if a philosophical problem succumbs to empirical methods, that shows it wasn't *really* philosophical to begin with. Either way, the facts seem clear enough: questions first mooted by philosophers are sometimes coopted by people who do experiments. This seems to be happening now to the question: "what are propositional attitudes?" and cognitive psychology is the science of note.

One way to elucidate this situation is to examine theories that cognitive psychologists endorse, with an eye to explicating the account of propositional attitudes that the theories presuppose. That was my strategy in Fodor (1975). In this paper, however, I'll take another tack. I want to outline a number of a priori conditions which, on my view, a theory of propositional attitudes (PAs) ought to meet. I'll argue that, considered together, these conditions pretty clearly demand a treatment of PAs as relations between organisms and internal representations; precisely the view that the psychologists have independently arrived at. I'll thus be arguing that we have good reasons to endorse the psychologists' theory even aside from the empirical exigencies that drove them to it. I take it that this convergence between what's plausible a priori and what's demanded ex post facto is itself a reason for believing that the theory is probably true.

Three preliminary remarks: first, I'm not taking 'a priori' all that seriously. Some of the points I'll be making are, I suppose, strictly conceptual, but others are merely self-evident. What I've got is a set of glaring facts about propositional attitudes. I don't doubt that we might rationally adopt an account of the attitudes which contravenes some, or maybe even all of them. But the independent evidence for such an account would have to be extremely persuasive or I, for one, would get the jitters. Second, practically everything I'll say about the attitudes has been said previously in the philo-sophical literature. All I've done is bring the stuff together. I do think, however, that the various constraints that I'll discuss illuminate each other; it is only when one attempts to satisfy them all at once that one sees how univocal their demands are. Finally, though I intend what I say to apply, mutatis mutandis, to PAs at large, I shall run the discussion pretty much exclusively on beliefs and wants. These seem to be the root cases for a systematic cognitive psychology; thus learning and perception are presumably to be treated as varieties of the fixation of belief, and the theory of action is presumably continuous with the theory of utility.[1]

Here, then, are my conditions, with comments.

I. Propositional attitudes should be analyzed as relations. In particular, the verb in a sentence like 'John believes it's raining' expresses a relation between John and something else, and a token of that sentence is true iff John stands in the belief-relation to that thing.[2] Equivalently, for these purposes, 'it's raining' is a term in 'John believes it's raining.'[3] I have three arguments for imposing condition I, all of them inconclusive.

I-a) It's intuitively plausible. 'Believes' looks like a two-place relation, and it would be nice if our theory of belief permitted us to save the appearances.

No doubt, appearances sometimes deceive. The "s" in 'Mary's sake' looks like expressing a relation (of possession) between Mary and a sake; but it doesn't, or so we're told. In fact, 'Mary's sake' doesn't look *very* relational, since *x's sake* would surely qualify as an idiom even if we had no ontological scruples to placate. There's something syntactically wrong with: ⌜Mary's sake is *Fer* than Bill's⌝, 'Mary has a (little) sake,' etc. For that matter, there's something syntactically wrong with 'a sake' *tout court*. Yet, we'd expect all such expressions to be well-formed if 'Mary's sake' contained a true possessive. 'Mary's sake' doesn't bear comparison with 'Mary's lamb.'

Still, there are some cases of *non*-idiomatic

From *The Monist*, 61:573–91, 1978. Copyright © 1978, *The Monist*, Peru, Illinois 61354. Reprinted with permission of the publisher.

expressions which appear to be relational, but which, upon reflection, maybe aren't. 'Mary's voice' goes through the transformations even if 'Mary's sake' does not (Dennett, 1969). Yet there aren't, perhaps, such *things* as voices; and, if there aren't, 'Mary's voice' can't refer in virtue of a relation between Mary and one of them.[4] I think it is fair to view the "surface" grammar as ontologically misleading in *these* cases, but only because we know how to translate into more parsimonious forms. 'Mary has a good voice (bad voice; little voice; better voice than Bill's)' goes over, pretty much without residue, into 'Mary sings well (badly, weakly, less well than Bill).' If, however, we were *unable* to provide (or, anyhow, to envision providing) the relevant translations, what right would we have to view such expressions as ontologically promiscuous? 'Bill believes it's raining' is not an idiom, and there is, so far as anybody knows, no way of translating sentences nominally about beliefs into sentences of reduced ontological load. (Behaviorists used to think such translations might be forthcoming, but they were wrong.) We must, then, either take the apparent ontological commitments seriously or admit to playing fast and loose.

I-b) Existential Generalization applies to the syntactic objects of verbs of propositional attitude; from 'John believes it's raining' we can infer 'John believes something' and 'there is something that John believes' (viz., that it's raining). *EG* may not be *criterial* for ontological commitment, but it is surely a straw in the wind.[5]

I-c) The only known alternative to the view that verbs of propositional attitude express relations is that they are (semantically) "fused" with their objects, and that view would seem to be hopeless.[6]

The fusion story is the proposal that sentences like 'John believes it's raining' ought really to be spelled 'John believes-it's-raining'; that the logical form of such sentences acknowledges a referring expression ('John') and a one-place predicate with no internal structure ('believes-it's-raining'). 'John believes it's raining' is thus an atomic sentence, similar *au fond* to 'John is purple.'

Talk about counter-intuitive! Moreover:

1. There are infinitely many (semantically distinct) sentences of the form *a believes complement*. If all such sentences are atomic, how is English learned? (Davidson, (1965)).

2. Different propositional attitudes are often "focused" on the same content; for example, one can both fear and believe that it will rain on Tuesday. But, on the fusion view, 'John fears that it will rain on Tuesday' has nothing in common with 'John believes that it will rain on Tuesday' save only the reference to John. In particular, it's an *accident* that the form of words 'it will rain on Tuesday' occurs in both.

3. Similarly, different beliefs can be related in such ways as the following: John thinks Sam is nice; Mary thinks Sam is nasty. Under ordinary English representation these beliefs overlap at the 'Sam' position, so the notation sustains the intuition that John and Mary disagree about Sam. But, if the fusion view is correct, 'John thinks Sam is nice' and 'Mary thinks Sam is nasty' have no more in common at the level of canonical notation than, say, 'John eats' and 'Mary swims.' Talk about imperspicuous! In respect of saving the intuitions, the recommended reconstruction does *worse* than the undisciplined orthography that we started with.[7] (For that matter, there's nothing in ⌜believes-that-S⌝ to suggest that it's about believing. Here too ⌜believes that S⌝ does much better.)

4. It could hardly be an accident that the declarative sentences of English constitute the (syntactic) objects of verbs like 'believe.' Whereas, on the fusion view it's *precisely* an accident; the complement of 'believes' in 'John believes it's raining' bears no more relation to the sentence 'It's raining' than, say, the word 'dog' bears to the first syllable of 'dogmatic.'

5. On the fusion view, it's a sheer accident that if 'John believes it's raining' is true, then what John believes is true iff 'it's raining' is true. But this, surely, is one accident too many. Surely the identity between the truth conditions on John's belief when he believes Fa, and those on the corresponding sentence ⌜a is F⌝ must be what connects the theory of sentence interpretation with the theory of PAs (and what explains our using 'it's raining', and not some other form of words, to specify *which* belief John has when he believes it's raining).

It's the mark of a bad theory that it makes the data look fortuitous. I conclude that the fusion story is not to be taken very seriously; that neither the philosophy of language nor the philosophy of mind is advanced just by proliferating hyphens. But the fusion story is (de facto) the only alternative to the view that 'believe' expresses a relation. Hence, first blush, we had better assume that 'believe' *does* express a relation and try to find an account of propositional attitudes which comports with that assumption.

II. A theory of PAs should explain the parallelism between verbs of PA and verbs of saying. ("Vendler's Condition").

Rather generally, the things we can be said to *believe* (want, hope, regret, etc.) are the very things that we can be said to *say* (assert, state, etc.). So, John can either believe or assert that it's about to blow; he can either hope that or inquire whether somebody has reefed the main; he can either doubt or demand that the crew should douse the Genny. Moreover, as Vendler (1972) has shown, there are interesting consequences of classifying verbs of PA (on the one hand) and verbs of saying (on the other) by reference to the syntax of their object complements. It turns out that the taxonomies thus engendered are isomorphic down to surprisingly fine levels of grain. Now, of course, this *could* be just an accident, as could the semantic and syntactic parallelisms between the complements of verbs of PA and free standing declaratives (see above). Certainly, it's a substantial inference from the syntactic similarities that Vendler observes to the conclusion he draws: that the object of assertion is identical with the object of belief. Suffice it for now to make the less ambitious point: we should prefer a theory which explains the facts to one which merely shrugs its shoulders; viz. a theory which satisfies Vendler's condition to a theory which does not.

III. A theory of propositional attitudes should account for their opacity ("Frege's Condition").

Thus far, I have stressed logico-syntactic analogies between the complements of belief clauses and the corresponding free-standing declaratives. However, it has been customary in the philosophical literature since Frege to stress one of their striking *dis*analogies: the former are, in general, opaque to inferential operations to which the latter are, in general, transparent. Since this aspect of the behavior of sentences that ascribe propositional attitudes has so dominated the philosophical discussion, I shall make the point quite briefly here. Sentences containing verbs of PA are not, normally, truth functions of their complements. Moreover, contexts subordinated to verbs of PA are normally themselves non-truth functional, and *EG* and substitution of identicals may apply at syntactic positions in a free-standing declarative while failing at syntactically comparable positions in belief sentences. A theory of PAs should explain why all this is so.

It should be acknowledged that, however gross the inadequacies of the fusion view, it does at least provide an account of propositional attitudes which meets Frege's condition. If *S* doesn't so much as occur in ⌜John believes S⌝ it's hardly surprising that the one should fail to be a truth function of the other; similarly, if 'Mary' doesn't occur in 'Bill believes that John bit Mary,' it's hardly surprising that the sentence doesn't behave the way it would if 'Mary' occurred referentially. The methodological moral is perhaps that Frege's condition underconstrains a theory of PAs; ideally, an acceptable account of opacity should follow from a theory that is independently plausible.

IV. The objects of propositional attitudes have logical form ("Aristotle's Condition").

Mental states (including, especially, token havings of propositional attitudes) interact causally. Such interactions constitute the mental processes which eventuate (inter alia) in the behaviors of organisms. Now, it is crucial to the whole program of explaining behavior by reference to mental states that the propositional attitudes belonging to these chains are typically *non*-arbitrarily related in respect of their content (taking the "content" of a propositional attitude, informally, to be whatever it is that the complement of the corresponding PA-ascribing sentence expresses).

This is not an a priori claim, though perhaps it is a transcendental one. For, though one can imagine the occurrence of causal chains of mental states which are not otherwise related (as, e.g., a thought that two is a prime number, causing a desire for tea, causing an intention to recite the alphabet backwards, causing an expectation of rain) and though such sequences doubtless actually occur (in dreams, say, and in madness) still if *all* our mental life were like this, it's hard to see what point ascriptions of contents to mental states would have. Even phenomenology presupposes some correspondence between the content of our beliefs and the content of our beliefs about our beliefs; else there would be no coherent introspections for phenomenologists to report.

The paradigm situation—the grist for the cognitivist's mill—is the one where propositional attitudes interact causally and do so *in virtue of* their content. And the paradigm of this paradigm is the practical syllogism. Since it is part of my point that the details matter not at all, I shall take liberties with Aristotle's text.

John believes that it will rain if he washes his car. John wants it to rain. So John acts in a manner intended to be a car-washing.

I take it that this might be a true, if informal, etiology of John's "car-washing behavior"; the car washing is an effect of the intention to car-wash, and the intention to car-wash is an effect of the causal interaction between John's beliefs and his utilities. Moreover, the etiological account might be counterfactual-supporting in at least the following sense: John wouldn't have car-washed had the content of his beliefs, utilities and intentions been other than they were. Or, if he did, he would have done so unintentionally, or for different reasons, or with other ends in view. To say that John's mental states interact causally *in virtue of* their content is, in part, to say that such counterfactuals hold.

If there are true, contingent counterfactuals which relate mental state *tokens* in virtue of their contents, that is presumably because there are true, contingent generalizations which relate mental state *types* in virtue of their contents. So, still following Aristotle at a distance, we can schematize etiologies like the one above to get the underlying generalization: if x believes that A is an action x can perform; and if x believes that a performance of A is sufficient to bring it about that Q; and if x wants it to be the case that Q; then x acts in a fashion intended be a performance of A.

I am not, for present purposes, interested in whether this is a plausible decision theory; still less in whether it is the decision theory that Aristotle thought plausible. What interests me here is rather: (a) that any decision theory we can now contemplate will surely look rather like this one in that (b) it will entail generalizations about the causal relations among content-related beliefs, utilities and intentions; and (c) such generalizations will be specified by reference to the form of the propositional attitudes which instantiate them. (This remains true even if, as some philosophers suppose, an adequate decision theory is irremediably in need of ceteris paribus clauses to flesh out its generalizations. See, for example, Grice (1975).) So, in particular, we can't state the theory-relevant generalization that is instantiated by the relations among John's mental states unless we allow reference to beliefs of the form *if X then Y,* desires of the form *that Y;* intentions of the form *that X should come about;* and so forth. Viewed one way (material mode) the recurrent schematic letters require identities of content among propositional attitudes. Viewed the other way (linguistically) they require formal iden-

tities among the complements of the PA-ascribing sentence which instantiate the generalizations of the theory that explains John's behavior. Either way, the form of the generalization determines how the theory relates to the events that it subsumes. There is nothing remarkable about this, of course, except that form is here being ascribed *inside* the scope of verbs of PA.

To summarize: our common-sense psychological generalizations relate mental states in virtue of their content, and canonical representation does what it can to reconstruct such content relations as relations of form. "Aristotle's condition" requires that our theory of propositional attitudes should rationalize this process by construing verbs of PA in a way that permits reference to the form of their objects. To do this is to legitimize the presuppositions of common-sense psychology and, for that matter, of real (viz. cognitive) psychology as well. (See Fodor, op. cit.)

In fact, we can state (and satisfy) Aristotle's condition in a still stronger version. Let anything be a *belief sentence* if it is of the form *a believes that S.* Define the *correspondent* of such a sentence as the formula which consists of S standing alone (i.e. the sentence #S#).[8] We remarked above that there is the following relation between the truth conditions on the belief that a belief sentence ascribes and the truth conditions on the correspondent of the belief sentence: the belief is true iff the correspondent is. This is, presumably, at least part of what is involved in viewing the correspondent of a belief sentence as *expressing* the ascribed belief.

It should not, therefore, be surprising to find that our intuitions about the form of the belief ascribed by a given belief sentence are determined by the logical form of its correspondent. So, intuitively, John's belief that Mary and Bill are leaving is a conjunctive belief (cf. the logical form of 'Mary and Bill are leaving'); John's belief that Alfred is a white swan is a singulary belief (cf. the logical form of 'Alfred is a white swan'); and so on. It is, of course, essential that we understand 'belief' *opaquely* in such examples; otherwise, the belief that P will have the logical form of any sentence equivalent to P. But this is as it should be: it is in virtue of its *opaque* content that John's belief that P plays its systematic role in John's mental life: e.g., in the determination of his actions and in the causation of his other mental states. Hence it is the opaque construal that operates in such patterns of explanation as the practical syllogism and its spiritual heirs.

We are now in position to state Aristotle's condition in its strongest (and final) version. A theory of propositional attitudes should legitimize the ascription of form to objects of propositional attitudes. In particular, it should explain why the form of a belief is identical to the logical form of the correspondent of a sentence which (opaquely) ascribes that belief.[9]

I digress: One may feel inclined to argue that the satisfaction of Aristotle's condition is incompatible with the satisfaction of Frege's condition; that the opacity of belief sentences shows the futility of assigning logical form to their objects. The argument might go as follows. Sentence have logical form in virtue of their behavior under logical transformations; the logical form of a sentence is that aspect of its structure in virtue of which it provides a domain for such transformations. But Frege shows us that the objects of verbs of propositional attitude are inferentially inert. Hence, it's a sort of charade to speak of the logical form of the objects of PAs; what's the force of saying that a sentence has the form $P \& Q$ if one must also say that simplification of conjunction does not apply?

Perhaps some such argument supplies the motive force of fusion theories. It is, in any event, misled. In particular, it muddles the distinction between what's entailed by what's believed, and what's entailed by believing what's believed. Less cryptically: if John believes that P & Q, then what John believes entails that P and what John believes entails that Q. This is surely incontestible; P & Q is what John believes, and P & Q entails P, Q. Full stop. It would thus be highly ill-advised to put Frege's condition as "P & Q is semantically inert when embedded to the context ⌜John believes . . .⌝ "; for this makes it sound as though P & Q sometimes doesn't entail P: viz. when it's in the scope of "believes." (A parallel bad argument: P & Q sometimes doesn't entail P, viz. when it's in the scope of the operator 'not'.) What falls under Frege's condition, then, is not the sentence that expresses what John believes (viz. P & Q) but the sentence that expresses John's believing what he believes (viz. the sentence ⌜John believes that P & Q⌝). Note that the inertia of this latter sentence isn't an exception to simplification of conjunction since simplification of conjunction isn't defined for sentences of the form *a believes that P & Q;* only for sentences of the form *P & Q.*

"Still," one might say, "if the form of words ⌜P & Q⌝ is logically inert when embedded to the form of words ⌜John believes . . .⌝, what's the *point* of talking about the logical form of the complement of belief sentences?" This isn't an argument, of course, but it's a fair question. Answers: (a) because we may want to satisfy Aristotle's condition (e.g., in order to be in a position to state the practical syllogism); (b) because we may want to compare beliefs in respect of their form (John's belief that (x) Fx → Gx is a generalization of Mary's belief that a is F and G; Sam's belief that P is incompatible with Bill's belief that not-P; etc.); (c) because we may wish to speak of the consequences of a belief, even while cheerfully admitting that the consequences of a belief may not themselves be objects of belief (viz. believed in). Indeed, we need the notion of the consequences of a belief if only in order to say that belief isn't closed under the consequence relation.

I cease to digress.

V. A theory of propositional attitudes should mesh with empirical accounts of mental processes.

We want a theory of PAs to say what (token) propositional attitudes *are;* or, at least, what the facts are in virtue of which PA ascriptions are true. It seems to me self-evident that no such theory could be acceptable unless it lent itself to explanations of the data—gross and commonsensical or subtle and experimental—about mental states and processes. This is not, of course, to require that a theory of PAs legitimize our current empirical psychology; only that it comport with some psychology or other that is independently warranted. I hear this as analogous to: the theory that water is H_2O couldn't be acceptable unless, taken together with appropriate empirical premises, it leads to explanations of the macro- and micro-properties of water. Hence, I hear it as undeniable.

I think, in fact, that the requirement that a theory of propositional attitudes should be empirically plausible can be made to do quite a lot of work; much more work than philosophers have usually realized. I'll return to this presently, when we have some theories in hand.

Those, then, are the conditions that I want a theory of propositional attitudes to meet. I shall argue that, taken together, they strongly suggest that propositional attitudes are relations between organisms and formulae in an internal language; between organisms and internal sentences, as it were. It's convenient, however, to give the arguments in two steps; first, to show that conditions I-V comport nicely with the view that the objects of PAs are sentences, and then to show that these sentences are plausibly internal.

I begin by anticipating a charge of false advertising. The arguments to be reviewed are explicitly non-demonstrative. All I claim for the internal language theory is that it works (a) surprisingly well, and (b) better than any of the available alternatives. The clincher comes at the end: even if we didn't need internal sentences for purposes of I-V, we'd need them to do our psychology. Another non-demonstrative argument, no doubt, but one I find terrifically persuasive.

Carnap's Theory

Carnap suggested, in *Meaning and Necessity* (1947), that PAs might be construed as relations between people and sentences they are disposed to utter; e.g., between people and sentences of English. What Carnap had primarily in mind was coping with the opacity problem, but it's striking and instructive that his proposal does pretty well with *all* the conditions I've enumerated. Consider:

I. If propositional attitudes are relations to sentences, then they are relations *tout court*. Moreover, assume that the relation ascribed by a sentence of the form *a believes* . . . holds between the individual denoted by 'a' and the correspondent of the complement clause. It is then immediately clear why the belief ascribed to *a* is true iff the correspondent is; the correspondent is the *object* of the belief (i.e., the correspondent is what's believed-true) if Carnap's story is right.

II. Vendler's condition is presumably satisfiable, though how the details go will depend on how we construe the objects of verbs of saying. A natural move for a neo-Carnapian to make would be to take 'John said that P' to be true in virtue of some relation between John and a token of the type P. Since, on this account, saying that P and believing that P involve relations to tokens of the very same sentence, it's hardly surprising that formulae which express the object of the *says-that* relation turn out to be logico-syntactically similar to formulae which express the object of the *believes-that* relation.

III. Frege's condition is satisfied; the opacity of belief is construed as a special case of the

opacity of quotation. To put it slightly differently; 'John said "Bill bit Mary"' expresses a relation between John and a (quoted) sentence, so we're unsurprised by the fact that John may bear *that* relation to *that* sentence, while not bearing it to some arbitrarily similar but distinct sentence; e.g., to the sentence 'somebody bit Mary' or to the sentence 'Bill bit somebody,' etc. But ditto, *mutatis mutandis,* if 'John believes Bill bit Mary' *also* expresses a relation between John and a quoted sentence.

IV. Aristotle's condition is satisfied in the strong form. The logical form of the object of a belief sentence is inherited from the logical form of the correspondent of the belief sentence. Of course it is, since on the Carnap view, the correspondent of the belief sentence *is* the object of the belief that it ascribes.

V. Whether you think that Carnap's theory can claim empirical plausibility depends on what you take the empirical facts about propositional attitudes to be and how ingenious you are in exploiting the theory to provide explanations of the facts. Here's one example of how such an explanation might go.

It's plausible to claim that there is a fairly general parallelism between the complexity of beliefs and the complexity of the sentences that express them. So, for example, I take it that 'the Second Punic War was fought under conditions which neither of the combatants could have desired or forseen' is a more complex sentence than, e.g., 'it's raining'; and, correspondingly, I take it that the thought that the Second Punic War was fought under conditions which neither of the combatants could have desired or forseen is a more complicated thought than the thought that it's raining. Carnap's theory explains this parallelism[10] since, according to the theory, what makes a belief ascription true is a relation between an organism and the correspondent of the belief-ascribing sentence. To hold the belief that the Second Punic War . . . , etc. is thus to be related to a more complex sentence than the one you are related to when you hold the belief that it's raining.

Some people need to count noses before they will admit to having one. In which case, see the discussion of "codability" in Brown and Lenneberg (1954) and Brown (1976). What the experiments showed is that the relative complexity of the descriptions which subjects supply for color chips predicts the relative difficulty that the subjects have in identifying the chips in a recognition-recall task. Brown and

Lenneberg explain the finding along strictly (though inadvertently) Carnapian lines: complex descriptions correspond to complex memories because it's the description which the subject (opaquely) remembers when he (transparently) remembers the color of the chip.

We can now begin to see *one* of the ways in which Condition V is supposed to work. A theory of propositional attitudes specifies a construal of the objects of the attitudes. It tells for such a theory if it can be shown to mesh with an independently plausible story about the "cost accounting" for mental processes. A cost accounting function is just a (partial) ordering of mental states by their relative complexity. Such an ordering is, in turn, responsive to a variety of types of empirical data, both intuitive and experimental. Roughly, one has a "mesh" between an empirically warranted cost accounting and a theory of the objects of PAs when one can predict the relative complexity of a mental state (or process) from the relative complexity of whatever the theory assigns as its object (or domain). (So, if Carnap is right, then the relative complexity of beliefs should be predictable from the relative linguistic complexity of the correspondents of belief ascribing sentences, all other things being equal.)

There's a good deal more to be said about all this than I have space for here. Again, roughly: to require that the complexity of the putative objects of PAs predict the cost accounting for the attitudes is to impose empirical constraints on the *notation* of (canonical) belief-ascribing sentences. So, for example, we would clearly get different predictions about the relative complexity of beliefs if we take the object of a PA to be the correspondent of the belief ascribing sentence than if we take it to be, e.g., the correspondent transformed into disjunctive form. The fact that there are empirical consequences of the notation we use to specify the objects of PAs is, of course, part and parcel of the fact that we are construing the attitude ascriptions *opaquely;* it is precisely under opaque construal that we distinguish (e.g.,) the mental state of believing that P & Q from the mental state of believing that neither not-P nor not-Q.

In short, Carnap's theory fares rather well with conditions I-V; there's more to be said in its favor than one might gather from the muted enthusiasm which philosophers have generally accorded it. Nevertheless, I think the philosophical consensus is warranted; Carnap's theory won't do. Here are some of the reasons.

1. Carnap has a theory about the objects of the propositional attitudes (viz., they're sentences) and a theory about the character of the relation to those objects in virtue of which one has a belief, desire, etc. Now, the latter theory is blatantly behavioristic; on Carnap's view, to believe that so-and-so is to be disposed (under presumably specifiable conditions) to utter tokens of the correspondent of the belief-ascribing sentence. But, patently, beliefs aren't behavioral dispositions; a fortiori, they aren't dispositions to utter. Hence, something's wrong with at least part of Carnap's account of the attitudes.

I put this objection first because it's the easiest to meet. So far as I can see, nothing prevents Carnap from keeping his account of the *objects* of belief while scuttling the behavioristic analysis of the belief relation. This would leave him wanting an answer to such questions as: what relation to the sentence 'it's raining' is such that you believe that it's raining iff you and it are in that relation? In particular, he'd want some answer other than the behavioristic: "It's the relation of being disposed to utter tokens of that sentence when. . . ."

The natural solution would be for Carnap to turn functionalist; to hold that to believe it's raining is to have a token of 'it's raining' play a certain role in the causation of your behavior and of your (other) mental states, said role eventually to be specified in the course of the detailed working out of empirical psychology . . . etc., etc. This is, perhaps, not much of a story, but it's fashionable, I know of nothing better, and it does have the virtue of explaining why propositional attitudes are opaque. Roughly, you wouldn't expect to be able to infer from 'tokens of the sentence S_1 have the causal role R' to 'tokens of the sentences S_2 have the causal role R' on the basis of any logical relation between S_1 and S_2 (except, of course, identity). More generally, so far as I can see, a functionalist account of the way quoted sentences figure in the having of PAs will serve as well as a disposition-to-utter account in coping with all of conditions I-V. From now on, I'll take this emendation for granted.

2. The natural way to read the Carnap theory is to take type identity of the correspondents of belief ascribing sentences as necessary and sufficient for type identity of the ascribed beliefs; and it's at least arguable that this cuts the PAs too thin. So, for example, one might plausibly hold that 'John believes Mary bit Bill' and 'John believes Bill was bitten by Mary' ascribe the

same belief (see n9). In effect, this is the sinister side of the strategy of inheriting the opacity of belief from the opacity of quotation. The strategy fails whenever the identity conditions on beliefs are *different* from the identity conditions on sentences.

A way to cope would be to allow that the objects of beliefs are, in effect, *translation sets* of sentences; something like this seems to be the impetus for Carnap's doctrine of intentional isomorphism. In any event, the problems in this area are well-known. It may well be, for example, that the right way to characterize a translation relation for sentences is by referring to the communicative intentions of speaker/hearers of whatever language the sentences belong to. (S_1 translates S_2 iff the two sentences are both standardly used with the same communicative intentions.) But, of course, we can't both identify translations by reference to intentions and individuate propositional attitudes (including, n.b., intentions) by reference to translations. This problem holds quite independent of epistemological worries about the facticity of ascriptions of propositional attitudes, the determinacy or otherwise of translations, etc; which suggests that it may be serious.

3. You can believe that it's raining even if you don't speak English. This is a variant of the thickness of slice problem just mentioned; it again suggests that the appropriate objects of belief are translation sets and raises the specters that haunt that treatment.

4. You can, surely, believe that it's raining even if you don't speak any language at all. To say this is to say that at least *some* human cognitive psychology generalizes to infra-human organisms; if it didn't, we would find the behavior of animals *utterly* bewildering, which, in fact, we don't.

Of course, relations are cheap; there must be *some* relation which a dog bears to 'it's raining' iff the dog believes that it's raining; albeit, perhaps, some not very interesting relation. So, why not choose *it* as the relation in virtue of which the belief-ascription holds of the dog? The problem is condition V. It would simply be a miracle if there were a relation between dogs and tokens of 'it's raining' such that any of the empirical facts about the propositional attitudinizing of dogs proved explicable in terms of that relation. (We can't, for example, choose any functional/causal relation because the behavior of dogs is surely not in any way caused by tokens of English sentences.) To put it generally if

crudely, satisfying condition V depends on assuming that whatever the theory takes to be the object of a PA plays an appropriate role in the mental processes of the organism to which the attitude is ascribed. But English sentences play no role in the mental life of dogs. (Excepting, perhaps, such sentences as 'Down, Rover!' which, in any event, don't play the kind of role envisaged.)

5. We argued that the truth conditions on beliefs are inherited from the truth conditions on the correspondents of belief ascribing sentences, but this won't work if, for example, there are inexpressible beliefs. This problem is especially serious for behaviorist (or functionalist) accounts of the belief relation; to believe that P can't be a question of being disposed to utter (or of having one's behavior caused by) tokens of the sentence P if, as a matter of fact, there is no such sentence. Yet it is the appeal to quoted sentences which does the work in such theories: which allows them to satisfy I–V.

6. We remarked that there's a rough correspondence between the complexity of thoughts and the complexity of the sentences which express them, and that the (neo-) Carnapian theory provides for this; more generally, that the view that the objects of PAs are natural-language sentences might mesh reasonably well with an empirically defensible cost accounting for mental states and processes. Unfortunately this argument cuts both ways if we assume—as seems plausible—that the correspondence is no better than partial. Whenever it fails, there's prima facie evidence *against* the theory that sentences are the objects of propositional attitudes.

In fact, we can do rather better than appealing to intuitions here. For example: we noted above that the "codability" (viz., mean simplicity of descriptions in English) of colors predicts their recallability in a population of English-speakers, and that this comports with the view that what one remembers when one remembers a color is (at least sometimes) its description: i.e., with the view that descriptions are the objects of (at least some) propositional attitudes. It thus comes as a shock to find that codability *in English* also predicts recall for a Dani subject population. We can't explain this by assuming a correlation between codability-in-English and codability-in-Dani (i.e., by assuming that the colors that English speakers find easy to describe are the ones that Dani-speakers also find easy to describe) since, as it turns out, Dani has no vocabulary *at all* for chromatic variation; all such variation is *infinitely* uncodable in Dani. This comes close to being the paradox dreaded above: how could *English* sentences be the objects of the propositional attitudes of (monolingual) Dani? And, if they are not, how could a property defined over English sentences mesh with a theory of cost accounting for the mental processes of the Dani? It looks as though either: (a) some propositional attitudes are *not* relations to sentences, or (b) if they are—if English sentences are somehow the objects of Dani PAs—then sentences which constitute the objects of PAs need play no functional/causal role in the having of the attitudes. (For discussion of the cross-cultural results on codability, see Brown op. cit. For details of the original studies, see Heider (1972) and Berlin and Kay (1969).)

7. If (token) sentences of a natural language are the objects of propositional attitudes, how are (first) languages learned? On any theory of language learning we can now imagine that process must involve the collection of data, the formulation of hypotheses, the checking of the hypotheses against the data, and the decision about which of the hypotheses the data best confirm. That is, it must involve such mental states and processes as beliefs, expectation and perceptual integration. It's important to realize that *no* account of language learning which does not thus involve propositional attitudes and mental processes has ever been proposed by anyone, barring only behaviorists. And behaviorist accounts of language learning are, surely, not tenable. So, on pain of circularity, there must be *some* propositional attitudes which are not functional/causal relations to natural language sentences. I see no way out of this which isn't a worse option than rejecting the Carnap theory.

So, the situation looks discouraging. On the one hand, we have a number of plausible arguments in favor of accepting the Carnap story (viz., I–V) and, on the other, we have a number of equally plausible arguments in favor of not (viz. 1–7). Never mind; for, at second blush, it seems we needn't accept the whole Carnap theory to satisfy I–V and we needn't reject the whole Carnap theory to avoid 1–7. Roughly, all that I–V require is the part of the story that says that the objects of PAs are *sentences* (hence have logical forms, truth conditions, etc.). Whereas what causes the trouble with 1–7 is only that part of the story which says that they are *natural language* sentences (hence raising problems about non-verbal organisms, first language learning, etc.). The recommended solution is thus to take the objects of PAs to be sentences of a *non*-natural language; in effect, formulae in an Internal Representational System.

The first point is to establish that this proposal does what it is supposed to: copes with I–V without running afoul of 1–7. In fact, I propose to do less than that since, so far as I can see, the details would be extremely complicated. Suffice it here to indicate the general strategy.

Conditions I and III are relatively easy to meet. I demands that propositional attitudes be relations, and so they are if they are relations to internal representations. III demands a construal of opacity. Carnap met this demand by reducing the opacity of belief to the opacity of quotation, and so do we: the only difference is that, whereas for Carnap, 'John believes it's raining' relates John to a sentence of English, for us it relates John to an internal formula.

Conditions II and IV stress logico/syntactic parallelism between the complements and the correspondents of belief-ascribing sentences; such relations are epitomized by the identity between the truth conditions on 'it's raining' and those on what is believed when it's believed that it's raining. (Neo-) Carnap explained these symmetries by taking the correspondents of belief ascriptions to be the objects of beliefs. The present alternative is spiritually similar but one step less direct: we assume that the correspondent of a belief-ascriber inherits its logico-semantic properties from the same internal formula which functions as the object of the belief ascribed.

There are three pieces in play: there are (a) *belief-ascribers* (like 'John believes it's raining'); (b) *complements* of belief ascribers (like ⌜it's raining⌝ in 'John believes it's raining'); and (c) *correspondents* of belief ascribers (like 'it's raining' standing free). The idea is to get all three to converge (though, of course, by different routes) on the same internal formula (call it 'F (it's raining)'[11]) thereby providing the groundwork for explaining the analogies that II and IV express.

To get this to work out right would be to supply detailed instructions for connecting the theory of PAs with the theory of sentence interpretation, and I have misplaced mine. But the general idea is apparent. Belief ascribers are true in virtue of functional/causal (call them 'belief making') relations between organisms and tokens of internal formulae. Thus, in particular, 'John believes it's raining' is true in virtue of a belief-making relation between John and a token of F (it's raining). It is, of course, the complement of a belief-ascriber that determines *which* internal formula is involved in its truth conditions; in effect 'it's raining' in 'John believes it's raining' functions as an index which picks out F (it's raining) and not, for example, F (elephants have wings) as the internal formula that John is related to iff 'John believes it's raining' is true.

So, viewed along one vector, the complement of a belief-ascriber connects it with an internal formula. But, viewed along another vector, the complement of a belief ascriber connects it to its correspondent: if the correspondent of 'John believes it's raining' is 'it's raining', that is because the form of words 'it's raining' constitutes its complement. And now we can close the circle, since, of course, F (it's raining) is *also* semantically connected with the correspondent of 'John believes it's raining' viz., by the principle that 'it's raining' is the sentence that English speakers use when they are in the belief-making relation to a token of F (it's raining) and wish to use a sentence of English to say what it is that they believe.

There are various ways of thinking about the relation between internal formulae and the correspondents of belief-ascribers. One is to think of the conventions of a natural language as functioning to establish a pairing of its verbal forms with the internal formulae that mediate the propositional attitudes of its users; in particular, as pairing the internal objects of beliefs with the form of words that speaker/hearers use to express their beliefs. This is a natural way to view the situation if you think of a natural language as a system of conventional vehicles for the expression of thoughts (a view to which I know of no serious objections). So in the present case, the conventions of English pair: 'it's raining' with F (it's raining) (viz., with the object of the belief that it's raining); 'elephants have wings' with F (elephants have wings) (viz., with the object of the belief that elephants have wings); and, generally, the object of each belief with the correspondent of some belief-ascribing sentence.[12]

Another option is to assume that F (it's raining) is distinguished by the fact that its tokens play a causal/functional role (not only as the object of the belief that it's raining, but also) in the production of linguistically regular utterances of 'it's raining.' Indeed, this option would plausibly be exercised in tandem with the one mentioned just above since it would be reasonable to construe "linguistically regular" utterances as the ones that are produced in light of the speak-

er's knowledge of the linguistic conventions. The basic idea, in any event, would be to implicate F (it's raining) as the object of the communicative intentions that utterances of 'it's raining' standardly function to express; hence, as among the mental causes of such utterances. I take it that, given this relation, it ought to be possible to work out detailed tactics for the satisfaction of conditions II and IV, but this is the bit I propose to leave to the ingenuity of the reader. What I want to emphasize here is the way the linguistic structure of the complement of a belief ascriber connects it with free declaratives (in one direction) and with internal formulae (in the other). Contrary to the fusion story, it's no accident that 'it's raining' occurs in 'John believes it's raining.' Rather, the availability of natural languages for saying *both* what one believes *and* that one believes it turns on the exploitation of this elegant symmetry.

What about condition V? I shall consider this in conjunction with 2–7, since what's noteworthy about the latter is that they all register *empirical* complaints against the Carnap account. For example, 3, 4 and 6 would be without force if only everybody (viz., every subject of true propositional attitude ascriptions) talked English. 2 and 5 depend upon the empirical likelihood that English sentences fail to correspond one-to-one to objects of propositional attitudes. 7 would be met if only English were innate. Indeed, I suppose an ultra-hard-line Neo-Carnapian might consider saving the bacon by claiming that—appearances to the contrary notwithstanding—English *is* innate, universal, just rich enough, etc. My point is that this is the right *kind* of move to make; all we have against it is its palpable untruth.

Whereas, it's part of the charm of the internal language story that, since practically nothing is known about the details of cognitive processes, we can make the corresponding assumptions about the internal representational system risking no more than gross implausibility at the very worst.

So, let's assume—what we don't, at any event, *know* to be false—that the internal language is innate, that its formulae correspond one-one with the contents of propositional attitudes (e.g., that 'John bit Mary' and 'Mary was bitten by John' correspond to the same "internal sentence"), and that it is *as* universal as human psychology; viz., that to the extent that an organism shares our mental processes, it also shares our system of internal representations.

On these assumptions, everything works. It's no longer paradoxical, for example, that codability *in English* predicts the relative complexity of the mental processes of the Dani; for, by assumption, it's not *really* the complexity of English sentences that predicts *our* cost accounting; we wouldn't expect *that* correspondence to be better than partial (see objection 6). What really predicts our cost accounting is the relative complexity of the internal representations that we use English sentences to express. And, again by assumption, the underlying system of internal representations is common to the Dani and to us. If you don't like this assumption, try and find some other hypothesis that accounts for the facts about the Dani.

Notice that to say that we can have our empirical assumptions isn't to say that we can have them for free. They carry a body of empirical commitments which, if untenable, will defeat the internal representation view. Imagine, for example, that cost accounting for English speakers proves utterly unrelated to cost accounting for (e.g.,) speakers of Latvian. (Imagine, in effect, that the Whorf-Sapir hypothesis turns out to be more or less true.) It's then hard to see how the system of internal representations could be universal. But if it's not universal, it's presumably not innate. And if it's not innate, it's not available to mediate the learning of first languages. And if it's not available to mediate the learning of first languages, we lose our means of coping with objection 7. There are plenty of ways in which we could find out that the theory's wrong if, in fact, it is.

Where we've gotten to is this: the general characteristics of propositional attitudes appear to demand sentence-like entities to be their objects. And broadly empirical conditions appear to preclude identifying these entities with sentences of *natural* languages; hence internal representations and private languages. How bad is it to have gotten here? I now want to argue that the present conclusion is independently required because it is presupposed by the best— indeed the only—psychology that we've got. Not just, as one philosopher has rather irresponsibly remarked, that "some psychologists like to talk that way," but that the best accounts of mental processes we have are quite unintelligible unless something like the internal representation story is true.

The long way of making this point is via a detailed discussion of such theories, but I've done that elsewhere and enough is enough. Suffice it here to consider a single example which is, however, prototypical. I claim again that the details don't matter; that one could make the same points by considering phenomena drawn from any area of congitive psychology which is sufficiently well worked out to warrant talk of a theory *in situ*.

So, consider a fragment of contemporary (psycho)linguistics; consider the explanation of the ambiguity of a sentence like 'they are flying planes' (hereinafter, frequently *S*). The conventional story goes as follows: the sentence is ambiguous because there are two ways of grouping the word sequence into phrases, two ways of "bracketing" it. One bracketing, corresponding to the reading of the sentence which answers 'what are those things?', goes: (they) (are) (flying planes). Viz., the sentence is copular, the main verb is 'are' and 'flying' is an adjectival modifier of 'planes.' Whereas, on the other bracketing, corresponding to the reading on which the sentence answers 'what are those guys doing?', the bracketing goes: (they) (are flying) (planes); viz. the sentence is transitive, the main verb is 'flying' and 'are' belongs to the auxiliary. I assume without argument that something like this is, or at least contributes to, the explanation of the ambiguity of *S*. The evidence for such treatments is overwhelming and there is, literally, no alternative theory in the field.

But what could it mean to speak of *S* as "having" two bracketings? I continue to tread the well-worn path: *S* has two bracketings in that there exists a function (call it *G-proper*) from (as it might be) the word 'sentence' onto precisely those bracketed word strings which constitute the sentences of English. And both '(they) (are) (flying planes)' and '(they) (are flying) (planes)' are in the range of that function. (Moreover, no other bracketing of that word sequence is in the range of G-proper . . . etc.)

Now, the trouble with this explanation, as it stands, is that it is either enthymemic or silly. For, one wants to ask, how *could* the mere, as it were Platonic, existence of G-proper account for the facts about the ambiguity of English sentences? Or, to put it another way, sure there is, Platonically, a function under which *S* gets two bracketings. But there is also, Platonically, a function G' under which it gets sixteen; and a function G'' under which it gets seven; and a function G''' under which it gets none. Since G', G'', and G''' are all, qua functions, just as good as G-proper, how could the mere *existence* of the latter explain the linguistic properties of *S?*

(You may feel inclined to say: "Ah, but G-proper is the [or perhaps is *the*] grammar of English, and that distinguishes it from G′, G″ and the rest." But this explanation takes one nowhere, since it invites the question: why does the grammar of English play a special role in the explanation of English sentences? Or, to put the same question minutely differently: call G′ the schmamar of English. We now want to know how come it's the bracketing assigned by English grammar and not the bracketing assigned by English schmamar, which predicts the ambiguity of 'they are flying planes'?)

So far as I can see, there's only one way such questions can conceivably be answered; viz., by holding that G-proper (not only exists but) is the very system of (internal [what else?]) formulae that English speaker/hearers use to represent the sentences of their language. But, then, if we accept this, we are willy-nilly involved in talking of at least *some* mental processes (processes of understanding and producing sentences) as involving at least some relations to at least some internal representations. And, if we have to have internal representations anyhow, why not take them to be the objects of propositional attitudes, thereby placating I–V? I say "if we accept this"; but really we have no choice. For the account is well-evidenced, not demonstrably incoherent, and, again, it's the only one in the field. A working science is ipso facto in philosophical good repute.

So, by a series of non-demonstrative arguments: there are internal representations and propositional attitudes are relations that we bear to them. It remains to discuss two closely related objections.

Objection 1: Why not take the object of propositional attitudes to be *propositions?*

This suggestion has, no doubt, a ring of etymological plausibility; in fact, for all I know, it may be right. The mistake is in supposing it somehow conflicts with the present proposal.

I am taking seriously the idea that the system of internal representations constitutes a (computational) language. Qua language, it presumably has a syntax and a semantics; specifying the language involves saying what the properties are in virtue of which its formulae are well-formed, and what relations(s) obtain between the formulae and things in the (non-linguistic) world. I have no idea what an adequate semantics for a system of internal representations would look like; suffice it that, if propositions come in at all, they come in here. In particular,

nothing stops us from specifying a semantics for the IRS by saying (inter alia) that some of its formulae express propositions. If we do say this, then we can make sense of the notion that propositional attitudes are relations to propositions; viz., they are *mediated* relations to propositions, with internal representations doing the mediating.

This is, quite generally, the way that representational theories of the mind work. So, in classical versions, thinking of John (construed opaquely) is a relation to an "idea"; viz., to an internal representation of John. But this is quite compatible with its also being (transparently) construable as a relation *to John*. In particular, when Smith is thinking of John, he (normally) stands in relation to John and does so *in virtue* of his standing in relation to an idea of John. Similarly, mutatis mutandis, if thinking that it will rain is standing in relation to a proposition, then, on the present account, you stand in that relation in virtue of your (functional/causal) relation to an internal formula which expresses the proposition. No doubt, the "expressing" bit is obscure; but that's a problem about propositions, not a problem about internal representations.

"Ah, but if you are going to allow propositions as the *mediate* objects of propositional attitudes, why bother with internal representations as their immediate objects? Why not just say: 'propositional attitudes are relations to propositions. Punkt!' " There's a small reason and a big reason. The small reason is that propositions don't have the right properties for our purposes. In particular, one anticipates problems of cost-accounting. Condition V, it will be remembered, permits us to choose among theories of PAs in virtue of the form of the entities they assign as objects of the attitudes. Now, the problem with propositions is that they are the sorts of things which, presumably, don't *have* forms. Propositions are sheer contents; they neutralize the lexico-syntactic differences between various ways of saying the same thing. That's what they're *for*. I say that this is a small problem but it looms prodigious if you hanker after a theory of the object of PAs which claims empirical repute. After all, it's not just cost-accounting which is supposed to be determined by formal aspects of the objects of PAs; it's *all* the mental processes and properties that cognitive psychology explains. That's what it *means* to speak of a *computational* psychology. Computational principles are ones that apply in virtue of the form of entities in their domain.

But my main reason for not saying "propositional attitudes are relations to propositions. Punkt." is that I don't understand it. I don't see how an organism can stand in an (interesting epistemic) relation to a proposition except by standing in a (causal/functional) relation to some token of a formula which expresses the proposition. I am aware that there is a philosophical tradition to the contrary. Plato says (I think) that there is a special intellectual faculty (theoria) wherewith one peers at abstract objects. Frege says that one *apprehends* (what I'm calling) propositions, but I can find no doctrine about what apprehension comes to beyond the remark (in "The Thought") that it's not sense perception because its objects are abstract and it's not introspection because its objects aren't mental. (He also says that grasping a thought isn't much like grasping a hammer. To be sure. As for me, I want a mechanism for the relation between organisms and propositions, and the only one I can think of is mediation by internal representations.[13])

Objection 2: Surely it's *conceivable* that propositional attitudes are *not* relations to internal representations.

I think it is; the theory that propositional attitudes are relations to internal representations is a piece of empirical psychology, not an analysis. For, there might have been angels, or behaviorism might have been true, and then the internal representation story would have been false. The moral is, I think, that we ought to give up asking for analyses; psychology is all the philosophy of mind that we are likely to get.

But, moreover, it may be *empirically* possible that there should be creatures which have the same propositional attitudes we do (e.g., the same beliefs) but *not* the same system of internal representations; creatures which, as it were, share our epistemic states but not our psychology. Suppose, for example, it turns out that Martians, or porpoises, believe what we do but have a very different sort of cost accounting. We might

then want to say that there are translation relations among systems of internal representation (viz., that formally distinct representations can express the same proposition). Whether we can make sense of saying this remains to be seen; we can barely think about the question prior to the elaboration of theories about how such systems are semantically interpreted; and as things now stand, we haven't got semantic theories for natural languages, to say nothing of languages of thought. Perhaps it goes without saying that it's no objection to a doctrine that it *may* run us into incoherencies. Or, rather, if it is an objection, there's an adequate reply: "Yes, but also it may not."

I'll end on the note just sounded. Contemporary cognitive psychology is, in effect, a revival of the representational theory of the mind. The favored treatment of PAs arises in this context. So, in particular, the mind is conceived of as an organ whose function is the manipulation of representations and these, in turn, provide the domain of mental processes and the (immediate) objects of mental states. That's what it is to see the mind as something like a computer. (Or rather, to put the horse back in front of the cart, that's what it is to see a computer as something like the mind. We give sense to the analogy by treating selected states of the machine as formulae and by specifying which semantic interpretations the formulae are to bear. It is in the context of such specifications that we speak of machine processes as computations and of machine states as intensional.)

If the representational theory of the mind is true, then we know what propositional attitudes are. But the net total of philosophical problems is surely not decreased thereby. We must now face what has always been *the* problem for representational theories to solve: what relates internal representations to the world? What is it for a system of internal representations to be semantically interpreted? I take it that this problem is now the main content of the philosophy of mind.[14]

NOTES

1. I shall have nothing at all to say about knowing, discovering, recognizing, or any other of the "factive" attitudes. The justification for this restriction is worth discussing, but not here.

2. I haven't space to discuss here the idea that 'John believes' should be construed as an operator on 'it's raining.' Suffice it (a) that it's going to be hard to square that account with such observations as I-b

below; and (b) that it seems quite implausible for such sentences as 'John believes what Mary said' (and what Mary said might *be* that it's raining). In general, the objects of propositional attitude verbs exhibit the syntax of object noun phrases, which is just what the operator account would not predict.

3. I assume that this is approximately correct: given a sentence of the syntactic form NP_1 (V (NP_2)) V

expresses a relation iff NP$_1$ and NP$_2$ refer. So, for present purposes, the question whether 'believes' expresses a relation in 'John believes it's raining' comes down to the question whether there are such things as objects of beliefs. I shan't, therefore, bother to distinguish among these various ways of putting the question in the discussion which follows.

4. Of course, it might refer in virtue of a relation between Mary and something other than a voice. 'John is taller than the average man' isn't true in virtue of a relation between John and the average man ('the average man' doesn't refer). But the sentence is relational for all that. It's for this sort of reason that such principles as the one announced in n3 hold only to a first approximation.

5. Nb., verbs of propositional attitude are transparent, in this sense, only when their objects are *complements;* one can't infer 'there is something Ponce de Leon sought' from 'Ponce de Leon sought the Fountain of Youth.' It may, however, be worth translating 'seek' to 'try to find' to save the generalization. This would give us: 'Ponce de Leon tried to find the Fountain of Youth,' which does, I suppose, entail that there is something that Ponce de Leon tried (viz., tried to do; viz., to find the Fountain of Youth).

Also, to say that *EG* applies *to* the complement of verbs of PA is, of course, not to say that it applies *in* the complement of verbs of PA. 'John wants to marry Marie of Rumania' implies that there is something that John wants (viz., to marry Marie of Rumania); it notoriously does *not* imply that there is someone whom John wants to marry (see III below).

6. Fusion has been contemplated as a remedy for untransparency in several philosophical contexts; see Goodman (1968); Dennett (1969); Nagel (1965). Nb., 'contemplated,' not 'embraced.'

7. 3 is not a point about *EG*. On the fusion view, there's no representation of the fact that 'the belief that Sam is nice' is about Sam even when 'belief' and 'about' are both construed *opaquely.*

8. Defining 'correspondent' gets complicated where verbs of PA take *transformed* sentences as their objects, but the technicalities needn't concern us here. Suffice it that we want the correspondent of 'John wants to leave' to be 'John leaves'; the correspondent of 'John objects to Mary and Bill being elected' to be 'Mary and Bill are elected', etc.

9. I am assuming that two sentences with correspondents of *different* logico-syntactic form cannot assign the same (opaque) belief, and someone might wish to challenge this; consider 'John believes that Mary bit Bill' and 'John believes that Bill was bitten by Mary.' This sort of objection is serious and will be accommodated later on.

10. In speaking of Carnap's theory, I don't wish to imply that Carnap would endorse the uses to which I'm putting it; quite the contrary, I should imagine.

11. Where *F* might be thought of as a function from (e.g., English) sentences onto internal formulae.

12. Assuming, as we may but now needn't do, that all beliefs are expressible in English. It is, of course, a consequence of the present view that all the beliefs we can entertain are expressible in the internal code.

13. The notion that the apprehension of propositions is mediated by linguistic objects is not entirely foreign even to the Platonistic tradition. Church says: ". . . the preference of (say) seeing over *understanding* as a method of observation seems to me capricious. For just as an opaque body may be seen, so a concept may be understood or grasped. . . . In both cases the observation is not direct but through intermediaries . . . linguistic expressions in the case of the concept" (1951a). See also the discussion in Dummett (1973, pp. 156–57).

14. All of the following helped: Professors Ned Block, Noam Chomsky, Dan Dennett, Hartry Field, Janet Dean Fodor, Keith Lehrer and Brian Loar. Many thanks.

REFERENCES

Berlin, B. and Kay, P. *Basic Color Terms.* Berkeley, California: University of California Press, 1969.

Brown, R. Reference—in memorial tribute to Eric Lenneberg. *Cognition,* 1976, *4,* 125–53.

Brown, R. and Lenneberg, E. A study in language and cognition. *J. Abnormal and Social Psychol.,* 1954, No. 49, 454–62.

Carnap, R. *Meaning and Necessity.* Chicago: Phoenix Books, University of Chicago Press, 1947.

Church, A. The need for abstract entities in semantic analysis. In *Contributions to the Analysis and Synthesis of Knowledge,* Proceedings of the American Academy of Arts and Sciences, 1951, No. 80, pp. 100–12.

Davidson, D. Theories of meaning and learnable languages. In *Logic, Methodology and Philosophy of Science,* Proceedings of the 1964 International Congress, Y. Bar-Hillel (ed.). Amsterdam, 1965, pp. 383–94.

Dennett, D. *Content and Consciousness.* New York: Routledge and Kegan Paul, 1969.

Dummett, M. *Frege.* London: Buckworth & Co., 1973.

Fodor, J. A. *The Language of Thought.* New York: Thomas Y. Crowell Co., 1975.

Goodman, N. *Languages of Art.* New York: Bobbs-Merrill, 1968.

Grice, H. P. Method in philosophical psychology. *Proceedings and Addresses of the American Philosophical Association,* 1975, Vol. XLVIII, pp. 23–53.

Heider, E. Universals in color naming and memory. *J. Exp. Psychol.,* 1972, No. 93, 10–20.

Nagel, T. Physicalism. *The Philosophical Review,* 1965, *74,* 339–56.

Vendler, Z. *Res Cogitans.* Ithaca, New York: Cornell University Press, 1972.

True Believers
The Intentional Strategy and Why It Works

52

Daniel C. Dennett

Death Speaks

There was a merchant in Baghdad who sent his servant to market to buy provisions and in a little while the servant came back, white and trembling, and said, Master, just now when I was in the marketplace I was jostled by a woman in the crowd and when I turned I saw it was Death that jostled me. She looked at me and made a threatening gesture; now, lend me your horse, and I will ride away from this city and avoid my fate. I will go to Samarra and there Death will not find me. The merchant lent him his horse, and the servant mounted it, and he dug his spurs in its flanks and as fast as the horse could gallop he went. Then the merchant went down to the market-place and he saw me standing in the crowd, and he came to me and said, why did you make a threatening gesture to my servant when you saw him this morning? That was not a threatening gesture, I said, it was only a start of surprise. I was astonished to see him in Baghdad, for I had an appointment with him tonight in Samarra.

W. Somerset Maugham

In the social sciences, talk about *belief* is ubiquitous. Since social scientists are typically self-conscious about their methods, there is also a lot of talk about *talk about belief*. And since belief is a genuinely curious and perplexing phenomenon, showing many different faces to the world, there is abundant controversy. Sometimes belief attribution appears to be a dark, risky, and imponderable business—especially when exotic, and more particularly religious or superstitious, beliefs are in the limelight. These are not the only troublesome cases; we also court argument and skepticism when we attribute beliefs to nonhuman animals, or to infants, or to computers or robots. Or when the beliefs we feel constrained to attribute to an apparently healthy, adult member of our own society are contradictory, or even just wildly false. A biologist colleague of mine was once called on the telephone by a man in a bar who wanted him to settle a bet. The man asked: "Are rabbits birds?" "No" said the biologist. "Damn!" said the man as he hung up. Now could he *really* have believed that rabbits were birds? Could anyone really and truly be attributed that belief? Perhaps, but it would take a bit of a story to bring us to accept it.

In all of these cases belief attribution appears beset with subjectivity, infected with cultural relativism, prone to "indeterminacy of radical translation"—clearly an enterprise demanding special talents: the art of phenomenological analysis, hermeneutics, empathy, *Verstehen,* and all that. On other occasions, normal occasions, when familiar beliefs are the topic, belief attribution looks as easy as speaking prose and as objective and reliable as counting beans in a dish. Particularly when these straightforward cases are before us, it is quite plausible to suppose that in principle (if not yet in practice) it would be possible to confirm these simple, objective belief attributions by *finding something inside the believer's head*—by finding the beliefs themselves, in effect. "Look," someone might say, "You either believe there's milk in the fridge or you don't believe there's milk in the fridge" (you might have no opinion, in the latter case). But if you do believe this, that's a perfectly objective fact about you, and it must come down in the end to your brain's being in some particular physical state. If we knew more about physiological psychology, we could in principle determine the facts about your brain state and thereby determine whether or not you believe there is milk in the fridge, even if you were determined to be silent or disingenuous on the topic. In principle, on this view physiological psychology could trump the results—or nonresults—of any "black box" method in the social sciences that divines beliefs (and other mental features) by behavioral, cultural, social, historical, *external* criteria.

These differing reflections congeal into two opposing views on the nature of belief attribution, and hence on the nature of belief. The latter, a variety of *realism,* likens the question of whether a person has a particular belief to the question of whether a person is infected with a particular virus—a perfectly objective internal matter of fact about which an observer can often make educated guesses of great reliability. The former, which we could call *interpretationism* if we absolutely had to give it a name, likens the question of whether a person has a particular belief to the question of whether a person is immoral, or has style, or talent, or would make a good wife. Faced with such questions, we preface our answers with "well, it all depends on what you're interested in," or make some similar acknowledgment of the relativity of the issue. "It's a matter of interpretation," we say. These two opposing views, so baldly stated, do not fairly represent any serious theorists' positions, but they do express views that are typically seen as mutually exclusive and exhaustive; the theorist must be friendly with one and only one of these themes.

I think this is a mistake. My thesis will be that while belief is a perfectly objective phenomenon (that apparently makes me a realist), it can be discerned only from the point of view of one who adopts a certain *predictive strategy,* and its existence can be confirmed only by an assessment of the success of that strategy (that apparently makes me an interpretationist).

First I will describe the strategy, which I call the intentional strategy or adopting the intentional stance. To a first approximation, the intentional strategy consists of treating the object whose behavior you want to predict as a rational agent with beliefs and desires and other mental stages exhibiting what Brentano and others call *intentionality.* The strategy has often been described before, but I shall try to put this very familiar material in a new light by showing *how* it works and by showing *how well* it works.

Then I will argue that any object—or as I shall say, any *system*—whose behavior is well predicted by this strategy is in the fullest sense of the word a believer. *What it is* to be a true believer is to be an *intentional system,* a system whose behavior is reliably and voluminously predictable via the intentional strategy. I have argued for this position before (Dennett 1971, 1976, 1978), and my arguments have so far garnered few converts and many presumed counterexamples. I shall try again here, harder, and shall also deal with several compelling objections.

The Intentional Strategy and How It Works

There are many strategies, some good, some bad. Here is a strategy, for instance, for predicting the future behavior of a person: determine the date and hour of the person's birth and then feed this modest datum into one or another astrological algorithm for generating predictions of the person's prospects. This strategy is deplorably popular. Its popularity is deplorable only because we have such good reasons for believing that it does not work (*pace* Feyerabend 1978). When astrological predictions come true this is sheer luck, or the result of such vagueness or ambiguity in the prophecy that almost any eventuality can be construed to confirm it. But suppose the astrological strategy did in fact work well on some people. We could call those people *astrological systems*—systems whose behavior was, as a matter of fact, predictable by the astrological strategy. If there were such people, such astrological systems, we would be more interested than most of us in fact are in *how the astrological strategy works*—that is, we would be interested in the rules, principles, or methods of astrology. We could find out how the strategy works by asking astrologers, reading their books, and observing them in action. But we would also be curious about *why* it worked. We might find that astrologers had no useful opinions about this latter question—they either had no theory of why it worked or their theories were pure hokum. Having a good strategy is one thing; knowing why it works is another.

So far as we know, however, the class of astrological systems is empty, so the astrological strategy is of interest only as a social curiosity. Other strategies have better credentials. Consider the physical strategy, or physical stance; if you want to predict the behavior of a system, determine its physical constitution (perhaps all the way down to the microphysical level) and the physical nature of the impingements upon it, and use your knowledge of the laws of physics to predict the outcome for any input. This is the grand and impractical strategy of Laplace for predicting the entire future of everything in the universe, but it has more modest, local, actually usable versions. The chemist or physicist in the laboratory can use this strategy to predict the behavior of exotic materials, but equally the cook in the kitchen can predict the effect of leaving the pot on the burner too long. The strategy is not always practically available, but that it will always work *in principle* is a dogma of the physical sciences (I ignore the minor complications raised by the subatomic indeterminacies of quantum physics).

Sometimes, in any event, it is more effective to switch from the physical stance to what I call the design stance, where one ignores the actual (possibly messy) details of the physical constitution of an object, and, on the assumption that it has a certain design, predicts that it will behave *as it is designed to behave* under various circumstances. For instance, most users of computers have not the foggiest idea what physical principles are responsible for the computer's highly reliable, and hence predictable, behavior. But if they have a good idea of what the computer is designed to do (a description of its operation at any one of the many possible levels of abstraction), they can predict its behavior with great accuracy and reliability, subject to disconfirmation only in cases of physical malfunction. Less dramatically, almost anyone can predict when an alarm clock will sound on the basis of the most casual inspection of its exterior. One does not know or care to know whether it is spring wound, battery driven, sunlight powered, made of brass wheels and jewel bearings or silicon chips—one just assumes that it is designed so that the alarm will sound when it is set to sound, and it is set to sound where it appears to be set to sound, and the clock will keep on running until that time and beyond, and is designed to run more or less accurately, and so forth. For more accurate and detailed design stance predictions of the alarm clock, one must descend to a less abstract level of description of its design; for instance, to the level at which gears are described, but their material is not specified.

Only the designed behavior of a system is predictable from the design stance, of course. If you want to predict the behavior of an alarm clock when it is pumped full of liquid helium, revert to the physical stance. Not just artifacts but also many biological objects (plants and animals, kidneys and hearts, stamens and pistils) behave in ways that can be predicted from the design stance. They are not just physical systems but designed systems.

Sometimes even the design stance is practically inaccessible, and then there is yet another stance or strategy one can adopt: the intentional stance. Here is how it works: first you decide to treat the object whose behavior is to be predicted as a rational agent; then you figure out what beliefs that agent ought to have, given its place in the world and its purpose. Then you figure out what desires it ought to have, on the same considerations, and finally you predict that this rational agent will act to further its goals in the light of its beliefs. A little practical reasoning from the chosen set of beliefs and desires will in many—but not all—instances yield a decision about what the agent ought to do; that is what you predict the agent *will* do.

The strategy becomes clearer with a little elaboration. Consider first how we go about populating each other's heads with beliefs. A few truisms: sheltered people tend to be ignorant; if you expose someone to something he comes to know all about it. In general, it seems, we come to believe all the truths about the parts of the world around us we are put in a position to learn about. Exposure to *x,* that is, sensory confrontation with *x* over some suitable period of time, is the *normally sufficient* condition for knowing (or having true beliefs) about *x.* As we say, we come to *know all about* the things around us. Such exposure is only *normally* sufficient for knowledge, but this is not the large escape hatch it might appear; our threshold for accepting abnormal ignorance in the face of exposure is quite high. "I didn't know the gun was loaded," said by one who was observed to be present, sighted, and awake during the loading, meets with a variety of utter skepticism that only the most outlandish supporting tale could overwhelm.

Of course we do not come to learn or remember all the truths our sensory histories avail us. In spite of the phrase "know all about," what we come to know, normally, are only all the *relevant* truths our sensory histories avail us. I do not typically come to know the ratio of spectacle-wearing people to trousered people in a room I inhabit, though if this interested me, it would be readily learnable. It is not just that some facts about my environment are below my thresholds of discrimination or beyond the integration and holding power of my memory (such as the height in inches of all the people present), but that many perfectly detectable, graspable, memorable facts are of no interest to me and hence do not come to be believed by me. So one rule for attributing beliefs in the intentional strategy is this: attribute as beliefs all the truths relevant to the system's interests (or desires) that the system's experience to date has made available. This rule leads to attributing somewhat too much—since we all are somewhat forgetful, even of important things. It also fails to capture the false beliefs we are all known to have. But the attribution of false belief, *any* false belief, requires a special genealogy, which will be seen to consist in the main in true beliefs. Two paradigm cases: *S* believes (falsely) that *p,* because *S* believes (truly) that Jones told him that *p,* that Jones is pretty clever, that Jones did not intend to deceive him, . . . etc. Second case: *S* believes (falsely) that there is a snake on the barstool, because *S* believes (truly) that he seems to see a snake on the barstool, is himself sitting in a bar not a yard from the barstool he sees, and so forth. The falsehood has to start somewhere; the seed may be sown in hallucination, illusion, a normal variety of simple misperception, memory deterioration, or deliberate fraud, for instance, but the false beliefs that are reaped grow in a culture medium of true beliefs.

Then there are the arcane and sophisticated beliefs, true and false, that are so often at the focus of attention in discussions of belief attribution. They do not arise directly, goodness knows, from exposure to mundane things and events, but their attribution requires tracing out a lineage of mainly good argument or reasoning from the bulk of beliefs already attributed. An implication of the intentional strategy, then, is that true believers mainly believe truths. If anyone could devise an agreed-upon method of individuating and counting beliefs (which I doubt very much), we would see that all but the smallest portion (say, less than ten percent) of a person's beliefs were attributable under our first rule.[1]

Note that this rule is a derived rule, an elaboration and further specification of the fundamental rule: attribute those beliefs the system *ought to have*. Note also that the rule interacts with the attribution of desires. How do we attribute the desires (preferences, goals, interests) on whose basis we will shape the list of beliefs? We attribute the desires the system *ought to have*. That is the fundamental rule. It dictates, on a first pass, that we attribute the familiar list of highest, or most basic, desires to people: survival, absence of pain, food, comfort, procreation, entertainment. Citing any one of these desires typically terminates the "Why?" game of reason giving. One is not supposed to need an ulterior motive for desiring comfort or pleasure or the prolongation of one's existence. Derived rules of desire attribution interact with belief attributions. Trivially, we have the rule: attribute desires for those things a system believes to be good for it. Somewhat more informatively, attribute desires for those things a system believes to be best means to other ends it desires. The attribution of bizarre and detrimental desires thus requires, like the attribution of false beliefs, special stories.

The interaction between belief and desire becomes trickier when we consider what desires we attribute on the basis of verbal behavior. The capacity to *express* desires in language opens the floodgates of desire attribution. "I want a two-egg mushroom omelette, some French bread and butter, and a half bottle of lightly chilled white Burgundy." How could one begin to attribute a desire for anything so specific in the absence of such verbal declaration? How, indeed, could a creature come to *contract* such a specific desire without the aid of language? Language *enables* us to formulate highly specific desires, but it also *forces* us on occasion to commit ourselves to desires altogether more stringent in their conditions of satisfaction than anything we would otherwise have any reason to endeavor to satisfy. Since in order to get what you want you often have to say what you want, and since you often cannot say what you want without saying something more specific than you antecedently mean, you often end up giving others evidence—the very best of evidence, your unextorted word—that you desire things or states of affairs far more particular than would satisfy you—or better, than would have satisfied you, for once you have declared, being a man of your word, you acquire an interest in satisfying exactly the desire you declared and no other.

"I'd like some baked beans, please."

"Yes sir. How many?"

You might well object to having such a specification of desire demanded of you, but in fact we are all socialized to accede to similar requirements in daily life—to the point of not noticing it, and certainly not feeling oppressed by it. I dwell on this because it has a parallel in the realm of belief, where our linguistic environment is forever forcing us to give—or concede—precise verbal expression to convictions that lack the hard edges verbalization endows them with (see Dennett 1969, pp. 184–85, and Dennett 1978, chapter 16). By concentrating on the *results* of this social force, while ignoring its distorting effect, one can easily be misled into thinking that it is *obvious* that beliefs and desires are rather like sentences stored in the head. Being language-using creatures, it is inevitable that we should often come to believe that some particular, actually formulated, spelled and punctuated sentence *is true,* and that on other occasions we should come to want such a sentence to *come true,* but these are special cases of belief and desire and as such may not be reliable models for the whole domain.

That is enough, on this occasion, about the principles of belief and desire attribution to be found in the intentional strategy. What about the rationality one attributes to an intentional system? One starts with the ideal of perfect rationality and revises downward as circumstances dictate. That is, one starts with the assumption that people believe all the implications of their beliefs and believe no contradictory pairs of beliefs. This does not create a practical problem of clutter (infinitely many implications, for instance), for one is interested only in ensuring that the system one is predicting is rational enough to get to the particular implications that are relevant to its behavioral predicament of the moment. Instances of irrationality, or of finitely powerful capacities of inferences, raise particularly knotty problems of interpretation, which I will set aside on this occasion (see Dennett 1987, chapter 4, and Cherniak 1986).

For I want to turn from the description of the strategy to the question of its use. Do people actually use this strategy? Yes, all the time. There may someday be other strategies for attributing belief and desire and for predicting behavior, but this is the only one we all know now. And when does it work? It works with people almost all the time. Why would it *not* be a good idea to allow individual Oxford colleges to create and grant academic degrees whenever they saw fit? The answer is a long story, but very easy to generate. And there would be widespread agreement about the major points. We have no difficulty thinking of the reasons people would then have for acting in such ways as to give others reasons for acting in such ways as to give others reasons for . . . creating a circumstance we would not want. Our use of the intentional strategy is so habitual and effortless that the role it plays in shaping our expectations about people is easily overlooked. The strategy also works on most other mammals most of the time. For instance, you can use it to design better traps to catch those mammals, by reasoning about what the creature knows or believes about various things, what it prefers, what it wants to avoid. The strategy works on birds, and on fish, and on reptiles, and on insects and spiders, and even on such lowly and unenterprising creatures as clams (once a clam believes there is danger about, it will not relax its grip on its closed shell until it is convinced that the danger has passed). It also works on some artifacts: the chess-playing computer will not take your knight because it knows that there is a line of ensuing play that would lead to losing its rook, and it does not want that to happen. More modestly, the thermostat will turn off the boiler as soon as it comes to believe the room has reached the desired temperature.

The strategy even works for plants. In a locale with late spring storms, you should plant apple varieties that are particularly *cautious* about *concluding* that it is spring—which is when they *want* to blossom, of course. It even works for such inanimate and apparently undesigned phenomena as lightning. An electrician once explained to me how he worked out how to protect my underground water pump from lightning damage: lightning, he said, always wants to find the best way to ground, but sometimes it gets tricked into taking second-best paths. You can protect the pump by making another, better path more *obvious* to the lightning.

True Believers as Intentional Systems

Now clearly this is a motley assortment of "serious" belief attributions, dubious belief attributions, pedagogically useful metaphors, *façons de parler,* and, perhaps worse, outright frauds. The next task would seem to be distinguishing those intentional systems that *really* have beliefs and desires from those we may find it handy to treat *as if* they had beliefs and desires. But that would be a Sisyphean labor, or else would be terminated by fiat. A better understanding of the phenomenon of belief begins with the observation that even in the worst of these cases, even when we are surest that the strategy works *for the wrong reasons,* it is nevertheless true that it does work, at least a little bit. This is an interesting fact, which distinguishes this class of objects, the class of *intentional systems,* from the class of objects for which the strategy never works. But is this so? Does our definition of an intentional system exclude any objects at all? For instance, it seems the lectern in this lecture room can be construed as an intentional system, fully rational, believing that it is currently located at the center of the civilized world (as some of you may also think), and desiring above all else to remain at that center. What should such a rational agent so equipped with belief and desire do? Stay put, clearly, which is just what the lectern does. I predict the lectern's behavior, accurately, from the intentional stance, so is it an intentional system? If it is, anything at all is.

What should disqualify the lectern? For one

thing, the strategy does not recommend itself in this case, for we get no predictive power from it that we did not antecedently have. We already knew what the lectern was going to do—namely nothing—and tailored the beliefs and desires to fit in a quite unprincipled way. In the case of people or animals or computers, however, the situation is different. In these cases often the only strategy that is at all practical is the intentional strategy; it gives us predictive power we can get by no other method. But, it will be urged, this is no difference in nature, but merely a difference that reflects upon our limited capacities as scientists. The Laplacean omniscient physicist could predict the behavior of a computer—or of a live human body, assuming it to be ultimately governed by the laws of physics—without any need for the risky, short-cut methods of either the design or intentional strategies. For people of limited mechanical aptitude, the intentional interpretation of a simple thermostat is a handy and largely innocuous crutch, but the engineers among us can quite fully grasp its internal operation without the aid of this anthropomorphizing. It may be true that the cleverest engineers find it practically impossible to maintain a clear conception of more complex systems, such as a time-sharing computer system or remote-controlled space probe, without lapsing into an intentional stance (and viewing these devices as asking and telling, trying and avoiding, wanting and believing), but this is just a more advanced case of human epistemic frailty. We would not want to classify these artifacts with the true believers—ourselves—on such variable and parochial grounds, would we? Would it not be intolerable to hold that some artifact or creature or person was a believer from the point of view of one observer, but not a believer at all from the point of view of another, cleverer observer? That would be a particularly radical version of interpretationism, and some have thought I espoused it in urging that belief be viewed in terms of the success of the intentional strategy. I must confess that my presentation of the view has sometimes invited that reading, but I now want to discourage it. The decision to adopt the intentional stance is free, but the facts about the success or failure of the stance, were one to adopt it, are perfectly objective.

Once the intentional strategy is in place, it is an extraordinarily powerful tool in prediction—a fact that is largely concealed by our typical concentration on the cases in which it yields dubious or unreliable results. Consider, for instance, predicting moves in a chess game. What makes chess an interesting game, one can see, is the *un*predictability of one's opponent's moves, except in those cases where moves are "forced"—where there is *clearly* one best move—typically the least of the available evils. But this unpredictability is put in context when one recognizes that in the typical chess situation there are very many perfectly legal and hence available moves, but only a few—perhaps half a dozen—with anything to be said for them, and hence only a few high-probability moves according to the intentional strategy. Even when the intentional strategy fails to distinguish a single move with a highest probability, it can dramatically reduce the number of live options.

The same feature is apparent when the intentional strategy is applied to "real world" cases. It is notoriously unable to predict the exact purchase and sell decisions of stock traders, for instance, or the exact sequence of words a politician will utter when making a scheduled speech, but one's confidence can be very high indeed about slightly less specific predictions: that the particular trader *will not buy utilities today,* or that the politician *will side with the unions against his party,* for example. This inability to predict fine-grained descriptions of actions, looked at another way, is a source of strength for the intentional strategy, for it is this neutrality with regard to details of implementation that permits one to exploit the intentional strategy in complex cases, for instance, in *chaining predictions* (see Dennett 1978). Suppose the US Secretary of State were to announce he was a paid agent of the KGB. What an unparalleled event! How unpredictable its consequences! Yet in fact we can predict dozens of not terribly interesting but perfectly salient consequences, and consequences of consequences. The President would confer with the rest of the Cabinet, which would support his decision to relieve the Secretary of State of his duties pending the results of various investigations, psychiatric and political, and all this would be reported at a news conference to people who would write stories that would be commented upon in editorials that would be read by people who would write letters to the editors, and so forth. None of that is daring prognostication, but note that it describes an arc of causation in space-time that could not be predicted under *any* description by any imaginable practical extension of physics or biology.

The power of the intentional strategy can be seen even more sharply with the aid of an objection first raised by Robert Nozick some years ago. Suppose, he suggested, some beings of vastly superior intelligence—from Mars, let us say—were to descend upon us, and suppose that we were to them as simple thermostats are to clever engineers. Suppose, that is, that they did not *need* the intentional stance—or even the design stance—to predict our behavior in all its detail. They can be supposed to be Laplacean super-physicists, capable of comprehending the activity on Wall Street, for instance, at the microphysical level. Where we see brokers and buildings and sell orders and bids, they see vast congeries of subatomic particles milling about—and they are such good physicists that they can predict days in advance what ink marks will appear each day on the paper tape labeled "Closing Dow Jones Industrial Average." They can predict the individual behaviors of all the various moving bodies they observe without ever treating any of them as intentional systems. Would we be right then to say that from *their* point of view we really were not believers at all (any more than a simple thermostat is)? If so, then our status as believers is nothing objective, but rather something in the eye of the beholder—provided the beholder shares our intellectual limitations.

Our imagined Martians might be able to predict the future of the human race by Laplacean methods, but if they did not also see us as intentional systems, they would be missing something perfectly objective: the *patterns* in human behavior that are describable from the intentional stance, and only from that stance, and that support generalizations and predictions. Take a particular instance in which the Martians observe a stockbroker deciding to place an order for 500 shares of General Motors. They predict the exact motions of his fingers as he dials the phone and the exact vibrations of his vocal cords as he intones his order. But if the Martians do not see that indefinitely many *different* patterns of finger motions and vocal cord vibrations—even the motions of indefinitely many different individuals—could have been substituted for the actual particulars without perturbing the subsequent operation of the market, then they have failed to see a real pattern in the world they are observing. Just as there are indefinitely many ways of *being a spark plug*—and one has not understood what an internal combustion engine is unless one realizes that a variety of different devices can be screwed into these sockets without affecting the performance of the engine—so there are indefinitely many ways of *ordering 500 shares of General Motors,* and there are societal sockets in which one of these ways will produce just about the same effect as any other. There are also societal pivot points, as it were, where which way people go depends on whether they *believe that p,* or *desire A,* and does not depend on any of the other infinitely many ways they may be alike or different.

Suppose, pursuing our Martian fantasy a little further, that one of the Martians were to engage in a predicting contest with an Earthling. The Earthling and the Martian observe (and observe each other observing) a particular bit of local physical transaction. From the Earthling's point of view, this is what is observed. The telephone rings in Mrs. Gardner's kitchen. She answers, and this is what she says: "Oh, hello dear. You're coming home early? Within the hour? And bringing the boss to dinner? Pick up a bottle of wine on the way home, then, and drive carefully." On the basis of this observation, our Earthling predicts that a large metallic vehicle with rubber tires will come to a stop in the drive within one hour, disgorging two human beings, one of whom will be holding a paper bag containing a bottle containing an alcoholic fluid. The prediction is a bit risky, perhaps, but a good bet on all counts. The Martian makes the same prediction, but has to avail himself of much more information about an extraordinary number of interactions of which, so far as he can tell, the Earthling is entirely ignorant. For instance, the deceleration of the vehicle at intersection *A,* five miles from the house, without which there would have been a collision with another vehicle—whose collision course had been laboriously calculated over some hundreds of meters by the Martian. The Earthling's performance would look like magic! How did the Earthling know that the human being who got out of the car and got the bottle in the shop would get back in? The coming true of the Earthling's prediction, after all the vagaries, intersections, and branches in the paths charted by the Martian, would seem to anyone bereft of the intentional strategy as marvelous and inexplicable as the fatalistic inevitability of the appointment in Samarra. Fatalists—for instance, astrologers—believe that there is a pattern in human affairs that is inexorable, that will impose itself *come what may,* that is, no matter how the victims scheme and second-guess, no matter how they twist and turn in their chains. These fatalists are wrong, but they are *almost* right. There *are* patterns in human affairs that impose themselves, not quite inexorably but with great vigor, absorbing physical perturbations and variations that might as well be considered random; these are the patterns that we characterize in terms of the beliefs, desires, and intentions of rational agents.

No doubt you will have noticed, and been distracted by, a serious flaw in our thought experiment: the Martian is presumed to treat his Earthling opponent as an intelligent being like himself, with whom communication is possible, a being with whom one can make a wager, against whom one can compete. In short, a being with beliefs (such as the belief he expressed in his prediction) and desires (such as the desire to win the prediction contest). So if the Martian sees the pattern in one Earthling, how can he fail to see it in the others? As a bit of narrative, our example could be strengthened by supposing that our Earthling cleverly learned Martian (which is transmitted by X-ray modulation) and disguised himself as a Martian, counting on the species-chauvinism of these otherwise brilliant aliens to permit him to pass as an intentional system while not giving away the secret of his fellow human beings. This addition might get us over a bad twist in the tale, but might obscure the moral to be drawn: namely, *the unavoidability of the intentional stance with regard to oneself and one's fellow intelligent beings.* This unavoidability is itself interest relative; it is perfectly possible to adopt a physical stance, for instance, with regard to an intelligent being, oneself included, but not to the exclusion of maintaining at the same time an intentional stance with regard to oneself at a minimum, and one's fellows *if* one intends, for instance, to learn what they know (a point that has been powerfully made by Stuart Hampshire in a number of writings). We can perhaps suppose our super-intelligent Martians fail to recognize *us* as intentional systems, but we cannot suppose them to lack the requisite concepts.[2] If they observe, theorize, predict, communicate, they view *themselves* as intentional systems.[3] Where there are intelligent beings, the patterns must be there to be described, whether or not we care to see them.

It is important to recognize the objective reality of the intentional patterns discernible in the activities of intelligent creatures, but also important to recognize the incompleteness and imperfections in the patterns. The objective fact is that the intentional strategy *works as well as it does,* which is not perfectly. No one is perfectly rational, perfectly unforgetful, all-observant, or invulnerable to fatigue, malfunction, or design imperfection. This leads inevitably to circumstances beyond the power of the intentional strategy to describe, in much the same way that physical damage to an artifact, such as a telephone or an automobile, may render it indescribable by the normal design terminology for that artifact. How do you draw the schematic wiring diagram of an audio amplifier that has been partially melted, or how do you characterize the program state of a malfunctioning computer? In cases of even the mildest and most familiar cognitive pathology—where people seem to hold contradictory beliefs or to be deceiving themselves, for instance—the canons of interpretation of the intentional strategy fail to yield clear, stable verdicts about which beliefs and desires to attribute to a person.

Now a *strong* realist position on beliefs and desires would claim that in these cases the person in question really does have some particular beliefs and desires which the intentional strategy, as I have described it, is simply unable to divine. On the milder sort of realism I am advocating, there is no fact of the matter of exactly which beliefs and desires a person has in these degenerate cases, but this is not a surrender to relativism or subjectivism, for *when* and *why* there is no fact of the matter is itself a matter of objective fact. On this view one can even acknowledge the *interest relativity* of belief attributions and grant that given the different interests of different cultures, for instance, the beliefs and desires one culture would attribute to a member might be quite different from the beliefs and desires another culture would attribute to that very same person. But supposing that were so in a particular case, there would be the further facts about *how well* each of the rival intentional strategies worked for predicting the behavior of that person. We can be sure in advance that no intentional interpretation of an individual will work to perfection, and it may be that two rival schemes are about equally good, and better than any others we can devise. That this is the case is itself something about which there can be a fact of the matter. The objective presence of one pattern (with whatever imperfections) does not rule out the objective presence of another pattern (with whatever imperfections).

The bogey of radically different interpretations with equal warrant from the intentional strategy is theoretically important—one might better say metaphysically important—but practically negligible once one restricts one's attention to the largest and most complex intentional systems we know: human beings.[4]

Until now I have been stressing our kinship to clams and thermostats, in order to emphasize a view of the logical status of belief attribution, but the time has come to acknowledge the obvious differences and say what can be made of them. The perverse claim remains: *all there is* to being a true believer is being a system whose behavior is reliably predictable via the intentional strategy, and hence *all there is* to really and truly believing that *p* (for any proposition *p*) is being an intentional system for which *p* occurs as a belief in the best (most predictive) interpretation. But once we turn our attention to the truly interesting and versatile intentional systems, we see that this apparently shallow and instrumentalistic criterion of belief puts a severe constraint on the internal constitution of a genuine believer, and thus yields a robust version of belief after all.

Consider the lowly thermostat, as degenerate a case of an intentional system as could conceivably hold our attention for more than a moment. Going along with the gag, we might agree to grant it the capacity for about half a dozen different beliefs and fewer desires—it can believe the room is too cold or too hot, that the boiler is on or off, and that if it wants the room warmer it should turn on the boiler, and so forth. But surely this is imputing too much to the thermostat; it has no concept of heat or of a boiler, for instance. So suppose we *de-interpret* its beliefs and desires: it can believe the *A* is too *F* or *G,* and if it wants the *A* to be more *F* it should do *K,* and so forth. After all, by attaching the thermostatic control mechanism to different input and output devices, it could be made to regulate the amount of water in a tank, or the speed of a train, for instance. Its attachment to a heat-sensitive transducer and a boiler is too impoverished a link to the world to grant any rich semantics to its belief-like states.

But suppose we then enrich these modes of attachment. Suppose we give it more than one way of learning about the temperature, for instance. We give it an eye of sorts that can distinguish huddled, shivering occupants of the room and an ear so that it can be told how cold it is. We give it some facts about geography so that it can conclude that it is probably in a cold place if it learns that its spatiotemporal location is Win-nipeg in December. Of course giving it a visual system that is multipurpose and general—not a mere shivering-object detector—will require vast complications of its inner structure. Suppose we also give our system more behavioral versatility: it chooses the boiler fuel, purchases it from the cheapest and most reliable dealer, checks the weather stripping, and so forth. This adds another dimension of internal complexity; it gives individual belief-like states *more to do,* in effect, by providing more and different occasions for their derivation or deduction from other states, and by providing more and different occasions for them to serve as premises for further reasoning. The cumulative effect of enriching these connections between the device and the world in which it resides is to enrich the semantics of its dummy predicates, *F* and *G* and the rest. The more of this we add, the less amenable our device becomes to serving as the control structure of anything other than a room-temperature maintenance system. A more formal way of saying this is that the class of indistinguishably satisfactory models of the formal system embodied in its internal states gets smaller and smaller as we add such complexities; the more we add, the richer or more demanding or specific the semantics of the system, until eventually we reach systems for which a unique semantic interpretation is practically (but never in principle) dictated (cf. Hayes 1979). At that point we say this device (or animal or person) has beliefs *about heat* and *about this very room,* and so forth, not only because of the system's actual location in, and operations on, the world, but because we cannot imagine another niche in which it could be placed *where it would work* (see also Dennett 1987, chapters 5 and 8).

Our original simple thermostat had a state we called a belief about a particular boiler, to the effect that it was on or off. Why about *that* boiler? Well, what other boiler would you want to say it was about? The belief is about the boiler because it is *fastened* to the boiler.[5] Given the actual, if mimimal, causal link to the world that happened to be in effect, we could endow a state of the device with *meaning* (of a sort) and *truth conditions,* but it was altogether too easy to substitute a different minimal link and completely change the meaning (in this impoverished sense) of that internal state. But as systems become perceptually richer and behaviorally more versatile, it becomes harder and harder to make substitutions in the actual links of the system to the world without changing the organization of the system itself. If you change its environment, it will *notice,* in effect, and make a change in its internal state in response. There comes to be a two-way constraint of growing specificity between the device and the environment. Fix the device in any one state and it demands a very specific environment in which to operate properly (you can no longer switch it easily from regulating temperature to regulating speed or anything else); but at the same time, if you do not *fix* the state it is in, but just plonk it down in a changed environment, its sensory attachments will be sensitive and discriminative enough to respond appropriately to the change, driving the system into a new state, in which it will operate effectively in the new environment. There is a familiar way of alluding to this tight relationship that can exist between the organization of a system and its environment: you say that the organism continuously *mirrors* the environment, or that there is a *representation* of the environment in—or implicit in—the organization of the system.

It is not that we attribute (or should attribute) beliefs and desires only to things in which we find internal representations, but rather that when we discover some object for which the intentional strategy works, we endeavor to interpret some of its internal states or processes as internal representations. What makes some internal feature of a thing a representation could only be its role in regulating the behavior of an intentional system.

Now the reason for stressing our kinship with the thermostat should be clear. There is no magic moment in the transition from a simple thermostat to a system that *really* has an internal representation of the world around it. The thermostat has a minimally demanding representation of the world, fancier thermostats have more demanding representations of the world, fancier robots for helping around the house would have still more demanding representations of the world. Finally you reach us. We are so multifariously and intricately connected to the world that almost no substitution is possible—though it is clearly imaginable in a thought experiment. Hilary Putnam imagines the planet Twin Earth, which is just like Earth right down to the scuff marks on the shoes of the Twin Earth replica of your neighbor, but which differs from Earth in some property that is entirely beneath the thresholds of your capacities to discriminate. (What they call water on Twin Earth has a different chemical analysis.) Were *you* to be whisked instantaneously to Twin Earth and exchanged for your Twin Earth replica, you would never be the wiser—just like the simple control system that cannot tell whether it is regulating temperature, speed, or volume of water in a tank. It is easy to devise radically different Twin Earths for something as simple and sensorily deprived as a thermostat, but your internal organization puts a much more stringent demand on substitution. Your Twin Earth and Earth must be virtual replicas or you will change state dramatically on arrival.

So which boiler are *your* beliefs about when you believe the boiler is on? Why, the boiler in your cellar (rather than its twin on Twin Earth, for instance). What other boiler would your beliefs be about? The completion of the semantic interpretation of your beliefs, fixing the referents of your beliefs, requires, as in the case of the thermostat, facts about your actual embedding in the world. The principles, and problems, of interpretation that we discover when we attribute beliefs to people are the *same* principles and problems we discover when we look at the ludicrous, but blessedly simple, problem of attributing beliefs to a thermostat. The differences are of degree, but nevertheless of such great degree that understanding the internal organization of a simple intentional system gives one very little basis for understanding the internal organization of a complex intentional system, such as a human being.

Why Does the Intentional Strategy Work?

When we turn to the question of *why* the intentional strategy works as well as it does, we find that the question is ambiguous, admitting of two very different sorts of answers. If the intentional system is a simple thermostat, one answer is simply this: the intentional strategy works because the thermostat is well designed; it was designed to be a system that could be easily and reliably comprehended and manipulated from this stance. That is true, but not very informative, if what we are after are the actual features of its design that explain its performance. Fortunately, however, in the case of a simple thermostat those features are easily discovered and understood, so the other answer to our *why* question, which is really an answer about *how the machinery works,* is readily available.

If the intentional system in question is a person, there is also an ambiguity in our question. The first answer to the question of why the intentional strategy works is that evolution has designed human beings to be rational, to believe what they ought to believe and want what they ought to want. The fact that we are products of a long and demanding evolutionary process guarantees that using the intentional strategy on us is a safe bet. This answer has the virtues of truth and brevity, and on this occasion the additional virtue of being an answer Herbert Spencer would applaud, but it is also strikingly uninformative. The more difficult version of the question asks, in effect, how the machinery which Nature has provided us works. And we cannot yet give a good answer to that question. We just do not know. We do know how the *strategy* works, and we know the easy answer to the question of why it works, but knowing these does not help us much with the hard answer.

It is not that there is any dearth of doctrine, however. A Skinnerian behaviorist, for instance, would say that the strategy works because its imputations of beliefs and desires are shorthand, in effect, for as yet unimaginably complex descriptions of the effects of prior histories of response and reinforcement. To say that someone wants some ice cream is to say that in the past the ingestion of ice cream has been reinforced in him by the results, creating a propensity under certain background conditions (also too complex to describe) to engage in ice-cream-acquiring behavior. In the absence of detailed knowledge of those historical facts we can nevertheless make shrewd guesses on inductive grounds; these guesses are embodied in our intentional stance claims. Even if all this were true, it would tell us very little about the way such propensities were regulated by the internal machinery.

A currently more popular explanation is that the account of how the strategy works and the account of how the mechanism works will (roughly) *coincide:* for each predictively attributable belief, there will be a functionally salient internal state of the machinery, decomposable into functional parts in just about the same way the sentence expressing the belief is decomposable into parts—that is, words or terms. The inferences we attribute to rational creatures will be mirrored by physical, causal processes in the hardware; the *logical* form of the propositions believed will be copied in the *structural* form of the states in correspondence with them. This is the hypothesis that there is a *language of thought* coded in our brains, and our brains will eventually be understood as symbol manipulating systems in at least rough analogy with computers. Many different versions of this view are currently being explored, in the new research program called cognitive science, and provided one allows great latitude for attenuation of the basic, bold claim, I think some version of it will prove correct.

But I do not believe that this is *obvious*. Those who think that it is obvious, or inevitable, that such a theory will prove true (and there are many who do), are confusing two different empirical claims. The first is that intentional stance description yields an objective, real pattern in the world—the pattern our imaginary Martians missed. This is an empirical claim, but one that is confirmed beyond skepticism. The second is that this real pattern is *produced by* another real pattern roughly isomorphic to it within the brains of intelligent creatures. Doubting the existence of the second real pattern is not doubting the existence of the first. There *are* reasons for believing in the second pattern, but they are not overwhelming. The best simple account I can give of the reasons is as follows.

As we ascend the scale of complexity from simple thermostat, through sophisticated robot, to human being, we discover that our efforts to design systems with the requisite behavior increasingly run foul of the problem of *combinatorial explosion*. Increasing some parameter by, say, ten percent—ten percent more inputs or more degrees of freedom in the behavior to be controlled or more words to be recognized or whatever—tends to increase the internal complexity of the system being designed by orders of magnitude. Things get out of hand very fast and, for instance, can lead to computer programs that will swamp the largest, fastest machines. Now somehow the brain has solved the problem of combinatorial explosion. It is a gigantic network of billions of cells, but still finite, compact, reliable, and swift, and capable of learning new behaviors, vocabularies, theories, almost without limit. Some elegant, *generative,* indefinitely extendable principles of representation must be responsible. We have only one model of such a representation system: a human language. So the argument for a language of thought comes down to this: what else could it be? We have so far been unable to imagine any plausible alternative in any detail. That is a good enough reason, I think, for recommending as a matter of scientific tactics that we pursue the hypothesis in its various forms as far as we can.[6] But we will engage in that exploration more circumspectly, and fruitfully, if we bear in mind that its inevitable rightness is far from assured. One does not well understand even a true empirical hypothesis so long as one is under the misapprehension that it is necessarily true.

NOTES

1. The idea that most of anyone's beliefs *must* be true seems obvious to some people. Support for the idea can be found in works by Quine, Putnam, Shoemaker, Davidson, and myself. Other people find the idea equally incredible—so probably each side is calling a different phenomenon belief. Once one makes the distinction between belief and opinion (in my technical sense—see "How to Change Your Mind" in Dennett 1978, chapter 16), according to which opinions are linguistically infected, relatively sophisticated cognitive states—*roughly* states of betting on the truth of a particular, formulated sentence—one can see the near triviality of the claim that most beliefs are true. A few reflections on peripheral matters should bring it out. Consider Democritus, who had a systematic, all-embracing, but (let us say, for the sake of argument) entirely false physics. He had things *all wrong,* though his views held together and had a sort of systematic utility. But even if every *claim* that scholarship permits us to attribute to Democritus (either explicit or implicit in his writings) is false, these represent a vanishingly small fraction of his *beliefs,* which include both the vast numbers of humdrum standing beliefs he must have had (about which house he lived in, what to look for in a good pair of sandals, and so forth) and also those occasional beliefs that came and went by the millions as his perceptual experience changed.

   But, it may be urged, this isolation of his humdrum beliefs from his science relies on an insupportable distinction between truths of observation and truths of theory; all Democritus's beliefs are theory-laden, and since his theory is false, they are false. The reply is as follows: Granted that all observation beliefs are theory laden, why should we choose Democritus's *explicit,* sophisticated theory (couched in his *opinions*) as the theory with which to burden his quotidian observations? Note that the least theoretical compatriot of Democritus also had myriads of theory-laden observation beliefs—and was, in one sense, none the wiser for it. Why should we not suppose Democritus's observations are laden with the same (presumably innocuous) theory? If Democritus forgot his theory, or changed his mind, his observational beliefs would be *largely* untouched. To the extent that his sophisticated theory played a discernible role in his routine behavior and expectations and so forth, it would be quite appropriate to couch his humdrum beliefs in terms of the sophisticated theory, but this will not yield a *mainly false* catalogue of beliefs, since so few of his beliefs will be affected. (The effect of theory on observation is nevertheless often underrated. See Churchland 1979 for dramatic and convincing examples of the tight relationship that can sometimes exist between theory and experience. [The discussion in this note was distilled from a useful conversation with Paul and Patricia Churchland and Michael Stack.])

2. A member of the audience in Oxford pointed out that if the Martian included the Earthling in his physical stance purview (a possibility I had not explicitly excluded), he would not be surprised by the Earthling's prediction. He would indeed have predicted exactly the pattern of X-ray modulations produced by the Earthling speaking Martian. True, but as the Martian wrote down the results of his calculations, his prediction of the Earthling's prediction would appear, word by Martian word, as on a Ouija board, and what would be baffling to the Martian was how this chunk of mechanism, the Earthling predictor dressed up like a Martian, was able to yield this *true* sentence of Martian when it was so informationally isolated from the events the Martian needed to know of in order to make his own prediction about the arriving automobile.

3. Might there not be intelligent beings who had no use for communicating, predicting, observing . . . ? There might be marvelous, nifty, invulnerable entities lacking these modes of action, but I cannot see what would lead us to call them *intelligent.*

4. John McCarthy's analogy to cryptography nicely makes this point. The larger the corpus of cipher text, the less chance there is of dual, systematically unrelated decipherings. For a very useful discussion of the principles and presuppositions of the intentional stance applied to machines—explicitly including thermostats—see McCarthy 1979.

5. This idea is the ancestor in effect of the species of different ideas lumped together under the rubric of *de re* belief. If one builds from this idea toward its scions, one can see better the difficulties with them, and how to repair them. (For more on this topic, see Dennett 1987, chapter 5.)

6. The fact that all *language of thought* models of mental representation so far proposed fall victim to combinatorial explosion in one way or another should temper one's enthusiasm for engaging in what Fodor aptly calls "the only game in town."

BIBLIOGRAPHY

Akins, K. A. 1986. On piranhas, narcissism, and mental representation. CCM-86-2, Center for Cognitive Studies, Tufts University.

Cherniak, C. 1986. *Minimal Rationality.* Cambridge, MA: MIT Press.

Churchland, P. M. 1979. *Scientific Realism and the Plasticity of Mind.* Cambridge: Cambridge University Press.

Dennett, D. C. 1971. Intentional systems. *Journal of Philosophy* 8:87:106. Reprinted in Dennett 1978.

Dennett, D. C. 1976. Conditions of personhood. In A. Rorty (ed.), *The Identities of Persons*. Berkeley: University of California Press. Reprinted in Dennett 1978.

Dennett, D. C. 1978. *Brainstorms: Philosophical Essays on Mind and Psychology*. Cambridge, MA: MIT Press.

Dennett, D. C. 1987. *The Intentional Stance*. Cambridge, MA: MIT Press.

Feyerabend, P. 1978. *Science in a Free Society*. London: New Left Bank Publishers.

Hayes, P. 1979. The naïve physics manifesto. In D. Michie (ed.), *Expert Systems in the Microelectronic Age*. Edinburgh: Edinburgh University Press.

McCarthy, J. 1979. Ascribing mental qualities to machines. In M. Ringle (ed.), *Philosophical Perspectives on Artificial Intelligence*. Atlantic Highlands, NJ: Humanities Press.

53 | Eliminative Materialism and the Propositional Attitudes
Paul M. Churchland

Eliminative materialism is the thesis that our common-sense conception of psychological phenomena constitutes a radically false theory, a theory so fundamentally defective that both the principles and the ontology of that theory will eventually be displaced, rather than smoothly reduced, by completed neuroscience. Our mutual understanding and even our introspection may then be reconstituted within the conceptual framework of completed neuroscience, a theory we may expect to be more powerful by far than the common-sense psychology it displaces, and more substantially integrated within physical science generally. My purpose in this paper is to explore these projections, especially as they bear on (1) the principal elements of common-sense psychology: the propositional attitudes (beliefs, desires, etc.), and (2) the conception of rationality in which these elements figure.

This focus represents a change in the fortunes of materialism. Twenty years ago, emotions, qualia, and "raw feels" were held to be the principal stumbling blocks for the materialist program. With these barriers dissolving,[1] the locus of opposition has shifted. Now it is the realm of the intentional, the realm of the propositional attitude, that is most commonly held up as being both irreducible to and ineliminable in favor of anything from within a materialist framework. Whether and why this is so, we must examine.

Such an examination will make little sense, however, unless it is first appreciated that the relevant network of common-sense concepts does indeed constitute an empirical theory, with all the functions, virtues, *and perils* entailed by that status. I shall therefore begin with a brief sketch of this view and a summary rehearsal of its rationale. The resistance it encounters still surprises me. After all, common sense has yielded up many theories. Recall the view that space has a preferred direction in which all things fall; that weight is an intrinsic feature of a body; that a force-free moving object will promptly return to rest; that the sphere of the heavens turns daily; and so on. These examples are clear, perhaps, but people seem willing to concede a theoretical component within common sense only if (1) the theory and the common sense involved are safely located in antiquity, and (2) the relevant theory is now so clearly false that its speculative nature is inescapable. Theories are indeed easier to discern under these circumstances. But the vision of hindsight is always 20/20. Let us aspire to some foresight for a change.

I. Why Folk Psychology Is a Theory

Seeing our common-sense conceptual framework for mental phenomena as a theory brings a simple and unifying organization to most of the major topics in the philosophy of mind, includ-

From *Journal of Philosophy* 78:67–90, 1981. Reprinted with permission of author and publisher.

ing the explanation and prediction of behavior, the semantics of mental predicates, action theory, the other-minds problem, the intentionality of mental states, the nature of introspection, and the mind-body problem. Any view that can pull this lot together deserves careful consideration.

Let us begin with the explanation of human (and animal) behavior. The fact is that the average person is able to explain, and even predict, the behavior of other persons with a facility and success that is remarkable. Such explanations and predictions standardly make reference to the desires, beliefs, fears, intentions, perceptions, and so forth, to which the agents are presumed subject. But explanations presuppose laws—rough and ready ones, at least—that connect the explanatory conditions with the behavior explained. The same is true for the making of predictions, and for the justification of subjunctive and counterfactual conditionals concerning behavior. Reassuringly, a rich network of common-sense laws can indeed be reconstructed from this quotidian commerce of explanation and anticipation; its principles are familiar homilies; and their sundry functions are transparent. Each of us understands others, as well as we do, because we share a tacit command of an integrated body of lore concerning the law-like relations holding among external circumstances, internal states, and overt behavior. Given its nature and functions, this body of lore may quite aptly be called "folk psychology."[2]

This approach entails that the semantics of the terms in our familiar mentalistic vocabulary is to be understood in the same manner as the semantics of theoretical terms generally: the meaning of any theoretical term is fixed or constituted by the network of laws in which it figures. (This position is quite distinct from logical behaviorism. We deny that the relevant laws are analytic, and it is the lawlike connections generally that carry the semantic weight, not just the connections with overt behavior. But this view does account for what little plausibility logical behaviorism did enjoy.)

More importantly, the recognition that folk psychology is a theory provides a simple and decisive solution to an old skeptical problem, the problem of other minds. The problematic conviction that another individual is the subject of certain mental states is not inferred deductively from his behavior, nor is it inferred by inductive analogy from the perilously isolated instance of one's own case. Rather, that conviction is a singular *explanatory hypothesis* of a perfectly

straightforward kind. Its function, in conjunction with the background laws of folk psychology, is to provide explanations/predictions/understanding of the individual's continuing behavior, and it is credible to the degree that it is successful in this regard over competing hypotheses. In the main, such hypotheses are successful, and so the belief that others enjoy the internal states comprehended by folk psychology is a reasonable belief.

Knowledge of other minds thus has no essential dependence on knowledge of one's own mind. Applying the principles of our folk psychology to our behavior, a Martian could justly ascribe to us the familiar run of mental states, even though his own psychology were very different from ours. He would not, therefore, be "generalizing from his own case."

As well, introspective judgments about one's own case turn out not to have any special status or integrity anyway. On the present view, an introspective judgment is just an instance of an acquired habit of conceptual response to one's internal states, and the integrity of any particular response is always contingent on the integrity of the acquired conceptual framework (theory) in which the response is framed. Accordingly, one's *introspective* certainty that one's mind is the seat of beliefs and desires may be as badly misplaced as was the classical man's *visual* certainty that the star-flecked sphere of the heavens turns daily.

Another conundrum is the intentionality of mental states. The "propositional attitudes," as Russell called them, form the systematic core of folk psychology; and their uniqueness and anomalous logical properties have inspired some to see here a fundamental contrast with anything that mere physical phenomena might conceivably display. The key to this matter lies again in the theoretical nature of folk psychology. The intentionality of mental states here emerges not as a mystery of nature, but as a structural feature of the concepts of folk psychology. Ironically, those same structural features reveal the very close affinity that folk psychology bears to theories in the physical sciences. Let me try to explain.

Consider the large variety of what might be called "numerical attitudes" appearing in the conceptual framework of physical science: '. . . has a mass$_{kg}$ of n', '. . . has a velocity of n', '. . . has a temperature$_K$ of n', and so forth. These expressions are predicate-forming expressions: when one substitutes a singular term for a number into the place held by '*n*', a determinate predicate results. More interestingly, the relations between the various "numerical attitudes" that result are precisely the relations between the numbers "contained" in those attitudes. More interesting still, the argument place that takes the singular terms for numbers is open to quantification. All this permits the expression of generalizations concerning the lawlike relations that hold between the various numerical attitudes in nature. Such laws involve quantification over numbers, and they exploit the mathematical relations holding in that domain. Thus, for example,

(1) $(x) (f) (m)[((x$ has a mass of $m)$ &
$(x$ suffers a net force of $f))$
$\qquad \supset (x$ accelerates at $f/m)]$

Consider now the large variety of propositional attitudes: '. . . believes that p', '. . . desires that p', '. . . fears that p', '. . . is happy that p', etc. These expressions are predicate-forming expressions also. When one substitutes a singular term for a proposition into the place held by 'p', a determinate predicate results, e.g., '. . . believes that Tom is tall.' (Sentences do not generally function as singular terms, but it is difficult to escape the idea that when a sentence occurs in the place held by 'p', it is there functioning as or like a singular term. On this, more below.) More interestingly, the relations between the resulting propositional attitudes are characteristically the relations that hold between the propositions "contained" in them, relations such as entailment, equivalence, and mutual inconsistency. More interesting still, the argument place that takes the singular terms for propositions is open to quantification. All this permits the expression of generalizations concerning the lawlike relations that hold among propositional attitudes. Such laws involve quantification over propositions, and they exploit various relations holding in that domain. Thus, for example,

(2) $(x) (p)[(x$ fears that $p)$
$\qquad \supset (x$ desires that $\sim p)]$
(3) $(x) (p)[((x$ hopes that $p)$ & $(x$ discovers
$\qquad$ that $p)) \supset (x$ is pleased that $p)]$
(4) $(x) (p) (q)[((x$ believes that $p)$ &
$(x$ believes that (if p then $q)))$
$\qquad \supset$ (barring confusion, distraction,
etc., x believes that $q)]$
(5) $(x) (p) (q)[((x$ desires that $p)$ & $(x$
believes that (if q then $p))$ & $(x$ is

able to bring it about that $q)) \supset$ (barring conflicting desires or preferred strategies, x brings it about that $q)]$[3]

Not only is folk psychology a theory, it is so *obviously* a theory that it must be held a major mystery why it has taken until the last half of the twentieth century for philosophers to realize it. The structural features of folk psychology parallel perfectly those of mathematical physics; the only difference lies in the respective domain of abstract entities they exploit—numbers in the case of physics, and propositions in the case of psychology.

Finally, the realization that folk psychology is a theory puts a new light on the mind–body problem. The issue becomes a matter of how the ontology of one theory (folk psychology) is, or is not, going to be related to the ontology of another theory (completed neuroscience); and the major philosophical positions on the mind–body problem emerge as so many different anticipations of what future research will reveal about the intertheoretic status and integrity of folk psychology.

The identity theorist optimistically expects that folk psychology will be smoothly *reduced* by completed neuroscience, and its ontology preserved by dint of transtheoretic identities. The dualist expects that it will prove *ir*reducible to completed neuroscience, by dint of being a nonredundant description of an autonomous, nonphysical domain of natural phenomena. The functionalist also expects that it will prove irreducible, but on the quite different grounds that the internal economy characterized by folk psychology is not, in the last analysis, a law-governed economy of natural states, but an abstract organization of functional states, an organization instantiable in a variety of quite different material substrates. It is therefore irreducible to the principles peculiar to any of them.

Finally, the eliminative materialist is also pessimistic about the prospects for reduction, but his reason is that folk psychology is a radically inadequate account of our internal activities, too confused and too defective to win survival through intertheoretic reduction. On his view it will simply be displaced by a better theory of those activities.

Which of these fates is the real destiny of folk psychology, we shall attempt to divine presently. For now, the point to keep in mind is that we shall be exploring the fate of a theory, a systematic, corrigible, speculative *theory*.

II. Why Folk Psychology Might (Really) Be False

Given that folk psychology is an empirical theory, it is at least an abstract possibility that its principles are radically false and that its ontology is an illusion. With the exception of eliminative materialism, however, none of the major positions takes this possibility seriously. None of them doubts the basic integrity or truth of folk psychology (hereafter, "FP"), and all of them anticipate a future in which its laws and categories are conserved. This conservatism is not without some foundation. After all, FP does enjoy a substantial amount of explanatory and predictive success. And what better grounds than this for confidence in the integrity of its categories?

What better grounds indeed? Even so, the presumption in FP's favor is spurious, born of innocence and tunnel vision. A more searching examination reveals a different picture. First, we must reckon not only with FP's successes, but with its explanatory failures, and with their extent and seriousness. Second, we must consider the long-term history of FP, its growth, fertility, and current promise of future development. And third, we must consider what sorts of theories are *likely* to be true of the etiology of our behavior, given what else we have learned about ourselves in recent history. That is, we must evaluate FP with regard to its coherence and continuity with fertile and well-established theories in adjacent and overlapping domains— with evolutionary theory, biology, and neuroscience, for example—because active coherence with the rest of what we presume to know is perhaps the final measure of any hypothesis.

A serious inventory of this sort reveals a very troubled situation, one which would evoke open skepticism in the case of any theory less familiar and dear to us. Let me sketch some relevant detail. When one centers one's attention not on what FP can explain, but on what it cannot explain or fails even to address, one discovers that there is a very great deal. As examples of central and important mental phenomena that remain largely or wholly mysterious within the framework of FP, consider the nature and dynamics of mental illness, the faculty of creative imagination, or the ground of intelligence differences between individuals. Consider our utter ignorance of the nature and psychological functions of sleep, that curious state in which a third of one's life is spent. Reflect on the common ability to catch an outfield fly ball on the run, or hit a moving car with a snowball. Consider the internal construction of a 3-D visual image from subtle differences in the 2-D array of stimulations in our respective retinas. Consider the rich variety of perceptual illusions, visual and otherwise. Or consider the miracle of memory, with its lightning capacity for relevant retrieval. On these and many other mental phenomena, FP sheds negligible light.

One particularly outstanding mystery is the nature of the learning process itself, especially where it involves large-scale conceptual change, and especially as it appears in its pre-linguistic or entirely nonlinguistic form (as in infants and animals), which is by far the most common form in nature. FP is faced with special difficulties here, since its conception of learning as the manipulation and storage of propositional attitudes founders on the fact that how to formulate, manipulate, and store a rich fabric of propositional attitudes is itself something that is learned, and is only one among many acquired cognitive skills. FP would thus appear constitutionally incapable of even addressing this most basic of mysteries.[4]

Failures on such a large scale do not (yet) show that FP is a false theory, but they do move that prospect well into the range of real possibility, and they do show decisively that FP is *at best* a highly superficial theory, a partial and unpenetrating gloss on a deeper and more complex reality. Having reached this opinion, we may be forgiven for exploring the possibility that FP provides a positively misleading sketch of our internal kinematics and dynamics, one whose success is owed more to selective application and forced interpretation on our part than to genuine theoretical insight on FP's part.

A look at the history of FP does little to allay such fears, once raised. The story is one of retreat, infertility, and decadence. The presumed domain of FP used to be much larger than it is now. In primitive cultures, the behavior of most of the elements of nature were understood in intentional terms. The wind could know anger, the moon jealousy, the river generosity, the sea fury, and so forth. These were not metaphors. Sacrifices were made and auguries undertaken to placate or divine the changing passions of the gods. Despite its sterility, this animistic approach to nature has dominated our history, and it is only in the last two or three thousand years that we have restricted FP's literal application to the domain of the higher animals.

Even in this preferred domain, however, both the content and the success of FP have not advanced sensibly in two or three thousand years. The FP of the Greeks is essentially the FP we use today, and we are negligibly better at explaining human behavior in its terms than was Sophocles. This is a very long period of stagnation and infertility for any theory to display, especially when faced with such an enormous backlog of anomalies and mysteries in its own explanatory domain. Perfect theories, perhaps, have no need to evolve. But FP is profoundly imperfect. Its failure to develop its resources and extend its range of success is therefore darkly curious, and one must query the integrity of its basic categories. To use Imre Lakatos' terms, FP is a stagnant or degenerating research program, and has been for millennia.

Explanatory success to date is of course not the only dimension in which a theory can display virtue or promise. A troubled or stagnant theory may merit patience and solicitude on other grounds; for example, on grounds that it is the only theory or theoretical approach that fits well with other theories about adjacent subject matters, or the only one that promises to reduce to or be explained by some established background theory whose domain encompasses the domain of the theory at issue. In sum, it may rate credence because it holds promise of theoretical integration. How does FP rate in this dimension?

It is just here, perhaps, that FP fares poorest of all. If we approach *homo sapiens* from the perspective of natural history and the physical sciences, we can tell a coherent story of his constitution, development, and behavioral capacities which encompasses particle physics, atomic and molecular theory, organic chemistry, evolutionary theory, biology, physiology, and materialistic neuroscience. That story, though still radically incomplete, is already extremely powerful, outperforming FP at many points even in its own domain. And it is deliberately and self-consciously coherent with the rest of our developing world picture. In short, the greatest theoretical synthesis in the history of the human race is currently in our hands, and parts of it already provide searching descriptions and explanations of human sensory input, neural activity, and motor control.

But FP is no part of this growing synthesis. Its intentional categories stand magnificently alone, without visible prospect of reduction to that larger corpus. A successful reduction cannot be ruled out, in my view, but FP's explanatory impotence and long stagnation inspire little faith that its categories will find themselves neatly reflected in the framework of neuroscience. On the contrary, one is reminded of how alchemy must have looked as elemental chemistry was taking form, how Aristotelean cosmology must have looked as classical mechanics was being articulated, or how the vitalist conception of life must have looked as organic chemistry marched forward.

In sketching a fair summary of this situation, we must make a special effort to abstract from the fact that FP is a central part of our current *lebenswelt,* and serves as the principal vehicle of our interpersonal commerce. For these facts provide FP with a conceptual inertia that goes far beyond its purely theoretical virtues. Restricting ourselves to this latter dimension, what we must say is that FP suffers explanatory failures on an epic scale, that it has been stagnant for at least twenty-five centuries, and that its categories appear (so far) to be incommensurable with or orthogonal to the categories of the background physical science whose long-term claim to explain human behavior seems undeniable. Any theory that meets this description must be allowed a serious candidate for outright elimination.

We can of course insist on no stronger conclusion at this stage. Nor is it my concern to do so. We are here exploring a possibility, and the facts demand no more, and no less, than it be taken seriously. The distinguishing feature of the eliminative materialist is that he takes it very seriously indeed.

III. Arguments against Elimination

Thus the basic rationale of eliminative materialism: FP is a theory, and quite probably a false one; let us attempt, therefore to transcend it.

The rationale is clear and simple, but many find it uncompelling. It will be objected that FP is not, strictly speaking, an *empirical* theory; that it is not false, or at least not refutable by empirical considerations; and that it ought not or cannot be transcended in the fashion of a defunct empirical theory. In what follows we shall examine these objections as they flow from the most popular and best-founded of the competing positions in the philosophy of mind: functionalism.

An antipathy toward eliminative materialism arises from two distinct threads running through contemporary functionalism. The first thread concerns the *normative* character of FP, or at least of that central core of FP which treats of the propositional attitudes. FP, some will say, is a characterization of an ideal, or at least praise-worthy mode of internal activity. It outlines not only what it is to have and process beliefs and desires, but also (and inevitably) what it is to be rational in their administration. The ideal laid down by FP may be imperfectly achieved by empirical humans, but this does not impugn FP as a normative characterization. Nor need such failures seriously impugn FP even as a descriptive characterization, for it remains true that our activities can be both usefully and accurately understood as rational *except for* the occasional lapse due to noise, interference, or other break-down, which defects empirical research may eventually unravel. Accordingly, though neuro-science may usefully augment it, FP has no pressing need to be displaced, even as a descriptive theory; nor could it be replaced, qua norma-tive characterization, by any descriptive theory of neural mechanisms, since rationality is de-fined over propositional attitudes like beliefs and desires. FP, therefore, is here to stay.

Daniel Dennett has defended a view along these lines.[5] And the view just outlined gives voice to a theme of the property dualists as well. Karl Popper and Joseph Margolis both cite the normative nature of mental and linguistic activ-ity as a bar to their penetration or elimination by any descriptive/materialist theory.[6] I hope to de-flate the appeal of such moves below.

The second thread concerns the *abstract* na-ture of FP. The central claim of functionalism is that the principles of FP characterize our inter-nal states in a fashion that makes no reference to their intrinsic nature or physical constitution. Rather, they are characterized in terms of the network of causal relations they bear to one an-other, and to sensory circumstances and overt behavior. Given its abstract specification, that internal economy may therefore be realized in a nomically heterogeneous variety of physical systems. All of them may differ, even radically, in their physical constitution, and yet at another level, they will all share the same nature. This view, says Fodor, "is compatible with very strong claims about the ineliminability of men-tal language from behavioral theories."[7] Given the real possibility of multiple instantiations in heterogeneous physical substrates, we cannot eliminate the functional characterization in favor of any theory peculiar to one such sub-strate. That would preclude our being able to de-scribe the (abstract) organization that any one instantiation shares with all the others. A func-tional characterization of our internal states is therefore here to stay.

This second theme, like the first, assigns a faintly stipulative character to FP, as if the onus were on the empirical systems to instantiate faithfully the organization that FP specifies, instead of the onus being on FP to describe faithfully the internal activities of a naturally distinct class of empirical systems. This impres-sion is enhanced by the standard examples used to illustrate the claims of functionalism—mousetraps, valve-lifters, arithmetical calcula-tors, computers, robots, and the like. These are artifacts, constructed to fill a preconceived bill. In such cases, a failure of fit between the physi-cal system and the relevant functional charac-terization impugns only the former, not the lat-ter. The functional characterization is thus removed from empirical criticism in a way that is most unlike the case of an empirical theory. One prominent functionalist—Hilary Putnam—has argued outright that FP is not a corrigible theory at all.[8] Plainly, if FP is construed on these models, as regularly it is, the question of its em-pirical integrity is unlikely ever to pose itself, let alone receive a critical answer.

Although fair to some functionalists, the pre-ceding is not entirely fair to Fodor. On his view the aim of psychology is to find the *best* func-tional characterization of ourselves, and what that is remains an empirical question. As well, his argument for the ineliminability of mental vocabulary from psychology does not pick out current FP in particular as ineliminable. It need claim only that *some* abstract functional charac-terization must be retained, some articulation or refinement of FP perhaps.

His estimate of eliminative materialism re-mains low, however. First, it is plain that Fodor thinks there is nothing fundamentally or inter-estingly wrong with FP. On the contrary, FP's central conception of cognitive activity—as consisting in the manipulation of propositional attitudes—turns up as the central element in Fodor's own theory on the nature of thought (*The Language of Thought,* op. cit.). And sec-ond, there remains the point that, whatever tidy-ing up FP may or may not require, it cannot be displaced by any naturalistic theory of our phys-ical substrate, since it is the abstract functional features of his internal states that make a per-son, not the chemistry of his substrate.

All of this is appealing. But almost none of it, I think, is right. Functionalism has too long en-joyed its reputation as a daring and *avant garde* position. It needs to be revealed for the short-sighted and reactionary position it is.

IV. The Conservative Nature of Functionalism

A valuable perspective on functionalism can be gained from the following story. To begin with, recall the alchemists' theory of inanimate matter. We have here a long and variegated tradition, of course, not a single theory, but our purposes will be served by a gloss.

The alchemists conceived the "inanimate" as entirely continuous with animated matter, in that the sensible and behavioral properties of the various substances are owed to the ensoulment of baser matter by various spirits or essences. These nonmaterial aspects were held to undergo development, just as we find growth and development in the various souls of plants, animals, and humans. The alchemist's peculiar skill lay in knowing how to seed, nourish, and bring to maturity the desired spirits enmattered in the appropriate combinations.

On one orthodoxy, the four fundamental spirits (for "inanimate" matter) were named "mercury," "sulphur," "yellow arsenic," and "sal ammoniac." Each of these spirits was held responsible for a rough but characteristic syndrome of sensible, combinatorial, and causal properties. The spirit mercury, for example, was held responsible for certain features typical of metallic substances—their shininess, liquefiability, and so forth. Sulphur was held responsible for certain residual features typical of metals, and for those displayed by the ores from which running metal could be distilled. Any given metallic substance was a critical orchestration principally of these two spirits. A similar story held for the other two spirits, and among the four of them a certain domain of physical features and transformations was rendered intelligible and controllable.

The degree of control was always limited, of course. Or better, such prediction and control as the alchemists possessed was owed more to the manipulative lore acquired as an apprentice to a master, than to any genuine insight supplied by the theory. The theory followed, more than it dictated, practice. But the theory did supply some rhyme to the practice, and in the absence of a developed alternative it was sufficiently compelling to sustain a long and stubborn tradition.

The tradition had become faded and frag-mented by the time the elemental chemistry of Lavoisier and Dalton arose to replace it for good. But let us suppose that it had hung on a little longer—perhaps because the four-spirit orthodoxy had become a thumb-worn part of everyman's common sense—and let us examine the nature of the conflict between the two theories and some possible avenues of resolution.

No doubt the simplest line of resolution, and the one which historically took place, is outright displacement. The dualistic interpretation of the four essences—as immaterial spirits—will appear both feckless and unnecessary given the power of the corpuscularian taxonomy of atomic chemistry. And a reduction of the old taxonomy to the new will appear impossible, given the extent to which the comparatively toothless old theory cross-classifies things relative to the new. Elimination would thus appear the only alternative—*unless* some cunning and determined defender of the alchemical vision has the wit to suggest the following defense.

Being "ensouled by mercury," or "sulphur," or either of the other two so-called spirits, is actually a *functional* state. The first, for example, is defined by the disposition to reflect light, to liquefy under heat, to unite with other matter in the same state, and so forth. And each of these four states is related to the others, in that the syndrome for each varies as a function of which of the other three states is also instantiated in the same substrate. Thus the level of description comprehended by the alchemical vocabulary is abstract: various material substances, suitably "ensouled," can display the features of a metal, for example, or even of gold specifically. For it is the total syndrome of occurrent and causal properties which matters, not the corpuscularian details of the substrate. Alchemy, it is concluded, comprehends a level of organization in reality distinct from and irreducible to the organization found at the level of corpuscularian chemistry.

This view might have had considerable appeal. After all, it spares alchemists the burden of defending immaterial souls that come and go; it frees them from having to meet the very strong demands of a naturalistic reduction; and it spares them the shock and confusion of outright elimination. Alchemical theory emerges as basically all right! Nor need they appear too obviously stubborn or dogmatic in this. Alchemy as it stands, they concede, may need substantial tidying up, and experience must be our guide. But we need not fear its naturalistic displacement, they remind us, since it is the particular orchestration of the syndromes of occurrent and causal properties which makes a piece of matter gold, not the idiosyncratic details of its corpuscularian substrate. A further circumstance would have made this claim even more plausible. For the fact is, the alchemists *did* know how to make gold, in this relevantly weakened sense of 'gold,' and they could do so in a variety of ways. Their "gold" was never as perfect, alas, as the "gold" nurtured in nature's womb, but what mortal can expect to match the skills of nature herself?

What this story shows is that it is at least possible for the constellation of moves, claims, and defenses characteristic of functionalism to constitute an outrage against reason and truth, and to do so with a plausibility that is frightening. Alchemy is a terrible theory, well-deserving of its complete elimination, and the defense of it just explored is reactionary, obfuscatory, retrograde, and wrong. But in historical context, that defense might have seemed wholly sensible, even to reasonable people.

The alchemical example is a deliberately transparent case of what might well be called "the functionalist strategem," and other cases are easy to imagine. A cracking good defense of the phlogiston theory of combustion can also be constructed along these lines. Construe being highly phlogisticated and being dephlogisticated as functional states defined by certain syndromes of causal dispositions; point to the great variety of natural substrates capable of combustion and calxification; claim an irreducible functional integrity for what has proved to lack any natural integrity; and bury the remaining defects under a pledge to contrive improvements. A similar recipe will provide new life for the four humors of medieval medicine, for the vital essence or archeus of pre-modern biology, and so forth.

If its application in these other cases is any guide, the functionalist strategem is a smokescreen for the preservation of error and confusion. Whence derives our assurance that in contemporary journals the same charade is not being played out on behalf of FP? The parallel with the case of alchemy is in all other respects distressingly complete, right down to the parallel between the search for artificial gold and the search for artificial intelligence!

Let me not be misunderstood on this last point. Both aims are worthy aims: thanks to nuclear physics, artificial (but real) gold is finally within our means, if only in submicroscopic quantities; and artificial (but real) intelligence eventually will be. But just as the careful orchestration of superficial syndromes was the wrong way to produce genuine gold, so may the careful orchestration of superficial syndromes be the wrong way to produce genuine intelligence. Just as with gold, what may be required is that our science penetrate to the underlying *natural* kind that gives rise to the total syndrome directly.

In summary, when confronted with the explanatory impotence, stagnant history, and systematic isolation of the intentional idioms of FP, it is not an adequate or responsive defense to insist that those idioms are abstract, functional, and irreducible in character. For one thing, this same defense could have been mounted with comparable plausibility no matter *what* haywire network of internal states our folklore had ascribed to us. And for another, the defense assumes essentially what is at issue: it assumes that it is the intentional idioms of FP, plus or minus a bit, that express the *important* features shared by all cognitive systems. But they may not. Certainly it is wrong to assume that they do, and then argue against the possibility of a materialistic displacement on grounds that it must describe matters at a level that is different from the important level. This just begs the question in favor of the older framework.

Finally, it is very important to point out that eliminative materialism is strictly *consistent* with the claim that the essence of a cognitive system resides in the abstract functional organization of its internal states. The eliminative materialist is not committed to the idea that the correct account of cognition *must* be a naturalistic account, though he may be forgiven for exploring the possibility. What he does hold is that the correct account of cognition, whether functionalistic or naturalistic, will bear about as much resemblance to FP as modern chemistry bears to four-spirit alchemy.

Let us now try to deal with the argument, against eliminative materialism, from the normative dimension of FP. This can be dealt with rather swiftly, I believe.

First, the fact that the regularities ascribed by the intentional core of FP are predicated on certain logical relations among propositions is not by itself grounds for claiming anything essentially normative about FP. To draw a relevant parallel, the fact that the regularities ascribed by the classical gas law are predicated on arithmetical relations between numbers does not imply anything essentially normative about the classical gas law. And logical relations between propositions are as much an objective matter of abstract fact as are arithmetical relations between numbers. In this respect, the law

(4) (x) (p) (q) [((x believes that p) &
        (x believes that (if p then q)))
        ⊃ (barring confusion, distraction, etc.,
                                x believes that q)]

is entirely on a par with the classical gas law

(6) (x) (P) (V) (μ) [((x has a pressure P) &
        (x has a volume V) & (x has a quantity
        μ)) ⊃ (barring very high pressure or
        density, x has a temperature of
                                $PV/\mu R$)]

A normative dimension enters only because we happen to *value* most of the patterns ascribed by FP. But we do not value all of them. Consider

(7) (x) (p) [((x desires with all his heart that
        p) & (x learns that $\sim p$))
        ⊃ (barring unusual strength of charac-
                                ter, x is shattered that $\sim p$)]

Moreover, and as with normative convictions generally, fresh insight may motivate major changes in what we value.

Second, the laws of FP ascribe to us only a very minimal and truncated rationality, not an ideal rationality as some have suggested. The rationality characterized by the set of all FP laws falls well short of an ideal rationality. This is not surprising. We have no clear or finished conception of ideal rationality anyway; certainly the ordinary man does not. Accordingly, it is just not plausible to suppose that the explanatory failures from which FP suffers are owed primarily to human failure to live up to the ideal standard it provides. Quite to the contrary, the conception of rationality it provides appears limping and superficial, especially when compared with the dialectical complexity of our scientific history, or with the ratiocinative virtuosity displayed by any child.

Third, even if our current conception of rationality—and more generally, of cognitive virtue—is largely constituted within the sentential/propositional framework of FP, there is no guarantee that this framework is adequate to the deeper and more accurate account of cognitive virtue which is clearly needed. Even if we concede the categorial integrity of FP, at least as applied to language-using humans, it remains far from clear that the basic parameters of intellec-tual virtue are to be found at the categorial level comprehended by the propositional attitudes. After all, language use is something that is learned, by a brain already capable of vigorous cognitive activity; language use is acquired as only one among a great variety of learned manipulative skills; and it is mastered by a brain that evolution has shaped for a great many functions, language use being only the very latest and perhaps the least of them. Against the background of these facts, language use appears as an extremely peripheral activity, as a racially idiosyncratic mode of social interaction which is mastered thanks to the versatility and power of a more basic mode of activity. Why accept then, a theory of cognitive activity that models its elements on the elements of human language? And why assume that the fundamental parameters of intellectual virtue are or can be defined over the elements at this superficial level?

A serious advance in our appreciation of cognitive virtue would thus seem to *require* that we go beyond FP, that we transcend the poverty of FP's conception of rationality by transcending its propositional kinematics entirely, by developing a deeper and more general kinematics of cognitive activity, and by distinguishing within this new framework which of the kinematically possible modes of activity are to be valued and encouraged (as more efficient, reliable, productive, or whatever). Eliminative materialism thus does not imply the end of our normative concerns. It implies only that they will have to be reconstituted at a more revealing level of understanding, the level that a matured neuroscience will provide.

What a theoretically informed future might hold in store for us, we shall now turn to explore. Not because we can foresee matters with any special clarity, but because it is important to try to break the grip on our imagination held by the propositional kinematics of FP. As far as the present section is concerned, we may summarize our conclusions as follows. FP is nothing more and nothing less than a culturally entrenched theory of how we and the higher animals work. It has no special features that make it empirically invulnerable, no unique functions that make it irreplaceable, no special status of any kind whatsoever. We shall turn a skeptical ear then, to any special pleading on its behalf.

V. Beyond Folk Psychology

What might the elimination of FP actually involve—not just the comparatively straightforward idioms for sensation, but the entire apparatus of propositional attitudes? That depends heavily on what neuroscience might discover, and on our determination to capitalize on it. Here follow three scenarios in which the operative conception of cognitive activity is progressively divorced from the forms and categories that characterize natural language. If the reader will indulge the lack of actual substance, I shall try to sketch some plausible form.

First suppose that research into the structure and activity of the brain, both fine-grained and global, finally does yield a new kinematics and correlative dynamics for what is now thought of as cognitive activity. The theory is uniform for all terrestrial brains, not just human brains, and it makes suitable conceptual contact with both evolutionary biology and non-equilibrium thermodynamics. It ascribes to us, at any given time, a set or configuration of complex states, which are specified within the theory as figurative "solids" within a four- or five-dimensional phase space. The laws of the theory govern the interaction, motion, and transformation of these "solid" states within that space, and also their relations to whatever sensory and motor transducers the system possesses. As with celestial mechanics, the exact specification of the "solids" involved and the exhaustive accounting of all dynamically relevant adjacent "solids" is not practically possible, for many reasons, but here also it turns out that the obvious approximations we fall back on yield excellent explanations/predictions of internal change and external behavior, at least in the short term. Regarding long-term activity, the theory provides powerful and unified accounts of the learning process, the nature of mental illness, and variations in character and intelligence across the animal kingdom as well as across individual humans.

Moreover, it provides a straightforward account of "knowledge," as traditionally conceived. According to the new theory, any declarative sentence to which a speaker would give confident assent is merely a one-dimensional *projection*—through the compound lens of Wernicke's and Broca's areas onto the idiosyncratic surface of the speaker's language—a one-dimensional projection of a four- or five-dimensional "solid" that is an element in his true kinematical state. (Recall the shadows on the wall of Plato's cave.) Being projections of that inner reality, such sentences do carry significant information regarding it and are thus fit to function as elements in a communication system. On the other hand, being *sub*dimensional

projections, they reflect but a narrow part of the reality projected. They are therefore *un*fit to represent the deeper reality in all its kinematically, dynamically, and even normatively relevant respects. That is to say, a system of propositional attitudes, such as FP, must inevitably fail to capture what is going on here, though it may reflect just enough superficial structure to sustain an alchemylike tradition among folk who lack any better theory. From the perspective of the newer theory, however, it is plain that there simply are no law-governed states of the kind FP postulates. The real laws governing our internal activities are defined over different and much more complex kinematical states and configurations, as are the normative criteria for developmental integrity and intellectual virtue.

A theoretical outcome of the kind just described may fairly be counted as a case of elimination of one theoretical ontology in favor of another, but the success here imagined for systematic neuroscience need not have any sensible effect on common practice. Old ways die hard, and in the absence of some practical necessity, they may not die at all. Even so, it is not inconceivable that some segment of the population, or all of it, should become intimately familiar with the vocabulary required to characterize our kinematical states, learn the laws governing their interactions and behavioral projections, acquire a facility in their first-person ascription, and displace the use of FP altogether, even in the marketplace. The demise of FP's ontology would then be complete.

We may now explore a second and rather more radical possibility. Everyone is familiar with Chomsky's thesis that the human mind or brain contains innately and uniquely the abstract structures for learning and using specifically human natural languages. A competing hypothesis is that our brain does indeed contain innate structures, but that those structures have as their original and still primary function the organization of perceptual experience, the administration of linguistic categories being an acquired and additional function for which evolution has only incidentally suited them.[9] This hypothesis has the advantage of not requiring the evolutionary saltation that Chomsky's view would seem to require, and there are other advantages as well. But these matters need not concern us here. Suppose, for our purposes, that this competing view is true, and consider the following story.

Research into the neural structures that fund the organization and processing of perceptual information reveals that they are capable of administering a great variety of complex tasks, some of them showing a complexity far in excess of that shown by natural language. Natural languages, it turns out, exploit only a very elementary portion of the available machinery, the bulk of which serves far more complex activities beyond the ken of the propositional conceptions of FP. The detailed unraveling of what that machinery is and of the capacities it has makes it plain that a form of language far more sophisticated than "natural" language, though decidedly "alien" in its syntactic and semantic structures, could also be learned and used by our innate systems. Such a novel system of communication, it is quickly realized, could raise the efficiency of information exchange between brains by an order of magnitude, and would enhance epistemic evaluation by a comparable amount, since it would reflect the underlying structure of our cognitive activities in greater detail than does natural language.

Guided by our new understanding of those internal structures, we manage to construct a new system of verbal communication entirely distinct from natural language, with a new and more powerful combinatorial grammar over novel elements forming novel combinations with exotic properties. The compounded strings of this alternative system—call them "übersatzen"—are not evaluated as true or false, nor are the relations between them remotely analogous to the relations of entailment, etc., that hold between sentences. They display a different organization and manifest different virtues.

Once constructed, this "language" proves to be learnable; it has the power projected; and in two generations it has swept the planet. Everyone uses the new system. The syntactic forms and semantic categories of so-called "natural" language disappear entirely. And with them disappear the propositional attitudes of FP, displaced by a more revealing scheme in which (of course) "übersatzenal attitudes" play the leading role. FP again suffers elimination.

This second story, note, illustrates a theme with endless variations. There are possible as many different "folk psychologies" as there are possible differently structured communication systems to serve as models for them.

A third and even stranger possibility can be outlined as follows. We know that there is considerable lateralization of function between the two cerebral hemispheres, and that the two hemispheres make use of the information they get from each other by way of the great cerebral commissure—the corpus callosum—a giant cable of neurons connecting them. Patients whose commissure has been surgically severed display a variety of behavioral deficits that indicate a loss of access by one hemisphere to information it used to get from the other. However, in people with callosal agenesis (a congenital defect in which the connecting cable is simply absent), there is little or no behavioral deficit, suggesting that the two hemisphere have learned to exploit the information carried in other less direct pathways connecting them through the subcortical regions. This suggests that, even in the normal case, a developing hemisphere *learns* to make use of the information the cerebral commissure deposits at its doorstep. What we have then, in the case of a normal human, is two physically distinct cognitive systems (both capable of independent function) responding in a systematic and learned fashion to exchanged information. And what is especially interesting about this case is the sheer amount of information exchanged. The cable of the commissure consists of $\approx$ 200 million neurons,[10] and even if we assume that each of these fibres is capable of one of only two possible states each second (a most conservative estimate), we are looking at a channel whose information capacity is $> 2 \times 10^8$ binary bits/second. Compare this to the $<$ 500 bits/second capacity of spoken English.

Now, if two distinct hemispheres can learn to communicate on so impressive a scale, why shouldn't two distinct brains learn to do it also? This would require an artificial "commissure" of some kind, but let us suppose that we can fashion a workable transducer for implantation at some site in the brain that research reveals to be suitable, a transducer to convert a symphony of neural activity into (say) microwaves radiated from an aerial in the forehead, and to perform the reverse function of converting received microwaves back into neural activation. Connecting it up need not be an insuperable problem. We simply trick the normal processes of dendritic arborization into growing their own myriad connections with the active microsurface of the transducer.

Once the channel is opened between two or more people, they can learn (*learn*) to exchange information and coordinate their behavior with the same intimacy and virtuosity displayed by your own cerebral hemispheres. Think what this might do for hockey teams, and ballet companies, and research teams! If the entire population were thus fitted out, spoken language of any kind might well disappear completely, a victim of the "why crawl when you can fly?" principle. Libraries become filled not with books, but with long recordings of exemplary bouts of neural activity. These constitute a growing cultural heritage, an evolving "Third World," to use Karl Popper's terms. But they do not consist of sentences or arguments.

How will such people understand and conceive of other individuals? To this question I can only answer, "In roughly the same fashion that your right hemisphere 'understands' and 'conceives of' your left hemisphere—intimately and efficiently, but not propositionally!"

These speculations, I hope, will evoke the required sense of untapped possibilities, and I shall in any case bring them to a close here. Their function is to make some inroads into the aura of inconceivability that commonly surrounds the idea that we might reject FP. The felt conceptual strain even finds expression in an argument to the effect that the thesis of eliminative materialism is incoherent since it denies the very conditions presupposed by the assumption that it is meaningful. I shall close with a brief discussion of this very popular move.

As I have received it, the reductio proceeds by pointing out that the statement of eliminative materialism is just a meaningless string of marks or noises, unless that string is the expression of a certain *belief*, and a certain *intention* to communicate, and a *knowledge* of the grammar of the language, and so forth. But if the statement of eliminative materialism is true, then there are no such states to express. The statement at issue would then be a meaningless string of marks or noises. It would therefore *not* be true. Therefore it is not true. Q.E.D.

The difficulty with any nonformal reductio is that the conclusion against the initial assumption is always no better than the material assumptions invoked to reach the incoherent conclusion. In this case the additional assumptions involve a certain theory of meaning, one that presupposes the integrity of FP. But formally speaking, one can as well infer, from the incoherent result, that this theory of meaning is what must be rejected. Given the independent critique of FP leveled earlier, this would even seem the preferred option. But in any case, one cannot simply assume that particular theory of meaning without begging the question at issue, namely, the integrity of FP.

The question-begging nature of this move is most graphically illustrated by the following analogue, which I owe to Patricia Churchland.[11] The issue here, placed in the seventeenth century, is whether there exists such a substance as *vital spirit*. At the time, this substance was held, without significant awareness of real alternatives, to be that which distinguished the animate from the inanimate. Given the monopoly enjoyed by this conception, given the degree to which it was integrated with many of our other conceptions, and given the magnitude of the revisions any serious alternative conception would require, the following refutation of any anti-vitalist claim would be found instantly plausible.

> The anti-vitalist says that there is no such thing as vital spirit. But this claim is self-refuting. The speaker can expect to be taken seriously only if his claim cannot. For if the claim is true, then the speaker does not have vital spirit and must be *dead*. But if he is dead, then his statement is a meaningless string of noises, devoid of reason and truth.

The question-begging nature of this argument does not, I assume, require elaboration. To those moved by the earlier argument, I commend the parallel for examination.

The thesis of this paper may be summarized as follows. The propositional attitudes of folk psychology do not constitute an unbreachable barrier to the advancing tide of neuroscience. On the contrary; the principled displacement of folk psychology is not only richly possible, it represents one of the most intriguing theoretical displacements we can currently imagine.

NOTES

An earlier draft of this paper was presented at the University of Ottawa, and to the *Brain, Mind, and Person* colloquium at SUNY/Oswego. My thanks for the suggestions and criticisms that have informed the present version.

1. See Paul Feyerabend, "Materialism and the Mind–Body Problem," *Review* of *Metaphysics,* XVII.

1, 65 (September 1963):49–66; Richard Rorty, "Mind–Body Identity, Privacy, and Categories," ibid., XIX. 1, 73 (September 1965): 24–54; and my *Scientific Realism and the Plasticity of Mind* (New York: Cambridge, 1979).

2. We shall examine a handful of these laws presently. For a more comprehensive sampling of the laws of

folk psychology, see my *Scientific Realism and Plasticity of Mind,* op. cit., ch. 4. For a detailed examination of the folk principles that underwrite action explanations in particular, see my "The Logical Character of Action Explanations," *Philosophical Review,* LXXIX, 2 (April 1970): 214–36.

3. Staying within an objectual interpretation of the quantifiers, perhaps the simplest way to make systematic sense of expressions like ⌜*x* believes that *p*⌝ and closed sentences formed therefrom is just to construe whatever occurs in the nested position held by '*p*', '*q*', etc. as there having the function of a singular term. Accordingly, the standard connectives, as they occur between terms in that nested position, must be construed as there functioning as operators that form compound singular terms from other singular terms, and not as sentence operators. The compound singular terms so formed denote the appropriate compound propositions. Substitutional quantification will of course underwrite a different interpretation, and there are other approaches as well. Especially appealing is the prosentential approach of Dorothy Grover, Joseph Camp, and Nuel Belnap, "A Prosentential Theory of Truth," *Philosophical Studies,* XXVII, 2 (February 1975): 73–125. But the resolution of these issues is not vital to the present discussion.

4. A possible response here is to insist that the cognitive activity of animals and infants is linguaformal in its elements, structures, and processing right from birth. J. A. Fodor, in *The Language of Thought* (New York: Crowell 1975), has erected a positive theory of thought on the assumption that the innate forms of cognitive activity have precisely the form here denied. For a critique of Fodor's view, see Patricia Churchland, "Fodor on Language Learning," *Synthese,* XXXVIII, 1 (May 1978): 149–59.

5. Most explicitly in "Three Kinds of Intentional Psychology" in R. Healey, ed., *Reduction, Time, and Reality* (Cambridge, 1981), pp. 37–61, but this theme of Dennett's goes all the way back to his "Intentional Systems," *The Journal of Philosophy,* LXVIII, 4 (Feb. 25, 1971): 87–106; reprinted in his *Brainstorms* (Montgomery, Vt.: Bradford Books, 1978).

6. Popper, *Objective Knowledge* (New York: Oxford, 1972); with J. Eccles, *The Self and Its Brain* (New York: Springer Verlag, 1978). Margolis, *Persons and Minds* (Boston: Reidel, 1978).

7. *Psychological Explanation* (New York: Random House, 1968) p. 116.

8. "Robots: Machines or Artificially Created Life?", *The Journal of Philosophy,* LXI, 21 (Nov. 12, 1964): 668–91, pp. 675, 681 ff.

9. Richard Gregory defends such a view in "The Grammar of Vision," *Listener,* LXXXIII, 2133 (February 1970): 242–46; reprinted in his *Concepts and Mechanisms of Perception* (London: Duckworth, 1975), pp. 622–29.

10. M. S. Gazzaniga and J. E. LeDoux, *The Integrated Mind* (New York: Plenum Press, 1975).

11. "Is Determinism Self-Refuting?", *Mind* 90:99–101, 1981.

54 | The Meaning of "Meaning"
Hilary Putnam

Meaning and Extension

. . . Since the Middle Ages at least, writers on the theory of meaning have purported to discover an ambiguity in the ordinary concept of meaning, and have introduced a pair of terms—*extension* and *intension,* or *Sinn* and *Bedeutung,* or whatever—to disambiguate the notion. The *extension* of a term, in customary logical parlance, is simply the set of things the term is true of. Thus, "rabbit," in its most common English sense, is true of all and only rabbits, so the extension of "rabbit" is precisely the set of rabbits. Even this notion—and it is the *least* problematical notion in this cloudy subject—has its problems, however. Apart from problems it inherits from its parent notion of *truth,* the foregoing example of "rabbit" *in its most common English sense* illustrates one such problem: strictly speaking, it is not a term, but an ordered pair consisting of a term and a "sense" (or an occasion of use, or something else that distinguishes a term in one sense from the same term used in a different sense) that has an extension. Another problem is this: a "set," in the mathematical sense, is a "yes–no" object; any given object either definitely belongs to S or definitely does not belong to S, if S is a set. But words in a natural language are not generally "yes–no": there are things of which the description "tree" is clearly true and things of which the description "tree" is clearly false, to be sure, but there are a host of borderline cases. Worse, the line between the clear cases and the borderline cases is itself fuzzy. Thus the idealization involved in the notion of *extension*—the idealization involved in supposing that there is such a thing as the set of things of which the term "tree" is true—is actually very severe.

Recently some mathematicians have investigated the notion of a *fuzzy set*— that is, of an object to which other things belong or do not belong with a given probability or to a given degree, rather than belong "yes–no." If one really wanted to formalize the notion of extension as applied to terms in a natural language, it would be necessary to employ "fuzzy sets" or something similar rather than sets in the classical sense.

The problem of a word's having more than one sense is standardly handled by treating each of the senses as a different word (or rather, by treating the word as if it carried invisible subscripts, thus: "rabbit$_1$"—animal of a certain kind; "rabbit$_2$"—coward; and as if "rabbit$_1$" and "rabbit$_2$" or whatever were different words entirely). This again involves two very severe idealizations (at least two, that is): supposing that words have discretely many senses, and supposing that the entire repertoire of senses is fixed once and for all. Paul Ziff has recently investigated the extent to which both of these suppositions distort the actual situation in natural language;[1] nevertheless, we will continue to make these idealizations here.

Now consider the compound terms "creature with a heart" and "creature with a kidney." Assuming that every creature with a heart possesses a kidney and vice versa, the extension of these two terms is exactly the same. But they obviously differ in meaning. Supposing that there is a sense of "meaning" in which meaning = extension, there must be another sense of "meaning" in which the meaning of a term is not its extension but something else, say the "concept" associated with the term. Let us call this "something else" the *intension* of the term. The concept of a creature with a heart is clearly a different concept from the concept of a creature with a kidney. Thus the two terms have different intension. When we say they have different "meaning," meaning = intension.

Intension and Extension

Something like the preceding paragraph appears in every standard exposition of the notions "intension" and "extension." But it is not at all satisfactory. Why it is not satisfactory is, in a sense, the burden of this entire essay. But some points can be made at the very outset: first of all, what evidence is there that "extension" is a sense of the word "meaning"? The canonical explanation of the notions "intension" and "extension" is very much like "in one sense 'meaning' means *extension* and in the other sense 'meaning' means *meaning*." The fact is that while the notion of "extension" is made quite precise, relative to the fundamental logical notion of *truth* (and under the severe idealizations remarked above), the notion of intension is made no more precise than the vague (and, as we shall see, misleading) notion "concept." It is as if someone explained the notion "probability" by saying: "in one sense 'probability' means frequency, and in the other sense it means *propensity*." "Probability" *never* means "frequency," and "propensity" is at least as unclear as "probability."

Unclear as it is, the traditional doctrine that the notion "meaning" possesses the extension/intension ambiguity has certain typical consequences. Most traditional philosophers thought of concepts as something *mental*. Thus the doctrine that the meaning of a term (the meaning "in the sense of intension," that is) is a concept carried the implication that meanings are mental entities. Frege and more recently Carnap and his followers, however, rebelled against this "psychologism," as they termed it. Feeling that meanings are *public* property—that the *same* meaning can be "grasped" by more than one person and by persons at different times—they identified concepts (and hence "intensions" or meanings) with abstract entities rather than mental entities. However, "grasping" these abstract entities was still an individual psychological act. None of these philosophers doubted that understanding a word (knowing its intension) was just a matter of being in a certain psychological state (somewhat in the way in which knowing how to factor numbers in one's head is just a matter of being in a certain very complex psychological state).

Second, the timeworn example of the two terms "creature with a kidney" and "creature with a heart" does show that two terms can have the same extension and yet differ in intension. But it was taken to be obvious that the reverse is impossible: two terms cannot differ in extension and have the same intension. Interestingly, no argument for this impossibility was ever offered. Probably it reflects the tradition of the ancient and medieval philosophers who assumed that the concept corresponding to a term was just a conjunction of predicates, and hence that the concept corresponding to a term must *always* provide a necessary and sufficient condition for falling into the extension of the term.[2] For philosophers like Carnap, who accepted the verifiability theory of meaning, the concept corresponding to a term provided (in the ideal case, where the term had "complete meaning") a *criterion* for belonging to the extension (not just in the sense of "necessary and sufficient condition," but in the strong sense of *way of recognizing* if a given thing falls into the extension or not). Thus these positivistic philosophers were perfectly happy to retain the traditional view on this point. So, theory of meaning came to rest on two unchallenged assumptions:

I. That knowing the meaning of a term is just a matter of being in a certain psychological state (in the sense of "psychological state," in which states of memory and psychological dispositions are "psychological states"; no one thought that knowing the meaning of a word was a continuous state of consciousness, of course).

II. That the meaning of a term (in the sense of "intension") determines its extension (in the sense that sameness of intension entails sameness of extension).

I shall argue that these two assumptions are not jointly satisfied by *any* notion, let alone any notion of meaning. The traditional concept of meaning is a concept which rests on a false theory.

"Psychological State" and Methodological Solipsism

In order to show this, we need first to clarify the traditional notion of a psychological state. In one sense a state is simply a two-place predicate whose arguments are an individual and a time. In this sense, *being 5 feet tall, being in pain, knowing the alphabet,* and even *being a thousand miles from Paris* are all states. (Note that the *time* is usually left implicit or "contextual"; the full form of an atomic sentence of these predicates would be "x *is five feet tall at time* t," "x *is in pain at time* t," etc.) In science, however, it is customary to restrict the term state to properties which are defined in terms of the parameters of the individual which are fundamental from the point of view of the given science. Thus, being five feet tall is a state (from the point of view of physics); being in pain is a state (from the point of view of mentalistic psychology, at least); knowing the alphabet might be a state (from the point of view of cognitive psychology), although it is hard to say; but being a thousand miles from Paris would *not* naturally be called a *state.* In one sense, a psychological state is simply a state which is studied or described by psychology. In this sense it may be trivially true that, say *knowing the meaning of the word "water"* is a "psychological state" (viewed from the standpoint of cognitive psychology). But this is not the sense of psychological state that is at issue in the above assumption (I).

When traditional philosophers talked about psychological states (or "mental" states), they made an assumption which we may call the assumption of methodological solipsism. This assumption is the assumption that no psychological state, properly so called, presupposes the existence of any individual other than the subject to whom that state is ascribed. (In fact, the assumption was that no psychological state presupposes the existence of the subject's *body* even: if *P* is a psychological state, properly so called, then it must be logically possible for a "disembodied mind" to be in *P.*) This assumption is pretty explicit in Descartes, but it is implicit in just about the whole of traditional philosophical psychology. Making this assumption is, of course, adopting a *restrictive program*—a program which deliberately limits the scope and nature of psychology to fit certain mentalistic preconceptions or, in some cases, to fit an idealistic reconstruction of knowledge and the world. Just *how* restrictive the program is, however, often goes unnoticed. Such common or garden variety psychological states as *being jealous* have to be reconstructed, for example, if the assumption of methodological solipsism is retained. For, in its ordinary use, *x is jealous of y* entails that *y* exists, and *x is jealous of y's regard for z* entails that both *y* and *z* exist (as well

as *x,* of course). Thus *being jealous* and *being jealous of someone's regard for someone else* are not psychological states permitted by the assumption of methodological solipsism. (We shall call them "psychological states in the wide sense" and refer to the states which are permitted by methodological solipsism as "psychological states in the narrow sense.") The reconstruction required by methodological solipsism would be to reconstrue *jealousy* so that I can be jealous of my own hallucinations, or of figments of my imagination, etc. Only if we assume that psychological states in the narrow sense have a significant degree of causal closure (so that restricting ourselves to psychological states in the narrow sense will facilitate the statement of psychological *laws*) is there any point in engaging in this reconstruction, or in making the assumption of methodological solipsism. But the three centuries of failure of mentalistic psychology is tremendous evidence against this procedure, in my opinion.

Be that as it may, we can now state more precisely what we claimed at the end of the preceding section. Let *A* and *B* be any two terms which differ in extension. By assumption (II) they must differ in meaning (in the sense of "intension"). By assumption (I), *knowing the meaning of A* and *knowing the meaning of B* are psychological states *in the narrow sense*—for this is how we shall construe assumption (I). *But these psychological states must determine the extension of the terms A and B just as much as the meanings ("intensions") do.*

To see this, let us try assuming the opposite. Of course, there cannot be two terms *A* and *B* such that *knowing the meaning of A* is the same state as *knowing the meaning of B* even though *A* and *B* have different extensions. For *knowing the meaning of A* isn't just "grasping the intension" of *A,* whatever that may come to; it is also knowing that the "intension" that one has "grasped" *is* the intension of *A.* Thus, someone who knows the meaning of "wheel" presumably "grasps the intension" of its German synonym *Rad;* but if he doesn't know that the "intension" in question is the intension of Rad he isn't said to "know the meaning of Rad." If *A* and *B* are different terms, then *knowing the meaning of A* is a different state from *knowing the meaning of B* whether the meanings of *A* and *B* be themselves the same or different. But by the same argument, if I_1 and I_2 are different *intensions* and *A* is a term, then *knowing that* I_1 *is the meaning of A* is a different psychological state from *knowing that* I_2 *is the meaning of A.* Thus, there cannot be two different logically possible worlds L_1 and L_2 such that, say, Oscar is in the *same* psychological state (in the narrow sense) in L_1 and in L_2 (in all respects), but in L_1 Oscar understands A as having the meaning I_1 and in L_2 Oscar understands A as having the meaning I_2. (For, if there were, then in L_1 Oscar would be in the psychological state *knowing that* I_1 *is the meaning of A* and in L_2 Oscar would be in the psychological state *knowing that* I_2 *is the meaning of A,* and these are different and even—assuming that A has just *one* meaning for Oscar in each world—incompatible psychological states in the narrow sense.)

In short, if S is the sort of psychological state we have been discussing—a psychological state of the form *knowing that* I *is the meaning of A,* where I is an "intension" and A is a term—then the *same* necessary and sufficient condition for falling into the extension of A "works" in *every* logically possible world in which the speaker is in the psychological state S. For the state S *determines* the intension $I,$ and by assumption (II) the intension amounts to a necessary and sufficient condition for membership in the *extension.*

If our interpretation of the traditional doctrine of intension and extension is fair to Frege and Carnap, then the whole psychologism/Platonism issue appears somewhat a tempest in a teapot, as far as meaning-theory is concerned. (Of course, it is a very important issue as far as general philosophy of mathematics is concerned.) For even if meanings are "Platonic" entities rather than "mental" entities on the Frege–Carnap view, "grasping" those entities is presumably a psychological state (in the narrow sense). Moreover, the psychological state uniquely determines the "Platonic" entity. So whether one takes the "Platonic" entity or the psychological state as the "meaning" would appear to be somewhat a matter of convention. And taking the psychological state to be the meaning would hardly have the consequence that Frege feared, that meanings would cease to be public. For psychological states are "public" in the sense that different people (and even people in different epochs) can be in the *same* psychological state. Indeed, Frege's argument against psychologism is only an argument against identifying concepts with mental particulars, not with mental entities in general.

The "public" character of psychological states entails, in particular, that if Oscar and Elmer understand a word A differently, then they must be in different psychological states. For the state of *knowing the intension of A to be, say,* I is the *same* state whether Oscar or Elmer be in it. Thus two speakers cannot be in the same psychological state in all respects and understand the term A differently; the psychological state of the speaker determines the intension (and hence, by assumption (II), the extension) of A.

It is this last consequence of the joint assumptions (I), (II) that we claim to be false. We claim that it is possible for two speakers to be in exactly the *same* psychological state (in the narrow sense), even though the extension of the term A in the idiolect of the one is different from the extension of the term A in the idiolect of the other. Extension is not determined by psychological state.

This will be shown in detail in later sections. If this is right, then there are two courses open to one who wants to rescue at least one of the traditional assumptions; to give up the idea that psychological state (in the narrow sense) determines *intension,* or to give up the idea that intension determines extension. We shall consider these alternatives later.

Are Meanings in the Head?

That psychological state does not determine extension will now be shown with the aid of a little science-fiction. For the purpose of the following science-fiction examples, we shall suppose that somewhere in the galaxy there is a planet we shall call Twin Earth. Twin Earth is very much like Earth; in fact, people on Twin Earth even speak *English.* In fact, apart from the differences we shall specify in our science-fiction examples, the reader may suppose that Twin Earth is *exactly* like Earth. He may even suppose that he has a *Doppelgänger*—an identical copy—on Twin Earth, if he wishes, although my stories will not depend on this.

Although some of the people on Twin Earth (say, the ones who call themselves "Americans" and the ones who call themselves "Canadians" and the ones who call themselves "Englishmen," etc.) speak English, there are, not surprisingly, a few tiny differences which we will now describe between the dialects of English spoken on Twin Earth and Standard English. These differences themselves depend on some of the peculiarities of Twin Earth.

One of the peculiarities of Twin Earth is that the liquid called "water" is not H_2O but a different liquid whose chemical formula is very long and complicated. I shall abbreviate this chemical formula simply as XYZ. I shall suppose that XYZ is indistinguishable from water at normal temperatures and pressures. In particular, it tastes like water and it quenches thirst like water. Also, I shall suppose that the oceans and lakes and seas of Twin Earth contain XYZ and not water, that it rains XYZ on Twin Earth and not water, etc.

If a spaceship from Earth ever visits Twin Earth, then the supposition at first will be that "water" has the same meaning on Earth and on Twin Earth. This supposition will be corrected when it is discovered that "water" on Twin Earth is XYZ, and the Earthian spaceship will report somewhat as follows:

"On Twin Earth the word 'water' means XYZ."

(It is this sort of use of the word "means" which accounts for the doctrine that extension is one sense of "meaning," by the way. But note that although "means" does mean something like *has as extension* in this example, one would *not* say

"On Twin Earth the meaning of the word 'water' is XYZ."

unless, possibly, the fact that "water is XYZ" was known to every adult speaker of English on Twin Earth. We can account for this in terms of the theory of meaning we develop below; for the moment we just remark that although the verb "means" sometimes means "has as extension," the nominalization "meaning" *never* means "extension.")

Symmetrically, if a spaceship from Twin Earth ever visits Earth, then the supposition at first will be that the word "water" has the same meaning on Twin Earth and on Earth. This supposition will be corrected when it is discovered that "water" on Earth is H_2O, and the Twin Earthian spaceship will report

"On Earth[3] the word 'water' means H_2O."

Note that there is no problem about the extension of the term "water." The word simply has two different meanings (as we say) in the sense in which it is used on Twin Earth, the sense of water$_{TE}$, what *we* call "water" simply isn't water; while in the sense in which it is used on Earth, the sense of water$_E$, what the Twin Earthians call "water" simply isn't water. The extension of "water" in the sense of water$_E$ is the set

of all wholes consisting of H_2O molecules, or something like that; the extension of water in the sense of water$_{TE}$ is the set of all wholes consisting of XYZ molecules, or something like that.

Now let us roll the time back to about 1750. At that time chemistry was not developed on either Earth or Twin Earth. The typical Earthian speaker of English did not know water consisted of hydrogen and oxygen, and the typical Twin Earthian speaker of English did not know "water" consisted of XYZ. Let Oscar$_1$ be such a typical Earthian English speaker, and let Oscar$_2$ be his counterpart on Twin Earth. You may suppose that there is no belief that Oscar$_1$ had about water that Oscar$_2$ did not have about "water." If you like, you may even suppose that Oscar$_1$ and Oscar$_2$ were exact duplicates in appearance, feelings, thoughts, interior monologue, etc. Yet the extension of the term "water" was just as much H_2O on Earth in 1750 as in 1950; and the extension of the term "water" was just as much XYZ on Twin Earth in 1750 as in 1950. Oscar$_1$ and Oscar$_2$ understood the term "water" differently in 1750 *although they were in the same psychological state,* and although, given the state of science at the time, it would have taken their scientific communities about fifty years to discover that they understood the term "water" differently. Thus the extension of the term "water" (and, in fact, its "meaning" in the intuitive preanalytical usage of that term) is *not* a function of the psychological state of the speaker by itself.

But, it might be objected, why should we accept it that the term "water" has the same extension in 1750 and in 1950 (on both Earths)? The logic of natural-kind terms like "water" is a complicated matter, but the following is a sketch of an answer. Suppose I point to a glass of water and say "this liquid is called water" (or "this is called water," if the marker "liquid" is clear from the context). My "ostensive definition" of water has the following empirical presupposition that the body of liquid I am pointing to bears a certain sameness relation (say, *x is the same liquid as y,* or *x is the same$_L$* as y) to most of the stuff I and other speakers in my linguistic community have on other occasions called "water." If this presupposition is false because, say, I am without knowing it pointing to a glass of gin and not a glass of water, then I do not intend my ostensive definition to be accepted. Thus the ostensive definition conveys what might be called a defeasible necessary and sufficient condition: the necessary and sufficient condition for being water is bearing the relation same$_L$ to the stuff in the glass; but this is the necessary and sufficient condition only if the empirical presupposition is satisfied. If it is not satisfied, then one of a series of, so to speak, "fallback" conditions becomes activated.

The key point is that the relation same$_L$ is a *theoretical* relation whether something is or is not the same liquid as *this* may take an indeterminate amount of scientific investigation to determine. Moreover, even if a "definite" answer has been obtained either through scientific investigation or through the application of some "common sense" test, the answer is *defeasible:* future investigation might reverse even the most "certain" example. Thus, the fact that an English speaker in 1750 might have called *XYZ* "water," while he or his successors would not have called *XYZ* water in 1800 or 1850 does not mean that the "meaning" of "water" changed for the average speaker in the interval. In 1750 or in 1850 or in 1950 one might have pointed to, say, the liquid in Lake Michigan as an example of "water." What changed was that in 1750 we would have mistakenly thought that *XYZ* bore the relation same$_L$ to the liquid in Lake Michigan, while in 1800 or 1850 we would have known that it did not (I am ignoring the fact that the liquid in Lake Michigan was only dubiously water in 1950, of course).

Let us now modify our science-fiction story. I do not know whether one can make pots and pans out of molybdenum; and if one can make them out of molybdenum, I don't know whether they could be distinguished easily from aluminum pots and pans (I don't know any of this even though I have acquired the word "molybdenum.") So I shall suppose that molybdenum pots and pans *can't* be distinguished from aluminum pots and pans save by an expert. (To emphasize the point, I repeat that this could be true for all I know, and *a fortiori* it could be true for all I know by virtue of "knowing the meaning" of the words *aluminum* and *molybdenum.*) We will now suppose that molybdenum is as common on Twin Earth as aluminum is on Earth, and that aluminum is as rare on Twin Earth as molybdenum is on Earth. In particular, we shall assume that "aluminum" pots and pans are made of molybdenum on Twin Earth. Finally, we shall assume that the words "aluminum" and "molybdenum" are *switched* on Twin Earth: "aluminum" is the name of *molybdenum* and "molybdenum" is the name of *aluminum.*

This example shares some features with the previous one. If a spaceship from Earth visited Twin Earth, the visitors from Earth probably would not suspect that the "aluminum" pots and pans on Twin Earth were not made of aluminum, especially when the Twin Earthians *said* they were. But there is one important difference between the two cases. An Earthian metallurgist could tell very easily that "aluminum" was molybdenum, and a Twin Earthian metallurgist could tell equally easily that aluminum was "molybdenum." (The shudder quotes in the preceding sentence indicate Twin Earthian usages.) Whereas in 1750 no one on either Earth or Twin Earth could have distinguished water from "water," the confusion of aluminum with "aluminum" involves only a part of the linguistic communities involved.

The example makes the same point as the preceding one. If Oscar$_1$ and Oscar$_2$ are standard speakers of Earthian English and Twin Earthian English respectively, and neither is chemically or metallurgically sophisticated, then there may be no difference at all in their psychological state when they use the word "aluminum"; nevertheless we have to say that "aluminum" has the extension *aluminum* in the idiolect of Oscar$_1$ and the extension *molybdenum* in the idiolect of Oscar$_2$. (Also we have to say that Oscar$_1$ and Oscar$_2$ mean different things by "aluminum," that "aluminum" has a different meaning on Earth than it does on Twin Earth, etc.) Again we see that the psychological state of the speaker does *not* determine the extension (*or* the "meaning," speaking preanalytically) of the word.

Before discussing this example further, let me introduce a *non*-science-fiction example. Suppose you are like me and cannot tell an elm from a beech tree. We still say that the extension of "elm" in my idiolect is the same as the extension of "elm" in anyone else's, viz., the set of all elm trees, and that the set of all beech trees is the extension of "beech" in *both* of our idiolects. Thus "elm" in my idiolect has a different extension from "beech" in your idiolect (as it should). Is it really credible that this difference in extension is brought about by some difference in our *concepts?* My concept of an elm tree is exactly the same as my concept of a beech tree (I blush to confess). (This shows that the identification of meaning "in the sense of intension" with *concept* cannot be correct, by the way.) If someone heroically attempts to maintain that the difference between the extension of "elm" and the extension of "beech" in *my* idiolect is explained by a difference in my psychological state, then we can always refute him by constructing a "Twin

Earth" example—just let the words "elm" and "beech" be switched on Twin Earth (the way "aluminum" and "molybdenum" were in the previous example). Moreover, I suppose I have a *Doppelgänger* on Twin Earth who is molecule for molecule "identical" with me (in the sense in which two neckties can be "identical"). If you are a dualist, then also suppose my *Doppelgänger* thinks the same verbalized thoughts I do, has the same sense data, the same dispositions, etc. It is absurd to think *his* psychological state is one bit different from mine: yet he "means" *beech* when he says "elm" and *I* "mean" *elm* when I say elm. Cut the pie any way you like, "meanings" just ain't in the *head!*

A Sociolinguistic Hypothesis

The last two examples depend upon a fact about language that seems, surprisingly, never to have been pointed out: that there is *division of linguistic labor.* We could hardly use such words as "elm" and "aluminum" if no one possessed a way of recognizing elm trees and aluminum metal; but not everyone to whom the distinction is important has to be able to make the distinction. Let us shift the example: consider *gold.* Gold is important for many reasons: it is a precious metal, it is a monetary metal, it has symbolic value (it is important to most people that the "gold" wedding ring they wear *really* consist of gold and not just *look* gold), etc. Consider our community as a "factory": in this "factory" some people have the "job" of *wearing gold wedding rings,* other people have the "job" of *selling gold wedding rings,* still other people have the "job" of *telling whether or not something is really gold.* It is not at all necessary or efficient that everyone who wears a gold ring (or a gold cufflink, etc.), or discusses the "gold standard," etc., engage in buying and selling gold. Nor is it necessary or efficient that everyone who buys and sells gold be able to tell whether or not something is really gold in a society where this form of dishonesty is uncommon (selling fake gold) and in which one can easily consult an expert in case of doubt. And it is *certainly* not necessary or efficient that everyone who has occasion to buy or wear gold be able to tell with any reliability whether or not something is really gold.

The foregoing facts are just examples of mundane division of labor (in a wide sense). But they engender a division of linguistic labor: everyone to whom gold is important for any rea-

son has to *acquire* the word "gold"; but he does not have to acquire the *method of recognizing* if something is or is not gold. He can rely on a special subclass of speakers. The features that are generally thought to be present in connection with a general name—necessary and sufficient conditions for membership in the extension, ways of recognizing if something is in the extension ("criteria"), etc.—are all present in the linguistic community *considered as a collective body;* but that collective body divides the "labor" of knowing and employing these various parts of the "meaning" of "gold."

This division of linguistic labor rests upon and presupposes the division of *non*linguistic labor, of course. If only the people who know how to tell if some metal is really gold or not have any reason to have the word "gold" in their vocabulary, then the word "gold" will be as the word "water" was in 1750 with respect to that subclass of speakers, and the other speakers just won't acquire it at all. And some words do not exhibit any division of linguistic labor: "chair," for example. But with the increase of division of labor in the society and the rise of science, more and more words begin to exhibit this kind of division of labor. "Water," for example, did not exhibit it at all prior to the rise of chemistry. Today it is obviously necessary for every speaker to be able to recognize water (reliably under normal conditions), and probably every adult speaker even knows the necessary and sufficient condition "water is H_2O," but only a few adult speakers could distinguish water from liquids which superficially resembled water. In case of doubt, other speakers would rely on the judgement of these "expert" speakers. Thus the way of recognizing possessed by these "expert" speakers is also, through them, possessed by the collective linguistic body, even though it is not possessed by each individual member of the body, and in this way the most recherché fact about water may become part of the *social* meaning of the word while being unknown to almost all speakers who acquire the word.

It seems to me that this phenomenon of division of linguistic labor is one which it will be very important for sociolinguistics to investigate. In connection with it, I should like to propose the following hypothesis:

HYPOTHESIS OF THE UNIVERSALITY OF THE DIVISION OF LINGUISTIC LABOR: Every linguistic community exemplifies the sort of division of linguistic labor just described: that is, possesses at least some terms whose associated "criteria" are known only to a subset of the speakers who acquire the terms, and whose use by the other speakers depends upon a structured cooperation between them and the speakers in the relevant subsets.

It would be of interest, in particular, to discover if extremely primitive peoples were sometimes exceptions to this hypothesis (which would indicate that the division of linguistic labor is a product of social evolution), or if even they exhibit it. In the latter case, one might conjecture that division of labor, including linguistic labor, is a fundamental trait of our species.

It is easy to see how this phenomenon accounts for some of the examples given above of the failure of the assumptions (I), (II). Whenever a term is subject to the division of linguistic labor, the "average" speaker who acquires it does not acquire anything that fixes its extension. In particular, his individual psychological state *certainly* does not fix its extension; it is only the sociolinguistic state of the collective linguistic body to which the speaker belongs that fixes the extension.

We may summarize this discussion by pointing out that there are two sorts of tools in the world: there are tools like a hammer or a screwdriver which can be used by one person; and there are tools like a steamship which require the cooperative activity of a number of persons to use. Words have been thought of too much on the model of the first sort of tool.

Indexicality and Rigidity[4]

The first of our science-fiction examples—"water" on Earth and on Twin Earth in 1750—does not involve division of linguistic labor, or at least does not involve it in the same way the examples of "aluminum" and "elm" do. There were not (in our story, anyway) any "experts" on water on Earth in 1750, nor any experts on "water" on Twin Earth. (The example *can* be construed as involving division of labor *across time,* however. I shall not develop this method of treating the example here.) The example *does* involve things which are of fundamental importance to the theory of reference and also to the theory of necessary truth, which we shall now discuss.

There are two obvious ways of telling someone what one means by a natural-kind term such as "water" or "tiger" or "lemon." One can give him a so-called ostensive definition—"this (liquid) is water"; "this (animal) is a tiger"; "this

(fruit) is a lemon"; where the parentheses are meant to indicate that the "markers" *liquid, animal, fruit,* may be either explicit or implicit. Or one can give him a *description*. In the latter case the description one gives typically consists of one or more markers together with a *stereotype*[5]—a standardized description of features of the kind that are typical, or "normal," or at any rate stereotypical. The central features of the stereotype generally are *criteria*—features which in normal situations constitute ways of recognizing if a thing belongs to the kind or, at least, necessary conditions (or probabilistic necessary conditions) for membership in the kind. Not all criteria used by the linguistic community as a collective body are included in the stereotype, and in some cases the stereotypes may be quite weak. Thus (unless I am a very atypical speaker), the stereotype of an elm is just that of a common deciduous tree. These features are indeed necessary conditions for membership in the kind (I mean "necessary" in a loose sense; I don't think "elm trees are deciduous" is *analytic*), but they fall far short of constituting a way of recognizing elms. On the other hand, the stereotype of a tiger does enable one to recognize tigers (unless they are albino, or some other atypical circumstance is present), and the stereotype of a lemon generally enables one to recognize lemons. In the extreme case, the stereotype may be *just* the marker: the stereotype of molybdenum might be *just* that molybdenum is a *metal.* Let us consider both of these ways of introducing a term into someone's vocabulary.

Suppose I point to a glass of liquid and say "*this* is water," in order to teach someone the word "water." We have already described some of the empirical presuppositions of this act, and the way in which this kind of meaning-explanation is defeasible. Let us now try to clarify further how it is supposed to be taken.

In what follows, we shall take the notion of "possible world" as primitive. We do this because we feel that in several senses the notion makes sense and is scientifically important even if it needs to be made more precise. We shall assume further that in at least some cases it is possible to speak of the same individual as existing in more than one possible world.[6] Our discussion leans heavily on the work of Saul Kripke, although the conclusions were obtained independently.

Let W_1 and W_2 be two possible worlds in which I exist and in which this glass exists and in which I am giving a meaning explanation by pointing to this glass and saying "this is water." (We do *not* assume that the *liquid* in the glass is the same in both worlds.) Let us suppose that in W_1 the glass is full of H_2O and in W_2 the glass is full of *XYZ*. We shall also suppose that W_1 is the actual world and that *XYZ* is the stuff typically called "water" in the world W_2 (so that the relation between English speakers in W_1 and English speakers in W_2 is exactly the same as the relation between English speakers on Earth and English speakers on Twin Earth). Then there are two theories one might have concerning the meaning of "water":

1. One might hold that "water" was *world-relative* but *constant* in meaning (i.e., the word has a *constant relative meaning*). In this theory, "water" *means the same* in W_1 and W_2; it's just that water is H_2O in W_1 and water is *XYZ* in W_2.
2. One might hold that water is H_2O in all worlds (the stuff called "water" in W_2 isn't water), but "water" doesn't have the same meaning in W_1 and W_2.

If what was said before about the Twin Earth case was correct, then (2) is clearly the correct theory. When I say *"this* (liquid) is water," the "this" is, so to speak, a *de re* "this"—i.e., the force of my explanation is that "water" is whatever bears a certain equivalence relation (the relation we called "same$_L$" above) to the piece of liquid referred to as "this" *in the actual world.*

We might symbolize the difference between the two theories as a "scope" difference in the following way. In theory (1), the following is true:

(1′) (For every world *W*) (For every *x* in *W*) (*x* is water $\equiv$ *x* bears same$_L$ to the entity referred to as "this" in *W*)

while on theory (2):

(2′) (For every world *W*) (For every *x* in *W*) (*x* is water $\equiv$ *x* bears same$_L$ to the entity referred to as "this" *in the actual world* W_1).

(I call this a "scope" difference because in (1′) "the entity referred to as 'this' " is within the scope of "For every world *W*"—as the qualifying phrase "in *W*" makes explicit, whereas in (2′) "the entity referred to as 'this' " means "the entity referred to as 'this' *in the actual world,"* and has thus a reference *independent* of the bound variable "*W*.")

Kripke calls a designator "rigid" (in a given sentence) if (in that sentence) it refers to the same individual in every possible world in which the designator designates. If we extend the notion of rigidity to substance names, then we may express Kripke's theory and mine by saying that the term "water" is *rigid*.

The rigidity of the term "water" follows from the fact that when I give the ostensive definition *"this* (liquid) is water" I intend (2′) and not (1′).

We may also say, following Kripke, that when I give the ostensive definition "this (liquid) is water," the demonstrative "this" is *rigid*.

What Kripke was the first to observe is that this theory of the meaning (or "use," or whatever) of the word "water" (and other natural-kind terms as well) has startling consequences for the theory of necessary truth.

To explain this, let me introduce the notion of a *cross-world relation*. A two term relation *R* will be called *cross-world* when it is understood in such a way that its extension is a set of ordered pairs of individuals *not all in the same possible world*. For example, it is easy to understand the relation *same height as* as a cross-world relation: just understand it so that, e.g., if *x* is an individual in a world W_1 who is five feet tall (in W_1) and *y* is an individual in W_2 who is five feet tall (in W_2), then the ordered pair *x, y* belongs to the extension of *same height as.* (Since an individual may have different heights in different possible worlds in which that same individual exists, strictly speaking it is not the ordered pair *x, y* that constitutes an element of the extension of *same height as,* but rather the ordered pair *x-in-world-*W_1, *y-in-world-*W_2.)

Similarly, we can understand the relation *same$_L$* (same liquid as) as a cross-world relation by understanding it so that a liquid in world W_1 which has the same important physical properties (in W_1) that a liquid in W_2 possesses (in W_2) bears *same$_L$* to the latter liquid.

Then the theory we have been presenting may be summarized by saying that an entity *x,* in an arbitrary possible world, is *water* if and only if it bears the relation *same$_L$* (construed as a cross-world relation) to the stuff *we* call "water" in the *actual* world.

Suppose, now, that I have not yet discovered what the important physical properties of water are (in the actual world)—i.e., I don't yet know that water is H_2O. I may have ways of *recognizing* water that are successful (of course, I may make a small number of mistakes that I won't be able to detect until a later stage in our scientific development) but not know the microstructure of water. If I agree that a liquid with the superficial properties of "water" but a different microstructure *isn't really water,* then my ways of recognizing water (my "operational definition," so to speak) cannot be regarded as an analytical specification of *what it is to be* water. Rather, the operational definition, like the ostensive one, is simply a way of pointing out a standard—pointing out the stuff *in the actual world* such that for *x* to be water, in *any* world, is for *x* to bear the relation same$_L$ to the *normal* members of the class of *local* entities that satisfy the operational definition. "Water" on Twin Earth is not water, even if it satisfies the operational definition, because it doesn't bear *same$_L$* to the *local* stuff that satisfies the operational definition, and local stuff that satisfies the operational definition but has a microstructure different from the rest of the local stuff that satisfies the operational definition isn't water either, because it doesn't bear *same$_L$* to the *normal* examples of the local "water."

Suppose, now, that I discover the microstructure of water—that water is H_2O. At this point I will be able to say that the stuff on Twin Earth that I earlier *mistook* for water isn't really water. In the same way if you describe not another planet in the actual universe, but another possible universe in which there is stuff with the chemical formula *XYZ* which passes the "operational test" for *water,* we shall have to say that that stuff isn't water but merely *XYZ.* You will not have described a possible world in which "water is *XYZ,*" but merely a possible world in which there are lakes of *XYZ,* people drink *XYZ* (and not water), or whatever. In fact, once we have discovered the nature of water, nothing counts as a possible world in which water doesn't have that nature. Once we have discovered that water (in the actual world) is H_2O, *nothing counts as a possible world in which water isn't H_2O.* In particular, if a "logically possible" statement is one that holds in some "logically possible world," *it isn't logically possible that water isn't H_2O.*

On the other hand, we can perfectly well imagine having experiences that would convince us (and that would make it rational to believe that) water *isn't* H_2O. In that sense, it is conceivable that water isn't H_2O. It is conceivable but it isn't logically possible! Conceivability is no proof of logical possibility.

Kripke refers to statements which are rationally unrevisable (assuming there are such) as *epistemically necessary.* Statements which are true in all possible worlds he refers to simply as necessary (or sometimes as "metaphysically necessary"). In this terminology, the point just made can be restated as: a statement can be (metaphysically) necessary and epistemically contingent. Human intuition has no privileged access to metaphysical necessity.

Since Kant there has been a big split between philosophers who thought that all necessary truths were analytic and philosophers who thought that some necessary truths were synthetic a priori. But none of these philosophers thought that a (metaphysically) necessary truth could fail to be a priori: the Kantian tradition was as guilty as the empiricist tradition of equating metaphysical and epistemic necessity. In this sense Kripke's challenge to received doctrine goes far beyond the usual empiricism/Kantianism oscillation.

In this paper our interest is in theory of meaning, however, and not in theory of necessary truth. Points closely related to Kripke's have been made in terms of the notion of *indexicality.*[7] Words like "now," "this," "here," have long been recognized to be *indexical,* or *token-reflexive*—i.e., to have an extension which varied from context to context or token to token. For these words no one has ever suggested the traditional theory that "intension determines extension." To take our Twin Earth example: if I have a *Doppelgänger* on Twin Earth, then when I think "I have a headache," *he* thinks " I have a headache." But the extension of the particular token of "I" in his verbalized thought is himself (or his unit class, to be precise), while the extension of the token of "I" in *my* verbalized thought is *me* (or my unit class, to be precise). So the same word, "I," has two different extensions in two different idiolects; but it does not follow that the concept I have of myself is in any way different from the concept my *Doppelgänger* has of himself.

Now then, we have maintained that indexicality extends beyond the *obviously* indexical words and morphemes (e.g., the tenses of verbs). Our theory can be summarized as saying that words like "water" have an unnoticed indexical component: "water" is stuff that bears a certain similarity relation to the water *around here.* Water at another time or in another place or even in another possible world has to bear the relation same$_L$ to *our* "water" *in order to be water.* Thus the theory that (1) words have "intensions," which are something like concepts associated with the words by speakers; and that (2) intension determines extension—cannot be true of natural-kind words like "water" for the same reason the theory cannot be true of obviously indexical words like "I."

The theory that natural-kind words like "water" are indexical leaves it open, however, whether to say that "water" in the Twin Earth dialect of English has the same *meaning* as "water" in the Earth dialect and a different extension (which is what we normally say about "I" in different idiolects), thereby giving up the doctrine that "meaning (intension) determines extension"; or to say, as we have chosen to do, that difference in extension is *ipso facto* a difference in meaning for natural-kind words, thereby giving up the doctrine that meanings are concepts, or, indeed, mental entities of *any* kind.

It should be clear, however, that Kripke's doctrine that natural-kind words are rigid designators and our doctrine that they are indexical are but two ways of making the same point. We heartily endorse what Kripke says when he writes:

> Let us suppose that we do fix the reference of a name by a description. Even if we do so, we do not then make the name synonymous with the description, but instead we use the name rigidly to refer to the object so named, even in talking about counterfactual situations where the thing named would not satisfy the description in question. Now, this is what I think is in fact true for those cases of naming where the reference is fixed by description. But, in fact, I also think, contrary to most recent theorists, that the reference of names is rarely or almost never fixed by means of description. And by this I do not just mean what Searle says: "It's not a single description, but rather a cluster, a family of properties that fixes the reference." I mean that properties in this sense are not used at all.[8]

Other Words

. . . So far we have only used natural-kind words as examples, but the points we have made apply to many other kinds of words as well. They apply to the great majority of all nouns, and to other parts of speech as well.

Let us consider for a moment the names of artifacts—words like "pencil," "chair," "bottle," etc. The traditional view is that these words are certainly defined by conjunctions, or possibly clusters, of properties. Anything with all of the properties in the conjunction (or sufficiently many of the properties in the cluster, on the cluster model) is necessarily a *pencil, chair, bottle,* or whatever. In addition, some of the properties in the cluster (on the cluster model) are usually held to be *necessary* (on the conjunction-of-properties model, *all* of the properties in the conjunction are necessary). *Being an artifact* is supposedly necessary, and belonging to a kind with a certain standard purpose—e.g., "pencils are artifacts," and "pencils are standardly intended to be written with" are supposed to be necessary. Finally, this sort of necessity is held to be *epistemic* necessity—in fact, analyticity.

Let us once again engage in science fiction. This time we use an example devised by Rogers Albritton. Imagine that we someday discover that *pencils are organisms.* We cut them open and examine them under the electron microscope, and we see the almost invisible tracery of nerves and other organs. We spy upon them, and we see them spawn, and we see the offspring grow into full-grown pencils. We discover that these organisms are not imitating other (artifactual) pencils—there are not and never were any pencils except these organisms. It is strange, to be sure, that there is *lettering* on many of these organisms—e.g., BONDED *Grants* DELUXE made in U.S.A. No. 2.—perhaps they are intelligent organisms, and this is their form of camouflage. (We also have to explain why no one ever attempted to manufacture pencils, etc., but this is clearly a possible world, in some sense.)

If this is conceivable, and I agree with Albritton that it is, then it is epistemically possible that *pencils could turn out to be organisms.* It follows that *pencils are artifacts* is not epistemically necessary in the strongest sense and, a fortiori, not analytic.

Let us be careful, however. Have we shown that there is a possible world in which pencils are organisms? I think not. What we have shown is that there is a possible world in which certain organisms are the *epistemic counterparts* of pencils (the phrase is Kripke's). To return to the device of Twin Earth: imagine this time that pencils on Earth are just what we think they are, artifacts manufactured to be written with, while "pencils" on Twin Earth are organisms à la Albritton. Imagine, further, that this is totally unsuspected by the Twin Earthians—they have exactly the beliefs about "pencils" that we have about pencils. When we discovered this, we would not say: "some pencils are organisms." We would be far more likely to say: "the things on Twin Earth that pass for pencils aren't really pencils. They're really a species of organism."

Suppose now the situation to be as in Albritton's example both on Earth and on Twin Earth. Then we would say "pencils are organisms." Thus, whether the "pencil-organisms" on Twin Earth (or in another possible universe) are really *pencils* or not is a function of whether or not the *local* pencils are organisms or not. If the local pencils are just what we think they are, then a possible world in which there are pencil-organisms is *not* a possible world in which *pencils are organisms;* there are *no* possible worlds in which pencils are organisms in this case (which is, of course, the actual one). That pencils are artifacts *is* necessary in the sense of true in all possible worlds—metaphysically necessary. But it doesn't follow that it's epistemically necessary.

It follows that "pencil" is not *synonymous* with any description—not even loosely synonymous with a *loose* description. When we use the word "pencil," we intend to refer to whatever has the same *nature* as the normal examples of the local pencils in the actual world. "Pencil" is just as *indexical* as "water" or "gold."

In a way, the case of pencils turning out to be organisms is complementary to the case we discussed some years ago[9] of cats turning out to be robots (remotely controlled from Mars). Katz[10] argues that we misdescribed this case: that the case should rather be described as its *turning out that there are no cats in this world.* Katz admits that we might *say* "Cats have turned out not to be animals, but robots"; but he argues that this is a semantically deviant sentence which is glossed as "the things I am referring to as 'cats' have turned out not to be animals, but robots." Katz's theory is bad linguistics, however. First of all, the explanation of how it is we can *say* "Cats are robots" is simply an all-purpose explanation of how we can say *anything.* More important, Katz's theory predicts that "Cats are robots" is *deviant,* while "There are no cats in the world" is nondeviant, in fact standard, in the case described. Now then, I don't deny that there *is* a case in which "There are not (and never were) any cats in the world" would be standard: we might (speaking epistemically) discover that we have been suffering from a collective hallucination. ("Cats" are like pink elephants.) But in the case I described, "Cats have turned out to be robots remotely controlled from Mars" is surely nondeviant, and "There are no cats in the world" is highly deviant.

Incidentally, Katz's account is not only bad linguistics; it is also bad as a rational reconstruction. The reason we *don't* use "cat" as synonymous with a description is surely that we know enough about cats to know that they do have a hidden structure, and it is good scientific methodology to use the name to refer rigidly to the things that possess that hidden structure, and not to whatever happens to satisfy some description. Of course, if we *knew* the hidden structure we could frame a description in terms of *it;* but we don't at this point. In this sense the use of natural-kind words reflects an important fact about our relation to the world: we know that there are kinds of things with common hidden structure, but we don't yet have the knowledge to describe all those hidden structures.

Katz's view has more plausibility in the "pencil" case than in the "cat" case, however. We think we *know* a necessary and sufficient condition for being a *pencil,* albeit a vague one. So it is possible to make "pencil" synonymous with a loose description. We *might* say, in the case that "pencils turned out to be organisms" *either* "Pencils have turned out to be organisms" *or* "There are no pencils in the world"—i.e., we might use "pencil" either as a natural-kind word or as a "one-criterion" word.[11]

On the other hand, we might doubt that there *are* any true one-criterion words in natural language, apart from stipulative contexts. Couldn't it turn out that pediatricians aren't doctors but Martian spies? Answer "yes," and you have abandoned the synonymy of "pediatrician" and "doctor specializing in the care of children." It seems that there is a strong tendency for words which are introduced as "one-criterion" words to develop a "natural-kind" sense, with all the concomitant rigidity and indexicality. In the case of artifact-names, this natural-kind sense seems to be the predominant one.

(There is a joke about a patient who is on the verge of being discharged from an insane asylum. The doctors have been questioning him for some time, and he has been giving perfectly sane responses. They decide to let him leave, and at the end of the interview one of the doctors inquires casually, "What do you want to be when you get out?" "A teakettle." The joke would not be intelligible if it were literally inconceivable that a person could be a teakettle.)

There are, however, words which retain an almost pure one-criterion character. These are words whose meaning derives from a transformation: *hunter = one who hunts.*

Not only does the account given here apply to most nouns, but it also applies to other parts of speech. Verbs like "grow," adjectives like "red," etc., all have indexical features. On the other hand, some syncategorematic words seem to have more of a one-criterion character. "Whole," for example, can be explained thus: *The army surrounded the town* could be true even if the A division did not take part. *The whole army surrounded the town* means every part of the army (of the relevant kind, e.g., the A Division) took part in the action signified by the verb.[12]

Meaning

Let us now see where we are with respect to the notion of meaning. We have now seen that the extension of a term is not fixed by a concept that the individual speaker has in his head, and this is true both because extension is, in general, determined *socially*—there is division of linguistic labor as much as of "real" labor—and because extension is, in part, determined *indexically*. The extension of our terms depends upon the actual nature of the particular things that serve as paradigms,[13] and this actual nature is not, in general, fully known to the speaker. Traditional semantic theory leaves out only two contributions to the determination of extension—the contribution of society and the contribution of the real world!

We saw at the outset that meaning cannot be identified with extension. Yet it cannot be identified with "intension" either, if intension is something like an individual speaker's *concept*. What are we to do?

There are two plausible routes that we might take. One route would be to retain the identification of meaning with concept and pay the price of giving up the idea that meaning determines extension. If we followed this route, we might say that "water" has the same *meaning* on Earth and on Twin Earth, but a different *extension*. (Not just a different *local* extension but a different *global* extension. The *XYZ* on Twin Earth isn't in the extension of the tokens of "water" that I utter, but it is in the extension of the tokens of "water" that my *Doppelgänger* utters, and this isn't just because Twin Earth is far away from me, since molecules of H_2O are in the extension of the tokens of "water" that I utter no matter how far away from me they are in space and time. Also, what I can counterfactually suppose water to be is different from what

my *Doppelgänger* can counterfactually suppose "water" to be.) While this is the correct route to take for an *absolutely* indexical word like "I," it seems incorrect for the words we have been discussing. Consider "elm" and "beech," for example. If these are "switched" on Twin Earth, then surely we would *not* say that "elm" has the same meaning on Earth and Twin Earth, even if my *Doppelgänger*'s stereotype of a beech (or an "elm," as he calls it) is identical with my stereotype of an elm. Rather, we would say that "elm" in my *Doppelgänger*'s idiolect means *beech*. For this reason, it seems preferable to take a different route and identify "meaning" with an ordered pair (or possibly an ordered *n-tuple*) of entities, *one of which is the extension*. (The other components of the, so to speak, "meaning vector" will be specified later.) Doing this makes it trivially true that *meaning determines extension* (i.e., difference in extension is ipso facto difference in meaning), but totally abandons the idea that if there is a difference in the meaning my *Doppelgänger* and I assign to a word, then there *must* be some difference in our concepts (or in our psychological state). Following this route, we can say that my *Doppelgänger* and *I mean something different* when we say "elm," but this will not be an assertion about our psychological states. All this means is that the tokens of the word he utters have a different extension than the tokens of the word I utter; but this difference in extension is not a reflection of any difference in our individual linguistic competence considered in isolation.

If this is correct, and I think it is, then the traditional problem of meaning splits into two problems. The first problem is to account for the *determination of extension*. Since, in many cases, extension is determined socially and not individually, owing to the division of linguistic labor, I believe that this problem is properly a problem for sociolinguistics. Solving it would involve spelling out in detail exactly how the division of linguistic labor works. The so-called "causal theory of reference," introduced by Kripke for proper names and extended by us to natural-kind words and physical-magnitude terms, falls into this province. For the fact that, in many contexts, we assign to the tokens of a name that I utter whatever referent we assign to the tokens of the same name uttered by the person from whom I acquired the name (so that the reference is transmitted from speaker to speaker, starting from the speakers who were present at the "naming ceremony," even though no fixed *description* is transmitted) is simply a special case of social cooperation in the determination of reference.

The other problem is to describe *individual competence*. Extension may be determined socially, in many cases, but we don't assign the standard extension to the tokens of a word *W* uttered by Jones *no matter how* Jones uses *W*. Jones has to have some particular ideas and skills in connection with *W* in order to play his part in the linguistic division of labor. Once we give up the idea that individual competence has to be so strong as to actually determine extension, we can begin to study it in a fresh frame of mind. . . .

The Meaning of "Meaning"

We may now summarize what has been said in the form of a proposal concerning how one might reconstruct the notion of "meaning." Our proposal is not the only one that might be advanced on the basis of these ideas, but it may serve to encapsulate some of the major points. In addition, I feel that it recovers as much of ordinary usage in common sense talk and in linguistics as one is likely to be able to conveniently preserve. Since, in my view something like the assumptions (I) and (II) listed in the first part of this paper are deeply embedded in ordinary meaning talk, and these assumptions are jointly inconsistent with the facts, no reconstruction is going to be without some counterintuitive consequences.

Briefly, my proposal is to define "meaning" not by picking out an object which will be identified with the meaning (although that might be done in the usual set-theoretic style if one insists), but by specifying a normal form (or, rather, a *type* of normal form) for the description of meaning. If we know what a "normal form description" of the meaning of a word should be, then, as far as I am concerned, we know what meaning is in any scientifically interesting sense.

My proposal is that the normal form description of the meaning of a word should be a finite sequence, or "vector," whose components should certainly include the following (it might be desirable to have other types of components as well): (1) the syntactic markers that apply to the word, e.g., "noun"; (2) the semantic markers that apply to the word, e.g., "animal," "period of time"; (3) a description of the additional fea-

tures of the stereotype, if any; (4) a description of the extension.

The following convention is a part of this proposal: the components of the vector all represent a hypothesis about the individual speaker's competence, *except the extension*. Thus the normal form description for "water" might be, in part:

Syntactic Markers
mass noun; concrete;

Semantic Markers
natural-kind; liquid;

Stereotype
colorless; transparent; tasteless; thirst-quenching; etc.

Extension
H_2O(give or take impurities)

—this does not mean that knowledge of the fact that water is H_2O is being imputed to the individual speaker or even to the society. It means that (*we* say) the extension of the term "water" as *they* (the speakers in question) use it is *in fact* H_2O. The objection "who are *we* to say what the extension of *their* term is in fact" has been discussed above. Note that this is fundamentally an objection to the notion of *truth,* and that extension is a relative of truth and inherits the family problems.

Let us call two descriptions *equivalent* if they are the same except for the description of the extension, and the two descriptions are coextensive. Then, if the set variously described in the two descriptions is, *in fact,* the extension of the word in question, and the other components in the description are correct characterizations of the various aspects of competence they represent, *both* descriptions count as correct. Equivalent descriptions are both correct or both incorrect. This is another way of making the point that, although we have to use a *description* of the extension to *give* the extension, we think of the component in question as being the *extension* (the *set*), not the description of the extension.

In particular the representation of the words "water" in Earth dialect and "water" in Twin Earth dialect would be the same except that in the last column the normal form description of the Twin Earth word "water" would have *XYZ* and not H_2O. This means, in view of what has just been said, that we are ascribing the *same* linguistic competence to the typical Earthling/Twin Earthian speaker, but a different extension to the word, nonetheless.

This proposal means that we keep assumption (II) of our early discussion. Meaning determines extension—by construction, so to speak. But (I) is given up; the psychological state of the individual speaker does not determine "what he means."

In most contexts this will agree with the way we speak, I believe. But one paradox: suppose Oscar is a German-English bilingual. In our view, in his total collection of dialects, the words "beech" and *Buche* are *exact synonyms*. The normal form descriptions of their meanings would be identical. But he might very well not know that they are synonyms! A speaker can have two synonyms in his vocabulary and not know that they are synonyms!

It is instructive to see how the failure of the apparently obvious "if S_1 and S_2 are synonyms and Oscar understands both S_1 and S_2 then Oscar knows that S_1 and S_2 are synonyms" is related to the falsity of (I), in our analysis. Notice that if we had chosen to omit the extension as a component of the "meaning-vector," which is David Lewis's proposal as I understand it, then we would have the paradox that "elm" and "beech" have the *same meaning* but different extensions!

On just about any materialist theory, believing a proposition is likely to involve processing some *representation* of that proposition, be it a sentence in a language, a piece of "brain code," a thought form, or whatever. Materialists, and not only materialists, are reluctant to think that one can believe propositions *neat*. But even materialists tend to believe that, if one believes a proposition, *which* representation one employs is (pardon the pun) immaterial. If S_1 and S_2 are both representations that are *available* to me, then if I believe the proposition expressed by S_1 under the representation S_1, I must also believe it under the representation S_2—at least, I must do this if I have any claim to rationality. But, as we have just seen, this isn't right. Oscar may well believe that *this* is a "beech" (it has a sign on it that says "beech"), but not believe or disbelieve that this is a "*Buche*." It is not just that belief is a process involving representations; he believes the proposition (if one wants to introduce "propositions" at all) under one representation and not under another.

The amazing thing about the theory of meaning is how long the subject has been in the grip of philosophical misconceptions, and how strong these misconceptions are. Meaning has been identified with a necessary and sufficient condition by philosopher after philosopher. In the empiricist tradition, it has been identified with a method of verification, again by philosopher after philosopher. Nor have these misconceptions had the virtue of exclusiveness; not a few philosophers have held that meaning = method of verification = necessary and sufficient condition.

On the other side, it is amazing how weak the grip of the facts has been. After all, what have been pointed out in this essay are little more than home truths about the way we use words and how much (or rather, how little) we actually know when we use them. My own reflection on these matters began after I published a paper in which I confidently maintained that the meaning of a word was "a battery of semantical rules,"[14] and then began to wonder how the meaning of the common word "gold" could be accounted for in this way. And it is not that philosophers had never considered such examples: Locke, for example, uses this word as an example and is not troubled by the idea that its meaning is a necessary and sufficient condition!

If there is a reason for both learned and lay opinion having gone so far astray with respect to a topic which deals, after all, with matters which are in everyone's experience, matters concerning which we all have more data than we know what to do with, matters concerning which we have, if we shed preconceptions, pretty clear intuitions, it must be connected to the fact that the grotesquely mistaken views of language which are and always have been current reflect two specific and very central philosophical tendencies: the tendency to treat cognition as a purely *individual* matter and the tendency to ignore the *world,* insofar as it consists of more than the individual's "observations." Ignoring the division of linguistic labor is ignoring the social dimension of cognition; ignoring what we have called the *indexicality* of most words is ignoring the contribution of the environment. Traditional philosophy of language, like much traditional philosophy, leaves out other people and the world; a better philosophy and a better science of language must encompass both.

NOTES

1. This is discussed by Ziff, *Understanding Understanding* (Cornell University Press, 1972), especially chapter VIII.

2. This tradition grew up because *the* term whose analysis provoked all the discussion in medieval philosophy was the term "God," and the term "God" was thought to be defined through the conjunction of the terms "Good," "Powerful," "Omniscient," etc.— the so-called "Perfections." There was a problem, however, because God was supposed to be a Unity, and Unity was thought to exclude His essence being complex in *any* way—i.e., "God" was defined through a conjunction of terms, but God (without quotes) could not be the logical product of properties, nor could He be the unique thing exemplifying the logical product of two or more *distinct* properties, because even this highly abstract kind of "complexity" was held to be incompatible with His perfection of Unity. This is a theological paradox with which Jewish, Arabic, and Christian theologians wrestled for centuries (e.g., the doctrine of the Negation of Privation in Maimonides and Aquinas). It is amusing that theories of contemporary interest, such as conceptualism and nominalism, were first proposed as solutions to the problem of predication in the case of God. It is also amusing that the favorite model of definition in all of this theology—the conjunction-of-properties model—should survive, at least through its consequences, in philosophy of language until the present day.

3. Rather, they will report: "On Twin Earth (*the Twin Earthian name for Terra*—H.P.), the word 'water' means H$_2$O."

4. The substance of this section was presented at a series of lectures I gave at the University of Washing-

ton (Summer Institute in Philosophy) in 1968, and at a lecture at the University of Minnesota.

5. See my 'Is Semantics Possible,' *Metaphilosophy,* 1, no. 3 (July 1970).

6. This assumption is not actually needed in what follows. What *is* needed is that the same *natural kind* can exist in more than one possible world.

7. These points were made in my 1968 lectures at the University of Washington and the University of Minnesota.

8. See Kripke's 'Identity and Necessity', in M. Munitz, ed. *Identity and Individuation* (New York University Press, 1972), p. 157.

9. See my "It Ain't Necessarily So," *Journal of Philosophy* 59 (1962):658–71.

10. See Katz, "Logic and Language: An Examination of Recent Criticisms of Intentionalism," in K. Gunderson, ed., *Language, Mind, and Knowledge* (University of Minnesota Press, 1975).

11. The idea of a "one-criterion" word, and a theory of analyticity based on this notion, appears in my "The Analytic and The Synthetic," in H. Feigl and G. Maxwell, eds., *Minnesota Studies in the Philosophy of Science,* vol. 3 (University of Minnesota Press, 1962).

12. This example comes from an analysis by Anthony Kroch (in his M.I.T. doctoral dissertation, 1974, Department of Linguistics).

13. I *don't* have in mind the Flewish notion of "paradigm" in which any paradigm of a *K* is *necessarily* a *K* (in reality).

14. 'How Not to Talk about Meaning', in R. Cohen and M. Wortofsky, eds., *Boston Studies in the Philosophy of Science,* vol. 2 (Humanities Press, 1965).

55 | Individualism and the Mental

Tyler Burge

Since Hegel's *Phenomenology of Spirit,* a broad, inarticulate division of emphasis between the individual and his social environment has marked philosophical discussions of mind. On one hand, there is the traditional concern with the individual subject of mental states and events. In the elderly Cartesian tradition, the spotlight is on what exists or transpires "in" the individual—his secret cogitations, his innate cognitive structures, his private perceptions and introspections, his grasping of ideas, concepts, or forms. More evidentially oriented movements, such as behaviorism and its liberalized progeny, have highlighted the individual's publicly observable behavior—his input-output relations and the dispositions, states, or events that mediate them. But both Cartesian and behaviorist viewpoints tend to feature the individual subject. On the other hand, there is the Hegelian preoccupation with the role of social institutions in shaping the individual and the content of his thought. This tradition has dominated the continent since Hegel. But it has found echoes in English-speaking philosophy during this century in the form of a concentration on language. Much philosophical work on language and mind has been in the interests of Cartesian or behaviorist viewpoints that I shall term "individualistic." But many of Wittgenstein's remarks about mental representation point up a social orientation that is discernible from his flirtations with behaviorism. And more recent work on the theory of reference has provided glimpses of the role of social cooperation in determining what an individual thinks.

In many respects, of course, these emphases within philosophy—individualistic and social—are compatible. To an extent, they may be regarded simply as different currents in the turbulent stream of ideas that has washed the intellectual landscape during the last hundred and some odd years. But the role of the social environment has received considerably less clear-headed philosophical attention (though perhaps not less philosophical attention) than the role of the states, occurrences, or acts in, on, or by the individual. Philosophical discussions of social factors have tended to be obscure, evocative, metaphorical, or platitudinous, or to be bent on establishing some large thesis about the course of history and the destiny of man. There remains much room for sharp delineation. I shall offer some considerations that stress social factors in descriptions of an individual's mental phenomena. These considerations call into question individualistic presuppositions of several traditional and modern treatments of mind. I shall conclude with some remarks about mental models.

I. Terminological Matters

Our ordinary mentalistic discourse divides broadly into two sorts of idiom. One typically makes reference to mental states or events in terms of sentential expressions. The other does not. A clear case of the first kind of idiom is "Alfred thinks that his friends' sofa is ugly." A clear case of the second sort is "Alfred is in pain." Thoughts, beliefs, intentions, and so forth are typically specified in terms of subordinate sentential clauses, that-clauses, which may be judged as true or false. Pains, feels, tickles, and so forth have no special semantical relation to sentences or to truth or falsity. There are intentional idioms that fall in the second category on this characterization, but that share important semantical features with expressions in the first—idioms like "Al worships Buicks." But I shall not sort these out here. I shall discuss only the former kind of mentalistic idiom. The extension of the discussion to other intentional idioms will not be difficult.

In an ordinary sense, the noun phrases that embed sentential expressions in mentalistic idioms provide the *content* of the mental state or event. We shall call that-clauses and their grammatical variants "*content-clauses.*" Thus, the expression "that sofas are more comfortable than pews" provides the content of Alfred's belief that sofas are more comfortable than pews.

My phrase "provides the content" represents an attempt at remaining neutral, at least for present purposes, among various semantical and metaphysical accounts of precisely how that-clauses function and precisely what, if anything, contents are.

Although the notion of content is, for present purposes, ontologically neutral, I do think of it as holding a place in a systematic *theory* of mentalistic language. The question of when to count contents different, and when the same, is answerable to theoretical restrictions. It is often remarked that in a given context we may ascribe to a person two that-clauses that are only loosely equivalent and count them as attributions of the "same attitude." We may say that Al's intention to climb Mt. McKinley and his intention to climb the highest mountain in the United States are the "same intention." (I intend the terms for the mountain to occur obliquely here. See later discussion.) This sort of point extends even to content clauses with extensionally nonequivalent counterpart notions. For contextually relevant purposes, we might count a thought that the glass contains some water as "the same thought" as a thought that the glass contains some thirst-quenching liquid, particularly if we have no reason to attribute either content as opposed to the other, and distinctions between them are irrelevant. Nevertheless, in both these examples, every systematic theory I know of would want to represent the semantical contribution of the content-clauses in distinguishable ways—as "providing different contents."

One reason for doing so is that the person himself is capable of having different attitudes described by the different content-clauses, even if these differences are irrelevant in a particular context. (Al might have developed the intention to climb the highest mountain before developing the intention to climb Mt. McKinley— regardless of whether he, in fact, did so.) A second reason is that the counterpart components of the that-clauses allude to distinguishable elements in people's cognitive lives. "Mt. McKinley" and "the highest mountain in the U.S." serve, or might serve, to indicate cognitively different notions. This is a vague, informal way of generalizing Frege's point: the thought that Mt. McKinley is the highest mountain in the U.S. is potentially interesting or informative. The thought that Mt. McKinley is Mt. McKinley is not. Thus, when we say in a given context that attribution of different contents is attribution of the "same attitude," we use "same attitude" in a way similar to the way we use "same car" when we say that people who drive Fords (or green 1970 Ford Mavericks) drive the "same car." For contextual purposes different cars are counted as "amounting to the same."

Although this use of "content" is theoretical, it is not, I think, theoretically controversial. In cases where we shall be counting contents different, the cases will be uncontentious: in any systematic theory, differences in the *extension*— the actual denotation, referent, or application— of counterpart expressions in that-clauses will be semantically represented, and will, in our terms, make for differences in content. I shall be avoiding the more controversial, but interesting, questions about the general conditions under which sentences in that-clauses can be expected to provide the same content.

I should also warn of some subsidiary terms. I shall be (and have been) using the term "*notion*" to apply to components or elements of contents. Just as whole that-clauses provide the content of a person's attitude, semantically relevant components of that-clauses will be taken to indicate notions that enter into the attitude (or the attitude's content). The term is supposed to be just as ontologically neutral as its fellow. When I talk of understanding or mastering the notion of contract, I am not relying on any special epistemic or ontological theory, except insofar as the earlier-mentioned theoretical restrictions on the notion of content are inherited by the notion of notion. The expression, "*understanding (mastering) a notion*" is to be construed more or less intuitively. Understanding the notion of contract comes roughly to knowing what a contract is. One can master the notion of contract without mastering the term "contract"—at the very least if one speaks some language other than English that has a term roughly synonymous with "contract." (An analogous point holds for my use of "mastering a content.") Talk of notions is roughly similar to talk of concepts in an informal sense. "Notion" has the advantage of being easier to separate from traditional theoretical commitments.

I speak of *attributing* an attitude, content, or notion, and of *ascribing* a that-clause or other piece of language. Ascriptions are the linguistic analogs of attributions. This use of "ascribe" is nonstandard, but convenient and easily assimilated.

There are semantic complexities involving the behavior of expressions in content-clauses, most of which we can skirt. But some must be touched on. Basic to the subject is the observation that expressions in content-clauses are often not intersubstitutable with extensionally equivalent expressions in such a way as to maintain the truth value of the containing sentence. Thus, from the facts that water is H_2O and that Bertrand thought that water is not fit to drink, it does not follow that Bertrand thought that H_2O is not fit to drink. When an expression like "water" functions in a content-clause so that it is not freely exchangeable with all extensionally equivalent expressions, we shall say that it has *oblique occurrence*. Roughly speaking, the reason why "water" and "H_2O" are not interchangeable in our report of Bertrand's thought is that "water" plays a role in characterizing a different mental act or state from that which "H_2O" would play a role in characterizing. In this context at least, thinking that water is not fit to drink is different from thinking that H_2O is not fit to drink.

By contrast, there are nonoblique occurrences of expressions in content-clauses. One might say that some water—say, the water in the glass over there—is thought by Bertrand to be impure; or that Bertrand thought that *that* water is impure. And one might intend to make no distinction that would be lost by replacing "water" with "H_2O,"—or "that water" with "that H_2O" or "that common liquid," or any other expression extensionally equivalent with "that water." We might allow these exchanges even though Bertrand had never heard of, say, H_2O. In such purely nonoblique occurrences, "water" plays *no role* in providing the *content* of Bertrand's thought, *on our use of "content,"* or (in any narrow sense) in characterizing Bertrand or his mental state. Nor is the water part of Bertrand's thought content. We speak of Bertrand *thinking his content of* the water. At its nonoblique occurrence, the term "that water" simply isolates, in one of many equally good ways, a portion of wet stuff to which Bertrand or his thought is related or applied. In certain cases, it may also mark a context in which Bertrand's thought is applied. But it is expressions at oblique occurrences within content clauses that primarily do the job of providing the content of mental states or events, and in characterizing the person.

Mentalistic discourse containing obliquely occurring expressions has traditionally been called *intentional discourse*. The historical reasons for this nomenclature are complex and partly confused. But roughly speaking, grammatical contexts involving oblique occurrences have been fixed upon as specially relevant to the representational character (sometimes called "intentionality") of mental states and events. Clearly oblique occurrences in mentalistic discourse have something to do with characterizing a person's epistemic perspective—how things seem to him, or in an informal sense, how they are represented to him. So without endorsing all the commitments of this tradition, I shall take over its terminology.

The crucial point in the preceding discussion is the assumption that obliquely occurring expressions in content-clauses are a primary means of identifying a person's intentional mental states or events. A further point is worth remarking here. It is normal to suppose that those content clauses correctly ascribable to a person that are not in general intersubstitutable *salva veritate*—and certainly those that involve extensionally nonequivalent counterpart expressions—identify different mental states or events.

I have cited contextual exceptions to this normal supposition, at least in a manner of speaking. We sometimes count distinctions in content irrelevant for purposes of a given attribution, particularly where our evidence for the precise content of a person or animal's attitude is skimpy. Different contents may contextually identify (what amount to) the "same attitude." I have indicated that even in these contexts, I think it best, strictly speaking, to construe distinct contents as describing different mental states or events that are merely equivalent for the purposes at hand. I believe that this view is widely accepted. But nothing I say will depend on it. For any distinct contents, there will be imaginable contexts of attribution in which, even in the loosest, most informal ways of speaking, those contents would be said to describe different mental states or events. This is a consequence of the theoretical role of contents, discussed earlier. Since our discussion will have an "in principle" character, I shall take these contexts to be the relevant ones. Most of the cases we discuss will involve *extensional* differences between obliquely occurring counterpart expressions in that-clauses. In such cases, it is particularly natural and normal to take different contents as identifying different mental states or events.

II. A Thought Experiment

IIa. First Case

We now turn to a three-step thought experiment. Suppose first that:

A given person has a large number of attitudes commonly attributed with content-clauses containing "arthritis" in oblique occurrence. For example, he thinks (correctly) that he has had arthritis for years, that his arthritis in his wrists and fingers is more painful than his arthritis in his ankles, that it is better to have arthritis than cancer of the liver, that stiffening joints is a symptom of arthritis, that certain sorts of aches are characteristic of arthritis, that there are various kinds of arthritis, and so forth. In short, he has a wide range of such attitudes. In addition to these unsurprising attitudes, he thinks falsely that he has developed arthritis in the thigh.

Generally competent in English, rational and intelligent, the patient reports to his doctor his fear that his arthritis has now lodged in his thigh. The doctor replies by telling him that this cannot be so, since arthritis is specifically an inflammation of joints. Any dictionary could have told him the same. The patient is surprised, but relinquishes his view and goes on to ask what might be wrong with his thigh.

The second step of the thought experiment consists of a counterfactual supposition. We are to conceive of a situation in which the patient proceeds from birth through the same course of physical events that he actually does, right to and including the time at which he first reports his fear to his doctor. Precisely the same things (nonintentionally described) happen to him. He has the same physiological history, the same diseases, the same internal physical occurrences. He goes through the same motions, engages in the same behavior, has the same sensory intake (physiologically described). His dispositions to respond to stimuli are explained in physical theory as the effects of the same proximate causes. All of this extends to his interaction with linguistic expressions. He says and hears the same words (word forms) at the same time he actually does. He develops the disposition to assent to "Arthritis can occur in the thigh" and "I have arthritis in the thigh" as a result of the same physically described proximate causes. Such dispositions might have arisen in a number of ways. But we can suppose that in both actual and counterfactual situations, he acquires the word "arthritis" from casual conversation or reading, and never hearing anything to prejudice him for or against applying it in the way that he does, he applies the word to an ailment in his thigh (or to ailments in the limbs of others) which seems to produce pains or other symptoms roughly similar to the disease in his hands and ankles. In both actual and counterfac-

tual cases, the disposition is never reinforced or extinguished up until the time when he expresses himself to his doctor. We further imagine that the patient's nonintentional, phenomenal experience is the same. He has the same pains, visual fields, images, and internal verbal rehearsals. The *counterfactuality* in the supposition touches only the patient's social environment. In actual fact, "arthritis," as used in his community, does not apply to ailments outside joints. Indeed, it fails to do so by a standard, nontechnical dictionary definition. But in our imagined case, physicians, lexicographers, and informed laymen apply "arthritis" not only to arthritis but to various other rheumatoid ailments. The standard use of the term is to be conceived to encompass the patient's actual misuse. We could imagine either that arthritis had not been singled out as a family of diseases, or that some other term besides "arthritis" were applied, though not commonly by laymen, specifically to arthritis. We may also suppose that this difference and those necessarily associated with it are the only differences between the counterfactual situation and the actual one. (Other people besides the patient will, of course, behave differently.) To summarize the second step:

> The person might have had the same physical history and nonintentional mental phenomena while the word "arthritis" was conventionally applied, and defined to apply, to various rheumatoid ailments, including the one in the person's thigh, as well as to arthritis.

The final step is an interpretation of the counterfactual case, or an addition to it as so far described. It is reasonable to suppose that:

> In the counterfactual situation, the patient lacks some—probably *all*—of the attitudes commonly attributed with content-clauses containing "arthritis" in oblique occurrence. He lacks the occurrent thoughts or beliefs that he has arthritis in the thigh, that he has had arthritis for years, that stiffening joints and various sorts of aches are symptoms of arthritis, that his father had arthritis, and so on.

We suppose that in the counterfactual case we cannot correctly ascribe any content-clause containing an oblique occurrence of the term "arthritis." It is hard to see how the patient could have picked up the notion of arthritis. The word "arthritis" in the counterfactual community does not mean *arthritis*. It does not apply only to inflammations of the joints. We suppose that no other word in the patient's repertoire means *arthritis*. "Arthritis," in the counterfactual situation, differs both in dictionary definition and in extension from "arthritis" as we use it. Our ascriptions of content-clauses to the patient (and ascriptions within his community) would not constitute attributions of the same contents we actually attribute. For counterpart expressions in the content clauses that are actually counterfactually ascribable are not even extensionally equivalent. However we describe the patient's attitudes in the counterfactual situation, it will not be with a term or phrase extensionally equivalent with "arthritis." So the patient's counterfactual-attitudes contents differ from his actual ones.

The upshot of these reflections is that the patient's mental contents differ while his entire physical and nonintentional mental histories, considered in isolation from their social context, remain the same. (We could have supposed that he dropped dead at the time he first expressed his fear to the doctor.) The differences seem to stem from differences "outside" the patient considered as an isolated physical organism, causal mechanism, or seat of consciousness. The difference in his mental contents is attributable to differences in his social environment. In sum, the patient's internal qualitative experiences, his physiological states and events, his behaviorally described stimuli and responses, his dispositions to behave, and whatever sequences of states (nonintentionally described) mediated his input and output—all these remain constant, while his attitude contents differ, even in the extensions of counterpart notions. As we observed at the outset, such differences are ordinarily taken to spell differences in mental states and events.

IIb. Further Exemplifications

The argument has an extremely wide application. It does not depend, for example, on the kind of word "arthritis" is. We could have used an artifact term, an ordinary natural-kind word, a color adjective, a social-role term, a term for a historical style, an abstract noun, an action verb, a physical-movement verb, or any of various other sorts of words. I prefer to leave open precisely how far one can generalize the argument. But I think it has a very wide scope. The argument can get under way in any case where it is intuitively possible to attribute a mental state or event whose content involves a notion that the subject incompletely understands. As will become clear, this possibility is the key to the thought experiment. I want to give a more concrete sense of the possibility before going further.

It is useful to reflect on the number and variety of intuitively clear cases in which it is normal to attribute a content that the subject incompletely understands. One need only thumb through a dictionary for an hour or so to develop a sense of the extent to which one's beliefs are infected by incomplete understanding.[1] The phenomenon is rampant in our pluralistic age.

(a.) Most cases of incomplete understanding that support the thought experiment will be fairly idiosyncratic. There is a reason for this. Common linguistic errors, if entrenched, tend to become common usage. But a generally competent speaker is bound to have numerous words in his repertoire, possibly even common words, that he somewhat misconstrues. Many of these misconstruals will not be such as to deflect ordinary ascriptions of that-clauses involving the incompletely mastered term in oblique occurrence. For example, one can imagine a generally competent, rational adult having a large number of attitudes involving the notion of sofa—including beliefs that *those* (some sofas) are sofas, that some sofas are beige, that his neighbors have a new sofa, that he would rather sit in a sofa for an hour than on a church pew. In addition, he might think that sufficiently broad (but single-seat) overstuffed armchairs are sofas. With care, one can develop a thought experiment parallel to the one in section IIa, in which at least some of the person's attitude contents (particularly, in this case, contents of occurrent mental events) differ, while his physical history, dispositions to behavior, and phenomenal experience—non-intentionally and asocially described—remain the same.

(b.) Although most relevant misconstruals are fairly idiosyncratic, there do seem to be certain types of error which are relatively common—but not so common and uniform as to suggest that the relevant terms take on new sense. Much of our vocabulary is taken over from others who, being specialists, understand our terms better than we do.[2] The use of scientific terms by laymen is a rich source of cases. As the arthritis example illustrates, the thought experiment does not depend on specially technical terms. I shall leave it to the imagination of the reader to spin out further examples of this sort.

(c.) One need not look to the laymen's acquisitions from science for examples. People used to buying beef brisket in stores or ordering it in restaurants (and conversant with it in a general way) probably often develop mistaken beliefs (or uncertainties) about just what brisket is. For example, one might think that brisket is a cut from the flank or rump, or that it includes not only the lower part of the chest but also the upper part, or that it is specifically a cut of beef and not of, say, pork. No one hesitates to ascribe to such people content-clauses with "brisket" in oblique occurrence. For example, a person may believe that he is eating brisket under these circumstances (where "brisket" occurs in oblique position); or he may think that brisket tends to be tougher than loin. Some of these attitudes may be false; many will be true. We can imagine a counterfactual case in which the person's physical history, his dispositions, and his nonintentional mental life, are all the same, but in which "brisket" is commonly applied in a different way—perhaps in precisely the way the person thinks it applies. For example, it might apply only to beef and to the upper and lower parts of the chest. In such a case, as in the sofa and arthritis cases, it would seem that the person would (or might) lack some or all of the propositional attitudes that are actually attributed with content clauses involving "brisket" in oblique position.

(d.) Someone only generally versed in music history, or superficially acquainted with a few drawings of musical instruments, might naturally but mistakenly come to think that clavichords included harpsichords without legs. He may have many other beliefs involving the notion of clavichord, and many of these may be true. Again, with some care, a relevant thought experiment can be generated.

(e.) A fairly common mistake among lawyers' clients is to think that one cannot have a contract with someone unless there has been a written agreement. The client might be clear in intending "contract" (in the relevant sense) to apply to agreements, not to pieces of paper. Yet he may take it as part of the meaning of the word, or the essence of law, that a piece of formal writing is a necessary condition for establishing a contract. His only experiences with contracts might have involved formal documents, and he undergeneralizes. It is not terribly important here whether one says that the client misunderstands the term's meaning, or alternatively that the client makes a mistake about the essence of contracts. In either case, he misconceives what a contract is, yet ascriptions involving the term in oblique position are made anyway.

It is worth emphasizing here that I intend the misconception to involve the subject's attaching counterfactual consequences to his mistaken belief about contracts. Let me elaborate this a bit. A common dictionary definition of "contract" is "legally binding agreement." As I am imagining the case, the client does not explicitly define "contract" to himself in this way (though he might use this phrase in explicating the term). And he is not merely making a mistake about what the law happens to enforce. If asked why unwritten agreements are not contracts, he is likely to say something like, "They just aren't" or "It is part of the nature of the law and legal practice that they have no force." He is not disposed without prodding to answer, "It would be possible but impractical to give unwritten agreements legal force." He might concede this. But he would add that such agreements would not be contracts. He regards a document as inseparable from contractual obligation, regardless of whether he takes this to be a matter of meaning or a metaphysical essentialist truth about contracts.

Needless to say, these niceties are philosophers' distinctions. They are not something an ordinary man is likely to have strong opinions about. My point is that the thought experiment is independent of these distinctions. It does not depend on misunderstandings of dictionary meaning. One might say that the client understood the term's dictionary meaning, but misunderstood its essential application in the law—misconceived the nature of contracts. The thought experiment still flies. In a counterfactual case in which the law enforces both written and unwritten agreements and in which the subject's behavior and so forth are the same, but in which "contract" *means* "legally binding agreement based on written document," we would not attribute to him a mistaken belief that a contract requires written agreement, although the lawyer might have to point out that there are other legally binding agreements that do not require documents. Similarly, the client's other propositional attitudes would no longer involve the notion of contract, but another more restricted notion.

(f.) People sometimes make mistakes about color ranges. They may correctly apply a color term to a certain color, but also mistakenly apply it to shades of a neighboring color. When asked to explain the color term, they cite the standard cases (for "red," the color of blood, fire engines, and so forth). But they apply the term somewhat beyond its conventionally established range—beyond the reach of its vague borders. They think that fire engines, including *that* one, are red. They observe that red roses are covering the trellis. But they also think that *those* things are a shade of red (whereas they are not). Second looks do not change their opinion. But they give in when other speakers confidently correct them in unison.

This case extends the point of the contract example. The error is linguistic or conceptual in something like the way that the shopper's mistake involving the notion of brisket is. It is not an ordinary empirical error. But one may reasonably doubt that the subjects misunderstand the dictionary meaning of the color term. Holding their nonintentional phenomenal experience, physical history, and behavioral dispositions constant, we can imagine that "red" were applied as they mistakenly apply it. In such cases, we would no longer ascribe content-clauses involving the term "red" in oblique position. The attribution of the correct beliefs about fire engines and roses would be no less affected than the attribution of the beliefs that, in the actual case, display the misapplication. Cases bearing out the latter point are common in anthropological reports on communities whose color terms do not match ours. Attributions of content typically allow for the differences in conventionally established color ranges.

Here is not the place to refine our rough distinctions among the various kinds of misconceptions that serve the thought experiment. Our philosophical purposes do not depend on how these distinctions are drawn. Still, it is important to see what an array of conceptual errors is common among us. And it is important to note that such errors do not always or automatically prevent attribution of mental content provided by the very terms that are incompletely understood or misapplied. The thought experiment is nourished by this aspect of common practice.

IIc. Expansion and Delineation of the Thought Experiment

As I have tried to suggest in the preceding examples, the relevant attributions in the first step of the thought experiment need not display the subject's error. They may be attributions of a true content. We can begin with a propositional attitude that involved the misconceived notion, but in a true, unproblematic application of it: for example, the patient's belief that he, like his fa-

ther, developed arthritis in the ankles and wrists at age 58 (where "arthritis" occurs obliquely).

One need not even rely on an underlying *misconception* in the thought experiment. One may pick a case in which the subject only partially understands an expression. He may apply it firmly and correctly in a range of cases, but be unclear or agnostic about certain of its applications or implications which, in fact, are fully established in common practice. Most of the examples we gave previously can be reinterpreted in this way. To take a new one, imagine that our protagonist is unsure whether his father has mortgages on the car and the house, or just one on the house. He is a little uncertain about exactly how the loan and collateral must be arranged in order for their to be a mortgage, and he is not clear about whether one may have mortgages on anything other than houses. He is sure, however, that Uncle Harry paid off his mortgage. Imagine our man constant in the ways previously indicated and that "mortgage" commonly applied only to mortgages on houses. But imagine banking practices themselves to be the same. Then the subject's uncertainty would plausibly not involve the notion of mortgage. Nor would his other propositional attitudes be correctly attributed with the term "mortgage" in oblique position. Partial understanding is as good as misunderstanding for our purposes.

On the other hand, the thought experiment does appear to depend on the possibility of someone's having a propositional attitude despite an incomplete mastery of some notion in its content. To see why this appears to be so, let us try to run through a thought experiment, attempting to avoid any imputation of incomplete understanding. Suppose the subject thinks falsely that all swans are white. One can certainly hold the features of swans and the subject's nonintentional phenomenal experience, physical history, and nonintentional dispositions constant, and imagine that "swan" meant "white swan" (and perhaps some other term, unfamiliar to the subject, meant what "swan" means). Could one reasonably interpret the subject as having different attitude contents without at some point invoking a misconception? The questions to be asked here are about the subject's dispositions. For example, in the actual case, if he were shown a black swan and told that he was wrong, would he fairly naturally concede his mistake? Or would he respond, "I'm doubtful that that's a swan" until we brought in dictionaries, encyclopedias, and other native speakers to correct his usage? In the latter case, his understanding of "swan" would be deviant. Suppose then that in the actual situation he would respond normally to the counterexample. Then there is reason to say that he understands the notion of swan correctly: and his error is not conceptual or linguistic, but empirical in an ordinary and narrow sense. (Of course, the line we are drawing here is pretty fuzzy.) When one comes to the counterfactual stage of the thought experiment, the subject has the same dispositions to respond pliably to the presentation of a black specimen. But such a response would suggest a misunderstanding of the term "swan" as counterfactually used. For in the counterfactual community what they call "swans" could not fail to be white. The mere presentation of a black swan would be irrelevant to the definitional truth "All swans are white." I have not set this case up as an example of the thought experiment's going through. Rather I have used it to support the conjecture that *if* the thought experiment is to work, one must at some stage find the subject believing (or having some attitude characterized by) a content, despite an incomplete understanding or misapplication. An ordinary empirical error appears not to be sufficient.

It would be a mistake, however, to think that incomplete understanding, in the sense that the argument requires, is in general an unusual or even deviant phenomenon. *What I have called "partial understanding" is common or even normal in the case of a large number of expressions in our vocabularies.* "Arthritis" is a case in point. Even if by the grace of circumstance a person does not fall into views that run counter to the term's meaning or application, it would not be the least deviant or "socially unacceptable" to have no clear attitude that would block such views. "Brisket," "contract," "recession," "sonata," "deer," "elm" (to borrow a well-known example), "ore-amplifier," "carburetor," "gothic," "fermentation" probably provide analogous cases. Continuing the list is largely a matter of patience. The sort of "incomplete understanding" required by the thought experiment includes quite ordinary, nondeviant phenomena.

It is worth remarking that the thought experiment as originally presented might be run in reverse. The idea would be to start with an ordinary belief or thought involving no incomplete understanding. Then we find the incomplete understanding in the second step. For example, properly understanding "arthritis," a patient may think (correctly) that he has arthritis. He happens to have heard of arthritis only occurring in joints, and he correctly believes that that is where arthritis always occurs. Holding his physical history, dispositions, and pain constant, we imagine that "arthritis" commonly applies to rheumatoid ailments of all sorts. Arthritis has not been singled out for special mention. If a patient were told by a doctor "You also have arthritis in the thigh," the patient would be disposed (as he is in the actual case) to respond, "Really? I didn't know that one could have arthritis except in joints." The doctor would answer, "No, arthritis occurs in muscles, tendons, bursas, and elsewhere." The patient would stand corrected. The notion that the doctor and patient would be operating with in such a case would not be that of arthritis.

My reasons for not having originally set out the thought experiment in this way are largely heuristic. As will be seen, discussion of the thought experiment will tend to center on the step involving incomplete understanding. And I wanted to encourage you, dear reader, to imagine actual cases of incomplete understanding in your own linguistic community. Ordinary intuitions in the domestic case are perhaps less subject to premature warping in the interests of theory. Cases involving not only mental-content attribution, but also translation of a foreign tongue, are more vulnerable to intrusion of side issues.

A secondary reason for not beginning with this "reversed" version of the thought experiment is that I find it doubtful whether the thought experiment always works in symmetric fashion. There may be special intuitive problems in certain cases—perhaps, for example, cases involving perceptual natural kinds. We may give special interpretations to individual misconceptions in imagined foreign communities, when those misconceptions seem to match our conceptions. In other words, there may be some systematic, intuitive bias in favor of at least certain of our notions for purposes of interpreting the misconceptions of imagined foreigners. I do not want to explore the point here. I think that any such bias is not always crucial, and that the thought experiment frequently works "symmetrically." We have to take account of a person's community in interpreting his words and describing his attitudes—and this holds in the foreign case as well as in the domestic case.

The reversal of the thought experiment brings home the important point that *even those propositional attitudes not infected by incomplete understanding* depend for their content on social factors that are independent of the individual, asocially and non-intentionally described. For if the social environment has been appropriately different, the contents of those attitudes would have been different.

Even *apart* from reversals of the thought experiment, it is plausible (in the light of its original versions) that our well-understood propositional attitudes depend partly for their content on social factors independent of the individual, asocially and nonintentionally construed. For each of us can reason as follows. Take a set of attitudes that involve a given notion and whose contents are well-understood by me. It is only contingent that I understand that notion as well as I do. Now holding my community's practices constant, imagine that I understand the given notion incompletely, but that the deficient understanding is such that it does not prevent my having attitude contents involving that notion. In fact, imagine that I am in the situation envisaged in the first step of one of the original thought experiments. In such a case, a proper subset of the original set of my actual attitude contents would, or might, remain the same—intuitively, at least those of my actual attitudes whose justification or point is untouched by my imagined deficient understanding. (In the arthritis case, an example would be a true belief that many old people have arthritis.) These attitude contents remain constant despite the fact that my understanding, inference patterns, behavior, dispositions, and so on would in important ways be different and partly inappropriate to applications of the given notion. What is it that enables these unaffected contents to remain applications of the relevant notion? It is not *just* that my understanding, inference patterns, behavior, and so forth are enough like my actual understanding, inference patterns, behavior, and so forth. For if communal practice had *also* varied so as to apply the relevant notion as I am imagining I misapply it, then my attitude contents would not involve the relevant notion at all. This argument suggests that communal practice is a factor (in addition to my understanding, inference patterns, and perhaps behavior, physical activity, and other features) in fixing the contents of my attitudes—even in cases where I fully understand the content.

IId. Independence from Factive-Verb and Indexical-Reference Paradigms

The thought experiment does not play on psychological "success" verbs or "factive" verbs—verbs like "know," "regret," "realize," "remember," "foresee," "perceive." This point is important for our purposes because such verbs suggest an easy and clearcut distinction between the contribution of the individual subject and the object, "veridical" contribution of the environment to making the verbs applicable. (Actually the matter becomes more complicated on reflection, but we shall stay with the simple cases.) When a person knows that snow is common in Greenland, his knowledge obviously depends on more than the way the person is; it depends on there actually being a lot of snow in Greenland. His mental state (belief that snow is common in Greenland) must be successful in a certain way (true). By changing the environment, one could change the truth value of the content, so that the subject could no longer be said to know the content. It is part of the burden of our argument that even intentional mental states of the individual like beliefs, which carry no implication of veridicality or success, cannot be understood by focusing purely on the individual's acts, dispositions, and "inner" goings-on.

The thought experiment also does not rest on the phenomenon of indexicality, or on *de re* attitudes, in any direct way. When Alfred refers to an apple, saying to himself "That is wholesome," what he refers to depends not just on the content of what he says or thinks, but on what apple is before him. Without altering the meaning of Alfred's utterance, the nature of his perceptual experiences, or his physical acts or dispositions, we could conceive an exchange of the actual apple for another one that is indistinguishable to Alfred. We would thereby conceive him as referring to something different and even as saying something with a different truth value.

This rather obvious point about indexicality has come to be seen as providing a model for understanding a certain range of mental states or events—*de re* attitudes. The precise characterization of this range is no simple philosophical task. But the clearest cases involve nonobliquely occurring terms in content clauses. When we say that Bertrand thinks of some water that it would not slake his thirst (where "water" occurs in purely nonoblique position), we attribute a *de re* belief to Bertrand. We assume that Bertrand has something like an indexical relation to the water. The fact that Bertrand believes something of some water, rather than of a portion of some other liquid that is indistinguishable to him, depends partly on the fact that it is water to which Bertrand is contextually, "indexically" related.

For intuitively we could have exchanged the liquids without changing Bertrand and thereby changed what Bertrand believed his belief content *of*—and even whether his belief was true of it.[3] It is easy to interpret such cases by holding that the subject's mental states and contents (with allowances for brute differences in the contexts in which he applies those contents) remain the same. The differences in the situations do not pertain in any fundamental way to the subject's mind or the nature of his mental content, but to how his mind or content is related to the world.

It seems to me clear that the thought experiment need not rely on *de re* attitudes at all. The subject need not have entered into special *en rapport* or quasi-indexical relations with objects that the misunderstood term applies to in order for the argument to work. We can appeal to attitudes that would usually be regarded as paradigmatic cases of *de dicto,* nonindexical, *non-de-re* mental attitudes or events. The primary mistake in the contract example is one such, but we could choose others to suit the reader's taste. To insist that such attitudes must all be indexically infected of *de re* would, I think, be to trivialize and emasculate these notions, making nearly all attitudes *de re.* All *de dicto* attitudes presuppose *de re* attitudes. But it does not follow that indexical or *de re* elements survive in every attitude (cf. notes 2 and 3).

I shall not, however, argue this point here. The claim that is crucial is not that our argument does not fix on *de re* attitudes. It is, rather, that the social differences between the actual and counterfactual situations affect the *content* of the subject's attitudes. That is, the difference affects standard cases of obliquely occurring, cognitive-content-conveying expressions in content-clauses. For example, still with his misunderstanding, the subject might think that this (referring to his disease in his hands) is arthritis. Or he might think *de re* of the disease in his ankle or of the disease in his thigh that his arthritis is painful. It does not really matter whether the relevant attitude is *de re* or purely *de dicto.* What is crucial to our argument is that the occurrence of "arthritis" is oblique and contributes to a characterization of the subject's mental content. One might even hold, implausibly I think, that all the subject's attitudes involving the notion of arthritis are *de re,* that "arthritis" in that-clauses *indexically* picks out the property of being arthritis, or something like that. The fact remains that the term occurs obliquely in the relevant cases and serves in characterizing the *dicta* or contents of the subject's attitudes. The thought experiment exploits this fact.

Approaches to the mental that I shall later criticize as excessively individualistic tend to assimilate environmental aspects of mental phenomena to either the factive-verb or indexical-reference paradigm (cf. note 2). This sort of assimilation suggests that one might maintain a relatively clearcut distinction between extramental and mental aspects of mentalistic attributions. And it may encourage the idea that the distinctively mental aspects can be understood fundamentally in terms of the individual's abilities, dispositions, states, and so forth, considered in isolation from his social surroundings. Our argument undermines this later suggestion. Social content infects even the distinctively mental features of mentalistic attributions. No man's intentional mental phenomena are insular. Every man is a piece of the social continent, a part of the social main. . . .

NOTES

1. Our examples suggest points about learning that need exploration. It would seem naive to think that we first attain a mastery of expressions or notions we use and then tackle the subject matters we speak and think about in using those expressions or notions. In most cases, the processes overlap. But while the subject's understanding is still partial, we sometimes attribute mental contents in the very terms the subject has yet to master. Traditional views take mastering a word to consist in matching it with an already mastered (or innate) concept. But it would seem, rather, that many concepts (or mental content components) are like words in that they may be employed before they are mastered. In both cases, employment appears to be an integral part of the process of mastery.

2. A development of a similar theme may be found in Hilary Putnam's notion of a division of linguistic labor [cf. "The Meaning of 'Meaning'," *Philosophical Papers* 2 (Cambridge, 1975), pp. 227 ff.]. Putnam's imaginative work is in other ways congenial with points I have developed. Some of his examples can be adapted in fairly obvious ways so as to give an argument with different premises, but a conclusion complementary to the one I arrive at in Section IIa:

    Consider Alfred's belief contents involving the notion of water. Without changing Alfred's (or his fellows') nonintentional phenomenal experiences, internal physical occurrences, or dispositions to respond to stimuli on sensory surfaces, we can imagine that not water (H_2O), but a different liquid with different structure but similar macro-properties (and identical phenomenal properties) played the role in his environment that water does in ours. In such a case, we could ascribe no content clauses to Alfred with "water" in oblique position. His belief contents would differ. The conclusion (with which I am in sympathy) is that mental contents are affected not only by the physical and qualitatively mental way the person is, but by the nature of his *physical environment.*

Putnam himself does not give quite this argument. He nowhere states the first and third steps, though he gives analogs of them for the meaning of "water." This is partly just a result of his concentration on meaning instead of propositional attitudes. But some of what he says even seems to oppose the argument's conclusion. He remarks in effect that the subject's *thoughts* remain constant between his actual and counterfactual cases (p. 224). In his own argument he explicates the difference between actual and counterfactual cases in terms of a difference in the extension of term, not a difference in those aspects of their meaning that play a role in the cognitive life of the subject. And he tries to explicate his examples in terms of indexicality—a mistake, I think, and one that tends to divert attention from major implications of the examples he gives (cf. Section IId). In my view, the examples do illustrate the fact that all attitudes involving natural-kind notions, including *de dicto* attitudes, presuppose *de re* attitudes. But the examples do not show that natural-kind linguistic expressions are in any ordinary sense indexical. Nor do they show that beliefs involving natural-kind notions are always *de re*. Even if they did, the change from actual to counterfactual cases would affect oblique occurrences of natural-kind terms in that-clauses—occurrences that are the key to attributions of cognitive content (cf. above and note 3). In the cited paper and earlier ones, much of what Putnam says about psychological states (and implies about mental states) has a distinctly individualistic ring. Below in Section IV (not reprinted here—*ed.*), I crit-

icize viewpoints about mental phenomena influenced by and at least strongly suggested in his earlier work on functionalism [cf. note 9 (not reprinted here—*ed.*)].

On the other hand, Putnam's articulation of social and environmental aspects of the meaning of natural-kind terms complements and supplements our viewpoint. For me, it has been a rich rewarder of reflection. More recent work of his seems to involve shifts in his viewpoint on psychological states. It may have somewhat more in common with our approach than the earlier work, but there is much that I do not understand about it.

The argument regarding the notion of water that I extracted from Putnam's paper is narrower in scope than our argument. The Putnam-derived argument seems to work only for natural-kind terms and close relatives. And it may seem not to provide as direct a threat to certain versions of functionalism that I discuss in Section IV: At least a few philosophers would claim that one could accommodate the Putnamian argument in terms of *non*intentional formulations of input-output relations (formulations that make reference to the specific nature of the physical environment). Our argument does not submit to this maneuver. In our thought experiment, the physical environment (sofas, arthritis, and so forth in our examples) and the subject's causal relations with it (at least as these are usually conceived) were held constant. The Putnamian argument, however, has fascinatingly different implications from our argument. I have not developed these comparisons and contrasts here because doing justice to Putnam's viewpoint would demand a distracting amount of space, as the ample girth of this footnote may suggest.

3. I have discussed *de re* mental phenomena in "Belief De Re," *Journal of Philosophy* 74(1977), 338–62. There I argue that all attitudes with content presuppose *de re* attitudes. Our discussion here may be seen as bearing on the details of this presupposition. But for reasons I merely sketch in the next paragraph, I think it would be a superficial viewpoint that tried to utilize our present argument to support the view that nearly all intentional mental phenomena are covertly indexical or *de re*.

56 | The Components of Content
David J. Chalmers

1. Introduction[1]

Here are six puzzles about the contents of thought.[2]

(1) *Is content in the head?* Oscar believes that water is wet. His twin on Twin Earth, which is just like Earth except that H_2O is replaced by the superficially identical XYZ, does not. His twin's thoughts concern not water but twin water: Oscar believes that water is wet, but Twin Oscar believes that twin water is wet. This suggests that what a subject believes is not wholly determined by the internal state of the believer. Nevertheless, the cognitive similarities between Oscar and his twin are striking. Is there some wholly internal aspect of content that they share?

(2) *Frege's puzzle.* In thinking that Hesperus is Hesperus, I think about the same objects as in thinking that Hesperus is Phosphorus. But the first thought is trivial and the second is not. How can this difference in cognitive significance be reflected in a theory of content?

(3) *Kripke's puzzle.* In France, Pierre is told (in French) that London is pretty, and he believes it. Later, he arrives in London and thinks it is ugly, never suspecting that "Londres" and "London" name the same city. It seems that Pierre simultaneously believes that London is pretty and that London is not pretty. Pierre is highly rational, however, and would never believe a contradiction. What is going on?

(4) *The problem of the essential indexical.* When I believe that I am in danger, I will take evasive action. This belief seems to be essentially indexical, or self-directed; if I merely believe that x is in danger, where (unbeknownst to me) I am x, I might do something else entirely. How can we square this indexical aspect with an account of the contents of thought?

(5) *The mode-of-presentation problem.* If Jimmy says "Lois believes that Superman can fly", he speaks truly. If he says "Lois believes that Clark Kent can fly", he speaks falsely. But on many accounts, the proposition that Clark Kent can fly is the same as the proposition that Superman can fly. If so, it seems that to believe that Clark Kent can fly, it is not enough to believe the corresponding proposition; one must

believe it under an appropriate mode of presentation. What is a mode of presentation, and how can these be integrated into an account of belief ascription?

(6) *The contingent a priori.* Say it is stipulated that one meter is the length of a certain stick in Paris. Then it seems that one knows a priori that the stick is one meter long, if it exists. But it seems contingent that the stick is one meter long, as it might have been that the stick was longer or shorter than one meter. How can one have a priori knowledge of a contingent truth?

These puzzles are not unrelated. All of them suggest incompleteness in a familiar view of thought content, on which the content of a thought is tied to the external objects one is thinking about. In particular, most of them raise questions about how well such an account of thought content reflects *rational* or *cognitive* aspects of thought. Because of the dependence on external factors, this sort of content often seems to be dissociated from the rational relationships between thoughts (as witnessed by puzzles 2, 3, and 6), and from their role in guiding cognition and action (as witnessed by puzzles 1 and 4).

To resolve these and other puzzles, many have postulated a separate dimension of content—so-called "narrow content"—that depends only on the internal state of a thinker, and that is more closely tied to cognition and action.[3] The road from intuition to theory has been a difficult one, however, and no account of narrow content has yet gained widespread acceptance. It is widely held that because narrow content is internal, it lacks the sort of relation to the external world that is required to qualify as *content*. For example, many have thought that narrow content is not the sort of thing that can be true or false, as the Twin Earth cases show us that truth-conditions are not determined internally.

I think that these problems are illusory, and that there is a robust and natural notion of narrow content such that narrow content has truth-conditions of its own. This can be seen by developing the idea that content has two dimensions. On the account I will give here the content of a thought can be decomposed into two components: its *epistemic* and *subjunctive* con-

This paper is in print for the first time.

tent. Subjunctive content is a familiar external variety of content. Epistemic content has the following properties: (1) it is determined by the internal state of a cognitive system; (2) it is itself a sort of truth-conditional content; (3) it reflects the rational relations between thoughts. The first property ensures that epistemic content is a variety of narrow content. The second ensures that it is a truly semantic variety of content. The third ensures that it is central to the dynamics of cognition and action. Because of these three properties, epistemic content can help to resolve many problems in the philosophy of mind and language.

2. Intensions

In what follows, a *thought* is a token propositional attitude that aims to represent the world: for example, a belief, an expectation, or a hypothesis. Thoughts have truth-values (truth, falsity, and possibly others), and are often expressed in language by sentences. Thoughts are often (perhaps always) composed of *concepts*. Concepts are mental tokens that are often expressed in language by terms. Where thoughts have truth-values, concepts have *extensions:* for example, individuals, classes, or properties.

The truth-value of a thought typically depends on the extension of the concepts involved: For example, the truth value of my thought *Hesperus is Phosphorus* depends on whether the object that is the extension of *Hesperus* is the same as the object that is the extension of *Phosphorus*. In the actual world, the extension of both concepts is the planet Venus, so the thought is true.

It is a familiar idea that concepts and thoughts can be associated with an *intension:* a function from possible worlds to extensions or truth-values. The intension of a concept maps a possible world to the concept's extension in that world: in a given world, the intension of my concept *renate* picks out the class of creatures with a kidney in that world. The intension of a thought maps a world to the thought's truth-value in that world: in a given world, the intension of my thought *all renates are cordates* will be true if every creature with a kidney in that world also has a heart.

In effect, a concept's intension captures the way that its extension depends on the nature of the world. A thought's intension captures its *application conditions:* the way that its truth-value depends on the nature of the world.

On the framework I will develop, a concept or thought can be associated with *two* intensions. First, there is an *epistemic* intension, picking out a thought or concept's extension across the space of *epistemic* possibilities. This intension captures the epistemic dependence of extension or truth-value on the way the actual world turns out. Second, there is a *subjunctive* intension, picking out a thought or concept's extension across the space of *subjunctive* or *counterfactual* possibilities. This intension captures the subjunctive dependence of extension or truth-value on counterfactual states of the world, given that the character of the actual world is already fixed. On this two-dimensional picture, a thought's epistemic intension is narrow content, while a thought's subjunctive intension is often wide content.

To give a quick illustration: for my concept *water,* the epistemic intension picks out H_2O in our world (the Earth world), and XYZ in a Twin Earth world. This reflects the fact that if I accept that my actual world is like the Twin Earth world (i.e., if I accept that the liquid in the oceans is and always has been XYZ), I should accept that water is XYZ. By contrast, the subjunctive intension of my concept *water* picks out H_2O in both the Earth world and the Twin Earth world. This reflects the fact that *given* that water is H_2O in the actual world, the counterfactual Twin Earth world is best described as one in which water is still H_2O, and in which XYZ is merely watery stuff.

As a rough approximation, we can say that the epistemic intension of *water* picks out a substance with certain superficial characteristics (e.g. a clear drinkable liquid) in any given world, while the subjunctive intension of *water* picks out H_2O in all worlds. Here the epistemic intension is tied to the way that a subject thinks of water, while subjunctive intension is tied to water's underlying nature. A similar pattern exists for many other concepts. The basis of the pattern is discussed in what follows.

3. Epistemic Possibilities

Let us say that a thought is *epistemically necessary* when it can be justified a priori: that is, when there is a possible reasoning process that conclusively justifies the thought with justification independent of experience. A thought is *epistemically possible* (in a broad sense, related to but distinct from the usual philosophical sense) when the thought cannot be ruled out by a priori reasoning: that is, when its negation is not epistemically necessary. Intuitively, this holds when the thought does not involve an a priori contradiction. More precisely, this holds when there is no possible reasoning process that can conclusively justify the thought's negation, with justification independent of experience. On this understanding, my thought *water is H_2O* is epistemically possible, as is my thought *water is XYZ*. No amount of a priori reasoning can lead to the justified rejection of either of these thoughts. For all I can know a priori, the world might be such as to make either of these thoughts true.[4]

When a thought is epistemically possible, it is natural to hold that there are various specific *scenarios* compatible with the thought. A scenario can be thought of as a maximally specific epistemic possibility: one with all the details filled in. For example, the mere thought that water is XYZ is compatible with many epistemically possible hypotheses about the precise distribution of XYZ in my environment and about everything else that is going on in the world. Each of these maximally specific epistemically possible hypotheses corresponds to a scenario.

To flesh out this intuition further, it seems reasonable to say that some scenarios (those involving XYZ in certain distributions in my environment) *verify* my thought that water is XYZ: if I accept that the scenario obtains, I should accept that water is XYZ. Other scenarios (e.g., those involving H_2O in my environment) *falsify* my thought that water is XYZ: if I accept that the scenario obtains, I should deny that water is XYZ. Equivalently, we can say that my thought that water is XYZ *endorses* scenarios in the first class, and *excludes* scenarios in the second class.

In effect, the space of scenarios constitutes my *epistemic space:* the space of specific epistemic possibilities that are open to me a priori. If I had no empirical beliefs, all of epistemic space would be open to me. As I acquire empirical beliefs, my epistemic space is narrowed down. Any given belief will typically *divide* epistemic space into those epistemic possibilities that it endorses and those that it excludes. The basic idea I will pursue is that the narrow content of a thought is given by the way that the thought divides epistemic space.

Scenarios are much like possible worlds. For now, we can represent scenarios using possible worlds, though I will consider potential differences later. For example, let the H_2O-world be a world like ours with H_2O in the oceans and lakes, and let the XYZ-world be a specific Twin Earth world with XYZ in the oceans and lakes. Then for all I can know a priori, my world might be qualitatively just like the H_2O world, or it might be just like the XYZ-world. So these two worlds each represent highly specific epistemic possibilities for me. We can put this by saying it is epistemically possible (in the broad sense) that the H_2O-world is actual, and that it is epistemically possible that the XYZ-world is actual.

For any given scenario, one can in principle consider the hypothesis that the scenario is actual. For any given world W (on the possible-worlds understanding), it is epistemically possible that W is actual: that is, it is epistemically possible that one's own world is qualitatively just like W. When one considers a world as an epistemic possibility in this way, one is *considering it as actual:* that is, one is thinking of it as a way one's own world may be.[5]

Any given scenario verifies some thoughts and falsifies others. Here, we can say that a scenario falsifies a thought T when the hypothesis that the scenario is actual is rationally inconsistent with T. A scenario verifies T when the hypothesis that the scenario is actual is rationally inconsistent with the negation of T. For our purposes here, it is natural to say that a thought and a hypothesis are rationally inconsistent when their conjunction is epistemically impossible: that is, when this conjunction can be ruled out by a priori reasoning. On this interpretation, a scenario verifies a thought when acceptance of the hypothesis that the scenario is actual *implies* the thought: that is, when this acceptance can lead by a priori reasoning to acceptance of the thought.

Take my thought *water is H_2O*. The H_2O-world verifies my thought: if I accept that the H_2O-world is actual, I must rationally conclude that water is H_2O. It would be rationally inconsistent to accept that the H_2O-world is actual (i.e., that the liquid surrounding me with a certain appearance and distribution is and always has been H_2O, and so on) but deny that water is H_2O. By contrast, if I accept that the XYZ-world is actual, I must rationally conclude that water is not H_2O. It would be rationally inconsistent to accept that the XYZ-world is actual (i.e. that the liquid surrounding me with a certain appearance and distribution is and always has been XYZ, and so on), and at the same time to accept that water is H_2O. So the XYZ-world falsifies my thought *water is H_2O*, and verifies thoughts such as *water is not H_2O* and *water is XYZ*.

There is nothing here that contradicts the claim by Kripke and Putnam that water is necessarily H_2O. Kripke and Putnam are dealing with what is often called "metaphysical" possibility and necessity, which is usually sharply distinguished from epistemic possibility and necessity. Even if it is not metaphysically possible that water is XYZ, it is epistemically possible that water is XYZ: we cannot rule out the hypothesis that water is XYZ a priori. If Kripke and Putnam are right, then when the XYZ-world is considered as a metaphysical possibility (in effect, considered as a counterfactual world different from ours), it is best described as a world where XYZ is not water. But it is clear that when it is considered as an *epistemic* possibility (i.e., considered as a way our own world may be), and when verification is defined as above, it verifies the hypothesis that water is XYZ.

The indexical character of some thoughts forces us to refine the possible-worlds understanding of scenarios. If we consider an objective world W as actual, this does not yield a fully determinate epistemic possibility. Take a world W containing both H_2O and XYZ, in the oceans and lakes of separate planets. If I consider W as actual, I am not in a position to determine whether water is H_2O or XYZ, since I do not know which planet I am on. In effect, a fully determinate hypothesis must include information about my *location* within a world. To handle this, we can represent a scenario by a *centered* world: a world marked with an individual and a time at its "center".[6] A centered world corresponds to a world from a perspective, marked with a viewpoint at its center. In the case above, there will be many centered worlds corresponding to W, some centered on individuals on the H_2O planet, and some centered on individuals on the XYZ planet. Now, when I consider the hypothesis that a centered world W' is actual, I consider the hypothesis that my world is qualitatively just like W', that I am the individual marked at the center of W', and that the current time is the time marked at the center of W'. Given that sort of information in the case above, I will be in a position to determine which planet I am on, and I will be in a position to determine whether water is H_2O or XYZ.

4. Epistemic Intensions

Given the above, we can naturally define a thought's *epistemic intension* as a function from scenarios to truth-values. The epistemic intension of a thought T is true at a scenario W when W verifies T, and is false at a scenario W when W falsifies T. As before, W verifies T when it is rationally inconsistent to accept that W is actual and deny T, and W falsifies T when it is rationally inconsistent to accept that W is actual and accept T.

For a more precise definition of epistemic intensions, we would need to be more precise about what it is to consider a scenario as actual. The informal understanding above suffices for many purposes, but a more detailed account can be given as follows. To consider a scenario W as actual is to consider the hypothesis that D is the case, where D is a *canonical description* of W. When scenarios are understood as centered worlds, a canonical description will conjoin an *objective* description of the character of W (including its physical and mental character, for example), with an *indexical* description of the center's location within W. The objective description will be restricted to *semantically neutral* terms: roughly, terms that are not themselves vulnerable to Twin Earth thought experiments (thus excluding most names, natural kind terms, indexicals, and terms used with semantic deference). The indexical description will allow in addition indexical terms such as 'I' and 'now', to specify the center's location. We can then say that W verifies a thought T when a hypothesis that D is the case epistemically necessitates T. Equivalently, where S is a linguistic expression of T: W verifies T when a material conditional 'if D, then S' is a priori. These matters are explored in greater depth in Chalmers (forthcoming a).[7]

In the case of *water is H_2O*, the thought's epistemic intension will be true at the H_2O-scenario (a scenario centered on Oscar surrounded by H_2O, say), and will be false at the XYZ-scenario (a scenario centered on Twin Oscar, surrounded by XYZ). On a first approximation, one might suggest that the thought's epistemic intension will be true in a scenario when the dominant clear, drinkable liquid around the center of that scenario has a certain molecular structure. This seems to capture *roughly* what it takes for us to judge that water is H_2O in the actual world, depending on how things turn out. But this sort of approximation is no replacement for the real intension. The intension itself is best evaluated by considering specific scenarios and determining the consequences for the truth-values of our thoughts.

The existence of epistemic intensions is

grounded in the fact that given sufficient information about the actual world, we are in a position to know whether our thoughts are true. For example, given sufficient information about the appearance, behavior, composition, and distribution of objects and substances in my environment, I am in a position to determine whether water is H_2O. Even if things had turned out differently, I would still have been in a position to determine whether water is H_2O. So given enough relevant information about a scenario, I am in a position to determine whether, *if* that information is correct in my own world, water is H_2O. The same goes for all sorts of other thoughts. It may be that in some cases (involving vague concepts such as *tall,* for example), a complete specification of a scenario does not settle a thought as true or false. In that case, we can say that the thought's epistemic intension is *indeterminate* at that world. But otherwise, the thought's epistemic intension will be true or false at the world.

To help evaluate an epistemic intension at a world, one can use various heuristics. One useful heuristic for evaluating the epistemic intensions of one's own thought T, expressible by a sentence S, is to intuitively evaluate an indicative conditional: 'if W is actual, is it the case that S?' As with other indicative conditionals, one evaluates this conditional epistemically (by the "Ramsey test"): one hypothetically accepts that W is actual, and uses this to reach a rational conclusion about whether or not S is true.[8] If yes, then W verifies T; if not, then W falsifies T. To stress the epistemic character of the conditional, one can also appeal to "turns-out" conditionals such as the following: 'if W turns out to be actual, will it turn out that S'? For example, it seems reasonable to say that if the XYZ-world *turns out* to be actual, then it will *turn out* that water is XYZ.

Some thoughts have a very straightforward epistemic intension. For example, it is plausible that the epistemic intension of my thought *I am a philosopher* will be true at precisely those scenarios where the individual at the center is a philosopher. The identity of the individual at the center does not matter: it might be David Chalmers, and it might be Immanuel Kant. After all, my knowledge that I am not Immanuel Kant is a posteriori, so a scenario centered on Kant represents an epistemic possibility for me in the broad sense. It seems clear that *if* I accept that the Kant scenario is my actual scenario (i.e., that I am Kant philosophizing at the center of that scenario), then I should conclude that I am a philosopher.

As for a thought such as *Hesperus is Phosphorus:* it is plausible that this thought will be verified by roughly those scenarios where the bright object visible in a certain position in the evening sky around the individual at the center is identical to the bright object visible in the morning sky around the individual at the center. Again, this captures roughly what it takes for us to judge that Hesperus is Phosphorus in the actual world, given sufficient empirical information.

With a mathematical thought such as *2 + 2 = 4,* or *pi is irrational,* the thought's epistemic intension will be true in all worlds. This reflects the fact that these thoughts can be justified a priori, so that the negations of these thoughts will not be rationally consistent with any a posteriori hypothesis (the conjunction will itself be epistemically impossible). The same goes even for complex mathematical thoughts whose truth we are not in a position to know ourselves. The notion of epistemic possibility and necessity involves a rational idealization away from our contingent cognitive limitations. By definition, if it is even possible for a thought to be conclusively justified a priori, then the thought is epistemically necessary. If so, the thought has a necessary epistemic intension.

(This idealization also helps to deal with a natural worry: that in practice human thinkers are too limited to entertain the complete hypothesis that a scenario W is actual. A thought T is verified by W if a *possible* conjunction of a hypothesis that W is actual with the negation of T is rationally inconsistent; that is, if it is possible for a material conditional thought *if D is the case, then T* to be conclusively justified a priori, where D is a canonical description of W. This possibility may idealize away from the cognitive limitations of the thinker. Intuitively, we can think of the thinker as using ideal reasoning to assess the status of the relevant conditional.[9] In practice one can often avoid this sort of idealization by appealing to a relevant *partial* description D of W, where the thinker can entertain the hypothesis that D is the case, and where this hypothesis rationally settles the status of T.)

It is tempting to say that the reverse is also the case: that when a thought has a necessary epistemic intension, it is knowable a priori. On the centered-worlds understanding of scenarios, this is equivalent to the claim that when a thought is epistemically possible, it is verified by some centered world. I think this claim is correct, and have argued for it elsewhere, but it is nontrivial, at least when the worlds in question are understood as metaphysically possible worlds. Some philosophical views entail counterexamples to this claim. For example, on some theist views it is metaphysically necessary that a god exists, but the existence of a god cannot be known a priori. If so, then *a god exists* is not a priori, but its epistemic intension will be true in all metaphysically possible worlds. In effect, there are not enough possible worlds on this view to represent all epistemic possibilities. A similar result follows from some views on which the laws of nature in our world are the laws of all worlds: there will be no worlds with different laws to represent the epistemic possibility of different laws. The same goes for some materialist views on which zombies are epistemically possible but not metaphysically possible: on some such views, no possible world will correspond to the zombie epistemic possibility.

All of these views are controversial, and I have argued elsewhere (Chalmers 2002a) that they rest on an incorrect conception of metaphysical possibility. Sometimes these views are presented as drawing support from Kripkean a posteriori necessities such as 'Hesperus is Phosphorus' and 'water is H_2O', but the Kripkean examples are all compatible with the thesis that every epistemic possibility is verified by a centered possible world. So these views require a posteriori necessities of a sort much stronger than those discussed by Kripke, and there is reason to doubt that "strong necessities" of this sort exist.

Still, one who accepts any of these views will deny the thesis that every epistemically possible thought is verified by a centered world. Such a theorist could nevertheless preserve the thesis that every epistemically possible thought is verified by a scenario, by understanding scenarios as something other than centered metaphysically possible worlds. For example, one can define a space of maximal epistemic possibilities in purely epistemic terms (perhaps using a construction from epistemically consistent thoughts or sentences), and one can then make the case that every epistemically possible thought is verified by a scenario of this sort. (For example, the theist view above entails that even if there is no godless world, there is still a godless scenario.) I have taken this purely epistemic approach to scenarios elsewhere (Chalmers forthcoming b), as it is more neutral and arguably more philosophically fundamental. For reasons of simplicity and familiarity, I will usually stay with the centered-world approach to scenarios in this paper, but it should be kept in mind that the alternative understanding is available.[10]

One important note: It is tempting to suppose that the epistemic intension of a thought T can be evaluated in a scenario W by asking: what is the truth-value of T, as thought in W? But this is not so. On the present proposal, T's epistemic intension can be evaluated in scenarios containing no copy of T; even when a copy of T is present, it usually plays no special role. For example, my thought *I am a philosopher* is verified by a scenario regardless of whether I think I am a philosopher there. To take a more extreme example, the epistemic intension of my thought *someone is thinking* is false in a scenario that contains no thoughts. In these cases, all that matters is the epistemic relation between the hypothesis that W is actual and the thought T. Nothing here requires that T be present in W. One might define a different intension (a "contextual intension"; see section 9 and Chalmers forthcoming a) using the heuristic above, but such an intension behaves in a quite different way, and will not have the same sort of epistemic properties as an epistemic intension. This will be important later.

One can define epistemic intensions for *concepts* as well as for thoughts. A concept's epistemic intension picks out its extension in a scenario considered as actual. A precise definition involves some tricky details (see Chalmers forthcoming a), so here I will simply illustrate the idea intuitively. Let us take a singular concept C expressible by a term B. To evaluate C's epistemic intension in a scenario W, one considers the hypothesis that W is actual, and uses B to ask: 'what is B?' (Here B is used rather than mentioned.) One can appeal to the indicative conditional 'if W is actual, what is B?' Alternatively, one can appeal to the rational consistency of judgments of the form *C is such-and-such* with the hypothesis that W is actual.

For example, in the XYZ-scenario, the epistemic intension of my concept *water* picks out XYZ. As before, I can say: *if* the XYZ- scenario is actual, then water is XYZ. In the H_2O-scenario, on the other hand, the epistemic intension of my concept *water* picks out H_2O. More generally, one might say as a first approximation that in a given scenario, the epistemic intension of my concept *water* picks out the dominant clear, drinkable liquid found in the oceans and lakes around the individual at the center. As before, however, this is just an approximation, and the true intension corresponds to the results of considering and evaluating arbitrary scenarios as epistemic possibilities.

One can do something like this for an arbitrary concept. Even for a seemingly nondescriptive concept, such as *Gödel,* it will still be the case that given full information about a scenario and given the hypothesis that this information obtains in the actual world, one will be in a position to make a rational judgment about the identity of Gödel under that hypothesis. This mirrors the fact that given relevant information about the *actual* world, one is in a position to determine the identity of Gödel, and more generally is in a position to determine the extension of arbitrary concepts. This rational dependence of judgments about extension on information about the character of the actual world can be encapsulated in an epistemic intension.[11]

These epistemic intensions are often difficult to characterize in independent terms, but for some concepts this characterization is straightforward. If we take a quasidescriptive concept such as *Hesperus* (where we assume this functions to rigidly pick out the evening star in the actual world), we can say that the epistemic intension of *Hesperus* picks out the evening star around the center of an arbitrary scenario. Or if *Julius* functions to rigidly pick out the inventor of the zip, the epistemic intension of *Julius* picks out the inventor of the zip in a scenario.

The epistemic intension for an indexical concept is also very simple. The epistemic intension of my concept *I* picks out the individual at the center of a scenario. The epistemic intension of *now* picks out the time at the center. The epistemic intension of *here* picks out the location of the individual at the center, at the time at the center. The epistemic intension of *today* picks out (roughly) the day that includes the time at the center. And so on.

When a thought is composed from concepts, its truth-value typically depends on the concepts' extensions. In such a case, the thought's epistemic intension will be determined by the concepts' epistemic intensions. For example, the epistemic intension of *A is B* will be true at a world when the epistemic intensions of *A* and *B* pick out the same individual there. One will find a similar compositionality of intensions wherever one finds compositionality of extensions.

5. Subjunctive Intensions

In contemporary philosophy, epistemic intensions are less familiar than what I will call *subjunctive intensions.* To evaluate a thought's subjunctive intension, one evaluates it in a world *considered as counterfactual.* To consider a world as counterfactual, one considers it as a *subjunctive possibility:* as a way things might

have been, given that the character of the actual world is already fixed. In our world as it actually is, the liquid in the oceans and lakes is H_2O. Nevertheless, the liquid in the oceans and lakes *might have been* XYZ. So we can say that the XYZ-world *might have* obtained, and that the XYZ-world represents a subjunctive possibility.[12]

The subjunctive intension of a thought T in a world W picks out the thought's truth-value in W when W is considered as counterfactual. Here, we grant that the character of the actual world is already fixed and ask what *would have been* the case if W had obtained. If T is expressible by a sentence S, we can evaluate T's subjunctive intension at W by using S to ask: 'if W had obtained, would it have been the case that S?' If yes, then T's subjunctive intension is true at W; if no, then T's subjunctive intension is false at W. When T's subjunctive intension is true at W, we can say that W *satisfies* T.

Take my thought *I am here now.* Given that I exist and am spatiotemporally located, I know this thought to be true. So its epistemic intension is true in (almost) all scenarios. But it *might have been* that I was not here now. I might have been in Sydney rather than Tucson now, for example, had I flown out last week. If W is a world in which David Chalmers is in Sydney at the current time, we can say: if W had obtained, it would not have been the case that I am here now. So the subjunctive intension of my thought *I am here now* is false at W: W satisfies *I am not here now,* not *I am here now.* More generally, the subjunctive intension of my thought is false at any world where David Chalmers is not in Tucson at the current time.

Or take *water is H_2O.* If the XYZ-world had obtained—that is, if the liquid in the oceans and lakes *had been* XYZ—then (if Kripke and Putnam are correct) XYZ would not have been water.[13] XYZ would merely have been watery stuff, and water would still have been H_2O. If so, then the XYZ-world satisfies my thought *water is H_2O,* and the subjunctive intension of my thought is true at the XYZ-world. More generally, if Kripke and Putnam are correct, then the subjunctive intension of my thought *water is H_2O* is true at all possible worlds.

It is clear that subjunctive intensions can behave quite differently from epistemic intensions. We have seen that the XYZ-world verifies *water is not H_2O,* but it satisfies *water is H_2O.* This difference is rooted in the difference between epistemic and subjunctive possibility, and the corresponding difference between considering a world as actual and as counterfactual. This is mirrored in the different behavior of indicative and subjunctive conditionals: it seems reasonable to say indicatively that if the liquid in the oceans and lakes is XYZ, then water is XYZ; but if Kripke and Putnam are right, it is not reasonable to say that if the liquid in the oceans and lakes *had been* XYZ, then water would have been XYZ. In considering a world as counterfactual, empirical facts about the actual world make a difference to how we describe it. In considering a world as actual, they do not.

Something similar goes for an indexical thought such as *I am David Chalmers*. If Kripke is right, it could not have been that I was not David Chalmers. If so, then *I am David Chalmers* is true in any world considered as counterfactual (or at least in any world where I exist). Note that there is no special need for a center in the world here: once we know all the objective facts about a counterfactual state of affairs, we know all that we need to know, even to settle indexical claims. So subjunctive possibilities can be represented by ordinary uncentered worlds, and subjunctive intensions are defined over uncentered worlds.

We can associate subjunctive intensions with concepts in a similar way. A concept's subjunctive intension picks out its extension in a world considered as counterfactual. For a concept C expressible by a term B, we can use B to ask: 'if W had been actual, what would B have been?' For example, in the case of *water,* we can say that if the XYZ-world had been actual, then water would still have been H_2O. So the subjunctive intension of *water* picks out H_2O at the XYZ-world, and plausibly picks out H_2O in all possible worlds.

For many concepts, the concept's subjunctive intension picks out its actual extension in all possible worlds. This applies in particular to *rigid* concepts: those expressible by rigid designators, such as names or indexicals, picking out the same object in all worlds. For example, Kripke argues that 'Hesperus' is a rigid designator: if Hesperus is actually Venus, then it could not have been that Hesperus was other than Venus. If so, then the subjunctive intension of *Hesperus* picks out Venus in all possible worlds. Similarly, given that 'I' is a rigid designator, the subjunctive intension of my concept *I* picks out David Chalmers in all possible worlds.

For a purely descriptive concept such as *circular* or *the inventor of the zip,* by contrast, the subjunctive intension is very similar to the epistemic intension. For example, both the epistemic and subjunctive intensions of *the inventor of the zip* plausibly pick out whoever invented the zip in a given world. Note the difference

with *Julius,* which has the same epistemic intension but whose subjunctive intension picks out the actual inventor in all worlds. The difference reflects the intuition that if (for example) Ned Kelly had invented the zip, he would have been the inventor of the zip, but he would not have been Julius. (Compare: if Ned Kelly actually invented the zip, then he is Julius.) Some concepts behave in an intermediate manner. For example, the subjunctive intension of *the discoverer of water* does not pick out the actual extension in all worlds, but it is nevertheless quite different from the epistemic intension, due to the presence of the rigid concept *water* as a constituent.

The subjunctive intension of a concept or thought always depends in some way on the concept's epistemic intension and the actual world. For a purely descriptive concept, the subjunctive intension may simply be a copy of the epistemic intension, across uncentered worlds. For a rigid concept, the subjunctive intension will correspond to the value of the epistemic intension at the actual world, projected across all possible worlds. In other cases, the dependence may be somewhat more complex, but it will still exist.

We can encapsulate this dependence by associating concepts and thoughts with a *two-dimensional intension.* This intension maps an ordered pair (V, W) consisting of a scenario and a world to an extension or a truth-value in W. When a thought T is evaluated at (V, W), it returns the truth-value of T in the counterfactual world W, under the assumption that V is actual. (If a sentence S expresses T, we can use this heuristic: 'if V is actual, then if W had obtained, would it have been the case that S'?) Like an epistemic intension, a two-dimensional intension can plausibly be evaluated without relying on empirical knowledge, since all the empirical knowledge one needs is given in the first parameter V. To evaluate a thought's subjunctive intension at W, one evaluates its two-dimensional intension at (A, W), where A is the actual scenario. If we understand scenarios as centered worlds, the value of a thought's epistemic intension at a scenario W will coincide with the value of its two-dimensional intension at (W, W'), where W' is an uncentered version of W.[14] This two-dimensional intension is useful for certain purposes, but most of the time we need only appeal to a thought's epistemic and subjunctive intensions.

Within this framework, we can analyze the Kripkean "necessary a posteriori". Let us say that a sentence S is *subjunctively possible* when it is possible in the familiar Kripkean sense: that is, when a modal sentence such as 'it might have been the case that S' is true. A thought is subjunctively possible when it is expressible by a subjunctively possible sentence. Subjunctive necessity is defined correspondingly. Then it is easy to see that when a thought is subjunctively necessary, its subjunctive intension is true in all worlds, and vice versa. Cases of the Kripkean "necessary a posteriori" (e.g., *water is H_2O*) arise when a thought has a necessary subjunctive intension (true in all worlds considered as counterfactual) but a contingent epistemic intension (false in some world considered as actual). Cases of the Kripkean "contingent a priori" (e.g., *Julius invented the zip*) arise when a thought has a contingent subjunctive intension but a necessary epistemic intension.

There should be no question of whether the epistemic or the subjunctive intension is *the* intension associated with a given concept. The full story can only be given two-dimensionally. One or the other may be more useful for various specific purposes. In matters of linguistic content across a community, the subjunctive intension often plays a central role: different users of a name or natural kind term often have quite different associated epistemic intensions while sharing the same subjunctive intension. For questions about the role of thought in reason and action, however, we will see that the epistemic intension is central.

6. Wide and Narrow Content

Let us call a thought or concept's epistemic intension its *epistemic content,* and a thought or concept's subjunctive intension its *subjunctive content.* Let us say that when a thought or concept's content depends only on the intrinsic state of the thinker (that is, when every possible intrinsic duplicate of the thinker has a corresponding thought or concept with the same content), the content is *narrow.* Let us say that when content does not depend only on a thinker's intrinsic state (that is, when an intrinsic duplicate could have a corresponding thought or concept with different content), the content is *wide.* One can make the case that epistemic content is narrow, while subjunctive content is often wide.

It is clear that subjunctive content is often wide. For example, Oscar (on Earth) and Twin Oscar (on Twin Earth) are more or less intrinsic duplicates (abstracting away from differences due to the presence of H_2O and XYZ in their bodies), and have corresponding concepts that they express by saying 'water'. But the subjunc-

tive intension of Oscar's concept *water* picks out H_2O in all worlds, while the subjunctive intension of Twin Oscar's concept *water* picks out XYZ in all worlds. Something similar applies to most rigid concepts, including *Hesperus* and even *I.* Here, a subjunctive intension depends on a concept's extension, which usually depends on a subject's environment; so two intrinsic duplicates can have different subjunctive intensions. In other cases, subjunctive content will not depend on the environment. For example, purely descriptive concepts such as *circular* and *the inventor of the zip* will plausibly have subjunctive intensions that are shared between duplicates. But in cases where a concept or thought's subjunctive intension depends not just on its epistemic intension but on the way the actual world turns out, we can expect that subjunctive content will be wide content.

This environment-dependence does not extend to epistemic content. A concept's epistemic content is usually quite independent of its actual extension, and of the way the actual world turns out more generally. An epistemic intension encapsulates the way in which our rational judgments about extension and truth-value depend on arbitrary empirical information; so the intension can be evaluated without knowing which epistemic possibility is actual. The factors that make subjunctive content wide content appear to be irrelevant to epistemic content.

This can be illustrated by looking at familiar cases. Take Oscar's and Twin Oscar's respective thoughts T_1 and T_2, expressed by saying 'there is water in my pool.' Let W_1 be the Earth scenario centered on Oscar, with H_2O in the oceans and lakes and H_2O in Oscar's pool. Let W_2 be the Twin Earth scenario centered on Twin Oscar, with XYZ in the oceans and lakes and XYZ in Twin Oscar's pool. Then clearly, W_1 verifies T_1 and W_2 verifies T_2. But also, W_2 verifies T_1: if Oscar hypothetically accepts that W_2 is actual, he must rationally accept T_1. Equally, W_1 verifies T_2: if Twin Oscar hypothetically accepts that W_1 is actual, he should rationally accept T_2. So the epistemic intensions of T_1 and T_2 are on a par with respect to these worlds.

Something similar applies to other scenarios. Let W_3 be a Twin Earth scenario centered on Twin Oscar with XYZ in the oceans and lakes, but an isolated amount of H_2O in Twin Oscar's pool. Then W_3 falsifies both T_1 and T_2. If Oscar accepts that W_3 is actual, he should reject T_1; if Twin Oscar accepts that W_3 is actual, he should reject T_2. The same goes for any other world: if

W verifies T_1, it will also verify T_2, and vice versa. The same goes equally for any intrinsic duplicate of Oscar. We can even imagine Vat Oscar, who is a brain in a vat receiving artificial stimulation. Vat Oscar can entertain the hypothesis that his environment is just like W_1 (or W_2 or W_3) and can reach rational conclusions on that basis, and the conclusions that he reaches will mirror those of Oscar and Twin Oscar. So Vat Oscar has a thought with the same epistemic intension as Oscar's.[15] The same holds for intrinsic duplicates in general; so the epistemic content of Oscar's thought is narrow.

The same goes for other thoughts and concepts. For example, even though I may have a twin whose concept expressed by 'Hesperus' has a different extension and subjunctive intension, his concept nevertheless has the same epistemic intension as mine, picking out roughly the evening star near the center of any scenario. Similarly, although the *I* concepts of my twins will have an extension and subjunctive intension that differs from mine, they will have the same epistemic intension, picking out the individual at the center of any scenario.

One can apply this analysis to the cases used by Burge (1979) to argue for the social nature of mental content. Bert has a belief that he expresses by saying 'arthritis sometimes occurs in the thighs.' In fact, arthritis is a disease of the joints and cannot occur in the thigh, so it seems that Bert has a false belief about arthritis. Twin Bert, an intrinsic duplicate of Bert, also has a belief that he expresses by saying 'Arthritis sometimes occurs in the thighs.' But Twin Bert lives in a community in which the word 'arthritis' is used for a different disease, one that affects the muscles as well as the joints: we might call it 'twarthritis'. It seems that Twin Bert has a true belief about twarthritis. Where Bert believes (falsely) that he has arthritis in his thigh, Twin Bert does not: Twin Bert believes (truly) that he has twarthritis in his thigh. Burge concludes that in this sort of case, belief content is not in the head.

Here, the crucial factor is that Bert uses the term 'arthritis' with *semantic deference,* intending (at least tacitly) to use the word for the same phenomenon for which others in the community use it. We might say that this term expresses a *deferential concept* for Bert: one whose extension depends on the way the corresponding term is used in a subject's linguistic community. It is clear that for deferential concepts, extension can depend on a subject's environment, as can

subjunctive intension. The subjunctive intension of Bert's concept *arthritis* picks out arthritis in all worlds, while the subjunctive intension of Twin Bert's concept picks out twarthritis in all worlds.

Let T_1 and T_2 be the thoughts that Bert and Twin Bert express by saying 'arthritis sometimes occurs in the thighs.' Let W_1 be Bert's own centered world, with a surrounding community that uses the term 'arthritis' to refer to a disease of the joints. Let W_2 be Twin Bert's centered world, with a surrounding community that uses 'arthritis' to refer to a disease that can occur in the thigh. Then clearly W_1 falsifies T_1 and W_2 verifies T_2. At the same time, W_2 verifies T_1: if Bert accepts that W_2 is actual—that is, if he accepts that his linguistic community uses 'arthritis' for a disease that can occur in the thighs—then (since his concept is deferential) he should rationally accept that arthritis can occur in the thighs, and so should accept T_1. Similarly, W_1 falsifies T_2: if Twin Bert accepts that W_1 is actual—that is, if he accepts that his community uses 'arthritis' only for a disease of the joints—then he should reject his thought T_2. So the epistemic intension of T_1 is false at W_1 and true at W_2, and exactly the same is true for T_2.

Something similar applies to any other scenarios that Bert and Twin Bert evaluate. In general, the epistemic intension of their *arthritis* concepts in those scenarios will pick out the extension of the term 'arthritis' as used in the linguistic community around the center of those scenarios. (In worlds where the term is not used, the epistemic intension will arguably be empty or indeterminate.) And the same goes for any intrinsic duplicate of Bert. Any such duplicate can entertain the hypothesis that a given scenario W is actual, and will rationally reach conclusions similar to Bert's.

One can apply the same reasoning to Putnam's case of 'elm' and 'beech', in which a subject can use the terms with different referents despite users having no substantive knowledge to differentiate the two. In this case, the terms are being used deferentially: the epistemic intension of the subject's concept *elm* picks out roughly whatever is called 'elm' around the center of a scenario, and the epistemic intension of her concept *beech* picks out roughly whatever is called 'beech' around the center of a scenario. Here again, the epistemic intension is independent of the environment. So we can see that semantic deference and "the division of linguistic labor" is quite compatible with thoughts and concepts having internally determined epistemic content.

Putnam suggests that terms such as 'water' and 'elm' show that if a concept's intension is internally determined, it cannot determine the concept's extension. The current analysis shows that this is only half-true. The epistemic intension of a concept determines its extension, and the epistemic intension is internally determined. Of course, the epistemic intension is a *centered intension,* taking a centered world as argument, at least on the possible-worlds understanding of scenarios. So Putnam's claim still holds for uncentered intensions. But any intension requires facts about the actual world to determine extension, and it is most natural to regard the actual environment of a thinker as centered, so an internally determined centered intension is very useful here.

Why is epistemic content narrow? On the surface, this is because a thought's epistemic content is rationally prior to any knowledge of a subject's environment: it captures the way a thought's truth-value *depends* on the character of the environment, and so is independent of the environment itself. More deeply, it may be because epistemic content is defined in terms of the rational properties of thoughts, where the relevant rational properties are internally determined. For example, if one subject has a thought that is justifiable a priori, a corresponding thought in any intrinsic duplicate of that subject will also be justifiable a priori; if so, a thought's epistemic necessity is determined by the internal state of the thinker. This observation can be combined with the observation that when one subject entertains the hypothesis that a scenario W is actual, a duplicate of that subject must also be entertaining the hypothesis that W is actual. This second observation can be grounded in the fact that these hypotheses involve semantically neutral descriptions of scenarios, so there is no possibility of a "Twin Earth" difference between thinkers here. Putting these two observations together, it follows that if the hypothesis that W is actual epistemically necessitates a thought in one subject, it will also epistemically necessitate the corresponding thought in any duplicate subject. So epistemic content is narrow.

(Of course, the epistemic content of a thought will almost always depend *causally* on the external world, but it will not depend *constitutively* on the external environment. Whenever the external environment affects the epistemic contents of our thoughts, it will do so by affecting the internal state of the thinker.)

As promised, this sort of narrow content is truth-conditional. The epistemic content of a thought delivers conditions that one's actual centered world must satisfy in order for one's thought to be true. We might think of these as a thought's *epistemic* truth-conditions, as opposed to a thought's *subjunctive* truth-conditions, which govern truth across counterfactual worlds. Of course these truth-conditions can come apart at a given world: at the XYZ-world, the epistemic truth-conditions of *water is XYZ* are satisfied, but the subjunctive truth-conditions are not. This is to be expected, given the different functions of epistemic and subjunctive evaluation. One might worry that because of this, a thought could turn out to be both true and false in the actual world, but this is impossible. When evaluated at the actual world, epistemic intensions and subjunctive intensions always give the same results.

7. The Advantages of Epistemic Content

In recent times, the "content" of a thought has usually been identified with something like its subjunctive content;[16] but the epistemic content seems to be an equally good candidate. As before, there is no need to decide which is *the* content. That being said, there are a number of ways in which the epistemic content of a thought is responsible for the explanatory work that we would expect a notion of content to do.

First, epistemic content reflects the rational relations between thoughts. If one thought implies another thought a priori, the epistemic intension associated with the first entails the epistemic intension associated with the second (that is, in all scenarios in which the first intension is true, the second intension is also true). If I know that it is hot where I am now, I know that it is hot here, and vice versa; this is reflected in the fact that the epistemic contents of the two thoughts are the same. The subjunctive contents of the thoughts are very different, however. The subjunctive intension of the first thought is true at a world if it is hot where DJC is at time t in that world; the subjunctive intension of the second thought is true at a world when it is hot in place p in that world (where t and p are the time and place of the actual thoughts). The epistemic contents of the thoughts reflect their rational relationship, but the subjunctive contents do not.

It is straightforward to see why this is so. If

one thought entails another a priori, then any scenario that verifies the first will verify the second. Conversely, it is plausible that if the epistemic intension of one thought entails that of another, a thinker should in principle be able to infer the second from the first by (idealized) a priori reasoning. (As before, if scenarios are identified with centered worlds and if strong necessities exist, this converse claim will be false. For example, the epistemic intension of *a god exists* might be entailed by any intension without the thought being a priori. Again, on such a view the claim can be preserved by moving to the purely epistemic understanding of scenarios.) This is not so for subjunctive intensions: entailments between these may turn on facts about the external world that are not accessible to the thinker.

This can be applied straightforwardly to explain the informativeness of a thought such as *Hesperus is Phosphorus.* Although its subjunctive intension is equivalent to that of the trivial *Hesperus is Hesperus,* its epistemic intension is quite distinct, so it is not cognitively trivial. In effect, epistemic intension here plays the role of Fregean sense. Again, it is epistemic intensions that reflect the rational properties of thoughts.

We can also invoke epistemic content in the case of Kripke's Pierre, who paradoxically seems to believe that London is pretty and that London is not pretty, without any breakdown in rationality. Pierre's concepts *Londres* and *London* have quite different epistemic intensions: in a given scenario, the first picks out (roughly) the famous city called 'Londres' that the individual at the center has heard about, whereas the second picks out (very roughly) the grimy city in which that individual has been living. The subjunctive intensions are identical, picking out London in every world. So Pierre's two beliefs *Londres is pretty* and *London is not pretty* have contradictory subjunctive intensions, but their epistemic intensions are quite compatible. Rational relations are determined by epistemic content, so contradictory subjunctive intensions support no charge of irrationality.

Intuitively, Pierre's two beliefs are rationally compatible because there are specific ways the actual world could be that are consistent with both. There is a scenario in which 'Londres' names a faraway, beautiful city (maybe it is in India), and in which the individual at the center inhabits an entirely distinct ugly city called 'London'. For all Pierre knows and believes, such a scenario could be actual: this scenario

verifies *both* of Pierre's beliefs. As long as there is such a scenario, satisfying the epistemic intensions of all of Pierre's thoughts, the *epistemic* contents of these thoughts will be compatible, and Pierre's rationality will not be in danger.

This brings out the relation between this account and Dennett's (1981) suggestion that the narrow content of a thought is reflected in the *notional world* of the thinker. We can take the notional world to be a scenario (really a class of scenarios) that verifies all of a subject's beliefs, or at least as many as possible.[17] Pierre's notional world is a world in which there is a beautiful faraway city called 'Londres', and a grimy city close at hand called 'London'. If Pierre really lived in his notional world, he would be right about everything and rarely surprised.

On similar grounds, one can make the case that epistemic content reflects the *cognitive* relations between thoughts. Here there is an important qualification: epistemic content as I have defined it does not distinguish the various cognitive relations that might hold between thoughts that are deductively equivalent. From the point of view of epistemic content, a complex mathematical proof is as trivial as modus ponens; the fine-grained cognitive dynamics of deduction lies beyond the reach of epistemic content as I have defined it here. I think a more fine-grained variety of epistemic content can handle these cases better (see Chalmers forthcoming b). I will set these issues aside here, as subjunctive content does not handle them any better, and they are largely independent of the issues at play in this paper.

A qualified thesis would be the following: insofar as epistemic content or subjunctive content reflect the cognitive relations between thoughts, the contribution of epistemic content *screens off* the contribution of subjunctive content. That is, in cases where two thoughts are cognitively related, then (1) in related cases where the epistemic content of the thoughts is held constant but the subjunctive content is varied, the cognitive relations are preserved (except insofar as cognitive relations can be affected by varying factors independent of *both* epistemic and subjunctive content, as in the deductive case); and (2) in related cases in which the subjunctive content is preserved but epistemic content is not, the cognitive relations are damaged. One can make this case straightforwardly by examining cases; the details parallel those of the discussion of the explanation of behavior, below, so I will not duplicate them here.

A third advantage of epistemic content is its suitability for a role in the explanation of behavior. It is often noted that subjunctive content seems slightly out of synchrony with what one would expect of an explanatory psychological state. To use an example of Kaplan's (1989), if you are watching me and my pants catch fire, our respective beliefs that my pants are on fire now will have the same subjunctive content (true in all worlds in which DJC's pants are on fire at time t), but will lead to very different actions (I might jump into a river, while you just sit there). The difference between our actions does not seem to be something that a characterization in terms of subjunctive content alone can explain. In a similar way, belief states can produce very similar behavior for apparently systematic reasons, even when the beliefs have very different subjunctive content: witness the behavior that my twin and I produce when we think about twin water and water respectively, or the similarity between the actions of two people who think *I am hungry*. It seems that a whole dimension of the explanation of behavior is hard for subjunctive content to explain.

These explanations can be easily handled in terms of epistemic content. If you and I think *I am hungry,* the epistemic contents of our thoughts are the same, and that similarity is reflected in the similarity of our actions. When you and I both believe that my pants are on fire, on the other hand, our epistemic contents are very different, and our actions differ correspondingly. Note that this provides a straightforward solution to Perry's problem of the essential indexical: it is epistemic content, not subjunctive content, that governs action, and epistemic content, consisting in a centered intension, is a sort of *indexical* content.[18]

Epistemic content also accounts for the similarity of action between twin cases; this similarity reflects the fact that my beliefs about water and my twin's beliefs about twin water have the same epistemic content. But we need not move to the realm of science fiction to see the point. Two thoughts can share epistemic content even when two thinkers are quite different, as our thoughts *I am hungry* show. Even in these cases, similarities in epistemic content will lead to similarities in action, other things being equal. Suppose I think that Superman is across the road, and I want to have Superman's autograph: then other things being equal, I will cross the road.[19] If you have thoughts with similar epis-

temic content to mine, then you will do the same. If your thoughts share only subjunctive content with mine, while having different epistemic content—perhaps you think that Clark Kent is across the road, but want Superman's autograph—then your corresponding behavior may be quite different.

In general, whenever the content of a thought is causally relevant to behavior, its contribution is screened off by that of epistemic content in the following sense. If an alternative thought had the same epistemic content but different subjunctive content, the resulting behavior would have been physically indiscernible (except insofar it might be affected by changing factors independent of both sorts of content); whereas if it had the same subjunctive content but different epistemic content, the resulting behavior might have been quite different.

To see the latter point, we need only examine cases like those above. The thoughts *I am hungry* and *The guy over there is hungry* (unknowingly looking in a mirror) will lead to very different behavior, even though their subjunctive content is the same. When Lois Lane is trying to cut Clark Kent's hair, her observation "Clark's hair breaks the scissors" will prompt a reaction very different from that provoked by a corresponding thought concerning Superman. If I hear that Cary Grant is starring in a movie, I might be more likely to watch than if I hear that the movie stars Archie Leach. In all these cases, different reactions are provoked by a different in the epistemic content of a thought. In general, whenever the epistemic content of a thought is varied, different consequences can be expected, even if subjunctive content is preserved throughout.[20] Given that epistemic content is central to cognitive relations and that cognition governs action, this is just what we would expect.

By contrast, if the subjunctive content of a thought is varied but epistemic content is kept constant, behavior stays indistinguishable throughout. Perhaps, unbeknownst to me, Cary Grant is an elaborate hoax, a co-operative construction by avant-garde animators and the mass media. In such a case, my thought about Cary Grant will have no nontrivial subjunctive content, but as long as it has the same epistemic content, my behavior will be indistinguishable from the case in which he is real. Or perhaps Cary Grant is really Ludwig Wittgenstein in disguise: if so, the thought has a very different subjunctive content, but the same behavior results.

Similarly, when my twin and I think *I need some more water for this pot,* the subjunctive contents of our thoughts differ, but we both go to the sink.

We can make a similar point within a single system. Take Evans' example of 'Julius', which functions to rigidly designate whoever invented the zip. Then the epistemic intensions of my concepts *Julius* and *the inventor of the zip* will be the same, but the subjunctive intensions will be very different. Despite the difference in subjunctive intensions, however, it is clear that any thoughts of the form *Julius is such-and-such* and *the inventor of the zip is such-and-such* will play very much the same role in directing cognition and action. The rigidification and consequent difference in subjunctive intension is largely irrelevant. One exception: the two concepts may behave differently in subjunctive thought, as when one judges that Julius might not have been the inventor of the zip, but not that Julius might not have been Julius. But even here the difference is accounted for by a difference in the internally determined two-dimensional intension, rather than by a difference in subjunctive content per se.

Some might object that there are cases in which we individuate behavior extrinsically—for example, Oscar drinks water while Twin Oscar drinks twin water—so there is a dimension of behavior that escapes epistemic content. But even in this sort of case, subjunctive content does not usually help. Even Twin Oscar, with his different subjunctive content, would drink water if he were in Oscar's present environment. What is relevant to behavior here is not subjunctive content but current environment, as we can see by an extension of the varying-factors strategy; and I certainly do not wish to deny that current environment is relevant in the explanation of behavior.

The only cases in which there is a direct tie between subjunctive content and behavior are cases in which behavior is individuated by an intentional object: for example, Oscar searches for a glass of water, whereas Twin Oscar searches for a glass of twin water. This connection holds across all environments, as behavior only counts as water-searching if it is caused by water-thoughts. But for the same reason, this is a very weak sort of relevance for subjunctive content: as Fodor (1991) notes, in these cases the subjunctive contents of thoughts are not *causally* relevant to action, but instead are *conceptually* relevant, in effect determining the cat-

egory the action falls under.[21] Subjunctive content gives us very little purchase in the *explanation* of action here, as we will only know that some behavior is water-searching if we already know that water-thoughts lie behind it. In a causal (as opposed to a conceptual) explanation of the action, epistemic content will still play the central role.

Why is epistemic content primary? To answer this question, it is useful to think of my belief contents as constituting a model of my world, a kind of map by which I steer. This is a model of the world as I find it, a centered world with me at the center, and my beliefs are constraints on that world. Beliefs constitute a model by constraining *epistemic space:* the space of epistemic possibilities that were open to me a priori. One belief rules out one group of epistemic possibilities as a candidate for the world where I am, another belief rules out another group, until only a limited class of worlds is left. I operate under the assumption that my world is one of those worlds, and if I am lucky I will not be too surprised.

My world-model is ultimately a *notional* world: a set of epistemic possibilities, such that none of these would overly surprise me if they turned out to be actual. The constraints on these possibilities are those of epistemic content. Any further constraints imposed by subjunctive content are not useful to me. The subjunctive content of my belief that the liquid in thermometers is mercury endorses only those worlds in which thermometers contain the element with atomic number x, but this constraint is so distant that if it turned out that the liquid has atomic number y, I would not be in the least surprised. In an important sense, this constraint is not reflected in my world-model at all. Insofar as my world-model is useful to me in guiding cognition and action, the constraints on it are entirely those of epistemic content.

In making a case for the primacy of epistemic content, I have not appealed to any a priori methodological principles such as the dictum that what governs behavior is in the head. The case for epistemic content has been made directly, independently of questions about physical realization. Indeed, nothing I have said implies that facts about a thinker's environment are irrelevant to the explanation of behavior. Facts about the proximal environment will clearly play an important role insofar as they affect a thinker;[22] facts about the current environment are crucial to explaining the success or failure of various actions; and facts about environmental history will at least be central to a causal explanation of a thinker's current cognitive state. All that follows from the present framework is that the environment is not relevant to the explanation of behavior *in virtue of its role in constituting subjunctive content*. The kind of *content* that governs behavior is purely epistemic.

8. Belief Ascription and Psychological Explanation

All this raises a puzzle about the role of belief ascriptions in psychological explanation. If what has gone before is correct, the kind of content that governs cognition and action is epistemic content, which is narrow. But at the same time, there is strong evidence that the kind of content attributed by belief ascriptions is often wide. Does this mean that the common-sense framework of explanation of behavior in terms of belief ascription should be discarded? Alternatively, is the success of the common-sense framework evidence that something in these arguments has gone badly wrong?

Neither conclusion is justified. The present framework shows how it can at once be true that (1) belief ascriptions ascribe wide content, (2) narrow content governs action, and (3) belief ascriptions explain action. In short: belief ascriptions ascribe a combination of epistemic and subjunctive content. It is in virtue of the subjunctive component that the ascribed content is wide, and it is in virtue of the epistemic component that the ascribed content is explanatory.

A full justification of this answer requires two things. First, we need an analysis of what is attributed in belief ascriptions, so that we can see precisely what sorts of epistemic and subjunctive content are attributed. Second, we need an analysis of the role of belief ascriptions in psychological explanation, so that we can see that even in ordinary practice, it is the epistemic content attributed that carries the explanatory burden. I cannot provide anything like a complete treatment of these matters—the analysis of belief ascriptions deserves entire volumes of its own—but I can provide a preliminary sketch.

It is easy to see that ordinary belief ascriptions ascribe both epistemic and subjunctive content. If I say 'Ralph believes that Clark Kent is muscular', then in order for my utterance to be true, Ralph must have a belief that satisfies two sorts of constraints. First, the belief must have the subjunctive content of the proposition that Clark Kent is muscular (perhaps we can allow a certain amount of variation in the subjunctive content, if for example his concept of muscularity is slightly different from the norm). But that alone is not enough: a belief that Superman is muscular would have the same subjunctive content, but would not make my ascription true. As is often noted (e.g., Schiffer 1990), for the ascription to be true, the belief must involve a concept that refers to its object (Clark Kent) under an appropriate mode of presentation.[23]

In the current framework, modes of presentation are naturally seen as epistemic intensions. If Ralph refers to Clark Kent under an epistemic intension that picks out whoever is called 'Clark Kent', or one that picks out whoever is that reporter with glasses at the Daily Planet, or some more complex intension in the vicinity, my belief ascription will be true. If Ralph refers to Clark Kent under an epistemic intension that picks out the guy in the cape, or one that picks out the strongest man in the world, my belief ascription will be false. One might say that for the ascription to be true, Ralph must refer to Clark Kent under a 'Clark Kent'–appropriate epistemic intension. Here, the conditions on a 'Clark Kent'–appropriate epistemic intension are somewhat vague and unclear, and they may well be context-dependent, but it is clear from an examination of cases that they are substantive.

To take another case, if I am right in saying 'Tom believes that he is hungry', then Tom must have a belief with more or less the appropriate subjunctive content, true of all those worlds in which Tom is hungry at time t. But there is also a strong constraint on epistemic content. In particular, Tom must refer to himself via the epistemic intension that picks out the individual at the center in every scenario. If he sees someone in the distance clutching their belly, without realizing that he is in fact looking into a mirror, then a thought that that person is hungry has the right subjunctive content, but on the most natural reading it does not make my ascription true. The ascription will only be true if Tom's belief refers to himself under a *self*-concept, which requires a very specific sort of epistemic content. One might say that here, Tom must refer to himself under a 'he'-appropriate epistemic intension, where in context the only 'he'-appropriate epistemic intension is the purely indexical intension.

The general principle here is something like

the following. A belief ascription 'x believes that S' is true when the ascribee has a belief with the subjunctive intension of S (in the mouth of the ascriber), and with an S-appropriate epistemic intension. Here, the epistemic intension is usually much less strongly constrained than the subjunctive intension. The conditions on S-appropriateness may well be complex and context-dependent; their precise nature is one of the hardest questions in the theory of belief ascriptions. Still, one can make a few generalizations. Much of the time, an epistemic intension that is not too different from the ascriber's will be S-appropriate, and much of the time, an epistemic intension that involves the terms in S itself will be S-appropriate. But this does not yield any sort of general condition. Rather, the appropriateness-conditions are best revealed by careful investigation of judgments of the ascription's truth in specific cases involving various different epistemic intensions.

In effect, this yields truth-conditions on belief ascriptions that parallel those of what Schiffer (1992) calls a "hidden-indexical" theory of belief ascription (although I have remained neutral on the ascriptions' logical form), with epistemic intensions playing the role of modes of presentation.[24] If something like this is correct, then epistemic intensions yield a solution to Schiffer's "mode of presentation" problem.[25] Epistemic intensions are perfectly suited to satisfy what Schiffer (1990, p. 252) calls "Frege's constraint" on modes of presentation: roughly, that a rational person may both believe and disbelieve that y is such-and-such only if the two beliefs involve different modes of presentation of y. If "rationality" is interpreted to involve idealized a priori reasoning, then the satisfaction of this constraint follows from the fact that epistemic intensions reflect a priori connections between thoughts.

We can apply this to the case of Pierre, and the ascriptions 'Pierre believes that London is pretty' and 'Pierre believes that London is not pretty.' To satisfy these ascriptions, Pierre must have beliefs with the specified subjunctive intension, referring to London under a 'London'-appropriate epistemic intension. Pierre's *London* and *Londres* concepts have different epistemic intensions, but both intensions are 'London'-appropriate. So by virtue of his belief *Londres is pretty,* Pierre satisfies the first ascription, and by virtue of his belief *London is not pretty* he satisfies the second. Before, we explained Pierre's *beliefs* by noting that his two beliefs have con-

tradictory subjunctive intensions but compatible epistemic intensions, where only the latter is relevant to rationality. Now, we can explain the apparent contradiction in the belief *ascriptions* by noting that two different epistemic intensions can both be 'London'-appropriate, so the two ascriptions do not in fact ascribe a rational contradiction to Pierre.[26]

We have seen that content decomposes naturally into epistemic and subjunctive content; we now see that belief ascription puts strong constraints on both. Ideally, a full theory of belief ascription will specify the nature of these constraints for any given ascription, telling us the conditions that beliefs' epistemic and subjunctive contents must satisfy in order to make the ascription true. We can think of a belief ascription as marking out a subspace in the space of ordered pairs of epistemic and subjunctive content.

Given that epistemic content governs action, it follows that if belief ascriptions are to causally explain action, it must be in virtue of the epistemic content ascribed; the subjunctive content ascribed is redundant to the explanation. To make this case properly requires examining many specific cases, but the general point can be straightforwardly illustrated. One way to see the primacy of epistemic content is to consider belief ascriptions involving empty names, such as 'Santa Claus'. These ascribe no nontrivial subjunctive content, but ascription of beliefs about Santa Claus seem to function in precisely the same way in the explanation of action as do ascriptions of beliefs about real people. We might explain Karen's agitation on Christmas Eve in terms of her belief that Santa Claus is coming, that he will not fit down the chimney, and so on. Santa's non-existence and the corresponding absence of subjunctive content make little difference to the success of such an explanation. What governs Karen's actions are her *notions* of Santa Claus; and what governs the success of the explanation is the epistemic content that these ascriptions ascribe to her. This is a *typical* case of the role of belief ascriptions in explanation: even when non-trivial subjunctive content is ascribed (as when the referent of the name exists), it makes little difference to the patterns of explanation.

In a very wide variety of cases in which content explains action, we can see that the explanation succeeds even if the subjunctive content attributed is ignored. For instance, if we explain my opening the refrigerator in terms of my belief that there is water in the refrigerator and my desire for a glass of water, we never need to invoke the H_2O-involving subjunctive content. The explanation gains sufficient purchase from the epistemic content ascribed alone—roughly, the content that there is some of the liquid with the appropriate properties in the refrigerator, and that I want some of that liquid, and so on.[27]

It might be objected that there are cases in which the constraints on the epistemic content ascribed by a belief ascription are weak, so that subjunctive content must be doing any explanatory work. I think that ascriptions putting weak constraints on epistemic content are rare, but let us assume they can occur: perhaps an attribution of a belief about Smith constrains the relevant epistemic intension very little.[28] Even so, if we look at explanatory practice, we see that epistemic content is still doing the real work. For example, perhaps we explain why Bev goes to the pub by saying that she wants to see Smith and believes that Smith is at the pub. Leaving aside constraints in the concepts of seeing, the pub, and so on, there is a constraint on epistemic content implicit in the 'Smith' attributions. It is implicit here that the two 'Smith' concepts in Bev's thoughts have the same epistemic intensions. If her belief and her desire had very different epistemic content associated with 'Smith'—perhaps she wants to see Batman and believes that Smith is at the pub, not knowing that Smith is Batman—the inference from those states to her action would fail. So there is a strong joint constraint on epistemic content: despite a lack of constraint on the individual beliefs, Bev is implicitly ascribed the belief that a person she wants to see is at the pub. It is *this* ascribed belief that is doing the real explanatory work, and this ascription clearly puts a heavy constraint on epistemic content. To make the case that all such examples can be similarly analyzed requires a detailed treatment, but this illustrates the general pattern.

It follows that the centrality of narrow factors in the causation of action need not overthrow the role of belief ascriptions in explaining behavior, as some (e.g., Stich 1983) have suggested it should. At most we have shown that belief ascriptions are a somewhat rough-edged tool: they wrap both components of content into a single parcel, bringing the idle subjunctive content into play alongside the epistemic content that does all the work. But this should not surprise us; we cannot expect a folk theory to be maximally efficient.[29]

In moving from common-sense psychology toward a developed cognitive science, we might expect that the kind of content that is invoked will become more purely epistemic, and that subjunctive content will be relegated to a secondary role or dropped entirely.[30] We might also expect that better tools will be developed to specify the epistemic contents of thoughts than the current rough-and-ready language of belief ascription. This might qualify as a revision of our folk notion of belief, emphasizing and refining the elements of epistemic content that are already present within it. But precisely because those elements are already present and playing a central role in our practices, such a development would fall well short of elimination.

9. Connections and Objections

The framework outlined here is related to a number of existing proposals. There is a clear structural resemblance to other broadly two-dimensional frameworks, such as proposals by Kaplan (1989) and Stalnaker (1978) for analyzing the content of language, and proposals by White (1982) and Fodor (1987) for analyzing the contents of thought. The idea that this sort of proposal can be used to yield a sort of narrow content has been criticized by Block (1991), Stalnaker (1989; 1990), and others, and extended to an earlier version of the present proposal by Block and Stalnaker (1999). So we need to examine the relationship between these proposals, to see whether the criticisms apply. I think that on examination, the current framework differs in fundamental respects from the others, so that their problems do not arise here.

The relationship can be brought out by contrasting epistemic intensions with *contextual intensions*. A thought's contextual intension is defined by the heuristic discussed earlier: T is true in a centered world W (with T present at the center) if T is true as thought at the center of W. Likewise, the contextual intension of a concept C will return C's extension in worlds with C at the center. (One can define contextual intensions for sentences and other linguistic expressions similarly.) There are various possible variations here: one might have different requirements for what counts as a token of T in a world, or one might require only a token of T's type (for some relevant type) rather than T itself. But however one does things, the centered worlds here are functioning as *contexts* in which a thought (or concept) occurs, and a contextual intension encapsulates the *context-dependence* of a thought's truth-value or a concept's extension.

As we saw before, contextual intensions are quite different from epistemic intensions. An obvious difference: epistemic intensions give no special role to thought tokens within a scenario, and can be evaluated in scenarios without any such tokens at the center. Thus the epistemic intension of *I am a philosopher* can be true at a scenario regardless of what the being at the center is thinking. A thought such as *someone is thinking* has an epistemic intension that is plausibly false at some centered worlds (e.g., those without any thoughts), although its contextual intension (on a natural understanding) is true at all centered worlds in which it is defined. A deeper difference: where contextual intensions represent context-dependence, with centered worlds representing contexts of thought, epistemic intensions represent *epistemic dependence,* with centered worlds representing epistemic possibilities. This is a very different conception, and yields quite different behavior.

The frameworks of Kaplan and Stalnaker illustrate this. Kaplan defines the character of a linguistic expression type as a function from a context of utterance to the expression's content (roughly, subjunctive intension) relative to that context. In some ways this resembles the two-dimensional intension discussed above (in effect a function from centered worlds to subjunctive intensions), but the underlying ideas and resulting behavior are quite different. For example, on Kaplan's framework names such as 'Hesperus' and 'Phosphorus' have identical characters, picking out the same content in all contexts. This happens because the referent of a name is essential to that name, so any use of the name in any context will have the same referent. For this reason, Kaplan notes that his framework cannot provide a solution to Frege's puzzle in the case of names, natural kind terms, and the like. But as we have seen, the epistemic intension associated with a subject's use of a name behaves very differently, often picking out different individuals in different centered worlds (whether a name has its referent essentially is irrelevant on a non-contextual understanding), and holds out much more hope of dealing with Frege's puzzle.

Stalnaker defines the diagonal proposition of an expression token as a function from a world containing the token to the truth-value of the proposition that the token expresses in that world, as evaluated in that world. This bears a formal resemblance to an epistemic intension, which can be seen as equivalent to the diagonal of a two-dimensional intension. But again, the underlying ideas and resulting behavior are different. On Stalnaker's framework, the diagonal proposition of an expression is defined at worlds where it has a very different meaning. At a world where 'water is solid' means that snow is white, for example, the diagonal proposition of 'water is solid' will be true if snow is white in that world. This is quite different from an epistemic intension: if my usage is nondeferential, the use of terms such as 'water' in a scenario will be irrelevant to epistemic intensions. Stalnaker (1999) notes that because of this, diagonal propositions are not closely connected to a priori truth. This seems correct, but the problem does not generalize to epistemic intensions, which have a built-in connection to a priori truth.

White (1982) and Fodor (1987) generalize these analyses to the contents of thought. Fodor defines the narrow content of a thought as a function from a context of thought to a thought's (wide) content in that context. White does something similar, although his account is slightly more complex and he requires that a functional duplicate of the original thinker be present in the relevant context. As before, these proposals are based on context-dependence, and give results that differ correspondingly: witness the intensions of *I am a philosopher* and *someone is thinking.*[31]

Block (1991) gives a number of objections to proposals of this sort. White's proposal is subject to a charge of *holism:* no two different subjects can have thoughts with the same narrow content, unless they are functional duplicates. Further, it seems that the narrow contents of a subject's thoughts all change every time the subject acquires a new belief, or indeed every time that anything happens in the mind of the subject. This problem does not apply to epistemic intensions. There is no problem with quite different thinkers having thoughts with the same epistemic intension: for example, very different people can have *I am a philosopher* thoughts with the same epistemic intension. Further, epistemic intensions will not usually change with the acquisition of new beliefs. A change in epistemic intension requires a change in a subject's rational pattern of judgments about scenarios considered as actual: a change in belief may change the subject's judgments about which scenarios are actual, but it will not usually change a subject's rational judgment about what will be the case *if* a given scenario is actual. It may be that epistemic intensions sometimes drift over time, or that corresponding thoughts of different thinkers sometimes have different epistemic intensions, but this falls well short of a general holism.

Block charges Fodor's proposal with underdetermination: it is left unclear how to evaluate the mapping across worlds. The main problem is that of "what is held constant". That is, to know which worlds fall in the domain of the intension, one needs to know just what features of the original thought must be present in the thought token at the center. If only a sort of mental syntax is held constant, the result will be an intension that delivers wildly varying results across worlds: there will be worlds where the mapping for *water* picks out steel, if a token with that mental syntax has a different meaning. If extension is held constant, then the intension will be trivial: the mapping for *water* picks out H_2O in all worlds. For better results, one might suggest that the token's *narrow content* be held constant, but that presupposes what we are trying to explain. So it seems very difficult to set things up so that the mapping yields a narrow content that behaves in an appropriate way.

Again, epistemic intensions do not have this problem. There is no issues concerning what to "hold constant" across worlds here, since there is no need for the original token to be present in different worlds. Rather, we simply appeal to the *original* thought, and to its epistemic relations with the hypothesis that a given world is actual. These epistemic relations are well-defined, being grounded in the idealized rational judgments of the subject. They also do not presuppose any theoretical notion of narrow content; but they can be used to ground such a theoretical notion.

Fodor himself (1987, p. 50) raises the problem that his sort of narrow content is not semantically evaluable (for truth and falsity), and so is not really content; rather, it is just *potential* content, delivering a content in a context. (He later rejects narrow content for this reason.) Again, epistemic content is immune to this problem. An epistemic intension is a sort of first-order content, placing direct constraints on the world, with truth-conditions of its own. Epistemic intensions can also stand in semantic relations such as entailment, and can be analyzed using semantic frameworks involving possible worlds, which allows for significant explanatory power.

Stalnaker (1990) considers the idea that some version of his diagonal proposition (or "realization conditions") might yield an account of narrow content, and raises three criticisms. First, he suggests that we cannot identify a thought independently of its content, so we cannot ask what the content of a belief *would* have been had it been a belief on twin earth. Second, he notes that diagonal propositions are defined only in worlds containing the relevant thought token, and cannot easily be extended to worlds without the thought token. Third, he notes that on this proposal narrow content is derivative on wide content (since a diagonal proposition is defined using a two-dimensional matrix which is defined using wide content), so it presupposes rather than explains wide content. In response, it is fairly clear that the first two objections apply only to contextually defined narrow content, and not to epistemically defined narrow content. On the epistemic proposal, we never need to ask what the content of a belief would have been if it had been a belief on twin earth, and narrow content is defined in a straightforward way at worlds that do not contain the relevant thought token.

In discussing his second objection, Stalnaker raises a case that is worth addressing. If Bert uses his semantically deferential concept to think *my father has arthritis in his thigh,* how can we evaluate this thought in a world in which there is no word 'arthritis' in Bert's language, and in which Bert has no thoughts about his father's health? On the epistemic framework, it is most natural to say that the epistemic intension of Bert's *arthritis* concept picks out nothing in this world. In effect, the use of a semantically deferential concept *presupposes* that one lives in a community that uses the relevant term, just as a notion such as *the present king of France* presupposes that there is a king of France. If I discover that those assumptions do not hold in my actual scenario, it is reasonable to judge that my thoughts involving these concepts lack truth-value. The same goes for alternative scenarios. In Bert's case, the epistemic intension of his thought is indeterminate in the relevant worlds. In effect, Bert's thought partitions the space of scenarios in which the background assumptions are satisfied, and says nothing about those worlds in which the assumptions are false.[32]

As for Stalnaker's third objection: narrow content may be derivative on wide content on the diagonal understanding, but not on the epistemic understanding. Epistemic content can be defined quite independently of subjunctive content, and our definition of epistemic intensions makes no appeal to subjunctive evaluation. For this reason, an epistemic intension is not fundamentally a diagonal intension. *After* the fact, one can see an epistemic intension as equivalent to the diagonal of a two-dimensional intension involving both epistemic and subjunctive notions; but this complex construction is quite unnecessary to define epistemic intensions. One can characterize the first dimension of the framework in entirely epistemic terms, independently of the second dimension.

If any sort of content is derivative in the current framework, it is wide content. We have already seen that the subjunctive intension of a concept is determined by the epistemic intension in conjunction with the environment. In some cases it is a near-copy of the epistemic intension, as for simple descriptive concepts; in other cases it is determined by rigidifying the actual-world extension of the epistemic intension. By contrast, we can tell the entire story about the epistemic intension without ever involving the subjunctive intension. It therefore seems that if either intension is more fundamental, it is the epistemic intension. Still, there is no need to make too strong a claim here: both epistemic and subjunctive content are important, and both have a role to play in different domains.

Block and Stalnaker (1999) give a number of objections to the version of this framework put forward in Chalmers (1996). Many of these objections echo the objections above, and turn on interpreting the proposal via a contextual rather than an epistemic understanding.[33] Another objection is that the formal two-dimensional apparatus alone does not yield intensions with the relevant properties. This is clearly correct; but on my approach it is a substantive characterization of the intensions, not just the formal apparatus, that yields the properties in question. Block and Stalnaker also argue that the two-dimensional approach cannot explain or ground a notion of a priori truth. I have not suggested that the framework can do this; rather, I have used the notion of apriority in defining the framework. The notion of apriority, and the specific uses of it in grounding the framework, can be defended on quite independent grounds. The use of apriority in capturing the dependence of

judgments about extension and truth-value on sufficient information about the world is defended at length by Chalmers and Jackson (2001).

The current proposal also bears a resemblance to "descriptive" accounts of narrow content. It has sometimes been suggested that the narrow content of a concept such as *water* corresponds to the content of an associated description such as 'the dominant clear drinkable liquid in the environment', or some such. In response, a number of philosophers (LePore and Loewer 1986; Taylor 1989; White 1982) have objected that even if such descriptions exist, terms such as 'liquid' are themselves susceptible to Twin Earth scenarios (e.g., where liquids are replaced by superficially identical masses of sand), so that the content of such a description is wide rather than narrow. One might think that this objection will apply to the present proposal, since I have used descriptions of this sort to characterize epistemic intensions. But importantly, the description merely provides a rough handle on the intension for the purposes of illustration. The real narrow content is a function from scenarios to extensions, and can be characterized fully only by specifying its value at specific scenarios. As soon as we move to a summarizing description in language, imperfections are introduced, and the narrowness of the content is impurified. But the intension itself remains narrow; we should not mistake the linguistic description for the real thing.[34]

One would obtain a more closely related sort of "description" theory of epistemic content if one abstracted away from linguistic characterizations and regarded the relevant "descriptions" simply as properties that a referent must satisfy, or better, as relations to the thinker. If we speak merely of properties and relations, the linguistic contamination is avoided. Schiffer (1978) suggests a description theory of this sort, on which there is irreducibly *de re* reference by a thinker to himself or herself, with reference to everything else mediated by a property or relation. If we map the irreducible self-reference here to the appeal to centered worlds, and map the properties and relations to epistemic intensions, the resemblance between the accounts is clear, although Schiffer does not define the relevant properties in epistemic terms, and addresses his proposal largely to the question of accounting for *de re* thought.

Another closely related idea is Lewis's (1979) proposal that belief involves the self-ascription of a property. The set of individuals satisfying a property corresponds directly to a class of centered worlds, as Lewis notes. Lewis (1994) argues that this sort of content is narrow and is primary in explanation. In effect, Lewis advocates a one-dimensional view of content, where apparent wide content is an artifact of belief ascriptions. While Lewis does not advocate understanding these contents in epistemic terms, and does not give a general characterization of the set of worlds associated with a belief, his examples suggest that these sets of worlds closely resemble those of an epistemic intension. So the present proposal appears to be highly compatible with Lewis's framework.

A residual problem for the present account is the problem of hyperintensionality. It seems that two beliefs—mathematical beliefs, for example—can have the same epistemic and subjunctive intensions, while nevertheless having intuitively different content, and playing quite different roles in cognition and action. To handle these issues, one needs a more fine-grained sort of epistemic content that goes beyond epistemic intensions as I have defined them. One might appeal to intensions over a more fine-grained space of epistemic possibilities, defined using a more demanding notion of epistemic necessity operator that requires more than mere apriority (see Chalmers forthcoming b for some ideas here).[35] One might also appeal to a more basic sort of content that lies behind and determines an epistemic intension. Epistemic and subjunctive intensions are aspects of the contents of thoughts, but I have not suggested that they exhaust these contents. The nature of a complete characterization of thought contents, if such a thing can be given, remains an open question.

Another open question: is it possible to reductively explain the epistemic content of a subject's thoughts in naturalistic terms, in the way that some have attempted to explain wide content in causal or teleological terms? Certainly no such explanation is currently available. A first attempt might exploit the idea that epistemic content is mirrored in the idealized rational dispositions of the subject: perhaps a subject's actual dispositions will yield epistemic content by idealization? The normative character of the idealization may pose an obstacle to reduction, however, as will the fact that these dispositions are themselves characterized by appeal to content. My own view is that epistemic content is ultimately determined by a combination of a subject's functional organiza-

tion and phenomenology.[36] If so, any attempt at explanation will need to appeal to these factors. In any case, it is arguable that if wide content depends heavily on narrow content, as the current account suggests, any adequate reductive theory of wide content will require a reductive theory of narrow content first.[37]

10. Conclusion

What of the six puzzles at the start? To summarize:

(1) A thought's content decomposes into epistemic and subjunctive content, given by its epistemic and subjunctive intensions. Oscar's and Twin Oscar's thoughts differ in their subjunctive contents, and as a result ground different belief ascriptions, but their epistemic contents are the same.

(2) My thoughts that Hesperus is Hesperus and that Hesperus is Phosphorus have the same subjunctive intension but distinct epistemic intensions, as the *Hesperus* and *Phosphorus* concepts have different epistemic intensions. The triviality of the former does not imply the triviality of the latter, as it is epistemic content that governs rational relations.

(3) Pierre's two beliefs have contradictory subjunctive intensions but compatible epistemic intensions. The apparently contradictory belief ascriptions arise because of the contradictory subjunctive intensions and because his two concepts of London have distinct epistemic intensions that can each make 'London'-involving belief ascriptions true. Rationality is governed by epistemic intensions, so there is no rational contradiction here.

(4) The essential indexicality of belief reflects the fact that epistemic content, not subjunctive content, governs action, and that epistemic content, unlike subjunctive content, is an indexical centered intension.

(5) The modes of presentation central to a theory of belief ascription are epistemic intensions. Belief ascriptions specify a believer's subjunctive content, and constrain the believer's epistemic content.

(6) Instances of the contingent a priori have a necessary epistemic intension but a contingent subjunctive intension. One's cognitive world-model is constrained by epistemic content, not by subjunctive content; so a contingent subjunctive intension does not indicate a cognitive achievement.

There are many problems about the contents of thought that are not resolved by this framework. These include the problems of hyperintensionality, of a full account of belief ascriptions, and of giving a naturalistic explanation of content. Some of these matters are likely to be much more difficult than the puzzles at issue in this paper, but the two-dimensional approach at least clarifies the lay of the land.

NOTES

Thanks to too many people to mention, but especially Ned Block, Curtis Brown, Frank Jackson, David Lewis, Mark Sainsbury, Robert Stalnaker, and two reviewers. Thanks also to audiences at talks between 1994 and 1997 at Arizona, Cornell, Memphis, Princeton, Rice, UCLA, UC Santa Barbara, UC Santa Cruz, Washington University, Yale, and the Australasian Association of Philosophy. For comments on the revised version, thanks to Torin Alter, Chris Evans, Brie Gertler, Terry Horgan, and Daniel Stoljar.

1. This is a heavily revised version of a paper first written in 1994 and revised in 1995. Sections 1, 7, 8, and 10 are similar to the old version, but the other sections are quite different. Because the old version has been widely cited, I have made it available (in its 1995 version) at http://consc.net/papers/content95.html.

   This paper is an application of a framework that I have developed in other papers. The discussion here often passes over details that are explored in more depth in those papers. (Chalmers 2002b gives the gentlest introduction; Chalmers forthcoming a and b give full details.) The framework presented here has much in common with existing ideas in the philosophy of mind and language, especially Kaplan's (1989) and Stalnaker's (1978) two-dimensional analyses of language, Lewis's (1979) analysis of the contents of thought, and various proposals that have been made about the nature of narrow content. For some connections between these ideas, see section 9 and Chalmers (forthcoming a).

2. For background on the six puzzles, see: (1) Putnam 1975, Burge 1979; (2) Frege 1892; (3) Kripke 1979; (4) Perry 1979; (5) Schiffer 1990; (6) Kripke 1980.

3. Arguments for narrow content can be found in Dennett 1981, Fodor 1987, Lewis 1994, Loar 1988, Segal 2000, and White 1982.

4. A few fine details here: (1) We can say that a thought is conclusively justified when it has the sort of justification that carries a guarantee of truth: the sort of justification carried by deduction or analysis, for example, as opposed to the non-conclusive justification carried by induction or abduction. The restriction to conclusive a priori justification is required to exclude, e.g., false mathematical beliefs that might be a priori justified by induction from true beliefs. (2) A priori indeterminate thoughts, if there are such, are neither epistemically possible nor epistemically necessary. To handle such cases, one should say that a thought is epistemically possible when its *determinate* negation is not epistemically necessary. (3) Certain theoretical views (e.g. Salmon 1986) hold that it is knowable a priori that water is H_2O, on the grounds that 'water is H_2O' expresses roughly the same proposition as 'H_2O is H_2O' (setting aside the structure in 'H_2O' for present purposes), where this proposition is knowable a priori. Even on these controversial views, however, it is clear that the token thought *water is H_2O* is not epistemically necessary as defined above: that is, there is no reasoning process that can justify this thought a priori.

5. The phrase "consider a world as actual" is due to Davies and Humberstone (1980), developing ideas presented by Evans (1979). The explication given here differs from that given by Davies and Humberstone, who do not talk explicitly about epistemic possibility, but it is in much the same spirit.

6. This notion is introduced by Quine (1968), who defines a centered world as a world with a marked space-time point. The definition above is due to Lewis (1979).

7. On a full account, a canonical description of a centered world is required to be an epistemically complete statement in an idealized language that uses only semantically neutral terms and indexicals. A statement D is epistemically complete when D is epistemically possible and there is no S such that both D∧S and D∧¬S are epistemically possible. A semantically neutral term is one that behaves in the same way under epistemic and subjunctive evaluation. The indexicals allowed include 'I', 'now', and any others required to characterize the center of the world. This treatment requires that for every centered world, there exists an epistemically complete description using only semantically neutral terms and indexicals. This claim can be supported by noting (i) that there will be an epistemically complete description for every world (a consequence of the idealization of the language), and (ii) that semantic non-neutrality does not in itself add expressive power in characterizing epistemic possibilities (at most, it affects the description of metaphysical possibilities). If we appeal to the epistemic construction of scenarios rather than the possible-worlds construction (as discussed in section 4), the restriction to semantic neutrality can be waived: any epistemically complete description of the scenario will suffice. See Chalmers (forthcoming a) for more on these issues.

   Note that there is no requirement that a canonical description be given in a purely microphysical vocabulary or in a purely phenomenal vocabulary, or in a combination of the two. I have defended elsewhere (Chalmers 2002a, Chalmers and Jackson 2001) the claim that a conjunction ('PQTI') of microphysical, phenomenal, indexical, and "that's all" truths about the actual world implies all truths about the actual world. If so, then this sort of description will provide a canonical description of the actual world (at least if we put the microphysical description in semantically neutral form), and an analogous description will plausibly suffice for many other worlds. But this is a substantive claim, and is not built into the definition of a canonical description. If PQTI is not epistemically complete, a canonical description will need to include further information about a world. Of course there may be many canonical descriptions for a single world, but all of these will imply each other, so all will yield the same epistemic intensions.

8. Note that this heuristic invokes the intuitive correctness conditions (or "assertibility conditions") of an indicative conditional, which are given by the Ramsey test, rather than the truth-conditions, whose nature is disputed. We might think of the intension defined by the indicative conditional heuristic as a "Ramsey intension". Ramsey intensions and epistemic intensions are very similar, but it is arguable that they come apart in some cases (see Yablo 2002, Chalmers 2002a). Ramsey intensions have the advantage that they do not invoke the notion of apriority, and so are available even to Quineans and others who reject this notion; this makes it clear that even a Quinean can accept a version of the general framework here. Still, my own view is that the definition in terms of apriority is more fundamental.

9. As an alternative aid to the imagination, we might suppose that the thinker is assessing T with the aid of a supercomputer that stores the relevant information about W and carries out necessary a priori calculations. See Chalmers and Jackson 2001, section 4, for more on this.

10. A terminological point: I generally use "epistemic intension" for the intension defined over the space of maximal epistemic possibilities (whether or not these coincide with centered metaphysically possible worlds), while I use "primary intension" for the same sort of intension defined over the space of centered metaphysically possible worlds (whether or not these exhaust the maximal epistemic possibilities). In applications of the two-dimensional framework to metaphysical questions, the restriction to metaphysically possible worlds is often crucial, so in these contexts the issues are cast in terms of primary intensions. A central issue here is the thesis that a thought is a priori iff it has a necessary primary intension; this thesis makes a plausible but substantive claim about metaphysical possibility (one that is false if *a god exists* is metaphysically necessary but not a priori, for example). In applications of the framework to epistemic and semantic questions (such as the current discussion), the restriction to metaphysically possible worlds is less crucial, so in these contexts the issues are cast in terms of epistemic intensions. Here the claim that a thought is a priori iff it has a necessary epistemic intension can be seen as closer to definitional (if *a god exists* is necessary but not a priori, we can construe scenarios epistemically so that there will be a godless scenario). Of course if the plausible but substantive thesis above is correct, then every maximal epistemic possibility corresponds to a centered world, and primary and epistemic intensions will come to much the same thing.

11. For this reason, the current framework can be seen as neutral between "causal" theories of reference (on which reference is determined by a causal chain) and "descriptive" theories of reference (on which reference is determined by a description). Even a causal theorist should allow that relevant information about the actual world dictates rational judgments about our concept's extension. This methodology underlies Kripke's own arguments for the causal theory: in effect, he considers epistemic possibilities that we could discover to obtain (e.g., that a man called 'Gödel' stole the proof of the incompleteness of arithmetic from a man called 'Schmidt'), and reaches judgments about a term's extension on that basis (here, we judge that 'Gödel' will pick out the stealer, not the prover). So even on the causal theory, a term will plausibly have an epistemic intension: it is just that this epistemic intension may have a causal element. For example, for the epistemic intension of my concept *Gödel* to pick out a given individual in a scenario, it may be required that that individual stand in the right sort of causal relation to the subject at the center of the scenario. See Chalmers 2002b for more here.

12. The term "subjunctive" is used because this sort of possibility is grounded in the semantically subjunctive notion of what might have been the case (Kripke is explicit about this), and because the evaluation of such possibilities reflects the use of subjunctive conditionals. See Chalmers 2002b here.

13. I think that it is not obvious that Kripke and Putnam are correct about this, and a case can be made that it might have been that water was XYZ. For the purposes of this discussion, however, I will go along with the common view that Kripke's and Putnam's intuitions are correct. I also think that even if Kripke and Putnam are right about language, it is not obvious that this extends to thought. But again, for the purposes of this discussion, I will go along with the common view that the modal properties of a term such as 'water' mirror modal properties of the underlying concept *water* that the term expresses.

14. In this way the epistemic intension can be seen as equivalent to the "diagonal" of the two-dimensional intension, in a manner reminiscent of the "diagonal proposition" of Stalnaker 1978. But see section 9 for reasons why epistemic intensions are not fundamentally diagonal intensions.

15. Thus even a brain in a vat might have thoughts with epistemic content. This can be used to address Putnam's (1981) anti-skeptical argument that if he were a brain in a vat, he could not think *I am a brain in a vat*. A brain in a vat could think a thought with the appropriate epistemic content, if not the appropriate subjunctive content. It could also think a thought such as *I am in a skeptical scenario,* which has more or less identical epistemic and subjunctive content. The epistemic contents of such a thought seems sufficient to express a significant skeptical possibility, true only in worlds in which the individual at the center lacks the usual sort of epistemic contact with the surrounding world.

16. Alternatively, content is often identified with a structured proposition composed from either subjunctive intensions of the concepts involved, or from the extensions of the concepts involved (when the concepts are rigid). This sort of structured content is more fine-grained than a subjunctive intension, but it has the same truth-conditions, and depends on the environment in a similar way. What I say below about subjunctive intensions applies equally to structured propositions. Likewise, what I say about

epistemic intensions can easily be adapted to a view on which the contents of thoughts are structures composed from epistemic intensions of concepts.

17. Dennett suggests that the relevant worlds are "the environment (or class of environments) to which the organism as currently constituted is best fitted." This class may be quite different from the class of worlds that verify all of a subject's beliefs: subjects are sometimes better fitted to worlds that falsify their beliefs (when they are pessimistic or altruistic, for example); they often have beliefs about distant matters that are irrelevant to fitness; and their fitness often turns on matters about which they have no beliefs. See also the criticisms in Stalnaker 1989 and White 1991, and White's more refined account. Dennett's and White's suggestions might be seen as a first attempt at giving a naturalistic reduction of something in the vicinity of epistemic content. Such a reduction is likely to be a major project in its own right.

18. Perry (1979) considers the possibility that centered ("relativized") propositions might provide a solution, but dismisses it on the grounds that believing that such a proposition P is "true for me" does not distinguish me from third parties who also believe that P is true for me, but act differently. The trouble is that Perry's locution "true for me" introduces an unnecessary extensional element. What distinguishes me from the third parties is rather that I believe P *simpliciter*, or better, that my belief has P as its epistemic content.

19. To simplify the discussion, I make the happy assumption that Superman is actual and is identical to Clark Kent.

20. Of course, thoughts like *Cary Grant is in the movie* and *Archie Leach is in the movie* might lead to the same actions despite their different epistemic content, if I know that Cary Grant is Archie Leach. But even here, there exist circumstances under which the thoughts might play a different role: imagine someone telling me that Cary Grant is not Archie Leach after all. In general, whenever two thoughts have different epistemic content, there are at least hypothetical circumstances under which the action-governing roles of the thoughts will differ.

21. See Fodor 1991 for a detailed argument along these lines. I note also that one can individuate this sort behavior intentionally but still narrowly if one individuates by epistemic content.

22. It may even be that in certain cases, epistemic content can itself be constituted by an organism's proximal environment, in cases where the proximal environment is regarded as part of the cognitive system: if a subject's notebook is taken to be part of a subject's memory, for example (see Clark and Chalmers 1998). Here, epistemic content remains internal to a cognitive system; it is just that the skin is not a God-given boundary of a cognitive system. This is another way in which the issue between epistemic and subjunctive content runs deeper than the issue between internalism and externalism.

23. Some views (e.g., Salmon 1986) take ascriptions such as 'Lois believes that Clark can fly' to be strictly speaking true, so that modes of presentation are irrelevant to truth. Even if these counterintuitive views are accepted, the current account can be viewed an account of the (pragmatic) intuitive correctness conditions of belief ascriptions. Either way, we need an account of these intuitive correctness conditions to explain the function of belief ascriptions in psychological explanation.

24. See also Crimmins 1991 and Richard 1990. Many of the insights of these and other philosophers on the semantics of belief ascription should be straightforwardly adaptable to the present framework.

25. This sort of candidate is not mentioned in Schiffer's (1990) otherwise thorough survey of potential modes of presentation.

26. So Kripke's "Principle of Non-Contradiction" is false: someone can rationally believe that S and believe that ¬S, as long as the beliefs involve different epistemic intensions both of which satisfy the appropriate constraints.

27. I leave aside here the important question of the epistemic content of desires, and the semantics of desire attributions. On my view, the epistemic content of a desire cannot in general be represented by a simple intension. Rather, it is a sort of two-dimensional intension that can endorse a different set of worlds depending on which scenario is actual. This is clearest in cases such as "I wish I were two inches taller" or "I want to be over there". The moral is that the content of desires is perhaps more deeply two-dimensional than the content of beliefs.

28. How should one analyze so-called *de re* belief attributions, of the form 'S believes of x that it is F'? In the current framework, one might adapt the proposals of Kaplan 1967 and Lewis 1979 by holding that such an ascription is true when S has a belief with the appropriate subjunctive intension, true in worlds where A has property P, where A is the referent of 'x' and P of 'F', and when the belief involves a concept that picks out A under a *de-re*-appropriate epistemic intension. Here, a *de-re*-appropriate intension is one that entails acquaintance: this requires that in any scenario in which the intension yields an extension, the subject at the center is acquainted (in the contemporary non-Russellian sense) with this extension.

29. Why is subjunctive content ascribed at all? I think the reasons are tied to language. First, we ascribe beliefs in the same language we use to describe the world, and when we use world-involving language to ascribe epistemic content, world-involving constraints come along naturally in the package. Second, subjunctive content is important to understanding the success of communication and of collective action. When I tell you that I have a cold, you acquire a thought whose epistemic content is different from mine, but whose subjunctive content is the same. Communication very frequently involves transmission of subjunctive content, and our collective cohesion (if not our individual actions) can often be understood in terms of shared subjunctive content. But both of these points deserve a much more extensive development.

30. It is arguable that cognitive psychology is already mostly concerned with epistemic content rather than subjunctive content, insofar as it is concerned with content at all. For example, the psychological literature on concepts seems to be largely concerned with how concepts are applied to the actual world, concentrating on something like the epistemic intensions of the concepts involved. See Smith and Medin 1981 and Patterson 1991.

31. Related proposals for understanding narrow content in broadly contextual terms are given by Brown 1986 and Loar 1988.

32. Other concepts whose epistemic intensions have a limited domain of determinacy include perceptual demonstratives. When I think something like *That is pretty,* the referent of my demonstrative is often picked out (very roughly) as the cause of such-and-such experience. In a centered world in which there is no appropriate experience at the center, the epistemic intension may lack truth-value. This raises another subtlety: to capture the content of perceptual demonstratives, one may need to build in a "marked" experience to the center of the class of actual-world candidates, as one builds in a marked individual and time. Building this into the center will sometimes be needed to secure reference to otherwise indistinguishable experiences and their perceptual objects, as with (perhaps) a speckle in a large field, or one of the symmetrical red spots in Austin's (1990) "Two Tubes" puzzle (to which the present framework then provides a solution). In certain cases, centers may also require more than one experience, and perhaps a marked thought ("this very thought"). One might suggest that the contents of a center involve objects of "unmediated" reference: oneself, the present moment, the current thought, and perhaps certain experiences and orientations. This matter is closely connected to Russell's suggestions about direct reference; I hope to explore it in more depth elsewhere (see also Chalmers 2002c).

33. At one point, Block and Stalnaker acknowledge (in effect) that Chalmers (1996) does not intend a contextual interpretation, but suggest that a version of the "what is held constant" problem nevertheless arises in using an actual-word thought or concept to evaluate worlds without that thought or concept. I think that when things are understood in the appropriate epistemic terms, this problem clearly disappears. In fairness, it should be noted that the discussion in Chalmers (1996) is not explicit about the difference between contextual and epistemic intensions, and although the discussion tends to suggest an epistemic intension, the precise definition is left unclear. See Chalmers (forthcoming a) for discussion.

34. This might suggest that epistemic content is "ineffable". But the real problem is simply that it is difficult to capture the *epistemic content* of one expression with the *subjunctive content* of another. Just as one can capture the subjunctive content of a concept such as *water* by appealing to the equivalent subjunctive content of an expression such as 'H_2O', one might capture its epistemic content by appealing to the equivalent epistemic content of an expression such as 'the clear, drinkable liquid . . .'. It is hard to see why the second is any more objectionable than the first, or why it makes epistemic content any more "ineffable". Thanks to Frank Jackson for discussion on this point.

35. For example, one might hold that a thought is (nonideally) epistemically necessary when it is *trivial,* in a sense to be elucidated. One could then use this notion to set up a more fine-grained epistemic space of non-ideal epistemic possibilities, and could then associate concepts and thoughts with non-ideal epistemic intensions over this space. Then two concepts or thoughts that are nontrivially a priori equivalent will have the same epistemic intension as defined in the paper, but different non-ideal epistemic intensions as defined here.

36. For an argument that phenomenology is essential to the epistemic content of at least some concepts, see Chalmers 2002c. See also Horgan and Tienson (this volume, chapter 49) for arguments for phenomenally constituted narrow content that can be seen as complementing the current approach.

37. Arguably, contemporary causal theories of content have been unsuccessful precisely because they attempt to account for wide content directly, without taking into account the crucial epistemic dimension involved in its determination.

BIBLIOGRAPHY

Austin, D. F. 1990. *What's the Meaning of "This"?* Cornell University Press.

Block, N. 1991. What narrow content is not. In B. Loewer and G. Rey, eds., *Meaning in Mind: Fodor and His Critics.* Blackwell.

Block, N., and Stalnaker, R. 1999. Conceptual analysis, dualism, and the explanatory gap. *Philosophical Review* 108:1–46.

Brown, C. 1986. What is a belief state? *Midwest Studies in Philosophy* 10:357–78.

Burge, T. 1979. Individualism and the mental. *Midwest Studies in Philosophy* 4:73–122.

Chalmers, D. J. 1996. *The Conscious Mind: In Search of a Fundamental Theory.* Oxford University Press.

Chalmers, D. J. 2002a. Does conceivability entail possibility? In T. Gendler and J. Hawthorne (eds.), *Conceivability and Possibility.* Oxford University Press. http://consc.net/papers/conceivability.html.

Chalmers, D. J. 2002b. On sense and intension. *Philosophical Perspectives* 16. http://consc.net/papers/intension.html.

Chalmers, D. J. 2002c. The content and epistemology of phenomenal belief. In Q. Smith and A. Jokic (eds.), *Consciousness: New Philosophical Essays.* Oxford University Press. http://consc.net/papers/belief.html.

Chalmers, D. J. (forthcoming a). The foundations of two-dimensional semantics. http://consc.net/papers/foundations.html.

Chalmers, D. J. (forthcoming b). The nature of epistemic space. http://consc.net/papers/espace.html.

Chalmers, D. J., and Jackson, F. 2001. Conceptual analysis and reductive explanation. *Philosophical Review* 110:315–61. http://consc.net/papers/analysis.html.

Clark, A., and Chalmers, D. J. 1998. The extended mind. *Analysis* 58:7–19.

Crimmins, M. 1991. *Talk about Beliefs.* MIT Press.

Davies, M. K., and Humberstone, I. L. 1980. Two notions of necessity. *Philosophical Studies* 38:1–30.

Dennett, D. C. 1981. Beyond belief. In A. Woodfield (ed.), *Thought and Object.* Oxford University Press.

Evans, G. 1979. Reference and contingency. *The Monist* 62:161–89.

Fodor, J. 1987. *Psychosemantics.* MIT Press.

Fodor. J. 1991. A modal argument for narrow content. *Journal of Philosophy* 88:5–26.

Frege, G. 1892. Über Sinn und Bedeutung. Translated in (P. Geach and M. Black (eds.), *Translations from the Philosophical Writings of Gottlob Frege.* Blackwell, 1952.

Horgan, T., and Tienson, J. (this volume). The intentionality of phenomenology and the phenomenology of intentionality.

Kaplan, D. 1967. Quantifying in. *Synthese* 19:178–214.

Kaplan, D. 1989. Demonstratives. In J. Almog, J. Perry, and H. Wettstein (eds.), *Themes from Kaplan.* Oxford University Press.

Kripke, S. A. 1979. A puzzle about belief. In A. Margalit (ed.), *Meaning and Use.* D. Reidel.

Kripke, S. A. 1980. *Naming and Necessity.* Harvard University Press.

LePore, E., and Loewer, B. 1986. Solipsistic semantics. *Midwest Studies in Philosophy* 10:595–614.

Lewis, D. 1979. Attitudes de dicto and de se. *Philosophical Review* 88:513–43.

Lewis, D. 1994. Reduction of mind. In S. Guttenplan (ed.), *Companion to the Philosophy of Mind.* Blackwell.

Loar, B. 1988. Social content and psychological content. In R.H. Grimm and D.D. Merrill (eds.), *Contents of Thought.* University of Arizona Press.

Patterson, S. 1991. Individualism and semantic development. *Philosophy of Science* 58:15–35.

Perry, J. 1977. Frege on demonstratives. *Philosophical Review* 86:474–97.

Perry, J. 1979. The problem of the essential indexical. *Nous* 13:3–21.

Putnam, H. 1975. The meaning of 'meaning'. In K. Gunderson (ed.), *Language, Mind, and Knowledge.* Minneapolis: University of Minnesota Press.

Putnam, H. 1981. *Reason, Truth, and History.* Cambridge University Press.

Quine, W. V. 1968. Propositional objects. *Critica* 2(5): 3–22.

Richard, M. 1990. *Propositional Attitudes: An Essay on Thoughts and How We Ascribe Them.* Cambridge University Press.

Salmon, N. 1986. *Frege's Puzzle.* MIT Press.

Schiffer, S. 1978. The basis of reference. *Erkenntnis* 13:171–206.

Schiffer, S. 1990. The mode-of-presentation problem. In C.A. Anderson and J. Owens (eds.), *Propositional Attitudes: The Role of Content in Logic, Language, and Mind.* CSLI Press.

Schiffer, S. 1992. Belief ascription. *Journal of Philosophy* 87:602–14.

Segal, G. 2000. *A Slim Book about Narrow Content.* MIT Press.

Smith, E. E., and Medin, D. L. 1981. *Categories and Concepts.* Harvard University Press.

Stalnaker, R. 1978. Assertion. In P. Cole (ed.), *Syntax and Semantics: Pragmatics, Vol. 9.* Academic Press.

Stalnaker, R. 1989. On what's in the head. *Philosophical Perspectives* 3:287–316.

Stalnaker, R. 1990. Narrow content. In C.A. Anderson and J. Owens (eds.), *Propositional Attitudes.* Stanford: Center for the Study of Language and Information.

Stalnaker, R. 1999. *Context and Content.* Oxford University Press.

Stich, S. 1983. *From Folk Psychology to Cognitive Science.* MIT Press.

Taylor, K. 1989. Narrow content functionalism and the mind-body problem. *Nous* 23:355–72.

White, S. 1982. Partial character and the language of thought. *Pacific Philosophical Quarterly* 63:347–65.

White, S. 1991. Narrow content and narrow interpretation. In *The Unity of the Self.* Cambridge, MA: MIT Press.

Yablo, S. 2002. Coulda, woulda, shoulda. In T. Gendler and J. Hawthorne (eds.), *Conceivability and Possibility.* Oxford University Press.

57

Anti-Individualism and Privileged Access

Michael McKinsey

It has been a philosophical commonplace, at least since Descartes, to hold that each of us can know the existence and content of his own mental states in a privileged way that is available to no one else. This has at least seemed true with respect to those 'neutral' cognitive attitudes such as thought, belief, intention, and desire, whose propositional contents may be false. The crucial idea is not that one's knowledge of these states in oneself is incorrigible, for surely one can make mistakes about what one believes, intends, or desires. Rather the idea is that we can in principle find out about these states in ourselves 'just by thinking,' without launching an empirical investigation or making any assumptions about the external physical world. I will call knowledge obtained independently of empirical investigation a priori knowledge. And I will call the principle that it is possible to have a priori knowledge of one's own neutral cognitive attitude states, the Principle of Privileged Access, or just 'privileged access' for short.

Although many philosophers would insist that privileged access is undeniable, a series of recent discoveries and arguments in the philosophy of language has, I believe, convinced a perhaps equally large number of philosophers that privileged access is a complete illusion. One of the most persuasive of these arguments was proposed by Tyler Burge (1982) as an application of Putnam's (1975) famous Twin Earth case. Oscar, a resident of Earth, believes that water is wet. On Twin Earth, there is no water; rather there is a qualitatively similar liquid with a different chemical composition, a liquid that we may call 'twater.' Toscar, who is Oscar's identical twin and a denizen of Twin Earth, does not believe that water is wet. For Toscar has no beliefs about water at all; rather, he believes that twater is wet, that twater fills the oceans, etc. Yet Oscar and Toscar, being absolutely identical twins, would certainly seem to be *internally* the same. In Putnam's terminology, Oscar and Toscar would share all the same 'narrow' psychological states. Thus, Burge concludes, Oscar's belief that water is wet must be a *wide* state: it must, that is, 'presuppose' or 'depend upon' the relations that Oscar bears to other speakers or objects in his external environment.

In general, Burge endorses a conclusion something like

(B) Some neutral cognitive states that are ascribed by *de dicto* attitude sentences (e.g., 'Oscar is thinking that water is wet') necessarily depend upon or presuppose the existence of objects external to the person to whom the state is ascribed.

Now (B) might certainly *appear* to conflict with privileged access. For (B) implies that sometimes, whether or not a person is in a given cognitive state is determined by external facts that the person himself could only know by empirical investigation. In such cases, it would seem, the person would therefore not be able to know a priori that he is in the cognitive state in question.

But interestingly enough, Burge (1988) has recently urged that despite appearances, his anti-individualism (that is, his conclusion (B)) is perfectly compatible with privileged access. And a similar point of view had earlier been expressed by Davidson (1987). I want to argue here that Burge and Davidson are wrong. Anti-individualism and privileged access as standardly understood are incompatible, and something has to give.[1]

I will first briefly discuss Davidson's defence of compatibilism. Davidson clearly accepts anti-individualism as formulated by (B), and like Burge he accepts (B) in part on the basis of Burge's persuasive application of Putnam's Twin Earth case. But Davidson insists that anti-individualism does not undermine first person authority about one's own mental states. He agrees with the anti-individualist thesis that some *de dicto* attitude ascriptions 'identify thoughts by relating them to things outside the head' (1987, p. 451). But he suggests that philosophers like Putnam who find a difficulty for privileged access in this thesis are in effect

From *Analysis* 51:9–16, 1991. Reprinted with permission of the author.

confusing thoughts with their descriptions. Such philosophers make the mistake, Davidson says, of inferring from the fact that a thought is identified or *described* by relating it to something outside the head, that the thought itself must therefore *be* outside the head and hence must be unavailable to privileged access (1987, p. 451).

Now I do not myself see any reason to believe that Putnam or anyone else has actually made this mistake. Certainly, as we shall see below, the most cogent reason for endorsing incompatibilism does not involve this mistake at all, so that Davidson's diagnosis is inconclusive at best. But what is most disconcerting about Davidson's remarks is the version of privileged access that he apparently takes himself to be defending. He explicitly accepts anti-individualism, understanding it as the thesis that thoughts are often *described* (in attitude ascriptions) by relating them to objects outside the head. Then he (quite correctly) points out that it does not follow from this thesis that the thoughts so described are *themselves* outside the head. But what is the relevance of this point to the issue at hand? Apparently Davidson is saying that since the thoughts in question are inner episodes that exist independently of our means of describing them, we can have privileged access to these episodes, whatever the external implications of our descriptions of the episodes might be.

But if this is what Davidson has in mind, then the version of privileged access that he is defending is too weak to be of much philosophical interest. He wishes to claim, apparently, that one could have privileged access to an episode of thought independently of having privileged access to any particular descriptions that the episode might satisfy. But then what would one have privileged access *to* in such a case? Perhaps one would be privileged to know only that the episode exists; given what Davidson says, there is no reason to suppose that the agent would have privileged access even to the fact that the episode is an episode of *thought,* as opposed to being, say, an episode of indigestion.

But surely, having access of this sort to one's thoughts is not much of a privilege. The traditional view, I should think, is not just that we have privileged access to the fact that our thoughts *occur,* rather the view is that we have privileged access to our thoughts *as satisfying certain descriptions.* In particular, the traditional view is that we have privileged access to our thoughts as having certain contents, or as satis-

fying certain *de dicto* cognitive attitude predicates. Thus, if Oscar is thinking that water is wet, the traditional view would be that Oscar has privileged access, not just to the fact that some episode or other is occurring in him, but to the fact that he is thinking that water is wet. Now apparently, Davidson would just *deny* that Oscar has privileged access to the latter sort of fact, since as he says, the fact relates Oscar to objects outside his head. But if he would deny this, then Davidson's claim to be defending first person authority seems misleading at best.[2]

In contrast to Davidson, Burge clearly means to defend privileged access in its traditional guise. Given what he says in 'Individualism and Self-Knowledge' (1988), Burge would maintain that the following three propositions are consistent:

(1) Oscar knows a priori that he is thinking that water is wet.

(2) The proposition that Oscar is thinking that water is wet necessarily depends upon E.

(3) The proposition E cannot be known a priori, but only by empirical investigation.

(Here I assume that E is the 'external proposition' whose presupposition makes Oscar's thought that water is wet a wide state.)

Whether (1)–(3) are consistent is determined by the sense that the phrase 'necessarily depends upon' is taken to have in (2). Unfortunately, Burge never explains or clarifies the concept of necessary dependency that he invokes throughout his paper. I will now argue that Burge is able to make his compatibility thesis appear plausible only by tacitly identifying the dependency relation with *metaphysical* necessity. But this identification is illegitimate in the present context, for a reason that I will explain below.

A clue to what Burge has in mind by dependency is provided by the analogy he chooses to undermine the incompatibilist's reasoning. One who reasons from the assumption that we can know our own mental states a priori to the conclusion that these states must be independent of any empirical propositions about physical objects is, says Burge, making the same mistake as was once made by Descartes and diagnosed by Arnaud (in Burge, 1988, pp. 650–51).

From the fact that he could know directly and incorrigibly the existence of himself and his own thoughts, while consistently doubting the existence of his body and the rest of the physical world, Descartes inferred that it was possible for him to exist as a disembodied mind in a non-physical universe. But this inference is illegitimate. The fact that Descartes could not correctly *deduce* the existence of the physical world from the existence of himself and his thoughts may show something significant about Descartes' *concepts* of himself and his thoughts. But as Arnaud pointed out, this failure of deduction shows nothing about the *nature* of either Descartes or his thoughts. It is perfectly consistent with this failure of deduction to suppose that both Descartes and his thoughts have an essentially physical nature, and that neither Descartes nor his thoughts could possibly have existed unless certain physical objects, including perhaps Descartes' body, Descartes' parents, and the sperm and egg cells from which Descartes developed, had also existed. For the fact, if it is a fact, that Descartes' existence is dependent upon the existence of these other physical objects would not be something that is knowable a priori. It would be a fact that is necessary but only knowable a posteriori. (As Kripke 1980 pointed out.) Thus the dependency would be a fact that is not deducible a priori from Descartes' incorrigible knowledge of himself and his thoughts.

Since metaphysical dependencies are often only knowable a posteriori, propositions that are knowable a priori might metaphysically depend upon other propositions that are only knowable a posteriori. Thus Oscar might know a priori that he exists, and his existence might metaphysically depend upon the existence of his mother, even though Oscar cannot know a priori that his mother exists.

The upshot of this discussion is that (1), (2), and (3) are all clearly consistent, provided that 'depends upon' in (2) is interpreted as meaning *metaphysical* dependency. When the material conditional 'if p then q' is metaphysically necessary, let us say that p *metaphysically entails q.* Then our result so far is that (1) and (3) are consistent with

(2a) The proposition that Oscar is thinking that water is wet metaphysically entails E.

Burge's main point in defence of the compatibility of anti-individualism and privileged access, then, seems to be that such triads as (1), (2a) and (3) are consistent. In other words, his point is that our having privileged access to our own mental states is compatible with those states being metaphysically dependent upon facts to which we have no privileged access.

But this point, though correct, is quite irrelevant to the main issue. For anti-individualism is the thesis that some neutral *de dicto* cognitive attitude states are wide states, and to say that a state is wide (not narrow) cannot mean *merely* that the state metaphysically entails the existence of external objects.[3] For if it did, then given certain materialistic assumptions that are pretty widely held, it would follow that probably *all* psychological states of *any* kind would be wide, so that the concept of a narrow state would have no application at all, and anti-individualism would be merely a trivial consequence of (token) materialism.

For instance, it is plausible to suppose that no human could (metaphysically) have existed without biological parents, and that no human could (metaphysically) have had biological parents other than the ones she in fact had. (See Kripke 1980, pp. 312–14.) If this is so, then Oscar's thinking that water is wet metaphysically entails that Oscar's mother exists. In fact, Oscar's having *any* psychological property (or any property at all) would metaphysically entail the existence of Oscar's mother. Thus if metaphysical entailment of external objects were what made a psychological state wide, then probably *all* of Oscar's—and everyone else's—psychological states would be wide.

But this is obviously *not* the sense of 'wide psychological state' that philosophers like Putnam and Burge have had in mind. While it may well be true that Oscar's thinking that water is wet entails the existence of Oscar's mother or the existence of the egg from which Oscar developed, it would nevertheless not be for *this* kind of reason that Oscar's mental state is wide! Clearly, to say that the state in question is wide is not to say something that is true by virtue of Oscar's *nature* or the *nature* of the particular event that is Oscar's thought that water is wet. Rather it is to say something about the *concept,* or property, that is expressed by the English predicate 'x is thinking that water is wet'; it is to say something about what it *means* to say that a given person is thinking that water is wet.

Let us say that a proposition p *conceptually implies* a proposition q if and only if there is a correct deduction of q from p, a deduction whose only premises other than p are necessary or conceptual truths that are knowable a priori, and each of whose steps follows from previous lines by a self-evident inference rule of some adequate system of natural deduction. I intend the relation of conceptual implication to be an appropriately *logical,* as opposed to a metaphysical, relation.

Our discussion shows, I believe, that the thesis of anti-individualism should be stated in terms of conceptual implication rather than metaphysical entailment.[4] In this connection, it is worth noting that when Putnam originally introduced the notions of narrow and wide psychological states, he did so in terms of *logical* possibility (1975, p. 141). Moreover, he introduced these notions as explicitly *Cartesian* concepts. Thus a narrow state should be (roughly) a state from which the existence of external objects cannot be *deduced,* and a wide state would be one from which the existence of external objects *can* be deduced.

On my proposal, Burge's thesis of anti-individualism should be understood as

(Ba) Some neutral cognitive states that are ascribed by *de dicto* attitude sentences (e.g., 'Oscar is thinking that water is wet') conceptually imply the existence of objects external to the person to whom the state is ascribed.

But, of course, now that we have made anti-individualism into the conceptual thesis that it should be, we also have our contradiction with privileged access back again.

For instance, (2) must now be understood as

(2b) The proposition that Oscar is thinking that water is wet conceptually implies E,

and it is easy to see that (1), (2b), and (3) form an inconsistent triad. The argument is this. Suppose (1) that Oscar knows a priori that he is thinking that water is wet. Then by (2b), Oscar can simply *deduce* E, using only premises that are knowable a priori, including the premiss that he is thinking that water is wet. Since Oscar can deduce E from premises that are knowable a priori, Oscar can know E itself a priori. But this contradicts (3), the assumption that E *cannot* be known a priori. Hence (1), (2b), and (3) are inconsistent. And so in general, it seems, anti-individualism is inconsistent with privileged access.

It is worth keeping the structure of this simple argument in mind, so as not to confuse it with another (bad) argument that Burge frequently alludes to in his paper (1988). Burge sometimes characterizes the person who thinks that anti-individualism is inconsistent with privileged access as reasoning on the basis of the following sort of assumption (see for instance 1988, p. 653):

(4) Since the proposition that Oscar is thinking that water is wet necessarily depends upon E, no one, including Oscar, could know that Oscar is thinking that water is wet without first knowing E.

One who assumes (4) could then reason that (1), (2), and (3) are inconsistent, as follows. (2) and (4) imply that Oscar could not know that he is thinking that water is wet without first knowing E. But by (3), E is not knowable a priori. Hence, Oscar could also not know a priori that he is thinking that water is wet. But this contradicts (1). Hence, (1), (2), and (3) are inconsistent.

Burge is certainly right when he objects to this line of reasoning. The reasoning is obviously bad when necessary dependency is interpreted as metaphysical entailment. For then, one would be assuming (4) on the basis of the principle that

(5) If *p* metaphysically entails *q,* then no one could know that *p* without first knowing that *q.*

But (5) is obviously false. For instance, even if Oscar's existence metaphysically entails the existence of Oscar's mother, Oscar can surely know that he exists without first knowing that his mother does!

Even when necessary dependency is interpreted as conceptual implication, the reasoning is bad. In this case, (4) would be assumed on the basis of

(6) If *p* conceptually implies *q,* then no one could know that *p* without first knowing that *q.*

But, of course, it is a well known fact that closure principles like (6) are false: certainly with respect to any proposition *p* that can be known at all, it is possible to know *p* without first knowing each of (the infinite number of) *p*'s logical consequences.

So Burge was certainly right to object to the kind of reason he imagined one might have for believing that anti-individualism and privileged access are incompatible. But, of course, this does not show that no good reason for the incompatibility can be given. The simple argument I gave above is in fact such a good reason, and it does *not* depend on any suspicious closure principles like (5) and (6).

Rather, the argument is much more straightforward. In effect it says, look, if you could know a priori that you are in a given mental state, and your being in that state conceptually or logically implies the existence of external objects, then you could know a priori that the external world exists. Since you obviously *can't* know a priori that the external world exists, you also can't know a priori that you are in the mental state in question. It's just that simple. I myself find it hard to understand why Burge and Davidson will not just accept this obvious and compelling line of reasoning.

NOTES

1. I have elsewhere discussed at length the problems for particular forms of anti-individualism that arise from these theses' apparent incompatibility with privileged access. See McKinsey (1978) and (1987).

2. It is, of course, possible that Davidson would be prepared to defend a view on which all our thoughts that fall under wide *de dicto* descriptions also fall under *other* descriptions of some important kind to which we have privileged access. Perhaps, for instance, he might be willing to say that every thought with a 'wide' content would also have another 'narrow' content to which we have privileged access. (I suggest such a 'two-content' view in my 1986.) But as far as I know, Davidson nowhere spells out or defends such a view. And, of course, the mere hypothetical fact that Davidson *might* be willing to develop a view on which privileged access is compatible with anti-individualism does not by itself provide us with any *argument* in favour of this compatibility.

3. Here I assume that, for Burge, metaphysical entailment of external objects must be a logically *sufficient* condition for a state to be wide. Perhaps it might be objected that this is unfair to Burge, since all he really needs is the assumption that metaphysical entailment of external objects is a *necessary* condition of wideness. But this objection is misconceived. Burge is trying to show that such triads as (1), (2), and (3) are consistent. His argument is that this is so because (1), (2a), and (3) are consistent. But this argument requires the assumption that (2a)—the claim concerning metaphysical entailment—is logically *sufficient* for (2)—the claim concerning wideness, or necessary dependency. For unless (2a) is sufficient for (2), the fact that (1), (2a), and (3) are consistent is quite irrelevant to the conclusion that (1), (2), and (3) are consistent. (The correct general principle for proving consistency is that, if p and q are consistent, and q logically implies r, then p and r are consistent. Note the difference between this principle and the false principle that if p and q are consistent and q is logically implied by r, then p and r are consistent: this is wrong, since r might for instance be an explicit contradiction that logically implies the consistent q.)

4. In McKinsey [8] I give a more thorough and detailed defence of the thesis that the concepts of narrow and wide psychological states must be understood in terms of conceptual implication rather than metaphysical necessity.

REFERENCES

Tyler Burge, 'Other Bodies,' in *Thought and Object: Essays on Intentionality,* edited by A. Woodfield (Oxford: Oxford University Press, 1982).

———, 'Individualism and Self-Knowledge,' *Journal of Philosophy* 85 (1988) 649–63.

Donald Davidson, 'Knowing One's Own Mind,' *Proceedings and Addresses of the American Philosophical Association* 60 (1987) 441–58.

Saul Kripke, *Naming and Necessity* (Oxford: Basil Blackwell, 1980).

Michael McKinsey, 'Names and Intentionality,' *Philosophical Review* 87 (1978) 171–200.

———, 'Mental Anaphora,' *Synthese* 66 (1986) 159–75.

———, 'Apriorism in the Philosophy of Language,' *Philosophical Studies* 52 (1987) 1–32.

———, 'The Internal Basis of Meaning,' forthcoming.

Hilary Putnam, 'The Meaning of "Meaning,"' in his *Philosophical Papers* Vol. 2 (Cambridge: Cambridge University Press, 1975).

58

What an Anti-Individualist Knows A Priori

Anthony Brueckner

Michael McKinsey argues in (1991) that the anti-individualist theory of content has the obviously false consequence that one has a priori knowledge of the external facts which, according to the theory, help determine the content of one's mental states. Most of McKinsey's critical efforts are directed against the views of Tyler Burge, and I will argue that the criticisms rest upon a misunderstanding of these views.

According to McKinsey, Burge in (1988) is concerned to defend the consistency of these three propositions:

(1) Oscar knows a priori that he is thinking that water is wet.

(2) The proposition that Oscar is thinking that water is wet necessarily depends upon E.

(3) The proposition E cannot be known a priori, but only by empirical investigation (1991, p. 12).

E is some 'external proposition' describing 'the relations that Oscar bears to other speakers or objects in his external environment' (1991, p. 10). McKinsey's main criticism of Burge is as follows. Burge's defence of privileged access commits him to (1), and his anti-individualist theory of content commits him to (2) and (3). But (2) has the consequence that Oscar *can* know E a priori. Not only does this consequence contradict (3), but, further, it embodies a claim about a priori knowledge which is obviously false on anyone's view.

To see whether this criticism of Burge is sound, we must first look at McKinsey's grounds for attributing (1) to (3) to Burge (or, more generally, to a theorist sympathetic to the main ideas of anti-individualism about content). The attribution of (1) is straightforward, given that McKinsey understands a priori knowledge to be 'knowledge obtained independently of empirical investigation' (1991, p. 9). On Burge's view, one's knowledge of the content of one's own states has a special self-verifying character. Such knowledge is not, and need not be, based

upon any kind of empirical investigation of one's external environment, on Burge's view (see 1988).

The question whether the anti-individualist theory of content commits Burge to (2) and (3) obviously depends upon what the proposition E is. McKinsey is rather vague on this question, and we must proceed carefully if we are to arrive at an accurate assessment of the force of his criticism. Anti-individualism is, roughly, the view that environmental factors external to the individual subject of mental states figure in the individuation of the contents of those states. It is therefore quite natural to suppose that McKinsey's proposition E describes these external, environmental factors. To get clearer on this, let us consider, as McKinsey does, the Twin Earth case originally described by Putnam in (1975) and subsequently interpreted by Burge in (1982) as bearing on the theory of content. Oscar and his counterfactual twin Toscar 'have the same qualitative perceptual intake and qualitative streams of consciousness, the same movements, the same behavioural dispositions and inner functional states (non-intentionally and individualistically described)', and with one exception involving the ingestion of liquid, 'we might even fix their physical states as identical' (1982, p. 100). But their environments differ in respect of the chemical composition of the clear liquid filling the oceans, lakes, bath tubs, etc. in their respective worlds. The liquid in Oscar's Earthly environment is H_2O, while the twin liquid in Toscar's Twin Earthly environment is XYZ, a liquid which, according to the anti-individualist, is not water (though it is superficially indistinguishable from water; we will call it 'twater'). When Oscar says 'Water is wet,' this sentence expresses his thought that water is wet, but when Toscar uses the same sentence, it expresses his thought that twater is wet. The difference in content between the two thoughts is due to the difference between the two thinkers' environments, says Burge. Obviously, the fact that Oscar's environment contains H_2O and not XYZ is not knowable a priori by Oscar or anybody else: empirical investiga-

From *Analysis* 52:111–18, 1992. Reprinted with permission of the author.

tion of Oscar's environment is required for knowledge of that external content-determining fact.

At this point, it is natural to suppose the McKinsey's proposition E, which, according to (3), cannot be known a priori, but only by empirical investigation, is a proposition describing the recently mentioned external, content-determining fact:

(E1) Oscar inhabits an environment containing H_2O and not XYZ.

Assuming for now that E1 is the proposition McKinsey had in mind, what are we to make of his attribution of (2) to Burge? Here is the only passage in (1988) in which Burge uses the language of 'necessary dependence': 'My view . . . is that many thoughts are individuated non-individualistically: individuating many of a person or animal's mental kinds—certainly including thoughts about physical objects and properties—is necessarily dependent upon relations that the person bears to the physical, or in some cases social, environment' (1988, p. 650).[1] He then proceeds to give an abstract characterization of the sort of thought experiment we have just reviewed. Thus the sense in which, for Burge, the proposition that Oscar is thinking that water is wet *necessarily depends upon* E (interpreted now as E1) is this: the thought experiment involving Toscar establishes that if E1 had been false and, instead, Oscar had inhabited a twin environment containing XYZ instead of H_2O, and if Oscar's phenomenology, functional structure, behaviour, etc., had been held fixed, then some of Oscar's thoughts would have differed in content (he would have thought that twater is wet rather than that water is wet). A thought experiment reveals this counterfactual dependence of content upon E1, and thus we can say that it is necessary that such dependences hold.[2] This necessity is 'indicative of underlying principles for individuating mental kinds' (1988, p. 656).

McKinsey's criticism of Burge rests upon his attribution of (2) to Burge and his reading of (2) as asserting an *entailment* or *implication* of E by the proposition that Oscar is thinking that water is wet. He holds that the implication is conceptual in nature, where *p conceptually implies q* if and only if 'there is a correct deduction of *q* from *p*, a deduction whose only premises other than *p* are necessary or conceptual truths that are knowable a priori, and each of whose steps follows from previous lines by a self-evident inference rule of some adequate system of natural

deduction' (1991, p. 14). McKinsey accordingly interprets (2) as

(2b) The proposition that Oscar is thinking that water is wet conceptually implies E.

Now if (2b) is true, and if we interpret E as E1, then given that Oscar knows a priori that he is thinking that water is wet, it appears to follow that Oscar can know a priori that E1 is true. But since Burge accepts (3), he must *deny* that Oscar can know a priori that E1 is true. Thus Burge cannot consistently hold (1)–(3) if (2) is interpreted as (2b) (as McKinsey requires) and if E is interpreted as E1 (as we are supposing). Further, it is obviously false on anyone's view that Oscar can know a priori that he inhabits an environment containing H_2O and not XYZ.

But if E is interpreted as E1, then McKinsey's (2b) is clearly not a consequence of Burge's anti-individualism, according to which the 'necessary dependence' of Oscar's thoughts upon E1 amounts to the counterfactual dependence of those thoughts' contents upon the environmental factors described by E1. Thus, Burge's anti-individualism does not commit him to the obviously false claim that Oscar can know E1 a priori. An anti-individualist can hold that (a) Oscar would not have been thinking that water is wet had he been in a Twin Earthly environment containing XYZ instead of H_2O, while denying that (b) every world in which Oscar thinks that water is wet is a world containing H_2O (i.e., while denying a consequence of the *much stronger* (2b)). Burge explicitly makes such a denial in the paper (1982) McKinsey cites as the source of Burge's view about Twin Earth's ramifications for the theory of content. When it comes to questions about what is *conceptually implied* by one's thinking that water is wet (or necessitated by such thinkings in a manner knowable a priori), Burge is rightly cautious. This is because such questions concern the possibility of a Kantian transcendental argument against scepticism proceeding from the assumption of anti-individualism about content.

Before discussing the relation between anti-individualism and such transcendental arguments, let us consider a way in which McKinsey's objection might be recast in the light of the foregoing criticisms. One might hold that reflection upon Burge's thought experiment affords Oscar a priori knowledge about such counterfactual dependences as this:

(2c) If Oscar's environment had been sufficiently different from the way it in fact is (for example, if it had contained XYZ instead of H_2O), then, even holding fixed Oscar's phenomenology, functional structure, behaviour, etc., Oscar would not have been thinking that water is wet.

Oscar knows a priori that he is thinking that water is wet. If he also knows (2c) a priori on the basis of a thought experiment, then he can know a priori that his environment does not contain XYZ instead of H_2O. Thus it appears that Burge's anti-individualism, even when viewed correctly as a theory about the counterfactual dependence of content upon the environment, still yields unacceptable consequences about a priori knowledge.

The recast objection fails, though. The anti-individualist does not hold that (2c) is knowable a priori. (2c) can be decomposed into

> (2c1) If Oscar's environment had been sufficiently different from the way it in fact is, then, even holding fixed Oscar's phenomenology, functional structure, behaviour, etc., Oscar would not have been thinking that water is wet.

and

> (2c2) Oscar's environment in fact contains H_2O instead of XYZ.

Of (2c1) and (2c2), (2c1) may be knowable a priori, on the anti-individualist theory of content-determination, given various thought experiments involving counterfactual variations from stipulated actual circumstances. (We will return later to the a priori commitments, if any, of anti-individualism.) But (2c2) is clearly not knowable a priori. So even if Oscar does have a priori knowledge of (2c1), this nevertheless does not allow him to deduce anything of interest from his a priori knowledge that he is thinking that water is wet. He can at best infer to the a priori knowledge that his environment is not different from the way it in fact is.[3]

Let us return to the connection between anti-individualism and transcendental arguments. In (1982) (the only paper where Burge discusses Kantian-style anti-sceptical arguments at any length), Burge maintains that 'it is logically possible for an individual to have beliefs involving the concept of water . . . even though there is no water . . . of which the individual holds those beliefs.' Otherwise the individual's beliefs would not be *de dicto* in the first place. He says, further, that 'it is logically possible for an individual to

have beliefs involving the concept of water . . . even though there exists no water' (1982, p. 114). In such a situation, though, there is the prima facie worry that there is nothing licensing the attribution of water-thoughts, rather than twater-thoughts, to the individual. But if the individual is part of a community of language-users, 'there might still be enough in the community's talk to distinguish the notion of water from that of twater and from other candidate notions'. The deluded, waterless community would still have its 'chemical analyses, despite the illusoriness of their object'. However, in such a situation, the existence of water-thoughts would be contingent upon the assumption that 'not *all* of the community's beliefs involve similar illusions' (1982, p. 116). Burge's idea seems to be that in such a waterless world, there must exist enough physical entities to fix an appropriate content for the community's (false) theoretical sentences.[4] In the case in which one is *alone* in a waterless world, one's solo chemical theorizing might well suffice for a correct attribution of water-thoughts, just as in the communal-illusion case (though Burge does not explicitly say this). But it 'seems incredible' to Burge 'to suppose that . . . [a thinker], in his relative ignorance and indifference about the nature of water, holds beliefs whose contents involve the notion [of water], even though neither water nor communal cohorts exist' (1982, p. 116).

So Burge's view seems to be that it is impossible for Oscar to think that water is wet in a world in which no water exists and in which neither he nor a community of speakers propounds a mistaken chemical theory according to which H_2O exists. This is the view that

> (N) It is necessary that if Oscar is thinking that water is wet, then either (i) water exists, or (ii) Oscar theorizes that H_2O exists, or (iii) Oscar is part of a community of speakers some of whom theorize that H_2O exists.[5]

What sort of necessity is involved in (N)? Burge does not explicitly say in the passages in (1982) from which (N) is extracted. But he nowhere maintains that he has in mind a *conceptual* necessity which is knowable a priori. Further, since the conditions (ii) and (iii) which figure in the consequent of (N) are derived from the principle that *chemical theory* reveals the nature of water, it is clear that (N) is intended to have the status of a *metaphysical* necessity. Unlike conceptual necessities, some metaphysical necessities are only knowable a posteriori. Knowledge that (N), in particular, depends upon a posteriori knowledge concerning the connection between chemical analysis and the nature of water.

Thus, Burge's anti-individualism does not commit him to the view that Oscar can know a priori that *either (i), or (ii), or (iii) is true,* even if Burge's theory does have the consequence that the disjunction in question is metaphysically necessitated by the proposition (knowable a priori by Oscar) that Oscar is thinking that water is wet.[6] Given anti-individualism, though, is there some interesting substantive proposition, 'weaker' or less specific than the disjunction in question, which *is* knowable a priori by Oscar, assuming that he knows a priori what he is thinking? This is a difficult question, since it is hard to tell how much of anti-individualist theory is derived from a posteriori considerations. The theory tells us, quite generally, that in order for Oscar to have water-thoughts, there must be enough in Oscar's world (*whatever* it is like) to rule out the attribution to him of various 'twin' thoughts (such as twater-thoughts). Maybe this is knowable a priori if anti-individualism is true (though there is the worry that the notion of a 'twin' thought is introduced in the course of thought experiments involving a posteriori considerations which concern chemical theory). Anti-individualist theory also seems to tell us, quite generally but more substantively, that the candidates for such content-determining states of affairs are physical in nature and are distinct from the individual subject of contentful states (e.g., liquids with which a speaker causally interacts, speech communities, physical entities sufficient to fix appropriate contents for false theoretical sentences). Thus, it may be that the following a priori consequence can be distilled from anti-individualist theory:

(P) It is necessary that if Oscar is thinking that water is wet, then there exist some physical entities distinct from Oscar.

Suppose (P) is knowable a priori, on the basis of reflection on the philosophy of mind and of lan-

guage. Then, given Oscar's a priori knowledge of what he is thinking, he can know a priori that there exist some physical entities distinct from himself. Supposing that Oscar can know this much a priori, would this mean that he can know anything a priori about the character of his physical environment? It seems that he can at best know that it contains physical entities sufficient to fix the contents of his thoughts. *Which* sorts of entities are required is an a posteriori matter.

It is far from clear that (P) is something which an anti-individualist knows a priori. There is not space to consider the question whether claims about the pertinence of physical environment to the determination of content are, if true, knowable a priori. We would need to consider the difficult question whether such claims, if true, are knowable only on the basis of a posteriori knowledge about causal relations between language and the physical world, and about the social character of language. But even if anti-individualism does afford a priori knowledge of (P), is this a problem for the theory?[7]

It is obviously wrong to suppose that one can know a priori that there exist some physical entities distinct from oneself? Towards the end of his paper, McKinsey takes to construing his proposition E as the proposition that 'the external world exists', and he says that 'you obviously *can't* know a priori that the external world exists' (1991, p. 16). This does seem obvious if the alleged a priori knowledge is said to contain much detail concerning the character of the external world distinct from oneself. But if the alleged a priori knowledge is simply knowledge that something or other physical exists distinct from oneself, it is not obvious that such knowledge is impossible. McKinsey's mere assertion of such an impossibility is plainly not enough to prove the impossibility of a successful Kantian transcendental argument. Such arguments must be examined individually on their merits, not rejected a priori simply on the basis of their ambitions.

NOTES

1. McKinsey says, 'Unfortunately, Burge never explains or clarifies the concept of necessary dependency that he invokes throughout his paper' (1991, p. 12). As just noted, Burge in fact uses the language of 'necessary dependence' only once in that paper (in the passage just quoted in the text). As will become apparent, it is fairly obvious what Burge has in mind when he says that the individuation of con-

tent necessarily depends upon relations between thinkers and their environment.

2. That is, for every possible thinker of water-thoughts in a world relevantly similar to Oscar's, a similar counterfactual dependence holds.

3. I would like to thank the Editor for discussion of the foregoing recast objection and the response to it.

4. Burge's idea may be that there must be enough phys-

ical entities to guarantee that some theoretical sentence expresses, e.g., the content that *compounds of two parts hydrogen and one part oxygen exist,* rather than some 'twin' content which is irrelevant to the thinking of water-thoughts (say, a content involving the notion of *twhydrogen*).

5. Prior to the publication of McKinsey's paper, Paul Boghossian suggested to me that Burge's theory has the unpalatable consequence that something like (N) is knowable a priori. This objection is subtler than McKinsey's and is not marred by any of the misunderstandings of Burge I have attributed to McKinsey. But I think that it can be answered by the considerations which follow in the text.

6. McKinsey considers the possibility that Burge's anti-individualism gives rise to metaphysical necessities which are not knowable a priori (1991, pp. 12–14). Instead of (N), though, he considers the metaphysical necessity that if Oscar is thinking that water is wet, then some external objects exist. He then argues that since this metaphysical necessity could be embraced by an individualist (e.g., one who accepted both materialism and certain Kripkean claims about the necessity of origin), the necessity in question cannot be definitive of *anti*-individualism. But, as we have seen, the metaphysical necessity McKinsey considers is not put forward as definitive of anti-individualism.

7. In (1988), p. 655, n. 6, Burge rejects the suggestion that 'if anti-individualism and the authority of self-knowledge are accepted, then one would have an anti-sceptical argument.' He says that 'there is no easy argument against scepticism from anti-individualism and authoritative self-knowledge'. This suggests that he does not endorse the view that anti-individualism affords a priori knowledge of (P), since if it *did,* this would make possible an a priori argument against certain forms of scepticism.

REFERENCES

Tyler Burge, 'Other Bodies,' in *Thought and Object: Essays on Intentionality,* edited by A. Woodfield (Oxford: Oxford University Press, 1982).

——— , 'Individualism and Self-Knowledge,' *Journal of Philosophy* 85 (1988) 649–63.

Michael McKinsey, 'Anti-Individualism and Privileged Access,' *Analysis* 51 (1991) 9–16.

Hilary Putnam, 'The Meaning of "Meaning",' in his *Philosophical Papers* Vol. 2 (Cambridge: Cambridge University Press, 1975).

59 | The Extended Mind
Andy Clark and David J. Chalmers[1]

1. Introduction

Where does the mind stop and the rest of the world begin? The question invites two standard replies. Some accept the demarcations of skin and skull, and say that what is outside the body is outside the mind. Others are impressed by arguments suggesting that the meaning of our words "just ain't in the head," and hold that this externalism about meaning carries over into an externalism about mind. We propose to pursue a third position. We advocate a very different sort of externalism: an *active externalism,* based on the active role of the environment in driving cognitive processes.

2. Extended Cognition

Consider three cases of human problem-solving:

1. A person sits in front of a computer screen which displays images of various two-dimensional geometric shapes and is asked to answer questions concerning the potential fit of such shapes into depicted "sockets." To assess fit, the person must mentally rotate the shapes to align them with the sockets.

2. A person sits in front of a similar computer screen, but this time can choose either to

From *Analysis* 58:10–23, 1998. Reprinted with permission of the authors.

physically rotate the image on the screen, by pressing a rotate button, or to mentally rotate the image as before. We can also suppose, not unrealistically, that some speed advantage accrues to the physical rotation operation.

3. Sometime in the cyberpunk future, a person sits in front of a similar computer screen. This agent, however, has the benefit of a neural implant which can perform the rotation operation as fast as the computer in the previous example. The agent must still choose which internal resource to use (the implant or the good old fashioned mental rotation), as each resource makes different demands on attention and other concurrent brain activity.

How much *cognition* is present in these cases? We suggest that all three cases are similar. Case (3) with the neural implant seems clearly to be on a par with case (1). And case (2) with the rotation button displays the same sort of computational structure as case (3), although it is distributed across agent and computer instead of internalized within the agent. If the rotation in case (3) is cognitive, by what right do we count case (2) as fundamentally different? We cannot simply point to the skin/skull boundary as justification, since the legitimacy of that boundary is precisely what is at issue. But nothing else seems different.

The kind of case just described is by no means as exotic as it may at first appear. It is not just the presence of advanced external computing resources which raises the issue, but rather the general tendency of human reasoners to lean heavily on environmental supports. Thus consider the use of pen and paper to perform long multiplication (McClelland et al 1986, Clark 1989), the use of physical re-arrangements of letter tiles to prompt word recall in Scrabble (Kirsh 1995), the use of instruments such as the nautical slide rule (Hutchins 1995), and the general paraphernalia of language, books, diagrams, and culture. In all these cases the individual brain performs some operations, while others are delegated to manipulations of external media. Had our brains been different, this distribution of tasks would doubtless have varied.

In fact, even the mental rotation cases described in scenarios (1) and (2) are real. The cases reflect options available to players of the computer game Tetris. In Tetris, falling geometric shapes must be rapidly directed into an appropriate slot in an emerging structure. A rotation button can be used. David Kirsh and Paul Maglio (1994) calculate that the physical rotation of a shape through 90 degrees takes about 100 milliseconds, plus about 200 milliseconds to select the button. To achieve the same result by mental rotation takes about 1000 milliseconds. Kirsh and Maglio go on to present compelling evidence that physical rotation is used not just to position a shape ready to fit a slot, but often to help *determine* whether the shape and the slot are compatible. The latter use constitutes a case of what Kirsh and Maglio call an 'epistemic action.' *Epistemic* actions alter the world so as to aid and augment cognitive processes such as recognition and search. Merely *pragmatic* actions, by contrast, alter the world because some physical change is desirable for its own sake (e.g., putting cement into a hole in a dam).

Epistemic action, we suggest, demands spread of *epistemic credit.* If, as we confront some task, a part of the world functions as a process which, *were it done in the head,* we would have no hesitation in recognizing as part of the cognitive process, then that part of the world *is* (so we claim) part of the cognitive process. Cognitive processes ain't (all) in the head!

3. Active Externalism

In these cases, the human organism is linked with an external entity in a two-way interaction, creating a *coupled system* that can be seen as a cognitive system in its own right. All the components in the system play an active causal role, and they jointly govern behavior in the same sort of way that cognition usually does. If we remove the external component the system's behavioral competence will drop, just as it would if we removed part of its brain. Our thesis is that this sort of coupled process counts equally well as a cognitive process, whether or not it is wholly in the head.

This externalism differs greatly from standard variety advocated by Putnam (1975) and Burge (1979). When I believe that water is wet and my twin believes that twin water is wet, the external features responsible for the difference in our beliefs are distal and historical, at the other end of a lengthy causal chain. Features of the *present* are not relevant: if I happen to be surrounded by XYZ right now (maybe I have teleported to Twin Earth), my beliefs still concern standard water, because of my history. In these cases, the relevant external features are *passive.* Because of their distal nature, they play no role in driving the cognitive process in the here-and-now. This is reflected by the fact that the actions performed by me and my twin are physically indistinguishable, despite our external differences.

In the cases we describe, by contrast, the relevant external features are *active,* playing a crucial role in the here-and-now. Because they are coupled with the human organism, they have a direct impact on the organism and on its behavior. In these cases, the relevant parts of the world are *in the loop,* not dangling at the other end of a long causal chain. Concentrating on this sort of coupling leads us to an *active externalism,* as opposed to the passive externalism of Putnam and Burge.

Many have complained that even if Putnam and Burge are right about the externality of content, it is not clear that these external aspects play a causal or explanatory role in the generation of action. In counterfactual cases where internal structure is held constant but these external features are changed, behavior looks just the same; so internal structure seems to be doing the crucial work. We will not adjudicate that issue here, but we note that active externalism is not threatened by any such problem. The external features in a coupled system play an ineliminable role—if we retain internal structure but change the external features, behavior may change completely. The external features here are just as causally relevant as typical internal features of the brain.[2]

By embracing an active externalism, we allow a more natural explanation of all sorts of actions. One can explain my choice of words in Scrabble, for example, as the outcome of an extended cognitive process involving the rearrangement of tiles on my tray. Of course, one could always try to explain my action in terms of internal processes and a long series of "inputs" and "actions," but this explanation would be needlessly complex. If an isomorphic process were going on in the head, we would feel no urge to characterize it in this cumbersome way.[3] In a very real sense, the re-arrangement of tiles on the tray is not part of action; it is part of *thought.*

The view we advocate here is reflected by a growing body of research in cognitive science. In areas as diverse as the theory of situated cognition (Suchman 1987), studies of real-world-robotics (Beer 1989), dynamical approaches to child development (Thelen and Smith 1994), and research on the cognitive properties of collectives of agents (Hutchins 1995), cognition is often taken to be continuous with processes in the environment.[4] Thus, in seeing cognition as extended one is not merely making a terminological decision; it makes a significant difference to the methodology of scientific investigation. In effect, explanatory methods that might once have been thought appropriate only for the analysis of "inner" processes are now being adapted for the study of the outer, and there is promise that our understanding of cognition will become richer for it.

Some find this sort of externalism unpalatable. One reason may be that many identify the cognitive with the conscious, and it seems far from plausible that consciousness extends outside the head in these cases. But not every cognitive process, at least on standard usage, is a conscious process. It is widely accepted that all sorts of processes beyond the borders of consciousness play a crucial role in cognitive processing: in the retrieval of memories, linguistic processes, and skill acquisition, for example. So the mere fact that external processes are external where consciousness is internal is no reason to deny that those processes are cognitive.

More interestingly, one might argue that what keeps real cognition processes in the head is the requirement that cognitive processes be *portable.* Here, we are moved by a vision of what might be called the Naked Mind: a package of resources and operations we can always bring to bear on a cognitive task, regardless of the local environment. On this view, the trouble with coupled systems is that they are too easily *decoupled.* The true cognitive processes are those that lie at the constant core of the system; anything else is an add-on extra.

There is something to this objection. The brain (or brain and body) comprises a package of basic, portable, cognitive resources that is of interest in its own right. These resources may incorporate bodily actions into cognitive processes, as when we use our fingers as working memory in a tricky calculation, but they will not encompass the more contingent aspects of our external environment, such as a pocket calculator. Still, mere contingency of coupling does not rule out cognitive status. In the distant future we may be able to plug various modules into our brain to help us out: a module for extra short-term memory when we need it, for example. When a module is plugged in, the processes involving it are just as cognitive as if they had been there all along.[5]

Even if one were to make the portability criterion pivotal, active externalism would not be undermined. Counting on our fingers has already been let in the door, for example, and it is easy to push things further. Think of the old image of the engineer with a slide rule hanging from his belt wherever he goes. What if people always carried a pocket calculator, or had them implanted? The real moral of the portability intuition is that for coupled systems to be relevant to the core of cognition, *reliable* coupling is required. It happens that most reliable coupling takes place within the brain, but there can easily be reliable coupling with the environment as well. If the resources of my calculator or my Filofax are always there when I need them, then they are coupled with me as reliably as we need. In effect, they are part of the basic package of cognitive resources that I bring to bear on the everyday world. These systems cannot be impugned simply on the basis of the danger of discrete damage, loss, or malfunction, or because of any occasional decoupling: the biological brain is in similar danger, and occasionally loses capacities temporarily in episodes of sleep, intoxication, and emotion. If the relevant capacities are generally there when they are required, this is coupling enough.

Moreover, it may be that the biological brain has in fact evolved and matured in ways which factor in the reliable presence of a manipulable external environment. It certainly seems that evolution has favored on-board capacities which are especially geared to parasitizing the local environment so as to reduce memory load, and even to transform the nature of the computational problems themselves. Our visual systems have evolved to rely on their environment in various ways: they exploit contingent facts about the structure of natural scenes (e.g. Ullman and Richards 1984), for example, and they take advantage of the computational shortcuts afforded by bodily motion and locomotion (e.g. Blake and Yuille, 1992). Perhaps there are other cases where evolution has found it advantageous to exploit the possibility of the environment being in the cognitive loop. If so, then external coupling is part of the truly basic package of cognitive resources that we bring to bear on the world.

Language may be an example. Language appears to be a central means by which cognitive processes are extended into the world. Think of a group of people brainstorming around a table, or a philosopher who thinks best by writing, developing her ideas as she goes. It may be that language evolved, in part, to enable such exten-

sions of our cognitive resources within actively coupled systems.

Within the lifetime of an organism, too, individual learning may have molded the brain in ways that rely on cognitive extensions that surrounded us as we learned. Language is again a central example here, as are the various physical and computational artifacts that are routinely used as cognitive extensions by children in schools and by trainees in numerous professions. In such cases the brain develops in a way that complements the external structures, and learns to play its role within a unified, densely coupled system. Once we recognize the crucial role of the environment in constraining the evolution and development of cognition, we see that extended cognition is a core cognitive process, not an add-on extra.

An analogy may be helpful. The extraordinary efficiency of the fish as a swimming device is partly due, it now seems, to an evolved capacity to couple its swimming behaviors to the pools of external kinetic energy found as swirls, eddies and vortices in its watery environment (see Triantafyllou and G. Triantafyllou 1995). These vortices include both naturally occurring ones (e.g., where water hits a rock) and self-induced ones (created by well-timed tail flaps). The fish swims by building these externally occurring processes into the very heart of its locomotion routines. The fish and surrounding vortices together constitute a unified and remarkably efficient swimming machine.

Now consider a reliable feature of the human environment, such as the sea of words. This linguistic surround envelops us from birth. Under such conditions, the plastic human brain will surely come to treat such structures as a reliable resource to be factored into the shaping of on-board cognitive routines. Where the fish flaps its tail to set up the eddies and vortices it subsequently exploits, we intervene in multiple linguistic media, creating local structures and disturbances whose reliable presence drives our ongoing internal processes. Words and external symbols are thus paramount among the cognitive vortices which help constitute human thought.

4. From Cognition to Mind

So far we have spoken largely about "cognitive processing," and argued for its extension into the environment. Some might think that the conclusion has been bought too cheaply. Perhaps some *processing* takes place in the environment, but what of *mind?* Everything we have said so far is compatible with the view that truly mental states—experiences, beliefs, desires, emotions, and so on—are all determined by states of the brain. Perhaps what is truly mental is internal, after all?

We propose to take things a step further. While some mental states, such as experiences, may be determined internally, there are other cases in which external factors make a significant contribution. In particular, we will argue that *beliefs* can be constituted partly by features of the environment, when those features play the right sort of role in driving cognitive processes. If so, the mind extends into the world.

First, consider a normal case of belief embedded in memory. Inga hears from a friend that there is an exhibition at the Museum of Modern Art, and decides to go see it. She thinks for a moment and recalls that the museum is on 53rd Street, so she walks to 53rd Street and goes into the museum. It seems clear that Inga believes that the museum is on 53rd Street, and that she believed this even before she consulted her memory. It was not previously an *occurrent* belief, but then neither are most of our beliefs. The belief was sitting somewhere in memory, waiting to be accessed.

Now consider Otto. Otto suffers from Alzheimer's disease, and like many Alzheimer's patients, he relies on information in the environment to help structure his life. Otto carries a notebook around with him everywhere he goes. When he learns new information, he writes it down. When he needs some old information, he looks it up. For Otto, his notebook plays the role usually played by a biological memory. Today, Otto hears about the exhibition at the Museum of Modern Art, and decides to go see it. He consults the notebook, which says that the museum is on 53rd Street, so he walks to 53rd Street and goes into the museum.

Clearly, Otto walked to 53rd Street because he wanted to go to the museum and he believed the museum was on 53rd Street. And just as Inga had her belief even before she consulted her memory, it seems reasonable to say that Otto believed the museum was on 53rd Street even before consulting his notebook. For in relevant respects the cases are entirely analogous: the notebook plays for Otto the same role that memory plays for Inga. The information in the notebook functions just like the information constituting an ordinary non-occurrent belief; it just happens that this information lies beyond the skin.

The alternative is to say that Otto has no belief about the matter until he consults his notebook; at best, he believes that the museum is located at the address in the notebook. But if we follow Otto around for a while, we will see how unnatural this way of speaking is. Otto is constantly using his notebook as a matter of course. It is central to his actions in all sorts of contexts, in the way that an ordinary memory is central in an ordinary life. The same information might come up again and again, perhaps being slightly modified on occasion, before retreating into the recesses of his artificial memory. To say that the beliefs disappear when the notebook is filed away seems to miss the big picture in just the same way as saying that Inga's beliefs disappear as soon as she is no longer conscious of them. In both cases the information is reliably there when needed, available to consciousness and available to guide action, in just the way that we expect a belief to be.

Certainly, insofar as beliefs and desires are characterized by their explanatory roles, Otto's and Inga's cases seem to be on a par: the essential causal dynamics of the two cases mirror each other precisely. We are happy to explain Inga's action in terms of her occurrent desire to go to the museum and her standing belief that the museum is on 53rd street, and we should be happy to explain Otto's action in the same way. The alternative is to explain Otto's action in terms of his occurrent desire to go to the museum, his standing belief that the Museum is on the location written in the notebook, and the accessible fact that the notebook says the Museum is on 53rd Street; but this complicates the explanation unnecessarily. If we must resort to explaining Otto's action this way, then we must also do so for the countless other actions in which his notebook is involved; in each of the explanations, there will be an extra term involving the notebook. We submit that to explain things this way is to take *one step too many*. It is pointlessly complex, in the same way that it would be pointlessly complex to explain Inga's actions in terms of beliefs about her memory. The notebook is a constant for Otto, in the same way that memory is a constant for Inga; to point to it in every belief/desire explanation would be redundant. In an explanation, simplicity is power.

If this is right, we can even construct the case of Twin Otto, who is just like Otto except that a while ago he mistakenly wrote in his notebook that the Museum of Modern Art was on 51st Street. Today, Twin Otto is a physical duplicate of Otto from the skin in, but his notebook differs. Consequently, Twin Otto is best characterized as believing that the museum is on 51st Street, where Otto believes it is on 53rd. In these cases, a belief is simply not in the head.

This mirrors the conclusion of Putnam and Burge, but again there are important differences. In the Putnam/Burge cases, the external features constituting differences in belief are distal and historical, so that twins in these cases produce physically indistinguishable behavior. In the cases we are describing, the relevant external features play an active role in the here-and-now, and have a direct impact on behavior. Where Otto walks to 53rd Street, Twin Otto walks to 51st. There is no question of explanatory irrelevance for this sort of external belief content; it is introduced precisely because of the central explanatory role that it plays. Like the Putnam and Burge cases, these cases involve differences in reference and truth-conditions, but they also involve differences in the dynamics of *cognition*.[6]

The moral is that when it comes to belief, there is nothing sacred about skull and skin. What makes some information count as a belief is the role it plays, and there is no reason why the relevant role can be played only from inside the body.

Some will resist this conclusion. An opponent might put her foot down and insist that as she uses the term "belief," or perhaps even according to standard usage, Otto simply does not qualify as believing that the museum is on 53rd Street. We do not intend to debate what is standard usage; our broader point is that the notion of belief *ought* to be used so that Otto qualifies as having the belief in question. In all *important* respects, Otto's case is similar to a standard case of (non-occurrent) belief. The differences between Otto's case and Inga's are striking, but they are superficial. By using the "belief" notion in a wider way, it picks out something more akin to a natural kind. The notion becomes deeper and more unified, and is more useful in explanation.

To provide substantial resistance, an opponent has to show that Otto's and Inga's cases differ in some important and relevant respect. But in what deep respect are the cases different? To make the case *solely* on the grounds that information is in the head in one case but not in the other would be to beg the question. If this difference is relevant to a difference in belief, it is surely not *primitively* relevant. To justify the different treatment, we must find some more basic underlying difference between the two.

It might be suggested that the cases are relevantly different in that Inga has more *reliable* access to the information. After all, someone might take away Otto's notebook at any time, but Inga's memory is safer. It is not implausible that constancy is relevant: indeed, the fact that Otto always uses his notebook played some role in our justifying its cognitive status. If Otto were consulting a guidebook as a one-off, we would be much less likely to ascribe him a standing belief. But in the original case, Otto's access to the notebook is very reliable—not perfectly reliable, to be sure, but then neither is Inga's access to her memory. A surgeon might tamper with her brain, or more mundanely, she might have too much to drink. The mere possibility of such tampering is not enough to deny her the belief.

One might worry that Otto's access to his notebook *in fact* comes and goes. He showers without the notebook, for example, and he cannot read it when it is dark. Surely his belief cannot come and go so easily? We could get around this problem by redescribing the situation, but in any case an occasional temporary disconnection does not threaten our claim. After all, when Inga is asleep, or when she is intoxicated, we do not say that her belief disappears. What really counts is that the information is easily available when the subject needs it, and this constraint is satisfied equally in the two cases. If Otto's notebook were often unavailable to him at times when the information in it would be useful, there might be a problem, as the information would not be able to play the action-guiding role that is central to belief; but if it is easily available in most relevant situations, the belief is not endangered.

Perhaps a difference is that Inga has *better* access to the information than Otto does? Inga's "central" processes and her memory probably have a relatively high-bandwidth link between them, compared to the low-grade connection between Otto and his notebook. But this alone does not make a difference between believing and not believing. Consider Inga's museum-going friend Lucy, whose biological memory has only a low-grade link to her central systems, due to nonstandard biology or past misadventures. Processing in Lucy's case might be less efficient, but as long as the relevant information is accessible, Lucy clearly believes that the museum is on 53rd Street. If the connection was too indirect—if Lucy had to struggle hard to retrieve the information with mixed results, or a psychotherapist's aid were needed—we might become more reluctant to ascribe the belief, but such cases are well beyond Otto's situation, in which the information is easily accessible.

Another suggestion could be that Otto has access to the relevant information only by *perception,* whereas Inga has more direct access—by introspection, perhaps. In some ways, however, to put things this way is to beg the question. After all, we are in effect advocating a point of view on which Otto's internal processes and his notebook constitute a single cognitive system. From the standpoint of this system, the flow of information between notebook and brain is not perceptual at all; it does not involve the impact of something outside the system. It is more akin to information flow within the brain. The only deep way in which the access is perceptual is that in Otto's case, there is a distinctly perceptual phenomenology associated with the retrieval of the information, whereas in Inga's case there is not. But why should the nature of an associated phenomenology make a difference to the status of a belief? Inga's memory may have some associated phenomenology, but it is still a belief. The phenomenology is not visual, to be sure. But for visual phenomenology consider the Terminator, from the Arnold Schwarzenegger movie of the same name. When he recalls some information from memory, it is "displayed" before him in his visual field (presumably he is conscious of it, as there are frequent shots depicting his point of view). The fact that standing memories are recalled in this unusual way surely makes little difference to their status as standing beliefs.

These various small differences between Otto's and Inga's cases are all *shallow* differences. To focus on them would be to miss the way in which for Otto, notebook entries play just the sort of role that beliefs play in guiding most people's lives.

Perhaps the intuition that Otto's is not a true belief comes from a residual feeling that the only true beliefs are occurrent beliefs. If we take this feeling seriously, Inga's belief will be ruled out too, as will many beliefs that we attribute in everyday life. This would be an extreme view, but it may be the most consistent way to deny Otto's belief. Upon even a slightly less extreme view—the view that a belief must be *available*

for consciousness, for example—Otto's notebook entry seems to qualify just as well as Inga's memory. Once dispositional beliefs are let in the door, it is difficult to resist the conclusion that Otto's notebook has all the relevant dispositions.

5. Beyond the Outer Limits

If the thesis is accepted, how far should we go? All sorts of puzzle cases spring to mind. What of the amnesic villagers in *100 Years of Solitude,* who forget the names for everything and so hang labels everywhere? Does the information in my Filofax count as part of my memory? If Otto's notebook has been tampered with, does he believe the newly-installed information? Do I believe the contents of the page in front of me before I read it? Is my cognitive state somehow spread across the Internet?

We do not think that there are categorical answers to all of these questions, and we will not give them. But to help understand what is involved in ascriptions of extended belief, we can at least examine the features of our central case that make the notion so clearly applicable there. First, the notebook is a constant in Otto's life—in cases where the information in the notebook would be relevant, he will rarely take action without consulting it. Second, the information in the notebook is directly available without difficulty. Third, upon retrieving information from the notebook he automatically endorses it. Fourth, the information in the notebook has been consciously endorsed at some point in the past, and indeed is there as a consequence of this endorsement.[7] The status of the fourth feature as a criterion for belief is arguable (perhaps one can acquire beliefs through subliminal perception, or through memory tampering?), but the first three features certainly play a crucial role.

Insofar as increasingly exotic puzzle cases lack these features, the applicability of the notion of "belief" gradually falls off. If I rarely take relevant action without consulting my Filofax, for example, its status within my cognitive system will resemble that of the notebook in Otto's. But if I often act without consultation—for example, if I sometimes answer relevant questions with "I don't know"—then information in it counts less clearly as part of my belief system. The Internet is likely to fail on multiple counts, unless I am unusually computer-reliant, facile with the technology, and trusting, but information in certain files on my computer may qualify. In intermediate cases, the question of whether a belief is present may be indeterminate, or the answer may depend on the varying standards that are at play in various contexts in which the question might be asked. But any indeterminacy here does not mean that in the central cases, the answer is not clear.

What about socially extended cognition? Could my mental states be partly constituted by the states of other thinkers? We see no reason why not, in principle. In an unusually interdependent couple, it is entirely possible that one partner's beliefs will play the same sort of role for the other as the notebook plays for Otto.[8] What is central is a high degree of trust, reliance, and accessibility. In other social relationships these criteria may not be so clearly fulfilled, but they might nevertheless be fulfilled in specific domains. For example, the waiter at my favorite restaurant might act as a repository of my beliefs about my favorite meals (this might even be construed as a case of extended desire). In other cases, one's beliefs might be embodied in one's secretary, one's accountant, or one's collaborator.[9]

In each of these cases, the major burden of the coupling between agents is carried by language. Without language, we might be much more akin to discrete Cartesian "inner" minds, in which high-level cognition relies largely on internal resources. But the advent of language has allowed us to spread this burden into the world. Language, thus construed, is not a mirror of our inner states but a complement to them. It serves as a tool whose role is to extend cognition in ways that on-board devices cannot. Indeed, it

may be that the intellectual explosion in recent evolutionary time is due as much to this linguistically-enabled extension of cognition as to any independent development in our inner cognitive resources.

What, finally, of the self? Does the extended mind imply an extended self? It seems so. Most of us already accept that the self outstrips the boundaries of consciousness; my dispositional beliefs, for example, constitute in some deep sense part of who I am. If so, then these boundaries may also fall beyond the skin. The information in Otto's notebook, for example, is a central part of his identity as a cognitive agent. What this comes to is that Otto *himself* is best regarded as an extended system, a coupling of biological organism and external resources. To consistently resist this conclusion, we would have to shrink the self into a mere bundle of occurrent states, severely threatening its deep psychological continuity. Far better to take the broader view, and see agents themselves as spread into the world.

As with any reconception of ourselves, this view will have significant consequences. There are obvious consequences for philosophical views of the mind and for the methodology of research in cognitive science, but there will also be effects in the moral and social domains. It may be, for example, that in some cases interfering with someone's environment will have the same moral significance as interfering with their person. And if the view is taken seriously, certain forms of social activity might be reconceived as less akin to communication and action, and as more akin to thought. In any case, once the hegemony of skin and skull is usurped, we may be able to see ourselves more truly as creatures of the world.

NOTES

1. Authors are listed in order of degree of belief in the central thesis.
2. Much of the appeal of externalism in the philosophy of mind may stem from the intuitive appeal of active externalism. Externalists often make analogies involving external features in coupled systems, and appeal to the arbitrariness of boundaries between brain and environment. But these intuitions sit uneasily with the letter of standard externalism. In most of the Putnam/Burge cases, the immediate environment is irrelevant; only the historical environment counts. Debate has focused on the question of whether mind must be in the head, but a more relevant question in assessing these examples might be: is mind in the present?

3. Herbert Simon (1981) once suggested that we view internal memory as, in effect, an external resource upon which "real" inner processes operate. "Search in memory," he comments, "is not very different from search of the external environment." Simon's view at least has the virtue of treating internal and external processing with the parity they deserve, but we suspect that on his view the mind will shrink too small for most people's tastes.
4. Philosophical views of a similar spirit can be found in Haugeland 1995, McClamrock 1985, Varela et al 1991, and Wilson 1994.
5. Or consider the following passage from a recent science fiction novel (McHugh 1992, p. 213): "I am taken to the system's department where I am attuned

to the system. All I do is jack in and then a technician instructs the system to attune and it does. I jack out and query the time. 10:52. The information pops up. Always before I could only access information when I was jacked in, it gave me a sense that I knew what I thought and what the system told me, but now, how do I know what is system and what is Zhang?"

6. In the terminology of Chalmers' "The Components of Content" (this volume, chapter 56): the twins in the Putnam and Burge cases differ only in their *subjunctive* content (or relational content), but Otto and his twin can be seen to differ in their *epistemic* content (or notional content), which is the sort of content that governs cognition. Epistemic content is generally internal to a cognitive system, but in this case the cognitive system is itself effectively extended to include the notebook.

7. The constancy and past-endorsement criteria may suggest that history is partly constitutive of belief. One might react to this by removing any historical component (giving a purely dispositional reading of the constancy criterion and eliminating the past-endorsement criterion, for example), or one might allow such a component as long as the main burden

is carried by features of the present.

8. From the *New York Times,* March 30, 1995, p. B7, in an article on former UCLA basketball coach John Wooden: "Wooden and his wife attended 36 straight Final Fours, and she invariably served as his memory bank. Nell Wooden rarely forgot a name—her husband rarely remembered one—and in the standing-room-only Final Four lobbies, she would recognize people for him."

9. Might this sort of reasoning also allow something like Burge's extended "arthritis" beliefs? After all, I might always defer to my doctor in taking relevant actions concerning my disease. Perhaps so, but there are some clear differences. For example, any extended beliefs would be grounded in an existing active relationship with the doctor, rather than in a historical relationship to a language community. And on the current analysis, my deference to the doctor would tend to yield something like a true belief that I have some other disease in my thigh, rather than the false belief that I have arthritis there. On the other hand, if I used medical experts solely as terminological consultants, the results of Burge's analysis might be mirrored.

REFERENCES

Beer, R. 1989. *Intelligence as Adaptive Behavior.* New York: Academic Press.

Blake, A. & Yuille, A. (eds.) 1992. *Active Vision.* Cambridge, MA: MIT Press.

Burge, T. 1979. Individualism and the mental. Midwest Studies in Philosophy 4:73–122.

Clark, A. 1989. *Microcognition.* MIT Press.

Haugeland, J. 1995. Mind embodied and embedded. In Y. Houng and J. Ho (eds.), *Mind and Cognition.* Taipei: Academia Sinica.

Hutchins, E. 1995. *Cognition in the Wild.* Cambridge, MA: MIT Press,

Kirsh, D. 1995. The intelligent use of space. *Artificial Intelligence* 73:31–68.

Kirsh, D. & Maglio, P. 1994. On distinguishing epistemic from pragmatic action. *Cognitive Science* 18: 513–49.

McClamrock, R. 1995. *Existential Cognition.* Chicago: University of Chicago Press.

McClelland, J. L, D. E. Rumelhart, & G. E. Hinton 1986. The appeal of parallel distributed processing. In McClelland & Rumelhart (eds.), *Parallel Distributed Processing,* Volume 2. Cambridge, MA: MIT Press.

McHugh, M. 1992. *China Mountain Zhang.* New York: Tom Doherty Associates.

Putnam, H. 1975. The meaning of 'meaning.' In K. Gunderson (ed.), *Language, Mind, and Knowledge.* Minneapolis: University of Minnesota Press.

Simon, H. 1981. *The Sciences of the Artificial.* MIT Press.

Suchman, L. 1987. *Plans and Situated Actions.* Cambridge, UK: Cambridge University Press.

Thelen, E. & Smith, L. 1994. *A Dynamic Systems Approach to the Development of Cognition and Action.* Cambridge, MA: MIT Press.

Triantafyllou, M. & Triantafyllou, G. 1995. An Efficient Swimming Machine. *Scientific American* 272(3): 64–70.

Ullman, S. & Richards, W. 1984. *Image Understanding.* Norwood, NJ: Ablex.

Varela, F., Thompson, E. & Rosch, E. 1991. *The Embodied Mind.* Cambridge, MA: MIT Press.

Wilson, R. 1994. Wide computationalism. *Mind* 103: 351–72.

Miscellaneous

There are many other major philosophical problems that are closely connected to issues about the mind. Four of these are the problems of personal identity, free will, other minds, and artificial intelligence. Each of these is represented by an article here.

What is the self? What makes each of us the person that we are? What makes us the same person over time? These are the central issues of the problem of personal identity. These problems are addressed here by Derek Parfit (chapter 60), who introduces the problem by considering cases of teletransportation, where questions about the identity of a resulting person are unclear. Parfit contrasts reductionist and non-reductionist views of personal identity and argues for a reductionist view on which there are no deep facts about personal identity over and above facts about physical and psychological continuity.

What is free will? Is free action compatible with determinism? What sort of freedom is required for moral responsibility? These are the central issues of the problem of free will. On first appearance, many hold that if the evolution of the world is determined, we cannot have free will. A. J. Ayer (chapter 61) argues that this is wrong, and that free will and determinism are compatible. He gives a somewhat deflationary treatment of free will, on which freedom involves the absence of constraints on action, and argues that determinism does not preclude free will in this sense.

How can we know whether others have minds? This is the problem of other minds. In everyday life, we accept that others have minds like ours, and this acceptance seems unproblematic. But philosophically, it is not obvious how the belief in other minds is grounded. How do we know that others are not mindless zombies? Bertrand Russell (chapter 62) argues that our belief in other minds in grounded in an *analogy* with our own case: roughly, that others are broadly similar to ourselves, that we have minds, so that others have minds. This raises many questions (should one accept an analogy based only on a single case?), but it is far from obvious what the alternatives are.

Can machines have minds? If we program a computer appropriately, will it think, feel, and understand? This is the central philosophical problem about artificial intelligence, the discipline of creating intelligent machines. John Searle (chapter 63) argues that while some machines might have minds (we may ourselves be machines), these minds cannot be grounded in computation alone: merely programming a computer in the right way will not suffice for a mind. He argues for this using a thought-experiment about a "Chinese room" in which an English speaker simulates a computer program for understanding Chinese, without any real understanding. Searle argues that computers are in the same situation: They have syntax, but no real semantics. The conclusion is that computers running programs cannot literally be said to have minds.

FURTHER READING

The problem of personal identity is addressed at length by Parfit (1984) and by the papers in Perry (1975). Dennett (1984) discusses free will, and Kane (2001) and Watson (1982) are excellent collections of articles on the topic. Avramides (2000) gives an overview of issues about other minds, and Buford (1972) is a collection of papers on the issue. Searle (1980) sets out his critique of artificial intelligence at more length, with responses by many critics. See also Searle (1991), Churchland (chapter 36), and the papers in Dietrich 1994. Hofstadter and Dennett (1981) contains many accessible articles on the topics in this section.

Avramides, A. 2000. *Other Minds.* Routledge.

Buford, T. O. 1982. *Essays on Other Minds.* University of Illinois Press.

Dennett, D. C. 1984. *Elbow Room: The Varieties of Free Will Worth Wanting.* MIT Press.

Dietrich, E. (ed.). 1994. *Thinking Computers and Virtual Persons.* Academic Press.

Hofstadter, D. R., & Dennett, D. C. 1981. *The Mind's I: Fantasies and Reflections on Self and Soul.* Basic Books.

Kane, R. 2001. *The Oxford Handbook of Free Will.* Oxford University Press.

Parfit, D. 1984. *Reasons and Persons.* Oxford University Press.

Perry, J. 1975. *Personal Identity.* University of California Press.

Searle, J. R. 1980. Minds, brains and programs. *Behavioral and Brain Sciences* 3:417–57.

Searle, J. R. 1991. *The Rediscovery of the Mind.* MIT Press.

Watson, G. (ed.). 1982. *Free Will.* Oxford University Press.

60 | Reductionism and Personal Identity[1]
Derek Parfit

We can start with some science fiction. Here on Earth, I enter the Teletransporter. When I press some button, a machine destroys my body, while recording the exact states of all my cells. The information is sent by radio to Mars, where another machine makes, out of organic materials, a perfect copy of my body. The person who wakes up on Mars seems to remember living my life up to the moment when I pressed the button, and he is in every other way just like me.

Of those who have thought about such cases, some believe that it would be I who would wake up on Mars. They regard Teletransportation as merely the fastest way of travelling. Others believe that, if I chose to be Teletransported, I would be making a terrible mistake. On their view, the person who wakes up would be a mere Replica of me.

I

That is a disagreement about personal identity. To understand such disagreements, we must distinguish two kinds of sameness. Two white billiard balls may be qualitatively identical, or exactly similar. But they are not numerically identical, or one and the same ball. If I paint one of these balls red, it will cease to be qualitatively identical with itself as it was; but it will still be one and the same ball. Consider next a claim like, 'Since her accident, she is no longer the same person.' That involves both senses of identity. It means that *she,* one and the same person, is *not* now the same person. That is not a contradiction. The claim is only that this person's character has changed. This numerically identical person is now qualitatively different.

When psychologists discuss identity, they are typically concerned with the kind of person someone is, or wants to be. That is the question involved, for example, in an identity crisis. But, when philosophers discuss identity, it is numerical identity they mean. And, in our concern about our own futures, that is what we have in mind. I may believe that, after my marriage, I shall be a different person. But that does not make marriage death. However much I change, I shall still be alive if there will be someone living who will be me. Similarly, if I was Teletransported, my Replica on Mars would be qualitatively identical to me; but, on the sceptic's view, he wouldn't *be* me. *I* shall have ceased to exist. And that, we naturally assume, is what matters.

Questions about our numerical identity all take the following form. We have two ways of referring to a person, and we ask whether these are ways of referring to the same person. Thus we might ask whether Boris Nikolayevich is Yeltsin. In the most important questions of this kind, our two ways of referring to a person pick out a person at different times. Thus we might ask whether the person to whom we are speaking now is the same as the person to whom we spoke on the telephone yesterday. These are questions about identity over time.

To answer such questions, we must know the *criterion* of personal identity: the relation between a person at one time, and a person at another time, which makes these one and the same person.

Different criteria have been advanced. On one view, what makes me the same, throughout my life, is my having the same body. This criterion requires uninterrupted bodily continuity. There is no such continuity between my body on Earth and the body of my Replica on Mars; so, on this view, my Replica would not be me. Other writers appeal to psychological continuity. Thus Locke claimed that, if I was conscious of a past life in some other body, I would be the person who lived that life. On some versions of this view, my Replica would be me.

Supporters of these different views often appeal to cases where they conflict. Most of these cases are, like Teletransportation, purely imaginary. Some philosophers object that, since our concept of a person rests on a scaffolding of facts, we should not expect this concept to apply in imagined cases where we think those facts away. I agree. But I believe that, for a different reason, it is worth considering such cases. We

Excerpted from "The Unimportance of Identity," in *Identity,* edited by H. Harris (1995), pp. 13–28, with permission from Oxford University Press. Copyright © 1995 Oxford University Press.

can use them to discover, not what the truth is, but what we believe. We might have found that, when we consider science fiction cases, we simply shrug our shoulders. But that is not so. Many of us find that we have certain beliefs about what kind of fact personal identity is.

These beliefs are best revealed when we think about such cases from a first-person point of view. So, when I imagine something's happening to me, you should imagine its happening to you. Suppose that I live in some future century, in which technology is far advanced, and I am about to undergo some operation. Perhaps my brain and body will be remodelled, or partially replaced. There will be a resulting person, who will wake up tomorrow. I ask, 'Will that person be me? Or am I about to die? Is this the end?' I may not know how to answer this question. But it is natural to assume that there must *be* an answer. The resulting person, it may seem, must be either me, or someone else. And the answer must be all-or-nothing. That person cannot be *partly* me. If that person is in pain tomorrow, this pain cannot be partly mine. So, we may assume, either I shall feel that pain, or I shan't.

If this is how we think about such cases, we assume that our identity must be *determinate*. We assume that, in every imaginable case, questions about our identity must have answers, which must be either, and quite simply, Yes or No.

Let us now ask: 'Can this be true?' There is one view on which it might be. On this view, there are immaterial substances: souls, or Cartesian Egos. These entities have the special properties once ascribed to atoms: they are indivisible, and their continued existence is, in its nature, all or nothing. And such an Ego is what each of us really is.

Unlike several writers, I believe that such a view might have been true. But we have no good evidence for thinking that it is, and some evidence for thinking that it isn't; so I shall assume here that no such view is true.

If we do not believe that there are Cartesian Egos, or other such entities, we should accept the kind of view which I have elsewhere called *Reductionist*. On this view

    (1) A person's existence just consists in the existence of a body, and the occurrence of a series of thoughts, experiences, and other mental and physical events.

Some Reductionists claim

    (2) Persons just *are* bodies.

This view may seem not to be Reductionist, since it does not reduce persons to something else. But that is only because it is hyper-Reductionist: it reduces persons to bodies in so strong a way that it doesn't even distinguish between them. We can call it *Identifying* Reductionism.

Such a view seems to me too simple. I believe that we should combine (1) with

    (3) A person is an entity that has a body, and has thoughts and other experiences.

On this view, though a person is distinct from that person's body, and from any series of thoughts and experiences, the person's existence just *consists* in them. So we can call this view *Constitutive* Reductionism.

It may help to have other examples of this kind of view. If we melt down a bronze statue, we destroy this statue, but we do not destroy this lump of bronze. So, though the statue just consists in the lump of bronze, these cannot be one and the same thing. Similarly, the existence of a nation just consists in the existence of a group of people, on some territory, living together in certain ways. But the nation is not the same as that group of people, or that territory.

Consider next *Eliminative* Reductionism. Such a view is sometimes a response to arguments against the Identifying view. Suppose we start by claiming that a nation just is a group of people on some territory. We are then persuaded that this cannot be so: that the concept of a nation is the concept of an entity that is distinct from its people and its territory. We may conclude that, in that case, there are really no such things as nations. There are only groups of people, living together in certain ways.

In the case of persons, some Buddhist texts take an Eliminative view. According to these texts

    (4) There really aren't such things as persons: there are only brains and bodies, and thoughts and other experiences.

For example:

> Buddha has spoken thus: 'O brethren, actions do exist, and also their consequences, but the person that acts does not. . . . There exists no Individual, it is only a conventional name given to a set of elements.'

Or:

> *The mental and the material are really here,*

But here there is no person to be found.
For it is void and merely fashioned like a
doll,
Just suffering piled up like grass and
sticks.

Eliminative Reductionism is sometimes justified. Thus we are right to claim that there were really no witches, only persecuted women. But Reductionism about some kind of entity is not often well expressed with the claim that there are no such entities. We should admit that there are nations, and that we, who are persons, exist.

Rather than claiming that there are no entities of some kind, Reductionists should distinguish kinds of entity, or ways of existing. When the existence of an X just consists in the existence of a Y, or Ys, though the X is *distinct* from the Y or Ys, it is not an *independent* or *separately existing* entity. Statues do not exist separately from the matter of which they are made. Nor do nations exist separately from their citizens and their territory. Similarly, I believe,

(5) Though persons are distinct from their bodies, and from any series of mental events, they are not independent or separately existing entities.

Cartesian Egos, if they existed, would not only be distinct from human bodies, but would also be independent entities. Such Egos are claimed to be like physical objects, except that they are wholly mental. If there were such entities, it would make sense to suppose that they might cease to be causally related to some body, yet continue to exist. But, on a Reductionist view, persons are not in that sense independent from their bodies. (That is not to claim that our thoughts and other experiences are merely changes in the states of our brains. Reductionists, while not believing in purely mental substances, may be dualists.)

We can now return to personal identity over time, or what constitutes the continued existence of the same person. One question here is this. What explains the unity of a person's mental life? What makes thoughts and experiences, had at different times, the thoughts and experiences of a single person? According to some Non-Reductionists, this question cannot be answered in other terms. We must simply claim that these different thoughts and experiences are all had by the same person. This fact does not consist in any other facts, but is a bare or ultimate truth.

If each of us was a Cartesian Ego, that might be so. Since such an Ego would be an independent substance, it could be an irreducible fact that different experiences are all changes in the states of the same persisting Ego. But that could not be true of persons, I believe, if, while distinct from their bodies, they are not separately existing entities. A person, so conceived, is not the kind of entity about which there could be such irreducible truths. When experiences at different times are all had by the same person, this fact must consist in certain other facts.

If we do not believe in Cartesian Egos, we should claim

(6) Personal identity over time just consists in physical and/or psychological continuity.

That claim could be filled out in different ways. On one version of this view, what makes different experiences the experiences of a single person is their being either changes in the states of, or at least directly causally related to, the same embodied brain. That must be the view of those who believe that persons just are bodies. And we might hold that view even if, as I think we should, we distinguish persons from their bodies. But we might appeal, either in addition or instead, to various psychological relations between different mental states and events, such as the relations involved in memory, or in the persistence of intentions, desires, and other psychological features. That is what I mean by psychological continuity.

On Constitutive Reductionism, the fact of personal identity is distinct from these facts about physical and psychological continuity. But, since it just consists in them, it is not an independent or separately obtaining fact. It is not a further difference in what happens.

To illustrate that distinction, consider a simpler case. Suppose that I already know that several trees are growing together on some hill. I then learn that, because that is true, there is a copse on this hill. That would not be new factual information. I would have merely learnt that such a group of trees can be called a 'copse.' My only new information is about our language. That those trees can be called a copse is not, except trivially, a fact about the trees.

Something similar is true in the more complicated case of nations. In order to know the facts about the history of a nation, it is enough to know what large numbers of people did and said. Facts about nations cannot be barely true:

they must consist in facts about people. And, once we know these other facts, any remaining questions about nations are not further questions about what really happened.

I believe that, in the same way, facts about people cannot be barely true. Their truth must consist in the truth of facts about bodies, and about various interrelated mental and physical events. If we knew these other facts, we would have all the empirical input that we need. If we understood the concept of a person, and had no false beliefs about what persons are, we would then know, or would be able to work out, the truth of any further claims about the existence or identity of persons. That is because such claims would not tell us more about reality.

That is the barest sketch of a Reductionist view. These remarks may become clearer if we return to the so-called 'problem cases' of personal identity. In such a case, we imagine knowing that, between me now and some person in the future, there will be certain kinds or degrees of physical and/or psychological continuity or connectedness. But, though we know these facts, we cannot answer the question whether that future person would be me.

Since we may disagree on which the problem cases are, we need more than one example. Consider first the range of cases that I have elsewhere called the *Physical Spectrum*. In each of these cases, some proportion of my body would be replaced, in a single operation, with exact duplicates of the existing cells. In the case at the near end of this range, no cells would be replaced. In the case at the far end, my whole body would be destroyed and replicated. That is the case with which I began: Teletransportation.

Suppose we believe that in that case, where my whole body would be replaced, the resulting person would not be me, but a mere Replica. If no cells were replaced, the resulting person would be me. But what of the cases in between, where the percentage of the cells replaced would be, say, 30, or 50, or 70 per cent? Would the resulting person here be me? When we consider some of these cases, we will not know whether to answer Yes or No.

Suppose next that we believe that, even in Teletransportation, my Replica would be me. We should then consider a different version of that case, in which the Scanner would get its information without destroying my body, and my Replica would be made while I was still alive. In this version of the case, we may agree that my Replica would not be me. That may shake our view that, in the original version of case, he *would* be me.

If we still keep that view, we should turn to what I have called the *Combined Spectrum*. In this second range of cases, there would be all the different degrees of both physical and psychological connectedness. The new cells would not be exactly similar. The greater the proportion of my body that would be replaced, the less like me would the resulting person be. In the case at the far end of this range, my whole body would be destroyed, and they would make a Replica of some quite different person, such as Greta Garbo. Garbo's Replica would clearly *not* be me. In the case at the near end, with no replacement, the resulting person would be me. On any view, there must be cases in between where we could not answer our question.

For simplicity, I shall consider only the Physical Spectrum, and I shall assume that, in some of the cases in this range, we cannot answer the question whether the resulting person would be me. My remarks could be transferred, with some adjustment, to the Combined Spectrum.

As I have said, it is natural to assume that, even if *we* cannot answer this question, there must always *be* an answer, which must be either Yes or No. It is natural to believe that, if the resulting person will be in pain, either I shall feel that pain, or I shan't. But this range of cases challenges that belief. In the case at the near end, the resulting person would be me. In the case at the far end, he would be someone else. How could it be true that, in all the cases in between, he must be either me, or someone else? For that to be true, there must be, somewhere in this range, a sharp borderline. There must be some critical set of cells such that, if only those cells were replaced, it would be me who would wake up, but that in the very next case, with only just a few more cells replaced, it would be, not me, but a new person. That is hard to believe.

Here is another fact, which makes it even harder to believe. Even if there were such a borderline, no one could ever discover where it is. I might say, 'Try replacing half of my brain and body, and I shall tell you what happens.' But we know in advance that, in every case, since the resulting person would be exactly like me, he would be inclined to believe that he was me. And this could not show that he *was* me, since any mere Replica of me would think that too.

Even if such cases actually occurred, we would learn nothing more about them. So it does not matter that these cases are imaginary.

We should try to decide now whether, in this range of cases, personal identity could be determinate. Could it be true that, in every case, the resulting person either would or would not be me?

If we do not believe that there are Cartesian Egos, or other such entities, we seem forced to answer No. It is not true that our identity must be determinate. We can always ask, 'Would that future person be me?' But, in some of these cases,

(7) This question would have no answer. It would be neither true nor false that this person would be me.

And

(8) This question would be *empty*. Even without an answer, we could know the full truth about what happened.

If our questions were about such entities as nations or machines, most of us would accept such claims. But, when applied to ourselves, they can be hard to believe. How could it be neither true nor false that I shall still exist tomorrow? And, without an answer to our question, how could I know the full truth about my future?

Reductionism gives the explanation. We naturally assume that, in these cases, there are different possibilities. The resulting person, we assume, might be me, or he might be someone else, who is merely like me. If the resulting person will be in pain, either I shall feel that pain, or I shan't. If these really were different possibilities, it would be compelling that one of them must be the possibility that would in fact obtain. How could reality fail to choose between them? But, on a Reductionist view,

(9) Our question is not about different possibilities. There is only a single possibility, or course of events. Our question is merely about different possible descriptions of this course of events.

That is how our question has no answer. We have not yet decided which description to apply. And, that is why, even without answering this question, we could know the full truth about what would happen.

Suppose that, after considering such examples, we cease to believe that our identity must be determinate. That may seem to make little difference. It may seem to be a change of view only about some imaginary cases, that will never actually occur. But that may not be so. We may be led to revise our beliefs about the nature of personal identity; and that would be a change of view about our own lives.

In nearly all actual cases, questions about personal identity have answers, so claim (7) does not apply. If we don't know these answers, there is something that we don't know. But claim (8) still applies. Even without answering these questions, we could know the full truth about what happens. We would know that truth if we knew the facts about both physical and psychological continuity. If, implausibly, we still didn't know the answer to a question about identity, our ignorance would only be about our language. And that is because claim (9) still applies. When we know the other facts, there are never different possibilities at the level of what happens. In all cases, the only remaining possibilities are at the linguistic level. Perhaps it would be correct to say that some future person would be me. Perhaps it would be correct to say that he would not be me. Or perhaps neither would be correct. I conclude that in *all* cases, if we know the other facts, we should regard questions about our identity as merely questions about language.

That conclusion can be misunderstood. First, when we ask such questions, that is usually because we *don't* know the other facts. Thus, when we ask if we are about to die, that is seldom a conceptual question. We ask that question because we don't know what will happen to our bodies, and whether, in particular, our brains will continue to support consciousness. Our question becomes conceptual only when we already know about such other facts.

Note next that, in certain cases, the relevant facts go beyond the details of the case we are considering. Whether some concept applies may depend on facts about other cases, or on a choice between scientific theories. Suppose we see something strange happening to an unknown animal. We might ask whether this process preserves the animal's identity, or whether the result is a new animal (because what we are seeing is some kind of reproduction). Even if we knew the details of this process, that question would not be merely conceptual. The answer would depend on whether this process is part of the natural development of this kind of animal. And that may be something we have yet to discover.

If we identify persons with human beings, whom we regard as a natural kind, the same would be true in some imaginable cases involving persons. But these are not the kind of case that I have been discussing. My cases all involve artificial intervention. No facts about natural development could be relevant here. Thus, in my Physical Spectrum, if we knew which of my cells would be replaced by duplicates, all of the relevant empirical facts would be in. In such cases any remaining questions would be conceptual.

Since that is so, it would be clearer to ask these questions in a different way. Consider the case in which I replace some of the components of my audio system, but keep the others. I ask, 'Do I still have one and the same system?' That may seem a factual question. But, since I already know what happened, that is not really so. It would be clearer to ask, 'Given that I have replaced those components, would it be correct to call this the same system?'

The same applies to personal identity. Suppose that I know the facts about what will happen to my body, and about any psychological connections that there will be between me now and some person tomorrow. I may ask, 'Will that person be me?' But that is a misleading way to put my question. It suggests that I don't know what's going to happen. When I know these other facts, I should ask, 'Would it be correct to call that person me?' That would remind me that, if there's anything that I don't know, that is merely a fact about our language.

I believe that we can go further. Such questions are, in the belittling sense, merely verbal. Some conceptual questions are well worth discussing. But questions about personal identity, in my kind of case, are like questions that we would all think trivial. It is quite uninteresting whether, with half its components replaced, I still have the same audio system. In the same way, we should regard it as quite uninteresting whether, if half of my body were simultaneously replaced, I would still exist. As questions about reality, these are entirely empty. Nor, as conceptual questions, do they need answers.

We might need, for legal purposes, to *give* such questions answers. Thus we might decide that an audio system should be called the same if its new components cost less than half its original price. And we might decide to say that I would continue to exist as long as less than half my body were replaced. But these are not answers to conceptual questions; they are mere decisions.

(Similar remarks apply if we are Identifying Reductionists, who believe that persons just are bodies. There are cases where it is a merely verbal question whether we still have one and the same human body. That is clearly true in the cases in the middle of the Physical Spectrum.)

It may help to contrast these questions with one that is not merely verbal. Suppose we are studying some creature which is very unlike ourselves, such as an insect, or some extraterrestrial being. We know all the facts about this creature's behaviour, and its neurophysiology. The creature wriggles vigorously, in what seems to be a response to some injury. We ask, 'Is it conscious, and in great pain? Or is it merely like an insentient machine?' Some Behaviourist might say, 'That is a merely verbal question. These aren't different possibilities, either of which might be true. They are merely different descriptions of the very same state of affairs.' That I find incredible. These descriptions give us, I believe, two quite different possibilities. It could not be an empty or a merely verbal question whether some creature was unconscious or in great pain.

It is natural to think the same about our own identity. If I know that some proportion of my cells will be replaced, how can it be a merely verbal question whether I am about to die, or shall wake up again tomorrow? It is because that is hard to believe that Reductionism is worth discussing. If we become Reductionists, that may change some of our deepest assumptions about ourselves.

These assumptions, as I have said, cover actual cases, and our own lives. But they are best revealed when we consider the imaginary problem cases. It is worth explaining further why that is so.

In ordinary cases, questions about our identity have answers. In such cases, there is a fact about personal identity, and Reductionism is one view about what kind of fact this is. On this view, personal identity just consists in physical and/or psychological continuity. We may find it hard to decide whether we accept this view, since it may be far from clear when one fact just consists in another. We may even doubt whether Reductionists and their critics really disagree.

In the problem cases, things are different. When we cannot answer questions about personal identity, it is easier to decide whether we accept a Reductionist view. We should ask: Do we find such cases puzzling? Or do we accept the Reductionist claim that, even without answering these questions, if we knew the facts about the continuities, we would know what happened?

Most of us do find such cases puzzling. We believe that, even if we knew those other facts, if we could not answer questions about our identity, there would be something that we didn't know. That suggests that, on our view, personal identity does *not* just consist in one or both of the continuities, but is a separately obtaining fact, or a further difference in what happens. The Reductionist account must then leave something out. So there is a real disagreement, and one that applies to all cases.

Many of us do not merely find such cases puzzling. We are inclined to believe that, in all such cases, questions about our identity must have answers, which must be either Yes or No. For that to be true, personal identity must be a separately obtaining fact of a peculiarly simple kind. It must involve some special entity, such as a Cartesian Ego, whose existence must be all-or-nothing.

When I say that we have these assumptions, I am *not* claiming that we believe in Cartesian Egos. Some of us do. But many of us, I suspect, have inconsistent beliefs. If we are asked whether we believe that there are Cartesian Egos, we may answer No. And we may accept that, as Reductionists claim, the existence of a person just involves the existence of a body, and the occurrence of a series of interrelated mental and physical events. But, as our reactions to the problem cases show, we don't fully accept that view. Or, if we do, we also seem to hold a different view.

Such a conflict of beliefs is quite common. At a reflective or intellectual level, we may be convinced that some view is true; but at another level, one that engages more directly with our emotions, we may continue to think and feel as if some different view were true. One example of this kind would be a hope, or fear, that we know to be groundless. Many of us, I suspect, have such inconsistent beliefs about the metaphysical questions that concern us most, such as free will, time's passage, consciousness, and the self. . . .

NOTE

1. Some of this essay draws from Part Three of my *Reasons and Persons* (Oxford University Press, 1984). The new material will be more fully developed in my contribution to Dancy, *Derek Parfit and His Critics: Vol. I. Persons* (Blackwell's, forthcoming).

61 | Freedom and Necessity

A. J. Ayer

When I am said to have done something of my own free will it is implied that I could have acted otherwise; and it is only when it is believed that I could have acted otherwise that I am held to be morally responsible for what I have done. For a man is not thought to be morally responsible for an action that it was not in his power to avoid. But if human behaviour is entirely governed by causal laws, it is not clear how any action that is done could ever have been avoided. It may be said of the agent that he would have acted otherwise if the causes of his action had been different, but they being what they were, it seems to follow that he was bound to act as he did. Now it is commonly assumed both that men are capable of acting freely, in the sense that is required to make them morally responsible, and that human behaviour is entirely governed by causal laws: and it is the apparent conflict between these two assumptions that gives rise to the philosophical problem of the freedom of the will.

Confronted with this problem, many people will be inclined to agree with Dr. Johnson: 'Sir, we *know* our will is free, and *there's* an end on't.' But, while this does very well for those who accept Dr. Johnson's premiss, it would hardly convince anyone who denied the freedom of the will. Certainly, if we do know that our wills are free, it follows that they are so. But the logical reply to this might be that since our wills are not free, it follows that no one can know that they are: so that if anyone claims, like Dr. Johnson, to know that they are, he must be mistaken. What is evident, indeed, is that people often believe themselves to be acting freely; and it is to this 'feeling' of freedom that some philosophers appeal when they wish, in the supposed interests of morality, to prove that not all human action is causally determined. But if these philosophers are right in their assumption that a man cannot be acting freely if his action is causally determined, then the fact that someone feels free to do, or not to do, a certain action does not prove that he really is so. It may prove that the agent does not himself know what it is that makes him act in one way rather than an-other: but from the fact that a man is unaware of the causes of his action, it does not follow that no such causes exist.

So much may be allowed to the determinist; but his belief that all human actions are subservient to causal laws still remains to be justified. If, indeed, it is necessary that every event should have a cause, then the rule must apply to human behaviour as much as to anything else. But why should it be supposed that every event must have a cause? The contrary is not unthinkable. Nor is the law of universal causation a necessary presupposition of scientific thought. The scientist may try to discover causal laws, and in many cases he succeeds; but sometimes he has to be content with statistical laws, and sometimes he comes upon events which, in the present state of his knowledge, he is not able to subsume under any law at all. In the case of these events he assumes that if he knew more he would be able to discover some law, whether causal or statistical, which would enable him to account for them. And this assumption cannot be disproved. For however far he may have carried his investigation, it is always open to him to carry it further; and it is always conceivable that if he carried it further he would discover the connection which had hitherto escaped him. Nevertheless, it is also conceivable that the events with which he is concerned are not systematically connected with any others: so that the reason why he does not discover the sort of laws that he requires is simply that they do not obtain.

Now in the case of human conduct the search for explanations has not in fact been altogether fruitless. Certain scientific laws have been established; and with the help of these laws we do make a number of successful predictions about the ways in which different people will behave. But these predictions do not always cover every detail. We may be able to predict that in certain circumstances a particular man will be angry, without being able to prescribe the precise form that the expression of his anger will take. We may be reasonably sure that he will shout, but not sure how loud his shout will be, or exactly

From *Philosophical Essays* (Macmillan, 1954). Reprinted with permission of the publisher.

what words he will use. And it is only a small proportion of human actions that we are able to forecast even so precisely as this. But that, it may be said, is because we have not carried our investigations very far. The science of psychology is still in its infancy and, as it is developed, not only will more human actions be explained, but the explanations will go into greater detail. The ideal of complete explanation may never in fact be attained: but it is theoretically attainable. Well, this may be so: and certainly it is impossible to show a priori that it is not so: but equally it cannot be shown that it is. This will not, however, discourage the scientist who, in the field of human behaviour, as elsewhere, will continue to formulate theories and test them by the facts. And in this he is justified. For since he has no reason a priori to admit that there is a limit to what he can discover, the fact that he also cannot be sure that there is no limit does not make it unreasonable for him to devise theories, nor, having devised them, to try constantly to improve them.

But now suppose it to be claimed that, so far as men's actions are concerned, there is a limit: and that this limit is set by the fact of human freedom. An obvious objection is that in many cases in which a person feels himself to be free to do, or not to do, a certain action, we are even now able to explain, in causal terms, why it is that he acts as he does. But it might be argued that even if men are sometimes mistaken in believing that they act freely, it does not follow that they are always so mistaken. For it is not always the case that when a man believes that he has acted freely we are in fact able to account for his action in causal terms. A determinist would say that we should be able to account for it if we had more knowledge of the circumstances, and had been able to discover the appropriate natural laws. But until those discoveries have been made, this remains only a pious hope. And may it not be true that, in some cases at least, the reason why we can give no causal explanation is that no causal explanation is available; and that this is because the agent's choice was literally free, as he himself felt it to be?

The answer is that this may indeed be true, inasmuch as it is open to anyone to hold that no explanation is possible until some explanation is actually found. But even so it does not give the moralist what he wants. For he is anxious to show that men are capable of acting freely in order to infer that they can be morally responsi-

ble for what they do. But if it is a matter of pure chance that a man should act in one way rather than another, he may be free but he can hardly be responsible. And indeed when a man's actions seem to us quite unpredictable, when, as we say, there is no knowing what he will do, we do not look upon him as a moral agent. We look upon him rather as a lunatic.

To this it may be objected that we are not dealing fairly with the moralist. For when he makes it a condition of my being morally responsible that I should act freely, he does not wish to imply that it is purely a matter of chance that I act as I do. What he wishes to imply is that my actions are the result of my own free choice: and it is because they are the result of my own free choice that I am held to be morally responsible for them.

But now we must ask how it is that I come to make my choice. Either it is an accident that I choose to act as I do or it is not. If it is an accident, then it is merely a matter of chance that I did not choose otherwise; and if it is merely a matter of chance that I did not choose otherwise, it is surely irrational to hold me morally responsible for choosing as I did. But if it is not an accident that I choose to do one thing rather than another, then presumably there is some causal explanation of my choice: and in that case we are led back to determinism.

Again, the objection may be raised that we are not doing justice to the moralist's case. His view is not that it is a matter of chance that I choose to act as I do, but rather that my choice depends upon my character. Nevertheless he holds that I can still be free in the sense that he requires; for it is I who am responsible for my character. But in what way am I responsible for my character? Only, surely, in the sense that there is a causal connection between what I do now and what I have done in the past. It is only this that justifies the statement that I have made myself what I am: and even so this is an oversimplification, since it takes no account of the external influences to which I have been subjected. But, ignoring the external influences, let us assume that it is in fact the case that I have made myself what I am. Then it is still legitimate to ask how it is that I have come to make myself one sort of person rather than another. And if it be answered that it is a matter of my strength of will, we can put the same question in another form by asking how it is that my will has the strength that it has and not some other degree of strength. Once more, either it is an accident or it is not. If it is an accident, then by the same argument as before, I am not morally responsible, and if it is not an accident we are led back to determinism.

Furthermore, to say that my actions proceed from my character or, more colloquially, that I act in character, is to say that my behaviour is consistent and to that extent predictable: and since it is, above all, for the actions that I perform in character that I am held to be morally responsible, it looks as if the admission of moral responsibility, so far from being incompatible with determinism, tends rather to presuppose it. But how can this be so if it is a necessary condition of moral responsibility that the person who is held responsible should have acted freely? It seems that if we are to retain this idea of moral responsibility, we must either show that men can be held responsible for actions which they do not do freely, or else find some way of reconciling determinism with the freedom of the will.

It is no doubt with the object of effecting this reconciliation that some philosophers have defined freedom as the consciousness of necessity. And by so doing they are able to say not only that a man can be acting freely when his action is causally determined, but even that his action must be causally determined for it to be possible for him to be acting freely. Nevertheless this definition has the serious disadvantage that it gives to the word 'freedom' a meaning quite different from any that it ordinarily bears. It is indeed obvious that if we are allowed to give the word 'freedom' any meaning that we please, we can find a meaning that will reconcile it with determinism: but this is no more a solution of our present problem than the fact that the word 'horse' could be arbitrarily used to mean what is ordinarily meant by 'sparrow' is a proof that horses have wings. For suppose that I am compelled by another person to do something 'against my will.' In that case, as the word 'freedom' is ordinarily used, I should not be said to be acting freely: and the fact that I am fully aware of the constraint to which I am subjected makes no difference to the matter. I do not become free by becoming conscious that I am not. It may, indeed, be possible to show that my being aware that my action is causally determined is not incompatible with my acting freely: but it by no means follows that it is in this that my freedom consists. Moreover, I suspect that one of the reasons why people are inclined to define freedom as the consciousness of necessity is that they think that if one is conscious of necessity one

may somehow be able to master it. But this is a fallacy. It is like someone's saying that he wishes he could see into the future, because if he did he would know what calamities lay in wait for him and so would be able to avoid them. But if he avoids the calamities then they don't lie in the future and it is not true that he foresees them. And similarly if I am able to master necessity, in the sense of escaping the operation of a necessary law, then the law in question is not necessary. And if the law is not necessary, then neither my freedom nor anything else can consist in my knowing that it is.

Let it be granted, then, that when we speak of reconciling freedom with determinism we are using the word 'freedom' in an ordinary sense. It still remains for us to make this usage clear: and perhaps the best way to make it clear is to show what it is that freedom, in this sense, is contrasted with. Now we began with the assumption that freedom is contrasted with causality: so that a man cannot be said to be acting freely if his action is causally determined. But this assumption has led us into difficulties and I now wish to suggest that it is mistaken. For it is not, I think, causality that freedom is to be contrasted with, but constraint. And while it is true that being constrained to do an action entails being caused to do it, I shall try to show that the converse does not hold. I shall try to show that from the fact that my action is causally determined it does not necessarily follow that I am constrained to do it: and this is equivalent to saying that it does not necessarily follow that I am not free.

If I am constrained, I do not act freely. But in what circumstances can I legitimately be said to be constrained? An obvious instance is the case in which I am compelled by another person to do what he wants. In a case of this sort the compulsion need not be such as to deprive one of the power of choice. It is not required that the other person should have hypnotized me, or that he should make it physically impossible for me to go against his will. It is enough that he should induce me to do what he wants by making it clear to me that, if I do not, he will bring about some situation that I regard as even more undesirable than the consequences of the action that he wishes me to do. Thus, if the man points a pistol at my head I may still choose to disobey him: but this does not prevent its being true that if I do fall in with his wishes he can legitimately be said to have compelled me. And if the circumstances are such that no reasonable person would be expected to choose the other alternative, then the action that I am made to do is not one for which I am held to be morally responsible.

A similar, but still somewhat different, case is that in which another person has obtained an habitual ascendancy over me. Where this is so, there may be no question of my being induced to act as the other person wishes by being confronted with a still more disagreeable alternative: for if I am sufficiently under his influence this special stimulus will not be necessary. Nevertheless I do not act freely, for the reason that I have been deprived of the power of choice. And this means that I have acquired so strong a habit of obedience that I no longer go through any process of deciding whether or not to do what the other person wants. About other matters I may still deliberate; but as regards the fulfilment of this other person's wishes, my own deliberations have ceased to be a causal factor in my behaviour. And it is in this sense that I may be said to be constrained. It is not, however, necessary that such constraint should take the form of subservience to another person. A kleptomaniac is not a free agent, in respect of his stealing, because he does not go through any process of deciding whether or not to steal. Or rather, if he does go through such a process, it is irrelevant to his behaviour. Whatever he resolved to do, he would steal all the same. And it is this that distinguishes him from the ordinary thief.

But now it may be asked whether there is any essential difference between these cases and those in which the agent is commonly thought to be free. No doubt the ordinary thief does go through a process of deciding whether or not to steal, and no doubt it does affect his behaviour. If he resolved to refrain from stealing, he could carry his resolution out. But if it be allowed that his making or not making this resolution is causally determined, then how can he be any more free than the kleptomaniac? It may be true that unlike the kleptomaniac he could refrain from stealing if he chose: but if there is a cause, or set of causes, which necessitate his choosing as he does, how can he be said to have the power of choice? Again, it may be true that no one now compels me to get up and walk across the room: but if my doing so can be causally explained in terms of my history or my environment, or whatever it may be, then how am I any more free than if some other person had compelled me? I do not have the feeling of constraint that I have when a pistol is manifestly pointed at my head; but the chains of causation by which I am bound are no less effective for being invisible.

The answer to this is that the cases I have mentioned as examples of constraint do differ from the others: and they differ just in the ways that I have tried to bring out. If I suffered from a compulsion neurosis, so that I got up and walked across the room, whether I wanted to or not, or if I did so because somebody else compelled me, then I should not be acting freely. But if I do it now, I shall be acting freely, just because these conditions do not obtain; and the fact that my action may nevertheless have a cause is, from this point of view, irrelevant. For it is not when my action has any cause at all, but only when it has a special sort of cause, that it is reckoned not to be free.

But here it may be objected that, even if this distinction corresponds to ordinary usage, it is still very irrational. For why should we distinguish, with regard to a person's freedom, between the operations of one sort of cause and those of another? Do not all causes equally necessitate? And is it not therefore arbitrary to say that a person is free when he is necessitated in one fashion but not when he is necessitated in another?

That all causes equally necessitate is indeed a tautology, if the word 'necessitate' is taken merely as equivalent to 'cause': but if, as the objection requires, it is taken as equivalent to 'constrain' or 'compel,' then I do not think that this proposition is true. For all that is needed for one event to be the cause of another is that, in the given circumstances, the event which is said to be the effect would not have occurred if it had not been for the occurrence of the event which is said to be the cause, or vice versa, according as causes are interpreted as necessary, or sufficient, conditions: and this fact is usually deducible from some causal law which states that whenever an event of the one kind occurs then, given suitable conditions, an event of the other kind will occur in a certain temporal or spatio-temporal relationship to it. In short, there is an invariable concomitance between the two classes of events; but there is no compulsion, in any but a metaphorical sense. Suppose, for example, that a psycho-analyst is able to account for some aspect of my behaviour by referring it to some lesion that I suffered in my childhood. In that case, it may be said that my childhood experience, together with certain other events, necessitates my behaving as I do. But all that this involves is that it is found to be true in general that when people have had certain experiences as children, they subsequently behave in certain specifiable ways; and my case is just another instance of this general law. It is in this way indeed that my behaviour is explained. But from the fact that my behaviour is capable of being explained, in the sense that it can be subsumed under some natural law, it does not follow that I am acting under constraint.

If this is correct, to say that I could have acted otherwise is to say, first, that I should have acted otherwise if I had so chosen; secondly, that my action was voluntary in the sense in which the actions, say, of the kleptomaniac are not; and thirdly, that nobody compelled me to choose as I did: and these three conditions may very well be fulfilled. When they are fulfilled, I may be said to have acted freely. But this is not to say that it was a matter of chance that I acted as I did, or, in other words, that my action could not be explained. And that my actions should be capable of being explained is all that is required by the postulate of determinism.

If more than this seems to be required it is, I think, because the use of the very word 'determinism' is in some degree misleading. For it tends to suggest that one event is somehow in the power of another, whereas the truth is merely that they are factually correlated. And the same applies to the use, in this context, of the word 'necessity' and even of the word 'cause' itself. Moreover, there are various reasons for this. One is the tendency to confuse causal with logical necessitation, and so to infer mistakenly that the effect is contained in the cause. Another is the uncritical use of a concept of force which is derived from primitive experiences of pushing and striking. A third is the survival of an animistic conception of causality, in which all causal relationships are modelled on the example of one person's exercising authority over another. As a result we tend to form an imaginative picture of an unhappy effect trying vainly to escape from the clutches of an overmastering cause. But, I repeat, the fact is simply that when an event of one type occurs, an event of another type occurs also, in a certain temporal or spatio-temporal relation to the first. The rest is only metaphor. And it is because of the metaphor, and not because of the fact, that we come to think that there is an antithesis between causality and freedom.

Nevertheless, it may be said, if the postulate of determinism is valid, then the future can be explained in terms of the past: and this means that if one knew enough about the past one would be able to predict the future. But in that case what will happen in the future is already decided. And how then can I be said to be free? What is going to happen is going to happen and nothing that I do can prevent it. If the determinist is right, I am the helpless prisoner of fate.

But what is meant by saying that the future course of events is already decided? If the implication is that some person has arranged it, then the proposition is false. But if all that is meant is that it is possible, in principle, to deduce it from a set of particular facts about the past, together with the appropriate general laws, then, even if this is true, it does not in the least entail that I am the helpless prisoner of fate. It does not even entail that my actions make no difference to the future: for they are causes as well as effects; so that if they were different their consequences would be different also. What it does entail is that my behaviour can be predicted: but to say that my behaviour can be predicted is not to say that I am acting under constraint. It is indeed true that I cannot escape my destiny if this is taken to mean no more than that I shall do what I shall do. But this is a tautology, just as it is a tautology that what is going to happen is going to happen. And such tautologies as these prove nothing whatsoever about the freedom of the will.

62 | Analogy

Bertrand Russell

The postulates hitherto considered have been such as are required for knowledge of the physical world. Broadly speaking, they have led us to admit a certain degree of knowledge as to the space–time structure of the physical world, while leaving us completely agnostic as regards its qualitative character. But where other human beings are concerned, we feel that we know more than this; we are convinced that other people have thoughts and feelings that are qualitatively fairly similar to our own. We are not content to think that we know only the space–time structure of our friends' minds, or their capacity for initiating causal chains that end in sensations of our own. A philosopher might pretend to think that he knew only this, but let him get cross with his wife and you will see that he does not regard her as a mere spatio-temporal edifice of which he knows the logical properties but not a glimmer of the intrinsic character. We are therefore justified in inferring that his skepticism is professional rather than sincere.

The problem with which we are concerned is the following. We observe in ourselves such occurrences as remembering, reasoning, feeling pleasure, and feeling pain. We think that sticks and stones do not have these experiences, but that other people do. Most of us have no doubt that the higher animals feel pleasure and pain, though I was once assured by a fisherman that "Fish have no sense nor feeling." I failed to find out how he had acquired this knowledge. Most people would disagree with him, but would be doubtful about oysters and starfish. However this may be, common sense admits an increasing doubtfulness as we descend in the animal kingdom, but as regards human beings it admits no doubt.

It is clear that belief in the minds of others requires some postulate that is not required in physics, since physics can be content with a knowledge of structure. My present purpose is to suggest what this further postulate may be.

It is clear that we must appeal to something that may be vaguely called "analogy." The behavior of other people is in many ways analogous to our own, and we suppose that it must have analogous causes. What people say is what we should say if we had certain thoughts, and so we infer that they probably have these thoughts. They give us information which we can sometimes subsequently verify. They behave in ways in which we behave when we are pleased (or displeased) in circumstances in which we should be pleased (or displeased). We may talk over with a friend some incident which we have both experienced, and find that his reminiscences dovetail with our own; this is particularly convincing when he remembers something that we have forgotten but that he recalls to our thoughts. Or again: you set your boy a problem in arithmetic, and with luck he gets the right answer; this persuades you that he is capable of arithmetical reasoning. There are, in short, very many ways in which my responses to stimuli differ from those of "dead" matter, and in all these ways other people resemble me. As it is clear to me that the causal laws governing my behavior have to do with "thoughts," it is natural to infer that the same is true of the analogous behavior of my friends.

The inference with which we are at present concerned is not merely that which takes us beyond solipsism, by maintaining that sensations have causes about which *something* can be known. This kind of inference, which suffices for physics, has already been considered. We are concerned now with a much more specific kind of inference, the kind that is involved in our knowledge of the thoughts and feelings of others—assuming that we have such knowledge. It is of course obvious that such knowledge is more or less doubtful. There is not only the general argument that we may be dreaming; there is also the possibility of ingenious automata. There are calculating machines that do sums much better than our schoolboy sons; there are gramophone records that remember impeccably what So-and-so said on such-and-such an occasion; there are people in the cinema who, though copies of real people, are not themselves alive. There is no theoretical limit to what

From *Human Knowledge: Its Scope and Limits* (George Allen and Unwin, 1948), pp. 482–86. Reprinted with permission of the publisher.

ingenuity could achieve in the way of producing the illusion of life where in fact life is absent.

But, you will say, in all such cases it was the thoughts of human beings that produced the ingenious mechanism. Yes, but how do you know this? And how do you know that the gramophone does *not* "think"?

There is, in the first place, a difference in the causal laws of observable behavior. If I say to a student, "Write me a paper on Descartes' reasons for believing in the existence of matter," I shall, if he is industrious, cause a certain response. A gramophone record might be so constructed as to respond to this stimulus, perhaps better than the student, but if so it would be incapable of telling me anything about any other philosopher, even if I threatened to refuse to give it a degree. One of the most notable peculiarities of human behavior is change of response to a given stimulus. An ingenious person could construct an automation which would always laugh at his jokes, however often it heard them; but a human being, after laughing a few times, will yawn, and end by saying, "How I laughed the first time I heard that joke."

But the difference in observable behavior between living and dead matter does not suffice to prove that there are "thoughts" connected with living bodies other than my own. It is probably possible theoretically to account for the behavior of living bodies by purely physical causal laws, and it is probably impossible to refute materialism by external observation alone. If we are to believe that there are thoughts and feelings other than our own, that must be in virtue of some inference in which our own thoughts and feelings are relevant, and such an inference must go beyond what is needed in physics.

I am, of course, not discussing the history of how we come to believe in other minds. We find ourselves believing in them when we first begin to reflect; the thought that Mother may be angry or pleased is one which rises in early infancy. What I am discussing is the possibility of a postulate which shall establish a rational connection between this belief and data, e.g., between the belief "Mother is angry" and the hearing of a loud voice.

The abstract schema seems to be as follows. We know, from observation of ourselves, a causal law of the form "A causes B," where A is a "thought" and B a physical occurrence. We sometimes observe a B when we cannot observe any A; we then infer an unobserved A. For example: I know that when I say, "I'm thirsty," I say so, usually, because I am thirsty, and therefore, when I hear the sentence "I'm thirsty" at a time when I am not thirsty, I assume that someone else is thirsty. I assume this the more readily if I see before me a hot, drooping body which goes on to say, "I have walked twenty desert miles in this heat with never a drop to drink." It is evident that my confidence in the "inference" is increased by increased complexity in the datum and also by increased certainty of the causal law derived from subjective observation, provided the causal law is such as to account for the complexities of the datum.

It is clear that in so far as plurality of causes is to be suspected, the kind of inference we have been considering is not valid. We are supposed to know "A causes B," and also to know that B has occurred; if this is to justify us in inferring A, we must know that *only* A causes B. Or, if we are content to infer that A is probable, it will suffice if we can know that in most cases it is A that causes B. If you hear thunder without having seen lightning, you confidently infer that there was lightning, because you are convinced that the sort of noise you heard is seldom caused by anything except lightning. As this example shows, our principle is not only employed to establish the existence of other minds but is habitually assumed, though in a less concrete form, in physics. I say "a less concrete form" because unseen lightning is only abstractly similar to seen lightning, whereas we suppose the similarity of other minds to our own to be by no means purely abstract.

Complexity in the observed behavior of another person, when this can all be accounted for by a simple cause such as thirst, increases the probability of the inference by diminishing the probability of some other cause. I think that in ideally favorable circumstances the argument would be formally as follows:

From subjective observation I know that A, which is a thought or feeling, causes B, which is a bodily act, e.g., a statement. I know also that, whenever B is an act of my own body, A is its cause. I now observe an act of the kind B in a body not my own, and I am having no thought or feeling of the kind A. But I still believe, on the basis of self-observation, that only A can cause B; I therefore infer that there was an A which caused B, though it was not an A that I could observe. On this ground I infer that other people's bodies are associated with minds, which resemble mine in proportion as their bodily behavior resembles my own.

In practice, the exactness and certainty of the above statement must be softened. We cannot be sure that, in our subjective experience, A is the only cause of B. And even if A is the only cause of B in our experience, how can we know that this holds outside our experience? It is not necessary that we should know this with any certainty; it is enough if it is highly probable. It is the assumption of probability in such cases that is our postulate. The postulate may therefore be stated as follows:

If, whenever we can observe whether A and B are present or absent, we find that every case of B has an A as a causal antecedent, then it is probable that most B's have A's as causal antecedents, even in cases where observation does not enable us to know whether A is present or not.

This postulate, if accepted, justifies the inference to other minds, as well as many other inferences that are made unreflectingly by common sense.

63 | Can Computers Think?
John R. Searle

In the previous chapter, I provided at least the outlines of a solution to the so-called 'mind–body problem.' Though we do not know in detail how the brain functions, we do know enough to have an idea of the general relationships between brain processes and mental processes. Mental processes are caused by the behaviour of elements of the brain. At the same time, they are realised in the structure that is made up of those elements. I think this answer is consistent with the standard biological approaches to biological phenomena. Indeed, it is a kind of commonsense answer to the question, given what we know about how the world works. However, it is very much a minority point of view. The prevailing view in philosophy, psychology, and artificial intelligence is one which emphasises the analogies between the functioning of the human brain and the functioning of digital computers. According to the most extreme version of this view, the brain is just a digital computer and the mind is just a computer program. One could summarise this view—I call it 'strong artificial intelligence', or 'strong AI'—by saying that the mind is to the brain, as the program is to the computer hardware.

This view has the consequence that there is nothing essentially biological about the human mind. The brain just happens to be one of an indefinitely large number of different kinds of hardware computers that could sustain the programs which make up human intelligence. On this view, any physical system whatever that had the right program with the right inputs and outputs would have a mind in exactly the same sense that you and I have minds. So, for example, if you made a computer out of old beer cans powered by windmills; if it had the right program, it would have to have a mind. And the point is not that for all we know it might have thoughts and feelings, but rather that it must have thoughts and feelings, because that is all there is to having thoughts and feelings: implementing the right program.

Most people who hold this view think we have not yet designed programs which are minds. But there is pretty much general agreement among them that it's only a matter of time until computer scientists and workers in artificial intelligence design the appropriate hardware and programs which will be the equivalent of human brains and minds. These will be artificial brains and minds which are in every way the equivalent of human brains and minds.

Many people outside of the field of artificial

intelligence are quite amazed to discover that anybody could believe such a view as this. So, before criticising it, let me give you a few examples of the things that people in this field have actually said. Herbert Simon of Carnegie-Mellon University says that we already have machines that can literally think. There is no question of waiting for some future machine, because existing digital computers already have thoughts in exactly the same sense that you and I do. Well, fancy that! Philosophers have been worried for centuries about whether or not a machine could think, and now we discover that they already have such machines at Carnegie-Mellon. Simon's colleague Alan Newell claims that we have now discovered (and notice that Newell says 'discovered' and not 'hypothesised' or 'considered the possibility', but we have *discovered*) that intelligence is just a matter of physical symbol manipulation; it has no essential connection with any specific kind of biological or physical wetware or hardware. Rather, any system whatever that is capable of manipulating physical symbols in the right way is capable of intelligence in the same literal sense as human intelligence of human beings. Both Simon and Newell, to their credit, emphasise that there is nothing metaphorical about these claims; they mean them quite literally. Freeman Dyson is quoted as having said that computers have an advantage over the rest of us when it comes to evolution. Since consciousness is just a matter of formal processes, in computers these formal processes can go on in substances that are much better able to survive in a universe that is cooling off than beings like ourselves made of our wet and messy materials. Marvin Minsky of MIT says that the next generation of computers will be so intelligent that we will 'be lucky if they are willing to keep us around the house as household pets.' My all-time favourite in the literature of exaggerated claims on behalf of the digital computer is from John McCarthy, the inventor of the term 'artificial intelligence.' McCarthy says even 'machines as simple as thermostats can be said to have beliefs.' And indeed, according to him, almost any machine capable of problem-solving can be said to have beliefs. I admire McCarthy's courage. I once asked him: 'What beliefs does your thermostat have?' And he said: 'My thermostat has three beliefs—it's too hot in here, it's too cold in here, and it's just right in here.' As a philosopher, I like all these claims for a simple reason. Unlike most philosophical theses, they

are reasonably clear, and they admit of a simple and decisive refutation. It is this refutation that I am going to undertake in this chapter.

The nature of the refutation has nothing whatever to do with any particular stage of computer technology. It is important to emphasise this point because the temptation is always to think that the solution to our problems must wait on some as yet uncreated technological wonder. But in fact, the nature of the refutation is completely independent of any state of technology. It has to do with the very definition of a digital computer, with what a digital computer is.

It is essential to our conception of a digital computer that its operations can be specified purely formally; that is, we specify the steps in the operation of the computer in terms of abstract symbols—sequences of zeroes and ones printed on a tape, for example. A typical computer 'rule' will determine that when a machine is in a certain state and it has a certain symbol on its tape, then it will perform a certain operation such as erasing the symbol or printing another symbol and then enter another state such as moving the tape one square to the left. But the symbols have no meaning; they have no semantic content; they are not about anything. They have to be specified purely in terms of their formal or syntactical structure. The zeroes and ones, for example, are just numerals; they don't even stand for numbers. Indeed, it is this feature of digital computers that makes them so powerful. One and the same type of hardware, if it is appropriately designed, can be used to run an indefinite range of different programs. And one and the same program can be run on an indefinite range of different types of hardwares.

But this feature of programs, that they are defined purely formally or syntactically, is fatal to the view that mental processes and program processes are identical. And the reason can be stated quite simply. There is more to having a mind than having formal or syntactical processes. Our internal mental states, by definition, have certain sorts of contents. If I am thinking about Kansas City or wishing that I had a cold beer to drink or wondering if there will be a fall in interest rates, in each case my mental state has a certain mental content in addition to whatever formal features it might have. That is, even if my thoughts occur to me in strings of symbols, there must be more to the thought than the abstract strings, because strings by themselves can't have any meaning. If my thoughts are to be *about* anything, then the strings must have a *meaning* which makes the thoughts about those things. In a word, the mind has more than a syntax, it has a semantics. The reason that no computer program can ever be a mind is simply that a computer program is only syntactical, and minds are more than syntactical. Minds are semantical, in the sense that they have more than a formal structure, they have a content.

To illustrate this point I have designed a certain thought-experiment. Imagine that a bunch of computer programmers have written a program that will enable a computer to simulate the understanding of Chinese. So, for example, if the computer is given a question in Chinese, it will match the question against its memory, or data base, and produce appropriate answers to the questions in Chinese. Suppose for the sake of argument that the computer's answers are as good as those of a native Chinese speaker. Now then, does the computer, on the basis of this, understand Chinese, does it literally understand Chinese, in the way that Chinese speakers understand Chinese? Well, imagine that you are locked in a room, and in this room are several baskets full of Chinese symbols. Imagine that you (like me) do not understand a word of Chinese, but that you are given a rule book in English for manipulating these Chinese symbols. The rules specify the manipulations of the symbols purely formally, in terms of their syntax, not their semantics. So the rule might say: 'Take a squiggle-squiggle sign out of basket number one and put it next to a squoggle-squoggle sign from basket number two.' Now suppose that some other Chinese symbols are passed into the room, and that you are given further rules for passing back Chinese symbols out of the room. Suppose that unknown to you the symbols passed into the room are called 'questions' by the people outside the room, and the symbols you pass back out of the room are called 'answers to the questions.' Suppose, furthermore, that the programmers are so good at designing the programs and that you are so good at manipulating the symbols, that very soon your answers are indistinguishable from those of a native Chinese speaker. There you are locked in your room shuffling your Chinese symbols and passing out Chinese symbols in response to incoming Chinese symbols. On the basis of the situation as I have described it, there is no way you could learn any Chinese simply by manipulating these formal symbols.

Now the point of the story is simply this: by virtue of implementing a formal computer program from the point of view of an outside observer, you behave exactly as if you understood Chinese, but all the same you don't understand a word of Chinese. But if going through the appropriate computer program for understanding Chinese is not enough to give *you* an understanding of Chinese, then it is not enough to give *any other digital computer* an understanding of Chinese. And again, the reason for this can be stated quite simply. If you don't understand Chinese, then no other computer could understand Chinese because no digital computer, just by virtue of running a program, has anything that you don't have. All that the computer has, as you have, is a formal program for manipulating uninterpreted Chinese symbols. To repeat, a computer has a syntax, but no semantics. The whole point of the parable of the Chinese room is to remind us of a fact that we knew all along. Understanding a language, or indeed, having mental states at all, involves more than just having a bunch of formal symbols. It involves having an interpretation, or a meaning attached to those symbols. And a digital computer, as defined, cannot have more than just formal symbols because the operation of the computer, as I said earlier, is defined in terms of its ability to implement programs. And these programs are purely formally specifiable—that is, they have no semantic content.

We can see the force of this argument if we contrast what it is like to be asked and to answer questions in English, and to be asked and to answer questions in some language where we have no knowledge of any of the meanings of the words. Imagine that in the Chinese room you are also given questions in English about such things as your age or your life history, and that you answer these questions. What is the difference between the Chinese case and the English case? Well again, if like me you understand no Chinese and you do understand English, then the difference is obvious. You understand the questions in English because they are expressed in symbols whose meanings are known to you. Similarly, when you give the answers in English you are producing symbols which are meaningful to you. But in the case of the Chinese, you have none of that. In the case of the Chinese, you simply manipulate formal symbols according to a computer program, and you attach no meaning to any of the elements.

Various replies have been suggested to this argument by workers in artificial intelligence and in psychology, as well as philosophy. They all have something in common; they are all in-adequate. And there is an obvious reason why they have to be inadequate, since the argument rests on a very simple logical truth, namely, syntax alone is not sufficient for semantics, and digital computers insofar as they are computers have, by definition, a syntax alone.

I want to make this clear by considering a couple of the arguments that are often presented against me.

Some people attempt to answer the Chinese room example by saying that the whole system understands Chinese. The idea here is that though I, the person in the room manipulating the symbols do not understand Chinese, I am just the central processing unit of the computer system. They argue that it is the whole system, including the room, the baskets full of symbols and the ledgers containing the programs and perhaps other items as well, taken as a totality, that understands Chinese. But this is subject to exactly the same objection I made before. There is no way that the system can get from the syntax to the semantics. I, as the central processing unit have no way of figuring out what any of these symbols means; but then neither does the whole system.

Another common response is to imagine that we put the Chinese understanding program inside a robot. If the robot moved around and interacted causally with the world, wouldn't that be enough to guarantee that it understood Chinese? Once again the inexorability of the semantics-syntax distinction overcomes this manoeuvre. As long as we suppose that the robot has only a computer for a brain then, even though it might behave exactly as if it understood Chinese, it would still have no way of getting from the syntax to the semantics of Chinese. You can see this if you imagine that I am the computer. Inside a room in the robot's skull I shuffle symbols without knowing that some of them come in to me from television cameras attached to the robot's head and others go out to move the robot's arms and legs. As long as all I have is a formal computer program, I have no way of attaching any meaning to any of the symbols. And the fact that the robot is engaged in causal interactions with the outside world won't help me to attach any meaning to the symbols unless I have some way of finding out about that fact. Suppose the robot picks up a hamburger and this triggers the symbol for hamburger to come into the room. As long as all I have is the symbol with no knowledge of its causes or how it got there, I have no way of knowing what it means. The causal interactions between the robot and the rest of the world are irrelevant unless those causal interactions are represented in some mind or other. But there is no way they can be if all that the so-called mind consists of is a set of purely formal, syntactical operations.

It is important to see exactly what is claimed and what is not claimed by my argument. Suppose we ask the question that I mentioned at the beginning: 'Could a machine think?' Well, in one sense, of course, we are all machines. We can construe the stuff inside our heads as a meat machine. And of course, we can all think. So, in one sense of 'machine,' namely that sense in which a machine is just a physical system which is capable of performing certain kinds of operations, in that sense, we are all machines, and we can think. So, trivially, there are machines that can think. But that wasn't the question that bothered us. So let's try a different formulation of it. Could an artefact think? Could a man-made machine think? Well, once again, it depends on the kind of artefact. Suppose we designed a machine that was molecule-for-molecule indistinguishable from a human being. Well then, if you can duplicate the causes, you can presumably duplicate the effects. So once again, the answer to that question is, in principle at least, trivially yes. If you could build a machine that had the same structure as a human being, then presumably that machine would be able to think. Indeed, it would be a surrogate human being. Well, let's try again.

The question isn't: 'Can a machine think?' or: 'Can an artefact think?' The question is: 'Can a digital computer think?' But once again we have to be very careful in how we interpret the question. From a mathematical point of view, anything whatever can be described *as if* it were a digital computer. And that's because it can be described as instantiating or implementing a computer program. In an utterly trivial sense, the pen that is on the desk in front of me can be described as a digital computer. It just happens to have a very boring computer program. The program says: 'Stay there.' Now since in this sense, anything whatever is a digital computer, because anything whatever can be described as implementing a computer program, then once again, our question gets a trivial answer. Of course our brains are digital computers, since they implement any number of computer programs. And of course our brains can think. So once again, there is a trivial answer to the question. But that wasn't really the question we were trying to ask. The question we wanted to ask is this: 'Can a digital computer, as defined, think?' That is to say: 'Is instantiating or implementing the right computer program with the right inputs and outputs, sufficient for, or constitutive of, thinking?' And to this question, unlike its predecessors, the answer is clearly 'no.' And it is 'no' for the reason that we have spelled out, namely, the computer program is defined purely syntactically. But thinking is more than just a matter of manipulating meaningless symbols, it involves meaningful semantic contents. These semantic contents are what we mean by 'meaning'.

It is important to emphasise again that we are not talking about a particular stage of computer technology. The argument has nothing to do with the forthcoming, amazing advances in computer science. It has nothing to do with the distinction between serial and parallel processes, or with the size of programs, or the speed of computer operations, or with computers that can interact causally with their environment, or even with the invention of robots. Technological progress is always grossly exaggerated, but even subtracting the exaggeration, the development of computers has been quite remarkable, and we can reasonably expect that even more remarkable progress will be made in the future. No doubt we will be much better able to simulate human behaviour on computers than we can at present, and certainly much better than we have been able to in the past. The point I am making is that if we are talking about having mental states, having a mind, all of these simulations are simply irrelevant. It doesn't matter how good the technology is, or how rapid the calculations made by the computer are. If it really is a computer, its operations have to be defined syntactically, whereas consciousness, thoughts, feelings, emotions, and all the rest of it involve more than a syntax. Those features, by definition, the computer is unable to *duplicate* however powerful may be its ability to *simulate*. The key distinction here is between duplication and simulation. And no simulation by itself ever constitutes duplication.

What I have done so far is give a basis to the sense that those citations I began this talk with are really as preposterous as they seem. There is a puzzling question in this discussion though, and that is: 'Why would anybody ever have thought that computers could think or have feelings and emotions and all the rest of it?' After all, we can do computer simulations of any process whatever that can be given a formal de-

scription. So, we can do a computer simulation of the flow of money in the British economy, or the pattern of power distribution in the Labour party. We can do computer simulation of rain storms in the home counties, or warehouse fires in East London. Now, in each of these cases, nobody supposes that the computer simulation is actually the real thing; no one supposes that a computer simulation of a storm will leave us all wet, or a computer simulation of a fire is likely to burn the house down. Why on earth would anyone in his right mind suppose a computer simulation of mental processes actually had mental processes? I don't really know the answer to that, since the idea seems to me, to put it frankly, quite crazy from the start. But I can make a couple of speculations.

First of all, where the mind is concerned, a lot of people are still tempted to some sort of behaviourism. They think if a system behaves as if it understood Chinese, then it really must understand Chinese. But we have already refuted this form of behaviourism with the Chinese room argument. Another assumption made by many people is that the mind is not a part of the biological world, it is not a part of the world of nature. The strong artificial intelligence view relies on that in its conception that the mind is purely formal; that somehow or other, it cannot be treated as a concrete product of biological processes like any other biological product. There is in these discussions, in short, a kind of residual dualism. AI partisans believe that the mind is more than a part of the natural biological world; they believe that the mind is purely formally specifiable. The paradox of this is that the AI literature is filled with fulminations against some view called 'dualism,' but in fact, the whole thesis of strong AI rests on a kind of dualism. It rests on a rejection of the idea that the mind is just a natural biological phenomenon in the world like any other.

I want to conclude this chapter by putting together the thesis of the last chapter and the thesis of this one. Both of these theses can be stated very simply. And indeed, I am going to state them with perhaps excessive crudeness. But if we put them together I think we get a quite powerful conception of the relations of minds, brains and computers. And the argument has a very simple logical structure, so you can see whether it is valid or invalid. The first premise is:

1. *Brains cause minds.*

Now, of course, that is really too crude. What we mean by that is that mental processes that we consider to constitute a mind are caused, entirely caused, by processes going on inside the brain. But let's be crude, let's just abbreviate that as three words—brains cause minds. And that is just a fact about how the world works. Now let's write proposition number two:

2. *Syntax is not sufficient for semantics.*

That proposition is a conceptual truth. It just articulates our distinction between the notion of what is purely formal and what has content. Now, to these two propositions—that brains cause minds and that syntax is not sufficient for semantics—let's add a third and a fourth:

3. *Computer programs are entirely defined by their formal, or syntactical, structure.*

That proposition, I take it, is true by definition; it is part of what we mean by the notion of a computer program.

4. *Minds have mental contents; specifically, they have semantic contents.*

And that, I take it, is just an obvious fact about how our minds work. My thoughts, and beliefs, and desires are about something, or they refer to something, or they concern states of affairs in the world; and they do that because their content directs them at these states of affairs in the world. Now, from these four premises, we can draw our first conclusion; and it follows obviously from premises 2, 3 and 4:

Conclusion 1. *No computer program by itself is sufficient to give a system a mind. Programs, in short, are not minds, and they are not by themselves sufficient for having minds.*

Now, that is a very powerful conclusion, because it means that the project of trying to create minds solely by designing programs is doomed from the start. And it is important to re-emphasise that this has nothing to do with any particular state of technology or any particular state of the complexity of the program. This is a purely formal, or logical, result from a set of axioms which are agreed to by all (or nearly all) of the disputants concerned. That is, even most of the hardcore enthusiasts for artificial intelligence agree that in fact, as a matter of biology, brain processes cause mental states, and they agree that programs are defined purely formally. But if you put these conclusions together with cer-

tain other things that we know, then it follows immediately that the project of strong AI is incapable of fulfilment.

However, once we have got these axioms, let's see what else we can derive. Here is a second conclusion:

Conclusion 2. *The way that brain functions cause minds cannot be solely in virtue of running a computer program.*

And this second conclusion follows from conjoining the first premise together with our first conclusion. That is, from the fact that brains cause minds and that programs are not enough to do the job, it follows that the way that brains cause minds can't be solely by running a computer program. Now that also I think is an important result, because it has the consequence that the brain is not, or at least is not just, a digital computer. We saw earlier that anything can trivially be described as if it were a digital computer, and brains are no exception. But the importance of this conclusion is that the computational properties of the brain are simply not enough to explain its functioning to produce mental states. And indeed, that ought to seem a commonsense scientific conclusion to us anyway because all it does is remind us of the fact that brains are biological engines; their biology matters. It is not, as several people in artificial intelligence have claimed, just an irrelevant fact about the mind that it happens to be realised in human brains.

Now, from our first premise, we can also derive a third conclusion:

Conclusion 3. *Anything else that caused minds would have to have causal powers at least equivalent to those of the brain.*

And this third conclusion is a trivial consequence of our first premise. It is a bit like saying that if my petrol engine drives my car at seventy-five miles an hour, then any diesel engine that was capable of doing that would have to have a power output at least equivalent to that of my petrol engine. Of course, some other system might cause mental processes using entirely different chemical or biochemical features from those the brain in fact uses. It might turn out that there are beings on other planets, or in other solar systems, that have mental states and use an entirely different biochemistry from ours. Suppose that Martians arrived on earth and we concluded that they had mental states. But suppose that when their heads were opened up, it was discovered that all they had inside was green slime. Well still, the green slime, if it functioned to produce consciousness and all the rest of their mental life, would have to have causal powers equal to those of the human brain. But now, from our first conclusion, that programs are not enough, and our third conclusion, that any other system would have to have causal powers equal to the brain, conclusion four follows immediately:

Conclusion 4. *For any artefact that we might build which had mental states equivalent to human mental states, the implementation of a computer program would not by itself be sufficient. Rather the artefact would have to have powers equivalent to the powers of the human brain.*

The upshot of this discussion I believe is to remind us of something that we have known all along: namely, mental states are biological phenomena. Consciousness, intentionality, subjectivity, and mental causation are all a part of our biological life history, along with growth, reproduction, the secretion of bile, and digestion.